| American Heritage | *A Reader* |

American Heritage	*A Reader*

EDITED BY THE HILLSDALE COLLEGE HISTORY FACULTY

Hillsdale College Press

Hillsdale, Michigan

HILLSDALE COLLEGE PRESS

American Heritage: A Reader
©2011 Hillsdale College Press, Hillsdale, Michigan 49242

Printed in the United States of America.

Cover design
Hesseltine & DeMason, Ann Arbor, Michigan

Library of Congress Control Number: 2009943958

ISBN 978-0-916308-28-5

Contents

VI   The Gilded Age   503

VII   America Between the Wars   629

Preface

In late September of 1787, after four toilsome months of the Constitutional Convention, the venerable Benjamin Franklin emerged from the Pennsylvania State House. The Philadelphia assembly of statesmen had wrapped up their work framing a new government and adjourned. Franklin had not walked far when one Mrs. Powel, a citizen anxious to hear about the fruit of their summer labors, accosted him to ask what sort of government he and his fellow delegates had crafted for the American people. "A republic, madam," he replied, "if you can keep it." Franklin's response is no less important today than it was when uttered, for it still demands that every serious student of the American Heritage consider two fundamental questions: What did the founders mean when they spoke of a "republic"? And what did a people have to know and do to keep it?

What did the founding fathers have in mind when they framed our American form of self-government and called it a republic? How new was this *novus ordo seclorum*—new order for the ages—that they created? Was the American Revolution a radical change and departure from the past, as some historians argue? Or was continuity with the past its chief feature, rendering it, as one contemporary observed, "a revolution not made, but prevented"? To what sources were these learned statesmen indebted as they undertook their political enterprise? Just as today we have a heritage—an inheritance of ideas, principles, commitments, and stories from our American past by which we make sense of our country, find our places in it, and order our lives—so, too, did the founders have a heritage. Theirs was the Western intellectual and spiritual heritage whose sources traced back through the histories of Jerusalem, Athens, Rome, and London.

The framers worked in the Philadelphia of the late eighteenth century, however, not ancient Greece, Rome, or medieval Christendom. Just what ingredients from their heritage did the founders weave into the new fabric of American self-government? Was their vision of a self-governing republic illuminated by "the lamp of experience" or had they set the past aside to begin something altogether new? Were they indebted principally to an old classical republicanism, to a new enlightenment liberalism or to something else? Was their government built chiefly upon newly expressed but timeless abstract truths, upon inferences distilled from inherited custom, or upon some combination of both? Further, what beliefs and customs animated and informed the American way of self-governed life? Were Americans rugged individualists who defined liberty as private autonomy and freedom from social restraints? Or were Americans substantially communitarian, rural, Protestant Christians who prized an ordered liberty while happily submitting to the bonds of family, Church, and local community? Finally, from what sources did the founders acquire their understanding of such concepts as liberty and equality, morality and virtue, citizenship and duty, natural rights and happiness?

Answers to these questions matter because they bear directly upon any effort to keep the republic that the founders had crafted. Keeping the republic meant facing the challenges of self-government. Whatever their differences, the founders knew that to endure, a self-governing republic must have self-governed citizens. That is, Americans had to be animated by civic virtue and possessed of souls ordered by right reason, not subject to the whims of passion and desire. As the world's most powerful and prosperous nation, the United States faces a recurring challenge with every generation. Will it retain its strength and continue to flourish as a self-governed land of liberty and prosperity? Preserving liberty requires that Americans identify, understand, and maintain liberty's chief sources and supports—the principles articulated by the founding generation.

Of course, there are many today with no genuine or even professed interest in keeping the founders' republic. They smugly dismiss the political wisdom of the eighteenth century as unworthy of an allegedly wiser postmodern age. Nobody denies that America has changed since its founding. Yet the founders' republican vision remains relevant, as is clear to any who understand how their ideals and contentions played out over the course of American history. If founding ideals have been challenged and undergone modification since the late eighteenth century, as undeniably they have, the stories of those challenges and changes are themselves key parts of the American Heritage. These are stories we must tell. Indeed, the stories we tell and the way we tell them shape our national character and serve either to cultivate or to undermine civic piety.

The course of a nation is set by its founding principles. The vicissitudes experienced by subsequent generations may challenge and even undermine founding principles; but a people will always tell their national story according to their understanding of its beginning. Successive generations of Americans have looked to the founding period through lenses colored by their own circumstances. Consequently, Americans have argued among themselves about the sources of their identity. They have disagreed about how to tell the stories that they tell themselves about themselves, about their past, and about the meaning of their past. Such disagreements and varying stories are part of the American Heritage—itself a human story of good and evil, gain and loss, addition and subtraction, honor and shame. So history is messy business and discerning its lessons hard work. Evidence—such as the documents in this volume—must be scrutinized with care. The contingencies and foibles of the human condition prove that men are not always animated by right reason and that timeless truths can be ignored. Such messiness does not obscure the fact that timeless truths, nevertheless, can be known and acted upon. One aim of the history student is to identify such timeless truths as they reveal themselves in the course of human events.

The primary role of this volume is to supply a rich sample of documents from the periods we examine. These primary sources provide portals into the American past. Reading them, we escape the provincialism of our own time and culture. We discover earlier manifestations of ideas and ideals that would become part of contemporary, often unanalyzed, belief systems. As artifacts of the past, these documents do not convey information merely, but are the sources that historians interpret to make sense of our past. Consequently, we invite students to engage in the same enterprise as they examine and interrogate these fragments of the American past as the primary means of understanding both the roots of American order and sources of contemporary disorders. This daunting task of viewing sympathetically ideas that, although part of our heritage, seem distant and alien is an important and exhilarating part of a proper education in which one seeks to make sense of oneself as an American. Properly understood, then, this book is a means toward American self-understanding, with all of the pride and shame that attends any such exploration.

Careful reading of and reflection upon the documents in this volume will highlight an inescapable fact about the American Heritage. However much its political and cultural order have evolved over time and been subjected to regional variations, the American political vision grew from a shared understanding that humans are religious beings subject to an order of Divine origin. Americans have succeeded best in living, working, worshipping, and playing together when they have shared a sufficiently common culture as the ground of their social order and stability. What have been the sources of that order? While reading this book, students should consider the following questions: What do shared cultural assumptions, traditions, and institutions have to do with obtaining and securing political stability? In what ways have Americans appropriated and modified the cultural components of earlier civilizations? In what ways do such social structures as the family, religious institutions, and local communities contribute to political stability? How is political stability fostered when law and custom function to limit the power and scope of government? In short, how is self-government achieved? To understand the answers to these questions is to grasp key themes in the story of American political culture.

Many twenty-first-century students may be tempted to ask about the utility of such an immersion in documents penned by departed Americans who were necessarily ignorant of our complicated post-9/11 world. The answer remains disarmingly simple. The highest things, the most noble ideals—the well-ordered soul, the furnished and disciplined mind—are valuable for their own sakes, not just for the alleged practicality they may have for getting a job or earning a dollar. In a world where so many see education as mere job training, too few tend to the purposes for which we work and live. Too few see education as preparation for living worthy and virtuous lives in which flourishing can be measured in nonmaterial ways. Consequently, too many colleges and universities have become places for focusing on means, and not upon ends—and as such, places where the confused and bewildered of the next generation acquire techniques and tools, but graduate having gained neither direction nor order to their souls. Such students become clever but not wise. They can make a dollar but have not the wisdom to spend it well. A liberal arts education is an education in those things that merit studying for their own sake, because they are beautiful, good, and true, because they help make us wise, prepare us to live well, and lead us to self-government. Learning the American Heritage is part of an American liberal education. While the practical utility of the documents in this book may elude immediate detection, the inheritance they offer is invaluable.

Nevertheless, as we have noted, there remains an intensely practical application of studying the American Heritage. If liberal education is to survive, if its priceless effect of turning hearts and minds toward the good and the true is to continue, then self-governed citizens must maintain the cultural conditions that foster liberal education. America is a land of liberty where liberal education has long prospered. Without such liberty, the very enterprise of liberal education in America may be imperiled. The starting place for any maintenance of American liberty is the study of the American Heritage, a necessary and practical duty for any self-governed member of a free society. Finally, there is nothing more practical than understanding the world in which one lives and knowing how to distinguish that which is timeless from the passing fads and fashions of the day. Perhaps C. S. Lewis expressed this notion best in his splendid essay "Learning in War-Time":

> We need intimate knowledge of the past. Not that the past has any magic about it, but because we . . . need something to set against the present, to remind us that the basic assumptions have been quite different in different periods and that much

which seems certain to the uneducated is merely temporary fashion. A man who has lived in many places is not likely to be deceived by the local errors of his native village; the scholar has lived in many times and is therefore in some degree immune from the great cataract of nonsense that pours from the press and microphone of his own age.

The study of history enables one to escape from the narrowness of "chronological snobbery" or "presentism," the culturally crippling condition of those who ignore wise voices from the past. Such folk trust, instead, only the ignorant set of fools described by G. K. Chesterton as the "arrogant oligarchy of those who merely happen to be walking about." Students of our heritage can escape that lot.

Just as the American Heritage unfolded over time and was the product of many minds, this book issued from the collective efforts of more than a dozen colleagues from the Hillsdale history faculty working and teaching together for over a decade. Some who worked on this volume at its inception have moved on. John Willson, who has retired from full-time teaching, and Ted McAllister, now at Pepperdine University in California, played important early roles, John as the senior member of the department in the early days of this project and Ted as an early contributor to the effort. Others, new faculty when we began, have matured into tenured and seasoned professors while teaching these documents. Although the documents in this volume were written by others, the process of their selection and editing was our own labor. Further, each document opens with an introduction written by a member of our history faculty, as does each chapter of the book. Recognition for such effort is owed to Thomas Conner, Lucy Moye, Paul Moreno, Paul Rahe, Harold Siegel, Burt Folsom, Richard Gamble, David Raney, and especially to Bradley Birzer and David Stewart whose tireless enthusiasm and remarkable organizational talents were conspicuous and invaluable.

MARK A. KALTHOFF
Chairman
Department of History
HILLSDALE COLLEGE
Hillsdale, Michigan

I
THE COLONIAL HERITAGE

Seventeenth-century Europeans left the lands of their fathers and braved the treacherous voyage across the Atlantic to the New World for a variety of reasons, but chief among them were religious liberty and economic opportunity. Although the English were not the first Europeans to explore and settle North America, their colonization efforts had a greater influence on the American heritage than those of any other nation or empire. English culture served as a template upon which succeeding generations have built a noble and enduring social structure based on religious liberty, individual rights, and the rule of law.

England's religious climate in the late sixteenth and early seventeenth centuries was unstable at best. As one monarch succeeded another, the Church of England alternately moved closer to and then further away from the practices of the Roman Catholic Church. As the Church of England was pulled one direction and then another, one constant remained: dissent from the Church was proscribed. English law prohibited so-called "Dissenters" or "Non-Conformists" from worshipping in a venue other than the Church of England, and these dissidents were persecuted to varying degrees depending upon the proclivities of the reigning monarch and local authorities. Puritans, Catholics, Quakers, and others frequently felt the oppressive hand of this persecution, and many ultimately chose to leave England to escape it. Countless Dissenters increasingly regarded North America as their best hope for religious freedom; the vast and untamed continent seemed to offer a haven for those who felt compelled to worship outside the Church of England.

Concurrent with this religious instability, an economic malaise gripped England. At the same time the nation's population was increasing markedly, a shift in agricultural practices toward wool production and away from crop cultivation produced significant food shortages. Tenant farmers who had lost their land wandered the countryside aimlessly, producing serious social problems. Even townsfolk felt the pinch, as skilled and unskilled workers alike often faced unemployment as a result of increasingly stiff foreign competition. In the midst of this economic turmoil, English theorists such as Richard Hakluyt (*c.* 1552–1616) and Francis Bacon (1561–1626) began to tout North America as a "safety valve" that would ameliorate social problems in England by siphoning off the nation's excess population. Removal to North America would be a boon to the emigrants as well, as the New World would give them seemingly limitless opportunities to improve their economic condition.

The first permanent English settlement in North America began as an economic and religious venture. The colony established at Jamestown, Virginia, in 1607 was the product of an arrangement known as a joint stock company. A small group of English investors pooled their resources and obtained a royal charter that granted exclusive rights to settle and exploit the resources of a vast region that included, in part, what is now the State of Virginia. Initially, the venture was a communal one; settlers were to labor on behalf of the so-called Virginia Company, and in turn they would be fed and otherwise provided for out of the common store. At the end of seven years, the company's investors were to split all profits generated by the enterprise.

It would be a grave error to regard the settlement of Virginia as a strictly economic undertaking. Richard Hakluyt, for one, regarded England's North American colonies as an opportunity to spread Protestantism—the "true and sincere religion," as he put it. No less an authority than the famed Captain John Smith (*c.* 1580–1631) echoed these sentiments, as he declared that a chief priority of Englishmen in the New World was to convert Indians to Christianity. The Virginia Company's backers shared these views, going so far as to announce that their primary objective was to save the heathen Indians from the wiles of the Devil. The Church of England, which was established by law as the colony's official church, was expected to advance these aims as part of its ministry.

Tragically, the Virginia colony foundered from its inception. Disease, malnourishment, and exposure all took their toll, as did the communal structure of the colony's economy, which provided little incentive for hard work and initiative. Although the introduction of private property and the establishment of tobacco as a viable cash crop eventually helped to place the colony on a solid economic footing, growth was slow and painful. Mortality rates remained at horrific levels throughout the seventeenth century, and the supply of English laborers (indentured servants) began to dry up as the image of Virginia as a death trap gained currency in England. By the 1670s, tobacco planters increasingly began turning to black slaves to cultivate their crops, taking advantage of greater access to that labor supply.

The founding of Maryland benefited greatly from the Virginia example, and the two colonies eventually developed strikingly similar economies based on tobacco cultivation and slave labor. Maryland was the brainchild of George Calvert (1579–1632), otherwise known as the first Lord Baltimore. A convert to Catholicism, Calvert was a successful English businessman who sought to establish a colony in North America for two significant purposes. First, Calvert wished to create a haven in the New World where English Catholics could worship without fear of retribution. Second, he wished to obtain title to a massive landholding that he could in turn sell or rent to others, thereby amassing a substantial fortune.

Unfortunately, George Calvert died before his goals achieved fruition, but his son Cecilius (1605–1675) (the second Lord Baltimore) carried on his father's legacy. Cecilius finally secured a charter from King Charles I (r. 1625–1649) in 1632, and with it he obtained title to a vast swath of territory that included not only what is now the state of Maryland but also parts of modern-day Virginia, Pennsylvania, and Delaware. This proprietary charter granted the proprietor, Cecilius Calvert, virtually unlimited authority over his new domain. While he had to recognize the sovereignty of the monarch, Calvert was otherwise given wide latitude in the government of his colony and in the distribution of its lands.

Unfortunately for Cecilius Calvert and his extended family, the subsequent growth and development of Maryland was in many respects disappointing. While Maryland avoided many of the serious pitfalls that befell neighboring Virginia in its early years, it soon became clear that few English Catholics desired to settle in Maryland. English Catholics were relatively few in number to begin with, and most of them felt reasonably satisfied with their station and therefore opted to remain in their native land. This undermined the economic underpinning of the colonial venture: to make money for the proprietor through the sale and rental of lands. Thus, to fulfill this objective, Calvert encouraged Protestants as well as Catholics to emigrate to Maryland, and soon Protestants constituted a significant majority in the colony. Aware that this development threatened the religious underpinning of the colony—the establishment of a haven for Catholics—Calvert admonished his fellow Catholics to avoid antagonizing Protestants and insisted that his co-religionists worship privately and quietly.

As Protestants became increasingly numerous in Maryland, Calvert felt the need to act boldly to protect the colony's Catholic minority. In 1649, he promulgated his "Act Concerning Religion," which promised religious toleration for all who worshipped Jesus Christ. This act demonstrates that in Maryland, as elsewhere in the American colonies, religious toleration was not absolute. Typically, only those who fell within the Judeo-Christian tradition could expect official sanction and protection, and often the parameters of toleration were far narrower.

Like Maryland before it, Pennsylvania was founded as a proprietary colony. In 1681, William Penn (1644–1708) received a massive land grant as payment for a debt that King Charles II owed Penn's father. Reminiscent of the Calverts, Penn conceived of his colony as a religious refuge and as a money-making

venture. As a Quaker who had been persecuted in England, Penn appreciated the value of religious toleration, and his colony welcomed all those who
worshipped "the one Almighty and eternal God." As such, religious liberty in
Pennsylvania was extensive but limited; only those who worshipped the God of
Abraham could expect toleration. Further, Penn's laws for the colony stipulated
that colonial officials and their electors must be professing Christians.

Also like the Calverts in Maryland, Penn hoped to amass a fortune by selling
and renting land to his colony's settlers. Much to his chagrin, these plans never
achieved fruition. He earned far less than he anticipated from the sale of his
lands, and he frequently experienced a great deal of difficulty in extracting rents
from tenant farmers. Penn's refusal to use heavy-handed tactics against these
delinquent renters contributed to his economic woes, and he died in penury.

Perhaps the most celebrated example of emigration to North America for
religious reasons is that of the Puritans of New England. During the first half
of the seventeenth century, two distinct groups of Puritans left England and
landed in what became Massachusetts—the "separating" Puritans of Plymouth
and the "non-separating" Puritans of Massachusetts Bay. Although both enterprises began as joint stock companies that intended to produce sizable returns
for their investors, they soon evolved into primarily religious missions.

In a general sense, the New England Puritans were escaping not only religious persecution but also the corrosive effects of a culture that they believed
was straying increasingly from the will of God as revealed in the Bible. Puritans
believed that every society possessed a covenant with God—a covenant that
God established and that He expected His people to uphold. God demanded
obedience, and if that obedience were forthcoming He would protect and bless
the faithful accordingly. In contrast, God did not hesitate to punish those who
did not adhere to His will.

During the opening decades of the seventeenth century, Puritans were
dismayed by the state of religion, politics, and society in England. They believed
that the Church of England bore little resemblance to the "True Church" as
outlined in the New Testament, and that it retained too many elements of the
despised Roman Catholic Church. Puritan attempts to reform the Church of
England bore little fruit, and most concluded that such efforts were doomed
to failure. Similarly, attempts to reform politics made little headway. Although
Puritans succeeded in establishing a substantial power base in Parliament, the
hostility of King Charles I prevented that body from meeting regularly and
accomplishing much of note. In addition, Puritans believed that English society
was becoming rotten to the core, and that the English government was derelict
in its duty to punish sinful behavior. If the English didn't adhere to God's will
and punish transgressions of it, they reasoned, God would step in and visit His

wrath upon the nation. Few Puritans wanted to experience this wrath when it came, and leaving England became an increasingly attractive option.

The Plymouth Puritans, who established their colony in 1620, emigrated to New England with the intention of severing all links with the Church of England, hence their designation as "separating" Puritans. They believed that further attempts to reform the Church were futile, and that remaining within the Church and within the broader English society would only corrupt them and their progeny. Thus, they resolved to remove themselves to North America where they could create a church and a society pleasing to God, based on His precepts as outlined in the Bible.

The so-called "non-separating" Puritans who founded the colony of Massachusetts Bay in 1630 agreed with their Plymouth brethren about the corruption within the Church of England and within English culture generally, but their response to this situation was markedly different. While the Massachusetts Bay group also thought it best to leave England so as to avoid God's wrath or, at the very least, the corruption of their youth, they were loath to abandon their spiritual brothers and sisters within the Church of England. Instead, they maintained a tenuous link with the Church by refusing to leave it officially while at the same time creating their own Congregational churches organized strictly upon biblical principles. The Massachusetts Bay Puritans and, to a lesser extent, their counterparts in Plymouth, hoped to fashion an example of a godly church and society that could serve as a blueprint for reform back in England.

As additional colonies were established and existing ones grew, religious life in English North America underwent a series of significant transformations, the most notable of which would come to be called the Great Awakening (see next chapter). Such spiritual change was not the only significant eighteenth-century cultural development. Colonists experienced notable political transformation as well. By the early 1700s, all of the colonies possessed assemblies that were, at least in part, popularly elected, and these assemblies began to assert increasing control over colonial affairs. They assumed unto themselves the powers to tax, control militias, and appoint certain colonial officials. While the royal governors in these colonies possessed a great deal of power, including an absolute veto over legislation, they found it prudent to exercise this power sparingly. Since the assemblies controlled the power of the purse, governors considered it wise to avoid antagonizing them whenever possible. Thus, royal governors rarely acted as an effective check upon legislative power in the colonies. As colonial assemblies increasingly considered themselves "mini-Parliaments" with powers that equaled or exceeded those of the House of Commons in England, royal governors did little or nothing to prevent them from exercising such powers.

Royal officials in England did little to check the growing power of colonial assemblies either. This was partially by default and partially by design. Government officers were notoriously ill-informed about colonial affairs, and many were pre-occupied with other matters that were regarded as more important. The concerns of the British Isles and Continental Europe, for example, almost always took precedence over the events in the American colonies. In addition, responsibility for colonial affairs was divided among a variety of governmental agencies, often resulting in overlapping jurisdictions and uncertain duties. This state of affairs was notoriously inefficient, but most astute British observers realized this and even supported it.

One such astute observer was the first British prime minister, Sir Robert Walpole (r. 1721–1742). Walpole realized that the colonial assemblies in America were aggrandizing their power, and he also realized that American merchants were routinely evading British trade laws. Rather than initiating a crackdown, Walpole believed it was best to ignore these troubling developments. To do otherwise, he argued, would invite conflict with the colonists—conflict that might result in boycotts of British goods or, even worse, armed rebellion that would be costly to suppress.

Walpole's strategy, which the British government maintained to a great degree until the French and Indian War, was dubbed "salutary neglect" by the British statesman Edmund Burke (1729–1792). Burke's description seemed to characterize accurately the widespread notion that Britain's "laissez-faire" policy was, for the most part, beneficial to a multiplicity of interests on both sides of the Atlantic. When Prime Minister George Grenville (r. 1763–1765) abandoned "salutary neglect" by attempting to impose novel revenue-raising measures on the American colonies in 1764, he forged ahead where Walpole had feared to tread. The consequences could scarcely have been more significant.

LAWS OF VIRGINIA

Sir Thomas Gates (c. 1585–1621), acting as Governor of the colony of Virginia, imposed the first American law code in the year following the infant colony's winter "starving time" of 1609–1610, when the Jamestown settlement was nearly extinguished. The colony continued to be plagued by typhoid fever, dysentery, and malaria, so that of 14,000 who migrated there, only 1,100 remained alive in 1622. The laws, which were implemented by Sir Thomas Dale (?–1619), marshal of the colony—for which reason they are sometimes known as "Dale's Code"—made no provision for liberty against government power or for local self-government, and they imposed religious orthodoxy and a biblical moral code.

1610

Whereas His Majesty, like himself a most zealous prince, has in his own realms a principal care of true religion and reverence to God, and has always strictly commanded his generals and governors, with all his forces wheresoever, to let their ways be like his ends, for the glory of God.

And forasmuch as no good service can be performed, or war well managed, 5 where military discipline is not observed, and military discipline cannot be kept where the rules, or chief parts thereof, be not certainly set down and generally known, have (with the advice and counsel of Sir Thomas Gates, Knight, Lieutenant-General) adhered unto the laws divine and orders politic and martial of his lordship (the same exemplified) an addition of such others as I have found 10 either the necessity of the present state of the colony to require, or the infancy and weakness of the body thereof as yet able to digest, and do now publish them to all persons in the colony, that they may as well take knowledge of the laws themselves as of the penalty and punishment, which without partiality shall be inflicted upon the breakers of the same. 15

William Strachey, *For the Colony in Virginea Britannia, Lawes Diuine, Morall and Martiall, &c.* (London: Walter Burre, 1612), 9–12, 19 in Peter Force, ed. *Tracts and Other Papers Relating to the Origin, Settlement, and Progress of Colonies in North America* (Washington, DC: William W. Force, 1844), volume III [modernized].

1. First, since we owe our highest and supreme duty, our greatest, and all our allegiance to Him from whom all power and authority is derived and flows as from the first, and only, fountain, and being special soldiers impressed in this sacred cause, we must alone expect our success from Him who is only the blesser of all good attempts, the King of kings, the Commander of commanders, and Lord of hosts, I do strictly command and charge all captains and officers, of what quality or nature soever, whether commanders in the field, or in town, or towns, forts, or fortresses, to have a care that the Almighty God be duly and daily served, and that they call upon their people to hear sermons, as that also they diligently frequent morning and evening prayer themselves by their own exemplar and daily life, and duty herein, encouraging others thereunto, and that such who shall often and willfully absent themselves be duly punished according to the martial law in that case provided.

2. That no man speak impiously or maliciously against the holy and blessed Trinity, or any of the three persons, that is to say, against God the Father, God the Son, and God the Holy Ghost, or against the known articles of the Christian faith, upon pain of death.

3. That no man blaspheme God's holy name, upon pain of death, or use unlawful oaths, taking the name of God in vain, curse, or ban, upon pain of severe punishment for the first offence so committed, and for the second, to have a bodkin thrust through his tongue, and if he continue the blaspheming of God's holy name, for the third time so offending, he shall be brought to a martial court, and there receive censure of death for his offence.

4. No man shall use any traitorous words against His Majesty's person or royal authority, upon pain of death.

5. No man shall speak any word, or do any act, which may tend to the derision or despite of God's holy word, upon pain of death. Nor shall any man unworthily demean himself unto any preacher or minister of the same, but generally hold them in all reverent regard and dutiful entreaty, otherwise he, the offender, shall openly be whipped three times, and ask public forgiveness in the assembly of the congregation three several Sabbath days.

6. Every man and woman duly twice a day upon the first tolling of the bell shall upon the working days repair unto the Church to hear divine service upon pain of losing his or her day's allowance for the first omission, for the

second to be whipped, and for the third to be condemned to the galleys for six months. Likewise no man or woman shall dare to violate or break the Sabbath by any gaming, public or private, abroad or at home, but duly sanctify and observe the same, both himself and his family, by preparing themselves at home with private prayer, that they may be the better fitted for the public, 5 according to the commandment of God, and the orders of our Church, as also every man and woman shall repair in the morning to the divine service, and sermons preached upon the Sabbath day, and in the afternoon to divine service, and catechizing, upon pain for the first fault to lose their provision and allowance for the whole week following, for the second to lose the said 10 allowance, and also to be whipped, and for the third to suffer death.

7. All preachers or ministers within this, our colony or colonies, shall in the forts where they are resident after divine service duly preach every Sabbath day in the forenoon, and catechize in the afternoon, and weekly say the divine service twice every day, and preach every Wednesday. Likewise every 15 minister where he is resident, within the same fort or fortress, towns or town, shall choose unto him four of the most religious and better disposed as well to inform of the abuses and neglects of the people in their duties and service to God, as also to the due reparation and keeping of the Church handsome and fitted with all reverent observances thereunto belonging. 20 Likewise every minister shall keep a faithful and true record, or church book, of all christenings, marriages, and deaths of such our people as shall happen within their fort or fortresses, towns or town at any time, upon the burden of a neglectful conscience, and upon pain of losing their entertainment.

8. He that upon pretended malice shall murder or take away the life of any 25 man shall be punished with death.

9. No man shall commit the horrible and detestable sins of sodomy, upon pain of death; and he or she that can be lawfully convicted of adultery shall be punished with death. No man shall ravish or force any woman, maid or Indian, or other, upon pain of death, and know that he or she that shall 30 commit fornication, and evident proof made thereof, for their first fault shall be whipped, for their second they shall be whipped, and for their third they shall be whipped three times a week for one month, and ask public forgiveness in the assembly of the congregation.

10. No man shall be found guilty of sacrilege, which is a trespass as well com- 35 mitted in violating and abusing any sacred ministry, duty, or office of the

Church irreverently or profanely, as by being a church robber, to filch, steal, or carry away anything out of the church appertaining thereunto, or unto any holy and consecrated place, to the divine service of God, which no man should do, upon pain of death. Likewise he that shall rob the store of any commodities therein, of what quality soever, whether provisions of victuals, or of arms, trucking stuff, apparel, linen or woolen, hose or shoes, hats or caps, instruments or tools of steel, iron, etc., or shall rob from his fellow soldier or neighbor anything that is his, victuals, apparel, household stuff, tool, or what necessary else soever, by water or land, out of boat, house, or knapsack, shall be punished with death.

11. He that shall take an oath untruly, or bear false witness in any cause, or against any man whatsoever, shall be punished with death.

37. ... Every minister or preacher shall every Sabbath day before catechizing read all these laws and ordinances, publicly in the assembly of the congregation, upon pain of his entertainment checked for that week.

TWO COLONIAL COVENANTS

The forty-one "freemen" (adult male voters) aboard the English emigrant ship MAYFLOWER *signed what later became known as their "compact" shortly before they disembarked near Plymouth in November 1620. As children of the Reformation they would probably have used the more familiar term "covenant" to describe their action in forming a "civil body politic." In the 1690s, John Locke's political writings made the terms "compact" and "contract" popular.*

This was the first of hundreds of covenants drawn up by Englishmen who planted colonies along the Atlantic seaboard in the seventeenth and eighteenth centuries. They all shared three great ideas: the consent of the freemen, the rule of law, and the grace of God. Consent *was perhaps ill-defined in 1620, but it had deep roots in such English documents as Magna Carta. The rule of law was primarily associated with the Common Law of England. Englishmen also regarded God as the author of all law. These medieval ideas, tempered and extended by the Reformation, laid the foundation for American political culture.*

The Salem Covenant of 1629 was the shortest of all the colonial covenants.

The Mayflower Compact

11 NOVEMBER 1620

In the name of God, amen. We, whose names are underwritten, the loyal subjects of our dread sovereign lord, King James, by the Grace of God, of Great Britain, France, and Ireland, King, Defender of the Faith, etc, having undertaken for the glory of God, and advancement of the Christian faith, and the honour of our king and country, a voyage to plant the first colony in the northern parts of Virginia, do by these presents solemnly and mutually in the presence of God, 5

"The Mayflower Compact," in Charles Deane, ed., *History of Plymouth Plantation by William Bradford* (Boston, 1856), 89–90 [modernized].

and one another, covenant and combine ourselves together into a civil body politic, for our better ordering and preservation, and furtherance of the ends aforesaid; and by virtue hereof to enact, constitute, and frame such just and equal laws, ordinances, acts, constitutions, and offices, from time to time, as
5   shall be thought most meet and convenient for the general good of the colony, unto which we promise all due submission and obedience. In witness whereof we have hereunto subscribed our names at Cape Cod, the eleventh of November, in the reign of our sovereign lord, King James, of England, France, and Ireland the eighteenth and of Scotland the fifty-fourth. Anno Domini 1620.

The Salem Covenant

1629

10   We covenant with the Lord and one with another, and do bind ourselves in the presence of God, to walk together in all his ways, according as he is pleased to reveal himself unto us in his blessed word of truth.

"The Salem Covenant," in Samuel Worcester, *Memorial of the Old and New Tabernacle, Salem, Mass* (Boston: Crocker and Brewster, 1855), 6.

A MODELL OF CHRISTIAN CHARITY
JOHN WINTHROP (1588–1649)

John Winthrop, first governor of Massachusetts Bay Colony, grew up in the tiny village of Groton in Suffolk, England, on the former abbey lands his grandfather had purchased at the time of Henry VIII's dissolution of the monasteries. Winthrop studied for a time at Trinity College, Cambridge, before pursuing a career in law. Swept up in the Puritan movement and seeing little hope in England for godly government and the "pure ordinances" of Christ's church, he sold the family estate and led the first large migration of Puritan refugees to New England.

In the spring of 1630, Winthrop sailed for Massachusetts aboard the ARBELLA, *a 35-ton ship with a crew of 52 and armed with 28 guns to defend itself from the privateers prowling the busy sea lanes of the North Atlantic. The* ARBELLA *served as the flagship of what was meant to be a flotilla of eleven ships, but only four set out together in early April, the others following close behind. By the end of 1630, seventeen ships in all had carried about 1,100 settlers to the Puritan settlements in and around Boston. In the decades ahead, the "plantation," as it was known, survived disease, Indian warfare, political and religious dissent, and the return migration of many clergymen and homesick settlers to flourish as a populous and prosperous colony in the slowly expanding empire of British North America.*

At some point, whether before or during the voyage is not known, Winthrop wrote "A Model of Christian Charity." Drawing heavily from the Old and New Testaments, he exhorted his fellow colonists to strengthen the "bonds of affection" that would enable the Puritan community to fulfill its divine mandate. He offered them a "model," or template, after

John Winthrop, "A Modell of Christian Charity" *Old South Leaflets* 207 (1916), 7–21 [modernized].

The original copy of Winthrop's lay sermon has not survived. An early copy, not in his handwriting, belongs to the New York Historical Society and includes on the cover page of the manuscript, in yet another hand, nearly all the historical evidence connecting it to Winthrop and to the voyage of the ARBELLA in 1630. The "Modell of Christian Charity" appeared in print for the first time in 1838.

*which they ought to pattern their lives as Christian brothers and sisters.
The document makes clear that Winthrop thought the stakes of failing
to do so were very high.*

*Over the past fifty years, the "Model of Christian Charity" has
become one of the most frequently quoted documents in American history. But it remained unpublished from 1630 until 1838 and only
gradually thereafter made its way into textbook accounts of America's
origins. No copy of the discourse in Winthrop's handwriting survives.
The earliest manuscript copy, held in the archives of the New York
Historical Society, includes a cover page that provides almost all of the
evidence we have linking the document to Governor Winthrop and to
the* ARBELLA's *voyage.*

1630

God Almighty, in His most holy and wise providence, has so disposed of the
condition of mankind as in all times some must be rich, some poor, some high
and eminent in power and dignity, others mean and in subjection.

The Reason Hereof

First, to hold conformity with the rest of His works, being delighted to show
5   forth the glory of His wisdom in the variety and difference of the creatures;
and the glory of His power in ordering all these differences for the preservation
and good of the whole; and the glory of His greatness, that as it is the glory
of princes to have many officers, so this great King will have many stewards,
counting Himself more honored in dispensing His gifts to man by man than
10   if He did it by His own immediate hands.

Secondly, that He might have the more occasion to manifest the work of His
Spirit: first upon the wicked in moderating and restraining them, so that the rich
and mighty should not eat up the poor, nor the poor and despised rise up against
their superiors and shake off their yoke; secondly in the regenerate, in exercising
15   His graces in them, as in the great ones, their love, mercy, gentleness, temperance
etc.; in the poor and inferior sort, their faith patience, obedience etc.

Thirdly, that every man might have need of other, and from hence they
might be all knit more nearly together in the bonds of brotherly affection. From
hence it appears plainly that no man is made more honorable than another or
20   more wealthy, etc. out of any particular and singular respect to himself, but for
the glory of his Creator and the common good of the creature, man. Therefore
God still reserves the property of these gifts to Himself as in Ezekiel 16:17.
He there calls wealth His gold and His silver. In Proverbs 3:9 He claims their
service as His due, honor the Lord with the riches, etc. All men being thus (by

divine providence) ranked into two sorts, rich and poor; under the first are comprehended all such as are able to live comfortably by their own means duly improved; and all others are poor according to the former distribution.

There are two rules whereby we are to walk one towards another: JUSTICE and MERCY. These are always distinguished in their act and in their object, yet may they both concur in the same subject in each respect; as sometimes there may be an occasion of showing mercy to a rich man in some sudden danger of distress, and also doing of mere justice to a poor man in regard of some particular contract, etc.

There is likewise a double law by which we are regulated in our conversation one towards another in both the former respects: the law of nature and the law of grace (that is, the moral law or the law of the gospel) to omit the rule of justice as not properly belonging to this purpose otherwise than it may fall into consideration in some particular cases. By the first of these laws man as he was enabled so withall is commanded to love his neighbor as himself. Upon this ground stands all the precepts of the moral law, which concerns our dealings with men. To apply this to the works of mercy, this law requires two things. First, that every man afford his help to another in every want or distress. Secondly, that he performed this out of the same affection which makes him careful of his own goods, according to that of our Savior, (Matt. 7:12) "Whatsoever ye would that men should do to you...." This was practiced by Abraham and Lot in entertaining the angels and the old man of Gibea.[1]

The law of grace or the gospel has some difference from the former as in these respects. First, the law of nature was given to man in the estate of innocency; this of the gospel in the estate of regeneracy. Secondly, the former propounds one man to another, as the same flesh and image of god; this as a brother in Christ also, and in the communion of the same spirit and so teaches us to put a difference between Christians and others. *Do good to all, especially to the household of faith*; upon this ground the Israelites were to put a difference between the brethren of such as were strangers though not of Canaanites. Thirdly, the law of nature could give no rules for dealing with enemies, for all are to be considered as friends in the state of innocency, but the Gospel commands love to an enemy. Proof: if your enemy hunger, feed him; love your enemies, do good to them that hate you.[2]

This law of the gospel propounds likewise a difference of seasons and occasions. There is a time when a Christian must sell all and give to the poor, as they did in the Apostles' times. There is a time also when a Christian (though they

[1]Genesis 18–19; Judges 19
[2]Matthew 5:44

give not all yet) must give beyond their ability, as they of Macedonia. Likewise community of perils calls for extraordinary liberality, and so does community in some special service for the Church. Lastly, when there is no other means whereby our Christian brother may be relieved in his distress, we must help
5   him beyond our ability, rather than tempt God in putting him upon help by miraculous or extraordinary means.

This duty of mercy is exercised in the kinds: *giving, lending,* and *forgiving.*

Question—What rule shall a man observe in giving in respect of the measure?

Answer—If the time and occasion be ordinary, he is to give out of his abun-
10   dance. Let him lay aside as God has blessed him. If the time and occasion be extraordinary, he must be ruled by them; taking this with all, that then a man cannot likely do too much, especially if he may leave himself and his family under probable means of comfortable subsistence.

Objection—A man must lay up for posterity, the fathers lay up for posterity and
15   children and he "is worse than an infidel" that "provides not for his own."[3]

Answer—For the first, it is plain that it being spoken by way of comparison, it must be meant of the ordinary and usual course of fathers and cannot extend to times and occasions extraordinary. For the other place, the Apostle speaks against such as walked inordinately, and it is without question that he is worse
20   than an infidel who through his own sloth and voluptuousness shall neglect to provide for his family.

Objection—"The wise man's eyes are in his head" says Solomon, "and foresees the plague;"[4] therefore we must forecast and lay up against evil times when he or his may stand in need of all he can gather.

25   *Answer*—This very argument Solomon uses to persuade to liberality, "Cast thy bread upon the waters"[5] and "for thou know not what evil may come upon the land."[6] "Make your friends of the riches of iniquity."[7] You will ask how this shall be? Very well. For first he that gives to the poor, lends to the Lord and He will repay him even in this life a hundred fold to him or his—The righteous is ever
30   merciful and lends and his seed enjoys the blessing; and besides we know what advantage it will be to us in the day of account when many such witnesses shall stand forth for us to witness the improvement of our talent. And I would know

---

[3]I Timothy 5:8
[4]Ecclesiastes 2:14
[5]Ecclesiastes 11:1
[6]Ecclesiastes 11:2
[7]Luke 16:9

of those who plead so much for laying up for time to come, whether they hold that to be Gospel, "Lay not up for yourselves treasures upon Earth,"[8] etc. If they acknowledge it, what extent will they allow it? If only to those primitive times, let them consider the reason whereupon our Savior grounds it. The first is that they are subject to the moth, the rust, the thief. Secondly, they will steal away 5 the heart; where the treasure is there will the heart be also. The reasons are of like force at all times. Therefore the exhortation must be general and perpetual, with always in respect of the love and affection to riches and in regard of the things themselves when any special service for the church or particular distress of our brother do call for the use of them; otherwise it is not only lawful but 10 necessary to lay up as Joseph did to have ready upon such occasions, as the Lord (whose stewards we are of them) shall call for them from us. Christ gives us an instance of the first when he sent his disciples for the ass, and bids them answer the owner thus, "the Lord has need of him." So when the Tabernacle was to be built, He sends to his people to call for their silver and gold, etc.; and yields them 15 no other reason but that it was for His work. When Elisha comes to the widow of Sareptah and finds her preparing to make ready her pittance for herself and family, he bids her first provide for him, he challenges first God's part which she must first give before she must serve her own family.[9] All these teach us that the Lord looks that when he is pleased to call for his right in any thing we 20 have, our own Interest we have must stand aside till his turn be served. For the other, we need look no further than to that of I John: "He who has this world's goods and sees his brother to need and shuts up his compassion from him, how dwell the love of God in him,"[10] which comes punctually to this conclusion: if our brother be in want and you can't help him, you need not make doubt what 25 you should do; if you love God you must help him.

Question—What rule must we observe in lending?

Answer—You must observe whether your brother has present, or probable, or possible means of re-paying you; if there be none of these, you must give him according to his necessity, rather than lend him as he requires. If he has present 30 means of re-paying you, you are to look at him not as an act of mercy, but by way of commerce, wherein you are to walk by the rule of justice; but if his means of re-paying you be only probable or possible, then is he an object of your mercy, you must lend him, though there be danger of losing it, "If any of thy brethren be poor," etc., "thou shall lend him sufficient."[11] That men might not shift off 35

---

[8]Matthew 6:19–21
[9]I Kings 17
[10]I John 3:17
[11]Deuteronomy 15:7

this duty by the apparent hazard, He tells them that though the year of Jubilee were at hand (when he must remit it, if he were not able to repay it before) yet he must lend him and that cheerfully: "It may not grieve thee to give him" says He; and because some might object, "why so I should soon impoverish myself and my family," He adds "with all your work," etc.; for our Savior, "From him that would borrow of thee turn not away."[12]

Question—What rule must we observe in forgiving?

Answer—Whether you did lend by way of commerce or in mercy, if he have nothing to pay, you must forgive (except in cause where you have a surety or a lawful pledge). Every seventh year the creditor was to quit that which he lent to his brother if he were poor as appears—"save when there shall be no poor with thee."[13] In all these and like cases, Christ was a general rule, "Whatsoever you would that men do to you, do you the same to them also."[14]

Question—What rule must we observe and walk by in cause of community of peril?

Answer—The same as before, but with more enlargement towards others and less respect towards ourselves and our own right. Hence it was that in the primitive Church they sold all, had all things in common, neither did any man say that which he possessed was his own. Likewise in their return out of the Captivity, because the work was great for the restoring of the church and the danger of enemies was common to all, Nehemiah exhorts the Jews to liberality and readiness in remitting their debts to their brethren, and disposing liberally of his own to such as wanted, and stand not upon his own due, which he might have demanded of them. Thus did some of our forefathers in times of persecution in England, and so did many of the faithful of other churches, whereof we keep an honorable remembrance of them; and it is to be observed that both in Scriptures and later stories of the churches that such as have been most bountiful to the poor saints, especially in these extraordinary times and occasions, God has left them highly commended to posterity, as Zaccheus,[15] Cornelius,[16] Dorcas,[17] Bishop Hooper,[18] the Cutler of Brussells[19] and diverse others. Observe again that the Scripture give no cause to restrain any from be-

---

[12]Matthew 5:42

[13]Deuteronomy 15:2–8

[14]Matthew 5:42

[15]Luke 19

[16]Acts 10

[17]Acts 9

[18]John Hooper, Bishop of Worcester, was martyred in 1555 for his faith by Queen Mary I.

[19]Giles Tillerman, a cutler (knife-maker), was martyred in 1544 at Brussels for his faith.

ing over liberal this way; but all men to the liberal and cheerful practice hereof
by the sweetest promises; as to instance one for many

> Is not this the fast I have chosen to loose the bonds of wickedness, to
> take off the heavy burdens, to let the oppressed go free and to break
> every yoke, to deal the bread to the hungry and to bring the poor that   5
> wander into your house, when you see the naked to cover them. And
> then shall the light break forth as the morning, and your health shall
> grow speedily, your righteousness shall go before God, and the glory
> of the Lord shall embrace you; then you shall call and the Lord shall
> answer you.... If you pour out thy soul to the hungry, then shall the   10
> light spring out in darkness, and the Lord shall guide you continually,
> and satisfy the soul in draught, and make fat the bones, you shall be
> like a watered garden, and they shall be of you that shall build the old
> waste places. [20]

On the contrary, most heavy curses are laid upon such as are straightened   15
towards the Lord and His people, "Curse you Meroshe because you came not to
help the Lord...."[21] "He who shuts his ears from hearing the cry of the poor, he
shall cry and shall not be heard."[22] "Go you cursed into everlasting fire.... I was
hungry and you fed me not."[23] "He that sows sparingly shall reap sparingly." [24]

Having already set forth the practice of mercy according to the rule of   20
God's law, it will be useful to lay open the grounds of it also, being the other
part of the Commandment, and that is the affection from which this exercise
of mercy must arise. The Apostle tells us that this love is the fulfilling of the
law, not that it is enough to love our brother and go no further; but in regard
of the excellency of his parts giving any motion to the other as the soul to the   25
body and the power it has to set all the faculties on work in the outward exercise
of this duty. As when we bid one make the clock strike, he does not lay hand
on the hammer, which is the immediate instrument of the sound, but sets on
work the first mover or main wheel, knowing that will certainly produce the
sound which he intends. So the way to draw men to works of mercy is not by   30
force of argument from the goodness or necessity of the work; for though this
course may enforce a rational mind to some present act of mercy, as is frequent
in experience, yet it cannot work such a habit in a soul as shall make it prompt
upon all occasions to produce the same effect, but by framing these affections

---

[20]Isaiah 58:6–12
[21]Judges 5:23
[22]Proverbs 21:13
[23]Matthew 25:41–42
[24]II Corinthians 9:6

of love in the heart which will as natively bring forth the other, as any cause does produce effect.

The definition which the Scripture gives us of love is this: "Love is the bond of perfection."[25] First, it is a bond or ligament. Secondly it makes the work perfect. There is no body but consists of parts and that which knit these parts together, gives the body its perfection, because it makes each part so contiguous to others as thereby they do mutually participate with each other, both in strength and infirmity, in pleasure and pain. To instance in the most perfect of all bodies: Christ and his church make one body. The several parts of this body, considered a part before they were united, were as disproportionate and as much disordering as so many contrary qualities or elements, but when Christ comes and by his spirit and love knits all these parts to himself and each to other, it is become the most perfect and best proportioned body in the world. "Christ, by whom all the body being knit together by every joint for the furniture thereof, according to the effectual power which is in the measure of every perfection of parts,"[26] "a glorious body without spot or wrinkle,"[27] the ligaments hereof being Christ, or his love, for Christ is love.[28] So this definition is right: "Love is the bond of perfection."

From hence we may frame these conclusions. First of all, true Christians are one body in Christ, "You are the body of Christ and members of their part."[29] Secondly, the ligaments of this body which knit together are love. Thirdly, no body can be perfect which wants its proper ligament. Fourthly, all the parts of this body being thus united are made so contiguous in a special relation as they must needs partake of each other's strength and infirmity: joy and sorrow, wealth and woe. "If one member suffers, all suffer with it, if one be in honor, all rejoice with it."[30] Fifthly, this sensibleness and sympathy of each other's conditions will necessarily infuse into each part a native desire and endeavor to strengthen, defend, preserve, and comfort the other.

To insist a little on this conclusion being the product of all the former, the truth hereof will appear both by precept and pattern. "You ought to lay down your lives for the brethren."[31] "Bear you one another's burdens and so fulfill the law of Christ."[32] For patterns we have that first of our Savior who out of his

---

[25]Colossians 3:14
[26]Ephesians 4:15–16
[27]Ephesians 5:27
[28]I John 4:8
[29]I Corinthians 12:27
[30]I Corinthians 12:26
[31]John 3:10
[32]Galatians 6:2

good will in obedience to his father, becoming a part of this body, and being knit with it in the bond of love, found such a native sensibleness of our infirmities and sorrows as he willingly yielded himself to death to ease the infirmities of the rest of his body, and so held their sorrows. From the like sympathy of parts did the Apostles and many thousands of the saints lay down their lives for Christ. Again, the like we may see in the members of this body among themselves. Paul could have been contented to have been separated from Christ, that the Jews might not be cut off from the body.[33] It is very observable what he professes of his affectionate partaking with every member: "who is weak" says he "and I am not weak? Who is offended and I burn not;"[34] and again, "therefore we are comforted because you were comforted."[35] Of Epaphroditus he speaks that he regarded not his own life to do him service.[36] So Phebe and others are called the servants of the church.[37] Now it is apparent that they served not for wages, or by constraint, but out of love. The like we shall find in the histories of the church in all ages, the sweet sympathy of affections which was in the members of this body one towards another, their cheerfulness in serving and suffering together, how liberal they were without repining, harborers without grudging and helpful without reproaching; and all from hence, because they had fervent love amongst them, which only make the practice of mercy constant and easy.

The next consideration is how this love comes to be wrought. Adam in his first estate was a perfect model of mankind in all their generations, and in him this love was perfected in regard of the habit. But Adam rent himself from his Creator, rent all his posterity also one from another; whence it comes that every man is born with this principle in him, to love and seek himself only, and thus a man continues till Christ comes and takes possession of the soul and infuses another principle, love to God and our brother. And this latter having continual supply from Christ, as the head and root by which he is united, gets the predomining in the soul, so by little and little expels the former. "Love comes of God and everyone that loves is born of God,"[38] so that this love is the fruit of the new birth, and none can have it but the new Creature. Now when this quality is thus formed in the souls of men, it works like the Spirit upon the dry bones. Ezek. 37: "Bone came to bone."[39] It gathers together the scattered bones, or perfect old man Adam, and knits them into one body again in Christ, whereby a man is become again a living soul.

[33]Romans 9
[34]II Corinthians 11:29
[35]II Corinthians 7:13
[36]Philippians 2:30
[37]Romans 16:1, 27
[38]I John 4:7
[39]Ezekiel 37:7

The third consideration is concerning the exercise of this love which is two-
fold, inward or outward. The outward has been handled in the former preface of
this discourse. For unfolding the other we must take in our way that maxim of
philosophy *Simile simili gaudet*, or like will do like; for as it is things which are
turned with disaffection to each other, the ground of it is from a dissimilitude arising from the contrary or different nature of the things themselves; for the ground
of love is an apprehension of some resemblance in things loved to that which
affects it. This is the cause why the Lord loves the creature, so far as it has any of
his Image in it; he loves his elect because they are like himself, he beholds them
in his beloved son. So a mother loves her child, because she thoroughly conceives
a resemblance of herself in it. Thus it is between the members of Christ. Each
discerns, by the works of the Spirit, his own Image and resemblance in another,
and therefore cannot but love him as he loves himself. Now when the soul, which
is of a sociable nature, finds anything like to itself, it is like Adam when Eve was
brought to him. She must have it one with herself. This is flesh of my flesh (says
the soul) and bone of my bone. She conceives a great delight in it, therefore she
desires nearness and familiarity with it. She has a great propensity to do it good and
receives such content in it, as fearing the miscarriage of her beloved, she bestows
it in the inmost closet of her heart. She will not endure that it shall want any
good which she can give it. If by occasion she be withdrawn from the company
of it, she is still looking towards the place where she left her beloved. If she heard
it groan, she is with it presently. If she find it sad and disconsolate, she sighs and
moans with it. She has no such joy as to see her beloved merry and thriving. If
she see it wronged, she cannot hear it without passion. She sets no bounds to
her affections, nor has any thought of reward. She finds recompense enough in
the exercise of her love towards it. We may see this acted to life in Jonathan and
David. Jonathan, a valiant man, endowed with the spirit of Christ, so soon as
he discovers the same spirit in David had presently his heart knit to him by this
ligament of love, so that it is said he loved him as his own soul. He takes so great
pleasure in him, that he strips himself to adorn his beloved. His father's kingdom
was not so precious to him as his beloved David. David shall have it with all his
heart, himself desires no more but that he may be near to him to rejoice in his
good. He chooses to converse with him in the wilderness even to the hazard of
his own life, rather than with the great courtiers in his father's palace. When he
sees danger towards him, he spares neither rare pains nor peril to direct it. When
injury was offered his beloved David, he would not bear it, though from his own
father; and when they must part for a season only, they thought their hearts would
have broke for sorrow, had not their affections found vent by abundance of tears.
Other instances might be brought to show the nature of this affection, as of Ruth
and Naomi, and many others; but this truth is cleared enough.

If any shall object that it is not possible that love should be bred or upheld without hope of requital, it is granted; but that is not our cause; for this love is always under reward. It never gives, but it always receives with advantage; first, in regard that among the members of the same body, love and affection are reciprocal in a most equal and sweet kind of commerce. Secondly, in regard of the pleasure and content that the exercise of love carries with it, as we may see in the natural body. The mouth is at all the pains to receive and mince the food which serves for the nourishment of all the other parts of the body, yet it has no cause to complain; for first the other parts send back by several passages a due proportion of the same nourishment, in a better form for the strengthening and comforting the mouth. Secondly the labor of the mouth is accompanied with such pleasure and content as far exceeds the pains it takes. So is it in all the labor of love among Christians. First, the party loving reaps love again, as was showed before, which the soul covets more than all the wealth in the world. Secondly, nothing yields more pleasure and content to the soul than when it finds that which it may love fervently, for to love and live beloved is the soul's paradise, both here and in heaven. In the state of wedlock there be many comforts to bear out the troubles of that condition; but let such as have tried the most say if there be any sweetness in that condition comparable to the exercise of mutual love.

From former considerations arise these conclusions.

First, this love among Christians is a real thing, not imaginary.

Secondly, this love is as absolutely necessary to the being of the body of Christ, as the sinews and other ligaments of a natural body are to the being of that body.

Thirdly, this love is a divine, spiritual nature free, active, strong, courageous, permanent; undervaluing all things beneath its proper object; and of all the graces, this makes us nearer to resemble the virtues of our heavenly father.

Fourthly, it rests in the love and welfare of its beloved. For the full and certain knowledge of these truths concerning the nature, use, and excellency of this grace, that which the Holy Ghost has left recorded may give full satisfaction,[40] which is needful for every true member of this lovely body of the Lord Jesus, to work upon their hearts by prayer, meditation, continual exercise at least of the special [influence] of this grace, till Christ be formed in them and they in him, all in each other, knit together by this bond of love.

It rests now to make some application of this discourse by the present design, which gave the occasion of writing of it. Herein are four things to be propounded: first the persons, secondly the work, thirdly the end, fourthly the means.

---

[40]I Corinthians 13

Firstly, for the persons. We are a company professing our selves fellow members of Christ, in which respect only though we were absent from each other many miles, and had our employments as far distant, yet we ought to account ourselves knit together by this bond of love, and live in the exercise of it, if we would have comfort of our being in Christ. This was notorious in the practice of the Christians in former times; as is testified of the Waldenses, from the mouth of one of the adversaries, Æneas Sylvius, "mutuo [ament] penè antequam norunt"—they used to love any of their own religion even before they were acquainted with them.

Secondly, for the work we have in hand. It is by a mutual consent, through a special overvaluing providence and a more than an ordinary approbation of the churches of Christ, to seek out a place of co-habitation and consortship under a due form of government both civil and ecclesiastical. In such cases as this, the care of the public must oversway all private respects, by which, not only conscience, but mere civil policy, does bind us. For it is a true rule that particular estates cannot subsist in the ruin of the public.

Thirdly, the end is to improve our lives to do more service to the Lord; the comfort and increase of the body of Christ whereof we are members; that ourselves and posterity may be the better preserved from the common corruptions of this evil world, to serve the Lord and work out our Salvation under the power and purity of His holy ordinances.

Fourthly, for the means whereby this must be effected. They are twofold, a conformity with the work and end we aim at. These we see are extraordinary, therefore we must not content ourselves with usual ordinary means. Whatsoever we did or ought to have done when we lived in England, the same must we do, and more also, where we go. That which the most in their churches maintain as a truth in profession only, we must bring into familiar and constant practice, as in this duty of love. We must love brotherly without dissimulation; we must love one another with a pure heart fervently. We must bear one another's burdens. We must not look only on our own things, but also on the things of our brethren, neither must we think that the Lord will bear with such failings at our hands as he does from those among whom we have lived; and that for three reasons.

Firstly, in regard of the more near bond of marriage between Him and us, wherein He has taken us to be His after a most strict and peculiar manner, which will make Him the more jealous of our love and obedience. So He tells the people of Israel, you only have I known of all the families of the Earth, therefore will I punish you for your transgressions. Secondly, because the Lord will be sanctified in them that come near Him. We know that there were many that corrupted the service of the Lord, some setting up altars before His own, others offering both strange fire and strange sacrifices also; yet there came no fire from heaven or other sudden judgment upon them, as did upon Nadab and Abihu, who yet we may think did not sin presumptuously. Thirdly, when God gives a special commission He looks to have it strictly observed in every article. When He gave Saul a commission to destroy Amaleck, He indented with him upon certain articles, and because he failed in one of the least, and that upon a fair pretence, it lost him the kingdom which should have been his reward if he had observed his commission.

Thus stands the cause between God and us. We are entered into covenant with Him for this work. We have taken out a commission, the Lord has given us leave to draw our own articles. We have professed to enterprise these actions, upon these and those ends, we have hereupon besought Him of favor and blessing. Now if the Lord shall please to hear us, and bring us in peace to the place we desire, then has He ratified this covenant and sealed our commission, [and] will expect a strict performance of the articles contained in it; but if we shall neglect the observation of these articles which are the ends we have propounded, and, dissembling without God, shall fall to embrace this present world and prosecute our carnal intentions, seeking great things for ourselves and our posterity, the Lord will surely break out in wrath against us; be revenged of such a perjured people, and make us know the price of the breach of such a covenant.

Now the only way to avoid this shipwreck, and to provide for our posterity, is to follow the counsel of Micah to do justly, to love mercy, to walk humbly with our God.[41] For this end, we must be knit together in this work as one man. We must entertain each other in brotherly affection, we must be willing to abridge ourselves of our superfluities for the supply of others necessities. We must uphold a familiar commerce together in all meekness, gentleness, patience, and liberality. We must delight in each other, make other's conditions our own, rejoice together, mourn together, labor and suffer together, always having before our eyes our commission and community in the work, our community as members of the same body. So shall we keep the unity of the spirit in the bond of peace. The Lord will be our God, and delight to dwell among us as His own people, and will command a blessing upon us in all our ways, so that we shall see much more of His wisdom, power, goodness, and truth than formerly we have been acquainted with. We shall find that the God of Israel is among us when ten of us shall be able to resist a thousand of our enemies; when He shall make us a praise and glory that men shall say of succeeding plantations, "the Lord make it like that of NEW ENGLAND," For we must consider that we shall be as a city upon a hill. The eyes of all people are upon us, so that if we shall

---

[41]Micah 6:8

deal falsely with our God in this work we have undertaken, and so cause Him to withdraw His present help from us, we shall be made a story and a by-word through the world. We shall open the mouths of enemies to speak evil of the ways of God, and all professors for God's sake. We shall shame the faces of many
5   of God's worthy servants, and cause their prayers to be turned into curses upon us till we be consumed out of the good land whither we are going.

And to shut up this discourse with that exhortation of Moses, that faithful servant of the Lord, in his last farewell to Israel.[42] Beloved, there is now set before us life and good, death and evil, in that we are commanded this day to
10 love the Lord our God, and to love one another, to walk in His ways and to keep his commandments and His ordinance and His laws, and the articles of our covenant with Him, that we may live and be multiplied, and that the Lord our God may bless us in the land whither we go to possess it. But if our hearts shall turn away, so that we will not obey, but shall be seduced, and worship
15 other gods, our pleasures and profits, and serve them; it is propounded unto us this day, we shall surely perish out of the good land whither we pass over this vast sea to possess it.

Therefore let us choose life, that we and our seed may live by obeying His voice and cleaving to Him, for He is our life and our prosperity.

---

[42]Deuteronomy 30

Speech to the General Court
John Winthrop (1588–1649)

Representative government was part of the New England Way from the beginning. Voters were termed "Freemen," a designation rooted in medieval England but having a special New England twist. In addition to being adult male property owners (and thus free, or independent of bondage to others), voters and office holders in Massachusetts Bay were required to be church members, which in effect certified that they were fit to uphold the covenant. The township was the basic unit of local government. Freemen in the towns elected Deputies to the General Court, the assembly charged with overseeing the commonwealth. Among the duties of the General Court was the annual election of a Governor.

John Winthrop was usually the Governor, often the watchdog of political orthodoxy, always the leading citizen of Boston. But even so prominent a man felt the effects of the "great questions that have troubled the country," which he defined as "the authority of the magistrates and the liberty of the people." In 1645 the General Court accused Winthrop of abusing his power by interfering in local matters. He was acquitted but humiliated, and he took the opportunity to speak to the Court about the fundamental problem of New England politics: liberty and authority in a covenantal culture.

1645

I suppose something may be expected from me upon this charge that is befallen me, which moves me to speak now to you; yet I intend not to intermeddle in the proceedings of the court, or with any of the persons concerned therein. Only I bless God that I see an issue of this troublesome business. I also acknowledge the justice of the court and, for mine own part, I am well satisfied, I was publicly charged, and I am publicly and legally acquitted, which is all I did expect or desire. And though this be sufficient for my justification before men, yet not so before the God, who has seen so much amiss in my dispensations (and

5

Robert C. Winthrop, *Life and Letters of John Winthrop* (Boston: Little, Brown and Company, 1869), II:339–42.

even in this affair) as calls me to be humble. For to be publicly and criminally charged in this court is matter of humiliation (and I desire to make a right use of it), notwithstanding I be thus acquitted. If her father had spit in her face (says the Lord concerning Miriam) should she not have been ashamed seven days?[1] Shame had lien upon her, whatever the occasion had been. I am unwilling to stay you from your urgent affairs, yet give me leave (upon this special occasion) to speak a little more to this assembly. It may be of some good use to inform and rectify the judgments of some of the people, and may prevent such distempers as have arisen amongst us.

The great questions that have troubled the country are about the authority of the magistrates and the liberty of the people. It is yourselves who have called us to this office, and being called by you, we have our authority from God, in way of an ordinance, such as has the image of God eminently stamped upon it, the contempt and violation whereof had been vindicated with examples of divine vengeance. I entreat you to consider that when you choose magistrates, you take them from among yourselves, men subject to like passions as you are. Therefore when you see infirmities in us, you should reflect upon your own, and that would make you bear the more with us, and not be severe censurers of the failings of your magistrates when you have continual experience of the like infirmities in yourselves and others.

We account him a good servant who breaks not his covenant. The covenant between you and us is the oath you have taken of us, which is to this purpose, that we shall govern you and judge your causes by the rules of God's laws and our own, according to our best skill. When you agree with a workman to build you a ship or house, etc., he undertakes as well for his skill as for his faithfulness, for it is his profession, and you pay him for both. But when you call one to be a magistrate, he does not profess nor undertake to have sufficient skill for that office, nor can you furnish him with gifts, etc., therefore you must run the hazard of his skill and ability. But if he fails in faithfulness, which by his oath he is bound unto, that he must answer for. If it fall out that the case be clear to common apprehension, and the rule clear also, if he transgress here, the error is not in the skill, but in the evil of the will: it must be required of him. But if the case be doubtful, or the rule doubtful, to men of such understanding and parts as your magistrates are, if your magistrates should err here, yourselves must bear it.

For the other point concerning liberty, I observe a great mistake in the country about that. There is a two-fold liberty, natural (I mean as our nature is now corrupt) and civil or federal. The first is common to man with beasts and other creatures. By this, man, as he stands in relation to man simply, has liberty

---

[1] Numbers 12:14

to do what he lists; it is a liberty to evil as well as to good. This liberty is incompatible and inconsistent with authority, and cannot endure the least restraint of the most just authority. The exercise and maintaining of this liberty makes men grow more evil, and in time to be worse than brute beasts: *omnes sumus licentiâ deteriores.*[2] This is that great enemy of truth and peace, that wild beast, which all the ordinances of God are bent against, to restrain and subdue it.

    The other kind of liberty I call civil or federal; it may also be termed moral, in reference to the covenant between God and man, in the moral law, and the politic covenants and constitutions amongst men themselves. This liberty is the proper end and object of authority, and cannot subsist without it; and it is a liberty to that only which is good, just, and honest. This liberty you are to stand for, with the hazard not only of your goods, but of your lives, if need be. Whatsoever crosses this is not authority, but a distemper thereof. This liberty is maintained and exercised in a way of subjection to authority; it is of the same kind of liberty wherewith Christ has made us free. The woman's own choice makes such a man her husband; yet being so chosen, he is her lord, and she is to be subject to him, yet in a way of liberty, not of bondage; and a true wife accounts her subjection her honor and freedom, and would not think her condition safe and free but in her subjection to her husband's authority. Such is the liberty of the church under the authority of Christ, her king and husband; his yoke is so easy and sweet to her as a bride's ornaments; and if through forwardness or wantonness, etc., she shake it off at any time, she is at no rest in her spirit until she takes it up again; and whether her lord smiles upon her and embraces her in his arms, or whether he frowns, or rebukes, or smites her, she apprehends the sweetness of his love in all, and is refreshed, supported, and instructed by every such dispensation of his authority over her. On the other side, you know who they are that complain of this yoke and say, let us break their bands, etc., we will not have this man to rule over us. Even so, brethren, it will be between you and your magistrates. If you stand for your natural corrupt liberties, and will do what is good in your own eyes, you will not endure the least weight of authority, but will murmur, and oppose, and be always striving to shake off that yoke; but if you will be satisfied to enjoy such civil and lawful liberties such as Christ allows you, then will you quietly and cheerfully submit unto that authority which is set over you, in all the administrations of it, for your good. Wherein, if we fail at any time, we hope we shall be willing (by God's assistance) to hearken to good advice from any of you, or in any other way of God; so shall your liberties be preserved, in upholding the honor and power of authority amongst you.

---

[2]"We all degenerate in the absence of control." Publius Terentius Afer, *Heauton Timorumenos* III, I:74.

Capital Lawes

In December 1641, the General Court approved a code of laws compiled by Nathaniel Ward (1578–1652), the minister of Ipswich. Ward was concerned that the Massachusetts Bay leadership tended to exercise authority arbitrarily. This "Body of Liberties" detailed offenses and punishments for all members of the community, and thus was a significant step in defining the Puritan understanding of the rule of law.

Ward was not alone in being suspicious of political power and the men who held it. John Cotton (1585–1652), the Bay Colony's most influential preacher, said, "Let all the world learn to give mortal men no greater power than they are content they shall use—for use it they will." Puritans checked power by a congregational form of church government and by granting most local political authority to the towns. They also relied on the family to provide nurture and good order and insulated the family from encroachments by church or state.

Ward drew much of the Body of Liberties from Scripture and especially from the Law of Moses (the Pentateuch). In 1647 the Bay Colony incorporated his work into a larger organic document, "The Laws and Liberties of Massachusetts," which served as a constitution for many years. The following selection, the "Capital Lawes," includes specific biblical references in support of the crimes prohibited and is a good illustration of the Puritans' devotion to Scripture, law, and the fundamental institutions of society.

1647

1. If any man, after legal conviction shall HAVE OR WORSHIP any other God, but the LORD GOD, he shall be put to death. Exod.22, 20. Deut. 13.6 & 10. Deut. 17 2. 6.

2. If any man or woman be a WITCH, that is, hath or consulteth with a familiar spirit, they shall be put to death. Exod. 22. 18. Levit. 20. 27. Deut. 18. 10. 11.   5

Colonial Origins of the American Constitution: A Documentary History, Donald S. Lutz, ed. (Indianapolis, IN: Liberty Fund, 1998), 102–3.

3. If any person within this Jurisdiction whether Christian or Pagan shall wittingly and willingly presume to BLASPHEME the holy Name of God, Father, Son or Holy-Ghost, with direct, expresse, presumptuous, or highhanded blasphemy, either by wilfull or obstinate denying the true God, or his Creation, or Government of the world: or shall curse God in like manner, or reproach the holy religion of God as if it were but a politick device to keep ignorant men in awe; or shal utter any other kinde of Blasphemy of the like nature & degree they shall be put to death. Levit. 24. 15. 16.

4. If any person shall commit any wilful MURTHER, which is Man-slaughter, committed upon premeditate malice, hatred, or crueltie not in a mans necessary and just defence, nor by meer casualty against his will, he shall be put to death. Exod. 21. 12. 13. Numb. 35. 31.

5. If any person slayeth another suddenly in his ANGER, OR CRUELTY of passion, he shall be put to death. Levit. 24. 17. Numb. 35. 20. 21.

6. If any person shall slay another through guile, either by POYSONING, or other such devilish practice, he shall be put to death. Exod. 21. 14.

7. If any man or woman shall LYE WITH ANY BEAST, or bruit creature, by carnall copulation; they shall surely be put to death: and the beast shall be slain, & buried, and not eaten. Lev. 20. 15. 16.

8. If any man LYETH WITH MAN-KINDE as he lieth with a woman, both of them have committed abomination, they both shal surely be put to death:unles the one partie were forced (or be under fourteen years of age in which case he shall be severely punished) Levit. 20. 13.

9. If any person commit ADULTERIE with a married or espoused wife; the Adulterer & Adulteress shall surely be put to death. Lev. 20. 19. & 18. 20 Deu. 22. 23. 27.

10. If any man STEALETH A MAN, or Man-kinde, he shall surely be put to death. Exodus 21. 16.

11. If any man rise up by FALSE-WITNES wittingly and of purpose to take away any mans life: he shal be put to death. Deut. 19. 16. 18. 16.

12. If any man shall CONSPIRE, and attempt any Invasion, Insurrection, or publick Rebellion against our Common-Wealth: or shall indeavour to surprize any town, or Townes, Fort, or Forts therin; or shall treacherously, & perfidiously attempt the Alteration and Subversion of our frame of Politie, or Government fundamentally he shall be put to death. Numb. 16. 2. Sam. 3. 2 Sam. 18. 2 Sam. 20.

13. If any child, or children, above sixteen years old, and of sufficient understanding, shall CURSE, OR SMITE their natural FATHER , OR MOTHER; he or
they shall be put to death: unless it can be sufficiently testified that the
Parents have been very unchristianly negligent in the education of such
children; or so provoked them by extream, and cruel correction: that they   5
have been forced therunto to preserve themselves from death or maiming.
Exod. 21. 17. Lev. 20.9. Exod. 21. 15.

14. If a man have a stubborn or REBELLIOUS SON, of sufficient years & understanding (viz) sixteen years of age, which will not obey the voice of
his Father, or the voice of his Mother, and that when they have chastened   10
him will not harken unto them: then shal his Father & Mother being his
natural parents, lay hold on him, & bring him to the Magistrates assembled
in Court & testifie unto them, that their Son is stubborn & rebellious &
will not obey their voice and chastisement, but lives in sundry notorious
crimes, such a son shal be put to death. Deut. 21. 20. 21   15

15. If any man shal RAVISH any maid or single woman, comitting carnal copulation with her by force, against her own will; that is above the age of ten
years he shal be punished either with death, or with some other greivous
punishment according to circumstances as the Judges, or General court
shal determin[e]....   20

FRAME OF GOVERNMENT
OF PENNSYLVANIA

William Penn (1644–1718) acquired what became Pennsylvania because of his, and especially his father's, loyalty to the Stuart King Charles II. He founded a colony that, because of proprietary rights, allowed him to dictate its constitution. The Frame of Government *outlined Penn's plans for a "holy experiment" granting religious toleration to everyone who believed in God, broad representation for freemen, separation of powers, a bill of rights, and free economic development. Pennsylvania attracted 23,000 Quakers from the north midlands of England and welcomed thousands of Germans and other Europeans. Philadelphia became the symbol of America as the "Land of Opportunity."*

Penn was a member of the Society of Friends (Quakers) who was himself persecuted for his beliefs. Although this experience seemed to him to call for toleration, he also affirmed the Greco-Roman (the one, the few, and the many; the rule of law) and the Christian (the divine origin of government) traditions in defining the purposes of government: "To support power in reverence with the people, and to secure the people from the abuse of power."

While the Frame of Government *expressed Penn's political theory, the* Laws Agreed Upon in England *(often referred to as the* Charter of Liberties*) gave expression to the more concrete "rights of Englishmen"—consent (especially to taxation, trial by jury, and Common Law guarantees against arbitrary deprivations of life, liberty, and property). Seventeenth-century Englishmen traced these back to Magna Carta, and every American colony had a charter with similar provisions.*

Francis Newton Thorpe, ed., *The Federal and State Constitution, Colonial Charters, and Other Organic Laws of the States, Territories, and Colonies Now or Heretofore Forming the United States of America* (Washington, DC: Government Printing Office, 1909), V:3052–54, 2059–63 [modernized].

5 MAY 1682

The frame of the government of the province of Pennsylvania, in America: together with certain laws agreed upon in England by the Governor and diverse freemen of the aforesaid province. To be further explained and confirmed there by the first provincial council that shall be held, if they see meet.

The Preface

5   When the great and wise God had made the world, of all his creatures, it pleased him to choose man his deputy to rule it; and to fit him for so great a charge and trust, he did not only qualify him with skill and power, but with integrity to use them justly. This native goodness was equally his honor and his happiness; and while he stood here, all went well; there was no need of coercive or compulsive
10   means; the precept of divine love and truth, in his bosom, was the guide and keeper of his innocency. But lust, prevailing against duty, made a lamentable breach upon it; and the law that before had no power over him took place upon him, and his dis-obedient posterity, that such as would not live conformable to the holy law within should fall under the reproof and correction of the just
15   law without, in a judicial administration.

This the Apostle teaches in diverse of his epistles: "The law (says he) was added because of transgression."[1] In another place, "Knowing that the law was not made for the righteous man, but for the dis-obedient and ungodly, for sinners, for unholy and profane, for murderers, for whoremongers, for them that
20   defile themselves with mankind, and for man-stealers, for liars, for perjured persons,"[2] etc., but this is not all; he opens and carries the matter of government a little further: "Let every soul be subject to the higher powers, for there is no power but of God. The powers that be are ordained of God: whosoever therefore resists the power, resists the ordinance of God. For rulers are not a
25   terror to good works, but to evil. Will you then not be afraid of the power? Do that which is good, and you shall have praise of the same." "He is the minister of God to you for good." "Wherefore you must needs be subject, not only for wrath, but for conscience sake."[3]

This settles the divine right of government beyond exception, and that for
30   two ends: first, to terrify evil doers. Secondly, to cherish those that do well; which gives government a life beyond corruption, and makes it as durable in the world as good men shall be. So that government seems to me a part of religion itself, a thing sacred in its institution and end. For, if it does not directly

---

[1]Romans 5:20
[2]I Timothy 1:9
[3]Romans 13:1–5

remove the cause, it crushes the effects of evil, and is as such (though a lower, yet) an emanation of the same Divine Power that is both author and object of pure religion; the difference lying here, that the one is more free and mental, the other more corporal and compulsive in its operations. But that is only to evil doers; government itself being otherwise as capable of kindness, goodness, 5 and charity as a more private society. They weakly err that think there is no other use of government than correction, which is the coarsest part of it. Daily experience tells us that the care and regulation of many other affairs, more soft and daily necessary, make up much of the greatest part of government; and which must have followed the peopling of the world, had Adam never fell, and 10 will continue among men, on earth, under the highest attainments they may arrive at, by the coming of the blessed Second Adam, the Lord from heaven. Thus much of government in general, as to its rise and end.

For particular frames and models, it will become me to say little; and comparatively I will say nothing. My reasons are: 15

First. That the age is too nice and difficult for it; there being nothing the wits of men are more busy and divided upon. It is true, they seem to agree to the end, to wit, happiness; but, in the means, they differ, as to divine, so to his human felicity; and the cause is much the same, not always want of light and knowledge, but want of using them rightly. 20 Men side with their passions against their reason, and their sinister interests have so strong a bias upon their minds that they lean to them against the good of the things they know.

Secondly. I do not find a model in the world that time, place, and some singular emergencies have not necessarily altered; nor is it easy to frame 25 a civil government that shall serve all places alike.

Thirdly. I know what is said by the several admirers of monarchy, aristocracy, and democracy, which are the rule of one, a few, and many, and are the three common ideas of government when men discourse on the subject. But I choose to solve the controversy with this small distinction, 30 and it belongs to all three: Any government is free to the people under it (whatever be the frame) where the laws rule, and the people are a party to those laws, and more than this is tyranny, oligarchy, or confusion.

But, lastly, when all is said, there is hardly one frame of government in the world so ill-designed by its first founders that, in good hands, would not do well 35 enough; and story tells us the best, in ill ones, can do nothing that is great or good; witness the Jewish and Roman states. Governments, like clocks, go from the motion men give them; and as governments are made and moved by men, so by them they are ruined, too. Wherefore governments rather depend upon men than men upon governments. Let men be good, and the government cannot be bad; if it be ill, they will cure it. But, if men be bad, let the government be never so good, they will endeavor to warp and spoil it to their turn.

I know some say, let us have good laws, and no matter for the men that execute them. But let them consider that though good laws do well, good men do better, for good laws may want good men, and be abolished or evaded by ill men; but good men will never want good laws, nor suffer ill ones. It is true, good laws have some awe upon ill ministers, but that is where they have not power to escape or abolish them, and the people are generally wise and good. But a loose and depraved people (which is the question) love laws and an administration like themselves. That, therefore, which makes a good constitution must keep it, *viz:* men of wisdom and virtue, qualities that, because they descend not with worldly inheritances, must be carefully propagated by a virtuous education of youth; for which after ages will owe more to the care and prudence of founders, and the successive magistracy, than to their parents for their private patrimonies.

These considerations of the weight of government, and the nice and various opinions about it, made it uneasy to me to think of publishing the ensuing frame and conditional laws, forseeing both the censures they will meet with, from men of differing humors and engagements, and the occasion they may give of discourse beyond my design.

But, next to the power of necessity (which is a solicitor that will take no denial), this induced me to a compliance, that we have (with reverence to God and good conscience to men) to the best of our skill, contrived and composed the frame and laws of this government, to the great end of all government, *viz:* To support power in reverence with the people, and to secure the people from the abuse of power; that they may be free by their just obedience, and the magistrates honorable, for their just administration. For liberty without obedience is confusion, and obedience without liberty is slavery. To carry this evenness is partly owing to the constitution, and partly to the magistracy. Where either of these fail, government will be subject to convulsions; but where both are wanting, it must be totally subverted; then where both meet, the government is like to endure, which I humbly pray and hope God will please to make the lot of this of Pennsylvania. Amen.

WILLIAM PENN...

Laws Agreed Upon in England, etc.

1. That the charter of liberties, declared, granted, and confirmed the five and twentieth day of the second month, called April, 1682, before diverse witnesses, by William Penn, Governor and chief proprietor of Pennsylvania, to all the freemen and planters of the said province, is hereby declared and approved, and shall be forever held for fundamental in the government 5 thereof, according to the limitations mentioned in the said charter.

2. That every inhabitant in the said province that is, or shall be, a purchaser of one hundred acres of land, or upwards, his heirs and assigns, and every person who shall have paid his passage and taken up one hundred acres of land at one penny an acre, and have cultivated ten acres thereof, and every 10 person that has been a servant or bonds-man, and is free by his service, that shall have taken up his fifty acres of land and cultivated twenty thereof, and every inhabitant, artificer, or other resident in the said province that pays scot and lot to the government shall be deemed and accounted a freeman of the said province. And every such person shall and may be capable of 15 electing, or being elected, representatives of the people, in provincial council, or General Assembly, in the said province.

3. That all elections of members or representatives of the people and freemen of the province of Pennsylvania to serve in provincial council, or General Assembly, to be held within the said province, shall be free and voluntary. 20 And that the elector that shall receive any reward or gift in meat, drink, monies, or otherwise shall forfeit his right to elect; and such person as shall directly or indirectly give, promise, or bestow any such reward as aforesaid to be elected shall forfeit his election, and be thereby incapable to serve as aforesaid. And the provincial council and General Assembly shall be the 25 sole judges of the regularity, or irregularity of the elections of their own respective members.

4. That no money or goods shall be raised upon, or paid by, any of the people of this province by way of public tax, custom, or contribution, but by a law for that purpose made; and whoever shall levy, collect, or pay any money 30 or goods contrary thereunto shall be held a public enemy to the province and a betrayer of the liberties of the people thereof.

5. That all courts shall be open, and justice shall neither be sold, denied, nor delayed.

6. That, in all courts all persons of all persuasions may freely appear in their own 35 way, and according to their own manner, and there personally plead their

own cause themselves; or, if unable, by their friends. And the first process shall be the exhibition of the complaint in court fourteen days before the trial; and that the party complained against may be fitted for the same, he or she shall be summoned no less than ten days before, and a copy of the complaint delivered him or her at his or her dwelling house. But before the complaint of any person be received, he shall solemnly declare in court that he believes, in his conscience, his cause is just.

7. That all pleadings, processes, and records in courts shall be short, and in English, and in an ordinary and plain character, that they may be understood and justice speedily administered.

8. That all trials shall be by twelve men, and as near as may be, peers or equals, and of the neighborhood, and men without just exception; in cases of life, there shall be first twenty-four returned by the sheriffs for a grand inquest, of whom twelve, at least, shall find the complaint to be true; and then the twelve men, or peers, to be likewise returned by the sheriff, shall have the final judgment. But reasonable challenges shall be always admitted against the said twelve men, or any of them.

9. That all fees in all cases shall be moderate, and settled by the provincial council, and General Assembly, and be hung up in a table in every respective court; and whosoever shall be convicted of taking more shall pay two-fold and be dismissed his employment; one moiety of which shall go to the party wronged.

10. That all prisons shall be work-houses for felons, vagrants, and loose and idle persons; whereof one shall be in every county.

11. That all prisoners shall be bailable by sufficient sureties, unless for capital offences, where the proof is evident, or the presumption great.

12. That all persons wrongfully imprisoned or prosecuted at law shall have double damages against the informer or prosecutor.

13. That all prisons shall be free as to fees, food, and lodging.

14. That all lands and goods shall be liable to pay debts, except where there is legal issue, and then all the goods, and one-third of the land only.

15. That all wills, in writing, attested by two witnesses, shall be of the same force as to lands as other conveyances, being legally proved within forty days, either within or without the said province.

16. That seven years quiet possession shall give an unquestionable right, except in cases of infants, lunatics, married women, or persons beyond the seas.

17. That all briberies and extortion whatsoever shall be severely punished.

18. That all fines shall be moderate, and saving men's contenements, merchandize, or wainage.

19. That all marriages (not forbidden by the law of God, as to nearness of blood and affinity by marriage) shall be encouraged; but the parents, or guardians, shall be first consulted, and the marriage shall be published before it be solemnized; and it shall be solemnized by taking one another as husband and wife, before credible witnesses; and a certificate of the whole, under the hands of parties and witnesses, shall be brought to the proper register of that county, and shall be registered in his office.

20. And, to prevent frauds and vexatious suits within the said province, that all charters, gifts, grants, and conveyances of (except leases for a year or under) and all bills, bonds, and specialties above five pounds, and not under three months, made in the said province, shall be enrolled, or registered in the public enrollment office of the said province, within the space of two months next after the making thereof, else to be void in law, and all deeds, grants, and conveyances of land (except as aforesaid) within the said province, and made out of the said province, shall be enrolled or registered, as aforesaid, within six months next after the making thereof, and settling and constituting an enrollment office or registry within the said province, else to be void in law against all persons whatsoever.

21. That all defacers or corrupters of charters, gifts, grants, bonds, bills, wills, contracts, and conveyances, or that shall deface or falsify any enrollment, registry, or record within this province shall make double satisfaction for the same; half whereof shall go to the party wronged, and they shall be dismissed of all places of trust and be publicly disgraced as false men.

22. That there shall be a register for births, marriages, burials, wills, and letters of administration, distinct from the other registry.

23. That there shall be a register for all servants, where their names, time, wages, and days of payment shall be registered.

24. That all lands and goods of felons shall be liable to make satisfaction to the party wronged twice the value; and for want of lands or goods, the felons shall be bondmen to work in the common prison, or work-house, or otherwise, till the party injured be satisfied.

25. That the estates of capital offenders, as traitors and murderers, shall go, one-third to the next of kin to the sufferer, and the remainder to the next of kin to the criminal.

26. That all witnesses, coming or called to testify their knowledge in or to any matter or thing, in any court or before any lawful authority within the said province, shall there give or deliver in their evidence or testimony by solemnly promising to speak the truth, the whole truth, and nothing but the truth to the matter or thing in question. And in case any person so called to evidence shall be convicted of willful falsehood, such person shall suffer and undergo such damage or penalty as the person, or persons, against whom he or she bore false witness did, or should, undergo; and shall also make satisfaction to the party wronged, and be publicly exposed as a false witness, never to be credited in any court, or before any magistrate, in the said province.

27. And, to the end that all officers chosen to serve within this province may, with more care and diligence, answer the trust reposed in them, it is agreed that no such person shall enjoy more than one public office at one time.

28. That all children within this province of the age of twelve years shall be taught some useful trade or skill, to the end none may be idle, but the poor may work to live, and the rich, if they become poor, may not want.

29. That servants be not kept longer than their time, and such as are careful be both justly and kindly used in their service, and put in fitting equipage at the expiration thereof, according to custom.

30. That all scandalous and malicious reporters, backbiters, defamers, and spreaders of false news, whether against magistrates or private persons, shall be accordingly severely punished as enemies to the peace and concord of this province.

31. That for the encouragement of the planters and traders in this province who are incorporated into a society, the patent granted to them by William Penn, Governor of the said province, is hereby ratified and confirmed....

33. That all factors or correspondents in the said province wronging their employers shall make satisfaction, and one-third over, to their said employers. And in case of the death of any such factor or correspondent, the committee of trade shall take care to secure so much of the deceased party's estate as belongs to his said respective employers.

34. That all treasurers, judges, masters of the rolls, sheriffs, justices of the peace, and other officers and persons whatsoever relating to courts, or trials of causes, or any other service in the government; and all members elected to serve in provincial council and General Assembly, and all that have right to elect such members, shall be such as possess faith in Jesus Christ, and that are not

convicted of ill fame, or un-sober and dis-honest conversation, and that are of one and twenty years of age, at least; and that all such so qualified shall be capable of the said several employments and privileges, as aforesaid.

35. That all persons living in this province who confess and acknowledge the one Almighty and eternal God to be the Creator, Upholder, and Ruler of the world, and that hold themselves obliged in conscience to live peaceably and justly in civil society, shall in no ways be molested or prejudiced for their religious persuasion, or practice in matters of faith and worship, nor shall they be compelled at any time to frequent or maintain any religious worship, place, or ministry whatever.

36. That, according to the good example of the primitive Christians, and the case of the creation, every first day of the week, called the Lord's Day, people shall abstain from their common daily labor that they may the better dispose themselves to worship God according to their understandings.

37. That as a careless and corrupt administration of justice draws the wrath of God upon magistrates, so the wildness and looseness of the people provoke the indignation of God against a country. Therefore, that all such offences against God as swearing, cursing, lying, profane talking, drunkenness, drinking of healths, obscene words, incest, sodomy, rapes, whoredom, fornication, and other uncleanness (not to be repeated), all treasons, misprisions, murders, duels, felony, seditions, maims, forcible entries, and other violences to the persons and estates of the inhabitants within this province; all prizes, stage-plays, cards, dice, May-games, gamesters, masques, revels, bull-baitings, cock-fightings, bear-baitings, and the like which excite the people to rudeness, cruelty, looseness, and irreligion, shall be respectively discouraged and severely punished, according to the appointment of the Governor and freemen in provincial council and General Assembly; as also all proceedings contrary to these laws, that are not here made expressly penal.

38. That a copy of these laws shall be hung up in the provincial council and in public courts of justice. And that they shall be read yearly at the opening of every provincial council and General Assembly and court of justice; and their assent shall be testified by their standing up after the reading thereof.

39. That there shall be at no time any alteration of any of these laws without the consent of the Governor, his heirs or assigns, and six parts of seven of the freemen, met in provincial council and General Assembly.

40. That all other matters and things not herein provided for which shall, and may, concern the public justice, peace, or safety of the said province; and

the raising and imposing taxes, customs, duties, or other charges whatsoever, shall be, and are, hereby referred to the order, prudence, and determination of the Governor and freemen, in provincial council and General Assembly, to be held, from time to time, in the said province.

THE SECRET DIARY
WILLIAM BYRD OF WESTOVER (1674–1744)

William Byrd of Westover profited greatly from the policies of Virginia's true founder, Sir William Berkeley (1605–1677). Berkeley recruited a royalist elite from the south and west of England, enticing them with huge grants of land and the prospect of respite from the Puritan control of England that followed the English Civil War. Berkeley envisioned a society that reflected the English countryside from which he came: royalist, Anglican, patriarchal, highly structured. He presided over the migration of 40,000 to 50,000 Englishmen between 1645 and 1670, most of them land-poor and of low position. William Byrd II rose to a position of high aristocracy in this setting. When he died, he had a library of almost 4,000 volumes and holdings in land of about 180,000 acres.

Byrd kept a diary for many years, in a shorthand that was not deciphered until the twentieth century. This selection, from November 1711, describes the daily activities of a Virginia aristocrat. His gambling (especially at cards and horses), dancing, drinking, and sex might seem both curiously modern and strangely anachronistic. But his self-revelation is necessary if we are to understand the political culture of the "Chesapeake Nation."

His dress, manners, command over "Tom" and others, and intimacy with relatives and rural neighbors may distract the reader from the structure of Virginia life. It was a hierarchy; it was also classical, sacramental, and based on a deep sense of responsibility for the good order of society. It would produce an idea of liberty quite different from that of New England, although having in common a devotion to the rule of law and representative government.

Louis B. Wright and Marion Tinling, eds., *The Secret Diary of William Byrd of Westover, 1709–1712* (Richmond, VA: Dietz Press, 1941), 431–47.

1 November 1711

I rose about 8 o'clock and read nothing because I had a great deal to say to my wife.[1] We sent some ducks and pigeons to the Governor[2] and my wife sent to Mrs. Dunn to come to her. I drank chocolate for breakfast and about 10 o'clock went to court but the Governor was not there. I sat till about 3 o'clock and
5 then went to my lodgings where I wrote in my journal till 4 o'clock, and then went to the Governor's to dinner and found my wife there. I ate venison pasty for dinner. In the evening we played at cards and I won. We put a trick [on] the Doctor, who left 10 shillings on the table and we took it when he turned his back and left it for the cards when we had done. About 10 o'clock we went
10 home in the Governor's coach. I neglected to say my prayers and had good health, good thoughts, and good humor, thank God Almighty.

2 November 1711

I rose about 7 o'clock and read nothing because my wife was there, nor did I say my prayers, but ate boiled milk[3] for breakfast. About 10 o'clock I went to the capitol and sat all day in court without once going away and by night we
15 made an end. Then I waited on the Governor home to dinner where we found Mrs. Churchill and several other ladies and my wife among them. The table was so full that the doctor and Mrs. Graeme and I had a little table to ourselves and were more merry than the rest of the company. I ate roast beef for supper. In the meantime the Doctor secured two fiddlers and candles were sent to the
20 capitol and then the company followed and we had a ball and danced till about 12 o'clock at night and then everybody went to their lodgings, but I neglected to say my prayers but had good health, good thoughts, and good humor, thank God Almighty. Mrs. Russell was my partner.

3 November 1711

I rogered my wife this morning and rose about 7 o'clock. I neglected to say my
25 prayers, but had boiled milk for breakfast. Mr. Beverley came to see my wife and breakfasted with us. About 10 o'clock I went to the capitol to write letters because I would not be disturbed, and my wife went to see her sister. The weather was grown warmer. I wrote three letters to England. About 1 o'clock I ate some gingerbread and drank sage and snakeroot, and then wrote more letters. About
30 5 o'clock I returned to my lodgings and put up my letters and because Mrs. Churchill and Mrs. Beverley were at Colonel Carter's lodgings. I went there and found the Colonel with the President and Mr. Clayton almost drunk. They would fain persuade me to drink with them but I refused and persuaded the Colonel

---

[1]Lucy Parke Byrd (*c.* 1690–1716)

[2]Alexander Spotswood (*c.* 1676–1740), Lieutenant-Governor of Virginia and acting Governor (1710–1722)

[3]In an age without refrigeration, it was common to boil milk to prevent disease.

not to suffer the ladies to wait on him so long. Then I went to the coffeehouse and had the misfortune to affront the President without saying anything to provoke a reasonable man. After that we went to [p–l–y] and I won £18 and got home before 11 o'clock. I neglected to say my prayers but had good health, good thoughts, and good humor, thank God Almighty. I let Mrs. Churchill know that   5
I owed her £40 of which her husband had kept no account.

4 NOVEMBER 1711

I rose about 7 o'clock and read a chapter in Hebrew and some Greek in Homer. I neglected to say my prayers, but ate boiled milk for breakfast. About 10 o'clock came my sister Custis[4] to dress here who told me the Major was better. About 11 the coach was sent by the Governor to carry the women to church   10
and I walked. Mr. Commissary[5] gave us an indifferent sermon. When church was done we went to the Governor's to dinner and I ate some boiled venison, though my stomach was not so good as usual. About 4 o'clock we went to see the new house and there we found Mrs. Blair and Mrs. Harrison. When we had tired ourselves there the coach sent the women home and the Governor and I   15
went to the coffeehouse, where we stayed about half an hour and then I went home to my lodgings and read some of the public news till about 9 o'clock. I neglected to say my prayers, but had good health, good thoughts, and good humor, thank God Almighty.

5 NOVEMBER 1711

I rose about 7 o'clock and read a chapter in Hebrew and some Greek in Lucian.   20
I said my prayers and ate boiled milk for breakfast. About 9 o'clock came Mrs. Bland and invited my wife and Mrs. Dunn to dinner and the Governor sent and invited me by Mr. Robinson, together with all the governors of the College[6] that were in town. The College presented their verses to the Governor by the hands of the Commissary and the master. About 11 o'clock I went to the capitol   25
and wrote a letter to England and set G–r–l to copying letters for me. About 2 o'clock I went to the Governor's to dinner and found there Mr. Commissary and the master of the College and Johnny Randolph as being the first scholar, who at dinner sat on the Governor's right hand. I ate roast mutton for dinner. The Governor was taken sick before we rose from table but it soon went over.   30
In the evening Mr. Bland took a walk to the College, and the Governor, Mrs. Russell, and several ladies came to see the bonfire made by the boys. At night

---

[4]Frances Parke Custis (c. 1686–1715), older sister of Byrd's wife and wife of Colonel John Custis (1678–1749). Their son, Daniel Custis, was the first husband of Martha Washington.
[5]James Blair (1656–1743), founder of William and Mary College and commissary (Representative of the Bishop of London) for Virginia
[6]The College of William and Mary at Williamsburg, of which Byrd was a member of the Board of Governors

we went to the Governor's to spend the rest of the evening till 10 o'clock and then we went home. I neglected to say my prayers but had good health, good thoughts, and indifferent humor, thank God Almighty.

6 NOVEMBER 1711

I rose about 7 o'clock and read two chapters in Hebrew and some Greek in
5 Homer. I said my prayers and ate boiled milk for breakfast. My wife and her sister and Mrs. Dunn waited on Mrs. Russell to Nat Burwell's, but I could not possibly go with them and therefore committed them to the care of the Doctor, who gallanted them. About 11 o'clock I went to the capitol, where I danced my dance and wrote several letters to England. The old Frenchman came to desire
10 me to get him a passage to England, which I promised to do when Captain H–n–t comes down. I stayed and wrote at the capitol till about 5 o'clock because it rained so hard that I could not get away. However at last I ran through it to the coffeehouse, where I sat an hour before anybody came. At last came Mr. Clayton from York but had no news. Soon after came Mr. Robinson and he
15 played at piquet with me and we neither won nor lost. About 10 I went home to my lodgings where I said my prayers and had good health, good thoughts, and good humor, thank God Almighty.

7 NOVEMBER 1711

I rose about 7 o'clock and read two chapters in Hebrew and some Greek in Homer. I said my prayers and ate boiled milk for breakfast. I paid £500 to Mr.
20 Tullitt for the College. About 10 I caused my secretary to be brought to my lodgings from the capitol. The wind blew very hard at northwest so that my wife and her company could not come from Gloucester. Some of the burgesses began to come and the House met and adjourned. I dined upon gingerbread because I could find no company to dine with. About 3 o'clock I went to the capitol and
25 wrote letters to England and danced my dance. About 5 o'clock Mr. Clayton came to me and told me my wife and the other gentlewomen were returned from Gloucester and were at my lodgings. I went to them and gave them some victuals and a bottle of wine from Marot's. My sister Custis and Mrs. Dunn went to Queen's Creek and my wife went to bed and I went to the coffeehouse where
30 I won 5 shillings and stayed till 9 o'clock. I neglected to say my prayers and had good health, good thoughts, and good humor, thank God Almighty.

8 NOVEMBER 1711

I rose about 7 o'clock and read nothing because my wife was preparing to go away home. I neglected to say my prayers and ate boiled milk for breakfast. About 9 we went to the Governor's who showed me his speech. I entreated for
35 Gilbert but could not prevail. I drank some tea till about 11 and then went in the Governor's coach to the capitol where he made his speech to the Council and Burgesses. Then I started a project of paying the ministers in money and

laying 3 shillings more on tobacco and everybody was pleased with the reason
of it. About 2 o'clock I dined with the Council at Marot's and ate mutton for
dinner. Harry W–l–s walked from hence to Jimmy Burwell's and back again in
less than three hours for a wager of two guineas, but was almost spent. I took a
walk to see the College and Governor's house and in the evening returned to the   5
coffeehouse where we played at cards and I won 20 shillings. I returned home
about 10 o'clock where I said my prayers and had good health, good humor,
and good thoughts, thank God Almighty.

9 November 1711

I rose about 7 o'clock and read two chapters in Hebrew and some Greek in
Homer. I said my prayers and had boiled milk for breakfast. Mr. Bland came to   10
see me and so did Frank [Ballard] and told me Mr. D–k was resolved to marry
Mrs. Young in spite of all his friends. I went to prayers with the Burgesses and
then we met as upper House but did nothing more than adjourn. Then I danced
my dance and wrote my proposal but learned that the Governor was against it
because it was no provision for more powers than are at present. About 2 o'clock   15
we dined at Marot's and I ate roast veal for dinner. In the afternoon we went to
the [?] coffeehouse where we fell into gaming and I won about £8 in all at piquet
and dice. About 10 o'clock I returned to my lodgings where I said my prayers
and had good health, good thoughts, and good humor, thank God Almighty.

10 November 1711

I rose about 7 o'clock and read nothing because of writing a letter to Mr. D–k to   20
endeavor to dissuade him from marrying Mrs. Young. I had several people come
to see me this afternoon; however I got ready about 9 and went to the Governor's
and found him [t–s] with the Commissary. I mentioned to him Mr. D–k's marriage, with which he was surprised because he had not heard of it before. I asked
the Governor if he had any service at Westover, and took my leave and went to   25
the capitol, where I danced my dance and wrote several things and stayed there
till 4 o'clock, and then took a walk. About 5 I went to Mr. Bland's and were
[sic] there about half an hour. My man Tom brought my horse and a letter from
home, by which I learned that all was well there, thank God. At night I went to
the coffeehouse where came some other gentlemen. I played at cards and won   30
5 shillings. Then I went to my lodgings where I said my prayers and had good
health, good thoughts, and good humor, thank God Almighty. At the coffeehouse
I ate some chicken pie and drank a bottle of the President's wine.

11 November 1711

I rose about 7 o'clock and read nothing because I prepared to go home. However
I said my prayers and ate some cranberry tart for breakfast. Mr. Graeme[7] came   35

---

[7]John Graeme, Lieutenant-Governor Spotswood's cousin

to go home with me and I gave him some Virginia wine. About 10 o'clock we
got on our horses and called at Green Springs where we drank tea and then
took our leave and proceeded to Frank Lightfoot's and were conducted there
by a dog which we found at the ferry. We designed to take Frank with us home
5   but he was obliged to go to court the next day but promised to dine with us
on Tuesday. I ate boiled beef for dinner. In the afternoon we sent to Major
Harrison to come to us and then took a walk and met a pretty girl and kissed
her and so returned. About 6 o'clock Major Harrison came to us but we could
not persuade him to go with us to Westover. We sat up and were merry till 11
10 o'clock and then we went to bed. I neglected to say my prayers but had good
health, good thoughts, and good humor, thank God Almighty.

12 NOVEMBER 1711

I rose about 7 o'clock and said my prayers. Then we ate our breakfast of milk
and took our leave and proceeded to Westover, where we found all well, thank
God Almighty. Mr. Graeme was pleased with the place exceedingly. I showed
15 him the library and then we walked in the garden till dinner and I ate some wild
duck. In the afternoon I paid money to several men on accounts of Captain
H–n–t and then we took a walk about the plantation and I was displeased with
John about the boat which he was building. In the evening we played at piquet
and I won a little. About 8 o'clock my wife was taken with the colic violently
20 but it was soon over. Then Mr. Graeme and I drank a bottle of pressed wine
which he liked very well, as he had done the white madeira. About 10 o'clock
I went to bed and rogered my wife. I neglected to say my prayers but had good
health, good thoughts, and good humor, thank God Almighty.

13 NOVEMBER 1711

I rose about 7 o'clock and read nothing because of my company. However I said
25 a short prayer and drank chocolate for breakfast and ate some cake. Then Mr.
Graeme and I went out with bows and arrows and shot at partridge and squirrel,
which gave us abundance of diversion, but we lost some of our arrows. We resumed
about one o'clock but found that Frank Lightfoot had broken his word by not
coming to us. About 2 o'clock we went to dinner and I ate some venison pasty
30 and were very merry. In the afternoon we played at billiards and I by accident
had almost lost some of my fore teeth by putting the stick in my mouth. Then
we went and took a walk with the women and Mr. Graeme diverted himself with
Mrs. Dunn. In the evening came Mr. Mumford who told me all was well again at
Appomattox.[8] We played at cards and drank some pressed wine and were merry
35 till 10 o'clock. I neglected to say my prayers but rogered my wife, and had good
health, good thoughts, and good humor, thank God Almighty.

---

[8]One of Byrd's plantations

14 November 1711

I rose about 7 o'clock and gave all the necessary orders to my people. I recommended myself and family to God and then ate some cold venison pasty for breakfast. I settled my business with Captain H–n–t and delivered my letters to him. Then we took our leave and were set over the creek and then proceeded on our journey and about 3 o'clock we got to Green Springs but neither the   5 Colonel nor his lady were at home and therefore we stayed but half an hour and then went on to Williamsburg, where we got about 5. I dressed myself and went to Colonel Bray's where the wedding had been kept and found abundance of company there. I dined and ate some chicken pie and then we went to dancing and the bride was my partner but because Colonel Bray was sick, we went away   10 before 10 o'clock to the coffeehouse where I won 5 shillings of the President. I said my prayers, and had good thoughts, good health, and good humor, thank God Almighty.

15 November 1711

I rose about 7 o'clock and read a chapter in Hebrew and some Greek in Homer. I said my prayers and ate boiled milk for breakfast. I wrote a letter to my wife and   15 sent Tom home. About 10 o'clock Colonel Ludwell [came] to my lodgings. He stayed about half an hour and then we went to the capitol where I danced my dance and wrote in my journal. Then I went into Council where our address to the Governor was read and Colonel Lewis and myself were ordered to wait on the Governor to know where and when the Council should wait on him with   20 it, and I walked him so fast that when he came there he could hardly speak. The Governor gave us some strong water to warm us and then we returned. About 2 o'clock we dined at Marot's and I won 5 shillings. I went home about 9 o'clock and read some Greek. I said my prayers and had good health, good thoughts, and good humor, thank God Almighty.   25

16 November 1711

I rose about 7 o'clock and read two chapters in Hebrew and some Greek in Homer. I said my prayers and ate boiled milk for breakfast. About 9 o'clock I went to the Governor's, where I stayed about an hour and then went to the capitol where we read a bill concerning rolling houses the first time. About 11 the Governor came and the President read our address to him with an indiffer-   30 ent grace. About 2 o'clock we dined at Marot's and I ate some fish for dinner. My mouth was sore with the blow I had with the billiard stick. About 4 o'clock Jimmy Burwell and I resolved to go to the wedding at Mr. Ingles' and went away in his coach and found all the company ready to go to supper but we ate nothing with them but some custard. After supper we began to dance, first   35 French dances and after country dances till about 11 o'clock, and then most of the company went to Williamsburg but I stayed with Jimmy Burwell and

Jimmy Roscow and James Bray, got drunk and went home by myself about 12 o'clock. I neglected to say my prayers but had good health, good thoughts, and good humor, thank God Almighty.

17 NOVEMBER 1711

I rose about 7 o'clock and neglected to say my prayers but ate boiled milk for 5 breakfast. Mr. Ingles entertained us very generously and is a very good and courteous man. We took our leave about 8 o'clock and returned in Jimmy Burwell's coach to Williamsburg and went away to the capitol where we read a bill concerning horses the first time. Then we adjourned and I went to Colonel Duke's who entertained me with good cider and toast. The weather threatened 10 rain or snow. About 1 o'clock I went again to the capitol and danced my dance and wrote in my journal. Then I read Italian for an hour. After which I took a walk round the town till about 5 o'clock, and then went to the coffeehouse and won 5 shillings of the President. About 9 I went to my lodgings where I read nothing but said my prayers and had good health, good thoughts, and good 15 humor, thank God Almighty.

18 NOVEMBER 1711

I rose about 7 o'clock and read two chapters in Hebrew and some Greek in Homer. I said my prayers and ate boiled milk for breakfast. About 11 o'clock the President called upon me with his coach to go to church, where Mr. Paxton gave us a sermon that was very good. After church Colonel Duke and I dined 20 with the Commissary and I ate roast turkey for dinner. Mrs. Blair was not very well. In the evening Colonel Duke and I took leave and walked to Colonel Bray's and found him much better but the design was to visit Mrs. B–r–d [bride?] before she went up to Captain Llewellyn [Eppes?]. We diverted ourselves with the girls till about 9 o'clock and then took our leave and wished them a good 25 journey the next day. I read some English at my lodgings and said my prayers and had good health, good thoughts, and good humor, thank God Almighty.

19 NOVEMBER 1711

I rose about 7 o'clock and read a chapter in Hebrew and some Greek in Homer. I said my prayers and ate boiled milk for breakfast. It rained a little in the morning. I went to the Governor's but he was gone to the new house and I went 30 there to him and found him putting up the arms. Captain H–n–t came over and could hardly prevail with the Governor to let him go; however I interceded for him and got leave. About 2 o'clock my sister Custis sent horses for me and about 3 I rode to make her a visit and found them pretty well and their whole family. About 6 o'clock we went to supper and I ate some roast beef. Then we 35 talked about dividing the land of old Colonel Parke between them and me. Some words were spoken concerning selling some of Colonel Parke's land to pay

his debts but my sister would not hear of it. I said my prayers, and had good
health, good thoughts, and good humor, thank God Almighty.

20 NOVEMBER 1711

I rose about 7 o'clock and my brother and I appointed Mr. Bland and Mr.
[Keeling] to divide the land of old Colonel Parke and agreed my sister should
have the choice. I said my prayers and ate boiled milk for breakfast. About 9   5
o'clock I took leave and rode to Williamsburg where I found my man Tom
with a letter from home, that told me all were well except my daughter, who
had fallen down and cut her forehead. I wrote a letter to my wife and sent Tom
home. Then I went to the capitol and read some bills. The Governor was there.
We sat till two o'clock and I went to dinner at the Governor's and ate roast beef.   10
About 4 we went away and I went and wrote in my journal and afterwards went
and recommended the business of the College to some of the burgesses and
then went to the coffeehouse, where I won of Dr. Cocke 45 shillings at piquet.
About 12 o'clock I went home and said a short prayer and had good thoughts,
good humor, and good health, thank God Almighty.   15

21 NOVEMBER 1711

I rose about 7 o'clock and read nothing because I went to the committee for
making the port bill and stayed there about an hour. Then I returned and said
my prayers and had boiled milk for breakfast. Then I went to the capitol and
danced my dance and did some business with Mr. Holloway. Then I went down
to the Council and read some law and the Governor came among us and stayed   20
about an hour. About 2 o'clock we rose and went to dinner and I ate fish. Then
Colonel Smith and I played at billiards and I won half a crown. Then we took
a walk and afterwards went to the coffeehouse and played at whisk, but lost 15
shillings. Then we played at dice and after losing £10 I recovered my money
and won £8, [by holding in 13 hands together]. About 12 o'clock we drank   25
a bottle of wine and then went home. I said my prayers and had good health,
good thoughts, and good humor, thank God Almighty.

22 NOVEMBER 1711

I rose about 7 o'clock and read a chapter in Hebrew and some Greek in Homer.
I said my prayers and ate boiled milk for breakfast. Mr. Bland came to see me
and told me he would go about the dividing of old Colonel Parke's land as we   30
desired. About 11 I went to the capitol, where I found the Governor, who had
letters from the Governor of North Carolina[9] which gave a terrible account of
the state of Carolina. He had also a letter from the Baron by which he had a
relation of his being taken with Mr. Lawson by the Indians and of Mr. Lawson's

---

[9]Edward Hyde (*c.* 1650–1712), Governor of North Carolina (1711–1712)

murder.[10] The House of Burgesses brought their address of thanks to which
the Governor answered them that he would thank them when he saw them act
with as little self interest as he had done. About 3 o'clock we went to dinner and
I ate some roast goose. Then I took a walk to the Governor's new house with
5   Frank W–l–s and then returned to the coffeehouse, where I lost 12 pounds 10
shillings and about 10 o'clock returned home very much out of humor to think
myself such a fool. I said my prayers and had good health, good thoughts, and
good humor, thank God Almighty. It was very hot till about 9 o'clock in the
evening and then it grew cold.

23 NOVEMBER 1711

10   I rose about 7 o'clock and read a chapter in Hebrew and some Greek in Homer.
I said my prayers and ate boiled milk for breakfast. Several gentlemen came to
my lodgings. About 10 o'clock I went to the capitol where I danced my dance
and then wrote in my journal. It was very cold this morning. About 11 o'clock
I went to the coffeehouse, where the Governor also came and from thence we
15   went to the capitol and read the bill concerning ports the first time. We stayed
till 3 o'clock and then went to dinner to Marot's, but could get none there and
therefore Colonel Lewis and I dined with Colonel Duke and I ate boiled chicken
for dinner. After dinner we went to Colonel Carter's room where we had a bowl
of punch of French brandy and oranges. We talked very lewdly and were almost
20   drunk and in that condition we went to the coffeehouse and played at dice and
I lost £12. We stayed at the coffeehouse till almost 4 o'clock in the morning
talking with Major Harrison. Then I went to my lodging, where I committed
uncleanness, for which I humbly beg God Almighty's pardon.

24 NOVEMBER 1711

I rose about 8 o'clock and read a chapter in Hebrew and some Greek in Homer.
25   I said my prayers and ate boiled milk for breakfast. Colonel Carter and several
others came to my lodgings to laugh at me for my disorder last night. About
10 I went to the coffeehouse and drank some tea, and then we went to the
President's and read the law about probate and administration. Then I went to
the capitol and danced my dance and wrote in my journal and read Italian. This
30   day I make a solemn resolution never at once to lose more than 50 shillings and
to spend less time in gaming, and I beg the God Almighty to give me grace to
keep so good a resolution if it be His holy will. I read some Italian and danced

---

[10]In 1710 Christoph von Graffenried (1661–1743), Baron of Bernberg, led a group of Swiss
and Palatine German settlers to North Carolina. Robbed by French privateers on their way
to America, they eventually settled New Bern on the site of a former Tuscarora Indian village.
Graffenried and John Lawson (1674–1711), Surveyor-General of North Carolina, were captured by the Indians in 1711 and sentenced to death. Graffenried was released, but Lawson was
executed. Graffenried returned to Switzerland.

again. Then I took a walk, notwithstanding I had a good cold on me and the
weather was also very cold. Then went to the coffeehouse but returned to my
lodgings about 5 o'clock and wrote two letters to England. I said my prayers
and had good health, good thoughts, and good humor, thank God Almighty.

25 NOVEMBER 1711

I rose about 7 o'clock and found my cold much worse. However I read a chapter   5
in Hebrew and some Greek in Homer. I said my prayers and ate boiled milk
for breakfast. I was so disordered with my cold that I could not go to church
but read some English. About 11 o'clock Mr. Clayton came to see me and I
desired him to lend me his horse to ride to Queen's Creek. About one my brother
Custis called on me and I went with him home and found all the family well.   10
Just before we sat to dinner Dr. Cocke came to us. I ate some roast beef for
dinner notwithstanding my cold, which continued violently. We were merry
till the evening and then we drank a bowl of punch made of French brandy and
oranges which I drank for my cold and ate roast apples with it. We sat up till
about 10 and then I said a short prayer and had good health, good thoughts,   15
and good humor, thank God Almighty.

26 NOVEMBER 1711

I rose about 8 o'clock and found myself much better, thank God. It rained and
thundered much in the night. I said my prayers and ate boiled milk for breakfast.
My sister agreed to divide her grandfather's land without any intervention of
[f–r–n] and she also agreed to the sale of some of the land and negroes of her   20
father to pay his debts. About 10 o'clock we took leave and went to Williamsburg
but there we did not meet to do business till almost 2 o'clock because we had not
enough in town. We read two bills and then went to dinner and I ate chicken
pie but was not well after it. In the evening we went to the coffeehouse where I
received a letter from Mr. Perry and an account of £5 a hogshead for tobacco.   25
About 9 o'clock I went to my lodgings where I said my prayers and had good
health, good thoughts, and good humor, thank God Almighty.

27 NOVEMBER 1711

I rose about 7 o'clock and read a chapter in Hebrew and some Greek in Homer.
I said my prayers and ate boiled milk for breakfast. The weather was very cold
and threatened snow. James Bray invited me to the wedding of his daughter this   30
day but the weather was so bad I made my excuses by the Commissary. We sat
at the President's house where we had a good fire. I received a letter from home
by my sloop that brought some coal on her way to Kiquotan with palisades. We
read several bills and the Governor came to us and made his exceptions to some
clauses in the bill concerning probate and administration, which we resolved to   35
amend. We sat till about 4 o'clock and then went to dinner and I ate some roast
mutton. In the evening we went to the coffeehouse where I played at cards and

won 25 shillings. About 9 I returned to my lodgings where I said my prayers and had good health, good thoughts, and good humor, thank God Almighty.

28 NOVEMBER 1711

I rose about 7 o'clock and found the weather extremely cold. I read a chapter in Hebrew and some Greek in Homer. I said my prayers and ate boiled milk for breakfast. I had a gentleman that came to buy the quitrents of Nansemond County but we could not agree. About 10 o'clock I went to the capitol where I wrote in my journal and danced my dance, and then went to the coffeehouse where I found several of the council but not ready to go to council, and so some of us took a walk to the Governor's house where we found the Governor looking over the workmen. It was exceedingly cold. Then we returned to the President's lodgings where we read some bills and afterwards adjourned to the capitol where the House of Burgesses brought an address to the Governor in which they desired him to make war on the Indians and the Council afterwards advised him if no other method would procure satisfaction from the Indians then to make war on them. About 4 o'clock we went to dinner and I ate some roast beef. In the evening we played at cards till 7 o'clock and then I went home and read some Greek and looked over several papers relating to the estate of old Colonel Parke. I said my prayers and had good health, good thoughts, and good humor, thank God Almighty.

29 NOVEMBER 1711

I rose about 7 o'clock and read some Hebrew, but no Greek because I intended to wait on the Governor. I said my prayers and ate boiled milk for breakfast. About 9 I went to the Governor but he was so busy nobody could speak with him. Then I returned to the coffeehouse where I ate some toast and butter and drank milk tea on it. Here I learned that Captain Smith, commander of the "Enterprise", was come and that Dr. [Barret's] house was burnt last night. It was cold and threatened snow. About 1 o'clock I went to the capitol, where I danced my dance and wrote in my journal and then went to the President's lodgings, with the rest of the Council, and there we read the law about probate of wills and administration, and the Governor came to us and I went in his coach with him to dinner, and I ate some fish. Captain Smith, commander of the "Enterprise", was there also. In the evening I went home, where I found Tom with a letter from my wife by which I learned that all was well there, thank God. Then I went to the coffeehouse where I played at cards and won […] shillings. Then I returned to my lodgings and said my prayers and had good health, good thoughts, and good humor, thank God Almighty. Tom brought a wild goose that was very fat and therefore I sent it to the Governor.

30 November 1711

I rose about 7 o'clock and read nothing because I prepared for my journey home. However I said my prayers and ate boiled milk for breakfast. I sold the quitrents to Mr. Bland and then took my leave of him and got on horseback about 9 o'clock when it was fair weather, but it was overcast before I got to the ferry. Sometimes I walked to get myself warm, and sometimes I rode, and got there about 3 o'clock in the afternoon, and found all my family well, thank God Almighty. My wife and Mrs. Dunn had worked very hard to put the house in order. In the evening I ate two partridges for my supper and spent the rest of the evening in talking about all the affairs of the neighborhood. My wife told me that Llewellyn Eppes' wife was like not to be very happy because he was cross already to her. I told them all the news of the town and about 8 o'clock we went to bed. I neglected to say my prayers but had good health, good thoughts, and good humor, thank God Almighty. I rogered my wife vigorously.

II
AWAKENINGS AND ENLIGHTENMENTS

Eer since Tertullian (*c.* 160–*c.* 220) famously asked what Athens had to do with Jerusalem, the challenge of properly relating faith to reason has remained a central theme of the Western heritage. The fact that episodes of both tension and accommodation between Christian enthusiasm and human rationalism have marked the American heritage should come, therefore, as no surprise. The eighteenth century, often called *The Age of Reason* or *The Enlightenment*, was also the century of intense American evangelical revivalism that historians have come to call *The Great Awakening*. Thus the 1700s witnessed both the rise of American evangelicalism and an American version of enlightenment rationalism. What were the principal themes and who played starring roles in the American episodes of awakening and enlightenment? Did Americans succeed in forging a reasonable evangelicalism? Or did the faith of American revivalism stand apart from or opposed to the enlightenment's skepticism and its emphasis upon science and reason? Of course, both Christian revivalism and Enlightenment rationalism were trans-Atlantic phenomena. Yet, despite their European versions, each found uniquely American expressions that together helped shape the ideas and ideals of the American Revolution and founding.

An intense Christian faith had motivated American colonists from the beginning. Varieties of that faith continued to inspire and define important aspects of American colonial life long after the 1649 death of John Winthrop. But beginning a generation later in the mid-1670s, and continuing unevenly for at least a century, American religious life underwent important changes, most notably those associated with periodic bursts of evangelical fervor called revivals or awakenings. The Great Awakening, as the phrase incorrectly suggests, was not a singular incident. Rather, it is the name that was given, only much later in the nineteenth century, to a series of eighteenth-century events that were first anticipated in the seventeenth century by revivalist preaching and calls for "covenant renewal." These earliest calls for repentance and experiential conversion first came from such New England pastors as Samuel Torrey (1632–1707), John Cotton, Jr. (1639–1699), and the famed Solomon Stoddard (1643–1729) of Northampton, Massachusetts, who had told his congregation, "I have made it my business to gain Souls to Christ." In that business he had no fewer than five major successes, which he called "harvests," in 1679, 1683, 1690, 1712, and 1718.

Then in the 1720s the preaching of German born, Dutch-educated, Theodore Jacob Frelinghuysen (1691–1748) in New Jersey sparked the first signs of a larger revival. A pietistic Calvinist who emphasized the necessity of a personal experiential conversion, Frelinghuysen's preaching provided an early model for others, including Presbyterian preachers in the middle colonies during the 1730s. Chief among this latter group was the Irish-born Scotsman William Tennent (1673–1746) and his four preaching sons, Gilbert, John, Charles, and William, Jr. Although critics derided these Presbyterian revival preachers as "backwoods half-educated enthusiasts," their zeal met with success. For example, young Gilbert Tennent (1703–1764) rapidly earned his reputation as a zealot for conversions after coming into contact with Frelinghuysen, whom he adopted as mentor and role model. With such published sermons as "The Danger of an Unconverted Ministry," it was hardly surprising that these early evangelical revivalists found critics among the traditionalist anti-revivalist clergy who were sometimes called "old lights."

The revival activity peaked in the 1730s and 1740s, particularly as it was associated in New England with the sermons of congregational minister Jonathan Edwards (1703–1758) and with the great preaching tour in 1739 and 1740 of America's first "media star" and cultural hero, the British Anglican evangelist George Whitefield (1714–1770). Edwards, who at the age of seventeen had graduated from Yale at the top of his class, would emerge as one of America's greatest theologians and philosophers. A deep-thinking Calvinist, Edwards's theology grew from his emphasis upon the sublime sovereignty of God and man's total depravity. Accordingly, sinful men could do nothing to save themselves. All rested upon being awakened to "the new birth" by the activity of God's Holy Spirit. As Edwards and all evangelical revivalists acknowledged, inspirational preaching would become the chief means by which God would affect the conversion experience—an event often accompanied by passionate emotions, wild excitement, or profoundly felt peace. But as Edwards reluctantly admitted, and as "Old-Light" detractors such as Boston's Charles Chauncey (1705–1787) insisted, over-emphasis upon cultivating of conversion feelings could be fraudulent. Reflecting on the fervor of the awakenings, Chauncey complained in 1743 of what he called "the first and Grand Delusion" of those caught up in the sentimental epistemology of revivalism: "People, in order to know whether the influences they are under are from the Spirit…hastily conclude such and such internal motions to be divine impressions, merely from the perception they have of them. They are ready, at once, if this is unusual or strong, to take it for some influence from above." Even

Edwards would acknowledge that pulpit sensationalism could churn popular passions and merely mimic genuine religious awakening. Thus he was a particularly keen observer of the revivals in New England during the 1730s. He wanted to explore the ways divine love had moved among people to instigate the conversion experience. His *Faithful Narrative of the Surprizing Work of God* offered Edwards's firsthand account of the 1734 revival in Northampton as he credited divine intervention, not the work of pulpit histrionics, for the revivals near the Massachusetts frontier.

If Edwards, who customarily sermonized with monotonic pulpit reading of carefully crafted theological treatises, could stir congregations to emotional frenzy, there is no wondering that the free-form performances of George Whitefield's open-air extemporizing attracted and entertained the religiously curious by the thousands. Whitefield first arrived in the New World in 1738 when he visited Georgia to assist with an orphanage project. But his return visit the following year for a barnstorming tour of the colonies triggered the greatest part of the Great Awakening. Whitefield abandoned the traditional social order in which preaching was done only in sacred spaces (the Church building) by the official person (the local minister) at appointed times (the Sunday meeting), and in defense of particular teachings (denominational orthodoxy and sacramental purity). Instead, Whitefield took advantage of the emerging modern economic climate and applied it to religion as he "marketed" a simple new birth and a gospel reduced to its bare basics. He made religion voluntary, entertaining, popular, and non-denominational. As a boy he had craved a stage career in acting. As a man he found his starring role wearing the clerical collar of a preaching deacon unplugged. He preached in public squares or country fields, wherever a crowd would assemble to hear him. It was said that he could reduce women to tears just by the way he pronounced the word "Mesopotamia." Thus Whitefield's religious authority came not from official sanction, but from the people who, moved by his words, made him the celebrity whose name recognition was surpassed only by George Washington later in the century. As he preached he appealed to the emotions, stirred the heart, and left people craving an experience of the new birth. Virginia's Edmond Randolph (1753–1813) later referred to him as "that stupendous master of the human passions." Whitefield also took advantage of the new popular printing enterprise as a tool for self-promotion. Just as Ben Franklin had been the publisher of Gilbert Tennent's sermons, so did Whitefield strike up an amazing friendship with the creator of *Poor Richard*. (See Franklin's observations of Whitefield's preaching later in this chapter.) Historians have estimated that Whitefield preached some 15,000 times in his thirty-three year career and had a voice that could be heard by tens of thousands at one time. Although popular with the people, he earned detractors from traditionalist naysayers. "Congregations were lifeless," bellowed Whitefield, "because dead men preach to them."

That such anti-establishment words could stir the masses of American colonists signaled an important change in the religious and social landscape. Religiously, the eighteenth century saw the rise of a new American evangelicalism that ever since the awakenings has heavily conditioned popular Protestantism. The twin emphases upon "conversionism" and the "activism" of converts in vocalizing their faith have become staples of evangelicalism, as has been a high regard for popular opinion and the unmediated experience of God through prayer and Bible reading. Evangelicalism signaled a new religious freedom and an emerging religious popular culture. These theological changes were in step with simultaneous shifts away from the traditional social order. As George Whitefield offered Americans a trans-colonial encounter with a pop culture hero, regional differences (which were considerable) began to diminish under the influence of this common religious experience. In the revivals Americans began to see the power inherent in a collective and voluntary association energized by free speech apart from the traditional order. The power to move people would now be available not just to those who asserted their authority, but to those who earned it from the people directly. The American tendency to equate celebrity with authority had begun. It was also significant that the revivals broke down ethnic differences—compare the diverse origins of Frelinghuysen and Tennent with those of Whitefield and Edwards—as they helped to create an American identity grounded in the emerging evangelicalism.

It might be a stretch to follow those historians who point to the Great Awakening as the first stage of the American Revolution. Nevertheless, before British colonists could declare and defend their status as an independent American nation, they would have to identify themselves as Americans and be willing to challenge the traditional social and political order. There seems no gainsaying the fact that the Great Awakening began that process in an important way with a trans-colonial religious outburst that resulted in Americans thinking about themselves and their neighbors in new ways.

Eighteenth-century Americans were thinking about more than just religion. Indeed, in the Age of Reason, Americans found themselves thinking deeply about all sorts of things, even about the meaning and value of thinking itself. The Enlightenment placed a new premium upon the power and importance of human reason. Following the remarkable successes of the seventeenth-century's scientific revolution, eighteenth-century intellects accentuated a faith in human ability to discover and comprehend a law-bound order in all things. Isaac Newton (1643–1727) had shown the way with his mathematically expressed universal law of gravitation. If, as Newton had shown, a single law could account for the regular motions of physical bodies, whether heavenly or earthbound, perhaps there were similar rationally discernable laws that governed the economic and political motions of man and society. This culture of Newtonianism combined with the scientific revolution's new empiricism and Baconianism to feed the eighteenth-century hope that human reason could be harnessed to know and control the world.

Just as the Great Awakening was no one event, it would be a mistake to regard the Enlightenment as a singular phenomenon. As the historian Henry May has capably shown in his history of *The Enlightenment in America,* the Enlightenment was a cultural fabric woven from no fewer than four principal strands. The first, which May called "The Moderate Enlightenment," took its cue from Isaac Newton and John Locke (1632–1704) and prevailed in England from 1688–1787. Its thinkers emphasized order, balance, religious tolerance, and compromise. May called the second strand, which dominated in France especially after 1750, "The Skeptical Enlightenment." Characterized by its brash dismissal of revealed religion and its cocky embrace of philosophical materialism, the Skeptical Enlightenment found its chief French spokesmen in Voltaire (1694–1778), Denis Diderot (1713–1784), the Baron d'Holbach (1723–1789), and the French *philosophes.* In Britain, David Hume (1711–1776) was its chief representative, as was Benjamin Franklin (1706–1790) in America. May's third strand was "The Revolutionary Enlightenment," a name derived from his characterization of the diverse ideas and ideals that, despite their differences, motivated both the American and French Revolutions. Thus the Revolutionary Enlightenment included those philosophical positions that fueled the French Revolution's hope for creating a new national order by wiping away the old. Grounded in a utopian belief in *Progress* and championing freedom from the restraints of tradition and authority, the Revolutionary Enlightenment found chief defenders in such names as Jean-Jacques Rousseau (1712–1778), Thomas Paine (1737–1809), and (especially in his earlier years) Thomas Jefferson (1743–1826). The fourth and final of May's enlightenment strands had the greatest long-term influence in America. He called it "The Didactic Enlightenment," for it would grow best in the late eighteenth- and nineteenth-century soils of American learning, American colleges. The Didactic Enlightenment originated in Scotland and is associated with the *Common Sense* philosophy of such thinkers as Thomas Reid (1710–1796). Squarely opposed to the skeptical and revolutionary dogmas of more radical enlightenment thinkers, representatives of the Didactic Enlightenment defended the harmony of faith and reason, and the reliability of plain sense experience and natural moral judgment. Sometimes called Scottish Common Sense Philosophy, the principles of the Didactic Enlightenment took root in America largely through the remarkable efforts of John Witherspoon (1723–1794), who arrived from Scotland to become president of Princeton in 1768 and would become the only clergyman to sign the Declaration of Independence. Witherspoon's most famous pupil was James Madison (1751–1836), but his students also included other delegates to the Constitutional Convention, forty-nine future congressmen, twenty-eight future senators, three future Supreme Court justices, a dozen members of the Continental Congress, and scores of other leaders and statesmen.

Given the variety of people and diversity of ideas that gather under the Enlightenment umbrella, sorting out all the details can be daunting. Still, it is probably fair to say that most intellectual leaders of the Enlightenment shared a set of common beliefs or principles. One shared principle was the belief in Progress. This is the conviction that C. S. Lewis labeled "chronological snobbery," the notion that intellectual achievements of bygone ages are necessarily inferior to those of the present merely because they are old. Time's arrow, according to this Enlightenment faith, necessarily points onward and upward toward intellectually superior advancement. Such achievement, Enlightenment thinkers believed, would be secured by harnessing human reason and common sense in service of social, political, and economic improvement. This fed the Enlightenment hope for practical educational reform, increased governmental efficiency, broadened economic prosperity, and especially for tolerance of intellectual and religious dissent. The flip side of this call for increased religious and intellectual freedom was the Enlightenment's broad skepticism regarding traditional religious dogma, formal creeds, and metaphysical doctrines of many sorts. In America, the popular writings of Benjamin Franklin offered one of the best widespread sources of these common Enlightenment themes.

But if many Enlightenment thinkers were confident skeptics ready to cashier the past and traditional orthodoxies, others were not. Perhaps such heterodox figures as Jefferson, Paine, and Voltaire were children of the Enlightenment, but other less radical eighteenth-century lights such as Edmund Burke (1729–1797), Adam Smith (1723–1790), and Jonathan Edwards were as well. If the French Revolution's leveling violence epitomized Enlightenment ideals run amuck, then the Declaration of Independence and Constitution reveal the power of enlightened human reason tethered to eternal verities.

Thus the eighteenth-century was a complicated time, a season of religious awakenings, passionate revivals, and evangelical fervor combined with and tempered by rationalist skepticism, utopian ideology, and optimistic trust in human reason. But in America the Enlightenment tended to be milder and less radical than in Europe, especially France. As one historian has observed, if the European Enlightenment tended to follow the French "ideology of reason," then the American Enlightenment found expression in the "politics of liberty."

Indeed, the language of liberty was the language of Enlightenment America. As George Whitefield and his fellow evangelists urged audiences to escape the tyranny of sin and find everlasting liberty in Christ, American patriots a generation later would fight against British tyranny in defense of their unalienable right to liberty. Eighteenth-century Americans did not, by and large, understand their Christian faith to be unreasonable. To the contrary, and Benjamin Franklin's heterodox deism notwithstanding, Americans typically followed the common sense Christianity of the patriot pastor and college president John Witherspoon. In the eighteenth-century American context, the answer to Tertullian's inquiry about the relation of Athens to Jerusalem was clear. The two had quite a lot to do with one another. As colonial church membership soared in the revival's wake, so did the need for well-trained clergy. The result was a merging of piety with reason in the founding of numerous denominational colleges and seminaries that would eventually grow into the country's most elite institutions of higher learning. The origins of Princeton, Columbia, Rutgers, Dartmouth, and Brown, to name just a few, are all traced to the eighteenth-century's revivalist impulse. It is the rare exception—in the Ivy League only Cornell and the University of Pennsylvania had non-sectarian origins—to find elite old colleges that were not formed to perpetuate the marriage of faith and learning. So if the eighteenth-century was an Age of Reason, in America it was equally an Age of Faith. Before long it would become the age of a revolution—a revolution born in the defense of *rationally* self-evident truths by *faithful* patriots waving battle flags bearing the motto "Rebellion to Tyrants is Obedience to God."

A Faithful Narrative of the Surprising Work of God
Jonathan Edwards (1703–1758)

Jonathan Edwards is widely considered America's greatest theologian. A Faithful Narrative *describes the three hundred or so "conversions" in the Connecticut River valley in 1734. It attracted international attention and influenced John Wesley (1703–1791) in his development of Methodism. Edwards was in most respects an ally of Whitefield and promoter of the Great Awakening. He was also one of the few Americans who had read and absorbed the writings of both John Locke (1632–1704) and Isaac Newton (1643–1727). These observations, empirical in method and traditionally Calvinist in theology, might be considered a scientific study of the New Birth.*

NORTHAMPTON, 6 NOVEMBER 1736

...But to give a clearer idea of the nature and manner of the operations of God's Spirit in this wonderful effusion of it, I would give an account of two particular instances. The first is an adult person, a young woman whose name was Abigail Hutchinson. I select her case especially because she is now dead, and so it may be more fit to speak freely of her than of living instances, though I am under 5 far greater disadvantages on other accounts to give a full and clear narrative of her experiences than I might of some others; nor can any account be given but what has been retained in the memories of her near friends and some others of what they have heard her express in her life-time.

She was of a rational, understanding family: there could be nothing in her 10 education that tended to enthusiasm, but rather to the contrary extreme. It is in no wise the temper of the family to be ostentatious of experiences, and it was far from being her temper. She was before her conversion, to the observation of her neighbors, of a sober and inoffensive conversation, and was a still, quiet, reserved person. She had long been infirm of body, but her infirmity had never 15 been observed at all to incline her to be notional or fanciful, or to occasion

Jonathan Edwards, *Edwards on Revivals, Containing a Faithful Narrative of the Surprising Work of God* (New York: Dunning and Spalding, 1832), 87–91, 97–111.

anything of religious melancholy. She was under awakenings scarcely a week before there seemed to be plain evidence of her being savingly converted.

She was first awakened in the winter season, on Monday, by something she heard her brother say of the necessity of being in good earnest in seeking
5   regenerating grace, together with the news of the conversion of the young woman before mentioned, whose conversion so generally affected most of the young people here. This news wrought much upon her, and stirred up a spirit of envy in her towards this young woman, whom she thought very unworthy of being distinguished from others by such a mercy; but withal it engaged her in a firm
10 resolution to do her utmost to obtain the same blessing; and considering with herself what course she should take, she thought that she had not a sufficient knowledge of the principles of religion, to render her capable of conversion; whereupon she resolved thoroughly to search the scriptures; and accordingly immediately began at the beginning of the Bible, intending to read it through.
15 She continued thus till Thursday; and then there was a sudden alteration, by a great increase of her concern, in an extraordinary sense of her own sinfulness, particularly the sinfulness of her nature, and wickedness of her heart, which came upon her (as she expressed it) as a flash of lightning, and struck her into an exceeding terror. Upon which she left-off reading the Bible in course as she
20 had begun, and turned to the New Testament, to see if she could not find some relief there for her distressed soul.

Her great terror, she said was, "that she had sinned against God." Her distress grew more and more for three days; until (as she said) she saw nothing but blackness of darkness before her, and her very flesh trembled for fear of
25 God's wrath: she wondered and was astonished at herself, that she had been so concerned for her body, and had applied so often to physicians to heal that, and had neglected her soul. Her sinfulness appeared with a very awful aspect to her, especially in three things, viz. her original sin, and her sin in murmuring at God's providence, in the weakness and afflictions she had been under, and in want of
30 duty to parents, though others had looked upon her to excel in dutifulness. On Saturday she was so earnestly engaged in reading the Bible and other books, that she continued in it, searching for something to relieve her, till her eyes were so dim, that she could not know the letters. While she was thus engaged in reading, prayer, and other religious exercises, she thought of those words of Christ
35 wherein he warns us not to be as the heathen, that think they shall be heard for their much speaking;[1] which, she said, led her to see that she had trusted to her own prayers and religious performances, and now she was put to a nonplus, and knew not which way to turn herself, or where to seek relief.

---

[1] Matthew 6:7

While her mind was in this posture, her heart, she said, seemed to fly to the minister for refuge, hoping that he could give her some relief. She came the same day to her brother, with the countenance of a person in distress, expostulating with him, why he had not told her more of her sinfulness, and earnestly inquiring of him what she should do. She seemed that day to feel in herself an enmity against the Bible, which greatly affrighted her. Her sense of her own exceeding sinfulness continued increasing from Thursday till Monday; and she gave this account of it, that it had been an opinion, which till now she had entertained, that she was not guilty of Adam's sin, nor any way concerned in it, because she was not active in it; but that now she saw she was guilty of that sin, and all over defiled by it; and that the sin which she brought into the world with her, was alone sufficient to condemn her.

On the sabbath-day she was so ill that her friends thought it not best that she should go to public worship, of which she seemed very desirous: but when she went to bed on the sabbath-day night, she took up a resolution that she would the next morning go to the minister, hoping to find some relief there. As she awaked on Monday morning, a little before day, she wondered within herself at the easiness and calmness she felt in her mind, which was of that kind she never felt before; as she thought of this, such words as these were in her mind: "The words of the Lord are pure words, health to the soul, and marrow to the bones." And then these words came to her mind, "the blood of Christ cleanses from all sin;"[2] which were accompanied with a lively sense of the excellency of Christ, and his sufficiency to satisfy for the sins of the whole world. She then thought of that expression, "It is a pleasant thing for the eyes to behold the sun;"[3] which words then seemed to her to be very applicable to Jesus Christ. By these things her mind was led into such contemplations and views of Christ as filled her exceedingly full of joy. She told her brother in the morning that she had seen (that is, in realizing views by faith) Christ the last night, and that she had really thought that she had not knowledge enough to be converted; but, says she, God can make it quite easy! On Monday she felt all day a constant sweetness in her soul. She had a repetition of the same discoveries of Christ three mornings together, that she had on Monday morning, and much in the same manner at each time, waking a little before day; but brighter and brighter every time.

At the last time on Wednesday morning, while in the enjoyment of a spiritual view of Christ's glory and fullness, her soul was filled with distress for Christ-less persons, to consider what a miserable condition they were in: and she felt in herself an inclination immediately to go forth to warn sinners; and

---

[2]I John 1:7
[3]Ecclesiastes 11:17

proposed it the next day to her brother to assist her in going from house to house; but her brother restrained her, by telling her of the unsuitableness of such a method. She told one of her sisters that day, that she loved all mankind, but especially the people of God. Her sister asked her why she loved all mankind?
5   She replied, because God had made them. After this there happened to come into the shop where she was at work, three persons that were thought to have been lately converted; her seeing them as they stepped in one after another into the door, so affected her, and so drew forth her love to them, that it overcame her, and she almost fainted: and when they began to talk of the things of religion,
10   it was more than she could bear; they were obliged to cease on that account. It was a very frequent thing with her to be overcome with a flow of affection to them that she thought godly, in conversation with them, and sometimes only at the sight of them.

She had many extraordinary discoveries of the glory of God and Christ;
15   sometimes in some particular attributes, and sometimes in many. She gave an account that once, as those four words passed through her mind, *Wisdom, Justice, Goodness,* and *Truth,* her soul was filled with a sense of the glory of each of these divine attributes, but especially the last: *Truth,* said she, sunk the deepest! And therefore, as these words passed, this was repeated, *Truth, Truth!* Her
20   mind was so swallowed up with a sense of the glory of God's truth and other perfections, that she said it seemed as though her life was going, and that she saw it was easy with God to take away her life by discoveries of himself. Soon after this, she went to a private religious meeting, and her mind was full of a sense and view of the glory of God all the time; and when the exercise was
25   ended, some asked her concerning what she had experienced; and she began to give them an account; but as she was relating it, it revived such a sense of the same things, that her strength failed, and they were obliged to take her and lay her upon the bed. Afterwards she was greatly affected, and rejoiced with these words, "Worthy is the Lamb that was slain...."[4]
30   But I now proceed to the other instance that I would give an account of, which is of the little child before mentioned. Her name is Phebe Bartlet, daughter of William Bartlet. I shall give the account as I took it from the mouths of her parents, whose veracity none that know them doubt of.

She was born in March, in the year 1731. About the latter end of April, or
35   the beginning of May 1735, she was greatly affected by the talk of her brother, who had been hopefully converted a little before, at about eleven years of age, and then seriously talked to her about the great things of religion. Her parents did not know of it at that time, and were not wont, in the counsels they gave

---

[4]Revelation 5:12

to their children, particularly to direct themselves to her, by reason of her being so young, and as they supposed, not capable of understanding: but after her brother had talked to her, they observed her very earnestly to listen to the advice they gave to the other children; and she was observed very constantly to retire, several times in a day, as was concluded, for secret prayer, and grew 5 more and more engaged in religion, and was more frequent in her closet, till at last she was wont to visit it five or six times in a day; and was so engaged in it, that nothing would at any time divert her from her stated closet exercises. Her mother often observed and watched her, when such things occurred as she thought most likely to divert her, either by putting it out of her thoughts, or 10 otherwise engaging her inclinations, but never could observe her to fail. She mentioned some very remarkable instances.

She once of her own accord spoke of her unsuccessfulness, in that she could not find God, or to that purpose. But on Thursday, the last day of July, about the middle of the day, the child being in the closet, where it used to retire, 15 its mother heard it speaking aloud, which was unusual, and never had been observed before: and her voice seemed to be as of one exceedingly importunate and engaged; but her mother could distinctly hear only these words (spoken in her childish manner, but seemed to be spoken with extraordinary earnestness and out of distress of soul), *Pray, blessed Lord, give me salvation! I pray, beg, pardon* 20 *all my sins!* When the child had done prayer, she came out of the closet, and sat down by her mother, and cried out aloud. Her mother very earnestly asked her several times, what the matter was, before she could make any answer; but she continued crying exceedingly, and writhing her body to and fro, like one in anguish of spirit. Her mother then asked her, whether she was afraid that God 25 would not give her salvation. She answered, 'Yes, I am afraid I shall go to hell!' Her mother then endeavored to quiet her; and told her she would not have her cry; she must be a good girl, and pray every day, and she hoped God would give her salvation. But this did not quiet her at all; but she continued thus earnestly crying, and taking on for some time, till at length she suddenly ceased crying, 30 and began to smile, and presently said with a smiling countenance, *'Mother, the kingdom of heaven is come to me!'* Her mother was surprised at the sudden alteration, and at the speech; and knew not what to make of it, but at first said nothing to her. The child presently spoke again, and said, 'There is another come to me, and there is another, there is three;' and being asked what she meant, she 35 answered, 'One is, Thy will be done, and there is another, Enjoy him forever;' by which it seems, that when the child said, 'There is three comes to me,' she meant three passages of her Catechism[5] that came to her mind.

---

[5]The Westminster Shorter Catechism

After the child had said this, she retired again into her closet; and her mother went over to her brother's, who was next neighbor; and when she came back, the child, being out of the closet, met her mother with this cheerful speech, 'I can find God now!' referring to what she had before complained of, that she could

5   not find God. Then the child spoke again and said, 'I love God!' Her mother asked her how well she loved God, whether she loved God better than her father and mother, she said, 'yes.' Then she asked her whether she loved God better than her little sister Rachel? She answered, 'Yes, better than anything!' Then her eldest sister, referring to her saying she could find God now, asked her where

10   she could find God. She answered, 'In heaven.' Why, said she, have you been in heaven? 'No,' said the child. By this it seems not to have been any imagination of anything seen with bodily eyes, that she called God, when she said, I can find God now. Her mother asked her whether she was afraid of going to hell, and that had made her cry. She answered, "Yes, I was, but now I shan't." Her mother

15   asked her whether she thought that God had given her salvation; she answered, "yes." Her mother asked her when. She answered, "today." She appeared all the afternoon exceedingly cheerful and joyful. One of her neighbors asked her how she felt herself? She answered, "I feel better than I did." The neighbor asked her, what made her feel better? She answered, "God makes me." That evening as

20   she lay in bed, she called one of her little cousins to her that was present in the room, as having something to say to him; and when he came, she told him that "heaven was better than earth." The next day being Friday, her mother asking her her catechism, asked her what God made her for. She answered, "To serve him," and added, "everybody should serve God, and get an interest in Christ."

25   The same day the elder children, when they came home from school, seemed much affected with the extraordinary change that seemed to be made in Phebe: and her sister Abigail standing by, her mother took occasion to counsel her now to improve her time to prepare for another world: on which Phebe burst out in tears, and cried out, "Poor Nabby!" Her mother told her she would not have

30   her cry, she hoped that God would give Nabby salvation; but that did not quiet her, but she continued earnestly crying for some time; and when she had in a measure ceased, her sister Eunice being by her, she burst out again, and cried, "Poor Eunice!" and cried exceedingly; and when she had almost done, she went into another room, and there looked up on her sister Naomi, and burst out

35   again, crying, "Poor Amy!" Her mother was greatly affected at such a behavior in the child, and knew not what to say to her. One of the neighbors coming in a little after, asked her what she had cried for. She seemed at first backward to tell the reason: her mother told her she might tell that person, for he had given her an apple; upon which she said, she "cried because she was afraid they

40   would go to hell."

At night a certain minister that was occasionally in the town, was at the house, and talked considerably with her of the things of religion; and after he was gone, she sat leaning on the table, with tears running out of her eyes: and being asked what made her cry, she said it was "thinking about God." The next day being Saturday, she seemed, great part of the day, to be in a very affection- 5 ate frame, had four turns of crying, and seemed to endeavor to curb herself and hide her tear, and was very backward to talk of the occasion of it. On the sabbath-day she was asked whether she believed in God; she answered "yes:" and being told that Christ was the son of God, she made ready answer, and said, "I know it." 10

From this time there has appeared a very remarkable, abiding change in the child: she has been very strict upon the sabbath, and seems to long for the sabbath-day before it comes, and will often in the week time be inquir-ing how long it is to the sabbath-day, and must have the days particularly counted over that are between, before she will be contented. And she seems 15 to love God's house, and is very eager to go thither. Her mother once asked her why she had such a mind to go? whether it was not to see fine folks? She said, "No, it was to hear Mr. Edwards preach." When she is in the place of worship, she is very far from spending her time there as children at her age usually do, but appears with an attention that is very extraordinary for such 20 a child. She also appears very desirous at all opportunities to go to private religious meetings; and is very still and attentive at home in prayer-time, and has appeared affected in time of family prayer. She seems to delight much in hearing religious conversation. When I once was there with some others that were strangers, and talked to her something of religion, she seemed more than 25 ordinarily attentive; and when we were gone, she looked out earnestly after us, and said, "I wish they would come again!" Her mother asked her why? says she, "I love to hear them talk."

She seems to have very much of the fear of God before her eyes, and an extraordinary dread of sin against him.... 30

She at sometimes appears greatly affected, and delighted with texts of scripture that come to her mind....

She has often manifested a great concern for the good of others' souls: and has been wont many times affectionately to counsel the other children....

She has discovered an uncommon degree of a spirit of charity.... 35

She has manifested great love to her minister; particularly when I returned from my long journey for my health, the last fall. When she heard of it she appeared very joyful at the news, and told the children of it, with an elevated voice, as the most joyful tidings: repeating it over and over, "Mr. Edwards is come home! Mr. Edwards is come home!"... 40

In the former part of this great work of God among us, till it got to its height, we seemed to be wonderfully smiled upon, and blest in all respects. Satan (as has been already observed) seemed to be unusually restrained. Persons that before had been involved in melancholy, seemed to be as it were waked up out of it; and those that had been entangled with extraordinary temptations, seemed wonderfully to be set at liberty; and not only so, but it was the most remarkable time of health that ever I knew since I have been in the town. We ordinarily have several bills put up every sabbath, for persons that are sick; but now we had not so much as one for many sabbaths together. But after this it seemed to be otherwise: when this work of God appeared to be at its greatest height, a poor weak man that belongs to the town, being in great spiritual trouble, was hurried with violent temptations to cut his own throat, and made an attempt, but did not do it effectually. He after this continued a considerable time exceedingly overwhelmed with melancholy; but has now of a long time been very greatly delivered by the light of God's countenance lifted up upon him,[6] and has expressed a great sense of his sin in so far yielding to temptation; and there are in him all hopeful evidences of his having been made a subject of saving mercy.

In the latter part of May it began to be very sensible that the Spirit of God was gradually withdrawing from us, and after this time Satan seemed to be more let loose, and raged in a dreadful manner. The first instance wherein it appeared was a person's putting an end to his own life, by cutting his throat.[7] He was a gentleman of more than common understanding, of strict morals, religious in his behavior, and a useful, honorable person in the town; but was of a family that are much prone to the disease of melancholy, and his mother was killed with it. He had, from the beginning of this extraordinary time, been exceedingly concerned about the state of his soul, and there were some things in his experience that appeared very hopefully; but he durst entertain no hope concerning his own good state. Towards the latter part of his time he grew much discouraged, and melancholy grew amain upon him, till he was wholly overpowered by it, and was in great measure past a capacity of receiving advice, or being reasoned with to any purpose: the devil took the advantage, and drove him into despairing thoughts. He was kept awake nights, meditating terror; so that he had scarce any sleep at all, for a long time together. And it was observed at last, that he was scarcely well capable of managing his ordinary business, and was judged delirious by the coroner's inquest. The news of this extraordinarily affected the minds of the people here, and struck them as it were with

---

[6]Numbers 6:26
[7]Joseph Hawley (1683–1735), Jonathan Edwards's uncle

astonishment. After this, multitudes in this and other towns seemed to have it strongly suggested to them, and pressed upon them, to do as this person had done. And many that seemed to be under no melancholy, some pious persons, that had no special darkness, or doubts about the goodness of their state, nor were under any special trouble or concern of mind about any thing spiritual or temporal, yet had it urged upon them, as if somebody had spoken to them, *Cut your own throat, now is a good opportunity. Now, now!* So that they were obliged to fight with all their might to resist it, and yet no reason suggested to them why they should do it.

About the same time there were two remarkable instances of persons led away with strange, enthusiastic delusions—one at Suffield, another at South Hadley. That which has made the greatest noise in the country was of the man at South Hadley, whose delusion was, that he thought himself divinely instructed to direct a poor man in melancholy and despairing circumstances, to say certain words in prayer to God, as recorded in Psalm 116:4 for his own relief. The man is esteemed a pious man. I have, since this error of his, had a particular acquaintance with him; and I believe none would question his piety, that had such an acquaintance. He gave me a particular account of the manner how he was deluded, which is too long to be here inserted. But in short, he was exceedingly rejoiced and elevated with this extraordinary work, so carried on in this part of the country; and was possessed with an opinion that it was the beginning of the glorious times of the church spoken of in scripture: and had read it as the opinion of some divines, that there would be many in these times that should be endued with extraordinary gifts of the Holy Ghost, and had embraced the notion; though he had at first no apprehensions that any besides ministers would have such gifts. But he since exceedingly laments the dishonor he has done to God, and the wound he has given religion in it, and has lain low before God and man for it.

After these things, the instances of conversion were rare here in comparison of what they had before been, (though that remarkable instance of the little child was after this), and the Spirit of God not long after this time appeared very sensibly withdrawing from all parts of the county; (though we have heard of its going on in some places of Connecticut, and that it continues to be carried on even to this day). But religion remained here, and I believe in some other places, the main subject of conversation for several months after this. And there were some turns, wherein God's work seemed something to revive, and we were ready to hope that all was going to be renewed again: yet in the main there was a gradual decline of that general, engaged, lively spirit in religion, which had been before. Several things have happened since, that have diverted people's minds, and turned their conversation more to others' affairs, particularly his Excellency,

the Governor, coming to this place, and the committee of General Court, on the treaty with the Indians;[8] and afterwards the Springfield controversy; and since that, our people in this town have been engaged in the building of a new meeting-house;[9] and some other occurrences might be mentioned that have
5 this effect. But as to those that have been thought to be converted among us, in this time, they generally seem to be persons that have had an abiding change wrought on them. I have had particular acquaintance with many of them since, and they generally appear to be persons that have a new sense of things, new apprehensions and views of God, of the divine attributes, and Jesus Christ, and
10 the great things of the gospel: they have a new sense of the truth of them, and they affect them in a new manner; though it is very far from being always alike with them, neither can they revive a sense of things when they please. Their hearts are often touched, and sometimes filled, with new sweetnesses and delights; there seems to be an inward ardor and burning of heart that they express, the
15 like to which they never experienced before; sometimes, perhaps, occasioned only by the mention of Christ's name, or some one of the divine perfections. There are new appetites, and a new kind of breathings and pantings of heart, and groanings that cannot be uttered. There is a new kind of inward labor and struggle of soul towards heaven and holiness.
20   Some, that before were very rough in their temper and manners, seem to be remarkably softened and sweetened. And some have had their souls exceedingly filled, and overwhelmed with light, love, and comfort, long since the work of God has ceased to be so remarkably carried on in a general way: and some have had much greater experiences of this nature than they had before. And there is
25 still a great deal of religious conversation continued in the town, among young and old; a religious disposition appears to be still maintained among our people, by their upholding frequent private religious meetings; and all sorts are generally worshiping God at such meetings, on sabbath-nights, and in the evening after our public lecture. Many children in the town do still keep up such meetings
30 among themselves. I know of no one young person in the town that has returned to former ways, or looseness and extravagancy in any respect; but we still remain a reformed people, and God has evidently made us a new people.
         I cannot say that there has been no instance of any one person that has carried himself so that others should justly be stumbled concerning his profession;
35 nor am I so vain as to imagine that we have not been mistaken concerning any that we have entertained a good opinion of, or that there are none pass among

---

[8] Jonathan Belcher (1682–1757), Governor of Massachusetts (1730–1741), met several tribes at Deerfield in 1735 to negotiate a treaty.
[9] The new meeting house was dedicated at Christmas 1737. The assigning of pews invariably caused controversy.

us for sheep, that are indeed wolves in sheep's clothing, who probably may some time or other discover themselves by their fruit. We are not so pure but that we have great cause to be humbled and ashamed that we are so impure, nor so religious but that those that watch for our halting may see things in us whence they may take occasion to reproach us and religion: but in the main there has been a great and marvelous work of conversion and sanctification among the people here; and they have paid all due respect to those who have been blest of God to be the instruments of it. Both old and young have shown a forwardness to hearken not only to my counsels, but even to my reproofs from the pulpit.

A great part of the country have not received the most favorable thoughts of this affair; and to this day many retain a jealousy concerning it, and prejudice against it. I have reason to think that the meanness and weakness of the instrument that has been made use of in this town, has prejudiced many against it; it does not appear to me strange that it should be so: but yet this circumstance of this great work of God is analogous to other circumstances of it. God has so ordered the manner of the work in many respects, as very signally and remarkably to show it to be his own peculiar and immediate work, and to secure the glory of it wholly to his own almighty power and sovereign grace. And whatever the circumstances and means have been, and though we are so unworthy, yet so hath it pleased God to work! And we are evidently a people blessed of the Lord! And here, in this corner of the world, God dwells, and manifests his glory.

Thus, Reverend Sir, I have given a large and particular account of this remarkable affair; and yet, considering how manifold God's works have been among us, that are worthy to be written, it is but a brief one. I should have sent it much sooner, had I not been greatly hindered by illness in my family, and also in myself. It is, probably, much larger than you expected, and it may be than you would have chosen. I thought that the extraordinariness of the thing, and the innumerable misrepresentations which have gone abroad of it, many of which have, doubtless, reached your ears, made it necessary that I should be particular. But I would leave it entirely to your wisdom to make what use of it you think best, to send a part of it to England, or all, or none, if you think it not worthy; or otherwise to dispose of it as you may think most for God's glory, and the interest of religion. If you are pleased to send anything to the Reverend Dr. Guyse, I should be glad to have it signified to him as my humble desire, that since he, and the congregation to which he preached, have been pleased to take so much notice of us as they have—that they would also think of us at the throne of grace, and seek there for us, that God would not forsake us, but enable us to bring forth fruit answerable to our profession and our mercies, and that our light may shine before men, that others seeing our good works, may glorify our Father who is in heaven.

When I first heard of the notice the Reverend Dr. Watts and Dr. Guyse took of God's mercies to us, I took occasion to inform our congregation of it in a discourse from these words: "A city that is set upon a hill cannot be hid." And having since seen a particular account of the notice the Reverend Dr. Guyse, 5 and the congregation he preached to, took of it, in a letter you wrote to my honored uncle Williams, I read that part of your letter to the congregation, and labored as much as in me lay to enforce their duty from it. The congregation were very sensibly moved and affected at both times.

I humbly request of you, Reverend Sir, your prayers for this county, in its 10 present melancholy circumstances, into which it is brought by the Springfield quarrel, which, doubtless, above all things that have happened, has tended to put a stop to the glorious work here, and to prejudice this country against it, and hinder the propagation of it. I also ask your prayers for this town, and would particularly beg an interest in them for him, who is, honored sir, with humble 15 respect, your obedient son and servant, Jonathan Edwards.

THE KINGDOM OF GOD
GEORGE WHITEFIELD (1714–1770)

One of the most unlikely friendships of the eighteenth century was Benjamin Franklin's with George Whitefield. Franklin was an exuberant materialist; Whitefield an enthusiastic spiritualist. Whitefield was the most visible and popular evangelist of the century, a dissenter against Enlightenment and all it seemed to stand for, and the embodiment of the Great Awakening. Yet Franklin was Whitefield's best American friend, and Whitefield was Franklin's only evangelical friend.

Whitefield preached the New Birth. John Bunyan's character Christian in Pilgrim's Progress *(by far the most widely read book in the colonies after the Bible) said, "I was delivered from the burden that so heavily oppressed me." The New Birth was the shattering recognition of sin and the need for repentance; the experience of God's grace. As Whitefield moved from colony to colony on several visits to America from England, tens of thousands came to hear and see him act out the evangelical message, and to experience grace for themselves. Franklin once calculated that Whitefield could be heard by 20,000 people in the open air.*

This selection represents the themes of Whitefield's preaching but cannot convey its power. His sermons were often given in "field meetings" since few churches could hold the crowds who flocked to hear him. Highly charged, emotional, and extemporaneous, they produced the experience of the New Birth.

1741

For the kingdom of God is not meat and drink; but righteousness, and peace, and joy in the Holy Ghost—Romans 14:17

...There are two things which those who call themselves Christians want much to be convinced of, namely, First, what religion is not; second, what religion positively is. Both these are in the words of the text plainly taught, and,   5

Henry C. Fish, ed., *History and Repository of Pulpit Eloquence* (New York: Dodd, Mead, and Company, 1856), I:333–48.

therefore, as God shall enable me, I shall endeavor, first, to explain what you are to understand by "the kingdom of God." Secondly, I shall endeavor to show that "the kingdom of God is not meat and drink;" and thirdly, I shall show you what "the kingdom of God" positively is, namely, "righteousness, and peace, and joy in the Holy Ghost."

First, I am to explain to you what you are to understand by "the kingdom of God." By the kingdom of God, in some places of Scripture, you are to understand no more than the outward preaching of the Gospel, as when the apostles went out and preached that "the kingdom of God and the kingdom of heaven was at hand."[1] In other places of Scripture you are to understand it as implying that work of grace, that inward holiness, which is wrought in the heart of every soul that is truly converted and brought home to God. The Lord Jesus Christ is King of His Church, and the Lord Jesus Christ has got a kingdom; and this kingdom is erected and set up in the hearts of sinners, when they are brought to be subject to the government of our dear Redeemer's laws. In this sense, therefore, we are to understand the kingdom of God, when Jesus Christ said, "The kingdom of God is within you,"[2] in your hearts; and when He tells Nicodemus that "unless a man be born again he cannot see the kingdom of God"[3] he can have no notion of the inward life of a Christian. In other places of Scripture, the kingdom of God not only signifies the kingdom of grace, but the kingdom of grace and of glory also; as when Jesus said, "It is easier for a camel to go through the eye of a needle than for a rich man to enter into the kingdom of God;"[4] that is, either to be a true member of His mystical Church here or a partaker of the glory of the Church triumphant hereafter. We are to take the kingdom of God in the text as signifying that inward work of grace, that kingdom which the Lord Jesus Christ sets up in the hearts of all that are truly brought home to God; so that when the Apostle tells us, "The kingdom of God is not meat and drink," it is the same as though he had said, "My dear friends, do not quarrel about outward things; for the kingdom of God, or true and undefiled religion, heart and soul religion, is not meat and drink."

Secondly, by meat and drink, if we compare the text with the context, we are to understand no more than this, that the kingdom of God, or true religion, does not consist in abstaining from a particular meat or drink. But I shall take the words in a more comprehensive sense, and shall endeavor to show you on this head that the kingdom of God, or true and undefiled religion, does not consist in any, no, not in all outward things, put them altogether. And,

---

[1]Matthew 10:7
[2]Luke 17:21
[3]John 3:3
[4]Matthew 19:24, Mark 10:25, Luke 18:25

First, The kingdom of God, or true and undefiled religion, does not consist in being of this or that particular sect or communion. Perhaps, my dear friends, were many of you asked what reason you can give for the hope that is in you, what title you have to call yourselves Christians—perhaps you could say no more for yourselves than this, namely, that you belong to such a church, and   5 worship God in the same way in which your fathers and mothers worshiped God before you; and perhaps, at the same time you are so narrow in your thoughts that you think none can worship God but those that worship God just in your way. It is certainly, my dear friends, a blessing to be born as you are, in a reformed Church; it is certainly a blessing to have the outward government   10 and discipline of the Church exercised; but then, if you place religion merely in being of this or that sect—if you contend to monopolize or confine the grace of God to your particular party—if you rest in that, you place the kingdom of God in something in which it does not consist—you had as good place it in meat and drink. There are certainly Christians among all sects and communions   15 that have learned the truth as it is in Christ Jesus. I do not mean that there are Christians among Arians, Socinians, or those that deny the divinity of Jesus Christ—I am sure the devil is priest of such congregations as these; but I mean there are Christians among other sects that may differ from us in the outward worship of God. Therefore, my dear friends, learn to be more catholic, more   20 unconfined in your notions; for if you place the kingdom of God merely in a sect, you place it in that in which it does not consist.

Again: as the kingdom of God does not consist in being of this or that sect, so neither does it consist in being baptized when you were young. Baptism is certainly an ordinance of the Lord Jesus Christ—it ought certainly to be ad-   25 ministered; but then, my dear friends, take care that you do not make a Christ of your baptism, for there have been many baptized with water, as you were, who were never savingly baptized with the Holy Ghost. Paul had a great value for circumcision; but when he saw the Jews resting upon their circumcision, he told them circumcision was nothing, and un-circumcision was nothing, but a   30 new creature. And yet most people live as if they thought it will be sufficient to entitle them to heaven to tell Jesus Christ that their name was in the register-book of such and such a parish. Your names may be in the register-book, and yet at the same time not be in the book of life. Ananias and Sapphira were bap-tized—Simon Magus was baptized: and, therefore, if you place religion merely   35 in being baptized, in having the outward washing of water, without receiving the baptism of the Holy Ghost, you place the kingdom of God in something in which it does not consist—in effect, you place it in meat and drink.

But further: as the kingdom of God and true religion does not consist in being baptized, neither does it consist in being orthodox in our notions, or   40 being able to talk fluently of the doctrines of the Gospel. There are a great many who can talk of free grace, of free justification, of final perseverance, of election, and God's everlasting love. All these are precious truths—they are all connected in a chain; take away one link and you spoil the whole chain of Gospel truths.

5   But then I am persuaded that there are many who talk of these truths, who preach up these truths, and yet at the same time never, never felt the power of these truths upon their hearts. It is a good thing to have a form of sound words; and I think you have got a form of sound words in your Larger and Shorter Catechism. But you may have orthodox heads, and yet you may have the devil

10   in your hearts; you may have clear heads, you may be able to speak, as it were, with the tongues of men and angels, the doctrines of the Gospel, but yet, at the same time, you may never have felt them upon your own souls. And if you have never felt the power of them upon your hearts, your talk of Christ and free justification, and having rational convictions of these truths, will but increase

15   your condemnation, and you will only go to hell with so much more solemnity. Take care, therefore, of resting in a form of knowledge—it is dangerous; if you do, you place the kingdom of God in meat and drink.

Again: as the kingdom of God does not consist in orthodox notions, much less does it consist in being sincere. I know not what sort of religion we have got

20   among us. I fear many ministers as well as people want to recommend themselves to God by their sincerity; they think, "If we do all we can, if we are but sincere, Jesus Christ will have mercy upon us." But pray what is there in our sincerity to recommend us to God? There is no natural man in the world sincere till God make us new creatures in Jesus Christ; and, therefore, if you depend upon your

25   sincerity for your salvation, your sincerity will damn you.

Further: as the kingdom of God does not consist merely in sincerity (for nothing will recommend us to God but the righteousness of Jesus Christ), neither does it consist in being negatively good, and yet I believe, my dear friends, if many of you were to be visited by a minister when you are upon a

30   death-bed, and if he were to ask you how you hope to be saved, why, you would say, "Yes, you hoped to be saved, you never did man, woman, nor child any harm in your life; you have done nobody any harm." And, indeed, I do not find that the unprofitable servant did one any harm; no, the poor man, be only innocently wrapped up his talent in a napkin, and when his lord came to call

35   him to account, he thought he should be applauded by his lord, and therefore introduces himself with the word lo—"Lo, there you have what is yours." But what says Jesus Christ? "Cast the unprofitable servant into outer darkness, there shall be weeping and gnashing of teeth."[5] Suppose it to be true that you had

---

[5]Matthew 25:14–30

done nobody harm, yet it will not avail you to salvation. If you bring forth only the fig-leaves of an outward profession, and bring not forth good fruit, it will not send you to heaven—it will send you to hell.

And some of you, perhaps, may think I have not reached you yet, therefore I go further, to show you that the kingdom of God does not consist in a dry, lifeless morality. I am not speaking against morality—it is a blessed thing when Jesus Christ is laid as the foundation of it, and I could heartily wish that you moral gentlemen, who are for talking so much of your morality, I wish we could see a little more of it than we do. I do not cry down morality, but so far as this, that you do not rest in your morality, that you do not think you are Christians because you are not vicious—because you now and then do some good action. Why, self-love will carry a man to perform all moral actions. A man, perhaps, will not get drunk for fear of making his head ache; a man may be honest because it would spoil his reputation to steal. And so a man who has not the love of God in his heart may do moral actions. But if you depend on morality, if you make a Christ of it, and go about to establish a righteousness of your own, and think your morality will recommend you to God, my dear friends, you are building upon a rotten foundation, you will find yourselves mistaken, and that the kingdom of God is not in your hearts.

Again: as the kingdom of God does not consist in doing nobody hurt, nor in doing moral actions, neither does it consist in attending upon all outward ordinances whatsoever. A great many of you may think that you go to church, and receive the sacrament once or twice a year (though I do think that is too seldom, by a great deal, to have it administered) you may read your Bibles, you may have family worship, you may say your prayers in your closets, and yet at the same time, my dear friends, know nothing of the Lord Jesus Christ in your hearts. You may have a token, and receive the sacrament, and perhaps at the same time be eating and drinking your own damnation. I speak this because it is a most fatal snare that poor professors are exposed to—we stop our consciences by our duties. Many of you, perhaps, lead a lukewarm, loose life—you are Gallio-like;[6] yet you will be very good the sacrament-week; you will attend all the sermons, and come to the sacrament, you will be very good for some time after that, and then afterward go on in your former way till the next sacrament. You are resting on the means of grace all the while, and placing religion in that which is only a mean of religion. I speak from my own experience. I know how much I was deceived with a form of godliness. I made conscience of fasting twice a week, I made conscience of praying sometimes nine times a day, and received the sacrament every Sabbath-day, and yet knew nothing of inward religion in

5

10

15

20

25

30

35

---

[6]Junius Annaeus Gallio, see Acts 18

my heart, till God was pleased to dart a ray of light into my soul, and show me I must be a new creature, or be damned for evermore. Being, therefore, so long deceived myself, I speak with more sympathy to you who are resting on a round of duties and model of performances. And now, my friends, if your

5   hearts were to be searched, and you were to speak your minds, I appeal to your own hearts whether you are not thinking within yourselves, though you may have so much charity as to think I mean well, yet I verily believe many of you think I have carried matters a little too far; and why is this but because I come close to some of your cases? The pride of your hearts does not care to admit

10   of conviction, therefore you would fain retort on the preacher, and say he is wrong, whereas it is your hearts that are wrong all the while.

     Others, again, perhaps may be saying, "Well, if a man may go thus far and not be a Christian, as I am sure he may, and a great deal further, you will be apt to cry out, 'Who, then, can be saved?'" And O that I could hear you

15   asking this question in earnest! For, my friends, I am obliged, wherever I go, to endeavor to plow up people's fallow ground, to bring them off from their duties, and making a Christ of them. There are so many shadows in religion that if you do not take care you will grasp at the shadow, and lose the substance. The Devil has so ordered the affairs of the Church now, and our hearts are so

20   desperately deceitful, that if we do not take a deal of care we shall come short of true religion—of the true kingdom of God in the soul. The great question then is, "Whether any of you are convinced of what has been said?" Does power come with the word? When I was reading a book entitled *The Life of God in the Soul of Man*[7] and reading that a man may read, pray, and go to church, and be

25   constant in the duties of the Sabbath, and yet not be a Christian, I wondered what the man would be at; I was ready to throw it from me, till at last he told me that religion was an union of the soul with God—the image of God wrought upon the heart, or Christ Jesus formed in us. Then God was pleased with these words to cast a ray of light into my soul; with the light there came

30   a power, and from that very moment I knew I must be a new creature. This, perhaps, may be your case, my dear hearers. Perchance many of you may be loving, good-natured people, and attend the duties of religion, but take care, for Christ's sake, that you do not rest on these things.

     I think I cannot sum up what has been said better than to give you the

35   character of the Apostle Paul. Are you a Christian, do you think, because you are of this or that sect? Paul was a Jew and a Pharisee. Are you a Christian because you are baptized, and enjoy Christian privileges? Then Paul was circumcised. Are you a Christian because you do nobody hurt, and are sincere? Paul was

---

[7]Henry Scougal (1650–1678), *The Life of God in the Soul of Man* (Edinburgh, 1677).

blameless before his conversion, and was not a Gallio in religion, as many of us are; he was so zealous for God that he persecuted the Church of Christ. But yet when God was pleased to reveal His Son in him, when God was pleased to strike him to the ground, and let him see what heart religion was, then Paul dropped his false confidence immediately; those things which he counted gain, 5 which he depended on before, he now counted loss, that he might win Christ, and be found in Him; not having his own righteousness, which is of the law, but that righteousness which is by faith in Christ Jesus. It is time, my dear friends, to proceed to

Thirdly, the next thing proposed, namely, to show you what the kingdom 10 of God, or true religion, positively is. I have told you what it is not; I shall now proceed to show you what it is. It is "righteousness, and peace, and joy in the Holy Ghost." But before I proceed to this, I must make a little digression. Perhaps curiosity has brought many here who have neither regard to God nor man. A man may be a member of the purest church, a man may be baptized, 15 do nobody harm, do a great deal of good, attend on all the ordinances of Christianity, and yet at the same time may be a child of the devil. If a man may go thus far, and yet at the same time miss salvation, what will become of you who do not keep up a form of religion, who scarcely know the time when you have been at church and attending sermons, unless curiosity brought you to 20 hear a particular stranger? What will become of you who, instead of believing the Gospel and reading the Bible, set up your corrupt religion in opposition to divine revelation? What will become of you, who count it your pleasure to riot in the daytime, to spend time in rioting and wantonness; who are sitting in the scorner's chair, and joining with your hellish companions, who love to 25 dress the children of God in bear-skins? What will become of you who live in acts of uncleanness, drunkenness, adultery, Sabbath-breaking? Surely, without repentance, you will be lost—your damnation slumbers not. God may bear with you long, but He will not forbear always. The time will come when He will ease Himself of His adversaries, and then you will be undone for evermore, 30 unless you come to Him as poor, lost sinners.

But I now go on to show you what true religion positively is; "it is righteousness," it is "peace," it is "joy in the Holy Ghost." And

First, the kingdom of God is "righteousness." By righteousness we are here to understand the complete, perfect, and all-sufficient righteousness of our Lord 35 Jesus Christ, as including both His active and His passive obedience. My dear friends, we have no righteousness of our own; our best righteousness, take them altogether, are but so many filthy rags; we can only be accepted for the sake of the righteousness of our Lord Jesus Christ. This righteousness must be imputed and made over to us, and applied to our hearts; and till we get this righteous- 40 ness brought home to our souls, we are in a state of death and damnation—the wrath of God abides on us.

Before I go further, I would endeavor to apply this. Give me leave to put this question to your hearts. You call yourselves Christians, and would count me uncharitable to call it in question; but I exhort you to let conscience speak out, do not bribe it any longer. Did you ever see yourselves as damned sinners? Did conviction ever fasten upon your hearts? And after you had been made to see your want of Christ, and made to hunger and thirst after righteousness, did you lay hold on Christ by faith? Did you ever close with Christ? Was Christ's righteousness ever put upon your naked souls? Was ever a feeling application of His righteousness made to your hearts? Was it, or was it not? If not, you are in a damnable state—you are out of Christ; for the Apostle says here, "The kingdom of God is righteousness;" that is, the righteousness of Christ applied and brought home to the heart.

It follows, "peace." "The kingdom of God is righteousness and peace." By peace I do not understand that false peace, or rather carnal security, into which so many are fallen. There are thousands who speak peace to themselves when there is no peace. Thousands have got a peace of the devil's making; the strong man armed has got possession of their hearts, and therefore their goods are all in peace. But the peace here spoken of is a peace that follows after a great deal of soul trouble; it is like that calm which the Lord Jesus Christ spoke to the wind; "Peace, be still; and immediately there was a great calm;"[8] it is like that peace which Christ spoke to His disciples, when He came and said, "Peace be unto you"[9], "My peace I leave with you."[10] It is a peace of God's making, it is a peace that can be felt, it is a peace that passes human understanding—it is a peace that results from a sense of having Christ's righteousness brought home to the soul. For a poor soul before this is full of trouble; Christ makes application of His righteousness to his heart; and then the poor creature, being justified by faith, has peace with God through our Lord Jesus Christ.

My dear friends, I am now talking of heart-religion, of an inward work of God, an inward kingdom in your hearts, which you must have, or you shall never sit with Jesus Christ in His kingdom. The most of you may have peace, but for Christ's sake examine upon what this peace is founded—see if Christ be brought home to your souls, if you have had a feeling application of the merits of Christ brought home to your souls. Is God at peace with you? Did Jesus Christ ever say, "Peace be to you"—"Be of good cheer"—"Go your way,

---

[8]Mark 4:39
[9]Luke 24:36, John 20:19
[10]John 14:27

your sins are forgiven"—"My peace I leave with you, My peace I give unto you?" Did God ever bring a comfortable promise with power to your soul? And after you have been praying, and fearing you would be damned, did you ever feel peace flow in like a river upon your soul so that you could say, Now I know that God is my friend, now I know that Jesus is my Savior, now I can call Him "My Lord, and my God;" now I know that Christ has not only died for others, but I know that Jesus has died for me in particular. O my dear friends, it is impossible to tell you the comfort of this peace, and I am astonished (only man's heart is desperately wicked) how you can have peace one moment and yet not know that God is at peace with you. How can you go to bed this night without this peace? It is a blessed thing to know when sin is forgiven; would you not be glad if an angel were to come and tell you so this night?

But there is something more—there is "joy in the Holy Ghost." I have often thought that if the Apostle Paul were to come and preach now he would be reckoned one of the greatest enthusiasts on earth. He talked of the Holy Ghost, of feeling the Holy Ghost; and so we must all feel it, all experience it, all receive it, or we can never see a holy God with comfort. We are not to receive the Holy Ghost so as to enable us to work miracles; for, "Many will say in that day, we have cast out devils in Your name, and in Your name done many wonderful works."[11] But we must receive the Holy Ghost to sanctify our nature, to purify our hearts, and make us meet for heaven. Unless we are born again, and have the Holy Ghost in our hearts, if we were in heaven we could take no pleasure there. The Apostle not only supposes we must have the Holy Ghost, but he supposes, as a necessary ingredient to make up the kingdom of God in a believer's heart, that he must have "joy in the Holy Ghost." There are a great many, I believe, who think religion is a poor melancholy thing, and they are afraid to be Christians. But, my dear friends, there is no true joy till you can joy in God and Christ. I know wicked men and men of pleasure will have a little laughter; but what is it but like the crackling of a few thorns under a pot? It makes a blaze, and soon goes out. I know what it is to take pleasure in sin; but I always found the smart that followed was ten thousand times more hurtful than any gratification I could receive. But they who joy in God have a joy that strangers intermeddle not with—it is a joy that no man can take from them; it amounts to a full assurance of faith that the soul is reconciled to God through Christ, that Jesus dwells in the heart; and when the soul reflects on itself, it magnifies the Lord, and rejoices in God its Savior. Thus we are told that "Zaccheus received Christ joyfully," that "the eunuch went on his way rejoicing," and that "the jailer rejoiced in God with all his house."[12] O, my friends, what

---

[11]Matthew 7:22
[12]Luke 19:6, Acts 8:39, Acts 16:34

joy have they that know their sins are forgiven them! What a blessed thing is it for a man to look forward and see an endless eternity of happiness before him, knowing that everything shall work together for his good!—it is joy unspeakable and full of glory. O may God make you all partakers of it!

5   Here, then, we will put the kingdom of God together. It is "righteousness," it is "peace," it is "joy in the Holy Ghost." When this is placed in the heart, God there reigns, God there dwells and walks—the creature is a son or daughter of the Almighty. But, my friends, how few are there here who have been made partakers of this kingdom! Perhaps the kingdom of the devil, instead of the
10 kingdom of God, is in most of our hearts. This has been a place much favored of God; may I hope some of you can go along with me and say "Blessed be God we have got righteousness, peace, and joy in the Holy Ghost?" Have you so? Then you are kings, though beggars; you are happy above all men in the world—you have got heaven in your hearts; and when the crust of your bodies
15 drops, your souls will meet with God, your souls will enter into the world of peace, and you shall be happy with God for evermore. I hope there is none of you who will fear death; fie for shame, if you do! What! afraid to go to Jesus, to your Lord? You may cry out, "O death, where is thy sting? O grave, where is thy victory?" You may go on your way rejoicing, knowing that God is your
20 friend; die when you will, angels will carry you safe to heaven.

    But, O, how many are here in this church-yard, who will be laid in some grave ere long, who are entire strangers to this work of God upon their souls! My dear friends, I think this is an awful sight. Here are many thousands of souls, that must shortly appear with me, a poor creature, in the general assembly of
25 all mankind before God in judgment. God Almighty knows whether some of you may not drop down dead before you go out of the church-yard; and yet, perhaps most are strangers to the Lord Jesus Christ in their hearts. Perhaps curiosity has brought you out to hear a poor babbler preach. But, my friends, I hope I came out of a better principle. If I know anything of my heart, I came
30 to promote God's glory; and if the Lord should make use of such a worthless worm, such a wretched creature, as I am, to do your precious souls good, nothing would rejoice me more than to hear that God makes the foolishness of preaching a means of making many believe. I was long myself deceived with a form of godliness, and I know what it is to be a factor for the devil, to
35 be led captive by the devil at his will, to have the kingdom of the devil in my heart; and I hope I can say, through free grace, I know what it is to have the kingdom of God erected in me. It is God's goodness that such a poor wretch as I am converted; though sometimes when I am speaking of God's goodness I am afraid he will strike me down dead. Let me draw out my soul and heart
40 to you, my dear friends, my dear guilty friends, poor bleeding souls, who must

shortly take your last farewell, and fly into endless eternity. Let me entreat you to lay these things seriously to heart this night. Now, when the Sabbath is over, the evening is drawing near, methinks the very sight is awful (I could almost weep over you, as our Lord did over Jerusalem) to think in how short a time every soul of you must die—some of you to go to heaven, and others to go to the devil for evermore.

O my dear friends, these are matters of eternal moment. I did not come to tickle your ears; if I had a mind to do so, I would play the orator; no, but I came, if God should be pleased, to touch your hearts. What shall I say to you? Open the door of your heart, that the King of glory, the blessed Jesus, may come in and erect His kingdom in your soul. Make room for Christ; the Lord Jesus desires to sup with you to-night; Christ is willing to come into any of your hearts, that will be pleased to open and receive Him. Are there any of you made willing Lydias? There are many women here, but how many Lydias are there here? Does power go with the word to open your heart? and find you a sweet melting in your soul? Are you willing? Then Christ Jesus is willing to come to you. But you may say, Will Christ come to my wicked, polluted heart? Yes, though you have many devils in your heart, Christ will come and erect His throne there; though the devils be in your heart, the Lord Jesus will scourge our a legion of devils, and His throne shall be exalted in thy soul. Sinners, be ye what you will, come to Christ, you shall have righteousness and peace. If you have no peace, come to Christ, and He will give you peace. When you come to Christ, you will feel such joy that it is impossible for you to tell. O may God pity you all! I hope this will be a night of salvation to some of your souls.

My dear friends, I would preach with all my heart till midnight, to do you good, till I could preach no more. Oh that this body might hold out to speak more for my dear Redeemer! Had I a thousand lives, had I a thousand tongues, they should be employed in inviting sinners to come to Jesus Christ! Come, then, let me prevail with some of you to come along with me. Come poor, lost, undone sinner, come just as you are to Christ, and say, If I be damned, I will perish at the feet of Jesus Christ, where never one perished yet. He will receive you with open arms; the dear Redeemer is willing to receive you all. Fly, then, for your lives. The devil is in you while unconverted; and will you go with the devil in your heart to bed this night? God Almighty knows if ever you and I shall see one another again. In one or two days more I must go, and, perhaps, I may never see you again till I meet you at the judgment-day. O my dear friends, think of that solemn meeting; think of that important hour, when the heavens shall pass away with a great noise, when the elements shall melt with fervent heat, when the sea and the grave shall be giving up their dead, and all shall be summoned to appear before the great God. What will you do then, if the kingdom of God is not erected in your hearts? You must go to the devil—like must go to like—if you are not converted Christ has asserted it in the strongest manner: "Verily, verily, I say unto you, Except a man be born again, he cannot enter into the kingdom of God." Who can dwell with devouring fire? Who can

5　dwell with everlasting burnings? O, my heart is melting with love to you. Surely God intends to do good to your poor souls. Will no one be persuaded to accept of Christ? If those who are settled Pharisees will not come, I desire to speak to you who are drunkards, Sabbath-breakers, cursers and swearers—will you come to Christ? I know that many of you come here out of curiosity: though you

10　come only to see the congregation, yet if you come to Jesus Christ, Christ will accept of you. Are there any cursing, swearing soldiers here? Will you come to Jesus Christ, and, list yourselves under the banner of the dear Redeemer? You are all welcome to Christ. Are there any little boys or little girls here? Come to Christ, and He will erect His kingdom in you. There are many little children

15　whom God is working on, both at home and abroad. O, if some of the little lambs would come to Christ, they shall have peace and joy in the day that the Redeemer shall set up His kingdom in their hearts. Parents tell them that Jesus Christ will take them in His arms, that He will dandle them on His knees. All of you, old and young, you that are old and gray-headed, come to Jesus Christ,

20　and you shall be kings and priests to your God. The Lord will abundantly pardon you at the eleventh hour. "Ho, every one of you that thirsts." If there be any of you ambitious of honor, do you want a crown, a scepter? Come to Christ, and the Lord Jesus Christ will give you a kingdom that no man shall take from you.

On George Whitefield
Benjamin Franklin (1706–1790)

In many ways the Great Awakening was a spiritual counterrevolution against the Enlightenment's worldliness. But just as Franklin's message transcended local cultures and limitations of time and space, so did White-field's. They also had in common a concern for mass communication, self-promotion, and popularity. They were both suspicious of local loyalties and traditional institutions, which they believed tended to be sectarian and thus to work against the universality of their messages. Their friendship was unusual, but important. Their movements had the effect of helping to produce an American culture that would emerge in the imperial crisis after the Great War for Empire.

1788

In 1739 arrived among us from Ireland the Reverend Mr. Whitefield, who had made himself remarkable there as an itinerant preacher. He was at first permitted to preach in some of our churches; but the clergy, taking a dislike to him, soon refused him their pulpits, and he was obliged to preach in the fields. The multitudes of all sects and denominations that attended his sermons were 5 enormous, and it was matter of speculation to me, who was one of the number, to observe the extraordinary influence of his oratory on his hearers, and how much they admired and respected him, notwithstanding his common abuse of them, by assuring them that they were naturally half beasts and half devils. It was wonderful to see the change soon made in the manners of our inhabitants. 10 From being thoughtless or indifferent about religion, it seemed as if all the world were growing religious, so that one could not walk thro' the town in an evening without hearing psalms sung in different families of every street.

And it being found inconvenient to assemble in the open air, subject to its inclemencies, the building of a house to meet in was no sooner proposed, 15 and persons appointed to receive contributions, but sufficient sums were soon

Autobiography of Benjamin Franklin (New York: The MacMillan Company, 1921), 103–7.

received to procure the ground and erect the building, which was one hundred feet long and seventy broad, about the size of Westminster Hall; and the work was carried on with such spirit as to be finished in a much shorter time than could have been expected. Both house and ground were vested in trustees,
5   expressly for the use of any preacher of any religious persuasion who might desire to say something to the people at Philadelphia; the design in building not being to accommodate any particular sect, but the inhabitants in general; so that even if the Mufti of Constantinople were to send a missionary to preach Mohammedanism to us, he would find a pulpit at his service.

10   Mr. Whitefield, on leaving us, went preaching all the way thro' the colonies to Georgia. The settlement of that province had lately been begun, but, instead of being made with hardy, industrious husbandmen, accustomed to labor, the only people fit for such an enterprise, it was with families of broken shop-keepers and other insolvent debtors, many of indolent and idle habits,
15   taken out of the jails, who, being set down in the woods, unqualified for clearing land, and unable to endure the hardships of a new settlement, perished in numbers, leaving many helpless children unprovided for. The sight of their miserable situation inspired the benevolent heart of Mr. Whitefield with the idea of building an Orphan House there, in which they might be supported
20   and educated. Returning northward, he preached up this charity, and made large collections, for his eloquence had a wonderful power over the hearts and purses of his hearers, of which I myself was an instance. I did not disapprove of the design, but, as Georgia was then destitute of materials and workmen, and it was proposed to send them from Philadelphia at a great expense, I thought
25   it would have been better to have built the house here, and brought the children to it. This I advised; but he was resolute in his first project, rejected my counsel, and I therefore refused to contribute. I happened soon after to attend one of his sermons, in the course of which I perceived he intended to finish with a collection, and I silently resolved he should get nothing from me, I had
30   in my pocket a handful of copper money, three or four silver dollars, and five *pistoles* in gold. As he proceeded I began to soften, and concluded to give the coppers. Another stroke of his oratory made me ashamed of that, and determined me to give the silver; and he finished so admirably that I emptied my pocket wholly into the collector's dish, gold and all. At this sermon there was
35   also one of our club, who, being of my sentiments respecting the building in Georgia, and suspecting a collection might be intended, had, by precaution, emptied his pockets before he came from home. Towards the conclusion of the discourse, however, he felt a strong desire to give, and applied to a neighbour, who stood near him, to borrow some money for the purpose. The application
40   was unfortunately [made] to perhaps the only man in the company who had

the firmness not to be affected by the preacher. His answer was, "At any other time, Friend Hopkinson, I would lend to thee freely; but not now, for thee seems to be out of thy right senses."

Some of Mr. Whitefield's enemies affected to suppose that he would apply these collections to his own private emolument; but I who was intimately acquainted with him (being employed in printing his Sermons and Journals, etc.), never had the least suspicion of his integrity, but am to this day decidedly of opinion that he was in all his conduct a perfectly honest man; and methinks my testimony in his favour ought to have the more weight, as we had no religious connection. He used, indeed, sometimes to pray for my conversion, but never had the satisfaction of believing that his prayers were heard. Ours was a mere civil friendship, sincere on both sides, and lasted to his death.

The following instance will show something of the terms on which we stood. Upon one of his arrivals from England at Boston, he wrote to me that he should come soon to Philadelphia, but knew not where he could lodge when there, as he understood his old friend and host, Mr. Benezet, was removed to Germantown. My answer was, "You know my house; if you can make shift with its scanty accommodations, you will be most heartily welcome." He replied that if I made that kind offer for Christ's sake, I should not miss of a reward. And I returned, "Don't let me be mistaken; it was not for Christ's sake, but for your sake." One of our common acquaintance jocosely remarked that, knowing it to be the custom of the saints, when they received any favour, to shift the burden of the obligation from off their own shoulders, and place it in heaven, I had contrived to fix it on earth.

The last time I saw Mr. Whitefield was in London, when he consulted me about his orphan house concern, and his purpose of appropriating it to the establishment of a college.

He had a loud and clear voice, and articulated his words and sentences so perfectly, that he might be heard and understood at a great distance, especially as his auditories, however numerous, observed the most exact silence. He preached one evening from the top of the Court-house steps, which are in the middle of Market-street, and on the west side of Second-street, which crosses it at right angles. Both streets were filled with his hearers to a considerable distance. Being among the hindmost in Market-street, I had the curiosity to learn how far he could be heard, by retiring backwards down the street towards the river; and I found his voice distinct till I came near Front-street, when some noise in that street obscured it. Imagining then a semi-circle, of which my distance should be the radius, and that it were filled with auditors, to each of whom I allowed two square feet, I computed that he might well be heard by more than thirty thousand. This reconciled me to the newspaper accounts of his having preached

5

10

15

20

25

30

35

40

to twenty-five thousand people in the fields, and to the ancient histories of generals haranguing whole armies, of which I had sometimes doubted.

By hearing him often, I came to distinguish easily between sermons newly composed, and those which he had often preached in the course of his travels. His delivery of the latter was so improved by frequent repetitions that every accent, every emphasis, every modulation of voice, was so perfectly well turned and well placed that, without being interested in the subject, one could not help being pleased with the discourse; a pleasure of much the same kind with that received from an excellent piece of music. This is an advantage itinerant preachers have over those who are stationary, as the latter can not well improve their delivery of a sermon by so many rehearsals.

His writing and printing from time to time gave great advantage to his enemies; unguarded expressions, and even erroneous opinions, delivered in preaching, might have been afterwards explained or qualified by supposing others that might have accompanied them, or they might have been denied; but *litera scripta manet*.[1] Critics attacked his writings violently, and with so much appearance of reason as to diminish the number of his votaries and prevent their increase; so that I am of opinion if he had never written anything, he would have left behind him a much more numerous and important sect, and his reputation might in that case have been still growing, even after his death, as there being nothing of his writing on which to found a censure and give him a lower character, his proselytes would be left at liberty to feign for him as great a variety of excellence as their enthusiastic admiration might wish him to have possessed.

---

[1] *Vox audita perit, littera scripta manet*—The spoken word perishes, but the written word endures.

ADVICE TO A YOUNG TRADESMAN
BENJAMIN FRANKLIN (1706–1790)

Benjamin Franklin was raised in a typical Puritan home in Boston, but migrated to Philadelphia as a teenager. In the freer atmosphere of the Quaker city he prospered; everything he touched became successful, including a printing business, the Pennsylvania Gazette, *and the little almanac he named* Poor Richard's. *He retired at forty-two, became famous for his scientific experiments and inventions, received an honorary doctorate from Oxford, and later somewhat reluctantly entered politics.*

Franklin grew with Philadelphia. He was the great American success story and did more than any one person to show the world that America was the "Land of Opportunity." He wrote this little occasional essay soon after his retirement from active management of his business affairs. It would be reprinted hundreds of times. Although much of its advice seems to later generations to be simple common sense, his ideas about time, money, and credit were new and wondrous to a world just awakening to entrepreneurial ways of thinking. The "way to wealth" reflects the celebration of material accumulation and concern for individual accomplishment that became culturally acceptable in the eighteenth century.

1748

As you have desired it of me, I write the following hints, which have been of service to me and may, if observed, be so to you.

Remember that time is money. He that can earn ten shillings a day by his labor and goes abroad, or sits idle, one-half of that day, though he spends but six-pence during his diversion or idleness, ought not to reckon that the only expense; he has really spent, or rather thrown away, five shillings besides. 5

Remember that credit is money. If a man lets his money lie in my hands after it is due, he gives me the interest, or so much as I can make of it during that time. This amounts to a considerable sum where a man has good and large credit, and makes good use of it. 10

John Bigelow, ed., *The Works of Benjamin Franklin* (New York: G. P. Putnam's, 1904), II: 234–37.

Remember that money is of the prolific, generating nature. Money can beget money, and its offspring can beget more, and so on. Five shillings turned is six, turned again it is seven and three-pence, and so on till it becomes an hundred pounds. The more there is of it, the more it produces every turning, so that the profits rise quicker and quicker. He that kills a breeding sow destroys all her offspring to the thousandth generation. He that murders a crown destroys all that it might have produced, even scores of pounds.

Remember that six pounds a year is but a groat a day. For this little sum (which may be daily wasted either in time or expense unperceived) a man of credit may, on his own security, have the constant possession and use of an hundred pounds. So much in stock, briskly turned by an industrious man, produces great advantage.

Remember this saying: The good paymaster is lord of another man's purse. He that is known to pay punctually and exactly to the time he promises may at any time, and on any occasion, raise all the money his friends can spare. This is sometimes of great use. After industry and frugality, nothing contributes more to the raising of a young man in the world than punctuality and justice in all his dealings; therefore, never keep borrowed money an hour beyond the time you promised, lest a disappointment shut up your friend's purse forever.

The most trifling actions that affect a man's credit are to be regarded. The sound of your hammer at five in the morning, or nine at night, heard by a creditor makes him easy six months longer; but if he sees you at a billiard-table or hears your voice at a tavern when you should be at work, he sends for his money the next day; demands it, before he can receive it, in a lump.

It shows, besides, that you are mindful of what you owe; it makes you appear a careful as well as an honest man, and that still increases your credit.

Beware of thinking all your own that you possess, and of living accordingly. It is a mistake that many people who have credit fall into. To prevent this, keep an exact account for some time, both of your expenses and your income. If you take the pains at first to mention particulars, it will have this good effect: you will discover how wonderfully small, trifling expenses mount up to large sums, and will discern what might have been and may for the future be saved, without occasioning any great inconvenience.

In short, the way to wealth, if you desire it, is as plain as the way to market. It depends chiefly on two words, industry and frugality—that is, waste neither time nor money, but make the best use of both. Without industry and frugality nothing will do, and with them everything. He that gets all he can honestly, and saves all he gets (necessary expenses excepted), will certainly become rich, if that Being who governs the world, to whom all should look for a blessing on their honest endeavors, does not, in his wise providence, otherwise determine.

—An Old Tradesman

Autobiography
Benjamin Franklin (1706–1790)

Franklin wrote his autobiography largely to teach his son William (1731–1813) and other young men how to become successful. What better example of success than his own life? This selection discusses his founding of the Junto (which we may think of as the first Rotary Club), his desire for education, the only extended comments he ever made about religion, and his plan for "the bold and arduous project of arriving at moral perfection." Notice how modern he sounds: voluntary community service, advancement through education, private and individualized religion, an almost scientific approach to virtue—all for useful reasons.

His writings practically defined the Enlightenment in America. All the old tensions were renewed: faith and reason (religion and science), spiritual and material, communal and individual; and the Enlightened thinkers tended to resolve them toward the latter. The Enlightenment also revived Classical Greek and Roman ideas of virtue and public service, well-illustrated in Franklin's list.

1784

It is some time since I received the above letters, but I have been too busy till now to think of complying with the request they contain. It might, too, be much better done if I were at home among my papers, which would aid my memory and help to ascertain dates; but my return being uncertain, and having just now a little leisure, I will endeavor to recollect and write what I can; if I live to get home, it may there be corrected and improved. 5

Not having any copy here of what is already written, I know not whether an account is given of the means I used to establish the Philadelphia public library, which, from a small beginning, is now become so considerable. Though I remember to have come down to near the time of that transaction. I will therefore begin here with an account of it, which may be struck out if found to have been already given. 10

Frank Woodworth Pine, ed., *Autobiography of Benjamin Franklin* (New York: Henry Holt and Company, 1916), 136–64.

At the time I established myself in Pennsylvania there was not a good bookseller's shop in any of the colonies to the southward of Boston. In New York and Philadelphia the printers were indeed stationers; they sold only paper, etc., almanacs, ballads, and a few common school-books. Those who loved reading were obliged to send for their books from England; the members of the Junto had each a few. We had left the ale-house, where we first met, and hired a room to hold our club in. I proposed that we should all of us bring our books to that room, where they would not only be ready to consult in our conferences, but become a common benefit, each of us being at liberty to borrow such as he wished to read at home. This was accordingly done, and for some time contented us.

Finding the advantage of this little collection, I proposed to render the benefit from books more common by commencing a public subscription library. I drew a sketch of the plan and rules that would be necessary, and got a skillful conveyancer, Mr. Charles Brockden, to put the whole in form of articles of agreement, to be subscribed, by which each subscriber engaged to pay a certain sum down for the first purchase of books, and an annual contribution for increasing them. So few were the readers at that time in Philadelphia, and the majority of us so poor, that I was not able, with great industry, to find more than fifty persons, mostly young tradesmen, willing to pay down for this purpose forty shillings each, and ten shillings per annum. On this little fund we began. The books were imported; the library was opened one day in the week for lending to the subscribers, on their promissory notes to pay double the value if not duly returned. The institution soon manifested its utility; was imitated by other towns, and in other provinces. The libraries were augmented by donations; reading became fashionable; and our people, having no public amusements to divert their attention from study, became better acquainted with books, and in a few years were observed by strangers to be better instructed and more intelligent than people of the same rank generally are in other countries.

When we were about to sign the above mentioned articles, which were to be binding on us, our heirs, etc., for fifty years, Mr. Brockden, the scrivener, said to us, "You are young men, but it is scarcely probable that any of you will live to see the expiration of the term fixed in the instrument." A number of us, however, are yet living; but the instrument was after a few years rendered null by a charter that incorporated and gave perpetuity to the company.

The objections and reluctances I met with in soliciting the subscriptions made me soon feel the impropriety of presenting one's self as the proposer of any useful project that might be supposed to raise one's reputation in the smallest degree above that of one's neighbors when one has need of their assistance to accomplish that project. I therefore put myself as much as I could out of sight, and stated it as a scheme of a number of friends, who had requested me to go about and propose it to such as they thought lovers of reading. In this way my affair went on more smoothly, and I ever after practiced it on such occasions and, from my frequent successes, can heartily recommend it. The present little sacrifice of your vanity will afterwards be amply re-paid. If it remains awhile uncertain to whom the merit belongs, someone more vain than yourself will be encouraged to claim it, and then even envy will be disposed to do you justice by plucking those assumed feathers and restoring them to their right owner.

This library afforded me the means of improvement by constant study, for which I set apart an hour or two each day, and thus repaired in some degree the loss of the learned education my father once intended for me. Reading was the only amusement I allowed myself. I spent no time in taverns, games, or frolics of any kind; and my industry in my business continued as indefatigable as it was necessary. I was indebted for my printing-house; I had a young family coming on to be educated, and I had to contend with for business two printers, who were established in the place before me. My circumstances, however, grew daily easier. My original habits of frugality continuing, and my father having, among his instructions to me when a boy, frequently repeated a proverb of Solomon, "Do you see a man diligent in his calling? He shall stand before kings; he shall not stand before mean men."[1] I from thence considered industry as a means of obtaining wealth and distinction, which encouraged me, though I did not think that I should ever literally stand before kings, which, however, has since happened; for I have stood before five, and even had the honor of sitting down with one, the King of Denmark,[2] to dinner.

We have an English proverb that says, "He that would thrive must ask his wife." It was lucky for me that I had one as much disposed to industry and frugality as myself. She assisted me cheerfully in my business, folding and stitching pamphlets, tending shop, purchasing old linen rags for the paper-makers, etc., etc., We kept no idle servants, our table was plain and simple, our furniture of the cheapest. For instance, my breakfast was a long time bread and milk (no tea), and I ate it out of a two-penny earthen porringer, with a pewter spoon. But mark how luxury will enter families and make a progress, in spite of principle: being called one morning to breakfast, I found it in a china bowl, with a spoon of silver! They had been bought for me without my knowledge by my wife, and had cost her the enormous sum of three-and-twenty shillings, for which she had no other excuse or apology to make but that she thought her husband deserved a silver spoon and china bowl as well as any of his neighbors.

5

10

15

20

25

30

35

---

[1]Proverbs 22:29
[2]King Christian VII (r. 1766–1808)

This was the first appearance of plate and china in our house, which afterward, in a course of years, as our wealth increased, augmented gradually to several hundred pounds in value.

I had been religiously educated as a Presbyterian; and though some of the dogmas of that persuasion, such as the eternal decrees of God, election, reprobation, etc., appeared to me unintelligible, others doubtful, and I early absented myself from the public assemblies of the sect, Sunday being my studying day, I never was without some religious principles. I never doubted, for instance, the existence of the Deity; that He made the world, and governed it by His providence; that the most acceptable service of God was the doing good to man; that our souls are immortal; and that all crime will be punished and virtue rewarded, either here or hereafter. These I esteemed the essentials of every religion; and, being to be found in all the religions we had in our country, I respected them all, though with different degrees of respect, as I found them more or less mixed with other articles, which, without any tendency to inspire, promote, or confirm morality, served principally to divide us and make us unfriendly to one another. This respect to all, with an opinion that the worst had some good effects, induced me to avoid all discourse that might tend to lessen the good opinion another might have of his own religion; and as our province increased in people, and new places of worship were continually wanted, and generally erected by voluntary contribution, my mite for such purpose, whatever might be the sect, was never refused.

Though I seldom attended any public worship, I had still an opinion of its propriety, and of its utility when rightly conducted, and I regularly paid my annual subscription for the support of the only Presbyterian minister or meeting we had in Philadelphia. He used to visit me sometimes as a friend, and admonish me to attend his administrations, and I was now and then prevailed on to do so, once for five Sundays successively. Had he been in my opinion a good preacher, perhaps I might have continued, notwithstanding the occasion I had for the Sunday's leisure in my course of study; but his discourses were chiefly either polemic arguments, or explications of the peculiar doctrines of our sect, and were all to me very dry, uninteresting, and unedifying, since not a single moral principle was inculcated or enforced, their aim seeming to be rather to make us Presbyterians than good citizens.

At length he took for his text that verse of the fourth chapter of Philippians, "Finally, brethren, whatsoever things are true, honest, just, pure, lovely, or of good report, if there be any virtue, or any praise, think on these things." And, I imagined, in a sermon on such a text we could not miss of having some morality. But he confined himself to five points only, as meant by the apostle, *viz.*: (1) Keeping holy the Sabbath day. (2) Being diligent in reading the Holy

Scriptures. (3) Attending duly the public worship. (4) Partaking of the sacrament. (5) Paying a due respect to God's ministers. These might be all good things, but, as they were not the kind of good things that I expected from the text, I despaired of ever meeting with them from any other, was disgusted, and attended his preaching no more. I had some years before composed a little liturgy, or form of prayer, for my own private use (*viz.*, in 1728), entitled "Articles of Belief and Acts of Religion." I returned to the use of this, and went no more to the public assemblies. My conduct might be blamable, but I leave it without attempting further to excuse it; my present purpose being to relate facts, and not to make apologies for them.

It was about this time I conceived the bold and arduous project of arriving at moral perfection. I wished to live without committing any fault at any time; I would conquer all that either natural inclination, custom, or company might lead me into. As I knew, or thought I knew, what was right and wrong, I did not see why I might not always do the one and avoid the other. But I soon found I had undertaken a task of more difficulty than I had imagined. While my care was employed in guarding against one fault, I was often surprised by another; habit took the advantage of inattention; inclination was sometimes too strong for reason. I concluded, at length, that the mere speculative conviction that it was our interest to be completely virtuous was not sufficient to prevent our slipping, and that the contrary habits must be broken, and good ones acquired and established, before we can have any dependence on a steady, uniform rectitude of conduct. For this purpose I therefore contrived the following method.

In the various enumerations of the moral virtues I met in my reading, I found the catalogue more or less numerous, as different writers included more or fewer ideas under the same name. Temperance, for example, was by some confined to eating and drinking, while by others it was extended to mean the moderating every other pleasure, appetite, inclination, or passion, bodily or mental, even to our avarice and ambition. I proposed to myself, for the sake of clearness, to use rather more names, with fewer ideas annexed to each, than a few names with more ideas; and I included under thirteen names of virtues all that at that time occurred to me as necessary or desirable, and annexed to each a short precept, which fully expressed the extent I gave to its meaning.

These names of virtues, with their precepts were:

1. *Temperance*—Eat not to dullness; drink not to elevation.
2. *Silence*—Speak not but what may benefit others or yourself; avoid trifling conversation.
3. *Order*—Let all your things have their places; let each part of your business have its time.

4. *Resolution*—Resolve to perform what you ought; perform without fail what you resolve.

5. *Frugality*—Make no expense but to do good to others or yourself, *i.e.*, waste nothing.

6. *Industry*—Lose no time; be always employed in something useful; cut off all unnecessary actions.

7. *Sincerity*—Use no hurtful deceit; think innocently and justly, and, if you speak, speak accordingly.

8. *Justice*—Wrong none by doing injuries or omitting the benefits that are your duty.

9. *Moderation*—Avoid extremes; forbear resenting injuries so much as you think they deserve.

10. *Cleanliness*—Tolerate no uncleanliness in body, clothes, or habitation.

11. *Tranquility*—Be not disturbed at trifles, or at accidents common or unavoidable.

12. *Chastity*—Rarely use venery but for health or offspring, never to dullness, weakness, or the injury of your own or another's peace or reputation.

13. *Humility*—Imitate Jesus and Socrates.

My intention being to acquire the habitude of all these virtues, I judged it would be well not to distract my attention by attempting the whole at once, but to fix it on one of them at a time, and, when I should be master of that, then to proceed to another, and so on, till I should have gone through the thirteen; and, as the previous acquisition of some might facilitate the acquisition of certain others, I arranged them with that view, as they stand above. Temperance first, as it tends to procure that coolness and clearness of head which is so necessary where constant vigilance was to be kept up, and guard maintained against the unremitting attraction of ancient habits and the force of perpetual temptations. This being acquired and established, silence would be more easy; and my desire being to gain knowledge at the same time that I improved in virtue, and considering that in conversation it was obtained rather by the use of the ears than of the tongue, and therefore wishing to break a habit I was getting into prattling, punning, and joking, which only made me acceptable to trifling company, I gave silence the second place. This and the next, order, I expected would allow me more time for attending to my project and my studies. Resolution, once become habitual, would keep me firm in my endeavors to obtain all the subsequent virtues; frugality and industry, freeing me from my remaining debt, and producing affluence and independence, would make more easy the practice of sincerity and justice, etc. Conceiving, then, that, agreeably to the advice of Pythagoras in his *Garden Verses*, daily examination would be necessary, I contrived the following method for conducting that examination.

I made a little book, in which I allotted a page for each of the virtues. I ruled each page with red ink, so as to have seven columns, one for each day of the week, marking each column with a letter for the day. I crossed these columns with thirteen red lines, marking the beginning of each line with the first letter of one of the virtues, on which line, and in its proper column, I might mark,   5 by a little black spot, every fault I found upon examination to have been committed respecting that virtue upon that day.

TEMPERANCE.

EAT NOT TO DULNESS; DRINK NOT TO ELEVATION.

	S.	M.	T.	W.	T.	F.	S.
T.							
S.	*	*		*		*	
O.	* *	*	*		*	*	*
R.			*			*	
F.		*	.		*		
I.			*				
S.							
J.							
M.							
C.							
T.							
C.							
H.							

I determined to give a week's strict attention to each of the virtues successively. Thus, in the first week, my great guard was to avoid every the least offense against Temperance, leaving the other virtues to their ordinary chance,   10 only marking every evening the faults of the day. Thus, if in the first week I could keep my first line, marked T, clear of spots, I supposed the habit of that virtue so much strengthened, and its opposite weakened, that I might venture extending my attention to include the next, and for the following week keep both lines clear of spots. Proceeding thus to the last, I could go through a   15 course complete in thirteen weeks, and four courses in a year. And like him who, having a garden to weed, does not attempt to eradicate all the bad herbs at once, which would exceed his reach and his strength, but works on one of the beds at a time, and, having accomplished the first, proceeds to a second, so I should have, I hoped, the encouraging pleasure of seeing on my pages the   20 progress I made in virtue, by clearing successively my lines of their spots, till in the end, by a number of courses, I should be happy in viewing a clean book, after a thirteen weeks' daily examination.

This, my little book, had for its motto these lines from Addison's "Cato":

Here will I hold. If there's a power above us
5 (And that there is, all nature cries aloud
Thro' all her works), He must delight in virtue;
And that which He delights in must be happy.

Another from Cicero:

O vitae Philosophia dux!
10 *O virtutum indagatrix expultrixque vitiorum!*
Unus dies, bene et ex praeceptis tuis actus, peccanti immortalitati
est anteponendus.

Another from the Proverbs of Solomon, speaking of wisdom or virtue, "Length of days is in her right hand; and in her left hand riches and honor. Her 15 ways are ways of pleasantness, and all her paths are peace."[3]

And conceiving God to be the fountain of wisdom, I thought it right and necessary to solicit His assistance for obtaining it; to this end I formed the following little prayer, which was prefixed to my tables of examination, for daily use:

20 O powerful Goodness! Bountiful Father! Merciful Guide! Increase in me that wisdom which discovers my truest interest. Strengthen my resolutions to perform what that wisdom dictates. Accept my kind offices to Your other children as the only return in my power for Your continual favors to me.

25 I used also sometimes a little prayer which I took from Thomson's "Poems," *viz.*:

Father of light and life, thou Good Supreme!
O teach me what is good; teach me Thyself!
Save me from folly, vanity, and vice,
From every low pursuit; and fill my soul
30 With knowledge, conscious peace, and virtue pure;
Sacred, substantial, never-fading bliss!

The precept of order requiring that every part of my business should have its allotted time, one page in my little book contained the following scheme of employment for the twenty-four hours of a natural day:

---

[3]Proverbs 3:16–17

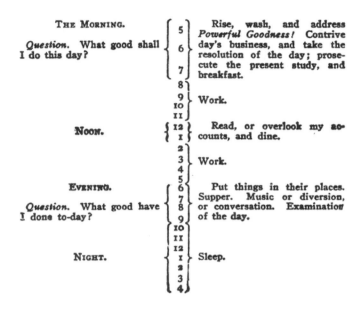

THE MORNING.	5	Rise, wash, and address *Powerful Goodness!* Contrive
Question. What good shall I do this day?	6	day's business, and take the resolution of the day; prose-
	7	cute the present study, and breakfast.
	8	
	9	Work.
	10	
	11	
NOON.	12	Read, or overlook my ac-
	1	counts, and dine.
	2	
	3	Work.
	4	
	5	
EVENING.	6	Put things in their places.
	7	Supper. Music or diversion,
Question. What good have I done to-day?	8	or conversation. Examination
	9	of the day.
	10	
	11	
	12	
NIGHT.	1	Sleep.
	2	
	3	
	4	

I entered upon the execution of this plan for self-examination, and continued it, with occasional intermissions, for some time. I was surprised to find myself so much fuller of faults than I had imagined; but I had the satisfaction of seeing them diminish. To avoid the trouble of renewing now and then my little book, which, by scraping out the marks on the paper of old faults to make room for new ones in a new course, became full of holes, I transferred my tables and precepts to the ivory leaves of a memorandum book, on which the lines were drawn with red ink that made a durable stain, and on those lines I marked my faults with a black leading pencil, which marks I could easily wipe out with a wet sponge. After a while I went through one course only in a year, and afterward only one in several years, till at length I omitted them entirely, being employed in voyages and business abroad, with a multiplicity of affairs that interfered; but I always carried my little book with me.

My scheme of order gave me the most trouble; and I found that, though it might be practicable where a man's business was such as to leave him the disposition of his time, that of a journeyman printer, for instance, it was not possible to be exactly observed by a master, who must mix with the world, and often receive people of business at their own hours. Order, too, with regard to places for things, papers, etc., I found extremely difficult to acquire. I had not been early accustomed to it, and, having an exceeding good memory, I was not so sensible of the inconvenience attending want of method. This article, therefore, cost me so much painful attention, and my faults in it vexed me so much, and I made so little progress in amendment, and had such frequent relapses, that I was almost ready to give up the attempt and content myself with a faulty character in that respect, like the man who, in buying an ax of a smith,

5   my neighbor, desired to have the whole of its surface as bright as the edge. The smith consented to grind it bright for him if he would turn the wheel; he turned, while the smith pressed the broad face of the ax hard and heavily on the stone, which made the turning of it very fatiguing. The man came every now and then from the wheel to see how the work went on, and at length would

10   take his ax as it was, without farther grinding. " No," said the smith; " turn on, turn on; we shall have it bright by and by; as yet, it is only speckled." "Yes," says the man, "but I think I like a speckled ax best." And I believe this may have been the case with many who, having, for want of some such means as I employed, found the difficulty of obtaining good and breaking bad habits in

15   other points of vice and virtue, have given up the struggle, and concluded that "a speckled ax was best" for something, that pretended to be reason, was every now and then suggesting to me that such extreme nicety as I exacted of myself might be a kind of foppery in morals, which, if it were known, would make me ridiculous; that a perfect character might be attended with the inconvenience

20   of being envied and hated; and that a benevolent man should allow a few faults in himself, to keep his friends in countenance.

In truth, I found myself incorrigible with respect to order; and now I am grown old, and my memory bad, I feel very sensibly the want of it. But, on the whole, though I never arrived at the perfection I had been so ambitious

25   of obtaining, but fell far short of it, yet I was, by the endeavor, a better and a happier man than I otherwise should have been if I had not attempted it; as those who aim at perfect writing by imitating the engraved copies, though they never reach the wished-for excellence of those copies, their hand is mended by the endeavor, and tolerable, while it continues fair and legible.

30   It may be well my posterity should be informed that to this little artifice, with the blessing of God, their ancestor owned the constant felicity of his life down to his seventy-ninth year, in which this is written. What reverses may attend the remainder is in the hand of Providence; but, if they arrive, the reflection on past happiness enjoyed ought to help his bearing them with

35   more resignation. To temperance he ascribes his long-continued health and what is still left to him of a good constitution; to industry and frugality, the early easiness of his circumstances and acquisition of his fortune, with all that knowledge that enabled him to be a useful citizen, and obtained for him some degree of reputation among the learned; to sincerity and justice, the confidence

40   of his country, and the honorable employs it conferred upon him; and to the

joint influence of the whole mass of the virtues, even in the imperfect state he was able to acquire them, all that evenness of temper, and that cheerfulness in conversation, which makes his company still sought for, and agreeable even to his younger acquaintance. I hope, therefore, that some of my descendants may follow the example and reap the benefit.

It will be remarked that, though my scheme was not wholly without religion, there was in it no mark of any of the distinguishing tenets of any particular sect. I had purposely avoided them; for, being fully persuaded of the utility and excellency of my method, and that it might be serviceable to people in all religions, and intending some time or other to publish it, I would not have anything in it that should prejudice anyone of any sect against it. I purposed writing a little comment on each virtue, in which I would have shown the advantages of possessing it, and the mischiefs attending its opposite vice; and I should have called my book *The Art of Virtue*, because it would have shown the means and manner of obtaining virtue, which would have distinguished it from the mere exhortation to be good, that does not instruct and indicate the means, but is like the apostle's man of verbal charity, who only, without showing to the naked and hungry how or where they might get clothes or victuals, exhorted them to be fed and clothed.[4]

But it so happened that my intention of writing and publishing this comment was never fulfilled. I did, indeed, from time to time, put down short hints of the sentiments, reasonings, etc., to be made use of in it, some of which I have still by me. But the necessary close attention to private business in the earlier part of life, and public business since, have occasioned my postponing it. For it being connected in my mind with a great and extensive project that required the whole man to execute, and which an unforeseen sucession of employs prevented my attending to, it has hitherto remained unfinished.

In this piece it was my design to explain and enforce this doctrine, that vicious actions are not hurtful because they are forbidden, but forbidden because they are hurtful, the nature of man alone considered; that it was, therefore, every one's interest to be virtuous who wished to be happy even in this world; and I should, from this circumstance (there being always in the world a number of rich merchants, nobility, states, and princes who have need of honest instruments for the management of their affairs, and such being so rare), have endeavored to convince young persons that no qualities were so likely to make a poor man's fortune as those of probity and integrity.

My list of virtues contained at first but twelve; but a Quaker friend having kindly informed me that I was generally thought proud, that my pride showed

---

[4]James 2:15–16

itself frequently in conversation, that I was not content with being in the right when discussing any point, but was overbearing and rather insolent, of which he convinced me by mentioning several instances, I determined endeavoring to cure myself, if I could, of this vice or folly among the rest, and I added Humility
5   to my list, giving an extensive meaning to the word.

I cannot boast of much success in acquiring the reality of this virtue, but I had a good deal with regard to the appearance of it. I made it a rule to forbear all direct contradiction to the sentiments of others, and all positive assertion of my own. I even forbid myself, agreeably to the old laws of our Junto, the use of
10   every word or expression in the language that imported a fixed opinion, such as certainly, undoubtedly, etc., and I adopted, instead of them, I conceive, I apprehend, or I imagine a thing to be so or so, or it so appears to me at present. When another asserted something that I thought an error, I denied myself the pleasure of contradicting him abruptly and of showing immediately some
15   absurdity in his proposition; and in answering, I began by observing that in certain cases or circumstances his opinion would be right, but in the present case there appeared or seemed to me some difference, etc. I soon found the advantage of this charge in my manner; the conversations I engaged in went on more pleasantly.
20   The modest way in which I proposed my opinions procured them a readier reception and less contradiction; I had less mortification when I was found to be in the wrong, and I more easily prevailed with other to give up their mistakes and join with me when I happened to be in the right.

And this mode, which I at first put on with some violence to natural
25   inclination, became at length so easy, and so habitual to me, that perhaps for these fifty years past no one has ever heard a dogmatical expression escape me. And to this habit (after my character of integrity) I think it principally owing that I had early so much weight with my fellow-citizens when I proposed new institutions, or alterations in the old, and so much influence in public councils
30   when I became a member; for I was but a bad speaker, never eloquent, subject to much hesitation in my choice of words, hardly correct in language, and yet I generally carried my points.

In reality, there is, perhaps, no one of our natural passions so hard to subdue as pride. Disguise it, struggle with it, beat it down, stifle it, mortify it as much as
35   one pleases, it is still alive, and will every now and then peep out and show itself; you will see it, perhaps, often in this history; for, even if I could conceive that I had completely overcome it, I should probably be proud of my humility.

[THUS FAR WRITTEN AT PASSY, 1784]

III
THE AMERICAN
FOUNDING

Until the American Revolution, most American colonists thought of themselves as Englishmen, with all of the "rights of Englishmen." England enjoyed a reputation for constitutional liberty and, while not without its mythological elements, the reputation was well-deserved on the whole. All of the principles of Greco-Roman, Judeo-Christian, and medieval constitutionalism contributed to it. Most important, England withstood the challenge of absolutism in the sixteenth and seventeenth centuries, and could celebrate a "Glorious Revolution" in 1688. In the midst of these political and constitutional struggles, England founded colonies in North America where the seeds of liberty struck still deeper roots.

The most significant development in English constitutional history during the American colonial period was the rise to power of Parliament. Twice in the seventeenth century, during the Civil War (1642–1660) and the Glorious Revolution (1688–1689), Parliament overthrew the English monarch and established itself as the ultimate power in England. The American colonists participated in the Glorious Revolution by overthrowing unpopular royalist governments in New England, New York, and Maryland. The English Bill of Rights and John Locke's *Second Treatise* provided the political and theoretical expressions of what seventeenth-century Anglo-Americans regarded as the "rights of Englishmen." Principal among these were the right to representation and consent to taxation, trial by jury, and habeas corpus—in short, not to be deprived of one's life, liberty, or property arbitrarily. Locke explained that individuals had rights derived from nature, and that the purpose of government was to secure these rights. When government became destructive of these ends, the people had a right to revolution.

It was during the tumultuous seventeenth century that the English established their first colonies in the New World. Today it is easy to see that the seeds of rebellion were sown very early, that America was conceived in liberty long before 1776. Edmund Burke (1729–1797) was among the few English statesmen to recognize it in the eighteenth century. The same forces of Protestantism

Used by kind permission, *National Association of Scholars*. "A Concise History of the American Constitution."

and parliamentary government that drove the English civil wars were planted along the Atlantic coast.

Almost all of the settlers were reformed Protestants, and even those who were Anglican became accustomed to a high degree of self-government in their churches. There were no bishops in America, just as there was no secular aristocracy. The first constitutions in America reflected this. The Mayflower Compact simply transferred the covenant that made a congregation into a constitution for civil government. Other colonies that were established as business corporations turned their charters into constitutions. This is how the Massachusetts Bay Company, a project undertaken by religious dissenters in England, evolved. The General Court (originally a meeting of stockholders) became a civil representative body, with membership based on membership in a Puritan congregation. In Virginia, the House of Burgesses was used as a promotional device to attract settlers, to assure Englishmen that they would have a say in the government of the colony. The charter of the Massachusetts Bay Company granted that every settler and his descendants "shall have and enjoy all liberties and immunities of free and natural subjects within any of the dominions of us, our heirs and successors, to all intents, constructions, and purposes whatsoever, as if they and every one of them were born within the realm of England."

Every colony had a charter from the king, and all of them guaranteed the settlers that they retained their rights as Englishmen in the New World. Every colony had a popular assembly that looked like a little parliament, most of which actually exercised more real power than the Parliament in London. Every American constitution also provided a great deal of local self-government. Most political action took place at the county and town level. There already was a great deal of "federalism" within the colonies. The word itself reflects these origins, derived from the Latin *foedus*, or "compact."

The colonists were the most highly educated people in the world, and legal knowledge was especially widely diffused among them. Lawyers were particularly important in politics, and every liberally educated man in America was familiar with legal principles and constitutional history. The colonies were also prosperous. They were little republics, and were also *commercial* republics. This made the common English hostility to taxation even more intense in America. Property rights were important in a country where property was widely held, and where business was not disdained as it was in the Old World, where deference to nobility of blood and office remained strong. Even in that part of British North America where these traits were least evident, among the great plantation owners of the South, the spirit of liberty was just as intense, because slaveholders had firsthand experience with tyranny.

All of this was reinforced by the fact that the British had largely left their American colonies to fend for themselves for a century and a half. The whole issue of the American Revolution was really laid out in the Glorious Revolution. The question was whether the principles of the Glorious Revolution, expressed in the Bill of Rights and Locke, applied to the colonies. Americans believed that they did. Americans had participated in the Glorious Revolution themselves, overthrowing King James's governors who, they believed, were going to establish "popery" and arbitrary government in America. They believed that they had vindicated the right to govern themselves by their assemblies just as Englishmen had established the supremacy of their Parliament in England. The British, on the other hand, never gave a direct answer to the question of whether colonial self-government was a right or a privilege. The charters and assemblies that James had dissolved were restored, but it was not clear whether this was a British gift or a colonial right. And for the next seventy years the British maintained their policy of salutary neglect, and the colonists continued to govern themselves. As long as no crisis brought the issue up, both sides were happy to leave it alone.

In the meantime, the American colonists were developing a distinctly modern political culture. They certainly maintained a great many features of traditional political thought: acceptance of monarchy, hierarchy, and deference; a belief that it is government's role to inculcate virtue and piety in the people; and a suspicion of democracy and faction or party. At the same time, American politics exhibited many traits of modern interest-group competition. With fifty percent of adult white males enfranchised, the colonies were the most democratic polities in the history of the world. The popular branches of their legislatures were the dominant ones, able to control finances especially and to resist the royal governors. These assemblies were often arenas for contests among a multitude of ethnic, cultural, religious, and economic groups. While the American Revolution would evoke the language of traditional republicanism, and while Americans would never be fully comfortable with partisanship, the latter was the prevailing trend in the eighteenth century. While these internal cleavages in American politics often threatened discord within and among the colonies, their common constitutional culture, expressed in their charters, institutions, traditions, and principles, united them more than these differences divided them.

The period of "salutary neglect" came to an end in 1763, when Great Britain won the Seven Years' War and had to pay for it and provide administration for the vast North American empire that it had won from France. The British annoyed the Americans by forbidding settlement beyond the Appalachian mountains, by keeping a standing army in the colonies, and especially by new taxes. These taxes were intended to establish a "civil list," a fund from which the

British could pay their officials without having to rely on appropriations from the colonial legislatures. This threatened the popular control of fiscal policy, which was the basis of the power of the colonial assemblies. Although colonial protests and boycotts caused Parliament to repeal many of the taxes, Parliament insisted on its sovereign power—that it, in the words of the 1766 Declaratory Act, "had, hath, and of right ought to have, full power and authority to make laws and statutes of sufficient force and validity to bind the colonies and people of America, subjects of the crown of Great Britain, in all cases whatsoever." The Americans, on the other hand, insisted that Parliament's power was not unlimited, and ultimately that the American colonial assemblies were the equals of Parliament, which had no legitimate position in the colonial constitutional system. They were connected to England only by a common monarch—thus the Declaration of Independence is addressed to the King and does not mention Parliament by name.

When the British moved to put down colonial resistance by force after the 1773 Boston Tea Party, the colonists rallied around Massachusetts in the First Continental Congress. After armed conflict began in April 1775, the Second Continental Congress issued the "Declaration of the Causes and Necessity of Taking Up Arms," and finally declared independence in 1776. The Congress also instructed the thirteen states to revise their colonial charters into new constitutions that reflected their independence. They did so along the lines of "republican" political theory.

In accord with republican principles, states made their constitutions more responsive to the people. The most radical of them, Pennsylvania's, did away with its upper house and relied on a unicameral legislature. They broadened the suffrage, lowering property qualifications. By the end of the century, Maryland became the first polity in history to provide universal male suffrage; even women (with property) could vote under New Jersey's revolutionary constitution, which made no sex qualification. Annual elections would keep legislators in touch with the people, and legislatures were reapportioned to make representation more equal. Governors had fewer powers, being seen as monarchical. Pennsylvania's constitution provided for a plural executive, a committee of delegates from each county. Rejecting the theory of "mixed government," the state constitutions strove for "separation of powers," wherein the executive would not influence legislation, for this was the mechanism of corruption in the English system. Not every state went as far as Pennsylvania—Connecticut and Rhode Island, for example, simply removed references to the King from their seventeenth-century corporation charters and carried on as usual. But there was on the whole a democratic tendency in the revolutionary era.

Politics under the state constitutions confirmed many of the historical fears of republican government. The fundamental problem was that the legislatures possessed overwhelming power and began to act in an unrestrained fashion. As James Madison (1751–1836) put it in *Federalist* 48, "The legislative department is everywhere extending the sphere of its authority and drawing all power into its impetuous vortex." Legislatures were unchecked by the state constitutions, because they had written them themselves. Before the Massachusetts constitution of 1780, there was an imperfect sense that a constitution was a "higher law," the work of the people, created outside of, and superior to, the legislature. In several cases where state judges attempted to protect rights against legislative encroachment—usually involving judicial process and jury trials—they were intimidated by overweening legislators. The most common abuse by legislative power involved property rights. The United States endured an economic depression after the War for Independence, and there was pressure from distressed debtors for relief. The legislatures responded with a variety of devices, inflationary paper money laws especially, that many regarded as violations of private, contractual rights and attempts to use force of numbers to redistribute the wealth. More generally, the laws of the states changed rapidly, sensitive to shifts in public opinion, and this further undermined the security of private rights.

At the same time, the national or continental government was even more defective. The Articles of Confederation were not ratified until 1781. While not completely feckless—it was able to arrange the Treaty of Paris in 1783 and to create the Northwest Ordinance in 1787—its main value was to provide an object lesson and experience for later constitution-makers. If the main defect of the state constitutions was that they were too close to the people, the Articles' main weakness was that it was not connected to the people at all. In short, it was not a genuinely republican government, and therefore lacked the essential element of legitimacy. Rather, the Articles established what it called "a firm league of friendship" among the states. The document was entitled "Articles of Confederation and Perpetual Union," implying unity, but was formed "between the states of New Hampshire, Massachusetts Bay, Rhode Island…," emphasizing their independence. Article 2 stated quite clearly, "Each state retains its sovereignty, freedom, and independence, and every power, jurisdiction, and right which is not by this confederation expressly delegated to the United States."

The state legislatures chose and controlled the delegates to the Congress, and each state had equal voting power. The powers surrendered by the states and granted to Congress principally involved diplomacy, but there was no real basis for national power. The Congress lacked any revenue of its own; it could only request money from the states, and relied on the state to collect the requisitions. Its executive was amorphous; a committee of delegates had power to act when the whole Congress was not assembled. It provided for a complicated judicial process to settle disputes among states, but it was never used. Most important decisions required the assent of nine of thirteen states, and amendment required the unanimous consent of all state legislatures.

Consequently, paralysis usually characterized the government. The weakness of the Confederation made it impossible for the United States to "assume among the powers of the earth the separate and equal station to which the laws of Nature and of Nature's God entitle them." It was unable to pay its debts. It could not compel the British to fulfill their promises under the Treaty of Paris, in part because it could not compel the states to fulfill theirs. Nor could the Congress secure a commercial treaty with Britain, nor prevent Spain from using its control of the Mississippi River against the United States. It was similarly powerless to stop the states from discriminating against one another in commerce. In the winter of 1787, debtor farmers in the western part of Massachusetts broke out in rebellion (Shays' Rebellion)—largely because the state constitution of 1780 did not produce the kind of legislative populism seen in other states—and the national government could render no assistance.

CAUSES AND NECESSITIES OF TAKING UP ARMS
SECOND CONTINENTAL CONGRESS

When the Second Continental Congress began its work in May of 1775, it was by no means clear that the American colonies were headed toward independence. The battles of Lexington and Concord prompted the Congress to organize an army and place George Washington in command of the colonial forces. The battle of Bunker Hill in June of 1775 further severed the political bands connecting the American colonies with the "mother country." Such martial resistance could be explained by the colonists as necessary for defending their rights as British subjects. Members of Congress were divided, however, on the inevitability and desirability of a separation from arguably the freest and most powerful nation in the world. While John Adams (1735–1826) labored to persuade delegates that attempts at reconciliation were illusory, John Dickinson of Pennsylvania (1732–1808) and fellow moderates held out hopes of prevailing on the King to come to reason. To justify military action against British troops, the Congress required the drafting of the following "Declaration," passed a year before the Declaration of Independence. *The work of a committee, it was written principally by John Dickinson and Thomas Jefferson (1743–1826), representing, respectively, the conciliatory and increasingly revolutionary camps. The document appeared the day after the so-called "Olive Branch Petition," also written by Dickinson, which professed continued loyalty to George III (r. 1760–1820).*

6 JULY 1775

A declaration by the representatives of the United colonies of North America, now met in General Congress at Philadelphia, setting forth the causes and necessity of their taking up arms.

If it was possible for men who exercise their reason to believe that the Divine Author of our existence intended a part of the human race to hold an absolute property in and an unbounded power over others, marked out by his infinite goodness and wisdom as the objects of a legal domination never rightfully resist-

5

Worthington Chauncey Ford, ed., *Journals of the Continental Congress, Volume II–10 May–20 September 1775* (Washington, DC: Government Printing Office, 1905), I:140–57 [modernized].

ible, however severe and oppressive, the inhabitants of these colonies might at least require from the Parliament of Great Britain some evidence that this dreadful authority over them has been granted to that body. But a reverence for our great Creator, principles of humanity, and the dictates of common sense must convince
5 all those who reflect upon the subject that government was instituted to promote the welfare of mankind, and ought to be administered for the attainment of that end. The legislature of Great Britain, however, stimulated by an inordinate passion for a power, not only unjustifiable, but which they know to be peculiarly reprobated by the very constitution of that Kingdom, and desperate of success in
10 any mode of contest where regard should be had to truth, law, or right, have at length, deserting those, attempted to effect their cruel and impolitic purpose of enslaving these colonies by violence, and have thereby rendered it necessary for us to close with their last appeal from reason to arms. Yet, however blinded that assembly may be by their intemperate rage for unlimited domination so to slight
15 justice and the opinion of mankind, we esteem ourselves bound, by obligations of respect to the rest of the world, to make known the justice of our cause.

Our forefathers, inhabitants of the island of Great Britain, left their native land to seek on these shores a residence for civil and religious freedom. At the expense of their blood, at the hazard of their fortunes, without the least charge to
20 the country from which they removed, by unceasing labor and an unconquerable spirit they effected settlements in the distant and inhospitable wilds of America, then filled with numerous and war-like nations of barbarians. Societies or governments, vested with perfect legislatures, were formed under charters from the Crown, and an harmonious intercourse was established between the colonies
25 and the kingdom from which they derived their origin. The mutual benefits of this union became in a short time so extraordinary as to excite astonishment. It is universally confessed that the amazing increase of the wealth, strength, and navigation of the realm arose from this source; and the minister who so wisely and successfully directed the measures of Great Britain in the late war publicly
30 declared that these colonies enabled her to triumph over her enemies. Towards the conclusion of that war, it pleased our sovereign to make a change in his counsels. From that fatal moment, the affairs of the British empire began to fall into confusion and, gradually sliding from the summit of glorious prosperity, to which they had been advanced by the virtues and abilities of one man, are
35 at length distracted by the convulsions that now shake it to its deepest foundations. The new ministry, finding the brave foes of Britain, though frequently defeated, yet still contending, took up the unfortunate idea of granting them a hasty peace, and of then subduing her faithful friends.

These devoted colonies were judged to be in such a state as to present victories without bloodshed, and all the easy emoluments of statuteable plunder.
40 The uninterrupted tenor of their peaceable and respectful behavior from the

beginning of colonization, their dutiful, zealous, and useful services during the war, though so recently and amply acknowledged in the most honorable manner by His Majesty, by the late King, and by Parliament, could not save them from the meditated innovations. Parliament was influenced to adopt the pernicious project, and assuming a new power over them, have, in the course of eleven years, given such decisive specimens of the spirit and consequences attending this power as to leave no doubt concerning the effects of acquiescence under it. They have undertaken to give and grant our money without our consent, though we have ever exercised an exclusive right to dispose of our own property; statutes have been passed for extending the jurisdiction of courts of Admiralty and Vice-Admiralty beyond their ancient limits; for depriving us of the accustomed and inestimable privilege of trial by jury, in cases affecting both life and property; for suspending the legislature of one of the colonies; for interdicting all commerce to the capital of another; and for altering fundamentally the form of government established by charter, and secured by acts of its own legislature solemnly confirmed by the crown; for exempting the "murderers" of colonists from legal trial, and in effect, from punishment; for erecting in a neighboring province, acquired by the joint arms of Great Britain and America, a despotism dangerous to our very existence; and for quartering soldiers upon the colonists in time of profound peace. It has also been resolved in Parliament that colonists charged with committing certain offences shall be transported to England to be tried.

But why should we enumerate our injuries in detail? By one statute it is declared that Parliament can "of right make laws to bind *us in all cases whatsoever.*" What is to defend us against so enormous, so unlimited a power? Not a single man of those who assume it is chosen by us, or is subject to our control or influence; but, on the contrary, they are all of them exempt from the operation of such laws, and an American revenue, if not diverted from the ostensible purposes for which it is raised, would actually lighten their own burdens in proportion as they increase ours. We saw the misery to which such despotism would reduce us. We for ten years incessantly and ineffectually besieged the Throne as supplicants; we reasoned, we remonstrated with Parliament in the most mild and decent language. But Administration, sensible that we should regard these oppressive measures as freemen ought to do, sent over fleets and armies to enforce them. The indignation of the Americans was roused, it is true; but it was the indignation of a virtuous, loyal, and affectionate people. A congress of delegates from the united colonies was assembled at Philadelphia, on the fifth day of last September. We resolved again to offer an humble and dutiful petition to the King, and also addressed our fellow-subjects of Great Britain. We have pursued every temperate, every respectful measure; we have even proceeded to break off our commercial intercourse with our fellow-subjects as the last peaceable admonition that our attachment to no nation upon earth should supplant our attachment to liberty. This, we flattered ourselves, was the ultimate step of the controversy: But subsequent events have shown how vain was this hope of finding moderation in our enemies.

Several threatening expressions against the colonies were inserted in His Majesty's speech; our petition, though we were told it was a decent one, and that His Majesty had been pleased to receive it graciously, and to promise laying it before his Parliament, was huddled into both Houses amongst a bundle of American papers, and there neglected. The Lords and Commons in their address, in the month of February, said that "a rebellion at that time actually existed within the province of Massachusetts Bay; and that those concerned in it had been countenanced and encouraged by unlawful combinations and engagements, entered into by His Majesty's subjects in several of the other colonies; and therefore they besought His Majesty that he would take the most effectual measures to enforce due obedience to the laws and authority of the supreme legislature."

Soon after, the commercial intercourse of whole colonies with foreign countries, and with each other, was cut off by an Act of Parliament; by another, several of them were entirely prohibited from the fisheries in the seas near their coasts, on which they always depended for their sustenance; and large re-enforcements of ships and troops were immediately sent over to General Gage.[1]

Fruitless were all the entreaties, arguments, and eloquence of an illustrious band of the most distinguished Peers and Commoners, who nobly and strenuously asserted the justice of our cause, to stay, or even to mitigate the heedless fury with which these accumulated and unexampled outrages were hurried on. Equally fruitless was the interference of the City of London, of Bristol, and many other respectable towns in our favor. Parliament adopted an insidious manoeuvre calculated to divide us, to establish a perpetual auction of taxations where colony should bid against colony, all of them un-informed what ransom would redeem their lives; and thus to extort from us, at the point of the bayonet, the unknown sums that should be sufficient to gratify, if possible to gratify, ministerial rapacity with the miserable indulgence left to us of raising, in our own mode, the prescribed tribute. What terms more rigid and humiliating could have been dictated by remorseless victors to conquered enemies? In our circumstances to accept them would be to deserve them.

Soon after the intelligence of these proceedings arrived on this continent, General Gage, who in the course of the last year had taken possession of the town of Boston, in the province of Massachusetts Bay, and still occupied it as a garrison, on the 19th day of April, sent out from that place a large detachment of his army, who made an unprovoked assault on the inhabitants of the said province

---

[1] Lieutenant-General Thomas Gage (1719–1787), Commander-in-Chief of British forces in North America (1763–1775) and military Governor of Boston (1774–1775)

at the town of Lexington, as appears by the affidavits of a great number of person, some of whom were officers and soldiers of that detachment, murdered eight of the inhabitants and wounded many others. From thence the troops proceeded in warlike array to the town of Concord, where they set upon another party of the inhabitants of the same province, killing several and wounding more, until 5 compelled to retreat by the country people suddenly assembled to repel this cruel aggression. Hostilities, thus commenced by the British troops, have been since prosecuted by them without regard to faith or reputation. The inhabitants of Boston being confined within that town by the General, their Governor, and having, in order to procure their dismission, entered into a treaty with him, it 10 was stipulated that the said inhabitants having deposited their arms with their own magistrates, should have liberty to depart, taking with them their other effects. They accordingly delivered up their arms, but in open violation of honor, in defiance of the obligation of treaties, which even savage nations esteemed sacred, the Governor ordered the arms deposited as aforesaid, that they might 15 be preserved for their owners, to be seized by a body of soldiers; detained the greatest part of the inhabitants in the town, and compelled the few who were permitted to retire, to leave their most valuable effects behind.

By this perfidy wives are separated from their husbands, children from their parents, the aged and the sick from their relations and friends, who wish to 20 attend and comfort them; and those who have been used to live in plenty, and even elegance, are reduced to deplorable distress.

The General, further emulating his ministerial masters, by a proclamation bearing date on the 12th day of June, after venting the grossest falsehoods and calumnies against the good people of these colonies, proceeds to "declare them 25 all, either by name or description, to be rebels and traitors, to supersede the course of the common law, and instead thereof to publish and order the use and exercise of the law martial." His troops have butchered our countrymen, have wantonly burnt Charles-Town, besides a considerable number of houses in other places; our ships and vessels are seized; the necessary supplies of provisions 30 are intercepted, and he is exerting his utmost power to spread destruction and devastation around him.

We have received certain intelligence that General Carleton, the Governor of Canada, is instigating the people of that province and the Indians to fall upon us; and we have but too much reason to apprehend that schemes have been formed 35 to excite domestic enemies against us. In brief, a part of these colonies now feels, and all of them are sure of feeling, as far as the vengeance of administration can inflict them, the complicated calamities of fire, sword, and famine.

We are reduced to the alternative of choosing an unconditional submission to the tyranny of irritated ministers, or resistance by force. The latter is our choice. 40

We have counted the cost of this contest, and find nothing so dreadful as voluntary slavery. Honor, justice, and humanity forbid us tamely to surrender that freedom which we received from our gallant ancestors, and which our innocent posterity have a right to receive from us. We cannot endure the infamy and guilt
5 of resigning succeeding generations to that wretchedness which inevitably awaits them if we basely entail hereditary bondage upon them.

Our cause is just. Our union is perfect. Our internal resources are great and, if necessary, foreign assistance is undoubtedly attainable. We gratefully acknowledge, as signal instances of the Divine favor towards us, that his Providence would
10 not permit us to be called into this severe controversy until we were grown up to our present strength, had been previously exercised in warlike operation, and possessed of the means of defending ourselves. With hearts fortified with these animating reflections, we most solemnly, before God and the world, declare that, exerting the utmost energy of those powers which our beneficent Creator has
15 graciously bestowed upon us, the arms we have been compelled by our enemies to assume, we will, in defiance of every hazard, with unabating firmness and perseverance, employ for the preservation of our liberties; being with our mind resolved to die freemen rather than live slaves.

Lest this declaration should disquiet the minds of our friends and fellow-
20 subjects in any part of the empire, we assure them that we mean not to dissolve that union which has so long and so happily subsisted between us, and which we sincerely wish to see restored. Necessity has not yet driven us into that desperate measure, or induced us to excite any other nation to war against them. We have not raised armies with ambitious designs of separating from Great Britain
25 and establishing independent states. We fight not for glory or for conquest. We exhibit to mankind the remarkable spectacle of a people attacked by unprovoked enemies, without any imputation or even suspicion of offence. They boast of their privileges and civilization, and yet proffer no milder conditions than servitude or death.

30 In our own native land, in defense of the freedom that is our birth-right, and which we ever enjoyed till the late violation of it—for the protection of our property, acquired solely by the honest industry of our fore-fathers and ourselves, against violence actually offered, we have taken up arms. We shall lay them down when hostilities shall cease on the part of the aggressors and all danger of their
35 being renewed shall be removed, and not before.

With an humble confidence in the mercies of the supreme and impartial Judge and Ruler of the universe, we most devoutly implore his divine goodness to protect us happily through this great conflict, to dispose our adversaries to reconciliation on reasonable terms, and thereby to relieve the empire from the
40 calamities of civil war.

DECLARATION OF INDEPENDENCE

Thomas Jefferson's Declaration of Independence *was the thirteen colonies' instrument of secession from the British Empire. Jefferson (1743–1826) later said that he was trying to present "the common sense of the subject," by which he meant that sense of the subject held in common by those men who had to live and die by its words. Its structure is a syllogism: these are the principles, ends, and purposes of government; the "King" has violated them systematically; therefore, we must separate from him and become independent. His list of violations was both the longest and the most controversial section and was probably the part of the Declaration that most interested his contemporaries. It contains four types of grievances, most of which had been used in documents of protest before and were deeply rooted in American experience:*

- *Interruptions of legislative self-government*
- *Administrative attempts to impose the King's agenda*
- *Offenses against historic liberties*
- *The King's abdication of the proper ends of government, especially in making war on his subjects.*

The short preamble laid out the principles, ends, and purposes of government in about three-hundred words. Jefferson relied heavily on constitutional themes Americans (as they now called themselves) had been discussing throughout the years of crisis since the end of the Great War for Empire. He later said that he had also drawn from "Aristotle, Cicero, Locke, Sidney," and other books familiar to American leaders. The "self-evident" principles Jefferson identified apparently were: More than ninety other American "declarations of independence" were produced in the years 1770–1776, most of them containing ideas and grievances that Jefferson had expressed. The Declaration did not offer a specific plan of government, but it did contain a pledge of unity and a name for the new country—The United States of America.

Worthington Chauncey Ford, ed., *Journals of the Continental Congress, 1774–1789* (Washington, DC: Government Printing Office, 1906), V:511–15.

The unanimous Declaration of the thirteen United States of America.

When, in the course of human events, it becomes necessary for one people to dissolve the political bands which have connected them with another, and to assume among the powers of the earth the separate and equal station to which
5   the laws of Nature and of Nature's God entitle them, a decent respect to the opinions of mankind requires that they should declare the causes which impel them to the separation.

We hold these truths to be self-evident, that all men are created equal, that they are endowed by their Creator with certain unalienable rights, that among
10   these are life, liberty, and the pursuit of happiness. That, to secure these rights, governments are instituted among men, deriving their just powers from the consent of the governed. That whenever any form of government becomes destructive of these ends, it is the right of the people to alter or to abolish it, and to institute new government, laying its foundation on such principles, and
15   organizing its powers in such form, as to them shall seem most likely to effect their safety and happiness. Prudence, indeed, will dictate that governments long established should not be changed for light and transient causes; and, accordingly, all experience hath shewn, that mankind are more disposed to suffer, while evils are sufferable, than to right themselves by abolishing the forms to which
20   they are accustomed. But, when a long train of abuses and usurpations, pursuing invariably the same object, evinces a design to reduce them under absolute despotism, it is their right, it is their duty, to throw off such government, and to provide new guards for their future security. Such has been the patient sufferance of these colonies; and such is now the necessity which constrains them
25   to alter their former systems of government. The history of the present King of Great Britain is a history of repeated injuries and usurpations, all having in direct object the establishment of an absolute tyranny over these states. To prove this, let facts be submitted to a candid world.

He has refused his assent to laws the most wholesome and necessary for the
30   public good.

He has forbidden his governors to pass laws of immediate and pressing importance, unless suspended in their operation till his assent should be obtained; and when so suspended, he has utterly neglected to attend to them.

He has refused to pass other laws for the accommodation of large districts of
35   people, unless those people would relinquish the right of representation in the legislature; a right inestimable to them and formidable to tyrants only.

He has called together legislative bodies at places unusual, uncomfortable, and distant from the depository of their public records, for the sole purpose of fatiguing them into compliance with his measures.

He has dissolved representative houses repeatedly for opposing, with manly firmness, his invasions on the rights of the people.

He has refused for a long time, after such dissolutions, to cause others to be elected; whereby the legislative powers, incapable of annihilation, have returned to the people at large for their exercise; the state remaining in the meantime exposed to all the dangers of invasion from without, and convulsions within.

He has endeavoured to prevent the population of these states; for that purpose obstructing the laws for naturalization of foreigners; refusing to pass others to encourage their migrations hither, and raising the conditions of new appropriations of lands.

He has obstructed the administration of justice by refusing his assent to laws for establishing judiciary powers.

He has made judges dependent on his will alone for the tenure of their offices, and the amount and payment of their salaries.

He has erected a multitude of new offices, and sent hither swarms of officers to harass our people and eat out their substance.

He has kept among us, in times of peace, standing armies, without the consent of our legislatures.

He has affected to render the military independent of and superior to the civil power.

He has combined with others to subject us to a jurisdiction foreign to our constitution, and unacknowledged by our laws; giving his assent to their acts of pretended legislation:

- For quartering large bodies of armed troops among us;
- For protecting them, by a mock trial, from punishment for any murders which they should commit on the inhabitants of these states;
- For cutting off our trade with all parts of the world;
- For imposing taxes on us without our consent;
- For depriving us, in many cases, of the benefits of trial by jury;
- For transporting us beyond seas to be tried for pretended offences;
- For abolishing the free system of English laws in a neighbouring province, establishing therein an arbitrary government, and enlarging its boundaries

so as to render it at once an example and fit instrument for introducing the same absolute rule into these colonies;

- For taking away our charters, abolishing our most valuable laws, and altering fundamentally the forms of our governments;

5 • For suspending our own legislatures, and declaring themselves invested with power to legislate for us in all cases whatsoever.

He has abdicated government here by declaring us out of his protection, and waging war against us.

He has plundered our seas, ravaged our coasts, burnt our towns, and destroyed 10 the lives of our people.

He is at this time transporting large armies of foreign mercenaries to complete the works of death, desolation, and tyranny, already begun with circumstances of cruelty and perfidy scarcely paralleled in the most barbarous ages, and totally unworthy the head of a civilized nation.

15 He has constrained our fellow citizens, taken captive on the high seas, to bear arms against their country, to become the executioners of their friends and brethren, or to fall themselves by their hands.

He has excited domestic insurrections amongst us, and has endeavoured to bring on the inhabitants of our frontiers the merciless Indian savages, whose known rule 20 of warfare is an undistinguished destruction of all ages, sexes, and conditions.

In every stage of these oppressions, we have petitioned for redress, in the most humble terms: our repeated petitions have been answered only by repeated injury. A prince whose character is thus marked by every act which may define a tyrant is unfit to be the ruler of a free people.

25 Nor have we been wanting in attentions to our British brethren. We have warned them from time to time of attempts by their legislature to extend an unwarrantable jurisdiction over us. We have reminded them of the circumstances of our emigration and settlement here. We have appealed to their native justice and magnanimity, and we have conjured them by the ties of our common kindred to disavow these 30 usurpations, which would inevitably interrupt our connections and correspondence. They too have been deaf to the voice of justice and of consanguinity. We must, therefore, acquiesce in the necessity, which denounces our separation, and hold them, as we hold the rest of mankind, enemies in war, in peace, friends.

We, therefore, the representatives of the united States of America, in general 35 Congress assembled, appealing to the Supreme Judge of the World for the rectitude of our intentions, do, in the name, and by authority of the good people of these colonies, solemnly *publish* and *declare* that these united colonies are, and of right ought to be, free and independent states; that they are absolved from all allegiance to the British Crown, and that all political connection between them and the state of Great Britain is and ought to be totally dissolved; and that, as free and independent states, they have full power to levy war, conclude peace, 5 contract alliances, establish commerce, and to do all other acts and things which independent states may of right do. And for the support of this declaration, with a firm reliance on the protection of divine Providence, we mutually pledge to each other our lives, our fortunes, and our sacred honour.

JOHN HANCOCK	JOHN WITHERSPOON	CHARLES CARROLL
JOSIAH BARTLETT	FRANCIS HOPKINSON	of CARROLLTON
WILLIAM WHIPPLE	JOHN HART	GEORGE WYTHE
SAMUEL ADAMS	ABRAHAM CLARK	RICHARD HENRY LEE
JOHN ADAMS	ROBERT MORRIS	THOMAS JEFFERSON
ROBERT TREAT PAINE	BENJAMIN RUSH	BENJAMIN HARRISON
ELBRIDGE GERRY	BENJAMIN FRANKLIN	THOMAS NELSON, JUNIOR
STEPHEN HOPKINS	JOHN MORTON	FRANCIS LIGHTFOOT LEE
WILLIAM ELLERY	GEORGE CLYMER	CARTER BRAXTON
ROGER SHERMAN	JAMES SMITH	WILLIAM HOOPER
SAMUEL HUNTINGTON	GEORGE TAYLOR	JOSEPH HEWES
WILLIAM WILLIAMS	JAMES WILSON	JOHN PENN
OLIVER WOLCOTT	GEORGE ROSS	EDWARD RUTLEDGE
MATTHEW THORNTON	CÆSAR RODNEY	THOMAS HEYWARD, JUNIOR
WILLIAM FLOYD	GEORGE READ	THOMAS LYNCH, JUNIOR
PHILIP LIVINGSTON	THOMAS M. KEAN	ARTHUR MIDDLETON
FRANCIS LEWIS	SAMUEL CHASE	BUTTON GWINNETT
LEWIS MORRIS	WILLIAM PACA	LYMAN HALL
RICHARD STOCKTON	THOMAS STONE	GEORGE WALTON

FAST DAY PROCLAMATIONS
CONTINENTAL CONGRESS

Whereas, the war in which the United States are engaged with Great Britain has not only been prolonged, but is likely to be carried to the greatest extremity; and whereas, it becomes all public bodies, as well as private persons, to reverence the Providence of God, and look up to Him as the supreme disposer of all events and the arbiter of the fate of nations; therefore,   5

Resolved, That it be recommended to all the United States, as soon as possible, to appoint a day of solemn fasting and humiliation; to implore of Almighty God the forgiveness of the many sins prevailing among all ranks, and to beg the countenance as assistance of His Providence in the prosecution of the present just and necessary war.   10

The Congress do also, in the most earnest manner, recommend to all the members of the United States, and particularly the officers civil and military under them, the exercise of repentance and reformation; and further, require of them the strict observation of the Articles of War, and particularly that part of the said Articles which forbids profane swearing and all immorality, of which all   15
such officers are desired to take notice.

It is left to each state to issue out proclamations fixing the days that appear most proper within their several bounds.

SATURDAY, 20 MARCH 1779

The committee appointed to prepare a recommendation to the several states to set apart a day of fasting, humiliation, and prayer, brought in a draft, which was   20
taken into consideration, and agreed to as follows:

Whereas, in just punishment of our manifold transgressions, it has pleased the Supreme Disposer of all events to visit these United States with a destructive, calamitous war, through which his divine Providence has, hitherto, in a wonderful manner, conducted us, so that we might acknowledge that the race is not to the   25

Worthington Chauncey Ford, ed., *Journals of the Continental Congress, 1774–1789* (Washington, DC: Government Printing Office, 1909), VI:1022, XIII:342–44.

swift, nor the battle to the strong. And whereas there is but too much reason to fear that notwithstanding the chastisements received and benefits bestowed, too few have been sufficiently awakened to a sense of their guilt, or warmed our bosoms with gratitude, or taught to amend their lives and turn from their sins,
5   that so he might turn from his wrath. And whereas, from a consciousness of what we have merited at his hands, and an apprehension that the malevolence of our disappointed enemies, like the incredulity of Pharaoh, may be used as the scourge of Omnipotence to vindicate his slighted Majesty, there is reason to fear that he may permit much of our land to become the prey of the spoiler,
10   and the blood of the innocent be poured out that our borders to be ravaged, and our habitations destroyed.

Resolved, that it be recommended to the several states to appoint the first Thursday in May next to be a day of fasting, thanksgiving, humiliation, and prayer to Almighty God that he will be pleased to avert those impending calamities which
15   we have but too well deserved. That he will grant us His grace to repent of our sins, and amend our lives, according to his holy word. That he will continue that wonderful protection which has led us through the paths of danger and distress. That he will be a husband to the widow and a father to the fatherless children, who weep over the barbarities of a savage enemy. That he will grant
20   us patience in suffering, and fortitude in adversity. That he will inspire us with humility and moderation, and gratitude in prosperous circumstances. That he will give wisdom to our councils, firmness to our resolutions, and victory to our arms. That he will have mercy on our foes, and graciously forgive them, and turn their hearts from enmity to love.

25   That he will bless the labours of the husbandman, and pour forth abundance, so that we may enjoy the fruits of the earth in due season. That he will cause union, harmony, and mutual confidence to prevail throughout these states. That he will bestow on our great ally all those blessings which may enable him to be gloriously instrumental in protecting the rights of mankind, and promoting
30   the happiness of his subjects and advancing the peace and liberty of nations. That he will give to both parties to this alliance grace to perform with honor and fidelity their national engagements. That he will bountifully continue his paternal care to the commander-in-chief, and the officers and soldiers of the United States. That he will grant the blessings of peace to all contending
35   nations, freedom to those who are in bondage, and comfort to the afflicted. That he will diffuse useful knowledge, extend the influence of true religion, and give us that peace of mind which the world cannot give. That he will be our shield in the day of battle, our comforter in the hour of death, and our kind parent and merciful judge through time and through eternity.

THE MEANING OF THE REVOLUTION

When the members of the Continental Congress appointed Benjamin Franklin (1706–1790), John Adams (1735–1826), and Thomas Jefferson (1743–1826) to draft the Declaration of Independence and then voted to adopt and promulgate that document, they had in mind two distinct aims and two distinct audiences. On the one hand, they wanted to attract foreign support for their separation from Great Britain and, to this end, they sought to justify that break in the eyes of the world in terms accepted in international law. On the other hand, they wanted to instruct the citizens of the nascent United States in the reasoning that underpinned the Revolution and to lay a principled foundation for the government that they would soon establish. That those who fought the Revolutionary War understood their cause to be that of liberty is evident in the unsigned broadside, found among the papers of the British general Sir Thomas Gage (1719–1787), that is printed below. That, in this regard, they looked to Aristotle, Cicero, John Locke, and Algernon Sidney for inspiration is suggested by Thomas Jefferson in his letter to Henry Lee. He also argues that the "harmonizing sentiments" contained within the Declaration were of universal significance and had profound consequences for peoples outside the borders of the United States. As it happens, he penned the letter on the eve of the fiftieth anniversary of America's Declaration of Independence, an event that coincided with the date of his death and that of his onetime collaborator John Adams.

AMERICA

FELLOW COUNTRYMEN

Be not intimidated at the sight of soldiers, mercenary soldiers, who for a penny a day addition to their wages would serve Mustaphay 3rd as soon as George the 3rd. You know their number: 1000 slaves are not to give laws to a brave and free people. They have already began to show their insolence. There is now no appeal but to God. Extirpate them root and branch, be sure their chiefs are the first victims; rise my countrymen. Throw off the first fetter of slavery, a standing army—remember your brave forefathers, men of whom the world was not

5   worthy. They purchased this land with much treasure and seas of their blood; let them not in this day rise up and see their posterity less brave, less resolute, and less virtuous. My countrymen, we either must unsheath our swords or be slaves. Your understandings would be affronted were the last to be put to you. The day is come. Strike these invaders of your liberty, these enemies of

10   your God, and not let them any longer pollute this *Insulam Sacram,*[1] ye that have got no swords, sell your garments and buy one. You fear not death, only slavery. The anniversary of our last stroke to their underhand plots was the 14th August. Let our last and effectual stroke to their open hostilities be the same. My countrymen, be freemen or slaves, or die.

---

[1] *Insulam Sacram*—Holy land

Gage Papers, William Clements Library, University of Michigan—Ann Arbor: unsigned broadside.

Thomas Jefferson (1743–1826)
to Henry Lee (1782–1867)

8 May 1825

15   …with respect to our rights, and the acts of the British government contravening those rights, there was but one opinion on this side of the water. All American Whigs thought alike on these subjects. When forced, therefore, to resort to arms for redress, an appeal to the tribunal of the world was deemed proper for our justification. This was the object of the Declaration of Independence.

20   Not to find out new principles, or new arguments, never before thought of, not merely to say things which had never been said before; but to place before mankind the common sense of the subject, in terms so plain and firm as to command their assent, and to justify ourselves in the independent stand we are compelled to take. Neither aiming at originality of principle or sentiment,

25   nor yet copied from any particular and previous writing, it was intended to be an expression of the American mind, and to give to that expression the proper tone and spirit called for by the occasion. All its authority rests then on the harmonizing sentiments of the day, whether expressed in conversation, in letters, printed essays, or in the elementary books of public right, as Aristotle,

30   Cicero, Locke, Sidney, &c."

H. A. Washington, ed., *The Writings of Thomas Jefferson* (1853–1854), VIII:407.

THE NORTHWEST ORDINANCE

The United States is the only country in modern history that began its independent history as an empire. The treaty ending the War for Independence transferred about 510,000 square miles of land west of the Appalachian Mountains and east of the Mississippi River to the new United States. Land policy relating to this vast territory therefore became one of the most pressing problems of the early republic. States that had western land claims under colonial charters ceded their lands to the national government by 1784. This cleared the way for a national land policy, which was effected by the passing of the Land Ordinance of 1785 and the Northwest Ordinance in July 1787, at the same time that delegates in Philadelphia were debating a new Constitution for the United States.

The Northwest Ordinance, which Congress later gave the force and status of constitutional law, was essentially a conserving law. It guaranteed the rule of law and all the "rights of Americans" to settlers in the colonies, or territories as they were called. It provided a process for achieving representative government and equal statehood. And it insisted that the original states be cloned in the wilderness—the basic condition for statehood was that they had to submit acceptable republican constitutions to the Congress.

The Ordinance was also innovative in a way that made it perhaps the most complete statement of liberty authored by the Founding generation. It banned slavery from the territory and so set the precedent for the nation to complete its promise that liberty applied equally to all men.

13 JULY 1787

An Ordinance for the Government of the Territory of the United States North West of the river Ohio

Be it ordained by the United States in Congress assembled that the said territory for the purposes of temporary government be one district, subject, however,

Roscoe R. Hill, ed., *Journals of the Continental Congress, 1774–1789* (Washington DC: Government Printing Office, 1936), XXXII: 334–43.

to be divided into two districts as future circumstances may in the opinion of
Congress make it expedient.

Be it ordained by the authority aforesaid that the estates both of resident and
non-resident proprietors in the said territory dying intestate shall descend to
5   and be distributed among their children and the descendants of a deceased child
in equal parts; the descendants of a deceased child or grand-child to take the
share of their deceased parent in equal parts among them; and where there shall
be no children or descendants, then in equal parts to the next of kin in equal
degree, and among collaterals the children of a deceased brother or sister of the
10 intestate shall have in equal parts among them their deceased parent's share, and
there shall in no case be a distinction between kindred of the whole and half
blood; saving in all cases to the widow of the intestate her third part of the real
estate for life, and one third part of the personal estate; and this law relative to
descents and dower shall remain in full force until altered by the legislature of
15 the district. And until the governor and judges shall adopt laws as hereinafter
mentioned estates in the said territory may be devised or bequeathed by wills
in writing signed and sealed by him or her in whom the estate may be, being
of full age, and attested by three witnesses, and real estates may be conveyed by
lease and release or bargain and sale signed, sealed, and delivered by the person
20 being of full age in whom the estate may be and attested by two witnesses
provided such wills be duly proved and such conveyances be acknowledged or
the execution thereof duly proved and be recorded within one year after proper
magistrates, courts, and registers shall be appointed for that purpose and personal property may be transferred by delivery saving, however, to the French
25 and Canadian inhabitants and other settlers of the Kaskaskies, Saint Vincent's,
and the neighboring villages who have heretofore professed themselves citizens
of Virginia, their laws and customs now in force among them relative to the
descent and conveyance of property.

Be it ordained by the authority aforesaid that there shall be appointed from
30 time to time by Congress a governor, whose commission shall continue in force
for the term of three years, unless sooner revoked by Congress; he shall reside
in the district and have a freehold estate therein in one thousand acres of land
while in the exercise of his office. There shall be appointed from time to time by
Congress a secretary, whose commission shall continue in force for four years,
35 unless sooner revoked; he shall reside in the district and have a freehold estate
therein in five hundred acres of land while in the exercise of his office. It shall be
his duty to keep and preserve the acts and laws passed by the legislature and the
public records of the district and the proceedings of the governor in his executive
department and transmit authentic copies of such acts and proceedings every

six months to the Secretary of Congress. There shall also be appointed a court, to consist of three judges, any two of whom to form a court, who shall have a common law jurisdiction and reside in the district and have each therein a freehold estate in five hundred acres of land while in the exercise of their offices, and their commissions shall continue in force during good behavior.   5

The governor and judges, or a majority of them, shall adopt and publish in the district such laws of the original states criminal and civil as may be necessary and best suited to the circumstances of the district and report them to Congress from time to time, which laws shall be in force in the district until the organization of the general assembly therein, unless disapproved of by Congress; but afterwards the legislature shall have authority to alter them as they shall think fit.   10

The governor for the time being shall be commander-in-chief of the militia, appoint and commission all officers in the same below the rank of general officers; all general officers shall be appointed and commissioned by Congress.

Previous to the organization of the general assembly, the governor shall appoint such magistrates and other civil officers in each county or township, as he shall   15
find necessary for the preservation of the peace and good order in the same. After the general assembly shall be organized, the powers and duties of magistrates and other civil officers shall be regulated and defined by the said assembly; but all magistrates and other civil officers, not herein otherwise directed shall during the continuance of this temporary government be appointed by the governor.   20

For the prevention of crimes and injuries, the laws to be adopted or made shall have force in all parts of the district and for the execution of process criminal and civil, the governor shall make proper divisions thereof, and he shall proceed from time to time as circumstances may require to lay out the parts of the district in which the Indian titles shall have been extinguished into counties   25
and townships subject, however, to such alterations as may thereafter be made by the legislature.

So soon as there shall be five thousand free male inhabitants of full age in the district upon giving proof thereof to the governor, they shall receive authority with time and place to elect representatives from their counties or townships to   30
represent them in the general assembly, provided that for every five hundred free male inhabitants there shall be one representative and so on progressively with the number of free male inhabitants shall the right of representation increase until the number of representatives shall amount to twenty-five, after which the number and proportion of representatives shall be regulated by the legislature;   35
provided that no person be eligible or qualified to act as a representative unless

he shall have been a citizen of one of the United States three years and be a resident in the district or unless he shall have resided in the district three years and in either case shall likewise hold in his own right in fee simple two hundred acres of land within the same; provided also that a freehold in fifty acres of land
5 in the district having been a citizen of one of the states and being resident in the district; or the like freehold and two years residence in the district shall be necessary to qualify a man as an elector of a representative.

The representatives thus elected shall serve for the term of two years, and in case
10 of the death of a representative or removal from office, the governor shall issue a writ to the county or township for which he was a member, to elect another in his stead to serve for the residue of the term.

The general assembly or legislature shall consist of the governor, legislative council, and a house of representatives. The legislative council shall consist
15 of five members to continue in office five years, unless sooner removed by Congress, any three of whom to be a quorum and the members of the council shall be nominated and appointed in the following manner, to wit: As soon as representatives shall be elected, the governor shall appoint a time and place for them to meet together, and when met they shall nominate ten persons, resi-
20 dents in the district, and each possessed of a freehold in five hundred acres of land and return their names to Congress; five of whom Congress shall appoint and commission to serve as aforesaid; and whenever a vacancy shall happen in the council by death or removal from office, the house of representatives shall nominate two persons, qualified as aforesaid, for each vacancy and return their
25 names to Congress, one of whom Congress shall appoint and commission for the residue of the term, and every five years, four months, at least, before the expiration of the time of service of the members of council, the said house shall nominate ten persons qualified as aforesaid, and return their names to Congress, five of whom Congress shall appoint and commission to serve as members of the
30 council five years, unless sooner removed. And the governor, legislative council, and house of representatives shall have authority to make laws in all cases for the good government of the district not repugnant to the principles and articles in this ordinance established and declared. And all bills having passed by a majority in the house, and by a majority in the council, shall be referred to the governor
35 for his assent; but no bill or legislative act whatever shall be of any force without his assent. The governor shall have power to convene, prorogue, and dissolve the general assembly, when in his opinion it shall be expedient.

The governor, judges, legislative council, secretary, and such other officers as Congress shall appoint in the district shall take an oath or affirmation of fidelity and of office, the governor before the President of Congress, and all other officers before the governor. As soon as a legislature shall be formed in the district, the council and house, assembled in one room, shall have authority by joint ballot to elect a delegate to Congress, who shall have a seat in Congress, with a right of debating, but not of voting, during this temporary government.   5

And for extending the fundamental principles of civil and religious liberty, which form the basis whereon these republics, their laws, and constitutions are erected; to fix and establish those principles as the basis of all laws, constitutions, and governments which forever hereafter shall be formed in the said territory; to provide also for the establishment of states and permanent government   10
therein, and for their admission to a share in the federal councils on an equal footing with the original states, at as early periods as may be consistent with the general interest,

It is hereby ordained and declared by the authority aforesaid that the following articles shall be considered as articles of compact between the original states   15
and the people and states in the said territory, and forever remain unalterable, unless by common consent, to wit,

Article the First. No person demeaning himself in a peaceable and orderly manner shall ever be molested on account of his mode of worship or religious sentiments in the said territory.   20

Article the Second. The inhabitants of the said territory shall always be entitled to the benefits of the writ of *habeas corpus* and of the trial by jury; of a proportionate representation of the people in the legislature, and of judicial proceedings according to the course of the common law; all persons shall be bailable unless for capital offences, where the proof shall be evident, or the presumption   25
great; all fines shall be moderate, and no cruel or unusual punishments shall be inflicted; no man shall be deprived of his liberty or property but by the judgment of his peers, or the law of the land; and should the public exigencies make it necessary for the common preservation to take any person's property, or to demand his particular services, full compensation shall be made for the   30
same; and in the just preservation of rights and property it is understood and declared; that no law ought ever to be made, or have force in the said territory, that shall in any manner whatever interfere with, or affect private contracts or engagements, bona fide and without fraud previously formed.

Article the Third. Religion, morality, and knowledge being necessary to good   35
government and the happiness of mankind, schools and the means of education shall forever be encouraged. The utmost good faith shall always be observed

towards the Indians; their lands and property shall never be taken from them without their consent, and in their property, rights, and liberty, they never shall be invaded or disturbed, unless in just and lawful wars authorized by Congress; but laws founded in justice and humanity shall from time to time
5 be made for preventing wrongs being done to them, and for preserving peace and friendship with them.

Article the Fourth. The said territory, and the states which may be formed therein shall forever remain a part of this Confederacy of the United States of America, subject to the Articles of Confederation, and to such alterations
10 therein as shall be constitutionally made; and to all the acts and ordinances of the United States in Congress assembled, conformable thereto. The inhabitants and settlers in the said territory shall be subject to pay a part of the federal debts contracted or to be contracted, and a proportional part of the expenses of government, to be apportioned on them by Congress, according to the same
15 common rule and measure by which apportionments thereof shall be made on the other states; and the taxes for paying their proportion shall be laid and levied by the authority and direction of the legislatures of the district or districts or new states, as in the original states, within the time agreed upon by the United States in Congress assembled. The legislatures of those districts, or new states,
20 shall never interfere with the primary disposal of the soil by the United States in Congress assembled, nor with any regulations Congress may find necessary for securing the title in such soil to the *bona fide* purchasers. No tax shall be imposed on lands the property of the United States; and in no case shall nonresident proprietors be taxed higher than residents. The navigable waters leading
25 into the Mississippi and Saint Lawrence, and the carrying places between the same, shall be common highways and forever free, as well to the inhabitants of the said territory as to the citizens of the United States, and those of any other states that may be admitted into the Confederacy, without any tax, impost, or duty therefor.

30 Article the Fifth. There shall be formed in the said territory not less than three nor more than five states, and the boundaries of the states, as soon as Virginia shall alter her act of cession and consent to the same, shall become fixed and established as follows, to wit: The western state in the said territory shall be bounded by the Mississippi, the Ohio, and Wabash rivers; a direct line drawn
35 from the Wabash and post Vincents due north to the territorial line between the United States and Canada, and by the said territorial line to the lake of the Woods and Mississippi. The middle state shall be bounded by the said direct line, the Wabash from post Vincents to the Ohio; by the Ohio, by direct line drawn due north from the mouth of the Great Miami to the said territorial

line, and by the said territorial line. The eastern state shall be bounded by the last mentioned direct line, the Ohio, Pennsylvania, and the said territorial line; provided however, and it is further understood and declared that the boundaries of these three states shall be subject so far to be altered, that if Congress shall hereafter find it expedient, they shall have authority to form one or two states 5 in that part of the said territory which lies north of an east and west line drawn through the southerly bend or extreme of Lake Michigan; and whenever any of the said states shall have sixty thousand free inhabitants therein, such state shall be admitted by its delegates into the Congress of the United States, on an equal footing with the original states in all respects whatever; and shall be 10 at liberty to form a permanent constitution and state government, provided the constitution and government so to be formed shall be republican, and in conformity to the principles contained in these articles; and so far as it can be consistent with the general interest of the Confederacy, such admission shall be allowed at an earlier period, and when there may be a less number of free 15 inhabitants in the state than sixty thousand.

Article the Sixth. There shall be neither slavery nor involuntary servitude in the said territory otherwise than in the punishment of crimes, whereof the party shall have been duly convicted; provided always that any person escaping into the same, from whom labor or service is lawfully claimed in any one of the 20 original states, such fugitive may be lawfully reclaimed and conveyed to the person claiming his or her labor or service as aforesaid.

Be it ordained by the authority aforesaid that the resolutions of the 23^{d} of April 1784 relative to the subject of this ordinance be, and the same are hereby, repealed and declared null and void.   25

CONSTITUTION OF THE UNITED STATES

Problems of public debt, western lands, and internal rebellion (especially Shays' Rebellion in Massachusetts) convinced many leaders that the United States could not survive under the Articles of Confederation. That constitution, ratified in 1781, provided for thirteen republics, confederated or covenanted into a union but leaving sovereignty clearly in the state governments. The Philadelphia Convention of 1787 was called to strengthen the Confederation; it ended by writing a new Constitution.

Nationalists dominated the Convention; that is, men who were determined to form "a more perfect Union" that had the power to tax and to hold a rather unruly nation together. There were many compromises—the most important over the question of representation in the legislature—but two broad principles of government emerged. The Republic would be "partly national, partly federal": the Convention divided sovereignty on a vertical axis, recognizing that legitimate authority should be exercised in national, state, and local governments. And power was also divided horizontally, according to the principle of separation of powers—legislative, executive, judicial—which snatched part of a power away every time it seemed to be located in one place. The Convention thus offered to the people and to the states truly limited government. The Constitution provided a government that could act, but only in carefully defined ways; it was a law created to limit law.

John Dickinson (1732–1808) of Pennsylvania and Delaware reminded the delegates that "Experience must be our only guide. Reason may mislead us." Attention to their heritage in the end controlled what they wrought. Their most immediate experience was as colonists, working out representative government in the American provinces of the British Empire. They drew heavily on their classical Greek and Roman heritage, since most of the world's

---

Signed Copy of the Constitution of the United States, National Archives and Records Administration; Miscellaneous Papers of the Continental Congress, 1774–1789; Records of the Continental and Confederation Congresses and the Constitutional Convention, 1774–1789, Record Group 360.

experience with republican government was in those cultures. They were also
Englishmen, devoted right up to independence to the "rights of Englishmen."
Much of their thinking about liberty and constitutions came from English
history—the tradition of Magna Carta, the Common Law, and the Glori-
ous Revolution. Finally, they looked to the highest level of "experience," that
revealed by God in Holy Scripture and the created order. The most frequently
quoted definition of liberty in the period of the Founding was, "But they shall
sit every man under his vine and under his fig tree; and none shall make
them afraid" (Micah 4:4). It was precisely this balance between freedom
and security that summed up the lessons of experience.

17 SEPTEMBER 1787

We the people of the United States, in order to form a more perfect union, establish justice, ensure domestic tranquility, provide for the common defense, promote the general welfare, and secure the blessings of liberty to ourselves and our posterity, do ordain and establish this Constitution for the United States
5   of America.

Article I

I§1 All legislative powers herein granted shall be vested in a Congress of the United States, which shall consist of a Senate and House of Representatives.

I§2 The House of Representatives shall be composed of members chosen every second year by the people of the several states, and the electors in each state
10   shall have the qualifications requisite for electors of the most numerous branch of the state legislature.

No person shall be a Representative who shall not have attained to the age of twenty-five years, and been seven years a citizen of the United States, and who shall not, when elected, be an inhabitant of that state in which
15   he shall be chosen.

Representatives and direct taxes shall be apportioned among the several states which may be included within this union, according to their respective numbers, which shall be determined by adding to the whole number of free persons, including those bound to service for a term of years, and
20   excluding Indians not taxed, three-fifths of all other persons. The actual enumeration shall be made within three years after the first meeting of the Congress of the United States, and within every subsequent term of ten years, in such manner as they shall by law direct. The number of representatives shall not exceed one for every thirty thousand, but each state
25   shall have at least one Representative; and until such enumeration shall be made, the state of New Hampshire shall be entitled to choose three, Massachusetts eight, Rhode Island and Providence Plantations one, Con-

necticut five, New York six, New Jersey four, Pennsylvania eight, Delaware one, Maryland six, Virginia ten, North Carolina five, South Carolina five, and Georgia three.

When vacancies happen in the representation from any state, the executive authority thereof shall issue writs of election to fill such vacancies.

The House of Representatives shall choose their Speaker and other officers; and shall have the sole power of impeachment.

I§3 The Senate of the United States shall be composed of two Senators from each state, chosen by the legislature thereof for six years; and each Senator shall have one vote.

Immediately after they shall be assembled in consequence of the first election, they shall be divided as equally as may be into three classes. The seats of the Senators of the first class shall be vacated at the expiration of the second year, of the second class at the expiration of the fourth year, and of the third class at the expiration of the sixth year, so that one third may be chosen every second year; and if vacancies happen by resignation, or otherwise, during the recess of the legislature of any state, the executive thereof may make temporary appointments until the next meeting of the legislature, which shall then fill such vacancies.

No person shall be a Senator who shall not have attained to the age of thirty years, and been nine years a citizen of the United States, and who shall not, when elected, be an inhabitant of that state for which he shall be chosen.

The Vice President of the United States shall be President of the Senate, but shall have no vote, unless they be equally divided.

The Senate shall choose their other officers, and also a president *pro tempore*, in the absence of the Vice President, or when he shall exercise the office of President of the United States.

The Senate shall have the sole power to try all impeachments. When sitting for that purpose, they shall be on oath or affirmation. When the President of the United States is tried, the Chief Justice shall preside. And no person shall be convicted without the concurrence of two thirds of the members present.

Judgment in cases of impeachment shall not extend further than to removal from office, and disqualification to hold and enjoy any office of honor, trust, or profit under the United States. But the party convicted shall nevertheless be liable and subject to indictment, trial, judgment, and punishment, according to law.

I§4 The times, places, and manner of holding elections for Senators and Representatives shall be prescribed in each state by the legislature thereof; but the Congress may at any time by law make or alter such regulations, except as to the places of choosing Senators.

5   The Congress shall assemble at least once in every year, and such meeting shall be on the first Monday in December, unless they shall by law appoint a different day.

I§5 Each House shall be the judge of the elections, returns, and qualifications of its own members, and a majority of each shall constitute a quorum
10   to do business; but a smaller number may adjourn from day to day, and may be authorized to compel the attendance of absent members, in such manner, and under such penalties as each House may provide.

Each House may determine the rules of its proceedings, punish its members for disorderly behavior, and, with the concurrence of two-thirds, expel a
15   member.

Each House shall keep a journal of its proceedings, and from time to time publish the same, excepting such parts as may in their judgment require secrecy; and the yeas and nays of the members of either House on any question shall, at the desire of one-fifth of those present, be entered on
20   the journal.

Neither House, during the session of Congress, shall, without the consent of the other, adjourn for more than three days, nor to any other place than that in which the two Houses shall be sitting.

I§6 The Senators and Representatives shall receive a compensation for their
25   services, to be ascertained by law, and paid out of the Treasury of the United States. They shall in all cases, except treason, felony, and breach of the peace, be privileged from arrest during their attendance at the session of their respective Houses, and in going to and returning from the same; and for any speech or debate in either House, they shall not be questioned
30   in any other place.

No Senator or Representative shall, during the time for which he was elected, be appointed to any civil office under the authority of the United States which shall have been created, or the emoluments whereof shall have been increased, during such time; and no person holding any office
35   under the United States shall be a member of either House during his continuance in office.

I§7 All bills for raising revenue shall originate in the House of Representatives; but the Senate may propose or concur with amendments as on other bills.

Every bill which shall have passed the House of Representatives and the Senate shall, before it become a law, be presented to the President of the United States. If he approve, he shall sign it; but if not, he shall return it, with his objections to that House in which it shall have originated, who shall enter the objections at large on their journal, and proceed to re-consider it. 5
If after such reconsideration, two-thirds of that House shall agree to pass the bill, it shall be sent, together with the objections, to the other House, by which it shall likewise be re-considered, and if approved by two-thirds of that House, it shall become a law. But in all such cases the votes of both Houses shall be determined by yeas and nays, and the names of the persons 10
voting for and against the bill shall be entered on the journal of each House respectively. If any bill shall not be returned by the President within ten days (Sundays excepted) after it shall have been presented to him, the same shall be a law, in like manner as if he had signed it, unless the Congress by their adjournment prevent its return, in which case it shall not be a law. 15

Every order, resolution, or vote to which the concurrence of the Senate and House of Representatives may be necessary (except on a question of adjournment) shall be presented to the President of the United States; and before the same shall take effect, shall be approved by him or, being disapproved by him, shall be re-passed by two-thirds of the Senate and House of Representatives, 20
according to the rules and limitations prescribed in the case of a bill.

I§8 The Congress shall have power to lay and collect taxes, duties, imposts, and excises, to pay the debts and provide for the common defense and general welfare of the United States; but all duties, imposts, and excises shall be uniform throughout the United States; 25

To borrow money on the credit of the United States;

To regulate commerce with foreign nations, and among the several states, and with the Indian tribes;

To establish an uniform rule of naturalization, and uniform laws on the subject of bankruptcies throughout the United States. 30

To coin money, regulate the value thereof, and of foreign coin, and fix the standard of weights and measures;

To provide for the punishment of counterfeiting the securities and current coin of the United States;

To establish post offices and post roads; 35

To promote the progress of science and useful arts, by securing for limited times to authors and inventors the exclusive right to their respective writings and discoveries;

To constitute tribunals inferior to the supreme court;

To define and punish piracies and felonies committed on the high seas, and offences against the law of nations;

To declare war, grant letters of marque and reprisal, and make rules concerning captures on land and water;

To raise and support armies, but no appropriation of money to that use shall be for a longer term than two years;

To provide and maintain a navy;

To make rules for the government and regulation of the land and naval forces;

To provide for calling forth the militia to execute the laws of the union, suppress insurrections, and repel invasions;

To provide for organizing, arming, and disciplining the militia, and for governing such part of them as may be employed in the service of the United States, reserving to the states respectively the appointment of the officers and the authority of training the militia according to the discipline prescribed by Congress;

To exercise exclusive legislation in all cases whatsoever over such district (not exceeding ten miles square) as may, by cession of particular states and the acceptance of Congress, become the seat of the government of the United States, and to exercise like authority over all places purchased by the consent of the legislature of the state in which the same shall be for the erection of forts, magazines, arsenals, dock-yards, and other needful buildings;—and

To make all laws which shall be necessary and proper for carrying into execution the foregoing powers, and all other powers vested by this Constitution in the government of the United States, or in any department or officer thereof.

I§9 The migration or importation of such persons as any of the states now existing shall think proper to admit shall not be prohibited by the Congress prior to the year one thousand eight hundred and eight, but a tax or duty may be imposed on such importation, not exceeding ten dollars for each person.

The privilege of the writ of *habeas corpus* shall not be suspended, unless when in cases of rebellion or invasion the public safety may require it.

No bill of attainder or *ex post facto* law shall be passed.

No capitation, or other direct tax, shall be laid, unless in proportion to the census or enumeration herein before directed to be taken.

No tax or duty shall be laid on articles exported from any state.

No preference shall be given by any regulation of commerce or revenue to the ports of one state over those of another; nor shall vessels bound to, or from, one state be obliged to enter, clear, or pay duties in another.

No money shall be drawn from the Treasury but in consequence of appropriations made by law; and a regular statement and account of the receipts and expenditures of all public money shall be published from time to time.

No title of nobility shall be granted by the United States. And no person holding any office of profit or trust under them shall, without the consent of the Congress, accept of any present, emolument, office, or title, of any kind whatever, from any king, prince, or foreign state.

I§10 No state shall enter into any treaty, alliance, or confederation; grant letters of marque and reprisal; coin money; emit bills of credit; make anything but gold and silver coin a tender in payment of debts; pass any bill of attainder, *ex post facto* law, or law impairing the obligation of contracts, or grant any title of nobility.

No state shall, without the consent of the Congress, lay any imposts or duties on imports or exports, except what may be absolutely necessary for executing its inspection laws. And the net produce of all duties and imposts laid by any state on imports or exports shall be for the use of the Treasury of the United States; and all such laws shall be subject to the revision and control of the Congress.

No state shall, without the consent of Congress, lay any duty of tonnage, keep troops or ships of war in time of peace, enter into any agreement or compact with another state, or with a foreign power, or engage in war, unless actually invaded, or in such imminent danger as will not admit of delay.

Article II

II§1 The executive power shall be vested in a President of the United States of America. He shall hold his office during the term of four years and, together with the Vice President, chosen for the same term, be elected, as follows:

Each state shall appoint, in such manner as the legislature thereof may direct, a number of electors, equal to the whole number of Senators and Representatives to which the state may be entitled in the Congress. But no Senator or Representative, or person holding an office of trust or profit under the United States, shall be appointed an elector.

The electors shall meet in their respective states, and vote by ballot for two persons, of whom one at least shall not be an inhabitant of the same state with themselves. And they shall make a list of all the persons voted for, and of the number of votes for each; which list they shall sign and certify, and transmit sealed to the seat of the government of the United States, directed to the President of the Senate. The President of the Senate shall, in the presence of the Senate and House of Representatives, open all the certificates, and the votes shall then be counted. The person having the greatest number of votes shall be the President, if such number be a majority of the whole number of electors appointed; and if there be more than one who have such majority, and have an equal number of votes, then the House of Representatives shall immediately choose by ballot one of them for President; and if no person have a majority, then from the five highest on the list the said House shall in like manner choose the President. But in choosing the President, the votes shall be taken by states, the representation from each state having one vote; a quorum for this purpose shall consist of a member or members from two-thirds of the states, and a majority of all the states shall be necessary to a choice. In every case, after the choice of the President, the person having the greatest number of votes of the electors shall be the Vice President. But if there should remain two or more who have equal votes, the Senate shall choose from them by ballot the Vice President.

The Congress may determine the time of choosing the electors, and the day on which they shall give their votes; which day shall be the same throughout the United States.

No person except a natural-born citizen, or a citizen of the United States at the time of the adoption of this Constitution, shall be eligible to the office of President; neither shall any person be eligible to that office who shall not have attained to the age of thirty five Years, and been fourteen years a resident within the United States.

In case of the removal of the President from office, or of his death, resignation, or inability to discharge the powers and duties of the said office, the same shall devolve on the Vice President, and the Congress may by law provide for the case of removal, death, resignation, or inability, both of the President and Vice President declaring what officer shall then act as President, and such officer shall act accordingly, until the disability be removed, or a President shall be elected.

The President shall, at stated times, receive for his services a compensation, which shall neither be increased nor diminished during the period for which he shall have been elected, and he shall not receive within that period any other emolument from the United States, or any of them.

Before he enter on the execution of his office, he shall take the following oath or affirmation: "I do solemnly swear (or affirm) that I will faithfully execute the office of President of the United States, and will to the best of 5 my ability preserve, protect, and defend the Constitution of the United States."

II§2 The President shall be commander-in-chief of the army and navy of the United States, and of the militia of the several states when called into the actual service of the United States; he may require the opinion, in writing, of 10 the principal officer in each of the executive departments upon any subject relating to the duties of their respective offices, and he shall have power to grant reprieves and pardons for offences against the United States, except in cases of impeachment.

He shall have power, by and with the advice and consent of the Senate, 15 to make treaties, provided two-thirds of the Senators present concur; and he shall nominate, and by and with the advice and consent of the Senate, shall appoint ambassadors, other public ministers, and consuls, judges of the supreme court, and all other officers of the United States whose appointments are not herein otherwise provided for, and which shall be 20 established by law. But the Congress may by law vest the appointment of such inferior offices, as they think proper, in the President alone, in the courts of law, or in the heads of departments.

The President shall have power to fill up all vacancies that may happen during the recess of the Senate by granting commissions which shall expire 25 at the end of their next session.

II§3 He shall from time to time give to the Congress information of the state of the union, and recommend to their consideration such measures as he shall judge necessary and expedient; he may, on extraordinary occasions, convene both Houses, or either of them, and in case of disagreement 30 between them, with respect to the time of adjournment, he may adjourn them to such time as he shall think proper; he shall receive ambassadors and other public ministers; he shall take care that the laws be faithfully executed, and shall commission all the officers of the United States.

II§4 The President, Vice President, and all civil officers of the United States shall 35 be removed from office on impeachment for, and conviction of, treason, bribery, or other high crimes and misdemeanors.

Article III

III§1 The judicial power of the United States shall be vested in one supreme court, and in such inferior courts as the Congress may from time to time ordain and establish. The judges, both of the supreme and inferior courts, shall hold their offices during good behavior, and shall, at stated times, receive for their services a compensation, which shall not be diminished during their continuance in office.

III§2 The judicial power shall extend to all cases, in law and equity, arising under this Constitution, the laws of the United States, and treaties made, or which shall be made, under their authority; to all cases affecting ambassadors, other public ministers, and consuls; to all cases of admiralty and maritime jurisdiction; to controversies to which the United States shall be a party; to controversies between two or more states; between a state and citizens of another state; between citizens of different states; between citizens of the same state claiming lands under grants of different states, and between a state, or the citizens thereof, and foreign states, citizens, or subjects.

In all cases affecting ambassadors, other public ministers, and consuls, and those in which a state shall be party, the supreme court shall have original jurisdiction. In all the other cases before mentioned, the supreme court shall have appellate jurisdiction, both as to law and fact, with such exceptions, and under such regulations, as the Congress shall make.

The trial of all crimes, except in cases of impeachment, shall be by jury; and such trial shall be held in the state where the said crimes shall have been committed; but when not committed within any state, the trial shall be at such place or places as the Congress may by law have directed.

III§3 Treason against the United States shall consist only in levying war against them, or in adhering to their enemies, giving them aid and comfort. No person shall be convicted of treason unless on the testimony of two witnesses to the same overt act, or on confession in open court.

The Congress shall have power to declare the punishment of treason, but no attainder of treason shall work corruption of blood, or forfeiture except during the life of the person attained.

Article IV

IV§1 Full faith and credit shall be given in each state to the public acts, records, and judicial proceedings of every other state. And the Congress may by general laws prescribe the manner in which such acts, records, and proceedings shall be proved, and the effect thereof.

IV§2 The citizens of each state shall be entitled to all privileges and immunities of citizens in the several states.

A person charged in any state with treason, felony, or other crime, who shall flee from justice, and be found in another state, shall on demand of the executive authority of the state from which he fled, be delivered up, to be removed to the state having jurisdiction of the crime.

No person held to service or labor in one state, under the laws thereof, escaping into another shall, in consequence of any law or regulation therein, be discharged from such service or labor, but shall be delivered up on claim of the party to whom such service or labor may be due.

IV§3 New states may be admitted by the Congress into this union; but no new state shall be formed or erected within the jurisdiction of any other state; nor any state be formed by the junction of two or more states, or parts of states, without the consent of the legislatures of the states concerned as well as of the Congress.

The Congress shall have power to dispose of and make all needful rules and regulations respecting the territory or other property belonging to the United States; and nothing in this Constitution shall be so construed as to prejudice any claims of the United States, or of any particular state.

IV§4 The United States shall guarantee to every state in this union a republican form of government, and shall protect each of them against invasion; and on application of the legislature, or of the executive (when the legislature cannot be convened), against domestic violence.

Article V

The Congress, whenever two thirds of both Houses shall deem it necessary, shall propose amendments to this Constitution or, on the application of the legislatures of two-thirds of the several states, shall call a convention for proposing amendments, which, in either case, shall be valid to all intents and purposes, as part of this Constitution, when ratified by the legislatures of three-fourths of the several states, or by conventions in three-fourths thereof, as the one or the other mode of ratification may be proposed by the Congress; provided that no amendment which may be made prior to the year One thousand eight hundred and eight shall in any manner affect the first and fourth clauses in the ninth section of the first article; and that no state, without its consent, shall be deprived of its equal suffrage in the Senate.

Article VI

All debts contracted and engagements entered into before the adoption of this Constitution shall be as valid against the United States under this Constitution as under the Confederation.

This Constitution, and the laws of the United States which shall be made in pursuance thereof; and all treaties made, or which shall be made, under the authority of the United States, shall be the supreme law of the land; and the judges in every state shall be bound thereby, anything in the constitution or laws of any state to the contrary notwithstanding.

The Senators and Representatives before mentioned, and the members of the several state legislatures, and all executive and judicial officers, both of the United States and of the several states, shall be bound by oath or affirmation to support this Constitution; but no religious test shall ever be required as a qualification to any office or public trust under the United States.

Article VII

The ratification of the conventions of nine states shall be sufficient for the establishment of this Constitution between the states so ratifying the same.

Done in convention by the unanimous consent of the states present the seventeenth day of September in the Year of our Lord one thousand seven hundred and eighty-seven and of the independence of the United States of America, the twelfth. In witness whereof we have hereunto subscribed our names.

George Washington, President and deputy from Virginia

Delaware	*South Carolina*	*Connecticut*
George Read	John Rutledge	William Samuel Johnson
Gunning Bedford, Junior	Charles Cotesworth Pinckney	Roger Sherman
John Dickinson	Charles Pinckney	
Richard Bassett	Pierce Butler	*New Jersey*
Jacob Broom		William Livingston
	Georgia	David Brearley
Maryland	William Few	William Paterson
James McHenry	Abraham Baldwin	Jonathan Dayton
Dan of Saint Thomas Jenifer		
Daniel Carroll	*New Hampshire*	*Pennsylvania*
	John Langdon	Benjamin Franklin
Virginia	Nicholas Gilman	Thomas Mifflin
John Blair		Robert Morris
James Madison, Junior	*Massachusetts*	George Clymer
	Nathaniel Gorham	Thomas FitzSimons
North Carolina	Rufus King	Jared Ingersoll
William Blount		James Wilson
Richard Dobbs Spaight	*New York*	Gouverneur Morris
Hugh Williamson	Alexander Hamilton	

THE BILL OF RIGHTS

15 DECEMBER 1791

The Preamble

The conventions of a number of the states, having at the time of their adopting the Constitution expressed a desire, in order to prevent misconstruction or abuse of its powers, that further declaratory and restrictive clauses should be added; and as extending the ground of public confidence in the government, will best ensure the beneficent ends of its institution.

Resolved, by the Senate and House of Representatives of the United States of America, in Congress assembled, two-thirds of both Houses concurring, that the following articles be proposed to the legislatures of the several states as amendments to the Constitution of the United States, all, or any of which articles, when ratified by three-fourths of the said legislatures, to be valid to all intents and purposes, as part of the said Constitution; viz.

Articles in addition to, and amendment of, the Constitution of the United States of America, proposed by Congress, and ratified by the legislatures of the several states, pursuant to the fifth Article of the original Constitution.

Amendment 1

Congress shall make no law respecting an establishment of religion, or prohibiting the free exercise thereof; or abridging the freedom of speech, or of the press; or the right of the people peaceably to assemble, and to petition the government for a redress of grievances.

Amendment 2

A well-regulated militia being necessary to the security of a free state, the right of the people to keep and bear arms shall not be infringed.

Amendment 3

No soldier shall, in time of peace, be quartered in any house without the consent of the owner, nor in time of war but in a manner to be prescribed by law.

Engrossed Bill of Rights (25 September 1789), National Archives and Records Administration, General Records of the United States Government, Record Group 11.

Amendment 4

The right of the people to be secure in their person, houses, papers, and effects against unreasonable searches and seizures shall not be violated, and no warrants shall issue but upon probable cause, supported by oath or affirmation, and particularly describing the place to be searched, and the persons or things
5 to be seized.

Amendment 5

No person shall be held to answer for a capital, or otherwise infamous, crime unless on a presentment or indictment of a grand jury, except in cases arising in the land or naval forces, or in the militia when in actual service in time of war or public danger; nor shall any person be subject for the same offence to
10 be twice put in jeopardy of life or limb; nor shall be compelled in any criminal case to be a witness against himself, nor be deprived of life, liberty, or property without due process of law; nor shall private property be taken for public use without just compensation.

Amendment 6

In all criminal prosecutions the accused shall enjoy the right to a speedy and
15 public trial, by an impartial jury of the state and district wherein the crime shall have been committed, which district shall have been previously ascertained by law, and to be informed of the nature and cause of the accusation; to be confronted with the witnesses against him; to have compulsory process for obtaining witnesses in his favor, and to have the assistance of counsel for his defense.

Amendment 7

20 In suits at common law where the value in controversy shall exceed twenty dollars, the right of trial by jury shall be preserved, and no fact tried by a jury shall be otherwise re-examined in any court of the United States than according to the rules of the common law.

Amendment 8

Excessive bail shall not be required, nor excessive fines imposed, nor cruel and
25 unusual punishments inflicted.

Amendment 9

The enumeration in the Constitution of certain rights shall not be construed to deny or disparage others retained by the people.

Amendment 10

The powers not delegated to the United States by the Constitution, nor prohibited by it to the states, are reserved to the states respectively, or to the people.

LETTER OF BRUTUS

The new Constitution was not at first widely perceived to be superior to the old one. Nationalists, or federalists *as they came to be called, mounted a vigorous campaign for its ratification.* Anti-federalists *responded and almost won; ratification votes were particularly close in Virginia and New York. The debates over ratification, conducted often in newspapers, produced some of the best and most enduring American political philosophy.*

John Dickinson's Letters of Fabius *helped Pennsylvanians decide for the Constitution. "Fabius" was a general who helped to save Rome from the armies of Hannibal, but his caution ultimately turned his own citizens against him. Dickinson's pen name thus signified prudence, looking at an issue from every side before acting. "Brutus," who was probably Robert Yates (1738–1801) of New York, a justice of the New York Supreme Court, implied sentiment against "Caesar," or centralized power. The names they chose thus advertised their principles as well as reflected their devotion to their classical heritage.*

Robert Yates (1738–1801) was a leader of the Revolution in New York and a justice on his state's highest court until 1798. He was convinced that the framers of the Constitution had exceeded their authority and that state sovereignty was the best safeguard of liberty. "This government is to possess absolute and uncontrollable powers," he said.

1787

... The first question that presents itself on the subject is whether a confederated government be the best for the united states or not? Or in other words, whether the thirteen united states should be reduced to one great republic, governed by one legislature, and under the direction of one executive and judiciary; or whether they should continue thirteen confederated republics, under the direction and control of a supreme Federal head for certain defined, national purposes only?

This inquiry is important, because, although the government reported by the Convention does not go to a perfect and entire consolidation, yet it

5

Debates and Proceedings in the Convention of the Commonwealth of Massachusetts Held in the Year 1788 (Boston: William White, 1856), 366–78.

approaches so near to it, that it must, if executed, certainly and infallibly terminate in it.

This government is to possess absolute and uncontrollable powers, legislative, executive, and judicial, with respect to every object to which it extends, for by the last clause of section eighth, article first, it is declared that the Congress shall have power "to make all laws which shall be necessary and proper for carrying into execution the foregoing powers, and all other powers vested by this Constitution in the government of the United States, or in any department or office thereof." And by the sixth article it is declared, "that this Constitution, and the laws of the United States, which shall be made in pursuance thereof, and the treaties made, or which shall be made, under the authority of the United States, shall be the supreme law of the land; and the judges in every state shall be bound thereby, anything in the Constitution or law of any state to the contrary notwithstanding."

It appears from these articles that there is no need of any intervention of the state governments between the Congress and the people, to execute any one power vested in the general government, and that the Constitution and laws of every state are nullified and declared void, so far as they are or shall be inconsistent with this Constitution, or the laws made in pursuance of it, or with treaties made under the authority of the United States. The government, then, so far as it extends, is a complete one, and not a confederation. It is as much one complete government as that of New York or Massachusetts; has as absolute and perfect powers to make and execute all laws, to appoint officers, institute courts, declare offences, and annex penalties, with respect to every object to which it extends, as any other in the world. So far, therefore, as its powers reach, all ideas of confederation are given up and lost....

...[T]he legislature of the United States are vested with the great and uncontrollable powers of laying and collecting taxes, duties, imposts, and excises; of regulating trade, raising and supporting armies, organizing, arming, and disciplining the militia, instituting courts, and other general powers; and are by this clause invested with the power of making all laws, proper and necessary, for carrying all these into execution; and they may so exercise this power as entirely to annihilate all the state governments, and reduce this country to one single government.

And if they may do it, it is pretty certain they will; for it will be found that the power retained by individual states, small as it is, will be a clog upon the wheels of the government of the United States; the latter, therefore, will be naturally inclined to remove it out of the way. Besides, it is a truth confirmed by the unerring experience of ages that every man, and every body of men, invested with power are ever disposed to increase it, and to acquire a superiority over everything that stands in their way. This disposition, which is implanted in human nature, will operate in the Federal legislature to lessen and ultimately

to subvert the state authority, and having such advantages, will most certainly succeed, if the Federal government succeeds at all. It must be very evident, then, that what this Constitution wants of being a complete consolidation of the several parts of the union into one complete government, possessed of perfect legislative, judicial, and executive powers, to all intents and purposes, it will   5
necessarily acquire in its exercise in operation.

Let us now proceed to inquire, as I at first purposed, whether it be best the thirteen united states should be reduced to one great republic, or not? It is here taken for granted, that all agree in this, that whatever government we adopt, it ought to be a free one; that it should be so framed as to secure the liberty of the   10
citizens of America, and such as one as to admit of a full, fair, and equal representation of the people. The question, then, will be, whether a government thus constituted, and founded on such principles, is practicable, and can be exercised over the whole United States, reduced into one state?

If respect is to be paid to the opinion of the greatest and wisest men who   15
have ever thought or wrote on the science of government, we shall be constrained to conclude that a free republic cannot succeed over a country of such immense extent, containing such a number of inhabitants, and these increasing in such rapid progression, as that of the whole United States. Among the many illustrious authorities which might be produced to this point, I shall content myself   20
with quoting only two. The one is the Baron de Montesquieu,[1] *Spirit of Laws*, Chapter 16, Volume 1. "It is natural to a republic to have only a small territory, otherwise it cannot long subsist. In a large republic there are men of large fortunes, and consequently of less moderation; there are trusts too great to be placed in any single subject; he has interest of his own; he soon begins to think   25
that he may be happy, great, and glorious, by oppressing his fellow-citizens; and that he may raise himself to grandeur on the ruins of his country. In a large republic, the public good is sacrificed to a thousand views; it is subordinate to exceptions, and depends on accidents. In a small one, the interest of the public is easier perceived, better understood, and more within the reach of every citizen;   30
abuses are of less extent, and of course are less protected." Of the same opinion is the Marquis Beccarari.[2]

History furnishes no example of a free republic, anything like the extent of the United States. The Grecian republics were of small extent; so also was that of the Romans. Both of these, it is true, in process of time, extended their   35
conquests over large territories of country; and the consequence was that their governments were changed from that of free governments to those of the most tyrannical that ever existed in the world.

---

[1] Charles de Secondat (1689–1755), Baron de Montesquieu, French author and political theorist
[2] Césare (1738–1794), Marquis of Beccaria, Italian political theorist most famous for his *On Crimes and Punishments* (1764)

Not only the opinion of the greatest men, and the experience of mankind, are against the idea of an extensive republic, but a variety of reasons may be drawn from the reason and nature of things, against it. In every government the will of the sovereign is the law. In despotic governments, the supreme authority being lodged in one, his will is law, and can be as easily expressed to a large, extensive territory as to a small one. In a pure democracy, the people are the sovereign, and their will is declared by themselves; for this purpose they must all come together to deliberate and decide. This kind of government cannot be exercised, therefore, over a country of any considerable extent; it must be confined to a single city, or at least limited to such bounds as that the people can conveniently assemble, be able to debate, understand the subject submitted to them, and declare their opinion concerning it.

In a free republic, although all laws are derived from the consent of the people, yet the people do not declare their consent by themselves in person, but by representatives, chosen by them, who are supposed to know the minds of their constituents, and to be possessed of integrity to declare this mind.

In every free government, the people must give their assent to the laws by which they are governed. This is the true criterion between a free government and an arbitrary one. The former are ruled by the will of the whole, expressed in any manner they may agree upon; the latter by the will of one, or a few. If the people are to give their assent to the laws by persons chosen and appointed by them, the manner of the choice and the number chosen must be such as to possess, be disposed, and consequently qualified to declare the sentiments of the people; for if they do not know, or are not disposed to speak, the sentiments of the people, the people do not govern, but the sovereignty is in a few. Now, in a large, extended country, it is impossible to have a representation possessing the sentiments, and of integrity to declare the minds of the people, without having it so numerous and unwieldy as to be subject, in great measure, to the inconveniency of a democratic government.

The territory of the United States is of vast extent; it now contains near three millions of souls, and is capable of containing much more than ten times that number. Is it practicable for a country, so large and numerous as they will soon become, to elect a representation that will speak their sentiments without their becoming so numerous as to be incapable of transacting public business? It certainly is not.

In a republic, the manners, sentiments, and interests of the people should be similar. If this be not the case, there will be a constant clashing of opinions; and the representatives of one part will be continually striving against those of the other. This will retard the operations of government, and prevent such conclusions as will promote the public good. If we apply this remark to the condition of the United States, we shall be convinced that it forbids that we should be one government. The United States includes a variety of climates. The productions of the different parts of the union are very variant, and their interests, of consequence, diverse. Their manners and habits differ as much as their climates and productions; and their sentiments are by no means coincident. The laws and customs of the several states are, in many respects, very diverse, and in some opposite; each would be in favor of its own interests and customs; and, of consequence, a legislature formed of representatives from the respective parts would not only be too numerous to act with any care or decision, but would be composed of such heterogeneous and discordant principles as would constantly be contending with each other.

The laws cannot be executed in a republic of an extent equal to that of the United States with promptitude.

The magistrates in every government must be supported in the execution of the laws, either by an armed force, maintained at the public expense for that purpose, or by the people turning out to aid the magistrate upon his command, in case of resistance.

In despotic governments, as well as in all the monarchies of Europe, standing armies are kept up to execute the commands of the prince or the magistrate, and are employed for this purpose when occasion requires; but they have always proved the destruction of liberty, and are abhorrent to the spirit of a free republic. In England, where they depend upon the Parliament for their annual support, they have always been complained of as oppressive and unconstitutional, and are seldom employed in executing the laws; never except on extraordinary occasions, and then under the direction of a civil magistrate.

A free republic will never keep a standing army to execute its laws. It must depend upon the support of its citizens. But when a government is to receive its support from the aid of the citizens, it must be so constructed as to have the confidence, respect, and affection of the people. Men who, upon the call of the magistrate, offer themselves to execute the laws, are influenced to do it either by affection to the government, or from fear; where a standing army is at hand to punish offenders, every man is actuated by the latter principle, and therefore, when the magistrate calls, will obey; but, where this is not the case, the government must rest for its support upon the confidence and respect which the people have for their government and laws. The body of the people being attached, the government will always be sufficient to support and execute its laws, and to operate upon the fears of any faction which may be opposed to it, not only to prevent any opposition to the execution of the laws themselves, but also to compel the most of them to aid the magistrate; but the people will not be likely to have such confidence in their rulers, in a republic so extensive as the United States, as is necessary for these purposes. The confidence which the people have in their rulers, in a free republic, arises from their knowing them,

from their being responsible to them for their conduct, and from the power they have of displacing them when they misbehave; but in a republic of the extent of this continent, the people in general would be acquainted with very few of their rulers; the people at large would know little of their proceedings, and it would be
5   extremely difficult to change them. The people in Georgia and New Hampshire would not know one another's mind, and therefore could not act in concert to enable them to effect a general change of representatives. The different parts of so extensive a country could not possibly be made acquainted with the conduct of their representatives, nor be informed of the reasons upon which measures
10   were founded. The consequence will be they will have no confidence in their legislature, suspect them of ambitious views, be jealous of every measure they adopt, and will not support the laws they pass. Hence the government will be nerveless and inefficient, and no way will be left to render it otherwise but by establishing an armed force to execute the laws at the point of the bayonet—a
15   government of all others the most to be dreaded.

In a republic of such vast extent as the United States, the legislature cannot attend to the various concerns and wants of its different parts. It cannot be sufficiently numerous to be acquainted with the local condition and wants of the different districts, and if it could, it is impossible it should have sufficient time
20   to attend to and provide for all the variety of cases of this nature that would be continually arising.

In so extensive a republic, the great officers of government would soon become above the control of the people, and abuse their powers to the purpose of aggrandizing themselves, and oppressing them. The trust committed to the
25   executive offices, in a country of the extent of the United States, must be various and of magnitude. The command of all the troops and navy of the republic, the appointment of officers, the power of pardoning offences, the collecting of all the public revenues, and the power of expending them, with a number of other powers, must be lodged and exercised in every state, in the hands of a
30   few. When these are attended with great honor and emolument, as they always will be in large states, so as greatly to interest men to pursue them, and to be proper objects for ambitious and designing men, such men will be ever restless in their pursuit after them. They will use the power, when they have acquired it, to the purposes of gratifying their own interest and ambition, and it is scarcely
35   possible, in a very large republic, to call them to account for their misconduct, or to prevent their abuse of power.

These are some of the reasons by which it appears that a free republic cannot long subsist over a country of the great extent of these states. If then this new Constitution is calculated to consolidate the thirteen states into one, as it
40   evidently is, it ought not to be adopted....

FEDERALIST 1
ALEXANDER HAMILTON (1755–1804)

Soon after 17 September 1787, when the constitution framed at the Philadelphia Convention was signed and dispatched to the Continental Congress, the ratification debate began. The most memorable and authoritative contribution to that debate was made up of a series of seventy-seven articles that first appeared in New York in The Independent Journal *and* The New York Packet *under the pseudonym Publius in the period stretching from 27 October 1787 to 2 April 1788, which were soon thereafter reprinted, along with eight additional articles, in a two-volume work titled* The Federalist. *Alexander Hamilton initiated the series and saw to the publication of the two volumes. He had hoped to work in tandem with John Jay (1745–1829), but soon after the project's inception Jay fell ill. He then recruited James Madison (1751–1836), whose contributions turned out to be no less important than those of Hamilton himself. In the first number of the* Federalist, *Hamilton explained why such an endeavor is necessary and outlined the argument that Publius will make on behalf of ratification. In the tenth number, Madison set out to disprove Montesquieu's claim that it is impossible to establish a viable republic on an extended territory. In the thirty-ninth number, he defended the republican character of the Constitution and specified that it is to be "neither wholly national nor wholly federal." In the fifty-first number, he explored the nature and purpose of the separation of powers provided for by the Constitution.*

INDEPENDENT JOURNAL, 27 OCTOBER 1787

After an unequivocal experience of the inefficiency of the subsisting federal government, you are called upon to deliberate on a new constitution for the United States of America. The subject speaks its own importance; comprehending in its consequences nothing less than the existence of the *union*, the safety and welfare of the parts of which it is composed, the fate of an empire in many respects the most interesting in the world. It has been frequently remarked that it

The Federalist (New York: Walter Dunne, 1901), I:9–13.

seems to have been reserved to the people of this country, by their conduct and example, to decide the important question whether societies of men are really capable or not of establishing good government from reflection and choice, or whether they are forever destined to depend for their political constitutions on
5   accident and force. If there be any truth in the remark, the crisis at which we are arrived may with propriety be regarded as the era in which that decision is to be made; and a wrong election of the part we shall act may, in this view, deserve to be considered as the general misfortune of mankind.

This idea will add the inducements of philanthropy to those of patriotism,
10   to heighten the solicitude which all considerate and good men must feel for the event. Happy will it be if our choice should be directed by a judicious estimate of our true interests, un-perplexed and un-biased by considerations not connected with the public good. But this is a thing more ardently to be wished than seriously to be expected. The plan offered to our deliberations affects too
15   many particular interests, innovates upon too many local institutions, not to involve in its discussion a variety of objects foreign to its merits, and of views, passions, and prejudices little favorable to the discovery of truth.

Among the most formidable of the obstacles which the new constitution will have to encounter may readily be distinguished the obvious interest of
20   a certain class of men in every state to resist all changes which may hazard a diminution of the power, emolument, and consequence of the offices they hold under the state establishments; and the perverted ambition of another class of men, who will either hope to aggrandize themselves by the confusions of their country, or will flatter themselves with fairer prospects of elevation from the
25   subdivision of the empire into several partial confederacies than from its union under one government.

It is not, however, my design to dwell upon observations of this nature. I am well aware that it would be disingenuous to resolve indiscriminately the opposition of any set of men (merely because their situations might subject them
30   to suspicion) into interested or ambitious views. Candor will oblige us to admit that even such men may be actuated by upright intentions; and it cannot be doubted that much of the opposition which has made its appearance, or may hereafter make its appearance, will spring from sources, blameless at least, if not respectable—the honest errors of minds led astray by preconceived jealousies
35   and fears. So numerous indeed and so powerful are the causes which serve to give a false bias to the judgment that we, upon many occasions, see wise and good men on the wrong as well as on the right side of questions of the first magnitude to society. This circumstance, if duly attended to, would furnish a lesson of moderation to those who are ever so much persuaded of their being
40   in the right in any controversy. And a further reason for caution, in this respect,

might be drawn from the reflection that we are not always sure that those who advocate the truth are influenced by purer principles than their antagonists. Ambition, avarice, personal animosity, party opposition, and many other motives not more laudable than these, are apt to operate as well upon those who support as those who oppose the right side of a question. Were there not even these inducements to moderation, nothing could be more ill-judged than that intolerant spirit which has, at all times, characterized political parties. For in politics, as in religion, it is equally absurd to aim at making proselytes by fire and sword. Heresies in either can rarely be cured by persecution.

And yet, however just these sentiments will be allowed to be, we have already sufficient indications that it will happen in this as in all former cases of great national discussion. A torrent of angry and malignant passions will be let loose. To judge from the conduct of the opposite parties, we shall be led to conclude that they will mutually hope to evince the justness of their opinions, and to increase the number of their converts by the loudness of their declamations and the bitterness of their invectives. An enlightened zeal for the energy and efficiency of government will be stigmatized as the offspring of a temper fond of despotic power and hostile to the principles of liberty. An over-scrupulous jealousy of danger to the rights of the people, which is more commonly the fault of the head than of the heart, will be represented as mere pretense and artifice, the stale bait for popularity at the expense of the public good. It will be forgotten, on the one hand, that jealousy is the usual concomitant of love, and that the noble enthusiasm of liberty is apt to be infected with a spirit of narrow and illiberal distrust. On the other hand, it will be equally forgotten that the vigor of government is essential to the security of liberty; that, in the contemplation of a sound and well-informed judgment, their interest can never be separated; and that a dangerous ambition more often lurks behind the specious mask of zeal for the rights of the people than under the forbidden appearance of zeal for the firmness and efficiency of government. History will teach us that the former has been found a much more certain road to the introduction of despotism than the latter, and that of those men who have overturned the liberties of republics, the greatest number have begun their career by paying an obsequious court to the people; commencing demagogues, and ending tyrants.

In the course of the preceding observations, I have had an eye, my fellow-citizens, to putting you upon your guard against all attempts, from whatever quarter, to influence your decision in a matter of the utmost moment to your welfare, by any impressions other than those which may result from the evidence of truth. You will, no doubt, at the same time, have collected from the general scope of them, that they proceed from a source not unfriendly to the new Constitution. Yes, my countrymen, I own to you that, after having given it

an attentive consideration, I am clearly of opinion it is your interest to adopt it. I am convinced that this is the safest course for your liberty, your dignity, and your happiness. I affect not reserves which I do not feel. I will not amuse you with an appearance of deliberation when I have decided. I frankly acknowledge
5   to you my convictions, and I will freely lay before you the reasons on which they are founded. The consciousness of good intentions disdains ambiguity. I shall not, however, multiply professions on this head. My motives must remain in the depository of my own breast. My arguments will be open to all, and may be judged of by all. They shall at least be offered in a spirit which will not
10   disgrace the cause of truth.

I propose, in a series of papers, to discuss the following interesting particulars:

The utility of the union to your political prosperity; the insufficiency of the present confederation to preserve that union; the necessity of a government at
15   least equally energetic with the one proposed, to the attainment of this object; the conformity of the proposed constitution to the true principles of republican government; its analogy to your own state constitution; and, lastly, the additional security which its adoption will afford to the preservation of that species of government, to liberty, and to property.
20   In the progress of this discussion I shall endeavor to give a satisfactory answer to all the objections which shall have made their appearance, that may seem to have any claim to your attention.

It may perhaps be thought superfluous to offer arguments to prove the utility of the *union*, a point, no doubt, deeply engraved on the hearts of the
25   great body of the people in every state, and one, which it may be imagined, has no adversaries. But the fact is that we already hear it whispered in the private circles of those who oppose the new constitution that the thirteen states are of too great extent for any general system, and that we must of necessity resort to separate confederacies of distinct portions of the whole. This doctrine will, in all
30   probability, be gradually propagated, till it has votaries enough to countenance an open avowal of it. For nothing can be more evident, to those who are able to take an enlarged view of the subject, than the alternative of an adoption of the new constitution or a dismemberment of the union. It will therefore be of use to begin by examining the advantages of that union, the certain evils, and
35   the probable dangers, to which every state will be exposed from its dissolution. This shall accordingly constitute the subject of my next address.

PUBLIUS

Federalist 10

James Madison (1751–1836)

The New York Packet, 23 November 1787

Among the numerous advantages promised by a well-constructed union, none deserves to be more accurately developed than its tendency to break and control the violence of faction. The friend of popular governments never finds himself so much alarmed for their character and fate, as when he contemplates their propensity to this dangerous vice. He will not fail, therefore, to set a 5 due value on any plan which, without violating the principles to which he is attached, provides a proper cure for it. The instability, injustice, and confusion introduced into the public councils, have, in truth, been the mortal diseases under which popular governments have everywhere perished; as they continue to be the favorite and fruitful topics from which the adversaries to 10 liberty derive their most specious declamations. The valuable improvements made by the American constitutions on the popular models, both ancient and modern, cannot certainly be too much admired; but it would be an unwarrantable partiality, to contend that they have as effectually obviated the danger on this side, as was wished and expected. Complaints are everywhere heard 15 from our most considerate and virtuous citizens, equally the friends of public and private faith, and of public and personal liberty, that our governments are too unstable, that the public good is disregarded in the conflicts of rival parties, and that measures are too often decided, not according to the rules of justice and the rights of the minor party, but by the superior force of an 20 interested and overbearing majority. However anxiously we may wish that these complaints had no foundation, the evidence of known facts will not permit us to deny that they are in some degree true. It will be found, indeed, on a candid review of our situation, that some of the distresses under which we labor have been erroneously charged on the operation of our governments; 25 but it will be found, at the same time, that other causes will not alone account

The Federalist (New York: Walter Dunne, 1901), I:62–70.

for many of our heaviest misfortunes; and, particularly, for that prevailing and increasing distrust of public engagements, and alarm for private rights, which are echoed from one end of the continent to the other. These must be chiefly, if not wholly, effects of the unsteadiness and injustice with which a
5   factious spirit has tainted our public administrations.

By a faction, I understand a number of citizens, whether amounting to a majority or a minority of the whole, who are united and actuated by some common impulse of passion, or of interest, adverse to the rights of other citizens, or to the permanent and aggregate interests of the community. There
10   are two methods of curing the mischiefs of faction: the one, by removing its causes; the other, by controlling its effects. There are again two methods of removing the causes of faction: the one, by destroying the liberty which is essential to its existence; the other, by giving to every citizen the same opinions, the same passions, and the same interests.

15   It could never be more truly said than of the first remedy, that it was worse than the disease. Liberty is to faction what air is to fire, an aliment without which it instantly expires. But it could not be less folly to abolish liberty, which is essential to political life, because it nourishes faction, than it would be to wish the annihilation of air, which is essential to animal life,
20   because it imparts to fire its destructive agency.

The second expedient is as impracticable as the first would be unwise. As long as the reason of man continues fallible, and he is at liberty to exercise it, different opinions will be formed. As long as the connection subsists between his reason and his self-love, his opinions and his passions will have
25   a reciprocal influence on each other; and the former will be objects to which the latter will attach themselves. The diversity in the faculties of men, from which the rights of property originate, is not less an insuperable obstacle to a uniformity of interests. The protection of these faculties is the first object of government. From the protection of different and unequal faculties of
30   acquiring property, the possession of different degrees and kinds of property immediately results; and from the influence of these on the sentiments and views of the respective proprietors, ensues a division of the society into different interests and parties.

The latent causes of faction are thus sown in the nature of man; and we
35   see them everywhere brought into different degrees of activity, according to the different circumstances of civil society. A zeal for different opinions concerning religion, concerning government, and many other points, as well of speculation as of practice; an attachment to different leaders ambitiously contending for pre-eminence and power; or to persons of other descriptions
40   whose fortunes have been interesting to the human passions, have, in turn,

divided mankind into parties, inflamed them with mutual animosity, and
rendered them much more disposed to vex and oppress each other than to
co-operate for their common good. So strong is this propensity of mankind
to fall into mutual animosities, that where no substantial occasion presents
itself, the most frivolous and fanciful distinctions have been sufficient to kindle 5
their unfriendly passions and excite their most violent conflicts. But the most
common and durable source of factions has been the various and unequal
distribution of property. Those who hold and those who are without property
have ever formed distinct interests in society. Those who are creditors, and
those who are debtors, fall under a like discrimination. A landed interest, a 10
manufacturing interest, a mercantile interest, a moneyed interest, with many
lesser interests, grow up of necessity in civilized nations, and divide them into
different classes, actuated by different sentiments and views. The regulation
of these various and interfering interests forms the principal task of modern
legislation, and involves the spirit of party and faction in the necessary and 15
ordinary operations of the government.

No man is allowed to be a judge in his own cause, because his interest
would certainly bias his judgment and, not improbably, corrupt his integrity.
With equal, nay with greater reason, a body of men are unfit to be both judges
and parties at the same time; yet what are many of the most important acts of 20
legislation, but so many judicial determinations, not indeed concerning the
rights of single persons, but concerning the rights of large bodies of citizens?
And what are the different classes of legislators but advocates and parties to
the causes which they determine? Is a law proposed concerning private debts?
It is a question to which the creditors are parties on one side and the debtors 25
on the other. Justice ought to hold the balance between them. Yet the parties
are, and must be, themselves the judges; and the most numerous party, or,
in other words, the most powerful faction must be expected to prevail. Shall
domestic manufactures be encouraged, and in what degree, by restrictions
on foreign manufactures? Are questions which would be differently decided 30
by the landed and the manufacturing classes, and probably by neither with
a sole regard to justice and the public good. The apportionment of taxes on
the various descriptions of property is an act which seems to require the most
exact impartiality; yet there is, perhaps, no legislative act in which greater
opportunity and temptation are given to a predominant party to trample on 35
the rules of justice. Every shilling with which they overburden the inferior
number, is a shilling saved to their own pockets. It is in vain to say that enlightened statesmen will be able to adjust these clashing interests, and render
them all subservient to the public good. Enlightened statesmen will not
always be at the helm. Nor, in many cases, can such an adjustment be made 40

at all without taking into view indirect and remote considerations, which will rarely prevail over the immediate interest which one party may find in disregarding the rights of another or the good of the whole.

The inference to which we are brought is that the *causes* of faction cannot be removed, and that relief is only to be sought in the means of controlling its *effects*.

If a faction consists of less than a majority, relief is supplied by the republican principle, which enables the majority to defeat its sinister views by regular vote. It may clog the administration, it may convulse the society; but it will be unable to execute and mask its violence under the forms of the Constitution. When a majority is included in a faction, the form of popular government, on the other hand, enables it to sacrifice to its ruling passion or interest both the public good and the rights of other citizens. To secure the public good and private rights against the danger of such a faction, and at the same time to preserve the spirit and the form of popular government, is then the great object to which our inquiries are directed. Let me add that it is the great desideratum by which this form of government can be rescued from the opprobrium under which it has so long labored, and be recommended to the esteem and adoption of mankind. By what means is this object attainable? Evidently by one of two only. Either the existence of the same passion or interest in a majority at the same time must be prevented, or the majority, having such coexistent passion or interest, must be rendered, by their number and local situation, unable to concert and carry into effect schemes of oppression. If the impulse and the opportunity be suffered to coincide, we well know that neither moral nor religious motives can be relied on as an adequate control. They are not found to be such on the injustice and violence of individuals, and lose their efficacy in proportion to the number combined together, that is, in proportion as their efficacy becomes needful.

From this view of the subject it may be concluded that a pure democracy, by which I mean a society consisting of a small number of citizens, who assemble and administer the government in person, can admit of no cure for the mischiefs of faction. A common passion or interest will, in almost every case, be felt by a majority of the whole; a communication and concert result from the form of government itself; and there is nothing to check the inducements to sacrifice the weaker party or an obnoxious individual. Hence it is that such democracies have ever been spectacles of turbulence and contention; have ever been found incompatible with personal security or the rights of property; and have in general been as short in their lives as they have been violent in their deaths. Theoretic politicians, who have patronized this species of government, have erroneously supposed that by reducing mankind to a perfect equality in their political rights, they would, at the same time, be perfectly equalized and assimilated in their possessions, their opinions, and their passions.

A republic, by which I mean a government in which the scheme of representation takes place, opens a different prospect, and promises the cure   5
for which we are seeking. Let us examine the points in which it varies from pure democracy, and we shall comprehend both the nature of the cure and the efficacy which it must derive from the union.

The two great points of difference between a democracy and a republic are: first, the delegation of the government, in the latter, to a small number   10
of citizens elected by the rest; secondly, the greater number of citizens, and greater sphere of country, over which the latter may be extended. The effect of the first difference is, on the one hand, to refine and enlarge the public views, by passing them through the medium of a chosen body of citizens, whose wisdom may best discern the true interest of their country, and whose   15
patriotism and love of justice will be least likely to sacrifice it to temporary or partial considerations. Under such a regulation, it may well happen that the public voice, pronounced by the representatives of the people, will be more consonant to the public good than if pronounced by the people themselves, convened for the purpose. On the other hand, the effect may be inverted.   20
Men of factious tempers, of local prejudices, or of sinister designs, may, by intrigue, by corruption, or by other means, first obtain the suffrages, and then betray the interests, of the people. The question resulting is, whether small or extensive republics are more favorable to the election of proper guardians of the public weal; and it is clearly decided in favor of the latter by two obvious   25
considerations:

In the first place, it is to be remarked that, however small the republic may be, the representatives must be raised to a certain number, in order to guard against the cabals of a few; and that, however large it may be, they must be limited to a certain number, in order to guard against the confusion of a   30
multitude. Hence, the number of representatives in the two cases not being in proportion to that of the two constituents, and being proportionally greater in the small republic, it follows that, if the proportion of fit characters be not less in the large than in the small republic, the former will present a greater option, and consequently a greater probability of a fit choice.   35

In the next place, as each representative will be chosen by a greater number of citizens in the large than in the small republic, it will be more difficult for unworthy candidates to practice with success the vicious arts by which elections are too often carried; and the suffrages of the people being more free, will be more likely to centre in men who possess the most attractive   40 merit and the most diffusive and established characters. It must be confessed that in this, as in most other cases, there is a mean, on both sides of which inconveniences will be found to lie. By enlarging too much the number of electors, you render the representatives too little acquainted with all their local circumstances and lesser interests; as by reducing it too much, you render him unduly attached to these, and too little fit to comprehend and pursue great and national objects. The federal Constitution forms a happy combination in this respect; the great and aggregate interests being referred to the national, the local and particular to the state legislatures.

The other point of difference is, the greater number of citizens and extent of territory which may be brought within the compass of republican than of democratic government; and it is this circumstance principally which renders factious combinations less to be dreaded in the former than in the latter. The smaller the society, the fewer probably will be the distinct parties and interests composing it; the fewer the distinct parties and interests, the more frequently will a majority be found of the same party; and the smaller the number of individuals composing a majority, and the smaller the compass within which they are placed, the more easily will they concert and execute their plans of oppression. Extend the sphere, and you take in a greater variety of parties and interests; you make it less probable that a majority of the whole will have a common motive to invade the rights of other citizens; or if such a common motive exists, it will be more difficult for all who feel it to discover their own strength, and to act in unison with each other. Besides other impediments, it may be remarked that, where there is a consciousness of unjust or dishonorable purposes, communication is always checked by distrust in proportion to the number whose concurrence is necessary.

Hence, it clearly appears, that the same advantage which a republic has over a democracy, in controlling the effects of faction, is enjoyed by a large over a small republic—is enjoyed by the union over the states composing it. Does the advantage consist in the substitution of representatives whose enlightened views and virtuous sentiments render them superior to local prejudices and schemes of injustice? It will not be denied that the representation of the Union will be most likely to possess these requisite endowments. Does it consist in the greater security afforded by a greater variety of parties, against the event of any one party being able to outnumber and oppress the rest? In an equal degree does the increased variety of parties comprised within the union, increase this security. Does it, in fine, consist in the greater obstacles opposed to the concert and accomplishment of the secret wishes of an unjust and interested majority? Here, again, the extent of the union gives it the most palpable advantage.

The influence of factious leaders may kindle a flame within their particular states, but will be unable to spread a general conflagration through the other states. A religious sect may degenerate into a political faction in a part of the Confederacy; but the variety of sects dispersed over the entire face of it must secure the national councils against any danger from that source. A rage for 5 paper money, for an abolition of debts, for an equal division of property, or for any other improper or wicked project, will be less apt to pervade the whole body of the Union than a particular member of it; in the same proportion as such a malady is more likely to taint a particular county or district, than an entire state. 10

In the extent and proper structure of the union, therefore, we behold a republican remedy for the diseases most incident to republican govern-ment. And according to the degree of pleasure and pride we feel in being republicans, ought to be our zeal in cherishing the spirit and supporting the character of Federalists.

Publius

FEDERALIST 39
JAMES MADISON (1751–1836)

INDEPENDENT JOURNAL, 16 JANUARY 1788

The last paper having concluded the observations which were meant to introduce a candid survey of the plan of government reported by the convention, we now proceed to the execution of that part of our undertaking.

The first question that offers itself is whether the general form and aspect of the government be strictly republican. It is evident that no other form would 5 be reconcilable with the genius of the people of America; with the fundamental principles of the Revolution; or with that honorable determination which animates every votary of freedom, to rest all our political experiments on the capacity of mankind for self-government. If the plan of the convention, therefore, be found to depart from the republican character, its advocates must abandon 10 it as no longer defensible.

What, then, are the distinctive characters of the republican form? Were an answer to this question to be sought, not by recurring to principles, but in the application of the term by political writers, to the constitution of different states, no satisfactory one would ever be found. Holland, in which no particle 15 of the supreme authority is derived from the people, has passed almost universally under the denomination of a republic. The same title has been bestowed on Venice, where absolute power over the great body of the people is exercised, in the most absolute manner, by a small body of hereditary nobles. Poland, which is a mixture of aristocracy and of monarchy in their worst forms, has 20 been dignified with the same appellation. The government of England, which has one republican branch only, combined with an hereditary aristocracy and monarchy, has, with equal impropriety, been frequently placed on the list of republics. These examples, which are nearly as dissimilar to each other as to a genuine republic, show the extreme inaccuracy with which the term has been 25 used in political disquisitions.

The Federalist (New York: Walter Dunne, 1901), I:256–63.

If we resort for a criterion to the different principles on which different forms of government are established, we may define a republic to be, or at least may bestow that name on, a government which derives all its powers directly or indirectly from the great body of the people, and is administered by persons holding their offices during pleasure, for a limited period, or during good behavior. It is *essential* to such a government that it be derived from the great body of the society, not from an inconsiderable proportion, or a favored class of it; otherwise a handful of tyrannical nobles, exercising their oppressions by a delegation of their powers, might aspire to the rank of republicans, and claim for their government the honorable title of republic. It is *sufficient* for such a government that the persons administering it be appointed, either directly or indirectly, by the people; and that they hold their appointments by either of the tenures just specified; otherwise every government in the United States, as well as every other popular government that has been or can be well organized or well executed, would be degraded from the republican character. According to the constitution of every state in the Union, some or other of the officers of government are appointed indirectly only by the people. According to most of them, the chief magistrate himself is so appointed. And according to one, this mode of appointment is extended to one of the co-ordinate branches of the legislature. According to all the constitutions, also, the tenure of the highest offices is extended to a definite period, and in many instances, both within the legislative and executive departments, to a period of years. According to the provisions of most of the constitutions, again, as well as according to the most respectable and received opinions on the subject, the members of the judiciary department are to retain their offices by the firm tenure of good behavior.

On comparing the Constitution planned by the convention with the standard here fixed, we perceive at once that it is, in the most rigid sense, conformable to it. The House of Representatives, like that of one branch at least of all the state legislatures, is elected immediately by the great body of the people. The Senate, like the present Congress, and the Senate of Maryland, derives its appointment indirectly from the people. The President is indirectly derived from the choice of the people, according to the example in most of the states. Even the judges, with all other officers of the union, will, as in the several states, be the choice, though a remote choice, of the people themselves, the duration of the appointments is equally conformable to the republican standard, and to the model of state constitutions The House of Representatives is periodically elective, as in all the states; and for the period of two years, as in the state of South Carolina. The Senate is elective, for the period of six years; which is but one year more than the period of the Senate of Maryland, and but two more than that of the Senates of New York and Virginia. The President is to continue in office for

the period of four years; as in New York and Delaware, the chief magistrate is elected for three years, and in South Carolina for two years. In the other states the election is annual. In several of the states, however, no constitutional provision is made for the impeachment of the chief magistrate. And in Delaware and Virginia he is not impeachable till out of office. The President of the United   5
States is impeachable at any time during his continuance in office. The tenure by which the judges are to hold their places, is, as it unquestionably ought to be, that of good behavior. The tenure of the ministerial offices generally, will be a subject of legal regulation, conformably to the reason of the case and the example of the state constitutions.   10

Could any further proof be required of the republican complexion of this system, the most decisive one might be found in its absolute prohibition of titles of nobility, both under the federal and the state governments; and in its express guaranty of the republican form to each of the latter.

"But it was not sufficient," say the adversaries of the proposed Constitu-   15
tion, "for the convention to adhere to the republican form. They ought, with equal care, to have preserved the *federal* form, which regards the Union as a *confederacy* of sovereign states; instead of which, they have framed a *national* government, which regards the union as a *consolidation* of the states." And it is asked by what authority this bold and radical innovation was undertaken?   20
The handle which has been made of this objection requires that it should be examined with some precision.

Without inquiring into the accuracy of the distinction on which the objection is founded, it will be necessary to a just estimate of its force, first, to ascertain the real character of the government in question; secondly, to inquire   25
how far the convention were authorized to propose such a government; and thirdly, how far the duty they owed to their country could supply any defect of regular authority.

First—In order to ascertain the real character of the government, it may be considered in relation to the foundation on which it is to be established; to   30
the sources from which its ordinary powers are to be drawn; to the operation of those powers; to the extent of them; and to the authority by which future changes in the government are to be introduced.

On examining the first relation, it appears, on one hand, that the Constitution is to be founded on the assent and ratification of the people of America,   35
given by deputies elected for the special purpose; but, on the other, that this assent and ratification is to be given by the people, not as individuals composing one entire nation, but as composing the distinct and independent states to which they respectively belong. It is to be the assent and ratification of the several states, derived from the supreme authority in each state, the authority   40

of the people themselves. The act, therefore, establishing the Constitution, will not be a *national*, but a *federal* act.

That it will be a federal and not a national act, as these terms are understood by the objectors; the act of the people, as forming so many independent states, not as forming one aggregate nation, is obvious from this single consideration, that it is to result neither from the decision of a *majority* of the people of the union, nor from that of a *majority* of the states. It must result from the *unanimous* assent of the several states that are parties to it, differing no otherwise from their ordinary assent than in its being expressed, not by the legislative authority, but by that of the people themselves. Were the people regarded in this transaction as forming one nation, the will of the majority of the whole people of the United States would bind the minority, in the same manner as the majority in each state must bind the minority; and the will of the majority must be determined either by a comparison of the individual votes, or by considering the will of the majority of the states as evidence of the will of a majority of the people of the United States. Neither of these rules have been adopted. Each state, in ratifying the Constitution, is considered as a sovereign body, independent of all others, and only to be bound by its own voluntary act. In this relation, then, the new Constitution will, if established, be a *federal*, and not a *national* constitution.

The next relation is, to the sources from which the ordinary powers of government are to be derived. The House of Representatives will derive its powers from the people of America; and the people will be represented in the same proportion, and on the same principle, as they are in the legislature of a particular state. So far the government is *national*, not *federal*. The Senate, on the other hand, will derive its powers from the states, as political and coequal societies; and these will be represented on the principle of equality in the Senate, as they now are in the existing Congress. So far the government is *federal*, not *national*. The executive power will be derived from a very compound source. The immediate election of the President is to be made by the states in their political characters. The votes allotted to them are in a compound ratio, which considers them partly as distinct and coequal societies, partly as unequal members of the same society. The eventual election, again, is to be made by that branch of the legislature which consists of the national representatives; but in this particular act they are to be thrown into the form of individual delegations, from so many distinct and co-equal bodies politic. From this aspect of the government it appears to be of a mixed character, presenting at least as many *federal* as *national* features.

The difference between a federal and national government, as it relates to the *operation of the government*, is supposed to consist in this, that in the former the powers operate on the political bodies composing the Confederacy, in their political capacities; in the latter, on the individual citizens composing the nation, in their individual capacities. On trying the Constitution by this criterion, it falls under the *national*, not the *federal* character; though perhaps not so completely as has been understood. In several cases, and particularly in the trial of controversies to which states may be parties, they must be viewed and proceeded against in their collective and political capacities only. So far the national countenance of the government on this side seems to be disfigured by a few federal features. But this blemish is perhaps unavoidable in any plan; and the operation of the government on the people, in their individual capacities, in its ordinary and most essential proceedings, may, on the whole, designate it, in this relation, a *national* government.

But if the government be national with regard to the *operation* of its powers, it changes its aspect again when we contemplate it in relation to the *extent* of its powers. The idea of a national government involves in it, not only an authority over the individual citizens, but an indefinite supremacy over all persons and things, so far as they are objects of lawful government. Among a people con- solidated into one nation, this supremacy is completely vested in the national legislature. Among communities united for particular purposes, it is vested partly in the general and partly in the municipal legislatures. In the former case, all local authorities are subordinate to the supreme; and may be controlled, directed, or abolished by it at pleasure. In the latter, the local or municipal authorities form distinct and independent portions of the supremacy, no more subject, within their respective spheres, to the general authority, than the general authority is subject to them, within its own sphere. In this relation, then, the proposed government cannot be deemed a *national* one; since its jurisdiction extends to certain enumerated objects only, and leaves to the several states a residuary and inviolable sovereignty over all other objects. It is true that in controversies relating to the boundary between the two jurisdictions, the tribunal which is ultimately to decide, is to be established under the general government. But this does not change the principle of the case. The decision is to be impartially made, according to the rules of the Constitution; and all the usual and most effectual precautions are taken to secure this impartiality. Some such tribunal is clearly essential to prevent an appeal to the sword and a dissolution of the compact; and that it ought to be established under the general rather than under the local governments, or, to speak more properly, that it could be safely established under the first alone, is a position not likely to be combated.

If we try the Constitution by its last relation to the authority by which amendments are to be made, we find it neither wholly *national* nor wholly *federal*. Were it wholly national, the supreme and ultimate authority would reside in the *majority* of the people of the union; and this authority would be competent at all times, like that of a majority of every national society, to alter or abolish its established government. Were it wholly federal, on the other hand, the concurrence of each state in the union would be essential to every alteration

5 that would be binding on all. The mode provided by the plan of the convention is not founded on either of these principles. In requiring more than a majority, and particularly in computing the proportion by *states*, not by *citizens*, it departs from the *national* and advances towards the *federal* character; in rendering the concurrence of less than the whole number of states sufficient, it loses again

10 the *federal* and partakes of the *national* character.

The proposed Constitution, therefore, is, in strictness, neither a national nor a federal constitution, but a composition of both. In its foundation it is federal, not national; in the sources from which the ordinary powers of the government are drawn, it is partly federal and partly national; in the operation

15 of these powers, it is national, not federal; in the extent of them, again, it is federal, not national; and, finally, in the authoritative mode of introducing amendments, it is neither wholly federal nor wholly national.

Publius

FEDERALIST 51
JAMES MADISON (1751–1836)

INDEPENDENT JOURNAL, 8 FEBRUARY 1788

To what expedient, then, shall we finally resort, for maintaining in practice the necessary partition of power among the several departments, as laid down in the Constitution? The only answer that can be given is that as all these exterior provisions are found to be inadequate, the defect must be supplied, by so contriving the interior structure of the government as that its several constituent parts may, by their mutual relations, be the means of keeping each other in their proper places. Without presuming to undertake a full development of this important idea, I will hazard a few general observations which may perhaps place it in a clearer light, and enable us to form a more correct judgment of the principles and structure of the government planned by the convention.

In order to lay a due foundation for that separate and distinct exercise of the different powers of government, which to a certain extent is admitted on all hands to be essential to the preservation of liberty, it is evident that each department should have a will of its own; and consequently should be so constituted that the members of each should have as little agency as possible in the appointment of the members of the others. Were this principle rigorously adhered to, it would require that all the appointments for the supreme executive, legislative, and judiciary magistracies should be drawn from the same fountain of authority, the people, through channels having no communication whatever with one another. Perhaps such a plan of constructing the several departments would be less difficult in practice than it may in contemplation appear. Some difficulties, however, and some additional expense would attend the execution of it. Some deviations, therefore, from the principle must be admitted. In the constitution of the judiciary department in particular, it might be inexpedient to insist rigorously on the principle: first, because peculiar qualifications being essential in the members, the primary consideration ought to be to select that mode of choice which best secures these qualifications; secondly, because the

The Federalist (New York: Walter Dunne, 1901), I:353–58.

permanent tenure by which the appointments are held in that department, must soon destroy all sense of dependence on the authority conferring them.

It is equally evident that the members of each department should be as little dependent as possible on those of the others for the emoluments annexed
5   to their offices. Were the executive magistrate, or the judges, not independent of the legislature in this particular, their independence in every other would be merely nominal. But the great security against a gradual concentration of the several powers in the same department, consists in giving to those who administer each department the necessary constitutional means and personal
10 motives to resist encroachments of the others. The provision for defense must in this, as in all other cases, be made commensurate to the danger of attack. Ambition must be made to counteract ambition. The interest of the man must be connected with the constitutional rights of the place. It may be a reflection on human nature, that such devices should be necessary to control the abuses
15 of government. But what is government itself, but the greatest of all reflections on human nature? If men were angels, no government would be necessary.

If angels were to govern men, neither external nor internal controls on government would be necessary. In framing a government which is to be administered by men over men, the great difficulty lies in this: you must first
20 enable the government to control the governed; and in the next place oblige it to control itself. A dependence on the people is, no doubt, the primary control on the government; but experience has taught mankind the necessity of auxiliary precautions. This policy of supplying, by opposite and rival interests, the defect of better motives, might be traced through the whole system of human affairs,
25 private as well as public.

We see it particularly displayed in all the subordinate distributions of power, where the constant aim is to divide and arrange the several offices in such a manner as that each may be a check on the other that the private interest of every individual may be a sentinel over the public rights. These inventions of
30 prudence cannot be less requisite in the distribution of the supreme powers of the state. But it is not possible to give to each department an equal power of self-defense. In republican government, the legislative authority necessarily predominates. The remedy for this inconveniency is to divide the legislature into different branches; and to render them, by different modes of election and
35 different principles of action, as little connected with each other as the nature of their common functions and their common dependence on the society will admit. It may even be necessary to guard against dangerous encroachments by still further precautions. As the weight of the legislative authority requires that it should be thus divided, the weakness of the executive may require, on the
40 other hand, that it should be fortified. An absolute negative on the legislature appears, at first view, to be the natural defense with which the executive mag-

istrate should be armed. But perhaps it would be neither altogether safe nor alone sufficient. On ordinary occasions it might not be exerted with the requisite firmness, and on extraordinary occasions it might be perfidiously abused. May not this defect of an absolute negative be supplied by some qualified connection between this weaker department and the weaker branch of the stronger department, by which the latter may be led to support the constitutional rights of the former, without being too much detached from the rights of its own department? If the principles on which these observations are founded be just, as I persuade myself they are, and they be applied as a criterion to the several state constitutions, and to the federal Constitution it will be found that if the latter does not perfectly correspond with them, the former are infinitely less able to bear such a test.

There are, moreover, two considerations particularly applicable to the federal system of America, which place that system in a very interesting point of view. First, in a single republic, all the power surrendered by the people is submitted to the administration of a single government; and the usurpations are guarded against by a division of the government into distinct and separate departments. In the compound republic of America, the power surrendered by the people is first divided between two distinct governments, and then the portion allotted to each subdivided among distinct and separate departments. Hence a double security arises to the rights of the people. The different governments will control each other, at the same time that each will be controlled by itself. Second, it is of great importance in a republic not only to guard the society against the oppression of its rulers, but to guard one part of the society against the injustice of the other part. Different interests necessarily exist in different classes of citizens. If a majority be united by a common interest, the rights of the minority will be insecure.

There are but two methods of providing against this evil: the one by creating a will in the community independent of the majority, that is, of the society itself; the other, by comprehending in the society so many separate descriptions of citizens as will render an unjust combination of a majority of the whole very improbable, if not impracticable. The first method prevails in all governments possessing an hereditary or self-appointed authority. This, at best, is but a precarious security; because a power independent of the society may as well espouse the unjust views of the major, as the rightful interests of the minor party, and may possibly be turned against both parties. The second method will be exemplified in the federal republic of the United States. Whilst all authority in it will be derived from and dependent on the society, the society itself will be broken into so many parts, interests, and classes of citizens, that the rights of individuals, or of the minority, will be in little danger from interested combinations of the majority. In a free government the security for civil rights must be the same as that for religious rights. It consists in the one case in the multiplicity of interests, and in the other in the multiplicity of sects. The degree of security in both cases will depend on the number of interests and sects; and this may be presumed to depend on the extent of country and number of people comprehended under the same government. This view of the subject must particularly recommend a proper federal system to all the sincere and considerate friends of republican government, since it shows that in exact proportion as the territory of the union may be formed into more circumscribed confederacies, or states oppressive combinations of a majority will be facilitated: the best security, under the republican forms, for the rights of every class of citizens, will be diminished: and consequently the stability and independence of some member of the government, the only other security, must be proportionately increased. Justice is the end of government. It is the end of civil society. It ever has been and ever will be pursued until it be obtained, or until liberty be lost in the pursuit. In a society under the forms of which the stronger faction can readily unite and oppress the weaker, anarchy may as truly be said to reign as in a state of nature, where the weaker individual is not secured against the violence of the stronger; and as, in the latter state, even the stronger individuals are prompted, by the uncertainty of their condition, to submit to a government which may protect the weak as well as themselves; so, in the former state, will the more powerful factions or parties be gradually induced, by a like motive, to wish for a government which will protect all parties, the weaker as well as the more powerful.

It can be little doubted that if the state of Rhode Island was separated from the Confederacy and left to itself, the insecurity of rights under the popular form of government within such narrow limits would be displayed by such re-iterated oppressions of factious majorities that some power altogether independent of the people would soon be called for by the voice of the very factions whose misrule had proved the necessity of it. In the extended republic of the United States, and among the great variety of interests, parties, and sects which it embraces, a coalition of a majority of the whole society could seldom take place on any other principles than those of justice and the general good; whilst there being thus less danger to a minor from the will of a major party, there must be less pretext, also, to provide for the security of the former, by introducing into the government a will not dependent on the latter, or, in other words, a will independent of the society itself. It is no less certain than it is important, notwithstanding the contrary opinions which have been entertained, that the larger the society, provided it lie within a practical sphere, the more duly capable it will be of self-government. And happily for the *republican cause*, the practicable sphere may be carried to a very great extent, by a judicious modification and mixture of the *federal principle*.

PUBLIUS

LETTERS OF FABIUS
JOHN DICKINSON (1732–1808)

The new Constitution was not at first widely perceived to be superior to the old one. Nationalists, or federalists *as they came to be called, mounted a vigorous campaign for its ratification.* Anti-federalists *responded and almost won; ratification votes were particularly close in Virginia and New York. The debates over ratification, conducted often in newspapers, produced some of the best and most enduring American political philosophy.*

John Dickinson's Letters of Fabius *helped Pennsylvanians decide for the Constitution. Fabius was a general who helped to save Rome from the armies of Hannibal, but his caution ultimately turned his own citizens against him. Dickinson's pen name thus signified prudence, looking at an issue from every side before acting. "Brutus," who was probably Robert Yates of New York, implied sentiment against "Caesar," or centralized power. The names they chose thus advertised their principles as well as reflected their devotion to their classical heritage.*

1788

Letter I

The Constitution proposed by the Federal Convention now engages the fixed attention of America.

Every person appears to be affected. Those who wish the adoption of the plan, consider its rejection as the source of endless contests, confusions, and misfortunes; and they also consider a resolution to alter, without previously adopting it, as a rejection.   5

Those who oppose the plan, are influenced by different views. Some of them are friends, others of them are enemies, to the United States. The latter are of two classes; either men without principles or fortunes, who think they may have a chance to mend their circumstances, with impunity, under a weak   10

Paul Leicester Ford, ed., *Pamphlets on the Constitution of the United States Published During Its Discussion by the People, 1787–1788* (Brooklyn, 1888), 165–67, 174–80, 200–204, 211–16.

government or in public convulsions, but cannot make them worse even by
the last—or men who have been always averse to the revolution; and though
at first confounded by that event, yet, their hopes reviving with the declension
of our affairs, have since persuaded themselves, that at length the people, tired
5   out with their continued distresses, will return to their former connection with
Great Britain. To argue with these opposers would be vain—the other opposers
of the plan deserve the highest respect.

What concerns all, should be considered by all; and individuals may injure a
whole society by not declaring their sentiments. It is therefore not only their
10   right, but their duty, to declare them. Weak advocates of a good cause or artful advocates of a bad one may endeavor to stop such communications, or to
discredit them by clamor and calumny. Men have suffered so severely by being
deceived upon subjects of the highest import, those of religion and freedom, that
truth becomes infinitely valuable to them, not as a matter of curious speculation,
15   but of beneficial practice—a spirit of inquiry is excited, information diffused,
judgment strengthened.

Before this tribunal of *the people*, let everyone freely speak what he thinks,
but with so sincere a reverence for the cause he ventures to discuss as to use the
utmost caution, lest he should lead any into errors upon a point of such sacred
20   concern as the public happiness....

...[S]ome inhabitants of large states may desire the system to be so altered
that they may possess more authority in the decisions of the government; or
some inhabitants of commercial states may desire it to be so altered that the
advantages of trade may center almost wholly among themselves; and this
25   predilection they may think compatible with the common welfare. Their judgment being thus warped at the beginning of their deliberations, objections are
accumulated as very important that, without this prepossession, would never
have obtained their approbation. Certain it is that strong understandings may
be so influenced by this insulated patriotism as to doubt—whether general
30   benefits can be communicated by a general government.

Probably nothing would operate so much for the correction of these errors
as the perusal of the accounts transmitted to us by the ancients of the calamities occasioned in Greece by a conduct founded on similar mistakes. They are
expressly ascribed to this cause—that each city meditated a part on its own
35   profit and ends—insomuch that those *who seemed to contend for union* could
never relinquish their own interests and advancement while they deliberated
for the public.

Heaven grant that our countrymen may pause in time—duly estimate the
present moment—and solemnly reflect—whether their measures may not tend
40   to draw down the same distractions upon us that desolated Greece.

They may now tolerably judge from the proceedings of the Federal Convention and of other conventions what are the sentiments of America upon her present and future prospects. Let the voice of her distress be venerated—and adhering to the generous Virginian declaration, let them resolve to "*cling to Union as the political Rock of our Salvation.*"   5

Letter III

The writer of this address hopes that he will now be thought so disengaged from the objections against the principle assumed that he may be excused for recurring to his assertion that—the power of the people pervading the proposed system, together with the strong confederation of the states, will form an adequate security against every danger that has been apprehended.   10

It is a mournful, but may be a useful, truth that the liberty of single republics has generally been destroyed by some of the citizens, and of confederated republics, by some of the associated states.

It is more pleasing, and may be more profitable to reflect, that their tranquility and prosperity have commonly been promoted in proportion to the strength   15
of their government for protecting the worthy against the licentious.

As in forming a political society, each individual contributes some of his rights in order that he may, from *a common stock* of rights, derive greater benefits than he could from merely *his own*; so, in forming a confederation, each political society should contribute such a share of their rights as will, from *a common*   20
stock of these rights, produce the largest quantity of benefits for them.

But, what is that share? And how to be managed? Momentous questions! Here, flattery is treason; and error, destruction.

Are they unanswerable? No. Our most gracious *Creator* does not condemn us to sigh for unattainable blessedness: But one thing he demands—that we   25
should seek for happiness in his way, and not in our own.

Humility and benevolence must take place of pride and overweening selfishness. Reason, rising above these mists, will then discover to us that we cannot be true to ourselves without being true to others—that to love our neighbors as ourselves is to love ourselves in the best manner—that to give is to gain—and   30
that we never consult our own happiness more effectually than when we most endeavor to correspond with *the divine designs* by communicating happiness, as much as we can, to our fellow-creatures. *Inestimable truth!* Sufficient, if they do not barely ask what it is to melt tyrants into men, and to soothe the inflamed minds of a multitude into mildness—*Inestimable truth!* which our Maker in   35
his providence enables us, not only to talk and write about, but to adopt in practice of vast extent, and of instructive example.

Let us now enquire if there be not some *principle*, simple as the laws of nature in other instances, from which, as from a *source*, the many benefits of society are deduced.

We may with reverence say that our *Creator* designed men for society because otherwise they cannot be happy. They cannot be happy without freedom, nor free without security; that is, without the absence of fear; nor thus secure without society. The conclusion is strictly syllogistic—that men cannot be free without society. Of course, they cannot be equally free without society, *which freedom produces the greatest happiness.*

As these premises are invincible, we have advanced a considerable way in our enquiry upon *this deeply interesting subject.* If we can determine what share of his rights every individual must contribute to *the common stock* of rights in forming a society for obtaining equal freedom, we determine at the same time what share of their rights each political society must contribute to *the common stock* or rights in forming a confederation, which is only a larger society, for obtaining equal freedom. For, if the deposit be not proportioned to the magnitude of the association in the latter case, it will generate the same mischief among the component parts of it, from their inequality, that would result from a defective contribution to association in the former case, among the component parts of it, from their inequality.

Each individual then must contribute such a share of his rights as is necessary for attaining that *security* that is essential to freedom; and he is bound to make this contribution by the law of his nature, which prompts him to a participated happiness; that is, by the command of his creator; therefore, he must submit his will, *in what concerns all*, to the will of all, that is of the whole society. What does he lose by this submission? The power of doing injuries to others—and the dread of suffering injuries from them. What does he gain by it? The aid of those associated with him for his relief from the incommodities of mental or bodily weakness—the pleasure for which his heart is formed—of doing good—*protection* against injuries—a capacity of enjoying his undelegated rights to the best advantage—a repeal of his fears—and tranquility of mind—or, in other words, that perfect liberty better described in the Holy Scriptures than anywhere else, in these expressions—"When every man shall sit under his vine and under his fig-tree, and *none shall make him afraid*."[1] ...

...In short, the government of each state is, and is to be, sovereign and supreme in all matters that relate to each state only. It is to be subordinate barely in those matters that relate to the whole; and it will be their *own faults* if the several states suffer the federal sovereignty to interfere in things of their respective

---

[1] Micah 4:4

jurisdictions. An instance of such interference with regard to any single state will be a dangerous precedent as to all, and therefore will be guarded against by all as the trustees or servants of the several states will not dare, if they retain their senses, so to violate the independent sovereignty of their respective states, *that justly darling object* of American affections, to which they are responsible,   5
besides being endeared by all the charities of life.

The common sense of mankind agrees to the devolutions of individual wills in society; and if it has not been as universally assented to in confederation, the reasons are evident, and worthy of being retained in remembrance by Americans. They were want of opportunities, or the loss of them, through   10
defects of knowledge and virtue. The principle, however, has been sufficiently vindicated in imperfect combinations, as their prosperity has generally been commensurate to its operation.

How beautifully and forcibly does the inspired Apostle Paul, argue upon a sublimer subject, with a train of reasoning strictly applicable to the present?   15
His words are, "If the foot shall say, because I am not the hand, I am not of the body; is it therefore not of the body? And if the ear shall say, because I am not the eye, I am not of the body; is it therefore not of the body?"[2] As plainly inferring as could be done in that allegorical manner the strongest censure of such partial discontents and dissentions, especially, as his meaning is enforced   20
by his description of the benefits of union in these expressions—"But, now they are many members, yet but one body: and the eye *cannot* say to the hand, I have no need of thee."[3]

When the commons of Rome upon a rupture with the Senate seceded in arms at the Mons sacer, Menemius Agrippa used the like allusion to the   25
human body in his famous apologue of a quarrel among some of the members. The unpolished but honest-hearted Romans of that day understood him, and were appeased.

Another comparison has been made by the learned between a natural and a political body; and no wonder indeed, when the title of the latter was   30
borrowed from the resemblance. It has therefore been justly observed that if a mortification takes place in one or some of the limbs, and the rest of the body is sound, remedies may be applied, and not only the contagion prevented from spreading, but the diseased part or parts saved by the connection with the body, and restored to former usefulness. When general putrefaction prevails, death is   35
to be expected. History sacred and profane tells us that *corruption of manners sinks nations into slavery.*

---

[2] I Corinthians 12:15–16
[3] I Corinthians 12:20–21

Letter VII

…How the liberty of this country is to be destroyed is another question. Here, the gentlemen assign a cause, in no manner proportioned, as it is apprehended, to the effect.

The uniform tenor of history is against them. That holds up the licentious-
5   ness of the people and turbulent temper of some of the states as the only causes to be dreaded, not the conspiracies of federal officers. Therefore, it is highly probable that, if our liberty is ever subverted, it will be by one of the two causes first mentioned. Our tragedy will then have the same acts with those of the nations that have gone before us; and we shall add one more example to the
10 number already too great of people that would not take warning, not "know the things which belong to their peace."…

Would this be doing justice to our country? The composition of her tem-per is excellent, and seems to be acknowledged equal to that of any nation in the world. Her prudence will guard its warmth against two faults, to which it
15 may be exposed—the one, an imitation of foreign fashions, which from small things may lead to great. May her citizens aspire at a national dignity in every part of conduct, private as well as public. This will be influenced by the former. May simplicity be the characteristic feature of their manners, which, inlaid with their other virtues and their forms of government, may then indeed be
20 compared, in the Eastern style, to "apples of gold in pictures of silver." Thus will they long, and may they, while their rivers run, escape the contagion of luxury—that motley issue of innocence debauched by folly, and the lineal predecessor of tyranny, prolific of guilt and wretchedness. The other fault, of which, as yet, there are no symptoms among us, is the thirst of empire. This
25 is a vice that ever has been, and from the nature of things ever must be, fatal to republican forms of government. Our wants are sources of happiness: our irregular desires, of misery. The abuse of prosperity is rebellion against Heaven, and succeeds accordingly.…

From the annals of mankind these conclusions are deducible—that confed-
30 erated states may act prudently and honestly, and apart foolishly and knavishly; but, that it is a defiance of all probability to suppose that states conjointly shall act with folly and wickedness, and yet separately with wisdom and virtue.

Letter IX

…Let the gentlemen be so good, on a subject so familiar to them, as to make a comparison between the British constitution and that proposed to us. Questions
35 like these will then probably present themselves: Is there more danger to our liberty from such a president as we are to have than to that of Britons from an

hereditary monarch with a vast revenue—absolute in the erection and disposal
of offices, and in the exercise of the whole executive power—in the command
of the militia, fleets, and armies, and the direction of their operations—in the
establishments of fairs and markets, the regulation of weights and measures,
and coining of money—who can call Parliaments with a breath, and dissolve 5
them with a nod—who can, at his will, make war, peace, and treaties irrevocably binding the nation—and who can grant pardons and titles of nobility as it
pleases him? Is there more danger to us from twenty-six senators, or double the
number, than to Britons from an hereditary aristocratic body, consisting of many
hundreds, possessed of enormous wealth in lands and money—strengthened 10
by a host of dependants—and who, availing themselves of defects in the constitution, send many of these into the House of Commons—who hold a third
part of the legislative power in their own hands—and who form the highest
court of judicature in the nation? Is there more danger to us from a house of
representatives to be chosen by all the freemen of the union, every two years, 15
than to Britons from such a sort of representation as they have in the House
of Commons, the members of which, too, are chosen but every seven years? Is
there more danger to us from the intended federal officers, than to Britons from
such a monarch, aristocracy, and House of Commons together? What bodies
are there in Britain vested with such capacities for enquiring into, checking, 20
and regulating the conduct of national affairs as our sovereign states? What
proportion does the number of free holders in Britain bear to the number of
people? And what is the proportion in united America?

If any person, after considering such questions, shall say there will be more
danger to our freedom under the proposed plan than to that of Britons under 25
their constitution, he must mean that Americans are, or will be, beyond all
comparison, inferior to Britons in understanding and virtue; otherwise, with a
constitution and government, every branch of which is so extremely popular,
they certainly might guard their rights, at least as well as Britons can guard
theirs under such political institutions as they have; unless the person has some 30
inclination to an opinion that monarchy and aristocracy are favorable to the
preservation of their rights. If he has, he cannot too soon recover himself. If
ever monarchy or aristocracy appears in this country, it must be in the hideous
form of despotism.

What an infatuated, depraved people must Americans become if, with 35
such unequalled advantages committed to their trust in a manner almost
miraculous, they lose their liberty? Through a single organ of representation,
in the legislature only, of the kingdom just mentioned, though that organ is
diseased, such portions of popular sense and integrity have been conveyed into
the national councils, as have purified other parts, and preserved the whole in 40

its present state of healthfulness. To their own vigor and attention, therefore, is that people, under providence, indebted for the blessings they enjoy. They have held, and now hold, the true balance in their government. While they retain their enlightened spirit, they will continue to hold it; and if they regard
5   what they owe to others, as well as what they owe to themselves, they will, most probably, continue to be happy....

Let us consider our affairs in another light. Our difference of government, participation in commerce, improvement in policy, and magnitude of power can be no favorite objects of attention to the monarchies and sovereignties
10   of Europe. Our loss will be their gain—our fall, their rise—our shame, their triumph. Divided, they may distract, dictate, and destroy. United, their efforts will be waves dashing themselves into foam against a rock. May our national character be—an animated moderation, that seeks only its own, and will not be satisfied with less.

15   To his beloved fellow-citizens of United America, the writer dedicates this imperfect testimony of his affection, with fervent prayers, for a perpetuity of freedom, virtue, piety, and felicity, to them and their posterity.

Declaration of the Rights of Man and of the Citizen

The American republic survived two great challenges in its infancy: the internal challenge of the terms of its union and the external challenge of the French Revolution. The principles declared by the French National Assembly at the beginning of its overthrow of the Ancien Régime *are often compared with the principles contained in the founding documents of the United States.*

26 August 1789

The representatives of the French people, organized as a National Assembly, believing that the ignorance, neglect, or contempt of the rights of man are the sole causes of public calamities and of the corruption of governments, have determined to set forth in a solemn declaration the natural, inalienable, and sacred rights of man, in order that this declaration, being constantly before all   5
the members of the social body, shall remind them continually of their rights and duties; in order that the acts of the legislative power, as well as those of the executive power, may be compared at any moment with the ends of all political institutions and may thus be more respected; in order that the grievances of the citizens, based hereafter upon simple and incontestable principles, shall   10
tend to the maintenance of the constitution and redound to the happiness of all. Therefore the National Assembly recognizes and proclaims in the presence and under the auspices of the Supreme Being the following rights of man and of the citizen:

1. Men are born and remain free and equal in rights. Social distinctions may   15
   only be founded upon the general good.

2. The aim of all political association is the preservation of the natural and imprescriptible rights of man. These rights are liberty, property, security, and resistance to oppression.

James Harvey Robinson, ed., *Translations and Reprints from the Original Sources of European History* I, 5 (Philadelphia: Department of History, University of Pennsylvania, 1902), 6–8.

3. The principle of all sovereignty resides essentially in the nation. No body nor individual may exercise any authority which does not proceed directly from the nation.

4. Liberty consists in the freedom to do everything which injures no one else; hence the exercise of the natural rights of each man has no limits, except those which assure to the other members of the society the enjoyment of the same rights. These limits can only be determined by law.

5. Law can only prohibit such actions as are hurtful to society. Nothing may be prevented which is not forbidden by law, and no one may be forced to do anything not provided for by law.

6. Law is the expression of the general will. Every citizen has a right to participate personally or through his representative in its formation. It must be the same for all, whether it protects or punishes. All citizens being equal in the eyes of the law are equally eligible to all dignities and to all public positions and occupations according to their abilities and without distinction except that of their virtues and talents.

7. No person shall be accused, arrested, or imprisoned except in the cases and according to the forms prescribed by law. Anyone soliciting, transmitting, executing, or causing to be executed any arbitrary order shall be punished. But any citizen summoned or arrested in virtue of the law shall submit without delay, as resistance constitutes an offence.

8. The law shall provide for such punishments only as are strictly and obviously necessary, and no one shall suffer punishment except it be legally inflicted in virtue of a law passed and promulgated before the commission of the offence.

9. As all persons are held innocent until they shall have been declared guilty; if arrest shall be deemed indispensable, all harshness not essential to the securing of the prisoner's person shall be severely repressed by law.

10. No one shall be disquieted on account of his opinions, including his religious views, provided their manifestation does not disturb the public order established by law.

11. The free communication of ideas and opinions is one of the most precious of the rights of man. Every citizen may, accordingly, speak, write, and print with freedom, but shall be responsible for such abuses of this freedom as shall be defined by law.

12. The security of the rights of man and of the citizen requires public military force. These forces are, therefore, established for the good of all and not for the personal advantage of those to whom they shall be entrusted.

13. A common contribution is essential for the maintenance of the public forces and for the cost of administration. This should be equitably distributed   5 among all the citizens in proportion to their means.

14. All the citizens have a right to decide, either personally or by their representatives, as to the necessity of the public contribution, to grant this freely, to know to what uses it is put, and to fix the proportion, the mode of assessment, and of collection, and the duration of the taxes.   10

15. Society has the right to require of every public agent an account of his administration.

16. A society in which the observance of the law is not assured nor the separation of powers defined has no constitution at all.

17. Since property is an inviolable and sacred right, no one shall be deprived   15 thereof except where public necessity, legally determined, shall clearly demand it, and then only on condition that the owner shall have been previously and equitably indemnified.

First Inaugural Address
George Washington (1732–1799)
President of the United States (1789–1797)

Washington felt summoned. This is the only presidential inaugural address that states the republican idea: "I would rather be at home tending my gardens." Since 1783 he had been president of the Society of the Cincinnati, an organization of former officers of the Continental Line devoted to protecting the liberty for which they had fought. Like Cincinnatus, Washington wanted to return to the plow. The people's call brought him back to duty, the "preservation of the sacred fire of liberty."

30 April 1789

Among the vicissitudes incident to life, no event could have filled me with greater anxieties than that of which the notification was transmitted by your order, and received on the 14th day of the present month. On the one hand, I was summoned by my country, whose voice I can never hear but with veneration and love, from a retreat which I had chosen with the fondest 5 predilection and, in my flattering hopes, with an immutable decision, as the asylum of my declining years; a retreat which was rendered every day more necessary as well as more dear to me by the addition of habit to inclination and of frequent interruptions in my health to the gradual waste committed on it by time. On the other hand, the magnitude and difficulty of the trust 10 to which the voice of my country called me being sufficient to awaken in the wisest and most experienced of her citizens a distrustful scrutiny into his qualifications could not but overwhelm with despondence one, who, inheriting inferior endowments from nature, and unpracticed in the duties of civil administration, ought to be peculiarly conscious of his own deficiencies. In 15 this conflict of emotions all I dare aver is that it has been my faithful study to collect my duty from a just appreciation of every circumstance by which it might be affected. All I dare hope is that if in executing this task I have been too much swayed by a grateful remembrance of former instances, or by an affectionate sensibility to this transcendent proof of the confidence of my 20

Worthington Chauncey Ford, ed., *The Writings of George Washington* (New York: G. P. Putnam's Sons, 1891), XI:381–86.

fellow-citizens; and have thence too little consulted my incapacity as well as disinclination for the weighty and untried cares before me; my error will be palliated by the motives which misled me, and its consequences be judged by my country with some share of the partiality in which they originated.

5   Such being the impressions under which I have, in obedience to the public summons, repaired to the present station, it would be peculiarly improper to omit in this first official act my fervent supplications to that Almighty Being who rules over the universe, who presides in the councils of nations, and whose providential aids can supply every human defect, that his benediction

10   may consecrate to the liberties and happiness of the people of the United States a government instituted by themselves for these essential purposes, and may enable every instrument employed in its administration to execute with success the functions allotted to his charge. In tendering this homage to the great Author of every public and private good, I assure myself that it expresses

15   your sentiments not less than my own; nor those of my fellow-citizens at large less than either. No people can be bound to acknowledge and adore the invisible hand which conducts the affairs of men more than the people of the United States. Every step by which they have advanced to the character of an independent nation seems to have been distinguished by some token

20   of providential agency. And, in the important revolution just accomplished in the system of their united government, the tranquil deliberations and vol-untary consent of so many distinct communities, from which the event has resulted, cannot be compared with the means by which most governments have been established without some return of pious gratitude along with an

25   humble anticipation of the future blessings which the past seem to presage. These reflections, arising out of the present crisis, have forced themselves too strongly on my mind to be suppressed. You will join with me, I trust, in thinking that there are none under the influence of which the proceedings of a new and free government can more auspiciously commence.

30   By the article establishing the executive department it is made the duty of the President "to recommend to your consideration such measures as he shall judge necessary and expedient." The circumstances under which I now meet you will acquit me from entering into that subject farther than to refer you to the great constitutional charter under which we are assembled; and

35   which, in defining your powers, designates the objects to which your atten-tion is to be given. It will be more consistent with those circumstances, and far more congenial with the feelings which actuate me, to substitute, in place of a recommendation of particular measures, the tribute that is due to the talents, the rectitude, and the patriotism which adorn the characters selected

40   to devise and adopt them. In these honorable qualifications I behold the surest

pledges that as, on one side, no local prejudices or attachments, no separate views or party animosities, will mis-direct the comprehensive and equal eye which ought to watch over this great assemblage of communities and interests; so, on another, that the foundations of our national policy will be laid in the pure and immutable principles of private morality, and the pre-eminence of a free government be exemplified by all the attributes, which can win the affections of its citizens, and command the respect of the world.

I dwell on this prospect with every satisfaction which an ardent love for my country can inspire; since there is no truth more thoroughly established than that there exists in the economy and course of nature an indissoluble union between virtue and happiness, between duty and advantage, between the genuine maxims of an honest and magnanimous policy, and the solid rewards of public prosperity and felicity, since we ought to be no less persuaded that the propitious smiles of Heaven can never be expected on a nation that disregards the eternal rules of order and right, which Heaven itself has ordained; and since the preservation of the sacred fire of liberty, and the destiny of the republican model of government, are justly considered as *deeply*, perhaps as *finally* staked, on the experiment entrusted to the hands of the American people.

Besides the ordinary objects submitted to your care, it will remain with your judgment to decide how far an exercise of the occasional power delegated by the fifth Article of the Constitution is rendered expedient at the present juncture by the nature of objections which have been urged against the system, or by the degree of inquietude which has given birth to them. Instead of undertaking particular recommendations on this subject, in which I could be guided by no lights derived from official opportunities, I shall again give way to my entire confidence in your discernment and pursuit of the public good; for I assure myself that, whilst you carefully avoid every alteration which might endanger the benefits of a united and effective government, or which ought to await the future lessons of experience; a reverence for the characteristic rights of freemen, and a regard for the public harmony, will sufficiently influence your deliberations on the question how far the former can be more impregnably fortified, or the latter be safely and advantageously promoted.

To the preceding observations I have one to add, which will be most properly addressed to the House of Representatives. It concerns myself, and will therefore be as brief as possible. When I was first honored with a call into the service of my country, then on the eve of an arduous struggle for its liberties, the light in which I contemplated my duty required that I should renounce every pecuniary compensation. From this resolution I have in no instance departed. And being still under the impressions which produced it, I must decline as inapplicable to myself any share in the personal emoluments which may be indispensably included in a permanent provision for the executive department; and must accordingly pray that the pecuniary estimates for the station in which I am placed may, during my continuance in it, be limited to such actual expenditures as the public good may be thought to require.

Having thus imparted to you my sentiments, as they have been awakened by the occasion which brings us together, I shall take my present leave; but not without resorting once more to the benign Parent of the human race, in humble supplication that, since he has been pleased to favor the American people with opportunities for deliberating in perfect tranquility, and dispositions for deciding with unparalleled unanimity on a form of government for the security of their union and the advancement of their happiness; so his divine blessing may be equally *conspicuous* in the enlarged views, the temperate consultations, and the wise measures on which the success of this government must depend.

SELECTIONS
EDMUND BURKE (1729–1797)

A great Anglo-Irish poet, philosopher, and statesman, Edmund Burke spent much of his life fighting corruption in the British government, working for the rights of American colonists, Roman Catholics, the Irish, and Asian Indians. Most famously, though, and certainly perplexing to many of his contemporaries, Burke vehemently attacked the French Revolutionaries in several of his works.

Though he had originally wanted to be a poet and private philosopher, he first entered Parliament in late 1765, becoming secretary to Prime Minister Rockingham. He remained in Parliament until 1794, three years prior to his death. Certainly, though, he had already built his reputation as a man of letters by the time he entered politics. In 1756, only age 26, Burke published his first work, A Vindication of Natural Society, *a satire on the teachings of Jean-Jacques Rousseau. The following year, he published a treatise on aesthetics and the imagination,* A Philosophical Inquiry into the Origin of Our Ideas of the Sublime and Beautiful. *In 1759, an important faction of the Whig party recruited him to be a man of ideas for the party, and Burke accepted the offer.*

Throughout the patriot cause, Burke defended the rights of Americans, calling them true Englishmen. "Leave the Americans as they anciently stood and these distinctions, born of our unhappy contest, will die along with it. They and we, and their and our ancestors, have been happy under that system.... Nobody will be argued into slavery."

Burke saw the French Revolution as a very different movement. From its origins in 1789, he feared, the revolution would devolve into a violent bloodbath, overturning all the traditions of Christendom. In his first response to it, Reflections on the Revolution in France, *Burke labeled it "most astonishing [thing] that has hitherto happened in the world." The following comes from Burke's second work on the French Revolution,* Further

Edmund Burke, *The Works of Edmund Burke, With a Memoir* (New York: George Dearborn, 1835), II:15–17, 23, 26.

*Reflections (1791) and its famous section, "An Appeal from the Old to the
New Whigs." Burke hoped the Whigs might reclaim the spirit of the 1688
Glorious Revolution.*

1790

At popular elections the most rigorous casuists will remit a little of their severity.
They will allow to a candidate some unqualified effusions in favor of freedom,
without binding him to adhere to them in their utmost extent. But Mr. Burke
put a more strict rule upon himself than most moralists would put upon others.
5   At his first offering himself to Bristol, where he was almost sure he should not
obtain, on that or any occasion, a single Tory vote (in fact he did obtain but one)
and rested wholly on the Whig interest, he thought himself bound to tell the
electors, both before and after his election, exactly what sort of representative
they had to expect in him.
10   "The distinguishing part of our constitution," he said, "is its liberty. To
preserve that liberty inviolate, is the peculiar duty and proper trust of a Member
of the House of Commons. But the liberty, the only liberty I mean, is a liberty
connected with order, and that not only exists with order and virtue, but cannot
exist at all without them. It inheres in good and steady government, as in its
15 substance and vital principle."
The liberty to which Mr. Burke declared himself attached is not French liberty. That liberty is nothing but the rein given to vice and confusion. Mr. Burke
was then, as he was at the writing of his *Reflections*, awfully impressed with the
difficulties arising from the complex state of our constitution and our empire,
20 and that it might require, in different emergencies, different sorts of exertions,
and the successive call upon all the various principles which uphold and justify
it. This will appear from what he said at the close of the poll.

To be a good Member of Parliament is, let me tell you, no easy task;
especially at this time, when there is so strong a disposition to run into
25   the perilous extremes of servile compliance or wild popularity. To unite
circumspection with vigor is absolutely necessary; but it is extremely
difficult. We are now Members for a rich commercial city; this city,
however, is but part of a rich commercial nation, the interests of which
are various, multi-form, and intricate. We are Members for that great
30   nation which, however, is itself but a part of a great-empire, extended
by our virtue and our fortune to the farthest limits of the east and of
the west. All these wide-spread interests must be considered; must be
compared; must be reconciled, if possible. We are Members for a free
country; and surely we all know that the machine of a free constitution
35   is no simple thing; but as intricate, and as delicate, as it is valuable. We
are members in a great and ancient MONARCHY; and we must preserve
religiously the true legal rights of the sovereign, which form the key-stone

that binds together the noble and well-constructed arch of our empire
and our constitution. A constitution made up of balanced powers must
ever be a critical thing. As such I mean to touch that part of it which
comes within my reach.

In this manner Mr. Burke spoke to his constituents seventeen years ago. He   5
spoke, not like a partisan of one particular member of our constitution, but as a
person strongly, and on principle, attached to them all. He thought these great
and essential members ought to be preserved, and preserved each in its place;
and that the monarchy ought not only to be secured in its peculiar existence, but
in its pre-eminence too, as the presiding and connecting principle of the whole.   10
Let it be considered whether the language of his book, printed in 1790, differs
from his speech at Bristol in 1774.

With equal justice his opinions on the American war are introduced, as if in
his late work he had belied his conduct and opinions in the debates which arose
upon that great event. On the American war he never had any opinions which   15
he has seen occasion to retract, or which he has ever retracted. He, indeed, differs
essentially from Mr. Fox[1] as to the cause of that war. Mr. Fox has been pleased
to say that the Americans rebelled, "because they thought they had not enjoyed
liberty enough." This cause of the war from him I have heard for the first time.
It is true that those who stimulated the nation to that measure did frequently   20
urge this topic. They contended that the Americans had, from the beginning,
aimed at independence; that from the beginning they meant wholly to throw
off the authority of the Crown, and to break their connection with the parent
country. This Mr. Burke never believed. When he moved his second conciliatory
proposition in the year 1776, he entered into the discussion of this point at very   25
great length; and from nine several heads of resumption, endeavored to prove
the charge upon that people not to be true.

If the principles of all he has said and wrote on the occasion be viewed with
common temper, the gentlemen of the party will perceive that on the supposition
that the Americans had rebelled merely in order to enlarge their liberty, Mr. Burke   30
would have thought very differently of the American cause. What might have been
in the secret thoughts of some of their leaders it is impossible to say. As far as a
man so locked up as Dr. Franklin could be expected to communicate his ideas, I
believe he opened them to Mr. Burke. It was, I think, the very day before he set
out for America that a very long conversation passed between them, and with a   35
greater air of openness on the doctor's side than Mr. Burke had observed in him
before. In this discourse Dr. Franklin lamented, and with apparent sincerity, the

---

[1]Charles James Fox (1749–1806) was a Member of Parliament and defender of the French
Revolution who urged liberal reforms in Britain. He had been a close friend of Burke until a
dramatic confrontation in May 1791.

separation which he feared was inevitable between Great Britain and her colonies. He certainly spoke of it as an event which gave him the greatest concern.
America, he said, would never again see such happy days as she had passed under
the protection of England. He observed that ours was the only instance of a great
5 empire in which the most distant parts and members had been as well governed
as the metropolis and its vicinage, but that the Americans were going to lose the
means which secured to them this rare and precious advantage. The question
with them was not whether they were to remain as they had been before the
troubles—for better, he allowed, they could not hope to be—but whether they
10 were to give up so happy a situation without a struggle? Mr. Burke had several
other conversations with him about that time, in none of which, soured and
exasperated as his mind certainly was, did he discover any other wish in favor of
America than for a security to its ancient condition. Mr. Burke's conversation
with other Americans was large indeed, and his inquiries extensive and diligent.
15 Trusting to the result of all these means of information, but trusting much more
in the public presumptive indications I have just referred to, and to the reiterated solemn declarations of their assemblies, he always firmly believed that they
were purely on the defensive in that rebellion. He considered the American as
standing at that time, and in that controversy, in the same relation to England as
20 England did to King James II in 1688. He believed that they had taken up arms
from one motive only; that is, our attempting to tax them without their consent;
to tax them for the purposes of maintaining civil and military establishments.
If this attempt of ours could have been practically established, he thought with
them, that their assemblies would become totally useless; that under the system
25 of policy which was then pursued, the Americans could have no sort of security
for their laws or liberties, or for any part of them; and, that the very circumstance
of *our* freedom would have augmented the weight of *their* slavery.

Considering the Americans on that defensive footing, he thought Great
Britain ought instantly to have closed with them by the repeal of the taxing act.
30 He was of opinion that our general rights over that country would have been
preserved by this timely concession. When, instead of this, a Boston port bill, a
Massachusetts charter bill, a fishery bill, an intercourse bill, I know not how many
hostile bills rushed out like so many tempests from all points of the compass,
and were accompanied first with great fleets and armies of English, and followed
35 afterwards with great bodies of foreign troops, he thought that their cause grew
daily better, because daily more defensive; and that ours, because daily more offensive, grew daily worse. He therefore, in two motions, in two successive years,
proposed in Parliament many concessions beyond what he had reason to think
in the beginning of the troubles would ever be seriously demanded.
40 So circumstanced, he certainly never could and never did wish the colonists to
be subdued by arms. He was fully persuaded that if such should be the event, they

must be held in that subdued state by a great body of standing forces, and perhaps of foreign forces. He was strongly of opinion that such armies, first victorious over Englishmen in a conflict for English constitutional rights and privileges, and afterwards habituated (though in America) to keep an English people in a state of abject subjection, would prove fatal in the end to the liberties of England itself;   5 that in the meantime this military system would lie as an oppressive burden upon the national finances; that it would constantly breed and feed new discussions, full of heat and acrimony, leading possibly to a new series of wars; and that foreign powers, whilst we continued in a state at once burdened and distracted, must at length obtain a decided superiority over us. On what part of his late publication,   10 or on what expression that might have escaped him in that work, is any man authorized to charge Mr. Burke with a contradiction to the line of his conduct, and to the current of his doctrines on the American war? The pamphlet is in the hands of his accusers, let them point out the passage if they can....

These new Whigs hold that the sovereignty, whether exercised by one or   15 many, did not only originate *from* the people (a position not denied, nor worth denying or assenting to), but that in the people the same sovereignty constantly and un-alienably resides; that the people may lawfully depose kings, not only for misconduct, but without any misconduct at all; that they may set up any new fashion of government for themselves, or continue without any government at   20 their pleasure; that the people are essentially their own rule, and their will the measure of their conduct; that the tenure of magistracy is not a proper subject of contract, because magistrates have duties, but no rights; and that if a contract *de facto* is made with them in one age, allowing that it binds at all, it only binds those who are immediately concerned in it, but does not pass to posterity. These   25 doctrines concerning the *people* (a term which they are far from accurately defining, but by which, from many circumstances, it is plain enough they mean their own faction, if they should grow by early arming, by treachery, or violence into the prevailing force) tend, in my opinion, to the utter subversion, not only of all government, in all modes, and to all stable securities to rational freedom, but to   30 all the rules and principles of morality itself.

I assert, that the ancient Whigs held doctrines totally different from those I have last mentioned. I assert that the foundation laid down by the Commons, on the trial of Dr. Sacheverell[2] for justifying the revolution of 1688, are the very same laid down in Mr. Burke's *Reflections*; that is to say, a breach of the original   35 contract, implied and expressed in the constitution of this country, as a scheme of government fundamentally and inviolably fixed in King, Lords, and Commons.

---

[2] Henry Sacheverell (1674–1724), a London minister, was found guilty in 1710 of seditious libel for publishing sermons charging that the Whigs had failed to defend the Church in England. His conviction led to riots across Englad and the fall of the Whig Ministry.

That the fundamental subversion of this ancient constitution by one of its parts having been attempted, and in effect accomplished, justified the Revolution. That it was justified *only* upon the *necessity* of the case; as the *only* means left for the recovery of that *ancient* constitution, formed by the *original contract* of the
5   British state; as well as for the future preservation of the *same* government. These are the points to be proved....

Taking it for granted that I do not write to the disciples of the Parisian philosophy, I may assume, that the awful Author of our being is the Author of our place in the order of existence; and that having disposed and marshaled
10 us by a divine tactic, not according to our will, but according to his, he has, in and by that disposition, virtually subjected us to act the part which belongs to the place assigned us. We have obligations to mankind at large, which are not in consequence of any special voluntary pact. They arise from the relation of man to man, and the relation of man to God, which relations are not matters
15 of choice. On the contrary, the force of all the pacts which we enter into with any particular person or number of persons among mankind depends upon those prior obligations. In some cases the subordinate relations are voluntary, in others they are necessary—but the duties are all compulsive. When we marry, the choice is voluntary, but the duties are not matter of choice. They are dictated
20 by the nature of the situation. Dark and inscrutable are the ways by which we come into the world. The instincts which give rise to this mysterious process of nature are not of our making. But of our physical causes, unknown to us, perhaps unknowable, arise moral relation; but consenting or not, they are bound to a long train of burdensome duties towards those with whom they have never made a
25 convention of any sort. Children are not consenting to their relation, but their relation, without their actual consent, binds them to their duties; or rather it implies their consent, because the presumed consent of every rational creature is in unison with the predisposed order of things. Men come in that manner into a community with the social state of their parents, endowed with all the benefits,
30 loaded with all the duties of their situation. If the social ties and ligaments, spun out of those physical relations which are the elements of the commonwealth, in most cases begin, and always continue, independently of our will, so without any stipulation on our own part, are we bound by that relation called our country, which comprehends (as it has been well said) "all the charities of all." Nor are we
35 left without powerful instincts to make this duty as dear and grateful to us, as it is awful and coercive. Our country is not a thing of mere physical locality. It consists, in a great measure, in the ancient order into which we are born. We may have the same geographical situation, but another country; as we may have the same country in another soil. The place that determines our duty to our country
40 is a social, civil relation....

ON THE PRINCIPLES OF POLITICAL MORALITY
MAXIMILIEN ROBESPIERRE (1758–1794)

Inspired by Enlightenment principles, a group of prominent Frenchmen in 1789 began the French Revolution. Although the reformers initially demanded only some legislative power and limited political reforms, over time they came to reject traditional political values and forms. By early 1794 the dominant political faction, known as Jacobins, insisted on a comprehensive application of Enlightenment reason to every facet of public life. They abolished the monarchy, altered the week to have ten days, replaced Christian public worship with the Cult of Reason, regulated prices and wages, and instituted universal manhood suffrage.

The most prominent facet of this "triumph of reason," however, was the Reign of Terror. An attempt to purify the French Republic through the systematic application of reason, it effected the execution of 20,000 to 40,000 people as counterrevolutionaries. As the leader of the Jacobins, Maximilien Robespierre, a lawyer from northern France, justified the Reign of Terror in the following speech to the French legislature.

18 PLUVIOSE, YEAR II (6 FEBRUARY 1794)

It is time to designate clearly the purposes of the revolution and the point which we wish to attain. It is time we should examine ourselves the obstacles which yet are between us and our wishes, and the means most proper to realize them: A consideration simple and important which appears not yet to have been contemplated.   5

Indeed, how could a base and corrupt government have dared to view themselves in the mirror of political rectitude? A king, a proud senate, a Caesar, a Cromwell; of these the first care was to cover their dark designs under the cloak of religion, to covenant with every vice, caress every party, destroy men of probity, oppress and deceive the people to attain the end of their perfidious   10
ambition. If we had not had a task of the first magnitude to accomplish; if all

Maximilien Robespierre, *Report upon the Principles of Political Morality which are to Form the Basis of the Administration of the Interior Concerns of the Republic* (Philadelphia, 1794).

our concern had been to raise a party or create a new aristocracy, we might have believed, as certain writers more ignorant than wicked asserted, that the plan of the French Revolution was to be found written in the works of Tacitus and of Machiavelli; we might have sought the duties of the representatives of the
5   people in the history of Augustus, of Tiberius, or of Vespasian, or even in that of certain French legislators; for tyrants are substantially alike and only differ by trifling shades of perfidy and cruelty.

For our part, we now come to make the whole world partake in your political secrets, that all friends of their country may rally at the voice of reason and
10   public interest, and that the French nation and her representatives be respected in all countries which may attain a knowledge of their true principles; and that intriguers who always seek to supplant other intriguers may be judged by public opinion upon settled and plain principles. Every precaution must early be used to place the interests of freedom in the hands of truth, which is eternal,
15   rather than in those of men who change; so that if the government forgets the interests of the people or falls into the hands of men corrupted, according to the natural course of things the light of acknowledged principles should unmask their treasons, and that every new faction may read its death in the very thought of a crime. Happy the people that attains this end; for, whatever new
20   machinations are plotted against their liberty, what resources does not public reason present when guaranteeing freedom!

What is the end of our revolution? The tranquil enjoyment of liberty and equality; the reign of that eternal justice, the laws of which are graven, not on marble or stone, but in the hearts of men, even in the heart of the slave who
25   has forgotten them, and in that of the tyrant who disowns them. We wish that order of things where all the low and cruel passions are enchained, all the beneficent and generous passions awakened by the laws; where ambition subsists in a desire to deserve glory and serve the country; where distinctions grow out of the system of equality, where the citizen submits to the authority
30   of the magistrate, the magistrate obeys that of the people, and the people are governed by a love of justice; where the country secures the comfort of each individual, and where each individual prides himself on the prosperity and glory of his country; where every soul expands by a free communication of republican sentiments, and by the necessity of deserving the esteem of a great
35   people: where the arts serve to embellish that liberty which gives them value and support, and commerce is a source of public wealth and not merely of immense riches to a few individuals.

We wish in our country that morality may be substituted for egotism, probity for false honor, principles for usages, duties for good manners, the
40   empire of reason for the tyranny of fashion, a contempt of vice for a contempt

of misfortune, pride for insolence, magnanimity for vanity, the love of glory for the love of money, good people for good company, merit for intrigue, genius for wit, truth for tinsel show, the attractions of happiness for the ennui of sensuality, the grandeur of man for the littleness of the great, a people magnanimous, powerful, happy, for a people amiable, frivolous and miserable; in a word, all the virtues and miracles of a republic instead of all the vices and absurdities of a monarchy.

We wish, in a word, to fulfill the intentions of nature and the destiny of man, realize the promises of philosophy, and acquit Providence of a long reign of crime and tyranny. That France, once illustrious among enslaved nations, may, by eclipsing the glory of all free countries that ever existed, become a model to nations, a terror to oppressors, a consolation to the oppressed, an ornament of the universe and that, by sealing the work with our blood, we may at least witness the dawn of the bright day of universal happiness. This is our ambition, this is the end of our efforts....

Since virtue and equality are the soul of the republic, and your aim is to found, to consolidate the republic, it follows that the first rule of your political conduct should be to let all your measures tend to maintain equality and encourage virtue, for the first care of the legislator should be to strengthen the principles on which the government rests. Hence all that tends to excite a love of country, to purify manners, to exalt the mind, to direct the passions of the human heart towards the public good you should adopt and establish. All that tends to concenter and debase them into selfish egotism, to awaken an infatuation for littlenesses, and a disregard for greatness, you should reject or repress.

In the system of the French revolution that which is immoral is impolitic, and what tends to corrupt is counter-revolutionary.

Weaknesses, vices, prejudices are the road to monarchy. Carried away, too often perhaps, by the force of ancient habits, as well as by the innate imperfection of human nature, to false ideas and pusillanimous sentiments, we have more to fear from the excesses of weakness than from excesses of energy. The warmth of zeal is not perhaps the most dangerous rock that we have to avoid; but rather that languor which ease produces and a distrust of our own courage. Therefore continually wind up the sacred spring of republican government, instead of letting it run down. I need not say that I am not here justifying any excess. Principles the most sacred may be abused. The wisdom of government should guide its operations according to circumstances, it should time its measures, choose its means; for the manner of bringing about great things is an essential part of the talent of producing them, just as wisdom is an essential attribute of virtue....

It is not necessary to detail the natural consequences of the principle of democracy, it is the principle itself, simple yet copious, which deserves to be developed. Republican virtue may be considered as it respects the people and as it respects the government. It is necessary in both. When however, the government alone want it, there exists a resource in that of the people; but when the people themselves are corrupted liberty is already lost. Happily virtue is natural in the people, despite aristocratic prejudices. A nation is truly corrupt when, after having by degrees lost its character and liberty, it slides from democracy into aristocracy or monarchy; this is the death of the political body by decrepitude....

But, when, by prodigious effects of courage and of reason, a whole people break asunder the fetters of despotism to make of the fragments trophies to liberty; when, by their innate vigor, they rise in a manner from the arms of death, to resume all the strength of youth when, in turns forgiving and inexorable, intrepid and docile, they can neither be checked by impregnable ramparts, nor by innumerable armies of tyrants leagued against them, and yet of themselves stop at the voice of the law; if then they do not reach the heights of their destiny it can only be the fault of those who govern. Again, it may be said, that to love justice and equality the people need no great effort of virtue; it is sufficient that they love themselves....

If virtue be the spring of a popular government in times of peace, the spring of that government during a revolution is virtue combined with terror; virtue, without which terror is destructive; terror, without which virtue is impotent. Terror is only justice prompt, severe, and inflexible—it is then an emanation of virtue; it is less a distinct principle than a natural consequence of the general principle of democracy, applied to the most pressing wants of the country.

It has been said that terror is the spring of despotic government. Does yours then resemble despotism? Yes, as the steel that glistens in the hands of the heroes of liberty resembles the sword with which the satellites of tyranny are armed. Let the despot govern by terror his debased subjects; he is right as a despot: conquer by terror the enemies of liberty and you will be right as founders of the republic. The government in a revolution is the despotism of liberty against tyranny. Is force only intended to protect crime? Is not the lightning of heaven made to blast vice exalted?

The law of self-preservation with every being, whether physical or moral, is the first law of nature. Crime butchers innocence to secure a throne, and innocence struggles with all its might against the attempts of crime. If tyranny reigned one single day not a patriot would survive it. How long yet will the madness of despots be called justice, and the justice of the people barbarity or rebellion? How tenderly oppressors and how severely the oppressed are treated! Nothing more natural; whoever does not abhor crime cannot love virtue. Yet one or the other must be crushed. Let mercy be shown the royalists exclaim some men. Pardon the villains! No; be merciful to innocence, pardon the unfortunate, show compassion for human weakness. The protection of government is only due to peaceable citizens; and all citizens in the republic are republicans. The royalists, the conspirators, are strangers, or rather enemies. Is not this dreadful contest, which liberty maintains against tyranny, indivisible? Are not the internal 5 enemies the allies of those in the exterior? The assassins who lay waste the interior; the intriguers who purchase the consciences of the delegates of the people: the traitors who sell them; the mercenary libelists paid to dishonor the cause of the people, to smother public virtue, to fan the flame of civil discord, and bring about a political counter revolution by means of a moral one; all these men, are 10 they less culpable or less dangerous than the tyrants whom they serve?...

To punish the oppressors of humanity is clemency; to forgive them is barbarity. The severity of tyrants has barbarity for its principle; that of a republican government is founded on beneficence. Therefore let him beware who should dare to influence the people by that terror which is made only for their 15 enemies! Let him beware, who, regarding the inevitable errors of civism in the same light, with the premeditated crimes of perfidiousness, or the attempts of conspirators, suffers the dangerous intriguer to escape and pursues the peaceable citizen! Death to the villain who dares abuse the sacred name of liberty or the powerful arms intended for her defense, to carry mourning or death to 20 the patriotic heart.

FAREWELL ADDRESS
GEORGE WASHINGTON (1732–1799)
PRESIDENT OF THE UNITED STATES (1789–1797)

*The first president set many precedents. Among the most lasting was his deci-
sion to retire after two terms, which every president honored until Franklin
Roosevelt in 1940. Washington worked on his farewell knowing that he
was regarded as the "Father of his country" and that his parting words
would add significantly to America's political legacy. His message—liberty
in unity and independence from foreign influence—became the cornerstone
of a conservative republic.*

19 SEPTEMBER 1796

The period for a new election of a Citizen, to Administer the Executive government of the United States, being not far distant, and the time actually arrived
when your thoughts must be employed in designating the person, who is to
be cloathed with that important trust, it appears to me proper, especially as it
may conduce to a more distinct expression of the public voice, that I should   5
now apprise you of the resolution I have formed, to decline being considered
among the number of those, out of whom a choice is to be made.

I beg you, at the same time, to do me the justice to be assured, that this
resolution has not been taken, without a strict regard to all the considerations
appertaining to the relation, which binds a dutiful Citizen to his country—and   10
that, in withdrawing the tender of service which silence in my Situation might
imply, I am influenced by no diminution of zeal for your future interest, no
deficiency of grateful respect for your past kindness; but am supported by a full
conviction that the step is compatible with both.

The acceptance of, & continuance hitherto in, the Office to which your   15
Suffrages have twice called me, have been a uniform sacrifice of inclination to
the opinion of duty, and to a deference for what appeared to be your desire. I
constantly hoped, that it would have been much earlier in my power, consistently

Victor Hugo Paltsits, ed., *Washington's Farewell Address: In Facsimile, wth Transliterations of all
the Drafts of Washington, Madison, and Hamilton, Together with their Correspondence and Other
Supporting Documents* (New York: New York Public Library, 1935), 105–36.

with motives, which I was not at liberty to disregard, to return to that retirement, from which I had been reluctantly drawn. The strength of my inclination to do this, previous to the last Election, had even led to the preparation of an address to declare it to you; but mature reflection on the then perplexed & 5 critical posture of our Affairs with foreign nations, and the unanimous advice of persons entitled to my confidence, impelled me to abandon the idea.

I rejoice, that the state of your concerns, external as well as internal, no longer renders the pursuit of inclination incompatible with the sentiment of duty, or propriety, & am persuaded whatever partiality may be retained for my 10 services, that in the present circumstances of our country, you will not disapprove my determination to retire.

The impressions with which I first undertook the arduous trust, were explained on the proper occasion. In the discharge of this trust, I will only say, that I have, with good intentions, contributed towards the Organization and 15 Administration of the government, the best exertions of which a very fallible judgment was capable. Not unconscious, in the outset, of the inferiority of my qualifications, experience in my own eyes, perhaps still more in the eyes of others, has strengthened the motives to diffidence of myself; and every day the encreasing weight of years admonishes me more and more, that the shade 20 of retirement is as necessary to me as it will be welcome. Satisfied that if any circumstances have given peculiar value to my services, they were temporary, I have the consolation to believe, that while choice and prudence invite me to quit the political scene, patriotism does not forbid it.

In looking forward to the moment, which is intended to terminate the career 25 of my public life, my feelings do not permit me to suspend the deep acknowledgment of that debt of gratitude which I owe to my beloved country, for the many honors it has conferred upon me; still more for the steadfast confidence with which it has supported me; and for the opportunities I have thence enjoyed of manifesting my inviolable attachment, by services faithful & persevering, though 30 in usefulness unequal to my zeal. If benefits have resulted to our country from these services, let it always be remembered to your praise, and as an instructive example in our annals, that, under circumstances in which the Passions agitated in every direction were liable to mislead, amidst appearances sometimes dubious, vicissitudes of fortune often discouraging, in situations in which not infrequently 35 want of Success has countenanced the spirit of criticism, the constancy of your support was the essential prop of the efforts, and a guarantee of the plans by which they were effected. Profoundly penetrated with this idea, I shall carry it with me to my grave, as a strong incitement to unceasing vows that Heaven may continue to you the choicest tokens of its beneficence—that your Union 40 & brotherly affection may be perpetual—that the free constitution, which is

the work of your hands, may be sacredly maintained—that its Administration
in every department may be stamped with wisdom and Virtue—that, in fine,
the happiness of the people of these States, under the auspices of liberty, may be
made complete, by so careful a preservation and so prudent a use of this blessing
as will acquire to them the glory of recommending it to the applause, the affec-   5
tion—and adoption of every nation which is yet a stranger to it.

Here, perhaps, I ought to stop. But a solicitude for your welfare, which
cannot end but with my life, and the apprehension of danger, natural to that
solicitude, urge me, on an occasion like the present, to offer to your solemn
contemplation, and to recommend to your frequent review, some sentiments,   10
which are the result of much reflection, of no inconsiderable observation, and
which appear to me all important to the permanency of your felicity as a People.
These will be offered to you with the more freedom as you can only see in them
the disinterested warnings of a parting friend, who can possibly have no personal
motive to bias his counsel. Nor can I forget, as an encouragement to it, your in-   15
dulgent reception of my sentiments on a former and not dissimilar occasion.

Interwoven as is the love of liberty with every ligament of your hearts, no
recommendation of mine is necessary to fortify or confirm the Attachment.

The Unity of Government which constitutes you one people is also now dear
to you. It is justly so; for it is a main Pillar in the Edifice of your real independence,   20
the support of your tranquility at home; your peace abroad; of your safety; of
your prosperity; of that very Liberty which you so highly prize. But as it is easy
to foresee, that from different causes & from different quarters, much pains will
be taken, many artifices employed, to weaken in your minds the conviction of
this truth; as this is the point in your political fortress against which the batter-   25
ies of internal & external enemies will be most constantly and actively (though
often covertly & insidiously) directed, it is of infinite moment, that you should
properly estimate the immense value of your national Union to your collective
& individual happiness; that you should cherish a cordial, habitual, & immove-
able attachment to it; accustoming yourselves to think and speak of it as of the   30
Palladium of your political safety and prosperity; watching for its preservation
with jealous anxiety; discountenancing whatever may suggest even a suspicion
that it can in any event be abandoned, and indignantly frowning upon the first
dawning of every attempt to alienate any portion of our Country from the rest,
or to enfeeble the sacred ties which now link together the various parts.   35

For this you have every inducement of sympathy and interest. Citizens by
birth or choice, of a common country, that country has a right to concentrate
your affections. The name of American, which belongs to you, in your national
capacity, must always exalt the just pride of Patriotism, more than any appellation derived from local discriminations. With slight shades of difference, you   40

have the same Religion, Manners, Habits, and Political Principles. You have in a common cause fought & triumphed together—the independence & liberty you possess are the work of joint councils, and joint efforts—of common dangers, sufferings and successes.

But these considerations, however powerfully they address themselves to your sensibility are greatly outweighed by those which apply more immediately to your Interest. Here every portion of our country finds the most commanding motives for carefully guarding & preserving the Union of the whole.

The *North*, in an unrestrained intercourse with the *South*, protected by the equal Laws of a common government, finds in the productions of the latter, great additional resources of maritime & commercial enterprise and—precious materials of manufacturing industry. The *South*, in the same Intercourse, benefitting by the Agency of the *North*, sees its agriculture grow & its commerce expand. Turning partly into its own channels the seamen of the *North*, it finds its particular navigation envigorated; and while it contributes, in different ways, to nourish & increase the general mass of the National navigation, it looks forward to the protection of a maritime strength, to which itself is unequally adapted. The *East*, in a like intercourse with the *West*, already finds, and in the progressive improvement of interior communications by land & water, will more & more find a valuable vent for the commodities which it brings from abroad, or manufactures at home. The *West* derives from the *East* supplies requisite to its growth & comfort—and, what is perhaps of still greater consequence, it must of necessity owe the Secure enjoyment of indispensable *outlets* for its own productions to the weight, influence, and the future maritime strength of the Atlantic side of the Union, directed by an indissoluble community of interest as *one Nation*. Any other tenure by which the *West* can hold this essential advantage, whether derived from its own separate strength, or from an apostate & unnatural connection with any foreign Power, must be intrinsically precarious.

While, then, every part of our country thus feels an immediate & particular Interest in Union, all the parts combined cannot fail to find in the united mass of means & efforts greater strength, greater resource, proportionably greater security from external danger, a less frequent interruption of their Peace by foreign Nations; and, what is of inestimable value, they must derive from Union an exemption from those broils and Wars between themselves, which so frequently afflict neighboring countries, not tied together by the same governments; which their own rival ships alone would be sufficient to produce, but which opposite foreign alliances, attachments & intrigues would stimulate & imbitter. Hence likewise they will avoid the necessity of those overgrown Military establishments, which under any form of Government are inauspicious to liberty, and which are to be regarded as particularly hostile to Republican

Liberty: In this sense it is, that your union ought to be considered as a main prop of your liberty, and that the love of the one ought to endear to you the preservation of the other.

These considerations speak a persuasive language to every reflecting & virtuous mind, and exhibit the continuance of the Union as a primary object of   5
Patriotic desire. Is there a doubt, whether a common government can embrace so large a sphere? Let experience solve it. To listen to mere speculation in such a case were criminal. We are authorized to hope that a proper organization of the whole, with the auxiliary agency of governments for the respective Subdivisions, will afford a happy issue to the experiment. 'Tis well worth a fair and full   10
experiment. With such powerful and obvious motives to Union, affecting all parts of our country, while experience shall not have demonstrated its impracticability, there will always be reason, to distrust the patriotism of those, who in any quarter may endeavor to weaken its bands.

In contemplating the causes which may disturb our Union, it occurs as matter of serious concern that any ground should have been furnished for characterizing parties by *Geographical* discriminations—*Northern* and *Southern, Atlantic* and *Western*; whence designing men may endeavor to excite a belief that there is a real difference of local interests and views. One of the expedients of party to acquire influence, within particular districts, is to misrepresent the opinions   20
& aims of other Districts. You cannot shield yourselves too much against the jealousies and heart burnings which spring from these misrepresentations. They tend to render Alien to each other those who ought to be bound together by fraternal Affection. The Inhabitants of our Western country have lately had a useful lesson on this head. They have seen, in the negotiation by the Executive,   25
and in the unanimous ratification by the Senate, of the Treaty with Spain,[1] and in the universal satisfaction at that event, throughout the United States, a decisive proof how unfounded were the suspicions propagated among them of a policy in the General Government and in the Atlantic States unfriendly to their Interests in regard to the Mississippi. They have been witnesses to the   30
formation of two Treaties, that with G. Britain and that with Spain, which secure to them everything they could desire, in respect to our Foreign relations, towards confirming their prosperity. Will it not be their wisdom to rely for the preservation of these advantages on the Union by which they were procured? Will they not henceforth be deaf to those Advisers, if such there are, who would   35
sever them from their Brethren and connect them with Aliens?

---

[1]The *Treaty of Friendship, Limits, and Navigation* resolved the boundary dispute between the Spanish colony of Florida and the United States, assured both parties that neither would incite Indians to war, and guaranteed both nations rights of navigation along the entire length of the Mississippi River.

To the efficacy and permanency of Your Union, a Government for the whole is indispensable. No Alliances however strict between the parts can be an adequate substitute. They must inevitably experience the infractions & interruptions which all Alliances in all times have experienced. Sensible of this momentous truth, you have improved upon your first essay, by the adoption of a Constitution of Government, better calculated than your former for an intimate Union, and for the efficacious management of your common concerns. This government, the offspring of our own choice uninfluenced and unawed, adopted upon full investigation & mature deliberation, completely free in its principles, in the distribution of its powers, uniting security with energy, and containing within itself a provision for its own amendment, has a just claim to your confidence and your support. Respect for its authority, compliance with its Laws, acquiescence in its measures, are duties enjoined by the fundamental maxims of true Liberty. The basis of our political Systems is the right of the people to make and to alter their Constitutions of Government. But the Constitution which at any time exists, 'till changed by an explicit and authentic act of the whole People, is sacredly obligatory upon all. The very idea of the power and the right of the People to establish Government presupposes the duty of every Individual to obey the established Government.

All obstructions to the execution of the Laws, all combinations and Associations, under whatever plausible character, with the real design to direct, control, counteract, or awe the regular deliberation and action of the Constituted authorities are destructive of this fundamental principle and of fatal tendency. They serve to organize Faction, to give it an artificial and extraordinary force—to put in the place of the delegated will of the Nation, the will of a party: often a small but artful and enterprising minority of the Community; and, according to the alternate triumphs of different parties, to make the public Administration the Mirror of the ill concerted and incongruous projects of faction, rather than the Organ of consistent and wholesome plans digested by common counsils and modified by mutual interests. However combinations or Associations of the above description may now & then answer popular ends, they are likely, in the course of time and things, to become potent engines, by which cunning, ambitious, and unprincipled men will be enabled to subvert the Power of the People, & to usurp for themselves the reins of Government, destroying afterwards the very engines which have lifted them to unjust dominion.

Towards the preservation of your Government, and the permanency of your present happy state, it is requisite, not only that you steadily discountenance irregular oppositions to its acknowledged authority, but also that you resist with care the spirit of innovation upon its principles however specious the pretexts. One method of assault may be to effect, in the forms of the Constitution, altera-

tions which will impair the energy of the system, and thus to undermine what cannot be directly overthrown. In all the changes to which you may be invited, remember that time and habit are at least as necessary to fix the true character of Governments, as of other human institutions—that experience is the surest standard, by which to test the real tendency of the existing Constitution of a   5
Country—that facility in changes, upon the credit of mere hypotheses and opinion, exposes to perpetual change, from the endless variety of hypotheses & opinion: and remember, especially, that for the efficient management of your common interests, in a country so extensive as ours, a Government of as much vigour as is consistent with the perfect security of Liberty is indispensable—Lib-   10
erty itself will find in such a Government, with powers properly distributed and adjusted, its surest Guardian. It is indeed little else than a name, where the government is too feeble to withstand the enterprises of faction, to confine each member of the Society within the limits prescribed by the laws, & to maintain all in the secure & tranquil enjoyment of the rights of person & property.   15

I have already intimated to you the danger of Parties in the State, with particular reference to the founding of them on Geographical discriminations. Let me now take a more comprehensive view, & warn you in the most solemn manner against the baneful effects of the Spirit of Party, generally.

This spirit, unfortunately, is inseperable from our nature, having its root in   20
the strongest passions of the human Mind. It exists under different shapes in all Governments, more or less stifled, controlled, or repressed; but, in those of the popular form, it is seen in its greatest rankness, and is truly their worst enemy.

The alternate domination of one faction over another, sharpened by the spirit of revenge natural to party dissension, which in different ages & countries   25
has perpetrated the most horrid enormities, is itself a frightful despotism. But this leads at length to a more formal and permanent despotism. The disorders & miseries, which result, gradually incline the minds of men to seek security & repose in the absolute power of an Individual: and sooner or later the chief of some prevailing faction more able or more fortunate than his competitors,   30
turns this disposition to the purposes of his own elevation, on the ruins of Public Liberty.

Without looking forward to an extremity of this kind (which nevertheless ought not to be entirely out of sight) the common & continual mischiefs of the spirit of party are sufficient to make it the interest and duty of a wise people to   35
discourage and restrain it.

It serves always to distract the Public Councils and enfeeble the Public Administration. It agitates the Community with ill founded Jealousies and false alarms, kindles the animosity of one part against another, foments occasion-ally riot & insurrection. It opens the door to foreign influence & corruption,   40 which finds a facilitated access to the government itself through the channels of party passions. Thus the policy and the will of one country, are subjected to the policy and will of another.

There is an opinion that parties in free countries are useful checks upon
5 the Administration of the Government and serve to keep alive the spirit of Liberty. This within certain limits is probably true—and in Governments of a Monarchical cast, Patriotism may look with indulgence, if not with favor, upon the spirit of party. But in those of the popular character, in Governments purely elective, it is a spirit not to be encouraged. From their natural tendency, it is
10 certain there will always be enough of that spirit for every salutary purpose. And there being constant danger of excess, the effort ought to be by force of public opinion, to mitigate and assuage it. A fire not to be quenched, it demands a uniform vigilance to prevent its bursting into a flame, lest, instead of warming, it should consume.

15 It is important, likewise, that the habits of thinking in a free Country should inspire caution in those entrusted with its Administration, to confine themselves within their respective Constitutional Spheres, avoiding in the exercise of the Powers of one department to encroach upon another. The spirit of encroachment tends to consolidate the powers of all the departments in one,
20 and thus to create whatever the form of government, a real despotism. A just estimate of that love of power, and proneness to abuse it, which predominates in the human heart, is sufficient to satisfy us of the truth of this position. The necessity of reciprocal checks in the exercise of political power, by dividing and distributing it into different depositaries, & constituting each the Guardian of
25 the Public Weal against invasions by the others, has been evinced by experiments ancient & modern; some of them in our country & under our own eyes. To preserve them must be as necessary as to institute them. If in the opinion of the People, the distribution or modification of the Constitutional powers be in any particular wrong, let it be corrected by an amendment in the way which the
30 Constitution designates. But let there be no change by usurpation; for though this, in one instance, may be the instrument of good, it is the customary weapon by which free governments are destroyed. The precedent must always greatly overbalance in permanent evil any partial or transient benefit, which the use can at any time yield.

35 Of all the dispositions and habits which lead to political prosperity, Religion and morality are indispensable supports. In vain would that man claim the tribute of Patriotism, who should labor to subvert these great pillars of human happiness, these firmest props of the duties of Men & citizens. The mere Politician, equally with the pious man ought to respect & to cherish them. A volume
40 could not trace all their connections with private & public felicity. Let it simply

be asked where is the security for property, for reputation, for life, if the sense of religious obligation *desert* the Oaths which are the instruments of investigation in Courts of Justice? And let us with caution indulge the supposition, that morality can be maintained without religion. Whatever may be conceded to the influence of refined education on minds of peculiar structure—reason &   5
experience both forbid us to expect that national morality can prevail in exclusion of religious principle.

'Tis substantially true, that virtue or morality is a necessary spring of popular government. The rule indeed extends with more or less force to every species of Free Government. Who that is a sincere friend to it, can look with indifference   10
upon attempts to shake the foundation of the fabric.

Promote then as an object of primary importance, Institutions for the general diffusion of knowledge. In proportion as the structure of a government gives force to public opinion, it is essential that public opinion should be enlightened.   15

As a very important source of strength & security, cherish public credit. One method of preserving it is to use it as sparingly as possible: avoiding occasions of expence by cultivating peace, but remembering also that timely disbursements to prepare for danger frequently prevent much greater disbursements to repel it—avoiding likewise the accumulation of debt, not only by shunning occasions   20
of expence but by vigorous exertion in time of Peace to discharge the Debts which unavoidable wars may have occasioned, not ungenerously throwing upon posterity the burthen—which we ourselves ought to bear. The execution of these maxims belongs to your Representatives, but it is necessary that public opinion should cooperate. To facilitate to them the performance of their duty, it is   25
essential that you should practically bear in mind, that towards the payment of debts there must be Revenue—that to have Revenue there must be taxes—that no taxes can be devised which are not more or less inconvenient & unpleasant—that the intrinsic embarrassment inseparable from the Selection of the proper objects (which is always a choice of difficulties) ought to be a decisive   30
motive for a candid construction of the Conduct of the Government in making it, and for a spirit of acquiescence in the measures for obtaining Revenue which the public exigencies may at any time dictate.

Observe good faith & justice towards all Nations. Cultivate peace &harmony with all—Religion & morality enjoin this conduct; and can it be that   35
good policy does not equally enjoin it? It will be worthy of a free, enlightened, and, at no distant period, a great Nation, to give to mankind the magnanimous and too novel example of a People always guided by an exalted justice & benevolence. Who can doubt that in the course of time and things the fruits of such a plan would richly repay any temporary advantages which might be   40

lost by a steady adherence to it? Can it be, that Providence has not connected the permanent felicity of a Nation with its virtue ? The experiment, at least, is recommended by every sentiment which ennobles human Nature. Alas! is it rendered impossible by its vices?

5   In the execution of such a plan nothing is more essential than that permanent inveterate antipathies against particular Nations and passionate attachments for others should be excluded; and that in place of them just & amicable feelings towards all should be cultivated. The Nation, which indulges towards another an habitual hatred or an habitual fondness is in some degree a slave.
10 It is a slave to its animosity or to its affection, either of which is sufficient to lead it astray from its duty and its interest. Antipathy in one Nation against another—disposes each more readily to offer insult and injury, to lay hold of slight causes of umbrage, and to be haughty and intractable, when accidental or trifling occasions of dispute occur. Hence frequent collisions, obstinate
15 envenomed and bloody contests. The Nation, prompted by ill will & resentment sometimes impels to War the Government, contrary to the best calculations of policy. The Government sometimes participates in the national propensity, and adopts through passion what reason would reject; at other times, it makes the animosity of the Nation subservient to projects of hostility instigated by pride,
20 ambition, and other sinister & pernicious motives. The peace often, sometimes perhaps the Liberty, of Nations has been the victim.

So likewise, a passionate attachment of one Nation for another produces a variety of evils. Sympathy for the favorite nation, facilitating the illusion of an imaginary common interest, in cases where no real common interest
25 exists, and infusing into one the enmities of the other, betrays the former into a participation in the quarrels and wars of the latter, without adequate inducement or justification. It leads also to concessions to the favorite Nation of priviledges denied to others which is apt doubly to injure the Nation making the concessions—by unnecessarily parting with what ought to have
30 been retained—& by exciting jealousy, ill will, and a disposition to retaliate, in the parties from whom equal priviledges are withheld: And it gives to ambitious, corrupted, or deluded citizens (who devote themselves to the favorite Nation), facility to betray, or sacrifice the interests of their own country, without odium, sometimes even with popularity; gilding with the appearances of
35 a virtuous sense of obligation a commendable deference for public opinion, or a laudable zeal for public good, the base or foolish compliances of ambition, corruption, or infatuation.

As avenues to foreign influence in innumerable ways, such attachments are particularly alarming to the truly enlightened and independent Patriot. How
40 many opportunities do they afford to tamper with domestic factions, to practice

the arts of seduction, to mislead public opinion, to influence or awe the public Councils? Such an attachment of a small or weak, towards a great & powerful Nation, dooms the former to be the satellite of the latter.

Against the insidious wiles of foreign influence (I conjure you to believe me fellow citizens) the jealousy of a free people ought to be *constantly* awake; since history and experience prove that foreign influence is one of the most baneful foes of Republican Government. But that jealousy to be useful must be impartial; else it becomes the instrument of the very influence to be avoided, instead of a defense against it. Excessive partiality for one foreign nation and excessive dislike of another cause those whom they actuate to see danger only on one side, and serve to veil and even second the arts of influence on the other. Real Patriots, who may resist the intrigues of the favorite, are liable to become suspected and odious; while its tools and dupes usurp the applause & confidence of the people, to surrender their interests.

The Great rule of conduct for us, in regard to foreign Nations is in extend- ing our commercial relations to have with them as little *political* connection as possible. So far as we have already formed engagements, let them be fulfilled with perfect good faith. Here let us stop.

Europe has a set of primary interests which to us have none, or a very remote relation. Hence she must be engaged in frequent controversies, the causes of which are essentially foreign to our concerns. Hence therefore it must be unwise in us to implicate ourselves, by artificial ties, in the ordinary vicissitudes of her politics, or the ordinary combinations & collisions of her friendships, or enmities.

Our detached & distant situation invites and enables us to pursue a different course. If we remain one People, under an efficient government, the period is not far off, when we may defy material injury from external annoyance; when we may take such an attitude as will cause the neutrality we may at any time resolve upon to be scrupulously respected; when belligerent nations, under the impossibility of making acquisitions upon us, will not lightly hazard the giving us provocation; when we may choose peace or War, as our interest guided by justice shall counsel.

Why forego the advantages of so peculiar a situation? Why quit our own to stand upon foreign ground? Why, by interweaving our destiny with that of any part of Europe, entangle our peace and prosperity in the toils of European Ambition, Rivalship, Interest, Humor or Caprice?

'Tis our true policy to steer clear of permanent Alliances, with any portion of the foreign World—so far, I mean, as we are now at liberty to do it—for let me not be understood as capable of patronizing infidelity to existing engage- ments, (I hold the maxim no less applicable to public than to private affairs, that honesty is always the best policy)—I repeat it therefore Let those engagements be observed in their genuine sense. But in my opinion, it is unnecessary and would be unwise to extend them.

Taking care always to keep ourselves, by suitable establishments, on a
5   respectable defensive posture, we may safely trust to temporary alliances for extraordinary emergencies.

Harmony, liberal intercourse with all Nations, are recommended by policy, humanity and interest. But even our Commercial policy should hold an equal and impartial hand: neither seeking nor granting exclusive favors or prefer-
10 ences; consulting the natural course of things; diffusing & diversifying by gentle means the streams of Commerce, but forcing nothing; establishing with Powers so disposed—in order to give trade a stable course, to define the rights of our Merchants, and to enable the government to support them—conventional rules of intercourse; the best that present circumstances and mutual opinion will
15 permit, but temporary, & liable to be from time to time abandoned or varied, as experience and circumstances shall dictate; constantly keeping in view, that 'tis folly in one Nation to look for disinterested favors from another—that it must pay with a portion of its Independence for whatever it may accept under that character—that by such acceptance, it may place itself in the condition of
20 having given equivalents for nominal favors and yet of being reproached with ingratitude for not giving more. There can be no greater error than to expect, or calculate upon real favors from Nation to Nation. 'Tis an illusion, which experience must cure, which a just pride ought to discard.

In offering to you, my Countrymen, these counsels of an old and affection-
25 ate friend, I dare not hope they will make the strong and lasting impression I could wish—that they will control the usual current of the passions, or prevent our Nation from running the course which has hitherto marked the Destiny of Nations: But if I may even flatter myself, that they may be productive of some partial benefit, some occasional good; that they may now & then recur
30 to moderate the fury of party spirit, to warn against the mischiefs of foreign Intriegue, to guard against the Impostures of pretended patriotism—this hope will be a full recompense for the solicitude for your welfare, by which they have been dictated.

How far in the discharge of my Official duties, I have been guided by the
35 principles which have been delineated, the public Records and other evidences of my conduct must witness to You and to the world. To myself, the assurance of my own conscience is, that I have at least believed myself to be guided by them.

In relation to the still subsisting War in Europe, my Proclamation of the 22d of April 1793, is the index of my Plan. Sanctioned by your approving voice
40 and by that of Your Representatives in both Houses of Congress, the spirit of

that measure has continually governed me, uninfluenced by any attempts to deter or divert me from it.

After deliberate examination with the aid of the best lights I could obtain I was well satisfied that our Country, under all the circumstances of the case, had a right to take, and was bound in duty and interest, to take a Neutral position. 5 Having taken it, I determined, as far as should depend upon me, to maintain it, with moderation, perseverance & firmness.

The considerations which respect the right to hold this conduct, it is not necessary on this occasion to detail. I will only observe, that according to my understanding of the matter, that right, so far from being denied by any of the 10 Belligerent Powers has been virtually admitted by all.

The duty of holding a neutral conduct may be inferred, without any thing more, from the obligation which justice and humanity impose on every Nation, in cases in which it is free to act, to maintain inviolate the relations of peace and amity towards other Nations. 15

The inducements of interest for observing that conduct will best be referred to your own reflections & experience. With me, a predominant motive has been to endeavor to gain time to our country to settle & mature its yet recent institutions, and to progress without interruption, to that degree of strength & consistency which is necessary to give it, humanly speaking, the command 20 of its own fortunes.

Though in reviewing the incidents of my Administration, I am unconscious of intentional error—I am nevertheless too sensible of my defects not to think it probable that I may have committed many errors. Whatever they may be I fervently beseech the Almighty to avert or mitigate the evils to which they may 25 tend. I shall also carry with me the hope that my Country will never cease to view them with indulgence; and that, after forty five years of my life dedicated to its Service with an upright zeal, the faults of incompetent abilities will be consigned to oblivion, as myself must soon be to the Mansions of rest.

Relying on its kindness in this as in other things, and actuated by that fervent 30 love towards it, which is so natural to a Man, who views in it the native soil of himself and his progenitors for several Generations; I anticipate with pleasing expectation that retreat, in which I promise myself to realize, without alloy, the sweet enjoyment of partaking, in the midst of my fellow Citizens, the benign influence of good Laws under a free Government—the ever-favorite object of 35 my heart, and the happy reward, as I trust, of our mutual cares, labors, and dangers.

KENTUCKY RESOLUTION
THOMAS JEFFERSON (1743–1826)
PRESIDENT OF THE UNITED STATES (1801–1809)

The great American political debate developed very early in the history of the republic. Once adopted, the Constitution became a secular form of Holy Scripture and Americans became political as well as spiritual "people of the Book." How literally does one read the Book? Thomas Jefferson took a rather fundamentalist stance. Reacting against Hamilton's financial plans and the broad reading of the Constitution they required, he proposed a "Revolution of 1800" to put political authority back where he thought it belonged—in the states.

The "Republican" party Jefferson inspired eventually became "The Democracy," today's Democratic Party. Although Jefferson himself was a patriarchal Virginia aristocrat and slaveholder, his party appealed to Americans whose loyalties were primarily local and who wished the "voice of the people" to be heard. Jefferson wrote the "Kentucky Resolution" in defense of state sovereignty and in reaction against the grants of power to the national government implied in the Alien and Sedition Acts. His opponents argued that "sovereignty" in the states had ended with the passing of the Articles of Confederation, that states' rights should be protected while recognizing that the Constitution was the fundamental law of the land.

10 NOVEMBER 1798

1. *Resolved,* That the several states composing the United States of America are not united on the principle of unlimited submission to their general government; but that, by compact, under the style and title of a Constitution for the United States, and of amendments thereto, they constituted a general government for special purposes, delegated to that government certain definite powers, reserving, each state to itself, the residuary mass of right to their own self-government; and that whensoever the general government assumes undelegated powers, its acts are un-authoritative, void,

5

Jonathan Elliot, ed., *The Debates in the Several State Conventions on the Adoption of the Federal Constitution* (Washington, DC, 1836), IV:540–44.

and of no force; that to this compact each state acceded as a state, and is an integral party; that this government, created by this compact, was not made the exclusive or final judge of the extent of the powers delegated to itself, since that would have made it discretion, and not the Constitution, the measure of its powers; but that, as in all other cases of compact among parties having no common judge, *each party has an equal right to judge for itself, as well of infractions as of the mode and measure of redress.*

2. *Resolved,* That the Constitution of the United States , having delegated to Congress a power to punish treason, counterfeiting the securities and current coin of the United States, piracies and felonies committed on the high seas, and offences against the laws of nations, and no other crimes whatever; and it being true, as a general principle, and one of the amendments to the Constitution having also declared "that the powers not delegated to the United States by the Constitution, nor prohibited by it to the states, are reserved to the states respectively, or to the people,"—therefore, also, the same act of Congress, passed on the 14th day of July, 1798, and entitled "An Act in Addition to the Act entitled 'An Act for the Punishment of certain Crimes against the United States;'" as also the act passed by them on the 27th day of June, 1798, entitled "An Act to punish Frauds committed on the Bank of the United States," (and all other their acts which assume to create, define, or punish crimes other than those enumerated in the Constitution,) are altogether void, and of no force; and that the power to create, define, and punish, such other crimes is reserved, and of right appertains, solely and exclusively, to the respective states, each within its own territory.

3. *Resolved,* That it is true, as a general principle, and is also expressly declared by one of the amendments to the Constitution, that "the powers not delegated to the United States by the Constitution, nor prohibited by it to the states, are reserved to the states respectively, or to the people;" and that, no power over the freedom of religion, freedom of speech, or freedom of the press, being delegated to the United States by the Constitution, nor prohibited by it to the states, all lawful powers respecting the same did of right remain, and were reserved to the states, or to the people; that thus was manifested their determination to retain to themselves the right of judging how far the licentiousness of speech, and of the press, may be abridged without lessening their useful freedom, and how far those abuses which cannot be separated from their use, should be tolerated rather than the use be destroyed; and thus also they guarded against all abridgment, by the United States, of the freedom of religious principles and exercises, and

retained to themselves the right of protecting the same, as this, stated by
a law passed on the general demand of its citizens, had already protected
them from all human restraint or interference; and that, in addition to
this general principle and express declaration, another and more special
provision has been made by one of the amendments to the Constitution,   5
which expressly declares, that "Congress shall make no law respecting
an establishment of religion, or prohibiting the free exercise thereof, or
abridging the freedom of speech, or of the press," thereby guarding, in
the same sentence, and under the same words, the freedom of religion, of
speech, and of the press, insomuch that whatever violates either throws   10
down the sanctuary which covers the others,—and that libels, falsehood,
and defamation, equally with heresy and false religion, are withheld from
the cognizance of federal tribunals. That therefore the act of the Congress
of the United States, passed on the 14th of July, 1798, entitled "An Act in
Addition to the Act entitled 'An Act for the Punishment of certain Crimes   15
against the United States,'" which does abridge the freedom of the press,
is not law, but is altogether void, and of no force.

4. *Resolved*, That alien friends are under the jurisdiction and protection of the
laws of the state wherein they are; that no power over them has been delegated to the United States, nor prohibited to the individual states, distinct   20
from their power over citizens; and it being true, as a general principle,
and one of the amendments to the Constitution having also declared, that
"the powers not delegated to the United States by the Constitution, nor
prohibited to the states, are reserved to the states, respectively, or to the
people," the act of the Congress of the United States, passed the 22d day of   25
June, 1798, entitled "An Act concerning Aliens," which assumes power over
alien friends not delegated by the Constitution, is not law, but is altogether
void and of no force.

5. *Resolved*, That, in addition to the general principle, as well as the express
declaration, that powers not delegated are reserved, another and more special   30
provision inserted in the Constitution from abundant caution, has declared,
"that the migration or importation of such persons as any of the states now
existing shall think proper to admit, shall not be prohibited by the Congress
prior to the year 1808." That this commonwealth does admit the migration
of alien friends described as the subject of the said act concerning aliens;   35
that a provision against prohibiting their migration is a provision against
all acts equivalent thereto, or it would be nugatory; that to remove them,
when migrated, is equivalent to a prohibition of their migration, and is,
therefore, contrary to the said provision of the Constitution, and *void*.

6. *Resolved*, That the imprisonment of a person under the protection of the laws of this commonwealth, on his failure to obey the simple order of the President to deport out of the United States, as is undertaken by the said act, entitled, "An Act concerning Aliens," is contrary to the Constitution, one amendment in which has provided, that "no person shall be deprived of liberty without due process of law;" and that another having provided, "that, in all criminal prosecutions, the accused shall enjoy the right of a public trial by an impartial jury, to be informed as to the nature and cause of the accusation, to be confronted with the witnesses against him, to have compulsory process for obtaining witnesses in his favor, and to have assistance of counsel for his defense," the same act undertaking to authorize the President to remove a person out of the United States who is under the protection of the law, on his own suspicion, without jury, without public trial, without confrontation of the witnesses against him, without having witnesses in his favor, without defense, without counsel—contrary to these provisions also of the Constitution—is therefore not law, but utterly void, and of no force.

That transferring the power of judging any person who is under the protection of the laws, from the courts to the President of the United States, as is undertaken by the same act concerning aliens, is against the article of the Constitution which provides, that "the judicial power of the United States shall be vested in the courts, the judges of which shall hold their office during good behavior," and that the said act is void for that reason also; and it is further to be noted that this transfer of judiciary power is to that magistrate of the general government who already possesses all the executive, and a qualified negative in all the legislative powers.

7. *Resolved*, That the construction applied by the general government (as is evident by sundry of their proceedings) to those parts of the Constitution of the United States which delegate to Congress power to lay and collect taxes, duties, imposts, excises, to pay the debts, and provide for the common defense and general welfare, of the United States, and to make all laws which shall be necessary and proper for carrying into execution the powers vested by the Constitution in the government of the United States, or any department thereof, goes to the destruction of all the limits prescribed to their power by the Constitution; that words meant by that instrument to be subsidiary only to the execution of the limited powers, ought not to be so construed as themselves to give unlimited powers, nor a part so to be taken as to destroy the whole residue of the instrument; that the proceedings of the general government, under color of those articles,

will be a fit and necessary subject for revisal and correction at a time of greater tranquility, while those specified in the preceding resolutions call for immediate redress.

8. *Resolved,* That the preceding resolutions be transmitted to the senators and representatives in Congress from this commonwealth, who are enjoined to present the same to their respective houses, and to use their best endeavors to procure, at the next session of Congress, a repeal of the aforesaid unconstitutional and obnoxious acts.

9. *Resolved,* lastly, That the governor of the commonwealth be, and is, authorized and requested to communicate the preceding resolutions to the legislatures of the several states, to assure them that this commonwealth considers union for special national purposes, and particularly for those specified in their late federal compact, to be friendly to the peace, happiness, and prosperity, of all the states; that, faithful to that compact according to the plain intent and meaning in which it was understood and acceded to by the several parties, it is sincerely anxious for its preservation.

That it does also believe that, to take from the states all the powers of self-government, and transfer them to a general and consolidated government, without regard to the special government, and reservations solemnly agreed to in that compact, is not for the peace, happiness, or prosperity of these states; and that, therefore, this commonwealth is determined, as it doubts not its co-states are, to submit to undelegated and consequently unlimited powers in no man, or body of men, on earth; that, if the acts before specified should stand, these conclusions would flow from them.

That the general government may place any act they think proper on the list of crimes, and punish it themselves, whether enumerated or not enumerated by the Constitution as cognizable by them; that they may transfer its cognizance to the President, or any other person, who may himself be the accuser, counsel, judge, and jury, whose suspicions may be the evidence, his order the sentence, his officer the executioner, and his breast the sole record of the transaction; that a very numerous and valuable description of the inhabitants of these states, being, by this precedent, reduced, as outlaws, to absolute dominion of one man, and the barriers of the Constitution thus swept from us all, no rampart now remains against the passions and the power of a majority of Congress, to protect from a like exportation, or other grievous punishment, the minority of the same body, the legislatures, judges, governors, and counselors of the states, nor their other peaceable inhabitants, who may venture to reclaim the constitutional rights and liberties of the states and people, or who, for other causes, good

or bad, may be obnoxious to the view, or marked by the suspicions, of
the President, or be thought dangerous to his or their elections, or other
interests, public or personal.

5   That the friendless alien has been selected as the safest subject of a first
experiment; but the citizen will soon follow, or rather has already followed;
for already has a Sedition Act marked him as a prey: That these and successive acts of the same character, unless arrested on the threshold, may tend to
drive these states into revolution and blood, and will furnish new calumnies
against republican governments, and new pretexts for those who wish it to
10   be believed that man cannot be governed but by a rod of iron; that it would
be a dangerous delusion were a confidence in the men of our choice to
silence our fears for the safety of our rights; that confidence is everywhere
the parent of despotism; free government is founded in jealousy, and not
in confidence; it is jealousy, and not confidence, which prescribes limited
15   constitutions to bind down those whom we are obliged to trust with power;
that our Constitution has accordingly fixed the limits to which, and no
farther, our confidence may go; and let the honest advocate of confidence
read the Alien and Sedition Acts, and say if the Constitution has not been
wise in fixing limits to the government it created, and whether we should
20   be wise in destroying those limits; let him say what the government is, if
it be not a tyranny, which the men of our choice have conferred on the
President, and the President of our choice has assented to and accepted,
over the friendly strangers, to whom the mild spirit of our country and its
laws had pledged hospitality and protection; that the men of our choice
25   have more respected the bare suspicions of the President than the solid
rights of innocence, the claims of justification, the sacred force of truth,
and the forms and substance of law and justice.

In questions of power, then, let no more be said of confidence in man, but
bind him down from mischief by the chains of the Constitution. That this
30   commonwealth does therefore call on its co-states for an expression of their
sentiments on the acts concerning aliens, and for the punishment of certain
crimes herein before specified, plainly declaring whether these acts are or are
not authorized by the federal compact. And it doubts not that their sense will
be so announced as to prove their attachment to limited government, whether
35   general or particular, and that the rights and liberties of their co-states will be
exposed to no dangers by remaining embarked on a common bottom with
their own; but they will concur with this commonwealth in considering the
said acts as so palpably against the Constitution as to amount to an undisguised
declaration, that the compact is not meant to be the measure of the powers

of the general government, but that it will proceed in the exercise over these states of all powers whatsoever. That they will view this as seizing the rights of the states, and consolidating them in the hands of the general government, with a power assumed to bind the states, not merely in cases made federal, but in all cases whatsoever, by laws made, not with their consent, but by others   5 against their consent; that this would be to surrender the form of government we have chosen, and live under one deriving its powers from its own will, and not from our authority; and that the co-states, recurring to their natural rights not made federal, will concur in declaring these void and of no force, and will each unite with this commonwealth in requesting their repeal at the next ses-   10 sion of Congress.

COUNTER-RESOLUTIONS

State of Delaware

1 FEBRUARY 1799

Resolved, by the Senate and House of Representatives of the State of Delaware, in General Assembly met, that they consider the resolutions from the State of Virginia as a very unjustifiable interference with the general government and constituted authorities of the United States, and of dangerous tendency, and therefore not fit subject for the further consideration of the General Assembly.   5

State of Rhode Island and Providence Plantations

FEBRUARY 1799

Certain resolutions of the legislature of Virginia, passed on 21st of December last, being communicated to this Assembly,

1. *Resolved*, that, in the opinion of this legislature, the second section of third Article of the Constitution of the United States, in these words, to wit—"The judicial power shall extend to all cases arising under the laws   10 of the United States"—vests in the federal courts, exclusively, and in the Supreme Court of the United States, ultimately, the authority of deciding on the constitutionality of any act or law of the Congress of the United States.

2. *Resolved,* that for any state legislature to assume that authority would be   15
   1. Blending together legislative and judicial powers;
   2. Hazarding an interruption of the peace of the states by civil discord, in case of a diversity of opinions among the state legislatures; each state having, in that case, no resort for vindicating its own opinions but the strength of its own arm;   20
   3. Submitting most important questions of law to less competent tribunals; and,

---

Jonathan Elliot, ed., *The Debates in the Several State Conventions on the Adoption of the Federal Constitution* (Washington, DC, 1836), IV:532–39.

4. An infraction of the Constitution of the United States, expressed in plain terms.

3. *Resolved,* that, although, for the above reasons, this legislature, in their public capacity, do not feel themselves authorized to consider and decide on the constitutionality of the Sedition and Alien laws (so called), yet they are called upon, by the exigency of this occasion, to declare that, in their private opinions, these laws are within the powers delegated to Congress, and promotive of the welfare of the United States.

4. *Resolved,* that the governor communicate these resolutions to the supreme executive of the State of Virginia, and at the same time express to him that this legislature cannot contemplate, without extreme concern and regret, the many evil and fatal consequences which may flow from the very unwarrantable resolutions aforesaid of the legislature of Virginia, passed on the twenty-first day of December last.

Commonwealth of Massachusetts
9 FEBRUARY 1799

The legislature of Massachusetts, having taken into serious consideration the resolutions of the State of Virginia, passed the 21st day of December last, and communicated by his excellency the governor, relative to certain supposed infractions of the Constitution of the United States by the government thereof; and being convinced that the Federal Constitution is calculated to promote the happiness, prosperity, and safety of the people of these United States, and to maintain that union of the several states so essential to the welfare of the whole; and being bound by solemn oath to support and defend that Constitution, feel it unnecessary to make any professions of their attachment to it, or of their firm determination to support it against every aggression, foreign or domestic.

But they deem it their duty solemnly to declare that, while they hold sacred the principle that consent of the people is the only pure source of just and legitimate power, they cannot admit the right of the state legislatures to denounce the administration of that government to which the people themselves, by a solemn compact, have exclusively committed their national concerns. That, although a liberal and enlightened vigilance among the people is always to be cherished, yet an unreasonable jealousy of the men of their choice, and a recurrence to measures of extremity upon groundless or trivial pretexts, have a strong tendency to destroy all rational liberty at home and to deprive the United States of the most essential advantages in relations abroad. That this legislature are persuaded that the decision of all cases in law and equity arising under the Constitution of the United States, and the construction of all laws made in pursuance thereof, are exclusively vested by the people in the judicial courts of the United States.

That the people, in that solemn compact which is declared to be the supreme law of the land, have not constituted the state legislatures the judges of the acts or measures of the federal government, but have confided to them the power of proposing such amendments of the Constitution as shall appear to them necessary to the interests, or conformable to the wishes, of the people   5
whom they represent.

That, by this construction of the Constitution, an amicable and dispassionate remedy is pointed out for any evil which experience may prove to exist, and the peace and prosperity of the United States may be preserved without interruption.

But, should the respectable State of Virginia persist in the assumption of   10
the right to declare the acts of the national government unconstitutional, and should she oppose successfully her force and will to those of the nation, the Constitution would be reduced to a mere cipher, to the form and pageantry of authority without the energy of power; every act of the federal government which thwarted the views or checked the ambitious projects of a particular state,   15
or of its leading and influential members, would be the object of opposition and of remonstrance; while the people, convulsed and confused by the conflict between two hostile jurisdictions, enjoying the protection of neither, would be wearied into a submission to some bold leader, who would establish himself on the ruins of both.   20

The legislature of Massachusetts, although they do not themselves claim the right nor admit the authority of any of the state governments to decide upon the constitutionality of the acts of the federal government, still, lest their silence should be construed into disapprobation, or at best into a doubt as to the constitutionality of the acts referred to by the State of Virginia; and as the   25
General Assembly of Virginia has called for an expression of their sentiments, do explicitly declare that they consider the acts of Congress, commonly called "the Alien and Sedition Acts," not only constitutional, but expedient and necessary. That the former act respects a description of persons whose rights were not particularly contemplated in the Constitution of the United States,   30
who are entitled only to a temporary protection while they yield a temporary allegiance—a protection which ought to be withdrawn whenever they become "dangerous to the public safety" or are found guilty of "treasonable machina-tion" against the government. That Congress, having been especially entrusted by the people with the general defense of the nation, had not only the right,   35
but were bound, to protect it against internal as well as external foes. That the United States, at the time of passing the *Act concerning Aliens*, were threatened with actual invasion; had been driven, by the unjust and ambitious conduct of the French government, into warlike preparations, expensive and burdensome; and had then, within the bosom of the country, thousands of aliens, who, we   40
doubt not, were ready to co-operate in any external attack.

It cannot be seriously believed that the United States should have waited till the poniard had in fact been plunged. The removal of aliens is the usual preliminary of hostility, and is justified by the invariable usages of nations. Actual hostility and unhappily long been experienced, and a formal declaration of it
5 the government had reason daily to expect. The law, therefore, was just and salutary; and no officer could with so much propriety be entrusted with the execution of it as the one in whom the Constitution has reposed the executive power of the United States.

The *Sedition Act*, so called, is, in the opinion of this legislature, equally
10 defensible. The General Assembly of Virginia, in their resolve under consideration, observe that when that state, by its Convention, ratified the Federal Constitution, it expressly declared, "that, among other essential rights, the liberty of conscience and of the press cannot be cancelled, abridged, restrained, or modified by any authority of the United States," and, from its extreme anxiety to
15 guard these rights from every possible attack of sophistry or ambition, with other states, recommended an amendment for that purpose; which amendment was, in due time, annexed to the Constitution; but they did not surely expect that the proceedings of their state Convention were to explain the amendment adopted by the Union. The words of that amendment, on this subject, are, "Congress
20 shall make no law abridging the freedom of speech or of the press."

The act complained of is no abridgment of the freedom of either. The genuine liberty of speech and the press is the liberty to utter and publish the truth; but the constitutional right of the citizens to utter and publish the truth is not to be confounded with the licentiousness, in speaking and writing, that is
25 only employed in propagating falsehood and slander. This freedom of the press has been explicitly secured by most, if not all the state constitutions; and of this provision there has been generally but one construction among enlightened men—that it is a security for the rational use, and not the abuse, of the press; of which the courts of law, the juries, and people will judge. This right is not
30 infringed, but confirmed and established by the late act of Congress.

By the Constitution, the legislative, executive, and judicial departments of government are ordained and established; and general enumerated powers vested in them respectively, including those which are prohibited to the several states. Certain powers are granted, in general terms, by the people, to
35 their general government, for the purposes of their safety and protection. The government is not only empowered, but it is made their duty, to repel invasions and suppress insurrections; to guaranty to the several states a republican form of government; to protect each state against invasion, and, when applied to, against domestic violence; to hear and decide all cases in law and equity arising
40 under the Constitution, and under any treaty or law made in pursuance thereof; and all cases of admiralty and maritime jurisdiction, and relating to the law of

nations. Whenever, therefore, it becomes necessary to effect any of the objects designated, it is perfectly consonant to all just rules of construction to infer that the usual means and powers necessary to the attainment of that object are also granted. But the Constitution has left no occasion to resort to implication for these powers; it has made an express grant of them, in the 8th Section of the 1st Article, which ordains, "that Congress shall have power to make all laws which shall be necessary and proper for carrying into execution the foregoing powers, and all other powers vested by the Constitution in the government of the United States, or in any department or officer thereof."

This Constitution has established a Supreme Court of the United States, but has made no provision for its protection, even against such improper conduct in its presence, as might disturb its proceedings, unless expressed in the section before recited. But as no statute has been passed on this subject, this protection is, and has been for nine years past, uniformly found in the application of the principles and usages of the common law. The same protection may unquestionably be afforded by a statute passed in virtue of the before-mentioned section, as necessary and proper for carrying into execution the powers vested in that department. A construction of the different parts of the Constitution, perfectly just and fair, will, on analogous principles, extend protection and security, against the offences in question, to the other departments of government, in discharge of their respective trusts.

The President of the United States is bound by his oath "to preserve, protect, and defend the Constitution"; and it is expressly made his duty "to take care that the laws be faithfully executed." But this would be impracticable by any created being if there could be no legal restraint of those scandalous misrepresentations of his measures and motives which directly tend to rob him of the public confidence; and equally impotent would be every other public officer, if thus left to the mercy of the seditious.

It is holden to be a truth most clear that the important trusts before enumerated cannot be discharged by the government to which they are committed without the power to restrain seditious practices and unlawful combinations against itself, and to protect the officers thereof from abusive misrepresentations. Had the Constitution withheld this power, it would have made the government responsible for the effects without any control over the causes which naturally produce them, and would have essentially failed of answering the great ends for which the people of the United States declare, in the first clause of that instrument, that they establish the same—viz., "to form a more perfect union, establish justice, insure domestic tranquility, provide for the common defense, promote the general welfare, and secure the blessings of liberty to ourselves and posterity."

Seditious practices and unlawful combinations against the federal government, or any officer thereof, in the performance of his duty, as well as

licentiousness of speech and of the press, were punishable, on the principles of common law, in the courts of the United States before the act in question was passed. This act, then, is an amelioration of that law in favor of the party accused, as it mitigates the punishment which that authorizes, and admits of
5 any investigation of public men and measures which is regulated by truth. It is not intended to protect men in office, only as they are agents of the people. Its object is to afford legal security to public offices and trusts created for the safety and happiness of the people, and therefore the security derived from it is for the benefit of the people, and is their right.
10 This construction of the Constitution, and of the existing law of the land, as well as the act complained of, the legislature of Massachusetts most deliberately and firmly believe, results from a just and full view of the several parts of the Constitution; and they consider that act to be wise and necessary, as an audacious and unprincipled spirit of falsehood and abuse had been too
15 long unremittingly exerted for the purpose of perverting public opinion, and threatened to undermine and destroy the whole fabric of government.

The legislature further declare that in the foregoing sentiments they have expressed the general opinion of their constituents, who have not only acquiesced without complaint in those particular measures of the federal government, but
20 have given their explicit approbation by re-electing those men who voted for the adoption of them. Nor is it apprehended that the citizens of this state will be accused of supineness, or of an indifference to their constitutional rights; for while, on the one hand, they regard with due vigilance the conduct of the government, on the other, their freedom, safety, and happiness required that
25 they should defend that government and its constitutional measures against the open or insidious attacks of any foe, whether foreign or domestic.

And, lastly, that the legislature of Massachusetts feel a strong conviction that the several United States are connected by a common interest, which ought to render their union indissoluble; and that this state will always co-operate with
30 its confederate states in rendering that union productive of mutual security, freedom, and happiness.

State of New York

5 MARCH 1799

Whereas the people of the United States have established for themselves a free and independent national government. And whereas it is essential to the existence of every government that it have authority to defend and preserve its
35 constitutional powers inviolate, inasmuch as every infringement thereof tends to its subversion. And whereas the judicial power extends expressly to all cases of law and equity arising under the Constitution and the laws of the United States, whereby the interference of the legislatures of the particular states in

those cases is manifestly excluded. And whereas our peace, prosperity, and happiness eminently depend on the preservation of the Union, in order to which a reasonable confidence in the constituted authorities and chosen representatives of the people is indispensable. And whereas every measure calculated to weaken that confidence has a tendency to destroy the usefulness of our public   5
functionaries, and to excite jealousies equally hostile to rational liberty, and the principles of a good republican government. And whereas the Senate, not perceiving that the rights of the particular states have been violated, nor any unconstitutional powers assumed by the general government, cannot forbear to express the anxiety and regret with which they observe the inflammatory and   10
pernicious sentiments and doctrines which are contained in the resolutions of the legislatures of Virginia and Kentucky—sentiments and doctrines no less repugnant to the Constitution of the United States, and the principles of their union, than destructive to the federal government and unjust to those whom the people have elected to administer it; wherefore   15

Resolved, that while the Senate feel themselves constrained to bear unequivocal testimony against such sentiments and doctrines, they deem it a duty no less indispensable explicitly to declare their incompetency, as a branch of the legislature of this state, to supervise the acts of the general government.

Resolved, that his excellency, the governor, be, and he is hereby, requested   20
to transmit a copy of the foregoing resolution to the executives of the states of Virginia and Kentucky, to the end that the same may be communicated to the legislatures thereof.

State of Connecticut

MAY 1799

At a General Assembly of the state of Connecticut, holden at Hartford, in the said state, on the second Thursday of May, *Anno Domini* 1799, his excellency,   25
the Governor, having communicated to this Assembly sundry resolutions of the legislature of Virginia, adopted in December 1798, which relate to the measure of the general government, and the said resolutions having been considered, it is

Resolved, that this Assembly views with deep regret, and explicitly disavows, the principles contained in the aforesaid resolutions, and particularly the opposi-   30
tion to the "alien and Sedition Acts"—acts which the Constitution authorized, which the exigency of the country rendered necessary, which the constituted authorities have enacted, and which merit the entire approbation of this Assembly. They, therefore, decidedly refuse to concur with the legislature of Virginia in promoting any of the objects attempted in the aforesaid resolutions.   35

And it is further resolved, that his excellency, the Governor, be requested to transmit a copy of the foregoing resolution to the governor of Virginia, that it may be communicated to the legislature of that state.

State of New Hampshire

14 JUNE 1799

The legislature of New Hampshire, having taken into consideration certain resolutions of the General Assembly of Virginia, dated December 21, 1798; also certain resolutions of the legislature of Kentucky, of the 10th of November 1798:

Resolved, that the legislature of New Hampshire unequivocally express a
5 firm resolution to maintain and defend the Constitution of the United States, and the Constitution of this state, against every aggression, either foreign or domestic, and that they will support the government of the United States in all measures warranted by the former.

That the state legislatures are not the proper tribunals to determine the
10 constitutionality of the laws of the general government; that the duty of such decision is properly and exclusively confided to the judicial department.

That, if the legislature of New Hampshire, for more speculative purposes, were to express an opinion on the acts of the general government, commonly called "the Alien and Sedition Bills," that opinion would unreservedly be that
15 those acts are constitutional and, in the present critical situation of our country, highly expedient.

That the constitutionality and expediency of the acts aforesaid have been very ably advocated and clearly demonstrated by many citizens of the United States, more especially by the minority of the General Assembly of Virginia. The
20 legislature of New Hampshire, therefore, deem it unnecessary, by any train of arguments, to attempt further illustration of the propositions, the truth of which, it is confidently believed, at this day, is very generally seen and acknowledged.

State of Vermont

30 OCTOBER 1799

The house proceeded to take under their consideration the resolutions of the General Assembly of Virginia, relative to certain measures of the general gov-
25 ernment, transmitted to the legislature of this state, for their consideration. Whereupon,

Resolved, that the General Assembly of the State of Vermont do highly disapprove of the resolutions of the General Assembly of Virginia as being unconstitutional in their nature, and dangerous in their tendency. It belongs
30 not to state legislatures to decide on the constitutionality of laws made by the general government, this power being exclusively vested in the judiciary courts of the Union. That his excellency, the Governor, be requested to transmit a copy of this resolution to the executive of Virginia, to be communicated to the General Assembly of that state. And that the same be sent to the governor and
35 council for their concurrence.

First Inaugural Address
Thomas Jefferson (1743–1826)
President of the United States (1801–1809)

Jefferson's point of view prevailed in the election of 1800. His Inaugu-
ral Address marked a crucial point in the nation's history—an orderly
transfer of power under the rule of law. It also outlined the principles of
republican government that dominated American politics for the next
fifty years. These principles—equal justice to all men, majority rule,
economy in government, freedom of the individual—were different from
Washington's only in emphasis, and the two agreed absolutely on the
need to remain free of "entangling alliances" with foreign governments.
Jefferson underscored the necessity for America's independence in his
instructions to Robert Livingston by pointing out the strategic importance
of New Orleans. When in 1803 the French offered the Louisiana Ter-
ritory for sale, Jefferson violated his most basic constitutional principles
to buy it. The most republican of Republicans put the national interest
ahead of his own ideals.

4 March 1801

Called upon to undertake the duties of the first executive office of our country;
I avail myself of the presence of that portion of my fellow-citizens which is
here assembled to express my grateful thanks for the favor with which they
have been pleased to look towards me, to declare a sincere consciousness that
the task is above my talents, and that I approach it with those anxious and   5
awful presentiments which the greatness of the charge, and the weakness of
my powers so justly inspire. A rising nation, spread over a wide and fruitful land, traversing all the seas with the rich productions of their industry,
engaged in commerce with nations who feel power and forget right, advancing rapidly to destinies beyond the reach of mortal eye; when I contemplate   10
these transcendant objects, and see the honor, the happiness, and the hopes
of this beloved country committed to the issue and the auspices of this day,
I shrink from the contemplation and humble myself before the magnitude

Maryland Gazette (12 March 1801):2–3.

of the undertaking. Utterly indeed should I despair, did not the presence of
many, whom I here see, remind me, that, in the other high authorities provided by our constitution, I shall find resources of wisdom, of virtue, and of
zeal, on which to rely under all difficulties. To you, then gentlemen, who are
5   charged with the sovereign functions of legislation, and to those associated
with you, I look with encouragement for that guidance and support which
may enable us to steer with safety the vessel in which we are all embarked,
amidst the conflicting elements of a troubled world.

     During the contest of opinion through which we have past, the animation
10 of discussion and of exertions has sometimes worn an aspect which might
impose on strangers unused to think freely, and to speak and to write what
they think; but this being now decided by the voice of the union, announced
according to the rules of the constitution, all will of course arrange themselves
under the will of the law, and unite in common efforts for the common good.
15 All too will bear in mind this sacred principle, that though the will of the
majority is in all cases to prevail, that will, to be rightful, must be reasonable;
that the minority possess their equal rights, which equal laws must protect,
and to violate would be oppression. Let us then, fellow-citizens, unite with
one heart and one mind, let us restore to social intercourse that harmony and
20 affection without which liberty, and even life itself, are but dreary things. And
let us reflect that having banished from our land that religious intolerance
under which mankind so long bled and suffered, we have yet gained little, if
we countenance a political intolerance, as despotic, as wicked, and capable
of as bitter and bloody persecutions. During the throes and convulsions of
25 the ancient world, during the agonizing spasm of infuriated man, seeking
through blood and slaughter his long lost liberty, it was not wonderful that
the agitation of the billows should reach even this distant and peaceful shore;
that this should be more felt and feared by some and less by others; and should
divide opinions as to measures of safety; but every difference of opinion is
30 not a difference of principle. We are all republicans: we are all federalists. If
there be any among us who would wish to dissolve this Union, or to change
its republican form, let them stand undisturbed as monuments of the safety
with which error of opinion may be tolerated, where reason is left free to
combat it. I know indeed that some honest men fear that a republican gov-
35 ernment cannot be strong; that this government is not strong enough. But
would the honest patriot, in the full tide of successful experiment, abandon
a government which has so far kept us free and firm, on the theoretic and
visionary fear, that this government, the world's best hope, may, by possibility, want energy to preserve itself? I trust not. I believe this, on the contrary,
40 the strongest government on earth—I believe it the only one, where every

man, at the call of the law, would fly to the standard of the law, and would meet invasions of the public order as his own personal concern. Sometimes it is said that man cannot be trusted with the government of himself. Can he then be trusted with the government of others? Or have we found angels, in the form of kings, to govern him? Let history answer this question.   5

Let us then, with courage and confidence, pursue our own federal and republican principles: our attachment to union and representative government. Kindly separated by nature and a wide ocean front the exterminating havoc of one quarter of the globe; too high minded to endure the degradations of the others, possessing a chosen country, with room enough for our   10
descendants to the thousandth and thousandth generation, entertaining a due sense of our equal right to the use of our own faculties, to the acquisitions of our own industry, to honor and confidence from our fellow-citizens, resulting not from birth, but from our actions and their sense of them, enlightened by a benign religion, professed indeed and practiced in various forms, yet   15
all of them inculcating honesty, truth, temperance, gratitude and the love of man, acknowledging and adoring an overruling Providence, which by all its dispensations proves that it delights in the happiness of man here, and his greater happiness hereafter; with all these blessings what more is necessary to make us a happy and a prosperous people? Still one thing more, fellow-   20
citizens, a wise and frugal government, which shall restrain men from injuring one another, shall leave them otherwise free to regulate their own pursuits of industry and improvement, and shall not take from the mouth of labor the bread it has earned. This is the sum of good government; and this is necessary to close the circle of our felicities.   25

About to enter, fellow-citizens, on the exercise of duties which comprehend every thing dear and valuable to you, it is proper you should understand what I deem the essential principles of our government, and consequently those which ought to shape its administration. I will compress them within the narrowest compass they will bear, stating the general principle, but not   30
all its limitations. Equal and exact justice to all men, of whatever state or persuasion, religious or political:—peace, commerce, and honest friendship with all nations, entangling alliances with none:—the support of the state governments in all their rights, as the most competent administrations for our domestic concerns, and the surest bulwarks against anti-republican tenden-   35
cies:—the preservation of the general government in its whole constitutional vigor, as the sheet anchor of our peace at home, and safety abroad; a zealous care of the right of election by the people, a mild and safe corrective of abuses which are lopped by the sword of revolution where peaceable remedies are unprovided:—absolute acquiescence in the decisions of the majority, the vital   40

principle of republics, from which is no appeal but to force, the vital principle and immediate parent of despotism: a well disciplined militia, our best reliance in peace, and for the first moments of war, till regulars may relieve them: the supremacy of the civil over the military authority: economy in the public expense, that labor may be lightly burthened: the honest payment of our debts and sacred preservation of the public faith: encouragement of agriculture, and of commerce as its handmaid: the diffusion of information, and arraignment of all abuses at the bar of the public reason: freedom of religion; freedom of the press; and freedom of person, under the protection of the habeas corpus: and trial by juries impartially selected. These principles form the bright constellation, which has gone before us, and guided our steps through an age of revolution and reformation. The wisdom of our sages, and blood of our heroes, have been devoted to their attainment; they should be the creed of our political faith; the text of civic instruction, the touchstone by which to try the services of those we trust; and should we wander from them in moments of error or of alarm, let us hasten to retrace our steps, and to regain the road which alone leads to peace, liberty and safety.

I repair then, fellow-citizens, to the post you have assigned me. With experience enough in subordinate offices to have seen the difficulties of this the greatest of all, I have learnt to expect that it will rarely fall to the lot of imperfect man to retire from this station with the reputation, and the favor, which bring him into it. Without pretensions to that high confidence you reposed in our first and greatest revolutionary character, whose pre-eminent services had entitled him to the first place in his country's love, and destined for him the fairest page in the volume of faithful history, I ask so much confidence only as may give firmness and effect to the legal administration of your affairs. I shall often go wrong through defect of judgment. When right, I shall often be thought wrong by those whose positions will not command a view of the whole ground. I ask your indulgence for my own errors, which will never be intentional; and your support against the errors of others, who may condemn what they would not if seen in all its parts. The approbation implied by your suffrage; is a great consolation to me for the past; and my future solicitude will be, to retain the good opinion of those who have bestowed it in advance, to conciliate that of others by doing them all the good in my power, and to be instrumental to the happiness and freedom of all.

Relying then on the patronage of your good will, I advance with obedience to the work, ready to resign from it whenever you become sensible how much better choice it is in your power to make. And may that Infinite Power, which rules the destinies of the universe, lead our councils to what is best, and give them a favorable issue for your peace and prosperity.

LETTER

THOMAS JEFFERSON (1743–1826)
PRESIDENT OF THE UNITED STATES (1801–1809)
TO ROBERT LIVINGSTON (1746–1813)
U.S. MINISTER TO FRANCE (1801–1804)

18 APRIL 1802

The cession of Louisiana and the Floridas by Spain to France works most sorely on the United States. On this subject the Secretary of State[1] has written to you fully, yet I cannot forbear recurring to it personally, so deep is the impression it makes on my mind. It completely reverses all the political relations of the United States, and will form a new epoch in our political course. 5

Of all nations, of any consideration, France is the one which, hitherto, has offered the fewest points on which we could have any conflict of right, and the most points of a communion of interests. From these causes, we have ever looked to her as our natural friend, as one with which we never could have an occasion of difference. Her growth, therefore, we viewed as our own—her 10 misfortunes ours.

There is on the globe one single spot, the possessor of which is our natural and habitual enemy. It is New Orleans, through which the produce of three-eighths of our territory must pass to market, and from its fertility it will ere long yield more than half of our whole produce, and contain more than half of our inhabitants. 15 France, placing herself in that door, assumes to us the attitude of defiance.

Spain might have retained it quietly for years. Her pacific dispositions, her feeble state, would induce her to increase our facilities there, so that her possession of the place would be hardly felt by us, and it would not, perhaps, be very long before some circumstance might arise which might make the cession 20 of it to us the price of something of more worth to her.

Not so can it ever be in the hands of France: the impetuosity of her temper, the energy and restlessness of her character, placed in a point of eternal friction with us, and our character, which, though quiet and loving peace and the pursuit of wealth, is high-minded, despising wealth in competition with insult or injury, 25 enterprising and energetic as any nation on earth; these circumstances render it

---

[1]James Madison (1751–1836), U.S. Secretary of State (1801–1809)

Henry S. Randall, *The Life of Thomas Jefferson* (New York: Derby and Jackson, 1858), III:6–7.

impossible that France and the United States can continue long friends, when they meet in so irritable a position. They, as well as we, must be blind if they do not see this; and we must be very improvident if we do not begin to make arrangements on that hypothesis.

5   The day that France takes possession of New Orleans fixes the sentence which is to restrain her forever within her low-water mark. It seals the union of two nations who, in conjunction, can maintain exclusive possession of the ocean. From that moment we must marry ourselves to the British fleet and nation. We must turn all our attentions to a maritime force, for which our resources place

10   us on very high ground, and having formed and connected together a power which may render reinforcement of her settlement here impossible to France, make the first cannon which shall be fired in Europe the signal for tearing up any settlement she may have made, and for holding the two continents of America in sequestration for the common purposes of the United British and

15   American nations.

The day that France takes possession of New Orleans is not a state of things we seek or desire. It is one which this measure, if adopted by France, forces on us, as necessarily as any other cause, by the laws of nature, brings on its necessary effect. It is not from a fear of France that we deprecate this measure proposed by her. For however greater her force is than

20   ours, compared in the abstract, it is nothing in comparison of ours when to be exerted on our soil.

But it is from a sincere love of peace, and a firm persuasion that bound to France by the interests and the strong sympathies still existing in the minds of our citizens, and holding relative positions which insure their continuance, we

25   are secure of a long course of peace. Whereas, the change of friends, which will be rendered necessary if France changes that position, embarks us necessarily as a belligerent power in the first war of Europe. In that case, France will have held possession of New Orleans during the interval of a peace, long or short, at the end of which it will be wrested from her. Will this short-lived posses-

30   sion have been an equivalent to her for the transfer of such a weight into the scale of her enemy? Will not the amalgamation of a young, thriving nation, continue to that enemy the health and force which are at present so evidently on the decline? And will a few years' possession of New Orleans add equally to the strength of France? She may say she needs Louisiana for the supply of her

35   West Indies. She does not need it in time of peace, and in war she could not depend on them, because they would be so easily intercepted.

I should suppose that all these considerations might, in some proper form, be brought into view of the government of France. Though stated by us, it ought not to give offence; because we do not bring them forward as a menace,

40   but as consequences not controllable by us, but inevitable from the course of

things. We mention them, not as things which we desire by any means, but as things we deprecate; and we beseech a friend to look forward and to prevent them for our common interests.

If France considers Louisiana, however, as indispensable for her views, she might perhaps be willing to look about for arrangements which might reconcile   5 it to our interests. If anything could do this, it would be the ceding to us the island of New Orleans and the Floridas. This would certainly, in a great degree, remove the causes of jarring and irritation between us, and perhaps for such a length of time as might produce other means of making the measure permanently conciliatory to our interests and friendships. It would, at any rate, relieve   10 us from the necessity of taking immediate measures for countervailing such an operation by arrangements in another quarter. But still we should consider New Orleans and the Floridas as no equivalent for the risk of a quarrel with France produced by her vicinage.

I have no doubt you have urged these considerations, on every proper   15 occasion, with the government where you are. They are such as must have effect, if you can find means of producing thorough reflection on them by that government. The idea here is that the troops sent to Saint Domingo were to proceed to Louisiana after finishing their work in that island. If this were the arrangement, it will give you time to return again and again to the charge. For   20 the conquest of Saint Domingo will not be a short work. It will take considerable time, and wear down a great number of soldiers. Every eye in the United States is now fixed on the affairs of Louisiana. Perhaps nothing since the Revolutionary War has produced more uneasy sensations through the body of the nation. Notwithstanding temporary bickerings have taken place with France, she has   25 still a strong hold on the affections of our citizens generally. I have thought it not amiss, by way of supplement to the letters of the Secretary of State, to write you this private one, to impress you with the importance we affix to this transaction.

THE PLEASURES OF AGRICULTURE
JOHN M. TAYLOR (1753–1824)

*In 1800 nearly nine-tenths of Americans lived on the land and were
dependent on its bounty for their livelihood. Today almost ninety-eight
out of a hundred Americans earn their livings from something other than
agriculture. If today's political culture is inspired by the business of business,
Jeffersonian America drew its moral capital from the land.*

*John Taylor of Caroline County, Virginia, was so much a strict con-
stitutional republican that he opposed Jefferson's purchase of Louisiana.
Taylor was first and last a farmer and believed that republics were based on
the virtues of agricultural life. To him the created order demanded private
property and the stewardship of the land. Agriculture united true religion
and patriotism. Taylor was an American Cato, and believed that the American republic should aspire to the* pietas *of the Roman republic. His veriest
enemies were strong government and standing armies, both of which he was
convinced produced heavy taxation, and thus destroyed agriculture.*

1813

In free countries are more, and in enslaved, fewer, than the pleasures of most
other employments. The reason of it is that agriculture both from its nature, and
also as being generally the employment of a great portion of a nation, cannot
be united with power, considered as an exclusive interest. It must of course be
enslaved wherever despotism exists, and its masters will enjoy more pleasures   5
in that case than it can ever reach. On the contrary, where power is not an
exclusive, but a general, interest, agriculture can employ its own energies for
the attainment of its own happiness.

Under a free government it has before it the inexhaustible sources of
human pleasure, of fitting ideas to substances, and substances to ideas; and of   10
a constant rotation of hope and fruition.

The novelty, frequency, and exactness of accommodations between our ideas
and operations constitutes the most exquisite source of mental pleasure. Agricul-

John Taylor, *Arator: Being a Series of Agricultural Essays, Practical and Political* (Baltimore:
J. Robinson, 1817), 178–81 [modernized].

ture feeds it with endless supplies in the natures of soils, plants, climates, manures, instruments of culture, and domestic animals. Their combinations are inexhaustible, the novelty of results is endless, discrimination and adaption are never idle, and an unsatiated interest receives gratifications in quick succession.

5 Benevolence is so closely associated with this interest that its exertion in numberless instances is necessary to foster it. Liberality in supplying its laborers with the comforts of life is the best sponsor for the prosperity of agriculture, and the practice of almost every moral virtue is amply remunerated in this world, whilst it is also the best surety for attaining the blessings of the next.

10 Poetry, in allowing more virtue to agriculture than to any other profession, has abandoned her privilege of fiction, and yielded to the natural moral effect of the absence of temptation. The same fact is commemorated by religion, upon an occasion the most solemn within the scope of the human imagination. At the awful day of judgment, the discrimination of the good from the wicked is

15 not made by the criterion of sects or of dogmas, but by one which constitutes the daily employment and the great end of agriculture. The judge upon this occasion has by anticipation pronounced that to feed the hungry, clothe the naked, and give drink to the thirsty are the passports to future happiness; and the divine intelligence which selected an agricultural state as a paradise for its

20 first favorites has here again prescribed the agricultural virtues as the means for the admission of their posterity into heaven.

With the pleasures of religion, agriculture unites those of patriotism, and among the worthy competitors for pre-eminence in the practice of this cardinal virtue, a profound author assigns a high station to him who has made two

25 blades of grass grow instead of one; an idea capable of a signal amplification by a comparison between a system of agriculture which doubles the fertility of a country and a successful war which doubles its territory. By the first the territory itself is also substantially doubled, without wasting the lives, the wealth, or the liberty of the nation which has thus subdued sterility, and drawn prosperity

30 from a willing source. By the second, the blood pretended to be enriched is split; the wealth pretended to be increased is wasted; the liberty said to be secured is immolated to the patriotism of a victorious army; and desolation in every form is made to stalk in the glittering garb of false glory throughout some neighboring country. Moral law decides the preference with undeviating consistency in

35 assigning to the nation which elects true patriotism the recompense of truth, and to the electors of the false, the expiation of error. To the respective agents, the same law assigns the remorses of a conqueror, and the quiet conscience of the agriculturist.

The capacity of agriculture for affording luxuries to the body is not less

40 conspicuous than its capacity for affording luxuries to the mind; it being a science

singularly possessing the double qualities of feeding with unbounded liberality both the moral appetites of the one and the physical wants of the other. It can even feed a morbid love of money, whilst it is habituating us to the practice of virtue; and whilst it provides for the wants of the philosopher, it affords him ample room for the most curious and yet useful researches. In short, by the exercise it gives both to the body and to the mind, it secures health and vigor to both; and by combining a thorough knowledge of the real affairs of life with a necessity for investigating the arcana of nature, and the strongest invitations to the practice of morality, it becomes the best architect of a complete man.

If this eulogy should succeed in awakening the attention of men of science to a skillful practice of agriculture, they will become models for individuals, and guardians for national happiness. The discoveries of the learned will be practiced by the ignorant; and a system which sheds happiness, plenty, and virtue all around will be gradually substituted for one which fosters vice, breeds want, and begets misery.

Politicians (who ought to know the most, and generally know the least, of a science in which the United States are more deeply interested than in any other) will appear of more practical knowledge, or at least of better theoretical instruction; and the hopeless habit of confiding our greatest interest to people most ignorant of it, will be abandoned.

The errors of politicians ignorant of agriculture, or their projects designed to oppress it, can only rob it of its pleasures, and consign it to contempt and misery. This revolution of its natural state is invariably affected by war, armies, heavy taxes, or exclusive privileges. In two cases alone have nations ever gained anything by war— those of repelling invasion and emigrating into a more fruitful territory. In every other case, the industrious of all professions suffer by war, the effects of which in its modern form are precisely the same to the victorious and the vanquished nation. The least evil to be apprehended from victorious armies is a permanent system of heavy taxation, than which nothing can more vitally wound or kill the pleasures of agriculture. Of the same stamp are exclusive privileges in every form; and to pillage or steal under the sanction of the statute books is no less fatal to the happiness of agriculture than the hierarchical tyranny over the soul under the pretended sanction of God, or the feudal tyranny over the body under the equally fraudulent pretense of defending the nation. In a climate and soil where good culture never fails to beget plenty, where bad cannot produce famine, begirt by nature against the risk of invasion, and favored by the accident with the power of self-government, agriculture can only lose its happiness by the folly or fraud of statesmen, or by its own ignorance.

IV
DEMOCRATIZATION AND EXPANSION

Historians of the American republic have often characterized the period after 1815 as an "Era of Good Feelings." The end of the War of 1812 and the settlement of the Napoleonic Wars at the Congress of Vienna brought several decades of relative peace to the Western world. This peace allowed millions of Europeans to emigrate to the United States, which helped to fuel the drive westward to the Pacific Ocean. Thomas Jefferson (1743–1826) believed that American acquisition and settlement of these vast territories might take a thousand years; in fact, it took only about fifty years from the time of the Louisiana Purchase (1803). Immigration and westward expansion were two aspects of a larger release of energy in the republic: Political, religious, and entrepreneurial energy began to challenge virtually all institutions of authority and to transform a small republic into a large democracy.

The outcome of the War of 1812 greatly affected the political climate in the United States for decades. General Andrew Jackson's lopsided victory over the British at the Battle of New Orleans in January 1815 (a battle fought after the peace treaty was signed, but before it was ratified) helped to convince Americans that the war was a success, and a flush of nationalistic sentiment swept over the republic. These developments spelled doom for the Federalist Party, which had opposed the war and thus appeared to be little more than a bitter and disloyal faction. In 1816 and again in 1820, the Republican Party captured the White House and also continued its domination of Congress. This so-called "Republican Ascendancy" ushered in an era of one-party rule on the national level, a period often dubbed by historians the "Era of Good Feelings" for its political stability and explosive economic growth.

The political comity of the "Era of Good Feelings" came to an abrupt end with the contentious presidential election of 1824. The Battle of New Orleans had transformed Andrew Jackson (1767–1845) of Tennessee into a national hero, and a group of skillful political handlers sought to parlay this renown into a stint in the White House for "Old Hickory." Jackson won a plurality of all electoral and popular votes cast, but he was denied the presidency when the election was decided in the House of Representatives. There, Congressman Henry Clay (1777–1852) of Kentucky (who had also been a candidate for president that year) used his influence to swing the election to John Quincy

Adams (1767–1848), the son of the nation's second president. Adams had been the runner-up to Jackson in both popular and electoral votes, and Jackson's supporters howled in protest when the diplomat from Massachusetts emerged as the victor. The protests became louder and more bitter when Adams selected Henry Clay as his Secretary of State—a position that had been traditionally regarded as a stepping-stone to the presidency. Jackson charged that Clay had obtained his position through "bargain and corruption," a claim that Clay and Adams plausibly denied. Jackson also insisted that the will of the people had been thwarted, and he and his supporters mobilized a widespread political effort to install the general in the White House four years later. Jackson realized his objective in 1828, but his hatred for Henry Clay did not subside with his political success.

While Jackson's long-running feud with Henry Clay was indeed personal, it also reflected competing visions of America's economic future. Clay was a devotee of Alexander Hamilton's nationalistic financial program, and he supported the national bank, protective tariffs, and national financing for internal improvements as a means for creating a unified national economy based on manufacturing and commerce. Clay's version of this agenda, his so-called "American System," served as the basis for his 1824 campaign for the presidency. Jackson, a self-styled Jeffersonian agrarian, vehemently opposed each element of Clay's program. While Jackson had qualms about the constitutionality of a national bank, his staunch opposition to it stemmed more from his sense that such an institution conveyed special privileges to a handful of investors at the expense of the American people as a whole. With the twin rallying cries of "monopoly" and "privilege," Jackson and his supporters embarked on a crusade to crush the Bank of the United States, which, ironically enough, had been re-authorized in 1816 by strict constructionist James Madison (r. 1809–1817). As in so many other battles, Jackson emerged victorious in this one, and the national bank ceased to exist when its twenty-year charter was allowed to expire in 1836.

Jackson also opposed the protective tariff on the grounds of fairness. While he did not object to tariffs intended strictly to raise revenue, he believed that protective tariffs conveyed special privileges to certain sectors of the economy at the expense of the rest. Likewise, with varying degrees of consistency he refused to support national funding for internal improvements. Jackson argued that the Constitution did not grant the national government the power to back such enterprises, and he insisted that the American people should not be compelled to support projects of a purely local character.

Underpinning Jackson's political philosophy was a deep-seated faith in the ability of free men to govern themselves wisely. Declaring that the first principle of the American political system is "that the majority is to govern," Jackson sought to remove all impediments to the direct expression of the popular will. One such impediment was the electoral college, which the Framers of the Constitution instituted as a check upon the turbulent passions of the electorate. Jackson believed that the president was the only legitimate and effective representative of the will of the American people as a whole, and he did not hesitate to use the powers of the presidency to implement that will.

Jackson's liberal use of presidential powers provoked a backlash among those who believed that the Old Hero was undermining the republic and attempting to install an executive tyranny. The president's imperious style and frequent use of the veto pen led detractors to dub him "King Andrew the First," and key senators such as Henry Clay, Daniel Webster (1782–1852), and John C. Calhoun (1782–1850) began to organize an anti-Jackson opposition. The president's political opponents acquired the name "Whigs" (derived from the party in England with the same name that traditionally worked to limit royal power), and consequently the so-called "Second Party System" of American politics emerged.

Jackson's Democrats tended to draw the majority of their support from yeomen, small businessmen, and the working classes, while the opposing Whigs could typically boast support from large planters, manufacturers, and commercial interests. However, these tendencies were just that—tendencies—and political support in the Jacksonian period was often fluid. It must be remembered that both the Democrats and the Whigs were national parties that attracted supporters from a wide cross-section of the populace, and the demise of these parties as national institutions in the 1850s did much to promote the forces of disunion.

Although Jackson is frequently credited (or charged) with fundamentally altering the republic by ushering in an era of democratization in American politics, he should be regarded more as a symbol of such trends than as their cause. Well before Jackson's arrival in the White House, the shift toward popular democracy was proceeding apace in the states. Property qualifications for voting were modified or abolished, and universal adult white male suffrage became the rule rather than the exception. The French reformer Alexis de Tocqueville (1805–1859) eyed these developments nervously, famously opining in his work *Democracy in America* that democratic government in the United States was trending toward a "tyranny of the majority" that might eviscerate liberty and the nation's most cherished institutions.

The democratization of American politics in the Jacksonian era resembled developments that were occurring within the nation's Christian churches. Protestant denominations in particular experienced a widespread and intense religious revival typically referred to as the "Second Great Awakening." While the origins of the revival can be traced back at least as far as the 1790s, when preachers such as Yale University president Timothy Dwight IV (1752–1817) defended orthodox Christian beliefs from the perceived threat of deism, the Second Great Awakening did not reach its apex until the opening decades of the nineteenth century.

Much like the First Great Awakening of the eighteenth century, the Second Great Awakening was pietistic and reflected a general disdain for liturgy, clerical authority, and theological purity. Traveling preachers known as itinerants roamed the countryside, drawing immense crowds to hear sermons that exhorted listeners to establish a personal relationship with God. Unlike the First Great Awakening, however, the Second Great Awakening was characterized by a broad rejection of traditional Calvinism. The Presbyterian minister Charles Grandison Finney (1792–1875), the revival's most influential leader, spoke for most of the movement's leading lights when he announced that God's gift of eternal life was available to all who were willing to accept it. In this democratic view of salvation, the doctrine of original sin was de-emphasized in favor of the belief that sin was a choice that people made freely. Consequently, people were not sinful by nature and thus could choose to live godly lives free of immoral behavior.

The Second Great Awakening's emphasis on sin as a choice had profound implications for social reform. Evangelists like Lyman Beecher (1775–1863), a student of Timothy Dwight, insisted that Christians could choose to eradicate sin from their own lives and, by extension, could assist in the eradication of sin in the broader society. According to many Christians, success in this endeavor would usher in the millennium—a thousand-year period of righteousness that would prepare the way for Christ's return to Earth. Thus, it is not surprising that Christian revivalists were often at the forefront of some of the most significant reform efforts of the Jacksonian period.

Christian millennial thinking, coupled with secular impulses toward social perfection spawned by the American Revolution and its aftermath, helped to produce a reform ferment without precedent in American history. Proponents of causes as varied as temperance, antislavery, and education shared an optimistic view of human nature that regarded social ills as consequences of moral failings that could be eradicated. These reformers argued that collective action was needed to encourage proper behavior as well as to eliminate environmental factors that led otherwise good people astray. Temperance advocates, for example, insisted that social problems such as poverty and domestic violence could be prevented or significantly reduced by removing alcohol from people's lives. Education reformers endorsed tax-supported public schools in large part to prepare the nation's youth to become informed citizens as well as to inculcate them with Protestant cultural values—supposed prerequisites for the success of an increasingly democratic government. Antislavery crusaders, for their part, hoped to eliminate an environmental force that prevented some humans from achieving their full potential—the institution of chattel slavery.

As America's political and religious institutions experienced a fundamental shift toward democracy, the nation's economy underwent a transformation as well. In the South, the exponential growth of cotton cultivation reinvigorated the demand for slave labor and enabled wealthy planters to wield disproportionate political, economic, and social power within their states and local communities. Concurrently, the North's economy was disproportionately affected by forces that historians have labeled the "Market Revolution." Farmers increasingly shifted away from subsistence agriculture and toward the production of crops that were to be sold locally, nationally, and even internationally. The region's manufacturing base grew slowly but steadily as well, with most production concentrated in the Northeast. Banking and commerce also advanced steadily in the North, fostered in part by the piecemeal implementation of the elements of Henry Clay's American System.

The fundamental political, religious, economic, and social shifts that occurred in the United States during the Jacksonian era found a common expression in the impulse to extend American culture to the far reaches of North America and beyond. This idea, commonly referred to as "Manifest Destiny," held that the United States had a God-sanctioned duty to spread Christianity and the other benefits of "white civilization" to the less fortunate peoples of the world. Influential figures ranging from Senators Thomas Hart Benton (1782–1858) and Stephen A. Douglas (1813–1861) to newspaper editor John L. O'Sullivan (1813–1895) argued that the United States was a nation of human progress—"the great nation of futurity," as O'Sullivan put it. As American culture spread westward, ignorance, poverty, and heathenism would recede in its path.

The acquisition of territory as a result of the Mexican War (1846–1848) provided the United States with a laboratory in which to test the doctrine of Manifest Destiny. Americans hoped to extend democracy and Protestant Christianity to regions that had long "suffered" under an illiberal and Catholic Mexican culture. Others sought economic opportunity in lands that had supposedly remained underutilized by an indolent population. Before these ideas could be implemented fully, however, the United States became embroiled in sectional discord that ultimately tore the nation asunder.

HISTORY OF COSMOPOLITE
LORENZO DOW (1777–1834)

The democratization and expansion of the republic may be dated from the beginning of the revival at Cane Ridge, Kentucky, August 6, 1801. We cannot understand the great release of energy without first appreciating the power of the Second Great Awakening. Evangelical revivals, often conducted in "camp-meetings," continued throughout the first two-thirds of the nineteenth century, creating controversy and division as well as sweeping institutional change. As in the first Great Awakening, their main evangelical theme was the personal experience of Christ. To an even greater extent than in the First Great Awakening, the revivals spilled over into American political culture.

Lorenzo Dow was an itinerant preacher loosely associated with the Methodist movement. He apparently thought of himself as a combination of John the Baptist and a radical Democrat. He defended revivals—even their most controversial emotional excesses—and preached to anyone who would listen from upper New York to the forests of Alabama. Like his fellow Methodists Francis Asbury and Peter Cartwright, he traveled perhaps 300,000 miles by horseback seeking new souls for the Lord.

He was also suspicious of religious and political authority, preferring to find equal rights for all men in nature. A major effect of the Second Great Awakening was the creation of scores of new denominations and the rapid movement of believers from one to another. To Dow and to many other reform-minded preachers, equal rights also meant new potential for the improvement of individual human beings and of society in general. It was often a short distance from the personal experience of Christ at a camp-meeting to a temperance crusade, a women's rights meeting, or an antislavery association.

Lorenzo Dow, *History of Cosmopolite* (New York: John C. Totten, 1814), 50–51, 195–99, 356–59 [modernized].

In Hampton and Skeinsborough, on the south end of Lake Champlain, was some revival, likewise.

Here was a woman who found fault with me for exhorting the wicked to pray, saying the prayers of the wicked were an abomination to the Lord. But I
5   told her that was home-made Scripture, for that there was no such expression in the Bible, and after bringing undeniable passages to prove it was their duty, I besought her to pray. She replied, I cannot get time. I then offered to buy the time, and for a dollar she promised she would spend one day as I should direct, if it were in a lawful way, provided she could get the day (she not thinking I was
10   in earnest). I then turned to her mistress, who promised to give her a day—then throwing a dollar into her lap, I called God and about thirty persons present to witness the agreement. She besought me to take the dollar again, which I refused, saying, if you go to hell, it may follow and enhance your damnation. About ten days elapsed, when her conscience roaring loud, she took the day, and read two
15   chapters in the Bible, and retired thrice to pray to God to show her what she was, and what she would have her to be, according to my directions.

Afterwards, I had the satisfaction to hear that before night she felt distressed on account of her soul, and before long found the comforts of religion. From thence I visited Kingsborough and Queensborough, where many were brought
20   to a sense of themselves, among whom was Solomon Moon.

One evening, just as I had dismissed the assembly, I saw a man to whom my mind was impressed to go; and before I was aware of it, I was breaking through the crowd; and when I had got to him, I said, "are you willing I should ask you a few serious questions?" to which he replied, yes. "Do you believe (said
25   I) there is a God?" Said he, "yes."

Q. Do you believe that there is a reality in religion?
A. I am uncertain; but think we ought to do as we would be done by.
Q. Are you willing for some good advice?
A. Yes.
30   Q. Supposing I shall give you some that you can find no fault with the tendency of it; are you willing, and will you try to follow it for four weeks?
A. Yes, if it is no unreasonable request.

I then desired him not to believe what authors, ministers, or people said because they said so; but to search the Scriptures to seek for light and instruction there;
35   to read but little at a time, and read it often, striving to take the sense of it.

Secondly, not to stumble over the unexemplary walk of professors of religion; nor the contradiction of ministers' sermons; but to forsake not what other people thought was wrong, but what he himself thought to be wrong.

And then to take his leisure time, and go where none would see him but God, twice or thrice a-day, and upon his knees beseech the Almighty to give him an evidence within that there was a heaven and a hell, and a reality in religion, and the necessity of enjoying it in order to die happy. And then, said I, I do not believe the time will expire before you will find an alteration in your mind, and that for the better.

Q. Is the advice good or bad?
A. I have no fault to find; the natural tendency of it is to good, if followed.

I then said, you promised, if the advice was good, and you had no fault to find with it, that you would follow it four weeks; and now I call God to witness to your promise; so left him.

He went away, and began to meditate how he was taken in the promise before he was aware of it, and for forty-eight hours neglected it—when his conscience condemned him, and for the ease of his mind was necessitated to go and pray.

From hence I went to Thermon's patent, and held several meetings, not in vain, and riding across the branches of Hudson's river, I called the inhabitants together, and we had a refreshing season from the presence of the Lord. In eternity, I believe, some will be thankful for that day....

I had heard about a singularity called the jerks or jerking exercise which appeared first near Knoxville, in August last to the great alarm of the people; which reports at first I considered as vague and false; but at length, like the Queen of Sheba, I set out, to go and see for myself; and sent over there appointments into this country accordingly.

When I arrived in sight of this town I saw hundreds of people collected in little bodies; and observing no place appointed for meeting, before I spoke to any, I got on a log and gave out an hymn; which caused them to assemble round in solemn attentive silence. I observed several involuntary motions in the course of the meeting, which I considered as a specimen of the jerks. I rode seven miles behind a man across streams of water; and held meeting in the evening, being ten miles on my way.

In the night I grew uneasy, being twenty-five miles from my appointment for next morning at eleven o'clock, I prevailed on a young man to attempt carrying me with horses until day, which he thought was impracticable, considering the darkness of the night, and the thickness of the trees. Solitary shrieks were heard in these woods, which he told me were said to be the cries of murdered persons; at day we parted, being still seventeen miles from the spot, and the ground covered with a white frost. I had not preceded far before I came to a stream of water, from the springs of the mountain, which made it dreadful cold;

in my heated state I had to wade this stream five times in the course of about an hour; which I perceived so affected my body that my strength began to fail. Fears began to arise that I must disappoint the people, till I observed some fresh tracks of horses which caused me to exert every nerve to overtake them, in hopes of aid or assistance on my journey, and soon I saw them on an eminence. I shouted for them to stop till I came up; they enquired what I wanted, I replied I had heard there was to be meeting at Severseville by a stranger, and was going to it; they replied that they had heard that a crazy-man was to hold forth there, and were going also; and perceiving that I was weary, they invited me to ride. And soon our company was increased to forty or fifty, who fell in with us on the road, from different plantations. At length I was interrogated whether I knew anything about the preacher. I replied, I have heard a good deal about him, and had heard him preach, but I had no great opinion of him. And thus the conversation continued for some miles before they found me out, which caused some color and smiles in the company. Thus I got on to meeting and, after taking a cup of tea gratis, I began to speak to a vast audience; and I observed about thirty to have the jerks; though they strove to keep still as they could, these emotions were involuntary and irresistible, as any unprejudiced eye might discern. Lawyer Porter (who had come a considerable distance) got his heart touched under the word, and being informed how I came to meeting, voluntarily lent me a horse to ride near one hundred miles and gave me a dollar, though he had never seen me before.

Hence to Marysville, where I spoke to about one thousand five hundred, and many appeared to feel the word, but about fifty felt the jerks. At night I lodged with one of the Nicholites, a kind of Quakers who do not feel free to wear colored clothes. I spoke to a number of people at his house that night. While at tea I observed his daughter (who sat opposite to me at table) to have the jerks, and dropped the tea cup from her hand in the violent agitation. I said to her, "Young woman, what is the matter?" She replied, "I have got the jerks." I asked her how long she had it? She observed, "a few days" and that it had been the means of the awakening and conversion of her soul, by stirring her up to serious consideration about her careless state, etc.

Sunday, February 19th, I spoke in Knoxville to hundreds more than could get into the court house, the Governor being present. About one hundred and fifty appeared to have the jerking exercise, amongst whom was a circuit preacher (Johnson) who had opposed them a little before, but he now had them powerfully; and I believe that he would have fallen over three times had not the auditory been so crowded that he could not, unless he fell perpendicularly.

After meeting I rode eighteen miles to hold meeting at night. The people of this settlement were mostly Quakers, and they had said (as I was informed) the

Methodists and Presbyterians have the jerks because they sing and pray so much, but we are a still peaceable people wherefore we do not have them. However, about twenty of them came to meeting to hear one, as was said, somewhat in a Quaker line. But their usual stillness and silence was interrupted, for about a dozen of them had the jerks as keen and powerful as any I had seen, so as to have occasioned a kind of grunt or groan when they would jerk. It appears that many have undervalued the great revival, and attempted to account for it altogether on natural principles; therefore it seems to me (from the best judgment I can form) that God has seen proper to take this method to convince people that he will work in a way to show his power, and sent the jerks as a sign of the times, partly in judgment for the people's unbelief, and yet as a mercy to convict people of divine realities.

I have seen Presbyterians, Methodists, Quakers, Baptists, Church of England, and Independents exercised with the jerks; gentlemen and lady, black and white, the aged and the youth, rich and poor, without exception; from which I infer, as it cannot be accounted for on natural principles and carries such marks of involuntary motion, that it is no trifling matter. I believe that those who are the most pious and given up to God are rarely touched with it, and also those naturalists, who wish and try to get it to philosophize upon it are excepted. But the lukewarm, lazy, half-hearted, indolent professor is subject to it, and many of them I have seen who, when it came upon them, would be alarmed and stirred up to redouble their diligence with God, and after they would get happy, were thankful it ever came upon them. Again, the wicked are frequently more afraid of it than the small-pox or yellow fever; these are subject to it. But the persecutors are more subject to it than any, and they sometimes have cursed, and swore, and damned it whilst jerking. There is no pain attending the jerks except they resist it, which if they do, it will weary them more in an hour than a day's labor; which shows that it requires the consent of the will to avoid suffering.

20th. I passed by a meeting-house, where I observed the undergrowth had been cut up for a camp-meeting, and from 50 to 100 saplings left breast high, which to me appeared so slovenish that I could not but ask my guide the cause, who observed they were topped so high and left for the people to jerk by. This so excited my attention that I went over the ground to view it, and found where the people had laid hold of them and jerked so powerfully that they had kicked up the earth as a horse stamping flies. I observed some emotion, both this day and night among the people; a Presbyterian minister (with whom I stayed) observed, "yesterday while I was preaching some had the jerks, and a young man from North Carolina mimicked them out of derision and soon was seized with them himself (which was the case with many others) he grew ashamed and on attempting to mount his horse to go off, his foot jerked about so that he could

not put it into the stirrup; some youngsters seeing this assisted him on, but he jerked so that he could not sit alone, and one got up to hold him on; which was done with difficulty. I observing this, went to him and asked him what he thought of it? Said he, 'I believe God sent it on me for my wickedness, and
5   making so light of it in others;' and he requested me to pray for him."

I observed his wife had it; she said she was first attacked with it in bed. Dr. Nelson said he had frequently strove to get it (in order to philosophize upon it), but could not, and observed they could not account for it on natural principles....

A Few Social Reflections

10   After several years absence, I met my old friend, Covel, at Brother Munson's, New York. He informed me of a promise that I had requested of him, viz. to visit from house to house, if he felt it a duty laid upon him from God. Some time passed, when he recollected it in a dull neighborhood—it came upon him—he visited—a glorious work ensued, and a good society was raised up. Though some
15   thought he was insane, but found the error was in themselves.

The different modes have varied in different countries and ages of the world amongst the truly pious. When the different "denominations," so called, judge of each other's religion, they judge that they are all wrong—but if they judge of their own religion, they judge that they are right. Hence, according to that
20   mode of reasoning and judging, it will follow of course, that they are all right, or else that they are all wrong. But the truth is there is good and bad among the whole—and these two classes comprise the whole world of mankind.

It is a self-evident truth that as all men descend from the same original stock, they are of one degree, and hence have the same natural rights—equally.
25   Therefore every generation of men have as good a right to govern itself as the generation that preceded it, by the same rule that every man is born equal in right with his contemporary—consequently, the difference of distinctions is rather the result of *art*, by which the order of things is inverted, than of any natural modification of things.

30   By what rule of right can one man exercise authorities with a command over others? Either it must be the gift of God or, secondly, it must be delegated by the people—or less, thirdly, it must be *assumed!*

A power without a right is assumption, and must be considered as a piece of unjust tyranny.

35   Kingly power had its origin and foundation in that of "Babel" or Babylon which met the Divine disapprobation, and whose curse, as a just retribution, scattered them abroad—and laid the foundation for the different nations and dialects! Likewise the case of Saul, was a striking example of "kingly power" not

being founded in Divine wisdom, nor agreeable to "moral order." But if there be kings, it would be better to have good men than bad ones—hence the Christians were to pray for them; as friends to society, who wish for peace in the land!

The power of the Pope, who is styled "universal Bishop," as the spurious "Vicegerent of the Almighty upon earth"—and *Kingly Power* and *Slavery* are all of a piece, though different modeled—the principle is the same, being founded in "moral evil," and requires terror and ignorance for it support—therefore tyrannical barbarity, and every species of cruelty that human nature could invent has been used to prevent the spirit of inquiry, that man might not see, feel, and detect the imposition—but quietly submit to the galling yoke of

Passive Obedience and Non-Resistance

without being permitted to think, and see, and judge, or *act* for themselves! Which shows that those governors "love darkness rather than light, because their deeds are evil!"

But if all men are *born equal,* and are endowed with unalienable *rights* by their *Creator,* in the blessings of life, liberty, and the pursuit of happiness—then there can be no just reason, as a cause, why he may or should not think, and judge, and act for himself in matters of religion, opinion, and private judgment.

For what right has any man to meddle with that which does not concern him?

If all men are "equal and independent" in their *individual* capacity—yet it is equally self-evident that they are dependent in a social capacity. Natural rights are by virtue of existence—social rights by virtue of being a member of society. Those rights imperfect in *power* are cast into the common stock by delegation—and he takes the arm of society, of which he is a part, in preference and in addition to his own.

A whole being composed of parts, the parts collectively form one whole.

The Constitution of the United States was framed by a delegated *confederation,* who were chosen by the people for that purpose. The Constitution, when framed, was recommended by the confederation to the different states—each of which voluntarily received it by their own proper legislative and sovereign authority, whose officers were chosen by the people for that purpose—all of which procedure is agreeable to natural justice, arising from the Creator's "law of nature!"

And as the Constitution admits of *amendment,* how different this from the old theory—"Can do no wrong, nor think any evil." How great is the contrast, which admits of "freedom of speech and of the press"—and the one *death* for *imagination*—death of the K* * *!

If the Creator made the ocean for the benefit of his creatures, as a common "highway" for all nations—by what right can one claim it for his own; and compel others to pay him for the privilege to use it?

Is it not assumption? A power without a just right, of course, an infringement upon natural justice—and must be considered as an unjust tyranny!

Universal rights of conscience should be established in every land, agreeable to the Creator's law of nature—that light may be disseminated, and the joyful sound extend to every clime—that the earth may revert to its original and proper owner—and his Kingdom come and rule over all!

It has been a matter of thankfulness with me to the wise and good Creator that my lot was cast in America. For had I existed in any other age or nation, it would have been naturally impossible for me to have enjoyed those privileges that I do now, because they did not then and there exist.

WHAT A REVIVAL OF RELIGION IS
CHARLES GRANDISON FINNEY (1792–1875)

Charles Grandison Finney earned the title "Father of Modern Revivalism" for his wildly successful revivalist techniques that helped transform American evangelicalism during the Second Great Awakening of the Jacksonian Era. Although he originally studied law and began a legal career as an apprentice in upstate New York's Adams County, Finney's life and career took a radical turn following his dramatic conversion experience on October 10, 1821. After studying briefly with his Calvinist pastor, Finney obtained a preaching license and was ordained in 1824, the year he began work as a missionary in upstate New York. His evangelistic enterprise grew as he staged ever-larger revival meetings throughout New York's "Burned-Over District." Recurring illnesses forced him, however, to leave the revival circuit in 1832. That year he became pastor of New York City's Chatham Street Chapel, the first in a series of three pastorates that would keep him occupying a pulpit until 1872.

Known for his controversial revival techniques which he called "New Measures," Finney detailed his methods of Christian revivalism in his Lectures on Revivals of Religion, *the first of which was published as an article in December 1834, and is reprinted below. Finney denied that a revival involved a miracle of any kind. Instead, he believed that a conversion was rational free choice—a view clearly evident in the title of his well-known sermon, "Sinners Bound to Change Their Own Hearts." Controversial and iconoclastic, Finney's theology motivated his idealistic belief in human perfectibility. Accordingly, he remained deeply committed to reform movements such as abolitionism and temperance that typified the progressive society of the antebellum North.*

In 1837 Finney moved to Oberlin, Ohio, where he became pastor of the First Congregational Church and professor of theology at the new Oberlin

Charles Grandison Finney, *Lectures on Revival of Religion* (New York: Leavitt, Lord, and Company, 1834), 9–20.

Collegiate Institute (now Oberlin College). From 1851 to 1866 he served as
Oberlin's second president. Although his work as an active traveling revivalist
had ended by mid-life, Finney's enduring legacy remains the degree to which
his career shaped the spirit of American evangelical revivalism.

1834

O Lord, revive thy work in the midst of the years, in the midst of the years
make known; in wrath remember mercy—Habakkuk 3:2

It is supposed that the prophet Habakkuk was contemporary with Jeremiah,
and that this prophecy was uttered in anticipation of the Babylonish captiv-
5   ity. Looking at the judgments which were speedily to come upon his nation,
the soul of the prophet was wrought up to an agony, and he cries out in his
distress, "O Lord, revive thy work." As if he had said, "O Lord, grant that thy
judgments may not make Israel desolate. In the midst of these awful years, let
the judgments of God be made the means of reviving religion among us. In
10   wrath remember mercy."

Religion is the work of man. It is something for man to do. It consists in
obeying God. It is man's duty. It is true, God induces him to do it. He influences him by his Spirit, because of his great wickedness and reluctance to obey.
If it were not necessary for God to influence men—if men were disposed to
15   obey God, there would be no occasion to pray, "O Lord, revive thy work."
The ground of necessity for such a prayer is, that men are wholly indisposed to
obey; and unless God interpose the influence of his Sprit, not a man on earth
will ever obey the commands of God.

A "Revival of Religion" presupposes a declension. Almost all the religion
20   in the world has been produced by revivals. God has found it necessary to take
advantage of the excitability there is in mankind, to produce powerful excitements among them, before he can lead them to obey. Men are so sluggish, there
are so many things to lead their minds off from religion, and to oppose the
influence of the gospel, that it is necessary to raise an excitement among them,
25   till the tide rises so high as to sweep away the opposing obstacles. They must
be so excited that they will break over these counteracting influences, before
they will obey God.

Look back at the history of the Jews, and you will see that God used to
maintain religion among them by special occasions, when there would be a great
30   excitement, and people would turn to the Lord. And after they had been thus
revived, it would be but a short time before there would be so many counteracting influences brought to bear upon them, that religion would decline, and
keep on declining, till God could have time—so to speak—to shape the course
of events so as to produce another excitement, and then pour out his Spirit
35   again to convert sinners. Then the counteracting causes would again operate,

and religion would decline, and the nation would be swept away in the vortex
of luxury, idolatry, and pride.

There is so little principle in the church, so little firmness and stability of
purpose, that unless they are greatly excited, they will not obey God. They have
so little knowledge, and their principles are so weak, that unless they are excited,   5
they will go back from the path of duty, and do nothing to promote the glory
of God. The state of the world is still such, and probably will be till the millennium is fully come, that religion must be mainly promoted by these excitements.
How long and how often has the experiment been tried, to bring the church
to act steadily for God, without these periodical excitements. Many good men   10
have supposed, and still suppose, that the best way to promote religion, is to go
along uniformly, and gather in the ungodly gradually, and without excitement.
But however such reasoning may appear in the abstract, facts demonstrate its
futility. If the church were far enough advanced in knowledge, and had stability
of principle enough to keep awake, such a course would do; but the church is so   15
little enlightened, and there are so many counteracting causes, that the church
will not go steadily to work without a special excitement. As the millennium
advances, it is probable that these periodical excitements will be unknown. Then
the church will be enlightened, and the counteracting causes removed, and the
entire church will be in a state of habitual and steady obedience to God. The   20
entire church will stand and take the infant mind, and cultivate it for God.
Children will be trained up in the way they should go, and there will be no such
torrents of worldliness, and fashion, and covetousness, to bear away the piety
of the church as soon as the excitement of a revival is withdrawn.

It is very desirable it should be so. It is very desirable that the church should   25
go on steadily in a course of obedience without these excitements. Such excitements are liable to injure the health. Our nervous system is so strung that any
powerful excitement, if long continued, injures our health and unfits us for duty.
If religion is ever to have a pervading influence in the world, it can't be so; this
spasmodic religion must be done away. Then it will be uncalled for. Christians   30
will not sleep the greater part of the time, and once in a while wake up, and rub
their eyes, and bluster about, and vociferate, a little while, and then go to sleep
again. Then there will be no need that ministers should wear themselves out, and
kill themselves, by their efforts to roll back the flood of worldly influence that sets
in upon the church. But as yet the state of the Christian world is such, that to   35
expect to promote religion without excitements is un-philosophical and absurd.
The great political, and other worldly excitements that agitate Christendom, are
all unfriendly to religion, and divert the mind from the interests of the soul. Now
these excitements can only be counteracted by religious excitements. And until
there is religious principle in the world to put down irreligious excitements, it   40

is in vain to try to promote religion, except by counteracting excitements. This is true in philosophy, and it is a historical fact.

It is altogether improbable that religion will ever make progress among heathen nations except through the influence of revivals. The attempt is now making to do it by education, and other cautions and gradual improvements. But so long as the laws of mind remain what they are, it cannot be done in this way. There must be excitement sufficient to wake up the dormant moral powers, and roll back the tide of degradation and sin. And precisely so far as our own land approximates to heathenism, it is impossible for God or man to promote religion in such a state of things but by powerful excitements.—This is evident from the fact that this has always been the way in which God has done it. God does not create these excitements, and choose this method to promote religion for nothing or without reason. Where mankind are so reluctant to obey God, they will not act until they are excited. For instance, how many there are who know that they ought to be religious, but they are afraid if they become pious they shall be laughed at by their companions. Many are wedded to idols, others are procrastinating repentance, until they are settled in life, or until they have secured some favorite worldly interest. Such persons never will give up their false shame, or relinquish their ambitious schemes, till they are so excited that they cannot contain themselves any longer.

These remarks are designed only as an introduction to the discourse. I shall now proceed with the main design, to show,

    I. What a revival of religion is not;
    II. What it is; and,
    III. The agencies employed in promoting it.

I. A Revival of Religion is Not a Miracle

1. A miracle has been generally defined to be a Divine interference, setting aside or suspending the laws of nature. It is not a miracle, in this sense. All the laws of matter and mind remain in force. They are neither suspended nor set aside in a revival.

2. It is not a miracle according to another definition of the term miracle— something above the powers of nature. There is nothing in religion beyond the ordinary powers of nature. It consists entirely in the right exercise of the powers of nature. It is just that, and nothing else. When mankind become religious, they are not enabled to put forth exertions which they were unable before to put forth. They only exert the powers they had before in a different way, and use them for the glory of God.

3. It is not a miracle, or dependent on a miracle, in any sense. It is a purely philosophical result of the right use of the constituted means—as much so as any other effect produced by the application of means. There may be a miracle among its antecedent causes, or there may not. The apostles employed miracles, simply as a means by which they arrested attention to their message, and established its Divine authority. But the miracle was not the revival. The miracle was one thing; the revival that followed it was quite another thing. The revivals in the apostles' days were connected with miracles, but they were not miracles.

I said that a revival is the result of the right use of the appropriate means. The means which God has enjoined for the production of a revival, doubtless have a natural tendency to produce a revival. Otherwise God would not have enjoined them. But means will not produce a revival, we all know, without the blessing of God. No more will grain, when it is sowed, produce a crop without the blessing of God. It is impossible for us to say that there is not as direct an influence or agency from God, to produce a crop of grain, as there is to produce a revival. What are the laws of nature according to which, it is supposed, that grain yields a crop? They are nothing but the constituted manner of the operations of God. In the Bible, the word of God is compared to grain, and preaching is compared to sowing seed, and the results to the springing up and growth of the crop. And the result is just as philosophical in the one case, as in the other, and is as naturally connected with the cause.

I wish this idea to be impressed on all your minds, for there has long been an idea prevalent that promoting religion has something very peculiar in it, not to be judged of by the ordinary rules of cause and effect; in short, that there is no connection of the means with the result, and no tendency in the means to produce the effect. No doctrine is more dangerous than this to the prosperity of the church, and nothing more absurd.

Suppose a man were to go and preach this doctrine among farmers, about their sowing grain. Let him tell them that God is a sovereign, and will give them a crop only when it pleases him, and that for them to plow and plant and labor as if they expected to raise a crop is very wrong, and taking the work out of the hands of God, that it interferes with his sovereignty, and is going on in their own strength; and that there is no connection between the means and the result on which they can depend. And now, suppose the farmers should believe such doctrine. Why, they would starve the world to death.

Just such results will follow from the church's being persuaded that promoting religion is somehow so mysteriously a subject of Divine sovereignty, that there is no natural connection between the means and the end. What are the

results? Why generation after generation have gone down to hell. No doubt more than five thousand millions have gone down to hell, while the church has been dreaming, and waiting for God to save them without the use of means. It has been the devil's most successful means of destroying souls. The connection
5   is as clear in religion as it is when the farmer sows his grain.

There is one fact under the government of God, worthy of universal notice, and of everlasting remembrance; which is, that the most useful and important things are most easily and certainly obtained by the use of the appropriate means. This is evidently a principle in the Divine administration. Hence, all
10   the necessaries of life are obtained with great certainty by the use of the simplest means. The luxuries are more difficult to obtain; the means to procure them are more intricate and less certain in their results; while things absolutely hurtful and poisonous, such as alcohol and the like, are often obtained only by torturing nature, and making use of a kind of infernal sorcery to procure the
15   death-dealing abomination.

This principle holds true in moral government, and as spiritual blessings are of surpassing importance, we should expect their attainment to be connected with great certainty with the use of the appropriate means; and such we find to be the fact; and I fully believe that could facts be known, it would be found
20   that when the appointed means have been rightly used, spiritual blessings have been obtained with greater uniformity than temporal ones.

II. I Am to Show What a Revival Is

It presupposes that the church is sunk down in a backslidden state, and a revival consists in the return of the church from her backslidings, and in the conversion of sinners.

25   1.   A revival always includes conviction of sin on the part of the church. Backslidden professors cannot wake up and begin right away in the service of God, without deep searchings of heart. The fountains of sin need to be broken up. In a true revival, Christians are always brought under such convictions; they see their sins in such a light, that often they find it
30   impossible to maintain a hope of their acceptance with God. It does not always go to that extent; but there are always, in a genuine revival, deep convictions of sin, and often cases of abandoning all hope.

2.   Backslidden Christians will be brought to repentance. A revival is nothing else than a new beginning of obedience to God. Just as in the case of a converted
35   sinner, the first step is a deep repentance, a breaking down of heart, a getting down into the dust before God, with deep humility, and forsaking of sin.

3. Christians will have their faith renewed. While they are in their backslidden state they are blind to the state of sinners. Their hearts are as hard as marble. The truths of the Bible only appear like a dream. They admit it to be all true; their conscience and their judgment assent to it; but their faith does not see it standing out in bold relief, in all the burning realities of eternity. But when they enter into a revival, they no longer see men as trees walking, but they see things in that strong light which will renew the love of God in their hearts. This will lead them to labor zealously to bring others to him. They will feel grieved that others do not love God, when they love him so much. And they will set themselves feelingly to persuade their neighbors to give him their hearts. So their love to men will be renewed. They will be filled with a tender and burning love for souls. They will have a longing desire for the salvation of the whole world. They will be in an agony for individuals whom they want to have saved; their friends, relations, enemies. They will not only be urging them to give their hearts to God, but they will carry them to God in the arms of faith, and with strong crying and tears beseech God to have mercy on them, and save their souls from endless burnings.

4. A revival breaks the power of the world and of sin over Christians. It brings them to such vantage ground that they get a fresh impulse towards heaven. They have a new foretaste of heaven, and new desires after union to God; and the charm of the world is broken, and the power of sin overcome.

5. When the churches are thus awakened and reformed, the reformation and salvation of sinners will follow, going through the same stages of conviction, repentance, and reformation. Their hearts will be broken down and changed. Very often the most abandoned profligates are among the subjects. Harlots, and drunkards, and infidels, and all sorts of abandoned characters, are awakened and converted. The worst part of human society are softened, and reclaimed, and made to appear as lovely specimens of the beauty of holiness.

III. I Am to Consider the Agencies Employed in Carrying Forward a Revival of Religion

Ordinarily, there are three agents employed in the work of conversion, and one instrument. The agents are God, some person who brings the truth to bear on the mind, and the sinner himself. The instrument is the truth. There are always two agents, God and the sinner, employed and active in every case of genuine conversion.

1. The agency of God is two-fold; by his Providence and by his Spirit.

(1) By his providential government, he so arranges events as to bring the sinner's mind and the truth in contact. He brings the sinner where the truth reaches his ears or his eyes. It is often interesting to trace the manner in which God arranges events so as to bring this about, and how he sometimes makes everything seem to favor a revival. The state of the weather, and of the public health, and other circumstances concur to make everything just right to favor the application of truth with the greatest possible efficacy. How he sometimes sends a minister along, just at the time he is wanted! How he brings out a particular truth, just at the particular time when the individual if fitted to reach is in the way to hear!

(2) God's special agency by his Holy Spirit. Having direct access to the mind, and knowing infinitely well the whole history and state of each individual sinner, he employs that truth which is best adapted to his particular case, and then sets it home with Divine power. He gives it such vividness, strength, and power, that the sinner quails, and throws down his weapons of rebellion, and turns to the Lord. Under his influence, the truth burns and cuts its way like fire. He makes the truth stand out in such aspects, that it crushes the proudest man down with the weight of a mountain. If men were disposed to obey God, the truth is given with sufficient clearness in the Bible; and from preaching they could learn all that is necessary for them to know. But because they are wholly disinclined to obey it, God clears it up before their minds, and pours in a blaze of convincing light upon their souls, which they cannot withstand, and they yield to it, and obey God, and are saved.

2. The agency of men is commonly employed. Men are not mere instruments in the hands of God. Truth is the instrument. The preacher is a moral agent in the work; he acts; he is not a mere passive instrument; he is voluntary in promoting the conversion of sinners.

3. The agency of the sinner himself. The conversion of a sinner consists in his obeying the truth. It is therefore impossible it should take place without his agency, for it consists in his acting right. He is influenced to this by the agency of God, and by the agency of men. Men act on their fellow-men, not only by language, but by their looks, their tears, their daily deportment. See that impenitent man there, who has a pious wife. Her very looks, her tenderness, her solemn, compassionate dignity, softened and moulded into the image of Christ, are a sermon to him all the time. He has to turn his mind away, because it is such a reproach to him. He feels a sermon ringing in his ears all day long.

Mankind are accustomed to read the countenances of their neighbors. Sinners often read the state of a Christian's mind in his eyes. If his eyes are full of levity, or worldly anxiety and contrivance, sinners read it. If they are full of the Spirit of God, sinners read it; and they are often led to conviction by barely seeing the countenance of Christians.

An individual once went into a manufactory to see the machinery. His mind was solemn, as he had been where there was a revival. The people who labored there all knew him by sight, and knew who he was. A young lady who was at work saw him, and whispered some foolish remark to her companion, and laughed. The person stopped and looked at her with a feeling of grief. She stopped, her thread broke, and she was so much agitated she could not join it. She looked out at the window to compose herself, and then tried again; again and again she strove to recover her self-command. At length she sat down, overcome with her feelings. The person then approached and spoke with her; she soon manifested a deep sense of sin. The feeling spread through the establishment like fire, and in a few hours almost every person employed there was under conviction, so much so, that the owners, though worldly men, were astounded, and requested to have the works stop and have a prayer meeting; for they said it was a great deal more important to have these people converted than to have the works go on. And in a few days, the owners and nearly every person employed in the establishment were hopefully converted. The eye of this individual, his solemn countenance, his compassionate feeling, rebuked the levity of the young woman, and brought her under conviction of sin: and this whole revival followed, probably in a great measure, from so small an incident.

If Christians have deep feeling on the subject of religion themselves, they will produce deep feeling wherever they go. And if they are cold, or light and trifling, they inevitably destroy all deep feeling, even in awakened sinners.

I knew a case, once, of an individual who was very anxious, but one day I was grieved to find that her convictions seemed to be all gone. I asked her what she had been doing. She told me she had been spending the afternoon at such a place, among some professors of religion, not thinking that it would dissipate her convictions to spend an afternoon with professors of religion. But they were trifling and vain, and thus her convictions were lost. And no doubt those professors of religion, by their folly, destroyed a soul, for her convictions did not return.

The church is required to use the means for the conversion of sinners. Sinners cannot properly be said to use the means of their own conversion. The church uses the means. What sinners do is to submit to the truth, or to resist it. It is a mistake of sinners, to think they are using means for their own conversion. The whole drift of a revival, and everything about it, is designed to present the truth to your mind, for your obedience or resistance.

Remarks

1. Revivals were formerly regarded as miracles. And it has been so by some
even in our day. And others have ideas on the subject so loose and unsatis-
factory, that if they would only think, they would see their absurdity. For
a long time, it was supposed by the church, that a revival was a miracle,
an interposition of Divine power which they had nothing to do with, and
which they had no more agency in producing, than they had in producing thunder, or a storm of hail, or an earthquake. It is only within a few
years that ministers generally have supposed revivals were to be promoted,
by the use of means designed and adapted specially to that object. Even
in New England, it has been supposed that revivals came just as showers
do, sometimes in one town, and sometimes in another, and that ministers
and churches could do nothing more to produce them, than they could to
make showers of rain come on their own town, when they are falling on a
neighboring town.

It used to be supposed that a revival would come about once in fifteen
years, and all would be converted that God intended to save, and then they
must wait until another crop came forward on the stage of life. Finally, the
time got shortened down to five years, and they supposed there might be
a revival about as often as that.

I have heard a fact in relation to one of these pastors, who supposed
revivals might come about once in five years. There had been a revival in
his congregation. The next year, there was a revival in a neighboring town,
and he went there to preach, and staid several days, till he got his soul all
engaged in the work. He returned home on Saturday, and went into his
study to prepare for the Sabbath. And his soul was in an agony. He thought
how many adult persons there were in his congregation at enmity with
God—so many still unconverted—so many persons die yearly—such a
portion of them unconverted—if a revival does not come under five years,
so many adult heads of families will be in hell. He put down his calculations on paper, and embodied them in his sermon for the next day, with
his heart bleeding at the dreadful picture. As I understood it, he did not
do this with any expectation of a revival, but he felt deeply, and poured out
his heart to his people. And that sermon awakened forty heads of families,
and a powerful revival followed; and so his theory about a revival once in
five years was all exploded.

Thus God has overthrown, generally, the theory that revivals are
miracles.

2. Mistaken notions concerning the sovereignty of God, have greatly hindered revivals.

   Many people have supposed God's sovereignty to be something very different from what it is. They have supposed it to be such an arbitrary disposal of events, and particularly of the gift of his Spirit, as precluded   5
   a rational employment of means for promoting a revival of religion. But there is no evidence from the Bible, that God exercises any such sovereignty as that. There are no facts to prove it. But everything goes to show, that God has connected means with the end through all the departments of his government—in nature and in grace. There is no natural event in which   10
   his own agency is not concerned. He has not built the creation like a vast machine, that will go on alone without his further care. He has not retired from the universe, to let it work for itself. This is mere atheism. He exercises a universal superintendence and control. And yet every event in nature has been brought about by means. He neither administers providence nor grace   15
   with that sort of sovereignty, that dispenses with the use of means. There is no more sovereignty in one than in the other.

   And yet some people are terribly alarmed at all direct efforts to promote a revival, and they cry out, "You are trying to get up a revival in your own strength. Take care, you are interfering with the sovereignty of God. Better   20
   keep along in the usual course, and let God give a revival when he thinks it is best. God is a sovereign, and it is very wrong for you to attempt to get up a revival, just because you think a revival is needed." This is just such preaching as the devil wants. And men cannot do the devil's work more effectually, than by preaching up the sovereignty of God, as a reason why   25
   we should not put forth efforts to produce a revival.

3. You see the error of those who are beginning to think that religion can be better promoted in the world without revivals, and who are disposed to give up all efforts to produce religious excitements. Because there are evils arising in some instances out of great excitements on the subject of religion,   30
   they are of opinion that it is best to dispense with them altogether. This cannot, and must not be. True, there is danger of abuses. In cases of great religious as well as all other excitements, more or less incidental evils may be expected of course. But this is no reason why they should be given up. The best things are always liable to abuses. Great and manifold evils have   35
   originated in the providential and moral governments of God. But these foreseen perversions and evils were not considered a sufficient reason for giving them up. For the establishment of these governments was on the

whole the best that could be done for the production of the greatest amount of happiness. So in revivals of religion, it is found by experience, that in the present state of the world, religion cannot be promoted to any considerable extent without them. The evils which are sometimes complained of, when they are real, are incidental, and of small importance when compared with the amount of good produced by revivals. The sentiment should not be admitted by the church for a moment, that revivals may be given up. It is fraught with all that is dangerous to the interests of Zion, is death to the cause of missions, and brings in its train the damnation of the world.

Finally, I have a proposal to make to you who are here present. I have not commenced this course of Lectures on Revivals to get up a curious theory of my own on the subject. I would not spend my time and strength merely to give you instructions, to gratify your curiosity, and furnish you something to talk about. I have no idea of preaching about revivals. It is not my design to preach so as to have you able to say at the close, "We understand all about revivals now," while you do nothing. But I wish to ask you a question. What do you hear lectures on revivals for? Do you mean that whenever you are convinced what your duty is in promoting a revival, you will go to work and practice it?

Will you follow the instructions I shall give you from the word of God, and put them in practice in your own hearts? Will you bring them to bear upon your families, your acquaintance, neighbors, and through the city? Or will you spend the winter in learning about revivals, and do nothing for them? I want you, as fast as you learn anything on the subject of revivals, to put it in practice, and go to work and see if you cannot promote a revival among sinners here. If you will not do this, I wish you to let me know at the beginning, so that I need not waste my strength. You ought to decide now whether you will do this or not. You know that we call sinners to decide on the spot whether they will obey the gospel. And we have no more authority to let you take time to deliberate whether you will obey God, than we have to let sinners do so. We call on you to unite now in a solemn pledge to God, that you will do your duty as fast as you learn what it is, and to pray that He will pour out his Spirit upon this church and upon all the city this winter.

First Annual Message
Andrew Jackson (1767–1845)
President of the United States (1829–1837)

*One of Andrew Jackson's biographers pointed out that Jackson never cham-
pioned the cause of the people; he merely invited the people to champion
him. Jackson embodied the people more than he represented them. He
came to the presidency in an atmosphere of growing democracy. Almost all
the states had adopted the principle of universal (white) male suffrage. A
major theme of his inaugural and of his first message to Congress (December
8, 1829) was that "the first principle of our system" is that "the majority is
to govern." He wanted a Constitutional innovation to make this a reality
in the election of the President. Perhaps Jackson's own first principle was a
deep faith in the judgment of free men.*

*In many ways Jackson was the heir of Jefferson. He called for low
taxes, control of the military, payment of the national debt, a small
national government, and preservation of state sovereignty. He attacked
and destroyed the National Bank, denied the use of federal monies for
"internal improvements" (including roads, canals, and railroads), and
used his veto power extensively, all in the name of protecting the people
against accumulations of power and privilege in Washington. He sincerely
believed that the best way to serve the people was to keep the states and the
people free to pursue their interests.*

*Jackson's principles and policies accelerated the release of energy in
the nation and promoted the sense of equality in an age that would bear
his name. They would also bring to light the contradictions in a system
that tried to promote majority rule, equality, and individual liberty all
at the same time. One of those contradictions was that Jackson favored an
Indian policy that allowed the majorities in several states to remove their
indigenous tribes west, beyond a "permanent Indian frontier."*

Messages of Gen. Andrew Jackson (Concord, NH: John F. Brown, 1837), 39–40, 46–50, 51–53,
59–62, 67–68.

8 December 1829

It affords me pleasure to tender my friendly greetings to you on the occasion of your assembling at the seat of government, to enter upon the important duties to which you have been called by the voice of our countrymen. The task devolves on me, under a provision of the Constitution, to present to you, as
5 the Federal legislature of twenty-four sovereign states, and twelve millions of happy people, a view of our affairs; and to propose such measures as, in the discharge of my official functions, have suggested themselves as necessary to promote the objects of our union.

In communicating with you for the first time, it is, to me, a source of
10 unfeigned satisfaction, calling for mutual gratulation and devout thanks to a benign Providence, that we are at peace with all mankind; and that our country exhibits the most cheering evidence of general welfare and progressive improvement. Turning our eyes to other nations, our great desire is to see our brethren of the human race secured in the blessings enjoyed by ourselves, and advancing
15 in knowledge, in freedom, and in social happiness.

Our foreign relations, although in their general character pacific and friendly, presents subjects of difference between us and other powers, of deep interest, as well to the country at large as to many of our citizens. To effect an adjustment of these shall continue to be the object of my earnest endeavors; and
20 notwithstanding the difficulties of the task, I do not allow myself to apprehend unfavorable results. Blessed as our country is with everything which constitutes national strength, she is fully adequate to the maintenance of all her interests. In discharging the responsible trust confided to the Executive in this respect, it is my settled purpose to ask nothing that is wrong; and I flatter myself, that,
25 supported by the other branches of the government, and by the intelligence and patriotism of the People, we shall be able, under the protection of Providence, to cause all our just rights to be respected....

I consider it one of the most urgent of my duties to bring to your attention the propriety of amending that part of our Constitution which relates to the
30 election of President and Vice President. Our system of government was, by its frames, deemed an experiment; and they, therefore, consistently provided a mode of remedying its defects.

To the People belongs the right of electing their Chief Magistrate: it was never designed that their choice should, in any case, be defeated, either by the
35 intervention of electoral colleges, or by the agency confided, under certain contingencies, to the House of Representatives. Experience proves, that, in proportion as agents to execute the will of the People are multiplied, there is danger of their wishes being frustrated. Some may be unfaithful: all are liable to err. So far, therefore, as the People can, with convenience, speak, it is safer
40 for them to express their own will.

The number of aspirants to the Presidency, and the diversity of the interests which may influence their claims, leave little reason to expect a choice in the first instance: and, in that event, the election must devolve on the House of Representatives, where, it is obvious, the will of the People may not be always ascertained; or, if ascertained, may not be regarded. From the mode of voting by states, the choice is to be made by twenty-four votes; and it may often occur, that one of these will be controlled by an individual representative. Honors and offices are at the disposal of the successful candidate. Repeated ballotings may make it apparent that a single individual holds the cast in his hand. May he not be tempted to name his reward? But even without corruption—supposing the probity of the Representative to be proof against the powerful motives by which it may be assailed—the will of the people is still constantly liable to be misrepresented. One may err from ignorance of the wishes of his constituents; another, from a conviction that it is his duty to be governed by his own judgment of the fitness of the candidates: finally, although all were inflexibly honest—all accurately informed of the wishes of their constituents—yet, under the present mode of election, a minority may often elect the President; and when this happens, it may reasonably be expected that efforts will be made on the part of the majority to rectify this injurious operation of their institutions. But although no evil of this character should result from such a perversion of the first principles of our system—*that the majority is to govern*—it must be very certain that a President elected by a minority cannot enjoy the confidence necessary to the successful discharge of his duties.

In this, as in all other matters of public concern, policy requires that as few impediments as possible should exist to the free operation of the public will. Let us then, endeavor so to amend our system, that the office of Chief Magistrate may not be conferred upon any citizen, but in pursuance of a fair expression of the will of the majority.

I would therefore recommend such an amendment of the Constitution as may remove all intermediate agency in the election of the President and Vice President. The mode may be so regulated as to preserve to each state its present relative weight in the election; and a failure in the first attempt may be provided for, by confining the second to a choice between the two highest candidates. In connection with such an amendment, it would seem advisable to limit the service of the Chief Magistrate to a single term, of either four or six years. If, however, it should not be adopted, it is worthy of consideration whether a provision disqualifying for office the Representatives in Congress on whom such an election may have devolved, would not be proper.

While members of Congress can be constitutionally appointed to offices of trust and profit, it will be the practice, even under the most conscientious adherence to duty, to select them for such stations as they are believed to be bet-

ter qualified to fill than other citizens; but the purity of our government would doubtless be promoted by their exclusion from all appointments in the gift of the President in whose election they may have been officially concerned. The nature of the judicial office, and the necessity of securing in the Cabinet and
5 diplomatic stations of the highest rank, the best talents and political experience, should, perhaps, except these from the exclusion.

There are perhaps few men who can for any great length of time enjoy office and power without being more or less under the influence of feelings unfavorable to the faithful discharge of their public duties. Their integrity may
10 be proof against improper considerations immediately addressed to themselves; but they are apt to acquire a habit of looking with indifference upon the public interests, and of tolerating conduct from which an unpracticed man would revolt. Office is considered as a species of property; and government rather as a means of promoting individual interest than as an instrument created solely
15 for the service of the People. Corruption in some, and, in others, a perversion of correct feelings and principles, divert government from its legitimate ends, and make it an engine for the support of the few at the expense of the many. The duties of all public officers are, or, at least, admit of being made, so plain and simple, that men of intelligence may readily qualify themselves for their
20 performance; and I cannot but believe that more is lost by the long continuance of men in office, than is generally to be gained by their experience. I submit therefore to your consideration, whether the efficiency of the government would not be promoted, and official industry and integrity better secured, by a general extension of the law which limits appointments to four years.

25 In a country where offices are created solely for the benefit of the People, no one man has any more intrinsic right to official station than another. Offices were not established to give support to particular men, at the public expense. No individual wrong is therefore done by removal, since neither appointment to, nor continuance in, office, is matter of right. The incumbent became an officer with
30 a view to public benefits; and when these require his removal, they are not to be sacrificed to private interests. It is the People, and they alone, who have a right to complain, when a bad officer is substituted for a good one. He who is removed has the same means of obtaining a living, that are enjoyed by the millions who never held office. The proposed limitation would destroy the idea of property, now
35 so generally connected with official station; and although individual distress may be sometimes produced, it would, by promoting that rotation which constitutes a leading principle in the republican creed, give healthful action to the system.

No very considerable change has occurred, during the recess of Congress, in the condition of either our agriculture, commerce, or manufactures. The
40 operation of the tariff has not proved so injurious to the two former, or as

beneficial to the latter, as was anticipated. Importations of foreign goods have not been sensibly diminished; while domestic competition, under an illusive excitement, has increased the production much beyond the demand for home consumption. The consequences have been low prices, temporary embarrassment, and partial loss. That such of our manufacturing establishments as are based upon capital, and are prudently managed, will survive the shock, and be ultimately profitable, there is no good reason to doubt.

To regulate its conduct, so as to promote equally the prosperity of these three cardinal interests, is one of the most difficult tasks of government; and it may be regretted that the complicated restrictions which now embarrass the intercourse of nations, could not by common consent be abolished; and commerce allowed to flow in those channels to which individual enterprise—always its surest guide—might direct it. But we must ever expect selfish legislation in other nations; and are therefore compelled to adapt our own to their regulations, in the manner best calculated to avoid serious injury, and to harmonize the conflicting interests of our agriculture, our commerce and our manufactures. Under these impressions, I invite your attention to the existing tariff, believing that some of its provisions require modification.

The general rule to be applied in graduating the duties upon the articles of foreign growth or manufacture, is that which will place our own in fair competition with those of other countries; and the inducements to advance even a step beyond this point, are controlling in regard to those articles which are of primary necessity in time of war. When we reflect upon the difficulty and delicacy of this operation, it is important that it should never be attempted but with the utmost caution. Frequent legislation in regard to any branch of industry, affecting its value, and by which its capital may be transferred to new channels, must always be productive of hazardous speculation and loss.

In deliberating, therefore, on these interesting subjects, local feelings and prejudices should be merged in the patriotic determination to promote the great interests of the whole. All the attempts to connect them with the party conflicts of the day are necessarily injurious, and should be discountenanced. Our action upon them should be under the control of higher and purer motives. Legislation, subjected to such influences, can never be just; and will not long retain the sanction of the People, whose active patriotism is not bounded by sectional limits, nor insensible to that spirit of concession and forbearance, which gave life to our political compact, and still sustains it. Discarding all calculations of political ascendency, the North, the South, the East, and the West should unite in diminishing any burden of which either may justly complain.

The agricultural interest of our country is so essentially connected with every other, and so superior in importance to them all, that it is scarcely necessary to invite to it your particular attention. It is principally as manufactures and commerce tend to increase the value of agricultural productions, and to extend their application to the wants and comforts of society, that they deserve the fostering care of government....

5   This state of the finances exhibits the resources of the nation in an aspect highly flattering to its industry; and auspicious of the ability of the government, in a very short time, to extinguish the public debt. When this shall be done, our population will be relieved from a considerable portion of its present burdens; and will find, not only new motives to patriotic affection, but additional means

10   for the display of individual enterprise. The fiscal power of the states will also be increased; and may be more extensively exerted in favor of education and other public objects; while ample means will remain in the Federal government to promote the general weal, in all the modes permitted to its authority.

After the extinction of the public debt, it is not probable that any adjustment

15   of the tariff, upon principles satisfactory to the People of the Union, will, until a remote period, if ever, leave the government without a considerable surplus in the Treasury, beyond what may be required for its current service. As then the period approaches when the application of the revenue to the payment of debt will cease, the disposition of the surplus will present a subject for the seri-

20   ous deliberation of Congress; and it may be fortunate for the country that it is yet to be decided. Considered in connection with the difficulties which have heretofore attended appropriations for purposes of internal improvement; and with those which this experience tells us will certainly arise, whenever power over such subjects may be exercised by the general government; it is hoped that

25   it may lead to the adoption of some plan which will reconcile the diversified interests of the states, and strengthen the bonds which unite them. Every member of the Union, in peace and in war, will be benefitted by the improvement of inland navigation and the construction of highways in the several states. Let us then endeavor to attain this benefit in a mode which will be satisfactory to

30   all. That hitherto adopted has, by many of our fellow-citizens, been deprecated as an infraction of the Constitution; while by others it has been viewed as inexpedient. All feel that it has been employed at the expense of harmony in the legislative councils.

To avoid these evils, it appears to me that the most safe, just and federal

35   disposition which could be made of the surplus revenue, would be its apportionment among the several states according to their ratio of representation; and should this measure not be found warranted by the Constitution, that it would be expedient to propose to the states an amendment authorizing it. I regard an appeal to the source of power, in all cases of real doubt, and where

40   its exercise is deemed indispensable to the general welfare, as among the most

sacred of all our obligations. Upon this country, more than any other, has, in the providence of God, been cast the special guardianship of the great principle of adherence to written constitutions. If it fail here, all hope in regard to it will be extinguished. That this was intended to be a government of limited and specific, and not general powers, must be admitted by all; and it is our duty to preserve 5 for it the character intended by its framers. If experience points out the necessity for an enlargement of these powers, let us apply for it to those for whose benefit it is to be exercised; and not undermine the whole system by a resort to overstrained constructions. The scheme has worked well. It has exceeded the hopes of those who devised it and become an object of admiration to the world. 10 We are responsible to our country, and to the glorious cause of self-government, for the preservation of so great a good. The great mass of legislation relating to our internal affairs, was intended to be left where the Federal Convention found it—in the state governments. Nothing is clearer, in my view, than that we are chiefly indebted for the success of the constitution under which we are now 15 acting, to the watchful and auxiliary operation of the state authorities. This is not the reflection of a day, but belongs to the most deeply rooted convictions of my mind. I cannot, therefore, too strongly or too earnestly, for my own sense of its importance, warn you against all encroachments upon the legitimate sphere of state sovereignty. Sustained by its healthful and invigorating influence, the 20 Federal system can never fall....

The condition and ulterior destiny of the Indian tribes within the limits of some of our states have become objects of much interest and importance. It has long been the policy of government to introduce among them the arts of civilization, in the hope of gradually reclaiming them from a wandering life. 25 This policy has, however, been coupled with another wholly incompatible with its success. Professing a desire to civilize and settle them, we have, at the same time, lost no opportunity to purchase their lands, and thrust them further into the wilderness. By this means they have not only been kept in a wandering state, but been led to look upon us as unjust and indifferent to their fate. Thus, though 30 lavish in its expenditures upon the subject, government has constantly defeated its own policy; and the Indians, in general, receding further and further to the West, have retained their savage habits. A portion, however, of the Southern tribes, having mingled much with the whites, and made some progress in the arts of civilized life, have lately attempted to erect an independent government, 35 within the limits of Georgia and Alabama. These states, claiming to be the only sovereigns within their territories, extended their laws over the Indians; which induced the latter to call upon the United States for protection.

Under these circumstances, the question presented was whether the general government had a right to sustain those people in their pretensions? The 40

Constitution declares that "no new state shall be formed or erected within the jurisdiction of any other state" without the consent of its legislature. If the general government is not permitted to tolerate the erection of a confederate state within the territory of one of the members of this Union against her consent;
5   much less could it allow a foreign and independent government to establish itself there. Georgia became a member of the Confederacy which eventuated in our Federal Union, as a sovereign state, always asserting her claim to certain limits; which having been originally defined in her colonial charter, and subsequently recognized in the treaty of peace, she has ever since continued to
10   enjoy, except as they have been circumscribed by her own voluntary transfer of a portion of her territory to the United States, in the articles of cession of 1802. Alabama was admitted into the Union on the same footing with the original states, with boundaries which were prescribed by Congress. There is no constitutional, conventional, or legal provision which allows them less power
15   over the Indians within their borders than is possessed by Maine or New York. Would the people of Maine permit the Penobscot tribe to erect an independent government within their state? And unless they did, would it not be the duty of the general government to support them in resisting such a measure? Would the people of New York permit each remnant of the Six Nations within her
20   borders to declare itself an independent people under the protection of the United States? Could the Indians establish a separate republic on each of their reservations in Ohio? And if they were so disposed, would it be the duty of this government to protect them in the attempt? If the principle involved in the obvious answer to these questions be abandoned, it will follow that the objects
25   of this government are reversed; and that it has become a part of its duty to aid in destroying the states which it was established to protect.

Actuated by this view of the subject, I informed the Indians inhabiting parts of Georgia and Alabama that their attempt to establish an independent government would not be countenanced by the Executive of the United States;
30   and advised them to emigrate beyond the Mississippi, or submit to the laws of those states.

Our conduct towards these people is deeply interesting to our national character. Their present condition, contrasted with what they once were, makes a most powerful appeal to our sympathies. Our ancestors found them the un-
35   controlled possessors of these vast regions. By persuasion and force, they have been made to retire from river to river, and from mountain to mountain; until some of the tribes have become extinct, and others have left but remnants, to preserve, for a while, their once terrible names. Surrounded by the whites, with their arts of civilization, which, by destroying the resources of the savage, doom
40   him to weakness and decay; the fate of the Mohegan, the Narragansett, and the

Delaware, is fast overtaking the Choctaw, the Cherokee, and the Creek. That this fate surely awaits them, if they remain within the limits of the states, does not admit of a doubt. Humanity and national honor demand that every effort should be made to avert so great a calamity. It is too late to inquire whether it was just in the United States to include them and their territory within the bounds of new states whose limits they could control. That step cannot be retraced. A state cannot be dismembered by Congress, or restricted in the exercise of her constitutional power. But the people of those states, and of every state, actuated by feelings of justice and a regard for our national honor, submit to you the interesting question, whether something cannot be done, consistently with the rights of the states, to preserve this much injured race?

As a means of effecting this end, I suggest, for your consideration, the propriety of setting apart an ample district West of the Mississippi, and without the limits of any state or territory now formed, to be guaranteed to the Indian tribes as long as they shall occupy it; each tribe having a distinct control over the portion designated for its use. There they may be secured in the enjoyment of governments of their own choice, subject to no other control from the United States than such as may be necessary to preserve peace on the frontier, and between the several tribes. There the benevolent may endeavor to teach them the arts of civilization; and, by promoting union and harmony among them, to raise up an interesting commonwealth, destined to perpetuate the race, and to attest the humanity and justice of this government.

This emigration should be voluntary, for it would be as cruel as unjust to compel the aborigines to abandon the graves of their fathers and seek a home in a distant land. But they should be distinctly informed that if they remain within the limits of the states, they must be subject to their laws. In return for their obedience, as individuals, they will, without doubt, be protected in the enjoyment of those possessions which they have improved by their industry. But it seems to me visionary to suppose that, in this state of things, claims can be allowed on tracts of country on which they have neither dwelt nor made improvements, merely because they have seen them from the mountain, or passed them in the chase. Submitting to the laws of the states, and receiving, like other citizens, protection in their persons and property, they will, ere long, become merged in the mass of our population....

The charter of the Bank of the United States expires in 1836, and its stockholders will most probably apply for a renewal of their privileges. In order to avoid the evils resulting from precipitancy in a measure involving such important principles, and such deep pecuniary interests, I feel that I cannot, in justice to the parties interested, too soon present it to the deliberate consideration of the Legislature and the People. Both the constitutionality and the expediency of the law creating this Bank are well questioned by a large portion of our fellow-citizens; and it must be admitted by all, that it has failed in the great end of establishing a uniform and sound currency.

Under these circumstances, if such an institution is deemed essential to the fiscal operations of the government, I submit to the wisdom of the Legislature whether a national one, founded upon the credit of the government and its revenues, might not be devised, which would avoid all constitutional difficulties; and, at the same time, secure all the advantages to the government and country that were expected to result from the present Bank.

I cannot close this communication without bringing to your view the just claim of the representatives of Commodore Decatur, his officers, and crew, arising from the re-capture of the frigate PHILADELPHIA under the heavy batteries of Tripoli.[1] Although sensible as a general rule, of the impropriety of Executive interference under a government like ours, where every individual enjoys the right of directly petitioning Congress; yet, viewing this case as one of very peculiar character, I deem it my duty to recommend it to your favorable consideration. Besides the justice of this claim, as corresponding to those which have been since recognized and satisfied, it is the fruit of a deed of patriotic and chivalrous daring, which infused life and confidence into our infant Navy, and contributed, as much as any exploit in its history, to elevate our national character. Public gratitude, therefore, stamps her seal upon it; and the mood should not be withheld which may hereafter operate as a stimulus to our gallant tars.

I now commend you, fellow citizens, to the guidance of Almighty God, with a full reliance on his merciful providence for the maintenance of our free institutions; and with an earnest supplication, that, whatever errors it may be my lot to commit, in discharging the arduous duties which have devolved on me, will find a remedy in the harmony and wisdom of your counsels.

---

[1]In 1803, the U.S. frigate PHILADELPHIA ran aground in Tripoli Harbor while combating pirates. In early 1804, Lieutenant Stephen Decatur led a raiding party that captured and blew up the frigate, which had been incorporated by the ruler of Tripoli into his navy. In 1826, Decatur's widow petitioned Congress to award her husband and his crew prize money for the capture of the PHILADELPHIA.

DEMOCRACY IN AMERICA
ALEXIS DE TOCQUEVILLE (1805–1859)

Alexis, Comte de Tocqueville, spent eighteen months traveling in America in 1831 to 1832 trying to figure out what made its liberties secure and its system hold together. He observed American law, government, religion, families, schools—all our institutions, with the eye of an anthropologist. He believed that in the United States lay the future: "The gradual development of the principle of equality is a Providential fact."

Tocqueville believed that equality as a condition was both a cause and effect of democracy. Whether Americans had planned it or not, democracy and equality had become the central characteristics of their political culture. In turn, both were dependent on religion and morality; his books are most lasting in their descriptions of the necessary connection between morality (what he calls "mores") and freedom. In these selections, Tocqueville presents his observations on several aspects of democracy and equality, leading up to an account of their chief dangers.

Building on Andrew Jackson's conviction, Tocqueville wrote that the "very essence of democratic government consists in the absolute sovereignty of the majority." This leads to its greatest weakness and danger, the "tyranny of the majority," that can pit equality against liberty and bring on the destruction of free institutions. His picture of a free, vital, energetic, moral, materialistic people threatened by the internal contradictions of their devotion to equality and democracy challenges us as much today as it did in the Age of Jackson.

1835

Introduction

Amongst the novel objects that attracted my attention during my stay in the United States, nothing struck me more forcibly than the general equality of

---

Alexis de Tocqueville, *Democracy in America*, Henry Reeve, trans. (London: Saunders and Otley, 1835), I:xiii–xiv, 49–68; II:143–71; (1840) III:36–53, 60–64, 193–206.

295

conditions. I readily discovered the prodigious influence which this primary fact exercises on the whole course of society, by giving a certain direction to public opinion, and a certain tenor to the laws; by imparting new maxims to the governing powers, and peculiar habits to the governed.

5   I speedily perceived that the influence of this fact extends far beyond the political character and the laws of the country, and that it has no less empire over civil society than over the government; it creates opinions, engenders sentiments, suggests the ordinary practices of life, and modifies whatever it does not produce.

10   The more I advanced in the study of American society, the more I perceived that the equality of conditions is the fundamental fact from which all others seem to be derived, and the central point at which all my observations constantly terminated.

I then turned my thoughts to our own hemisphere, where I imagined that I
15 discerned something analogous to the spectacle which the New World presented to me. I observed that the equality of conditions is daily progressing towards those extreme limits which it seems to have reached in the United States; and that the democracy which governs the American communities appears to be rapidly rising into power in Europe.

20   I hence conceived the idea of the book which is now before the reader....

Book I, Part I, Chapter III
Social Condition of the Anglo-Americans

A social condition is commonly the result of circumstances, sometimes of laws, oftener still of these two causes united; but wherever it exists, it may justly be considered as the source of almost all the laws, the usages, and the ideas which regulate the conduct of nations: whatever it does not produce, it modifies.

25   It is therefore necessary, if we would become acquainted with the legislation and the manners of a nation, to begin by the study of its social condition.

The Striking Characteristic of the Social Condition of the Anglo-Americans is Its Essential Democracy

Many important observations suggest themselves upon the social condition of the Anglo-Americans; but there is one which takes precedence of all the rest. The social condition of the Americans is eminently democratic; this was its
30 character at the foundation of the colonies, and is still more strongly marked at the present day.

I have stated in the preceding chapter that great equality existed among the emigrants who settled on the shores of New England. The germ of aristocracy was never planted in that part of the union. The only influence which obtained there was that of intellect; the people were used to reverence certain names as the emblems of knowledge and virtue. Some of their fellow-citizens acquired a power over the rest which might truly have been called aristocratic, if it had been capable of transmission from father to son.   5

This was the state of things to the east of the Hudson: to the south-west of that river, and in the direction of the Floridas, the case was different. In most of the states situated to the south-west of the Hudson some great English proprietors had settled, who had imported with them aristocratic principles and the English law of descent. I have explained the reasons why it was impossible ever to estab-   10
lish a powerful aristocracy in America; these reasons existed with less force to the south-west of the Hudson. In the South, one man, aided by slaves, could cultivate a great extent of country: it was therefore common to see rich landed proprietors. But their influence was not altogether aristocratic as that term is understood in Europe, since they possessed no privileges; and the cultivation of their estates being   15
carried on by slaves, they had no tenants depending on them, and consequently no patronage. Still, the great proprietors south of the Hudson constituted a superior class, having ideas and tastes of its own, and forming the centre of political action. This kind of aristocracy sympathized with the body of the people, whose passions and interests it easily embraced; but it was too weak and too short-lived to excite   20
either love or hatred for itself. This was the class which headed the insurrection in the South, and furnished the best leaders of the American revolution.

At the period of which we are now speaking society was shaken to its centre: the people, in whose name the struggle had taken place, conceived the desire of exercising the authority which it had acquired; its democratic tendencies were   25
awakened; and having thrown off the yoke of the mother-country, it aspired to independence of every kind. The influence of individuals gradually ceased to be felt, and custom and law united together to produce the same result.

But the law of descent was the last step to equality. I am surprised that ancient and modern jurists have not attributed to this law a greater influence on   30
human affairs.[1] It is true that these laws belong to civil affairs; but they ought nevertheless to be placed at the head of all political institutions; for, whilst political laws are only the symbol of a nation's condition, they exercise an incredible influence upon its social state. They have, moreover, a sure and uniform manner of operating upon society, affecting, as it were, generations yet unborn.   35

---

[1] I understand by the law of descent all those laws whose principal object it is to regulate the distribution of property after the death of its owner. The law of entail is of this number: it certainly prevents the owner from disposing of his possessions before his death; but this is solely with the view of preserving them entire for the heir. The principal object, therefore, of the law of entail is to regulate the descent of property after the death of its owner: its other provisions are merely means to this end.

Through their means man acquires a kind of preternatural power over the future lot of his fellow-creatures. When the legislator has regulated the law of inheritance, he may rest from his labor. The machine once put in motion will go on for ages, and advance, as if self-guided, towards a given point. When framed
5   in a particular manner, this law unites, draws together, and vests property and power in a few hands: its tendency is clearly aristocratic. On opposite principles its action is still more rapid; it divides, distributes, and disperses both property and power. Alarmed by the rapidity of its progress, those who despair of arresting its motion endeavor to obstruct it by difficulties and impediments; they vainly seek to
10 counteract its effect by contrary efforts: but it gradually reduces or destroys every obstacle, until by its incessant activity the bulwarks of the influence of wealth are ground down to the fine and shifting sand which is the basis of democracy. When the law of inheritance permits, still more when it decrees, the equal division of a father's property amongst all his children, its effects are of two kinds: it is important
15 to distinguish them from each other, although they tend to the same end.

In virtue of the law of partible inheritance, the death of every proprietor brings about a kind of revolution in property: not only do his possessions change hands, but their very nature is altered; since they are parceled into shares, which become smaller and smaller at each division. This is the direct and, as it were,
20 the physical effect of the law. It follows, then, that in countries where equality of inheritance is established by law, property, and especially landed property, must have a tendency to perpetual diminution. The effects, however, of such legislation would only be perceptible after a lapse of time, if the law was abandoned to its own working; for supposing a family to consist of two children,
25 (and in a country peopled as France is the average number is not above three,) these children, sharing amongst them the fortune of both parents, would not be poorer than their father or mother.

But the law of equal division exercises its influence not merely upon the property itself, but it affects the minds of the heirs, and brings their passions
30 into play. These indirect consequences tend powerfully to the destruction of large fortunes, and especially of large domains.

Among nations whose law of descent is founded upon the right of primogeniture, landed estates often pass from generation to generation without undergoing division. The consequence of which is that family feeling is to a
35 certain degree incorporated with the estate. The family represents the estate, the estate the family; whose name, together with its origin, its glory, its power, and its virtues, is thus perpetuated in an imperishable memorial of the past, and a sure pledge of the future.

When the equal partition of property is established by law, the intimate con-
40 nection is destroyed between family feeling and the preservation of the paternal

estate; the property ceases to represent the family; for, as it must inevitably be divided after one or two generations, it has evidently a constant tendency to diminish, and must in the end be completely dispersed. The sons of the great landed proprietor, if they are few in number, or if fortune befriends them, may indeed entertain the hope of being as wealthy as their father, but not that of possessing the same property as he did; their riches must necessarily be composed of elements different from his.

Now, from the moment that you divest the landowner of that interest in the preservation of his estate which he derives from association, from tradition, and from family pride, you may be certain that sooner or later he will dispose of it; for there is a strong pecuniary interest in favor of selling, as floating capital produces higher interest than real property, and is more readily available to gratify the passions of the moment.

Great landed estates which have once been divided never come together again; for the small proprietor draws from his land a better revenue in proportion, than the large owner does from his; and of course he sells it at a higher rate. The calculations of gain, therefore, which decided the rich man to sell his domain, will still more powerfully influence him against buying small estates to unite them into a large one.

What is called family-pride is often founded upon an illusion of self-love. A man wishes to perpetuate and immortalize himself, as it were, in his great-grandchildren. Where the *esprit de famille* ceases to act, individual selfishness comes into play. When the idea of family becomes vague, indeterminate, and uncertain, a man thinks of his present convenience; he provides for the establishment of the succeeding generation, and no more.

Either a man gives up the idea of perpetuating his family, or at any rate he seeks to accomplish it by other means than that of a landed estate. Thus not only does the law of partible inheritance render it difficult for families to preserve their ancestral domains entire, but it deprives them of the inclination to attempt it, and compels them in some measure to co-operate with the law in their own extinction.

The law of equal distribution proceeds by two methods: by acting upon things, it acts upon persons; by influencing persons, it affects things. By these means the law succeeds in striking at the root of landed property, and dispersing rapidly both families and fortunes.

Most certainly it is not for us Frenchmen of the nineteenth century, who daily witness the political and social changes which the law of partition is bringing to pass, to question its influence. It is perpetually conspicuous in our country, overthrowing the walls of our dwellings and removing the landmarks of our fields. But although it has produced great effects in France, much still remains for it to do. Our recollections, opinions, and habits present powerful obstacles to its progress.

In the United States it has nearly completed its work of destruction, and there we can best study its results. The English laws concerning the transmission
5 of property were abolished in almost all the states at the time of the Revolution. The law of entail was so modified as not to interrupt the free circulation of property. The first generation having passed away, estates began to be parceled out; and the change became more and more rapid with the progress of time. At this moment, after a lapse of little more than sixty years, the aspect of soci-
10 ety is totally altered; the families of the great landed proprietors are almost all commingled with the general mass. In the State of New York, which formerly contained many of these, there are but two who still keep their heads above the stream; and they must shortly disappear. The sons of these opulent citizens are become merchants, lawyers, or physicians. Most of them have lapsed into
15 obscurity. The last trace of hereditary ranks and distinctions is destroyed—the law of partition has reduced all to one level.

I do not mean that there is any deficiency of wealthy individuals in the United States; I know of no country, indeed, where the love of money has taken stronger hold on the affections of men, and where a profounder contempt is
20 expressed for the theory of the permanent equality of property. But wealth circulates with inconceivable rapidity, and experience shows that it is rare to find two succeeding generations in the full enjoyment of it.

This picture, which may perhaps be thought to be overcharged, still gives a very imperfect idea of what is taking place in the new states of the West and
25 Southwest. At the end of the last century a few bold adventurers began to penetrate into the valleys of the Mississippi: and the mass of the population very soon began to move in that direction: communities unheard of till then were seen to emerge from the wilds: states, whose names were not in existence a few years before, claimed their place in the American Union: and in the Western
30 settlements we may behold democracy arrived at its utmost extreme. In these states, founded offhand and as it were by chance, the inhabitants are but of yesterday. Scarcely known to one another, the nearest neighbors are ignorant of each other's history. In this part of the American continent, therefore, the population has not experienced the influence of great names and great wealth,
35 nor even that of the natural aristocracy of knowledge and virtue. None are there to wield that respectable power which men willingly grant to the remembrance of a life spent in doing good before their eyes. The new states of the West are already inhabited; but society has no existence among them.

It is not only the fortunes of men which are equal in America; even their
40 acquirements partake in some degree of the same uniformity. I do not believe

that there is a country in the world where, in proportion to the population, there are so few uninstructed, and at the same time so few learned individuals. Primary instruction is within the reach of everybody; superior instruction is scarcely to be obtained by any. This is not surprising; it is in fact the necessary consequence of what we have advanced above. Almost all the Americans are in easy circumstances, 5 and can therefore obtain the first elements of human knowledge.

In America there are comparatively few who are rich enough to live without a profession. Every profession requires an apprenticeship, which limits the time of instruction to the early years of life. At fifteen they enter upon their calling, and thus their education ends at the age when ours begins. Whatever is done 10 afterwards, is with a view to some special and lucrative object; a science is taken up as a matter of business, and the only branch of it which is attended to is such as admits of an immediate practical application.

In America most of the rich men were formerly poor: most of those who now enjoy leisure were absorbed in business during their youth; the consequence of 15 which is that when they might have had a taste for study, they had no time for it, and when the time is at their disposal they have no longer the inclination.

There is no class, then, in America in which the taste for intellectual pleasures is transmitted with hereditary fortune and leisure, and by which the labors of the intellect are held in honor. Accordingly there is an equal want of the desire 20 and the power of application to these objects.

A middling standard is fixed in America for human knowledge. All approach as near to it as they can; some as they rise, others as they descend. Of course, an immense multitude of persons are to be found who entertain the same number of ideas on religion, history, science, political economy, legisla- 25 tion, and government. The gifts of intellect proceed directly from God, and man cannot prevent their unequal distribution. But in consequence of the state of things which we have here represented, it happens that although the capacities of men are widely different, as the Creator has doubtless intended they should be, they are submitted to the same method of treatment. 30

In America the aristocratic element has always been feeble from its birth; and if at the present day it is not actually destroyed, it is at any rate so completely disabled that we can scarcely assign to it any degree of influence in the course of affairs.

The democratic principle, on the contrary, has gained so much strength by 35 time, by events, and by legislation, as to have become not only predominant but all-powerful. There is no family or corporate authority, and it is rare to find even the influence of individual character enjoy any durability.

America, then, exhibits in her social state a most extraordinary phenomenon. Men are there seen on a greater equality in point of fortune and intellect, 40 or, in other words, more equal in their strength, than in any other country of the world, or in any age of which history has preserved the remembrance.

Political Consequences of the Social Condition of the Anglo-Americans

The political consequences of such a social condition as this are easily deducible. It is impossible to believe that equality will not eventually find its way into the
5   political world as it does everywhere else. To conceive of men remaining for ever unequal upon one single point, yet equal on all others, is impossible; they must come in the end to be equal upon all.

Now I know of only two methods of establishing equality in the political world; every citizen must be put in possession of his rights, or rights must be
10   granted to no one. For nations which are arrived at the same stage of social existence as the Anglo-Americans, it is therefore very difficult to discover a medium between the sovereignty of all and the absolute power of one man: and it would be vain to deny that the social condition which I have been describing is equally liable to each of these consequences.

15   There is, in fact, a manly and lawful passion for equality which excites men to wish all to be powerful and honored. This passion tends to elevate the humble to the rank of the great; but there exists also in the human heart a depraved taste for equality, which impels the weak to attempt to lower the powerful to their own level, and reduces men to prefer equality in slavery to inequality with
20   freedom. Not that those nations whose social condition is democratic naturally despise liberty; on the contrary, they have an instinctive love of it. But liberty is not the chief and constant object of their desires; equality is their idol: they make rapid and sudden efforts to obtain liberty; and if they miss their aim, resign themselves to their disappointment; but nothing can satisfy them except
25   equality, and rather than lose it they resolve to perish.

On the other hand, in a state where the citizens are nearly on an equality, it becomes difficult for them to preserve their independence against the aggressions of power. No one among them being strong enough to engage in the struggle with advantage, nothing but a general combination can protect
30   their liberty. And such a union is not always to be found.

From the same social position, then, nations may derive one or the other of two great political results; these results are extremely different from each other, but they may both proceed from the same cause.

The Anglo-Americans are the first nations who, having been exposed to
35   this formidable alternative, have been happy enough to escape the dominion of absolute power. They have been allowed by their circumstances, their origin, their intelligence, and especially by their moral feeling, to establish and maintain the sovereignty of the people.

The Principle of the Sovereignty of the People in America

Whenever the political laws of the United States are to be discussed, it is with the doctrine of the sovereignty of the people that we must begin.

The principle of the sovereignty of the people, which is to be found, more or less, at the bottom of almost all human institutions, generally remains concealed from view. It is obeyed without being recognized, or if for a moment it 5
be brought to light, it is hastily cast back into the gloom of the sanctuary.

"The will of the nation" is one of those expressions which have been most profusely abused by the wily and the despotic of every age. To the eyes of some it has been represented by the venal suffrages of a few of the satellites of power; to others, by the votes of a timid or an interested minority; and some have 10
even discovered it in the silence of a people, on the supposition that the fact of submission established the right of command.

In America, the principle of the sovereignty of the people is not either barren or concealed, as it is with some other nations; it is recognized by the customs and proclaimed by the laws; it spreads freely, and arrives without impediment 15
at its most remote consequences. If there be a country in the world where the doctrine of the sovereignty of the people can be fairly appreciated, where it can be studied in its application to the affairs of society, and where its dangers and its advantages may be foreseen, that country is assuredly America.

I have already observed that, from their origin, the sovereignty of the people 20
was the fundamental principle of the greater number of British colonies in America. It was far, however, from then exercising as much influence on the government of society as it now does. Two obstacles, the one external, the other internal, checked its invasive progress.

It could not ostensibly disclose itself in the laws of colonies which were still 25
constrained to obey the mother-country; it was therefore obliged to spread secretly, and to gain ground in the provincial assemblies, and especially in the townships.

American society was not yet prepared to adopt it with all its consequences. The intelligence of New England, and the wealth of the country to the south of the Hudson, (as I have shown in the preceding chapter) long exercised a sort of 30
aristocratic influence, which tended to retain the exercise of social authority in the hands of a few. The public functionaries were not universally elected, and the citizens were not all of them electors. The electoral franchise was everywhere placed within certain limits, and made dependent on a certain qualification, which was exceedingly low in the north and more considerable in the south. 35

The American revolution broke out, and the doctrine of the sovereignty of the people, which had been nurtured in the townships and municipalities, took possession of the state: every class was enlisted in its cause; battles were fought, and victories obtained for it; until it became the law of laws.

A no less rapid change was effected in the interior of society, where the law of descent completed the abolition of local influences.

At the very time when this consequence of the laws and of the revolution was apparent to every eye, victory was irrevocably pronounced in favor of the democratic cause. All power was, in fact, in its hands, and resistance was no longer possible. The higher orders submitted without a murmur and without a struggle to an evil which was thenceforth inevitable. The ordinary fate of falling powers awaited them; each of their several members followed his own interest; and as it was impossible to wring the power from the hands of a people which they did not detest sufficiently to brave, their only aim was to secure its good-will at any price. The most democratic laws were consequently voted by the very men whose interests they impaired: and thus, although the higher classes did not excite the passions of the people against their order, they accelerated the triumph of the new state of things; so that, by a singular change, the democratic impulse was found to be most irresistible in the very states where the aristocracy had the firmest hold.

The State of Maryland, which had been founded by men of rank, was the first to proclaim universal suffrage, and to introduce the most democratic forms into the conduct of its government.

When a nation modifies the elective qualification, it may easily be foreseen that sooner or later that qualification will be entirely abolished. There is no more invariable rule in the history of society: the further electoral rights are extended, the greater is the need of extending them; for after each concession the strength of the democracy increases, and its demands increase with its strength. The ambition of those who are below the appointed rate is irritated in exact proportion to the great number of those who are above it. The exception at last becomes the rule, concession follows concession, and no stop can be made short of universal suffrage.

At the present day the principle of the sovereignty of the people has acquired, in the United States, all the practical development which the imagination can conceive. It is unencumbered by those fictions which have been thrown over it in other countries, and it appears in every possible form according to the exigency of the occasion. Sometimes the laws are made by the people in a body, as at Athens; and sometimes its representatives, chosen by universal suffrage, transact business in its name, and almost under its immediate control.

In some countries a power exists which, though it is in a degree foreign to the social body, directs it, and forces it to pursue a certain track. In others the ruling force is divided, being partly within and partly without the ranks of the people. But nothing of the kind is to be seen in the United States; there society governs itself for itself. All power centres in its bosom; and scarcely an individual is to be met with who would venture to conceive, or, still less, to express, the idea of seeking it elsewhere. The nation participates in the making of its laws by the choice of its legislators, and in the execution of them by the choice of the agents of the executive government; it may almost be said to govern itself, so feeble and so restricted is the share left to the administration, so little do the authorities forget their popular origin and the power from which they emanate....

Book I, Part I, Chapter XV
Unlimited Power of the Majority in the United States, and its Consequences

The very essence of democratic government consists in the absolute sovereignty of the majority; for there is nothing in democratic states which is capable of resisting it. Most of the American Constitutions have sought to increase this natural strength of the majority by artificial means.

The legislature is, of all political institutions, the one which is most easily swayed by the wishes of the majority. The Americans determined that the members of the legislature should be elected by the people immediately, and for a very brief term, in order to subject them, not only to the general convictions, but even to the daily passions of their constituents. The members of both Houses are taken from the same class in society, and are nominated in the same manner; so that the modifications of the legislative bodies are almost as rapid and quite as irresistible as those of a single assembly. It is to a legislature thus constituted that almost all the authority of the government has been entrusted.

But whilst the law increased the strength of those authorities which of themselves were strong, it enfeebled more and more those which were naturally weak. It deprived the representatives of the executive of all stability and independence; and by subjecting them completely to the caprices of the legislature, it robbed them of the slender influence which the nature of a democratic government might have allowed them to retain. In several states, the judicial power was also submitted to the elective discretion of the majority; and in all of them its existence was made to depend on the pleasure of the legislative authority, since the representatives were empowered annually to regulate the stipend of the judges.

Custom, however, has done even more than law. A proceeding which will in the end set all the guarantees of representative government at naught, is becoming more and more general in the United States: it frequently happens that the electors, who choose a delegate, point out a certain line of conduct to him, and impose upon him a certain number of positive obligations which he is pledged to fulfill. With the exception of the tumult, this comes to the same thing as if the majority of the populace held its deliberations in the marketplace.

Several other circumstances concur in rendering the power of the majority
5 in America, not only preponderant, but irresistible. The moral authority of the majority is partly based upon the notion that there is more intelligence and more wisdom in a great number of men collected together than in a single individual, and that the quantity of legislators is more important than their quality. The theory of equality is in fact applied to the intellect of man; and human pride
10 is thus assailed in its last retreat, by a doctrine which the minority hesitate to admit, and in which they very slowly concur. Like all other powers, and perhaps more than all other powers, the authority of the many requires the sanction of time; at first it enforces obedience by constraint; but its laws are not respected until they have long been maintained.

15 The right of governing society, which the majority supposes itself to derive from its superior intelligence, was introduced into the United States by the first settlers; and this idea, which would be sufficient of itself to create a free nation, has now been amalgamated with the manners of the people, and the minor incidents of social intercourse.

20 The French, under the old monarchy, held it for a maxim (which is still a fundamental principle of the English Constitution) that the King could do no wrong; and if he did do wrong, the blame was imputed to his advisers. This notion was highly favorable to habits of obedience; and it enabled the subject to complain of the law, without ceasing to love and honor the lawgiver. The
25 Americans entertain the same opinion with respect to the majority.

The moral power of the majority is founded upon yet another principle, which is that the interests of the many are to be preferred to those of the few. It will readily be perceived that the respect here professed for the rights of the majority must naturally increase or diminish according to the state of parties. When a
30 nation is divided into several irreconcilable factions, the privilege of the majority is often overlooked, because it is intolerable to comply with its demands.

If there existed in America a class of citizens whom the legislating majority sought to deprive of exclusive privileges, which they had possessed for ages, and to bring down from an elevated station to the level of the ranks of the multitude,
35 it is probable that the minority would be less ready to comply with its laws. But as the United States were colonized by men holding an equal rank amongst themselves, there is as yet no natural or permanent source of dissension between the interests of its different inhabitants.

There are certain communities in which the persons who constitute the
40 minority can never hope to draw over the majority to their side, because they

must then give up the very point which is at issue between them. Thus, an aristocracy can never become a majority whilst it retains its exclusive privileges, and it cannot cede its privileges without ceasing to be an aristocracy.

In the United States, political questions cannot be taken up in so general and absolute a manner; and all parties are willing to recognize the rights of the majority, because they all hope to turn those rights to their own advantage at some future time. The majority therefore in that country exercises a prodigious actual authority, and a moral influence which is scarcely less preponderant; no obstacles exist which can impede, or so much as retard its progress, or which can induce it to heed the complaints of those whom it crushes upon its path. This state of things is fatal in itself and dangerous for the future.

How the Unlimited Power of the Majority Increases in America, The Instability of Legislation and the Administration Inherent in Democracy

I have already spoken of the natural defects of democratic institutions, and they all of them increase in the exact ratio of the power of the majority. To begin with the most evident of them all; the mutability of the laws is an evil inherent in democratic government, because it is natural to democracies to raise men to power in very rapid succession. But this evil is more or less sensible in proportion to the authority and the means of action which the legislature possesses.

In America the authority exercised by the legislative bodies is supreme; nothing prevents them from accomplishing their wishes with celerity, and with irresistible power, whilst they are supplied by new representatives every year. That is to say, the circumstances which contribute most powerfully to democratic instability, and which admit of the free application of caprice to every object in the state, are here in full of operation. In conformity with this principle, America is, at the present day, the country in the world where laws last the shortest time. Almost all the American constitutions have been amended within the course of thirty years: there is therefore not a single American state which has not modified the principles of its legislation in that lapse of time. As for the laws themselves, a single glance upon the archives of the different states of the Union suffices to convince one that in America the activity of the legislator never slackens. Not that the American democracy is naturally less stable than any other, but that it is allowed to follow its capricious propensities in the formation of the laws.

The omnipotence of the majority, and the rapid as well as absolute manner in which its decisions are executed in the United States, has not only the effect of rendering the law unstable, but it exercises the same influence upon the execution of the law and the conduct of the public administration. As the majority is the only power which it is important to court, all its projects are taken up with the greatest ardor; but no sooner is its attention distracted, than all this ardor ceases; whilst in the free states of Europe, the administration is at once independent and secure, so that the projects of the legislature are put into execution, although its immediate attention may be directed to other objects.

5   In America certain ameliorations are undertaken with much more zeal and activity than elsewhere; in Europe the same ends are promoted by much less social effort, more continuously applied.

Some years ago several pious individuals undertook to ameliorate the condition of the prisons. The public was excited by the statements which they put 10 forward, and the regeneration of criminals became a very popular undertaking. New prisons were built; and, for the first time, the idea of reforming as well as of punishing the delinquent, formed a part of prison discipline. But his happy alteration, in which the public had taken so hearty an interest, and which the exertions of the citizens had irresistibly accelerated, could not be completed in 15 a moment. Whilst the new penitentiaries were being erected (and it was the pleasure of the majority that they should be terminated with all possible celerity) the old prisons existed, which still contained a great number of offenders. These gaols became more unwholesome and more corrupt in proportion as the new establishments were beautified and improved, forming a contrast which 20 may readily be understood. The majority was so eagerly employed in founding the new prisons that those which already existed were forgotten; and as the general attention was diverted to a novel object, the care which had hitherto been bestowed upon the others ceased. The salutary regulations of discipline were first relaxed, and afterwards broken; so that in the immediate neighbor- 25 hood of a prison which bore witness to the mild and enlightened spirit of our time, dungeons might be met with which reminded the visitor of the barbarity of the Middle Ages.

Tyranny of the Majority

I hold it to be an impious and an execrable maxim that, politically speaking, a people has a right to do whatsoever it pleases; and yet I have asserted that all 30 authority originates in the will of the majority. Am I, then, in contradiction with myself?

A general law—which bears the name of Justice—has been made and sanctioned, not only by a majority of this or that people, but by a majority of mankind. The rights of every people are consequently confined within the 35 limits of what is just. A nation may be considered in the light of a jury which is empowered to represent society at large, and to apply the great and general law of Justice. Ought such a jury, which represents society, to have more power than the society in which the laws it applies originate?

When I refuse to obey an unjust law, I do not contest the right which the majority has of commanding, but I simply appeal from the sovereignty of the people to the sovereignty of mankind. It has been asserted that a people can never entirely out-step the boundaries of justice and of reason in those affairs which are more peculiarly its own; and that consequently full power may fear-lessly be given to the majority by which it is represented. But this language is that of a slave.

A majority taken collectively may be regarded as a being whose opinions, and most frequently whose interests, are opposed to those of another being, which is styled a minority. If it be admitted that a man, possessing absolute power, may misuse that power by wronging his adversaries, why should a majority not be liable to the same reproach? Men are not apt to change their characters by agglomeration; nor does their patience in the presence of obstacles increase with the consciousness of their strength. And for these reasons I can never willingly invest any number of my fellow-creatures with that unlimited authority which I should refuse to any one of them.

I do not think that it is possible to combine several principles in the same government so as at the same time to maintain freedom, and really to oppose them to one another. The form of government which is usually termed *mixed* has always appeared to me to be a mere chimera. Accurately speaking there is no such thing as a mixed government (with the meaning usually given to that word) because in all communities some one principle of action may be discov-ered which preponderates over the others. England in the last century, which has been more especially cited as an example of this form of government, was in point of fact an essentially aristocratic state, although it comprised very powerful elements of democracy: for the laws and customs of the country were such that the aristocracy could not but preponderate in the end, and subject the direc-tion of public affairs to its own will. The error arose from too much attention being paid to the actual struggle which was going on between the nobles and the people, without considering the probable issue of the contest, which was in reality the important point. When a community really has a mixed government, that is to say, when it is equally divided between two adverse principles, it must either pass through a revolution, or fall into complete dissolution.

I am therefore of opinion that some one social power must always be made to predominate over the others; but I think that liberty is endangered when this power is checked by no obstacles which may retard its course, and force it to moderate its own vehemence.

Unlimited power is in itself a bad and dangerous thing; human beings are not competent to exercise it with discretion; and God alone can be omnipotent, because his wisdom and his justice are always equal to his power. But no power

upon earth is so worthy of honor for itself, or of reverential obedience to the
rights which it represents, that I would consent to admit its uncontrolled and
all-predominant authority. When I see that the right and the means of absolute
command are conferred on a people or upon a king, upon an aristocracy or a
5   democracy, a monarchy or a republic, I recognize the germ of tyranny, and I
journey onwards to a land of more hopeful institutions.

In my opinion the main evil of the present democratic institutions of the
United States does not arise, as is often asserted in Europe, from their weakness, but from their overpowering strength; and I am not so much alarmed
10 at the excessive liberty which reigns in that country, as at the very inadequate
securities which exist against tyranny.

When an individual or a party is wronged in the United States, to whom
can he apply for redress? If to public opinion, public opinion constitutes the
majority; if to the legislature, it represents the majority, and implicitly obeys
15 its injunctions; if to the executive power, it is appointed by the majority and
remains a passive tool in its hands; the public troops consist of the majority
under arms; the jury is the majority invested with the right of hearing judicial
cases; and in certain states even the judges are elected by the majority. However
iniquitous or absurd the evil of which you complain may be, you must submit
20 to it as well as you can.

If, on the other hand, a legislative power could be so constituted as to
represent the majority without necessarily being the slave of its passions; an
executive, so as to retain a certain degree of uncontrolled authority; and a
judiciary, so as to remain independent of the two other powers; a government
25 would be formed which would still be democratic, without incurring any risk
of tyrannical abuse.

I do not say that tyrannical abuses frequently occur in America at the present
day; but I maintain that no such barrier is established against them, and that
the causes which mitigate the government are to be found in the circumstances
30 and the manners of the country more than in its laws.

Effects of the Unlimited Power of the Majority Upon
the Arbitrary Authority of the American Public Officers

A distinction must be drawn between tyranny and arbitrary power. Tyranny may
be exercised by means of the law, and in that case it is not arbitrary: arbitrary
power may be exercised for the good of the community at large, in which case
it is not tyrannical. Tyranny usually employs arbitrary means, but, if necessary,
35 it can rule without them.

In the United States the unbounded power of the majority, which is favorable to the legal despotism of the legislature, is likewise favorable to the arbitrary

authority of the magistrate. The majority has an entire control over the law when it is made and when it is executed; and as it possesses an equal authority over those who are in power, and the community at large, it considers public officers as its passive agents, and readily confides the task of serving its designs to their vigilance. The details of their office and the privileges which they are to enjoy   5 are rarely defined beforehand; but the majority treats them, as a master does his servants, when they are always at work in his sight, and he has the power of directing or reprimanding them at every instant.

In general the American functionaries are far more independent than the French civil officers within the sphere which is prescribed to them. Sometimes,   10 even, they are allowed by the popular authority to exceed those bounds; and as they are protected by the opinion, and backed by the co-operation, of the majority, they venture upon such manifestations of their power as astonish a European. By this means habits are formed in the heart of a free country which may someday prove fatal to its liberties.   15

Power Exercised by the Majority in America Upon Opinion

It is in the examination of the display of public opinion in the United States that we clearly perceive how far the power of the majority surpasses all the powers with which we are acquainted in Europe. Intellectual principles exercise an influence which is so invisible and often so inappreciable that they baffle the toils of oppression. At the present time the most absolute monarchs in Europe   20 are unable to prevent certain notions, which are opposed to their authority, from circulating in secret throughout their dominions, and even in their courts. Such is not the case in America; as long as the majority is still undecided, discussion is carried on; but as soon as its decision is irrevocably pronounced, a submissive silence is observed; and the friends, as well as the opponents, of the   25 measure, unite in assenting to its propriety. The reason of this is perfectly clear: no monarch is so absolute as to combine all the powers of society in his own hands, and to conquer all opposition, with the energy of a majority, which is invested with the right of making and of executing the laws.

The authority of a king is purely physical, and it controls the actions of   30 the subject without subduing his private will; but the majority possesses a power which is physical and moral at the same time; it acts upon the will as well as upon the actions of men, and it represses not only all contest, but all controversy.

I know no country in which there is so little true independence of mind   35 and freedom of discussion as in America. In any constitutional state in Europe every sort of religious and political theory may be advocated and propagated abroad; for there is no country in Europe so subdued by any single authority, as not to contain citizens who are ready to protect the man who raises his voice in the cause of truth, from the consequences of his hardihood. If he is unfortunate enough to live under an absolute government, the people is upon his side; if he inhabits a free country, he may find a shelter behind the authority of the throne, if he require one. The aristocratic part of society supports him in some countries, and the democracy in others. But in a nation where democratic institutions exist, organized like those of the United States, there is but one sole authority, one single element of strength and of success, with nothing beyond it.

In America, the majority raises very formidable barriers to the liberty of opinion: within these barriers an author may write whatever he pleases, but he will repent it if he ever step beyond them. Not that he is exposed to the terrors of an *auto-de-fé*,[2] but he is tormented by the slights and persecutions of daily obloquy. His political career is closed for ever, since he has offended the only authority which is able to promote his success. Every sort of compensation, even that of celebrity, is refused to him. Before he published his opinions, he imagined that he held them in common with many others; but no sooner has he declared them openly, than he is loudly censured by his overbearing opponents, whilst those who think, without having the courage to speak, like him, abandon him in silence. He yields at length, oppressed by the daily efforts he has been making, and he subsides into silence, as if he was tormented by remorse for having spoken the truth.

Fetters and headsmen were the coarse instruments which tyranny formerly employed; but the civilization of our age has refined the arts of despotism, which seemed however to have been sufficiently perfected before. The excesses of monarchical power had devised a variety of physical means of oppression; the democratic republics of the present day have rendered it as entirely an affair of the mind, as that will which it is intended to coerce. Under the absolute sway of an individual despot, the body was attacked in order to subdue the soul; and the soul escaped the blows which were directed against it, and rose superior to the attempt; but such is not the course adopted by tyranny in democratic republics; there the body is left free, and the soul is enslaved. The sovereign can no longer say, "You shall think as I do on pain of death;" but he says, "You are free to think differently from me, and to retain your life, your property, and all that you possess; but if such be your determination, you are henceforth an alien among your people. You may retain your civil rights, but they will be useless to you, for you will never be chosen by your fellow-citizens if you solicit their suffrages; and they will affect to scorn you, if you solicit their esteem. You will

---

[2]An *auto-de-fé* (literally, *act of faith*) was a public penance performed after condemnation by the Spanish Inquisition.

remain among men, but you will be deprived of the rights of mankind. Your fellow-creatures will shun you like an impure being; and those who are most persuaded of your innocence will abandon you too, lest they should be shunned in their turn. Go in peace! I have given you your life, but it is an existence incomparably worse than death."   5

Monarchical institutions have thrown an odium upon despotism; let us beware lest democratic republics should restore oppression, and should render it less odious and less degrading in the eyes of the many, by making it still more onerous to the few.

Works have been published in the proudest nations of the Old World,   10 expressly intended to censure the vices and deride the follies of the times: La Bruyère[3] inhabited the palace of Louis XIV when he composed his chapter upon the Great, and Molière[4] criticized the courtiers in the very pieces which were acted before the Court. But the ruling power in the United States is not to be made game of; the smallest reproach irritates its sensibility, and the lightest   15 joke which has any foundation in truth renders it indignant; from the style of its language to the more solid virtues of its character, everything must be made the subject of encomium. No writer, whatever be his eminence, can escape from this tribute of adulation to his fellow-citizens. The majority lives in the perpetual practice of self-applause; and there are certain truths which the Americans can   20 only learn from strangers or from experience.

If great writers have not at present existed in America, the reason is very simply given in these facts; there can be no literary genius without freedom of opinion, and freedom of opinion does not exist in America. The Inquisition has never been able to prevent a vast number of anti-religious books from   25 circulating in Spain. The empire of the majority succeeds much better in the United States, since it actually removes the wish of publishing them. Unbelievers are to be met with in America, but, to say the truth, there is no public organ of infidelity. Attempts have been made by some governments to protect the morality of nations by prohibiting licentious books. In the United States   30 no one is punished for this sort of works, but no one is induced to write them; not because all the citizens are immaculate in their manners, but because the majority of the community is decent and orderly.

In these cases the advantages derived from the exercise of this power are unquestionable; and I am simply discussing the nature of the power itself. This   35

---

[3]Jean de la Bruyére (1645–1696), a French essayist who routinely caricatured leading literary figures
  of his day
[4]Jean-Baptiste Poquelin (1622–1673), who wrote many comedies under the pseudonym Molière,
  including *The Misanthrope* and *Tartuffe*

irresistible authority is a constant fact, and its judicious exercise is an accidental occurrence.

Effects of the Tyranny of the Majority Upon the National Character of the Americans

The tendencies which I have just alluded to are as yet very slightly perceptible in political society; but they already begin to exercise an unfavorable influence
5   upon the national character of the Americans. I am inclined to attribute the singular paucity of distinguished political characters to the ever-increasing activity of the despotism of the majority in the United States.

When the American Revolution broke out, they arose in great numbers; for public opinion then served, not to tyrannize over, but to direct the exertions
10   of individuals. Those celebrated men took a full part in the general agitation of mind common at that period, and they attained a high degree of personal fame, which was reflected back upon the nation, but which was by no means borrowed from it.

In absolute governments, the great nobles who are nearest to the throne
15   flatter the passions of the sovereign, and voluntarily truckle to his caprices. But the mass of the nation does not degrade itself by servitude; it often submits from weakness, from habit, or from ignorance, and sometimes from loyalty. Some nations have been known to sacrifice their own desires to those of the sovereign with pleasure and with pride; thus exhibiting a sort of independence
20   in the very act of submission. These peoples are miserable, but they are not degraded. There is a great difference between doing what one does not approve, and feigning to approve what one does; the one is the necessary case of a weak person, the other befits the temper of a lackey.

In free countries, where everyone is more or less called upon to give his
25   opinion in the affairs of state; in democratic republics, where public life is incessantly commingled with domestic affairs, where the sovereign authority is accessible on every side, and where its attention can almost always be attracted by vociferation, more persons are to be met with who speculate upon its foibles, and live at the cost of its passions, than in absolute monarchies. Not because
30   men are naturally worse in these states than elsewhere, but the temptation is stronger, and of easier access at the same time. The result is a far more extensive debasement of the characters of citizens.

Democratic republics extend the practice of currying favor with the many, and they introduce it into a greater number of classes at once: this is one of the
35   most serious reproaches that can be addressed to them. In democratic states organized on the principles of the American republics, this is more especially the case, where the authority of the majority is so absolute and so irresistible

that a man must give up his rights as a citizen, and almost abjure his quality as a human being, if he intends to stray from the track which it lays down.

In that immense crowd which throngs the avenues to power in the United States, I found very few men who displayed any of that manly candor and that masculine independence of opinion which frequently distinguished the Americans in former times, and which constitutes the leading feature in distinguished characters wheresoever they may be found. It seems, at first sight, as if all the minds of the Americans were formed upon one model, so accurately do they correspond in their manner of judging. A stranger does, indeed, sometimes meet with Americans who dissent from these rigorous formularies; with men who deplore the defects of the laws, the mutability and the ignorance of democracy; who even go so far as to observe the evil tendencies which impair the national character, and to point out such remedies as it might be possible to apply; but no one is there to hear these things besides yourself, and you, to whom these secret reflections are confided, are a stranger and a bird of passage. They are very ready to communicate truths which are useless to you, but they continue to hold a different language in public.

If ever these lines are read in America, I am well assured of two things: in the first place, that all who peruse them will raise their voices to condemn me; and in the second place, that very many of them will acquit me at the bottom of their conscience.

I have heard of patriotism in the United States, and it is a virtue which may be found among the people, but never among the leaders of the people. This may be explained by analogy; despotism debases the oppressed much more than the oppressor: in absolute monarchies the king has often great virtues, but the courtiers are invariably servile. It is true that the American courtiers do not say "Sire" or "Your Majesty"—a distinction without a difference. They are forever talking of the natural intelligence of the populace they serve; they do not debate the question as to which of the virtues of their master is pre-eminently worthy of admiration; for they assure him that he possesses all the virtues under heaven without having acquired them, or without caring to acquire them: they do not give him their daughters and their wives to be raised at his pleasure to the rank of his concubines, but, by sacrificing their opinions, they prostitute themselves. Moralists and philosophers in America are not obliged to conceal their opinions under the veil of allegory; but, before they venture upon a harsh truth, they say, "We are aware that the people which we are addressing is too superior to all the weaknesses of human nature to lose the command of its temper for an instant; and we should not hold this language if we were not speaking to men, whom their virtues and their intelligence render more worthy of freedom than all the rest of the world."

It would have been impossible for the sycophants of Louis XIV to flatter more dexterously. For my part, I am persuaded that in all governments, whatever their nature may be, servility will cower to force, and adulation will cling to power. The only means of preventing men from degrading themselves, is to invest no one
5   with that unlimited authority which is the surest method of debasing them.

The Greatest Dangers of the American Republics Proceed From the Unlimited Power of the Majority

Governments usually fall a sacrifice to impotence or to tyranny. In the former case their power escapes from them; it is wrested from their grasp in the latter. Many observers who have witnessed the anarchy of democratic states have imagined that the government of those states was naturally weak and impotent. The truth is that when once hostilities are begun between parties, the govern-
10   ment loses its control over society. But I do not think that a democratic power is naturally without force or without resources: say rather that it is almost always by the abuse of its force, and the misemployment of its resources that a democratic government fails. Anarchy is almost always produced by its tyranny or its mistakes, but not by its want of strength.
15   It is important not to confound stability with force, or the greatness of a thing with its duration. In democratic republics, the power which directs society is not stable; for it often changes hands and assumes a new direction. But whichever way it turns, its force is almost irresistible. The governments of the American republics appear to me to be as much centralized as those of the
20   absolute monarchies of Europe, and more energetic than they are. I do not, therefore, imagine that they will perish from weakness.
      If ever the free institutions of America are destroyed, that event may be attributed to the unlimited authority of the majority, which may at some future time urge the minorities to desperation, and oblige them to have recourse to
25   physical force. Anarchy will then be the result, but it will have been brought about by despotism.
      Mr. Madison expresses the same opinion in the Federalist, No. 51. "It is of great importance in a republic not only to guard the society against the oppression of its rulers, but to guard one part of the society against the injustice
30   of the other part. Justice is the end of government. It is the end of civil society. It ever has been, and ever will be pursued until it be obtained, or until liberty be lost in the pursuit. In a society, under the forms of which the stronger faction can readily unite and oppress the weaker, anarchy may as truly be said to reign as in a state of nature, where the weaker individual is not secured against the
35   violence of the stronger: and as in the latter state even the stronger individuals are prompted by the uncertainty of their condition to submit to a government

which may protect the weak as well as themselves, so in the former state will the more powerful factions be gradually induced by a like motive to wish for a government which will protect all parties, the weaker as well as the more power- ful. It can be little doubted that if the State of Rhode Island was separated from the Confederacy and left to itself, the insecurity of rights under the popular form of government within such narrow limits, would be displayed by such reiterated oppressions of the factious majorities, that some power altogether independent of the people, would soon be called for by the voice of the very factions whose misrule had proved the necessity of it."

Jefferson has also thus expressed himself in a letter to Madison, "The execu- tive power in our government is not the only, perhaps not even the principal object of my solicitude. The tyranny of the legislature is really the danger most to be feared, and will continue to be so for many years to come. The tyranny of the executive power will come in its turn, but at a more distant period."

I am glad to cite the opinion of Jefferson upon this subject rather than that of another, because I consider him to be the most powerful advocate democracy has ever sent forth....

BOOK I, PART II, CHAPTER V
Of the Manner in Which Religion in the United States Avails Itself of Democratic Tendencies

I have laid it down in a preceding chapter that men cannot do without dogmati- cal belief; and even that it is very much to be desired that such belief should exist amongst them. I now add that of all the kinds of dogmatical belief, the most desirable appears to me to be dogmatical belief in matters of religion; and this is a very clear inference, even from no higher consideration than the interests of this world.

There is hardly any human action, however particular a character be assigned to it, which does not originate in some very general idea men have conceived of the Deity, of His relation to mankind, of the nature of their own souls, and of their duties to their fellow-creatures. Nor can anything prevent these ideas from being the common spring from which everything else emanates.

Men are therefore immeasurably interested in acquiring fixed ideas of God, of the soul, and of their common duties to their Creator and to their fellow- men; for doubt on these first principles would abandon all their actions to the impulse of chance, and would condemn them to live, to a certain extent, powerless and undisciplined.

This is then the subject on which it is most important for each of us to entertain fixed ideas; and unhappily it is also the subject on which it is most difficult for each of us, left to himself, to settle his opinions by the sole force of his reason. None but minds singularly free from the ordinary anxieties of life—minds at once penetrating, subtle, and trained by thinking—can, even with the assistance of much time and care, sound the depth of these most

5   necessary truths. And, indeed, we see that these philosophers are themselves almost always enshrouded in uncertainties; that at every step the natural light which illuminates their path grows dimmer and less secure; and that, in spite of all their efforts, they have as yet only discovered a small number of conflicting notions, on which the mind of man has been tossed about for thousands of

10   years, without either laying a firmer grasp on truth, or finding novelty even in its errors. Studies of this nature are far above the average capacity of men; and even if the majority of mankind were capable of such pursuits, it is evident that leisure to cultivate them would still be wanting.

Fixed ideas of God and human nature are indispensable to the daily prac-

15   tice of men's lives; but the practice of their lives prevents them from acquiring such ideas.

The difficulty appears to me to be without a parallel. Amongst the sciences there are some which are useful to the mass of mankind, and which are within its reach; others can only be approached by the few, and are not cultivated by

20   the many, who require nothing beyond their more remote applications: but the daily practice of the science I speak of is indispensable to all, although the study of it is inaccessible to the far greater number.

General ideas respecting God and human nature are therefore the ideas above all others which it is most suitable to withdraw from the habitual action

25   of private judgment, and in which there is most to gain and least to lose by recognizing a principle of authority.

The first object and one of the principal advantages of religions is to furnish to each of these fundamental questions a solution which is at once clear, precise, intelligible to the mass of mankind, and lasting. There are religions

30   which are very false and very absurd; but it may be affirmed that any religion which remains within the circle I have just traced, without aspiring to go beyond it (as many religions have attempted to do, for the purpose of inclosing on every side the free progress of the human mind), imposes a salutary restraint on the intellect; and it must be admitted that, if it do not save men

35   in another world, such religion is at least very conducive to their happiness and their greatness in this.

This is more especially true of men living in free countries. When the religion of a people is destroyed, doubt gets hold of the highest portions of the intellect, and half paralyses all the rest of its powers. Every man accustoms himself to

40   entertain none but confused and changing notions on the subjects most interest-

ing to his fellow-creatures and himself. His opinions are ill-defended and easily abandoned; and despairing of ever resolving, by himself, the hardest problems of the destiny of man, he ignobly submits to think no more about them.

Such a condition cannot but enervate the soul, relax the springs of the will, and prepare a people for servitude. Nor does it only happen, in such a case, that they allow their freedom to be wrested from them; they frequently themselves surrender it. When there is no longer any principle of authority in religion any more than in politics, men are speedily frightened at the aspect of this unbounded independence. The constant agitation of all surrounding things alarms and exhausts them. As everything is at sea in the sphere of the intellect, they determine at least that the mechanism of society should be firm and fixed; and as they cannot resume their ancient belief, they assume a master.

For my own part, I doubt whether man can ever support at the same time complete religious independence and entire public freedom. And I am inclined to think that if faith be wanting in him, he must serve; and if he be free, he must believe.

Perhaps, however, this great utility of religions is still more obvious amongst nations where equality of conditions prevails than amongst others. It must be acknowledged that equality, which brings great benefits into the world, nevertheless suggests to men (as will be shown here-after) some very dangerous propensities. It tends to isolate them from each other, to concentrate every man's attention upon himself; and it lays open the soul to an inordinate love of material gratification.

The greatest advantage of religion is to inspire diametrically contrary principles. There is no religion which does not place the object of man's desires above and beyond the treasures of earth, and which does not naturally raise his soul to regions far above those of the senses. Nor is there any which does not impose on man some sort of duties to his kind, and thus draws him at times from the contemplation of himself. This occurs in religions the most false and dangerous.

Religious nations are therefore naturally strong on the very point on which democratic nations are weak; which shows of what importance it is for men to preserve their religion as their conditions become more equal.

I have neither the right nor the intention of examining the supernatural means which God employs to infuse religious belief into the heart of man. I am at this moment considering religions in a purely human point of view: my object is to inquire by what means they may most easily retain sway in the democratic ages upon which we are entering.

It has been shown that, at times of general cultivation and equality, the human mind does not consent to adopt dogmatical opinions without reluctance, and feels their necessity acutely in spiritual matters only. This proves, in the first place, that at such times religions ought, more cautiously than at any other, to confine themselves within their own precincts; for in seeking to extend their power beyond religious matters, they incur a risk of not being believed at all. The circle within which they seek to bound the human intellect ought therefore to be carefully traced, and beyond its verge the mind should be left in entire freedom to its own guidance.

Mohammed professed to derive from Heaven, and he has inserted in the Koran, not only a body of religious doctrines, but political maxims, civil and criminal laws, and theories of science. The Gospel, on the contrary, only speaks of the general relations of men to God and to each other—beyond which it inculcates and imposes no point of faith. This alone, besides a thousand other reasons, would suffice to prove that the former of these religions will never long predominate in a cultivated and democratic age, whilst the latter is destined to retain its sway at these as at all other periods.

But in continuation of this branch of the subject, I find that in order for religions to maintain their authority, humanly speaking, in democratic ages, they not only must confine themselves strictly within the circle of spiritual matters: their power also depends very much on the nature of the belief they inculcate, on the external forms they assume, and on the obligations they impose.

The preceding observation, that equality leads men to very general and very extensive notions, is principally to be understood as applied to the question of religion. Men living in a similar and equal condition in the world readily conceive the idea of the one God, governing every man by the same laws, and granting to every man future happiness on the same conditions. The idea of the unity of mankind constantly leads them back to the idea of the unity of the Creator; whilst, on the contrary, in a state of society, where men are broken up into very unequal ranks, they are apt to devise as many deities as there are nations, castes, classes, or families, and to trace a thousand private roads to Heaven.

It cannot be denied that Christianity itself has felt, to a certain extent, the influence which social and political conditions exercise on religious opinions.

At the epoch at which the Christian religion appeared upon earth, Providence, by whom the world was doubtless prepared for its coming, had gathered a large portion of the human race, like an immense flock, under the scepter of the Caesars. The men of whom this multitude was composed were distinguished by numerous differences; but they had thus much in common, that they all obeyed the same laws, and that every subject was so weak and insignificant in relation to the imperial potentate, that all appeared equal when their condition was contrasted with his.

This novel and peculiar state of mankind necessarily predisposed men to listen to the general truths which Christianity teaches, and may serve to explain the facility and rapidity with which they then penetrated into the human mind.

The counterpart of this state of things was exhibited after the destruction of the Empire. The Roman world being then as it were shattered into a thousand fragments, each nation resumed its pristine individuality. An infinite scale of ranks very soon grew up in the bosom of these nations; the different races were more sharply defined, and each nation was divided by castes into several peoples. In the midst of this common effort, which seemed to be urging human society to the greatest conceivable amount of voluntary subdivision, Christianity did not lose sight of the leading general ideas which it had brought into the world. But it appeared, nevertheless, to lend itself, as much as was possible, to those new tendencies to which the fractional distribution of mankind had given birth. Men continued to worship an only God, the Creator and Preserver of all things; but every people, every city, and, so to speak, every man, thought to obtain some distinct privilege, and win the favor of an especial patron at the foot of the throne of Grace. Unable to subdivide the Deity, they multiplied and improperly enhanced the importance of the divine agents. The homage due to Saints and Angels became an almost idolatrous worship amongst the majority of the Christian world; and apprehensions might be entertained for a moment lest the religion of Christ should retrograde towards the superstitions which it had subdued.

It seems evident that the more the barriers are removed which separate nation from nation amongst mankind, and citizen from citizen amongst a people, the stronger is the bent of the human mind, as if by its own impulse, towards the idea of an only and all-powerful Being, dispensing equal laws in the same manner to every man. In democratic ages then it is more particularly important not to allow the homage paid to secondary agents to be confounded with the worship due to the Creator alone.

Another truth is no less clear—that religions ought to assume fewer external observances in democratic periods than at any others.

In speaking of philosophical method among the Americans, I have shown that nothing is more repugnant to the human mind in an age of equality than the idea of subjection to forms. Men living at such times are impatient of figures; to their eyes symbols appear to be the puerile artifice which is used to conceal or to set off truths, which should more naturally be bared to the light of open day: they are unmoved by ceremonial observances, and they are predisposed to attach a secondary importance to the details of public worship.

Those whose care it is to regulate the external forms of religion in a democratic age should pay a close attention to these natural propensities of the human mind, in order not unnecessarily to run counter to them.

I firmly believe in the necessity of forms, which fix the human mind in the contemplation of abstract truths, and stimulate its ardor in the pursuit of them, whilst they invigorate its powers of retaining them steadfastly. Nor do I suppose that it is possible to maintain a religion without external observances; but, on the other hand, I am persuaded that, in the ages upon which we are entering, it would be peculiarly dangerous to multiply them beyond measure; and that they ought rather to be limited to as much as is absolutely necessary to perpetuate the doctrine itself, which is the substance of religions of which the ritual is only the form. A religion of which should become more minute, more peremptory, and more surcharged with small observances at a time in which men are becoming more equal, would soon find itself reduced to a band of fanatical zealots in the midst of an infidel people.

I anticipate the objection that as all religions have general and eternal truths for their object, they cannot thus shape themselves to the shifting spirit of every age, without forfeiting their claim to certainty in the eyes of mankind.

To this I reply again that the principal opinions which constitute belief, and which theologians call articles of faith, must be very carefully distinguished from the accessories connected with them. Religions are obliged to hold fast to the former, whatever be the peculiar spirit of the age; but they should take good care not to bind themselves in the same manner to the latter, at a time when everything is in transition, and when the mind, accustomed to the moving pageant of human affairs, reluctantly endures the attempt to fix it to any given point. The fixity of external and secondary things can only afford a chance of duration when civil society is itself fixed; under any other circumstances I hold it to be perilous.

We shall have occasion to see that, of all the passions which originate in, or are fostered by, equality, there is one which it renders peculiarly intense, and which it infuses at the same time into the heart of every man: I mean the love of well-being. The taste for well-being is the prominent and indelible feature of democratic ages.

It may be believed that a religion which should undertake to destroy so deep-seated a passion, would meet its own destruction thence in the end; and if it attempted to wean men entirely from the contemplation of the good things of this world, in order to devote their faculties exclusively to the thought of another, it may be foreseen that the soul would at length escape from its grasp, to plunge into the exclusive enjoyment of present and material pleasures.

The chief concern of religions is to purify, to regulate, and to restrain the excessive and exclusive taste for well-being which men feel at periods of equality; but they would err in attempting to control it completely or to eradicate it. They will not succeed in curing men of the love of riches; but they may still persuade men to enrich themselves by none but honest means.

This brings me to a final consideration, which comprises, as it were, all the others. The more the conditions of men are equalized and assimilated to each other, the more important is it for religions, whilst they carefully abstain from the daily turmoil of secular affairs, not needlessly to run counter to the ideas which generally prevail, and the permanent interests which exist in the mass of the people. For as public opinion grows to be more and more evidently the first and most irresistible of existing powers, the religious principle has no external support strong enough to enable it long to resist its attacks. This is not less true of a democratic people, ruled by a despot, than in a republic. In ages of equality, kings may often command obedience, but the majority always commands belief: to the majority therefore deference is to be paid in whatsoever is not contrary to the faith.

I showed in my former volumes how the American clergy stand aloof from secular affairs. This is the most obvious, but it is not the only, example of their self-restraint. In America religion is a distinct sphere, in which the priest is sovereign, but out of which he takes care never to go. Within its limits he is the master of the mind; beyond them, he leaves men to themselves, and surrenders them to the independence and instability which belong to their nature and their age. I have seen no country in which Christianity is clothed with fewer forms, figures and observances than in the United States; or where it presents more distinct, more simple, or more general notions to the mind. Although the Christians of America are divided into a multitude of sects, they all look upon their religion in the same light. This applies to Roman Catholicism as well as to the other forms of belief. There are no Romish priests who show less taste for the minute individual observances, for extraordinary or peculiar means of salvation, or who cling more to the spirit, and less to the letter, of the law than the Roman Catholic priests of the United States. Nowhere is that doctrine of the Church, which prohibits the worship reserved to God alone from being offered to the saints, more clearly inculcated or more generally followed. Yet the Roman Catholics of America are very submissive and very sincere.

Another remark is applicable to the clergy of every communion. The American ministers of the Gospel do not attempt to draw or to fix all the thoughts of man upon the life to come; they are willing to surrender a portion of his heart to the cares of the present; seeming to consider the goods of this world as important, although as secondary, objects. If they take no part themselves in productive labor, they are at least interested in its progression and ready to applaud its results; and whilst they never cease to point to the other world as the great object of the hopes and fears of the believer, they do not forbid him honestly to court prosperity in this. Far from attempting to show that these things are distinct and contrary to one another, they study rather to find out on what point they are most nearly and closely connected.

All the American clergy know and respect the intellectual supremacy exercised by the majority; they never sustain any but necessary conflicts with it. They take no share in the altercations of parties, but they readily adopt the general opinions of their country and their age; and they allow themselves to be borne away without opposition in the current of feeling and opinion by which everything around them is carried along. They endeavor to amend their contemporaries, but they do not quit fellowship with them. Public opinion is therefore never hostile to them: it rather supports and protects them; and their belief owes its authority at the same time to the strength which is its own, and to that which they borrow from the opinions of the majority.

Thus it is that by respecting all democratic tendencies not absolutely contrary to herself, and by making use of several of them for her own purposes, Religion sustains an advantageous struggle with that spirit of individual independence which is her most dangerous antagonist....

Book I, Part II, Chapter VIII
The Principle of Equality Suggests to the Americans the Idea of the Indefinite Perfectibility of Man

Equality suggests to the human mind several ideas which would not have originated from any other source, and it modifies almost all those previously entertained. I take as an example the idea of human perfectibility, because it is one of the principal notions that the intellect can conceive, and because it constitutes of itself a great philosophical theory, which is every instant to be traced by its consequences in the practice of human affairs.

Although man has many points of resemblance with the brute creation, one characteristic is peculiar to himself—he improves; they are incapable of improvement. Mankind could not fail to discover this difference from its earliest period. The idea of perfectibility is therefore as old as the world: equality did not give birth to it, although it has imparted to it a novel character.

When the citizens of a community are classed according to their rank, their profession or their birth, and when all men are constrained to follow the career which happens to open before them, everyone thinks that the utmost limits of human power are to be discerned in proximity of himself, and none seeks any longer to resist the inevitable law of his destiny. Not indeed that an aristocratic people absolutely contests man's faculty of self-improvement, but they do not hold it to be indefinite; amelioration they conceive, but not change: they imagine that the future condition of society may be better, but not essentially different; and whilst they admit that mankind has made vast strides in improvement, and may still have some to make, they assign to it beforehand certain impassable limits.

Thus they do not presume that they have arrived at the supreme good or at absolute truth (what people or what man was ever wild enough to imagine it?) but they cherish a persuasion that they have pretty nearly reached that degree of greatness and knowledge which our imperfect nature admits of; and, as nothing moves about them, they are willing to fancy that everything is in its fit place. Then it is that the legislator affects to lay down eternal laws; that kings and nations will raise none but imperishable monuments; and that the present generation undertakes to spare generations to come the care of regulating their destinies.

In proportion as castes disappear and the classes of society approximate—as manners, customs and laws vary, from the tumultuous intercourse of men—as new facts arise—as new truths are brought to light—as ancient opinions are dissipated and others take their place—the image of an ideal perfection, forever on the wing, presents itself to the human mind. Continual changes are then every instant occurring under the observation of every man: the position of some is rendered worse; and he learns but too well that no people and no individual, how enlightened soever they may be, can lay claim to infallibility—the condition of others is improved; whence he infers that man is endowed with an indefinite faculty of improvement. His reverses teach him that none may hope to have discovered absolute good—his success stimulates him to the never-ending pursuit of it. Thus, forever seeking—forever falling, to rise again—often disappointed, but not discouraged—he tends unceasingly towards that unmeasured greatness so indistinctly visible at the end of the long track which humanity has yet to tread.

It can hardly be believed how many facts naturally flow from the philosophical theory of the indefinite perfectibility of man, or how strong an influence it exercises even on men who, living entirely for the purposes of action and not of thought, seem to conform their actions to it, without knowing anything about it.

I accost an American sailor, and I inquire why the ships of his country are built so as to last but for a short time; he answers without hesitation that the art of navigation is every day making such rapid progress that the finest vessel would become almost useless if it lasted beyond a certain number of years. In these words, which fell accidentally and on a particular subject from a man of rude attainments, I recognize the general and systematic idea upon which a great people directs all its concerns.

Aristocratic nations are naturally too apt to narrow the scope of human perfectibility; democratic nations to expand it beyond compass.

Book II, Part II, Chapter I
Why Democratic Nations Show a More Ardent and Enduring Love of Equality than of Liberty

The first and most intense passion which is engendered by the equality of conditions is, I need hardly say, the love of that same equality. My readers will therefore not be surprised that I speak of it before all others.

5   Everybody has remarked that in our time, and especially in France, this passion for equality is every day gaining ground in the human heart. It has been said a hundred times that our contemporaries are far more ardently and tenaciously attached to equality than to freedom; but, as I do not find that the causes of the fact have been sufficiently analyzed, I shall endeavor to point them out.

It is possible to imagine an extreme point at which freedom and equality would meet and be confounded together. Let us suppose that all the members
10   of the community take a part in the government, and that each one of them has an equal right to take a part in it. As none is different from his fellows, none can exercise a tyannical power: men will be perfectly free, because they will all be entirely equal; and they will all be perfectly equal, because they will be entirely
15   free. To this ideal state democratic nations tend. Such is the completest form that equality can assume upon earth; but there are a thousand others which, without being equally perfect, are not less cherished by those nations.

The principle of equality may be established in civil society, without prevailing in the political world. Equal rights may exist in indulging in the same
20   pleasures, of entering the same professions, of frequenting the same places—in a word, of living in the same manner and seeking wealth by the same means, although all men do not take an equal share in the government.

A kind of equality may even be established in the political world, though there should be no political freedom there. A man may be the equal of all his
25   countrymen save one, who is the master of all without distinction, and who selects equally from among them all the agents of his power.

Several other combinations might be easily imagined by which very great equality would be united to institutions more or less free, or even to institutions wholly without freedom.

30   Although men cannot become absolutely equal unless they be entirely free, and consequently equality, pushed to its furthest extent, may be confounded with freedom, yet there is good reason for distinguishing the one from the other. The taste which men have for liberty, and that which they feel for equality, are, in fact two different things; and I am not afraid to add that, amongst democratic
35   nations, they are two unequal things.

Upon close inspection, it will be seen that there is in every age some peculiar and preponderating fact with which all others are connected; this fact almost always gives birth to some pregnant idea or some ruling passion, which attracts to itself, and bears away in its course, all the feelings and opinions of the time: it is like a great stream, towards which each of the surrounding rivulets seems 5 to flow.

Freedom has appeared in the world at different times and under various forms; it has not been exclusively bound to any social condition, and it is not confined to democracies. Freedom cannot, therefore, form the distinguishing characteristic of democratic ages. The peculiar and preponderating fact which marks those ages 10 as its own is the equality of conditions; the ruling passion of men in those periods is the love of this equality. Ask not what singular charm the men of democratic ages find in being equal, or what special reasons they may have for clinging so tenaciously to equality rather than to the other advantages which society holds out to them: equality is the distinguishing characteristic of the age they live in; 15 that, of itself, is enough to explain that they prefer it to all the rest.

But independently of this reason there are several others, which will at all times habitually lead men to prefer equality to freedom.

If a people could ever succeed in destroying, or even in diminishing, the equality which prevails in its own body, this could only be accomplished by long 20 and laborious efforts. Its social condition must be modified, its laws abolished, its opinions superseded, its habits changed, its manners corrupted. But political liberty is more easily lost; to neglect to hold it fast, is to allow it to escape.

Men therefore not only cling to equality because it is dear to them; they also adhere to it because they think it will last forever. 25

That political freedom may compromise in its excesses the tranquility, the property, the lives of individuals, is obvious to the narrowest and most unthinking minds. But, on the contrary, none but attentive and clear-sighted men perceive the perils with which equality threatens us, and they commonly avoid pointing them out. They know that the calamities they apprehend are 30 remote, and flatter themselves that they will only fall upon future generations, for which the present generation takes but little thought. The evils which freedom sometimes brings with it are immediate; they are apparent to all, and all are more or less affected by them. The evils which extreme equality may produce are slowly disclosed; they creep gradually into the social frame; they are only 35 seen at intervals, and at the moment at which they become most violent, habit already causes them to be no longer felt.

The advantages which freedom brings are only shown by length of time; and it is always easy to mistake the cause in which they originate. The advantages of equality are instantaneous, and they may constantly be traced from their source.

Political liberty bestows exalted pleasures, from time to time, upon a certain number of citizens. Equality every day confers a number of small enjoyments
5   on every man. The charms of equality are every instant felt, and are within the reach of all: the noblest hearts are not insensible to them, and the most vulgar souls exult in them. The passion which equality engenders must therefore be at once strong and general. Men cannot enjoy political liberty un-purchased by some sacrifices, and they never obtain it without great exertions. But the
10 pleasures of equality are self-proffered: each of the petty incidents of life seems to occasion them, and in order to taste them nothing is required but to live.

Democratic nations are at all times fond of equality, but there are certain epochs at which the passion they entertain for it swells to the height of fury. This occurs at the moment when the old social system, long menaced, com-
15 pletes its own destruction after a last intestine struggle, and when the barriers of rank are at length thrown down. At such times men pounce upon equality as their booty, and they cling to it as to some precious treasure which they fear to lose. The passion for equality penetrates on every side into men's hearts, ex-pands there, and fills them entirely. Tell them not that by this blind surrender
20 of themselves to an exclusive passion, they risk their dearest interests: they are deaf. Show them not freedom escaping from their grasp, whilst they are looking another way: they are blind—or rather, they can discern but one sole object to be desired in the universe.

What I have said is applicable to all democratic nations: what I am about to
25 say concerns the French alone. Amongst most modern nations, and especially amongst all those of the continent of Europe, the taste and the idea of freedom only began to exist and to extend itself at the time when social conditions were tending to equality, and as a consequence of that very equality. Absolute kings were the most efficient levelers of ranks amongst their subjects. Amongst these
30 nations equality preceded freedom: equality was therefore a fact of some standing, when freedom was still a novelty: the one had already created customs, opinions, and laws belonging to it, when the other, alone and for the first time, came into actual existence. Thus the latter was still only an affair of opinion and of taste, whilst the former had already crept into the habits of the people, possessed itself
35 of their manners, and given a particular turn to the smallest actions in their lives. Can it be wondered that the men of our own time prefer the one to the other?

I think that democratic communities have a natural taste for freedom: left to themselves, they will seek it, cherish it, and view any privation of it with regret. But for equality, their passion is ardent, insatiable, incessant, invincible:
40 they call for equality in freedom; and if they cannot obtain that, they still call

for equality in slavery. They will endure poverty, servitude, barbarism—but they will not endure aristocracy.

This is true at all times, and especially true in our own. All men and all powers seeking to cope with this irresistible passion, will be overthrown and destroyed by it. In our age, freedom cannot be established without it, and   5
despotism itself cannot reign without its support.

BOOK II, PART II, CHAPTER II
Of Individualism in Democratic Countries

I have shown how it is that in ages of equality every man seeks for his opinions within himself: I am now about to show how it is that, in the same ages, all his feelings are tuned towards himself alone. *Individualism* is a novel expression to which a novel idea has given birth. Our fathers were only acquainted   10
with egotism. Egotism is a passionate and exaggerated love of self, which leads a man to connect everything with his own person, and to prefer himself to everything in the world. Individualism is a mature and calm feeling, which disposes each member of the community to sever himself from the mass of his fellow-creatures, and to draw apart with his family and his friends; so that,   15
after he has thus formed a little circle of his own, he willingly leaves society at large to itself. Egotism originates in blind instinct: individualism proceeds from erroneous judgment more than from depraved feelings; it originates as much in the deficiencies of the mind as in the perversity of the heart.

Egotism blights the germ of all virtue: individualism, at first, only saps the   20
virtues of public life; but, in the long run, it attacks and destroys all others, and is at length absorbed in downright egotism. Egotism is a vice as old as the world, which does not belong to one form of society more than to another: individualism is of democratic origin, and it threatens to spread in the same ratio as the equality of conditions.   25

Amongst aristocratic nations, as families remain for centuries in the same condition, often on the same spot, all generations become as it were contemporaneous. A man almost always knows his forefathers, and respects them: he thinks he already sees his remote descendants, and he loves them. He willingly imposes duties on himself towards the former and the latter; and he will fre-   30
quently sacrifice his personal gratifications to those who went before and to those who will come after him.

Aristocratic institutions have, moreover, the effect of closely binding every man to several of his fellow-citizens. As the classes of an aristocratic people are strongly marked and permanent, each of them is regarded by its own members   35
as a sort of lesser country, more tangible and more cherished than the country

at large. As in aristocratic communities all the citizens occupy fixed positions, one above the other, the result is that each of them always sees a man above himself whose patronage is necessary to him, and below himself another man whose co-operation he may claim.

Men living in aristocratic ages are therefore almost always closely attached to something placed out of their own sphere, and they are often disposed to forget themselves. It is true that in those ages the notion of human fellowship is faint, and that men seldom think of sacrificing themselves for mankind; but they often sacrifice themselves for other men. In democratic ages, on the contrary, when the duties of each individual to the race are much more clear, devoted service to any one man becomes more rare; the bond of human affection is extended, but it is relaxed.

Amongst democratic nations new families are constantly springing up, others are constantly falling away, and all that remain change their condition; the woof of time is every instant broken, and the track of generations effaced. Those who went before are soon forgotten; of those who will come after no one has any idea: the interest of man is confined to those in close propinquity to himself.

As each class approximates to other classes, and intermingles with them, its members become indifferent and as strangers to one another. Aristocracy had made a chain of all the members of the community, from the peasant to the king: democracy breaks that chain, and severs every link of it.

As social conditions become more equal, the number of persons increases who, although they are neither rich enough nor powerful enough to exercise any great influence over their fellow-creatures, have nevertheless acquired or retained sufficient education and fortune to satisfy their own wants. They owe nothing to any man, they expect nothing from any man; they acquire the habit of always considering themselves as standing alone, and they are apt to imagine that their whole destiny is in their own hands.

Thus not only does democracy make every man forget his ancestors, but it hides his descendants, and separates his contemporaries from him; it throws him back for ever upon himself alone, and threatens in the end to confine him entirely within the solitude of his own heart.

REMARKS ON SENECA FALLS
ELIZABETH CADY STANTON (1815–1902)

The perfectionist strain Tocqueville noticed surfaced in a bewildering variety of reform movements. The 1840s were not unlike the 1960s in producing challenges to existing authority on behalf of Progress and a better world. Ralph Waldo Emerson wrote, "What is man born for, but to be a Reformer, a Remaker of what man has made?"

The reform movements were of three main types: (1) voluntary, utopian, perfectionist communities dedicated to both religious and secular goals ("Shaking Quakers," Brook Farm, Oneida Community, New Harmony, and Fourier Phalanxes, among others); (2) voluntary associations committed to reforming individual behavior (Temperance crusade, observance of the Sabbath, care of "unfortunates"); and (3) political movements designed to change social institutions or mass behavior (public education, prisons, asylums, abolition of slavery).

The movement for women's rights embodied all three, although it began more modestly than the others during this era. The small western New York village of Seneca Falls hosted the first convention on behalf of women's rights. One of the most prominent women's rights leaders, Elizabeth Cady Stanton, offered this speech after the convention concluded, encapsulating the position of many suffragettes.

1848

…Among the many important questions which have been brought before the public, there is none that more vitally affects the whole human family than that which is technically called woman's rights. Every allusion to the degraded and inferior position occupied by women all over the world has been met by scorn and abuse. From the man of highest mental cultivation to the most degraded wretch who staggers in the streets do we meet ridicule and coarse jests, freely bestowed upon those who dare assert that woman stands by the side of man, his   5

Elizabeth Cady Stanton, *Address of Mrs. Elizabeth Cady Stanton Delivered at Seneca Falls and Rochester, N.Y.* (New York: Robert J. Johnston, 1870), 3–12, 14–16, 19.

equal, placed here by her God, to enjoy with him the beautiful earth, which is
her home as it is his, having the same sense of right and wrong, and looking to
the same Being for guidance and support. So long has man exercised tyranny
over her, injurious to himself and benumbing to her faculties, that few can
5   nerve themselves to meet the storm; and so long has the chain been about her
that she knows not there is a remedy.

The whole social, civil, and religious condition of woman is a subject too
vast to be brought within the limits of one short lecture. Suffice it to say, for the
present, wherever we turn, the history of woman is sad and dark, without any
10   alleviating circumstances, nothing from which we can draw consolation.

As the nations of the earth emerge from a state of barbarism, the sphere
of woman gradually becomes wider; but not even under what is thought to
be the full blaze of the sun of civilization is it what God designed it to be. In
every country and clime does man assume the responsibility of marking out the
15   path for her to tread. In every country does he regard her as a being inferior to
himself, and one whom he is to guide and control....

There is a class of men who believe in their natural, inborn, inbred superiority, and their heaven-descended right to dominion over the fish of the sea, the
fowl of the air, and last, though not least, the immortal being called woman. I
20   would recommend this class to the attentive perusal of their Bibles—Genesis
1:28; to historical research, to foreign travel, to a closer observation of the
manifestations of mind about them, and to a humble comparison of themselves
with such women as Catherine of Russia,[1] Elizabeth of England,[2] distinguished
for their statesmanlike qualities; Harriet Martineau[3] and Madame de Stael,[4]
25   for their literary attainments; or Caroline Herschel[5] and Mary Somerville[6]
for their scientific researches, or for physical equality, to that whole nation of
famous women, the Amazons. We seldom find this class of objectors among
liberally-educated persons, who have the advantage of observing the race in
different countries, climes, and phases. But barbarians though they may be, in
30   entertaining such an opinion, they must be met and fairly vanquished. Let us
consider, then, man's superiority—intellectually, morally, physically.

Man's intellectual superiority cannot be a question until woman has had
a fair trial. When we shall have had our freedom to find out our own sphere,
when we shall have had our colleges, our professions, our trades for a century, a
35   comparison then may be justly instituted. When woman, instead of being taxed

---

[1]Catherine II (1729–1792), Empress of Russia (1762–1792)
[2]Elizabeth II (1533–1603), Queen of England (1558–1603)
[3]Harriet Martineau (1802–1876), English author and abolitionist
[4]Anne Louise de Staël-Holstein (1766–1817), prominent French author & hostess of intellectual salons
[5]Caroline Herschel (1750–1848), English astronomer and discoverer of several comets
[6]Mary Somerville (1780–1872), Scottish scientist and member of the Royal Astronomical Society

to endow colleges where she is forbidden to enter—instead of forming sewing societies to educate "poor, but pious" young men, shall first educate herself, when she shall be just to herself before she is generous to others; improving the talents God has given her, and leaving her neighbor to do the same for himself, we shall not then hear so much about this boasted superiority. How often, now, we see young men carelessly throwing away the intellectual food their sisters crave. A little music, that she may while an hour away pleasantly, a little French, a smattering of the sciences, and in rare instances, some slight classical knowledge, and woman is considered highly educated. She leaves her books and studies just as a young man is entering thoroughly into his. Then comes the gay routine of fashionable life, courtship and marriage, the perplexities of house and children, and she knows nothing beside. Her sphere is home. And whatever yearning her spirit may have felt for a higher existence, whatever may have been the capacity she well knew she possessed for more elevated enjoyments, enjoyments which would not conflict with those holy duties, but add new luster to them, all, all is buried beneath the weight of these undivided cares....

In consideration of man's claim to moral superiority, glance now at our theological seminaries, our divinity students, the long line of descendants from our Apostolic fathers, the immaculate priesthood, and what do we find here? Perfect moral rectitude in every relation of life, a devoted spirit of self-sacrifice, a perfect union of thought, opinion, and feeling among those who profess to worship one God, and whose laws they feel themselves called upon to declare to a fallen race? Far from it. These persons, all so thoroughly acquainted with the character of God, and of His designs, made manifest by His words and works, are greatly divided among themselves. Every sect has its God, every sect has its Bible, and there is as much bitterness, envy, hatred, and malice between those contending sects, yea, even more, than in our political parties during the periods of their greatest excitement. Now the leaders of these sects—are they distinguished among men for their holy aspirations, their virtue, purity, and chastity? Do they keep themselves unspotted from the world? Is the moral and religious life of this class what we might expect from minds said to be fixed on such mighty themes? By no means. Not a year passes but we hear of some sad, soul-sickening deed perpetrated by some of this class. If such be the state of the most holy, we need not pause now to consider those classes who claim of us less reverence and respect. The lamentable want of principle among our lawyers, generally, is too well known to need comment. The everlasting back-biting and bickering of our physicians is proverbial. The disgraceful riots at our polls, where man, in performing the highest duty of citizenship, ought surely to be sober-minded, the perfect rowdyism that now characterizes the debates in our national Congress—all these are great facts which rise up against man's claim for moral superiority. In my opinion, he is infinitely woman's inferior in every moral quality, not by nature, but made so by a false education....

Let us now consider man's claims to physical superiority. Methinks I hear some say, surely you will not contend for equality here. Yes, we must not give an inch lest you claim an ell, we cannot accord to man even this much and he has no right to claim it until the fact be fully demonstrated, until the physical

5   education of the boy and the girl shall have been the same for many years. If you claim the advantage of size merely, why it may be that under any course of training in ever so perfect a development of the physique in woman, man might still be the larger of the two, though we do not grant even this. But the perfection of the physique is great power combined with endurance. Now

10   your strongest men are not always the tallest men, nor the broadest, nor the most corpulent, but very often the small, elastic man who is well-built, tightly put together, and possessed of an indomitable will.... We cannot say what the woman might be physically if the girl were allowed all the freedom of the boy in romping, climbing, swimming, playing whoop and ball.... Physically, as well

15   as intellectually, it is use that produces growth and development....

But there is a class of objectors who say they do not claim superiority, they merely assert a difference. But you will find by following them up closely that they soon run this difference into the old groove of superiority....

We have met here today to discuss our rights and wrongs, civil and political

20   and not, as some have supposed, to go into the detail of social life alone.... But we are assembled to protect against a form of government, existing without the consent of the governed—to declare our right to be free as man is free, to be represented in the government which we are taxed to support, to have such disgraceful laws as give man the power to chastise and imprison his wife, to take the wages which she

25   earns, the property which she inherits, and, in case of separation, the children of her love; laws which makes her the mere dependent on his bounty. It is to protest against such unjust laws as these that we are assembled today, and to have them, if possible, forever erased from our statute-books, deeming them a shame and a disgrace to a Christian republic in the nineteenth century. We have met

30   *To uplift woman's fallen divinity*
                    Upon an even pedestal with man's

And, strange as it may seem to many, we now demand our right to vote accord-ing to the declaration of the government under which we live. This right no one pretends to deny. We need not prove ourselves equal to Daniel Webster to

35   enjoy this privilege, for the ignorant Irishman in the ditch has all the civil rights he has. We need not prove our muscular power equal to this same Irishman to enjoy this privilege, for the most tiny, weak, ill-shaped stripling of twenty-one has all the civil rights of the Irishman. We have no objection to discuss the question of equality, for we feel that the weight of argument lies wholly with us,

40   but we wish the question of equality kept distinct from the question of rights,

for the proof of the one does not determine the truth of the other. All men in this country have the same rights, however they may differ in mind, body, or estate. The right is ours. The question now is how shall we get possession of what rightfully belongs to us. We should not feel so sorely grieved if no man who had not attained the full stature of a Webster, Van Buren, Clay, or Gerrit Smith could claim the right of the elective franchise, but to have the rights of drunkards, idiots, horse-racing, rum-selling rowdies, ignorant foreigners, and silly boys fully recognized, whilst we ourselves are thrust out from all the rights that belong to citizens—it is too grossly insulting to the dignity of woman to be longer quietly submitted to. The right is ours, have it we must—use it we will. The pens, the tongues, the fortunes, the indomitable wills of many women are already pledged to secure this right. The great truth that no just government can be formed without the consent of the governed, we shall echo and re-echo in the ears of the unjust judge until by continual coming we shall weary him.

But say some would you have woman vote? What? Refined, delicate woman at the polls, mingling in such scenes of violence and vulgarity—most certainly. Where there is so much to be feared for the pure, the innocent, the noble, the mother surely should be there to watch and guard her sons, who must encounter such stormy dangerous scenes at the tender age of 21. Much is said of woman's influence; might not her presence do much towards softening down this violence—refining this vulgarity? Depend upon it that places that by their impure atmosphere are rendered unfit for woman cannot but be dangerous to her sires and sons....

But what would woman gain by voting? Men must know the advantages of voting, for they all seem very tenacious about the right. Think you if woman had a voice in this government that all those laws affecting her interests would so entirely violate every principle of right and justice? Had woman a vote to give, might not the office-holders and seekers propose some change in her condition? Might not woman's rights become as great a question as free soil?

But are you not already sufficiently represented by your fathers, husbands, brothers, and sons? Let your statute books answer the question. We have had enough of such representation. In nothing is woman's true happiness consulted. Men like to call her an angel—to feed her with what they think sweet food nourishing her vanity, to induce her to believe her organization is so much finer more delicate than theirs, that she is not fitted to struggle with the tempests of public life but needs their care and protection. Care and protection? Such as the wolf gives the lamb; such as the eagle the hare he carries to his eyrie. Most cunningly he entraps her and then takes from her all those rights which are dearer to him than life itself, rights which have been baptized in blood and the maintenance of which is even now rocking to their foundations the kingdoms of the old world.

The most discouraging, the most lamentable aspect our cause wears is the indifference, indeed, the contempt with which women themselves regard our

movement. When the subject is introduced among our young ladies, among those even who claim to be intelligent and educated, it is met by the scornful curl of the lip and by expressions of disgust and ridicule. But we shall hope better things of them when they are enlightened in regard to their present
5   position, to the laws under which they live—they will not then publish their degradation by declaring themselves satisfied nor their ignorance by declaring they have all the rights they want....

One common objection to this movement is that if the principles of freedom and equality which we advocate were put into practice, it would destroy all
10   harmony in the domestic circle. Here let me ask, how many truly harmonious households have we now? Look round your circle of friends. On the one hand you will find the meek, sad-looking, thoroughly-subdued wife, with no freedom of thought or action, her days passed in the dull routine of household cares, and her nights half perchance in making tattered garments whole, and the other half
15   in slumbers oft disturbed by sick and restless children. She knows nothing of the great world without; she has no time for reading and her husband finds more pleasure in discussing politics with men in groceries, taverns, or depots than he could in reading or telling his wife the news whilst she sits mending his stockings and shirts through many a lonely evening, nor thinks he, selfish being, that he
20   owes any duty to that perishing soul beyond providing a house to cover her head, food to sustain life, raiment to put on, and plenty of wood to burn....

On the other hand, in these "harmonious households" you sometimes find the so-called "hen-pecked husband"—oftentimes a kind, generous, noble-minded man who hates contention and is willing to do anything for peace. He
25   having unwarily caught a Tartar, tries to make the best of her. He can absent himself from home as much as possible, but he does not feel like a free man.... The only happy households we now see are those in which husband and wife share equally in counsel and government. There can be no true dignity or independence where there is subordination to the absolute will of another, no
30   happiness without freedom. Let us then have no fears that this movement will disturb what is seldom found a truly united and happy family....

In every generation God calls some men and women for the utterance of truth, a heroic action. We do not expect our path will be strewn with the flowers of popular applause, but over the thorns of bigotry and prejudice will be our
35   way, and on our banners will beat the dark storm-clouds of opposition from those who have entrenched themselves behind the stormy bulwarks of custom and authority, and who have fortified their position by every means, holy and unholy. But we will steadfastly abide the result. Unmoved we will bear it aloft. Undauntedly we will unfurl it to the gale, for we know that the storm cannot
40   rend from it a shred, that the electric flash will but more clearly show to us the glorious words inscribed upon it, "Equality of Rights."

Letter from the Alamo
Lieutenant-Colonel William Barret Travis
(1809–1836)

No policy, opportunity, or idea was more popular in the early republic than the desirability of westward expansion. Between 1783 and 1853, the United States doubled in size, then doubled and nearly doubled again. By 1853, it was the largest republic and the largest free trade area in the history of the world.

The West nurtured the ideal of the free individual, the free man limited only by his courage, strength, or vision. From Daniel Boone to John Wayne, no more powerful myth has influenced American political culture. The West was a major issue during the Age of Jackson and after. Davy Crockett was at the Alamo with Colonel Travis; they did not surrender or retreat, but died there so Texas could become part of the United States. The fact of expansion was that the West was a vast battleground as well as a nurturing place for heroic individualism.

Commandancy of the Alamo, Bejar, 24 February 1836

To the people of Texas and all Americans in the world.

Fellow citizens and compatriots. I am besieged, by a thousand or more of the Mexicans under Santa Anna. I have sustained a continual bombardment and cannonade for 24 hours and have not lost a man. The enemy has demanded a surrender at discretion; otherwise, the garrison are to be put to the sword if the fort is taken. I have answered the demand with a cannon shot, and our flag   5
still waves proudly from the walls. I shall never surrender or retreat. Then, I call on you in the name of Liberty, of patriotism, and everything dear to the American character to come to our aid with all dispatch. The enemy is receiving reinforcements daily and will no doubt increase to three or four thousand in four or five days.   10

William Barret Travis, "To the People of Texas and All Americans," 24 February 1836. From the John G. Davidson Collection, Texas State Library, Austin, Texas.

If this call is neglected, I am determined to sustain myself as long as possible and die like a soldier who never forgets what is due to his own honor and that of his country. Victory or Death

PS—The Lord is on our side. When the enemy appeared in sight we had not three bushels of corn. We have since found in deserted houses 80 or 90 bushels and got into the walls 20 or 30 head of beeves.

THE GREAT NATION OF FUTURITY
JOHN LOUIS O'SULLIVAN (1813–1895)
EDITOR, *DEMOCRATIC REVIEW*

*John Louis O'Sullivan garnered a well-deserved reputation as a lead-
ing proponent of Jacksonian democracy in the United States during the
1830s and 1840s, as he insisted on equality of opportunity for all adult
white males and special privileges for no one. After graduating from New
York City's Columbia College in 1831 at the age of eighteen, O'Sullivan
studied law and was admitted to the bar in 1835. During these formative years he was drawn to the politics of the Jacksonian Democrats,
and he identified with the more radical members of that party who
supported hard currency (specie) and loathed monopoly. Like many of
his contemporaries, he embraced a broad reform agenda that advocated
gradual progress toward greater political, economic, and social equality. With the assistance of his brother-in-law, Dr. Samuel D. Langtree,
O'Sullivan launched the* United States Magazine and Democratic
Review *(usually referred to as simply the* Democratic Review*) in*
October 1837. *The journal featured political opinion and literature,
and its objective was twofold: to promote Jacksonian Democracy and
to foster the growth of a distinctly American literature consistent with
democratic principles. In November 1839, O'Sullivan wrote "The Great
Nation of Futurity"—one of the most significant editorials to appear in
the* Democratic Review. *At the time, the United States was still suffering from the effects of the Panic of 1837, the worst economic depression
the nation had experienced in its brief history. Despite the prevailing
economic distress and widespread gloom, O'Sulllivan's piece offered a
beacon of optimism to his fellow countrymen by outlining a prescription for national progress. The editorial articulated his boundless faith
in America's expansive yet peaceful democratic mission.*

John Louis O'Sullivan, "The Great Nation of Futurity," *The United States Democratic Review*
(6 November 1839):426–30.

November 1839

The American people having derived their origin from many other nations, and the Declaration of National Independence being entirely based on the great principle of human equality, these facts demonstrate at once our disconnected position as regards any other nation; that we have, in reality, but little connec-
5   tion with the past history of any of them, and still less with all antiquity, its glories, or its crimes. On the contrary, our national birth was the beginning of a new history, the formation and progress of an untried political system, which separates us from the past and connects us with the future only; and so far as regards the entire development of the natural rights of man, in moral, political,
10   and national life, we may confidently assume that our country is destined to be *the great nation* of futurity.

It is so destined, because the principle upon which a nation is organized fixes its destiny, and that of equality is perfect, is universal. It presides in all the operations of the physical world, and it is also the conscious law of the
15   soul—the self-evident dictate of morality, which accurately defines the duty of man to man, and consequently man's rights as man. Besides, the truthful annals of any nation furnish abundant evidence, that its happiness, its great-ness, its duration, were always proportionate to the democratic equality in its system of government.

20   How many nations have had their decline and fall because the equal rights of the minority were trampled on by the despotism of the majority; or the interests of the many sacrificed to the aristocracy of the few; or the rights and interests of all given up to the monarchy of one? These three kinds of government have figured so frequently and so largely in the ages that have passed away, that their
25   history, through all time to come, can only furnish a resemblance. Like causes produce like effects, and the true philosopher of history will easily discern the principle of equality, or of privilege, working out its inevitable result. The first is regenerative, because it is natural and right; the latter is destructive to society, because it is unnatural and wrong.

30   What friend of human liberty, civilization, and refinement can cast his view over the past history of the monarchies and aristocracies of antiquity and not deplore that they ever existed? What philanthropist can contemplate the oppressions, the cruelties, and injustice inflicted by them on the masses of mankind and not turn with moral horror from the retrospect?

35   America is destined for better deeds. It is our unparalleled glory that we have no reminiscences of battle fields but in defense of humanity, of the oppressed of all nations, of the rights of conscience, the rights of personal enfranchisement. Our annals describe no scenes of horrid carnage, where men were led on by hundreds of thousands to slay one another, dupes and victims to emperors,

kings, nobles, demons in the human form called heroes. We have had patriots to defend our homes, our liberties, but no aspirants to crowns or thrones; nor have the American people ever suffered themselves to be led on by wicked ambition to de-populate the land, to spread desolation far and wide, that a human being might be placed on a seat of supremacy. 5

We have no interest in the scenes of antiquity, only as lessons of avoidance of nearly all their examples. The expansive future is our arena, and for our history. We are entering on its untrodden space, with the truths of God in our minds, beneficent objects in our hearts, and with a clear conscience unsullied by the past. We are the nation of human progress, and who will, what can, set 10 limits to our onward march? Providence is with us, and no earthly power can. We point to the everlasting truth on the first page of our national declaration, and we proclaim to the millions of other lands, that "the gates of hell"—the powers of aristocracy and monarchy—"shall not prevail against it."

The far-reaching, the boundless future will be the era of American 15 greatness. In its magnificent domain of space and time, the nation of many nations is destined to manifest to mankind the excellence of divine principles; to establish on earth the noblest temple ever dedicated to the worship of the Most High—the Sacred and the True. Its floor shall be a hemisphere—its roof the firmament of the star-studded heavens, and its congregation an Union of 20 many Republics, comprising hundreds of happy millions, calling, owning no man master, but governed by God's natural and moral law of equality, the law of brotherhood—of "peace and good will amongst men."

But although the mighty constituent truth upon which our social and political system is founded will assuredly work out the glorious destiny herein 25 shadowed forth, yet there are many untoward circumstances to retard our progress, to procrastinate the entire fruition of the greatest good to the human race. There is a tendency to imitativeness, prevailing amongst our professional and literary men, subversive of originality of thought, and wholly unfavorable to progress. Being in early life devoted to the study of the laws, institutions, 30 and antiquities of other nations, they are far behind the mind and movement of the age in which they live: so much so, that the spirit of improvement, as well as of enfranchisement, exists chiefly in the great masses—the agricultural and mechanical population.

This propensity to imitate foreign nations is absurd and injurious. It is 35 absurd, for we have never yet drawn on our mental resources that we have not found them ample and of unsurpassed excellence; witness our constitutions of government, where we had no foreign ones to imitate. It is injurious, for never have we followed foreign examples in legislation; witness our laws, our charters of monopoly, that we did not inflict evil on ourselves, subverting common right, 40

in violation of common sense and common justice. The halls of legislation and the courts of law in a Republic are necessarily the public schools of the adult population. If, in these institutions, foreign precedents are legislated, and foreign decisions adjudged over again, is it to be wondered at that an imitative propensity
5   predominates amongst professional and business men. Taught to look abroad from the highest standards of law, judicial wisdom, and literary excellence, the native sense is subjugated to a most obsequious idolatry of the tastes, sentiments, and prejudices of Europe. Hence our legislation, jurisprudence, literature, are more reflective of foreign aristocracy than of American democracy.
10   European governments have plunged themselves in debt, designating burdens on the people "national blessings." Our state legislatures, humbly imitating their pernicious example, have pawned, bonded the property, labor, and credit of their constituents to the subjects of monarchy. It is by our own labor, and with our own materials, that our internal improvements are constructed, but
15   our British-law-trained legislators have enacted that we shall be in debt for them, paying interest, but never to become owners. With various climates, soils, natural resources, and products, beyond any other country, and producing more real capital annually than any other sixteen millions of people on earth, we are, nevertheless borrowers, paying tribute to the money powers of Europe.
20   Our business men have also conned the lesson of example, and devoted themselves body and mind to the promotion of foreign interests. If states can steep themselves in debt with any propriety in times of peace, why may not merchants import merchandise on credit? If the one can bond the labor and property of generations yet unborn, why may not the other contract debts against
25   the yearly crops and daily labor of their contemporary fellow citizens?
And our literature!—Oh, when will it breathe the spirit of our republican institutions? When will it be imbued with the God-like aspiration of intellectual freedom—the elevating principle of equality? When will it assert *its* national independence, and speak the soul—the heart of the American people?
30   Why cannot our literati comprehend the matchless sublimity of our position amongst the nations of the world—our high destiny—and cease bending the knee to foreign idolatry, false tastes, false doctrines, false principles? When will they be inspired by the magnificent scenery of our own world, imbibe the fresh enthusiasm of a new heaven and a new earth, and soar upon the
35   expanded wings of truth and liberty? Is not nature as original—her truths as captivating—her aspects as various, as lovely, as grand—her promethean fire as glowing in this, our Western hemisphere, as in that of the East? And above all, is not our private life as morally beautiful and good—is not our public life as politically right, as indicative of the brightest prospects of
40   humanity, and therefore as inspiring of the highest conceptions? Why, then,

do our authors aim at no higher degree of merit, than a successful imitation of English writers of celebrity?

But with all the retrograde tendencies of our laws, our judicature, our colleges, our literature, still they are compelled to follow the mighty impulse of the age; they are carried onward by the increasing tide of progress; and though they 5 cast many a longing look behind, they cannot stay the glorious movement of the masses, nor induce them to venerate the rubbish, the prejudices, the superstitions of other times and other lands, the theocracy of priests, the divine right of kings, the aristocracy of blood, the metaphysics of colleges, the irrational stuff of law libraries. Already the brightest hopes of philanthropy, the most enlarged 10 speculations of true philosophy, are inspired by the indications perceptible amongst the mechanical and agricultural population. There, with predominating influence, beats the vigorous national heart of America, propelling the onward march of the multitude, propagating and extending, through the present and the future, the powerful purpose of soul, which, in the seventeenth century, 15 sought a refuge among savages, and reared in the wilderness the sacred altars of intellectual freedom. This was the seed that produced individual equality, and political liberty, as its natural fruit; and this is our true nationality. American patriotism is not of soil; we are not aborigines, nor of ancestry, for we are of all nations; but it is essentially personal enfranchisement, for "where liberty dwells," 20 said Franklin, the sage of the Revolution, "there is my country."

Such is our distinguishing characteristic, our popular instinct, and never yet has any public functionary stood forth for the rights of conscience against any, or all, sects desirous of predominating over such right, that he was not sustained by the people. And when a venerated patriot of the Revolution appealed to his 25 fellow-citizen against the over-shadowing power of a monarch institution, they came in their strength, and the moneyed despot was brought low. Corporate powers and privileges shrink to nothing when brought in conflict against the rights of individuals. Hence it is that our professional, literary, or commercial aristocracy, have no faith in the virtue, intelligence or capability of the people. 30 The latter have never responded to their exotic sentiments, nor promoted their views of a strong government irresponsible to the popular majority, to the will of the masses.

Yes, we are the nation of progress, of individual freedom, of universal enfranchisement. Equality of rights is the cynosure of our union of states, the 35 grand exemplar of the correlative equality of individuals; and while truth sheds its effulgence, we cannot retrograde, without dissolving the one and subverting the other. We must onward to the fulfillment of our mission—to the entire development of the principle of our organization—freedom of conscience, freedom of person, freedom of trade and business pursuits, universality of freedom 40

of person, freedom of trade and business pursuits, universality of freedom and
equality. This is our high destiny, and in nature's eternal, inevitable decree of
cause and effect we must accomplish it. All this will be our future history, to
establish on earth the moral dignity and salvation of man—the immutable
5   truth and beneficence of God. For this blessed mission to the nations of the
world, which are shut out from the life-giving light of truth, has America been
chosen; and her high example shall smite unto death the tyranny of kings, hi-
erarchs, and oligarchs, and carry the glad tidings of peace and good will where
myriads now endure an existence scarcely more enviable than that of beasts of
10 the field. Who, then, can doubt that our country is destined to be *the great
nation* of futurity?

THE DESTINY OF THE RACE
THOMAS HART BENTON (1782–1858)

The West was a battleground between red men and white; between Mexicans and Americans; and between North and South over the issue of the expansion of slavery. Thomas Hart Benton, Senator from Missouri for thirty years, father-in-law of the explorer John C. Frémont (1813–1890), and avid promoter of westward expansion, delivered his speech on "The Destiny of the Race" the year the Mexican War began. Comparisons among the "races" of men were fashionable all over the Western world; his conviction that white Christians ("the Celtic-Anglo-Saxon division") were destined to bring "civilization" to the rest of the world was an attitude that helped to complete the conquest of the continent and touched off a new round of European and American imperialism later in the century.

28 MAY 1846

…Since the dispersion of man upon earth, I know of no human event, past or to come, which promises a greater and more beneficent change upon earth than the arrival of the van of the Caucasian race (the Celtic-Anglo-Saxon division) upon the border of the sea which washes the shore of the eastern Asia. The Mongolian, or Yellow, race is there, four hundred millions in number, 5 spreading almost to Europe; a race once the foremost of the human family in the arts of civilization, but torpid and stationary for thousands of years. It is a race far above the Ethiopian, or Black—above the Malay, or Brown (if we must admit five races)—and above the American Indian, or Red; it is a race far above all these, but still, far below the White; and, like all the rest, must receive an 10 impression from the superior race whenever they come in contact.

It would seem that the White race alone received the divine command to subdue and replenish the earth,[1] for it is the only race that has obeyed it—the

---

[1] Genesis 1:28

Thomas Hart Benton, "Speech of Mr. Benton of Missouri," *The Congressional Globe* 58(6 June 1846):917–18.

only one that hunts out new and distant lands, and even a New World, to subdue and replenish. Starting from Western Asia, taking Europe for their field and the Sun for their guide, and leaving the Mongolians behind, they arrived, after many ages, on the shores of the Atlantic, which they lit up with the lights of science and religion, and adorned with the useful and the elegant arts. Three-and-a-half centuries ago, this race, in obedience to the great command, arrived in the New World, and found new lands to subdue and replenish. For a long time it was confined to the border of the new field, (I now mean the Celtic-Anglo-Saxon division) and even four score years ago the philosophic Burke[2] was considered a rash man because he said the English colonists would top the Alleghenies, and descend into the valley of the Mississippi, and occupy without parchment if the Crown refused to make grants of land.

What was considered a rash declaration eighty years ago is old history in our young country at this day. Thirty years ago I said the same thing of the Rocky Mountains and the Columbia; it was ridiculed then; it is becoming history today. The venerable Mr. Mason[3] has often told me that he remembered a line low down in North Carolina, fixed by a royal governor as a boundary between the whites and the Indians; where is that boundary now? The van of the Caucasian race now top the Rocky Mountains, and spread down to the shores of the Pacific. In a few years a great population will grow up there, luminous with the accumulated lights of European and American civilization.

Their presence in such a position cannot be without its influence upon eastern Asia. The sun of civilization must shine across the sea: socially and commercially the van of the Caucasians and the rear of the Mongolians must intermix. They must talk together, and trade together, and marry together. Commerce is a great civilizer—social intercourse as great—and marriage greater. The White and Yellow races can marry together, as well as eat and trade together. Moral and intellectual superiority will do the rest: the White race will take the ascendant, elevating what is susceptible of improvement—wearing out what is not.

The Red race has disappeared from the Atlantic coast; the tribes that resisted civilization met extinction. This is a cause of lamentation with many. For my part, I cannot murmur at what seems to be the effect of divine law. I cannot repine that this Capitol has replaced the wigwam—this Christian people replaced the savages—white matrons, the red squaws—and that such men as Washington, Franklin, and Jefferson have taken the place of Powhattan, Opechonecanough, and other red men, howsoever respectable they may have been as savages.

Civilization, or extinction, has been the fate of all people who have found themselves in the track of the advancing Whites and civilization, always the

[2]Edmund Burke (1729–1797)

[3]James Murray Mason (1798–1871), U.S. Senator from Virginia (1847–1861)

preference of the Whites has been pressed as an object, while extinction has followed as a consequence of its resistance. The Black and the Red races have often felt their ameliorating influence. The Yellow race, next to themselves in the scale of mental and moral excellence, and in the beauty of form, once their superiors in the useful and elegant arts and in learning, and still respect- 5
able though stationary; this race cannot fail to receive a new impulse from the approach of the Whites, improved so much since so many ages ago they left the western borders of Asia. The apparition of the van of the Caucasian race, rising upon them in the east after having left them on the west, and after hav- ing completed the circumnavigation of the globe, must wake up and reanimate 10
the torpid body of old Asia. Our position and policy will commend us to their hospitable reception; political considerations will aid the action of social and commercial influence. Pressed upon by the great powers of Europe—the same that press upon us—they must in our approach hail the advent of friends, not of foes—of benefactors, not of invaders. The moral and intellectual superiority 15
of the White race will do the rest; and thus, the youngest people, and the newest land will become the reviver and the regenerator of the oldest.

It is in this point of view, and as acting upon the social, political, and religious condition of Asia, and giving a new point of departure to her ancient civilization, that I look upon the settlement of the Columbia river by the van 20
of the Caucasian race as the most momentous human event in the history of man since his dispersion over the face of the earth....

EARTH'S HOLOCAUST
NATHANIEL HAWTHORNE (1804–1864)

By the early 1850s, novelist and short-story writer Nathaniel Hawthorne had established himself as one of America's leading men of letters. A descendant of early Puritan settlers and a native of Salem, Massachusetts, Hawthorne used his narrative gifts to explore some of deepest tensions in American thought and culture. His most enduring novels include The Scarlet Letter *(1850),* The House of the Seven Gables *(1851), and* The Blithedale Romance *(1852).*

Hawthorne's distinguished literary circle included the transcendentalist Ralph Waldo Emerson, novelist Herman Melville, essayist Henry David Thoreau, feminist Margaret Fuller, education reformer Horace Mann, utopian prophet Bronson Alcott, and his former college classmate Henry Wadsworth Longfellow. Democratic President Franklin Pierce, another classmate from Bowdoin College, remained a lifelong friend, and Hawthorne wrote his 1852 campaign biography.

The short story "Earth's Holocaust" first appeared in Graham's Magazine *in May 1844 and later in* Mosses From an Old Manse *(1846). The narrator calls his story "a parable," and as a parable it teaches something fundamental about man's efforts to transform his social institutions. Nearly every reform enthusiasm of the 1840s appears in this story. The "Washingtonians," for example, founded in Baltimore in 1840 and famous for staging mass processions through major American cities, fought to promote temperance. Much of the humor of this otherwise dark story may be easily lost on a modern audience. A case in point is Hawthorne's reference to the radical British reformer Sydney Smith (1771–1845), founder of the* Edinburgh Review *and advocate of utilitarian education. Smith invested heavily in bonds issued by Pennsylvania and other states. The states defaulted, and Smith petitioned the U.S. Congress in 1843 to force the bankrupt states to pay him.*

Nathaniel Hawthorne, "Earth's Holocaust," *Graham's Lady's and Gentleman's Magazine* 25 (May 1844):193–200.

Once upon a time—but whether in the time past or time to come is a matter of little or no moment—this wide world had become so overburdened with an accumulation of worn-out trumpery that the inhabitants determined to rid themselves of it by a general bonfire. The site fixed upon at the representation
5   of the insurance companies, and as being as central a spot as any other on the globe, was one of the broadest prairies of the West, where no human habitation would be endangered by the flames, and where a vast assemblage of spectators might commodiously admire the show. Having a taste for sights of this kind, and imagining, likewise, that the illumination of the bonfire might reveal some
10   profundity of moral truth heretofore hidden in mist or darkness, I made it convenient to journey thither and be present. At my arrival, although the heap of condemned rubbish was as yet comparatively small, the torch had already been applied. Amid that boundless plain, in the dusk of the evening, like a far off star alone in the firmament, there was merely visible one tremulous gleam,
15   whence none could have anticipated so fierce a blaze as was destined to ensue. With every moment, however, there came foot travelers, women holding up their aprons, men on horseback, wheelbarrows, lumbering baggage-wagons, and other vehicles, great and small, and from far and near, laden with articles that were judged fit for nothing but to be burned.
20   "What materials have been used to kindle the flame?" inquired I of a bystander; for I was desirous of knowing the whole process of the affair from beginning to end.
        The person whom I addressed was a grave man, fifty years old or thereabout, who had evidently come thither as a looker-on. He struck me immediately as
25   having weighed for himself the true value of life and its circumstances, and therefore as feeling little personal interest in whatever judgment the world might form of them. Before answering my question, he looked me in the face by the kindling light of the fire.
        "O, some very dry combustibles," replied he, "and extremely suitable to the
30   purpose—no other, in fact, than yesterday's newspapers, last month's magazines, and last year's withered leaves. Here now comes some antiquated trash that will take fire like a handful of shavings."
        As he spoke, some rough-looking men advanced to the verge of the bonfire and threw in, as it appeared, all the rubbish of the herald's office—the blazonry of
35   coat armor, the crests and devices of illustrious families, pedigrees that extended back, like lines of light, into the mist of the dark ages, together with stars, garters, and embroidered collars, each of which, as paltry a bauble as it might appear to the uninstructed eye, had once possessed vast significance, and was still, in truth, reckoned among the most precious of moral or material facts by the worship-
40   pers of the gorgeous past. Mingled with this confused heap, which was tossed

into the flames by armfuls at once, were innumerable badges of knighthood, comprising those of all the European sovereignties, and Napoleon's decoration of the Legion of Honor, the ribbons of which were entangled with those of the ancient order of Saint Louis. There, too, were the medals of our own Society of Cincinnati, by means of which, as history tells us, an order of hereditary   5 knights came near being constituted out of the king quellers of the Revolution. And besides, there were the patents of nobility of German counts and barons, Spanish grandees, and English peers, from the worm-eaten instruments signed by William the Conqueror down to the brand-new parchment of the latest lord who has received his honors from the fair hand of Victoria.   10

At sight of the dense volumes of smoke, mingled with vivid jets of flame, that gushed and eddied forth from this immense pile of earthly distinctions, the multitude of plebeian spectators set up a joyous shout, and clapped their hands with an emphasis that made the welkin echo. That was their moment of triumph, achieved, after long ages, over creatures of the same clay and the same spiritual   15 infirmities, who had dared to assume the privileges due only to Heaven's better workmanship. But now there rushed towards the blazing heap a gray-haired man, of stately presence, wearing a coat, from the breast of which a star, or other badge of rank, seemed to have been forcibly wrenched away. He had not the tokens of intellectual power in his face; but still there was the demeanor, the habitual and   20 almost native dignity, of one who had been born to the idea of his own social superiority, and had never felt it questioned till that moment.

"People," cried he, gazing at the ruin of what was dearest to his eyes with grief and wonder, but nevertheless with a degree of stateliness, "people, what have you done? This fire is consuming all that marked your advance from bar-   25 barism, or that could have prevented your relapse thither. We, the men of the privileged orders, were those who kept alive from age to age the old chivalrous spirit; the gentle and generous thought; the higher, the purer, the more refined and delicate life. With the nobles, too, you cast off the poet, the painter, the sculptor—all the beautiful arts; for we were their patrons, and created the   30 atmosphere in which they flourish. In abolishing the majestic distinctions of rank, society loses not only its grace, but its steadfastness—"

More he would doubtless have spoken; but here there arose an outcry, sportive, contemptuous, and indignant, that altogether drowned the appeal of the fallen nobleman, insomuch that, casting one look of despair at his own   35 half-burned pedigree, he shrunk back into the crowd, glad to shelter himself under his new-found insignificance.

"Let him thank his stars that we have not flung him into the same fire!" shouted a rude figure, spurning the embers with his foot. "And henceforth let no man dare to show a piece of musty parchment as his warrant for lording it   40 over his fellows. If he have strength of arm, well and good; it is one species of superiority. If he have wit, wisdom, courage, force of character, let these attributes do for him what they may; but from this day forward no mortal must hope for place and consideration by reckoning up the moldy bones of his ancestors. That nonsense is done away."

5   "And in good time," remarked the grave observer by my side, in a low voice, however, "if no worse nonsense comes in its place; but, at all events, this species of nonsense has fairly lived out its life."

There was little space to muse or moralize over the embers of this time-honored rubbish; for, before it was half burned out, there came another multi-
10   tude from beyond the sea, bearing the purple robes of royalty, and the crowns, globes, and scepters of emperors and kings. All these had been condemned as useless baubles, playthings at best, fit only for the infancy of the world or rods to govern and chastise it in its nonage, but with which universal manhood at its full-grown stature could no longer brook to be insulted.

15   Into such contempt had these regal insignia now fallen that the gilded crown and tinseled robes of the player king from Drury Lane Theatre had been thrown in among the rest, doubtless as a mockery of his brother monarchs on the great stage of the world. It was a strange sight to discern the crown jewels of England glowing and flashing in the midst of the fire. Some of them had
20   been delivered down from the time of the Saxon princes; others were purchased with vast revenues, or perchance ravished from the dead brows of the native potentates of Hindustan; and the whole now blazed with a dazzling luster, as if a star had fallen in that spot and been shattered into fragments. The splendor of the ruined monarchy had no reflection save in those inestimable precious
25   stones. But enough on this subject. It were but tedious to describe how the Emperor of Austria's mantle was converted to tinder, and how the posts and pillars of the French throne became a heap of coals, which it was impossible to distinguish from those of any other wood. Let me add, however, that I noticed one of the exiled Poles stirring up the bonfire with the Czar of Russia's scepter,
30   which he afterwards flung into the flames.

"The smell of singed garments is quite intolerable here," observed my new acquaintance, as the breeze enveloped us in the smoke of a royal wardrobe. "Let us get to windward and see what they are doing on the other side of the bonfire."
35   We accordingly passed around, and were just in time to witness the arrival of a vast procession of Washingtonians—as the votaries of temperance call themselves nowadays—accompanied by thousands of the Irish disciples of Father Mathew,[1] with that great apostle at their head. They brought a rich contribution

---

[1]Theobald Metthew (1790–1856), a Capuchin friar who founded a very influential temper-ance society in Ireland and, later, America (1849)

to the bonfire, being nothing less than all the hogsheads and barrels of liquor
in the world, which they rolled before them across the prairie.

"Now, my children," cried Father Mathew, when they reached the verge of
the fire, "one shove more, and the work is done. And now let us stand off and
see Satan deal with his own liquor."   5

Accordingly, having placed their wooden vessels within reach of the flames,
the procession stood off at a safe distance, and soon beheld them burst into
a blaze that reached the clouds and threatened to set the sky itself on fire.
And well it might; for here was the whole world's stock of spirituous liquors,
which, instead of kindling a frenzied light in the eyes of individual topers as   10
of yore, soared upwards with a bewildering gleam that startled all mankind. It
was the aggregate of that fierce fire which would otherwise have scorched the
hearts of millions. Meantime numberless bottles of precious wine were flung
into the blaze, which lapped up the contents as if it loved them, and grew, like
other drunkards, the merrier and fiercer for what it quaffed. Never again will   15
the insatiable thirst of the fire-fiend be so pampered. Here were the treasures
of famous bon vivants—liquors that had been tossed on ocean, and mellowed
in the sun, and hoarded long in the recesses of the earth—the pale, the gold,
the ruddy juice of whatever vineyards were most delicate—the entire vintage
of Tokay—all mingling in one stream with the vile fluids of the common pot   20
house, and contributing to heighten the self-same blaze. And while it rose in
a gigantic spire that seemed to wave against the arch of the firmament and
combine itself with the light of stars, the multitude gave a shout as if the broad
earth were exulting in its deliverance from the curse of ages.

But the joy was not universal. Many deemed that human life would be   25
gloomier than ever when that brief illumination should sink down. While the
reformers were at work I overheard muttered expostulations from several respectable gentlemen with red noses and wearing gouty shoes; and a ragged worthy,
whose face looked like a hearth where the fire is burned out, now expressed his
discontent more openly and boldly.   30

"What is this world good for," said the last toper, "now that we can never
be jolly anymore? What is to comfort the poor man in sorrow and perplexity?
How is he to keep his heart warm against the cold winds of this cheerless earth?
And what do you propose to give him in exchange for the solace that you take
away? How are old friends to sit together by the fireside without a cheerful   35
glass between them? A plague upon your reformation! It is a sad world, a cold
world, a selfish world, a low world, not worth an honest fellow's living in, now
that good fellowship is gone forever!"

This harangue excited great mirth among the bystanders; but, preposterous
as was the sentiment, I could not help commiserating the forlorn condition of   40

the last toper, whose boon companions had dwindled away from his side, leaving the poor fellow without a soul to countenance him in sipping his liquor, nor indeed any liquor to sip. Not that this was quite the true state of the case; for I had observed him at a critical moment filch a bottle of fourth-proof brandy that fell beside the bonfire and hide it in his pocket.

The spirituous and fermented liquors being thus disposed of, the zeal of the reformers next induced them to replenish the fire with all the boxes of tea and bags of coffee in the world. And now came the planters of Virginia, bringing their crops of tobacco. These, being cast upon the heap of inutility, aggregated it to the size of a mountain, and incensed the atmosphere with such potent fragrance that methought we should never draw pure breath again. The present sacrifice seemed to startle the lovers of the weed more than any that they had hitherto witnessed.

"Well, they've put my pipe out," said an old gentleman, flinging it into the flames in a pet. "What is this world coming to? Everything rich and racy—all the spice of life—is to be condemned as useless. Now that they have kindled the bonfire, if these nonsensical reformers would fling themselves into it, all would be well enough!"

"Be patient," responded a stanch conservative; "it will come to that in the end. They will first fling us in, and finally themselves."

From the general and systematic measures of reform I now turn to consider the individual contributions to this memorable bonfire. In many instances these were of a very amusing character. One poor fellow threw in his empty purse, and another a bundle of counterfeit or insolvable bank notes. Fashionable ladies threw in their last season's bonnets, together with heaps of ribbons, yellow lace, and much other half-worn milliner's ware, all of which proved even more evanescent in the fire than it had been in the fashion. A multitude of lovers of both sexes—discarded maids or bachelors and couples mutually weary of one another—tossed in bundles of perfumed letters and enamored sonnets. A hack politician, being deprived of bread by the loss of office, threw in his teeth, which happened to be false ones. The Reverend Sydney Smith—having voyaged across the Atlantic for that sole purpose—came up to the bonfire with a bitter grin and threw in certain repudiated bonds, fortified though they were with the broad seal of a sovereign state. A little boy of five years old, in the premature manliness of the present epoch, threw in his playthings; a college graduate, his diploma; an apothecary, ruined by the spread of homeopathy, his whole stock of drugs and medicines; a physician, his library; a parson, his old sermons; and a fine gentleman of the old school, his code of manners, which he had formerly written down for the benefit of the next generation. A widow, resolving on a second marriage, slyly threw in her dead husband's miniature. A young man, jilted by his mistress, would willingly have flung his own desperate heart into the flames, but could find no means to wrench it out of his bosom. An American author, whose works were neglected by the public, threw his pen and paper into the bonfire and betook himself to some less discouraging occupation. It somewhat startled me to overhear a number of ladies, highly respectable in appearance, proposing to fling their gowns and petticoats into the flames, and assume the garb, together with the manners, duties, offices, and responsibilities, of the opposite sex.

What favor was accorded to this scheme I am unable to say, my attention being suddenly drawn to a poor, deceived, and half-delirious girl, who, exclaiming that she was the most worthless thing alive or dead, attempted to cast herself into the fire amid all that wrecked and broken trumpery of the world. A good man, however, ran to her rescue.

"Patience, my poor girl!" said he, as he drew her back from the fierce embrace of the destroying angel. "Be patient, and abide Heaven's will. So long as you possess a living soul, all may be restored to its first freshness. These things of matter and creations of human fantasy are fit for nothing but to be burned when once they have had their day; but your day is eternity!"

"Yes," said the wretched girl, whose frenzy seemed now to have sunk down into deep despondency, "yes, and the sunshine is blotted out of it!"

It was now rumored among the spectators that all the weapons and munitions of war were to be thrown into the bonfire with the exception of the world's stock of gunpowder, which, as the safest mode of disposing of it, had already been drowned in the sea. This intelligence seemed to awaken great diversity of opinion. The hopeful philanthropist esteemed it a token that the millennium was already come; while persons of another stamp, in whose view mankind was a breed of bulldogs, prophesied that all the old stoutness, fervor, nobleness, generosity, and magnanimity of the race would disappear—these qualities, as they affirmed, requiring blood for their nourishment. They comforted themselves, however, in the belief that the proposed abolition of war was impracticable for any length of time together.

Be that as it might, numberless great guns, whose thunder had long been the voice of battle—the artillery of the Armada, the battering trains of Marlborough, and the adverse cannon of Napoleon and Wellington—were trundled into the midst of the fire. By the continual addition of dry combustibles it had now waxed so intense that neither brass nor iron could withstand it. It was wonderful to behold how these terrible instruments of slaughter melted away like playthings of wax. Then the armies of the earth wheeled around the mighty furnace, with their military music playing triumphant marches,—and flung in their muskets and swords. The standard-bearers, likewise, cast one look upward at their banners, all tattered with shot-holes and inscribed with the names of victorious fields; and, giving them a last flourish on the breeze, they lowered them into the flame, which snatched them upward in its rush towards the clouds. This ceremony being over, the world was left without a single weapon in its hands, except possibly a few old king's arms and rusty swords and other trophies of the Revolution in some of our state armories. And now the drums were beaten and the trumpets brayed all together, as a prelude to the proclamation of universal and eternal peace and the announcement that glory was no longer to be won by blood, but that it would henceforth be the contention of the human race to work out the greatest mutual good, and that beneficence, in the future annals of the earth, would claim the praise of valor. The blessed tidings were accordingly promulgated, and caused infinite rejoicings among those who had stood aghast at the horror and absurdity of war.

But I saw a grim smile pass over the seared visage of a stately old commander,—by his war-worn figure and rich military dress, he might have been one of Napoleon's famous marshals,—who, with the rest of the world's soldiery, had just flung away the sword that had been familiar to his right hand for half a century.

"Ay! ay!" grumbled he. "Let them proclaim what they please; but, in the end, we shall find that all this foolery has only made more work for the armorers and cannon-founders."

"Why, sir," exclaimed I, in astonishment, "do you imagine that the human race will ever so far return on the steps of its past madness as to weld another sword or cast another cannon?"

"There will be no need," observed, with a sneer, one who neither felt benevolence nor had faith in it. "When Cain wished to slay his brother, he was at no loss for a weapon."

"We shall see," replied the veteran commander. "If I am mistaken, so much the better; but in my opinion, without pretending to philosophize about the matter, the necessity of war lies far deeper than these honest gentlemen suppose. What! Is there a field for all the petty disputes of individuals? And shall there be no great law court for the settlement of national difficulties? The battle-field is the only court where such suits can be tried."

"You forget, general," rejoined I, "that, in this advanced stage of civilization, Reason and Philanthropy combined will constitute just such a tribunal as is requisite."

"Ah, I had forgotten that, indeed!" said the old warrior, as he limped away.

The fire was now to be replenished with materials that had hitherto been considered of even greater importance to the well-being of society than the warlike munitions which we had already seen consumed. A body of reformers had travelled all over the earth in quest of the machinery by which the different nations were accustomed to inflict the punishment of death. A shudder passed

through the multitude as these ghastly emblems were dragged forward. Even
the flames seemed at first to shrink away, displaying the shape and murderous
contrivance of each in a full blaze of light, which of itself was sufficient to convince mankind of the long and deadly error of human law. Those old implements
of cruelty; those horrible monsters of mechanism; those inventions which it   5
seemed to demand something worse than man's natural heart to contrive, and
which had lurked in the dusky nooks of ancient prisons, the subject of terror-
stricken legend, were now brought forth to view. Headsmen's axes, with the rust
of noble and royal blood upon them, and a vast collection of halters that had
choked the breath of plebeian victims, were thrown in together. A shout greeted   10
the arrival of the guillotine, which was thrust forward on the same wheels that
had borne it from one to another of the bloodstained streets of Paris. But the
loudest roar of applause went up, telling the distant sky of the triumph of the
earth's redemption, when the gallows made its appearance. An ill-looking fellow,
however, rushed forward, and, putting himself in the path of the reformers,   15
bellowed hoarsely, and fought with brute fury to stay their progress.

It was little matter of surprise, perhaps, that the executioner should thus
do his best to vindicate and uphold the machinery by which he himself had
his livelihood and worthier individuals their death; but it deserved special note
that men of a far different sphere—even of that consecrated class in whose   20
guardianship the world is apt to trust its benevolence—were found to take the
hangman's view of the question.

"Stay, my brethren!" cried one of them. "You are misled by a false philanthropy; you know not what you do. The gallows is a Heaven-ordained instrument. Bear it back, then, reverently, and set it up in its old place, else the world   25
will fall to speedy ruin and desolation!"

"Onward! Onward!" shouted a leader in the reform. "Into the flames with
the accursed instrument of man's bloody policy! How can human law inculcate benevolence and love while it persists in setting up the gallows as its chief
symbol? One heave more, good friends, and the world will be redeemed from   30
its greatest error."

A thousand hands, that nevertheless loathed the touch, now lent their assistance, and thrust the ominous burden far, far into the centre of the raging
furnace. There its fatal and abhorred image was beheld, first black, then a red
coal, then ashes.   35

"That was well done!" exclaimed I.

"Yes, it was well done," replied, but with less enthusiasm than I expected,
the thoughtful observer, who was still at my side; "well done, if the world be
good enough for the measure. Death, however, is an idea that cannot easily be
dispensed with in any condition between the primal innocence and that other   40

purity and perfection which perchance we are destined to attain after travelling round the full circle; but, at all events, it is well that the experiment should now be tried."

"Too cold! Too cold!" impatiently exclaimed the young and ardent leader
5   in this triumph. "Let the heart have its voice here as well as the intellect. And as for ripeness, and as for progress, let mankind always do the highest, kindest, noblest thing that, at any given period, it has attained the perception of; and surely that thing cannot be wrong nor wrongly timed."

I know not whether it were the excitement of the scene, or whether the good
10 people around the bonfire were really growing more enlightened every instant; but they now proceeded to measures in the full length of which I was hardly prepared to keep them company. For instance, some threw their marriage certificates into the flames, and declared themselves candidates for a higher, holier, and more comprehensive union than that which had subsisted from the birth
15 of time under the form of the connubial tie. Others hastened to the vaults of banks and to the coffers of the rich—all of which were opened to the first comer on this fated occasion—and brought entire bales of paper-money to enliven the blaze, and tons of coin to be melted down by its intensity. Henceforth, they said, universal benevolence, un-coined and exhaustless, was to be the golden
20 currency of the world. At this intelligence the bankers and speculators in the stocks grew pale, and a pickpocket, who had reaped a rich harvest among the crowd, fell down in a deadly fainting fit. A few men of business burned their day-books and ledgers, the notes and obligations of their creditors, and all other evidences of debts due to themselves; while perhaps a somewhat larger
25 number satisfied their zeal for reform with the sacrifice of any uncomfortable recollection of their own indebtment. There was then a cry that the period was arrived when the title-deeds of landed property should be given to the flames, and the whole soil of the earth revert to the public, from whom it had been wrongfully abstracted and most unequally distributed among individuals.
30 Another party demanded that all written constitutions, set forms of government, legislative acts, statute-books, and everything else on which human invention had endeavored to stamp its arbitrary laws, should at once be destroyed, leaving the consummated world as free as the man first created.

Whether any ultimate action was taken with regard to these propositions
35 is beyond my knowledge; for, just then, some matters were in progress that concerned my sympathies more nearly.

"See! see! What heaps of books and pamphlets!" cried a fellow, who did not seem to be a lover of literature. "Now we shall have a glorious blaze!"

"That's just the thing!" said a modern philosopher. "Now we shall get rid
40 of the weight of dead men's thought, which has hitherto pressed so heavily on

the living intellect that it has been incompetent to any effectual self-exertion. Well done, my lads! Into the fire with them! Now you are enlightening the world indeed!"

"But what is to become of the trade?" cried a frantic bookseller.

"O, by all means, let them accompany their merchandise," coolly observed an author. "It will be a noble funeral-pile!"

The truth was that the human race had now reached a stage of progress so far beyond what the wisest and wittiest men of former ages had ever dreamed of, that it would have been a manifest absurdity to allow the earth to be any longer encumbered with their poor achievements in the literary line. Accordingly a thorough and searching investigation had swept the booksellers' shops, hawkers' stands, public and private libraries, and even the little book-shelf by the country fireside, and had brought the world's entire mass of printed paper, bound or in sheets, to swell the already mountain bulk of our illustrious bonfire. Thick, heavy folios, containing the labors of lexicographers, commentators, and encyclopedists, were flung in, and, falling among the embers with a leaden thump, smoldered away to ashes like rotten wood. The small, richly gilt French tomes of the last age, with the hundred volumes of Voltaire among them, went off in a brilliant shower of sparkles and little jets of flame; while the current literature of the same nation burned red and blue, and threw an infernal light over the visages of the spectators, converting them all to the aspect of party-colored fiends. A collection of German stories emitted a scent of brimstone. The English standard authors made excellent fuel, generally exhibiting the properties of sound oak logs. Milton's works, in particular, sent up a powerful blaze, gradually reddening into a coal, which promised to endure longer than almost any other material of the pile. From Shakespeare there gushed a flame of such marvelous splendor that men shaded their eyes as against the sun's meridian glory; nor even when the works of his own elucidators were flung upon him did he cease to flash forth a dazzling radiance from beneath the ponderous heap. It is my belief that he is still blazing as fervidly as ever.

"Could a poet but light a lamp at that glorious flame," remarked I, "he might then consume the midnight oil to some good purpose."

"That is the very thing which modern poets have been too apt to do, or at least to attempt," answered a critic. "The chief benefit to be expected from this conflagration of past literature undoubtedly is, that writers will henceforth be compelled to light their lamps at the sun or stars."

"If they can reach so high," said I; "but that task requires a giant, who may afterwards distribute the light among inferior men. It is not every one that can steal the fire from heaven like Prometheus; but, when once he had done the deed, a thousand hearths were kindled by it."

It amazed me much to observe how indefinite was the proportion between the physical mass of any given author and the property of brilliant and long-continued combustion. For instance, there was not a quarto volume of the last century—nor, indeed, of the present—that could compete in that particular
5 with a child's little gilt-covered book containing Mother Goose's *Melodies. The Life and Death of Tom Thumb* outlasted the biography of Marlborough. An epic, indeed a dozen of them, was converted to white ashes before the single sheet of an old ballad was half consumed. In more than one case, too, when volumes of applauded verse proved incapable of anything better than a stifling
10 smoke, an un-regarded ditty of some nameless bard—perchance in the corner of a newspaper—soared up among the stars with a flame as brilliant as their own. Speaking of the properties of flame, methought Shelley's poetry emitted a purer light than almost any other productions of his day, contrasting beautifully with the fitful and lurid gleams and gushes of black vapor that flashed
15 and eddied from the volumes of Lord Byron. As for Tom Moore, some of his songs diffused an odor like a burning pastil.

I felt particular interest in watching the combustion of American authors, and scrupulously noted by my watch the precise number of moments that changed most of them from shabbily printed books to indistinguishable ashes.
20 It would be invidious, however, if not perilous, to betray these awful secrets; so that I shall content myself with observing that it was not invariably the writer most frequent in the public mouth that made the most splendid appearance in the bonfire. I especially remember that a great deal of excellent inflammability was exhibited in a thin volume of poems by Ellery Channing; although, to
25 speak the truth, there were certain portions that hissed and spluttered in a very disagreeable fashion. A curious phenomenon occurred in reference to several writers, native as well as foreign. Their books, though of highly respectable figure, instead of bursting into a blaze or even smoldering out their substance in smoke, suddenly melted away in a manner that proved them to be ice.
30 If it be no lack of modesty to mention my own works, it must here be confessed that I looked for them with fatherly interest, but in vain. Too probably they were changed to vapor by the first action of the heat; at best, I can only hope that, in their quiet way, they contributed a glimmering spark or two to the splendor of the evening.
35 "Alas! And woe is me!" thus bemoaned himself a heavy-looking gentleman in green spectacles. "The world is utterly ruined, and there is nothing to live for any longer. The business of my life is snatched from me. Not a volume to be had for love or money!"

"This," remarked the sedate observer beside me, "is a bookworm—one
40 of those men who are born to gnaw dead thoughts. His clothes, you see, are

covered with the dust of libraries. He has no inward fountain of ideas; and, in good earnest, now that the old stock is abolished, I do not see what is to become of the poor fellow. Have you no word of comfort for him?"

"My dear sir," said I to the desperate bookworm, "is not nature better than a book? Is not the human heart deeper than any system of philosophy? Is not 5 life replete with more instruction than past observers have found it possible to write down in maxims? Be of good cheer. The great book of Time is still spread wide open before us; and, if we read it aright, it will be to us a volume of eternal truth."

"O, my books, my books, my precious printed books!" re-iterated the 10 forlorn bookworm. "My only reality was a bound volume; and now they will not leave me even a shadowy pamphlet!"

In fact, the last remnant of the literature of all the ages was now descending upon the blazing heap in the shape of a cloud of pamphlets from the press of the New World. These likewise were consumed in the twinkling of an eye, leaving 15 the earth, for the first time since the days of Cadmus,[2] free from the plague of letters—an enviable field for the authors of the next generation.

"Well, and does anything remain to be done?" inquired I, somewhat anxiously. "Unless we set fire to the earth itself, and then leap boldly off into infinite space, I know not that we can carry reform to any farther point." 20

"You are vastly mistaken, my good friend," said the observer. "Believe me, the fire will not be allowed to settle down without the addition of fuel that will startle many persons who have lent a willing hand thus far."

Nevertheless there appeared to be a relaxation of effort for a little time, during which, probably, the leaders of the movement were considering what should 25 be done next. In the interval, a philosopher threw his theory into the flames— a sacrifice which, by those who knew how to estimate it, was pronounced the most remarkable that had yet been made. The combustion, however, was by no means brilliant. Some indefatigable people, scorning to take a moment's ease, now employed themselves in collecting all the withered leaves and fallen 30 boughs of the forest, and thereby recruited the bonfire to a greater height than ever. But this was mere by-play.

"Here comes the fresh fuel that I spoke of," said my companion.

To my astonishment the persons who now advanced into the vacant space around the mountain fire bore surplices and other priestly garments, mitres, 35 crosiers, and a confusion of Popish and Protestant emblems with which it seemed their purpose to consummate the great act of faith. Crosses from the spires of old cathedrals were cast upon the heap with as little remorse as if the reverence

---

[2]Cadmus—a mythic hero who introduced the alphabet to Greece

of centuries passing in long array beneath the lofty towers had not looked up to them as the holiest of symbols. The font in which infants were consecrated to God, the sacramental vessels whence piety received the hallowed draught, were given to the same destruction. Perhaps it most nearly touched my heart to see
5   among these devoted relics fragments of the humble communion-tables and undecorated pulpits which I recognized as having been torn from the meeting-houses of New England. Those simple edifices might have been permitted to retain all of sacred embellishment that their Puritan founders had bestowed, even though the mighty structure of Saint Peter's had sent its spoils to the fire of this
10 terrible sacrifice. Yet I felt that these were but the externals of religion, and might most safely be relinquished by spirits that best knew their deep significance.

"All is well," said I, cheerfully. "The wood-paths shall be the aisles of our cathedral—the firmament itself shall be its ceiling. What needs an earthly roof between the Deity and his worshippers? Our faith can well afford to lose all
15 the drapery that even the holiest men have thrown around it, and be only the more sublime in its simplicity."

"True," said my companion; "but will they pause here?"

The doubt implied in his question was well founded. In the general destruction of books already described, a holy volume, that stood apart from the
20 catalogue of human literature, and yet, in one sense, was at its head, had been spared. But the Titan of innovation—angel or fiend, double in his nature, and capable of deeds befitting both characters—at first shaking down only the old and rotten shapes of things, had now, as it appeared, laid his terrible hand upon the main pillars which supported the whole edifice of our moral and spiritual
25 state. The inhabitants of the earth had grown too enlightened to define their faith within a form of words, or to limit the spiritual by any analogy to our material existence. Truths which the heavens trembled at were now but a fable of the world's infancy. Therefore, as the final sacrifice of human error, what else remained to be thrown upon the embers of that awful pile, except the book which, though
30 a celestial revelation to past ages, was but a voice from a lower sphere as regarded the present race of man? It was done! Upon the blazing heap of falsehood and worn-out truth—things that the earth had never needed, or had ceased to need, or had grown childishly weary of—fell the ponderous church Bible, the great old volume that had lain so long on the cushion of the pulpit, and whence the
35 pastor's solemn voice had given holy utterance on so many a Sabbath day. There, likewise, fell the family Bible, which the long-buried patriarch had read to his children—in prosperity or sorrow, by the fireside and in the summer shade of trees—and had bequeathed downward as the heirloom of generations. There fell the bosom Bible, the little volume that had been the soul's friend of some sorely
40 tried child of dust, who thence took courage, whether his trial were for life or death, steadfastly confronting both in the strong assurance of immortality.

All these were flung into the fierce and riotous blaze; and then a mighty wind came roaring across the plain with a desolate howl, as if it were the angry lamentation of the earth for the loss of heaven's sunshine; and it shook the gigantic pyramid of flame and scattered the cinders of half-consumed abominations around upon the spectators.

"This is terrible!" said I, feeling that my check grew pale, and seeing a like change in the visages about me.

"Be of good courage yet," answered the man with whom I had so often spoken. He continued to gaze steadily at the spectacle with a singular calmness, as if it concerned him merely as an observer. "Be of good courage, nor yet exult too much; for there is far less both of good and evil in the effect of this bonfire than the world might be willing to believe."

"How can that be?" exclaimed I, impatiently. "Has it not consumed everything? Has it not swallowed up or melted down every human or divine appendage of our mortal state that had substance enough to be acted on by fire? Will there be anything left us tomorrow morning better or worse than a heap of embers and ashes?"

"Assuredly there will," said my grave friend. "Come hither tomorrow morning, or whenever the combustible portion of the pile shall be quite burned out, and you will find among the ashes everything really valuable that you have seen cast into the flames. Trust me, the world of tomorrow will again enrich itself with the gold and diamonds which have been cast off by the world of today. Not a truth is destroyed nor buried so deep among the ashes but it will be raked up at last."

This was a strange assurance. Yet I felt inclined to credit it, the more especially as I beheld among the wallowing flames a copy of the Holy Scriptures, the pages of which, instead of being blackened into tinder, only assumed a more dazzling whiteness as the finger marks of human imperfection were purified away. Certain marginal notes and commentaries, it is true, yielded to the intensity of the fiery test, but without detriment to the smallest syllable that had flamed from the pen of inspiration.

"Yes; there is the proof of what you say," answered I, turning to the observer; "but if only what is evil can feel the action of the fire, then, surely, the conflagration has been of inestimable utility. Yet, if I understand aright, you intimate a doubt whether the world's expectation of benefit would be realized by it."

"Listen to the talk of these worthies," said he, pointing to a group in front of the blazing pile; "possibly they may teach you something useful, without intending it."

The persons whom he indicated consisted of that brutal and most earthy figure who had stood forth so furiously in defense of the gallows—the hangman, in short—together with the last thief and the last murderer, all three of whom were clustered about the last toper. The latter was liberally passing the brandy bottle, which he had rescued from the general destruction of wines and spirits. This little convivial party seemed at the lowest pitch of despondency, as considering that the purified world must needs be utterly unlike the sphere that they had hitherto known, and therefore but a strange and desolate abode for gentlemen of their kidney.

"The best counsel for all of us is," remarked the hangman, "that, as soon as we have finished the last drop of liquor, I help you, my three friends, to a comfortable end upon the nearest tree, and then hang myself on the same bough. This is no world for us any longer."

"Poh, poh, my good fellows!" said a dark-complexioned personage, who now joined the group—his complexion was indeed fearfully dark, and his eyes glowed with a redder light than that of the bonfire; "be not so cast down, my dear friends; you shall see good days yet. There is one thing that these wiseacres have forgotten to throw into the fire, and without which all the rest of the conflagration is just nothing at all; yes, though they had burned the earth itself to a cinder."

"And what may that be?" eagerly demanded the last murderer.

"What but the human heart itself?" said the dark-visaged stranger, with a portentous grin. "And, unless they hit upon some method of purifying that foul cavern, forth from it will reissue all the shapes of wrong and misery—the same old shapes or worse ones—which they have taken such a vast deal of trouble to consume to ashes. I have stood by this livelong night and laughed in my sleeve at the whole business. O, take my word for it, it will be the old world yet!"

This brief conversation supplied me with a theme for lengthened thought. How sad a truth, if true it were, that man's age-long endeavor for perfection had served only to render him the mockery of the evil principle, from the fatal circumstance of an error at the very root of the matter! The heart, the heart—there was the little yet boundless sphere wherein existed the original wrong of which the crime and misery of this outward world were merely types. Purify that inward sphere, and the many shapes of evil that haunt the outward, and which now seem almost our only realities, will turn to shadowy phantoms and vanish of their own accord; but if we go no deeper than the intellect, and strive, with merely that feeble instrument, to discern and rectify what is wrong, our whole accomplishment will be a dream, so unsubstantial that it matters little whether the bonfire, which I have so faithfully described, were what we choose to call a real event and a flame that would scorch the finger, or only a phosphoric radiance and a parable of my own brain.

V
SECTIONALISM AND CIVIL WAR

The South "was established not by witch-burning Puritans, by cruel persecuting fanatics, who implanted in the North the standard of Torquemada, and breathed in the nostrils of their newly-born colonies all the ferocity, bloodthirstiness, and rapid intolerance of the Inquisition," some South Carolinian citizens assured the *London Times* correspondent William Howard Russell (1820–1907) in 1861, shortly after the first shots of the war had been fired in Charleston Harbor. Confusing its own bigotry with Christianity, Puritanism birthed "impurity of mind among men" and "unchastity in women," the Southerners continued. Evil, corrupt, and dark, Northerners "know how to read and write, but they don't know how to think, and they are the easy victims of the wretched imposters on all the 'ologies and 'isms who swarm over the region." Such hateful and ignorant people had recently just elected Abraham Lincoln (1809–1865) as president. The Illinois lawyer symbolized everything the South resented. An anonymous correspondent for the *Atlantic Monthly* recalled a telling conversation with a Charlestonian. "Is Lincoln considered here to be a bad or dangerous man?" the *Atlantic* man asked. "Not personally," the Charlestonian answered. "I understand that he is a man of excellent private character, and I have nothing to say against him as a ruler, inasmuch as he has never been tried." The president-elect "is simply a sign to us that we are in danger, and must provide for our own safety." The *Atlantic* writer pushed the Charlestonian a bit further: "You secede, then, solely because you think his election proves that the mass of the Northern people is adverse to you and your interests." The response was simple and direct: "Yes."

While these charges are nothing short of absurd, they reveal intense cultural misunderstandings between the North and the South. During 1860 and 1861, Southerners saw only John Brown (1800–1859) when they looked North. In turn, most Northerners saw only the bravado and arrogance of a Preston Brooks (1819–1857), (in)famous for caning Massachusetts Senator Charles Sumner (1811–1874) in 1856. By 1860, neither side understood the other. And, indeed, there are significant reasons for this, dating back to the founding of the republic. Most importantly, the American founders had never formed a consensus regarding the role of sovereignty in the interplay of the federal, state, and local governments. Even the means by which decisions could be made proved a compromise, for example, at the Constitutional Convention, where the nationalists dominated. But even in Philadelphia, each state represented at the convention received only one vote. Additionally, though the Constitution's preamble speaks in the language of "the people," the ratification process demanded that each state form a constitutional convention—separate from the state legislature that could initially vote for and, later, just as easily repeal its support—to ratify the Constitution itself. In other words, "the people" voting for or against the U.S. Constitution did not do so as a national aggregate of Americans, but rather as citizens of a particular state. Finally, as historian Forrest McDonald has pointed out, when the language of the Constitution speaks of the United States, it does so in the plural.

The years between 1787 and 1846 witnessed intense political and intellectual discussion and division over the issue of sovereignty. The Kentucky and the Virginia Resolutions of the late 1790s, the Hartford Federalist Resolutions of 1814, and the Missouri Compromise debates of 1819 and 1820 each revealed a fundamental disagreement among a variety of Americans, though the lines of contention were generally drawn at the Mason-Dixon Line. The most ardent supporter of state sovereignty, at least after 1820, was upland South Carolinian John C. Calhoun (1782–1850). In the minds of the South Carolinians, Calhoun held the status of a Founding Father. There was, first and foremost, George Washington (1732–1799) and, as a close second, there was John C. Calhoun. When some natives of the state took a visiting Northern student to Calhoun's grave in 1860, they treated the site as a medieval Roman Catholic would have reverenced a shrine or reliquary. "And the culmination of this sentiment was reached when the Northern visitor was taken to the grave of John C. Calhoun," E. G. Mason remembered. "Then, if never before," the visiting student continued, the Charlestonians expected the would-be pilgrim "to feel a due sense of his inferiority to the natives of the soil, which the presence of that superhuman individual had made more sacred than aught else of Mother Earth." William Howard Russell, the *London Times* correspondent mentioned above, remarked that he could not enter into a conversation with a South Carolinian in the spring of 1861 without Calhoun's name being invoked. "The founder of the school was Saint Calhoun," Russell recorded. "Here his pupils carry out their teaching in thunder and fire." Though Calhoun articulated his vision—derived from, among others, the works of John Calvin, Adam Smith, Jeremy Bentham, and Frederick Hegel—in a number of places, "A Disquisition on Government" served as his fullest treatment of the matter.

And yet, despite Calhoun's arguments, and despite popular memory, one could readily find more supporters of local and state sovereignty—in practice, if not in theory—north of the Mason-Dixon Line. Northern states, for example, passed a series of Personal Liberty Laws, protecting the rights of blacks and runaway slaves by preventing the use of state resources, funds, or personnel to comply with federal provisions of the Constitution. The Supreme Court upheld these laws in 1842 in *Prigg* v. *Pennsylvania*. It was in the North that the Abolitionist societies flourished. It was, however, in the South where one found the greatest demands for the use of federal money and power to protect the rights of southern slaveholding. The Fugitive Slave Law of 1850 was a part of the Compromise (or "Armistice," as one prominent historian put it) of 1850. The law, heinous and oppressive in every aspect, created the first federal police force and a new profession: the slave catcher. More than any other law, the Fugitive Slave Law brought the atrocities of slavery home to the North, creating awareness and horror. Figures such as Frederick Douglass (1818–1895) and Harriett Beecher Stowe (1811–1896) made their reputations fighting the law. It also radicalized many Americans. In response to the law, Douglass stated "the only way to make the Fugitive Slave Law a dead letter is to make a dozen or more dead kidnapers." Blacks themselves, he continued, "would hew their way to Liberty, despite the pale and puny opposition of their oppressors."

The fourteen years prior to the election of Abraham Lincoln witnessed some of the most tumultuous times in American history. The years of decision, 1846 to 1848, saw Americans embrace a blatant militant imperialism at the expense of republican familial expansion. Catholics, Lutherans, Germans, and Irish flooded into America, and Mormons moved West. Young Southern men, privately armed and trained, filibustered their way through much of Mexico and Central America. The U.S. Cavalry implemented the so-called "Big Reservation Policy" with the Indians of the Great Plains and went to war against the Indians of the Pacific Northwest. Stephen Douglas's Kansas-Nebraska Bill of 1854 destroyed, ultimately, the Whig Party and seriously damaged the Northern Democrats. It also led, in Jackson, Michigan, and Ripon, Wisconsin, to the formation of the Republican Party, dedicated to preventing the spread of slavery in the territories and the spread of the polygamy of the gnostic Christian sect of Mormonism. The cavalry also prevented any serious bloodshed when Jayhawkers, Northern abolitionists centered in Topeka and Lawrence, and Missouri Pukes (politely known as Border Ruffians) faced off in November 1855 along the Wakarusa River in eastern Kansas. The U.S. Cavalry and the fierce Kansas winter delayed but failed to prevent violence, which erupted during the first sacking of Lawrence in May 1856. Almost simultaneously, Representative Preston Brooks of South Carolina beat the brains out of Senator Charles Sumner of Massachusetts on the Senate floor, knocking him into a coma. In the minds of many in the North, "Bleeding Kansas" would always be associated with "Bleeding Sumner." In turn, a radicalized and murderous John Brown attacked a federal arsenal in

Virginia in 1859. Much to the surprise of Southerners, Ralph Waldo Emerson (1803–1882) claimed Brown's execution would "make the gallows as glorious as the cross." Brown, in his last statement, had said ominously: "I, John Brown, am now quite certain that the crimes of this guilty land will never be purged away but with blood." On December 20, 1860, a little over a month after Lincoln's fully constitutional election to the presidency, the State of South Carolina seceded from the Union, declaring itself an independent republic. Several other states followed, and, in convention, representatives from these states formed the Confederate States of America between February 7 and 9, 1861.

When Lincoln became president in early March 1861, he inherited an almost unimaginable situation. The head of a party only seven years old and with a cabinet that would not fully respect him until December 1862, Lincoln had to deal with the chaos of Charleston harbor and Fort Sumter, where President James Buchanan (r. 1857–1861) had failed in his presidential duty to protect federal property, leaving Major Robert Anderson (1805–1871) and his command under siege for months. The new president also had to deal with the secessionist states, declaring themselves collectively a power equal to the United States. When Lincoln decided to back the federal troops against the secessionists, the Confederacy opened fire on Fort Sumter at 4:27 AM, April 12,1861. On April 15, President Lincoln called for 75,000 volunteers to quell the rebellion. Four days later, Lincoln ordered a blockade around the Confederacy.

Lincoln himself seems not to have decided what the war was ultimately for until the late summer of 1862. After a number of military disasters with the eastern Army of the Potomac (Grant was leading the federal western armies to great success), Lincoln had a spiritual (or, so it seems) revelation, remembered as his "Meditation on the Divine Will." On September 22, 1862, Lincoln told his cabinet of the Emancipation Proclamation, to go into effect on January 1, 1863. That spring, Lincoln commissioned (through Massachusetts) the first black regiments, the 54th and 55th Massachusetts, both of which performed nobly, opening the way for nearly 178,000 blacks to serve the Union as soldiers, joining the nearly 1.4 million whites who served (94 percent of whom volunteered). In November of the same year, at Gettysburg, Lincoln offered his nationalist vision for America, one in which equality would rule. He reinforced this vision, in undeniably beautiful language, during his second inaugural.

Ulysses S. Grant (1822–1885) had experienced fine success in the western theater and, in the spring of 1864, President Lincoln, convinced he would not be re-elected to the presidency, appointed Grant head of all Union armies. He wasted no time consolidating martial power and setting into action a plan that would force General Robert E. Lee (1807–1870), and, consequently, all Confederate military forces, to surrender by the middle of 1865. Lee's troops turned over their weapons and flags, peaceably, on April 12, 1865, exactly four years to the day after the firing on Fort Sumter. This was "honor answering honor," the Bowdoin College classicist, Joshua Chamberlain (1828–1914), wrote, with men "of near blood born, made nearer by bloodshed.... On our part not a sound or a trumpet more, nor roll of drum; nor a cheer, nor word nor whisper of vain-glory, nor motion of man standing again at the order, but an awed stillness rather, and breath-holding, as if it were the passing of the dead." Jefferson Davis (1808–1889) ordered all Confederate forces to go underground, becoming a ceaseless terrorist force against the United States, but Lee countermanded the order. Amazingly enough—due to the republican, agrarian, and Christian character of most Americans, north and south—most soldiers simply went home to their families and readjusted to normal life. "When I returned home I found that the farm work my father was then engaged in was cutting and shucking corn," one Illinois solider remembered. "So, the morning after my arrival, September 29th, I doffed my uniform of first lieutenant, put on some of my father's old cloths, and proceeded to wage war on the standing corn. The feeling I had while engaged in this work was sort of queer. It almost seemed, sometimes, as if I had been away only a day or two, and had just taken up the farm work where I had left off."

Two days after the surrender of Lee's forces, John Wilkes Booth (1838–1865), a southern actor, yelled "Sic semper tyrannis," (thus always to tyrants) and shot President Lincoln. On Holy Saturday, the president died. Prior to his death, Lincoln, in what has been remembered as the River Queen Doctrine, called for a complete reconciliation with the South and its citizens. Desiring a so-called "soft peace," Lincoln told Generals Grant and Sherman in early 1865 that he only wanted

> to get the deluded men of the rebel armies disarmed and back to their homes.... Let them once surrender and reach their homes, [and] they won't take up arms again.... Let them all go, officers and all, I want submission and no more bloodshed.... I want no one punished; treat them liberally all around. We want those people to return to their allegiance to the Union and submit to the laws.

The radicals of Lincoln's party—such as Charles Sumner, Benjamin Wade (1800–1878), George Julian (1817–1899), and Thaddeus Stevens (1792–1868)—had hated Lincoln from the beginning, and they had attempted to usurp his power wherever and whenever possible. They were also more than willing to use the martyrdom of Lincoln as a pretext for remaking the South in the image of the North. Beginning in December 1865, under the auspices of the Joint Committee on Reconstruction, the radicals led the fight for a reconstructed South until roughly 1871. The reconstruction laws were repealed, and northern troops finally removed from the South, during the so-called "Compromise of 1877."

DISQUISITION ON GOVERNMENT
JOHN C. CALHOUN (1782–1850)
U.S. SENATOR FROM SOUTH CAROLINA (1832–1843, 1845–1850)

The Calhouns arrived in America in 1733, part of the large migration from Scotland via Ulster. They eventually settled in the South Carolina highlands and were a large, influential clan by the time of Jefferson's Presidency. John Caldwell Calhoun was born with brains, good looks, and a fierce will not uncommon among the men of the southern uplands. An old prayer in the region went, "Lord, grant that I may always be right, for You know I am hard to turn." He transformed himself from a rough frontiersman into the model of a gentleman and aristocrat. Yale provided much of his formal education, classical and literary, but he became a political philosopher out of his determination to defend both South Carolina and the Union.

Calhoun became one of America's greatest public men. He served in the House, Senate, Cabinet, and Vice-Presidency over the course of thirty-nine years, during which time he saw the balance of power in the United States tip northward and toward the national government. He undertook to defend state sovereignty by defending the South, and to defend the South by defending slavery. To do this he knew he had to confront the dominant political faith of his age: Equality.

Calhoun's "disquisitions and discourses" were published the year after his death. In them he tried to solve the great problem of American political life: how to protect and preserve local (or regional) communities against centralized democratic power.

1840

But government, although intended to protect and preserve society, has itself a strong tendency to disorder and abuse of its powers, as all experience and almost every page of history testify. The cause is to be found in the same constitution of our nature which makes government indispensable. The powers which it is

Richard K. Cralle, ed., *A Disquisition on Government and a Discourse on the Constitution and Government of the United States by John C. Calhoun* (Columbia, SC: A. S. Johnston, 1851), 7–8, 12–17, 24–31, 35–36, 45–49, 55–59.

necessary for government to possess, in order to repress violence and preserve order, cannot execute themselves. They must be administered by men in whom, like others, the individual are stronger than the social feelings. And hence, the powers vested in them to prevent injustice and oppression on the part of oth-
5 ers, will, if left unguarded, be by them converted into instruments to oppress the rest of the community. That, by which this is prevented, by whatever name called, is what is meant by CONSTITUTION, in its most comprehensive sense, when applied to GOVERNMENT.

Having its origin in the same principle of our nature, *constitution* stands to
10 *government*, as *government* stands to *society*; and, as the end for which society is ordained, would be defeated without government, so that for which government is ordained would, in a great measure, be defeated without constitution. But they differ in this striking particular. There is no difficulty in forming government. It is not even a matter of choice, whether there shall be one or not. Like
15 breathing, it is not permitted to depend on our volition. Necessity will force it on all communities in some one form or another. Very different is the case as to constitution. Instead of a matter of necessity, it is one of the most difficult tasks imposed on man to form a constitution worthy of the name; while, to form a perfect one—one that would completely counteract the tendency of govern-
20 ment to oppression and abuse, and hold it strictly to the great ends for which it is ordained—has thus far exceeded human wisdom, and possibly ever will. From this, another striking difference results. Constitution is the contrivance of man, while government is of Divine ordination. Man is left to perfect what the wisdom of the Infinite ordained, as necessary to preserve the race....
25 How government, then, must be constructed, in order to counteract, through its organism, this tendency on the part of those who make and execute the laws to oppress those subject to their operation, is the next questions which claims attention.

There is but one way in which this can possibly be done; and that is, by
30 such an organism as will furnish the ruled with the means of resisting success-fully this tendency on the part of the rulers to oppression and abuse. Power can only be resisted by power—and tendency by tendency. Those who exercise power and those subject to its exercise—the rulers and the ruled—stand in antagonistic relations to each other. The same constitution of our nature which
35 leads rulers to oppress the ruled—regardless of the object for which government is ordained—will, with equal strength, lead the ruled to resist, when possessed of the means of making peaceable and effective resistance. Such an organism, then, as will furnish the means by which resistance may be systematically and peaceably made on the part of the ruled, to oppression and abuse of power
40 on the part of the rulers, is the first and indispensable step forwards *forming* a

constitutional government. And as this can only be effected by or through the right of suffrage—(the right on the part of the ruled to choose their rulers at proper intervals, and to hold them thereby responsible for their conduct)—the responsibility of the rulers to the ruled, through the right of suffrage, is the indispensable and primary principle in the *foundation* of a constitutional government. When this right is properly guarded, and the people sufficiently enlightened to understand their own rights and the interests of the community, and duly to appreciate the motives and conduct of those appointed to make and execute the laws, it is all-sufficient to give to those who elect, effective control over those they have elected.

I call the right of suffrage the indispensable and primary principle; for it would be a great and dangerous mistake to suppose, as many do, that it is, of itself, sufficient to form constitutional governments. To this erroneous opinion may be traced one of the causes, why so few attempts to form constitutional governments have succeeded; and why, of the few which have, so small a number have had durable existence. It has led, not only to mistakes in the attempts to form such governments, but to their overthrow, when they have, by some good fortune, been correctly formed. So far from being, of itself, sufficient—however well guarded it might be, and however enlightened the people—it would, un-aided by other provisions, leave the government as absolute, as it would be in the hands of irresponsible rulers; and with a tendency, at least as strong, towards oppression and abuse of its powers; as I shall next proceed to explain.

The right of suffrage, of itself, can do no more than give complete control to those who elect, over the conduct of those they have elected. In doing this, it accomplishes all it possibly can accomplish. This is its aim—and when this is attained, its end is fulfilled. It can do no more, however enlightened the people, or however widely extended or well guarded the right may be. The sum total, then, of its effects, when most successful, is, to make those elected, the true and faithful representatives of those who elected them—instead of irresponsible rulers—as they would be without it; and thus, by converting it into an agency, and the rulers into agents, to divest government of all claims to sovereignty, and to retain it unimpaired to the community. But it is manifest that the right of suffrage, in making these changes, transfers, in reality, the actual control over the government, from those who make and execute the laws, to the body of the community; and, thereby, places the powers of the government as fully in the mass of the community, as they would be if they, in fact, had assembled, made, and executed the laws themselves, without the intervention of representatives or agents. The more perfectly it does this, the more perfectly it accomplishes its ends; but in doing so, it only changes the seat of authority, without counteracting, in the least, the tendency of the government to oppression and abuse of its powers.

If the whole community had the same interests, so that the interests of each and every portion would be so affected by the action of the government, that the laws which oppressed or impoverished one portion, would necessarily oppress and impoverish all others—or the reverse—then the right of suffrage, of itself, would be all-sufficient to counteract the tendency of the government

5   to oppression and abuse of its powers; and, of course, would form, of itself, a perfect constitutional government. The interest of all being the same, by supposition, as far as the action of the government was concerned, all would have like interests as to what laws should be made, and how they should be executed. All strife and struggle would cease as to who should be elected to make and

10   execute them. The only question would be, who was most fit; who the wisest and most capable of understanding the common interest of the whole. This decided, the election would pass off quietly, and without party discord; as no one portion could advance its own peculiar interest without regard to the rest, by electing a favorite candidate.

15   But such is not the case. On the contrary, nothing is more difficult than to equalize the action of the government, in reference to the various and diversified interests of the community; and nothing more easy than to pervert its powers into instruments to aggrandize and enrich one or more interests by oppressing and impoverishing the others; and this too, under the operation of laws,

20   couched in general terms;—and which, on their face, appear fair and equal. Nor is this the case in some particular communities only. It is so in all; the small and the great—the poor and the rich—irrespective of pursuits, productions, or degrees of civilization;—with, however, this difference, that the more extensive and populous the country, the more diversified the condition and pursuits of

25   its population, and the richer, more luxurious, and dissimilar the people, the more difficult is it to equalize the action of the government—and the more easy for one portion of the community to pervert its powers to oppress, and plunder the other.

Such being the case, it necessarily results, that the right of suffrage, by

30   placing the control of the government in the community, must, from the same constitution of our nature which makes government necessary to preserve society, lead to conflict among its different interests—each striving to obtain possession of its powers, as the means of protecting itself against the

35   others;—or of advancing its respective interests, regardless of the interests of others. For this purpose, a struggle will take place between the various interests to obtain a majority, in order to control the government. If no one interest be strong enough, of itself, to obtain it, a combination will be formed between those whose interests are most alike—each conceding something to the others,

40   until a sufficient number is obtained to make a majority. The process may be

slow, and much time may be required before a compact, organized majority can be thus formed; but formed it will be in time, even without preconcert or design, by the sure workings of that principle of constitution of our nature in which government itself originates. When once formed, the community will be divided into two great parties—a major and minor—between which there will be incessant struggles on the one side to retain, and on the other to obtain the majority—and, thereby, the control of the government and the advantages it confers.

So deeply seated, indeed, is the tendency to conflict between the different interests or portions of the community, that it would result from the action of the government itself, even though it were possible to find a community, where the people were all of the same pursuits, placed in the same condition of life, and in every respect, so situated, as to be without inequality of condition or diversity of interests. The advantages of possessing the control of the powers of the government, and, thereby, of its honors and emoluments, are, of themselves, exclusive of all other considerations, ample to divide even such a community into two great hostile parties....

As, then, the right of suffrage, without some other provision, cannot counteract this tendency of government, the next question for consideration is—What is that other provision? This demands the most serious consideration; for of all the questions embraced in the science of government, it involves a principle, the most important, and the least understood; and when understood, the most difficult of application in practice. It is, indeed, emphatically, that principle which *makes* the constitution, in its strict and limited sense.

From what has been said, it is manifest, that this provision must be of a character calculated to prevent any one interest, or combination of interests, from using the powers of government to aggrandize itself at the expense of the others. Here lies the evil: and just in proportion as it shall prevent, or fail to prevent it, in the same degree it will effect, or fail to effect the end intended to be accomplished. There is but one certain mode in which this result can be secured; and that is, by the adoption of some restriction or limitation, which shall so effectually prevent any one interest, or combination of interests, from obtaining the exclusive control of the government, as to render hopeless all attempts directed to that end. There is, again, but one mode in which this can be effected; and that is, by taking the sense of each interest or portion of the community, which may be unequally and injuriously affected by the action of the government, separately, through its own majority, or in some other way by which its voice may be fairly expressed; and to require the consent of each interest, either to put or to keep the government in action. This, too, can be accomplished only in one way—and that is, by such an organism of the govern-

ment—and, if necessary for the purpose, of the community also—as will, by dividing and distributing the powers of government, give to each division or interest, through its appropriate organ, either a concurrent voice in making and executing the laws, or a veto on their execution. It is only by such an organism,
5 that the assent of each can be made necessary to put the government in motion; or the power made effectual to arrest its action, when put in motion—and it is only by the one or the other that the different interests, orders, classes, or portions, into which the community may be divided, can be protected, and all conflict and struggle between them prevented—by rendering it impossible to
10 put or to keep it in action, without the concurrent consent of all.

Such an organism as this, combined with the right of suffrage, constitutes, in fact, the elements of constitutional government. The one, by rendering those who make and execute the laws responsible to those on whom they operate, prevents the rulers from oppressing the ruled; and the other, by making it im-
15 possible for any one interest or combination of interests or class, or order, or portion of the community, to obtain exclusive control, prevents any one of them from oppressing the other. It is clear, that oppression and abuse of power must come, if at all, from the one or the other quarter. From no other can they come. It follows, that the two, suffrage and proper organism combined, are sufficient
20 to counteract the tendency of government to oppression and abuse of power; and to restrict it to the fulfillment of the great ends for which it is ordained.

In coming to this conclusion, I have assumed the organism to be perfect, and the different interests, portions, or classes of the community, to be sufficiently enlightened to understand its character and object, and to exercise, with due
25 intelligence, the right of suffrage. To the extent that either may be defective, to the same extent the government would fall short of fulfilling its end. But this does not impeach the truth of the principles on which it rests. In reducing them to proper form, in applying them to practical uses, all elementary principles are liable to difficulties; but they are not, on this account, the less true, or valuable.
30 Where the organism is perfect, every interest will be truly and fully represented, and of course the whole community must be so. It may be difficult, or even impossible, to make a perfect organism—but, although this be true, yet even when, instead of the sense of each and of all, it takes that of a few great and prominent interests only, it would still, in a great measure, if not altogether, fulfill
35 the end intended by a constitution. For, in such case, it would require so large a portion of the community, compared with the whole, to concur, or acquiesce in the action of the government, that the number to be plundered would be too few, and the number to be aggrandized too many, to afford adequate motives to oppression and the abuse of its powers. Indeed, however imperfect the organism,
40 it must have more or less effect in diminishing such tendency.

It may be readily inferred, from what has been stated, that the effect of organism is neither to supersede nor diminish the importance of the right of suffrage; but to aid and perfect it. The object of the latter is to collect the sense of the community. The more fully and perfectly it accomplishes this, the more fully and perfectly it fulfills its end. But the most it can do, of itself, is to collect the sense of the greater number; that is, of the stronger interests, or combination of interests; and to assume this to be the sense of the community. It is only when aided by a proper organism, that it can collect the sense of the entire community—of each and all its interests; of each, through its appropriate organ, and of the whole, through all of them united. This would truly be the sense of the entire community; for whatever diversity each interest might have within itself—as all would have the same interest in reference to the action of the government, the individuals composing each would be fully and truly represented by its own majority or appropriate organ, regarded in reference to the other interests. In brief, every individual of every interest might trust, with confidence, its majority or appropriate organ, against that of every other interest.

It results, from what has been said, that there are two different modes in which the sense of the community may be taken; one, simply by the right of suffrage, unaided; the other, by the right through a proper organism. Each collects the sense of the majority. But one regards numbers only, and considers the whole community as a unit, having but one common interest throughout; and collects the sense of the greater number of the whole, as that of the community. The other, on the contrary, regards interests as well as numbers—considering the community as made up of different and conflicting interests, as far as the action of the government is concerned; and takes the sense of each, through its majority or appropriate organ, and the united sense of all, as the sense of the entire community. The former of these I shall call the numerical, or absolute majority; and the latter, the concurrent, or constitutional majority. I call it the constitutional majority, because it is an essential element in every constitutional government—be its form what it may. So great is the difference, politically speaking, between the two majorities, that they cannot be confounded, without leading to great and fatal errors; and yet the distinction between them has been so entirely overlooked, that when the term *majority* is used in political discussions, it is applied exclusively to designate the numerical—as if there were no other. Until this distinction is recognized, and better understood, there will continue to be great liability to error in properly constructing constitutional governments, especially of the popular form, and of preserving them when properly constructed. Until then, the latter will have a strong tendency to slide, first, into the government of the numerical majority, and, finally, into absolute government of some other form. To show that such must be the case, and at the same time to mark more strongly the difference between the two, in order to guard against the danger of overlooking it, I propose to consider the subject more at length.

    The first and leading error which naturally arises from overlooking the distinction referred to, is, to confound the numerical majority with the people; and this so completely as to regard them as identical. This is a consequence that necessarily results from considering the numerical as the only majority. All admit, that a popular government, or democracy, is the government of the people; for the terms imply this. A perfect government of the kind would be one which would embrace the consent of every citizen or member of the community; but as this is impracticable, in the opinion of those who regard the numerical as the only majority, and who can perceive no other way by which the sense of the people can be taken—they are compelled to adopt this as the only true basis of popular government, in contradistinction of governments of the aristocrati-cal or monarchical form. Being thus constrained, they are, in the next place, forced to regard the numerical majority, as, in effect, the entire people; that is, the greater part as the whole; and the government of the greater part as the government of the whole. It is thus the two come to be confounded, and a part made identical with the whole. And it is thus, also, that all the rights, powers, and immunities of the whole people come to be attributed to the numerical majority; and, among others, the supreme, sovereign authority of establishing and abolishing governments at pleasure.

    This radical error, the consequence of confounding the two, and of regard-ing the numerical as the only majority, has contributed more than any other cause, to prevent the formation of popular constitutional governments—and to destroy them even when they have been formed. It leads to the conclusion that, in their formation and establishment, nothing more is necessary than the right of suffrage—and the allotment to each division of the community a representation in the government, in proportion to numbers. If the numerical majority were really the people; and if, to take its sense truly, were to take the sense of the people truly, a government so constituted would be a true and perfect model of a popular constitutional government; and every departure from it would detract from its excellence. But, as such is not the case—as the numerical majority, instead of being the people, is only a portion of them—such a government, instead of being a true and perfect model of the people's govern-ment, that is, a people self-governed, is but the government of a part, over a part—the major over the minor portion.

    But this misconception of the true elements of constitutional government does not stop here. It leads to others equally false and fatal, in reference to the best means of preserving and perpetuating them, when, from some fortunate combination of circumstances, they are correctly formed. For they who fall into these errors regard the restrictions which organism imposes on the will of the numerical majority as restrictions on the will of the people, and, therefore, as not only useless, but wrongful and mischievous. And hence they endeavor to destroy organism, under the delusive hope of making government more democratic.

Such are some of the consequences of confounding the two, and of regarding the numerical as the only majority. And in this may be found the reason why so few popular governments have been properly constructed, and why, of these few, so small a number have proved durable. Such must continue to be the result, so long as these errors continue to be prevalent....

The necessary consequence of taking the sense of the community by the concurrent majority is, as has been explained, to give to each interest or portion of the community a negative on the others. It is this mutual negative among its various conflicting interests, which invests each with the power of protecting itself;--and places the rights and safety of each, where only they can be securely placed, under its own guardianship. Without this there can be no systematic, peaceful, or effective resistance to the natural tendency of each to come into conflict with the others: and without this there can be no constitution. It is this negative power—the power of preventing or arresting the action of the government—be it called by what term it may—veto, interposition, nullification, check, or balance of power—which, in fact, forms the constitution. They are all but different names for the negative power. In all its forms, and under all its names, it results from the concurrent majority. Without this there can be no negative; and, without a negative, no constitution. The assertion is true in reference to all constitutional governments, be their forms what they may. It is, indeed, the negative power which makes the constitution—and the positive which makes the government. The one is the power of acting—and the other the power of preventing or arresting action. The two, combined, make constitutional governments.

But, as there can be no constitution without the negative power, and no negative power without the concurrent majority—it follows, necessarily, that where the numerical majority has the sole control of the government, there can be no constitution; as constitution implies limitation or restriction—and, of course, is inconsistent with the idea of sole or exclusive power. And hence, the numerical, unmixed with the concurrent majority, necessarily forms, in all cases, absolute government....

Among the other advantages which governments of the concurrent have over those of the numerical majority—and which strongly illustrates their more popular character, is—that they admit, with safety, a much greater extension of the right of suffrage. It may be safely extended in such governments to universal suffrage: that is—to every male citizen of mature age, with few ordinary exceptions; but it cannot be so far extended in those of the numerical majority, without placing them ultimately under the control of the more ignorant and dependent portions of the community. For, as the community becomes populous, wealthy, refined, and highly civilized, the difference between the rich and the poor will become more strongly marked; and the number of the ignorant and dependent greater in proportion to the rest of the community. With the increase of this difference, the tendency to conflict between them will become stronger; and, as the poor and dependent become more numerous in proportion, there will be, in governments of the numerical majority, no want of leaders among the wealthy and ambitious, to excite and direct them in their efforts to obtain the control.

The case is different in governments of the concurrent majority. There, mere numbers have not the absolute control; and the wealthy and intelligent being identified in interest with the poor and ignorant, of their respective portions or interests of the community, become their leaders and protectors. And hence, as the latter would have neither hope nor inducement to rally the former in order to obtain the control, the right of suffrage, under such a government, may be safely enlarged to the extent stated, without incurring the hazard to which such enlargement would expose governments of the numerical majority.

In another particular, governments of the concurrent majority have greatly the advantage. I allude to the difference in their respective tendency, in reference to dividing or uniting the community. That of the concurrent, as has been shown, is to unite the community, let its interests be ever so diversified or opposed; while that of the numerical is to divide it into two conflicting portions, let its interests be, naturally, ever so united and identified.

That the numerical majority will divide the community, let it be ever so homogeneous, into two great parties, which will be engaged in perpetual struggles to obtain the control of the government, has already been established. The great importance of the object at stake, must necessarily form strong party attachments and party antipathies—attachments on the part of the members of each to their respective parties, through whose efforts they hope to accomplish an object dear to all; and antipathies to the opposite party, as presenting the only obstacle to success.

In order to have a just conception of their force, it must be taken into consideration, that the object to be won or lost appeals to the strongest passions of the human heart—avarice, ambition, and rivalry. It is not then wonderful, that a form of government, which periodically stakes all its honors and emoluments, as prizes to be contended for, should divide the community into two great hostile parties; or that party attachments, in the progress of the strife, should become so strong among the members of each respectively, as to absorb almost every feeling of our nature, both social and individual; or that their mutual antipathies should be carried to such an excess as to destroy, almost entirely, all sympathy between them, and to substitute in its place the strongest aversion. Nor is it surprising, 5 that under their joint influence, the community should cease to be the common centre of attachment, or that each party should find that centre only in itself. It is thus, that, in such governments, devotion to party becomes stronger than devotion to country—the promotion of the interests of party more important than the promotion of the common good of the whole, and its triumph and 10 ascendency, objects of far greater solicitude, than the safety and prosperity of the community. It is thus, also, that the numerical majority, by regarding the community as a unit, and having, as such, the same interests throughout all its parts, must, by its necessary operation, divide it into two hostile parts, waging, under the forms of law, incessant hostilities against each other. 15

The concurrent majority, on the other hand, tends to unite the most opposite and conflicting interests, and to blend the whole in one common attachment to the country. By giving to each interest, or portion, the power of self-protection, all strife and struggle between them for ascendency, is prevented; and, thereby, not only every feeling calculated to weaken the attachment to the 20 whole is suppressed, but the individual and the social feelings are made to unite in one common devotion to country. Each sees and feels that it can best promote its own prosperity by conciliating the goodwill, and promoting the prosperity of the others. And hence, there will be diffused throughout the whole community kind feelings between its different portions; and, instead of antipathy, 25 a rivalry amongst them to promote the interests of each other, as far as this can be done consistently with the interest of all. Under the combined influence of these causes, the interests of each would be merged in the common interests of the whole; and thus, the community would become a unit, by becoming the common centre of attachment of all its parts. And hence, instead of faction, 30 strife, and struggle for party ascendency, there would be patriotism, nationality, harmony, and a struggle only for supremacy in promoting the common good of the whole....

It follows, from what has been stated, that it is a great and dangerous error to suppose that all people are equally entitled to liberty. It is a reward 35 to be earned, not a blessing to be gratuitously lavished on all alike—a reward reserved for the intelligent, the patriotic, the virtuous and deserving—and not a boon to be bestowed on a people too ignorant, degraded and vicious, to be capable either of appreciating or of enjoying it. Nor is it any disparagement to liberty, that such is, and ought to be the case. On the contrary, its greatest 40

praise—its proudest distinction is, that an all-wise Providence has reserved it, as the noblest and highest reward for the development of our faculties, moral and intellectual. A reward more appropriate than liberty could not be conferred on the deserving;--nor a punishment inflicted on the undeserving more
5   just, than to be subject to lawless and despotic rule. This dispensation seems to be the result of some fixed law—and every effort to disturb or defeat it, by attempting to elevate a people in the scale of liberty, above the point to which they are entitled to rise, must ever prove abortive, and end in disappointment. The progress of a people rising from a lower to a higher point in the scale of
10 liberty, is necessarily slow—and by attempting to precipitate, we either retard, or permanently defeat it.

There is another error, not less great and dangerous, usually associated with the one which has just been considered. I refer to the opinion, that liberty and equality are so intimately united, that liberty cannot be perfect without
15 perfect equality.

That they are united to a certain extent—and that equality of citizens, in the eyes of the law, is essential to liberty in a popular government, is conceded. But to go further, and make equality of *condition* essential to liberty, would be to destroy both liberty and progress. The reason is, that inequality of condition,
20 while it is a necessary consequence of liberty, is, at the same time, indispensable to progress. In order to understand why this is so, it is necessary to bear in mind, that the main spring to progress is, the desire of individuals to better their condition; and that the strongest impulse which can be given to it is, to leave individuals free to exert themselves in the manner they may deem best for that
25 purpose, as far at least as it can be done consistently with the ends for which government is ordained—and to secure to all the fruits of their exertions. Now, as individuals differ greatly from each other, in intelligence, sagacity, energy, perseverance, skill, habits of industry and economy, physical power, position and opportunity—the necessary effect of leaving all free to exert themselves to
30 better their condition, must be a corresponding inequality between those who may possess these qualities and advantages in a high degree, and those who may be deficient in them. The only means by which this result can be prevented are, either to impose such restrictions on the exertions of those who may possess them in a high degree, as will place them on a level with those who do not; or
35 to deprive them of the fruits of their exertions. But to impose such restrictions on them would be destructive of liberty—while, to deprive them of the fruits of their exertions, would be to destroy the desire of bettering their condition. It is, indeed, this inequality of condition between the front and rear ranks, in the march of progress, which gives so strong an impulse to the former to
40 maintain their position, and to the latter to press forward into their files. This

gives to progress its greatest impulse. To force the front rank back to the rear, or attempt to push forward the rear into line with the front, by the interposition of the government, would put an end to the impulse, and effectually arrest the march of progress.

These great and dangerous errors have their origin in the prevalent opin- 5
ion that all men are born free and equal—than which nothing can be more unfounded and false. It rests upon the assumption of a fact, which is contrary to universal observation, in whatever light it may be regarded. It is, indeed, difficult to explain how an opinion so destitute of all sound reason, ever could have been so extensively entertained, unless we regard it as being confounded 10
with another, which has some semblance of truth;—but which, when properly understood, is not less false and dangerous. I refer to the assertion, that all men are equal in the state of nature; meaning, by a state of nature, a state of individuality, supposed to have existed prior to the social and political state; and in which men lived apart and independent of each other. If such a state 15
ever did exist, all men would have been, indeed, free and equal in it; that is, free to do as they pleased, and exempt from the authority or control of others—as, by supposition, it existed anterior to society and government. But such a state is purely hypothetical. It never did, nor can exist; as it is inconsistent with the preservation of perpetuation of the race. It is, therefore, a great misnomer to 20
call it *the state of nature*. Instead of being the natural state of man, it is, of all conceivable states, the most opposed to his nature—most repugnant to his feelings, and most incompatible with his wants. His natural state is, the social and political—the one for which his Creator made him, and the only one in which he can preserve and perfect his race. As, then, there never was such a state as 25
the, so called, state of nature, and never can be, it follows, that men, instead of being born in it, are born in the social and political state; and of course, instead of being born free and equal, are born subject, not only to parental authority, but to the laws and institutions of the country where born, and under whose protection they draw their first breath…. 30

SOCIOLOGY FOR THE SOUTH
GEORGE FITZHUGH (1806–1881)

George Fitzhugh, a Virginia planter and lawyer, was one of the most vigorous defenders of slavery in the 1850s. He insisted that slavery as practiced in the American South was a moral institution, especially if compared with the "low, selfish, atheistic and material" system of free society in the North. That comparison was at the heart of his defense.

Earlier defenses of slavery had usually emphasized that it was a practical necessity, or that it could be justified on grounds of the backwardness of African societies. Fitzhugh drew on these older arguments; he also added a deep knowledge of Greek and Roman sources and more recent theories of the biological inferiority of black Africans. What was new in his "sociology" was his moral comparison between free and slave societies. Calhoun questioned the progressive faith in equality. Fitzhugh denied the central proposition of progressives—that progress exists at all in human history. "We maintain," he said, "that man has not improved."

Fitzhugh was probably not typical of agrarian thinking. He embarrassed Southern unionists and was the counterpart of radical abolitionists in making civil discourse between the sections more difficult. But he presents as clearly as any writer of the time the moral distance that had developed between progressives and agrarians: patriarchy versus equality, tradition versus progress, slave versus free.

1854

We have already stated that we should not attempt to introduce any new theories of government and of society, but merely try to justify old ones, so far as we could deduce such theories from ancient and almost universal practices. Now it has been the practice in all countries and in all ages, in some degree, to accommodate the amount and character of government control to the wants, intelligence, and 5 moral capacities of the nations or individuals to be governed. A highly moral and

George Fitzhugh, *Sociology for the South, or The Failure of Free Society* (Richmond, VA: A. Morris, 1854), 82–95.

intellectual people, like the free citizens of ancient Athens, are best governed by a democracy. For a less moral and intellectual one, a limited and constitutional monarchy will answer. For a people either very ignorant or very wicked, nothing short of military despotism will suffice. So among individuals, the most moral
5   and well-informed members of society require no other government than law. They are capable of reading and understanding the law, and have sufficient self-control and virtuous disposition to obey it. Children cannot be governed by mere law; first, because they do not understand it, and secondly, because they are so much under the influence of impulse, passion and appetite, that
10   they want sufficient self-control to be deterred or governed by the distant and doubtful penalties of the law. They must be constantly controlled by parents or guardians, whose will and orders shall stand in the place of law for them. Very wicked men must be put into penitentiaries; lunatics into asylums, and the most wild of them into straight jackets, just as the most wicked of the sane
15   are manacled with irons; and idiots must have committees to govern and take care of them. Now, it is clear the Athenian democracy would not suit a negro nation, nor will the government of mere law suffice for the individual negro. He is but a grown up child, and must be governed as a child, not as a lunatic or criminal. The master occupies towards him the place of parent or guardian. We
20   shall not dwell on this view, for no one will differ with us who thinks as we do of the negro's capacity, and we might argue till dooms-day, in vain, with those who have a high opinion of the negro's moral and intellectual capacity.

      Secondly. The negro is improvident; will not lay up in summer for the wants of winter; will not accumulate in youth for the exigencies of age. He would
25   become an insufferable burden to society. Society has the right to prevent this, and can only do so by subjecting him to domestic slavery.

      In the last place, the negro race is inferior to the white race, and living in their midst, they would be far outstripped or outwitted in the chase of free competition. Gradual but certain extermination would be their fate. We presume
30   the maddest abolitionist does not think the negro's providence of habits and money-making capacity at all to compare to those of the whites. This defect of character would alone justify enslaving him, if he is to remain here. In Africa or the West Indies, he would become idolatrous, savage and cannibal, or be devoured by savages and cannibals. At the North he would freeze or starve.
35   We would remind those who deprecate and sympathize with negro slavery, that his slavery here relieves him from a far more cruel slavery in Africa, or from idolatry and cannibalism, and every brutal vice and crime that can disgrace humanity; and that it Christianizes, protects, supports, and civilizes him; that it governs him far better than free laborers at the North are governed. There,
40   wife-murder has become a mere holiday pastime; and where so many wives are

murdered, almost all must be brutally treated. Nay, more: men who kill their
wives or treat them brutally must be ready for all kinds of crime, and the calendar of crime at the North proves the inference to be correct. Negroes never
kill their wives. If it be objected that legally they have no wives, then we reply
that in an experience of more than forty years, we never yet heard of a negro   5
man killing a negro woman. Our negroes are not only better off as to physical
comfort than free laborers, but their moral condition is better.

    But abolish negro slavery, and how much of slavery still remains. Soldiers
and sailors in Europe enlist for life; here, for five years. Are they not slaves who
have not only sold their liberties, but their lives also? And they are worse treated   10
than domestic slaves. No domestic affection and self-interest extend their ægis
over them. No kind mistress, like a guardian angel, provides for them in health,
tends them in sickness, and soothes their dying pillow. Wellington[1] at Waterloo
was a slave. He was bound to obey, or would, like Admiral Byng,[2] have been shot
for gross misconduct, and might not, like a common laborer, quit his work at   15
any moment. He had sold his liberty, and might not resign without the consent
of his master, the king. The common laborer may quit his work at any moment,
whatever his contract; declare that liberty is an inalienable right, and leave his
employer to redress by a useless suit for damages. The highest and most honorable
position on earth was that of the slave Wellington; the lowest, that of the free   20
man who cleaned his boots and fed his hounds. The African cannibal, caught,
Christianized, and enslaved, is as much elevated by slavery as was Wellington.
The kind of slavery is adapted to the men enslaved. Wives and apprentices are
slaves; not in theory only, but often in fact. Children are slaves to their parents,
guardians and teachers. Imprisoned culprits are slaves. Lunatics and idiots are   25
slaves also. Three-fourths of free society are slaves, no better treated, when their
wants and capacities are estimated, than negro slaves. The masters in free society,
or slave society, if they perform properly their duties, have more cares and less
liberty than the slaves themselves. "In the sweat of thy face shalt thou earn thy
bread!"[3] made all men slaves, and such all *good men* continue to be.   30

    Negro slavery would be changed immediately to some form of peonage,
serfdom, or villienage if the negroes were sufficiently intelligent and provident
to manage a farm. No one would have the labor and trouble of management if
his negroes would pay in hires and rents one-half what free tenants pay in rent
in Europe. Every negro in the South would be soon liberated if he would take   35

---

[1]Arthur Wellesley (1769–1852), Duke of Wellington, commander of the army that defeated
  Napoleon at the Battle of Watterloo (1815)

[2]Admiral John Byng (1704–1757), British admiral executed for "failing to do his utmost" at
  the Battle of Menorca (1756)

[3]God's curse on Adam when expelling him from Eden (Genesis 3:19)

liberty on the terms that white tenants hold it. The fact that he cannot enjoy liberty on such terms seems conclusive that he is only fit to be a slave.

But for the assaults of the abolitionists, much would have been done ere this to regulate and improve Southern slavery. Our negro mechanics do not work so hard, have many more privileges and holidays, and are better fed and clothed than field hands, and are yet more valuable to their masters. The slaves of the South are cheated of their rights by the purchase of Northern manufactures which they could produce. Besides, if we would employ our slaves in the coarser processes of the mechanic arts and manufactures, such as brick making, getting and hewing timber for ships and houses, iron mining and smelting, coal mining, grading railroads and plank roads, in the manufacture of cotton, tobacco, etc., we would find a vent in new employments for their increase, more humane and more profitable than the vent afforded by new states and territories. The nice and finishing processes of manufactures and mechanics should be reserved for the whites, who only are fitted for them, and thus, by diversifying pursuits and cutting off dependence on the North, we might benefit and advance the interests of our whole population. Exclusive agriculture has depressed and impoverished the South. We will not here dilate on this topic, because we intend to make it the subject of a separate essay. Free trade doctrines, not slavery, have made the South agricultural and dependent, given her a sparse and ignorant population, ruined her cities, and expelled her people.

Would the abolitionists approve of a system of society that set white children free, and remitted them at the age of fourteen, males and females, to all the rights, both as to person and property, which belong to adults? Would it be criminal or praiseworthy to do so? Criminal, of course. Now, are the average of negroes equal in information, in native intelligence, in prudence or providence, to well-informed white children of fourteen? We who have lived with them for forty years, think not. The competition of the world would be too much for the children. They would be cheated out of their property and debased in their morals. Yet they would meet everywhere with sympathizing friends of their own color, ready to aid, advise and assist them. The negro would be exposed to the same competition and greater temptations, with no greater ability to contend with them, with these additional difficulties. He would be welcome nowhere; meet with thousands of enemies and no friends. If he went North, the white laborers would kick him and cuff him, an drive him out of employment. If he went to Africa, the savages would cook him and eat him. If he went to the West Indies, they would not let him in, or if they did, they would soon make of him a savage and idolater.

We have a further question to ask. If it be right and incumbent to subject children to the authority of parents and guardians, and idiots and lunatics to committees, would it not be equally right and incumbent to give the free negroes masters, until at least they arrive at years of discretion, which very few ever did or will attain? What is the difference between the authority of a parent and of a master? Neither pay wages, and each is entitled to the services of those subject to him. The father may not sell his child forever, but may hire him out till he is twenty-one. The free negro's master may also be restrained from selling. Let him stand *in loco parentis*, and call him papa instead of master. Look closely into slavery, and you will see nothing so hideous in it; or if you do, you will find plenty of it at home in its most hideous form.

The earliest civilization of which history gives account is that of Egypt. The negro was always in contact with that civilization. For four thousand years he has had opportunities of becoming civilized. Like the wild horse, he must be caught, tamed and domesticated. When his subjugation ceases he again runs wild, like the cattle on the Pampas of the South, or the horses on the prairies of the West. His condition in the West Indies proves this.

It is a common remark that the grand and lasting architectural structures of antiquity were the results of slavery. The mighty and continued association of labor requisite to their construction, when mechanic art was so little advanced and labor-saving processes unknown, could only have been brought about by a despotic authority, like that of the master over his slaves. It is, however, very remarkable that whilst in taste and artistic skill the world seems to have been retrograding ever since the decay and abolition of feudalism, in mechanical invention and in great utilitarian operations requiring the wielding of immense capital and much labor, its progress has been unexampled. Is it because capital is more despotic in its authority over free laborers than Roman masters and feudal lords were over their slaves and vassals?

Free society has continued long enough to justify the attempt to generalize its phenomena, and calculate its moral and intellectual influences. It is obvious that, in whatever is purely utilitarian and material, it incites invention and stimulates industry. Benjamin Franklin, as a man and a philosopher, is the best exponent of the working of the system. His sentiments and his philosophy are low, selfish, atheistic, and material. They tend directly to make man a mere "featherless biped", well-fed, well-clothed, and comfortable, but regardless of his soul as "the beasts that perish".

Since the Reformation the world has as regularly been retrograding in whatever belongs to the departments of genius, taste, and art as it has been progressing in physical science and its application to mechanical construction. Medieval Italy rivaled, if it did not surpass, ancient Rome in poetry, in sculpture, in painting, and many of the fine arts. Gothic architecture reared its monuments of skill and genius throughout Europe till the 15th century; but Gothic architecture died

with the Reformation. The age of Elizabeth was the Augustan age of England. The men who lived then acquired their sentiments in a world not yet deadened and vulgarized by puritanical cant and leveling demagoguism. Since then men have arisen who have been the fashion and the go for a season, but none have
5   appeared whose names will descend to posterity. Liberty and equality made slower advances in France. The age of Louis XIV was the culminating point of French genius and art. It then shed but a flickering and lurid light. Frenchmen are servile copyists of Roman art, and Rome had no art of her own. She borrowed from Greece; distorted and deteriorated what she borrowed; and France imitates and
10   falls below Roman distortions. The genius of Spain disappeared with Cervantes; and now the world seems to regard nothing as desirable except what will make money and what costs money. There is not a poet, an orator, a sculptor, or painter in the world. The tedious elaboration necessary to all the productions of high art would be ridiculed in this money-making, utilitarian, charlatan age. Nothing now
15   but what is gaudy and costly excites admiration. The public taste is debased.

But far the worst feature of modern civilization, which is the civilization of free society, remains to be exposed. Whilst labor-saving processes have probably lessened by one half, in the last century, the amount of work needed for comfortable support, the free laborer is compelled by capital and competition
20   to work more than he ever did before, and is less comfortable. The organization of society cheats him of his earnings, and those earnings go to swell the vulgar pomp and pageantry of the ignorant millionaires, who are the only great of the present day. These reflections might seem, at first view, to have little connection with negro slavery; but it is well for us of the South not to be deceived
25   by the tinsel glare and glitter of free society, and to employ ourselves in doing our duty at home, and studying the past, rather than in insidious rivalry of the expensive pleasures and pursuits of men who sentiments and whose aims are low, sensual, and groveling.

Human progress, consisting in moral and intellectual improvement, and
30   there being no agreed and conventional standard weights or measures of moral and intellectual qualities and quantities, the question of progress can never be accurately decided. We maintain that man has not improved, because in all save the mechanic arts he reverts to the distant past for models to imitate, and he never imitates what he can excel.

35   We need never have white slaves in the South because we have black ones. Our citizens, like those of Rome and Athens, are a privileged class. We should train and educate them to deserve the privileges and to perform the duties which society confers on them. Instead, by a low demagoguism depressing their self-respect by discourses on the equality of man, we had better excite their pride by
40   reminding them that they do not fulfill the menial offices which white men do in

other countries. Society does not feel the burden of providing for the few helpless paupers in the South. And we should recollect that here we have but half the people to educate, for half are negroes; whilst at the North they profess to educate all. It is in our power to spike this last gun of the abolitionists. We should educate all the poor. The abolitionists say that it is one of the necessary consequences of slavery that the poor are neglected. It was not so in Athens and in Rome, and should not be so in the South. If we had less trade with and less dependence on the North, all our poor might be profitably and honorably employed in trades, professions, and manufactures. Then we should have a rich and denser population. Yet we but marshal her in the way that she was going. The South is already aware of the necessity of a new policy, and has begun to act on it. Every day more and more is done for education, the mechanic arts, manufactures and internal improvements. We will soon be independent of the North.

We deem this peculiar question of negro slavery of very little importance. The issue is made throughout the world on the general subject of slavery in the abstract. The argument has commenced. One set of ideas will govern and control after awhile the civilized world. Slavery will everywhere be abolished, or everywhere be reinstituted. We think the opponents of practical, existing slavery are estopped by their own admission; nay, that unconsciously, as socialists, they are the defenders and propagandists of slavery, and have furnished the only sound arguments on which its defense and justification can be rested. We have introduced the subject of negro slavery to afford us a better opportunity to disclaim the purpose of reducing the white man anywhere to the condition of negro slaves here. It would be very unwise and unscientific to govern white men as you would negroes. Every shade and variety of slavery has existed in the world. In some cases there has been much of legal regulation, much restraint of the master's authority; in others, none at all. The character of slavery necessary to protect the whites in Europe should be much milder than negro slavery, for slavery is only needed to protect the white man, whilst it is more necessary for the government of the negro even than for his protection. But even negro slavery should not be outlawed. We might and should have laws in Virginia, as in Louisiana, to make the master subject to presentment by the grand jury and to punishment, for any inhuman or improper treatment or neglect of his slave.

We abhor the doctrine of the "Types of Mankind"; first, because it is at war with Scripture, which teaches us that the whole human race is descended from a common parentage; and, secondly, because it encourages and incites brutal masters to treat negroes, not as weak, ignorant, and dependent brethren, but as wicked beasts, without the pale of humanity. The Southerner is the negro's friend, his only friend. Let no intermeddling, abolitionist, no refined philosophy, dissolve this friendship.

WHAT TO THE SLAVE IS THE FOURTH OF JULY?
FREDERICK DOUGLASS (1818–1895)

The movement to abolish slavery gained momentum during the reform-minded 1840s. In many ways it was the reform of the era. It combined commitment to democracy and equality with the desire to remake an entire social order—that of the Agrarian South.

Frederick Douglass was born a slave in rural Maryland. His father was probably white, but as Douglass said, "Genealogical trees do not flourish among slaves." He learned to read and acquired a trade during an interlude as an urban slave in Baltimore. At the age of twenty he escaped, married Anna Murray, and soon ended up among the free black population in New Bedford, Massachusetts. Douglass planned to earn a living as a ship's caulker in the port town, but discovered the Boston abolitionist movement and was absorbed into its activities in the early 1840s. The first version of his autobiography (1845) earned him considerable fame and a speaking tour of Great Britain; eventually British friends bought his freedom for $711. He returned to the United States and moved to Rochester, New York, where he edited his own newspaper, and where he delivered the famous speech reprinted here. Among the thousands of speeches he delivered against the evils of slavery was one at Hillsdale College (January 21, 1863).

Douglass represented the Enlightenment side of abolitionism, which emphasized rights rather than religion, and he did not mince words. If the Constitution condoned slavery, then so much the worse for the Constitution. If the churches supported slavery, then the churches were not worth supporting. In fact, most major Protestant churches (including Methodist and Baptist) split into Northern and Southern branches by the mid-1840s. In the name of progress and equality Douglass was willing to sacrifice the past for a better future. His rhetoric is revolutionary: "For it is not light that is needed, but fire; it is not the gentle shower, but thunder. We need the storm, the whirlwind and the earthquake."

Frederick Douglass, *Oration Delivered in Corinthian Hall, Rochester* (Rochester, NY: Lee, Mann, and Company, 1852), 3–5, 9–39.

5 July 1852

The papers and placards say that I am to deliver a 4th of July oration. This certainly sounds large, and out of the common way, for me. It is true that I have often had the privilege to speak in this beautiful Hall, and to address many who now honor me with their presence. But neither their familiar faces, nor the perfect gage I

5   think I have for Corinthian Hall, seems to free me from embarrassment.

The fact is, ladies and gentlemen, the distance between this platform and the slave plantation, from which I escaped, is considerable—and the difficulties to be overcome in getting from the latter to the former are by no means slight. That I am here today is, to me, a matter of astonishment as well as of

10   gratitude. You will not, therefore, be surprised, if in what I have to say, I evince no elaborate preparation, nor grace my speech with any high sounding exordium. With little experience and with less learning, I have been able to throw my thoughts hastily and imperfectly together; and trusting to your patient and generous indulgence, I will proceed to lay them before you.

15   This, for the purpose of this celebration, is the 4th of July. It is the birthday of your national independence, and of your political freedom. This, to you, is what the Passover was to the emancipated people of God. It carries your minds back to the day and to the act of your great deliverance; and to the signs, and to the wonders, associated with that act and that day. This celebration also marks

20   the beginning of another year of your national life; and reminds you that the Republic of America is now 76 years old. I am glad, fellow-citizens, that your nation is so young. Seventy-six years, though a good old age for a man, is but a mere speck in the life of a nation. Three score years and ten is the allotted time for individual men; but nations number their years by thousands. According to

25   this fact, you are even now only in the beginning of your national career, still lingering in the period of childhood. I repeat, I am glad this is so. There is hope in the thought, and hope is much needed under the dark clouds which lower above the horizon. The eye of the reformer is met with angry flashes, portending disastrous times; but his heart may well beat lighter at the thought that America

30   is young, and that she is still in the impressible stage of her existence.

Citizens, your fathers made good that resolution. They succeeded; and today you reap the fruits of their success. The freedom gained is yours; and you, therefore, may properly celebrate this anniversary. The 4th of July is the first great fact in your nation's history—the very ring-bolt in the chain of your

35   yet undeveloped destiny.

Pride and patriotism, not less than gratitude, prompt you to celebrate and to hold it in perpetual remembrance. I have said that the Declaration of Independence is the ringbolt to the chain of your nation's destiny; so, indeed, I regard it. The principles contained in that instrument are saving principles.

Stand by those principles, be true to them on all occasions, in all places, against all foes, and at whatever cost.

From the round top of your ship of state, dark and threatening clouds may be seen. Heavy billows, like mountains in the distance, disclose to the leeward huge forms of flinty rocks! That *bolt* drawn, that *chain* broken, and all is lost. *Cling to this day—cling to it,* and to its principles, with the grasp of a storm-tossed mariner to a spar at midnight....

Fellow citizens, I am not wanting in respect for the fathers of this republic. The signers of the Declaration of Independence were brave men. They were great men too—great enough to give fame to a great age. It does not often happen to a nation to raise, at one time, such a number of truly great men. The point from which I am compelled to view them is not, certainly the most favorable; and yet I cannot contemplate their great deeds with less than admiration. They were statesmen, patriots and heroes, and for the good they did, and the principles they contended for, I will unite with you to honor their memory.

They loved their country better than their own private interests; and, though this is not the highest form of human excellence, all will concede that it is a rare virtue, and that when it is exhibited, it ought to command respect. He who will, intelligently, lay down his life for his country, is a man whom it is not in human nature to despise. Your fathers staked their lives, their fortunes, and their sacred honor, on the cause of their country. In their admiration of liberty, they lost sight of all other interests.

They were peace men; but they preferred revolution to peaceful submission to bondage. They were quiet men; but they did not shrink from agitating against oppression. They showed forbearance; but that they knew its limits. They believed in order; but not in the order of tyranny. With them, nothing was "settled" that was not right. With them, justice, liberty, and humanity were "final;" not slavery and oppression. You may well cherish the memory of such men. They were great in their day and generation. Their solid manhood stands out the more as we contrast it with these degenerate times.

How circumspect, exact, and proportionate were all their movements! How unlike the politicians of an hour! Their statesmanship looked beyond the passing moment, and stretched away in strength into the distant future. They seized upon eternal principles, and set a glorious example in their defense. Mark them!

Fully appreciating the hardships to be encountered, firmly believing in the right of their cause, honorably inviting the scrutiny of an on-looking world, reverently appealing to heaven to attest their sincerity, soundly comprehending the solemn responsibility they were about to assume, wisely measuring the terrible odds against them, your fathers, the fathers of this republic did, most deliberately, under the inspiration of a glorious patriotism, and with a sublime faith in the great principles of justice and freedom, lay deep the corner-stone of the national super-structure, which has risen and still rises in grandeur around you.

Of this fundamental work, this day is the anniversary. Our eyes are met with demonstrations of joyous enthusiasm. Banners and pennants wave exultingly on
5   the breeze. The din of business, too, is hushed. Even mammon seems to have quitted his grasp on this day. The ear-piercing fife and the stirring drum unite their accents with the ascending peal of a thousand church bells. Prayers are made, hymns are sung, and sermons are preached in honor of this day; while the quick martial tramp of a great and multitudinous nation, echoed back by
10 all the hills, valleys and mountains of a vast continent, bespeak the occasion one of thrilling and universal interest—a nation's jubilee.

Friends and citizens, I need not enter further into the causes which led to this anniversary. Many of you understand them better than I do. You could instruct me in regard to them. That is a branch of knowledge in which you
15 feel, perhaps, a much deeper interest than your speaker. The causes which led to the separation of the colonies from the British crown have never lacked for a tongue. They have all been taught in your common schools, narrated at your firesides, unfolded from your pulpits, and thundered from your legislative halls, and are as familiar to you as household words. They form the staple of your
20 national poetry and eloquence.

I remember, also, that, as a people, Americans are remarkably familiar with all facts which make in their own favor. This is esteemed by some as a national trait—perhaps a national weakness. It is a fact, that whatever makes for the wealth or for the reputation of Americans, and can be had CHEAP, will be found
25 by Americans. I shall not be charged with slandering Americans if I say I think the American side of any question may be safely left in American hands.

I leave, therefore, the great deeds of your fathers to other gentlemen whose claim to have been regularly descended will be less likely to be disputed than mine!

The Present

My business, if I have any here today, is with the present. The accepted time
30 with God and His cause is the ever-living now.

> Trust no future, however pleasant,
>   Let the dead past bury its dead;
> Act, act in the living present,
>   Heart within, and God overhead.

35   We have to do with the past only as we can make it useful to the present and to the future. To all-inspiring motives, to noble deeds which can be gained from the past, we are welcome. But now is the time, the important time. Your

fathers have lived, died, and have done their work, and have done much of it well. You live and must die, and you must do your work. You have no right to enjoy a child's share in the labor of your fathers, unless your children are to be blest by your labors. You have no right to wear out and waste the hard-earned fame of your fathers to cover your indolence. Sydney Smith tells us that men seldom eulogize the wisdom and virtues of their fathers but to excuse some folly or wickedness of their own. This truth is not a doubtful one. There are illustrations of it near and remote, ancient and modern. It was fashionable, hundreds of years ago, for the children of Jacob to boast we have "Abraham to our father" when they had long lost Abraham's faith and spirit. That people contented themselves under the shadow of Abraham's great name, while they repudiated the deeds which made his name great. Need I remind you that a similar thing is being done all over this country today? Need I tell you that the Jews are not the only people who built the tombs of the prophets, and garnished the speculchres of the righteous? Washington could not die till he had broken the chains of his slaves. Yet his monument is built up by the price of human blood, and the traders in the bodies and souls of men shout—"We have Washington to our father." Alas! That it should be so; yet so it is.

> The evil that men do, lives after them,
> The good is oft' interred with their bones.

Fellow-citizens, pardon me, allow me to ask, why am I called upon to speak here today? What have I, or those I represent, to do with your national independence? Are the great principles of political freedom and of natural justice, embodied in that Declaration of Independence, extended to us? And am I, therefore, called upon to bring our humble offering to the national altar, and to confess the benefits and express devout gratitude for the blessings resulting from your independence to us?

Would to God, both for your sakes and ours, that an affirmative answer could be truthfully returned to these questions! Then would my task be light, and my burden easy and delightful. For *who* is there so cold that a nation's sympathy could not warm him? Who so obdurate and dead to the claims of gratitude that would not thankfully acknowledge such priceless benefits? Who so stolid and selfish that would not give his voice to swell the hallelujahs of a nation's jubilee when the chains of servitude had been torn from his limbs? I am not that man. In a case like that, the dumb might eloquently speak, and the "lame man leap as an hart."

But, such is not the state of the case. I say it with a sad sense of the disparity between us. I am not included within the pale of this glorious anniversary! Your high independence only reveals the immeasurable distance between us.

The blessings in which you, this day, rejoice, are not enjoyed in common. The rich inheritance of justice, liberty, prosperity, and independence, bequeathed by your fathers, is shared by you, not by me. The sunlight that brought life and healing to you has brought stripes and death to me. This Fourth July is
5   *yours*, not *mine*. *You* may rejoice, *I* must mourn. To drag a man in fetters into the grand illuminated temple of liberty, and call upon him to join you in joyous anthems, were inhuman mockery and sacrilegious irony. Do you mean, citizens, to mock me, by asking me to speak today? If so, there is a parallel to your conduct. And let me warn you that it is dangerous to copy the example
10   of a nation whose crimes, towering up to heaven, were thrown down by the breath of the Almighty, burying that nation in irrecoverable ruin! I can today take up the plaintive lament of a peeled and woe-smitten people!

"By the rivers of Babylon, there we sat down. Yea! we wept when we remembered Zion. We hanged our harps upon the willows in the midst thereof.
15   For there, they that carried us away captive, required of us a song; and they who wasted us required of us mirth, saying, Sing us one of the songs of Zion. How can we sing the Lord's song in a strange land? If I forget thee, O Jerusalem, let my right hand forget her cunning. If I do not remember thee, let my tongue cleave to the roof of my mouth."

20   Fellow-citizens; above your national, tumultous joy, I hear the mournful wail of millions! Whose chains, heavy and grievous yesterday, are, today, rendered more intolerable by the jubilee shouts that reach them. If I do forget, if I do not faithfully remember those bleeding children of sorrow this day, "may my right hand forget her cunning, and may my tongue cleave to the roof of my mouth!" To forget them,
25   to pass lightly over their wrongs, and to chime in with the popular theme, would be treason most scandalous and shocking, and would make me a reproach before God and the world. My subject, then, fellow-citizens, is AMERICAN SLAVERY. I shall see, this day, and its popular characteristics, from the slave's point of view. Standing, there, identified with the American bondman, making his wrongs mine,
30   I do not hesitate to declare with all my soul that the character and conduct of this nation never looked blacker to me than on this 4th of July! Whether we turn to the declarations of the past, or to the professions of the present, the conduct of the nation seems equally hideous and revolting. America is false to the past, false to the present, and solemnly binds herself to be false to the future. Standing
35   with God and the crushed and bleeding slave on this occasion, I will, in the name of humanity which is outraged, in the name of liberty which is fettered, in the name of the constitution and the Bible, which are disregarded and trampled upon, dare to call in question and to denounce, with all the emphasis I can command, everything that serves to perpetuate slavery—the great sin and shame of America!
40   "I will not equivocate; I will not excuse;" I will use the severest language I can

command; and yet not one word shall escape me that any man, whose judgment is not blinded by prejudice, or who is not at heart a slaveholder, shall not confess to be right and just.

But I fancy I hear some one of my audience say it is just in this circumstance that you and your brother abolitionists fail to make a favorable impression on the public mind. Would you argue more, and denounce less, would you persuade more, and rebuke less, your cause would be much more likely to succeed. But, I submit, where all is plain there is nothing to be argued. What point in the anti-slavery creed would you have me argue? On what branch of the subject do the people of this country need light? Must I undertake to prove that the slave is a man? That point is conceded already. Nobody doubts it. The slave-holders themselves acknowledge it in the enactment of laws for their government. They acknowledge it when they punish disobedience on the part of the slave. There are seventy-two crimes in the state of Virginia, which, if committed by a black man (no matter how ignorant he be) subject him to the punishment of death; while only two of the same crimes will subject a white man to the like punishment. What is this but the acknowledgement that the slave is a moral, intellectual, and responsible being? The manhood of the slave is conceded. It is admitted in the fact that Southern statute books are covered with enactments forbidding, under severe fines and penalties, the teaching of the slave to read or to write. When you can point to any such laws, in reference to the beasts of the field, then I may consent to argue the manhood of the slave. When the dogs in your streets, when the fowls of the air, when the cattle on your hills, when the fish of the sea, and the reptiles that crawl shall be unable to distinguish the slave from a brute, *then* will I argue with you that the slave is a man!

For the present, it is enough to affirm the equal manhood of the negro race. Is it not astonishing that, while we are ploughing, planting, and reaping, using all kinds of mechanical tools, erecting houses, constructing bridges, building ships, working in metals of brass, iron, copper, silver, and gold; that, while we are reading, writing, and ciphering, acting as clerks, merchants, and secretaries, having among us lawyers, doctors, ministers, poets, authors, editors, orators, and teachers; that, while we are engaged in all manner of enterprises common to other men, digging gold in California, capturing the whale in the Pacific, feeding sheep and cattle on the hill-side, living, moving, acting, thinking, planning, living in families as husbands, wives, and children, and, above all, confessing and worshipping the Christian's God, and looking hopefully for life and immortality beyond the grave, we are called upon to prove that we are men!

Would you have me argue that man is entitled to liberty? That he is the rightful owner of his own body? You have already declared it. Must I argue the wrongfulness of slavery? Is that a question for republicans? Is it to be settled

by the rules of logic and argumentation, as a matter beset with great difficulty, involving a doubtful application of the principle of justice, hard to be understood? How should I look today, in the presence of Americans, dividing and sub-dividing a discourse to show that men have a natural right to freedom?
5   Speaking of it relatively, and positively, negatively, and affirmatively. To do so, would be to make myself ridiculous, and to offer an insult to your understanding. There is not a man beneath the canopy of heaven that does not know that slavery is wrong *for him*.

What, am I to argue that it is wrong to make men brutes, to rob them
10 of their liberty, to work them without wages, to keep them ignorant of their relations to their fellow men, to beat them with sticks, to flay their flesh with the lash, to load their limbs with irons, to hunt them with dogs, to sell them at auction, to sunder their families, to knock out their teeth, to burn their flesh, to starve them into obedience and submission to their masters? Must I argue
15 that a system thus marked with blood, and stained with pollution, is *wrong*? No I will not. I have better employment for my time and strength, than such arguments would imply.

What, then, remains to be argued? Is it that slavery is not divine; that God did not establish it; that our doctors of divinity are mistaken? There is
20 blasphemy in the thought. That which is inhuman cannot be divine! *Who* can reason on such a proposition? They that can, may; I cannot. The time for such argument is past.

At a time like this, scorching irony, not convincing argument, is needed. O, had I the ability, and could I reach the nation's ear, I would, today, pour
25 out a fiery stream of biting ridicule, blasting reproach, withering sarcasm, and stern rebuke. For it is not light that is needed, but fire; it is not the gentle shower, but thunder. We need the storm, the whirlwind, and the earthquake. The feeling of the nation must be quickened; the conscience of the nation must be roused; the propriety of the nation must be startled; the hypocrisy
30 of the nation must be exposed; and its crimes against God and man must be proclaimed and denounced.

What, to the American slave, is your 4th of July? I answer; a day that reveals to him, more than all other days in the year, the gross injustice and cruelty to which he is the constant victim. To him, your celebration is a sham; your boasted
35 liberty, an unholy license; your national greatness, swelling vanity; your sounds of rejoicing are empty and heartless; your denunciations of tyrants, brass-fronted impudence; your shouts of liberty and equality, hollow mockery; your prayers and hymns, your sermons and thanksgivings, with all your religious parade and solemnity are, to him, mere bombast, fraud, deception, impiety, and hypoc-
40 risy—a thin veil to cover up crimes which would disgrace a nation of savages.

There is not a nation on the earth guilty of practices more shocking and bloody than are the people of these United States at this very hour.

Go where you may, search where you will, roam through all the monarchies and despotisms of the old world, travel through South America, search out every abuse, and when you have found the last, lay your facts by the side of the every day practices of this nation, and you will say with me that, for revolting barbarity and shameless hypocrisy, America reigns without a rival.

THE INTERNAL SLAVE TRADE

Take the American slave-trade, which we are told by the papers is especially prosperous just now. Ex-Senator Benton tells us that the price of men was never higher than now. He mentions the fact to show that slavery is in no danger. This trade is one of the peculiarities of American institutions. It is carried on in all the large towns and cities in one half of this confederacy; and millions are pocketed every year, by dealers in this horrid traffic. In several states, this trade is a chief source of wealth. It is called (in contradistinction to the foreign slave-trade) "the internal slave-trade." It is, probably, called so, too, in order to divert from it the horror with which the foreign slave-trade is contemplated. That trade has long since been denounced by this government as piracy. It has been denounced with burning words, from the high places of the nation, as an execrable traffic. To arrest it, to put an end to it, this nation keeps a squadron, at immense cost, on the coast of Africa. Everywhere, in this country, it is safe to speak of this foreign slave-trade as a most inhuman traffic, opposed alike to the laws of God and of man. The duty to extirpate and destroy it, is admitted even by our DOCTORS OF DIVINITY. In order to put an end to it, some of these last have consented that their colored brethren (nominally free) should leave this country and establish themselves on the western coast of Africa! It is, however, a notable fact that, while so much execration is poured out by Americans upon those engaged in the foreign slave-trade, the men engaged in the slave-trade between the states pass without condemnation, and their business is deemed honorable.

Behold the practical operation of this internal slave-trade, the American slave-trade, sustained by American politics and American religion. Here you will see men and women reared like swine for the market. You know what is a swine-drover? I will show you a man-drover. They inhabit all our Southern states. They perambulate the country, and crowd the highways of the nation, with droves of human stock. You will see one of these human flesh jobbers, armed with pistol, whip, and bowie-knife, driving a company of a hundred men, women, and children from the Potomac to the slave market at New Orleans. These wretched people are to be sold singly, or in lots, to suit purchasers. They

are food for the cotton-field and the deadly sugar-mill. Mark the sad procession
as it moves wearily along, and the inhuman wretch who drives them. Hear his
savage yells and his blood-chilling oaths as he hurries on his affrighted captives!
There, see the old man with locks thinned and gray. Cast one glance, if you
5 please, upon that young mother, whose shoulders are bare to the scorching sun,
her briny tears falling on the brow of the babe in her arms. See, too, that girl
of thirteen, weeping, *yes!* weeping, as she thinks of the mother from whom she
has been torn! The drove moves tardily. Heat and sorrow have nearly consumed
their strength; suddenly you hear a quick snap, like the discharge of a rifle; the
10 fetters clank, and the chain rattles simultaneously; your ears are saluted with
a scream that seems to have torn its way to the centre of your soul! The crack
you heard was the sound of the slave-whip; the scream you heard was from
the woman you saw with the babe. Her speed had faltered under the weight
of her child and her chains! That gash on her shoulder tells her to move on.
15 Follow this drove to New Orleans. Attend the auction; see men examined like
horses; see the forms of women rudely and brutally exposed to the shocking
gaze of American slave-buyers. See this drove sold and separated forever; and
never forget the deep, sad sobs that arose from that scattered multitude. Tell
me citizens, WHERE, under the sun, you can witness a spectacle more fiendish
20 and shocking. Yet this is but a glance at the American slave-trade, as it exists at
this moment in the ruling part of the United States.

I was born amid such sights and scenes. To me the American slave-trade
is a terrible reality. When a child, my soul was often pierced with a sense of
its horrors. I lived on Philpot Street, Fell's Point, Baltimore, and have watched
25 from the wharves the slave ships in the Basin, anchored from the shore, with
their cargoes of human flesh, waiting for favorable winds to waft them down
the Chesapeake. There was, at that time, a grand slave mart kept at the head
of Pratt Street by Austin Woldfolk. His agents were sent into every town and
county in Maryland, announcing their arrival, through the papers, and on
30 flaming "hand-bills" headed CASH FOR NEGROES. These men were generally
well-dressed men, and very captivating in their manners. Ever ready to drink,
to treat, and to gamble. The fate of many a slave has depended upon the turn of
a single card; and many a child has been snatched from the arms of its mother
by bargains arranged in a state of brutal drunkenness.

35 The flesh-mongers gather up their victims by dozens, and drive them,
chained, to the general depot at Baltimore. When a sufficient number have
been collected here, a ship is chartered for the purpose of conveying the forlorn
crew to Mobile, or to New Orleans. From the slave prison to the ship, they are
usually driven in the darkness of night; for since the anti-slavery agitation, a
40 certain caution is observed.

In the deep still darkness of midnight, I have been often aroused by the dead heavy footsteps, and the piteous cries of the chained gangs that passed our door. The anguish of my boyish heart was intense; and I was often consoled when speaking to my mistress in the morning to hear her say that the custom was very wicked; that she hated to hear the rattle of the chains, and the heart-rending cries. I was glad to find one who sympathized with me in my horror.

Fellow-citizens, this murderous traffic is, today, in active operation in this boasted republic. In the solitude of my spirit, I see clouds of dust raised on the highways of the South; I see the bleeding footsteps; I hear the doleful wail of fettered humanity, on the way to the slave-markets, where the victims are to be sold like *horses, sheep*, and *swine*, knocked off to the highest bidder. There I see the tenderest ties ruthlessly broken, to gratify the lust, caprice and rapacity of the buyers and sellers of men. My soul sickens at the sight.

> Is this the land your Fathers loved,
>   The freedom which they toiled to win?
> Is this the earth whereon they moved?
>   Are these the graves they slumber in?

But a still more inhuman, disgraceful, and scandalous state of things remains to be presented.

By an act of the American Congress, not yet two years old, slavery has been nationalized in its most horrible and revolting form. By that act, Mason and Dixon's line has been obliterated; New York has become as Virginia; and the power to hold, hunt, and sell men, women, and children as slaves remains no longer a mere state institution, but is now an institution of the whole United States. The power is co-extensive with the star-spangled banner, and American Christianity. Where these go, may also go the merciless slave-hunter. Where these are, man is not sacred. He is a bird for the sportsman's gun. By that most foul and fiendish of all human decrees, the liberty and person of every man are put in peril. Your broad republican domain is hunting ground for *men. Not* for thieves and robbers, enemies of society, merely, but for men guilty of no crime. Your law-makers have commanded all good citizens to engage in this hellish sport. Your President, your Secretary of State, your lords, nobles, and ecclesiastics enforce, as a duty you owe to your free and glorious country, and to your God, that you do this accursed thing. Not fewer than forty Americans have, within the past two years, been hunted down and, without a moment's warning, hurried away in chains, and consigned to slavery and excruciating torture. Some of these have had wives and children, dependent on them for bread; but of this, no account was made. The right of the hunter to his prey stands superior to the right of marriage, and to *all* rights in this republic, the

rights of God included! For black men there are neither law, justice, humanity, nor religion. The Fugitive Slave Law makes MERCY TO THEM A CRIME; and
bribes the judge who tries them. An American JUDGE GETS TEN DOLLARS FOR
EVERY VICTIM HE CONSIGNS to slavery, and five when he fails to do so. The oath
5   of any two villains is sufficient, under this hell-black enactment, to send the
most pious and exemplary black man into the remorseless jaws of slavery! His
own testimony is nothing. He can bring no witnesses for himself. The minister
of American justice is bound, by the law to hear but *one* side; and *that* side is
the side of the oppressor. Let this damning fact be perpetually told. Let it be
10   thundered around the world that, in tyrant-killing, king-hating, people-loving,
democratic, Christian America, the seats of justice are filled with judges who
hold their offices under an open and palpable *bribe*, and are bound, in deciding
in the case of a man's liberty, *to hear only his accusers!*

In glaring violation of justice, in shameless disregard of the forms of admin-
15   istering law, in cunning arrangement to entrap the defenseless, and in diabolical
intent, this Fugitive Slave Law stands alone in the annals of tyrannical legislation.
I doubt if there be another nation on the globe having the brass and the baseness to put such a law on the statute-book. If any man in this assembly thinks
differently from me in this matter, and feels able to disprove my statements, I
20   will gladly confront him at any suitable time and place he may select.

RELIGIOUS LIBERTY

I take this law to be one of the grossest infringements of Christian liberty and,
if the churches and ministers of our country were not stupidly blind, or most
wickedly indifferent, they, too, would so regard it.

At the very moment that they are thanking God for the enjoyment of civil
25   and religious liberty, and for the right to worship God according to the dictates
of their own consciences, they are utterly silent in respect to a law which robs
religion of its chief significance, and makes it utterly worthless to a world lying
in wickedness. Did this law concern the "mint, anise, and cummin"—abridge
the right to sing psalms, to partake of the sacrament, or to engage in any of
30   the ceremonies of religion, it would be smitten by the thunder of a thousand
pulpits. A general shout would go up from the church, demanding *repeal,*
repeal, instant repeal! And it would go hard with that politician who presumed
to solicit the votes of the people without inscribing this motto on his banner.
Further, if this demand were not complied with, another Scotland would be
35   added to the history of religious liberty, and the stern old covenanters would
be thrown into the shade. A John Knox would be seen at every church door,
and heard from every pulpit, and Fillmore would have no more quarter than
was shown by Knox to the beautiful, but treacherous Queen Mary of Scotland.

The fact that the church of our country (with fractional exceptions) does not esteem "the Fugitive Slave Law" as a declaration of war against religious liberty implies that that church regards religion simply as a form of worship, an empty ceremony, and *not* a vital principle, requiring active benevolence, justice, love, and good will towards man. It esteems sacrifice above mercy; psalm-singing above right doing; solemn meetings above practical righteousness. A worship that can be conducted by persons who refuse to give shelter to the houseless, to give bread to the hungry, clothing to the naked, and who enjoin obedience to a law forbidding these acts of mercy, is a curse, not a blessing to mankind. The Bible addresses all such persons as "scribes, Pharisees, hypocrites who pay tithe of mint, anise, and cummin, and have omitted the weightier-matters of the law, judgment, mercy, and faith."

THE CHURCH RESPONSIBLE

But the church of this country is not only indifferent to the wrongs of the slave, it actually takes sides with the oppressors. It has made itself the bulwark of American slavery, and the shield of American slave-hunters. Many of its most eloquent Divines, who stand as the very lights of the church, have shamelessly given the sanction of religion, and the Bible, to the whole slave system. They have taught that man may properly be a slave; that the relation of master and slave is ordained of God; that to send back an escaped bondman to his master is clearly the duty of all the followers of the Lord Jesus Christ; and this horrible blasphemy is palmed off upon the world for Christianity.

For my part, I would say, welcome infidelity! Welcome atheism! Welcome anything in preference to the gospel as preached by those Divines! They convert the very name of religion into an engine of tyranny, and barbarous cruelty, and serve to confirm more infidels in this age than all the infidel writings of Thomas Paine, Voltaire, and Bolingbroke put together have done. These ministers make religion a cold and flinty-hearted thing, having neither principles of right action, nor bowels of compassion. They strip the love of God of its beauty, and leave the throne of religion a huge, horrible, repulsive form. It is a religion for oppressors, tyrants, man-stealers, and thugs. It is not that "pure and undefiled religion" which is from above, and which is "first pure, then peaceable, easy to be entreated, full of mercy and good fruits, without partiality, and without hypocrisy," but a religion which favors the rich against the poor; which exalts the proud above the humble; which divides mankind into two classes, tyrants and slaves; which says to the man in chains, *stay there*; and to the oppressor, *oppress on*; it is a religion which may be professed and enjoyed by all the robbers and enslavers of mankind; it makes God a respecter of persons, denies His fatherhood of the race, and tramples in the dust the great truth of the brotherhood of man. All this we affirm to be

true of the popular church, and the popular worship of our land and nation—a religion, a church, and a worship which, on the authority of inspired wisdom, we pronounce to be an abomination in the sight of God. In the language of Isaiah, the American church might be well addressed, "Bring no more vain oblations;
5   incense is an abomination unto me: the new moons and Sabbaths, the calling of assemblies, I cannot away with; it is iniquity, even the solemn meeting. Your new moons, and your appointed feasts my soul hates. They are a trouble to me; I am weary to bear them; and when you spread forth your hands I will hide my eyes from you. Yea! when you make many prayers, I will not hear. YOUR HANDS
10   ARE FULL OF BLOOD; cease to do evil, learn to do well; seek judgment; relieve the oppressed; judge for the fatherless; plead for the widow."

     The American church is guilty, when viewed in connection with what it is doing to uphold slavery; but it is superlatively guilty when viewed in connection with its ability to abolish slavery.

15   The sin of which it is guilty is one of omission as well as of commission. Albert Barnes but uttered what the common sense of every man at all observant of the actual state of the case will receive as truth when he declared that "There is no power out of the church that could sustain slavery an hour if it were not sustained in it."

20   Let the religious press, the pulpit, the Sunday school, the conference meeting, the great ecclesiastical, missionary, Bible, and tract associations of the land array their immense powers against slavery and slave-holding, and the whole system of crime and blood would be scattered to the winds, and that they do not do this involves them in the most awful responsibility of which the mind
25   can conceive.

     In prosecuting the anti-slavery enterprise, we have been asked to spare the church, to spare the ministry; but *how*, we ask, could such a thing be done? We are met on the threshold of our efforts for the redemption of the slave by the church and ministry of the country, in battle arrayed against us; and we are
30   compelled to fight or flee. From *what* quarter, I beg to know, has proceeded a fire so deadly upon our ranks, during the last two years, as from the Northern pulpit? As the champions of oppressors, the chosen men of American theology have appeared—men honored for their so-called piety and their real learning. The LORDS of Buffalo, the SPRINGS of New York, the LATHROPS of Auburn,
35   the COXES and SPENCERS of Brooklyn, the GANNETS and SHARPS of Boston, the DEWEYS of Washington, and other great religious lights of the land have, in utter denial of the authority of Him by whom they professed to be called to the ministry, deliberately taught us, against the example of the Hebrews, and against the remonstrance of the Apostles, they teach *that we ought to obey man's*
40   *law before the law of God.*

My spirit wearies of such blasphemy; and how such men can be supported as the "standing types and representatives of Jesus Christ" is a mystery which I leave others to penetrate. In speaking of the American church, however, let it be distinctly understood that I mean the *great mass* of the religious organizations of our land. There are exceptions, and I thank God that there are. Noble men may be found, scattered all over these Northern states, of whom Henry Ward Beecher of Brooklyn, Samuel J. May of Syracuse, and my esteemed friend on the platform are shining examples; and let me say further that upon these men lies the duty to inspire our ranks with high religious faith and zeal, and to cheer us on in the great mission of the slave's redemption from his chains.

Religion in England and Religion in America

One is struck with the difference between the attitude of the American church towards the anti-slavery movement and that occupied by the churches in England towards a similar movement in that country. There the church, true to its mission of ameliorating, elevating, and improving the condition of mankind, came forward promptly, bound up the wounds of the West Indian slave, and restored him to his liberty. There, the question of emancipation was a high religious question. It was demanded, in the name of humanity and according to the law of the living God. The Sharps, the Clarksons, the Wilberforces, the Buxtons, the Burchells, and the Knibbs were alike famous for their piety and for their philanthropy. The anti-slavery movement *there* was not an anti-church movement, for the reason that the church took its full share in prosecuting that movement: and the anti-slavery movement in this country will cease to be an anti-church movement when the church of this country shall assume a favorable, instead of a hostile position towards that movement.

Americans! Your republican politics, not less than your republican religion, are flagrantly inconsistent. You boast of your love of liberty, your superior civilization, and your pure Christianity while the whole political power of the nation, as embodied in the two great political parties, is solemnly pledged to support and perpetuate the enslavement of three millions of your countrymen. You hurl your anathemas at the crowned headed tyrants of Russia and Austria, and pride yourselves on your democratic institutions, while you yourselves consent to be the mere *tools* and *body-guards* of the tyrants of Virginia and Carolina. You invite to your shores fugitives of oppression from abroad, honor them with banquets, greet them with ovations, cheer them, toast them, salute them, protect them, and pour out your money to them like water; but the fugitives from your own land you advertise, hunt, arrest, shoot, and kill. You glory in your refinement and your universal education; yet you maintain a system as barbarous and dreadful as ever stained the character of a nation—a system begun in avarice, supported

in pride, and perpetuated in cruelty. You shed tears over fallen Hungary, and make the sad story of her wrongs the theme of your poets, statesmen, and orators till your gallant sons are ready to fly to arms to vindicate her cause against her oppressors; but, in regard to the ten thousand wrongs of the American slave,
5   you would enforce the strictest silence, and would hail him as an enemy of the nation who dares to make those wrongs the subject of public discourse! You are all on fire at the mention of liberty for France or for Ireland; but are as cold as an iceberg at the thought of liberty for the enslaved of America. You discourse eloquently on the dignity of labor; yet, you sustain a system which, in its very
10   essence, casts a stigma upon labor. You can bare your bosom to the storm of British artillery to throw off a three-penny tax on tea; and yet wring the last hard-earned farthing from the grasp of the black laborers of your country. You profess to believe "that, of one blood, God made all nations of men to dwell on the face of all the earth," and has commanded all men everywhere to love one
15   another; yet you notoriously hate (and glory in your hatred) all men whose skins are not colored like your own. You declare before the world, and are understood by the world to declare, that you 'hold these truths to be self evident, that all men are created equal; and are endowed by their Creator with certain inalienable rights; and that among these are life, liberty, and the pursuit of happiness;"
20   and yet you hold securely in a bondage, which according to your own Thomas Jefferson "is worse than ages of that which your fathers rose in rebellion to oppose," a seventh part of the inhabitants of your country.

Fellow-citizens! I will not enlarge further on your national inconsistencies. The existence of slavery in this country brands your republicanism as a sham,
25   your humanity as a base pretence, and your Christianity as a lie. It destroys your moral power abroad; it corrupts your politicians at home. It saps the foundation of religion; it makes your name a hissing and a bye-word to a mocking earth. It is the antagonistic force in your government, the only thing that seriously disturbs and endangers your union. It fetters your progress; it is the enemy of
30   improvement, the deadly foe of education; it fosters pride; it breeds insolence; it promotes vice; it shelters crime; it is a curse to the earth that supports it; and yet, you cling to it, as if it were the sheet anchor of all your hopes. Oh! Be warned! Be warned! A horrible reptile is coiled up in your nation's bosom; the venomous creature is nursing at the tender breast of your youthful republic;
35   *for the love of God, tear away* and fling from you the hideous monster, and *let the weight of twenty millions, crush and destroy it forever!*

THE CONSTITUTION

But it is answered in reply to all this that precisely what I have now denounced is, in fact, guaranteed and sanctioned by the Constitution of the United States;

that the right to hold and to hunt slaves is a part of that Constitution framed by the illustrious Fathers of this Republic.

Then, I dare to affirm, notwithstanding all I have said before, your fathers stooped, basely stooped.

> To palter with us in a double sense: 5
>   And keep the word of promise to the ear,
> But break it to the heart.

And instead of being the honest men I have before declared them to be, they were the veriest imposters that ever practiced on mankind. *This* is the in-evitable conclusion, and from it there is no escape; but I differ from those who   10
charge this baseness on the framers of the Constitution of the United States. *It is a slander upon their memory*, at least, so I believe. There is not time now to argue the constitutional question at length; nor have I the ability to discuss it as it ought to be discussed. The subject has been handled with masterly power by Lysander Spooner, Esquire, by William Goodell, by Samuel E. Sewall,   15
Esquire, and last, though not least, by Gerritt Smith, Esquire. These gentlemen have, as I think, fully and clearly vindicated the Constitution from any design to support slavery for an hour.

Fellow-citizens! There is no matter in respect to which the people of the North have allowed themselves to be so ruinously imposed upon as that of the   20
pro-slavery character of the Constitution. In *that* instrument I hold there is neither warrant, license, nor sanction of the hateful thing; but interpreted as it *ought* to be interpreted, the Constitution is a GLORIOUS LIBERTY DOCUMENT. Read its preamble, consider its purposes. Is slavery among them? Is it at the gateway? Or is it in the temple? It is neither. While I do not intend to argue this question   25
on the present occasion, let me ask if it be not somewhat singular that, if the Constitution were intended to be by its framers and adopters a slave-holding instrument, why neither *slavery, slaveholding*, nor *slave* can anywhere be found in it. What would be thought of an instrument drawn up, *legally* drawn up, for the purpose of entitling the city of Rochester to a tract of land in which no mention   30
of land was made? Now, there are certain rules of interpretation for the proper understanding of all legal instruments. These rules are well established. They are plain, common-sense rules, such as you and I, and all of us, can understand and apply, without having passed years in the study of law. I scout the idea that the questions of the constitutionality, or unconstitutionality of slavery, is not a   35
question for the people. I hold that every American citizen has a right to form an opinion of the Constitution, and to propagate that opinion, and to use all honorable means to make his opinion the prevailing one. Without this right, the liberty of an American citizen would be as insecure as that of a Frenchman.

Ex-Vice-President Dallas tells us that the constitution is an object to which no American mind can be too attentive, and no American heart too devoted. He further says the Constitution, in its words, is plain and intelligible, and is meant for the home-bred, unsophisticated understandings of our fellow-citizens. Senator
5   Berrien tells us that the Constitution is the fundamental law, that which controls all others. The charter of our liberties, which every citizen has a personal interest in understanding thoroughly. The testimony of Senator Breese, Lewis Cass, and many others that might be named, who are everywhere esteemed as sound lawyers, so regard the Constitution. I take it, therefore, that it is not presumption
10   in a private citizen to form an opinion of that instrument.

Now, take the Constitution according to its plain reading, and I defy the presentation of a single pro-slavery clause in it. On the other hand it will be found to contain principles and purposes, entirely hostile to the existence of slavery.

I have detained my audience entirely too long already. At some future
15   period I will gladly avail myself of an opportunity to give this subject a full and fair discussion.

Allow me to say, in conclusion, notwithstanding the dark picture I have this day presented of the state of the nation, I do not despair of this country. There are forces in operation which must inevitably work the downfall of slavery. "The
20   arm of the Lord is not shortened," and the doom of slavery is certain. I, therefore, leave off where I began, with *hope*. While drawing encouragement from "the Declaration of Independence," the great principles it contains, and the genius of American institutions, my spirit is also cheered by the obvious tendencies of the age. Nations do not now stand in the same relation to each other that they
25   did ages ago. No nation can now shut itself up from the surrounding world, and trot round in the same old path of its fathers without interference. The time *was* when such could be done. Long-established customs of hurtful character could formerly fence themselves in and do their evil work with social impunity. Knowledge was then confined and enjoyed by the privileged few, and the multi-
30   tude walked on in mental darkness. But a change has now come over the affairs of mankind. Walled cities and empires have become unfashionable. The arm of commerce has borne away the gates of the strong city. Intelligence is penetrating the darkest corners of the globe. It makes its pathway over and under the sea, as well as on the earth. Wind, steam, and lightning are its chartered agents. Oceans
35   no longer divide, but link nations together. From Boston to London is now a holiday excursion. Space is comparatively annihilated. Thoughts expressed on one side of the Atlantic, are distinctly heard on the other.

The far off and almost fabulous Pacific rolls in grandeur at our feet. The Celestial Empire, the mystery of ages, is being solved. The fiat of the Almighty,
40   "Let there be Light," has not yet spent its force. No abuse, no outrage whether in taste, sport, or avarice, can now hide itself from the all-pervading light. The

iron shoe and crippled foot of China must be seen, in contrast with nature. *Africa must rise and put on her yet unwoven garment.* "Ethiopia shall stretch out her hand unto God." In the fervent aspirations of William Lloyd Garrison, I say, and let every heart join in saying it:

> God speed the year of jubilee 5
>   The wide world o'er!
> When from their galling chains set free,
> Th' oppress'd shall vilely bend the knee,
> And wear the yoke of tyranny
>   Like brutes no more. 10
> That year will come, and freedom's reign,
> To man his plundered rights again
>   Restore.
>
> God speed the day when human blood
>   Shall cease to flow! 15
> In every clime be understood,
> The claims of human brotherhood,
> And each return for evil, good,
>   Now blow for blow;
> That day will come all feuds to end, 20
> And change into a faithful friend
>   Each foe.
>
> God speed the hour, the glorious hour,
>   When none on earth
> Shall exercise a lordly power, 25
> Nor in a tyrant's presence cower;
> But all to manhood's stature tower,
>   By equal birth!
> That hour will come, to each, to all,
> And from his prison-house, the thrall 30
>   Go forth.
>
> Until that year, day, hour, arrive,
> With head, and heart, and hand I'll strive,
> To break the rod, and rend the gyve,
> The spoiler of his prey deprive— 35
>   So witness Heaven!
> And never from my chosen post,
> Whate'er the peril or the cost,
>   Be driven.

THE COLLEGE AND THE REPUBLIC
EDMUND BURKE FAIRFIELD (1821–1904)
PRESIDENT OF HILLSDALE COLLEGE (1848–1869)

Edmund Burke Fairfield made these remarks at the laying of the corner-stone of Hillsale College's Central Hall. The extemporaneous twenty-minute speech was later written down. In his notes, Fairfield explained the following was an attempt to recapture the spirit of that day. The publisher of this pamphlet claimed that President Fairfield delivered the message to a congregation of between 7,000 to 10,000.

4 JULY 1853

I must confess to the reluctance which I have felt in consenting to occupy your attention at this hour, as well as during the next. But circumstances, and your committee of arrangements have imposed upon me the necessity, to which I submit. But I may also as well acknowledge that my embarrassment finds no little relief in seeing before me so large a gathering of the citizens of the County at   5
large, with whom it has been my privilege to form a most agreeable acquaintance in connection with the enterprise which has called us to this spot to day. The cordiality, the unanimity, and the liberality with which they have contributed to the erection of the building whose cornerstone is now to be laid, have not often been paralleled in the history of such institutions. And we have before us   10
in this immense concourse of people, from all parts of the county, only another manifestation of the same spirit and of the same lively interest which has from the first pervaded this whole movement.

Fellow citizens—it were a vain thing for me to say that you have the cordial thanks of the Trustees and officers of the College for what you have done, and   15
are still doing in its behalf. This you know full well. And what is more, you have already given yourselves a hearty vote of thanks for the interest you have taken in this work; and your presence and countenances to-day assure us that you are not yet ready to re-consider that vote. It is not merely the money which you have furnished and engaged to furnish for this work, but the cordial good-will   20
with which it has been done, that has cheered us on.

Edmund Fairfield, *True National Greatness. An Oration Delivered at the Celebration of the 77th Anniversary of American Independence* (Buffalo, NY: D.D. Waite, 1853), 19–27.

415

The law of custom imposes upon me the duty of saying a few things appropriate to the occasion. That duty I shall aim to discharge to the best of my ability, only premising that however deficient my words shall be in other respects, they shall not be wanting in brevity. There are many suitable topics that naturally
5   suggest themselves; but, convened as we are, to lay the cornerstone of a College edifice on this anniversary of our national independence, none presents itself to my mind more naturally than this—*the connection between our republican and our educational institutions*. This, then, is my text for a few brief utterances.

The history of Liberty has been the history of Intelligence. "The fathers"
10   brought with them to this goodly land the Common School and the College. These had prepared the way for national civil and religious liberty; and they were ever to stand as its reliable fortifications. Ignorance is rightly deemed an essential prerequisite to Slavery. The more the ignorance, the better the slave, and when the bondman becomes possessed of intelligence, his oppressor will tell you that
15   the devil is in him. Too much intelligence is the worst devil that oppression knows. The process of education is continually cherishing an independence of thought that is in close alliance with civil liberty. Give freedom to mind, and you will not easily put chains upon the body. Education gives to each man an individual personality that well enough prepares him to be a freeman, but sadly
20   disqualifies him from being a slave. It is a continual process of self-revelation: introducing him into the hidden arcana of his own intellectual nature, making him acquainted with his own powers and capacities.

Whatever else he may study—whether the heavens above him, or the earth beneath him, or the world around him, there is continually a reflection of himself,
25   and he who knows himself, knows that he was not made to be a slave; and the next thing that he knows is, that no human arm is strong enough to make him one. The victim of despotic oppression must as far as possible be stripped of all consciousness of personality: he must be hidden from himself; his noble nature must be unseen by his own eyes, that he may be content to be a thing—that
30   he may be stupidly submissive when the tyrant oppressor despoils him of his rights and crushes out of him his soul. Our educational institutions furnish a poor preparation for such a despotic rule. Intelligence, at the same time that it prepares a man for the enjoyment of his liberty, cultivates a sad distaste for the sweets of slavery. The man who knows not what he is or what he was made to
35   be, may tacitly consent to be a mere appendage to another; but as the process of intellectual development goes on, he discovers in himself the equal of his lord; he has revealed to him the fundamental doctrine of human equality, and he can no longer consent to be but a fraction of a unit. He sees in himself *a whole man*; and in another he sees no more. He recognizes in himself a separate responsible
40   agent; and as said Webster, "The greatest thought of my life is that of my individual responsibility to God." So with every man. And when once inspired with

such a thought as this, he is forever above that level where the tyrant may find a facile subject. The self-respect which such a man feels, and cannot but feel, illy qualifies him for the place of a menial, or to do the bidding of a haughty lord; he respects other men as men, and himself as a man too, and he thinks too highly of his manhood to consent to lose it, or allow it to be absorbed in that of another.   5

But Educational Institutions are not only invaluable in preparing for the enjoyment of national liberty, but they are equally so in perpetuating it; they are the constant allies and the eternal bulwarks of all the institutions of Republicanism. No nation approaching the confines of civilization but deems it important to educate their princes. The heir of sovereignty must be qualified   10 to meet the responsibilities of his kingly office. In a Republic the people are the kings. I speak to-day to those who either are, or are to be, the sovereigns of the land. You are not merely law-makers, but you make those that are law-makers. If you wear not the insignia of an aristocratic nobility—in the shape of ribbons, red and green and blue—you may remember that the inhabitants   15 of Lilliput did, and you are not over-anxious to imitate the little six-inch men of that far-famed land. The insignia of nature's nobility are the hand-hardened by toil, and the face radiant with intelligence and manly virtue.

You, fellow-citizens, are not merely dukes and lords, and barons and knights; but kings and the sons of kings, and the fathers of kings. The crowns   20 that have come down to you from the heads of those who lie low in the grave, will soon rest upon the heads of these princes of the blood whom I see before me. It is for the fathers to see that the sons are qualified for the responsibilities of American citizenship, and it is for the sons to see to it that they do not dis-honor the crowns that the Republic has placed upon their heads. The elements   25 of power and stability in a nation of freemen are the intelligence and virtue of the people who bear rule.

> What constitutes a state?
> Not high-raised battlement, or labored mound,
> Thick wall, or moated gate;   30
> Not cities proud with spires and turrets crowned;
> Not bays and broad-armed ports,
> Where laughing at the storm rich navies ride;
> Not starred and spangled court,
> Where low-browed baseness wafts perfume to pride;   35
> No—Men, high-minded *men*,
> With powers as far above dull brutes endued,
> In forest, brake or den,
> As beasts excel cold rocks and brambles rude,
> Men who their duties know,   40

But know their rights, and knowing dare maintain;
Prevent the long-aimed blow,
And crush the tyrant while they rend the chain:
These constitute a state.[1]

5   If there is in a Republican government a power behind the throne, that power is to be found in public sentiment. And in the formation of public sentiment, our educational institutions exert an influence beyond the power of computation. Happily for the interests of liberty and Republicanism, Colleges have almost universally ranged themselves on the side of popular rights. In every
10 contest between the prerogatives of the ruler and the rights of the ruled, they have defended the right against the might.

     Again: the strength of a Republican government is to be found not so much in the rigid enforcement by arms of the laws of the state, as in the fact that these laws are self-imposed by the intelligent perception on the part of the people
15 of their wisdom and of their necessity. Let the law be written not merely upon the statute book, but upon the hearts and minds of intelligent citizens, and the willing homage which they pay to its mandates is liberty itself in its highest form and truest type; while the constrained obedience rendered only at the point of the bayonet, even to wise and necessary laws, is little else than slavery.
20 The one is Republicanism; the other is Despotism. The one is Liberty, regulated by intelligence; the other is the recklessness of ignorance and the restlessness of insubordination, restrained by force. Not long can a Republic maintain its existence as such without at least that measure of general intelligence that perceives and acknowledges the necessity of just laws, and that for the public
25 good yields a cheerful and unconstrained obedience to them.

     Unrestrained freedom is anarchy. Restrained only by force and arms, is despotism; self-restraint is Republicanism. Wherever there is wanting the intelligence and virtue requisite for the latter, Republicanism expires. The complicated machinery of free institutions must have an adequate regulator; and that is to
30 be found in an enlightened public conscience. This our Educational institutions—teaching as well the laws of social morality as of physical science—are omnipotent in forming. And as we cherish the heritage of civil and religious liberty which has come down to us, so it becomes us to cherish the College, the Academy, and the Common School, permeated by Christian influence, which
35 alone have secured us this inheritance, prepared us for enjoying and appreciating it, or can prove its efficient conservators.

     But more than this: our Educational Institutions are eminently Republican in their very nature. Here are brought together the sons of wealth and of poverty,

---

[1]Sir William Jones, "An Ode In Imitation of Alcaeus" (1781)

of patrician and plebeian descent, to meet upon the same arena, to wrestle in
the same intellectual gymnasium, run in the same race, and contend for the
same honors, upon equal terms, and with equal chances of success, only as the
gifts of nature, or the vigorous industry, the close application, or the determined
perseverance of each individual candidate shall vary the equation; and this varia-   5
tion, justice requires us to say, is often in favor of the inheritor of poverty and
toil rather than of riches and titles. Within College walls aristocratic dignities,
aristocratic pretensions, or aristocratic airs, avail their possessor but little.—Woe
to the luckless youth that puts them on. Here, if no where else, the mind is the
measure of the man. Long genealogies and endless pedigrees are a sorry offset   10
for short memories and shallow brains. Here is valued not so much the crown
as the head that wears it. Lace and ribbons, and purple and fine linen, are a poor
compensation for a deficient cranium. Nor does a full purse make any amends
for an empty head. Gold is not a legal tender for college honors. A soft hand is
no passport for a soft head. The sun-burnt farmer's boy, with his inheritance of   15
poverty, hardships and toil, stands side by side with the fair-browed youth who
is the heir of millions, and who eats the bread of another's sweat; only that like
Saul among his fellows, he is not unfrequently higher than any of the sons of
wealth and luxury, "from his shoulders and upward." For an illustration of true
Republicanism, give us such a community as is found at the Common School   20
and the College, and you may find a better if you can. And the Republic owes
it to itself to open wide to all its sons the doors of the Common School, the
Academy, and the College. She has an interest in her children that a monarch
can never have. Her life is identified with theirs. They constitute the essential
parts of her own vital organism; and such and so many are the sympathies of this   25
complicated and living machinery, that if one member suffer, all the members
suffer with it. She may so rear her sons, that they shall be her honor and her
ornament not only, but her strength and her support; or, on the other hand,
she may, by a criminal recklessness, not only lose the strength and the glory
which they might impart to her, but virtually train them to inflict upon her the   30
bitterest curses, and in the end prove her remediless destruction.

   No nation, but least of all a Republic, can afford to lose from her garden of
beauty and her crown of glory, those of whom the Poet has so pensively sung:

>   Full many a flower is born to blush unseen,
>   And waste its fragrance on the desert air;   35
>   Full many a gem of purest ray serene,
>   The dark unfathomed caves of ocean bear.[2]

---

[2]Thomas Gray, "Elegy Witten in a Country Churchyard" (1751)

Still less can she long survive the suicidal policy of so abandoning her children to ignorance and to vice that they shall not only be ciphers in the account, but positive factors, whose product is gangrene and death.

The College is the friend of the Republic, and the Republic should be the
5   friend of the College. Our Educational establishments have ever been the faithful allies and firm supporters of all that is ennobling in our free institutions, and every lover of the Republic should see to it that they are nurtured and guarded with a sleepless vigilance.

Let it be deemed no sacrilege, therefore, that we are convened upon this
10   day, sacred to liberty, to human rights, and to patriotism, to lay the cornerstone of this College edifice. I deem it an auspicious coincidence. May it prove a significant prophecy. Upon this anniversary of the day on which our fathers laid the foundations of the beautiful temple of our National Liberties, we come to lay the corner-stone of this spacious temple of Science. May the walls
15   reared upon this foundation, stand for ages to come, sacred as well to freedom and humanity, to philanthropy and true patriotism, as to sound science, pure morality and true religion. The cornerstone will now be laid.

DRED SCOTT V. SANFORD

Dred Scott (c. 1795–1858) was an African-American slave. His owner, a U.S. Army doctor, took him from the slave state of Missouri to the free state of Illinois and then to the free territory of Wisconsin, then back to Missouri, where the doctor died. In 1846, abolitionist lawyers helped Scott sue for his freedom in state court, claiming he should be free since he had lived on free soil for a long time. The Missouri court applied the principle of "once free, always free" and gave Scott his freedom. His owners appealed and the Missouri Supreme Court, saying "times now are not what they were," reversed the decision. Scott then brought suit in federal court in 1854, lost, and appealed to the U.S. Supreme Court. The case was argued in February 1856, re-argued in December, and a decision handed down in March 1857.

6 MARCH 1857

The question is simply this: Can a negro, whose ancestors were imported into this country, and sold as slaves, be a citizen of the United States, and as such become entitled to all the rights, and privileges, and immunities, guaranteed by that instrument to the citizen? One of which rights is the privilege of suing in a court of the United States in the cases specified in the Constitution.... 5

The words "people of the United States" and "citizens" are synonymous terms, and mean the same thing. They both describe the political body who, according to our republican institutions, form the sovereignty, and who hold the power and conduct the government through their representatives. They are what we familiarly call the "sovereign people," and every citizen is one of this people, 10 and a constituent member of this sovereignty. The question before us is, whether [blacks] compose a portion of this people, and are constituent members of this sovereignty? We think they are not, and that they are not included, and were not intended to be included, under the word "citizens" in the Constitution, and can therefore claim none of the rights and privileges which that instrument provides 15 for and secures to citizens of the United States. On the contrary, they were [in

---

Dred Scott v. Sanford, 60 U.S. 393 (1856).

1787] considered as a subordinate and inferior class of beings, who had been subjugated by the dominant race, and, whether emancipated or not, yet remained subject to their authority, and had no rights or privileges but such as those who held the power and the government might choose to grant them....

5   In discussing this question, we must not confound the rights of citizenship which a state may confer within its own limits, and the rights of citizenship as a member of the Union. [A citizen of a state is not perforce] a citizen of the United States. He may have all of the rights and privileges of the citizen of a state, and yet not be entitled to the rights and privileges of a citizen in any other state. For,

10   previous to the adoption of the Constitution of the United States, every state had the undoubted right to confer on whomsoever it pleased the character of citizen, and to endow him with all its rights. But this character of course was confined to the boundaries of the state, and gave him no rights or privileges in other states beyond those secured to him by the laws of nations and the comity

15   of states. Nor have the several states surrendered the power of conferring these rights and privileges by adopting the Constitution of the United States. Each state may still confer them upon an alien, or any one it thinks proper, or upon any class or description of persons; yet he would not be a citizen in the sense in which that word is used in the Constitution of the United States, nor entitled to

20   sue as such in one of its courts, nor to the privileges and immunities of a citizen in the other states. The rights which he would acquire would be restricted to the state which gave them....

       The question then arises, whether the provisions of the Constitution, in relation to the personal rights and privileges to which the citizen of a state should be

25   entitled, embraced the negro African race, at that time in this country, or who might afterwards be imported, who had then or should afterwards be made free in any state; and to put it in the power of a single state to make him a citizen of the United States, and endue him with the full rights of citizenship in every other state without their consent? Does the Constitution of the United States act

30   upon him whenever he shall be made free under the laws of a state, and raised there to the rank of a citizen, and immediately cloth him with all the privileges of a citizen in every other state, and in its own courts?

       ...[T]hese propositions cannot be maintained. And if [they] cannot...[Dred Scott] could not be a citizen of the State of Missouri, within the meaning of

35   the Constitution of the United States, and, consequently, was not entitled to sue in its courts....

       It is difficult at this day to realize the state of public opinion in relation to that unfortunate race, which prevailed in the civilized and enlightened portions of the world at the time of the Declaration of Independence....

40   ...[I]t is too clear for dispute that the enslaved African race was not intended to be included, and formed no part of the people who framed and adopted

this declaration; for if the language, as understood in that day, would embrace them, the conduct of the distinguished men who framed the Declaration of Independence would have been utterly and flagrantly inconsistent with the principles they asserted....

But there are two clauses in the Constitution which point directly and   5
specifically to the negro race as a separate class of persons, and show clearly that they were not regarded as a portion of the people or citizens of the government then formed.

One of these clauses[1] reserves to each of the thirteen states the right to import slaves until 1808, if it thinks proper. And the importation which it thus   10
sanctions was unquestionably of persons of the race of which we are speaking, as the traffic in slaves in the United States had always been confined to them. And by the other provision[2] the states pledge themselves to each other to maintain the right of property of the master, by delivering up to him any slave who may have escaped from his service, and be found within their respective territories....   15
And these two provisions show, conclusively, that neither the description of persons therein referred to, nor their descendants, were embraced in any of the other provisions of the Constitution; for certainly these two clauses were not intended to confer on them or their posterity the blessings of liberty, or any of the personal rights so carefully provided for the citizen....   20

Indeed, when we look to the condition of this race in the several states at the time, it is impossible to believe that these rights and privileges were intended to be extended to them....

...[The Missouri Compromise] declares that slavery and involuntary servi-tude, except as a punishment for crime, shall be forever prohibited in all that part   25
of the territory.... And the difficulty which meets us at the threshold of this part of the inquiry is whether Congress was authorized to pass this law under any of the powers granted to it by the Constitution, for if the authority is not given by that instrument, it is the duty of this court to declare it void and inoperative, and incapable of conferring freedom upon any one who is held as a slave under   30
the laws of any one of the states.

The counsel for the plaintiff has laid much stress upon that article in the Constitution which confers on Congress the power "to dispose of and make all needful rules and regulations respecting the territory or other property belonging to the United States...." That provision had no bearing on the present controversy,   35
and the power there given, whatever it may be, is confined, and was intended to be confined, to the territory which at that time belonged to, or was claimed by, the United States, and was within their boundaries as settled by the treaty with

---

[1] Article I, Section 9
[2] Article IV, Section 2

Great Britain, and can have no influence upon a territory afterwards acquired from a foreign government. It was a special provision for a known and particular territory, and to meet a present emergency, and nothing more....

5 [Rather, Congress' power in the territories derives from Article IV, section 1, which gives Congress power to admit new states into the union.]

...[W]hen a territory becomes a part of the United States, the Federal government enters into possessions in the character impressed upon it by those who created it. It enters upon it with its powers over the citizen are strictly defined, and limited by the Constitution, from which it derives its own existence, and by 10 virtue of which alone it continues to exist and act as a government and sovereignty. It has no power of any kind beyond it.... [I]t cannot...assume discretionary or despotic powers which the Constitution has denied to it....

[T]he rights of property are united with the rights of person, and placed on the same ground by the fifth amendment to the Constitution, which provides that 15 no person shall be deprived of life, liberty, and property without due process of law. An act of Congress which deprives a citizen of the United States of his liberty or property merely because he came himself or brought his property into a particular territory of the United States, and who had committed no offence against the laws, could hardly be dignified with the name of due process of law....

20 It seems, however, to be supposed, that there is a difference between property in a slave and other property, and different rules may be applied to it in expounding the Constitution of the United States.... And if the Constitution recognizes the right of property of the master in a slave, and makes no distinction between that description of property and other property owned by a citizen, no tribunal, 25 acting under the authority of the United States, whether it be legislative, executive, or judicial, has a right to draw such a distinction, or deny to it the benefit of the provisions and guarantees which have been provided for the protection of private property against the encroachments of the government....

[T]he right of property in a slave is distinctly and expressly affirmed in the 30 Constitution. The right to traffic in it, like an ordinary article of merchandise and property, was guaranteed to the citizens of the United States, in every state that might desire it, for twenty years. And the government in express terms pledged to protect it in all future time if the slave escapes from his owner. This is done in plain words—too plain to be misunderstood.... The only power conferred is the power, 35 coupled with the duty, of guarding and protecting the owner in his rights.

Upon these considerations, it is the opinion of the court that...[the Missouri Compromise] is not warranted by the Constitution, and is therefore void; and that neither Dred Scott himself, nor any of his family, were made free by being carried into this territory; even if they had been carried there by the owner with 40 the intention of becoming a permanent resident....

Lincoln–Douglas Debates
Abraham Lincoln (1809–1865)
Stephen A. Douglas (1813–1861)

The Republican Party nominated Abraham Lincoln (1809–1865) as its candidate for Senate from Illinois in 1858. The party began in opposition to the repeal of the Missouri Compromise and the opening of the territories to slavery under the principle of "popular sovereignty" championed by incumbent Illinois Senator Stephen Douglas (1813–1861). Lincoln argued that the Supreme Court's Dred Scott decision prohibited the people of a territory from exercising such a right. Lincoln suggested that the decision was part of a campaign to nationalize slavery, and that a "second Dred Scott decision" would declare that no state could prohibit slavery. He claimed that Douglas was a party to this conspiracy, that Douglas's popular sovereignty was an unreliable doctrine to prevent the spread of slavery into the territories; and, even more, that Douglas himself was not reliable because of his moral indifference to slavery. Lincoln and the Republicans proposed to repeal the Kansas–Nebraska Act, prohibit slavery in the territories, and reverse the Dred Scott decision.

Douglas staked all on his popular sovereignty principle. While personally opposed to slavery, he believed the national government should allow local majorities to decide whether slavery was permissible for them. He claimed that he had stood up for it against abolitionists who would deny the right of territories to have slavery, and against the administration when it tried to impose a pro-slavery constitution on Kansas against the will of the majority. Lincoln and the Republicans called for a war on slavery, and would impose national uniformity and destroy states rights and local self-government. Douglas further accused the Republicans of not respecting the final authority of the Supreme Court to interpret the Constitution, while Douglas accepted Dred Scott and saw no appeal of the decision above the

Political Debates Between Honorable Abraham Lincoln and Honorable Stephen Douglas in the Celebrated Campaign of 1858… (Columbus, OH: Follett, Foster, and Company, 1860), 70–73, 74, 76–77, 82–83, 95, 119, 127–28, 135, 155, 176–78, 179, 181–82, 184–85, 197–98, 225, 232–33, 234, 235, 238, 239.

Supreme Court. He believed popular sovereignty remained possible under
Dred Scott, and agreed with the Court that blacks had no rights beyond
those that whites might extend to them, while he accused the Republicans
of favoring social and political equality for inferior races.

The candidates met in a series of seven debates across the state. The
first candidate spoke for an hour, his opponent gave a ninety-minute reply,
and the opening speaker had a half-hour rejoinder.

In the state legislative elections (U.S. Senators were chosen by state
legislatures until 1913), Republicans won more votes than the Democrats
but, due to pro-Democratic apportionment, the Democrats got a majority
of seats and returned Douglas to the Senate.

OTTAWA, 21 AUGUST 1858

Stephen Douglas: ...Mr. Lincoln, in the extract from which I have read, says
that this government cannot endure permanently in the same condition in
which it was made by its framers—divided into free and slave states. He says
that it has existed for about seventy years thus divided, and yet he tells you that
5   it cannot endure permanently on the same principles and in the same relative
condition in which our fathers made it. Why can it not exist divided into free
and slave states? Washington, Jefferson, Franklin, Madison, Hamilton, Jay, and
the great men of that day, made this government divided into free states and
slave states, and left each state perfectly free to do as it pleased on the subject of
10 slavery. Why can it not exist on the same principles on which our fathers made
it? They knew when they framed the Constitution that in a country as wide and
broad as this, with such a variety of climate, production and interest, the people
necessarily required different laws and institutions in different localities. They
knew that the laws and regulations which would suit the granite hills of New
15 Hampshire would be unsuited to the rice plantations of South Carolina, and
they, therefore, provided that each state should retain its own legislature and
its own sovereignty, with the full and complete power to do as it pleased within
its own limits, in all that was local and not national. One of the reserved rights
of the states was the right to regulate the relations between master and servant
20 on the slavery question. At the time the Constitution was framed, there were
thirteen states in the union, twelve of which were slaveholding states and one
a free state. Suppose this doctrine of uniformity preached by Mr. Lincoln, that
the states should all be free or all be slave had prevailed, and what would have
been the result? Of course, the twelve slaveholding states would have over-ruled
25 the one free state, and slavery would have been fastened by a Constitutional
provision on every inch of the American republic, instead of being left as our
fathers wisely left it, to each state to decide for itself. Here I assert that uniformity
in the local laws and institutions of the different states is neither possible or

desirable. If uniformity had been adopted when the government was established, it must inevitably have been the uniformity of slavery everywhere, or else the uniformity of Negro citizenship and Negro equality everywhere.

We are told by Lincoln that he is utterly opposed to the Dred Scott decision, and will not submit to it, for the reason that he says it deprives the Negro of   5
the rights and privileges of citizenship. That is the first and main reason which he assigns for his warfare on the Supreme Court of the United States and its decision. I ask you, are you in favor of conferring upon the Negro the rights and privileges of citizenship? Do you desire to strike out of our state constitution that clause which keeps slaves and free Negroes out of the state, and allow the   10
free Negroes to flow in, and cover your prairies with black settlements? Do you desire to turn this beautiful state into a free Negro colony, in order that when Missouri abolishes slavery she can send one hundred thousand emancipated slaves into Illinois, to become citizens and voters, on an equality with yourselves? If you desire Negro citizenship, if you desire to allow them to come into the   15
state and settle with the white man, if you desire them to vote on an equality with yourselves, and to make them eligible to office, to serve on juries, and to adjudge your rights, then support Mr. Lincoln and the Black Republican party, who are in favor of the citizenship of the Negro. For one, I am opposed to Negro citizenship in any and every form. I believe this government was made   20
on the white basis. I believe it was made by white men, for the benefit of white men and their posterity forever, and I am in favor of confining citizenship to white men, men of European birth and descent, instead of conferring it upon negroes, Indians, and other inferior races.

Mr. Lincoln, following the example and lead of all the little abolition   25
orators, who go around and lecture in the basements of schools and churches, reads from the Declaration of Independence that all men were created equal, and then asks how can you deprive a Negro of that equality which God and the Declaration of Independence awards to him? He and they maintain that Negro equality is guaranteed by the laws of God, and that it is asserted in the   30
Declaration of Independence. If they think so, of course they have a right to say so, and so vote. I do not question Mr. Lincoln's conscientious belief that the Negro was made his equal, and hence is his brother; but for my own part, I do not regard the Negro as my equal, and positively deny that he is my brother or any kin to me whatever. Lincoln has evidently learned by heart Parson Lovejoy's   35
catechism.[1] He can repeat it as well as Farnsworth,[2] and he is worthy of a medal

---

[1]Owen Lovejoy (1811–1864), a Congregational minister, U.S. Representative from Illinois (1857–1864), and an active abolitionist. His phrase "Slavery is a sin against the laws of God" became known as Lovejoy's catechism.

[2]John F. Farnsworth (1820–1897), U.S. Representative from Illinois (1857–1861) and abolitionist

from Father Giddings[3] and Fred Douglass[4] for his abolitionism. He holds that the Negro was born his equal and yours, and that he was endowed with equality by the Almighty, and that no human law can deprive him of these rights which were guaranteed to him by the Supreme ruler of the Universe. Now, I do not believe that the Almighty ever intended the Negro to be the equal of the white man. If He did, He has been a long time demonstrating the fact. For thousands of years the Negro has been a race upon the earth, and during all that time, in all latitudes and climates, wherever he has wandered or been taken, he has been inferior to the race which he has there met. He belongs to an inferior race, and must always occupy an inferior position.

I do not hold that because the Negro is our inferior that therefore he ought to be a slave. By no means can such a conclusion be drawn from what I have said. On the contrary, I hold that humanity and Christianity both require that the Negro shall have and enjoy every right, every privilege, and every immunity consistent with the safety of the society in which he lives. On that point, I presume, there can be no diversity of opinion. You and I are bound to extend to our inferior and dependent beings every right, every privilege, every facility and immunity consistent with the public good.

The question then arises, what rights and privileges are consistent with the public good? This is a question which each state and each territory must decide for itself—Illinois has decided it for herself. We have provided that the Negro shall not be a slave, and we have also provided that he shall not be a citizen, but protect him in his civil rights, in his life, his person, and his property, only depriving him of all political rights whatsoever, and refusing to put him on an equality with the white man. That policy of Illinois is satisfactory to the Democratic party and to me, and if it were to the Republicans, there would then be no question upon the subject; but the Republicans say that he ought to be made a citizen, and when he becomes a citizen he becomes your equal, with all your rights and privileges. They assert the Dred Scott decision to be monstrous because it denies that the Negro is or can be a citizen under the Constitution.

Now, I hold that Illinois had a right to abolish and prohibit slavery as she did, and I hold that Kentucky has the same right to continue and protect slavery that Illinois had to abolish it. I hold that New York had as much right to abolish slavery as Virginia has to continue it, and that each and every state of this union is a sovereign power, with the right to do as it pleases upon this question of

---

[3]Joshua Reed Giddings (1795–184). As U.S. Representative from Ohio (1838–1859), he was a leader of the anti-slavery movement in Congress.
[4]Frederick Douglass (1818–1895)

slavery, and upon all its domestic institutions. Slavery is not the only question which comes up in this controversy. There is a far more important one to you, and that is what shall be done with the free Negro? We have settled the slavery question as far as we are concerned; we have prohibited it in Illinois forever, and in doing so, I think we have done wisely, and there is no man in the state 5 who would be more strenuous in his opposition to the introduction of slavery than I would; but when we settled it for ourselves, we exhausted all our power over that subject. We have done our whole duty, and can do no more. We must leave each and every other state to decide for itself the same question.

In relation to the policy to be pursued toward the free negroes, we have 10 said that they shall not vote; whilst Maine, on the other hand, has said that they shall vote. Maine is a sovereign state, and has the power to regulate the qualifications of voters within her limits. I would never consent to confer the right of voting and of citizenship upon a Negro, but still I am not going to quarrel with Maine for differing from me in opinion. Let Maine take care of 15 her own Negroes and fix the qualifications of her own voters to suit herself, without interfering with Illinois, and Illinois will not interfere with Maine. So with the state of New York. She allows the Negro to vote provided he owns two hundred and fifty dollars' worth of property, but not otherwise. While I would not make any distinction whatever between a Negro who held property 20 and one who did not; yet if the sovereign state of New York chooses to make that distinction, it is her business and not mine, and I will not quarrel with her for it. She can do as she pleases on this question if she minds her own business, and we will do the same thing.

Now, my friends, if we will only act conscientiously and rigidly upon this 25 great principle of popular sovereignty, which guarantees to each state and territory the right to do as it pleases on all things, local and domestic, instead of Congress interfering, we will continue at peace one with another. Why should Illinois be at war with Missouri, or Kentucky with Ohio, or Virginia with New York, merely because their institutions differ? Our fathers intended that our 30 institutions should differ. They knew that the North and the South, having different climates, productions and interests, required different institutions. This doctrine of Mr. Lincoln, of uniformity among the institutions of the different states, is a new doctrine, never dreamed of by Washington, Madison, or the framers of this government. 35

Mr. Lincoln and the Republican party set themselves up as wiser than these men who made this government, which has flourished for seventy years under the principle of popular sovereignty, recognizing the right of each state to do as it pleased. Under that principle, we have grown from a nation of three or four millions to a nation of about thirty millions of people; we have crossed the 40

Allegheny Mountains and filled up the whole Northwest, turning the prairie into a garden, and building up churches and schools, thus spreading civilization and Christianity where before there was nothing but savage barbarism. Under that principle we have become, from a feeble nation, the most powerful on the face of
5   the earth, and if we only adhere to that principle, we can go forward increasing in territory, in power, in strength, and in glory until the Republic of America shall be the North Star that shall guide the friends of freedom throughout the civilized world. And why can we not adhere to the great principle of self-government, upon which our institutions were originally based? I believe that this
10 new doctrine preached by Mr. Lincoln and his party will dissolve the union if it succeeds. They are trying to array all the Northern states in one body against the South, to excite a sectional war between the free states and the slave states, in order that the one or the other may be driven to the wall....

Abraham Lincoln: ... This *declared* indifference, but, as I must think, covert *real*
15 zeal for the spread of slavery, I cannot but hate. I hate it because of the monstrous injustice of slavery itself. I hate it because it deprives our republican example of its just influence in the world—enables the enemies of free institutions, with plausibility, to taunt us as hypocrites—causes the real friends of freedom to doubt our sincerity, and especially because it forces so many really good men
20 amongst ourselves into an open war with the very fundamental principles of civil liberty—criticizing the Declaration of Independence, and insisting that there is no right principle of action but *self-interest*.

Before proceeding, let me say I think I have no prejudice against the Southern people. They are just what we would be in their situation. If slavery
25 did not now exist among them, they would not introduce it. If it did now exist amongst us, we should not instantly give it up. This I believe of the masses North and South. Doubtless there are individuals on both sides who would not hold slaves under any circumstances; and others who would gladly introduce slavery anew, if it were out of existence. We know that some Southern men
30 do free their slaves, go North, and become tip-top abolitionists; while some Northern ones go South, and become most cruel slave-masters.

When Southern people tell us they are no more responsible for the origin of slavery than we, I acknowledge the fact. When it is said that the institution exists, and that it is very difficult to get rid of it, in any satisfactory way, I can
35 understand and appreciate the saying. I surely will not blame them for not doing what I should not know how to do myself. If all earthly power were given me, I should not know what to do, as to the existing institution. My first impulse would be to free all the slaves, and send them to Liberia—to their own native land. But a moment's reflection would convince me that whatever of high hope

(as I think there is) there may be in this, in the long run, its sudden execution is impossible. If they were all landed there in a day, they would all perish in the next ten days; and there are not surplus shipping and surplus money enough in the world to carry them there in many times ten days. What then? Free them all, and keep them among us as underlings? Is it quite certain that this betters their condition? I think I would not hold one in slavery at any rate; yet the point is not clear enough to me to denounce people upon. What next? Free them, and make them politically and socially our equals? My own feelings will not admit of this; and if mine would, we well know that those of the great mass of white people will not. Whether this feeling accords with justice and sound judgment, is not the sole question, if, indeed, it is any part of it. A universal feeling, whether well or ill-founded, cannot be safely disregarded. We cannot, then, make them equals. It does seem to me that systems of gradual emancipation might be adopted; but for their tardiness in this, I will not undertake to judge our brethren of the South....

Now, my friends, I ask your attention to this matter for the purpose of saying something seriously. I know that the Judge may readily enough agree with me that the maxim which was put forth by the Savior is true, but he may allege that I misapply it; and the Judge has a right to urge that, in my application, I do misapply it, and then I have a right to show that I do *not* misapply it. When he undertakes to say that because I think this nation, so far as the question of slavery is concerned, will all become one thing or all the other, I am in favor of bringing about a dead uniformity in the various states, in all their institutions, he argues erroneously.

The great variety of the local institutions in the states, springing from differences in the soil, differences in the face of the country, and in the climate, are bonds of union. They do not make "a house divided against itself," but they make a house united. If they produce in one section of the country what is called for by the wants of another section, and this other section can supply the wants of the first, they are not matters of discord but bonds of union, true bonds of union. But can this question of slavery be considered as among *these* varieties in the institutions of the country?

I leave it to you to say whether, in the history of our government, this institution of slavery has not always failed to be a bond of union and, on the contrary, been an apple of discord, and an element of division in the house. I ask you to consider whether, so long as the moral constitution of men's minds shall continue to be the same, after this generation and assemblage shall sink into the grave, and another race shall arise, with the same moral and intellectual development we have—whether, if that institution is standing in the same irritating position in which it now is, it will not continue an element of division? If so, then I have a right to say that, in regard to this question, the union is a house divided against itself; and when the Judge reminds me that I have often said to him that the institution of slavery has existed for eighty years in some states, and yet it does not exist in some others, I agree to the fact, and I account for it by looking at the position in which our fathers originally placed it—restricting it from the new territories where it had not gone, and legislating to cut off its source by the abrogation of the slave-trade, thus putting the seal of legislation *against its spread*. The public mind *did* rest in the belief that it was in the course of ultimate extinction.

But lately, I think—and in this I charge nothing on the Judge's motives— lately, I think, that he, and those acting with him, have placed that institution on a new basis, which looks to the *perpetuity and nationalization of slavery*. And while it is placed upon this new basis, I say, and I have said, that I believe we shall not have peace upon the question until the opponents of slavery arrest the further spread of it, and place it where the public mind shall rest in the belief that it is in the course of ultimate extinction; or, on the other hand, that its advocates will push it forward until it shall become alike lawful in all the states, old as well as new, North as well as South. Now, I believe if we could arrest the spread, and place it where Washington, and Jefferson, and Madison placed it, it *would be* in the course of ultimate extinction, and the public mind *would*, as for eighty years past, believe that it was in the course of ultimate extinction. The crisis would be past and the institution might be let alone for a hundred years, if it should live so long, in the states where it exists, yet it would be going out of existence in the way best for both the black and the white races.

A Voice: Then do you repudiate Popular Sovereignty?

Abraham Lincoln: Well, then, let us talk about Popular Sovereignty! What is Popular Sovereignty? Is it the right of the people to have slavery or not have it, as they see fit, in the territories? I will state—and I have an able man to watch me—my understanding is that Popular Sovereignty, as now applied to the ques- tion of slavery, does allow the people of a territory to have slavery if they want to, but does not allow them *not* to have it if they *do not* want it. I do not mean that if this vast concourse of people were in a territory of the United States, any one of them would be obliged to have a slave if he did not want one; but I do say that, as I understand the Dred Scott decision, if any one man wants slaves, all the rest have no way of keeping that one man from holding them....

There is no danger that the people of Kentucky will shoulder their muskets and, with a young nigger stuck on every bayonet, march into Illinois and force them upon us. There is no danger of our going over there and making war upon them. Then what is necessary for the nationalization of slavery? It is simply the next Dred Scott decision. It is merely for the Supreme Court to decide that no *state* under the Constitution can exclude it, just as they have already decided that under the Constitution neither Congress nor the territorial legislature can do it. When that is decided and acquiesced in, the whole thing is done.   5

This being true, and this being the way, as I think, that slavery is to be made national, let us consider what Judge Douglas is doing every day to that end. In the first place, let us see what influence he is exerting on public sentiment. In this and like communities, public sentiment is everything. With public sentiment, nothing can fail; without it nothing can succeed. Consequently he who   10 moulds public sentiment, goes deeper than he who enacts statutes or pronounces decisions. He makes statutes and decisions possible or impossible to be executed. This must be borne in mind, as also the additional fact that Judge Douglas is a man of vast influence, so great that it is enough for many men to profess to believe anything, when they once find out that Judge Douglas professes to believe   15 it. Consider also the attitude he occupies at the head of a large party—a party which he claims has a majority of all the voters in the country.

This man sticks to a decision which forbids the people of a territory from excluding slavery, and he does so not because he says it is right in itself—he does not give any opinion on that—but because it has been *decided by the court*, and   20 being decided by the court, he is, and you are bound to take it in your political action as *law*—not that he judges at all of its merits, but because a decision of the court is to him a *Thus saith the Lord*. He places it on that ground alone, and you will bear in mind that, thus committing himself unreservedly to this decision, *commits him to the next one* just as firmly as to this. He did not commit   25 himself on account of the merit or demerit of the decision, but it is a *Thus saith the Lord*. The next decision, as much as this, will be a *Thus saith the Lord*.

There is nothing that can divert or turn him away from this decision. It is nothing that I point out to him that his great prototype, General Jackson, did not believe in the binding force of decisions. It is nothing to him that Jefferson   30 did not so believe. I have said that I have often heard him approve of Jackson's course in disregarding the decision of the Supreme Court pronouncing a national bank constitutional. He says I did not hear him say so. He denies the accuracy of my recollection. I say he ought to know better than I, but I will make no question about this thing, though it still seems to me that I heard   35 him say it twenty times. I will tell him though, that he now claims to stand on the Cincinnati platform, which affirms that Congress *cannot* charter a national bank, in the teeth of that old standing decision that Congress *can* charter a bank. And I remind him of another piece of history on the question of respect for judicial decisions, and it is a piece of Illinois history, belonging to a time   40

when the large party to which Judge Douglas belonged were displeased with
a decision of the Supreme Court of Illinois, because they had decided that a
governor could not remove a secretary of state. You will find the whole story in
Ford's *History of Illinois*, and I know that Judge Douglas will not deny that he
5   was then in favor of overslaughing that decision by the mode of adding five new
judges, so as to vote down the four old ones. Not only so, but it ended in *the*
Judge's sitting down on that very bench as one of the five new judges to break down
the four old ones. It was in this way precisely that he got his title of Judge. Now,
when the Judge tells me that men appointed conditionally to sit as members
10   of a court will have to be catechised beforehand upon some subject, I say, "You
know, Judge; you have tried it." When he says a court of this kind will lose the
confidence of all men, will be prostituted and disgraced by such a proceeding,
I say, "You know best, Judge; you have been through the mill."…
        …Now, having spoken of the Dred Scott decision, one more word and
15   I am done. Henry Clay, my beau ideal of a statesman, the man for whom I
fought all my humble life—Henry Clay once said of a class of men who would
repress all tendencies to liberty and ultimate emancipation that they must,
if they would do this, go back to the era of our Independence, and muzzle
the cannon which thunders its annual joyous return; they must blow out the
20   moral lights around us; they must penetrate the human soul, and eradicate
there the love of liberty; and then, and not till then, could they perpetuate
slavery in this country!
        To my thinking, Judge Douglas is, by his example and vast influence,
doing that very thing in this community when he says that the Negro has
25   nothing in the Declaration of Independence. Henry Clay plainly understood
the contrary. Judge Douglas is going back to the era of our Revolution and,
to the extent of his ability, muzzling the cannon which thunders its annual
joyous return. When he invites any people willing to have slavery to establish it, he is blowing out the moral lights around us. When he says he "cares
30   not whether slavery is voted down or voted up"—that it is a sacred right of
self-government—he is, in my judgment, penetrating the human soul and
eradicating the light of reason and the love of liberty in this American people.
And now I will only say that when, by all these means and appliances, Judge
Douglas shall succeed in bringing public sentiment to an exact accordance
35   with his own views—when these vast assemblages shall echo back all these
sentiments—when they shall come to repeat his views and to avow his principles, and to say all that he says on these mighty questions—then it needs
only the formality of the second Dred Scott decision, which he endorses in
advance, to make slavery alike lawful in all the states—old as well as new,
40   North as well as South.…

Stephen Douglas: …The next question propounded to me by Mr. Lincoln is can the people of a territory in any lawful way, against the wishes of any citizen of the United States, exclude slavery from their limits prior to the formation of a state constitution? I answer emphatically, as Mr. Lincoln has heard me answer a hundred times from every stump in Illinois, that in my opinion the people of   5
a territory can, by lawful means, exclude slavery from their limits prior to the formation of a state constitution. Mr. Lincoln knew that I had answered that question over and over again. He heard me argue the Nebraska Bill on that principle all over the state in 1854, in 1855, and in 1856, and he has no excuse for pretending to be in doubt as to my position on that question.   10

It matters not what way the Supreme Court may hereafter decide as to the abstract question whether slavery may or may not go into a territory under the Constitution, the people have the lawful means to introduce it or exclude it as they please, for the reason that slavery cannot exist a day or an hour anywhere unless it is supported by local legislature, and if the people are opposed to slavery   15
they will elect representatives to that body who will by unfriendly legislation effectually prevent the introduction of it into their midst. If, on the contrary, they are for it, their legislation will favor its extension. Hence, no matter what the decision of the Supreme Court may be on that abstract question, still the right of the people to make a slave territory or a free territory is perfect and   20
complete under the Nebraska Bill. I hope Mr. Lincoln deems my answer satisfactory on that point.…

Abraham Lincoln: …While I am upon this subject, I will make some answers briefly to certain propositions that Judge Douglas has put. He says, "Why can't this union endure permanently half slave and half free?" I have said that I sup-   25
posed it could not, and I will try, before this new audience, to give briefly some of the reasons for entertaining that opinion. Another form of his question is, "Why can't we let it stand as our fathers placed it?" That is the exact difficulty between us. I say that Judge Douglas and his friends have changed them from the position in which our fathers originally placed it. I say, in the way our fathers   30
originally left the slavery question, the institution was in the course of ultimate extinction, and the public mind rested in the belief that it *was* in the course of ultimate extinction. I say when this government was first established, it was the policy of its founders to prohibit the spread of slavery into the new territories of the United States, where it had not existed. But Judge Douglas and his friends   35
have broken up that policy, and placed it upon a new basis by which it is to become national and perpetual. All I have asked or desired any where is that it

should be placed back again upon the basis that the fathers of our government originally placed it upon. I have no doubt that it *would* become extinct, for all time to come, if we but readopted the policy of the fathers by restricting it to the limits it has already covered—restricting it from the new territories.

5   I do not wish to dwell at great length on this branch of the subject at this time, but allow me to repeat one thing that I have stated before. Brooks, the man who assaulted Senator Sumner on the floor of the Senate, and who was complimented with dinners, and silver pitchers, and gold-headed canes, and a good many other things for that fact, in one of his speeches declared that when this government was
10   originally established, nobody expected that the institution of slavery would last until this day. That was but the opinion of one man, but it was such an opinion as we can never get from Judge Douglas or anybody in favor of slavery in the North at all. You *can* sometimes get it from a Southern man. He said at the same time that the framers of our government did not have the knowledge that experience
15   has taught us—that experience and the invention of the cotton-gin have taught us that the perpetuation of slavery is a necessity. He insisted, therefore, upon its being changed from the basis upon which the fathers of the government left it to the basis of its perpetuation and nationalization....

      In the Senate of the United States, in 1850, Judge Trumbull,[5] in a speech,
20   substantially, if not directly, put the same interrogatory to Judge Douglas, as to whether the people of a territory had the lawful power to exclude slavery prior to the formation of a Constitution?... I appeal to you whether he did not say it was a question for the Supreme Court? Has not the Supreme Court decided that question? When he now says the people *may* exclude slavery, does he not
25   make it a question for the people? Does he not virtually shift his ground and say that it is *not* a question for the court, but for the people?...

      Again, I will ask you, my friends, if you were elected members of the legislature, what would be the first thing you would have to do before entering upon your duties? *Swear to support the Constitution of the United States.* Suppose
30   you believe, as Judge Douglas does, that the Constitution of the United States guaranties to your neighbor the right to hold slaves in that territory—that they are his property—how can you clear your oaths unless you give him such legislation as is necessary to enable him to enjoy that property? What do you understand by supporting the constitution of a state, or of the United States?
35   Is it not to give such constitutional helps to the rights established by that Constitution as may be practically needed? Can you, if you swear to support the Constitution, and believe that the Constitution established a right, clear your oath without giving it support? Do you support the Constitution if, knowing or believing there is a right established under it which needs specific legislation,

[5]Lyman Trumbull (1813–1896), U.S. Senator from Illinois (1855–1873)

you withhold that legislation? Do you not violate and disregard your oath? I can conceive of nothing plainer in the world. There can be nothing in the words "support the Constitution" if you may run counter to it by refusing support to any right established under the Constitution. And what I say here will hold with still more force against the Judge's doctrine of "unfriendly Legislation." 5 How could you, having sworn to support the Constitution, and believing it guaranteed the right to hold slaves in the territories, assist in legislation *intended to defeat that right?* That would be violating your own view of the Constitution. Not only so, but if you were to do so, how long would it take the courts to hold your votes unconstitutional and void? Not a moment. 10

Lastly I would ask—is not Congress, itself, under obligation to give legislative support to any right that is established under the United States Constitution? I repeat the question—is not Congress, itself, bound to give legislative support to any right that is established in the United States Constitution?...

Stephen Douglas: ...My doctrine is, that even taking Mr. Lincoln's view that 15 the decision recognizes the right of a man to carry his slaves into the territories of the United States, if he pleases, yet after he gets there he needs affirmative law to make that right of any value. The same doctrine not only applies to slave property, but all other kinds of property. Chief Justice Taney[6] places it upon the ground that slave property is on an equal footing with other property. Suppose 20 one of your merchants should move to Kansas and open a liquor store; he has a right to take groceries and liquors there, but the mode of selling them, and the circumstances under which they shall be sold, and all the remedies must be prescribed by local legislation, and if that is unfriendly it will drive him out just as effectually as if there was a Constitutional provision against the sale 25 of liquor. So the absence of local legislation to encourage and support slave property in a territory excludes it practically just as effectually as if there was a positive Constitutional provision against it. Hence, I assert that under the Dred Scott decision you cannot maintain slavery a day in a territory where there is an unwilling people and unfriendly legislation. If the people are opposed to 30 it, our right is a barren, worthless, useless right, and if they are for it, they will support and encourage it....

Charleston, 18 September 1858

Stephen Douglas: ...Mr. Lincoln said in his first remarks that he was not in favor of the social and political equality of the Negro with the white man. Everywhere up north he has declared that he was not in favor of the social and 35 political equality of the Negro, but he would not say whether or not he was opposed to Negroes voting and Negro citizenship. I want to know whether

---

[6]Roger B. Taney (1777–1864), Chief Justice of the United States (1836–1864)

he is for or against Negro citizenship? He declared his utter opposition to the Dred Scott decision, and advanced as a reason that the court had decided that it was not possible for a Negro to be a citizen under the Constitution of the United States. If he is opposed to the Dred Scott decision for that reason, he
5   must be in favor of conferring the right and privilege of citizenship upon the Negro! I have been trying to get an answer from him on that point, but have never yet obtained one, and I will show you why. In every speech he made in the north he quoted the Declaration of Independence to prove that all men were created equal, and insisted that the phrase "all men" included the Negro
10   as well as the white man, and that the equality rested upon Divine law. Here is what he said on that point:

> I should like to know if, taking this old Declaration of Independence, which declares that all men are equal upon principle, and making exceptions to it, where will it stop? If one man says it does not mean
> 15   a Negro, why may not another say it does not mean some other man? If that declaration is not the truth, let us get the statute book in which we find it and tear it out.

Lincoln maintains there that the Declaration of Independence asserts that the Negro is equal to the white man, and that under Divine Law, and if
20   he believes so it was rational for him to advocate Negro citizenship, which, when allowed, puts the Negro on an equality under the law. I say to you in all frankness, gentlemen, that in my opinion a Negro is not a citizen, cannot be, and ought not to be, under the Constitution of the United States. I will not even qualify my opinion to meet the declaration of one of the Judges of
25   the Supreme Court in the Dred Scott case, "that a Negro descended from African parents, who was imported into this country as a slave is not a citizen, and cannot be." I say that this government was established on the white basis. It was made by white men, for the benefit of white men and their posterity forever, and never should be administered by any except white men. I declare
30   that a Negro ought not to be a citizen, whether his parents were imported into this country as slaves or not, or whether or not he was born here. It does not depend upon the place a Negro's parents were born, or whether they were slaves or not, but upon the fact that he is a negro, belonging to a race incapable of self-government, and for that reason ought not to be on an
35   equality with white men....

GALESBURGH, 7 OCTOBER 1858

Stephen Douglas: ...Chief Justice Taney has said in his opinion in the Dred Scott case that a Negro slave, being property, stands on an equal footing with other property, and that the owner may carry them into United States territory the same as he does other property. Suppose any two of you, neighbors, should conclude to go to Kansas, one carrying $100,000 worth of Negro slaves and the other $100,000 worth of mixed merchandise, including quantities of liquors. You both agree that under that decision you may carry your property to Kansas, but when you get it there, the merchant who is possessed of the liquors is met by the Maine liquor law, which prohibits the sale or use of his property, and the owner of the slaves is met by equally unfriendly legislation, which makes his property worthless after he gets it there. What is the right to carry your property into the territory worth to either when unfriendly legislation in the territory renders it worthless after you get it there? The slave-holder when he gets his slaves there finds that there is no local law to protect him in holding them, no slave code, no police regulation maintaining and supporting him in his right, and he discovers at once that the absence of such friendly legislation excludes his property from the territory, just as irresistibly as if there was a positive Constitutional prohibition excluding it. Thus you find it is with any kind of property in a territory, it depends for its protection on the local and municipal law. If the people of a territory want slavery, they make friendly legislation to introduce it, but if they do not want it, they withhold all protection from it, and then it cannot exist there....

Abraham Lincoln: ...The Judge has alluded to the Declaration of Independence, and insisted that Negroes are not included in that Declaration; and that it is a slander upon the framers of that instrument to suppose that Negroes were meant therein; and he asks you, Is it possible to believe that Mr. Jefferson, who penned the immortal paper, could have supposed himself applying the language of that instrument to the Negro race, and yet held a portion of that race in slavery? Would he not at once have freed them? I only have to remark upon this part of the Judge's speech (and that, too, very briefly, for I shall not detain myself, or you, upon that point for any great length of time), that I believe the entire records of the world, from the date of the Declaration of Independence up to within three years ago, may be searched in vain for one single affirmation, from one single man, that the Negro was not included in the Declaration of Independence; I think I may defy Judge Douglas to show that he ever said so, that Washington ever said so, that any President ever said so, that any member of Congress ever said so, or that any living man upon the whole earth ever said so, until the necessities of the present policy of the Democratic party, in regard to slavery, had to invent that affirmation. And I will remind Judge Douglas and this audience, that while Mr. Jefferson was the owner of slaves, as undoubtedly he was, in speaking upon this very subject, he used the strong language that "he trembled for his country when he remembered that God was just;" and I will

offer the highest premium in my power to Judge Douglas if he will show that
he, in all his life, ever uttered a sentiment at all akin to that of Jefferson....

 ...But the Judge will have it that if we do not confess that there is a sort
of inequality between the white and black races, which justifies us in making
5　them slaves, we must, then, insist that there is a degree of equality that requires
us to make them our wives. Now, I have all the while taken a broad distinction in regard to that matter; and that is all there is in these different speeches
which he arrays here, and the entire reading of either of the speeches will show
that that distinction was made. Perhaps by taking two parts of the same speech
10　he could have got up as much of a conflict as the one he has found. I have all
the while maintained that in so far as it should be insisted that there was an
equality between the white and black races that should produce a perfect social
and political equality, it was an impossibility. This you have seen in my printed
speeches, and with it I have said that in their right to "life, liberty, and the pur-
15　suit of happiness," as proclaimed in that old Declaration, the inferior races are
our equals. And these declarations I have constantly made in reference to the
abstract moral question, to contemplate and consider when we are legislating
about any new country which is not already cursed with the actual presence of
the evil—slavery. I have never manifested any impatience with the necessities
20　that spring from the actual presence of black people amongst us, and the actual
existence of slavery amongst us where it does already exist; but I have insisted
that, in legislating for new countries, where it does not exist, there is no just
rule other than that of moral and abstract right!...

 ...I suppose that the real difference between Judge Douglas and his friends,
25　and the Republicans on the contrary, is that the Judge is not in favor of making
any difference between slavery and liberty—that he is in favor of eradicating,
of pressing out of view, the questions of preference in this country for free or
slave institutions; and consequently every sentiment he utters discards the idea
that there is any wrong in slavery. Everything that emanates from him or his
30　co-adjutors in their course of policy carefully excludes the thought that there is
anything wrong in slavery. All their arguments, if you will consider them, will be
seen to exclude the thought that there is anything whatever wrong in slavery.

 If you will take the Judge's speeches, and select the short and pointed sentences expressed by him—as his declaration that he "don't care whether slavery
35　is voted up or down"—you will see at once that this is perfectly logical, if you
do not admit that slavery is wrong. If you do admit that it is wrong, Judge
Douglas cannot logically say he don't care whether a wrong is voted up or voted
down. Judge Douglas declares that if any community wants slavery they have
a right to have it. He can say that logically, if he says that there is no wrong in
40　slavery; but if you admit that there is a wrong in it, he cannot logically say that

anybody has a right to do wrong. He insists that, upon the score of equality, the owners of slaves and owners of property—of horses and every other sort of property—should be alike and hold them alike in a new territory. That is perfectly logical, if the two species of property are alike and are equally founded in right. But if you admit that one of them is wrong, you cannot institute any   5
equality between right and wrong.

And from this difference of sentiment—the belief on the part of one that the institution is wrong, and a policy springing from that belief which looks to the arrest of the enlargement of that wrong; and this other sentiment, that it is no wrong, and a policy sprung from that sentiment which will tolerate no   10
idea of preventing that wrong from growing larger, and looks to there never being an end of it through all the existence of things—arises the real difference between Judge Douglas and his friends on the one hand, and the Republicans on the other. Now, I confess myself as belonging to that class in the country who contemplate slavery as a moral, social, and political evil, having due regard   15
for its actual existence amongst us and the difficulties of getting rid of it in any satisfactory way, and to all the Constitutional obligations which have been thrown about it; but, nevertheless, desire a policy that looks to the prevention of it as a wrong, and looks hopefully to the time when as a wrong it may come to an end....   20

...I think it follows, and I submit to the consideration of men capable of argu-ing, whether as I state it, in syllogistic form, the argument has any fault in it?

- Nothing in the Constitution or laws of any state can destroy a right distinctly and expressly affirmed in the Constitution of the United States.   25
- The right of property in a slave is distinctly and expressly affirmed in the Constitution of the United States.
- Therefore, nothing in the Constitution or laws of any state can destroy the right of property in a slave.

I believe that no fault can be pointed out in that argument; assuming the   30
truth of the premises, the conclusion, so far as I have capacity at all to under-stand it, follows inevitably. There is a fault in it as I think, but the fault is not in the reasoning; but the falsehood in fact is a fault of the premises. I believe that the right of property in a slave *is not* distinctly and expressly affirmed in the Constitution, and Judge Douglas thinks it *is*. I believe that the Supreme   35
Court and the advocates of that decision may search in vain for the place in the Constitution where the right of a slave is distinctly and expressly affirmed. I say, therefore, that I think one of the premises is not true in fact. But it is true with Judge Douglas. It is true with the Supreme Court who pronounced it. They are

stopped from denying it, and being stopped from denying it, the conclusion follows that the Constitution of the United States being the supreme law, no constitution or law can interfere with it.

It being affirmed in the decision that the right of property in a slave is distinctly and expressly affirmed in the Constitution, the conclusion inevitably follows that no state law or constitution can destroy that right. I then say to Judge Douglas and to all others that I think it will take a better answer than a sneer to show that those who have said that the right of property in a slave is distinctly and expressly affirmed in the Constitution are not prepared to show that no constitution or law can destroy that right. I say I believe it will take a far better argument than a mere sneer to show to the minds of intelligent men that whoever has so said is not prepared, whenever public sentiment is so far advanced as to justify it, to say the other.

This is but an opinion, and the opinion of one very humble man; but it is my opinion that the Dred Scott decision, as it is, never would have been made in its present form if the party that made it had not been sustained previously by the elections. My own opinion is that the new Dred Scott decision, deciding against the right of the people of the states to exclude slavery, will never be made if that party is not sustained by the elections. I believe, further, that it is just as sure to be made as tomorrow is to come, if that party shall be sustained. I have said upon a former occasion, and I repeat it now, that the course of argument that Judge Douglas makes use of upon this subject (I charge not his motives in this) is preparing the public mind for that new Dred Scott decision. I have asked him again to point out to me the reasons for his first adherence to the Dred Scott decision as it is. I have turned his attention to the fact that General Jackson differed with him in regard to the political obligation of a Supreme Court decision. I have asked his attention to the fact that Jefferson differed with him in regard to the political obligation of a Supreme Court decision. Jefferson said that "Judges are as honest as other men, and not more so." And he said, substantially, that "whenever a free people should give up in absolute submission to any department of government, retaining for themselves no appeal from it, their liberties were gone." I have asked his attention to the fact that the Cincinnati platform, upon which he says he stands, disregards a time-honored decision of the Supreme Court in denying the power of Congress to establish a national bank. I have asked his attention to the fact that he himself was one of the most active instruments at one time in breaking down the Supreme Court of the state of Illinois, because it had made a decision distasteful to him—a struggle ending in the remarkable circumstance of his sitting down as one of the new Judges who were to overslaugh that decision—getting his title of Judge in that very way....

Abraham Lincoln: ...We have in this nation this element of domestic slavery. It is a matter of absolute certainty that it is a disturbing element. It is the
opinion of all the great men who have expressed an opinion upon it that it is a
dangerous element. We keep up a controversy in regard to it. That controversy
necessarily springs from difference of opinion, and if we can learn exactly—can   5
reduce to the lowest elements—what that difference of opinion is, we perhaps
shall be better prepared for discussing the different systems of policy that we
would propose in regard to that disturbing element.

    I suggest that the difference of opinion, reduced to its lowest terms, is no
other than the difference between the men who think slavery a wrong and   10
those who do not think it wrong. The Republican party think it wrong—we
think it is a moral, a social, and a political wrong. We think it as a wrong not
confining itself merely to the persons or the states where it exists, but that it
is a wrong in its tendency, to say the least, that extends itself to the existence
of the whole nation. Because we think it wrong, we propose a course of policy   15
that shall deal with it as a wrong. We deal with it as with any other wrong, in
so far as we can prevent its growing any larger, and so deal with it that in the
run of time there may be some promise of an end to it. We have a due regard
to the actual presence of it amongst us and the difficulties of getting rid of it in
any satisfactory way, and all the Constitutional obligations thrown about it. I   20
suppose that in reference both to its actual existence in the nation, and to our
Constitutional obligations, we have no right at all to disturb it in the states
where it exists, and we profess that we have no more inclination to disturb it
than we have the right to do it. We go further than that; we don't propose to
disturb it where, in one instance, we think the Constitution would permit us.   25
We think the Constitution would permit us to disturb it in the District of
Columbia. Still we do not propose to do that, unless it should be in terms which
I don't suppose the nation is very likely soon to agree to—the terms of making
the emancipation gradual and compensating the unwilling owners. Where we
suppose we have the Constitutional right, we restrain ourselves in reference to   30
the actual existence of the institution and the difficulties thrown about it. We
also oppose it as an evil so far as it seeks to spread itself. We insist on the policy
that shall restrict it to its present limits. We don't suppose that in doing this we
violate any thing due to the actual presence of the institution, or anything due
to the Constitutional guarantees thrown around it.   35

    We oppose the Dred Scott decision in a certain way, upon which I ought
perhaps address you a few words. We do not propose that when Dred Scott
has been decided to be a slave by the court, we, as a mob, will decide him to be
free. We do not propose that, when any other one, or one thousand, shall be

decided by that court to be slaves, we will in any violent way disturb the rights of property thus settled; but we nevertheless do oppose that decision as a political rule, which shall be binding on the voter to vote for nobody who thinks it wrong, which shall be binding on the members of Congress or the President to favor no measure that does not actually concur with the principles of that decision. We do not propose to be bound by it as a political rule in that way, because we think it lays the foundation not merely of enlarging and spreading out what we consider an evil, but it lays the foundation for spreading that evil into the states themselves. We propose so resisting it as to have it reversed if we can, and a new judicial rule established upon this subject....

ALTON, 15 OCTOBER 1858

Abraham Lincoln: ...I think the authors of that notable instrument intended to include *all* men, but they did not mean to declare all men equal *in all respects*. They did not mean to say all men were equal in color, size, intellect, moral development, or social capacity. They defined with tolerable distinctness in what they did consider all men created equal—equal in certain inalienable rights, among which are life, liberty, and the pursuit of happiness. This they said, and this they meant. They did not mean to assert the obvious untruth that all were then actually enjoying that equality, or yet, that they were about to confer it immediately upon them. In fact they had no power to confer such a boon. They meant simply to declare the *right*, so that the *enforcement* of it might follow as fast as circumstances should permit.

They meant to set up a standard maxim for free society which should be familiar to all: constantly looked to, constantly labored for, and even, though never perfectly attained, constantly approximated, and thereby constantly spreading and deepening its influence and augmenting the happiness and value of life to all people, of all colors, everywhere....

At Galesburg the other day, I said in answer to Judge Douglas that three years ago there never had been a man, so far as I knew or believed, in the whole world, who had said that the Declaration of Independence did not include Negroes in the term "all men".... Do not let me be misunderstood. I know that more than three years ago there were men who, finding this assertion constantly in the way of their schemes to bring about the ascendancy and perpetuation of slavery, *denied the truth of it*.... I believe the first man who ever said it was Chief Justice Taney in the Dred Scott case, and the next to him was our friend, Stephen A. Douglas. And now it has become the catch-word of the entire party....

I have stated upon former occasions, and I may as well state again, what I understand to be the real issue in this controversy between Judge Douglas and myself. On the point of my wanting to make war between the free and the slave states, there has been no issue between us. So, too, when he assumes that I am in favor of introducing a perfect social and political equality between the white and black races. These are false issues, upon which Judge Douglas has tried to force the controversy. There is no foundation in truth for the charge that I maintain either of these propositions. The real issue in this controversy—the one pressing upon every mind—is the sentiment on the part of one class that looks upon the institution of slavery *as a wrong*, and of another class that *does not* look upon it as a wrong. The sentiment that contemplates the institution of slavery in this country as a wrong is the sentiment of the Republican Party. It is the sentiment around which all their actions—all their arguments circle—from which all their propositions radiate. They look upon it as being a moral, social, and political wrong; and while they contemplate it as such, they nevertheless have due regard for its actual existence among us, and the difficulties of getting rid of it in any satisfactory way and to all the constitutional obligations thrown about it. Yet having a due regard for these, they desire a policy in regard to it that looks to its not creating any more danger. They insist that it should as far as may be, *be treated* as a wrong, and one of the methods of treating it as a wrong is to *make provision that it shall grow no larger*. They also desire a policy that looks to a peaceful end of slavery at sometime, as being wrong....

On this subject of treating it as a wrong, and limiting its spread, let me say a word. Has anything ever threatened the existence of this union save and except this very institution of slavery? What is it that we hold most dear amongst us? Our own liberty and prosperity. What has ever threatened our liberty and prosperity save and except this institution of slavery? If this is true, how do you propose to improve the condition of things by enlarging slavery—by spreading it out and making it bigger? You may have a wen or cancer upon your person and not be able to cut it out lest you bleed to death; but surely it is no way to cure it, to engraft it and spread it over your whole body. That is no proper way of treating what you regard a wrong....

That is the real issue. That is the issue that will continue in this country when these poor tongues of Judge Douglas and myself shall be silent. It is the eternal struggle between these two principles—right and wrong—throughout the world. They are the two principles that have stood face to face from the beginning of time; and will ever continue to struggle. The one is the common right of humanity and the other the divine right of kings. It is the same principle in whatever shape it develops itself. It is the same spirit that says, "You work and toil and earn bread, and I'll eat it." No matter in what shape it comes, whether from the mouth of a king who seeks to bestride the people of his own nation and live by the fruit of their labor, or from one race of men as an apology for enslaving another race, it is the same tyrannical principle....

...I say if that Dred Scott decision is correct, then the right to hold slaves in a territory is equally a Constitutional right with the right of a slave-holder to have his runaway returned. No one can show the distinction between them. The one is express, so that we cannot deny it. The other is construed to be in the Constitution, so that he who believes the decision to be correct believes in the right. And the man who argues that by unfriendly legislation, in spite of that Constitutional right, slavery may be driven from the territories, cannot avoid furnishing an argument by which abolitionists may deny the obligation to return fugitives, and claim the power to pass laws unfriendly to the right of the slave-holder to reclaim his fugitive. I do not know how such an argument may strike a popular assembly like this, but I defy anybody to go before a body of men whose minds are educated to estimating evidence and reasoning, and show that there is an iota of difference between the Constitutional right to reclaim a fugitive, and the Constitutional right to hold a slave, in a territory, provided this Dred Scott decision is correct. I defy any man to make an argument that will justify unfriendly legislation to deprive a slave-holder of his right to hold his slave in a territory, that will not equally, in all its length, breadth and thickness, furnish an argument for nullifying the Fugitive Slave Law. Why, there is not such an abolitionist in the nation as Douglas, after all.

Stephen Douglas: ...He says that he looks forward to a time when slavery shall be abolished everywhere. I look forward to a time when each state shall be allowed to do as it pleases. If it chooses to keep slavery forever, it is not my business, but its own; if it chooses to abolish slavery, it is its own business—not mine. I care more for the great principle of self-government, the right of the people to rule, than I do for all the Negroes in Christendom. I would not endanger the perpetuity of this Union, I would not blot out the great inalienable rights of the white men for all the Negroes that ever existed....

...Let us examine for a moment and see what principle it was that overthrew the Divine right of George the Third to govern us. Did not these colonies rebel because the British Parliament had no right to pass laws concerning our property and domestic and private institutions without our consent? We demanded that the British government should not pass such laws unless they gave us representation in the body passing them—and this the British government insisting on doing—we went to war on the principle that the home government should not control and govern distant colonies without giving them a representation. Now, Mr. Lincoln proposes to govern the territories without giving them a representation, and calls on Congress to pass laws controlling their property and domestic concerns without their consent and against their will. Thus, he asserts for his party the identical principle asserted by George III and the Tories of the Revolution....

King Cotton

James Henry Hammond (1807–1864)
U.S. Senator from South Carolina (1857–1860)

*On March 4, 1858, Senator James Hammond of South Carolina said
on the floor of the United States Senate what Agrarians had been saying
to each other for many years—"Cotton is King!" He was right, in a way.
Cotton was America's only significant export, and it had helped to trigger
the release of energy that would be called the "Industrial Revolution" in
England and the United States. Hammond's speech, however, is perhaps
more interesting in how it sums up the Agrarian argument, emphasizing
the "harmony of her political and social institutions."*

4 March 1858

But if there were no other reason why we should never have war, would any
sane nation make war on cotton? Without firing a gun, without drawing a
sword, should they make war on us we could bring the whole world to our feet.
The South is perfectly competent to go on, one, two, or three years without
planting a seed of cotton. I believe that if she was to plant but half her cotton   5
for three years to come, it would be an immense advantage to her. I am not so
sure but that after three years' entire abstinence she would come out stronger
than ever she was before, and better prepared to enter afresh upon her great
career of enterprise. What would happen if no cotton was furnished for three
years? I will not stop to depict what every one can imagine, but this is certain: 10
England would topple headlong and carry the whole civilized world with her,
save the South. No, you dare not make war on cotton. No power on earth dares
to make war upon it.

Cotton *is* king. Until lately the Bank of England was king; but she tried to
put her screws as usual, the fall before the last, upon the cotton crop, and was   15
utterly vanquished. The last power has been conquered. Who can doubt, that has
looked at recent events, that cotton is supreme? When the abuse of credit had
destroyed credit and annihilated confidence; when thousands of the strongest

---

Selections from the Letters and Speeches of the Honorable James H. Hammond of South Carolina
(New York: John F. Trow and Company, 1866), 316–20.

447

commercial houses in the world were coming down, and hundreds of millions of dollars of supposed property evaporating in thin air; when you came to a dead lock, and revolutions were threatened, what brought you up? Fortunately for you it was the commencement of the cotton season, and we have poured in upon you one million six hundred thousand bales of cotton just at the crisis to save you from destruction. That cotton, but for the bursting of your speculative bubbles in the North, which produced the whole of this convulsion, would have brought us $100,000,000. We have sold it for $65,000,000, and saved you. Thirty-five million dollars we, the slaveholders of the South, have put into the charity box for your magnificent financiers, your "cotton lords," your "merchant princes."

But, sir, the greatest strength of the South arises from the harmony of her political and social institutions. This harmony gives her a frame of society, the best in the world, and an extent of political freedom, combined with entire security, such as no other people ever enjoyed upon the face of the earth. Society precedes government; creates it, and ought to control it; but as far as we can look back in historic times we find the case different; for government is no sooner created than it becomes too strong for society, and shapes and moulds, as well as controls it. In later centuries the progress of civilization and of intelligence has made the divergence so great as to produce civil wars and revolutions; and it is nothing now but the want of harmony between governments and societies which occasions all the uneasiness and trouble and terror that we see abroad. It was this that brought on the American Revolution. We threw off a government not adapted to our social system, and made one for ourselves. The question is, how far have we succeeded? The South, so far as that is concerned, is satisfied, harmonious, and prosperous, but demands to be let alone.

In all social systems there must be a class to do the menial duties, to perform the drudgery of life. That is, a class requiring but a low order of intellect and but little skill. Its requisites are vigor, docility, fidelity. Such a class you must have, or you would not have that other class which leads progress, civilization, and refinement. It constitutes the very mud-sill of society and of political government; and you might as well attempt to build a house in the air, as to build either the one or the other, except on this mud-sill. Fortunately for the South, she found a race adapted to that purpose to her hand. A race inferior to her own, but eminently qualified in temper, in vigor, in docility, in capacity to stand the climate, to answer all her purposes. We use them for our purpose, and call them slaves. We found them slaves by the common "consent of mankind," which, according to Cicero, "*lex naturæ est.*" The highest proof of what is Nature's law. We are old-fashioned at the South yet; slave is a word discarded now by "ears polite"; I will not characterize that class at the North by that term; but you have it; it is there; it is everywhere; it is eternal.

The Senator from New York said yesterday that the whole world had abolished slavery. Aye, the *name*, but not the *thing*; all the powers of the earth cannot
abolish that. God only can do it when he repeals the *fiat*, "the poor ye always
have with you;" for the man who lives by daily labor, and scarcely lives at that,
and who has to put out his labor in the market, and take the best he can get   5
for it; in short, your whole hireling class of manual laborers and "operatives," as
you call them, are essentially slaves. The difference between us is that our slaves
are hired for life and well compensated; there is no starvation, no begging, no
want of employment among our people, and not too much employment either.
Yours are hired by the day, not cared for, and scantily compensated, which may   10
be proved in the most painful manner, at any hour in any street in any of your
large towns. Why, you meet more beggars in one day, in any single street of
the city of New York, than you would met in a lifetime in the whole South.
We do not think that whites should be slaves either by law or necessity. Our
slaves are black, of another and inferior race. The *status* in which we have placed 15
them is an elevation. They are elevated from the condition in which God first
created them, by being made our slaves. None of that race on the whole face
of the globe can be compared with the slaves of the South. They are happy,
content, un-aspiring, and utterly incapable, from intellectual weakness, ever
to give us any trouble by their aspirations. Yours are white, of your own race;   20
you are brothers of one blood. They are your equals in natural endowment of
intellect, and they feel galled by their degradation. Our slaves do not vote. We
give them no political power. Yours do vote, and, being the majority, they are
the depositaries of all your political power. If they knew the tremendous secret,
that the ballot-box is stronger than "an army with banners," and could combine, 25
where would you be? Your society would be reconstructed, your government
overthrown, your property divided, not as they have mistakenly attempted to
initiate such proceedings by meeting in parks, with arms in their hands, but by
the quiet process of the ballot-box. You have been making war upon us to our
very hearthstones. How would you like for us to send lecturers and agitators   30
North, to teach these people this, to aid in combining, and to lead them?…

Declaration of Causes
South Carolina

The election of Abraham Lincoln precipitated secession. The legislature of South Carolina called for a state convention, which was the method by which the state had ratified the Constitution of the United States. The convention passed a resolution dissolving "the union now subsisting between South Carolina and other states." It also issued the following Declaration, which the delegates considered analogous to the Declaration of Independence. Mississippi followed South Carolina's lead in early January.

Both statements contained a theory of the nature of the Union and a list of charges against the people of the Northern states, which the Mississippi convention said had "assumed a revolutionary position toward the Southern states." The Constitution, both conventions claimed, was a compact among completely sovereign states. Implicit in this claim was that the Constitution did not create a nation, but a federal union that could be dissolved if a state or states concluded that the terms of the compact had been violated.

20 December 1860

The people of the State of South Carolina, in convention assembled, on the 26th day of April, A.D. 1852, declared that the frequent violations of the Constitution of the United States by the federal government, and its encroachments upon the reserved rights of the states, fully justified this state in then withdrawing from the federal union; but in deference to the opinions and wishes of the other slave-holding states, she forbore at that time to exercise this right. Since that time, these encroachments have continued to increase, and further forbearance ceases to be a virtue.

And now the State of South Carolina having resumed her separate and equal place among nations, deems it due to herself, to the remaining United States of America, and to the nations of the world, that she should declare the immediate causes which have led to this act.

Journal of the Convention of the People of South Carolina Held in 1860, 1861, and 1862... (Columbia, SC: R. W. Gibbes, 1862), 461–66.

In the year 1765, that portion of the British Empire embracing Great Britain undertook to make laws for the government of that portion composed of the thirteen American colonies. A struggle for the right of self-government ensued, which resulted, on the 4th of July 1776, in a declaration by the colonies "that they are, and of right ought to be, FREE AND INDEPENDENT STATES; and that, as free and independent states, they have full power to levy war, conclude peace, contract alliances, establish commerce, and to do all other acts and things which independent states may of right do."

They further solemnly declared that whenever any "form of government becomes destructive of the ends for which it was established, it is the right of the people to alter or abolish it, and to institute a new government." Deeming the government of Great Britain to have become destructive of these ends, they declared that the colonies "are absolved from all allegiance to the British Crown, and that all political connection between them and the state of Great Britain is, and ought to be, totally dissolved."

In pursuance of this Declaration of Independence, each of the thirteen states proceeded to exercise its separate sovereignty; adopted for itself a con-stitution, and appointed officers for the administration of government in all its departments—legislative, executive, and judicial. For purposes of defense, they united their arms and their counsels; and, in 1778, they entered into a league known as the Articles of Confederation, whereby they agreed to entrust the administration of their external relations to a common agent, known as the Congress of the United States, expressly declaring, in the first Article "that each state retains its sovereignty, freedom, and independence, and every power, jurisdiction, and right which is not, by this Confederation, expressly delegated to the United States in Congress assembled."

Under this Confederation the war of the Revolution was carried on, and on the 8th September 1783, the contest ended, and a definite treaty was signed by Great Britain, in which she acknowledged the independence of the colonies in the following terms:

Article 1—His Britannic Majesty acknowledges the said United States, viz: New Hampshire, Massachusetts Bay, Rhode Island and Provi-dence Plantation, Connecticut, New York, New Jersey, Pennsylvania, Delaware, Maryland, Virginia, North Carolina, South Carolina and Georgia, to be FREE, SOVEREIGN, AND INDEPENDENT STATES; that he treats with them as such; and for himself, his heirs, and successors, relinquishes all claims to the government, propriety, and territorial rights of the same and very part thereof.

Thus were established the two great principles asserted by the colonies, namely: the right of a state to govern itself; and the right of a people to abolish a government when it becomes destructive of the ends for which it was instituted. And concurrent with the establishment of these principles was the fact that each colony became and was recognized by the mother country as a FREE, SOVEREIGN, AND INDEPENDENT STATE.

In 1787, deputies were appointed by the states to revise the Articles of Confederation, and on 17th September 1787, these deputies recommended, for the adoption of the states, the articles of union known as the Constitution of the United States.

The parties to whom this Constitution was submitted were the several sovereign states; they were to agree or disagree, and when nine of them agreed the compact was to take effect among those concurring; and the general government, as the common agent, was then to be invested with their authority.

If only nine of the thirteen states had concurred, the other four would have remained as they then were—separate, sovereign states, independent of any of the provisions of the Constitution. In fact, two of the states did not accede to the Constitution until long after it had gone into operation among the other eleven; and during that interval, they each exercised the functions of an independent nation.

By this Constitution, certain duties were imposed upon the several states, and the exercise of certain of their powers was restrained, which necessarily implied their continued existence as sovereign states. But to remove all doubt, an amendment was added, which declared that the powers not delegated to the United States by the Constitution, nor prohibited by it to the states, are reserved to the states, respectively, or to the people. On 23d May 1788, South Carolina, by a convention of her people, passed an ordinance assenting to this Constitution, and afterwards altered her own constitution to conform herself to the obligations she had undertaken.

Thus was established, by compact between the states, a government, with defined objects and powers, limited to the express words of the grant. This limitation left the whole remaining mass of power subject to the clause reserving it to the states or to the people, and rendered unnecessary any specification of reserved rights.

We hold that the government thus established is subject to the two great principles asserted in the Declaration of Independence; and we hold further, that the mode of its formation subjects it to a third fundamental principle, namely: the law of compact. We maintain that in every compact between two or more parties, the obligation is mutual; that the failure of one of the contracting parties to perform a material part of the agreement, entirely releases the obligation of the other; and that where no arbiter is provided, each party is remitted to his own judgment to determine the fact of failure, with all its consequences.

In the present case, that fact is established with certainty. We assert that fourteen of the states have deliberately refused, for years past, to fulfill their constitutional obligations, and we refer to their own statutes for the proof.

The Constitution of the United States, in its fourth Article, provides as follows: "No person held to service or labor in one state, under the laws thereof, escaping into another, shall, in consequence of any law or regulation therein, be discharged from such service or labor, but shall be delivered up, on claim of the party to whom such service or labor may be due."

This stipulation was so material to the compact that without it that compact would not have been made. The greater number of the contracting parties held slaves, and they had previously evinced their estimate of the value of such a stipulation by making it a condition in that ordinance for the government of the territory ceded by Virginia, which now composes the states north of the Ohio River.

The same article of the Constitution stipulates also for rendition by the several states of fugitives from justice from the other states.

The general government, as the common agent, passed laws to carry into effect these stipulations of the states. For many years these laws were executed. But an increasing hostility on the part of the non-slaveholding states to the institution of slavery has led to a disregard of their obligations, and the laws of the general government have ceased to effect the objects of the Constitution. The states of Maine, New Hampshire, Vermont, Massachusetts, Connecticut, Rhode Island, New York, Pennsylvania, Illinois, Indiana, Michigan, Wisconsin, and Iowa have enacted laws which either nullify the acts of Congress or render useless any attempt to execute them. In many of these states the fugitive is discharged from the service or labor claimed, and in none of them has the state government complied with the stipulation made in the Constitution. The state of New Jersey, at an early day, passed a law in conformity with her constitutional obligations; but the current of anti-slavery feeling has led her more recently to enact laws which render inoperative the remedies provided by her own law and by the laws of Congress. In the state of New York even the right of transit for a slave has been denied by her tribunals; and the states of Ohio and Iowa have refused to surrender to justice fugitives charged with murder, and with inciting servile insurrection in the state of Virginia. Thus the constituted compact has been deliberately broken and disregarded by the non-slaveholding states, and the consequences follows that South Carolina is released from her obligation.

The ends for which this Constitution was framed are declared by itself to be "to form a more perfect union, establish justice, insure domestic tranquility, provide for the common defense, promote the general welfare, and secure the blessings of liberty to ourselves and our posterity."

These ends it endeavored to accomplish by a federal government in which each state was recognized as an equal, and had separate control over its own institutions. The right of property in slaves was recognized by giving to free persons distinct political rights, by giving them the right to represent, and burdening them with direct taxes for three-fifths of their slaves; by authorizing the importation of slaves for twenty years; and by stipulating for the rendition of fugitives from labor.

We affirm that these ends for which this government was instituted have been defeated, and the government itself has been made destructive of them by the action of the non-slaveholding states. Those states have assumed the right of deciding upon the propriety of our domestic institutions; and have denied the rights of property established in fifteen of the states and recognized by the Constitution; they have denounced as sinful the institution of slavery; they have permitted the open establishment among them of societies, whose avowed object is to disturb the peace and to eloign the property of the citizens of other states. They have encouraged and assisted thousands of our slaves to leave their homes; and those who remain, have been incited by emissaries, books and pictures to servile insurrection.

For twenty-five years this agitation has been steadily increasing, until it has now secured to its aid the power of the common government. Observing the *forms* of the Constitution, a sectional party has found within that Article establishing the executive department the means of subverting the Constitution itself. A geographical line has been drawn across the Union, and all the states north of that line have united in the election of a man to the high office of President of the United States whose opinions and purposes are hostile to slavery. He is to be entrusted with the administration of the common government, because he has declared that that "Government cannot endure permanently half slave, half free," and that the public mind must rest in the belief that slavery is in the course of ultimate extinction.

This sectional combination for the subversion of the Constitution, has been aided in some of the states by elevating to citizenship persons who, by the supreme law of the land, are incapable of becoming citizens: and their votes have been used to inaugurate a new policy, hostile to the South, and destructive of its peace and safety.

On the 4th of March next, this party will take possession of the government. It has announced that the South shall be excluded from the common territory, that the judicial tribunals shall be made sectional, and that a war must be waged against slavery until it shall cease throughout the United States.

The guaranties of the Constitution will then no longer exist; the equal rights of the states will be lost. The slaveholding states will no longer have the

power of self-government, or self-protection, and the federal government will
have become their enemy.

Sectional interest and animosity will deepen the irritation, and all hope of
remedy is rendered vain, by the fact that public opinion at the North has invested
5   a great political error with the sanctions of a more erroneous religious belief.

We, therefore, the people of South Carolina, by our delegates in Convention assembled, appealing to the Supreme Judge of the world for the rectitude
of our intentions, have solemnly declared that the union heretofore existing
between this state and the other states of North America, is dissolved, and
10   that the state of South Carolina has resumed her position among the nations
of the world, as a separate and independent state; with full power to levy war,
conclude peace, contract alliances, establish commerce, and to do all other acts
and things which independent states may of right do.

Secession Resolutions
State of Mississippi

30 November 1860

Whereas, the Constitutional union was formed by the several states in their separate sovereign capacity, for the purpose of actual advantage and protection;

That the several states are distinct sovereignties, whose supremacy is limited so far only as the same has been delegated by voluntary compact to a federal government, and when it fails to accomplish the ends for which it was established, the parties to the compact have the right to resume, each state for itself such delegated powers;

That the institution of slavery existed prior to the formation of the Federal Constitution, and is recognized by the letter, and all efforts to impair its value or lessen its duration by Congress, or any of the free states, is a violation of the compact of union, and is destructive of the ends for which it was ordained, but in defiance of the principles of the union thus established, the people of the Northern states have assumed a revolutionary position towards the Southern states;

That they have set at defiance that provision of the Constitution which was intended to secure domestic tranquility among the states and promote their general welfare, namely, "No person held to service or labor in one state, under the laws thereof, escaping into another shall in consequence of any law or regulation therein be discharged from such service or labor, but shall be delivered up on claim of the party to whom such service or labor may be due;

That they have by voluntary associations, individual agencies and state legislation, interfered with slavery as it prevails in the slaveholding states;

That they have enticed our slaves from us, and by state intervention, obstructed and prevented their rendition under the Fugitive Slave Law;

That they continue their system of agitation obviously for the purpose of encouraging other slaves to escape from service, to weaken the institution in

---

Laws of the State of Mississippi Passed at a Called Session of the Mississippi Legislature (Jackson, MS: 1860), 43–45.

the slaveholding states, by rendering the holding of such property insecure, and as a consequence its ultimate abolition certain;

That they claim the right, and demand its execution by Congress, to exclude slavery from the territories, but claim the right of protection for every species of property owned by themselves;

That they declare in every manner in which public opinion is expressed, their unalterable determination to exclude from admittance into the union any new state that tolerates slavery in its constitution and thereby force Congress to a condemnation of that species of property;

That they thus seek by an increase of abolition states "to acquire two-thirds of both houses" for the purpose of preparing an amendment to the Constitution of the United States abolishing slavery in the states, and so continue the agitation, that the proposed amendment shall be ratified by the legislatures of three-fourths of the states;

That they have in violation of the comity of all civilized nations, and in violation of the comity established by the Constitution of the United States, insulted and outraged our citizens when travelling among them for pleasure, health, or business, by taking their servants and liberating the same, under the forms of state laws, and subjecting their owners to degrading and ignominious punishment;

That to encourage the stealing of our property they have put at defiance that provision of the Constitution which declares that fugitives from justice into another state, on demand of the executive authority of the state from which he fled, shall be delivered up;

That they have sought to create domestic discord in the Southern states by incendiary publications;

That they encouraged a hostile invasion of a Southern state to excite insurrection, murder, and rapine;

That they have deprived Southern citizens of their property and continue an unfriendly agitation of their domestic institutions, claiming for themselves perfect immunity from external interference with their domestic policy;

We of the Southern states alone made an exception to that universal quiet;

That they have elected a majority of electors for President and Vice-President on the ground that there exists an irreconcilable conflict between the two sections of the confederacy in reference to their respective systems of labor and in pursuance of their hostility to us and our institutions, thus declaring to the civilized world that the powers of this government are to be used for the dishonor and overthrow of the Southern section of this great confederacy.

Therefore, Be it resolved by the legislature of the State of Mississippi that in the opinion of these who now constitute the said legislature, the secession of each aggrieved state is the proper remedy for these injuries.

SECESSION ORDINANCES
SOUTH CAROLINA, MISSISSIPPI, FLORIDA

Within the first three months after the legitimate and constitutional election of Abraham Lincoln to the presidency of the United States, seven southern states—South Carolina, Mississippi, Florida, Alabama, Georgia, Louisiana, and Texas—seceded from the Union and created the Confederate States of America (February 7, 1861). To many a Southerner, the North seemed nothing short of decadent, its freedom not standing for anything but a loss of purpose and direction, its people confused, running in many directions, chasing nothing of importance. "The parties in this conflict are not merely abolitionists and slave-holders—they are atheists, socialists, communists, red republicans, Jacobins on the one side and the friends of order and regulated freedom on the other," a famous southern theologian, James Henley Thornwell, had written. "In one word, the world is the battleground, Christianity and atheism the combatants, and the progress of humanity is at stake."

Written with great confidence, the secession ordinances claimed the states—through a compact, as understood by men such as John C. Calhoun—had a right, and perhaps a duty, to leave the compact when the Union no longer served its original purpose. "At first I was extremely reluctant to join in, and was even opposed to the secession movement; I doubted its necessity and dreaded the impending conflict and its result. A large number of the best and most thoughtful men all over the South felt as I did," Joseph LeConte remembered. But, "gradually a change came about—how, who can say? It was in the atmosphere; we breathed it in the air; it reverberated from heart to heart; it was like a spiritual contagion—good or bad, who could say? But the final result was enthusiastic unanimity of sentiment throughout the South."

Two sticking points, however, remained. First, what to do with federal property? The seceding states immediately formed committees to deal with

Journal of the Convention of the People of South Carolina Held in 1860, 1861, and 1862… (Columbia, SC: R. W. Gibbes, 1862), 42.

459

the peaceful transfer of such property. Second, though, the Southerners had to defend their very controversial position to each other as well as to the world.

SOUTH CAROLINA, 20 DECEMBER 1860

We the people of the State of South Carolina, in convention assembled, do declare and ordain, and it is hereby declared and ordained, that the ordinance adopted by us in convention on the twenty-third day of May, in the year of our Lord one thousand seven hundred and eighty-eight, whereby the Constitution of the United
5   States of America was ratified and also all acts and parts of acts of the General Assembly of this state ratifying amendments of the said Constitution, are hereby repealed; and that the union now subsisting between South Carolina and other states, under the name of the "United States of America," is hereby dissolved.

MISSISSIPPI, 9 JANUARY 1861

The people of the State of Mississippi, in convention assembled, do ordain and
10   declare, and it is hereby ordained and declared, as follows, to wit:

1.   That all the laws and ordinances by which the said State of Mississippi became a member of the Federal Union of the United States of America be, and the same are hereby, repealed, and that all obligations on the part of the said state or the people thereof to observe the same be withdrawn, and
15   that the said state do hereby resume all the rights, functions, and powers which by any of said laws or ordinances were conveyed to the government of the said United States, and is absolved from all the obligations, restraints, and duties incurred to the said Federal Union, and shall from henceforth be a free, sovereign, and independent state.

20   2.   That so much of the first section of the seventh article of the constitution of this state as requires members of the legislature and all officers, executive and judicial, to take an oath or affirmation to support the Constitution of the United States be, and the same is hereby, abrogated and annulled.

3.   That all rights acquired and vested under the Constitution of the United
25   States, or under any act of Congress passed, or treaty made, in pursuance thereof, or under any law of this state, and not incompatible with this ordinance, shall remain in force and have the same effect as if this ordinance had not been passed.

4.   That the people of the State of Mississippi hereby consent to form a Federal
30   Union with such of the states as may have seceded or may secede from

the Union of the United States of America, upon the basis of the present Constitution of the said United States, except such parts thereof as embrace other portions than such seceding states.

FLORIDA, 10 JANUARY 1861

We, the people of the State of Florida, in convention assembled, do solemnly ordain, publish, and declare that the State of Florida hereby withdraws herself   5 from the confederacy of states existing under the name of the United States of America and from the existing government of the said states; and that all political connection between her and the government of said states ought to be, and the same is hereby, totally annulled, and said union of states dissolved; and the State of Florida is hereby declared a sovereign and independent nation; and that all   10 ordinances heretofore adopted, in so far as they create or recognize said union, are rescinded; and all laws or parts of laws in force in this state, in so far as they recognize or assent to said union, be, and they are hereby, repealed.

Address to the People of the Slave-Holding States

Robert Barnwell Rhett (1800–1876)
Member, South Carolina Secession Convention

The fire-eating editor of the Charleston Mercury, *R. B. Rhett, defended John C. Calhoun's theories. Following closely Calhoun's "Disquisition on Government," Rhett claimed the United States had become a consolidated democracy rather than a republic. Consequently, the ever-increasingly democratic United States, in contrast to its founding, now stood for despotism, not free government. Indeed, Rhett claimed, drawing upon history and patriotic sentiment, "the Southern States now stand exactly in the same position toward the Northern States that our ancestors in the colonies did toward Great Britain."*

24 December 1860

It is seventy-three years since the union between the United States was made by the Constitution of the United States. During this time, their advance in wealth, prosperity, and power has been with scarcely a parallel in the history of the world. The great object of their union was defense against external aggression; which object is now attained from their mere progress in power. Thirty-one 5
millions of people, with a commerce and navigation which explore every sea, and with agricultural productions which are necessary to every civilized people, command the friendship of the world. But unfortunately, our internal peace has not grown with our external prosperity. Discontent and contention have moved in the bosom of the confederacy for the last thirty-five years. During this time, 10
South Carolina has twice called her people together in solemn convention, to take into consideration the aggression and unconstitutional wrongs perpetrated by the people of the North on the people of the South. These wrongs were submitted to by the people of the South, under the hope and expectation that they would be final. But such hope and expectation have proved to be vain. 15
Instead of producing forbearance, our acquiescence has only instigated to new forms of aggression and outrage; and South Carolina, having again assembled

Journal of the Convention of the People of South Carolina Held in 1860, 1861, and 1862… (Columbia, SC: R. W. Gibbes, 1862), 467–76.

her people in convention, has this day dissolved her connection with the states constituting the United States.

The one great evil, from which all other evils have flowed, is the overthrow of the Constitution of the United States. The government of the United States is no longer the government of confederated republics, but of a consolidated democracy. It is no longer a free government, but a despotism. It is, in fact, such a government as Great Britain attempted to set over our fathers; and which was resisted and defeated by a seven years' struggle for independence.

The Revolution of 1776 turned upon one great principle, self-government—and self-taxation, the criterion of self-government. Where the interests of two people united together under one government, are different, each must have the power to protect its interests by the organization of the government, or they cannot be free. The interests of Great Britain and of the colonies were different and antagonistic. Great Britain was desirous of carrying out the policy of all nations towards their colonies, of making them tributary to her wealth and power. She had vast and complicated relations with the whole world. Her policy towards her North American colonies was to identify them with her in all these complicated relations; and to make them bear, in common with the rest of the Empire, the full burden of her obligations and necessities. She had a vast public debt; she had an European policy and an Asiatic policy, which had occasioned the accumulation of her public debt; and which kept her in continual wars. The North American colonies saw their interests, political and commercial, sacrificed by such a policy. Their interest required that they should not be identified with the burdens and wars of the mother country. They had been settled under charters, which gave them self-government; at least so far as their property was concerned. They had taxed themselves, and had never been taxed by the government of Great Britain. To make them a part of a consolidated empire, the Parliament of Great Britain determined to assume the power of legislating for the colonies in all cases whatsoever. Our ancestors resisted the pretension. They refused to be a part of the consolidated government of Great Britain.

The Southern states now stand exactly in the same position towards the Northern states that the colonies did towards Great Britain. The Northern states, having the majority in Congress, claim the same power of omipotence in legislation as the British Parliament. "The General Welfare" is the only limit to the legislation of either; and the majority in Congress, as in the British Parliament, are the sole judges of the expediency of the legislation this "General Welfare" requires. Thus, the government of the United States has become a consolidated government; and the people of the Southern states are compelled to meet the very despotism their fathers threw off in the Revolution of 1776.

The consolidation of the government of Great Britain over the colonies was attempted to be carried out by the taxes. The British Parliament undertook to tax the colonies to promote British interests. Our fathers resisted this pretension. They claimed the right of self-taxation *through their colonial legislatures.* They were not represented in the British Parliament and, therefore, could not rightly be taxed by its legislation. The British government however, offered them a representation in Parliament; but it was not sufficient to enable them to protect themselves from the majority, and they refused the offer. Between taxation without any representation, and taxation without a representation adequate to protection, there was no difference. In neither case would the colonies tax themselves. Hence, they refused to pay the taxes laid by the British Parliament.

And so with the Southern states, towards the Northern states, in the vital matter of taxation. They are in a minority in Congress. Their representation in Congress is useless to protect them against unjust taxation; and they are taxed by the people of the North *for their benefit*, exactly as the people of Great Britain taxed our ancestors in the British Parliament for their benefit. For the last forty years, the taxes laid by the Congress of the United States, have been laid with a view of subserving the interests of the North. The people of the South have been taxed by duties on imports, not for revenue, but for an object inconsistent with revenue—to promote, by prohibitions, Northern interests in the productions of their mines and manufactures.

There is another evil, in the condition of the Southern towards the Northern states, which our ancestors refused to bear towards Great Britain. Our ancestors not only taxed themselves, but all the taxes collected from them were expended amongst them. Had they submitted to the pretensions of the British government, the taxes collected from them would have been expended in other parts of the British Empire. They were fully aware of the effect of such a policy in impoverishing the people from whom taxes are collected, and in enriching those who receive the benefit of their expenditure. To prevent the evils of such a policy was one of the motives which drove them on to revolution. Yet this British policy has been fully realized towards the Southern states by the Northern states. The people of the Southern states are not only taxed for the benefit of the Northern states, but after the taxes are collected, three-fourths of them are expended at the North. This cause, with others, connected with the operation of the General Government, has made the cities of the South provincial. Their growth is paralyzed; they are mere suburbs of Northern cities. The agricultural productions of the South are the basis of the foreign commerce of the United States; yet Southern cities do not carry it on. Our foreign trade is almost annihilated. In 1740, there were five ship-yards in South Carolina, to build ships to carry on our direct trade with Europe. Between 1740 and 1779, there were built in these yards twenty-five square rigged vessels, besides a great number of sloops and schooners, to carry on our coast and West India trade. In the half century immediately preceding the Revolution from 1725 to 1775, the population of South Carolina increased seven-fold.

No man can, for a moment, believe that our ancestors intended to establish over their posterity exactly the same sort of government they had overthrown. The great object of the Constitution of the United States, in its internal operation, was, doubtless, to secure the great end of the Revolution—a limited free government—a government limited to those matters only, which were general and common to all portions of the United States. All sectional or local interests were to be left to the states. By no other arrangement would they obtain free government, by a Constitution common to so vast a confederacy. Yet, by gradual and steady encroachments on the part of the people of the North, and aquiescence on the part of the South, the limitations in the Constitution have been swept away; and the government of the United States has become consolidated, with a claim of limitless powers in its operations.

It is not at all surprising, such being the character of the government of the United States, that it should assume to possess power over all the institutions of the country. The agitations on the subject of slavery are the natural results of the consolidation of the government. Responsibility follows power; and if the people of the North have the power by Congress "to promote the general welfare of the United States" by any means they deem expedient—why should they not assail and overthrow the institution of slavery in the South? They are responsible for its continuance or existence, in proportion to their power. A majority in Congress, according to their interested and perverted views, is omnipotent. The inducements to act upon the subject of slavery, under such circumstances, were so imperious, as to amount almost to a moral necessity. To make, however, their numerical power available to rule the union, the North must consolidate their power. It would not be united, on any matter common to the whole union—in other words, on any constitutional subject—for on such subjects divisions are as likely to exist in the North as in the South. Slavery was strictly a sectional interest. If this could be made the criterion of parties at the North, the North could be united in its power; and thus carry out its measures of sectional ambition, encroachment, and aggrandizement. To build up their sectional predominance in the union, the Constitution must be first abolished by counteractions; but that being done, the consolidation of the North, to rule the South, by the tariff and slavery issues, was in the obvious course of things.

The Constitution of the United States was an experiment. The experiment consisted in uniting under one government peoples living in different climates, and having different pursuits and institutions. It matters not how carefully the limitations of such a government be laid down in the Constitution—its success must, at least, depend upon the good faith of the parties to the constitutional compact in enforcing them. It is not in the power of human language to exclude false inferences, constructions, and perversions in any constitution; and when vast sectional interests are to be subserved, involving the appropriation of countless millions of money, it has not been the usual experience of mankind that words on parchments can arrest power. The Constitution of the United States, irrespective of the interposition of the states, rested on the assumption that power would yield to faith—that integrity would be stronger than interest; and that thus, the limitations of the Constitution would be observed. The experiment has been fairly made. The Southern states, from the commencement of the government, have striven to keep it within the orbit prescribed by the Constitution. The experiment has failed. The whole Constitution, by the constructions of the Northern people, has been absorbed by its preamble. In their reckless lust for power, they seem unable to comprehend that seeming paradox—that the more power is given to the General Government, the weaker it becomes. Its strength consists in the limitation of its agency to objects of common interests to all sections. To extend the scope of its power over sectional or local interests, is to raise up against it opposition and resistance. In all such matters, the General Government must necessarily be a despotism, because all sectional or local interests must ever be represented by a minority in the councils of the General Government—having no power to protect itself against the rule of the majority. The majority, constituted from those who do not represent these sectional or local interests, will control and govern them. A free people cannot submit to such a government. And the more it enlarges the sphere of its power, the greater must be the dissatisfaction it must produce, and the weaker it must become. On the contrary, the more it abstains from usurped powers, and the more faithfully it adheres to the limitations of the Constitution, the stronger it is made. The Northern people have had neither the wisdom nor the faith to perceive, that to observe the limitations of the Constitution was the only way to its perpetuity.

Under such a government, there must, of course, be many and endless "irrepressible conflicts," between the two great sections of the union. The same faithlessness which has abolished the Constitution of the United States will not fail to carry out the sectional purposes for which it has been abolished. There must be conflict; and the weaker section of the union can only find peace and liberty in an independence of the North. The repeated efforts made by South Carolina, in a wise conservatism, to arrest the program of the General Government in its fatal progress to consolidation, have been unsupported, and she has

been denounced as faithless to the obligations of the Constitution by the very men and states who were destroying it by their usurpations. It is now too late to reform or restore the government of the United States. All confidence in the North is lost by the South. The faithlessness of the North for half a century,
5   has opened a gulf of separation between the North and the South which no promises nor engagements can fill.

     It cannot be believed that our ancestors would have assented to any union whatever with the people of the North, if the feelings and opinions now existing amongst them had existed when the Constitution was framed. There was then
10   no tariff—no fanaticism concerning negroes. It was the delegates from New England who proposed in the Convention which framed the Constitution, to the delegates from South Carolina and Georgia, that if they would agree to give Congress the power of regulating commerce *by a majority*, that they would support the extension of the African slave trade for twenty years. African slavery
15   existed in all the states but one. The idea that the Southern states would be made to pay that tribute to their northern confederates which they had refused to pay to Great Britain; or that the institution of African slavery would be made the grand basis of a sectional organization of the North to rule the South, never crossed the imaginations of our ancestors. The union of the Constitution was a
20   union of slave-holding states. It rests on slavery, by prescribing a representation in Congress for three-fifths of our slaves. There is nothing in the proceedings of the convention which framed the Constitution to show that the Southern states would have formed any other union; and still less, that they would have formed a union with more powerful non-slave-holding states having majority in
25   both branches of the legislature of the government. They were guilty of no such folly. Time and the progress of things have totally altered the relations between the Northern and Southern states since the union was established. That identity of feelings, interests, and institutions which once existed is gone. They are now divided between agricultural and manufacturing and commercial states; between
30   slave-holding and non-slave-holding states. Their institutions and industrial pursuits have made them totally different peoples. That equality in the government between the two sections of the union which once existed no longer exists. We but imitate the policy of our fathers in dissolving a union with non-slave-holding confederates, and seeking a confederation with slave-holding states.
35   Experience has proved that slave-holding states cannot be safe in subjection to non-slave-holding states. Indeed, no people can ever expect to preserve its rights and liberties, unless these be in its own custody. To plunder and oppress, where plunder and oppression can be practiced with impunity, seems to be the natural order of things. The fairest portions of the world elsewhere have been
40   turned into wildernesses, and the most civilized and prosperous communities

have been impoverished and ruined by anti-slavery fanaticism. The people of the North have not left us in doubt as to their designs and policy. United as a section in the late Presidential election, they have elected as the exponent of their policy, one who has openly declared that all the states of the United States must be made *free states or slave states*. It is true that amongst those who aided 5 in his election, there are various shades of anti-slavery hostility. But if African slavery in the Southern states be the evil their political combination affirms it to be, the requisitions of an inexorable logic must lead them to emancipation. If it is right to preclude or abolish slavery in a territory, why should it be allowed to remain in the states? The one is not at all more unconstitutional than the 10 other, according to the decisions of the Supreme Court of the United States. And when it is considered that the Northern states will soon have the power to make that Court what they please, and that the Constitution never has been any barrier whatever to their exercise of power, what check can there be, in the unrestrained counsels of the North, to emancipation? There is sympathy 15 in association, which carries men along without principle; but when there is principle, and that principle is fortified by long existing prejudices and feelings, association is omnipotent in party influences.

In spite of all disclaimers and professions, there can be but one end by the submission of the South to the rule of a sectional anti-slavery government at 20 Washington; and that end, directly or indirectly, must be—the emancipation of the slaves of the South. The hypocrisy of thirty years—the faithlessness of their whole course from the commencement of our union with them, show that the people of the non-slave-holding North are not and cannot be safe associates of the slave-holding South, under a common government. 25

Not only their fanaticism, but their erroneous views of the principles of free governments, render it doubtful whether, if separated from the South, they can maintain a free government amongst themselves. Numbers, with them, is the great element of free government. A majority is infallible and omnipotent. "The right divine to rule in kings" is only transferred to their majority. The very 30 object of all constitutions, in free popular government, is to restrain the majority. Constitutions, therefore, according to their theory, must be most unrighteous inventions, restricting liberty. None ought to exist; but the body politic ought simply to have a political organization to bring out and enforce the will of the majority. This theory may be harmless in a small community, having identity of 35 interests and pursuits; but over a vast state—still more, over a vast confederacy, having various and conflicting interests and pursuits, it is a remorseless despotism. In resisting it, as applicable to ourselves, we are vindicating the great cause of free government, more important, perhaps, to the world, than the existence of all the United States. Nor in resisting it do we intend to depart from the 40 safe instrumentality the system of government we have established with them requires. In separating from them, we invade no rights—no interest of theirs. We violate no obligation or duty to them.

As separate, independent states in convention we made the Constitu-
5 tion of the United States with them; and as separate independent states, each state acting for itself, we adopted it. South Carolina, acting in her sovereign capacity, now thinks proper to secede from the union. She did not part with her sovereignty in adopting the Constitution. The last thing a state can be presumed to have surrendered is her sovereignty. Her sovereignty is her life.
10 Nothing but a clear express grant can alienate it. Inference is inadmissible. Yet it is not at all surprising that those who have construed away all the limitations of the Constitution should also by construction claim the annihilation of the sovereignty of the states. Having abolished all barriers to their omnipotence, by their faithless constructions in the operations of the General Government,
15 it is most natural that they should endeavor to do the same towards us in the states. The truth is, they have violated the express provisions of the Constitu-tion; it is at an end as a compact. It is morally obligatory only on those who choose to accept its perverted terms. South Carolinas, deeming the compact not only violated in particular features, but virtually abolished by her Northern
20 confederates, withdraws herself as a party from its obligations. The right to do so is denied by her Northern confederates. They desire to establish a sectional despotism, not only omnipotent in Congress, but omnipotent over the states; and as if to manifest the imperious necessity of our secession, they threaten us with the sword, to coerce submission to their rule.

25 Citizens of the slave-holding states of the United States! Circumstances beyond our control have placed us in the van of the great controversy between the Northern and Southern states. We would have preferred that other states should have assumed the position we now occupy. Independent ourselves, we disclaim any design or desire to lead the counsels of the other Southern states.
30 Providence has cast our lot together, by extending over us an identity of pursuits, interests, and institutions. South Carolina desires no destiny separated from yours. To be one of a great slave-holding confederacy, stretching its arms over a territory larger than any power in Europe possesses—with a population four times greater than that of the whole United States when they achieved their in-
35 dependence of the British Empire—with productions which make our existence more important to the world than that of any other people inhabiting it—with common institutions to defend, and common dangers to encounter—we ask your sympathy and confederation.

Whilst constituting a portion of the United States, it has been *your* states-
40 manship which has guided it, in its mighty strides to power and expansion. In

the field, as in the cabinet, *you* have led the way to its renown and grandeur. You have loved the union in whose service your great statesmen have labored, and your great soldiers have fought and conquered—not for the material benefits it conferred, but with the faith of a generous and devoted chivalry. You have long lingered in hope over the shattered remains of a broken Constitution.   5
Compromise after compromise, formed by your concessions, has been trampled underfoot by your Northern confederates.

All fraternity of feeling between the North and the South is lost, or has been converted into hate; and we, of the South, are at last driven together by the stern destiny which controls the existence of nations. Your bitter experi-   10
ence of the faithlessness and rapacity of your Northern confederates may have been necessary to evolve those great principles of free government, upon which the liberties of the world depend, and to prepare you for the grand mission of vindicating and re-establishing them. We rejoice that other nations should be satisfied with their institutions. Contentment is a great element of happiness,   15
with nations as with individuals. We are satisfied with ours. If they prefer a system of industry, in which capital and labor are in perpetual conflict—and chronic starvation keeps down the natural increase of population—and a man is worked out in eight years—and the law ordains that children shall be worked only *ten hours a day*—and the saber and the bayonet are the instruments of   20
order—be it so. It is their affair, not ours.

We prefer, however, our system of industry, by which labor and capital are identified in interest, and capital, therefore, protects labor—by which our population doubles every twenty years—by which starvation is unknown, and abundance crowns the land—by which order is preserved by an unpaid police,   25
and many fertile regions of the world, where the white man cannot labor, are brought into usefulness by the labor of the African, and the whole world is blessed by our productions. All we demand of other peoples is to be left alone, to work out our own high destinies. United together, and we must be the most independent, as we are among the most important, of the nations of the world.   30
United together, and we require no other instrument to conquer peace, than our beneficent productions. United together, and we must be a great, free and prosperous people, whose renown must spread throughout the civilized world, and pass down, we trust, to the remotest ages. We ask you to join us in forming a confederacy of slaveholding states.   35

First Inaugural Address
Abraham Lincoln (1809–1865)
President of the United States (1861–1865)

No American president has faced a national crisis of the magnitude Abraham Lincoln confronted upon assuming office. To most observers of the time, Lincoln seemed ill-prepared for the momentous challenges that lay ahead. Born in a log cabin in Kentucky, he later moved with his family to Indiana and then to Illinois, receiving little formal education along the way. Nonetheless, Lincoln possessed a prodigious intelligence, and while in New Salem, Illinois, he began to study law on his own. In 1834 he was elected to the first of several terms in the Illinois legislature, and he gravitated toward the Whig party and its prominent leader, Henry Clay. Lincoln became a staunch proponent of law and order, an attribute that guided his thinking during the secession crisis of 1860–1861.

In 1846 Lincoln was elected to the U.S. House of Representatives from Springfield, Illinois, and while serving a single term in that body he became a vocal critic of President James K. Polk's decision to lead the United States into war with Mexico. During and after the Mexican War, Lincoln asserted that any people "sufficiently numerous for national independence" possessed the right to "revolutionize" or throw off their existing government and to replace it with a government of their choosing. In later years, Lincoln was careful to insist that the right to revolution was a moral, not a legal, right—a right that could be exercised only on behalf of "a morally justifiable cause." During the secession crisis, Lincoln maintained that secession was not revolution and was thus illegitimate and illegal—a point that he made clear in his first inaugural address. Lincoln aimed his speech at Unionists throughout the South, whom he believed had been tempted to embrace secession by a vocal minority of Southern nationalists. Lincoln believed most Southerners, even those in the states that had claimed to secede, were loyal to the Union and would, with proper encouragement, wrest political power from the rebels. Thus, his address contained a care-

"First Inaugural Address," The Papers of Abraham Lincoln, Library of Congress, Manuscript Division.

ful blend of conciliation and coercion. While the Northern press generally approved of Lincoln's remarks, Southern papers—even those in the Upper South—tended to regard them as a declaration of war.

In compliance with a custom as old as the government itself, I appear before you to address you briefly and to take in your presence the oath prescribed by the Constitution of the United States to be taken by the President "before he enters on the execution of this office."

5   I do not consider it necessary at present for me to discuss those matters of administration about which there is no special anxiety or excitement.

Apprehension seems to exist among the people of the Southern states that by the accession of a Republican administration their property and their peace and personal security are to be endangered. There has never been any reasonable

10   cause for such apprehension. Indeed, the most ample evidence to the contrary has all the while existed and been open to their inspection. It is found in nearly all the published speeches of him who now addresses you. I do but quote from one of those speeches when I declare that

> I have no purpose, directly or indirectly, to interfere with the institu-
15   > tion of slavery in the states where it exists. I believe I have no lawful
> right to do so, and I have no inclination to do so.

Those who nominated and elected me did so with full knowledge that I had made this and many similar declarations and had never recanted them; and more than this, they placed in the platform for my acceptance, and as a law to

20   themselves and to me, the clear and emphatic resolution which I now read:

> Resolved, that the maintenance inviolate of the rights of the states, and
> especially the right of each state to order and control its own domestic
> institutions according to its own judgment exclusively, is essential to
> that balance of power on which the perfection and endurance of our
25   > political fabric depend; and we denounce the lawless invasion by armed
> force of the soil of any state or territory, no matter what pretext, as
> among the gravest of crimes.

I now re-iterate these sentiments, and in doing so I only press upon the public attention the most conclusive evidence of which the case is susceptible

30   that the property, peace, and security of no section are to be in any wise endangered by the now incoming administration. I add, too, that all the protection which, consistently with the Constitution and the laws, can be given will be cheerfully given to all the states when lawfully demanded, for whatever cause—as cheerfully to one section as to another.

There is much controversy about the delivering up of fugitives from service or labor. The clause I now read is as plainly written in the Constitution as any other of its provisions:

> No person held to service or labor in one state, under the laws thereof, escaping into another, shall in consequence of any law or regulation   5
> therein be discharged from such service or labor, but shall be delivered
> up on claim of the party to whom such service or labor may be due.

It is scarcely questioned that this provision was intended by those who made it for the reclaiming of what we call fugitive slaves; and the intention of the law-giver is the law. All members of Congress swear their support to the   10
whole Constitution—to this provision as much as to any other. To the proposition, then, that slaves whose cases come within the terms of this clause "shall be delivered up" their oaths are unanimous. Now, if they would make the effort in good temper, could they not with nearly equal unanimity frame and pass a law by means of which to keep good that unanimous oath?   15

There is some difference of opinion whether this clause should be enforced by national or by state authority, but surely that difference is not a very material one. If the slave is to be surrendered, it can be of but little consequence to him or to others by which authority it is done. And should anyone in any case be content that his oath shall go unkept on a merely unsubstantial controversy as   20
to how it shall be kept?

Again: In any law upon this subject ought not all the safeguards of liberty known in civilized and humane jurisprudence to be introduced, so that a free man be not in any case surrendered as a slave? And might it not be well at the same time to provide by law for the enforcement of that clause in the Consti-   25
tution which guarantees that "the citizens of each state shall be entitled to all privileges and immunities of citizens in the several states"?

I take the official oath today with no mental reservations and with no purpose to construe the Constitution or laws by any hypercritical rules; and while I do not choose now to specify particular acts of Congress as proper to   30
be enforced, I do suggest that it will be much safer for all, both in official and private stations, to conform to and abide by all those acts which stand unrepealed than to violate any of them trusting to find impunity in having them held to be unconstitutional.

It is seventy-two years since the first inauguration of a President under our   35
national Constitution. During that period fifteen different and greatly distinguished citizens have in succession administered the executive branch of the government. They have conducted it through many perils, and generally with great success. Yet, with all this scope of precedent, I now enter upon the same

task for the brief constitutional term of four years under great and peculiar difficulty. A disruption of the federal union, heretofore only menaced, is now formidably attempted.

I hold that in contemplation of universal law and of the Constitution the union of these states is perpetual. Perpetuity is implied, if not expressed, in the fundamental law of all national governments. It is safe to assert that no government proper ever had a provision in its organic law for its own termination. Continue to execute all the express provisions of our national constitution, and the union will endure forever, it being impossible to destroy it except by some action not provided for in the instrument itself.

Again: If the United States be not a government proper, but an association of states in the nature of contract merely, can it, as a contract, be peaceably unmade by less than all the parties who made it? One party to a contract may violate it—break it, so to speak—but does it not require all to lawfully rescind it?

Descending from these general principles, we find the proposition that in legal contemplation the union is perpetual confirmed by the history of the union itself. The union is much older than the Constitution. It was formed, in fact, by the Articles of Association in 1774. It was matured and continued by the Declaration of Independence in 1776. It was further matured, and the faith of all the then thirteen states expressly plighted and engaged that it should be perpetual, by the Articles of Confederation in 1778. And finally, in 1787, one of the declared objects for ordaining and establishing the Constitution was "to form a more perfect union."

But if destruction of the Union by one or by a part only of the states be lawfully possible, the Union is less perfect than before the Constitution, having lost the vital element of perpetuity.

It follows from these views that no state upon its own mere motion can lawfully get out of the Union; that resolves and ordinances to that effect are legally void, and that acts of violence within any state or states against the authority of the United States are insurrectionary or revolutionary, according to circumstances.

I therefore consider that in view of the Constitution and the laws the Union is unbroken, and to the extent of my ability, I shall take care, as the Constitution itself expressly enjoins upon me, that the laws of the Union be faithfully executed in all the states. Doing this I deem to be only a simple duty on my part, and I shall perform it so far as practicable unless my rightful masters, the American people, shall withhold the requisite means or in some authoritative manner direct the contrary. I trust this will not be regarded as a menace, but only as the declared purpose of the union that it will constitutionally defend and maintain itself.

In doing this there needs to be no bloodshed or violence, and there shall be none unless it be forced upon the national authority. The power confided to me will be used to hold, occupy, and possess the property and places belonging to the government and to collect the duties and imposts; but beyond what may be necessary for these objects, there will be no invasion, no using of force against or among the people anywhere. Where hostility to the United States in any interior locality shall be so great and universal as to prevent competent resident citizens from holding the Federal offices, there will be no attempt to force obnoxious strangers among the people for that object. While the strict legal right may exist in the government to enforce the exercise of these offices, the attempt to do so would be so irritating and so nearly impracticable withal that I deem it better to forego for the time the uses of such offices.

The mails, unless repelled, will continue to be furnished in all parts of the union. So far as possible the people everywhere shall have that sense of perfect security which is most favorable to calm thought and reflection. The course here indicated will be followed unless current events and experience shall show a modification or change to be proper, and in every case and exigency my best discretion will be exercised, according to circumstances actually existing and with a view and a hope of a peaceful solution of the national troubles and the restoration of fraternal sympathies and affections.

That there are persons in one section or another who seek to destroy the Union at all events and are glad of any pretext to do it, I will neither affirm nor deny; but if there be such, I need address no word to them. To those, however, who really love the Union may I not speak?

Before entering upon so grave a matter as the destruction of our national fabric, with all its benefits, its memories, and its hopes, would it not be wise to ascertain precisely why we do it? Will you hazard so desperate a step while there is any possibility that any portion of the ills you fly from have no real existence? Will you, while the certain ills you fly to are greater than all the real ones you fly from, will you risk the commission of so fearful a mistake?

All profess to be content in the Union if all constitutional rights can be maintained. Is it true, then, that any right plainly written in the Constitution has been denied? I think not. Happily, the human mind is so constituted that no party can reach to the audacity of doing this. Think, if you can, of a single instance in which a plainly-written provision of the Constitution has ever been denied. If by the mere force of numbers a majority should deprive a minority of any clearly-written constitutional right, it might in a moral point of view justify revolution; certainly would if such right were a vital one. But such is not our case. All the vital rights of minorities and of individuals are so plainly assured to them by affirmations and negations, guaranties and prohibitions, in the Constitution that controversies never arise concerning them. But no organic law can ever be framed with a provision specifically applicable to every question which may occur in practical administration. No foresight can anticipate nor any document of reasonable length contain express provisions for all possible questions. Shall fugitives from labor be surrendered by national or by state authority? The Constitution does not expressly say. May Congress prohibit slavery in the territories? The Constitution does not expressly say. Must Congress protect slavery in the territories? The Constitution does not expressly say.

From questions of this class spring all our constitutional controversies, and we divide upon them into majorities and minorities. If the minority will not acquiesce, the majority must, or the government must cease. There is no other alternative, for continuing the government is acquiescence on one side or the other. If a minority in such case will secede rather than acquiesce, they make a precedent which in turn will divide and ruin them, for a minority of their own will secede from them whenever a majority refuses to be controlled by such minority. For instance, why may not any portion of a new confederacy a year or two hence arbitrarily secede again, precisely as portions of the present Union now claim to secede from it? All who cherish dis-union sentiments are now being educated to the exact temper of doing this.

Is there such perfect identity of interests among the states to compose a new union as to produce harmony only and prevent renewed secession?

Plainly the central idea of secession is the essence of anarchy. A majority held in restraint by constitutional checks and limitations, and always changing easily with deliberate changes of popular opinions and sentiments, is the only true sovereign of a free people. Whoever rejects it does of necessity fly to anarchy or to despotism. Unanimity is impossible. The rule of a minority, as a permanent arrangement, is wholly inadmissible; so that, rejecting the majority principle, anarchy or despotism in some form is all that is left.

I do not forget the position assumed by some that constitutional questions are to be decided by the Supreme Court, nor do I deny that such decisions must be binding in any case upon the parties to a suit as to the object of that suit, while they are also entitled to very high respect and consideration in all parallel cases by all other departments of the government. And while it is obviously possible that such decision may be erroneous in any given case, still the evil effect following it, being limited to that particular case, with the chance that it may be over-ruled and never become a precedent for other cases, can better be borne than could the evils of a different practice. At the same time, the candid citizen must confess that if the policy of the government upon vital questions affecting the whole people is to be irrevocably fixed by decisions of the Supreme Court, the instant they are made in ordinary litigation between parties in personal actions the people will have ceased to be their own rulers, having to that extent practically resigned their government into the hands of that eminent tribunal. Nor is there in this view any assault upon the court or the judges. It is a duty from which they may not shrink to decide cases properly brought before them, and it is no fault of theirs if others seek to turn their decisions to political purposes.

One section of our country believes slavery is right and ought to be extended, while the other believes it is wrong and ought not to be extended. This is the only substantial dispute. The fugitive-slave clause of the Constitution and the law for the suppression of the foreign slave trade are each as well enforced, perhaps, as any law can ever be in a community where the moral sense of the people imperfectly supports the law itself. The great body of the people abide by the dry legal obligation in both cases, and a few break over in each. This, I think, cannot be perfectly cured, and it would be worse in both cases after the separation of the sections than before. The foreign slave trade, now imperfectly suppressed, would be ultimately revived without restriction in one section, while fugitive slaves, now only partially surrendered, would not be surrendered at all by the other.

Physically speaking, we cannot separate. We cannot remove our respective sections from each other nor build an impassable wall between them. A husband and wife may be divorced and go out of the presence and beyond the reach of each other, but the different parts of our country cannot do this. They cannot but remain face to face, and intercourse, either amicable or hostile, must continue between them. Is it possible, then, to make that intercourse more advantageous or more satisfactory after separation than before? Can aliens make treaties easier than friends can make laws? Can treaties be more faithfully enforced between aliens than laws can among friends? Suppose you go to war, you cannot fight always; and when, after much loss on both sides and no gain on either, you cease fighting, the identical old questions, as to terms of intercourse, are again upon you.

This country, with its institutions, belongs to the people who inhabit it. Whenever they shall grow weary of the existing government, they can exercise their constitutional right of amending it or their revolutionary right to dis-member or overthrow it. I cannot be ignorant of the fact that many worthy and patriotic citizens are desirous of having the national Constitution amended. While I make no recommendation of amendments, I fully recognize the rightful authority of the people over the whole subject, to be exercised in either of the modes prescribed in the instrument itself; and I should, under existing circumstances, favor rather than oppose a fair opportunity being afforded the people to act upon it.

I will venture to add that to me the convention mode seems preferable, in that it allows amendments to originate with the people themselves, instead of only permitting them to take or reject propositions originated by others, not especially chosen for the purpose, and which might not be precisely such as they would wish to either accept or refuse. I understand a proposed amendment to the Constitution—which amendment, however, I have not seen—has passed Congress, to the effect that the federal government shall never interfere with the domestic institutions of the states, including that of persons held to service. To avoid misconstruction of what I have said, I depart from my purpose not to speak of particular amendments so far as to say that, holding such a provision to now be implied constitutional law, I have no objection to its being made express and irrevocable.

The Chief Magistrate derives all his authority from the people, and they have conferred none upon him to fix terms for the separation of the states. The people themselves can do this if also they choose, but the Executive as such has nothing to do with it. His duty is to administer the present government as it came to his hands and to transmit it unimpaired by him to his successor.

Why should there not be a patient confidence in the ultimate justice of the people? Is there any better or equal hope in the world? In our present differences, is either party without faith of being in the right? If the Almighty Ruler of Nations, with His eternal truth and justice, be on your side of the North, or on yours of the South, that truth and that justice will surely prevail by the judgment of this great tribunal of the American people.

By the frame of the government under which we live this same people have wisely given their public servants but little power for mischief, and have with equal wisdom provided for the return of that little to their own hands at very short intervals. While the people retain their virtue and vigilance no administration by any extreme of wickedness or folly can very seriously injure the government in the short space of four years.

My countrymen, one and all, think calmly and well upon this whole subject. Nothing valuable can be lost by taking time. If there be an object to hurry any of you in hot haste to a step which you would never take deliberately, that object will be frustrated by taking time; but no good object can be frustrated by it. Such of you as are now dissatisfied still have the old Constitution unimpaired and, on the sensitive point, the laws of your own framing under it; while the new administration will have no immediate power, if it would, to change either. If it were admitted that you who are dissatisfied hold the right side in the dispute, there still is no single good reason for precipitate action. Intelligence, patriotism, Christianity, and a firm reliance on Him who has never yet forsaken this favored land are still competent to adjust in the best way all our present difficulty.

In your hands, my dissatisfied fellow-countrymen, and not in mine, is the momentous issue of civil war. The government will not assail you. You can have no conflict without being yourselves the aggressors. You have no oath registered in heaven to destroy the government, while I shall have the most solemn one to "preserve, protect, and defend it."

I am loath to close. We are not enemies, but friends. We must not be enemies. Though passion may have strained it must not break our bonds of affection. The mystic chords of memory, stretching from every battlefield and patriot grave to every living heart and hearthstone all over this broad land, will yet swell the chorus of the Union, when again touched, as surely they will be, by the better angels of our nature.

CORNERSTONE SPEECH
ALEXANDER HAMILTON STEPHENS (1812–1883)
VICE-PRESIDENT OF THE CONFEDERACY (1861–1865)

Alexander Hamilton Stephens was born and raised on a cotton farm near Crawfordville, Georgia. His father, whom he adored, and his stepmother, whom he did not, died when Stephens was fourteen, and he was sent to live with his uncle. In 1832, after imbibing a classical curriculum that included Homer, Virgil, Cicero, and the Greek Testament, Stephens graduated first in his class from Franklin College in Athens, Georgia. After a brief stint as a teacher, he turned to the study of law and established a successful legal practice. Stephens honed his impressive oratorical skills in the courtroom, and in 1836 he won the first of several terms in the Georgia legislature. In 1843, running as a Whig, he won a seat in Congress, where he went on to befriend a little-known colleague from Illinois named Abraham Lincoln. By the early 1850s, Congressman Stephens had drifted into the Democratic Party, leaving behind a Whig organization that, in his view, had become a tool of the Free Soil movement. He began to espouse increasingly radical Southern views on slavery and the question of its extension. Although Stephens opposed secession, he defended its legitimacy and ultimately sided with his home state when it claimed to leave the Union in January 1861. Shortly after having been selected Vice-President of the Confederate States of America, he delivered the following address in Savannah, Georgia, to a frenzied crowd of Southern partisans. With its unambiguous assertion that the "cornerstone" of the Confederacy rested on white supremacy and slavery, Stephens's speech undermined the efforts of Jefferson Davis and other Southern radicals who were attempting to justify the rebellion on the basis of states' rights.

SAVANNAH, 21 MARCH 1861

When perfect quiet is restored, I shall proceed. I cannot speak so long as there is any noise or confusion. I shall take my time—I feel quite prepared to spend

Henry Cleveland, *Alexander H. Stephens in Public and Private with Letters and Speeches Before, During, and Since the War* (Philadelphia: National Publishing Company, 1866), 718–29.

the night with you if necessary. I very much regret that everyone who desires cannot hear what I have to say. Not that I have any display to make, or anything very entertaining to present, but such views as I have to give, I wish all, not only in this city, but in this state, and throughout our Confederate Republic,
5   could hear who have a desire to hear them.

I was remarking that we are passing through one of the greatest revolutions in the annals of the world. Seven states have within the last three months thrown off an old government and formed a new. This revolution has been signally marked, up to this time, by the fact of its having been accomplished
10   without the loss of a single drop of blood.

This new constitution, or form of government, constitutes the subject to which your attention will be partly invited. In reference to it, I make this first general remark: it amply secures all our ancient rights, franchises, and liberties. All the great principles of Magna Carta are retained in it. No citizen is deprived
15   of life, liberty, or property, but by the judgment of his peers under the laws of the land. The great principle of religious liberty, which was the honor and pride of the old constitution, is still maintained and secured. All the essentials of the old constitution, which have endeared it to the hearts of the American people, have been preserved and perpetuated. Some changes have been made. Some
20   of these I should have preferred not to have seen made; but other important changes do meet my cordial approbation. They form great improvements upon the old constitution. So, taking the whole new constitution, I have no hesitancy in giving it as my judgment that it is decidedly better than the old.

Allow me briefly to allude to some of these improvements. The question of
25   building up class interests, or fostering one branch of industry to the prejudice of another under the exercise of the revenue power, which gave us so much trouble under the old constitution, is put at rest forever under the new. We allow the imposition of no duty with a view of giving advantage to one class of persons, in any trade or business, over those of another. All, under our system, stand
30   upon the same broad principles of perfect equality. Honest labor and enterprise are left free and unrestricted in whatever pursuit they may be engaged. This old thorn of the tariff, which was the cause of so much irritation in the old body politic, is removed forever from the new.

Again, the subject of internal improvements, under the power of Congress
35   to regulate commerce, is put at rest under our system. The power, claimed by construction under the old constitution, was at least a doubtful one; it rested solely upon construction. We of the South, generally apart from considerations of constitutional principles, opposed its exercise upon grounds of its inexpediency and injustice. Notwithstanding this opposition, millions of money, from
40   the common treasury had been drawn for such purposes. Our opposition sprang

from no hostility to commerce, or to all necessary aids for facilitating it. With us it was simply a question upon whom the burden should fall. In Georgia, for instance, we have done as much for the cause of internal improvements as any other portion of the country, according to population and means. We have stretched out lines of railroads from the seaboard to the mountains; dug   5 down the hills, and filled up the valleys at a cost of not less than $25,000,000. All this was done to open an outlet for our products of the interior, and those to the west of us, to reach the marts of the world. No state was in greater need of such facilities than Georgia, but we did not ask that these works should be made by appropriations out of the common treasury. The cost of the grading,   10 the super-structure, and the equipment of our roads was borne by those who had entered into the enterprise. Nay, more—not only the cost of the iron, no small item in the aggregate cost, was borne in the same way—but we were compelled to pay into the common treasury several millions of dollars for the privilege of importing the iron, after the price was paid for it abroad. What   15 justice was there in taking this money, which our people paid into the common treasury on the importation of our iron, and applying it to the improvement of rivers and harbors elsewhere?

The true principle is to subject the commerce of every locality, to whatever burdens may be necessary to facilitate it. If Charleston harbor needs improve-   20 ment, let the commerce of Charleston bear the burden. If the mouth of the Savannah river has to be cleared out, let the sea-going navigation which is benefited by it, bear the burden. So with the mouths of the Alabama and Mississippi river. Just as the products of the interior, our cotton, wheat, corn, and other articles, have to bear the necessary rates of freight over our railroads to   25 reach the seas. This is again the broad principle of perfect equality and justice, and it is especially set forth and established in our new constitution.

Another feature to which I will allude is that the new constitution provides that cabinet ministers and heads of departments may have the privilege of seats upon the floor of the Senate and House of Representatives and may have the   30 right to participate in the debates and discussions upon the various subjects of administration. I should have preferred that this provision should have gone further, and required the President to select his constitutional advisers from the Senate and House of Representatives. That would have conformed entirely to the practice in the British Parliament, which, in my judgment, is one of the   35 wisest provisions in the British constitution. It is the only feature that saves that government. It is that which gives it stability in its facility to change its administration. Ours, as it is, is a great approximation to the right principle.

Under the old constitution, a Secretary of the Treasury for instance, had no opportunity, save by his annual reports, of presenting any scheme or plan   40

of finance or other matter. He had no opportunity of explaining, expounding, enforcing, or defending his views of policy; his only resort was through the medium of an organ. In the British Parliament, the premier brings in his budget and stands before the nation responsible for its every item. If it
5   is indefensible, he falls before the attacks upon it, as he ought to. This will now be the case to a limited extent under our system. In the new constitution, provision has been made by which our heads of departments can speak for themselves and the administration, in behalf of its entire policy, without resorting to the indirect and highly objectionable medium of a newspaper.
10   It is to be greatly hoped that under our system we shall never have what is known as a government organ.

Another change in the constitution relates to the length of the tenure of the presidential office. In the new constitution it is six years instead of four, and the President rendered ineligible for a re-election. This is certainly a decid-
15   edly conservative change. It will remove from the incumbent all temptation to use his office or exert the powers confided to him for any objects of personal ambition. The only incentive to that higher ambition which should move and actuate one holding such high trusts in his hands, will be the good of the people, the advancement, prosperity, happiness, safety, honor, and true glory
20   of the confederacy.

But not to be tedious in enumerating the numerous changes for the better, allow me to allude to one other—though last, not least. The new constitution has put at rest, forever, all the agitating questions relating to our peculiar institution—African slavery as it exists amongst us; the proper status of the negro in our
25   form of civilization. This was the immediate cause of the late rupture and present revolution. Jefferson in his forecast, had anticipated this, as the "rock upon which the old Union would split." He was right. What was conjecture with him is now a realized fact. But whether he fully comprehended the great truth upon which that rock stood and stands, may be doubted. The prevailing ideas entertained by
30   him and most of the leading statesmen at the time of the formation of the old constitution, were that the enslavement of the African was in violation of the laws of nature; that it was wrong in principle, socially, morally, and politically. It was an evil they knew not well how to deal with, but the general opinion of the men of that day was that, somehow or other in the order of Providence, the
35   institution would be evanescent and pass away. This idea, though not incorporated in the constitution, was the prevailing idea at that time. The constitution, it is true, secured every essential guarantee to the institution while it should last, and hence no argument can be justly urged against the constitutional guarantees thus secured, because of the common sentiment of the day. Those ideas, however, were
40   fundamentally wrong. They rested upon the assumption of the equality of races.

This was an error. It was a sandy foundation, and the government built upon it fell when the "storm came and the wind blew."

Our new government is founded upon exactly the opposite idea; its foundations are laid, its corner-stone rests upon the great truth that the negro is not equal to the white man; that slavery—subordination to the superior race—is his natural and normal condition.

This, our new government, is the first, in the history of the world, based upon this great physical, philosophical, and moral truth. This truth has been slow in the process of its development, like all other truths in the various departments of science. It has been so even amongst us. Many who hear me, perhaps, can recollect well that this truth was not generally admitted, even within their day. The errors of the past generation still clung to many as late as twenty years ago. Those at the North who still cling to these errors, with a zeal above knowledge, we justly denominate fanatics.

All fanaticism springs from an aberration of the mind—from a defect in reasoning. It is a species of insanity. One of the most striking characteristics of insanity, in many instances, is forming correct conclusions from fancied or erroneous premises; so with the anti-slavery fanatics. Their conclusions are right if their premises were. They assume that the negro is equal, and hence conclude that he is entitled to equal privileges and rights with the white man. If their premises were correct, their conclusions would be logical and just—but their premise being wrong, their whole argument fails. I recollect once of having heard a gentleman from one of the northern states, of great power and ability, announce in the House of Representatives, with imposing effect, that we of the South would be compelled, ultimately, to yield upon this subject of slavery, that it was as impossible to war successfully against a principle in politics as it was in physics or mechanics. That the principle would ultimately prevail. That we, in maintaining slavery as it exists with us, were warring against a principle, a principle founded in nature, the principle of the equality of men. The reply I made to him was, that upon his own grounds, we should, ultimately, succeed and that he and his associates in this crusade against our institutions would ultimately fail. The truth announced that it was as impossible to war successfully against a principle in politics as it was in physics and mechanics, I admitted; but told him that it was he, and those acting with him, who were warring against a principle. They were attempting to make things equal which the Creator had made unequal.

In the conflict thus far, success has been on our side, complete throughout the length and breadth of the Confederate States. It is upon this, as I have stated, our social fabric is firmly planted; and I cannot permit myself to doubt the ultimate success of a full recognition of this principle throughout the civilized and enlightened world.

As I have stated, the truth of this principle may be slow in development, as all truths are and ever have been, in the various branches of science. It was so with the principles announced by Galileo—it was so with Adam Smith and his principles of political economy. It was so with Harvey, and his theory of
5   the circulation of the blood. It is stated that not a single one of the medical profession living at the time of the announcement of the truths made by him admitted them. Now they are universally acknowledged. May we not, therefore, look with confidence to the ultimate universal acknowledgment of the truths upon which our system rests?
10   It is the first government ever instituted upon the principles in strict conformity to nature, and the ordination of Providence, in furnishing the materials of human society. Many governments have been founded upon the principle of the sub-ordination and serfdom of certain classes of the same race; such were and are in violation of the laws of nature. Our system commits no such viola-
15   tion of nature's laws. With us, all of the white race, however high or low, rich or poor, are equal in the eye of the law. Not so with the negro. Subordination is his place. He, by nature, or by the curse against Canaan, is fitted for that condition which he occupies in our system. The architect, in the construction of buildings, lays the foundation with the proper material—the granite; then
20   comes the brick or the marble. The substratum of our society is made of the material fitted by nature for it, and by experience we know that it is best, not only for the superior, but for the inferior race, that it should be so.

It is, indeed, in conformity with the ordinance of the Creator. It is not for us to inquire into the wisdom of His ordinances, or to question them. For His
25   own purposes, He has made one race to differ from another, as He has made "one star to differ from another star in glory." The great objects of humanity are best attained when there is conformity to His laws and decrees, in the formation of governments as well as in all things else. Our confederacy is founded upon principles in strict conformity with these laws. This stone which was rejected by
30   the first builders "is become the chief of the corner"—the real "corner-stone"—in our new edifice. I have been asked, what of the future? It has been apprehended by some that we would have arrayed against us the civilized world. I care not who or how many they may be against us, when we stand upon the eternal principles of truth, if we are true to ourselves and the principles for which we
35   contend, we are obliged to, and must triumph.

Thousands of people who begin to understand these truths are not yet completely out of the shell; they do not see them in their length and breadth. We hear much of the civilization and Christianization of the barbarous tribes of Africa. In my judgment, those ends will never be attained, but by first
40   teaching them the lesson taught to Adam, that "in the sweat of his brow

he should eat his bread," and teaching them to work, and feed, and clothe themselves.

But to pass on: Some have propounded the inquiry whether it is practicable for us to go on with the confederacy without further accessions? Have we the means and ability to maintain nationality among the powers of the earth? On this point I would barely say, that as anxiously as we all have been, and are, for the border states, with institutions similar to ours, to join us, still we are abundantly able to maintain our position, even if they should ultimately make up their minds not to cast their destiny with us. That they ultimately will join us—be compelled to do it—is my confident belief; but we can get on very well without them, even if they should not.

We have all the essential elements of a high national career. The idea has been given out at the North, and even in the border states, that we are too small and too weak to maintain a separate nationality. This is a great mistake. In extent of territory we embrace five hundred and sixty-four thousand square miles and upward. This is upward of two hundred thousand square miles more than was included within the limits of the original thirteen states. It is an area of country more than double the territory of France or the Austrian empire. France, in round numbers, has but two hundred and twelve thousand square miles. Austria, in round numbers, has two hundred and forty-eight thousand square miles. Ours is greater than both combined. It is greater than all France, Spain, Portugal, and Great Britain, including England, Ireland, and Scotland, together. In population we have upward of five millions, according to the census of 1860; this includes white and black. The entire population, including white and black, of the original thirteen states, was less than four millions in 1790, and still less in '76, when the independence of our fathers was achieved. If they, with a less population, dared maintain their independence against the greatest power on earth, shall we have any apprehension of maintaining ours now?

In point of material wealth and resources, we are greatly in advance of them. The taxable property of the Confederate States cannot be less than twenty-two hundred millions of dollars! This, I think I venture but little in saying, may be considered as five times more than the colonies possessed at the time they achieved their independence. Georgia, alone, possessed last year, according to the report of our comptroller-general, six hundred and seventy-two millions of taxable property. The debts of the seven Confederate States sum up in the aggregate less than eighteen millions, while the existing debts of the other of the late United States sum up in the aggregate the enormous amount of one hundred and seventy-four millions of dollars. This is without taking into account the heavy city debts, corporation debts, and railroad debts which press, and will continue to press, as a heavy incubus upon the resources of those states. These debts, added to others, make a sum total not much under five hundred millions of dollars. With such an area of territory as we have, with such an amount of population, with a climate and soil unsurpassed by any on the face of the earth, with such resources already at our command, with productions which control the commerce of the world—who can entertain any apprehensions as to our ability to succeed, whether others join us or not?

It is true, I believe I state but the common sentiment, when I declare my earnest desire that the border states should join us. The differences of opinion that existed among us anterior to secession related more to the policy in securing that result by co-operation than from any difference upon the ultimate security we all looked to in common.

These differences of opinion were more in reference to policy than principle, and as Mr. Jefferson said in his inaugural, in 1801, after the heated contest preceding his election, that there might be differences of opinion without dif- ferences on principle, and that all, to some extent, had been Federalists and all Republicans; so it may now be said of us, that whatever differences of opinion as to the best policy in having a co-operation with our border sister slave states, if the worst came to the worst, that as we were all co-operationists, we are now all for independence, whether they come or not.

In this connection I take this occasion to state that I was not without grave and serious apprehensions that if the worst came to the worst, and cutting loose from the old government should be the only remedy for our safety and security, it would be attended with much more serious ills than it has been as yet. Thus far we have seen none of those incidents which usually attend revolutions. No such material as such convulsions usually throw up has been seen. Wisdom, prudence, and patriotism have marked every step of our progress thus far. This augurs well for the future, and it is a matter of sincere gratification to me that I am enabled to make the declaration. Of the men I met in the Congress at Mont- gomery, I may be pardoned for saying this, an abler, wiser, a more conservative, deliberate, determined, resolute, and patriotic body of men, I never met in my life. Their works speak for them; the provisional government speaks for them; the constitution of the permanent government will be a lasting monument of their worth, merit, and statesmanship.

But to return to the question of the future. What is to be the result of this revolution?

Will everything, commenced so well, continue as it has begun? In reply to this anxious inquiry, I can only say it all depends upon ourselves. A young man starting out in life on his majority with health, talent, and ability, under a favoring Providence, may be said to be the architect of his own fortunes. His destinies are in his own hands. He may make for himself a name, of honor or dishonor, according to his own acts. If he plants himself upon truth, integrity, honor, and uprightness, with industry, patience, and energy he cannot fail of success. So it is with us. We are a young republic, just entering upon the arena of nations; we will be the architects of our own fortunes. Our destiny, under Providence, is in our own hands. With wisdom, prudence, and statesmanship on the part of our public men, and intelligence, virtue, and patriotism on the part of the people, success, to the full measures of our most sanguine hopes, may be looked for. But if unwise counsels prevail, if we become divided, if schisms arise, if dissentions spring up, if factions are engendered, if party spirit, nourished by unholy personal ambition shall rear its hydra head, I have no good to prophesy for you. Without intelligence, virtue, integrity, and patriotism on the part of the people, no republic or representative government can be durable or stable.

We have intelligence, and virtue, and patriotism. All that is required is to cultivate and perpetuate these. Intelligence will not do without virtue. France was a nation of philosophers. These philosophers become Jacobins. They lacked that virtue, that devotion to moral principle, and that patriotism which is essential to good government. Organized upon principles of perfect justice and right-seeking amity and friendship with all other powers—I see no obstacle in the way of our upward and onward progress. Our growth, by accessions from other states, will depend greatly upon whether we present to the world, as I trust we shall, a better government than that to which neighboring states belong. If we do this, North Carolina, Tennessee, and Arkansas cannot hesitate long; neither can Virginia, Kentucky, and Missouri. They will necessarily gravitate to us by an imperious law. We made ample provision in our constitution for the admission of other states; it is more guarded, and wisely so, I think, than the old constitution on the same subject, but not too guarded to receive them as fast as it may be proper. Looking to the distant future, and, perhaps, not very far distant either, it is not beyond the range of possibility, and even probability, that all the great states of the north-west will gravitate this way, as well as Tennessee, Kentucky, Missouri, Arkansas, etc. Should they do so, our doors are wide enough to receive them, but not until they are ready to assimilate with us in principle.

The process of disintegration in the old Union may be expected to go on with almost absolute certainty if we pursue the right course. We are now the nucleus of a growing power which, if we are true to ourselves, our destiny, and high mission, will become the controlling power on this continent. To what extent accessions will go on in the process of time, or where it will end, the future will determine. So far as it concerns states of the old Union, this process will be upon no such principles of reconstruction as now spoken of, but upon reorganization and new assimilation. Such are some of the glimpses of the future as I catch them.

But at first we must necessarily meet with the inconveniences and difficulties and embarrassments incident to all changes of government. These will be felt in our postal affairs and changes in the channel of trade. These inconveniences, it is to be hoped, will be but temporary, and must be borne with patience and
5   forbearance.

As to whether we shall have war with our late confederates, or whether all matters of differences between us shall be amicably settled, I can only say that the prospect for a peaceful adjustment is better, so far as I am informed, than it has been. The prospect of war is, at least, not so threatening as it has been. The
10   idea of coercion, shadowed forth in President Lincoln's inaugural, seems not to be followed up thus far so vigorously as was expected. Fort Sumter, it is believed, will soon be evacuated. What course will be pursued toward Fort Pickens and the other forts on the Gulf is not so well understood. It is to be greatly desired that all of them should be surrendered. Our object is peace, not only with the
15   North, but with the world. All matters relating to the public property, public liabilities of the Union when we were members of it, we are ready and willing to adjust and settle upon the principles of right, equity, and good faith. War can be of no more benefit to the North than to us. Whether the intention of evacuating Fort Sumter is to be received as an evidence of a desire for a peace-
20   ful solution of our difficulties with the United States, or the result of necessity, I will not undertake to say. I would feign hope the former. Rumors are afloat, however, that it is the result of necessity. All I can say to you, therefore, on that point is, keep your armor bright and your powder dry.

The surest way to secure peace is to show your ability to maintain your
25   rights. The principles and position of the present administration of the United States—the Republican Party—present some puzzling questions. While it is a fixed principle with them never to allow the increase of a foot of slave territory, they seem to be equally determined not to part with an inch "of the accursed soil." Notwithstanding their clamor against the institution, they seemed to be
30   equally opposed to getting more, or letting go what they have got. They were ready to fight on the accession of Texas, and are equally ready to fight now on her secession. Why is this? How can this strange paradox be accounted for? There seems to be but one rational solution—and that is, notwithstanding their professions of humanity, they are disinclined to give up the benefits they derive
35   from slave labor. Their philanthropy yields to their interest. The idea of enforcing the laws, has but one object, and that is a collection of the taxes, raised by slave labor to swell the fund necessary to meet their heavy appropriations. The spoils is what they are after—though they come from the labor of the slave....

Our fathers had guarded the assessment of taxes by insisting that repre-
40   sentation and taxation should go together. This was inherited from the mother

country, England. It was one of the principles upon which the Revolution had been fought. Our fathers also provided in the old constitution that all appropriation bills should originate in the representative branch of Congress, but our new constitution went a step further, and guarded not only the pockets of the people, but also the public money after it was taken from their pockets.... 5

That as the admission of states by Congress under the constitution was an act of legislation, and in the nature of a contract or compact between the states admitted and the others admitting, why should not this contract or compact be regarded as of like character with all other civil contracts—liable to be rescinded by mutual agreement of both parties? The seceding states have rescinded it on 10 their part, they have resumed their sovereignty. Why cannot the whole question be settled, if the north desire peace, simply by the Congress, in both branches, with the concurrence of the President, giving their consent to the separation, and a recognition of our independence?...

If...we are true to ourselves, true to our cause, true to our destiny, true to 15 our high mission, in presenting to the world the highest type of civilization ever exhibited by man—there will be found in our lexicon no such word as fail.

LETTER TO HIS WIFE
MAJOR SULLIVAN BALLOU (1829–1861)
2ND REGIMENT, RHODE ISLAND VOLUNTEERS, TO
SARAH HUNT SHUMWAY BALLOU (1836–1917)

Both Northern and Southern Civil War soldiers knew what they fought for. They said so. With remarkable eloquence they articulated the patriotic commitments that led them from their homes to the battlefield. This was especially true of the volunteer soldiers, those who fought for reasons of their own. Although we know little about his background, we do know that Sullivan Ballou was a Major in the Second Rhode Island Volunteers, and that he wrote this letter to his wife, Sarah, one week before the battle of Bull Run. We also know that he died fighting in that battle. The letter stands as a remarkable statement of the sentiments animating the Northern soldier and of his ability to give voice to the conflicting passions of his heart.

14 JULY 1861

My very dear wife:

The indications are very strong that we shall move in a few days, perhaps tomorrow. Lest I should not be able to write you again, I feel impelled to write a few lines that may fall under your eye when I shall be no more.

Our movement may be one of a few days' duration and full of pleasure—and 5 it may be one of severe conflict and death to me. Not my will, but thine, O God, be done. If it is necessary that I should fall on the battlefield for my country, I am ready. I have no misgivings about, or lack of confidence in, the cause in which I am engaged, and my courage does not halt or falter. I know how strongly American civilization now leans upon the triumph of the government, and how 10 great a debt we owe to those who went before us through the blood and suffering of the Revolution. And I am willing, perfectly willing, to lay down all my joys in this life to help maintain this government, and to pay that debt.

But, my dear wife, when I know that with my own joys I lay down nearly all of yours, and replace them in this life with cares and sorrows—when, after 15 having eaten for long years the bitter fruit of orphanage myself, I must offer it as their only sustenance to my dear little children, is it weak or dishonorable, while the banner of my purpose floats calmly and proudly in the breeze, that my

---

H. S. Burrage, ed., *Brown University in the Civil War* (Providence, RI: Providence Press Company,

495

unbounded love for you, my darling wife and children, should struggle in fierce, though useless, contest with my love of country?

I cannot describe to you my feelings on this calm summer night, when two thousand men are sleeping around me, many of them enjoying the last, perhaps, 5 before that of death—and I, suspicious that Death is creeping behind me with his fatal dart, am communing with God, my country, and thee.

I have sought most closely and diligently, and often in my breast, for a wrong motive in thus hazarding the happiness of those I loved, and I could not find one. A pure love of my country and of the principles I have often advocated before 10 the people and "the name of honor that I love more than I fear death" have called upon me, and I have obeyed.

Sarah, my love for you is deathless. It seems to bind me to you with mighty cables that nothing but Omnipotence can break; and yet my love of country comes over me like a strong wind and bears me irresistibly on with all these chains 15 to the battlefield. The memories of the blissful moments I have spent with you come creeping over me, and I feel most gratified to God and to you that I have enjoyed them so long. And hard it is for me to give them up and burn to ashes the hopes of future years, when God willing, we might still have lived and loved together, and seen our sons grow up to honorable manhood around us.

20 I have, I know, but few claims upon Divine Providence, but something whispers to me, perhaps it is the wafted prayer of my little Edgar, that I shall return to my loved ones unharmed. If I do not, my dear Sarah, never forget how much I love you, and when my last breath escapes me on the battlefield, it will whisper your name.

Forgive my many faults, and the many pains I have caused you. How thought- 25 less and foolish I have oftentimes been! How gladly would I wash out with my tears every little spot upon your happiness, and struggle with all the misfortune of this world to shield you and my children from harm. But I cannot. I must watch you from the spirit land and hover near you, while you buffet the storms with your precious little freight, and wait with sad patience till we meet to part no more.

30 But, O Sarah! If the dead can come back to this earth and flit unseen around those they loved, I shall always be near you—in the garish day and in the darkest night—amidst your happiest scenes and gloomiest hours—always, always; and if there be a soft breeze upon your cheek, it shall be my breath; or the cool air fans your throbbing temples, it shall be my spirit passing by. Sarah, do not mourn me 35 dead; think I am gone and wait for me, for we shall meet again.

As for my little boys, they will grow as I have done, and never know a father's love and care. Little Willie is too young to remember me long, and my blue-eyed Edgar will keep my frolics with him among the dimmest memories of his child- hood. Sarah, I have unlimited confidence in your maternal care and your develop- 40 ment of their characters. Tell my two mothers I call God's blessing upon them. O Sarah, I wait for you there! Come to me, and lead thither my children.

MEDITATION ON THE DIVINE WILL
ABRAHAM LINCOLN (1809–1865)
PRESIDENT OF THE UNITED STATES (1861–1865)

As Lincoln's views on the nature of the war shifted in 1862, his outlook regarding God's role in the struggle seemed to evolve as well. By September of that year, the North and South were locked in a bloody stalemate that showed no sign of abating. A sense of gloom pervaded Washington, DC, and Lincoln mused about the significance of the seemingly interminable nature of the war in a memorandum which, according to his secretaries, "was not written to be seen of men." The so-called Meditation on the Divine Will *reveals a man wrestling with the nature of God—a God who has, for His own inscrutable reasons, allowed the war to continue indefinitely. Lincoln shows signs of jettisoning his earlier conception of God (a remote entity that governs human affairs only through natural laws) in favor of an active Deity who intervenes directly in human affairs, guiding the destinies of men and nations.*

SEPTEMBER [30?], 1862

The will of God prevails. In great contests each party claims to act in accordance with the will of God. Both may be, and one must be, wrong. God cannot be for and against the same thing at the same time. In the present civil war it is quite possible that God's purpose is something different from the purpose of either party; and yet the human instrumentalities, working 5 just as they do, are of the best adaptation to effect his purpose. I am almost ready to say that this is probably true; that God wills this contest, and wills that it shall not end yet. By his mere great power on the minds of the now contestants, he could have either saved or destroyed the Union without a human contest. Yet the contest began. And, having begun, he could give the 10 final victory to either side any day. Yet the contest proceeds.

Gettysburg Address
Abraham Lincoln (1809–1865)
President of the United States (1861–1865)

19 November 1863

Four score and seven years ago our fathers brought forth on this continent a new nation, conceived in liberty, and dedicated to the proposition that all men are created equal.

Now we are engaged in a great civil war, testing whether that nation, or any nation so conceived and so dedicated, can long endure. We are met on a great battle-field of that war. We have come to dedicate a portion of that field as a final resting place for those who here gave their lives that that nation might live. It is altogether fitting and proper that we should do this. 5

But, in a larger sense, we cannot dedicate—we cannot consecrate—we cannot hallow—this ground. The brave men, living and dead, who struggled here have consecrated it, far above our poor power to add or detract. The world will little note nor long remember what we say here, but it can never forget what they did here. It is for us the living, rather, to be dedicated here to the unfinished work which they who fought here have thus far so nobly advanced. It is rather for us to be here dedicated to the great task remaining before us—that from these honored dead we take increased devotion to that cause for which they gave the last full measure of devotion—that we here highly resolve that these dead shall not have died in vain—that this nation, under God, shall have a new birth of freedom—and that government of the people, by the people, for the people, shall not perish from the earth. 10 15 20

"Gettysburg Address," Bliss Copy, The Papers of Abraham Lincoln, Library of Congress, Manuscript Division.

Second Inaugural Address
Abraham Lincoln (1809–1865)
President of the United States (1861–1865)

4 March 1865

At this second appearing to take the oath of the presidential office there is less occasion for an extended address than there was at the first. Then a statement, somewhat in detail, of a course to be pursued seemed fitting and proper. Now, at the expiration of four years, during which public declarations have been constantly called forth on every point and phase of the great contest which 5 still absorbs the attention, and engrosses the energies of the nation, little that is new could be presented. The progress of our arms, upon which all else chiefly depends, is as well known to the public as to myself; and it is, I trust, reasonably satisfactory and encouraging to all. With high hope for the future, no prediction in regard to it is ventured. 10

On the occasion corresponding to this four years ago, all thoughts were anxiously directed to an impending civil war. All dreaded it; all sought to avert it. While the inaugural address was being delivered from this place, devoted altogether to saving the Union without war, insurgent agents were in the city seeking to destroy it without war—seeking to dissolve the Union, and divide 15 effects, by negotiation. Both parties deprecated war; but one of them would make war rather than let the nation survive; and the other would accept war rather than let it perish. And the war came.

One eighth of the whole population were colored slaves, not distributed generally over the Union, but localized in the southern half of it. These slaves 20 constituted a peculiar and powerful interest. All knew that this interest was, somehow, the cause of the war. To strengthen, perpetuate, and extend this interest was the object for which the insurgents would rend the Union, even by war; while the government claimed no right to do more than to restrict the territorial enlargement of it. Neither party expected for the war the magnitude 25 or the duration which it has already attained. Neither anticipated that the cause

"Second Inaugural Address," The Papers of Abraham Lincoln, Library of Congress, Manuscript Division.

of the conflict might cease with, or even before, the conflict itself should cease. Each looked for an easier triumph, and a result less fundamental and astounding. Both read the same Bible, and pray to the same God; and each invokes His aid against the other. It may seem strange that any men should dare to ask a just God's assistance in wringing their bread from the sweat of other men's faces; but let us judge not that we be not judged. The prayers of both could not be answered; that of neither has been answered fully. The Almighty has His own purposes. "Woe unto the world because of offences! For it must needs be that offences come; but woe to that man by whom the offence comes!"[1] If we shall suppose that American slavery is one of those offences which, in the providence of God, must needs come, but which, having continued through His appointed time, He now wills to remove, and that He gives to both North and South this terrible war as the woe due to those by whom the offence came, shall we discern therein any departure from those divine attributes which the believers in a living God always ascribe to Him? Fondly do we hope—fervently do we pray—that this mighty scourge of war may speedily pass away. Yet, if God wills that it continue until all the wealth piled by the bond-man's two hundred and fifty years of unrequited toil shall be sunk, and until every drop of blood drawn with the lash shall be paid by another drawn with the sword, as was said three thousand years ago, so still it must be said "the judgments of the Lord, are true and righteous altogether."[2]

With malice toward none; with charity for all; with firmness in the right, as God gives us to see the right, let us strive on to finish the work we are in; to bind up the nation's wounds; to care for him who shall have borne the battle, and for his widow, and his orphan—to do all which may achieve and cherish a just, and a lasting peace, among ourselves, and with all nations.

---

[1]Matthew 18:7
[2]Psalm 19:9

VI
THE GILDED AGE

After the Civil War, Americans seemed to have trouble deciding whether their nation's dramatically increasing wealth and power amounted to a Gilded Age or a Golden Age. In 1873, novelists Mark Twain (1835–1910) and Charles Dudley Warner (1829–1900) published their best-selling satire, *The Gilded Age*, stamping late nineteenth-century America with an indelible identity. Their epithet "gilded" suggested that there was something cheap, vulgar, or even fraudulent about American civilization during Reconstruction. Calling their novel "a tale of today," the authors took deadly aim at the pretense of comfortable middle-class morality that to their minds masked political corruption, feverish land speculation, and raw greed. In the next decade, the United States looked no better to Henry Adams (1838–1918), the grandson and great-grandson of two American presidents. In his 1880 novel, *Democracy*, Adams's main character, exasperated by political corruption in Washington, demanded to know if "a respectable government [is] impossible in a democracy." "Half of our wise men declare that the world is going straight to perdition; the other half that it is fast becoming perfect," she continued. "Both cannot be right. There is only one thing in life...that I must and will have before I die. I must know whether America is right or wrong."

While Twain and Adams had no trouble seeing what was wrong with the United States after the Civil War, others saw incontrovertible evidence that the nation was very right. America stood, in fact, on the brink of a millennium of peace and prosperity. Congregationalist minister Henry Ward Beecher (1813–1887) (famous for shipping "Beecher's Bibles" to the Kansas Territory back in 1856) told his Brooklyn church in 1870 that he could "look forward into that 'golden' future, literally, which is opening before us, and marvel whether the most poetic dreams of growing wealth may not fall short of the reality. In 1874, Republican Senator Charles Sumner (1811–1874) called the expectation of a Golden Age the "prevailing faith" of his time. He predicted a bright future marked by an expanding population, abundant natural resources, refinement in the arts, and nothing less than the "conquest of the world" by America's irresistible example.

Whether or not the condition of American civilization in the 1870s justified this breathless optimism, the half-century between Reconstruction and the First

World War witnessed a turbulent epoch of economic expansion, technological innovation, intellectual ferment, mass immigration, ethnic and religious conflict, reform agitation, and war. While no period in American history has been static, the post-Civil War generation watched a once-provincial republic transform itself at dizzying speed into a colossus of unprecedented wealth and energy. A nation of thirty-two million, shattered by war in the 1860s, had more than tripled its population by 1920. Rural and small-town America gave way to the cultural, economic, and political dominance of great urban centers. Veterans, North and South, lived to see their sons fight in Cuba and the Philippines and their grandsons fight in the trenches of France.

Struck by the nation's energy and productivity on a speaking tour of the United States in 1876, the British naturalist Thomas Huxley (1825–1895) challenged his audience at the new Johns Hopkins University to face an inescapable decision: "What are you going to do with all these things? What is to be the end to which these things are to be the means?" For many Americans, the answer to Huxley's question about ends and means seemed obvious: Unprecedented wealth provided the resources to do unprecedented good in the world. The Reverend Beecher told his prosperous congregation that same decade that "there must be prosperity in material things if there is to be prosperity in moral things in the last estate." All about him he saw evidence of increasing luxury, comfort, and power for every social class. Likewise, Russell H. Conwell (1843–1925), Baptist minister and founder of Temple University, preached an inspirational message he called "Acres of Diamonds." Delivered over 6,000 times in the late-nineteenth and early-twentieth centuries and still in print, "Acres of Diamonds" made Conwell a wealthy man. "I say that you ought to get rich, and it is your duty to get rich," he instructed countless listeners. "Money is power, and you ought to be reasonably ambitious to have it. You ought [to] because you can do more good with it than you could without it." For industrialist Andrew Carnegie (1835–1919), the "Gospel of Wealth," as he called it, required the rich to administer their resources in the way "best calculated to produce the most beneficial results for the community."

By quantitative measures, America in the late nineteenth century did indeed appear to be making spectacular progress in its aggregate material well-being. Five transcontinental railways bound east to west in a single national market for farm goods and industrial products. The "New South" began to build mills and factories. America's ports shipped grain, petroleum, and machinery around the world. Department stores, such as Macy's in New York, Wanamaker's in Philadelphia, and Marshall Fields in Chicago, became landmarks of urban convenience and sophistication. Mail-order giants Montgomery Ward and Sears-Roebuck made every conceivable consumer good available through their catalogs. Sod farmers in Nebraska could order any of these products and have them delivered by rail. Chain stores such as A&P and Woolworth appeared on every Main Street in America. European and American investors pumped millions of dollars into the new steel and petroleum industries dominated by such tycoons as Andrew Carnegie (1835–1919) and John D. Rockefeller (1839–1937).

Many technological innovations that now seem commonplace or archaic made their debut between the Civil War and the First World War. Fixing an exact date for an invention, or even identifying its true inventor, can be difficult, but the thousands of patents issued in these years told the story of America's conquest of time and space. Alexander Graham Bell (1847–1922) patented his telephone in 1876, and by 1884 customers in New York and Boston could talk to each other. The city of Philadelphia installed electric arc lamps on its streets in 1878. Thomas Edison (1847–1931) invented a practical, mass-produced electric bulb the next year. Soon, modern American homes and businesses enjoyed the novelty and convenience of phonographs, typewriters, "Kodak" cameras, radios, and countless electric appliances, from vacuum cleaners to washing machines and stoves. The practice of medicine benefited from X-ray imaging, developments in anesthesia, and improved surgical techniques. In 1903, the Wright brothers made their first flight at Kitty Hawk, North Carolina. And by 1914, Henry Ford's (1863–1947) assembly line began to make the automobile affordable to average workers, changing how and where most Americans lived and worked and vacationed.

Despite such tangible benefits, the modern industrial age placed new strains on the traditional family, farm communities, and booming cities and towns. Some blamed industrialization for unpredictable cycles of boom and bust, for dehumanizing labor through the factory system and assembly line, for attracting immigrant laborers faster than they could be assimilated, and for increasing the noise, crime, and blight of urban America. Much of the debate centered on government's proper role in shaping the direction of the nation's economy and providing humanitarian relief. To some, the older "liberalism" of limited government and individual rights seemed to be under systematic assault. Defenders of laissez-faire, whether inspired by the eighteenth-century Scottish economist and moral philosopher Adam Smith (1723–1790), by the nineteenth-century British sociologist Herbert Spencer (1820–1903), or by so-called "Social Darwinists," advocated minimal government regulation of banking, industry, markets, trade, and labor. Such intervention smacked of "paternalism." Government acted for the greater good when it confined itself to securing property rights and maintaining the rule of law. National planning would lead only to distortions in the market's efficient operation. Smith's "invisible hand" of the self-regulating marketplace seemed up to the challenge of the new industrial economy. Spencer's doctrine of "survival of the fittest" seemed to promise indefinite material and moral progress. And to Andrew Carnegie, the "truth of evolution" assured man's "march to perfection." In the 1890s, Yale sociologist William Graham Sumner (1840–1910) argued that it was pointless to try to control the inevitable growth of industry and big business and the concentration of great fortunes in the hands of a few entrepreneurs. Industrial organization had simply become the great fact of modern life. Man had to adjust himself to these material forces rather than try to direct their trajectory. Efforts to "democratize" industry, he claimed, betrayed a naïve sentimentalism ignorant of history, human nature, and the operation of natural laws.

A number of critics of laissez-faire principles believed in government's capacity and moral obligation to manage the American economy. They envisioned an alternative America remade by human intelligence and sympathy. Prominent social-gospel ministers and activist evangelicals urged the churches to put aside age-old fights over doctrine and the Bible to devote themselves to the urgent task of remaking the social order into the Kingdom of God on Earth. Some political economists believed that human and social evolution could be directed by wise policies and not left to blind chance and natural laws. They called for direct action to ensure social justice, harmony, and equitable distribution of wealth. Two of the best-selling books of the 1870s and 1880s shaped the national reform debate for the generation that came of age after the Civil War: Henry George's *Poverty and Progress* and Edward Bellamy's *Looking Backward*. George (1839–1897) blamed poverty's persistence in a world of plenty on the private ownership of land and proposed sweeping tax reforms to keep land out the hands of speculators. Bellamy (1850–1898) used his utopian novel about a twentieth-century Golden Age to preach his message of brotherhood, co-operation, and abundance for all through scientific management and government ownership of all the means of production.

Despite the radicalism of these popular authors, the reform impulse in late nineteenth century America can be hard to place on a simple spectrum from Left to Right. While some of the most ideologically driven advocates of change looked to Karl Marx (1818–1883) and German state-socialism, others drew from America's own past to create an unlikely mix of traditionalism and big government to address the problems of industrial society. The People's Party, founded in 1892, tried to give greater political power to the "producers" in the American economy: the farmers and factory workers who, by the sweat of their brow, cultivated the land and made things with their hands. The "Populists," as they were commonly known, appealed to familiar and enduring principles of Jeffersonian republicanism and Jacksonian democracy to defend the common man and majority rule against monopoly power and governance by political and economic elites. To their minds, big business constituted the new tyrant whose arbitrary powers needed to be checked by the state in the name of individual liberty. Doing so, however, required an unprecedented role for government in the economy. The Populist agenda called for government regulation or outright ownership of the railroads and telegraph and telephone lines, a graduated income tax, and an inflationary monetary policy. They looked to more democracy as the key to a just economy. To that end, the Populists called for the direct election of U.S. Senators, the referendum, and the initiative.

Reform agitation culminated in what historians have dubbed the "Progressive Era." The Progressives dominated American thought, culture, and politics in the first two decades of the twentieth century. Through journalism, the churches, colleges and universities, national and international conferences, and public office, they promoted and enacted sweeping changes in government policy at the local, state, and national level, in both private and public institutions. In the words of Herbert Croly (1869–1930), whose *Promise of American Life* (1909) likely influenced Teddy Roosevelt's "New Nationalism," the government ought to use Hamiltonian means to Jeffersonian ends, combining nationalist centralization and democratic idealism to fulfill America's destiny. The Progressives' reforms touch nearly every aspect of American life: women's suffrage, race relations, worker safety, alcohol, regulation of monopolies, birth control, food safety, child labor, immigration restriction, and eugenics. The "muckraker" journalists, as Teddy Roosevelt (1858–1919) called them, boosted magazine sales by exposing such sensations as political graft, organized crime, prostitution, and Wall Street conspiracies. Walter Lippmann (1889–1974) praised this "business of exposure" as "one of the hopeful signs of the age"; it showed that Americans still held their leaders to a high ethical standard.

On the national level, the Progressives' reforms touched the fabric of the Constitution itself, changing the national charter for the first time since Reconstruction. Despite hundreds of proposed amendments, the Constitution had remained untouched for over forty years. But in 1913, after a four-year effort, the states ratified the Sixteenth Amendment, making the national income tax constitutional. Within a few months, the Seventeenth Amendment changed Article I of the Constitution to require the direct election of U.S. Senators by the people. The Eighteenth Amendment, ratified in 1919, prohibited the manufacture, sale, and distribution of alcohol. And in 1920, women nationwide gained the right to vote with passage of the Nineteenth Amendment.

Reformers also focused on the record number of immigrants coming to America in search of work and opportunity. A generous federal land policy, most notably the Homestead Act of 1862, drew immigrant farmers from

Scandinavia, Bohemia, and Germany to the frontier West. The expanding industrial economy attracted a seemingly endless labor supply from Europe. Europe in the late nineteenth century was a world in motion. Workers moved from less industrialized parts of Europe to more industrialized. Railroads made internal migration cheap and efficient while modern steamship lines made ocean transportation over great distances relatively fast and affordable. People who in previous generations would not have been able to relocate now found it possible. Many millions of Europeans migrated to Argentina, Brazil, and Canada, broadening out the more familiar textbook picture of refugees disembarking at Ellis Island. Millions also came intending to stay only a few years and soon returned to their families and communities in Italy, Poland, or Germany. Nevertheless, from 1901 to 1920 alone, over fourteen million aliens came to the United States.

Along with this scale and pace of immigration came ethnic and religious conflict, especially with those who were eager to keep the nation as rooted as possible in its British and Protestant heritage. And at a time when ethnicity and religion offered the best predictors of how a man would vote, immigration became a heated political debate. The "wrong" kind of immigration meant the loss of political power, most likely for the Republicans. Various efforts to limit immigration tended at first to focus on one group, such as the Chinese, and Congress did not enact comprehensive restrictions until the mid-1920s. In the meantime, a number of high-profile reformers offered sweeping proposals to bar the "unfit" from entering the U.S. Former superintendent of the census and president of the Massachusetts Institute of Technology, Francis A. Walker (1840–1897), proposed in 1896 "to exclude hundreds of thousands" of immigrants with the intention "of protecting the American rate of wages, the American standard of living, and the quality of American citizenship from degradation through the tumultuous access of vast throngs of ignorant and brutalized peasantry from the countries of eastern and southern Europe." These paupers "represent[ed] the worst failures in the struggle for existence." In 1904, the noted sociologist E. A. Ross (1866–1951) lamented that the "Great Killing" of the Civil War had been followed by the "Great Dilution" of southern and eastern European immigrants who watered down the American stock.

In the same years that Americans faced questions about industrialization and the size and scope of government, they also wrestled with the United States' role in world affairs. Economically, America had never been isolated from the rest of the world. Diplomatically and militarily, it had engaged Europe, Latin America, and Asia from time to time. But the nation had followed Washington's advice from his Farewell Address and had avoided permanent alliances while pursuing a unilateral policy of national interests. By the 1890s, a number of prominent Americans argued that the United States had left its infancy behind as a nation and therefore had to assume the responsibilities of adulthood and recognize its status as a great power. It could no longer pretend it was an eighteenth-century republic of farmers and merchants. It had become an industrial Titan. America's economic interests and security demanded that it defend itself in a hostile world. America's mission demanded that it rescue the oppressed and promote democracy and the cause of civilization. In 1898, the United States waged a brief war against the crumbling Spanish empire. Quickly subduing Cuba and seizing Puerto Rico, Guam, and the Philippine Islands, America became a world colonial power for the first time in its history. The popular British author Rudyard Kipling (1865–1936) urged America to "take up the White Man's burden." But as the nation did so, it faced the dilemma of whether it could acquire territories that it had no intention of incorporating into its system of self-governing states and at the same time remain a constitutional republic. In short, did 1898 mark the fulfillment or the betrayal of America's founding principles?

Within twenty years, the United States faced a far greater challenge to its traditional conception of its role in the world. In 1917, President Woodrow Wilson (r. 1913–1921) stood before a joint session of Congress and asked for a declaration of war against Germany. He pledged that the United States would wage war to "make the world safe for democracy." The U.S. fought alongside Britain, France, and Russia for the next two and a half years. Its financial resources, industrial capacity, abundant crops, and fresh manpower proved indispensable to the Allied victory over Germany and the other Central Powers. Wilson personally led the American peace delegation to Paris and helped craft the Treaty of Versailles and the Covenant of the League of Nations. Ultimately, the United States Senate would not ratify the treaty or join the League. But the nation had unmistakably become a key player in world politics. A people that had emerged from the debris of civil war a half century before, now stood poised on the verge of what Henry Luce would one day call the "American Century."

THE NEW SOUTH
HENRY WOODFIN GRADY (1850–1889)
EDITOR, *ATLANTA CONSTITUTION*, TO THE
NEW ENGLAND SOCIETY

Henry Woodfin Grady emerged as the leading spokesman in post-Civil War America for an industrialized and progressive "New South." He rose to national prominence after Reconstruction as an editor and part owner of the Atlanta Constitution. *A native Georgian, he attended the University of Georgia and the University of Virginia, and then worked as a reporter in his home state, covering the Florida election results in the disputed presidential election of 1876.*

On December 22, 1886, the anniversary of the Pilgrims' landing at Plymouth Rock, Grady delivered his vision for the "New South" to members of the New England Society of New York who had gathered at the city's fashionable Delmonico's Restaurant for their annual dinner. Grady's appearance there marked the first time a Southerner had ever addressed this enclave of the Northern elite. His audience included none other than General William Tecumseh Sherman, future Secretary of State Elihu Root, railroad magnate Henry Morrison Flagler, financier James Pierpont Morgan, and Social Gospel pioneer Lyman Abbott. Harper's Weekly *acclaimed Grady's eloquence, calling his speech "one of the most striking that have been delivered by any citizen of a southern state since the war." Grady's New South, the journal rejoiced, was the South of "emancipation, and secession settled forever, and free schools, and active industry, and generous and sincere patriotism." Grady's speech brought him such fame that he was soon talked about as a Democratic candidate for vice president on a ticket with Grover Cleveland.*

NEW YORK, 22 DECEMBER 1886

"There was a South of slavery and secession—that South is dead. There is a South of union and freedom— that South, thank God, is living, breathing, growing every hour." These words, delivered from the immortal lips of Benjamin

Joel Chandler Harris, ed., *Life of Henry W. Grady, Including the Writings and Speeches* (New York: Cassell Publishing Company, 1890), 83–93.

H. Hill, at Tammany Hall in 1866, true then, and truer now, I shall make my
text tonight.

    Mr. President and Gentlemen: Let me express to you my appreciation
of the kindness by which I am permitted to address you. I make this abrupt
5   acknowledgment advisedly, for I feel that if, when I raise my provincial voice
in this ancient and august presence, I could find courage for no more than the
opening sentence, it would be well if, in that sentence, I had met in a rough
sense my obligation as a guest, and had perished, so to speak, with courtesy on
my lips and grace in my heart. [Laughter.] Permitted through your kindness to
10 catch my second wind, let me say that I appreciate the significance of being the
first Southerner to speak at this board, which bears the substance, if it surpasses
the semblance, of original New England hospitality [Applause], and honors a
sentiment that in turn honors you, but in which my personality is lost, and the
compliment to my people made plain. [Laughter.]

15   I bespeak the utmost stretch of your courtesy to-night. I am not troubled
about those from whom I come. You remember the man whose wife sent him
to a neighbor with a pitcher of milk, and who, tripping on the top step, fell,
with such casual interruptions as the landing afforded, into the basement; and
while picking himself up had the pleasure of hearing his wife call out: "John,
20 did you break the pitcher?"

    "No, I didn't," said John, "but I be dinged if I don't!" [Laughter.]

    So, while those who call to me from behind may inspire me with energy if
not with courage, I ask an indulgent hearing from you. I beg that you will bring
your full faith in American fairness and frankness of judgment upon what I shall
25 say. There was an old preacher once who told some boys of the Bible lesson he
was going to read in the morning. The boys finding the place, glued together the
connecting pages. [Laughter.] The next morning he read on the bottom of one
page: "When Noah was one hundred and twenty years old he took unto himself
a wife, who was"—then turning the page—"one hundred and forty cubits long
30 [Laughter], forty cubits wide, built of gopher-wood [Laughter], and covered
with pitch inside and out." [Loud and continued laughter.] He was naturally
puzzled at this. He read it again, verified it, and then said: "My friends, this is
the first time I ever met this in the Bible, but I accept it as an evidence of the
assertion that we are fearfully and wonderfully made." [Immense laughter.] If I
35 could get you to hold such faith tonight I could proceed cheerfully to the task
I otherwise approach with a sense of consecration.

    Pardon me one word, Mr. President, spoken for the sole purpose of get-
ting into the volumes that go out annually freighted with the rich eloquence
of your speakers—the fact that the Cavalier as well as the Puritan was on the
40 continent in its early days, and that he was "up and able to be about." [Laugh-

ter.] I have read your books carefully and I find no mention of that fact, which seems to me an important one for preserving a sort of historical equilibrium if for nothing else.

Let me remind you that the Virginia Cavalier first challenged France on this continent—that Cavalier John Smith gave New England its very name, 5 and was so pleased with the job that he has been handing his own name around ever since—and that while Miles Standish was cutting off men's ears for courting a girl without her parents' consent, and forbade men to kiss their wives on Sunday, the Cavalier was courting everything in sight, and that the Almighty had vouchsafed great increase to the Cavalier colonies, the huts in the wilderness 10 being full as the nests in the woods.

But having incorporated the Cavalier as a fact in your charming little books I shall let him work out his own salvation, as he has always done with engaging gallantry, and we will hold no controversy as to his merits. Why should we? Neither Puritan nor Cavalier long survived as such. The virtues and traditions 15 of both happily still live for the inspiration of their sons and the saving of the old fashion. [Applause.] But both Puritan and Cavalier were lost in the storm of the first Revolution; and the American citizen, supplanting both and stronger than either, took possession of the Republic bought by their common blood and fashioned to wisdom, and charged himself with teaching men government 20 and establishing the voice of the people as the voice of God. [Applause.]

My friends, Dr. Talmage[1] has told you that the typical American has yet to come. Let me tell you that he has already come. [Applause.] Great types like valuable plants are slow to flower and fruit. But from the union of these colonist Puritans and Cavaliers, from the straightening of their purposes and the 25 crossing of their blood, slow perfecting through a century, came he who stands as the first typical American, the first who comprehended within himself all the strength and gentleness, all the majesty and grace of this Republic— Abraham Lincoln. [Loud and continued applause.] He was the sum of Puritan and Cavalier, for in his ardent nature were fused the virtues of both, and in the 30 depths of his great soul the faults of both were lost. [Renewed applause.] He was greater than Puritan, greater than Cavalier, in that he was American [renewed applause], and that in his homely form were first gathered the vast and thrilling forces of his ideal government— charging it with such tremendous meaning and so elevating it above human suffering that martyrdom, though infamously 35 aimed, came as a fitting crown to a life consecrated from the cradle to human liberty. [Loud and prolonged cheering.] Let us, each cherishing the traditions and honoring his fathers, build with reverent hands to the type of this simple

---

[1]Thomas DeWitt Talmage (1832–1902), prominent Presbyterian preacher

but sublime life, in which all types are honored; and in our common glory as Americans there will be plenty and to spare for your forefathers and for mine. [Renewed cheering.]

5   In speaking to the toast with which you have honored me, I accept the term, "The New South," as in no sense disparaging to the old. Dear to me, sir, is the home of my childhood and the traditions of my people. I would not, if I could, dim the glory they won in peace and war, or by word or deed take aught from the splendor and grace of their civilization—never equaled and, perhaps, never to be equaled in its chivalric strength and grace. There is a New
10 South, not through protest against the Old, but because of new conditions, new adjustments and, if you please, new ideas and aspirations. It is to this that I address myself, and to the consideration of which I hasten lest it become the Old South before I get to it. Age does not endow all things with strength and virtue, nor are all new things to be despised. The shoemaker who put over his
15 door "John Smith's shop. Founded in 1760," was more than matched by his young rival across the street who hung out this sign: "Bill Jones. Established 1886. No old stock kept in this shop."

Dr. Talmage has drawn for you, with a master's hand, the picture of your returning armies. He has told you how, in the pomp and circumstance of war,
20 they came back to you, marching with proud and victorious tread, reading their glory in a nation's eyes! Will you bear with me while I tell you of another army that sought its home at the close of the late war—an army that marched home in defeat and not in victory—in pathos and not in splendor, but in glory that equaled yours, and to hearts as loving as ever welcomed heroes home. Let me
25 picture to you the footsore Confederate soldier, as, buttoning up in his faded gray jacket the parole which was to bear testimony to his children of his fidelity and faith, he turned his face southward from Appomattox in April 1865. Think of him as ragged, half-starved, heavy-hearted, enfeebled by want and wounds; having fought to exhaustion, he surrenders his gun, wrings the hands of his
30 comrades in silence, and lifting his tear-stained and pallid face for the last time to the graves that dot the old Virginia hills, pulls his gray cap over his brow and begins the slow and painful journey. What does he find—let me ask you, who went to your homes eager to find in the welcome you had justly earned, full payment for four years' sacrifice—what does he find when, having followed
35 the battle-stained cross against overwhelming odds, dreading death not half so much as surrender, he reaches the home he left so prosperous and beautiful? He finds his house in ruins, his farm devastated, his slaves free, his stock killed, his barns empty, his trade destroyed, his money worthless; his social system, feudal in its magnificence, swept away; his people without law or legal status,
40 his comrades slain, and the burdens of others heavy on his shoulders. Crushed

by defeat, his very traditions are gone. Without money, credit, employment, material or training; and beside all this, confronted with the gravest problem that ever met human intelligence—the establishing of a status for the vast body of his liberated slaves.

What does he do—this hero in gray with a heart of gold? Does he sit 5
down in sullenness and despair? Not for a day. Surely God, who had stripped him of his prosperity, inspired him in his adversity. As ruin was never before so overwhelming, never was restoration swifter. The soldier stepped from the trenches into the furrow; horses that had charged Federal guns marched before the plow, and fields that ran red with human blood in April were green with 10
the harvest in June; women reared in luxury cut up their dresses and made breeches for their husbands, and, with a patience and heroism that fit women always as a garment, gave their hands to work. There was little bitterness in all this. Cheerfulness and frankness prevailed. Bill Arp[2] struck the keynote when he said: "Well, I killed as many of them as they did of me, and now I am going 15
to work." [Laughter and applause.] Or the soldier returning home after defeat and roasting some corn on the roadside, who made the remark to his comrades: "You may leave the South if you want to, but I am going to Sandersville, kiss my wife and raise a crop, and if the Yankees fool with me any more I will whip 'em again." [Renewed applause.] I want to say to General Sherman—who is 20
considered an able man in our hearts, though some people think he is a kind of careless man about fire—that from the ashes he left us in 1864 we have raised a brave and beautiful city; that somehow or other we have caught the sunshine in the bricks and mortar of our homes, and have builded therein not one ignoble prejudice or memory. [Applause.] 25

But in all this what have we accomplished? We have found out that in the general summary the free Negro counts more than he did as a slave. We have planted the schoolhouse on the hilltop and made it free to white and black. We have sowed towns and cities in the place of theories and put business above politics. [Applause.] We have challenged your spinners in Massachusetts and 30
your iron-makers in Pennsylvania. We have learned that the $400,000,000 annually received from our cotton crop will make us rich, when the supplies that make it are home-raised. We have reduced the commercial rate of interest from twenty-four to six per cent, and are floating four per cent bonds. We have learned that one Northern immigrant is worth fifty foreigners, and have smoothed the 35
path to southward, wiped out the place where Mason and Dixon's line used to be, and hung our latch-string out to you and yours. [Prolonged cheers.] We have reached the point that marks perfect harmony in every household, when

---

[2]Charles Henry Smith (1826–1903), a humor writer from Georgia

the husband confesses that the pies which his wife cooks are as good as those
his mother used to bake; and we admit that the sun shines as brightly and the
moon as softly as it did before the war. [Laughter.] We have established thrift
in city and country. We have fallen in love with work. We have restored com-
5   fort to homes from which culture and elegance never departed. We have let
economy take root and spread among us as rank as the crabgrass which sprang
from Sherman's cavalry camps, until we are ready to lay odds on the Georgia
Yankee, as he manufactures relics of the battlefield in a one-story shanty and
squeezes pure olive oil out of his cotton-seed, against any downeaster that ever
10 swapped wooden nutmegs for flannel sausages in the valleys of Vermont. [Loud
and continuous laughter.] Above all, we know that we have achieved in these
"piping times of peace" a fuller independence for the South than that which
our fathers sought to win in the forum by their eloquence or compel on the
field by their swords. [Loud applause.]
15   It is a rare privilege, sir, to have had part, however humble, in this work.
Never was nobler duty confided to human hands than the uplifting and upbuild-
ing of the prostrate and bleeding South, misguided perhaps, but beautiful in
her suffering, and honest, brave and generous always. [Applause.] In the record
of her social, industrial, and political illustrations we await with confidence the
20 verdict of the world.
          But what of the negro? Have we solved the problem he presents or pro-
gressed in honor and equity towards the solution? Let the record speak to
the point. No section shows a more prosperous laboring population than the
Negroes of the South; none in fuller sympathy with the employing and land-
25 owning class. He shares our school fund, has the fullest protection of our laws
and the friendship of our people. Self-interest, as well as honor, demand that he
should have this. Our future, our very existence depend upon our working out
this problem in full and exact justice. We understand that when Lincoln signed
the Emancipation Proclamation, your victory was assured; for he then commit-
30 ted you to the cause of human liberty, against which the arms of man cannot
prevail [Applause]; while those of our statesmen who trusted to make slavery
the cornerstone of the Confederacy doomed us to defeat as far as they could,
committing us to a cause that reason could not defend or the sword maintain
in the sight of advancing civilization. [Renewed applause.] Had Mr. Toombs[3]
35 said, which he did not say, that he would call the roll of his slaves at the foot of
Bunker Hill, he would have been foolish, for he might have known that whenever
slavery became entangled in war it must perish, and that the chattel in human
flesh ended forever in New England when your fathers—not to be blamed for

---

[3]Robert Augustus Toombs (1810–1885), first Secretary of State for the Confederacy

parting with what didn't pay—sold their slaves to our fathers—not to be praised
for knowing a paying thing when they saw it. [Laughter.] The relations of the
Southern people with the Negro are close and cordial. We remember with what
fidelity for four years he guarded our defenseless women and children, whose
husbands and fathers were fighting against his freedom. To his eternal credit   5
be it said that whenever he struck a blow for his own liberty he fought in open
battle, and when at last he raised his black and humble hands that the shackles
might be struck off, those hands were innocent of wrong against his helpless
charges, and worthy to be taken in loving grasp by every man who honors
loyalty and devotion. [Applause.] Ruffians have maltreated him, rascals have   10
misled him, philanthropists established a bank for him, but the South, with the
North, protests against injustice to this simple and sincere people. To liberty and
enfranchisement is as far as law can carry the Negro. The rest must be left to
conscience and common sense. It should be left to those among whom his lot
is cast, with whom he is indissolubly connected and whose prosperity depends   15
upon their possessing his intelligent sympathy and confidence. Faith has been
kept with him in spite of calumnious assertions to the contrary by those who
assume to speak for us or by frank opponents. Faith will be kept with him in
the future, if the South holds her reason and integrity. [Applause.]

But have we kept faith with you? In the fullest sense, yes. When Lee sur-   20
rendered—I don't say when Johnston surrendered, because I understand he
still alludes to the time when he met General Sherman last as the time when he
"determined to abandon any further prosecution of the struggle"—when Lee
surrendered, I say, and Johnston quit, the South became, and has since been,
loyal to this Union. We fought hard enough to know that we were whipped,   25
and in perfect frankness accepted as final the arbitrament of the sword to
which we had appealed. The South found her jewel in the toad's head of
defeat. The shackles that had held her in narrow limitations fell forever when
the shackles of the Negro slave were broken. [Applause.] Under the old regime
the Negroes were slaves to the South, the South was a slave to the system. The   30
old plantation, with its simple police regulation and its feudal habit, was the
only type possible under slavery. Thus was gathered in the hands of a splendid
and chivalric oligarchy the substance that should have been diffused among
the people, as the rich blood, under certain artificial conditions, is gathered
at the heart, filling that with affluent rapture, but leaving the body chill and   35
colorless. [Applause.]

The Old South rested everything on slavery and agriculture, unconscious
that these could neither give nor maintain healthy growth. The New South
presents a perfect democracy, the oligarchs leading in the popular movement—a
social system compact and closely knitted, less splendid on the surface but   40

stronger at the core—a hundred farms for every plantation, fifty homes for every palace, and a diversified industry that meets the complex needs of this complex age.

The New South is enamored of her new work. Her soul is stirred with the
5   breath of a new life. The light of a grander day is falling fair on her face. She is thrilling with the consciousness of growing power and prosperity. As she stands upright, full-statured and equal among the people of the earth, breathing the keen air and looking out upon the expanding horizon, she understands that her emancipation came because in the inscrutable wisdom of God her honest
10   purpose was crossed and her brave armies were beaten. [Applause.]

This is said in no spirit of time-serving or apology. The South has nothing for which to apologize. She believes that the late struggle between the states was war and not rebellion, revolution and not conspiracy, and that her convictions were as honest as yours. I should be unjust to the dauntless spirit of the South
15   and to my own convictions if I did not make this plain in this presence. The South has nothing to take back. In my native town of Athens is a monument that crowns its central hills—a plain, white shaft. Deep cut into its shining side is a name dear to me above the names of men, that of a brave and simple man who died in brave and simple faith. Not for all the glories of New Eng-
20   land—from Plymouth Rock all the way—would I exchange the heritage he left me in his soldier's death. To the foot of that shaft I shall send my children's children to reverence him who ennobled their name with his heroic blood. But, sir, speaking from the shadow of that memory, which I honor as I do nothing else on earth, I say that the cause in which he suffered and for which he gave
25   his life was adjudged by higher and fuller wisdom than his or mine, and I am glad that the omniscient God held the balance of battle in His Almighty hand, and that human slavery was swept forever from American soil—the American Union saved from the wreck of war. [Loud applause.]

This message, Mr. President, comes to you from consecrated ground. Every
30   foot of the soil about the city in which I live is as sacred as a battleground of the Republic. Every hill that invests it is hallowed to you by the blood of your brothers, who died for your victory, and doubly hallowed to us by the blood of those who died hopeless, but undaunted, in defeat—sacred soil to all of us—rich with memories that make us purer and stronger and better—silent but
35   stanch witnesses in its red desolation of the matchless valor of American hearts and the deathless glory of American arms—speaking an eloquent witness in its white peace and prosperity to the indissoluble union of American states and the imperishable brotherhood of the American people. [Immense cheering.]

Now, what answer has New England to this message? Will she permit the
40   prejudices of war to remain in the hearts of the conquerors, when it has died in

the hearts of the conquered? [Cries of "No! No!"] Will she transmit this prejudice to the next generation, that in their hearts, which never felt the generous
ardor of conflict, it may perpetuate itself? ["No! No!"] Will she withhold, save
in strained courtesy, the hand which straight from his soldier's heart Grant
offered to Lee at Appomattox? Will she make the vision of a restored and happy   5
people, which gathered above the couch of your dying captain, filling his heart
with grace, touching his lips with praise and glorifying his path to the grave;
will she make this vision on which the last sight of his expiring soul breathed
a benediction, a cheat and a delusion? [Tumultuous cheering and shouts of
"No! No!"] If she does, the South, never abject in asking for comradeship, must   10
accept with dignity its refusal; but if she does not; if she accepts in frankness
and sincerity this message of goodwill and friendship, then will the prophecy
of Webster, delivered in this very Society forty years ago amid tremendous
applause, be verified in its fullest and final sense, when he said: "Standing hand
to hand and clasping hands, we should remain united as we have been for sixty   15
years, citizens of the same country, members of the same government, united
all, united now, and united forever. There have been difficulties, contentions,
and controversies, but I tell you that in my judgment

> Those opposed eyes,
> Which like the meteors of a troubled heaven,   20
> All of one nature, of one substance bred,
> Did lately meet in th' intestine shock,
> Shall now, in mutual well beseeming ranks,
> March all one way.

WEALTH
ANDREW CARNEGIE (1835–1919)

Andrew Carnegie was a Scottish immigrant who began as a helper in a textile factory and rose to become the master of an enormous steel company. He sold his company to the organizers of the United States Steel Company for $450 million, and devoted the rest of his life and money to philanthropy, building libraries and schools, providing 4,000 churches with organs, and establishing the Carnegie Foundation for International Peace.

Carnegie defended industrial capitalism and accepted many of the principles of classical liberal political economy—individualism, competition that promoted the "survival of the fittest," the sanctity of private property, inequality. At the same time, he maintained the biblical demand that the wealthy provide for the common good. His "gospel of wealth" was meant to provide an alternative to the "science of wealth" advanced by atheist-materialists of the laissez-faire school as well as the "social gospel" of collectivism.

1889

The problem of our age is the proper administration of wealth so that the ties of brotherhood may still bind together the rich and poor in harmonious relationship. The conditions of human life have not only been changed, but revolutionized, with the past few hundred years. In former days there was little difference between the dwelling, dress, food, and environment of the chief and those of his retainers. The Indians are today where civilized man then was. When visiting the Sioux, I was led to the wigwam of the chief. It was just like the others in external appearance, and even within the difference was trifling between it and those of the poorest of his braves. The contrast between the palace of the millionaire and the cottage of the laborer with us today measures the change which has come with civilization.

This change, however, is not to be deplored, but welcomed as highly beneficial. It is well, nay, essential for the progress of the race, that the houses of

Andrew Carnegie, "Wealth," *The North American Review* 148 (June 1889):653–64.

some should be homes for all that is highest and best in literature and the arts, and for all the refinements of civilization rather than that none should be so. Much better this great irregularity than universal squalor. Without wealth there can be no Maecenas. The "good old times" were not good old times. Neither
5   master nor servant was as well situated then as today. A relapse to old conditions would be disastrous to both—not the least so to him who serves—and would sweep away civilization with it. But whether the change be for good or ill, it is upon us, beyond our power to alter, and therefore to be accepted and made the best of. It is a waste of time to criticize the inevitable.

10   It is easy to see how the change has come. One illustration will serve for almost every phase of the cause. In the manufacture of products we have the whole story. It applies to all combinations of human industry, as stimulated and enlarged by the inventions of this scientific age. Formerly articles were manufactured at the domestic hearth or in small shops which formed part of
15   the household. The master and his apprentices worked side by side, the latter living with the master, and therefore subject to the same conditions. When these apprentices rose to be masters, there was little or no change in their mode of life, and they, in turn, educated in the same routine succeeding apprentices. There was, substantially, social equality, and even political equality, for those engaged
20   in industrial pursuits had then little or no political voice in the state.

          But the inevitable result of such a mode of manufacture was crude articles at high prices. Today the world obtains commodities of excellent quality at prices which even the generation preceding this would have deemed incredible. In the commercial world similar causes have produced similar results, and the
25   race is benefited thereby. The poor enjoy what the rich could not before afford. What were the luxuries have become the necessaries of life. The laborer has now more comforts than the farmer had a few generations ago. The farmer has more luxuries than the landlord had, and is more richly clad and better housed. The landlord has books and pictures rarer, and appointments more artistic, than
30   the king could then obtain.

          The price we pay for this salutary change is, no doubt, great. We assemble thousands of operatives in the factory, in the mine, and in the counting-house, of whom the employer can know little or nothing, and to whom the employer is little better than a myth. All intercourse between then is at an end. Rigid castes
35   are formed and, as usual, mutual ignorance breeds mutual distrust. Each caste is without sympathy for the other, and ready to credit anything disparaging in regard to it. Under the law of competition, the employer of thousands is forced into the strictest economies, among which the rates paid to labor figure prominently, and often there is friction between the employer and the employed, between capital
40   and labor, between rich and poor. Human society loses homogeneity.

The price which society pays for the law of competition, like the price it pays for cheap comforts and luxuries, is also great; but the advantages of this law are also greater still, for it is to this law that we owe our wonderful material development, which brings improved conditions in its train. But, whether the law be benign or not, we must say of it, as we say of the change in the conditions of men to which we have referred: It is here; we cannot evade it; no substitutes for it have been found; and while the law may be sometimes hard for the individual, it is best for the race, because it ensures the survival of the fittest in every department. We accept and welcome, therefore, as conditions to which we must accommodate ourselves, great inequality of environment, the concentration of business, industrial and commercial, in the hands of a few, and the law of competition between these as being not only beneficial, but essential for the future progress of the race.

Having accepted these, it follows that there must be great scope for the exercise of special ability in the merchant and in the manufacturer who has to conduct affairs upon a great scale. That this talent for organization and management is rare among men is proved by the fact that it invariably secures for its possessor enormous rewards, no matter where or under what laws or conditions. The experienced in affairs always rate the *man* whose services can be obtained as a partner as not only the first consideration, but such as to render the question of his capital scarcely worth considering, for such men soon create capital; while, without the special talent required, capital soon takes wings. Such men become interested in firms or corporations using millions; and estimating only simple interest to be made upon the capital invested, it is inevitable that their income must exceed their expenditures, and that they must accumulate wealth. Nor is there any middle ground which such men can occupy, because the great manufacturing or commercial concern which does not earn at least interest upon its capital soon becomes bankrupt. It must either go forward or fall behind: to stand still is impossible. It is a condition essential for its successful operation that it should be thus far profitable, and even that, in addition to interest on capital, it should make profit. It is a law, as certain as any of the others named, that men possessed of this peculiar talent for affairs, under the free play of economic forces, must, of necessity, soon be in receipt of more revenue than can be judiciously expended upon themselves; and this law is as beneficial for the race as the others.

Objections to the foundations upon which society is based are not in order, because the condition of the race is better with these than it has been with any others which have been tried. Of the effect of any new substitutes proposed we cannot be sure. The socialist or anarchist who seeks to overturn present conditions is to be regarded as attacking the foundation upon which

civilization itself rests, for civilization took its start from the day that the capable, industrious workman said to his incompetent and lazy fellow, "If thou dost not sow, thou shalt not reap," and thus ended primitive communism by separating the drones from the bees. One who studies this subject will soon be
5   brought face to face with the conclusion that upon the sacredness of property civilization itself depends—the right of the laborer to his hundred dollars in the savings bank, and equally the legal right of the millionaire to his millions. To those who propose to substitute communism for this intense individualism the answer, therefore, is: The race has tried that. All progress from that barbarous
10   day to the present time has resulted from its displacement. Not evil, but good, has come to the race from the accumulation of wealth by those who have the ability and energy that produce it.

But even if we admit for a moment that it might be better for the race to discard its present foundation, individualism—that it is a nobler ideal that
15   man should labor, not for himself alone, but in and for a brotherhood of his fellows, and share with them all in common, realizing Swedenborg's idea of Heaven, where, as he says, the angels derive their happiness, not from laboring for self, but for each other—even admit all this, and a sufficient answer is, this is not evolution, but revolution. It necessitates the changing of human nature
20   itself—a work of eons, even if it were good to change it, which we cannot know. It is not practicable in our day or in our age. Even if desirable theoretically, it belongs to another and long-succeeding sociological stratum. Our duty is with what is practicable now; with the next step possible in our day and generation. It is criminal to waste our energies in endeavoring to uproot, when all we can
25   profitably or possibly accomplish is to bend the universal tree of humanity a little in the direction most favorable to the production of good fruit under existing circumstances. We might as well urge the destruction of the highest existing type of man because he failed to reach our ideal as to favor the destruction of individualism, private property, the law of accumulation of wealth, and the
30   law of competition; for these are the highest results of human experience, the soil in which society so far has produced the best fruit. Unequally or unjustly, perhaps, as these laws sometimes operate, and imperfect as they appear to the idealist, they are, nevertheless, like the highest type of man, the best and most valuable of all that humanity has yet accomplished.
35   We start, then, with a condition of affairs under which the best interests of the race are promoted, but which inevitably gives wealth to the few. Thus far, accepting conditions as they exist, the situation can be surveyed and pronounced good. The question then arises—and, if the foregoing be correct, it is the only question with which we have to deal—what is the proper mode of administering
40   wealth after the laws upon which civilization is founded have thrown it into the

hands of the few? And it is of this great question that I believe I offer the true solution. It will be understood that *fortunes* are here spoken of, not moderate sums saved by many years of effort, the returns from which are required for the comfortable maintenance and education of families. This is not *wealth*, but only *competence*, which it should be the aim of all to acquire. 5

There are but three modes in which surplus wealth can be disposed of. It can be left to the families of the decedents; or it can be bequeathed for public purposes; or, finally, it can be administered during their lives by its possessors. Under the first and second modes most of the wealth of the world that has reached the few has hitherto been applied. Let us in turn consider each of these 10 modes. The first is the most injudicious. In monarchical countries, the estates and the greatest portion of the wealth are left to the first son that the vanity of the parent may be gratified by the thought that his name and title are to descend to succeeding generations un-impaired. The condition of this class in Europe today teaches the futility of such hopes or ambitions. The successors 15 have become impoverished through their follies or from the fall in the value of land. Even in Great Britain the strict law of entail has been found inadequate to maintain the status of an hereditary class. Its soil is rapidly passing into the hands of the stranger. Under republican institutions the division of property among the children is much fairer, but the question which forces itself upon 20 thoughtful men in all lands is: Why should men leave great fortunes to their children? If this is done from affection, is it not misguided affection? Observation teaches that, generally speaking, it is not well for the children that they should be so burdened. Neither is it well for the state. Beyond providing for the wife and daughters moderate sources of income, and very moderate allow- 25 ances indeed, if any, for the sons, men may well hesitate, for it is no longer questionable that great sums bequeathed oftener work more for the injury than for the good of the recipients. Wise men will soon conclude that, for the best interests of the members of their families and of the state, such bequests are an improper use of their means. 30

It is not suggested that men who have failed to educate their sons to earn a livelihood shall cast them adrift in poverty. If any man has seen fit to rear his sons with a view to their living idle lives or, what is highly commendable, has instilled in them the sentiment that they are in a position to labor for public ends without reference to pecuniary considerations, then, of course, the duty of 35 the parent is to see that such are provided for *in moderation*. There are instances of millionaires' sons unspoiled by wealth, who, being rich, still perform great services in the community. Such are the very salt of the earth, as valuable as, unfortunately, they are rare; still it is not the exception, but the rule, that men must regard and, looking at the usual result of enormous sums conferred upon 40 legatees, the thoughtful man must shortly say, "I would as soon leave to my son a curse as the almighty dollar," and admit to himself that it is not the welfare of the children, but family pride, which inspires these enormous legacies.

As to the second mode, that of leaving wealth at death for public uses, it may be said that this is only a means for the disposal of wealth, provided a man is content to wait until he is dead before it becomes of much good in the world. Knowledge of the results of legacies bequeathed is not calculated to inspire the brightest hopes of much posthumous good being accomplished. The cases are not few in which the real object sought by the testator is not attained, nor are they few in which his real wishes are thwarted. In many cases the bequests are so used as to become only monuments of his folly. It is well to remember that it requires the exercise of not less ability than that which acquired the wealth to use it so as to be really beneficial to the community. Besides this, it may fairly be said that no man is to be extolled for doing what he cannot help doing, nor is he to be thanked by the community to which he only leaves wealth at death. Men who leave vast sums in this way may fairly be thought men who would not have left it at all, had they been able to take it with them. The memories of such cannot be held in grateful remembrance, for there is no grace in their gifts. It is not to be wondered at that such bequests seem so generally to lack the blessing.

The growing disposition to tax more and more heavily large estates left at death is a cheering indication of the growth of a salutary change in public opinion. The state of Pennsylvania now takes—subject to some exceptions—one-tenth of the property left by its citizens. The budget presented in the British Parliament the other day proposes to increase the death-duties; and, most significant of all, the new tax is to be a graduated one. Of all forms of taxation, this seems the wisest. Men who continue hoarding great sums all their lives, the proper use of which for public ends would work to the community, should be made to feel that the community, in the form of the state, cannot thus be deprived of its proper share. By taxing estates heavily at death the state marks its condemnation of the selfish millionaire's unworthy life.

It is desirable that nations should go much further in this direction. Indeed, it is difficult to set bounds to the share of a rich man's estate which should go at his death to the public through the agency of the state, and by all means such taxes should be graduated, beginning at nothing upon moderate sums to dependents, and increasing rapidly as the amounts swell, until of the millionaire's hoard, as of Shylock's, at least.

> ... *The other half*
> *Comes to the privy coffer of the state*[1]

---

[1]Portia, in Shakespeare's *The Merchant of Venice*, Act 4, Scene 1

This policy would work powerfully to induce the rich man to attend to the administration of wealth during his life, which is the end that society should always have in view, as being that by far most fruitful for the people. Nor need it be feared that this policy would sap the root of enterprise and render men less anxious to accumulate, for to the class whose ambition it is to leave great fortunes and be talked about after their death, it will attract even more attention and, indeed, be a somewhat nobler ambition to have enormous sums paid over to the state from their fortunes.

There remains, then, only one mode of using great fortunes; but in this we have the true antidote for the temporary unequal distribution of wealth, the reconciliation of the rich and the poor—a reign of harmony—another ideal, differing, indeed, from that of the communist in requiring only the further evolution of existing conditions, not the total overthrow of our civilization. It is founded upon the present most intense individualism, and the race is prepared to put it in practice by degrees whenever it pleases. Under its sway we shall have an ideal state, in which the surplus wealth of the few will become, in the best sense, the property of the many, because administered for the common good, and this wealth, passing through the hands of the few, can be made a much more potent force for the elevation of our race than if it had been distributed in small sums to the people themselves. Even the poorest can be made to see this, and to agree that great sums gathered by some of their fellow-citizens and spent for public purposes, from which the masses reap the principal benefit, are more valuable to them than if scattered among them through the course of many years in trifling amounts.

If we consider what results flow from the Cooper Institute,[2] for instance, to the best portion of the race in New York not possessed of means, and compare these with those which would have arisen for the good of the masses from an equal sum distributed by Mr. Cooper in his lifetime in the form of wages, which is the highest form of distribution, being for work done and not for charity, we can form some estimate of the possibilities for the improvement of the race which lie embedded in the present law of the accumulation of wealth. Much of this sum, if distributed in small quantities among the people, would have been wasted in the indulgence of appetite, some of it in excess, and it may be doubted whether even the part put to the best use, that of adding to the comforts of the home, would have yielded results for the race, as a race, at all comparable to those which are flowing and are to flow from the Cooper Institute from generation to generation. Let the advocate of violent or radical change ponder well this thought.

[2]The Cooper Union was founded by the industrialist Peter Cooper in 1859 as a center of education in New York City.

We might even go so far as to take another instance, that of Mr. Tilden's bequest of five millions of dollars for a free library in the city of New York, but in referring to this one cannot help saying involuntarily, how much better if Mr. Tilden had devoted the last years of his own life to the proper administration
5   of this immense sum; in which case neither legal contest nor any other cause of delay could have interfered with his aims.[3] But let us assume that Mr. Tilden's millions finally become the means of giving to this city a noble public library, where the treasures of the world contained in books will be open to all forever, without money and without price. Considering the good of that part of the
10   race which congregates in and around Manhattan Island, would its permanent benefit have been better promoted had these millions been allowed to circulate in small sums through the hands of the masses? Even the most strenuous advocate of communism must entertain a doubt upon this subject. Most of those who think will probably entertain no doubt whatever.

15   Poor and restricted are our opportunities in this life; narrow our horizon; our best work most imperfect; but rich men should be thankful for one inestimable boon. They have it in their power during their lives to busy themselves in organizing benefactions from which the masses of their fellows will derive lasting advantage, and thus dignify their own lives. The highest life is probably
20   to be reached, not by such imitation of the life of Christ as Count Tolstoi gives us, but, while animated by Christ's spirit, by recognizing the changed conditions of this age, and adopting modes of expressing this spirit suitable to the changed conditions under which we live; still laboring for the good of our fellows, which was the essence of his life and teaching, but laboring in a different manner.

25   This, then, is held to be the duty of the man of wealth: First, to set an example of modest, unostentatious living, shunning display or extravagance; to provide moderately for the legitimate wants of those dependent upon him; and after doing so to consider all surplus revenues which come to him simply as trust funds, which he is called upon to administer, and strictly bound as a matter
30   of duty to administer in the manner which, in his judgment, is best calculated to produce the most beneficial results for the community—the man of wealth thus becoming the mere agent and trustee for his poorer brethren, bringing to their service his superior wisdom, experience, and ability to administer, doing for them better than they would or could do for themselves.

35   We are met here with the difficulty of determining what are moderate sums to leave to members of the family; what is modest, unostentatious living;

---

[3]Samuel J. Tilden (1814–1886) left millions of dollars to found a public library in New York City. His heirs, however, successfully contested the will, leaving a reduced sum available for the library. In 1901, Carnegie added $5.2 million to Tilden's bequest to create the New York Public Library System.

what is the test of extravagance. There must be different standards for different conditions. The answer is that it is as impossible to name exact amounts or actions as it is to define good manners, good taste, or the rules of propriety; but, nevertheless, these are verities, well known although undefinable. Public sentiment is quick to know and to feel what offends these. So in the case of wealth. 5
The rule in regard to good taste in the dress of men or women applies here. Whatever makes one conspicuous offends the canon. If any family be chiefly known for display, for extravagance in home, table, equipage, for enormous sums ostentatiously spent in any form upon itself—if these be its chief distinctions, we have no difficulty in estimating its nature or culture. So likewise in regard 10 to the use or abuse of its surplus wealth, or to generous, freehanded co-operation in good public uses, or to unabated efforts to accumulate and hoard to the last, whether they administer or bequeath. The verdict rests with the best and most enlightened public sentiment. The community will surely judge, and its judgments will not often be wrong. 15

The best uses to which surplus wealth can be put have already been indicated. Those who would administer wisely must, indeed, be wise, for one of the serious obstacles to the improvement of our race is indiscriminate charity. It were better for mankind that the millions of the rich were thrown into the sea than so spent as to encourage the slothful, the drunken, the unworthy. Of 20 every thousand dollars spent in so called charity today, it is probable that $950 is unwisely spent; so spent, indeed, as to produce the very evils which it proposes to mitigate or cure. A well-known writer of philosophic books admitted the other day that he had given a quarter of a dollar to a man who approached him as he was coming to visit the house of his friend. He knew nothing of the habits 25 of this beggar; knew not the use that would be made of this money, although he had every reason to suspect that it would be spent improperly. This man professed to be a disciple of Herbert Spencer; yet the quarter-dollar given that night will probably work more injury than all the money which its thoughtless donor will ever be able to give in true charity will do good. He only gratified 30 his own feelings, saved himself from annoyance—and this was probably one of the most selfish and very worst actions of his life, for in all respects he is most worthy.

In bestowing charity, the main consideration should be to help those who will help themselves; to provide part of the means by which those who desire 35 to improve may do so; to give those who desire to rise the aids by which they may rise; to assist, but rarely or never to do all. Neither the individual nor the race is improved by alms-giving. Those worthy of assistance, except in rare cases, seldom require assistance. The really valuable men of the race never do, except in cases of accident or sudden change. Everyone has, of course, cases of 40

individuals brought to his own knowledge where temporary assistance can do genuine good, and these he will not overlook. But the amount which can be wisely given by the individual for individuals is necessarily limited by his lack of knowledge of the circumstances connected with each. He is the only true
5   reformer who is as careful and as anxious not to aid the unworthy as he is to aid the worthy, and, perhaps, even more so, for in alms-giving more injury is probably done by rewarding vice than by relieving virtue.

The rich man is thus almost restricted to following the examples of Peter Cooper, Enoch Pratt[4] of Baltimore, Mr. Pratt[5] of Brooklyn, Senator Stanford[6],
10   and others, who know that the best means of benefiting the community is to place within its reach the ladders upon which the aspiring can rise—parks and means of recreation, by which men are helped in body and mind; works of art, certain to give pleasure and improve the public taste; and public institutions of various kinds, which will improve the general condition of the people;—in
15   this manner returning their surplus wealth to the mass of their fellows in the forms best calculated to do them lasting good.

Thus is the problem of rich and poor to be solved. The laws of accumulation will be left free; the laws of distribution free. Individualism will continue, but the millionaire will be but a trustee for the poor; entrusted for a season with a
20   great part of the increased wealth of the community, but administering it for the community far better than it could or would have done for itself. The best minds will thus have reached a stage in the development of the race in which it is clearly seen that there is no mode of disposing of surplus wealth creditable to thoughtful and earnest men into whose hands it flows save by using it year
25   by year for the general good. This day already dawns. But a little while, and although, without incurring the pity of their fellows, men may die sharers in great business enterprises from which their capital cannot be or has not been withdrawn, and is left chiefly at death for public uses, yet the man who dies leaving behind him millions of available wealth, which was his to administer
30   during life, will pass away "unwept, unhonored, and unsung," no matter to what uses he leaves the dross which he cannot take with him. Of such as these the public verdict will then be: "The man who dies thus rich dies disgraced."

Such, in my opinion, is the true Gospel concerning Wealth, obedience to which is destined some day to solve the problem of the rich and the poor, and
35   to bring "Peace on earth, among men good-will."

---

[4]Enoch Pratt (1808–1896) built and endowed a free library in Baltimore.
[5]Charles Pratt (1830–1891) created an art school in New York.
[6]Leland Stanford (1824–1893), having made a fotune in transportation industries, served as
   U.S. Senator from California (1885–1893) and founded Stanford University.

THE CREED OF
THE OLD SOUTH
BASIL LANNEAU GILDERSLEEVE (1831–1924)

Basil Lanneau Gildersleeve's amazing longevity is easily grasped when one considers that at the time of his birth James Madison was alive, and when he died Ronald Reagan was 13 years old. Born in Charleston, South Carolina, and educated at the College of Charleston, he went to Germany for further study, receiving his Ph.D. from the University of Gottingen in 1853. Upon returning to the United States, Gildersleeve began his professional career at the University of Virginia. During the Civil War he served in the Confederate Army every summer throughout the War. In 1876 Gildersleeve was called to the newly founded Johns Hopkins University in Baltimore, Maryland, where he helped establish the classics department, which he chaired until his death.

It is no exaggeration to say that Gildersleeve is the greatest classicist America has produced. He was renown worldwide, and many of his articles and books on classical subjects have yet to be superseded. His text of the Greek poet Pindar, for example, is still considered a model of what such things should be. But as the attentive reader will discover in the excerpts reprinted here, Gildersleeve is always a loyal son of the South and his perceptions of the terrible conflict of 1861 to 1865 have a universal validity because he saw the War through the eyes of the foundations of Western culture: the Greek and Latin Classics.

1892

...[W]hat was to all true Confederates beyond a question "a holy cause," "the holiest of causes," this fight in defense of "the sacred soil" of our native land, was to the other side "a wicked rebellion" and "damnable treason," and both parties to the quarrel were not sparing of epithets which, at this distance of time, may seem to our children unnecessarily undignified; and no doubt some 5 of these *epitheta ornantia* continue to flourish in remote regions, just as picto-

Basil Gildersleeve, "The Creed of the Old South," *Atlantic Monthly* 69 (January 1892):77–83, 85–87.

rial representations of Yankees and rebels in all their respective fiendishness are
still cherished here and there. At the Centennial Exposition of 1876, by way of
conciliating the sections, the place of honor in the Art Annex, or by whatever
un-English name they called it, was given to Rothermel's painting of the battle
5   of Gettysburg, in which the face of every dying Union soldier is lighted up with
a celestial smile, while guilt and despair are stamped on the wan countenances of
the moribund rebels. At least such is my recollection of the painting; and I hope
that I may be pardoned for the malicious pleasure I felt when I was informed
of the high price that the State of Pennsylvania had paid for that work of art.
10   The dominant feeling was amusement, not indignation. But as I looked at it I
recalled another picture of a battle scene, painted by a friend of mine, a French
artist, who had watched our life with an artist's eye. One of the figures in the
foreground was a dead Confederate boy, lying in the angle of a worm fence.
His uniform was worn and ragged, mud-stained as well as blood-stained; the
15   cap which had fallen from his head was a tatter, and the torn shores were ready
to drop from his stiffening feet; but in a buttonhole of his tunic was stuck the
inevitable toothbrush, which continued even to the end of the war to be the
distinguishing mark of gentle nurture—the souvenir that the Confederate so
often received from fair sympathizers in border towns. I am not a realist, but I
20   would not exchange that homely toothbrush in the Confederate's button hole
for the most angelic smile that Rothermel's brush could have conjured up.

   Now I make no doubt that most of the readers of *The Atlantic* have got
beyond the Rothermel stage, and yet I am not certain that all of them appreciate the entire clearness of conscience with which we of the South went into
25   the war. A new patriotism is one of the results of the great conflict, and the
power of local patriotism is no longer felt to the same degree. In one of his
recent deliverances Mr. Carnegie, a canny Scot who has constituted himself the
representative of American patriotism, not without profit, says, "The citizen of
the republic today is prouder of being an American than he is of being a native
30   of any state in the country." What it is to be a native of any state in the country,
especially an old state with an ancient and honorable history, is something that
Mr. Carnegie cannot possibly understand. But the "today" is superfluous. The
Union was a word of power in 1861 as it is in 1891. Before the secession of
Virginia, a Virginian Breckinridge asked, "If exiled in a foreign land, would
35   the heart turn back to Virginia, or South Carolina, or New York, or to any
one state as the cherished home of its pride? No. We would remember only
that we were Americans." Surely this seems quite as patriotic as Mr. Carnegie's
utterance; and yet, to the native Virginian just quoted, so much stronger was
the state than the central government that, a few weeks after this bold speech,
40   he went into the war, and finally perished in the war. "A Union man," says his

biographer, "fighting for the rights of his old mother Virginia." And there were many men of his mind, noted generals, valiant soldiers. The *University Memorial*, which records the names and lives of the alumni of the University of Virginia who fell in the Confederate war, two hundred in number—this volume, full "of memories and of sighs" to every Southern man of my age, lies open before me as I write, and some of the noblest men who figure in its pages were Union men; and the Memorial of the Virginia Military Institute tells the same story with the same eloquence. The state was imperiled, and parties disappeared; and of the combatants in the field, some of the bravest and the most conspicuous belonged to those whose love of the old Union was warm and strong, to whom the severance of the tie that bound the states together was a personal grief. But even those who prophesied the worst, who predicted a long and bloody struggle and a doubtful result, had no question about the duty of the citizen; shared the common burden and submitted to the individual sacrifice as readily as the veriest fire-eater—nay, as they claimed, more readily. The most intimate friend I ever had, who fell after heroic services, was known by all our circle to be utterly at variance with the prevalent Southern view of the quarrel, and died upholding a right which was not a right to him except so far as the mandate of his state made it a right; and while he would have preferred to see "the old flag" floating over a united people, he restored the new banner to its place time after time when it had been cut down by shot and shell.

Those who were bred in the opposite political faith, who read their right of withdrawal in the Constitution, had less heart-searching to begin with than the Union men of the South; but when the state called there were no parties, and the only trace of the old difference was a certain rivalry which should do the better fighting. This ready response to the call of the state showed very clearly that, despite varying theories of government, the people of the Southern states were practically of one mind as to the seat of the paramount obligation. Adherence to the Union was a matter of sentiment, a matter of interest. The arguments urged on the South against secession were addressed to the memories of the glorious struggle for independence, to the anticipation of the glorious future that awaited the united country, to the difficulties and the burdens of a separate life. Especial stress was laid on the last argument; and the expense of a separate government, of a standing army, was set forth in appalling figures. A Northern student of the war once said to me, "If the Southern people had been of a statistical turn, there would have been no secession, there would have been no war." But there were men enough of a statistical turn in the South to warn the people against the enormous expense of independence, just as there are men enough of a statistical turn in Italy to remind the Italians of the enormous cost of national unity. "Counting the cost" is in things temporal the

only wise course, as in the building of a tower; but there are times in the life
of an individual, of a people, when the things that are eternal force themselves
into the calculation, and the abacus is nowhere. "Neither count I my life dear
unto myself" is a sentiment that does not enter into the domain of statistics.
5   The great Athenian statesman who saw the necessity of the Peloponnesian war
was not above statistics, as he showed when he passed in review the resources
of the Athenian empire, the tribute from the allies, the treasure laid up in the
House of the Virgin. But when he addressed the people in justification of the
war, he based his argument not on a calculation of material resources, but on
10   a simple principle of right. Submission to any encroachment, the least as well
as the greatest, on the rights of a state means slavery. To us submission meant
slavery, as it did to Pericles and the Athenians; as it did to the great historian of
Greece, who had learned this lesson from the Peloponnesian war, and who took
sides with the Southern states, to the great dismay of his fellow-radicals who
15   could not see, as George Grote saw, the real point at issue in the controversy.
Submission is slavery, and the bitterest taunt in the vocabulary of those who
advocated secession was "submissionist."…

There is such a thing as fighting for a principle, an idea; but principle and
idea must be incarnate, and the principle of states' rights was incarnate in the
20   historical life of the Southern people. Of the thirteen original states, Virginia,
North Carolina, South Carolina, and Georgia were openly and officially upon
the side of the South. Maryland as a state was bound hand and foot. We counted
her as ours, for the Potomac and Chesapeake Bay united as well as divided. Each
of these states had a history, had an individuality. Every one was something more
25   than a certain aggregate of square miles wherein dwelt an uncertain number of
uncertain inhabitants, something more than a territory transformed into a state
by the magic of political legerdemain; a creature of the central government, and
duly loyal to its creator.…

The cohesive power of the Revolutionary war was not sufficiently strong to
30   make the states sink their contributions to the common cause in the common
glory. Washington was the one national hero, and yet the Washington Light
Infantry of Charleston was named not after the illustrious George, but after his
kinsman, William[1]. The story of Lexington and Concord and Bunker Hill did
not thrill the South Carolinian of an earlier day, and those great achievements
35   were actually criticized. Who were Putnam[2] and Stark[3] that South Carolinians

---

[1]William Washington (1752–1810), Revolutionary War general and cousin of George
Washington
[2]Israel Putnam (1718–1790), prominent Revolutionary War general from Massachussetts
[3]John Stark (1728–1822), prominent Revolutionary War general from New Hampshire

should worship them, when they had a Marion[4] and a Sumter[5] of their own? Vermont went wild, the other day, over Bennington as she did not over the centenary of the surrender at Yorktown. Take away this local patriotism and you take out all the color that is left in American life. That the local patriotism may not only consist with a wider patriotism, but may serve as a most important element in wider patriotism, is true. Witness the strong local life in the old provinces of France. No student of history, no painter of manners, can neglect it. In *Gerfaut*, a novel written before the Franco-Prussian war, Charles de Bernard represents an Alsatian shepherd as saying, "I am not French; I am Alsatian"—"trait de patriotisme de clocher assez commun dans la belle province du Rhin"[6] adds the author, little dreaming of the national significance of that "patriotisme de clocher." The Breton's love of his home is familiar to everyone who has read his Renan, and Blanche Willis Howard, in *Guenn*, makes her priest exclaim, "Monsieur, I would fight with France against any other nation, but I would fight with Brittany against France. I love France. I am a Frenchman. But first of all I am a Breton." The Provencal speaks of France as if she were a foreign country, and fights for her as if she were his alone. What is true of France is true in a measure of England. Devonshire men are notoriously Devonshire men first and last. If this is true of what have become integral parts of kingdom or republic by centuries of incorporation, what is to be said of the states that had never renounced their sovereignty, that had only suspended it in part?

The example of state pride set by the older states was not lost on the younger Southern states, and the Alabamian and the Mississippian lived in the same faith as did the stock from which they sprang; and the community of views, of interest, of social order, soon made a larger unit and prepared the way for a true nationality, and with the nationality a great conflict. The heterogeneousness of the elements that made up the confederacy did not prove the great source of weakness that was expected. The border states looked on the world with different eyes from the Gulf states. The Virginia farmer and the Creole planter of Louisiana were of different strains; and yet there was a solidarity that has never failed to surprise the few Northerners who penetrated the South for study and pleasure. There was an extraordinary ramification of family and social ties throughout the Southern states, and a few minutes' conversation sufficed to place any member of the social organism from Virginia to Texas. Great schools, like the University of Virginia, within the Southern border did much to foster the community of feeling, and while there were not a few Southerners at Harvard

---

[4]Francis Marion (1732–1795), prominent Revolutionary War general from South Carolina
[5]Thomas Sumter (1734–1832), prominent Revolutionary War general from South Carolina
[6]"A nice feature of local patriotism so common in the beautiful province of the Rhine."

and Yale, and while Princeton was almost a Southern college, an education in the North did not seem to nationalize the Southerner. On the contrary, as in the universities of the Middle Ages, groups were formed in accordance with nativity; and sectional lines, though effaced at certain points, were strength-
5 ened at others. There may have been a certain broadening of view; there was no weakening of the home ties. West Point made fewer converts to this side and to that than did the Northern wives of Southern husbands, the Southern wives of Northern husbands....

I have tried in this paper to reproduce the past and its perspective, to show
10 how the men of my time and of my environment looked at the problems that confronted us. It has been a painful and I fear a futile task. So far as I have reproduced the perspective for myself it has been a revival of sorrows such as this generation cannot understand; it has recalled the hours when it gave one a passion for death, a shame of life, to read our bulletins. And how could I
15 hope to reproduce that perspective for others, for men who belong to another generation and another region, when so many men who lived the same life and fought on the same side have themselves lost the point of view not only of the beginning of the war, but also of the end of the war, not only of the inexpress-ible exaltation, but of the unutterable degradation? They have forgotten what
20 a strange world the survivors of the conflict had to face. If the state had been ours still, the foundations of the earth would not have been out of course; but the state was a military district, and the Confederacy had ceased to exist. The generous policy which would have restored the state and made a new union possible, which would have disentwined much of the passionate clinging to
25 the past, was crossed by the death of the only man who could have carried it through, if even he could have carried it through; and years of trouble had to pass before the current of national life ran freely through the Southern states. It was before this circuit was complete that the principal of one of the chief schools of Virginia set up a tablet to the memory of the "old boys" who had
30 perished in the war—it was a list the length of which few Northern colleges could equal—and I was asked to furnish a motto. Those who know classic literature at all know that for patriotism and friendship mottoes are not far to seek, but during the war I felt as I had never felt before the meaning of many a classic sentence. The motto came from Ovid, whom many call a frivolous
35 poet; but the frivolous Roman was after all a Roman, and he was young when he wrote the line—too young not to feel the generous swell of true feeling. It was written of the dead brothers of Briseis:

Qui bene pro patria cum patriaque iacent[7]

---

[7]"They died well for and with their country." (Ovid, *Heriodes* III:106)

The sentiment found an echo at the time, deserved an echo at the time. Now it is a sentiment without an echo, and last year a valued personal friend of mine, in an eloquent oration, a noble tribute to the memory of our great captain, a discourse full of the glory of the past, the wisdom of the present, the hope of the future, rebuked the sentiment as idle in its despair. As well rebuke 5 a cry of anguish, a cry of desolation out of the past. For those whose names are recorded on that tablet the line is but too true. For those of us who survive it has ceased to have the import that it once had, for we have learned to work resolutely for the furtherance of all that is good in the wider life that has been opened to us by the issue of the war, without complaining, without repining. 10 That the cause we fought for and our brothers died for was the cause of civil liberty, and not the cause of human slavery, is a thesis which we feel ourselves bound to maintain whenever our motives are challenged or misunderstood, if only for our children's sake. But even that will not long be necessary, for the vindication of our principles will be made manifest in the working out of the 15 problems with which the republic has to grapple. If, however, the effacement of state lines and the complete centralization of the government shall prove to be the wisdom of the future, the poetry of life will still find its home in the old order, and those who loved their state best will live longest in song and legend—song yet unsung, legend not yet crystallized. 20

People's Party Platform

The national election of 1892 was a contest of two presidents—one, the incumbent Benjamin Harrison (1833–1901), and the other Grover Cleveland (1827–1908), whose re-election bid Harrison had defeated in 1888. The 1892 campaign unfolded against a backdrop of difficult economic conditions and enflamed social divisions. Across the country, farmers were particularly agitated about the low prices they were getting for their crops, the high rates they had to pay to ship and store their produce, and credit that was either too hard to get or too expensive to afford. By 1892, in short, farmers and other working-class people were feeling victimized for many years by the operation of the free market; yet, when they looked to the two major political parties for relief, they found little support for the reforms they sought. During the 1880s, grassroots organizations known as Farmers' Alliances began to spring up in the great agricultural areas of the Midwest and South. By 1890, the white and black chapters of the racially segregated Alliance movement claimed between two and three million members nationwide and became the political spearhead of a major farm protest movement. In state after state, especially in the South, the Alliance either ran candidates for office under its own banner, or pressured the Democratic Party to nominate sympathetic candidates.

With the presidential campaign of 1892 in the offing, many from within the Alliance movement began to promote the establishment of a new party that would work for change benefitting "the people," as opposed to "big business" or other "special interests." A national convention of the "People's Party" (also known as the Populist Party) met in Omaha and nominated for president of the United States a former general in the Union Army and unsuccessful third-party candidate for president twelve years earlier, James B. Weaver (1833–1912). Weaver ran on the platform below, won over a million votes, or eight percent of the total, and carried four states

The National Economist 7 (9 July 1892):257–58.

(Colorado, Kansas, Nevada, and Idaho). Populism, as a political movement,
did not end with the election of 1892, although this was the only time the
People's Party nominated its own third-party candidate in a national elec-
tion. In 1900, the Democratic nominee William Jennings Bryan also had
the Populist endorsement. Soon, Progressivism would supersede Populism
as the principal reformist strain in American politics.

4 July 1892

Assembled upon the 116th anniversary of the declaration of Independence, the
People's Party of America, in their first national convention, invoking upon their
action the blessing of Almighty God, puts forth, in the name and on behalf of the
people of this country, the following preamble and declaration of principles:

5   The conditions which surround us best justify our co-operation. We meet
in the midst of a nation brought to the verge of moral, political, and material
ruin. Corruption dominates the ballot box, the legislatures, the Congress, and
touches even the ermine of the bench. The people are demoralized; most of the
states have been compelled to isolate the voters at the polling places to prevent
10   universal intimidation or bribery. The newspapers are largely subsidized or
muzzled, public opinion silenced, business prostrated, our homes covered with
mortgages, labor impoverished, and the land concentrating in the hands of the
capitalists. The urban workmen are denied the right of organization for self-protection, imported pauperized labor beats down their wages, a hireling standing
15   army, unrecognized by our laws, is established to shoot them down, and they are
rapidly degenerating into European conditions. The fruits of the toil of millions
are boldly stolen to build up colossal fortunes for a few unprecedented in the
history of mankind, and the possessors of these, in turn, despise the Republic
and endanger liberty. From the same prolific womb of governmental injustice
20   we breed the two great classes—tramps and millionaires.

The national power to create money is appropriated to enrich bond-holders;
a vast public debt payable in legal tender currency has been funded into gold-
bearing bonds, thereby adding millions to the burdens of the people.

Silver, which has been accepted as coin since the dawn of history, has been
25   de-monetized to add to the purchasing power of gold by decreasing the value
of all forms of property as well as human labor and the supply of currency is
purposely abridged to fatten usurers, bankrupt enterprise, and enslave industry.
A vast conspiracy against mankind has been organized on two continents, and
it is rapidly taking possession of the world, if not met and overthrown at once
30   it forbodes terrible social convulsions, the destruction of civilization, or the
establishment of an absolute despotism.

We have witnessed for more than a quarter of a century the struggles of
the two great political parties for power and plunder, while grievous wrongs

have been inflicted upon the suffering people. We charge that the controlling influences dominating both these parties have permitted the existing dreadful conditions to develop without serious effort to prevent or restrain them. Neither do they now promise us any substantial reform. They have agreed together to ignore, in the coming campaign, every issue but one. They propose to drown the outcries of a plundered people with the uproar of a sham-battle over the tariff, so that capitalists, corporations, national banks, rings, trusts, watered stock, the de-monetization of silver, and the oppressions of the usurers may all be lost sight of. They propose to sacrifice our homes, lives, and children on the altar of mammon, to destroy the multitude in order to secure corruption funds from the millionaires.

Assembled on the anniversary of the birthday of the nation and filled with the spirit of the grand general and chief, who established our independence, we seek to restore the government of the Republic to the hands of "the plain people" with whose class it originated. We assert our purposes to be identical with the purposes of the national Constitution, to form a more perfect union and establish justice, ensure domestic tranquility, provide for the common defense, protect the general welfare, and secure the blessings of liberty for ourselves and our posterity.

We declare that this Republic can only endure as a free government while built upon the love of the whole people for each other and for the nation; that it cannot be pinned together by bayonets; that the Civil War is over and that every passion and resentment which grew out of it must die with it and that we must be in fact, as we are in name, one united brotherhood of free men.

Our country finds itself confronted by conditions for which there is no precedent in the history of the world. Our annual agricultural productions amount to billions of dollars in value, which must within a few weeks or months be exchanged for billions of dollars worth of commodities consumed in their production; the existing currency supply is wholly inadequate to make this exchange. The results are falling prices, the formation of combines and rings, the impoverishment of the producing class. We pledge ourselves that, if given power, we will labor to contest these evils by wise and reasonable legislation, in accordance with the terms of our platform.

We believe that the powers of government—in other words, of the people—should be expanded (as in the case of the postal service) as rapidly and as far as the good sense of an intelligent people and the teachings of experience shall justify, to the end that oppression, injustice, and poverty shall eventually cease in the land.

While our sympathies as a party of reform are naturally upon the side of every proposition which will tend to make men intelligent, virtuous, and

temperate, we nevertheless regard these questions—important as they are—as secondary to the great issues now pressing for solution, and upon which not only our individual prosperity, but the very existence of free institution depend, and we ask all men to first help us to determine whether we are to have
5   a Republic to administer before we differ as to the conditions upon which it is to be administered, believing that the forces of reform this day organized will never cease to move forward until every wrong is righted and equal privileges securely established for all the men and women of this country.

We declare, therefore,

10 First, that the union of the labor forces of the United States this day consummated shall be permanent and perpetual; may its spirit enter into all hearts for the salvation of the Republic and the uplifting of mankind.

Second, wealth belongs to him who creates it, and every dollar taken from industry without an equivalent is robbery; "if any will not work, neither shall he eat."
15 The interests of rural and civic labor are the same; their enemies are identical.

Third, we believe that the time has come when the railroad corporations will either own the people or the people must own the railroads; and should the government enter upon the work of owning and managing all railroads, we should favor an amendment to the Constitution by which all persons engaged
20 in the government service shall be placed under a civil service regulation of the most rigid character, so as to prevent the increase of the power of the national administration by the use of such additional government employees.

The Question of Finance

We demand a national currency, safe, sound, and flexible, issued by the general government only, a full legal tender for all debts, public and private, and that
25 without the use of banking corporations, a just, equitable, and efficient means of distribution direct to the people at a tax not to exceed 2 percent per annum, to be provided as set forth in the sub-treasury plan of the Farmers' Alliance, or a better system; also by payments in discharge of its obligations for public improvements.

30 We demand free and unlimited coinage of silver and gold at the present legal ratio of 16 to 1.

We demand that the amount of circulating medium be speedily increased to not less than $50 per capita.

We demand a graduated income tax.

We believe that the money of the country should be kept as much as possible in the hands of the people, and hence we demand that all states and national revenues shall be limited to the necessary expenses of the government, economically and honestly administered.

We demand that postal savings banks be established by the government for the safe deposit of the earnings of the people and to facilitate exchange.

Control of Transportation

Transportation being a means of exchange and a public necessity, the government should own and operate the railroads in the interest of the people.

The telegraph and telephone, like the post-office system, being a necessity for the transmission of news, should be owned and operated by the government in the interest of the people.

Reclaiming the Land

The land, including all the natural sources of wealth, is the heritage of the people, and should not be monopolized for speculative purposes, and alien ownership of land should be prohibited. All land now held by railroads and other corporations in excess of their actual needs and all lands now owned by aliens should be re-claimed by the government and held for actual settlers only.

Expression of Sentiments

The following resolutions were offered independent of the platform, and were adopted as expressive of the sentiment of the convention:

Resolved, that we demand a free ballot and a fair count in all elections, and pledge ourselves to secure it to every legal voter without Federal intervention through the adoption by the states of the un-perverted Australian secret ballot system.

Resolved, that the revenue derived from a graduated income tax should be supplied to the reduction of the burden of taxation now levied upon the domestic industries of this country.

Resolved, that we pledge our support to fair and liberal pensions to ex-Union soldiers and sailors.

Resolved, that we condemn the fallacy of protecting American labor under the present system, which opens our ports to the pauper and criminal classes of the world and crowds out our wage-earners, and we denounce the present ineffective law against contract labor, and demand the further restriction of undesirable immigration.

Resolved, that we cordially sympathize with the efforts of organized working men to shorten the hours of labor, and demand a rigid enforcement of the existing eight-hour law on government work, and ask that a penalty clause be added to the said law.

Resolved, that we regard the maintenance of a large standing army of mercenaries, known as the Pinkerton system, as a menace to our liberties, and we demand its abolition, and we condemn the recent invasion of the Territory of Wyoming by the hired assassins of plutocracy, assisted by Federal officers.

Resolved, that we favor a constitutional provision limiting the office of President and Vice-President to one term, and providing for the election of the Senators by a direct vote of the people.

Resolved, that we oppose any subsidy or national aid to any private corporation for any purpose....

THE FRONTIER IN AMERICAN HISTORY
FREDERICK JACKSON TURNER (1861–1932)

Frederick Jackson Turner delivered his famous essay, "The Significance of the Frontier in American History" on July 12, 1893, at the Columbian Exposition. Only blocks away on that sweltering Chicago afternoon, Buffalo Bill Cody and his Congress of Rough Riders performed their "Wild West" show. Though Turner delivered his paper to an academic audience and Bill Cody to a popular audience, both told the same story—the pioneer remade the landscape, establishing a new nation. In the process, the settler exchanged many of his European habits with those of the Indian, becoming neither European nor Indian. Instead, he became something wholly new, the American.

12 JULY 1893

In a recent bulletin of the superintendent of the census for 1890 appear these significant words: "Up to and including 1880 the country had a frontier of settlement, but at present the unsettled area has been so broken into by isolated bodies of settlement that there can hardly be said to be a frontier line. In the discussion of its extent, its westward movement, etc., it cannot, therefore, any 5 longer have a place in the census reports." This brief official statement marks the closing of a great historic movement. Up to our own day American history has been in a large degree the history of the colonization of the Great West. The existence of an area of free land, its continuous recession, and the advance of American settlement westward, explain American development. Behind institu- 10 tions, behind constitutional forms and modifications, lie the vital forces that call these organs into life, and shape them to meet changing conditions. Now, the peculiarity of American institutions is the fact that they have been compelled to adapt themselves to the changes of an expanding people—to the changes involved in crossing a continent, in winning a wilderness, and in developing 15 at each area of this progress out of the primitive economic and political condi-

Frederick Jackson Turner, *The Significance of the Frontier in American History* (Madison: State Historical Society of Wisconsin, 1894), 1–4, 13–14, 20–22, 27–29, 33–34.

tions of the frontier into the complexity of city life. Said Calhoun in 1817, "We are great, and rapidly—I was about to say fearfully—growing!" So saying, he touched the distinguishing feature of American life. All peoples show development: the germ theory of politics has been sufficiently emphasized. In the case
5　of most nations, however, the development has occurred in a limited area; and if the nation has expanded, it has met other growing peoples whom it has conquered. But in the case of the United States we have a different phenomenon. Limiting our attention to the Atlantic coast, we have the familiar phenomenon of the evolution of institutions in a limited area, such as the rise of representative
10　government: the differentiation of simple colonial governments into complex organs; the progress from primitive industrial society, without division of labor, up to manufacturing civilization. But we have in addition to this *a recurrence of the process of evolution in each western area reached in the process of expansion.* Thus American development has exhibited not merely advance along a single line,
15　but a return to primitive conditions on a continually advancing frontier line, and a new development for that area. American social development has been continually beginning over again on the frontier. This perennial re-birth, this fluidity of American life, this expansion westward with its new opportunities, its continuous touch with the simplicity of primitive society, furnish the forces
20　dominating American character. The true point of view in the history of this nation is not the Atlantic coast, it is the Great West. Even the slavery struggle, which is made so exclusive an object of attention by writers like Professor von Holst, occupies its important place in American history because of its relation to westward expansion.
25　　　In this advance, the frontier is the outer edge of the wave—the meeting point between savagery and civilization. Much has been written about the frontier from the point of view of border warfare and the chase, but as a field for the serious study of the economist and the historian it has been neglected.
　　　What is the frontier? It is not the European frontier—a fortified boundary
30　line running through dense populations. The most significant thing about it is, that it lies at the hither edge of free land. In the census reports it is treated as the margin of that settlement which has a density of two or more to the square mile. The term is an elastic one, and for our purposes does not need sharp definition. We shall consider the whole frontier belt, including the Indian
35　country and the outer margin of the "settled area" of the census reports. This paper will make no attempt to treat the subject exhaustively; its aim, is simply to call attention to the frontier as a fertile field for investigation, and to suggest some of the problems which arise in connection with it.
　　　In the settlement of America we have to observe how European life entered
40　the continent, and how America modified and developed that life, and reacted

on Europe. Our early history is the study of European germs developing in an American environment. Too exclusive attention has been paid by institutional students to the Germanic origins, too little to the American factors. Now, the frontier is the line of most rapid and effective Americanization. The wilderness masters the colonist. It finds him a European in dress, industries, tools, modes 5 of travel, and thought. It takes him from the railroad car and puts him in the birch canoe. It strips off the garments of civilization, and arrays him in the hunting shirt and the moccasin. It puts him in the log cabin of the Cherokee and the Iroquois, and runs an Indian palisade around him. Before long he has gone to planting Indian corn and plowing with a sharp stick; he shouts the war 10 cry and takes the scalp in orthodox Indian fashion. In short, at the frontier the environment is at first too strong for the man. He must accept the conditions which it furnishes, or perish, and so he fits himself into the Indian clearings and follows the Indian trails. Little by little he transforms the wilderness, but the outcome is not the old Europe, not simply the development of Germanic 15 germs, any more than the first phenomenon was a case of reversion to the Germanic mark. The fact is that here is a new product that is American. At first, the frontier was the Atlantic coast. It was the frontier of Europe in a very real sense. Moving westward, the frontier became more and more American. *As successive terminal moraines result from successive glaciations, so each frontier leaves* 20 *its traces behind it, and when it becomes a settled area the region still partakes of the frontier characteristics.* Thus the advance of the frontier has meant a steady movement away from the influence of Europe, a steady growth of independence on American lines. And to study this advance, the men who grew up under these conditions, and the political, economic and social results of it, is to study 25 the really American part of our history....

And yet, in spite of this opposition of the interests of the trader and the farmer, the Indian trade pioneered the way for civilization. The buffalo trail became the Indian trail, and this became the trader's "trace": the trails widened into roads, and the roads into turnpikes, and these in turn were transformed 30 into railroads. The same origin can be shown for the railroads of the South, the far West, and the Dominion of Canada. The trading posts reached by these trails were on the sites of Indian villages which had been placed in positions suggested by nature; and these trading posts, situated so as to command the water systems of the country, have grown into such cities as Albany, Pittsburg, 35 Detroit, Chicago, Saint Louis, Council Bluffs, and Kansas City. Thus civilization in America has followed the arteries made by geology, pouring an ever richer tide through them, until at last the slender paths of aboriginal intercourse have been broadened and interwoven into the complex mazes of modern commercial lines; the wilderness has been interpenetrated by lines of civilization, growing 40 ever more numerous. It is like the steady growth of a complex nervous system for the originally simple, inert continent. If one would understand why we are to-day one nation, rather than a collection of isolated states, he must study this economic and social consolidation of the country. In this progress from savage conditions lie topics for the evolutionist.

The effect of the Indian frontier as a consolidating agent in our history is important. From the close of the seventeenth century various inter-colonial congresses have been called to treat with Indians and establish common measures of defense. Particularism was strongest in colonies with no Indian frontier. This frontier stretched along the western border like a cord of union. The Indian was a common danger, demanding united action. Most celebrated of these conferences was the Albany congress of 1754, called to treat with the Six Nations, and to consider plans of union. Even a cursory reading of the plan proposed by the congress reveals the importance of the frontier. The powers of the general council and the officers were, chiefly, the determination of peace and war with the Indians, the regulation of Indian trade, the purchase of Indian lands, and the creation and government of new settlements as a security against the Indians. It is evident that the unifying tendencies of the Revolutionary period were facilitated by the previous co-operation in the regulation of the frontier. In this connection may be mentioned the importance of the frontier, from that day to this, as a military training school, keeping alive the power of resistance to aggression, and developing the stalwart and rugged qualities of the frontiersman....

Composite Nationality

First, we note that the frontier promoted the formation of a composite nationality for the American people. The coast was preponderantly English, but the later tides of continental immigration flowed across to the free lands. This was the case from the early colonial days. The Scotch-Irish and the Palatine Germans, or "Pennsylvania Dutch," furnished the stock of the colonial frontier. With these peoples were also the freed indented servants, or redemptioners, who at the expiration of their time of service passed to the frontier. Governor Spottswood of Virginia writes in 1717, "The inhabitants of our frontiers are composed generally of such as have been transported hither as servants, and, being out of their time, settle themselves where land is to be taken up and that will produce the necessaries of life with little labor." Very generally these redemptioners were of non-English stock. In the crucible of the frontier the immigrants were Americanized, liberated and fused into a mixed race, English in neither nationality or characteristics. The process has gone on from the early days to our own. Burke and other writers in the middle of the eighteenth century believed that Pennsylvania was "threatened with the danger of being wholly foreign in language, manners, and perhaps even inclinations." The German and Scotch-Irish elements in the frontier of the South were only less great. In the middle of the present century the German element in Wisconsin was already so considerable that leading publicists looked to the creation of a German state 5 out of the commonwealth by concentrating their colonization. Such examples teach us to beware of misinterpreting the fact that there is a common English speech in America into a belief that the stock is also English.

Industrial Independence

In another way the advance of the frontier decreased our dependence on England. The coast, particularly of the South, lacked diversified industries, and was 10 dependent on England for the bulk of its supplies. In the South there was even a dependence on the Northern colonies for articles of food. Governor Glenn of South Carolina writes in the middle of the eighteenth century: "Our trade with New York and Philadelphia was of this sort, draining us of all the little money and bills we could gather from other places for their bread, flour, beer, 15 hams, bacon, and other things of their produce, all which, except beer, our new townships begin to supply us with, which are settled with very industrious and thriving Germans. This no doubt diminishes the number of shipping and the appearance of our trade, but it is far from being a detriment to us." Before long the frontier created a demand for merchants. As it retreated from the coast it 20 became less and less possible for England to bring her supplies directly to the consumer's wharfs, and carry away staple crops, and staple crops began to give way to diversified agriculture for a time. The effect of this phase of the frontier action upon the northern section is perceived when we realize how the advance of the frontier aroused seaboard cities like Boston, New York, and Baltimore, to 25 engage in rivalry for what Washington called "the extensive and valuable trade of a rising empire."...

Growth of Democracy

But the most important effect of the frontier has been in the promotion of democracy here and in Europe. As has been pointed out, the frontier is productive of individualism. Complex society is precipitated by the wilderness into a 30 kind of primitive organization based on the family. The tendency is anti-social. It produces antipathy to control, and particularly to any direct control. The tax-gatherer is viewed as a representative of oppression. Professor Osgood, in an able article, has pointed out that the frontier conditions prevalent in the colonies are important factors in the explanation of the American revolution, 35 where individual liberty was sometimes confused with absence of all effective

government. The same conditions aid in explaining the difficulty of instituting a
strong government in the period of the confederacy. The frontier individualism
has from the beginning promoted democracy.

5   The frontier states that came into the Union in the first quarter of a century
of its existence came in with democratic suffrage provisions, and had reactive
effects of the highest importance upon the other states whose peoples were being
attracted there. It was *western* New York that forced an extension of suffrage in
the constitutional convention of that state in 1820; and it was *western* Virginia
that compelled the tide-water region to put a more liberal suffrage provision
10   in the constitution framed in 1830, and to give to the frontier region a more
nearly proportionate representation with the tide-water aristocracy. The rise of
democracy as an effective force in the nation came in with western preponderance under Jackson and William Henry Harrison, and it meant the triumph of
the frontier—with all of its good and with all of its evil elements. An interesting
15   illustration of the tone of frontier democracy in 1830 comes from the same
debates in the Virginia convention already referred to. A representative from
western Virginia declared: "But, sir, it is not the increase of population in the
West which this gentleman ought to fear. It is the energy which the mountain
breeze and western habits impart to those emigrants. They are regenerated,
20   politically I mean, sir. They soon become *working politicians*; and the difference,
sir, between a *talking* and a *working* politician is immense. The Old Dominion
has long been celebrated for producing great orators; the ablest metaphysicians
in policy; men that can split hairs in all abstruse questions of political economy.
But at home, or when they return from congress, they have negroes to fan them
25   asleep. But a Pennsylvania, a New York, an Ohio, or a western Virginia statesman, though far inferior in logic, metaphysics and rhetoric to an old Virginia
statesman, has this advantage, that when he returns home he takes off his coat
and takes hold of the plough. This gives him bone and muscle, sir, and preserves
his republican principles pure and uncontaminated."

30   So long as free land exists, the opportunity for a competency exists, and
economic power secures political power. But the democracy born of free land,
strong in selfishness and individualism, intolerant of administrative experience
and education, and pressing individual liberty beyond its proper bounds, has
its dangers as well as its benefits. Individualism in America has allowed a laxity
35   in regard to governmental affairs which has rendered possible the spoils system,
and all the manifest evils that follow from the lack of a highly developed civic
spirit. In this connection may be noted also the influence of frontier conditions
in permitting lax business honor, inflated paper currency and wild-cat banking.
The colonial and revolutionary frontier was the region whence emanated many
40   of the worst forms of an evil currency. The West in the War of 1812 repeated

the phenomenon on the frontier of that day, while the speculation and wild-cat banking of the period of the crisis of 1837 occurred on the new frontier belt of the next tier of states. Thus each one of the periods of lax financial integrity coincides with periods when a new set of frontier communities had arisen, and coincides in area with these successive frontiers, for the most part. The recent 5 Populist agitation is a case in point. Many a state that now declines any connection with the tenets of the Populists, itself adhered to such ideas in an earlier stage of the development of the state. A primitive society can hardly be expected to show the intelligent appreciation of the complexity of business interests in a developed society. The continual recurrence of these areas of paper-money 10 agitation is another evidence that the frontier can be isolated and studied as a factor in American history of the highest importance....

Intellectual Traits

From the conditions of frontier life came intellectual traits of profound importance. The works of travelers along each frontier from colonial days onward describe for each certain traits, and these traits have, while softening down, 15 still persisted as survivals in the place of their origin, even when a higher social organization succeeded. The result is that to the frontier the American intellect owes its striking characteristics. That coarseness and strength combined with acuteness and inquisitiveness, that practical, inventive turn of mind, quick to find expedients, that masterful grasp of material things, lacking in the artistic 20 but powerful to effect great ends, that restless, nervous energy, that dominant individualism, working for good and for evil, and withal that buoyancy and exuberance which comes with freedom—these are traits of the frontier, or traits called out elsewhere because of the existence of the frontier. Since the days when the fleet of Columbus sailed into the waters of the New World, America has 25 been another name for opportunity, and the people of the United States have taken their tone from the incessant expansion which has not only been open but has even been forced upon them. He would be a rash prophet who should assert that the expansive character of American life has now entirely ceased. Movement has been its dominant fact, and, unless this training has no effect 30 upon a people, the American intellect will continually demand a wider field for its exercise. But never again will such gifts of free land offer themselves. For a moment at the frontier the bonds of custom are broken, and unrestraint is triumphant. There is not *tabula rasa*. The stubborn American environment is there with its imperious summons to accept its conditions; the inherited ways 35 of doing things are also there; and yet, in spite of environment, and in spite of custom, each frontier did indeed furnish a new field of opportunity, a gate of escape from the bondage of the past; and freshness, and confidence, and scorn

of older society, impatience of its restraints and its ideas, and indifference to its lessons, have accompanied the frontier. What the Mediterranean Sea was to the Greeks, breaking the bond of custom, offering new experiences, calling out new institutions and activities, that, and more, the ever retreating frontier has been
5   to the United States directly, and to the nations of Europe more remotely. And now, four centuries from the discovery of American, at the end of a hundred years of life under the Constitution, the frontier has gone, and with its going has closed the first period of American history.

AUTOBIOGRAPHY
THEODORE ROOSEVELT (1858–1919)
POLICE COMMISSIONER OF NEW YORK CITY (1895–1897)

*Following the Civil War, New York City witnessed a vast expansion in
its number of gambling halls, houses of prostitution, and saloons. Police
corruption was widespread, and virtually institutionalized by the bosses of
Tammany Hall. Theodore Roosevelt, fresh from his service on the United
States Civil Service Commission, gained appointment in 1895 as president
of the Board of the New York City Police Commission. Roosevelt had a
reputation for his "unimpeachable honesty, reforming zeal, and strict and
fair enforcement of law." He established new disciplinary rules, appointed
police recruits according to mental and physical qualifications rather than
political connections, and walked the late-night "beats" to make sure that
the officers were on duty. He also tangled with the city's liquor interests over
the issue of Sunday closings.*

1895

One of the perennially serious and difficult problems, and one of the chief
reasons for police blackmail and corruption, is to be found in the excise situation in New York. When I was Police Commissioner, New York was a city
with twelve or fifteen thousand saloons, with a state law which said they should
be closed on Sundays, and with a local sentiment which put a premium on   5
violating the law by making Sunday the most profitable day in the week to the
saloon-keeper who was willing to take chances. It was this willingness to take
chances that furnished to the corrupt politician and the corrupt police officer
their opportunities.

There was in New York City a strong sentiment in favor of honesty in   10
politics; there was also a strong sentiment in favor of opening the saloons on
Sundays; and, finally, there was a strong sentiment in favor of keeping the
saloons closed on Sunday. Unfortunately, many of the men who favored honest
government nevertheless preferred keeping the saloons open to having honest
government; and many others among the men who favored honest government   15

Theodore Roosevelt, *An Autobiography* (New York: The Macmillan Company, 1913), 207–11.

put it second to keeping the saloons closed. Moreover, among the people who wished the law obeyed and the saloons closed there were plenty who objected strongly to every step necessary to accomplish the result, although they also insisted that the result should be accomplished.

5   Meanwhile the politicians found an incredible profit in using the law as a club to keep the saloons in line; all except the biggest, the owners of which, or the owners of the breweries back of which, sat in the inner councils of Tammany, or controlled Tammany's allies in the Republican organization. The police used the partial and spasmodic enforcement of the law as a means of collecting
10 blackmail. The result was that the officers of the law, the politicians, and the saloon-keepers became inextricably tangled in a network of crime and connivance at crime. The most powerful saloon-keepers controlled the politicians and the police, while the latter in turn terrorized and blackmailed all the other saloon-keepers. It was not a case of non-enforcement of the law. The law was
15 very actively enforced, but it was enforced with corrupt discrimination.

    It is difficult for men who have not been brought into contact with that side of political life which deals with the underworld to understand the brazen openness with which this blackmailing of lawbreakers was carried out. A further very dark fact was that many of the men responsible for putting the law
20 on the statute-books in order to please one element of their constituents, also connived at or even profited by the corrupt and partial non-enforcement of the law in order to please another set of their constituents, or to secure profit from themselves. The organ of the liquor-sellers at that time was the *Wine and Spirit Gazette*. The editor of this paper believed in selling liquor on Sunday,
25 and felt that it was an outrage to forbid it. But he also felt that corruption and blackmail made too big a price to pay for the partial non-enforcement of the law. He made in his paper a statement, the correctness of which was never questioned, which offers a startling commentary on New York politics of that period. In this statement he recited the fact that the system of blackmail had
30 been brought to such a state of perfection, and had become so oppressive to the liquor dealers themselves, that they communicated at length on the subject with Governor Hill[1] (the state Democratic boss) and then with Mr. Croker[2] (the city Democratic boss). Finally the matter was formally taken up by a committee of the Central Association of Liquor Dealers in an interview they held
35 with Mr. Martin,[3] my Tammany predecessor as President of the police force.

---

[1]David Bennett Hill (1843–1910), Democratic Governor of New York (1885–1891) and U.S. Senator from New York (1892–1897)

[2]Richard Croker (1841–1922) held a a series of minor political jobs in New York City and was head of Tammany Hall (1866–1902).

[3]James J. Martin, New York City Police Commissioner (1889–1895)

In matter-of-course way the editor's statement continues, "An agreement was made between the leaders of Tammany Hall and the liquor dealers according to which the monthly blackmail paid to the force should be discontinued in return for political support."

Not only did the big bosses, state and local, treat this agreement, and the corruption to which it was due, as normal and proper, but they never even took the trouble to deny what had been done when it was made public. Tammany and the police, however, did not fully live up to the agreement; and much discrimination of a very corrupt kind, and of a very exasperating kind to liquor-sellers who wished to be honest, continued in connection with the enforcing of the law.

In short, the agreement was kept only with those who had "pull." These men with "pull" were benefited when their rivals were bullied and blackmailed by the police. The police, meanwhile, who had bought appointment or promotion, and the politicians back of them, extended the black-mailing to include about everything from the pushcart peddler and the big or small merchant who wished to use the sidewalk illegally for his goods, up to the keepers of the brothel, the gambling-house, and the policy-shop. The total blackmail ran into millions of dollars. New York was a wide-open town. The big bosses rolled in wealth, and the corrupt policemen who ran the force lost all sense of decency and justice. Nevertheless, I wish to insist on the fact that the honest men on the patrol posts, "the men with the night-sticks," remained desirous to see honesty obtained, although they were losing courage and hope.

This was the situation that confronted me when I came to Mulberry Street. The saloon was the chief source of mischief. It was with the saloon that I had to deal, and there was only one way to deal with it. That was to enforce the law. The howl that rose was deafening. The professional politicians raved. The yellow press surpassed themselves in clamor and mendacity. A favorite assertion was that I was enforcing a "blue" law, an obsolete law that had never before been enforced. As a matter of fact, I was only enforcing honestly a law that had hitherto been enforced dishonestly. There was very little increase in the number of arrests made for violating the Sunday law. Indeed, there were weeks when the number of arrests went down. The only difference was that there was no protected class. Everybody was arrested alike, and I took especial pains to see that there was no discrimination, and that the big men and the men with political influence were treated like everyone else. The immediate effect was wholly good. I had been told that it was not possible to close the saloons on Sunday and that I could not succeed. The warden of Bellevue Hospital reported, two or three weeks after we had begun, that for the first time in its existence there had not been a case due to a drunken brawl in the hospital all Monday. The police

courts gave the same testimony, while savings banks recorded increased deposits
and pawnshops hard times. The most touching of all things was the fact that we
received letters, literally by the hundred, from mothers in tenement-houses who
had never been allowed to take their children to the country in the wide-open
days, and who now found their husbands willing to take them and their families
for an outing on Sunday. Jake Riis[4] and I spent one Sunday from morning till
night in the tenement districts, seeing for ourselves what had happened.

During the two years that we were in office things never slipped back to
anything like what they had been before. But we did not succeed in keeping
them quite as highly keyed as during these first weeks. As regards the Sunday-
closing law, this was partly because public sentiment was not really with us. The
people who had demanded honesty, but who did not like to pay for it by the
loss of illegal pleasure, joined the openly dishonest in attacking us. Moreover,
all kinds of ways of evading the law were tried, and some of them were successful. The statute, for instance, permitted any man to take liquor with meals.
After two or three months a magistrate was found who decided judicially that
seventeen beers and one pretzel made a meal—after which decision joy again
became unconfined in at least some of the saloons, and the yellow press gleefully
announced that my "tyranny" had been curbed. But my prime object, that of
stopping blackmail, was largely attained.

---

[4]Jacob Riis (1849–1914) was a photographer, journalist, and social reformer. His most famous
book was *How the Other Half Lives* (1890).

The Fallacy of
Territorial Extension
William Graham Sumner (1840–1910)

Sociologist William Graham Sumner (1840–1910), the son of English immigrants, graduated from Yale during the Civil War before studying at Geneva, Gottingen, and Oxford. After a brief but active career as an Episcopal priest, he left the ministry to become a professor of political economy at his alma mater, where he remained for forty years. His thought became more secular over time and more thoroughly grounded on scientific materialism, and his work bears the imprint of Herbert Spencer, Charles Darwin, and Thomas Huxley. A prolific author, Sumner published a number of books, including What Social Classes Owe to Each Other *(1883),* The Absurd Effort to Make the World Over *(1894), and* Folkways *(1906), as well as biographies of Alexander Hamilton, Andrew Jackson, and Robert Morris, the financier of the American Revolution.*

As the titles of some of his works suggest, Sumner harbored no sympathy for his generation's visionary reformers. He preferred stubborn facts and the laws of nature, he said, to utopian speculation. He took aim at the sentimental humanitarianism of such reformers as Henry George, Edward Bellamy, and Upton Sinclair and continued to defend the free market and minimal government during the Progressive Era. Though a staunch defender of laissez-faire economics, Sumner at the same time feared the growth of a wealthy and politically powerful "plutocracy" in American life.

Ranging beyond economics and politics, Sumner also devoted his analytical and polemical skills to opposing American imperialism. He published "The Fallacy of Territorial Extension" in 1896, two years before the Spanish-American War and the United States' acquisition of the Philippine Islands, Guam, and Puerto Rico.

1896

The traditional belief is that a state aggrandizes itself by territorial extension, so that winning new land is gaining in wealth and prosperity, just as an individual

---

William Graham Sumner, "The Fallacy of Territorial Expansion," in *War and Other Essays*, Albert Gallloway Keller, ed. (1919), 285–96.

would gain if he increased his land possessions. It is undoubtedly true that a state may be so small in territory and population that it cannot serve the true purposes of a state for its citizens, especially in international relations with neighboring states which control a large aggregate of men and capital. There is,
5 therefore, under given circumstances, a size of territory and population which is at the maximum of advantage for the civil unit. The unification of Germany and Italy was apparently advantageous for the people affected. In the nineteenth century there has been a tendency to create national states, and nationality has been advocated as the true basis of state unity. The cases show, however, that
10 the national unit does not necessarily coincide with the most advantageous state unit, and that the principle of nationality cannot override the historical accidents which have made the states. Sweden and Norway, possessing unity, threaten to separate. Austro-Hungary, a conglomerate of nationalities largely hostile to each other, will probably be held together by political necessity. The
15 question of expedient size will always be one for the judgment and good sense of statesmen. The opinion may be risked that Russia has carried out a policy of territorial extension which has been harmful to its internal integration. For three hundred years it has been reaching out after more territory and has sought the grandeur and glory of conquest and size. To this it has sacrificed the elements of
20 social and industrial strength. The autocracy has been confirmed and established because it is the only institution which symbolizes and maintains the unity of the great mass, and the military and tax burdens have distorted the growth of the society to such an extent as to produce disease and weakness.

Territorial aggrandizement enhances the glory and personal importance of
25 the man who is the head of a dynastic state. The fallacy of confusing this with the greatness and strength of the state itself is an open pitfall close at hand. It might seem that a republic, one of whose chief claims to superiority over a monarchy lies in avoiding the danger of confusing the king with the state, ought to be free from this fallacy of national greatness, but we have plenty of examples to prove
30 that the traditional notions are not cut off by changing names and forms.

The notion that gain of territory is gain of wealth and strength for the state, after the expedient size has been won, is a delusion. In the Middle Ages the beneficial interest in land and the jurisdiction over the people who lived on it were united in one person. The modern great states, upon their formation,
35 took to themselves the jurisdiction, and the beneficial interest turned into full property in land. The confusion of the two often reappears now, and it is one of the most fruitful causes of fallacy in public questions. It is often said that the United States owns silver-mines, and it is inferred that the policy of the state in regard to money and currency ought to be controlled in some way by
40 this fact. The "United States," as a subject of property rights and of monetary

claims and obligations, may be best defined by calling it the *Fiscus*. This legal person owns no silver mines. If it did, it could operate them by farming them or by royalties. The revenue thus received would lower taxes. The gain would inure to all the people in the United States. The body politic named the United States has nothing to do with the silver-mines except that it exercises jurisdiction over the territory in which they lie. If it levies taxes on them it also incurs expenses for them, and as it wins no profits on its total income and outgo, these must be taken to be equal. It renders services for which it exacts only the cost thereof. The beneficial and property interest in the mines belongs to individuals, and they win profits only by conducting the exploitation of the mines with an expenditure of labor and capital. These individuals are of many nationalities.

They alone own the product and have the use and enjoyment of it. No other individuals, American or others, have any interest, right, duty, or responsibility in the matter. The United States has simply provided the protection of its laws and institutions for the mine-workers while they were carrying on their enterprise. Its jurisdiction was only a burden to it, not a profitable good. Its jurisdiction was a boon to the mine-workers and certainly did not entail further obligation.

It is said that the boundary between Alaska and British America runs through a gold field, and some people are in great anxiety as to who will "grab it." If an American can go over to the English side and mine gold there for his profit, under English laws and jurisdiction, and an Englishman can come over to the American side and mine gold there for his profit, under American laws and jurisdiction, what difference does it make where the line falls? The only case in which it would make any difference is where the laws and institutions of the two states were not on equal stages of enlightenment.

This case serves to bring out distinctly a reason for the old notion of territorial extension which is no longer valid. In the old colonial system, states conquered territories or founded colonies in order to shut them against all other states and to exploit them on principles of subjugation and monopoly. It is only under this system that the jurisdiction is anything but a burden.

If the United States should admit Hawaii to the Union, the *Fiscus* of the former state would collect more taxes and incur more expenses. The circumstances are such that the latter would probably be the greater. The United States would not acquire a square foot of land in property unless it paid for it. Individual Americans would get no land to till without paying for it and would win no products from it except by wisely expending their labor and capital on it. All that they can do now. So long as there is a government on the islands, native or other, which is competent to guarantee peace, order, and security, no more is necessary, and for any outside power to seize the jurisdiction is an unjustifiable aggression. That jurisdiction would be the best founded which was the most

liberal and enlightened, and would give the best security to all persons who
sought the islands upon their lawful occasions. The jurisdiction would, in any
case, be a burden, and any state might be glad to see any other state assume
the burden, provided that it was one which could be relied upon to execute the
5   charge on enlightened principles for the good of all. The best case is, therefore,
always that in which the resident population produce their own state by the
institutions of self-government.

What private individuals want is free access, under order and security, to any
part of the earth's surface, in order that they may avail themselves of its natural
10   resources for their use, either by investment or commerce. If, therefore, we could
have free trade with Hawaii while somebody else had the jurisdiction, we should
gain all the advantages and escape all the burdens. The Constitution of the United
States establishes absolute free trade between all parts of the territory under its
jurisdiction. A large part of our population was thrown into indignant passion
15   because the Administration rejected the annexation of Hawaii, regarding it like
the act of a man who refuses the gift of a farm. These persons were generally those
who are thrown into excitement by any proposition of free trade. They will not,
therefore, accept free trade with the islands while somebody else has the trouble
and burden of the jurisdiction, but they would accept free trade with the islands
20   eagerly if they could get the burden of the jurisdiction too.

Canada has to deal with a race war and a religious war, each of great viru-
lence, which render governmental jurisdiction in the Dominion difficult and
hazardous. If we could go to Canada and trade there our products for those of
that country, we could win all for our private interests which that country is
25   able to contribute to the welfare of mankind, and we should have nothing to do
with the civil and political difficulties which harass the government. We refuse
to have free trade with Canada. Our newspaper and congressional economists
prove to their own satisfaction that it would be a great harm to us to have free
trade with her now, while she is outside the jurisdiction under which we live;
30   but, within a few months, we have seen an eager impulse of public opinion
toward a war of conquest against Canada. If, then, we could force her to come
under the same jurisdiction, by a cruel and unprovoked war, thus bringing on
ourselves the responsibility for all her civil discords and problems, it appears to
be believed that free trade with her would be a good thing.

35   The case of Cuba is somewhat different. If we could go to the island and
trade with the same freedom with which we can go to Louisiana, we could make
all the gains, by investment and commerce, which the island offers to industry
and enterprise, provided that either Spain or a local government would give the
necessary security, and we should have no share in political struggles there. It
40   may be that the proviso is not satisfied, or soon will not be. Here is a case, then,

which illustrates the fact that states are often forced to extend their jurisdiction whether they want to do so or not. Civilized states are forced to supersede the local jurisdiction of uncivilized or half-civilized states, in order to police the territory and establish the necessary guarantees of industry and commerce. It is idle to set up absolute doctrines of national ownership in the soil which would 5 justify a group of population in spoiling a part of the earth's surface for themselves and everybody else. The island of Cuba may fall into anarchy. If it does, the civilized world may look to the United States to take the jurisdiction and establish order and security there. We might be compelled to do it. It would, however, be a great burden, and possibly a fatal calamity to us. Probably any 10 proposition that England should take it would call out a burst of jingo passion against which all reasoning would be powerless. We ought to pray that England would take it. She would govern it well, and everybody would have free access to it for the purposes of private interest, while our Government would be free from all complications with the politics of the island. If we take the jurisdiction 15 of the island, we shall find ourselves in a political dilemma, each horn of which is as disastrous as the other: either we must govern it as a subject province, or we must admit it into the Union as a state or group of states. Our system is unfit for the government of subject provinces. They have no place in it. They would become seats of corruption, which would react on our own body politic. If we 20 admitted the island as a state or group of states, we should have to let it help govern us. The prospect of adding to the present senate a number of Cuban senators, either native or carpet-bag, is one whose terrors it is not necessary to unfold. Nevertheless it appears that there is a large party which would not listen to free trade with the island while any other nation has the jurisdiction of it, 25 but who are ready to grab it at any cost and to take free trade with it, provided that they can get the political burdens too.

   This confederated state of ours was never planned for indefinite expansion or for an imperial policy. We boast of it a great deal, but we must know that its advantages are won at the cost of limitations, as is the case with most things 30 in this world. The fathers of the Republic planned a confederation of free and peaceful industrial commonwealths, shielded by their geographical position from the jealousies, rivalries, and traditional policies of the Old World and bringing all the resources of civilization to bear for the domestic happiness of the population only. They meant to have no grand state-craft or "high politics," no "balance 35 of power" or "reasons of state," which had cost the human race so much. They meant to offer no field for what Benjamin Franklin called the "pest of glory." It is the limitation of this scheme of the state that the state created under it must forego a great number of the grand functions of European states; especially that it contains no methods and apparatus of conquest, extension, domination, and 40 imperialism. The plan of the fathers would have no controlling authority for us if it had been proved by experience that that plan was narrow, inadequate, and mistaken. Are we prepared to vote that it has proved so? For our territorial extension has reached limits which are complete for all purposes and leave no

5 necessity for "rectification of boundaries." Any extension will open questions, not close them. Any extension will not make us more secure where we are, but will force us to take new measures to secure our new acquisitions. The preservation of acquisitions will force us to re-organize our internal resources, so as to make it possible to prepare them in advance and to mobilize them with promptitude.

10 This will lessen liberty and require discipline. It will increase taxation and all the pressure of government.

It will divert the national energy from the provision of self-maintenance and comfort for the people, and will necessitate stronger and more elaborate governmental machinery. All this will be disastrous to republican institutions

15 and to democracy. Moreover, all extension puts a new strain on the internal cohesion of the pre-existing mass, threatening a new cleavage within. If we had never taken Texas and Northern Mexico we should never have had secession.

The sum of the matter is that colonization and territorial extension are burdens, not gains. Great civilized states cannot avoid these burdens. They are

20 the penalty of greatness because they are the duties of it. No state can success-fully undertake to extend its jurisdiction unless its internal vitality is high, so that it has surplus energy to dispose of. Russia, as already mentioned, is a state which has taken upon itself tasks of this kind beyond its strength, and for which it is in no way competent. Italy offers at this moment the strongest instance

25 of a state which is imperiling its domestic welfare for a colonial policy which is beyond its strength, is undertaken arbitrarily, and has no proper motive. Germany has taken up a colonial policy with great eagerness, apparently from a notion that it is one of the attributes of a great state. To maintain it she must add a great navy to her great military establishment and increase the burdens

30 of a population which is poor and heavily taxed and which has not in its ter-ritory any great natural resources from which to draw the strength to bear its burdens. Spain is exhausting her last strength to keep Cuba, which can never repay the cost unless it is treated on the old colonial plan as a subject province to be exploited for the benefit of the mother-country. If that is done, however,

35 the only consequence will be another rebellion and greater expenditure. Eng-land, as a penalty of her greatness, finds herself in all parts of the world face to face with the necessity of maintaining her jurisdiction and of extending it in order to maintain it. When she does so she finds herself only extending law and order for the benefit of everybody. It is only in circumstances like hers that

40 the burdens have any compensation.

THE MARCH OF THE FLAG
ALBERT BEVERIDGE (1862–1927)

The United States went to war with Spain in April 1898 over the issue of Cuban independence. By the time the fighting stopped in August, the Spaniards had not only surrendered Cuba, but had lost their hold on the Philippine Islands and other overseas territories as well. An American army occupied Manila, but Spain had not yet formally ceded control of the islands to the United States. The fate of the Philippines would be determined by the diplomats who were meeting in Paris to write a peace treaty.

While running for the United States Senate from Indiana, the progressive Albert Beveridge delivered this speech to pressure the administration of President William McKinley (1843–1901) to annex the Philippines and move the Republican party to adopt a pro-imperialist stance. He expanded the old theme of America as a "Redeemer Nation" to insist that we should be "the propagandists and not the misers of liberty"—to be imperial, as "a greater England with a nobler destiny." Beveridge and other progressives such as Theodore Roosevelt (1858–1919), the theorist of naval power Alfred Thayer Mahan (1840–1914), and Senator Henry Cabot Lodge (1850–1924) wanted the United States to take its place in the world as a major power: to keep order, to expand the nation's economic interests, to proclaim liberty everywhere.

The progressives began America's great foreign policy debate: Should the nation hold true to the principles of Washington's Farewell Address, retain its independence from foreign political alliances and limit its expansion to the continental acquisitions of the nineteenth century, or should it assume a place among the great imperial powers of the world?

16 SEPTEMBER 1898

It is a noble land that God has given us; a land that can feed and clothe the world; a land whose coastlines would enclose half the countries of Europe; a

Albert J. Beveridge, *The Meaning of the Times and Other Speeches* (Indianapolis: Bobbs-Merrill, 1908), 47–57.

land set like a sentinel between the two imperial oceans of the globe, a greater England with a nobler destiny.

It is a mighty people that He has planted on this soil; a people sprung from the most masterful blood of history; a people perpetually revitalized by the virile, man-producing working-folk of all the earth; a people imperial by virtue of their power, by right of their institutions, by authority of their Heaven-directed purposes—the propagandists and not the misers of liberty.

It is a glorious history our God has bestowed upon His chosen people; a history heroic with faith in our mission and our future; a history of statesmen who flung the boundaries of the Republic out into unexplored lands and savage wilderness; a history of soldiers who carried the flag across blazing deserts and through the ranks of hostile mountains, even to the gates of sunset; a history of a multiplying people who overran a continent in half a century; a history of prophets who saw the consequences of evils inherited from the past and of martyrs who died to save us from them; a history divinely logical, in the process of whose tremendous reasoning we find ourselves today.

Therefore, in this campaign, the question is larger than a party question. It is an American question. It is a world question. Shall the American people continue their march toward the commercial supremacy of the world? Shall free institutions broaden their blessed reign as the children of liberty wax in strength, until the empire of our principles is established over the hearts of all mankind?

Have we a mission to perform, no duty to discharge to our fellow-man? Has God endowed us with gifts beyond our deserts and marked us as the people of His peculiar favor, merely to rot in our own selfishness, as men and nations must, who take cowardice for their companion and self for their deity—as China has, as India has, as Egypt has?

Shall we be as the man who had one talent and hid it, or as he who had ten talents and used them until they grew to riches? And shall we reap the reward that waits on our discharge of our high duty; shall we occupy new markets for what our farmers raise, our factories make, our merchants sell—aye, and, please God, new markets for what our ships shall carry?

Hawaii is ours; Porto Rico is to be ours; at the prayer of her people Cuba finally will be ours; in the islands of the East, even to the gates of Asia, coaling stations are to be ours at the very least; the flag of a liberal government is to float over the Philippines, and may it be the banner that Taylor[1] unfurled in Texas and Fremont[2] carried to the coast.

---

[1] General Zachary Taylor (1784–1850), commander of U.S. forces during the Mexican-American War (1846–1848)

[2] John Charles Fremont (1813–1890), U.S. Army officer who accepted the surrender of the Mexican army in California during the Mexican-American War

The Opposition tells us that we ought not to govern a people without their consent. I answer, The rule of liberty that all just government derives its authority from the consent of the governed applies only to those who are capable of self-government. We govern the Indians without their consent, we govern our territories without their consent, we govern our children without their consent.   5
How do they know that our government would be without their consent? Would not the people of the Philippines prefer the just, humane, civilizing government of this Republic to the savage, bloody rule of pillage and extortion from which we have rescued them?

And, regardless of this formula of words made only for enlightened, self-   10
governing people, do we owe no duty to the world? Shall we turn these peoples back to the reeking hands from which we have taken them? Shall we abandon them, with Germany, England, Japan, hungering for them? Shall we save them from those nations, to give them a self-rule of tragedy?

They ask us how we shall govern these new possessions. I answer: Out of   15
local conditions and the necessities of the case methods of government will grow. If England can govern foreign lands, so can America. If Germany can govern foreign lands, so can America. If they can supervise protectorates, so can America. Why is it more difficult to administer Hawaii than New Mexico or California? Both had a savage and an alien population; both were more remote   20
from the seat of government when they came under our dominion than the Philippines are today.

Will you say by your vote that American ability to govern has decayed; that a century's experience in self-rule has failed of a result? Will you affirm by your vote that you are an infidel to American power and practical sense? Or   25
will you say that ours is the blood of government; ours the heart of dominion; ours the brain and genius of administration? Will you remember that we do but what our fathers did—we but pitch the tents of liberty farther westward, farther southward—we only continue the march of the flag?

The march of the flag! In 1789 the flag of the Republic waved over 4,000,000   30
souls in thirteen states, and their savage territory which stretched to the Mississippi, to Canada, to the Floridas. The timid minds of that day said that no new territory was needed, and, for the hour, they were right. But Jefferson, through whose intellect the centuries marched; Jefferson, who dreamed of Cuba as an American state; Jefferson, the first Imperialist of the Republic—Jefferson   35
acquired that imperial territory which swept from the Mississippi to the mountains, from Texas to the British possessions, and the march of the flag began!

The infidels to the gospel of liberty raved, but the flag swept on! The title to that noble land out of which Oregon, Washington, Idaho, and Montana have been carved was uncertain; Jefferson, strict constructionist of constitu-   40 tional power though he was, obeyed the Anglo-Saxon impulse within him, whose watchword then and whose watchword throughout the world today is, "Forward!": another empire was added to the Republic, and the march of the flag went on!

5   Those who deny the power of free institutions to expand urged every argument, and more, that we hear, today; but the people's judgment approved the command of their blood, and the march of the flag went on!

A screen of land from New Orleans to Florida shut us from the Gulf, and over this and the Everglade Peninsula waved the saffron flag of Spain; Andrew

10   Jackson seized both, the American people stood at his back and, under Monroe, the Floridas came under the dominion of the Republic, and the march of the flag went on! The Cassandras prophesied every prophecy of despair we hear, today, but the march of the flag went on!

Then Texas responded to the bugle calls of liberty, and the march of the

15   flag went on! And, at last, we waged war with Mexico, and the flag swept over the southwest, over peerless California, past the Gate of Gold to Oregon on the north, and from ocean to ocean its folds of glory blazed.

And, now obeying the same voice that Jefferson heard and obeyed, that Jackson heard and obeyed, that Monroe heard and obeyed, that Seward[3] heard

20   and obeyed, that Grant[4] heard and obeyed, that Harrison heard and obeyed, our President today plants the flag over the islands of the seas, outposts of commerce, citadels of national security, and the march of the flag goes on!

Distance and oceans are no arguments. The fact that all the territory our fathers bought and seized is contiguous, is no argument. In 1819 Florida was

25   farther from New York than Porto Rico is from Chicago today; Texas, farther from Washington in 1845 than Hawaii is from Boston in 1898; California, more inaccessible in 1847 than the Philippines are now. Gibraltar is farther from London than Havana is from Washington; Melbourne is farther from Liverpool than Manila is from San Francisco.

30   The ocean does not separate us from lands of our duty and desire—the oceans join us, rivers never to be dredged, canals never to be repaired. Steam joins us; electricity joins us—the very elements are in league with our destiny. Cuba not contiguous! Porto Rico not contiguous! Hawaii and the Philippines not contiguous! The oceans make them contiguous. And our navy will make

35   them contiguous.

---

[3]William H. Seward (1801–1872) negotiated the purchase of Alaska as Lincoln's Secretary of State.
[4]During his presidency (1869–1877), Ulysses S. Grant (1822–1885) proposed the annexation of Santo Domingo. The Senate rejected the proposal.

But the Opposition is right—there is a difference. We did not need the western Mississippi Valley when we acquired it, nor Florida, nor Texas, nor California, nor the royal provinces of the far northwest. We had no emigrants to people this imperial wilderness, no money to develop it, even no highways to cover it. No trade awaited us in its savage fastnesses. Our productions were not greater than our trade. There was not one reason for the land-lust of our statesmen from Jefferson to Grant, other than the prophet and the Saxon within them. But, today, we are raising more than we can consume, making more than we can use. Therefore we must find new markets for our produce.

And so, while we did not need the territory taken during the past century at the time it was acquired, we do need what we have taken in 1898, and we need it now. The resources and the commerce of these immensely rich dominions will be increased as much as American energy is greater than Spanish sloth. In Cuba, alone, there are 15,000,000 acres of forest unacquainted with the ax, exhaustless mines of iron, priceless deposits of manganese, millions of dollars' worth of which we must buy, today, from the Black Sea districts. There are millions of acres yet unexplored.

The resources of Porto Rico have only been trifled with. The riches of the Philippines have hardly been touched by the finger-tips of modern methods. And they produce what we consume, and consume what we produce—the very predestination of reciprocity—a reciprocity "not made with hands, eternal in the heavens." They sell hemp, sugar, cocoanuts, fruits of the tropics, timber of price like mahogany; they buy flour, clothing, tools, implements, machinery, and all that we can raise and make. Their trade will be ours in time. Do you endorse that policy with your vote?

Cuba is as large as Pennsylvania, and is the richest spot on the globe. Hawaii is as large as New Jersey; Porto Rico half as large as Hawaii; the Philippines larger than all New England, New York, New Jersey and Delaware combined. Together they are larger than the British Isles, larger than France, larger than Germany, larger than Japan.

If any man tells you that trade depends on cheapness and not on government influence, ask him why England does not abandon South Africa, Egypt, India. Why does France seize South China, Germany the vast region whose port is Kiaochow[5]?

Our trade with Porto Rico, Hawaii, and the Philippines must be as free as between the states of the Union, because they are American territory, while every other nation on earth must pay our tariff before they can compete with

---

[5]In 1897, Germany used military action to compel the Chinese government to agree to a 99-year lease of Jiaozhou Bay (Kiaochow), which the Germans used as a commercial center.

us. Until Cuba shall ask for annexation, our trade with her will, at the very least, be like the preferential trade of Canada with England. That, and the excellence of our goods and products; that, and the convenience of traffic; that, and the kinship of interests and destiny, will give the monopoly of these markets to the
5   American people.

The commercial supremacy of the Republic means that this nation is to be the sovereign factor in the peace of the world. For the conflicts of the future are to be conflicts of trade—struggles for markets—commercial wars for existence. And the golden rule of peace is impregnability of position and invincibility of
10   preparedness. So, we see England, the greatest strategist of history, plant her flag and her cannon on Gibraltar, at Quebec, in the Bermudas, at Vancouver, everywhere.

So Hawaii furnishes us a naval base in the heart of the Pacific; the Ladrones another, a voyage further on; Manila another, at the gates of Asia—Asia, to
15   the trade of whose hundreds of millions American merchants, manufacturers, farmers, have as good right as those of Germany or France or Russia or England; Asia, whose commerce with the United Kingdom alone amounts to hundreds of millions of dollars every year; Asia, to whom Germany looks to take her surplus products; Asia, whose doors must not be shut against American trade.
20   Within five decades the bulk of Oriental commerce will be ours.

No wonder that, in the shadows of coming events so great, free-silver is already a memory. The current of history has swept past that episode. Men understand, today, that the greatest commerce of the world must be conducted with the steadiest standard of value and most convenient medium of exchange
25   human ingenuity can devise. Time, that unerring reasoner, has settled the silver question. The American people are tired of talking about money—they want to make it. Why should the farmer get a half-measure dollar of money any more that he should give a half-measure bushel of grain?

Why should not the proposition for the free coinage of silver be as dead as
30   the proposition of irredeemable paper money? It is the same proposition in a different form. If the government stamp can make a piece of silver, which you can buy for 45 cents, pass for 100 cents, the government stamp can make a piece of pewter, worth one cent, pass for 100 cents, and a piece of paper, worth a fraction of a cent, pass for 100 cents. Free-silver is the principle of fiat money
35   applied to metal. If you favor fiat silver, you necessarily favor fiat paper.

If the government can make money with a stamp, why does the government borrow money? If the government can create value out of nothing, why not abolish all taxation?

And if it is not the stamp of the government that raises the value, but the
40   demand which free coinage creates, why has the value of silver gone down at

a time when more silver was bought and coined by the government than ever before? Again, if the people want more silver, why do they refuse what we already have? And if free silver makes money more plentiful, how will *you* get any of it? Will the silver-mine owner give it to you? Will he loan it to you? Will the government give or loan it to you? Where do you or I come in on this free-silver proposition?

The American people want this money question settled forever. They want a uniform currency, a convenient currency, a currency that grows as business grows, a currency based on science and not on chance.

And now, on the threshold of our new and great career, is the time permanently to adjust our system of finance. The American people have the mightiest commerce of the world to conduct. They cannot halt to unsettle their money system every time some ardent imagination sees a vision and dreams a dream. Think of Great Britain becoming the commercial monarch of the world with her financial system periodically assailed! Think of Holland or Germany or France bearing their burdens, and, yet, sending their flag to every sea, with their money at the mercy of politicians-out-of-an-issue. Let us settle the whole financial system on principles so sound that no agitation can shake it. And then, like men and not like children, let us on to our tasks, our mission and our destiny.

There are so many real things to be done—canals to be dug, railways to be laid, forests to be felled, cities to be builded, fields to be tilled, markets to be won, ships to be launched, peoples to be saved, civilization to be proclaimed and the flag of liberty flung to the eager air of every sea. Is this an hour to waste upon triflers with nature's laws? Is this a season to give our destiny over to word-mongers and prosperity-wreckers? No! It is an hour to remember our duty to our homes. It is a moment to realize the opportunities fate has opened to us. And so it is an hour for us to stand by the government.

Wonderfully has God guided us. Yonder at Bunker Hill and Yorktown His providence was above us. At New Orleans and on ensanguined seas His hand sustained us. Abraham Lincoln was His minister and His was the altar of freedom the nation's soldiers set up on a hundred battle-fields. His power directed Dewey in the East and delivered the Spanish fleet into our hands, as He delivered the elder Armada into the hands of our English sires two centuries ago. The American people cannot use a dishonest medium of exchange; it is ours to set the world its example of right and honor. We cannot fly from our world duties; it is ours to execute the purpose of a fate that has driven us to be greater than our small intentions. We cannot retreat from any soil where Providence has unfurled our banner; it is ours to save that soil for liberty and civilization.

PLATFORM
AMERICAN ANTI-IMPERIALIST LEAGUE

Opposition to the progressive position coalesced in the Anti-Imperialist League, founded in the Boston office of insurance mogul Edward Atkinson in June 1898, shortly after the United States went to war with Spain. Its leading spokesmen were an unlikely coalition of businessmen, professors, politicians, and writers. They included Massachusetts Republican George F. Hoar (1826–1904) and unsuccessful Democratic presidential candidate William Jennings Bryan (1860–1925); classical liberal editor E. L. Godkin (1831–1902); millionaire steel magnate Andrew Carnegie (1835–1919) and labor leader Samuel Gompers (1850–1924); professors William James (1842–1910) and William Graham Sumner (1840–1910); and Mark Twain (1835–1910). Although the motives of the League's members varied, they had in common a primary concern for American independence and uniqueness—her moral and spiritual health, constitutional integrity, prosperity.

Initially, the League's purpose was to focus the American effort in the Spanish-American War on liberating oppressed Spanish colonies rather than acquiring an empire in Hawaii, Puerto Rico, Cuba, and especially the Philippines. After the fighting stopped in August 1898, the League's objective became the defeat of the Treaty of Paris, which ceded the islands of the Philippines and other overseas territories to the United States. When the Senate approved the Treaty in February 1899 and war broke out in the Philippines, the League opposed the policy of the McKinley administration, which had resulted in the Filipinos rebelling against the United States and which required American troops to fight far from home against people seeking their own independence.

The League's Program was published October 17, 1899, and, together with Senator Beveridge's speech, reveals what it was about the Filipino war and the question of overseas imperialism that so polarized Americans.

"Platform of the American Anti-Imperialist League," *The Land of Sunshine: The Magazine of California and the Old West* 12 (December 1899–May 1900):126–27.

1899

We hold that the policy known as imperialism is hostile to liberty and tends toward militarism, an evil from which it has been our glory to be free. We regret that it has become necessary in the land of Washington and Lincoln to re-affirm that all men, of whatever race or color, are entitled to life, liberty,
5   and the pursuit of happiness. We maintain that governments derive their just powers from the consent of the governed. We insist that the subjugation of any people is "criminal aggression" and open disloyalty to the distinctive principles of our government.

We earnestly condemn the policy of the present national administration
10   in the Philippines. It seeks to extinguish the spirit of 1776 in those islands. We deplore the sacrifice of our soldiers and sailors, whose bravery deserves admiration even in an unjust war. We denounce the slaughter of the Filipinos as a needless horror. We protest against the extension of American sovereignty by Spanish methods.

15   We demand the immediate cessation of the war against liberty, begun by Spain and continued by us. We urge that Congress announce to the Filipinos our purpose to concede to them the independence for which they have so long fought and which of right is theirs.

The United States have always protested against the doctrine of international
20   law which permits the subjugation of the weak by the strong. A self-governing state cannot accept sovereignty over an unwilling people. The United States cannot act upon the ancient heresy that might makes right.

Imperialists assume that with the destruction of self-government in the Philippines by American hands, all opposition here will cease. This is a grievous
25   error. Much as we abhor the war of "criminal aggression" in the Philippines, greatly as we regret that the blood of the Filipinos is on American hands, we more deeply resent the betrayal of American institutions at home. The real firing line is not in the suburbs of Manila. The foe is of our own household. The attempt of 1861 was to divide the country. That of 1899 is to destroy its
30   fundamental principles and noblest ideals.

Whether the ruthless slaughter of the Filipinos shall end next month or next year is but an incident in a contest that must go on until the Declaration of Independence and the Constitution of the United States are rescued from the hands of their betrayers. Those who dispute about standards of value while
35   the foundation of the republic is undermined will be listened to as little as those who would wrangle about the small economies of the household while the house is on fire. The training of a great people for a century, the aspiration for liberty of a vast immigration, are forces that will hurl aside those who in the delirium of conquest seek to destroy the character of our institutions.

We deny that the obligation of all citizens to support their government in times of grave national peril applies to the present situation. If an administration may with impunity ignore the issues upon which it was chosen, deliberately create a condition of war anywhere on the face of the globe, debauch the civil service for spoils to promote the adventure, organize a truth-suppressing censor- 5 ship, and demand of all citizens a suspension of judgment and their unanimous support while it chooses to continue the fighting, representative government itself is imperiled.

We propose to contribute to the defeat of any person or party that stands for the forcible subjugation of any people. We shall oppose for re-election all 10 who in the White House or in Congress betray American liberty in pursuit of un-American ends. We still hope that both of our great political parties will support and defend the Declaration of Independence in the closing campaign of the century.

We hold with Abraham Lincoln that "no man is good enough to govern 15 another man without that other's consent. When the white man governs him-self, that is self-government, but when he governs himself and also governs another man that is more than self-government—that is despotism." "Our reliance is in the love of liberty which God has planted in us. Our defense is in the spirit which prizes liberty as a heritage of all men in all lands. Those who 20 deny freedom to others deserve it not for themselves, and under a just God cannot long retain it."

We cordially invite the co-operation of all men and women who remain loyal to the Declaration of Independence and the Constitution of the United States.   25

The Eclipse of Liberalism
Edwin Lawrence Godkin (1831–1902)

Founder and chief editor of The Nation, *Edwin Lawrence Godkin shaped
public opinion during much of the two generations after the Civil War.
Godkin was "the towering influence in all thought concerning public
affairs," philosopher William James said. "He influenced other writers who
never quoted him, and determined the whole current of discussion."[1] This
editorial, written at the end of the nineteenth century and Godkin's career,
expressed the anxiety experienced by many classical liberal and conservative
intellectuals. With the rise of the Populist party, the agitation for an inflated
currency, the ousting of the Clevelandite forces from the Democratic party,
the rise of American imperialism, and continued labor strife, many persons
such as Godkin rightly feared that the twentieth century would be a much
bloodier and oppressive century than the nineteenth.*

1900

As the nineteenth century draws to its close it is impossible not to contrast the
political ideals now dominant with those of the preceding era. It was the rights
of man which engaged the attention of the political thinkers of the eighteenth
century. The world had suffered so much misery from the results of dynastic
ambitions and jealousies, the masses of mankind were everywhere so burdened   5
by the exactions of the superior classes, as to bring about a universal revulsion
against the principle of authority. Government, it was plainly seen, had become
the vehicle of oppression; and the methods by which it could be subordinated
to the needs of individual development, and could be made to foster liberty
rather than to suppress it, were the favorite study of the most enlightened   10
philosophers. In opposition to the theory of divine right, whether of kings or
demagogues, the doctrine of natural rights was set up. Humanity was exalted
above human institutions, man was held superior to the state, and universal
brotherhood supplanted the ideals of national power and glory.

[1]"The Most Influential Newspaper Editor That This Country Has Known," *Current Literature*
43 (July 1907):50.

E. L. Godkin, "The Eclipse of Liberalism," *The Nation* (9 August 1900):105–6.

These eighteenth-century ideas were the soil in which modern Liberalism flourished. Under their influence the demand for Constitutional Government arose. Rulers were to be the servants of the people, and were to be restrained and held in check by bills of rights and fundamental laws which defined the liberties proved by experience to be most important and most vulnerable. Hence arose the movement for Parliamentary reform in England, with its great outcome, the establishment of what was called free trade, but which was really the overthrow of many privileges besides those of the landlords. Hence arose the demands for Constitutional reform in all the countries of Europe; abortive and unsuccessful in certain respects, but frightening despots into a semblance of regard for human liberty, and into practical concessions which at least curbed despotic authority. Republics were established and constitutions were ordained. The revolutions of 1848 proved the power of the spirit of Liberalism, and where despotism re-asserted itself, it did so with fear and trembling.

To the principles and precepts of Liberalism the prodigious material progress of the age was largely due. Freed from the vexatious meddling of governments, men devoted themselves to their natural task, the bettering of their condition, with the wonderful results which surround us. But it now seems that its material comfort has blinded the eyes of the present generation to the cause which made it possible. In the politics of the world, Liberalism is a declining, almost a defunct force. The condition of the Liberal party in England is indeed parlous. There is actually talk of organizing a Liberal-Imperialist party; a combination of repugnant tendencies and theories as impossible as that of fire and water. On the other hand, there is a faction of so-called Liberals who so little understand their traditions as to make common cause with the Socialists. Only a remnant, old men for the most part, still uphold the Liberal doctrine, and when they are gone, it will have no champions.

True Liberalism has never been understood by the masses of the French people; and while it has no more consistent and enlightened defenders than the select group of orthodox economists that still reverence the principles of Turgot and Say, there is no longer even a Liberal faction in the Chamber. Much the same is true of Spain, of Italy, and of Austria, while the present condition of Liberalism in Germany is in painful contrast with what it was less than a generation ago. In our country recent events show how much ground has been lost. The Declaration of Independence no longer arouses enthusiasm; it is an embarrassing instrument which requires to be explained away. The Constitution is said to be "outgrown"; and at all events the rights which it guarantees must be carefully reserved to our own citizens, and not allowed to human beings over whom we have purchased sovereignty. The great party which boasted that it had secured for the negro the rights of humanity and of citizenship, now listens in silence to the proclamation of white supremacy and makes no protest against the nullification of the Fifteenth Amendment. Its mouth is closed, for it has become "patriot only in pernicious toils," and the present boasts of this "champion of human kind" are

> *To mix with Kings in the low lust of sway.* 5
> *Yell in the hunt, and share the murderous prey;*
> *To insult the shrine of Liberty with spoils*
> *From freemen torn, to tempt and to betray.*

Nationalism in the sense of national greed has supplanted Liberalism. It is an old foe under a new name. By making the aggrandizement of a particular nation 10 a higher end than the welfare of mankind, it has sophisticated the moral sense of Christendom. Aristotle justified slavery, because Barbarians were "naturally" inferior to Greeks, and we have gone back to his philosophy. We hear no more of natural rights, but of inferior races, whose part it is to submit to the government of those whom God has made their superiors. The old fallacy of divine 15 right has once more asserted its ruinous power, and before it is again repudiated there must be international struggles on a terrific scale. At home all criticism of the foreign policy of our rulers is denounced as unpatriotic. They must not be changed, for the national policy must be continuous. Abroad, the rulers of every country must hasten to every scene of territorial plunder, that they may 20 secure their share. To succeed in these predatory expeditions the restraints of parliamentary, even of party, government must be cast aside. The Czar of Russia and the Emperor of Germany have a free hand in China; they are not hampered by constitutions or by representatives of the common people. Lord Salisbury[1] is more embarrassed, and the President of the United States is, according to 25 our Constitution, helpless without the support of Congress. That is what our Imperialists mean by saying that we have outgrown the Constitution.

---

[1]Robert Cecil, Marques of Salisbury, Prime Minister of the United Kingdom (1885–1892, 1895–1902)

PLUNKITT OF TAMMANY HALL
WILLIAM L. RIORDAN (1861–1909)
REPORTER, *NEW YORK EVENING POST*

George Washington Plunkitt (1843–1924) was one of the few high officials of a political machine ever to go on record about its operations. He allowed newspaperman William Riordan to become his "Boswell," and his Series of Very Plain Talks on Very Practical Politics *was published in New York while Plunkitt and the machine were still very much in action.*

"Political machine" was a metaphor for the transformation of politics in an age of transforming technology and a product of rapidly expanding cities. The party replaced ineffective city governments as the locus of real political authority. Tammany Hall in New York City, where Plunkitt worked for forty years, learned how to gain power and hold onto it—and how to make it pay for loyal party workers. It also served as a welfare agency for the millions of immigrants who came to New York after 1870, and claimed to introduce them to American representative government. The Machine was the "politics of loyalty"—to one's party, neighborhood, ethnic identity—and of patronage, reminiscent of the clientage of ancient Rome. And it was big business. Tammany ran an empire with a larger payroll than Carnegie Steel.

The problem was that much of what the machines did was illegal. Plunkitt's namesake did not foresee the rise of political parties and would have disapproved of them if he had. Theodore Roosevelt, heir to the older tradition and an anti-Tammany reformer ("mornin' glory" to Plunkitt), pointed out in his 1914 autobiography that Tammany made a mockery of the rule of law.

Honest Graft and Dishonest Graft

1905

Everybody is talkin' these days about Tammany men growin' rich on graft, but nobody thinks of drawin' the distinction between honest graft and dishonest graft. There's all the difference in the world between the two. Yes, many of our

William L. Riordan, *Plunkitt of Tammany Hall* (New York: McClure, Phillips, and Company, 1905), 3–10, 30–37, 167–83.

men have grown rich in politics. I have myself. I've made a big fortune out of the game, and I'm gettin' richer every day, but I've not gone in for dishonest graft—blackmailin' gamblers, saloon-keepers, disorderly people, etc.—and neither has any of the men who have made big fortunes in politics.

5　　There's an honest graft, and I'm an example of how it works. I might sum up the whole thing by sayin': "I seen my opportunities and I took 'em."

Just let me explain by examples. My party's in power in the city, and it's goin' to undertake a lot of public improvements. Well, I'm tipped off, say, that they're goin' to lay out a new park at a certain place.

10　　I see my opportunity and I take it. I go to that place and I buy up all the land I can in the neighborhood. Then the board of this or that makes its plan public, and there is a rush to get my land, which nobody cared particular for before.

Ain't it perfectly honest to charge a good price and make a profit on my investment and foresight? Of course, it is. Well, that's honest graft.

15　　Or, supposin' it's a new bridge they're going to build. I get tipped off and I buy as much property as I can that has to be taken for approaches. I sell at my own price later on and drop some more money in the bank.

Wouldn't you? It's just like looking ahead in Wall Street or in the coffee or cotton market. It's honest graft, and I'm lookin' for it every day in the year. I

20　will tell you frankly that I've got a good lot of it, too.

I'll tell you of one case. They were going to fix up a big park, no matter where. I got on to it, and went lookin' about for land in that neighborhood.

I could get nothing at a bargain but a big piece of swamp, but I took it fast enough and held on to it. What turned out was just what I counted on. They

25　couldn't make the park complete without Plunkitt's swamp, and they had to pay a price for it. Anything dishonest in that?

Up in the watershed I made some money, too. I bought up several bits of land there some years ago and made a pretty good guess that they would be bought up for water purposes later by the city.

30　　Somehow, I always guessed about right, and shouldn't I enjoy the profit of my foresight? It was rather amusin' when the condemnation commissioners came along and found piece after piece of the land in the name of George Plunkitt of the Fifteenth Assembly District, New York City. They wondered how I knew just what to buy. The answer is—I seen my opportunity and I took it. I haven't

35　confined myself to land; anything that pays is in my line.

For instance, the city is repavin' a street and has several hundred thousand old granite blocks to sell. I am on hand to buy, and I know just what they are worth. How? Never mind that. I had a sort of monopoly of this business for a while, but once a newspaper tried to do me. It got some outside men to come

40　over from Brooklyn and New Jersey to bid against me.

Was I done? Not much. I went to each of the men and said, "How many of these 250,000 stones do you want?" One said 20,000, and another wanted 15,000, and another wanted 10,000. I said, "All right, let me bid for the lot, and I'll give each of you all you want for nothin'."

They agreed, of course. Then the auctioneer yelled: "How much am I bid for these 250,000 fine pavin' stones?"

"Two dollars and fifty cents," says I.

"Two dollars and fifty cents!" screamed the auctioneer. "Oh, that's a joke! Give me a real bid."

He found the bid was real enough. My rivals stood silent. I got the lot for $2.50 and gave them their share. That's how the attempt to do Plunkitt ended, and that's how all such attempts end.

I've told you how I got rich by honest graft. Now, let me tell you that most politicians who are accused of robbin' the city get rich the same way. They didn't steal a dollar from the city treasury. They just seen their opportunities and took them. That is why, when a reform administration comes in and spends a half million dollars in trying to find the public robberies they talked about in the campaign, they don't find them.

The books are always all right. The money in the city treasury is all right. Everything is all right. All they can show is that the Tammany heads of departments looked after their friends, within the law, and gave them what opportunities they could to make honest graft. Now, let me tell you that's never going to hurt Tammany with the people. Every good man looks after his friends, and any man who doesn't isn't likely to be popular. If I have a good thing to hand out in private life, I give it to a friend. Why shouldn't I do the same in public life?

Another kind of honest graft. Tammany has raised a good many salaries. There was an awful howl by the reformers, but don't you know that Tammany gains ten votes for every one it lost by salary raisin'? The Wall Street banker thinks it shameful to raise a department clerk's salary from $1500 to $1800 a year, but every man who draws a salary himself says, "That's all right. I wish it was me." And he feels very much like voting the Tammany ticket on election day, just out of sympathy.

Tammany was beat in 1901 because the people were deceived into believin' that it worked dishonest graft. They didn't draw a distinction between dishonest and honest graft, but they saw that some Tammany men grew rich, and supposed they had been robbin' the city treasury or levyin' blackmail on disorderly houses, or workin' in with the gamblers and lawbreakers. As a matter of policy, if nothing else, why should the Tammany leaders go into such dirty business, when there is so much honest graft lyin' around when they are in power? Did you ever consider that?

Now, in conclusion, I want to say that I don't own a dishonest dollar. If my worst enemy was given the job of writin' my epitaph when I'm gone, he couldn't do more than write: "George W. Plunkitt. He Seen His Opportunities, and He Took 'Em.".…

Reformers Only Mornin' Glories

5 College professors and philosophers who go up in a balloon to think are always discussin' the question, "Why Reform Administrations Never Succeed Themselves!" The reason is plain to anybody who has learned the ABC of politics.

I can't tell just how many of these movements I've seen started in New York during my forty years in politics, but I can tell you how many have lasted more
10 than a few years—none. There have been reform committees of fifty, of sixty, of seventy, of one hundred, and all sorts of numbers that started out to do up the regular political organizations. They were mornin' glories—looked lovely in the morning and withered up in a short time, while the regular machines went on flourishin' forever, like fine old oaks. Say, that's the first poetry I ever
15 worked off. Ain't it great?

Just look back a few years. You remember the People's Municipal League that nominated Frank Scott for mayor in 1890? Do you remember the reformers that got up that league? Have you ever heard of them since? I haven't. Scott himself survived because he had always been a first-rate politician, but you'd
20 have to look in the newspaper almanacs of 1891 to find out who made up the People's Municipal League. Oh, yes! I remember one name—Ollie Teall; dear, pretty Ollie and his big dog. They're about all that's left of the League.

Now take the reform movement of 1894. A lot of good politicians joined in that—the Republicans, the state Democrats, the Stecklerites, and the
25 O'Brienites, and they gave us a lickin', but the real reform part of the affair, the Committee of Seventy that started the thing goin', what's become of those reformers? What's become of Charles Stewart Smith? Where's Bangs? Do you ever hear of Cornell, the iron man, in politics now? Could a search party find R. W. G. Welling? Have you seen the name of Fulton McMahon or McMahon
30 Fulton—I ain't sure which—in the papers lately? Or Preble Tucker? Or—but it's no use to go through the list of the reformers who said they sounded in the death knell of Tammany in 1894. They're gone for good, and Tammany's pretty well, thank you. They did the talkin' and posin', and the politicians in the movement got all the plums. It's always the case.
35 The Citizens' Union has lasted a little bit longer than the reform crowd that went before them, but that's because they learned a thing or two from us. They learned how to put up a pretty good bluff—and bluff counts a lot in politics. With only a few thousand members, they had the nerve to run the

whole Fusion movement, make the Republicans and other organizations come to their headquarters to select a ticket and dictate what every candidate must do or not do. I love nerve, and I've had a sort of respect for the Citizens' Union lately, but the Union can't last. Its people haven't been trained to politics, and whenever Tammany calls their bluff they lay right down. You'll never hear of the Union again after a year or two.

And, by the way, what's become of the good government clubs, the political nurseries of a few years ago? Do you ever hear of Good Government Club D and P and Q and Z anymore? What's become of the infants who were to grow up and show us how to govern the city? I know what's become of the nursery that was started in my district. You can find pretty much the whole outfit over in my headquarters, Washington Hall.

The fact is that a reformer can't last in politics. He can make a show for a while, but he always comes down like a rocket. Politics is as much a regular business as the grocery or the dry-goods or the drug business. You've got to be trained up to it or you're sure to fall. Suppose a man who knew nothing about the grocery trade suddenly went into the business and tried to conduct it according to his own ideas. Wouldn't he make a mess of it? He might make a splurge for a while, as long as his money lasted, but his store would soon be empty. It's just the same with a reformer. He hasn't been brought up in the difficult business of politics and he makes a mess of it every time.

I've been studyin' the political game for forty-five years, and I don't know it all yet. I'm learnin' something all the time. How, then, can you expect what they call "business men" to turn into politics all at once and make a success of it? It is just as if I went up to Columbia University and started to teach Greek. They usually last about as long in politics as I would last at Columbia.

You can't begin too early in politics if you want to succeed at the game. I began several years before I could vote, and so did every successful leader in Tammany Hall. When I was twelve years old I made myself useful around the district headquarters and did work at all the polls on election day. Later on, I hustled about getting out voters who had jags on or who were too lazy to come to the polls. There's a hundred ways that boys can help, and they get an experience that's the first real step in statesmanship. Show me a boy that hustles for the organization on election day, and I'll show you a comin' statesman.

That's the ABC of politics. It ain't easy work to get up to Y and Z. You have to give nearly all your time and attention to it. Of course, you may have some business or occupation on the side, but the great business of your life must be politics if you want to succeed in it. A few years ago Tammany tried to mix politics and business in equal quantities, by having two leaders for each district, a politician and a business man. They wouldn't mix. They were like oil and water. The politician looked after the politics of his district; the business man looked after his grocery store or his milk route, and whenever he appeared at an executive meeting, it was only to make trouble. The whole scheme turned out to be a farce and was abandoned mighty quick.

5   Do you understand now, why it is that a reformer goes down and out in the first or second round, while a politician answers to the gong every time? It is because the one has gone into the fight without training, while the other trains all the time and knows every fine point of the game....

Strenuous Life of the Tammany District Leader

Note—This chapter is based on extracts from Plunkitt's diary and on my daily
10   observation of the work of the district leaders.—W.L.R.

The life of the Tammany district leader is strenuous. To his work is due the wonderful recuperative power of the organization. One year it goes down in defeat and the prediction is made that it will never again raise its head. The district leader, undaunted by defeat, collects his scattered forces, organizes them
15   as only Tammany knows how to organize, and in a little while the organization is as strong as ever.

No other politician in New York or elsewhere is exactly like the Tammany district leader or works as he does. As a rule, he has no business or occupation other than politics. He plays politics every day and night in the year, and his
20   headquarters bears the inscription "Never closed."

Everybody in the district knows him. Everybody knows where to find him, and nearly everybody goes to him for assistance of one sort or another, especially the poor of the tenements.

He is always obliging. He will go to the police courts to put in a good
25   word for the "drunks and disorderlies" or pay their fines, if a good word is not effective. He will attend christenings, weddings, and funerals. He will feed the hungry and help bury the dead.

A philanthropist? Not at all. He is playing politics all the time.

Brought up in Tammany Hall, he has learned how to reach the hearts of
30   the great mass of voters. He does not bother about reaching their heads. It is his belief that arguments and campaign literature have never gained votes.

He seeks direct contact with the people, does them good turns when he can, and relies on their not forgetting him on election day. His heart is always in his work, too, for his subsistence depends on its results.

35   If he holds his district and Tammany is in power, he is amply rewarded by a good office and the opportunities that go with it. What these opportunities are has been shown by the quick rise to wealth of so many Tammany district leaders. With the examples before him of Richard Croker, once leader of the

Twentieth District; John F. Carroll, formerly leader of the Twenty-Ninth; Timothy ("Dry Dollar") Sullivan, late leader of the Sixth, and many others, he can always look forward to riches and ease while he is going through the drudgery of his daily routine.

This is a record of a day's work by Plunkitt: 5

2 AM   Aroused from sleep by the ringing of his door bell; went to the door and found a bartender, who asked him to go to the police station and bail out a saloon-keeper who had been arrested for violating the excise law. Furnished bail and returned to bed at three o'clock.   10

6 AM   Awakened by fire engines passing his house. Hastened to the scene of the fire, according to the custom of the Tammany district leaders, to give assistance to the fire sufferers, if needed. Met several of his election district captains who are always under orders to look out for fires, which are considered great vote-getters. Found several   15 tenants who had been burned out, took them to a hotel, supplied them with clothes, fed them, and arranged temporary quarters for them until they could rent and furnish new apartments.

8:30 AM Went to the police court to look after his constituents. Found six "drunks." Secured the discharge of four by a timely word with   20 the judge, and paid the fines of two.

9 AM   Appeared in the Municipal District Court. Directed one of his district captains to act as counsel for a widow against whom dispossess proceedings had been instituted and obtained an extension of time. Paid the rent of a poor family about to be   25 dispossessed and gave them a dollar for food.

11 AM   At home again. Found four men waiting for him. One had been discharged by the Metropolitan Railway Company for neglect of duty, and wanted the district leader to fix things. Another wanted a job on the road. The third sought a place on the Subway and the   30 fourth, a plumber, was looking for work with the Consolidated Gas Company. The district leader spent nearly three hours fixing things for the four men, and succeeded in each case.

3 PM   Attended the funeral of an Italian as far as the ferry. Hurried back to make his appearance at the funeral of a Hebrew constituent.   35 Went conspicuously to the front both in the Catholic church and the synagogue, and later attended the Hebrew confirmation ceremonies in the synagogue.

7 PM   Went to district headquarters and presided over a meeting of election district captains. Each captain submitted a list of all the voters in his district, reported on their attitude toward Tammany, suggested who might be won over and how they could be won, told who were in need, and who were in trouble of any kind and the best way to reach them. District leader took notes and gave orders.

8 PM   Went to a church fair. Took chances on everything, bought ice-cream for the young girls and the children. Kissed the little ones, flattered their mothers and took their fathers out for something down at the corner.

9 PM   At the club-house again. Spent $10 on tickets for a church excursion and promised a subscription for a new church-bell. Bought tickets for a base-ball game to be played by two nines from his district. Listened to the complaints of a dozen push-cart peddlers who said they were persecuted by the police and assured them he would go to Police Headquarters in the morning and see about it.

10:30 PM   Attended a Hebrew wedding reception and dance. Had previously sent a handsome wedding present to the bride.

12 PM   In bed.

That is the actual record of one day in the life of Plunkitt. He does some of the same things every day, but his life is not so monotonous as to be wearisome.

Sometimes the work of a district leader is exciting, especially if he happens to have a rival who intends to make a contest for the leadership at the primaries. In that case, he is even more alert, tries to reach the fires before his rival, sends out runners to look for "drunks and disorderlies" at the police stations, and keeps a very close watch on the obituary columns of the newspapers.

PRAGMATISM
WILLIAM JAMES (1842–1910)

One of America's most widely read philosophers, William James traveled widely in Europe as a youth and pursued in fits and starts a scientific education and medical career. He followed Louis Agassiz to the Amazon to collect zoological specimens, and taught anatomy and physiology at Harvard, where he began to integrate biology, psychology, and philosophy. Though he was an ardent opponent of "Social Darwinism," the impact of Darwinian evolutionary theory on his thinking is clear.

Pragmatism attempts to apply the principles and methods of the positive, natural sciences to philosophy. It emphasizes the primacy of fact, observation, empiricism, and experiment—in short, the primacy of phenomena. James avoided first principles and deductive reasoning, or the idea that things have essential properties or "natures" that we can know prior to acts and events. He proffered a philosophy of action—knowledge is the product of deeds; ideas and words are consequences of experience; knowledge is a tool rather than an end to be obtained.

Pragmatism is often regarded as reflecting the Anglo-American aversion to abstraction, speculation, and rationalism, or as taking those tendencies to the point of rejecting philosophy altogether. James's goal of escaping interminable metaphysical problems suggests to some an abandonment of metaphysics. James's defenders deny his theory is equivalent to subjectivism, relativism, or existentialism, or that pragmatism promotes a moral and political calculation of short-term expediency. Its opponents believe that his war against rationalism led to the rationalization of every convenient belief, and that James facilitated a morally corrosive easy-going ethics, what Allan Bloom calls "nihilism American-style."

William James, *Pragmatism: A New Name for Some Old Ways of Thinking* (New York: Longmans, Green, and Company, 1907), 45–47, 48–50, 51–54, 54–55, 55, 55–58, 59–60, 63–64, 64–65, 67–68, 69–70, 72–73, 75–80, 198–205, 212–17, 222–26, 298–301.

1907

...The pragmatic method is primarily a method of settling metaphysical disputes that otherwise might be interminable. Is the world one or many? Fated or free? Material or spiritual? Here are notions either of which may or may not hold good of the world; and disputes over such notions are unending. The
5   pragmatic method in such cases is to try to interpret each notion by tracing its respective practical consequences. What difference would it practically make to any one if this notion rather than that notion were true? If no practical difference whatever can be traced, then the alternatives mean practically the same thing, and all dispute is idle. Whenever a dispute is serious, we ought to be
10 able to show some practical difference that must follow from one side or the other's being right.

A glance at the history of the idea will show you still better what pragmatism means. The term is derived from the same Greek word meaning action, from which our words "practice" and "practical" come. It was first introduced into
15 philosophy by Mr. Charles Peirce in 1878. In an article entitled "How to Make Our Ideas Clear," in the *Popular Science Monthly* for January of that year Mr. Peirce, after pointing out that our beliefs are really rules for action, said that, to develop a thought's meaning, we need only determine what conduct it is fitted to produce: that conduct is for us its sole significance. And the tangible
20 fact at the root of all our thought-distinctions, however subtle, is that there is no one of them so fine as to consist in anything but a possible difference of practice. To attain perfect clearness in our thoughts of an object, then, we need only consider what conceivable effects of a practical kind the object may involve—what sensations we are to expect from it, and what reactions we must
25 prepare. Our conception of these effects, whether immediate or remote, is then for us the whole of our conception of the object, so far as that conception has positive significance at all....

To take in the importance of Peirce's principle, one must get accustomed to applying it to concrete cases. I found a few years ago that Ostwald, the illus-
30 trious Leipzig chemist, had been making perfectly distinct use of the principle of pragmatism in his lectures on the philosophy of science, though he had not called it by that name.

"All realities influence our practice," he wrote me, "and that influence is their meaning for us. I am accustomed to put questions to my classes in this
35 way: In what respects would the world be different if this alternative or that were true? If I can find nothing that would become different, then the alternative has no sense."

That is, the rival views mean practically the same thing, and meaning, other than practical, there is for us none. Ostwald in a published lecture gives this example of what he means. Chemists have long wrangled over the inner constitution of certain bodies called "tautomerous". Their properties seemed equally consistent with the notion that an instable hydrogen atom oscillates inside of them, or that they are instable mixtures of two bodies. Controversy raged, but never was decided. "It would never have begun," says Ostwald, "if the combatants had asked themselves what particular experimental fact could have been made different by one or the other view being correct. For it would then have appeared that no difference of fact could possibly ensue; and the quarrel was as unreal as if, theorizing in primitive times about the raising of dough by yeast, one party should have invoked a 'brownie', while another insisted on an 'elf' as the true cause of the phenomenon."

It is astonishing to see how many philosophical disputes collapse into insignificance the moment you subject them to this simple test of tracing a concrete consequence. There can be no difference anywhere that doesn't *make* a difference elsewhere—no difference in abstract truth that doesn't express itself in a difference in concrete fact and in conduct consequent upon that fact, imposed on somebody, somehow, somewhere, and somewhen. The whole function of philosophy ought to be to find out what definite difference it will make to you and me, at definite instants of our life, if this world-formula or that world-formula be the true one....

Pragmatism represents a perfectly familiar attitude in philosophy, the empiricist attitude, but it represents it, as it seems to me, both in a more radical and in a less objectionable form than it has ever yet assumed. A pragmatist turns his back resolutely and once for all upon a lot of inveterate habits dear to professional philosophers. He turns away from abstraction and insufficiency, from verbal solutions, from bad *a priori* reasons, from fixed principles, closed systems, and pretended absolutes and origins. He turns toward concreteness and adequacy, towards facts, towards action and towards power. That means the empiricist temper regnant and the rationalist temper sincerely given up. It means the open air and possibilities of nature, as against dogma, artificiality, and the pretence of finality in truth.

At the same time it does not stand for any special results. It is a method only. But the general triumph of that method would mean an enormous change in what I called in my last lecture the "temperament" of philosophy. Teachers of the ultra-rationalistic type would be frozen out, much as the courtier type is frozen out in republics, as the ultramontane type of priest is frozen out in protestant lands. Science and metaphysics would come much nearer together, would in fact work absolutely hand in hand.

Metaphysics has usually followed a very primitive kind of quest. You know how men have always hankered after unlawful magic, and you know what a great

part in magic *words* have always played. If you have his name, or the formula of incantation that binds him, you can control the spirit, genie, afrite, or whatever the power may be. Solomon knew the names of all the spirits, and having their names, he held them subject to his will. So the universe has always appeared
5   to the natural mind as a kind of enigma, of which the key must be sought in the shape of some illuminating or power-bringing word or name. That word names the universe's *principle*, and to possess it is after a fashion to possess the universe itself. "God", "Matter", "Reason", "the Absolute", "Energy" are so many solving names. You can rest when you have them. You are at the end of
10   your metaphysical quest.

    But if you follow the pragmatic method, you cannot look on any such word as closing your quest. You must bring out of each word its practical cash-value, set it at work within the stream of your experience. It appears less as a solution, then, than as a program for more work, and more particularly as an indication
15   of the ways in which existing realities may be *changed*.

    Theories thus become instruments, not answers to enigmas, in which we can rest. We don't lie back upon them, we move forward, and, on occasion, make nature over again by their aid. Pragmatism un-stiffens all our theories, limbers them up and sets each one at work. Being nothing essentially new, it harmonized with
20   many ancient philosophic tendencies. It agrees with nominalism for instance, in always appealing to particulars; with utilitarianism in emphasizing practical aspects; with positivism in its disdain for verbal solutions, useless questions and metaphysical abstractions....

    No particular results then, so far, but only an attitude of orientation, is
25   what the pragmatic method means. *The attitude of looking away from first things, principles, "categories", supposed necessities; and of looking towards last things, fruits, consequences, facts....*

    ...Meanwhile the word pragmatism has come to be used in a still wider sense, as meaning also a certain *theory of truth....*
30   One of the most successfully cultivated branches of philosophy in our time is what is called inductive logic, the study of the conditions under which our sciences have evolved. Writers on this subject have begun to show a singular unanimity as to what the laws of nature and elements of fact mean, when formulated by mathematicians, physicists and chemists. When the first mathemati-
35   cal, logical, and natural uniformities, the first *laws*, were discovered, men were so carried away by the clearness, beauty and simplification that resulted, that they believed themselves to have deciphered authentically the eternal thoughts of the Almighty. His mind also thundered and reverberated in syllogisms. He also thought in conic sections, squares and roots and ratios, and geometrized
40   like Euclid. He made Kepler's laws for the planets to follow; he made velocity

increase proportionally to the time in falling bodies; he made the law of the sines for light to obey when refracted; he established the classes, orders, families and genera of plants and animals, and fixed the distances between them. He thought the archetypes of all things, and devised their variations; and when we rediscover any one of these his wondrous institutions, we seize his mind in its very literal intention.

But as the sciences have developed farther, the notion has gained ground that most, perhaps all, of our laws are only approximations. The laws themselves, moreover, have grown so numerous that there is no counting them; and so many rival formulations are proposed in all the branches of science that investigators have become accustomed to the notion that no theory is absolutely a transcript of reality, but that any one of them may from some point of view be useful. Their great use is to summarize old facts and to lead to new ones. They are only a man-made language, a conceptual short-hand, as someone calls them, in which we write our reports of nature; and languages, as is well known, tolerate much choice of expression and many dialects.

Thus human arbitrariness has driven divine necessity from scientific logic. If I mention the names of Sigwart, Mach, Ostwald, Pearson, Milhaud, Poincaré, Duhem, Heymans, those of you who are students will easily identify the tendency I speak of, and will think of additional names.

Riding now on the front of this wave of scientific logic Messrs. Schiller and Dewey appear with their pragmatistic account of what truth everywhere signifies. Everywhere, these teachers say, "truth" in our ideas and beliefs means the same thing that it means in science. It means, they say, nothing but this, *that ideas (which themselves are but parts of our experience) become true just in so far as they help us to get into satisfactory relation with other parts of our experience*, to summarize them and get about among them by conceptual short-cuts instead of following the interminable succession of particular phenomena. Any idea upon which we can ride, so to speak; any idea that will carry us prosperously from any one part of our experience to any other part, linking things satisfactorily, working securely, simplifying, saving labor; is true for just so much, true in so far forth, true *instrumentally*. This is the "instrumental" view of truth taught so successfully at Chicago, the view that truth in our ideas means their power to "work", promulgated so brilliantly at Oxford....

The observable process which Schiller and Dewey particularly singled out for generalization is the familiar one by which any individual settles into *new opinions*. The process here is always the same. The individual has a stock of old opinions already, but he meets a new experience that puts them to a strain. Somebody contradicts them; or in a reflective moment he discovers that they contradict each other; or he hears of facts with which they are incompatible; or

desires arise in him which they cease to satisfy. The result is an inward trouble to which his mind till then had been a stranger, and from which he seeks to escape by modifying his previous mass of opinions. He saves as much of it as he can, for in this matter of belief we are all extreme conservatives. So he tries to change
5 first this opinion, and then that (for they resist change very variously), until at last some new idea comes up which he can graft upon the ancient stock with a minimum of disturbance of the latter, some idea that mediates between the stock and the new experience and runs them into one another most felicitously and expediently....
10   A new opinion counts as "true" just in proportion as it gratifies the individual's desire to assimilate the novel in his experience to his beliefs in stock. It must both lean on old truth and grasp new fact; and its success (as I said a moment ago) in doing this, is a matter for the individual's appreciation. When old truth grows, then, by new truth's addition, it is for subjective reasons. We
15 are in the process and obey the reasons. That new idea is truest which performs most felicitously its function of satisfying our double urgency. It makes itself true, gets itself classed as true, by the way it works; grafting itself then upon the ancient body of truth, which thus grows much as a tree grows by the activity of a new layer of cambium....
20   The trail of the human serpent is thus over everything. Truth independent; truth that we *find* merely; truth no longer malleable to human need; truth incorrigible, in a word; such truth exists indeed superabundantly—or is supposed to exist by rationalistically minded thinkers; but then it means only the dead heart of the living tree, and its being there means only that truth also has its
25 paleontology, and its "prescription", and may grow stiff with years of veteran service and petrified in men's regard by sheer antiquity. But how plastic even the oldest truths nevertheless really are has been vividly shown in our day by the transformation of logical and mathematical ideas, a transformation which seems even to be invading physics. The ancient formulas are reinterpreted as
30 special expressions of much wider principles, principles that our ancestors never got a glimpse of in their present shape and formulation....
    ...Pragmatism is uncomfortable away from facts. Rationalism is comfortable only in the presence of abstractions. This pragmatist talk about truths in the plural, about their utility and satisfactoriness, about the success with which
35 they 'work,' etc., suggests to the typical intellectualist mind a sort of coarse lame second-rate makeshift article of truth. Such truths are not real truth. Such tests are merely subjective. As against this, objective truth must be something nonutilitarian, haughty, refined, remote, august, exalted. It must be an absolute correspondence of our thoughts with an equally absolute reality. It must be what
40 we *ought* to think unconditionally. The conditioned ways in which we *do* think

are so much irrelevance and matter for psychology. Down with psychology, up with logic, in all this question!

See the exquisite contrast of the types of mind! The pragmatist clings to facts and concreteness, observes truth at its work in particular cases, and generalizes. Truth, for him, becomes a class-name for all sorts of definite working-values in experience. For the rationalist it remains a pure abstraction, to the bare name of which we must defer. When the pragmatist undertakes to show in detail just *why* we must defer, the rationalist is unable to recognize the concretes from which his own abstraction is taken. He accuses us of *denying* truth; whereas we have only sought to trace exactly why people follow it and always ought to follow it. Your typical ultra-abstractionist fairly shudders at concreteness: other things equal, he positively prefers the pale and spectral. If the two universes were offered, he would always choose the skinny outline rather than the rich thicket of reality. It is so much purer, clearer, nobler....

Men who are strongly of the fact-loving temperament, you may remember me to have said, are liable to be kept at a distance by the small sympathy with facts which that philosophy from the present-day fashion of idealism offers them. It is far too intellectualistic. Old fashioned theism was bad enough, with its notion of God as an exalted monarch, made up of a lot of un-intelligible or preposterous "attributes"; but, so long as it held strongly by the argument from design, it keep some touch with concrete realities. Since, however, Darwinism has once for all displaced design from the minds of the "scientific", theism has lost that foothold; and some kind of an immanent or pantheistic deity working *in* things rather than above them is, if any, the kind recommended to our contemporary imagination. Aspirants to a philosophic religion turn, as a rule, more hopefully nowadays towards idealistic pantheism than towards the older dualistic theism, in spite of the fact that the latter still counts able defenders.

But, as I said in my first lecture, the brand of pantheism offered is hard for them to assimilate if they are lovers of facts, or empirically minded....

Now pragmatism, devoted though she be to facts, has no such materialistic bias as ordinary empiricism labors under. Moreover, she has no objection whatever to the realizing of abstractions, so long as you get about among particulars with their aid and they actually carry you somewhere. Interested in no conclusions but those which our minds and our experiences work out together, she has no *a priori* prejudices against theology. *If theological ideas prove to have a value for concrete life, they will be true, for pragmatism, in the sense of being good for so much. For how much more they are true, will depend entirely on their relations to the other truths that also have to be acknowledged....*

I am well aware how odd it must seem to some of you to hear me say that an idea is "true" so long as to believe it is profitable to our lives. That it is *good*, for as much as it profits, you will gladly admit. If what we do by its aid is good, you will allow the idea itself to be good in so far forth, for we are the better for possessing it. But is it not a strange misuse of the word "truth", you will say, to call ideas also "true" for this reason?

5   To answer this difficulty fully is impossible at this stage of my account. You touch here upon the very central point of Messrs. Schiller's, Dewey's, and my own doctrine of truth, which I cannot discuss with detail until my sixth lecture. Let me now say only this, that truth is *one species of good*, and not, as is usually supposed, a category distinct from good, and co-ordinate with it. *The*
10   *true is the name of whatever proves itself to be good in the way of belief, and good, too, for definite, assignable reasons.* Surely you must admit this, that if there were *no* good for life in true ideas, or if the knowledge of them were positively disadvantageous and false ideas the only useful ones, then the current notion that truth is divine and precious, and its pursuit a duty, could never have grown
15   up or become a dogma. In a world like that, our duty would be to *shun* truth, rather. But in this world, just as certain foods are not only agreeable to our taste, but good for our teeth, our stomach, and our tissues; so certain ideas are not only agreeable to think about, or agreeable as supporting other ideas that we are fond of, but they are also helpful in life's practical struggles. If there be
20   any life that it is really better we should lead, and if there be any idea which, if believed in, would help us to lead that life, then it would be really *better for us* to believe in that idea, *unless, indeed, belief in it incidentally clashed with other greater vital benefits.*

        "What would be better for us to believe"! This sounds very like a definition
25   of truth. It comes very near to saying "what we *ought* to believe": and in *that* definition none of you would find any oddity. Ought we ever not to believe what it is *better for us* to believe? And can we then keep the notion of what is better for us, and what is true for us, permanently apart?

        Pragmatism says no, and I fully agree with her. Probably you also agree,
30   so far as the abstract statement goes, but with a suspicion that if we practically did believe everything that made for good in our own personal lives, we should be found indulging all kinds of fancies about this world's affairs, and all kinds of sentimental superstitions about a world hereafter. Your suspicion here is undoubtedly well founded, and it is evident that something happens when you
35   pass from the abstract to the concrete that complicates the situation.

        I said just now that what is better for us to believe is true *unless the belief incidentally clashes with some other vital benefit.* Now in real life what vital benefits is any particular belief of ours most liable to clash with? What indeed except the vital benefits yielded by *other beliefs* when these prove incompatible
40   with the first ones? In other words, the greatest enemy of any one of our truths

may be the rest of our truths. Truths have once for all this desperate instinct of self-preservation and of desire to extinguish whatever contradicts them. My belief in the Absolute, based on the good it does me, must run the gauntlet of all my other beliefs. Grant that it may be true in giving me a moral holiday. Nevertheless, as I conceive it—and let me speak now confidentially, as it were, and merely in my own private person—it clashes with other truths of mine whose benefits I hate to give up on its account. It happens to be associated with a kind of logic of which I am the enemy, I find that it entangles me in metaphysical paradoxes that are inacceptable, etc, etc. But as I have enough trouble in life already without adding the trouble of carrying these intellectual inconsistencies, I personally just give up the Absolute. I just *take* my moral holidays; or else as a professional philosopher, I try to justify them by some other principle.

If I could restrict my notion of the Absolute to its bare holiday-giving value, it wouldn't clash with my other truths. But we cannot easily thus restrict our hypotheses. They carry supernumerary features, and these it is that clash so. My disbelief in the Absolute means then disbelief in those other supernumerary features, for I fully believe in the legitimacy of taking moral holidays.

You see by this what I meant when I called pragmatism a mediator and reconciler and said, borrowing the word from Papini, that she "un-stiffens" our theories. She has in fact no prejudices whatever, no obstructive dogmas, no rigid canons of what shall count as proof. She is completely genial. She will entertain any hypothesis, she will consider any evidence. It follows that in the religious field she is at a great advantage both over positivistic empiricism, with its anti-theological bias, and over religious rationalism, with its exclusive interest in the remote, the noble, the simple, and the abstract in the way of conception.

In short, she widens the field of search for God. Rationalism sticks to logic and the empyrean. Empiricism sticks to the external senses. Pragmatism is willing to take anything, to follow either logic or the senses and to count the humblest and most personal experiences. She will count mystical experiences if they have practical consequences. She will take a God who lives in the very dirt of private fact—if that should seem a likely place to find him.

Her only test of probable truth is what works best in the way of leading us, what fits every part of life best and combines with the collectivity of experience's demands, nothing being omitted. If theological ideas should do this, if the notion of God, in particular, should prove to do it, how could pragmatism possibly deny God's existence? She could see no meaning in treating as "not true" a notion that was pragmatically so successful. What other kind of truth could there be, for her, than all this agreement with concrete reality?...

I fully expect to see the pragmatist view of truth run through the classic stages of a theory's career. First, you know, a new theory is attacked as absurd;

then it is admitted to be true, but obvious and insignificant; finally it is seen to be so important that its adversaries claim that they themselves discovered it. Our doctrine of truth is at present in the first of these three stages, with symptoms of the second stage having begun in certain quarters. I wish that this lecture
5   might help it beyond the first stage in the eyes of many of you.

Truth, as any dictionary will tell you, is a property of certain of our ideas. It means their "agreement", as falsity means their disagreement, with "reality". Pragmatists and intellectualists both accept this definition as a matter of course. They begin to quarrel only after the question is raised as to what may precisely
10 be meant by the term "agreement", and what by the term "reality", when reality is taken as something for our ideas to agree with.

In answering these questions the pragmatists are more analytic and pains-taking, the intellectualists more offhand and irreflective. The popular notion is that a true idea must copy its reality. Like other popular views, this one follows
15 the analogy of the most usual experience. Our ideas of sensible things do indeed copy them. Shut your eyes and think of yonder clock on the wall, and you get just such a true picture or copy of its dial. But your idea of its "works" (unless you are a clock-maker) is much less of a copy, yet it passes muster, for it in no way clashes with the reality. Even though it should shrink to the mere word
20 "works", that word still serves you truly; and when you speak of the "time-keep-ing function" of the clock, or of its spring's "elasticity", it is hard to see exactly what your ideas can copy.

You perceive that there is a problem here. Where our ideas cannot copy definitely their object, what does agreement with that object mean? Some ide-
25 alists seem to say that they are true whenever they are what God means that we ought to think about that object. Others hold the copy-view all through, and speak as if our ideas possessed truth just in proportion as they approach to being copies of the Absolute's eternal way of thinking.

These views, you see, invite pragmatistic discussion. But the great assump-
30 tion of the intellectualists is that truth means essentially an inert static relation. When you've got your true idea of anything, there's an end of the matter. You're in possession; you *know*; you have fulfilled your thinking destiny. You are where you ought to be mentally; you have obeyed your categorical imperative; and nothing more need follow on that climax of your rational destiny. Epistemo-
35 logically you are in stable equilibrium.

Pragmatism, on the other hand, asks its usual question. "Grant an idea or belief to be true," it says, "what concrete difference will its being true make in any one's actual-life? How will the truth be realized? What experiences will be different from those which would obtain if the belief were false? What, in short,
40 is the truth's cash value in experiential terms?"

The moment pragmatism asks this question, it sees the answer: *True ideas are those that we can assimilate, validate, corroborate, and verify. False ideas are those that we cannot.* That is the practical difference it makes to us to have true ideas; that, therefore, is the meaning of truth, for it is all that truth is known-as.

This thesis is what I have to defend. The truth of an idea is not a stagnant property inherent in it. Truth *happens* to an idea. It *becomes* true, is *made* true by events. Its verity *is* in fact an event, a process: the process namely of its verifying itself, its veri-*fication.* Its validity is the process of its valid-*ation.*

But what do the words verification and validation themselves pragmatically mean? They again signify certain practical consequences of the verified and validated idea. It is hard to find any one phrase that characterizes these consequences better than the ordinary agreement-formula—just such consequences being what we have in mind whenever we say that our ideas 'agree' with reality. They lead us, namely, through the acts and other ideas which they instigate, into or up to, or towards, other parts of experience with which we feel all the while—such feeling being among our potentialities—that the original ideas remain in agreement. The connections and transitions come to us from point to point as being progressive, harmonious, satisfactory. This function of agreeable leading is what we mean by an idea's verification. Such an account is vague and it sounds at first quite trivial, but it has results which it will take the rest of my hour to explain.

Let me begin by reminding you of the fact that the possession of true thoughts means everywhere the possession of invaluable instruments of action; and that our duty to gain truth, so far from being a blank command from out of the blue, or a "stunt" self-imposed by our intellect, can account for itself by excellent practical reasons.

The importance to human life of having true beliefs about matters of fact is a thing too notorious. We live in a world of realities that can be infinitely useful or infinitely harmful. Ideas that tell us which of them to expect count as the true ideas in all this primary sphere of verification, and the pursuit of such ideas is a primary human duty. The possession of truth, so far from being here an end in itself, is only a preliminary means towards other vital satisfactions. If I am lost in the woods and starved, and find what looks like a cow-path, it is of the utmost importance that I should think of a human habitation at the end of it, for if I do so and follow it, I save myself. The true thought is useful here because the house which is its object is useful. The practical value of true ideas is thus primarily derived from the practical importance of their objects to us. Their objects are, indeed, not important at all times. I may on another occasion have no use for the house; and then my idea of it, however verifiable, will be practically irrelevant, and had better remain latent. Yet since almost any

object may someday become temporarily important, the advantage of having a general stock of *extra* truths, of ideas that shall be true of merely possible situations, is obvious. We store such extra truths away in our memories, and with the overflow we fill our books of reference. Whenever such an extra truth
5   becomes practically relevant to one of our emergencies, it passes from cold-storage to do work in the world and our belief in it grows active. You can say of it then either that "it is useful because it is true" or that "it is true because it is useful." Both these phrases mean exactly the same thing, namely that here is an idea that gets fulfilled and can be verified. True is the name for whatever idea
10   starts the verification-process, useful is the name for its completed function in experience. True ideas would never have been singled out as such, would never have acquired a class-name, least of all a name suggesting value, unless they had been useful from the outset in this way.

     From this simple cue pragmatism gets her general notion of truth as some-
15   thing essentially bound up with the way in which one moment in our experience may lead us towards other moments which it will be worthwhile to have been led to. Primarily, and on the common-sense level, the truth of a state of mind means this function of *a leading that is worthwhile*. When a moment in our experience, of any kind whatever, inspires us with a thought that is true, that
20   means that sooner or later we dip by that thought's guidance into the particulars of experience again and make advantageous connection with them. This is a vague enough statement, but I beg you to retain it, for it is essential....

     Realities mean, then, either concrete facts, or abstract kinds of thing and re-lations perceived intuitively between them. They furthermore and thirdly mean,
25   as things that new ideas of ours must no less take account of, the whole body of other truths already in our possession. But what now does "agreement" with such threefold realities mean?—to use again the definition that is current.

     Here it is that pragmatism and intellectualism begin to part company. Primarily, no doubt, to agree means to copy, but we saw that the mere word
30   'clock' would do instead of a mental picture of its works, and that of many realities our ideas can only be symbols and not copies. "Past time", "power", "spontaneity"—how can our mind copy such realities?

     To "agree" in the widest sense with a reality *can only mean to be guided either straight up to it or into its surroundings, or to be put into such working touch with*
35   *it as to handle either it or something connected with it better than if we disagreed.* Better either intellectually or practically! And often agreement will only mean the negative fact that nothing contradictory from the quarter of that reality comes to interfere with the way in which our ideas guide us elsewhere. To copy a reality is, indeed, one very important way of agreeing with it, but it is far from
40   being essential. The essential thing is the process of being guided. Any idea that

helps us to *deal*, whether practically or intellectually, with either the reality or its belongings, that doesn't entangle our progress in frustrations, that *fits*, in fact, and adapts our life to the reality's whole setting, will agree sufficiently to meet the requirement. It will hold true of that reality.

Thus, *names* are just as "true" or "false" as definite mental pictures are. 5
They set up similar verification-processes, and lead to fully equivalent practical results.

All human thinking gets discursified; we exchange ideas; we lend and borrow verifications, get them from one another by means of social intercourse. All truth thus gets verbally built out, stored up, and made available for everyone. 10
Hence, we must *talk* consistently just as we must *think* consistently: for both in talk and thought we deal with kinds. Names are arbitrary, but once understood they must be kept to. We mustn't now call Abel "Cain" or Cain "Abel". If we do, we un-gear ourselves from the whole book of Genesis, and from all its connections with the universe of speech and fact down to the present time. 15
We throw ourselves out of whatever truth that entire system of speech and fact may embody.

The overwhelming majority of our true ideas admit of no direct or face-to-face verification—those of past history, for example, as of Cain and Abel. The stream of time can be remounted only verbally, or verified indirectly by 20
the present prolongations or effects of what the past harbored. Yet if they agree with these verbalities and effects, we can know that our ideas of the past are true. *As true as past time itself was*, so true was Julius Caesar, so true were antediluvian monsters, all in their proper dates and settings. That past time itself was, is guaranteed by its coherence with everything that's present. True as the 25
present *is*, the past *was* also.

Agreement thus turns out to be essentially an affair of leading—leading that is useful because it is into quarters that contain objects that are important. True ideas lead us into useful verbal and conceptual quarters as well as directly up to useful sensible termini. They lead to consistency, stability and flowing human 30
intercourse. They lead away from excentricity and isolation, from foiled and barren thinking. The un-trammelled flowing of the leading-process, its general freedom from clash and contradiction, passes for its indirect verification; but all roads lead to Rome, and in the end and eventually, all true processes must lead to the face of directly verifying sensible experiences *somewhere*, which 35
somebody's ideas have copied.

Such is the large loose way in which the pragmatist interprets the word agreement. He treats it altogether practically. He lets it cover any process of conduction from a present idea to a future terminus, provided only it run prosperously. It is only thus that "scientific" ideas, flying as they do beyond common 40 sense, can be said to agree with their realities. It is, as I have already said, *as if* reality were made of ether, atoms or electrons, but we mustn't think so literally. The term "energy" doesn't even pretend to stand for anything "objective". It is only a way of measuring the surface of phenomena so as to string their changes on a simple formula.

Yet in the choice of these man-made formulas we cannot be capricious with impunity any more than we can be capricious on the common-sense practical level. We must find a theory that will *work*; and that means something extremely difficult; for our theory must mediate between all previous truths and certain new experiences. It must derange common sense and previous belief as little as possible, and it must lead to some sensible terminus or other that can be verified exactly. To "work" means both these things; and the squeeze is so tight that there is little loose play for any hypothesis. Our theories are wedged and controlled as nothing else is. Yet sometimes alternative theoretic formulas are equally compatible with all the truths we know, and then we choose between them for subjective reasons. We choose the kind of theory to which we are already partial; we follow "elegance" or "economy." Clerk-Maxwell somewhere says would be "poor scientific taste" to choose the more complicated of two equally well-evidenced conceptions; and you will all agree with him. Truth is science is what gives us the maximum possible sum of satisfactions, taste included, but consistency both with previous truth and with novel fact is always the most imperious claimant....

"The true", to put it very briefly, is only the expedient in the way of our thinking, just as "the right" is only the expedient in the way of our behaving. Expedient in almost any fashion; and expedient in the long run and on the whole of course; for what meets expediently all the experience in sight won't necessarily meet all farther experiences equally satisfactorily. Experience, as we know, has ways of *boiling over*, and making us correct our present formulas.

The "absolutely" true, meaning what no farther experience will ever alter, is that ideal vanishing-point towards which we imagine that all our temporary truths will someday converge. It runs on all fours with the perfectly wise man, and with the absolutely complete experience; and, if these ideals are ever realized, they will all be realized together. Meanwhile we have to live today by what truth we can get today, and be ready tomorrow to call it falsehood. Ptolemaic astronomy, Euclidean space, Aristotelian logic, scholastic metaphysics were expedient for centuries, but human experience has boiled over those limits, and we now call these things only relatively true, or true within those borders of experience. "Absolutely" they are false; for we know that those limits were casual, and might have been transcended by past theorists just as they are by present thinkers.

When new experiences lead to retrospective judgments, using the past tense, what these judgments utter *was* true, even though no past thinker had been led there. We live forwards, a Danish thinker has said, but we understand backwards. The present sheds a backward light on the world's previous processes. They may have been truth-processes for the actors in them. They are not so for one who knows the later revelations of the story.

This regulative notion of a potential better truth to be established later, possibly to be established someday absolutely, and having powers of retroactive legislation, turns its face, like all pragmatist notions, towards concreteness of fact, and towards the future. Like the half-truths, the absolute truth will have to be *made*, made as a relation incidental to the growth of a mass of verification-experience, to which the half-true ideas are all along contributing their quota.

I have already insisted on the fact that truth is made largely out of previous truths. Men's beliefs at any time are so much experience *funded*. But the beliefs are themselves parts of the sum total of the world's experience, and become matter, therefore, for the next day's funding operations. So far as reality means experienceable reality, both it and the truths men gain about it are everlastingly in process of mutation—mutation towards a definite goal, it may be—but still mutation.

Mathematicians can solve problems with two variables. On the Newtonian theory, for instance, acceleration varies with distance, but distance also varies with acceleration. In the realm of truth-processes facts come independently and determine our beliefs provisionally. But these beliefs make us act, and as fast as they do so, they bring into sight or into existence new facts which re-determine the beliefs accordingly. So the whole coil and ball of truth, as it rolls up, is the product of a double influence. Truths emerge from facts; but they dip forward into facts again and add to them; which facts again create or reveal new truth (the word is indifferent) and so on indefinitely. The "facts" themselves meanwhile are not *true*. They simply *are*. Truth is the function of the beliefs that start and terminate among them.

The case is like a snowball's growth, due as it is to the distribution of the snow on the one hand, and to the successive pushes of the boys on the other, with these factors co-determining each other incessantly....

I fear that my previous lectures, confined as they have been to human and humanistic aspects, may have left the impression on many of you that pragmatism means methodically to leave the superhuman out. I have shown small respect indeed for the Absolute, and I have until this moment spoken of no other superhuman hypothesis but that. But I trust that you see sufficiently that the Absolute has nothing but its superhumanness in common with the theistic God. On pragmatistic principles, if the hypothesis of God works satisfactorily in the widest sense of the word, it is true. Now whatever its residual difficulties may be, experience shows that it certainly does work, and that the problem is to build it out and determine it so that it will combine satisfactorily with all the other working truths. I cannot start upon a whole theology at the end of this last lecture; but when I tell you that I have written a book on men's religious experience, which on the whole has been regarded as making for the reality of God, you will perhaps exempt my own pragmatism from the charge of being an atheistic system. I firmly disbelieve, myself, that our human experience is the highest form of experience extant in the universe. I believe rather that we stand in much the same relation to the whole of the universe as our canine and feline pets do to the whole of human life. They inhabit our drawing-rooms and libraries. They take part in scenes of whose significance they have no inkling. They are merely tangent to curves of history the beginnings and ends and forms of which pass wholly beyond their ken. So we are tangent to the wider life of things. But, just as many of the dog's and cat's ideals coincide with our ideals, and the dogs and cats have daily living proof of the fact, so we may well believe, on the proofs that religious experience affords, that higher powers exist and are at work to save the world on ideal lines similar to our own.

You see that pragmatism can be called religious, if you allow that religion can be pluralistic or merely melioristic in type. But whether you will finally put up with that type of religion or not is a question that only you yourself can decide. Pragmatism has to postpone dogmatic answer, for we do not yet know certainly which type of religion is going to work best in the long run. The various overbeliefs of men, their several faith-ventures, are in fact what are needed to bring the evidence in. You will probably make your own ventures severally. If radically tough, the hurly-burly of the sensible facts of nature will be enough for you, and you will need no religion at all. If radically tender, you will take up with the more monistic form of religion: the pluralistic form, with its reliance on possibilities that are not necessities, will not seem to afford you security enough....

The New Nationalism
Theodore Roosevelt (1858–1919)
President of the United States (1901–1909)

Theodore Roosevelt was an energetic progressive Republican reformer who served on the U.S. Civil Service Commission, the New York City Police Commission, and as assistant secretary of the Navy, where he was an enthusiastic supporter of the war with Spain. He organized a volunteer regiment (the "Rough Riders") to fight in Cuba. The scandal-plagued New York Republican state machine nominated him for governor in 1898, and was glad to see him move to the national stage as vice-presidential candidate in 1900. The assassination of President McKinley in 1901 made Roosevelt president. He pursued a mild progressive agenda and was easily re-elected in 1904.

He was severely disappointed in the conservative administration of his successor and friend, William Howard Taft, and challenged him for the Republican nomination in 1912. His campaign for a "New Nationalism" marked a dramatic leap ahead in his belief in the power of the national government's role in the nation's political economy.

Osawatomie, Kansas, 31 August 1910

We come here today to commemorate one of the epoch-making events of the long struggle for the rights of man—the long struggle for the uplift of humanity. Our country—this great republic—means nothing unless it means the triumph of a real democracy, the triumph of popular government, and, in the long run, of an economic system under which each man shall be guaranteed   5
the opportunity to show the best that there is in him. That is why the history of America is now the central feature of the history of the world; for the world has set its face hopefully toward our democracy; and, O my fellow citizens, each one of you carries on your shoulders not only the burden of doing well for the sake of your own country, but the burden of doing well and of seeing that this   10
nation does well for the sake of mankind.

Theodore Roosevelt, *The New Nationalism* (New York: The Outlook Company, 1911), 3–33.

There have been two great crises in our country's history: first, when it was formed, and then, again, when it was perpetuated; and, in the second of these great crises—in the time of stress and strain which culminated in the Civil War, on the outcome of which depended the justification of what had been done earlier, you men of the Grand Army, you men who fought through the Civil War, not only did you justify your generation, not only did you render life worth living for our generation, but you justified the wisdom of Washington and Washington's colleagues. If this republic had been founded by them only to be split asunder into fragments when the strain came, then the judgment of the world would have been that Washington's work was not worth doing. It was you who crowned Washington's work, as you carried to achievement the high purpose of Abraham Lincoln.

Now, with this second period of our history the name of John Brown[1] will be forever associated; and Kansas was the theater upon which the first act of the second of our great national life dramas was played. It was the result of the struggle in Kansas which determined that our country should be in deed as well as in name devoted to both union and freedom; that the great experiment of democratic government on a national scale should succeed and not fail. In name we had the Declaration of Independence in 1776; but we gave the lie by our acts to the words of the Declaration of Independence until 1865; and words count for nothing except in so far as they represent acts. This is true everywhere; but, O my friends, it should be truest of all in political life. A broken promise is bad enough in private life. It is worse in the field of politics. No man is worth his salt in public life who makes on the stump a pledge which he does not keep after election; and, if he makes such a pledge and does not keep it, hunt him out of public life. I care for the great deeds of the past chiefly as spurs to drive us onward in the present. I speak of the men of the past partly that they may be honored by our praise of them, but more that they may serve as examples for the future.

It was a heroic struggle; and, as is inevitable with all such struggles, it had also a dark and terrible side. Very much was done of good, and much also of evil; and, as was inevitable in such a period of revolution, often the same man did both good and evil. For our great good fortune as a nation, we, the people of the United States as a whole, can now afford to forget the evil, or, at least, to remember it without bitterness, and to fix our eyes with pride only on the good that was accomplished. Even in ordinary times there are very few of us who do not see the problems of life as through a glass, darkly; and when the

---

[1]John Brown (1800–1859) was a violent abolitionist who massacred pro-slavery settlers in Kansas and led a failed slave rising at Harper's Ferry, Virginia.

glass is clouded by the murk of furious popular passion, the vision of the best
and the bravest is dimmed. Looking back, we are all of us now able to do justice
to the valor and the disinterestedness and the love of the right, as to each it
was given to see the right, shown both by the men of the North and the men
of the South in that contest which was finally decided by the attitude of the   5
West. We can admire the heroic valor, the sincerity, the self-devotion shown
alike by the men who wore the blue and the men who wore the gray; and our
sadness that such men should have had to fight one another is tempered by the
glad knowledge that ever hereafter their descendants shall be found fighting
side by side, struggling in peace as well as in war for the uplift of their common   10
country, all alike resolute to raise to the highest pitch of honor and usefulness
the nation to which they all belong. As for the veterans of the Grand Army of
the Republic, they deserve honor and recognition such as is paid to no other
citizens of the republic; for to them the republic owes its all; for to them it owes
its very existence. It is because of what you and your comrades did in the dark   15
years that we of today walk, each of us, head erect, and proud that we belong,
not to one of a dozen little squabbling contemptible commonwealths, but to
the mightiest nation upon which the sun shines.

I do not speak of this struggle of the past merely from the historic standpoint. Our interest is primarily in the application today of the lessons taught   20
by the contest of half a century ago. It is of little use for us to pay lip loyalty
to the mighty men of the past unless we sincerely endeavor to apply to the
problems of the present precisely the qualities which in other crises enabled
the men of that day to meet those crises. It is half melancholy and half amusing to see the way in which well-meaning people gather to do honor to the   25
men who, in company with John Brown, and under the lead of Abraham
Lincoln, faced and solved the great problems of the nineteenth century, while,
at the same time, these same good people nervously shrink from, or frantically
denounce, those who are trying to meet the problems of the twentieth century
in the spirit which was accountable for the successful solution of the problems   30
of Lincoln's time.

Of that generation of men to whom we owe so much, the man to whom we
owe most is, of course, Lincoln. Part of our debt to him is because he forecast
our present struggle and saw the way out. He said:

> I hold that while man exists it is his duty to improve not only his own   35
> condition, but to assist in ameliorating mankind.[2]

And again:

---

[2]Speech at Cincinnati, Ohio, 12 February 1861

> Labor is prior to, and independent of, capital. Capital is only the fruit of
> labor, and could never have existed if labor had not first existed. Labor is
> the superior of capital, and deserves much the higher consideration.[3]

5   If that remark was original with me, I should be even more strongly
denounced as a communist agitator than I shall be anyhow. It is Lincoln's. I am
only quoting it; and that is one side; that is the side the capitalist should hear.
Now, let the workingman hear his side.

> Capital has its rights, which are as worthy of protection as any other
> rights.... Nor should this lead to a war upon the owners of property.
10   Property is the fruit of labor... property is desirable; is a positive good
> in the world.[4]

And then comes a thoroughly Lincoln-like sentence:

> Let not him who is houseless pull down the house of another, but let
> him work diligently and build one for himself, thus by example assur-
15   ing that his own shall be safe from violence when built.[5]

It seems to me that, in these words, Lincoln took substantially the attitude
that we ought to take; he showed the proper sense of proportion in his relative
estimates of capital and labor, of human rights and property rights. Above all,
in this speech, as in many others, he taught a lesson in wise kindliness and
20   charity; an indispensable lesson to us of today. But this wise kindliness and
charity never weakened his arm or numbed his heart. We cannot afford weakly
to blind ourselves to the actual conflict which faces us today. The issue is joined,
and we must fight or fail.
     In every wise struggle for human betterment one of the main objects, and
25   often the only object, has been to achieve in large measure equality of opportunity. In the struggle for this great end, nations rise from barbarism to civilization,
and through it people press forward from one stage of enlightenment to the
next. One of the chief factors in progress is the destruction of special privilege.
The essence of any struggle for healthy liberty has always been, and must always
30   be, to take from some one man or class of men the right to enjoy power, or
wealth, or position, or immunity, which has not been earned by service to his
or their fellows. That is what you fought for in the Civil War, and that is what
we strive for now.

---

[3]Speech to the Workingmen's Association of the City of New York, 12 March 1864
[4]Ibid.
[5]Ibid.

At many stages in the advance of humanity, this conflict between the men who possess more than they have earned and the men who have earned more than they possess is the central condition of progress. In our day it appears as the struggle of free men to gain and hold the right of self-government as against the special interests, who twist the methods of free government into machinery 5 for defeating the popular will. At every stage, and under all circumstances, the essence of the struggle is to equalize opportunity, destroy privilege, and give to the life and citizenship of every individual the highest possible value both to himself and to the commonwealth. That is nothing new. All I ask in civil life is what you fought for in the Civil War. I ask that civil life be carried on 10 according to the spirit in which the army was carried on. You never get perfect justice, but the effort in handling the army was to bring to the front the men who could do the job. Nobody grudged promotion to Grant, or Sherman, or Thomas, or Sheridan, because they earned it. The only complaint was when a man got promotion which he did not earn. 15

Practical equality of opportunity for all citizens, when we achieve it, will have two great results. First, every man will have a fair chance to make of himself all that in him lies; to reach the highest point to which his capacities, unassisted by special privilege of his own and unhampered by the special privilege of others, can carry him, and to get for himself and his family substantially what he has 20 earned. Second, equality of opportunity means that the commonwealth will get from every citizen the highest service of which he is capable. No man who carries the burden of the special privileges of another can give to the commonwealth that service to which it is fairly entitled.

I stand for the square deal. But when I say that I am for the square deal, I 25 mean not merely that I stand for fair play under the present rules of the game, but that I stand for having those rules changed so as to work for a more substantial equality of opportunity and of reward for equally good service. One word of warning, which, I think, is hardly necessary in Kansas. When I say I want a square deal for the poor man, I do not mean that I want a square deal for the 30 man who remains poor because he has not got the energy to work for himself. If a man who has had a chance will not make good, then he has got to quit. And you men of the Grand Army, you want justice for the brave man who fought, and punishment for the coward who shirked his work. Is not that so?

Now, this means that our government, national and state, must be freed 35 from the sinister influence or control of special interests. Exactly as the special interests of cotton and slavery threatened our political integrity before the Civil War, so now the great special business interests too often control and corrupt the men and methods of government for their own profit. We must drive the special interests out of politics. That is one of our tasks today. Every special 40

interest is entitled to justice—full, fair, and complete—and, now, mind you, if there were any attempt by mob violence to plunder and work harm to the special interest, whatever it may be, that I most dislike, and the wealthy man, whomsoever he may be, for whom I have the greatest contempt, I would fight
5   for him, and you would if you were worth your salt. He should have justice. For every special interest is entitled to justice, but not one is entitled to a vote in Congress, to a voice on the bench, or to representation in any public office. The Constitution guarantees protection to property, and we must make that promise good. But it does not give the right of suffrage to any corporation.
10   The true friend of property, the true conservative, is he who insists that property shall be the servant and not the master of the commonwealth; who insists that the creature of man's making shall be the servant and not the master of the man who made it. The citizens of the United States must effectively control the mighty commercial forces which they have themselves called into being.
15   There can be no effective control of corporations while their political activity remains. To put an end to it will be neither a short nor an easy task, but it can be done.
         We must have complete and effective publicity of corporate affairs, so that the people may know beyond peradventure whether the corporations obey
20   the law and whether their management entitles them to the confidence of the public. It is necessary that laws should be passed to prohibit the use of corporate funds directly or indirectly for political purposes; it is still more necessary that such laws should be thoroughly enforced. Corporate expenditures for political purposes, and especially such expenditures by public service corporations, have
25   supplied one of the principal sources of corruption in our political affairs.
         It has become entirely clear that we must have government supervision of the capitalization, not only of public service corporations, including, particularly, railways, but of all corporations doing an interstate business. I do not wish to see the nation forced into the ownership of the railways if it can possibly be avoided,
30   and the only alternative is thoroughgoing and effective regulation, which shall be based on a full knowledge of all the facts, including a physical valuation of property. This physical valuation is not needed, or, at least, is very rarely needed, for fixing rates; but it is needed as the basis of honest capitalization.
         We have come to recognize that franchises should never be granted except
35   for a limited time, and never without proper provision for compensation to the public. It is my personal belief that the same kind and degree of control and supervision which should be exercised over public service corporations should be extended also to combinations which control necessaries of life, such as meat, oil, and coal, or which deal in them on an important scale. I have no doubt
40   that the ordinary man who has control of them is much like ourselves. I have

no doubt he would like to do well, but I want to have enough supervision to help him realize that desire to do well.

I believe that the officers, and, especially, the directors, of corporations should be held personally responsible when any corporation breaks the law.

Combinations in industry are the result of an imperative economic law which cannot be repealed by political legislation. The effort at prohibiting all combination has substantially failed. The way out lies, not in attempting to prevent such combinations, but in completely controlling them in the interest of the public welfare. For that purpose the Federal Bureau of Corporations is an agency of first importance. Its powers, and, therefore, its efficiency, as well as that of the Interstate Commerce Commission, should be largely increased. We have a right to expect from the Bureau of Corporations and from the Interstate Commerce Commission a very high grade of public service. We should be as sure of the proper conduct of the interstate railways and the proper management of interstate business as we are now sure of the conduct and management of the national banks, and we should have as effective supervision in one case as in the other. The Hepburn Act, and the amendment to the Act in the shape in which it finally passed Congress at the last session, represent a long step in advance, and we must go yet further.

There is a widespread belief among our people that, under the methods of making tariffs which have hitherto obtained, the special interests are too influential. Probably this is true of both the big special interests and the little special interests. These methods have put a premium on selfishness, and, naturally, the selfish big interests have gotten more than their smaller, though equally selfish, brothers. The duty of Congress is to provide a method by which the interest of the whole people shall be all that receives consideration. To this end there must be an expert tariff commission, wholly removed from the possibility of political pressure or of improper business influence. Such a commission can find the real difference between cost of production, which is mainly the difference of labor cost here and abroad. As fast as its recommendations are made, I believe in revising one schedule at a time. A general revision of the tariff almost inevitably leads to log-rolling and the subordination of the general public interest to local and special interests.

The absence of effective state, and, especially, national, restraint upon unfair money getting has tended to create a small class of enormously wealthy and economically powerful men, whose chief object is to hold and increase their power. The prime need is to change the conditions which enable these men to accumulate power which it is not for the general welfare that they should hold or exercise. We grudge no man a fortune which represents his own power and sagacity, when exercised with entire regard to the welfare of his fellows. Again, comrades over there, take the lesson from your own experience. Not only did you not grudge, but you gloried in the promotion of the great generals who gained their promotion by leading the army to victory. So it is with us. We grudge no man a fortune in civil life if it is honorably obtained and well used.

5 It is not even enough that it should have been gained without doing damage to the community. We should permit it to be gained only so long as the gaining represents benefit to the community. This, I know, implies a policy of a far more active governmental interference with social and economic conditions in this country than we have yet had, but I think we have got to face the fact that

10 such an increase in governmental control is now necessary.

No man should receive a dollar unless that dollar has been fairly earned. Every dollar received should represent a dollar's worth of service rendered—not gambling in stocks, but service rendered. The really big fortune, the swollen fortune, by the mere fact of its size acquires qualities which differentiate it

15 in kind as well as in degree from what is possessed by men of relatively small means. Therefore, I believe in a graduated income tax on big fortunes, and in another tax which is far more easily collected and far more effective—a graduated inheritance tax on big fortunes, properly safeguarded against evasion and increasing rapidly in amount with the size of the estate.

20 The people of the United States suffer from periodical financial panics to a degree substantially unknown among the other nations which approach us in financial strength. There is no reason why we should suffer what they escape. It is of profound importance that our financial system should be promptly investigated, and so thoroughly and effectively revised as to make it certain that

25 hereafter our currency will no longer fail at critical times to meet our needs.

It is hardly necessary for me to repeat that I believe in an efficient army and a navy large enough to secure for us abroad that respect which is the surest guarantee of peace. A word of special warning to my fellow citizens who are as progressive as I hope I am. I want them to keep up their interest in our internal

30 affairs; and I want them also continually to remember Uncle Sam's interests abroad. Justice and fair dealing among nations rest upon principles identical with those which control justice and fair dealing among the individuals of which nations are composed, with the vital exception that each nation must do its own part in international police work. If you get into trouble here, you

35 can call for the police; but if Uncle Sam gets into trouble, he has got to be his own policeman, and I want to see him strong enough to encourage the peaceful aspirations of other peoples in connection with us. I believe in national friendships and heartiest good will to all nations; but national friendships, like those between men, must be founded on respect as well as on liking, on forbearance

40 as well as upon trust. I should be heartily ashamed of any American who did

not try to make the American government act as justly toward the other nations in international relations as he himself would act toward any individual
in private relations. I should be heartily ashamed to see us wrong a weaker
power, and I should hang my head forever if we tamely suffered wrong from
a stronger power.   5

Of conservation I shall speak more at length elsewhere. Conservation means
development as much as it does protection. I recognize the right and duty of
this generation to develop and use the natural resources of our land; but I do
not recognize the right to waste them, or to rob, by wasteful use, the generations
that come after us. I ask nothing of the nation except that it so behave as each   10
farmer here behaves with reference to his own children. That farmer is a poor
creature who skins the land and leaves it worthless to his children. The farmer is
a good farmer who, having enabled the land to support himself and to provide
for the education of his children, leaves it to them a little better than he found
it himself. I believe the same thing of a nation.   15

Moreover, I believe that the natural resources must be used for the benefit
of all our people, and not monopolized for the benefit of the few, and here again
is another case in which I am accused of taking a revolutionary attitude. People
forget now that one hundred years ago there were public men of good character
who advocated the nation selling its public lands in great quantities, so that the   20
nation could get the most money out of it, and giving it to the men who could
cultivate it for their own uses. We took the proper democratic ground that the
land should be granted in small sections to the men who were actually to till
it and live on it. Now, with the water power, with the forests, with the mines,
we are brought face to face with the fact that there are many people who will   25
go with us in conserving the resources only if they are to be allowed to exploit
them for their benefit. That is one of the fundamental reasons why the special
interests should be driven out of politics. Of all the questions which can come
before this nation, short of the actual preservation of its existence in a great
war, there is none which compares in importance with the great central task of   30
leaving this land even a better land for our descendants than it is for us, and
training them into a better race to inhabit the land and pass it on. Conservation
is a great moral issue, for it involves the patriotic duty of insuring the safety
and continuance of the nation. Let me add that the health and vitality of our
people are at least as well worth conserving as their forests, waters, lands, and   35
minerals, and in this great work the national government must bear a most
important part.

I have spoken elsewhere also of the great task which lies before the farmers of the country to get for themselves and their wives and children not only
the benefits of better farming, but also those of better business methods and   40

better conditions of life on the farm. The burden of this great task will fall, as it should, mainly upon the great organizations of the farmers themselves. I am glad it will, for I believe they are all well able to handle it. In particular, there are strong reasons why the Departments of Agriculture of the various states,
5   the United States Department of Agriculture, and the agricultural colleges and experiment stations should extend their work to cover all phases of farm life, instead of limiting themselves, as they have far too often limited themselves in the past, solely to the question of the production of crops. And now a special word to the farmer. I want to see him make the farm as fine a farm as it can be
10 made; and let him remember to see that the improvement goes on indoors as well as out; let him remember that the farmer's wife should have her share of thought and attention just as much as the farmer himself.

   Nothing is more true than that excess of every kind is followed by reaction; a fact which should be pondered by reformer and reactionary alike. We are face
15 to face with new conceptions of the relations of property to human welfare, chiefly because certain advocates of the rights of property as against the rights of men have been pushing their claims too far. The man who wrongly holds that every human right is secondary to his profit must now give way to the advocate of human welfare, who rightly maintains that every man holds his
20 property subject to the general right of the community to regulate its use to whatever degree the public welfare may require it.

   But I think we may go still further. The right to regulate the use of wealth in the public interest is universally admitted. Let us admit also the right to regulate the terms and conditions of labor, which is the chief element of wealth,
25 directly in the interest of the common good. The fundamental thing to do for every man is to give him a chance to reach a place in which he will make the greatest possible contribution to the public welfare. Understand what I say there. Give him a chance, not push him up if he will not be pushed. Help any man who stumbles; if he lies down, it is a poor job to try to carry him; but if
30 he is a worthy man, try your best to see that he gets a chance to show the worth that is in him. No man can be a good citizen unless he has a wage more than sufficient to cover the bare cost of living, and hours of labor short enough so that after his day's work is done he will have time and energy to bear his share in the management of the community, to help in carrying the general load.
35 We keep countless men from being good citizens by the conditions of life with which we surround them. We need comprehensive workmen's compensation acts, both state and national laws to regulate child labor and work for women, and, especially, we need in our common schools not merely education in book learning, but also practical training for daily life and work. We need to enforce
40 better sanitary conditions for our workers and to extend the use of safety

appliances for our workers in industry and commerce, both within and between the states. Also, friends, in the interest of the workingman himself we need to set our faces like flint against mob violence just as against corporate greed; against violence and injustice and lawlessness by wage workers just as much as against lawless cunning and greed and selfish arrogance of employers. If I could ask but one thing of my fellow countrymen, my request would be that, whenever they go in for reform, they remember the two sides, and that they always exact justice from one side as much as from the other. I have small use for the public servant who can always see and denounce the corruption of the capitalist, but who cannot persuade himself, especially before election, to say a word about lawless mob violence. And I have equally small use for the man, be he a judge on the bench, or editor of a great paper, or wealthy and influential private citizen, who can see clearly enough and denounce the lawlessness of mob violence, but whose eyes are closed so that he is blind when the question is one of corruption in business on a gigantic scale. Also remember what I said about excess in reformer and reactionary alike. If the reactionary man, who thinks of nothing but the rights of property, could have his way, he would bring about a revolution; and one of my chief fears in connection with progress comes because I do not want to see our people, for lack of proper leadership, compelled to follow men whose intentions are excellent, but whose eyes are a little too wild to make it really safe to trust them. Here in Kansas there is one paper which habitually denounces me as the tool of Wall Street, and at the same time frantically repudiates the statement that I am a Socialist on the ground that that is an unwarranted slander of the Socialists.

National efficiency has many factors. It is a necessary result of the principle of conservation widely applied. In the end it will determine our failure or success as a nation. National efficiency has to do, not only with natural resources and with men, but it is equally concerned with institutions. The state must be made efficient for the work which concerns only the people of the state; and the nation for that which concerns all the people. There must remain no neutral ground to serve as a refuge for lawbreakers, and especially for lawbreakers of great wealth, who can hire the vulpine legal cunning which will teach them how to avoid both jurisdictions. It is a misfortune when the national legislature fails to do its duty in providing a national remedy, so that the only national activity is the purely negative activity of the judiciary in forbidding the state to exercise power in the premises.

I do not ask for over-centralization; but I do ask that we work in a spirit of broad and far-reaching nationalism when we work for what concerns our people as a whole. We are all Americans. Our common interests are as broad as the continent. I speak to you here in Kansas exactly as I would speak in New

York or Georgia, for the most vital problems are those which affect us all alike. The national government belongs to the whole American people, and where the whole American people are interested, that interest can be guarded effectively only by the national government. The betterment which we seek must be
5 accomplished, I believe, mainly through the national government.

The American people are right in demanding that New Nationalism, without which we cannot hope to deal with new problems. The New Nationalism puts the national need before sectional or personal advantage. It is impatient of the utter confusion that results from local legislatures attempting to treat
10 national issues as local issues. It is still more impatient of the impotence which springs from over-division of governmental powers, the impotence which makes it possible for local selfishness or for legal cunning, hired by wealthy special interests, to bring national activities to a deadlock. This New Nationalism regards the executive power as the steward of the public welfare. It demands of
15 the judiciary that it shall be interested primarily in human welfare rather than in property, just as it demands that the representative body shall represent all the people rather than any one class or section of the people.

I believe in shaping the ends of government to protect property as well as human welfare. Normally, and in the long run, the ends are the same; but
20 whenever the alternative must be faced, I am for men and not for property, as you were in the Civil War. I am far from underestimating the importance of dividends; but I rank dividends below human character. Again, I do not have any sympathy with the reformer who says he does not care for dividends. Of course, economic welfare is necessary, for a man must pull his own weight and
25 be able to support his family. I know well that the reformers must not bring upon the people economic ruin, or the reforms themselves will go down in the ruin. But we must be ready to face temporary disaster, whether or not brought on by those who will war against us to the knife. Those who oppose all reform will do well to remember that ruin in its worst form is inevitable if our national
30 life brings us nothing better than swollen fortunes for the few and the triumph in both politics and business of a sordid and selfish materialism.

If our political institutions were perfect, they would absolutely prevent the political domination of money in any part of our affairs. We need to make our political representatives more quickly and sensitively responsive to the people
35 whose servants they are. More direct action by the people in their own affairs under proper safeguards is vitally necessary. The direct primary is a step in this direction, if it is associated with a corrupt practices act effective to prevent the advantage of the man willing recklessly and unscrupulously to spend money over his more honest competitor. It is particularly important that all moneys
40 received or expended for campaign purposes should be publicly accounted for,

not only after election, but before election as well. Political action must be made simpler, easier, and freer from confusion for every citizen. I believe that the prompt removal of unfaithful or incompetent public servants should be made easy and sure in whatever way experience shall show to be most expedient in any given class of cases.   5

One of the fundamental necessities in a representative government such as ours is to make certain that the men to whom the people delegate their power shall serve the people by whom they are elected, and not the special interests. I believe that every national officer, elected or appointed, should be forbidden to perform any service or receive any compensation, directly or indirectly,   10 from interstate corporations; and a similar provision could not fail to be useful within the states.

The object of government is the welfare of the people. The material progress and prosperity of a nation are desirable chiefly so far as they lead to the moral and material welfare of all good citizens. Just in proportion as the average man   15 and woman are honest, capable of sound judgment and high ideals, active in public affairs—but, first of all, sound in their home life, and the father and mother of healthy children whom they bring up well—just so far, and no farther, we may count our civilization a success. We must have—I believe we have already—a genuine and permanent moral awakening, without which no   20 wisdom of legislation or administration really means anything; and, on the other hand, we must try to secure the social and economic legislation without which any improvement due to purely moral agitation is necessarily evanescent. Let me again illustrate by a reference to the Grand Army. You could not have won simply as a disorderly and disorganized mob. You needed generals; you needed   25 careful administration of the most advanced type; and a good commissary—the cracker line. You well remember that success was necessary in many different lines in order to bring about general success. You had to have the administration at Washington good, just as you had to have the administration in the field; and you had to have the work of the generals good. You could not have triumphed   30 without that administration and leadership; but it would all have been worthless if the average soldier had not had the right stuff in him. He had to have the right stuff in him, or you could not get it out of him. In the last analysis, therefore, vitally necessary though it was to have the right kind of organization and the right kind of generalship, it was even more vitally necessary that the average   35 soldier should have the fighting edge, the right character. So it is in our civil life. No matter how honest and decent we are in our private lives, if we do not have the right kind of law and the right kind of administration of the law, we cannot go forward as a nation. That is imperative; but it must be an addition to, and not a substitution for, the qualities that make us good citizens. In the last   40 analysis, the most important elements in any man's career must be the sum of those qualities which, in the aggregate, we speak of as character. If he has not got it, then no law that the wit of man can devise, no administration of the law by the boldest and strongest executive, will avail to help him. We must have the

5   right kind of character—character that makes a man, first of all, a good man in the home, a good father, a good husband—that makes a man a good neighbor. You must have that, and, then, in addition, you must have the kind of law and the kind of administration of the law which will give to those qualities in the private citizen the best possible chance for development. The prime problem of

10   our nation is to get the right type of good citizenship, and, to get it, we must have progress, and our public men must be genuinely progressive.

THE NEW FREEDOM
WOODROW WILSON (1856–1924)
PRESIDENT OF THE UNITED STATES (1913–1921)

*Historians have struggled to give a clear definition to the progressive move-
ment. In general, it was a mood among middle-class professionals that
order needed to be imposed on the chaotic American free enterprise system.
Progressives addressed most of the same concerns as the Populists, but did
so from a broader base, in a less angry, alienated, and apocalyptic way,
for many progressives were themselves the products of the economic system
that they sought to reform. Thus, the progressive movement was thoroughly
ambivalent, and progressives frequently took opposite sides on many issues,
and produced contradictory legislation, and often faced unintended consequences. But the one unifying theme of progressivism was statism: At one
level or another, progressives called for increased governmental power to
deal with social problems. It was in this period that the term "liberal" was
inverted from its nineteenth century laissez-faire to its twentieth century
big-government definition.*

*Progressives usually favored the expansion of executive power, seeing
nineteenth-century politics dominated by legislatures and courts, and
above all by corrupt parties in cahoots with business interests. Woodrow
Wilson, an academic political scientist before entering politics, was a pivotal
progressive theorist. Wilson was the first prominent thinker to argue that
the founders' constitutional system had become obsolete and needed to be
radically altered. Reflecting the evolutionary ethos of the era, Wilson argued
that a constitution was an organism that must grow and adapt, or die.
Federalism, separation of powers, checks-and-balances—the various devices
by which the Constitution limited government power—now rendered the
government incapable of dealing with contemporary problems.*

Woodrow Wilson, *The New Freedom: A Call for the Emancipation of the Generous Energies of a
People* (New York: Doubleday, Page and Company, 1913), 3–7, 18–22, 41–54.

There is one great basic fact which underlies all the questions that are discussed on the political platform at the present moment. That singular fact is that nothing is done in this country as it was done twenty years ago.

5 We are in the presence of a new organization of society. Our life has broken away from the past. The life of America is not the life that it was twenty years ago; it is not the life that it was ten years ago. We have changed our economic conditions, absolutely, from top to bottom; and, with our economic society, the organization of our life. The old political formulas do not fit the present problems; they read now like documents taken out of a forgotten age. The older 10 cries sound as if they belonged to a past age which men have almost forgotten. Things which used to be put into the party platforms of ten years ago would sound antiquated if put into a platform now. We are facing the necessity of fitting a new social organization, as we did once fit the old organization, to the happiness and prosperity of the great body of citizens; for we are conscious that 15 the new order of society has not been made to fit and provide the convenience or prosperity of the average man. The life of the nation has grown infinitely varied. It does not centre now upon questions of governmental structure or of the distribution of governmental powers. It centers upon questions of the very structure and operation of society itself, of which government is only the instru- 20 ment. Our development has run so fast and so far along the lines sketched in the earlier day of constitutional definition, has so crossed and interlaced those lines, has piled upon them such novel structures of trust and combination, has elaborated within them a life so manifold, so full of forces which transcend the boundaries of the country itself and fill the eyes of the world, that a new 25 nation seems to have been created which the old formulas do not fit or afford a vital interpretation of.

We have come upon a very different age from any that preceded us. We have come upon an age when we do not do business in the way in which we used to do business—when we do not carry on any of the operations of manufacture, 30 sale, transportation, or communication as men used to carry them on. There is a sense in which in our day the individual has been submerged. In most parts of our country men work, not for themselves, not as partners in the old way in which they used to work, but generally as employees—in a higher or lower grade—of great corporations. There was a time when corporations played a very 35 minor part in our business affairs, but now they play the chief part, and most men are the servants of corporations.

You know what happens when you are the servant of a corporation. You have in no instance access to the men who are really determining the policy of the corporation. If the corporation is doing the things that it ought not to do, you really have no voice in the matter and must obey the orders, and you have oftentimes with deep mortification to co-operate in the doing of things which you know are against the public interest. Your individuality is swallowed up in the individuality and purpose of a great organization.

It is true that, while most men are thus submerged in the corporation, a   5
few, a very few, are exalted to a power which as individuals they could never have wielded. Through the great organizations of which they are the heads, a few are enabled to play a part unprecedented by anything in history in the control of the business operations of the country and in the determination of the happiness of great numbers of people.   10

Yesterday, and ever since history began, men were related to one another as individuals. To be sure there were the family, the Church, and the state, institutions which associated men in certain wide circles of relationship. But in the ordinary concerns of life, in the ordinary work, in the daily round, men dealt freely and directly with one another. Today, the everyday relationships of   15
men are largely with great impersonal concerns, with organizations, not with other individual men.

Now this is nothing short of a new social age, a new era of human relationships, a new stage-setting for the drama of life....

There has come over the land that un-American set of conditions which   20
enables a small number of men who control the government to get favors from the government; by those favors to exclude their fellows from equal business opportunity; by those favors to extend a network of control that will presently dominate every industry in the country, and so make men forget the ancient time when America lay in every hamlet, when America was to be seen in every   25
fair valley, when America displayed her great forces on the broad prairies, ran her fine fires of enterprise up over the mountain-sides and down into the bowels of the earth, and eager men were everywhere captains of industry, not employees; not looking to a distant city to find out what they might do, but looking about among their neighbors, finding credit according to their character, not according   30
to their connections, finding credit in proportion to what was known to be in them and behind them, not in proportion to the securities they held that were approved where they were not known. In order to start an enterprise now, you have to be authenticated, in a perfectly impersonal way, not according to yourself, but according to what you own that somebody else approves of your owning. You   35
cannot begin such an enterprise as those that have made America until you are so authenticated, until you have succeeded in obtaining the good-will of large allied capitalists. Is that freedom? That is dependence, not freedom.

We used to think in the old-fashioned days when life was very simple that all that government had to do was to put on a policeman's uniform, and   40 say, "Now don't anybody hurt anybody else." We used to say that the ideal of government was for every man to be left alone and not interfered with, except when he interfered with somebody else; and that the best government was the government that did as little governing as possible. That was the idea that obtained in Jefferson's time. But we are coming now to realize that life is so complicated that we are not dealing with the old conditions, and that the law has to step in and create new conditions under which we may live, the conditions which will make it tolerable for us to live.

Let me illustrate what I mean: It used to be true in our cities that every family occupied a separate house of its own, that every family had its own little premises, that every family was separated in its life from every other family. That is no longer the case in our great cities. Families live in tenements, they live in flats, they live on floors; they are piled layer upon layer in the great tenement houses of our crowded districts, and not only are they piled layer upon layer, but they are associated room by room, so that there is in every room, sometimes, in our congested districts, a separate family. In some foreign countries they have made much more progress than we in handling these things. In the city of Glasgow, for example (Glasgow is one of the model cities of the world), they have made up their minds that the entries and the hallways of great tenements are public streets. Therefore, the policeman goes up the stairway and patrols the corridors; the lighting department of the city sees to it that the halls are abundantly lighted. The city does not deceive itself into supposing that great building is a unit from which the police are to keep out and the civic authority to be excluded, but it says: "These are public highways, and light is needed in them, and control by the authority of the city."

I liken that to our great modern industrial enterprises. A corporation is very like a large tenement house; it isn't the premises of a single commercial family; it is just as much a public affair as a tenement house is a network of public highways....

...I used to say, when I had to do with the administration of an educational institution,[1] that I should like to make the young gentlemen of the rising generation as unlike their fathers as possible. Not because their fathers lacked character or intelligence or knowledge or patriotism, but because their fathers, by reason of their advancing years and their established position in society, had lost touch with the processes of life; they had forgotten what it was to begin; they had forgotten what it was to rise; they had forgotten what it was to be dominated by the circumstances of their life on their way up from the bottom to the top, and, therefore, they were out of sympathy with the creative, formative, and progressive forces of society.

[1]Wilson was president of Princeton University (1902–1910).

Progress! Did you ever reflect that that word is almost a new one? No word comes more often or more naturally to the lips of modern man, as if the thing it stands for were almost synonymous with life itself, and yet men through many thousand years never talked or thought of progress. They thought in the other direction. Their stories of heroisms and glory were tales of the past. The ancestor wore the heavier armor and carried the larger spear. "There were giants in those days." Now all that has altered. We think of the future, not the past, as the more glorious time in comparison with which the present is nothing. Progress, development—those are modern words. The modern idea is to leave the past and press onward to something new.

But what is progress going to do with the past, and with the present? How is it going to treat them? With ignominy, or respect? Should it break with them altogether, or rise out of them, with its roots still deep in the older time? What attitude shall progressives take toward the existing order, toward those institutions of conservatism, the Constitution, the laws, and the courts?

Are those thoughtful men who fear that we are now about to disturb the ancient foundations of our institutions justified in their fear? If they are, we ought to go very slowly about the processes of change. If it is indeed true that we have grown tired of the institutions which we have so carefully and sedulously built up, then we ought to go very slowly and very carefully about the very dangerous task of altering them. We ought, therefore, to ask ourselves, first of all, whether thought in this country is tending to do anything by which we shall retrace our steps, or by which we shall change the whole direction of our development?

I believe, for one, that you cannot tear up ancient rootages and safely plant the tree of liberty in soil which is not native to it. I believe that the ancient traditions of a people are its ballast; you cannot make a *tabula rasa*[2] upon which to write a political program. You cannot take a new sheet of paper and determine what your life shall be tomorrow. You must knit the new into the old. You cannot put a new patch on an old garment without ruining it; it must be not a patch, but something woven into the old fabric, of practically the same pattern, of the same texture and intention. If I did not believe that to be progressive was to preserve the essentials of our institutions, I for one could not be a progressive.

One of the chief benefits I used to derive from being president of a university was that I had the pleasure of entertaining thoughtful men from all over the world. I cannot tell you how much has dropped into my granary by their presence. I had been casting around in my mind for something by which to draw

---

[2] *Tabula rasa*—blank slate

several parts of my political thought together when it was my good fortune to entertain a very interesting Scotsman who had been devoting himself to the philosophical thought of the seventeenth century. His talk was so engaging that it was delightful to hear him speak of anything, and presently there came out
5   of the unexpected region of his thought the thing I had been waiting for. He called my attention to the fact that in every generation all sorts of speculation and thinking tend to fall under the formula of the dominant thought of the age. For example, after the Newtonian Theory of the universe had been developed, almost all thinking tended to express itself in the analogies of the Newtonian
10 Theory, and since the Darwinian Theory has reigned amongst us, everybody is likely to express whatever he wishes to expound in terms of development and accommodation to environment.

     Now, it came to me, as this interesting man talked, that the Constitution of the United States had been made under the dominion of the Newtonian
15 Theory. You have only to read the papers of *The Federalist* to see that fact written on every page. They speak of the "checks and balances" of the Constitution, and use to express their idea the simile of the organization of the universe, and particularly of the solar system—how by the attraction of gravitation the various parts are held in their orbits; and then they proceeded to represent Congress,
20 the judiciary, and the President as a sort of imitation of the solar system.

     They were only following the English Whigs, who gave Great Britain its modern constitution. Not that those Englishmen analyzed the matter, or had any theory about it; Englishmen care little for theories. It was a Frenchman, Montesquieu, who pointed out to them how faithfully they had copied Newton's
25 description of the mechanism of the heavens.

     The makers of our Federal Constitution read Montesquieu with true scientific enthusiasm. They were scientists in their way—the best way of their age—those fathers of the nation. Jefferson wrote of "the laws of Nature"—and then by way of afterthought—"and of Nature's God." And they constructed a
30 government as they would have constructed an orrery—to display the laws of nature. Politics in their thought was a variety of mechanics. The Constitution was founded on the law of gravitation. The government was to exist and move by virtue of the efficacy of "checks and balances."

     The trouble with the theory is that government is not a machine, but a
35 living thing. It falls not under the theory of the universe, but under the theory of organic life. It is accountable to Darwin, not to Newton. It is modified by its environment, necessitated by its tasks, shaped to its functions by the sheer pressure of life. No living thing can have its organs offset against each other as checks and live. On the contrary, its life is dependent upon their quick co-
40 operation, their ready response to the commands of instinct or intelligence, their

amicable community of purpose. Government is not a body of blind forces; it is a body of men, with highly differentiated functions, no doubt, in our modern day, of specialization, with a common task and purpose. Their co-operation is indispensable, their warfare fatal. There can be no successful government without the intimate, instinctive co-ordination of the organs of life and action. This is not theory, but fact, and displays its force as fact, whatever theories may be thrown across its track. Living political constitutions must be Darwinian in structure and in practice. Society is a living organism and must obey the laws of life, not of mechanics; it must develop.

All that progressives ask or desire is permission—in an era when "development," "evolution," is the scientific word—to interpret the Constitution according to the Darwinian principle; all they ask is recognition of the fact that a nation is a living thing and not a machine.

Some citizens of this country have never got beyond the Declaration of Independence, signed in Philadelphia, July 4th, 1776. Their bosoms swell against George III, but they have no consciousness of the war for freedom that is going on today.

The Declaration of Independence did not mention the questions of our day. It is of no consequence to us unless we can translate its general terms into examples of the present day and substitute them in some vital way for the examples it itself gives, so concrete, so intimately involved in the circumstances of the day in which it was conceived and written. It is an eminently practical document, meant for the use of practical men; not a thesis for philosophers, but a whip for tyrants; not a theory of government, but a program of action. Unless we can translate it into the questions of our own day, we are not worthy of it, we are not the sons of the sires who acted in response to its challenge.

What form does the contest between tyranny and freedom take today? What is the special form of tyranny we now fight? How does it endanger the rights of the people, and what do we mean to do in order to make our contest against it effectual? What are to be the items of our new declaration of independence?

By tyranny, as we now fight it, we mean control of the law, of legislation, and adjudication by organizations which do not represent the people, by means which are private and selfish. We mean, specifically, the conduct of our affairs and the shaping of our legislation in the interest of special bodies of capital and those who organize their use. We mean the alliance, for this purpose, of political machines with selfish business. We mean the exploitation of the people by legal and political means. We have seen many of our governments under these influences cease to be representative governments, cease to be governments representative of the people, and become governments representative of special interests, controlled by machines, which in their turn are not controlled by the people.

Sometimes, when I think of the growth of our economic system, it seems to me as if, leaving our law just about where it was before any of the modern
5   inventions or developments took place, we had simply at haphazard extended the family residence, added an office here and a workroom there, and a new set of sleeping rooms there, built up higher on our foundations, and put out little lean-tos on the side, until we have a structure that has no character whatever. Now, the problem is to continue to live in the house and yet change it.

10   Well, we are architects in our time, and our architects are also engineers. We don't have to stop using a railroad terminal because a new station is being built. We don't have to stop any of the processes of our lives because we are re-arranging the structures in which we conduct those processes. What we have to undertake is to systematize the foundations of the house, then to thread
15   all the old parts of the structure with the steel which will be laced together in modern fashion, accommodated to all the modern knowledge of structural strength and elasticity, and then slowly change the partitions, relay the walls, let in the light through new apertures, improve the ventilation; until finally, a generation or two from now, the scaffolding will be taken away, and there
20   will be the family in a great building whose noble architecture will at last be disclosed, where men can live as a single community, co-operative as in a per- fected, co-ordinated beehive, not afraid of any storm of nature, not afraid of any artificial storm, any imitation of thunder and lightning, knowing that the foundations go down to the bedrock of principle, and knowing that whenever
25   they please they can change that plan again and accommodate it as they please to the altering necessities of their lives.

But there are a great many men who don't like the idea. Some wit recently said, in view of the fact that most of our American architects are trained in a certain École in Paris, that all American architecture in recent years was either
30   bizarre or "Beaux Arts." I think that our economic architecture is decidedly bizarre; and I am afraid that there is a good deal to learn about matters other than architecture from the same source from which our architects have learned a great many things. I don't mean the School of Fine Arts at Paris, but the experience of France; for from the other side of the water men can now hold up against us
35   the reproach that we have not adjusted our lives to modern conditions to the same extent that they have adjusted theirs. I was very much interested in some of the reasons given by our friends across the Canadian border for being very shy about the reciprocity arrangements. They said: "We are not sure whither these arrangements will lead, and we don't care to associate too closely with the
40   economic conditions of the United States until those conditions are as modern

as ours." And when I resented it, and asked for particulars, I had, in regard to many matters, to retire from the debate. Because I found that they had adjusted their regulations of economic development to conditions we had not yet found a way to meet in the United States.

Well, we have started now at all events. The procession is under way. The stand-patter doesn't know there is a procession. He is asleep in the back part of his house. He doesn't know that the road is resounding with the tramp of men going to the front. And when he wakes up, the country will be empty. He will be deserted, and he will wonder what has happened. Nothing has happened. The world has been going on. The world has a habit of going on. The world has a habit of leaving those behind who won't go with it. The world has always neglected stand-patters. And, therefore, the stand-patter does not excite my indignation; he excites my sympathy. He is going to be so lonely before it is all over. And we are good fellows, we are good company; why doesn't he come along? We are not going to do him any harm. We are going to show him a good time. We are going to climb the slow road until it reaches some upland where the air is fresher, where the whole talk of mere politicians is stilled, where men can look in each other's faces and see that there is nothing to conceal, that all they have to talk about they are willing to talk about in the open and talk about with each other; and whence, looking back over the road, we shall see at last that we have fulfilled our promise to mankind. We had said to all the world, "America was created to break every kind of monopoly, and to set men free, upon a footing of equality, upon a footing of opportunity, to match their brains and their energies." And now we have proved that we meant it.

VII
AMERICA BETWEEN
THE WARS

The 1920s and 1930s—the inter-war years—offer an interesting, if not unique, contrast in American history. One could readily label the decade of the 1920s politically and economically conservative. Presidents Harding (*r.* 1921–1923) and Coolidge (*r.* 1923–1929) undid much of the progressive experimentation of the previous three presidents, returning America to what Harding called "normalcy." Simultaneously, the 1920s saw a culture war of sorts, with the trend moving steadily toward a liberal and progressive exploration of the arts. Freudian theory, jazz, and sexual experimentation ruled college campuses. Authors such as Ernest Hemingway (1899–1961), F. Scott Fitzgerald (1896–1940), and Sinclair Lewis (1885–1951) predominated the literary scene, with older proponents of the liberal arts—Irving Babbitt (1865–1933) and Paul Elmer More (1864–1937)—defending traditional thought in politics and arts through their so-called "New Humanism." The biggest cultural event of the decade, without question, was the Scopes Trial, which pitted fundamentalist and evangelical America against progressive America.

The 1930s, by great contrast, witnessed radical political experimentation, progressivism, and liberalism, at home and abroad. Across the Atlantic and Pacific Oceans, fascism, communism, and National Socialism spread rapidly. At home, the Democratic party, under the leadership of Franklin D. Roosevelt (*r.* 1933–1945), embraced what Christopher Dawson at the time called "constitutional dictatorship." The best articulation of the longings for political and economic experimentation came from John Steinbeck (1902–1968) in his brilliant *Grapes of Wrath*. With the Great Depression of the 1930s, the average American became much more conservative in his lifestyle, and sexual mores, for example, returned to their pre-1920s norms.

America's years between the world wars were marked by strong prosperity during the 1920s followed by the Great Depression of the 1930s—the most cataclysmic economic collapse in U.S. history.

After World War I, President Warren Harding (1865–1923) and Vice-President Calvin Coolidge (1872–1933) won the 1920 election with a promise to cut the high tax rates of the war years, reduce government spending on the military, and, most importantly to the American people, return the republic to "normalcy." In 1921, unemployment stood at 11.7 percent and Harding appointed Andrew Mellon (1855–1937), a banker and founder of Alcoa, to head the Treasury department. Mellon, also with favor from Coolidge, who became president when Harding died in 1923, recommended that Congress cut income tax rates across the board to give investors incentives to start businesses and hire the veterans returning home from the war. Existing marginal tax rates on top incomes stood at 73 percent, and Mellon said that such taxes were causing businesses to stagnate. The Mellon Plan, as it was called, cut tax rates across the board from 73 to 24 percent on top incomes and from 4 to 0.5 percent on the lowest incomes. In part as a result of these cuts, businessmen plowed capital into the American economy during the decade. The American auto industry, for example, dominated the world in the 1920s and new inventions flourished—from air conditioning and radios to zippers and scotch tape. Unemployment plummeted to an average annual rate of 3.3 percent during the Coolidge presidency (1923–1929), and the American gross national product expanded by roughly 25 percent during the 1920s. No one benefitted more from this economic growth than American workers.

"Wealth is the product of industry, ambition, character and untiring effort," President Coolidge observed. "In all experience, the accumulation of wealth means the multiplication of schools, the increase of knowledge, the dissemination of intelligence, the encouragement of science, the broadening of outlook, the expansion of liberties, the widening of culture." Coolidge concluded: "Of course, the accumulation of wealth cannot be justified as the chief end of existence. But we are compelled to recognize it as a means to well-nigh every desirable achievement."

Coolidge believed that limited government and the protection of natural rights, as understood and expressed in the Declaration of Independence, would keep the U.S. strong. Coolidge was the last U.S. president to have budget surpluses every year. Indeed, during the Harding and Coolidge presidencies, almost one-third of the entire U.S. national debt was paid off.

What ended the strong prosperity of the 1920s? Economists have increasingly concluded that misplaced government intervention is the starting point to understanding the unraveling of the American economy during the 1930s. Herbert Hoover (r. 1929–1933), Coolidge's Secretary of Commerce, became the next president and Hoover did not have Coolidge's commitment to limited government. Not all of the problems were Hoover's fault. For example, the Federal Reserve, which is not directly controlled by the president, raised interest rates and that made it harder for Americans to borrow money to start businesses. Milton Friedman (1912–2006), who won a Nobel Prize in Economics, argued that Federal Reserve policy triggered the Great Depression.

Hoover's attempt to fix the economic crisis failed. First, he signed into law the largest tariff in U.S. history, the Smoot-Hawley Tariff, which effectively closed off trade with much of the world. If the U.S. would not buy products from the Europeans, the Europeans decided they would no longer buy American cars, typewriters, and radios. Second, Hoover increased income tax rates—back to 63 percent on top incomes. This scared investors and stifled economic expansion. Third, he promoted federal subsidies to targeted farmers (through the Farm Board) and to businesses (through the Reconstruction Finance Corporations). As one historian has put it, Hoover was a "forgotten progressive."

Finally, Europeans had problems of their own, and every European country except Finland reneged on more than $10 billion (total) in loans that the U.S. made to them during World War I. Unemployment reached 25 percent in the U.S. and American voters elected Democrat Franklin D. Roosevelt (1882–1945), Governor of New York, to the presidency in 1932.

Franklin Roosevelt, the son of an old, elite Dutch New York family, was a cousin of Theodore Roosevelt (1858–1919). Franklin emulated his cousin as a progressive. Just as Theodore once served as Assistant Secretary of the Navy, Franklin held this position as well under President Woodrow Wilson. In 1920, Franklin was the Democratic nominee for vice-president, but lost to the Harding–Coolidge ticket. Roosevelt was stricken with polio the following year, but he was persistent and determined to continue his political career. In 1928, a Republican year, Roosevelt won election as governor of New York, then the largest state in the union. He won re-election handily in 1930 and began his upbeat campaign to become president.

During the presidential campaign in 1932, and hoping to placate the laissez-faire wing of his party, Roosevelt promised to reduce taxes, cut federal spending, and lower the tariff. Despite such campaign promises, he increased tax rates dramatically and raised federal spending more than any previous president had done. He called his programs the "New Deal" which included a bureaucratic alphabet soup: subsidies for farmers (AAA), jobs for the unemployed to build roads (WPA), and massive public works (TVA). Because the government absorbed available cash and resources in the economy through its demand for taxes, entrepreneurs could not raise the capital to start businesses, and few were willing to take the risks inherent in start-up ventures if government would simply tax away all of the profits. Perhaps even more importantly, Roosevelt's new taxes and programs—such as Social Security—nearly drove to extinction the American tradition of voluntary associations that had traditionally provided insurance, medical benefits, and funerary benefits. A working man, even if still employed in the Depression, could simply not afford to pay taxes to the government and pay membership dues to his lodge or mutual aid associations.

Roosevelt's efforts to end the depression only exacerbated it. Unemployment in Roosevelt's first seven years in office, for example, never dropped below 14 percent; the rate averaged over 17 percent. Henry Morgenthau (1891–1967), Roosevelt's Secretary of Treasury, was frantic at the persistent unemployment. "We have tried spending money," Morgenthau said in May 1939. "We are spending more than we have ever spent before and it does not work.... I want to see people get enough to eat. We have never made good on our promises.... I say after eight years of this Administration we have just as much unemployment as when we started.... And an enormous debt to boot!" Indeed, the U.S. national debt more than doubled during Roosevelt's first two terms in the White House.

Despite such failures, Roosevelt remained incredibly popular in America. He remains the only person to have received the popular and electoral votes to win four terms to the presidency. But, Roosevelt also earned as much scorn as almost any president in history. Critics at home and abroad feared his intentions. Psychologist Carl Jung (1875–1961), for example, claimed in *Time* magazine, that Roosevelt "has the most amazing power complex, the Mussolini substance, the stuff of a dictator absolutely." Many associated Roosevelt with fascism. After a long interview with Adolf Hitler, the correspondent for the *New York Times* noted in her byline, "Chancellor admires Roosevelt for Marching to Objectives over Congress and Lobbies." The opening to the article read: "There is at least one official voice in Europe that expresses understanding of the methods and motives of President Roosevelt. This voice is that of Germany, as represented by Chancellor Adolf Hitler." With the bombing of Pearl Harbor on 7 December 1941, the U.S. entered World War II.

WAR MESSAGE
WOODROW WILSON (1856–1924)
PRESIDENT OF THE UNITED STATES (1913–1921)

Thomas Woodrow Wilson served two terms as president of the United States, from 1913 to 1921. He had been in the White House seventeen months when the First World War began in Europe. Determined to keep the United States out of the fight, Wilson declared shortly after the conflict began that Americans would be "neutral in thought as well as deed." The president did not believe, however, that being neutral should deprive Americans of any rights to trade or travel on the high seas that they would enjoy during peacetime. Thus, trans-Atlantic commerce continued in spite of efforts made by the warring Europeans to cut their enemies' trade.

Beginning in October 1914, British authorities enforced a blockade which over time cut American trade with Germany to a trickle. But, because Great Britain possessed the world's largest fleet of surface ships to steer offending vessels to port without destroying them, American "rights" were thus abused without loss of life. The Germans, forced to rely on submarines to enforce their blockade of the British Isles and France, were not able to be so delicate. Indeed, the German U-boat attack on the British liner Lusitania *in May 1915, which killed over a hundred American citizens, proved the most dramatic signal that Wilson's affirmation of "neutral rights" was not going to go unchallenged. While this incident outraged American opinion, the Germans were able to avoid a rupture of relations by assuring Wilson that they would cease attacking passenger ships and endeavor to warn merchant vessels before sinking them. During the next eighteen months, an uneasy peace was maintained with Germany on this basis, and Wilson won re-election in November 1916 on the slogan, "He Kept Us Out of War."*

In January 1917, desperate to defeat its foes, the German government announced a policy of "unrestricted submarine warfare" against

Woodrow Wilson, "Address of the President of the United States," *Senate Documents*, 65th Congress, First Session (Washington, DC: Government Printing Office, 1917), X:3–8.

*any and all vessels seeking to traverse the sea approaches to Great Britain
and France. American vessels were immediately attacked and sunk, and
Wilson broke diplomatic relations with Berlin. Within a couple of months,
the president had mustered his arguments for war, and he delivered the
address below before a joint session of Congress on April 2, 1917. By votes
of 82–6 in the Senate, and 373–50 in the House, Congress declared
war against Germany on April 6. The president's message not only made
a forceful case for war, but unveiled many of the principles that would
comprise "Wilsonian internationalism," a decidedly new understanding
of the United States' role in the world.*

2 APRIL 1917

I have called the Congress into extraordinary session because there are serious, very serious, choices of policy to be made, and made immediately, which
it was neither right nor constitutionally permissible that I should assume the
responsibility of making.

5   On the third of February last I officially laid before you the extraordinary
announcement of the Imperial German Government that on and after the first
day of February it was its purpose to put aside all restraints of law or of humanity and use its submarines to sink every vessel that sought to approach either
the ports of Great Britain and Ireland or the western coasts of Europe or any

10   of the ports controlled by the enemies of Germany within the Mediterranean.
That had seemed to be the object of the German submarine warfare earlier in
the war, but since April of last year the Imperial Government had somewhat
restrained the commanders of its undersea craft in conformity with its promise
then given to us that passenger boats should not be sunk and that due warning

15   would be given to all other vessels which its submarines might seek to destroy,
when no resistance was offered or escape attempted, and care taken that their
crews were given at least a fair chance to save their lives in their open boats.
The precautions taken were meagre and haphazard enough, as was proved in
distressing instance after instance in the progress of the cruel and unmanly

20   business, but a certain degree of restraint was observed. The new policy has
swept every restriction aside. Vessels of every kind, whatever their flag, their
character, their cargo, their destination, their errand, have been ruthlessly sent
to the bottom without warning and without thought of help or mercy for
those on board, the vessels of friendly neutrals along with those of belligerents.

25   Even hospital ships and ships carrying relief to the sorely bereaved and stricken
people of Belgium, though the latter were provided with safe conduct through
the proscribed areas by the German Government itself and were distinguished
by unmistakable marks of identity, have been sunk with the same reckless lack
of compassion or of principle.

I was for a little while unable to believe that such things would in fact be done by any government that had hitherto subscribed to the humane practices of civilized nations. International law had its origin in the attempt to set up some law which would be respected and observed upon the seas, where no nation had right of dominion and where lay the free highways of the world. By painful stage after stage has that law been built up, with meagre enough results, indeed, after all was accomplished that could be accomplished, but always with a clear view, at least, of what the heart and conscience of mankind demanded. This minimum of right the German Government has swept aside under the plea of retaliation and necessity and because it had no weapons which it could use at sea except these which it is impossible to employ as it is employing them without throwing to the winds all scruples of humanity or of respect for the understandings that were supposed to underlie the intercourse of the world. I am not now thinking of the loss of property involved, immense and serious as that is, but only of the wanton and wholesale destruction of the lives of non-combatants, men, women, and children, engaged in pursuits which have always, even in the darkest periods of modern history, been deemed innocent and legitimate. Property can be paid for; the lives of peaceful and innocent people cannot be. The present German submarine warfare against commerce is a warfare against mankind.

It is a war against all nations. American ships have been sunk, American lives taken, in ways which it has stirred us very deeply to learn of, but the ships and people of other neutral and friendly nations have been sunk and overwhelmed in the waters in the same way. There has been no discrimination. The challenge is to all mankind. Each nation must decide for itself how it will meet it. The choice we make for ourselves must be made with a moderation of counsel and a temperateness of judgment befitting our character and our motives as a nation. We must put excited feeling away. Our motive will not be revenge or the victorious assertion of the physical might of the nation, but only the vindication of right, of human right, of which we are only a single champion.

When I addressed the Congress on the twenty-sixth of February last I thought that it would suffice to assert our neutral rights with arms, our right to use the seas against unlawful interference, our right to keep our people safe against unlawful violence. But armed neutrality, it now appears, is impracticable. Because submarines are in effect outlaws when used as the German submarines have been used against merchant shipping, it is impossible to defend ships against their attacks as the law of nations has assumed that merchantmen would defend themselves against privateers or cruisers, visible craft giving chase upon the open sea.

There is one choice we cannot make, we are incapable of making; we will not choose the path of submission and suffer the most sacred rights of our nation and our people to be ignored or violated. The wrongs against which we now array ourselves are no common wrongs; they cut to the very roots of human life.

5 With a profound sense of the solemn and even tragical character of the step I am taking and of the grave responsibilities which it involves, but in unhesitating obedience to what I deem my constitutional duty, I advise that the Congress declare the recent course of the Imperial German Government to be in fact nothing less than war against the government and people of the United States; that it formally accept the status of belligerent which has thus been 10 thrust upon it; and that it take immediate steps not only to put the country in a more thorough state of defense but also to exert all its power and employ all its resources to bring the Government of the German Empire to terms and end the war.

What this will involve is clear. It will involve the utmost practicable co-op-15 eration in counsel and action with the governments now at war with Germany, and, as incident to that, the extension to those governments of the most liberal financial credits, in order that our resources may so far as possible be added to theirs. It will involve the organization and mobilization of all the material resources of the country to supply the materials of war and serve the incidental 20 needs of the nation in the most abundant and yet the most economical and efficient way possible. It will involve the immediate full equipment of the navy in all respects but particularly in supplying it with the best means of dealing with the enemy's submarines. It will involve the immediate addition to the armed forces of the United States already provided for by law in case of war at least 25 five hundred thousand men, who should, in my opinion, be chosen upon the principle of universal liability to service, and also the authorization of subsequent additional increments of equal force so soon as they may be needed and can be handled in training. It will involve also, of course, the granting of adequate credits to the government, sustained, I hope, so far as they can equitably be 30 sustained by the present generation, by well conceived taxation.

Our object now, as then, is to vindicate the principles of peace and justice in the life of the world as against selfish and autocratic power and to set up amongst the really free and self-governed peoples of the world such a concert of purpose and of action as will henceforth ensure the observance of those principles. Neu-35 trality is no longer feasible or desirable where the peace of the world is involved and the freedom of its peoples, and the menace to that peace and freedom lies in the existence of autocratic governments backed by organized force which is controlled wholly by their will, not by the will of their people. We have seen the last of neutrality in such circumstances. We are at the beginning of an age in 40 which it will be insisted that the same standards of conduct and of responsibility for wrong done shall be observed among nations and their governments that are observed among the individual citizens of civilized states.

We have no quarrel with the German people. We have no feeling towards them but one of sympathy and friendship. It was not upon their impulse that their government acted in entering this war. It was not with their previous knowledge   5
or approval. It was a war determined upon as wars used to be determined upon in the old, unhappy days when peoples were nowhere consulted by their rulers and wars were provoked and waged in the interest of dynasties or of little groups of ambitious men who were accustomed to use their fellow men as pawns and tools. Self-governed nations do not fill their neighbor states with spies or set the   10
course of intrigue to bring about some critical posture of affairs which will give them an opportunity to strike and make conquest. Such designs can be successfully worked out only under cover and where no one has the right to ask questions. Cunningly contrived plans of deception or aggression, carried, it may be, from generation to generation, can be worked out and kept from the light only within   15
the privacy of courts or behind the carefully guarded confidences of a narrow and privileged class. They are happily impossible where public opinion commands and insists upon full information concerning all the nations affairs.

A steadfast concert for peace can never be maintained except by a part-nership of democratic nations. No autocratic government could be trusted to   20
keep faith within it or observe its covenants. It must be a league of honor, a partnership of opinion. Intrigue would eat its vitals away; the plottings of inner circles who could plan what they would and render account to no one would be a corruption seated at its very heart. Only free peoples can hold their purpose and their honor steady to a common end and prefer the interests of mankind   25
to any narrow interest of their own.

Does not every American feel that assurance has been added to our hope for the future peace of the world by the wonderful and heartening things that have been happening within the last few weeks in Russia? Russia was known by those who knew it best to have been always in fact democratic at heart, in all the   30
vital habits of her thought, in all the intimate relationships of her people that spoke their natural instinct, their habitual attitude towards life. The autocracy that crowned the summit of her political structure, long as it had stood and ter-rible as was the reality of its power, was not in fact Russian in origin, character, or purpose; and now it has been shaken off and the great, generous Russian   35
people have been added in all their naive majesty and might to the forces that are fighting for freedom in the world, for justice, and for peace. Here is a fit partner for a League of Honour.

One of the things that has served to convince us that the Prussian autoc-racy was not and could never be our friend is that from the very outset of the   40

present war it has filled our unsuspecting communities and even our offices of
government with spies and set criminal intrigues everywhere afoot against our
national unity of counsel, our peace within and without, our industries and
our commerce. Indeed it is now evident that its spies were here even before
5   the war began; and it is unhappily not a matter of conjecture but a fact proved
in our courts of justice that the intrigues which have more than once come
perilously near to disturbing the peace and dislocating the industries of the
country have been carried on at the instigation, with the support, and even
under the personal direction of official agents of the Imperial Government
10 accredited to the Government of the United States. Even in checking these
things and trying to extirpate them we have sought to put the most generous
interpretation possible upon them because we knew that their source lay, not
in any hostile feeling or purpose of the German people towards us (who were,
no doubt as ignorant of them as we ourselves were), but only in the selfish
15 designs of a Government that did what it pleased and told its people nothing. But they have played their part in serving to convince us at last that that
Government entertains no real friendship for us and means to act against our
peace and security at its convenience. That it means to stir up enemies against
us at our very doors the intercepted note to the German Minister at Mexico
20 City is eloquent evidence.

We are accepting this challenge of hostile purpose because we know that in
such a government, following such methods, we can never have a friend; and
that in the presence of its organized power, always lying in wait to accomplish
we know not what purpose, there can be no assured security for the democratic
25 governments of the world. We are now about to accept gauge of battle with
this natural foe to liberty and shall, if necessary, spend the whole force of the
nation to check and nullify its pretensions and its power. We are glad, now that
we see the facts with no veil of false pretence about them, to fight thus for the
ultimate peace of the world and for the liberation of its peoples, the German
30 peoples included: for the rights of nations great and small and the privilege of
men everywhere to choose their way of life and of obedience. The world must be
made safe for democracy. Its peace must be planted upon the tested foundations
of political liberty. We have no selfish ends to serve. We desire no conquest, no
dominion. We seek no indemnities for ourselves, no material compensation
35 for the sacrifices we shall freely make. We are but one of the champions of the
rights of mankind. We shall be satisfied when those rights have been made as
secure as the faith and the freedom of nations can make them.

Just because we fight without rancor and without selfish object, seeking
nothing for ourselves but what we shall wish to share with all free peoples, we
40 shall, I feel confident, conduct our operations as belligerents without passion

and ourselves observe with proud punctilio the principles of right and of fair play we profess to be fighting for.

It will be all the easier for us to conduct ourselves as belligerents in a high spirit of right and fairness because we act without animus, not in enmity towards a people or with the desire to bring any injury or disadvantage upon them, but only in armed opposition to an irresponsible government which has thrown aside all considerations of humanity and of right and is running amuck. We are, let me say again, the sincere friends of the German people, and shall desire nothing so much as the early re-establishment of intimate relations of mutual advantage between us—however hard it may be for them, for the time being, to believe that this is spoken from our hearts. We have borne with their present government through all these bitter months because of that friendship—exercising a patience and forbearance which would otherwise have been impossible. We shall, happily, still have an opportunity to prove that friendship in our daily attitude and actions towards the millions of men and women of German birth and native sympathy who live amongst us and share our life, and we shall be proud to prove it towards all who are in fact loyal to their neighbors and to the Government in the hour of test. They are, most of them, as true and loyal Americans as if they had never known any other fealty or allegiance. They will be prompt to stand with us in rebuking and restraining the few who may be of a different mind and purpose. If there should be disloyalty, it will be dealt with a firm hand of stern repression; but, if it lifts its head at all, it will lift it only here and there and without countenance except from a lawless and malignant few.

It is a distressing and oppressive duty, Gentlemen of the Congress, which I have performed in thus addressing you. There are, it may be, many months of fiery trial and sacrifice ahead of us. It is a fearful thing to lead this great peaceful people into war, into the most terrible and disastrous of all wars, civilization itself seeming to be in the balance. But the right is more precious than peace, and we shall fight for the things which we have always carried nearest our hearts—for democracy, for the right of those who submit to authority to have a voice in their own governments, for the rights and liberties of small nations, for a universal dominion of right by such a concert of free peoples as shall bring peace and safety to all nations and make the world itself at last free. To such a task we can dedicate our lives and our fortunes, everything that we are and everything that we have, with the pride of those who know that the day has come when America is privileged to spend her blood and her might for the principles that gave her birth and happiness and the peace which she has treasured. God helping her, she can do no other.

Fourteen Points
Woodrow Wilson (1856–1924)
President of the United States (1913–1921)

Woodrow Wilson delivered his "Fourteen Points Address" to the Congress on January 8, 1918. The First World War continued for ten more months, but the president did not await a cessation of fighting to reveal his peace program to the world. After commenting at length on the negotiations just begun between Germany and Soviet Russia at Brest-Litovsk (talks which ultimately led to Russia's withdrawal from the war upon accepting immense territorial losses), Wilson recounted his own prescription for a just settlement of the four-year old struggle. Although he presumed to speak for an aggrieved humanity, the Fourteen Points found incomplete expression in the peace treaty finalized with Germany in June 1919—a document that the United States Senate refused to ratify after bitter and protracted debate. Still, the address below is vitally important as a refinement of Wilson's vision of a new and expanded role for the United States in international affairs.

8 January 1918

Gentlemen of the Congress: Once more, as repeatedly before, the spokesmen of the Central Empires have indicated their desire to discuss the objects of the war and the possible bases of a general peace. Parleys have been in progress at Brest-Litovsk between representatives of the Central Powers to which the attention of all the belligerents has been invited for the purpose of ascertaining whether it   5
may be possible to extend these parleys into a general conference with regard to terms of peace and settlement. The Russian representatives presented not only a perfectly definite statement of the principles upon which they would be willing to conclude peace, but also an equally definite programme of the concrete application of those principles. The representatives of the Central Powers, on   10
their part, presented an outline of settlement which, if much less definite, seemed

---

Woodrow Wilson, "Address of the President of the United States," *Journal of the Senate of the United States*, 65th Congress, Second Session (Washington, DC: Government Printing Office, 1919), 35–35.

susceptible of liberal interpretation until their specific programme of practical terms was added. That programme proposed no concessions at all either to the sovereignty of Russia or to the preferences of the populations with whose fortunes it dealt, but meant, in a word, that the Central Empires were to keep
5 every foot of territory their armed forces had occupied—every province, every city, every point of vantage—as a permanent addition to their territories and their power. It is a reasonable conjecture that the general principles of settlement which they at first suggested originated with the more liberal statesmen of Germany and Austria, the men who have begun to feel the force of their own
10 peoples' thought and purpose, while the concrete terms of actual settlement came from the military leaders who have no thought but to keep what they have got. The negotiations have been broken off. The Russian representatives were sincere and in earnest. They cannot entertain such proposals of conquest and domination.
15 The whole incident is full of significance. It is also full of perplexity. With whom are the Russian representatives dealing? For whom are the representatives of the Central Empires speaking? Are they speaking for the majorities of their respective parliaments or for the minority parties, that military and imperialistic minority which has so far dominated their whole policy and controlled the
20 affairs of Turkey and of the Balkan states which have felt obliged to become their associates in this war? The Russian representatives have insisted, very justly very wisely, and in the true spirit of modern democracy, that the conferences they have been holding with the Teutonic and Turkish statesmen should be held within open, not closed, doors, and all the world has been audience, as was
25 desired. To whom have we been listening, then? To those who speak the spirit and intention of the Resolutions of the German Reichstag of the ninth of July last, the spirit and intention of the liberal leaders and parties of Germany, or to those who resist and defy that spirit and intention and insist upon conquest and subjugation? Or are we listening, in fact, to both, un-reconciled and in
30 open and hopeless contradiction? These are very serious and pregnant questions. Upon the answer to them depends the peace of the world.

But, whatever the results of the parleys at Brest-Litovsk, whatever the confusions of counsel and of purpose in the utterances of the spokesmen of the Central Empires, they have again attempted to acquaint the world with their
35 objects in the war and have again challenged their adversaries to say what their objects are and what sort of settlement they would deem just and satisfactory. There is no good reason why that challenge should not be responded to, and responded to with the utmost candor. We did not wait for it. Not once, but again and again, we have laid our whole thought and purpose before the world,
40 not in general terms only, but each time with sufficient definition to make it

clear what sort of definitive terms of settlement must necessarily spring out of them. Within the last week Mr. Lloyd George has spoken with admirable candor and in admirable spirit for the people and Government of Great Britain. There is no confusion of counsel among the adversaries of the Central Powers, no uncertainty of principle, no vagueness of detail. The only secrecy of counsel, the only lack of fearless frankness, the only failure to make definite statement of the objects of the war, lies with Germany and her Allies. The issues of life and death hang upon these definitions. No statesman who has the least conception of his responsibility ought for a moment to permit himself to continue this tragical and appalling out-pouring of blood and treasure unless he is sure beyond a per-adventure that the objects of the vital sacrifice are part and parcel of the very life of Society and that the people for whom he speaks think them right and imperative as he does.

There is, moreover, a voice calling for these definitions of principle and of purpose which is, it seems to me, more thrilling and more compelling than any of the many moving voices with which the troubled air of the world is filled. It is the voice of the Russian people. They are prostrate and all but helpless, it would seem, before the grim power of Germany, which has hitherto known no relenting and no pity. Their power, apparently, is shattered. And yet their soul is not subservient. They will not yield either in principle or in action. Their conception of what is right, of what it is humane and honorable for them to accept, has been stated with a frankness, a largeness of view, a generosity of spirit, and a universal human sympathy which must challenge the admiration of every friend of mankind; and they have refused to compound their ideals or desert others that they themselves may be safe. They call to us to say what it is that we desire, in what, if in anything, our purpose and our spirit differ from theirs; and I believe that the people of the United States would wish me to respond, with utter simplicity and frankness. Whether their present leaders believe it or not, it is our heartfelt desire and hope that some way may be opened whereby we may be privileged to assist the people of Russia to attain their utmost hope of liberty and ordered peace.

It will be our wish and purpose that the processes of peace, when they are begun, shall be absolutely open and that they shall involve and permit henceforth no secret understandings gone by; so is also the day of secret covenants entered into in the interest of particular governments and likely at some unlooked-for moment to upset the peace of the world. It is this happy fact, now clear to the view of every public man whose thoughts do not still linger in an age that is dead and gone, which makes it possible for every nation whose purposes are consistent with justice and the peace of the world to avow now or at any other time the objects it has in view.

We entered this war because violations of right had occurred which touched us to the quick and made the life of our own people impossible unless they were corrected and the world secured once for all against their recurrence. What we demand in this war, therefore, is nothing peculiar to ourselves. It is that the world
5 be made fit and safe to live in; and particularly that it be made safe for every peace-loving nation which, like our own, wishes to live its own life, determine its own institutions, be assured of justice and fair dealing by the other peoples of the world as against force and selfish aggression. All the peoples of the world are in effect partners in this interest, and four our own part we see very clearly
10 that unless justice be done to others it will not be done to us. The programme of the world's peace, therefore, is our programme; and that programme, the only possible programme, as we see it, is this:

    I.   Open covenants of peace, openly arrived at, after which there shall be no private international understandings of any kind but diplomacy
15   shall proceed always frankly and in the public view.

    II.   Absolute freedom of navigation upon the seas, outside territorial waters, alike in peace and in war, except as the seas may be closed in whole or in part by international action for the enforcement of international covenants.

20   III. The removal, so far as possible, of all economic barriers and the establishment of an equality of trade conditions among all the nations consenting to the peace and associating themselves for its maintenance.

    IV. Adequate guarantees given and taken that national armaments will be reduced to the lowest point consistent with domestic safety.

25   V.   A free, open-minded, and absolutely impartial adjustment of all colonial claims, based upon a strict observance of the principle that in determining all such questions of sovereignty the interests of the populations concerned must have equal weight with the equitable claims of the government whose title is to be determined....

30   XIV. A general association of nations must be formed under specific covenants for the purpose of affording mutual guarantees of political independence and territorial integrity to great and small states alike.

In regard to these essential rectifications of wrong and assertions of right we feel ourselves to be intimate partners of all the governments and peoples associated
35 together against the Imperialists. We cannot be separated in interest or divided in purpose. We stand together until the end.

For such arrangements and covenants we are willing to fight and to continue to fight until they are achieved; but only because we wish the right to prevail and desire a just and stable peace such as can be secured only by removing the chief provocations to war, which this programme does remove. We have no jealousy of German greatness, and there is nothing in this programme that impairs it. We grudge her no achievement or distinction of learning or of pacific enterprise such as have made her record very bright and very enviable. We do not wish to injure her or to block in any way her legitimate influence or power. We do not wish to fight her either with arms or with hostile arrangements of trade if she is willing to associate herself with us and the other peace-loving nations of the world in covenants of justice and law and fair dealing. We wish her only to accept a place of equality among the peoples of the world,—the new world in which we now live,—instead of a place of mastery.

Neither do we presume to suggest to her any alteration or modification of her institutions. But it is necessary, we must frankly say, and necessary as a preliminary to any intelligent dealings with her on our part, that we should know whom her spokesman speak for when they speak to us, whether for the Reichstag majority or for the military party and the men whose creed is imperial domination.

We have spoken now, surely, in terms too concrete to admit of any further doubt or question. An evident principle runs through the whole programme I have outlined. It is the principle of justice to all peoples and nationalities, and their right to live on equal terms of liberty and safety with one another, whether they be strong or weak. Unless this principle be made its foundation no part of the structure of international justice can stand. The people of the United States could act upon no other principle; and to the vindication of this principle they are ready to devote their lives, their honor, and everything that they possess. The moral climax of this the culminating and final war for human liberty has come, and they are ready to put their own strength, their own highest purpose, their own integrity and devotion to the test.

THE AGE OF PLAY
ROBERT L. DUFFUS (1888–1972)

Why do American go to work? When wages were sufficiently low and efficiency-enhancing machinery sufficiently scarce, a typical American had to spend nearly all his working hours on the job simply to feed his family. The answer to the question then was simple: We worked to stay alive, literally. Hence, in 1860 the average work week was sixty-six hours. Many worked much longer. By 1920, however, the length of the average work week had fallen to forty-seven hours and was still dropping. This meant many things for American life, perhaps the most significant of which was the creation of "free time" in previously unimagined quantities. Accompanying this free time was a rapid growth in expendable income.

These changes presented new opportunities to engage in a variety of pastimes, both good and bad, worthwhile and worthless. How should one spend his "extra" time and money? Rather than pausing to reflect seriously on the proper meaning and uses of "leisure," most Americans instinctively followed their urges and opted for amusement and commercial entertainment—from crossword puzzles to theme parks, from spectator sports to playgrounds. Americans worked so they could play. They still do. In an insightful essay first published in December of 1924 in The Independent, *historian and social critic Robert Duffus described what he called the "final clause in the charter of democracy." This was the alleged American "right to play." Although people have always played games, the new twentieth-century commitment to commercial amusements marked a profound change in the American heritage, while it signaled an important shift in how people defined "the good life."*

1924

. . . It is difficult to assign an exact date for the beginning of the Age of Play. If we seek the influences which brought it about, we may go back half a century or more with profit; if we are looking for its external symptoms, a quarter of

Robert L. Duffus, "The Age of Play," *The Independent* 113 (20 December 1924):539–40, 556.

a century is nearly enough. Obviously, the first prerequisite for play is leisure, although animal spirits and some economic leeway are desirable. Play on anything like the American scale would have been impossible except for the short working day, the Saturday holiday or half holiday, and the annual vacation.
5   These are gifts of a century which also presented us with the World War and the newer pessimism.

With a decrease in the amount of human energy required for earning a living has gone a prodigious increase in wealth, thus upsetting what was once held to be an ethical as well as a mathematical law. In 1850, the national income
10   per capita was $95, in 1918, $586—a rate of progress which far outruns any inflation of the currency. In 1900, according to Mr. Julius Barnes,[1] the average American family spent 60 per cent of its income for the basic necessities of life but in 1920 had to devote only 50 per cent to the same purpose. Thus there was not only leisure to devote to play but money to spend on it. There was also,
15   no doubt, an increasing restlessness, growing out of the uninteresting nature of the mechanical tasks to which larger and larger armies of workers were being assigned. So the stage was amply set for the Age of Play.

The first unmistakable sign of the coming era was the development of interest in games, a phenomenon faintly manifested in the United States for a
20   decade or two prior to the Civil War and slowly gathering strength thereafter. Baseball first appeared in something like its modern form about 1845 but did not produce its first professionals and thus start on its career as a great national spectacle until 1871. Lawn tennis, first played in America in 1875, and golf, introduced early in the last decade of the century, remained games for the few
25   until very recently. Now there are said to be 2 million golfers and from a quarter to one-half as many tennis players. These are conspicuous instances of a general tendency. The playing of outdoor games was formerly either a juvenile or an aristocratic diversion; it has now become practically universal. There are golf links upon which horny-handed men in overalls play creditable games. And
30   the number of onlookers at professional sports is legion. In a single year there are said to have been 17 million admissions to college football games and 27 million to big-league baseball games.

A second phase of the development of play in America is the community recreation movement, which arose from the discovery by social workers that
35   training and organization for leisure were becoming as necessary as training and organization for work. In 1895, the city of Boston took the radical step of providing three sandpiles for the entertainment of young children, model playgrounds came about ten years later, and the first recreation centers were not

---

[1]Julius Howland Barnes (1873–1959), president of the U.S. Chamber of Commerce (1921–1924)

established until the middle of the first decade of the budding century. As late as 1903 only 18 cities had public playgrounds of any description. Then the growth of such facilities began with a rush. Last year there were 6,601 playgrounds in 80 cities, with an average daily attendance of about a million and a half.

In eighty-nine cities there were municipal golf courses on which any man   5
or woman who could afford clubs, balls, and a small green fee could play. Besides golf courses and tennis courts, upon which many a commoner became proficient in what had been "gentlemen's" games, there were municipal swimming pools, ball grounds, theatres, and, in forty-five instances, summer camps under municipal auspices. Municipal expenditures for public recreation have   10
nearly trebled since 1913, though they are as yet only about one-third of the national chewing-gum bill.

But no spontaneous play and no disinterestedly organized recreation program can for a moment be compared in magnitude with what are commonly known as the commercialized amusements—"the greatest industry in America,"   15
as James Edward Rogers of the Playground and Recreation Association has called them. The motion picture, the phonograph, and the cheap automobile came into existence, like the cheap newspaper, because a public had been created which (consciously or not) wanted them and could pay for them. Each had been the object of experimentation during the last quarter of the nineteenth century,   20
but each attained social significance only after the opening of the twentieth, when multitudes, for the first time in history, had money and leisure they did not know how to use....

The most significant aspect of the Age of Play, however, is not in its inventions, good and bad, but in an alteration of an ancient attitude—a veritable   25
change in one of the most fundamental of folkways. For uncounted generations man has survived and made progress, in the temperate zones, only by unceasing industry; in tropical and sub-tropical areas, where climatic conditions did not encourage industry, he survived without progress. At first the Industrial Revolution did not seem to break down this antique scheme of nature; but in   30
this country, at least, and within this generation, it has become evident that unremitting toil is not necessarily a law of human destiny, and that a thimbleful of brains is worth at any time an ocean of sweat. The mechanical multiplication of labor power by ten, twenty, forty, or a hundred, the replacement of a man by 2 cents' worth of coal, has struck a fatal blow at the ancestral faith in   35
mere hard work.

Less than a hundred years ago the merchants and shipowners of Boston were able to answer the demand of their employees for a ten-hour day with the argument that "the habits likely to be generated by this indulgence in idleness... will be very detrimental to the journeymen individually and very costly to us   40 as a community." Fifty years ago a United States Commissioner of Patents, Mortimer D. Leggett, declared amid the applause of well-meaning persons that "idleness…stimulates vice in all its forms and throttles every attempt at intellectual, moral, and religious culture."

5   The first break in this armor of conservatism occurred when it was discovered that play added to the worker's efficiency and was, therefore, of economic value. Through this chink, heresy has crept in, and it is now apparent that play is coming to be looked upon, whether athletic in character or not, whether "commercialized" or not, as an end justifiable in itself. Blindly, blunderingly, yet with 10 more intense conviction than appears on the surface, the masses of the people are uttering a new moral law. The chains of necessity have been loosened; they are nearer a frank and full enjoyment of life than any people that ever lived.

    I do not maintain that all their amusements are wholesome, nor that the excessive standardization and mechanization of work and play alike are without 15 their dangers. I do maintain that such evils as exist are minor in comparison with the great gain for civilization that took place when millions learned to play where only thousands played before. These evils are not to be cured by curbing the spirit of play. Reformers and educators must accept this spirit as more sacred than anything they have to give; they can help by guiding, not by 20 restraining.

    The right to play is the final clause in the charter of democracy. The people are king—*et le roi s'amuse.*

WHAT IT MEANS TO BE A BOY SCOUT
CALVIN COOLIDGE (1872–1933)
PRESIDENT OF THE UNITED STATES (1923–1929)

President Calvin Coolidge calmly restored a shattered presidency after the Harding scandals. He was perhaps the last fully "constitutional" president; that is, he was scrupulous in his respect for limited government, the rule of law, separation of powers, and federalism. He presided over an administration that cut government spending, lowered taxes, reduced the size of the bureaucracy, and entered into no foreign wars. There was greater general prosperity in America during his presidency than in any country in human history.

Calvin Coolidge was well known for controlling his tongue; the newspapers often called him "Silent Cal." But he believed that the president should be the nation's teacher. His carefully crafted speeches (he was the last president to write all his own speeches) reflect a deep knowledge of the roots of the American heritage, and almost all of them encouraged his countrymen to hold fast to those roots. Those excerpted here are concerned with voluntary associations, a free press and free business, and local self-government.

25 JULY 1924

There was no Boy Scout organization in my boyhood, but every boy who has the privilege of growing up on a farm learns instinctively the three fundamentals of scouthood.

The first is a reverence for nature. Boys should never lose their love of the fields and the streams, the mountains and the plains, the open places and the forests. That love will be a priceless possession as your years lengthen out. There is an instructive myth about the giant Antæus. Whenever in a contest he was thrown down, he drew fresh strength from his mother, the earth, and so was thought invincible. But Hercules lifted him away from the earth and so destroyed him. There is new life in the soil for every man. There is healing in the trees for 10

Calvin Coolidge, *Foundations of the Republic: Speeches and Addresses* (New York: Charles Scribner's Sons, 1926), 67–68.

tired minds and for our overburdened spirits, there is strength in the hills, if only we will lift up our eyes. Remember that nature is your great restorer.

The second is a reverence for law. I remember the town meetings of my boyhood, when the citizens of our little town met to levy taxes on themselves,
5   and to choose from their own number those who should be their officers. There is something in every town meeting, in every election, that approaches very near to the sublime. I am thrilled at the thought of my audience tonight, for I never address boys without thinking, among them may be a boy who will sit in this White House. Somewhere there are boys who will be presidents of our
10   railroads, presidents of colleges, of banks, owners of splendid farms and useful industries, members of Congress, representatives of our people in foreign lands. That is the heritage of the American boy.

It was an act of magnificent courage when our ancestors set up a nation wherein any boy may aspire to anything. That great achievement was not
15   wrought without blood and sacrifice. Make firm your resolution to carry on nobly what has been so nobly begun. Let this nation, under your influence, be a finer nation. Resolve that the sacrifices by which your great opportunities have been purchased will be matched by a sacrifice, on your part, that will give your children even a better chance.
20   The third is a reverence for God. It is hard to see how a great man can be an atheist. Without the sustaining influence of faith in a divine power we could have little faith in ourselves. We need to feel that behind us is intelligence and love. Doubters do not achieve; skeptics do not contribute; cynics do not create. Faith is the great motive power, and no man realizes his full possibilities unless
25   he has the deep conviction that life is eternally important, and that his work, well done, is a part of an unending plan.

These are not only some of the fundamentals of the teachings of the Boy Scouts, they are the fundamentals of our American institutions. If you will take them with you, if you will be living examples of them abroad, you will make a
30   great contribution toward a better understanding of our country, and receive in return a better understanding of other countries; for you will find in foreign lands, to a very large extent, exactly what you carry there yourselves. I trust that you can show to your foreign associates in the great scout movement that you have a deep reverence for the truth and are determined to live by it; that
35   you wish to protect and cherish your own country and contribute to the well being, right thinking and true living of the whole world.

Ordered Liberty and World Peace

Calvin Coolidge (1872–1933)
President of the United States (1923–1929)

Despite the nation's decisive participation in World War I, the Republican administrations of the 1920s mostly disengaged from Europe's internal power struggles. President Coolidge added to the earlier arguments for American independence the image of the United States as "Samaritan." Rather than attempt to "make over" Europe, he said, we should become the magnanimous republic. Foreign policy always reflects domestic policy; Coolidge's convictions about limited government applied to his international initiatives as well as to his strict constitutionalism at home.

6 September 1924

The Constitution of the United States has for its almost sole purpose the protection of the freedom of the people. We must combat every attempt to break down or to make it easy, under the pretended guise of legal procedure, to throw open the way to reaction or revolution. To adopt any other course is to put in jeopardy the sacred right to life, liberty, property, and the pursuit of happiness. 5

Lafayette was always an interested student of our affairs. Though he distrusted the effort to make France a republic, he believed greatly in our Republic and our Constitution. He had fought to establish American independence, in order that these might come into being. That independence to which he contributed has come to be with us a national axiom. We have always guarded it with the utmost 10 jealousy. We have sought to strengthen it with the Monroe Doctrine. We have refrained from treaties of offensive and defensive alliance. We have kept clear from political entanglements with other countries. Under this wise and sound policy America has been a country on the whole dedicated to peace, through honorable and disinterested relations with the other peoples of the earth. We have 15 always been desirous not to participate in controversies, but to compose them. What a success this has brought to us at home, and what a place of respect and moral power it has gained for us abroad, is known of all men.

Calvin Coolidge, *Foundations of the Republic: Speeches and Addresses* (New York: Charles Scribner's Sons, 1926), 97–100.

To continue to be independent we must continue to be whole-hearted American. We must direct our policies and lay our course with the sole consideration of serving our own people. We cannot become the partisans of one nation, or the opponents of another. Our domestic affairs should be entirely
5   free from foreign interference, whether such attempt be made by those who are without or within our own territory. America is a large country. It is a tolerant country. It has room within its borders for many races and many creeds. But it has no room for those who would place the interests of some other nation above the interests of our own nation.
10   To be independent to my mind does not mean to be isolated, to be the priest or the Levite, but rather to be the good Samaritan. There is no real independence save only as we secure it through the law of service.

The course of our country in recent years has been an example of these principles. We have avoided entanglements by reserving to our own decision
15   when and how we should help. We have not failed to help. We have contributed hundreds of millions of dollars to foreign charities. We have given freely of our counsel to the settlement of difficulties in Latin America and the adjustment of war problems in Europe. We are still pursuing that course. It has been a practical course, and it has secured practical results. One of these most important results
20   is found in the disarmament treaties, which have saved our own country to date about $300,000,000, and likewise relieved other nations. Another important result has been the adoption of the Dawes plan for the settlement of reparations. The effect these will have in averting war and promoting peace cannot possibly be overestimated. They stand out as great monuments, truly directing
25   the course of men along the way to more civilization, more enlightenment, and more righteousness. They appear to me properly to mark the end of the old order, and the beginning of a new era. We hope they are the end of aggressive war and the beginning of permanent peace.

Great changes have come over the world since Lafayette first came here
30   desirous of aiding the cause of freedom. His efforts in behalf of an American republic have been altogether successful. In no other country in the world was economic opportunity for the people ever so great as it is here. In no other country was it ever possible in a like degree to secure equality and justice for all. Just as he was passing off the stage, the British adopted their reform measures
35   giving them practically representative government. His own France has long since been welcomed into the family of republics. Many others have taken a like course. The cause of freedom has been triumphant. We believe it to be, likewise, the cause of peace.

But peace must have other guarantees than constitutions and covenants.
40   Laws and treaties may help, but peace and war are attitudes of mind. American

citizens, with the full sympathy of our Government, have been attempting with apparent success to restore stricken Europe. We have acted in the name of world peace and of humanity. Always the obstacles to be encountered have been distrust, suspicion and hatred. The great effort has been to allay and remove these sentiments. I believe that America can assist the world in this direction by her example. We have never forgotten the service done us by Lafayette, but we have long ago ceased to bear an enmity toward Great Britain by reason of two wars that were fought out between us. We want Europe to compose its difficulties and liquidate its hatreds. Would it not be well if we set the example and liquidated some of our own? The war is over. The militarism of Central Europe which menaced the security of the world has been overthrown. In its place have sprung up peaceful republics. Already we have assisted in refinancing Austria. We are about to assist refinancing Germany. We believe that such action will be helpful to France, but we can give further and perhaps even more valuable assistance both to ourselves and to Europe by bringing to an end our own hatreds. The best way for us who wish all our inhabitants to be single-minded in their Americanism is for us to bestow upon each group of our inhabitants that confidence and fellowship which is due to all Americans. If we want to get the hyphen out of our country, we can best begin by taking it out of our own minds. If we want France paid, we can best work towards that end by assisting in the restoration of the German people, now shorn of militarism, to their full place in the family of peaceful mankind.

I want to see America set the example to the world both in our domestic and foreign relations of magnanimity.

We cannot make over the people of Europe. We must help them as they are, if we are to help them at all. I believe that we should help, not at the sacrifice of our independence, not for the support of imperialism, but to restore to those great peoples a peaceful civilization. In that course lies the best guarantee of freedom. In that course lies the greatest honor which we can bestow upon the memory of Lafayette.

The Press Under a
Free Government
Calvin Coolidge (1872–1933)
President of the United States (1923–1929)

There does not seem to be cause for alarm in the dual relationship of the press
to the public, whereby it is on one side a purveyor of information and opinion
and on the other side a purely business enterprise. Rather, it is probable that
a press which maintains an intimate touch with the business currents of the
nation, is likely to be more reliable than it would be if it were a stranger to   5
these influences. After all, the chief business of the American people is business. They are profoundly concerned with producing, buying, selling, investing
and prospering in the world. I am strongly of opinion that the great majority
of people will always find these are moving impulses of our life. The opposite
view was oracularly and poetically set forth in those lines of Goldsmith which   10
everybody repeats, but few really believe:

> *Ill fares the land, to hastening ills a prey,*
> *Where wealth accumulates, and men decay.*

Excellent poetry, but not a good working philosophy. Goldsmith would have
been right, if, in fact, the accumulation of wealth meant the decay of men. It is   15
rare indeed that the men who are accumulating wealth decay. It is only when they
cease production, when accumulation stops, that an irreparable decay begins.
Wealth is the product of industry, ambition, character and untiring effort. In all
experience, the accumulation of wealth means the multiplication of schools, the
increase of knowledge, the dissemination of intelligence, the encouragement of   20
science, the broadening of outlook, the expansion of liberties, the widening of
culture. Of course, the accumulation of wealth cannot be justified as the chief
end of existence. But we are compelled to recognize it as a means to well-nigh
every desirable achievement. So long as wealth is made the means and not the
end, we need not greatly fear it. And there never was a time when wealth was   25
so generally regarded as a means, or so little regarded as an end, as today.

Calvin Coolidge, *Foundations of the Republic: Speeches and Addresses* (New York: Charles Scribner's
Sons, 1926), 187–90.

Just a little time ago we read in your newspapers that two leaders of American business, whose efforts at accumulation had been most astonishingly successful, had given fifty or sixty million dollars as endowments to educational works. That was real news. It was characteristic of our American experience with
5   men of large resources. They use their power to serve, not themselves and their own families, but the public. I feel sure that the coming generations, which will benefit by those endowments, will not be easily convinced that they have suffered greatly because of these particular accumulations of wealth.

So there is little cause for the fear that our journalism, merely because it is
10   prosperous, is likely to betray us. But it calls for additional effort to avoid even the appearance of the evil of selfishness. In every worthy profession, of course, there will always be a minority who will appeal to the baser instinct. There always have been, and probably always will be some who will feel that their own temporary interest may be furthered by betraying the interest of others.
15   But these are becoming constantly a less numerous and less potent element in the community. Their influence, whatever it may seem at a particular moment, is always ephemeral. They will not long interfere with the progress of the race which is determined to go its own forward and upward way. They may at times somewhat retard and delay its progress, but in the end their opposition will
20   be overcome. They have no permanent effect. They accomplish no permanent result. The race is not traveling in that direction. The power of the spirit always prevails over the power of the flesh. These furnish us no justification for interfering with the freedom of the press, because all freedom, though it may sometime tend toward excesses, bears within it those remedies which will finally effect a
25   cure for its own disorders.

American newspapers have seemed to me to be particularly representative of this practical idealism of our people. Therefore, I feel secure in saying that they are the best newspapers in the world. I believe that they print more real news and more reliable and characteristic news than any other newspaper. I
30   believe their editorial opinions are less colored in influence by mere partisanship or selfish interest, than are those of any other country. Moreover, I believe that our American press is more independent, more reliable and less partisan today than at any other time in its history. I believe this of our press, precisely as I believe it of those who manage our public affairs. Both are cleaner, finer, less
35   influenced by improper considerations, than ever before. Whoever disagrees with this judgment must take the chance of marking himself as ignorant of conditions which notoriously affected our public life, thoughts and methods, even within the memory of many men who are still among us.

It can safely be assumed that self-interest will always place sufficient
40   emphasis on the business side of newspapers, so that they do not need any out-

side encouragement for that part of their activities. Important, however, as this factor is, it is not the main element which appeals to the American people. It is only those who do not understand our people, who believe that our national life is entirely absorbed by material motives. We make no concealment of the fact that we want wealth, but there are many other things that we want very much more. We want peace and honor, and that charity which is so strong an element of all civilization. The chief ideal of the American people is idealism. I cannot repeat too often that America is a nation of idealists. That is the only motive to which they ever give any strong and lasting reaction. No newspaper can be a success which fails to appeal to that element of our national life. It is in this direction that the public press can lend its strongest support to our Government. I could not truly criticize the vast importance of the counting room, but my ultimate faith I would place in the high idealism of the editorial room of the American newspaper.

THE REIGN OF LAW
CALVIN COOLIDGE (1872–1933)
PRESIDENT OF THE UNITED STATES (1923–1929)

30 MAY 1925

…What America needs is to hold to its ancient and well-charted course. Our country was conceived in the theory of local self-government. It has been dedicated by long practice to that wise and beneficent policy. It is the foundation principle of our system of liberty. It makes the largest promise to the freedom and development of the individual. Its preservation is worth all the effort and all the sacrifice that it may cost. 5

It cannot be denied that the present tendency is not in harmony with this spirit. The individual, instead of working out his own salvation and securing his own freedom by establishing his own economic and moral independence by his own industry and his own self-mastery, tends to throw himself on some vague influence which he denominates society and to hold that in some way responsible for the sufficiency of his support and the morality of his actions. The local political units likewise look to the states, the states look to the nation, and nations are beginning to look to some vague organization, some nebulous concourse of humanity, to pay their bills and tell them what to do. This is not local self-government. It is not American. It is not the method which has made this country what it is. We cannot maintain the western standard of civilization on that theory. If it is supported at all, it will have to be supported on the principle of individual responsibility. If that principle be maintained, the result which I believe America wishes to see produced inevitably will follow. 10 15

There is no other foundation on which freedom has ever found a permanent abiding place. We shall have to make our decision whether we wish to maintain our present institutions, or whether we wish to exchange them for something else. If we permit someone to come to support us, we cannot prevent someone coming to govern us. If we are too weak to take charge of our own mortality, we shall not be strong enough to take charge of our own liberty. If we cannot govern 20 25

Calvin Coolidge, *Foundations of the Republic: Speeches and Addresses* (New York: Charles Scribner's Sons, 1926), 230–33.

ourselves, if we cannot observe the law, nothing remains but to have someone
else govern us, to have the law enforced against us, and to step down from the
honorable abiding place of freedom to the ignominious abode of servitude.

   If these principles are sound, two conclusions follow. The individual and
5   the local, state, and national political units ought to be permitted to assume
their own responsibilities. Any other course in the end will be subversive both
of character and liberty. But it is equally clear that they in their turn must meet
their obligations. If there is to be a continuation of individual and local self-
government, and of state sovereignty, the individual and locality must govern
10   themselves and the state must assert its sovereignty. Otherwise these rights and
privileges will be confiscated under the all-compelling pressure of public necessity
for a better maintenance of order and morality. The whole world has reached
a stage in which, if we do not set ourselves right, we may be perfectly sure that
an authority will be asserted by others for the purpose of setting us right.

15   But before we attempt to set ourselves up as exponents of universal reform,
it would be wise to remember that progress is of slow growth, and also to remember that moderation, patience, forbearance, and charity are virtues in their
own right. The only action which can be effective in the long run is that which
helps others to help themselves. Before we assume too great responsibilities
20   in the governing of others, it would be the part of wisdom very completely
to discharge our responsibilities for governing ourselves. A large amount of
work has to be done at home before we can start in on the neighbors, and very
considerable duties have to be performed in America before we undertake the
direction of the rest of the world. But we must at all times do the best we can
25   for ourselves without forgetting others, and the best we can for our own country
without forgetting other nations.

   Ours is a new land. It has had an almost unbelievable task to perform, and
has performed it well. We have been called to fit the institutions of ancient
civilization to the conditions of a new country. In that task the leaders of the
30   Nation have been supported by a deep devotion to the essentials of freedom.
At the bottom of the national character has been a strain of religious earnestness and moral determination which has never failed to give color and quality
to our institutions. Because our history shows us these things, we dare make
honest appraisal of our shortcomings. We have not failed. We have succeeded.
35   Because we have been privileged to rely upon generations of men and women
ready to serve and to sacrifice, we have magnificently succeeded.

   Our gathering here today is in testimony of supreme obligation to those
who have given most to make and preserve the Nation. They established it upon
the dual system of state government and Federal Government, each supreme
40   in its own sphere. But they left to the states the main powers and functions of

determining the form and course of society. We have demonstrated in the time of war that under the Constitution we possess an indestructible union. We must not fail to demonstrate in the time of peace that we are likewise determined to possess and maintain indestructible states. This policy can be greatly advanced by individual observance of the law. It can be strongly supplemented by a vigorous 5 enforcement of the law. The war which established Memorial Day had for its main purpose the enforcement of the Constitution. The peace which followed that war rests upon the universal observance of the Constitution. This union can only be preserved, the states can only be maintained, under a reign of national, local, and moral law, under the Constitution established by Washington, under 10 the peace provided by Lincoln.

The Inspiration of the Declaration

Calvin Coolidge (1872–1933)
President of the United States (1923–1929)

5 July 1926

We meet to celebrate the birthday of America. The coming of a new life always excites our interest. Although we know in the case of the individual that it has been an infinite repetition reaching back beyond our vision, that only makes it the more wonderful. But how our interest and wonder increase when we behold the miracle of the birth of a new nation. It is to pay our tribute of reverence 5
and respect to those who participated in such a mighty event that we annually observe the fourth day of July. Whatever may have been the impression created by the news which went out from this city on that summer day in 1776, there can be no doubt as to the estimate which is now placed upon it. At the end of 150 years the four corners of the earth unite in coming to Philadelphia as 10
to a holy shrine in grateful acknowledgment of a service so great, which a few inspired men here rendered to humanity, that it is still the preeminent support of free government throughout the world.

Although a century and a half measured in comparison with the length of human experience is but a short time, yet measured in the life of governments and 15
nations it ranks as a very respectable period. Certainly enough time has elapsed to demonstrate with a great deal of thoroughness the value of our institutions and their dependability as rules for the regulation of human conduct and the advancement of civilization. They have been in existence long enough to become very well seasoned. They have met, and met successfully, the test of experience. 20

It is not so much then for the purpose of undertaking to proclaim new theories and principles that this annual celebration is maintained, but rather to re-affirm and re-establish those old theories and principles which time and the unerring logic of events have demonstrated to be sound. Amid all the clash of conflicting interests, amid all the welter of partisan politics, every American 25
can turn for solace and consolation to the Declaration of Independence and

Calvin Coolidge, *Foundations of the Republic: Speeches and Addresses* (New York: Charles Scribner's Sons, 1926), 441–54.

the Constitution of the United States with the assurance and confidence that those two great charters of freedom and justice remain firm and unshaken. Whatever perils appear, whatever dangers threaten, the Nation remains secure in the knowledge that the ultimate application of the law of the land will provide

5 an adequate defense and protection.

It is little wonder that people at home and abroad consider Independence Hall as hallowed ground and revere the Liberty Bell as a sacred relic. That pile of bricks and mortar, that mass of metal, might appear to the uninstructed as only the outgrown meeting place and the shattered bell of a former time, use-

10 less now because of more modern conveniences, but to those who know they have become consecrated by the use which men have made of them. They have long been identified with a great cause. They are the framework of a spiritual event. The world looks upon them, because of their associations of one hundred and fifty years ago, as it looks upon the Holy Land because of what took place

15 there nineteen hundred years ago. Through use for a righteous purpose they have become sanctified.

It is not here necessary to examine in detail the causes which led to the American Revolution. In their immediate occasion they were largely economic. The colonists objected to the navigation laws which interfered with their trade,

20 they denied the power of Parliament to impose taxes which they were obliged to pay, and they therefore resisted the royal governors and the royal forces which were sent to secure obedience to these laws. But the conviction is inescapable that a new civilization had come, a new spirit had arisen on this side of the Atlantic more advanced and more developed in its regard for the rights of the

25 individual than that which characterized the Old World. Life in a new and open country had aspirations which could not be realized in any subordinate position. A separate establishment was ultimately inevitable. It had been decreed by the very laws of human nature. Man everywhere has an unconquerable desire to be the master of his own destiny.

30 We are obliged to conclude that the Declaration of Independence repre- sented the movement of a people. It was not, of course, a movement from the top. Revolutions do not come from that direction. It was not without the support of many of the most respectable people in the Colonies, who were entitled to all the consideration that is given to breeding, education, and possessions. It had

35 the support of another element of great significance and importance to which I shall later refer. But the preponderance of all those who occupied a position which took on the aspect of aristocracy did not approve of the Revolution and held toward it an attitude either of neutrality or open hostility. It was in no sense a rising of the oppressed and downtrodden. It brought no scum to the

40 surface, for the reason that colonial society had developed no scum. The great

body of the people were accustomed to privations, but they were free from depravity. If they had poverty, it was not of the hopeless kind that afflicts great cities, but the inspiring kind that marks the spirit of the pioneer. The American Revolution represented the informed and mature convictions of a great mass of independent, liberty-loving, God-fearing people who knew their rights, and 5 possessed the courage to dare to maintain them.

The Continental Congress was not only composed of great men, but it represented a great people. While its members did not fail to exercise a remarkable leadership, they were equally observant of their representative capacity. They were industrious in encouraging their constituents to instruct them to support 10 independence. But until such instructions were given they were inclined to withhold action.

While North Carolina has the honor of first authorizing its delegates to concur with other Colonies in declaring independence, it was quickly followed by South Carolina and Georgia, which also gave general instructions broad 15 enough to include such action. But the first instructions which unconditionally directed its delegates to declare for independence came from the great Commonwealth of Virginia. These were immediately followed by Rhode Island and Massachusetts, while the other Colonies, with the exception of New York, soon adopted a like course. 20

This obedience of the delegates to the wishes of their constituents, which in some cases caused them to modify their previous positions, is a matter of great significance. It reveals an orderly process of government in the first place; but more than that, it demonstrates that the Declaration of Independence was the result of the seasoned and deliberate thought of the dominant portion of the 25 people of the Colonies. Adopted after long discussion and as the result of the duly authorized expression of the preponderance of public opinion, it did not partake of dark intrigue or hidden conspiracy. It was well advised. It had about it nothing of the lawless and disordered nature of a riotous insurrection. It was maintained on a plane which rises above the ordinary conception of rebellion. 30 It was in no sense a radical movement but took on the dignity of a resistance to illegal usurpations. It was conservative and represented the action of the colonists to maintain their constitutional rights which from time immemorial had been guaranteed to them under the law of the land.

When we come to examine the action of the Continental Congress in 35 adopting the Declaration of Independence in the light of what was set out in that great document and in the light of succeeding events, we can not escape the conclusion that it had a much broader and deeper significance than a mere secession of territory and the establishment of a new nation. Events of that nature have been taking place since the dawn of history. One empire after another 40 has arisen, only to crumble away as its constituent parts separated from each other and set up independent governments of their own. Such actions long ago became commonplace. They have occurred too often to hold the attention of the world and command the admiration and reverence of humanity. There is something beyond the establishment of a new nation, great as that event would be, in the Declaration of Independence which has ever since caused it to be regarded as one of the great charters that not only was to liberate America but was everywhere to ennoble humanity.

It was not because it was proposed to establish a new nation, but because it was proposed to establish a nation on new principles, that July 4, 1776, has come to be regarded as one of the greatest days in history. Great ideas do not burst upon the world unannounced. They are reached by a gradual development over a length of time usually proportionate to their importance. This is especially true of the principles laid down in the Declaration of Independence. Three very definite propositions were set out in its preamble regarding the nature of mankind and therefore of government. These were the doctrine that all men are created equal, that they are endowed with certain inalienable rights, and that therefore the source of the just powers of government must be derived from the consent of the governed.

If no one is to be accounted as born into a superior station, if there is to be no ruling class, and if all possess rights which can neither be bartered away nor taken from them by any earthly power, it follows as a matter of course that the practical authority of the Government has to rest on the consent of the governed. While these principles were not altogether new in political action, and were very far from new in political speculation, they had never been assembled before and declared in such a combination. But remarkable as this may be, it is not the chief distinction of the Declaration of Independence. The importance of political speculation is not to be under-estimated, as I shall presently disclose. Until the idea is developed and the plan made there can be no action.

It was the fact that our Declaration of Independence containing these immortal truths was the political action of a duly authorized and constituted representative public body in its sovereign capacity, supported by the force of general opinion and by the armies of Washington already in the field, which makes it the most important civil document in the world. It was not only the principles declared, but the fact that therewith a new nation was born which was to be founded upon those principles and which from that time forth in its development has actually maintained those principles, that makes this pronouncement an incomparable event in the history of government. It was an assertion that a people had arisen determined to make every necessary sacrifice for the support of these truths and by their practical application bring the War of Independence to a successful conclusion and adopt the Constitution of the United States with all that it has meant to civilization.

The idea that the people have a right to choose their own rulers was not new in political history. It was the foundation of every popular attempt to depose an undesirable king. This right was set out with a good deal of detail by the Dutch when as early as July 26, 1581, they declared their independence of Philip of Spain. In their long struggle with the Stuarts the British people asserted the same principles, which finally culminated in the Bill of Rights deposing the last of that house and placing William and Mary on the throne. In each of these cases sovereignty through divine right was displaced by sovereignty through the consent of the people. Running through the same documents, though expressed in different terms, is the clear inference of inalienable rights. But we should search these charters in vain for an assertion of the doctrine of equality. This principle had not before appeared as an official political declaration of any nation. It was profoundly revolutionary. It is one of the corner stones of American institutions.

But if these truths to which the declaration refers have not before been adopted in their combined entirety by national authority, it is a fact that they had been long pondered and often expressed in political speculation. It is generally assumed that French thought had some effect upon our public mind during Revolutionary days. This may have been true. But the principles of our declaration had been under discussion in the Colonies for nearly two generations before the advent of the French political philosophy that characterized the middle of the eighteenth century. In fact, they come from an earlier date. A very positive echo of what the Dutch had done in 1581, and what the English were preparing to do, appears in the assertion of the Reverend Thomas Hooker of Connecticut as early as 1638, when he said in a sermon before the General Court that

The foundation of authority is laid in the free consent of the people.
The choice of public magistrates belongs unto the people by God's own allowance.

This doctrine found wide acceptance among the nonconformist clergy who later made up the Congregational Church. The great apostle of this movement was the Reverend John Wise, of Massachusetts. He was one of the leaders of the revolt against the royal governor Andros in 1687, for which he suffered imprisonment. He was a liberal in ecclesiastical controversies. He appears to have been familiar with the writings of the political scientist, Samuel Pufendorf, who was born in Saxony in 1632. Wise published a treatise, entitled "The Church's Quarrel Espoused," in 1710, which was amplified in another publication in 1717. In it he dealt with the principles of civil government. His works were reprinted in 1772 and have been declared to have been nothing less than a textbook of liberty for our Revolutionary fathers.

While the written word was the foundation, it is apparent that the spoken word was the vehicle for convincing the people. This came with great force and wide range from the successors of Hooker and Wise. It was carried on with a missionary spirit which did not fail to reach the Scotch-Irish of North Caro-
5   lina, showing its influence by significantly making that Colony the first to give instructions to its delegates looking to independence. This preaching reached the neighborhood of Thomas Jefferson, who acknowledged that his "best ideas of democracy" had been secured at church meetings.

That these ideas were prevalent in Virginia is further revealed by the
10   Declaration of Rights, which was prepared by George Mason and presented to the general assembly on May 27, 1776. This document asserted popular sovereignty and inherent natural rights, but confined the doctrine of equality to the assertion that "All men are created equally free and independent." It can scarcely be imagined that Jefferson was unacquainted with what had been done
15   in his own Commonwealth of Virginia when he took up the task of drafting the Declaration of Independence. But these thoughts can very largely be traced back to what John Wise was writing in 1710. He said, "Every man must be acknowledged equal to every man." Again, "The end of all good government is to cultivate humanity and promote the happiness of all and the good of every
20   man in all his rights, his life, liberty, estate, honor, and so forth...."

And again, "For as they have a power every man in his natural state, so upon combination they can and do bequeath this power to others and settle in ac-cording as their united discretion shall determine." And still again, "Democracy is Christ's government in church and state." Here was the doctrine of equality,
25   popular sovereignty, and the substance of the theory of inalienable rights clearly asserted by Wise at the opening of the eighteenth century, just as we have the principle of the consent of the governed stated by Hooker as early as 1638.

When we take all these circumstances into consideration, it is but natural that the first paragraph of the Declaration of Independence should open with a
30   reference to Nature's God and should close in the final paragraphs with an appeal to the Supreme Judge of the world and an assertion of a firm reliance on Divine Providence. Coming from these sources, having as it did this background, it is no wonder that Samuel Adams could say "The people seem to recognize this resolution as though it were a decree promulgated from heaven."

35   No one can examine this record and escape the conclusion that in the great outline of its principles the Declaration as the result of the religious teachings of the preceding period. The profound philosophy which Jonathan Edwards applied to theology, the popular preaching of George Whitefield, had aroused the thought and stirred the people of the Colonies in preparation for this great
40   event. No doubt the speculations which had been going on in England, and

especially on the Continent, lent their influence to the general sentiment of the times. Of course, the world is always influenced by all the experience and all the thought of the past. But when we come to a contemplation of the immediate conception of the principles of human relationship which went into the Declaration of Independence we are not required to extend our search 5 beyond our own shores. They are found in the texts, the sermons, and the writings of the early colonial clergy who were earnestly undertaking to instruct their congregations in the great mystery of how to live. They preached equality because they believed in the fatherhood of God and the brotherhood of man. They justified freedom by the text that we are all created in the divine image, 10 all partakers of the divine spirit.

Placing every man on a plane where he acknowledged no superiors, where no one possessed any right to rule over him, he must inevitably choose his own rulers through a system of self-government. This was their theory of democracy. In those days such doctrines would scarcely have been permitted to flourish and 15 spread in any other country. This was the purpose which the fathers cherished. In order that they might have freedom to express these thoughts and opportunity to put them into action, whole congregations with their pastors had migrated to the colonies. These great truths were in the air that our people breathed. Whatever else we may say of it, the Declaration of Independence was profoundly American. 20

If this apprehension of the facts be correct, and the documentary evidence would appear to verify it, then certain conclusions are bound to follow. A spring will cease to flow if its source be dried up; a tree will wither if its roots be destroyed. In its main features the Declaration of Independence is a great spiritual document. It is a declaration not of material but of spiritual concep- 25 tions. Equality, liberty, popular sovereignty, the rights of man—these are not elements which we can see and touch. They are ideals. They have their source and their roots in the religious convictions. They belong to the unseen world. Unless the faith of the American people in these religious convictions is to endure, the principles of our Declaration will perish. We can not continue to 30 enjoy the result if we neglect and abandon the cause.

We are too prone to overlook another conclusion. Governments do not make ideals, but ideals make governments. This is both historically and logically true. Of course the government can help to sustain ideals and can create institutions through which they can be the better observed, but their source by their very 35 nature is in the people. The people have to bear their own responsibilities. There is no method by which that burden can be shifted to the government. It is not the enactment, but the observance of laws, that creates the character of a nation.

About the Declaration there is a finality that is exceedingly restful. It is often asserted that the world has made a great deal of progress since 1776, that 40

we have had new thoughts and new experiences which have given us a great advance over the people of that day, and that we may therefore very well discard their conclusions for something more modern. But that reasoning cannot be applied to this great charter. If all men are created equal, that is final. If they are
5   endowed with inalienable rights, that is final. If governments derive their just powers from the consent of the governed, that is final. No advance, no progress can be made beyond these propositions. If anyone wishes to deny their truth or their soundness, the only direction in which he can proceed historically is not forward, but backward toward the time when there was no equality, no rights
10   of the individual, no rule of the people. Those who wish to proceed in that direction can not lay claim to progress. They are reactionary. Their ideas are not more modern, but more ancient, than those of the Revolutionary fathers.

In the development of its institutions America can fairly claim that it has remained true to the principles which were declared 150 years ago. In all the
15   essentials we have achieved an equality which was never possessed by any other people. Even in the less important matter of material possessions we have secured a wider and wider distribution of wealth. The rights of the individual are held sacred and protected by constitutional guaranties, which even the Government itself is bound not to violate. If there is any one thing among us that is established
20   beyond question, it is self-government—the right of the people to rule. If there is any failure in respect to any of these principles, it is because there is a failure on the part of individuals to observe them. We hold that the duly authorized expression of the will of the people has a divine sanction. But even in that we come back to the theory of John Wise that "Democracy is Christ's government...." The ultimate
25   sanction of law rests on the righteous authority of the Almighty.

On an occasion like this a great temptation exists to present evidence of the practical success of our form of democratic republic at home and the ever-broadening acceptance it is securing abroad. Although these things are well known, their frequent consideration is an encouragement and an inspiration.
30   But it is not results and effects so much as sources and causes that I believe it is even more necessary constantly to contemplate. Ours is a government of the people. It represents their will. Its officers may sometimes go astray, but that is not a reason for criticizing the principles of our institutions. The real heart of the American Government depends upon the heart of the people. It is from
35   that source that we must look for all genuine reform. It is to that cause that we must ascribe all our results.

It was in the contemplation of these truths that the fathers made their declaration and adopted their Constitution. It was to establish a free government, which must not be permitted to degenerate into the unrestrained authority of
40   a mere majority or the unbridled weight of a mere influential few. They under-

took to balance these interests against each other and provide the three separate independent branches, the executive, the legislative, and the judicial departments of the Government, with checks against each other in order that neither one might encroach upon the other. These are our guaranties of liberty. As a result of these methods enterprise has been duly protected from confiscation, the 5 people have been free from oppression, and there has been an ever-broadening and deepening of the humanities of life.

Under a system of popular government there will always be those who will seek for political preferment by clamoring for reform. While there is very little of this which is not sincere, there is a large portion that is not well informed. In 10 my opinion very little of just criticism can attach to the theories and principles of our institutions. There is far more danger of harm than there is hope of good in any radical changes. We do need a better understanding and comprehension of them and a better knowledge of the foundations of government in general. Our forefathers came to certain conclusions and decided upon certain courses 15 of action which have been a great blessing to the world. Before we can under-stand their conclusions we must go back and review the course which they fol-lowed. We must think the thoughts which they thought. Their intellectual life centered around the meeting-house. They were intent upon religious worship. While there were always among them men of deep learning, and later those 20 who had comparatively large possessions, the mind of the people was not so much engrossed in how much they knew, or how much they had, as in how they were going to live. While scantily provided with other literature, there was a wide acquaintance with the Scriptures. Over a period as great as that which measures the existence of our independence they were subject to this discipline 25 not only in their religious life and educational training, but also in their political thought. They were a people who came under the influence of a great spiritual development and acquired a great moral power.

No other theory is adequate to explain or comprehend the Declaration of Independence. It is the product of the spiritual insight of the people. We live 30 in an age of science and of abounding accumulation of material things. These did not create our Declaration. Our Declaration created them. The things of the spirit come first. Unless we cling to that, all our material prosperity, over-whelming though it may appear, will turn to a barren sceptre in our grasp. If we are to maintain the great heritage which has been bequeathed to us, we must 35 be like-minded as the fathers who created it. We must not sink into a pagan materialism. We must cultivate the reverence which they had for the things that are holy. We must follow the spiritual and moral leadership which they showed. We must keep replenished, that they may glow with a more compelling flame, the altar fires before which they worshipped. 40

SCOPES TRIAL

It takes little effort to summon from the twentieth century's episodic legal sensationalism a roster of candidates for "Trial of the Century": Sacco and Vanzetti, Ethel and Julius Rosenberg, O. J. Simpson, the impeachment of William Jefferson Clinton. There are others. None, however, captured so dramatically, so completely, and with such ballyhoo, the multiple dimensions of the century's cultural tensions as did the Scopes "Monkey" Trial.

In early 1925, Tennessee governor Austin Peay had signed into law the Butler Act, which made it a misdemeanor for a public school instructor "to teach any theory that denies the story of the Divine Creation of Man as taught in the Bible, and to teach instead that man had descended from a lower order of animal." As soon as they learned about it, lawyers for the fledgling American Civil Liberties Union moved into action looking for a way to challenge the law. The search ended with John Thomas Scopes (1900–1970), a twenty-four-year-old part-time football coach and science teacher who had substitute taught the high school biology class in rural Dayton, Tennessee. Because he had used the state-approved textbook, Hunter's Civic Biology, *which included material on evolution, all interested parties were satisfied that he could be charged in a test case with breaking the law.*

The interested parties were many. Town boosters and Fundamentalist anti-evolutionists joined with urban lawyers and visiting journalists to put Dayton on the map. When three-time presidential candidate William Jennings Bryan (1860–1925) came to town to assist the prosecution and Clarence Darrow (1857–1938), the nation's most famous courtroom attorney, joined the defense team, the stage was set for a media circus that would display the emerging American culture wars to all the world. The

---

John Thomas Scopes vs. *State of Tennessee*, Supplemental Original Transcript Appealed from the Circuit Court of Rhea County (16 July 1925), I:432–84.

677

first event of its kind in the history of radio, the trial riveted American attention upon rural Tennessee through live broadcasts by Chicago's WGN and daily coverage in over 2,300 newspapers. The trial began on Friday, July 10, 1925, and lasted for only eight days, during which participants and observers alike roasted in a mid-summer heat wave. At the end, when the jury returned its guilty verdict after only nine minutes of deliberation, few were surprised.

After all, the trial really was not about Scopes at all. In addition to the lawyers, the real celebrity in the trial was the set of issues at stake, not the defendant. The issues stemmed from tensions inherent in the American heritage. First, how could the conservative Christianity of the American evangelical heritage reckon with and reconcile itself to the conclusions of modern biology that seemed to have no room for God? In the most Christian and most scientific country of the world, the question had to be asked. Second, American political culture had been shaped by dual and potentially conflicting commitments to majoritarian democratic rule and to rights of minorities. If, for example, the minority was an educated elite claiming the "right" to teach unpopular ideas in publicly funded institutions, then these two commitments could come into conflict. How should the conflict be resolved? Third, as the United States entered a new modern era after World War I, those called Modernists forcefully embraced a new worldly culture shaped by secular consumerism and the rejection of traditional Christian supernaturalism. Those who militantly opposed such Modernist cultural and religious tendencies in defense of traditional Christian supernaturalism called themselves Fundamentalists. Could the United States preserve its self-identity as a nation "under God" amidst the culture conflict of the Fundamentalist–Modernist Controversy? These three conflicts—the imagined battle between science and religion, the potential conflict between majoritarian rule and minority rights, and the real conflict between Fundamentalism and Modernism—mixed explosively in Dayton to render the Scopes Trial the "Trial of the Century." Rather than resolving any of the three issues, however, the trial became a crystal ball for the century as it brought into focus themes that would shape the American culture wars for the rest of the millennium.

The following text reproduces selections of the trial transcript from the important Thursday, July 16, afternoon session. This portion features key testimony by Bryan, Darrow, and Dudley Field Malone, a slick international divorce lawyer who joined with Darrow in the defense of Scopes.

The Court:[1]   Now, as I announced this morning, the floor on which we are now
assembled is burdened with a great weight. I do not know how well
it is supported, but sometime buildings and floors give away when
they are unduly burdened. So, I suggest to you that you be as quiet   5
in the courtroom as you can, have no more emotion than you can
avoid, especially have no more emotion than you can avoid, especially no applause because it isn't proper in the court room. Now,
I regret very much that there are many people here who cannot
get inside and hear the speaking, but of course it isn't within my   10
power, physical power, to enlarge the courtroom. Mr. Counsel for
the defense, has Mr. Darrow[2] decided to speak or not?

Mr. Darrow: No, Mr. Malone[3] is the only other.

The Court: The only other counsel to speak for that side?

Mr. Darrow: Yes.   15

The Court: Well, I believe Mr. Bryan[4] then will speak next for the state.

Mr. Bryan: If the Court please, we are now approaching the end of the first
week of this trial, and I haven't thought it proper until this time
to take part in the discussion that has been dealing with phases
of this question or case where the state laws and the state rules   20
of practice were under discussion, and I felt that those who were
versed in the law of the state and who were used to the customs
of the court might better taken the burden of the case. But, today,
we come to the discussion of a very important part of this case. A
question so important that upon its decision will determine the   25
length of this trial. If the Court holds, as we believe the Court
should hold, that the testimony that the defense is now offering
is not competent and not proper testimony, then I assume we
are near the end of this trial. And, because the question involved
is not confined to local questions, but is the broadest that will   30
possibly arise, I have felt justified in submitting my views on the
case for the consideration of the Court.

I have been tempted to speak at former times, but I have
been able to withstand the temptation. I have been drawn into
the case by, I think, nearly all the lawyers on the other side. The   35

---

[1]John T. Raulston (1869–1956), presiding judge
[2]Clarence Seward Darrow (1857–1938), defense lawer
[3]Dudley Field Malone (1882–1950), defense lawyer
[4]William Jennings Bryan (1860–1925), prosecution lawyer

principal attorney has often suggested that I am the arch-conspira-
tor and that I am responsible for the presence of this case and I
have almost been credited with leadership of the ignorance and
bigotry which he thinks could alone inspire a law like this. Then,
Mr. Malone has seen fit to honor me by quoting my opinion on
religious liberty. I assume he means that that is the most important
opinion on religious liberty that he has been able to find in this
country, and I feel complimented that I should be picked out
from all the men, living and dead, as the one whose expressions
are most vital to the welfare of our country. And this morning I
was credited with being the cause of the presence of these so-called
experts. Mr. Hays[5] says that before he got here he read that I said
this was to be a duel to the death, between science, was it—and
revealed religion. I don't know who the other duelist was but I
was representing one of them, and because of that, they went to
the trouble and the expense of several thousand dollars to bring
down their witnesses. Well, my friend, if you said that this was
important enough to be regarded as a duel between two great
ideas or groups, I certainly will be given credit for foreseeing
what I could not then know, and that is that this question is so
important between religion and irreligion that even the invoking
of the Divine blessing upon it might seem partisan and partial.

I think when we come to consider the importance of this
question that all of us who are interested as lawyers on either side
could claim what we, what your Honor so graciously grants, a hearing. I have got it down here for fear I might forget them, certain
points that I desire to present for your Honor's consideration.

In the first place, the statute—our position is that the statute
is sufficient. The statute defines exactly what the people of Tennessee desired and intended and did declare unlawful and it needs no
interpretation. The caption speaks of the evolutionary theory and
the statute specifically states that teachers are forbidden to teach
in the schools supported by taxation in this state any theory of
creation of man that denies the divine record of man's creation as
found in the Bible, and that there might be no difference of opinion—there might be no ambiguity—that there might be no such
confusion of thought as our learned friends attempt to inject into
it, the legislature was careful to define what it meant by the first part
of the statute. It says to teach that man is descended from a lower

[5]Arthur Garfield Hays (1881–1954), defense lawyer

form of life—if that had not been there, if the first sentence had been the only sentence in the statute, then these gentlemen might come and ask to define what that meant or to explain whether the thing that was taught was contrary to the language of the statute in the first sentence. But the second sentence removes all doubt as 5 has been stated by my colleague. The second sentence points out specifically what is meant and that is the teaching that man is the descendant of any lower form of life, and if the defendant taught that, as we have proven by the textbook that he used, and as we have proven by the students that went to hear him—if he taught 10 that man is a descendant of any lower form of life, he violated the statute and the more than that, we have his own confession that he knew he was violating the statute.

We have the testimony here of Mr. White, the superintendent of schools, who says that Mr. Scopes told him he could not teach 15 that book without violating the law. We have the testimony of Mr. Robinson—the head of the Board of Education—who talked with Mr. Scopes just at the time the schools closed, or a day or two afterward, and Mr. Scopes told him that he had reviewed that book just before the school closed and that he could not teach 20 it without teaching evolution and without violating the law and we have Mr. Robinson's statement that Mr. Scopes told him that he and one of the teachers, Mr. Ferguson, had talked it over after the law was passed and had decided that they could not teach it without the violation of the law, and yet while Mr. Scopes knew 25 what the law was and knew what evolution was and knew that it violated the law, he proceeded to violate the law.

That is the evidence before this court and we do not need any expert to tell us what that law means. An expert cannot be permitted to come in here and try to defeat the enforcement of a 30 law by testifying that it isn't a bad law and it isn't—I mean a bad doctrine—no matter how these people praise the doctrine, no matter how they eulogize it. This is not the place to try to prove that the law ought never to have been passed. The place to prove that, or teach that, was to the legislature. If these people were so 35 anxious to keep the State of Tennessee from disgracing itself, if they were so afraid that by this action taken by the legislature, the state would put itself before the people of the nation as ignorant people and bigoted people—if they had half the affection for Tennessee that you would think they had, as they come here 40 to testify, they would have come at a time when their testimony would have been valuable and not at this time to ask you to refuse to enforce a law because they did not think the law ought to have been passed. And, my friends, if the people of Tennessee were to go into a state, into New York, the one from which this impulse comes, to resist this law, or go into any state, if they went into any state and tried to convince the people that a law they had passed ought not to be enforced, just because the people who went there didn't think it ought to have been passed, don't you think it would be resented as an impertinence? They passed a law up in New York repealing the enforcement of prohibition. Suppose the people of Tennessee had sent attorneys up there to fight that law, or to oppose it after it was passed, and experts to testify how good a thing prohibition is to New York and to the nation, I wonder if there would have been any lack of determination in the papers in speaking out against the offensiveness of such testimony?

The people of this state passed the law. The people of this state knew what they were doing when they passed the law, and they knew the dangers of the doctrine that they did not want it taught to their children. And, my friends, it isn't—your Honor, it isn't proper to bring experts in here to try to defeat the purpose of the people of this state by trying to show that this thing that they denounce and outlaw is a beautiful thing that everybody ought to believe in. If, for instance, and I think this is a fair illustration, if a man had made a contract with somebody to bring rain in a dry season down here, and if he was to have $500 for an inch of rain, and if the rain did not come and he sued to enforce his contract and collect the money, could he bring experts in to prove that a drought was better than a rain? And get pay for bringing a drought when he contracted to bring rain?

These people want to come here with experts and make your Honor believe that the law should never have been passed and because in their opinion it ought not to be enforced. It isn't a place for expert testimony. We have sufficient proof in the book—doesn't the book state the very thing that is objected to and outlawed in this state. Who has a copy of that book?

The Court: Do you mean the Bible?

Mr. Bryan: No, sir; the *Biology*.

A Voice: Here it is, Hunter's *Biology*.

Mr. Bryan:	No, not the Bible. You see in this state they cannot teach the Bible. They can only teach things that declare it to be a lie, according to the learned counsel. These people in the state, Christian people, have tied their hands by their constitution. They say we all believe in the Bible for it is the overwhelming belief in the state, but we will not teach that Bible which we believe even to our children through teachers that we pay without money. No, no, it isn't the teaching of the Bible, and we are not asking it.

The question is, can a minority in this state come in and compel a teacher to teach that the Bible is not true and make the parents of these children pay the expenses of the teacher to tell their children what these people believe is false and dangerous? Has it come to a time when the minority can take charge of a state like Tennessee and compel the majority to pay their teachers while they take religion out of the heart of the children and the parents who pay the teachers?

So, my friends, if that were true, if man and monkey were in the same class called primates, it would mean they did not come up from the same order. It might mean that instead of one being the ancestor of the other, they were all cousins. But, it does not mean they did not come up from the lower animals, if this is the only place they could come from, and the Christian believes man came from above, but the evolutionist believes he must have come from below; that is, from a lower order of animals.

Your Honor, I want to show you that we have evidence enough here, we do not need any experts to come in here and tell us about this thing. Here we have Mr. Hunter. Mr. Hunter is the author of this biology, and this is the man who wrote the book Mr. Scopes was teaching. And here we have the diagram. Has the court seen this diagram?

The Court:	No, sir; I have not.
Mr. Bryan:	Well, you must see it. (Handing book to the Court)
Mr. Bryan:	I will give you the family tree according to Darwin. If we are going to have family trees here, let us have something that is reliable. I will give you the only family tree that any believer in evolution has ever dared to outline—no other family tree that any evolutionist has ever proposed has as many believers as Darwin has in his family tree. Some of them have discarded his explanations. Natural selection. People confuse evolution with Darwinism.

They did not used to complain. It was not until Darwin was brought out into the open; it was not until the absurdities of Darwin had made his explanations the laughing stock that they began to try to distinguish between Darwinism and evolution. They explained that evolutionists had discarded Darwin's idea of sexual selection—I should think they would discard it—and they are discarding the doctrine of natural selection.

But, my friends, when they discard his explanations, they still teach his doctrines. Not one of these evolutionists has discarded Darwin's doctrine that makes life begin with one cell in the sea and continue in one unbroken line to man. Not one of them has discarded that.

My contention is that the evolutionary hypothesis is not a theory, your Honor.

The Court: Well, hypothesis.

Mr. Bryan: The legislature paid evolution a higher honor than it deserves. Evolution is not a theory, but a hypothesis. Huxley[6] said it could not raise to the dignity of a theory until they found some species that had developed according to the hypothesis, and at that time, Huxley's time, there had never been found a single species the origin of which could be traced to another species. Darwin, himself said he thought it was strange that with two or three million species they had not been able to find one that they could trace to another. About three years ago, Bateson[7] of London, who came all the way to Toronto at the invitation of the American Academy for the Advancement of Science, which, if the gentlemen will brace themselves for a moment while I say I am a member of the American Academy for the Advancement of Science—they invited Mr. Bateson to come over and speak to them on evolution, and he came, and his speech on evolution was printed in *Science* magazine, and *Science* is the organ of the society, and I suppose is the outstanding organ of science in this country, and I bought a copy so that if any of the learned counsel for the plaintiff had not had the pleasure of reading Bateson's speech that they could regale themselves during the odd hours. And, Bateson told those people after having taken up every effort that had been made to

---

[6]Thomas Henry Huxley (1825–1895), an English biologist who described himself as "Darwin's bulldog" for his defense of Darwin's theories

[7]William Bateson (1861–1926), an English geneticist

show the origin of species and find it, he declared that everyone had failed, everyone, everyone. And, it is true today, never have they traced one single species to any other, and that is why it was that this so-called expert stated that while the fact of evolution, they think, is established, that the various theories of how it came about—that every theory has failed. And, today, there is not a scientist in all the world who can trace one single species to any other, and yet they call us ignoramuses and bigots because we do not throw away our Bible and accept it as proved that out of two or three million species not a one is traceable to another. And they say that evolution is a fact when they can prove one species came from another and, if there is such a thing, all species must have come, commencing as they say, commencing in that one lonely little cell down there in the bottom of the ocean that just evolved and evolved until it got to be a man. And, they cannot find a single species that came from another, and yet they demand that we allow them to teach this stuff to our children, that they may come home with their imaginary family tree and scoff at their mother's and their father's Bible.

Now, my friends, I want you to know that they not only have no proof, but they cannot find the beginning. I suppose this distinguished scholar who came here shamed them all by his number of degrees. He did not shame me, for I have more than he has, but I can understand how my friends felt when he unrolled degree after degree. Did he tell you where life began? Did he tell you that back of all these that there was a God? Not a word about it. Did he tell you how life began? Not a word, and not one of them can tell you how life began. The atheists say it came some way without a God; the agnostics say it came in some way, they know not whether with a God or not. And the Christian evolutionists say we came away back there somewhere, but they do not know how far back, they do not give you the beginning. Not that gentleman that tried to qualify as an expert, he did not tell you how life began. He did not tell you whether it began with God or how. No, they take up life as a mystery that nobody can explain, and they want you to let them commence there and ask no questions. They want to come in with their little padded-up evolution that commences with nothing and ends nowhere. They do not dare to tell you that it began with God, and do not dare to tell you that it ended with God. They come here with this bunch of stuff that they call evolution, that they tell you that everybody believes in, but do not know that everybody knows as a fact, and nobody can tell how it came, and they do not explain the great riddle of the universe; they do not deal with the problems of life; they do not teach the great science of how to live; and yet they would undermine the faith of these little children in that God who stands back of everything and whose promise we have that we shall live with Him forever bye and bye. They shut God out of the world. They do not talk about God. Darwin says the beginning of all things is a mystery unsolvable by us. He does not pretend to say how these things started.

The Court: Well, if the theory is, Colonel Bryan, that God did not create the cell, then it could not be reconcilable with the Bible.

Mr. Bryan: Of course, it could not be reconcilable with the Bible.

The Court: Before it could be reconcilable with the Bible it would have to be admitted that God created the cell.

Mr. Bryan: There would be no contention about that, but our contention is even if they put God back there, it does not make it harmonious with the Bible. The Court is right that unless they put God back there, it must dispute the Bible, and this witness who has been questioned whether he was qualified or not, and they could ask him every question they wanted told, but they did not ask him how life began; they did not ask whether back of all, whether if in the beginning there was God. They did not tell us where immortality began. They did not tell us where in this long period of time between the cell at the bottom of the sea, and man, where man became endowed with the hope of immortality. They did not, if you please, and most of them do not go to the place to hunt for it, because more than half of the scientists of this country—Professor James H. Labell, one of them and he bases it on thousands of letters they sent to him, says more than half do not believe there is a God or personal immortality—and they want to teach that to these children, and take that from them, to take from them their belief in a God who stands ready to welcome His children.

And, your Honor asked me whether it has anything to do with the virgin birth. Yes, because this principle of evolution disputes the miracles—there is no place for the miracles in this train of evolution, and the Old Testament and New are filled with miracles, and if this doctrine is true, this logic eliminates every

mystery in the Old Testament and the New, and eliminates everything supernatural, and that means they eliminate the virgin birth;
that means that they eliminate the resurrection of the body; that
means that they eliminate the doctrine of atonement. And they
believe man has been rising all the time; that man never fell; that
when the Savior came there was not any reason for His coming;
there was no reason why He should not go as soon as He could;
that He was born of Joseph or some other co-respondent, and
that He lies in His grave. And when the Christians of this state
have tied their hands and said, "we will not take advantage of our
power to teach religion to our children, but teachers paid by us,
these people come in from the outside of the state and force upon
the people of this state and upon the children of the taxpayers of
this state a doctrine that refutes not only their belief in God, but
their belief in a Savior and belief in Heaven, and takes from them
every moral standard that the Bible gives us." It is this doctrine
that gives us Nietzsche,[8] the only great author who tried to carry
this to its logical conclusion. And, we have the testimony of my
distinguished friend from Chicago, in his speech in the Loeb
and Leopold[9] case, that 50,000 volumes had been written about
Nietzsche, and he is the greatest philosopher in the last hundred
years; and have him pleading that because Leopold read Nietzsche
and adopted Nietzsche's philosophy of the superman that he is not
responsible for the taking of human life. We have the doctrine—I
should not characterize it as I should like to characterize it—the
doctrine that the universities that had it taught, and the professors who taught it, are much more responsible for the crime that
Leopold committed than Leopold himself.

That is the doctrine, my friends, that they have tried to bring
into existence. They commence in the high schools with their
foundation in the evolutionary theory, and we have the word of
the distinguished lawyer that this is more read than any other
philosopher, and more read than any other in a hundred years,
and the statement of that distinguished man that the teachings
of Nietzsche made Leopold a murderer.

Mr. Darrow: Your Honor, I want to object; there is not a word of truth in
it. Nietzsche never taught that. Anyhow, there was not a word

---

[8]Friedrich Nietzsche (1844–1900), a German philosopher
[9]Nathan Leopold and Richard Loeb, sons of leading Chicago families, were in 1924 convicted
of murdering Bobby Franks in an effort to commit the perfect crime.

of criticism of the professors nor of the colleges in reference to that, nor was there a word of criticism of the theological colleges when that clergyman in southern Illinois killed his wife in order to marry someone else.[10] But, again, I say, the statement is not correct, and I object.

Mr. Bryan: We do not ask to have taught in the schools any doctrine that teaches a clergyman killed his wife—

The Court: Of course, I cannot pass on the question of fact.

Mr. Darrow: I want to take an exception.

Mr. Bryan: I will read you what you said in that speech here.

Mr. Darrow: If you will read it all.

Mr. Bryan: I will read that part I want; you read the rest. This book is for sale.

Mr. Darrow: First of all I want to say, of course, this argument is presumed to be made to the Court, but it is not; and I want to object to injecting any other case into this proceeding, no matter what the case is. I want to take exception to it, if the Court will permit it.

The Court: Well, Colonel Bryan, I doubt you are making reference to what Colonel Darrow has said in any other case, since he has not argued this case, except to verify what you have said, it cannot be an issue here. Perhaps you have the right—

Mr. Bryan: Yes, I would like very much to give you this.

Mr. Darrow: If your Honor permits, I want to take an exception.

The Court: You may do so.

To which ruling of the court defendant by his counsel then and there duly excepted.

Mr. Bryan: If I do not find what I say, I want to tender an apology, because I have never in my life misquoted a man intentionally.

Mr. Darrow: I am not intimating you did, Mr. Bryan, but you will find a thorough explanation in it. I am willing for him to refer to what he wants, to look it up, and I will refer the Court to what I want, later.

The Court: All right.

Mr. Darrow: It will only take up time.

Mr. Bryan: I want to find what he said, where he says the professors and universities were more responsible than Leopold was.

---

[10]In 1924, Lawrence M. Hight, a pastor of the local Methodist Episcopal Church, and Elsie Sweetin confessed to poisoning their spouses in Ina, Illinois, so they might wed one another.

Mr. Darrow:	All right; I will show you what I said, that the professors and the universities were not responsible at all.
Mr. Bryan:	You added after that, that you did not believe in excluding the reading of it, that you thought that was one of the things—
Mr. Darrow:	The fellow that invented the printing press did some mischief as 5 well as some good.
Mr. Bryan:	Here it is, page 84, and this is on sale here in town, I got four copies the other day; cost me $2.00. Anybody can get it for fifty cents apiece, but he cannot buy mine, they are valuable.
Mr. Malone:	I will pay $1.50 for yours! 10
Mr. Bryan:	"I will guarantee that you can go down to the University of Chicago today—into its big library and find over a thousand volumes of Nietzsche, and I am sure I speak moderately. If this boy is to blame for this, where did he get it? Is there any blame attached because somebody took Nietzsche's philosophy seriously 15 and fashioned his life on it? And there is not a question in this case but what it is true. Then who is to blame? The university would be more to blame than he is. The scholars of the world would be more to blame than he is. The publishers of the world—and Nietzsche's books are published by one of the biggest publishers 20 in the world—are more to blame than he. Your Honor, it is hardly fair to hang a nineteen year old boy for the philosophy that was taught him at the university." Now, there is the university and there is the scholar.
Mr. Darrow:	Will you let me see it? 25
Mr. Bryan:	Oh, yes, but let me have it back.
Mr. Darrow:	I'll give you a new one autographed for you.
Mr. Bryan:	Now, my friends, Mr. Darrow asked Howard Morgan[11] "Did it hurt you?" "Did it do you any harm?" "Did it do you any harm?" Why did he not ask the boy's mother? 30
Mr. Darrow:	She did not testify.
Mr. Bryan:	No, but why did you not bring her here to testify?
Mr. Darrow:	I fancy that his mother might have hurt him.
Mr. Bryan:	Your Honor, it is the mothers who find out what is being done. It is the fathers who find out what is being done. It is not neces- 35

---

[11]Howard Morgan, one of the pupils in John Scopes's class

sary that a boy, whose mind is poisoned by this stuff, poisoned by the stuff administered without ever having the precaution to write poison on the outside; it is the parents that are doing that, and here we have the testimony of the greatest criminal lawyer in the United States, defending some of the most dastardly crimes in the United States, stating that the universities—

Mr. Darrow: I object, your Honor, to an injection of that case into this one.

The Court: It is argument before the court period. I do not see how—

Mr. Darrow: If it does not prejudice you, it does not do any good.

The Court: No, sir; it does not prejudice me.

Mr. Darrow: Then it does not do any good.

The Court: Well.

Mr. Bryan: If your Honor please; let me submit, we have a different idea of the purpose of argument, my idea is that it is to inform the court, not merely to prejudice the Court.

The Court: Yes.

Mr. Darrow: I am speaking of this particular matter.

The Court: Suppose you get through with Colonel Darrow as soon as you can, Mr. Bryan.

Mr. Bryan: Yes, I will. I think I am through with the Colonel now. The gentleman was called as an expert, I say, and did not tell us where life began, or how. He did not tell us anything about the end of this series; he did not tell us about the logical consequences of it, and the implications based upon it. He did not qualify even as an expert in science, and not at all as an expert in the Bible. If a man is going to come as an expert to reconcile this definition of evolution with the Bible, he must be an expert on the Bible also, as well as on evolution, and he did not qualify as an expert on the Bible, except to say he taught a Sunday School class.

Mr. Malone: We were not offering him for that purpose; we expect to be able to call experts on the Bible.

Mr. Bryan: Oh, you did not count him as an expert?

Mr. Malone: We count him as a Christian, possibly not as good as Mr. Bryan.

Mr. Bryan: Oh, you have three kinds to be called.

Mr. Malone: No, just Americans; it is not a question of citizenship and not a distinction.

Mr. Bryan:	We are to have three kinds of people called; we are to have the expert scientist, the expert Bible men, and then just Christians.
Mr. Malone:	We will give you all the information you want, Mr. Bryan.
Mr. Bryan:	Thank you, sir. I think we have all we want now. Now, your Honor, when it comes to Bible experts, do they think that they can bring them in here to instruct the members of the jury, eleven of whom are members of the church? I submit that of the eleven members of the jury, more of the jurors are experts on what the Bible is than any Bible expert who does not subscribe to the true spiritual influences or spiritual discernments of what our Bible says.
Voices:	Amen.
Mr. Bryan:	And the man may discuss the Bible all he wants to, but he does not want to find out anything about the Bible until he accepts God and the Christ of whom he tells.
Mr. Darrow:	I hope the reporters got the Amens in the record. I want somewhere, at some time, to find some sort of a picture which will be painted.
Mr. Bryan:	Your Honor, we first pointed out that we do not need any experts in science. Here is one plain fact, and the statute defines itself, and it tells the kind of evolution it does not want taught, and the evidence says that this is the kind of evolution that was taught, and no number of scientists could come in here, my friends, and override that statute or take from the jury its right to decide this question, so that all the experts that they could bring would mean nothing. And, when it comes to Bible experts, every member of the jury is as good an expert on the Bible as any man that they could bring, or that we could bring. The one beauty about the Word of God is, it does not take an expert to understand it. They have translated that Bible into five hundred languages, they have carried it into nations where but few can read a word, or write, to people who never saw a book, who never read, and yet can understand that Bible, and they can accept the salvation that that Bible offers, and they can know more about that Book by accepting Jesus and feeling in their hearts the sense of their sins forgiven than all of the skeptical outside Bible experts that could come in here to talk to the people of Tennessee about the construction that they place upon the Bible, that is foreign to the construction that the people here place upon it.

Line numbers in right margin: 5, 10, 15, 20, 25, 30, 35

Therefore, your Honor, we believe that this evidence is not competent; it is not a mock trial; this is not a convocation brought here to allow men to come and stand for a time in the limelight, and speak to the world from the platform at Dayton. If we must have a mock trial to give these people a chance to get before the public with their views, then let us convene it after this case is over, and let people stay as long as they want to listen. But, let this Court, which is here supported by the law, and by the taxpayers, pass upon this law, and when the legislature passes a law and makes it so plain that even though a fool need not err therein, let us sustain it in our interpretation.

We have a book here that shows everything that is needed to make one understand evolution, and to show that the man violated the law. Then why should we prolong this case? We can bring our experts here for the Christians, forever, more than they can bring who don't believe in Christianity. We can bring more than one who believes in the Bible and rejects evolution, and our witnesses will be just as good experts as theirs on a question of that kind. We could have a thousand or a million witnesses, but this case as to whether evolution is true or not, is not going to be tried here, within this city. If it is carried to the state Courts, it will not be tried there, and if it is taken to the great court at Washington, it will not be tried there. No, my friends, no court, or the law, and no jury, great or small, is going to destroy the issue between the believer and the unbeliever. The Bible is the Word of God. The Bible is the only expression of man's hope of salvation. The Bible, the record of the Son of God, the Savior of the world, born of the Virgin Mary, crucified and risen again; that Bible, is not going to be driven out of this court by experts who come hundreds of miles to testify that they can reconcile evolution, with its ancestor in the jungle, or man made by God in His image, and put here for the purposes as a part of the Divine plan!

No, we are not going to settle that question here, and I think we ought to confine ourselves to the law and to the evidence that can be admitted in accordance with the law. Your Court is an office of this state, and we who represent the State as counsel are officers of the Court, and we cannot humiliate the great State of Tennessee by admitting for a moment that people can come from anywhere and protest against the enforcement of this state's laws on the ground that they do not conform with their ideas or because it banishes from our schools a thing that they believe in, and think ought to be taught in spite of the protest of those who employ the teacher and pay him his salary.

The facts are simple, the case is plain, and if these gentlemen want to enter upon a larger field of educational work on the subject of evolution, let us get through with this case and then convene a mock court, or it will deserve the title of mock court if its purpose is to banish from the hearts of the people the Word of God as revealed!

The Court: We will take a short recess.

(Thereupon a short recess was taken, after which the following proceedings were had.)

The Court: Colonel Darrow, did you say you had a statement you wanted to make?

Mr. Darrow: I want to read what I said. I shall not include an argument.

The Court: There is no objection, Colonel.

Mr. Darrow: I shall not include argument; I don't think I have the right. Following what Mr. Bryan said—

(Commotion near Judge's stand)

Officer: Just a picture machine fallen over.

Mr. Darrow: Following what he used is a paragraph explanatory of it that I want to quote:

"Now, I do not want to be misunderstood about this. Even for the sake of saving the lives of my clients, I do not want to be dishonest, and tell the court something I do not honestly think in this case. I do not believe that the universities are to blame. I do not think they should be held responsible , I do think, however, that they are too large, and that they should keep a closer watch, if possible, upon the individual. But you cannot destroy thought because, forsooth, some brain may be deranged by thought. It is the duty of the university, as I conceive it, to be the great store house of the wisdom of the ages, and to let students go there, and learn, and choose. I have no doubt but that it has meant the death of many; that we cannot help. Every changed idea in the world has had its consequences. Every new religious doctrine has created its victims. Every new philosophy has caused suffering and death. Every new machine has carved up men while it served the world. No railroad can be built without the destruction of human life.

No great building can be erected but that unfortunate workmen fall to the earth and die. No great movement that does not bear its toll of life and death; no great ideal but does good and harm, and we cannot stop because it may do harm.

5   In connection with Nietzsche, he was not connected with a university at all; he was a disciple of the doctrine of the superman"

Mr. Bryan: I want to show that Nietzsche did praise Darwin. He put him as one the three great men of his century. He put Napoleon first, because Napoleon had made war respectable. And he put Darwin

10   among the three great men, and his supermen were merely the logical outgrowth of the survival of the fittest with will and power, the only natural, logical outcome of evolution. And Nietzsche himself became an atheist following that doctrine, and became insane, and his father and mother and an uncle were among the

15   people he tried to kill.

Mr. Darrow: He didn't make half as many insane people as Jonathan Edwards, your great theologian. And he did not preach the doctrine of evolution. He said that Darwin had a great mind. I suppose Colonel Bryan would say that. And, Napoleon, though neither

20   Mr. Bryan nor I admire Napoleon; I know I don't and I don't think he does; he did not teach the doctrine of evolution.

The Court: All right, Colonel; be certain to return the book.

Mr. Malone: If the Court please, it does seem to me that we have gone far afield in this discussion. However, probably this is the time to discuss

25   everything that bears on the issues that have been raised in this case, because, after all, whether Mr. Bryan knows it or not, he is a mammal; he is an animal, and he is a man. But, your Honor, I would like to advert to the law and to remind the court that the heart of the matter is the question of whether there is liability

30   under this law.

               I have been puzzled and interested at one and the same time at the psychology of the prosecution, and I find it hard to distinguish between Mr. Bryan the lawyer in this case, Mr. Bryan the propagandist outside of this case, and the Mr. Bryan who made

35   a speech against science and for religion just now, and Mr. Bryan my old chief and friend. I know Mr. Bryan. I don't know Mr. Bryan as well as Mr. Bryan knows Mr. Bryan, but I know this, that he does believe, and Mr. Bryan, your Honor, is not the only one who believes; he is not the only one who believes in God; he

is not the only one who believes in the Bible. As a matter of fact there has been much criticism, by indirection and implication, of this text, or synopsis, if you please, that does not agree with their ideas on evolution, while, if our religious philosophy depended on the agreement of theologians, we would all be infidels.

I think it is in poor taste for the leader of the prosecution to cast reflection or aspersions upon the men and women of the teaching profession in this country. God knows, the poorest paid profession in America is the teaching profession; who devote themselves to science, forego the gifts of God, consecrate themselves, their brains to study, and eke out their lives as pioneers in the fields of study, fondly hoping that mankind will profit by their efforts, and to pen the doors of truth.

Mr. Bryan quoted Mr. Darwin. That theory was evolved and explained by Mr. Darwin seventy-five years ago. Have we learned nothing in seventy-five years? Here we have learned the truth of theology; we have learned the truth of anthropology; and we have learned more of archeology. Not very long since the archeological museum in London established that a city existed, showing a high degree of civilization in Egypt, fourteen thousand years old, showing that on the banks of the Nile River there was a civilization much older than ours. Are we to hold mankind to a literal understanding of the claim that the world is six thousand years old because of the limited vision of men who believed the world was flat, and that the earth was the center of the universe, and that man is the center of the earth? It is a dignified position for man to be the center of the universe, that the earth is the center of the universe, and that the heavens revolve about us. And, the theory or psychology of the prosecution, and the theory of ignorance and superstition for which they stood are identical, a psychology and ignorance which made it possible for theologians to take old and learned Galileo, who proposed to prove the theory of Copernicus, that the earth was round and did not stand still, and to bring old Galileo to trial, for what purpose? For the purpose of proving a literal construction of the Bible against truth which is revealed.

Haven't we learned anything in seventy-five years? Are we to have our children know nothing about science except what the church says they shall know? I have never seen harm in learning and understanding, in humility and open-mindedness, and I have never seen clearer the need of that learning than when I see the attitude of the prosecution, who attack and refuse to accept the information and intelligence which expert witnesses will give them.

Mr. Bryan may be satisfactory to thousands of people. It is in so many ways that he is satisfactory to me; his enthusiasm, his vigor, his courage, his fighting ability these long years for the things he thought were right. And, many a time I have fought with him, and for him, and when I did not think he was right, I fought just as hard against him.

This is not a conflict of personalities, of personages; it is a conflict of ideas, and I think this case has developed by men of two frames of mind. Your Honor, there is a difference between theological and scientific men. Theology deals with something that is established and revealed; it seeks to gather material which they claim should not be changed. It is the Word of God, and that cannot be changed; it is literal; it is not to be interpreted. That is the theological mind. It deals with theology.

And, the scientific fact is a modern thing, your Honor. I am not sure that Galileo was the one who brought relief to the scientific mind; because theretofore Aristotle and Plato had reached their conclusions and processes by metaphysical reasoning, because they had no telescope, and no microscope. Those were things that were invented by Galileo. The difference between the theological mind and the scientific mind is that the theological mind is closed, because that is what is revealed and is settled. But, the scientist says, no, the Bible is the book of revealed religion, with rules of conduct, and with aspirations, that is the Bible. The scientist says, take the Bible as guide, as an inspiration, as a set of philosophies, and preachments, in the world of theology.

And, what does this law do? We have been told here that this was not a religious question. I defy anybody, after Mr. Bryan's speech, to believe that this was not a religious question. Mr. Bryan brought all of the foreigners into this case. Mr. Bryan had offered his services from Miami, Florida; he does not belong to Tennessee. If it be wrong for American citizens from other parts of this country to come to Tennessee to discuss issues which we believe, then Mr. Bryan has no right here either. But, it was only when Mr. Darrow and I had heard that Mr. Bryan had offered his name and his reputation to the prosecution of this young teacher that we said, "Well, we will offer our services to the defense." And, as I said in the beginning, we feel at home in Tennessee; we have been received with hospitality, personally. Our ideas have not taken effect yet; we have corrupted no morals so far as I know. And, I would like to ask the court if there was any evidence in the witnesses produced by the prosecution, of moral deterioration due to the course of biology which Professor Scopes taught these children; the little boy who said he had been hurt by it, and who slipped out of the chair possibly and went to the swimming pool. And, the other who said that the theory he was taught had not taken him out of the church. This theory of evolution, in one form or another, has been up in Tennessee since 1832, and I think it is incumbent on the prosecution to introduce at least one person in the State of Tennessee whose morals have been affected by the teaching of this theory.

After all, we of the defense contend, and it has been my experience, your Honor, in my twenty years, as Mr. Bryan said, as a criminal lawyer, that the prosecution had to prove its case; that the defense did not have to prove it for them.

We have a defendant here charged with a crime. The prosecution is trying to get your Honor to take the theory of the prosecution as the theory of our defense. We maintain our right to present our own defense, and present our own theory of our defense, and to present our own theory of this law, because we maintain, your Honor, that if everything that the State has said in its testimony be true, and we admit it is true, that under this law the defendant Scopes has not violated that statute. Haven't we the right to prove it by our witnesses if that is our theory, if that is so? Moreover, let us take the law: *Be it enacted by the State of Tennessee that it shall be unlawful for any teacher in any universities, normals, or any other schools in the state which are supported in whole or in part by public funds of the state, to teach any theory that denies the story of divine creation of man as taught in the Bible, and to teach him that man is descended from a lower order of animals.*

If that word had been "or" instead of "and" then the prosecution would only have to prove half of its case. But, it must prove, according to our contention, that Scopes not only taught a theory that man had descended from a lower order of animal life, but at the same time, instead of that theory, he must teach the theory that denies the story of divine creation set forth in the Bible.

And we maintain that we have a right to introduce evidence by these witnesses that the theory of the defendant is not in conflict with the theory of creation in the Bible. And, moreover, your

Honor, we maintain, we have the right to call witnesses to show that there is more than one theory of the creation in the Bible. Mr. Bryan is not the only one who has spoken for the Bible; Judge McKenzie is not the only defender of the Word of God. There are other people in this country who have given their whole lives to God. Mr. Bryan, to my knowledge, with a very passionate spirit and enthusiasm, has given most of his life to politics.

I would like to say, your Honor, as personal information, that probably no man in the United States has done more to establish certain standards of conduct in the world of politics than Mr. Bryan. But is that any reason that I should fall down when Mr. Bryan speaks of theology? Is he the last word on the subject of theology?

Well, well do I remember in my history the story of the burning of the great library at Alexandria, and just before it was burned to the ground that the heathen, the Mohammedans and Egyptians went to the hostile general and said: "Your Honor, do not destroy this great library, because it contains all the truth that has been gathered." And the Mohammedan general said, "But, the Koran contains all the truth. If the library contains the truth that the Koran contains we do not need the library and if the library does not contain the truth that the Koran contains, then we must destroy the library anyway."

But, these gentlemen say the Bible contains the truth. "If the world of science can produce any truth or facts not in the Bible, as we understand it, then destroy science, but keep our Bible." And we say, "Keep your Bible. Keep it as your consolation, keep it as your guide, but keep it where it belongs, in the world of your own conscience, in the world of your individual judgment, in the world of the Protestant conscience that I heard so much about when I was a boy. Keep your Bible in the world of theology where it belongs, and do not try to tell an intelligent world and the intelligence of this country that these books written by men who knew none of the accepted fundamental facts of science can be put into a course of science," because what are they doing here?

This law says what? It says that no theory of creation can be taught in a course of science, except one which conforms with the theory of divine creation as set forth in the Bible. In other words, it says that only the Bible shall be taken as an authority on the subject of evolution in a course on biology.

The Court:	Let me ask you a question, Colonel. It is not within the province of this Court to determine which is true, is it?
Mr. Malone:	No, but it is within the province of the Court to listen to the evidence we wish to submit, to make up its own mind, because here is the issue—
The Court:	I am going to follow that with another question. Is it your theory; is it your opinion that the theory of evolution is reconcilable with the story of the divine creation as taught in the Bible?
Mr. Malone:	Yes.
The Court:	In other words, you believe, when it says, when the Bible says that God created man, you believe that God created the life cells and that then out of that one single life cell that God created man by a process of growth or development, is that your theory?
Mr. Malone:	Yes.
The Court:	And in that you think that it doesn't mean that He just completed him, complete all at once?
Mr. Malone:	Yes, I might think that and I might think he created him serially; I might think he created him any way. Our opinion is this, we have the right it seems to us to submit evidence to the Court of men without question who are God-fearing and believe in the Bible and who are students of the Bible and authorities on the Bible and authorities on the scientific world, they have a right to be allowed to testify in support of our view that the Bible is not to be taken literally as an authority in a court of science.
The Court:	That is what I am trying to get your position on. Here was my idea. I wanted to get your theory as to whether you thought it was in the province of the Court to determine which was true, or whether it was your theory that there was no conflict and that you had a right to introduce proof to show that the Bible—what the true construction or interpretation of the Bible story was.
Mr. Malone:	Yes.
The Court:	That is your opinion?
Mr. Darrow:	Yes. And also from scientists who believe in the Bible.
Mr. Malone:	And who belong to churches and who are God-fearing men; what they think about this subject of the reconcilment of science and religion. Of all science and the Bible. Your Honor, because yesterday I made a remark your Honor which might have been

Line numbers: 5, 10, 15, 20, 25, 30, 35

interpreted as personal to Mr. Bryan. I said that the defense believed we must keep a clear distinction between the Bible, the church, religion and Mr. Bryan. Mr. Bryan, like all of us, is just an individual, but like himself, he is a great leader. The danger from the viewpoint of the defense is this, that when any great leader goes out of his field and speaks as an authority on other subjects his doctrines are quite likely to be far more dangerous than the doctrines of experts in their field who we are ready and willing to follow, but, what I don't understand is this, your Honor, the prosecution inside and outside of the court has been ready to try the case and this is the case.

What is the issue that has gained the attention not only of the American people, but people everywhere? Is it a mere technical question as to whether the defendant Scopes taught the paragraph in the book of science? You think, your Honor, that the News Association in London, which sent you that very complimentary telegram you were good enough to show me for your kindness to the foreign correspondents, is interested in this case, because the issue is whether John Scopes taught a couple of paragraphs out of this book? Oh, no, the issue is as broad as Mr. Bryan himself has made it. The issue is as broad as Mr. Bryan has published it and why the fear? If the issue is as broad as they make it, why the fear of meeting the issue? Why, where issues are drawn by evidence, where the truth and nothing but the truth is scrutinized, and where statements can be answered by expert witnesses on the other side; what is this psychology of fear? I don't understand it. My old chief—I never saw him back away from a great issue before. I feel that the prosecution here is filled with a needless fear. I believe that if they withdrew their objection and heard the evidence of our experts their minds would not only be improved, but their souls would be purified. I believe and we believe that men who are God-fearing, who are giving their lives to study and observation, to the teaching of the young, are the teachers and scientists of this country, in a combination to destroy the morals of the children to whom they have dedicated their lives? Are preachers the only ones in America who care about our youth? Is the church the only source of morality in this country? And, I would like to say something for the children of the country.

We have no fears about the young people of America. They are a pretty smart generation. Any teacher who teaches the boys or the girls of today, an incredible theory—we need not worry about those children of this generation paying much attention to it. The children of this generation are pretty wise. People as a matter of fact—I feel that the children of this generation are probably much wiser than many of their elders. The least that this generation can do, your Honor, is to give to the next generation all the facts, all the available data, all the theories, all the information that learning, that study, that observation has produced; give it to the children in the hope to Heaven that they will make a better world of this than we have been able to make of it.

We have just had a war with twenty million dead. Civilization is not so proud of the work of the adults. Civilization need not be so proud of what the grown-ups have done. For God's sake, let the children have their minds kept open—close no doors to their knowledge; shut no doors from them. Make the distinction between theology and science. Let them have both. Let them both be taught. Let them both live. Let them be revered. But, we come here to say that the defendant is not guilty of violating this law. We have a defendant whom we contend could not violate this law. We have a defendant whom we can prove by witnesses whom we have brought here and are proud to have brought here, to prove, we say, that there is no conflict between the Bible and whatever he taught.

Your Honor, in a criminal case we think the defendant has a right to put in his own case, on his own theory, in his own way. Why, because your Honor after you hear the evidence, if it is inadmissible if it is not informing to the Court and informing to the jury, what can you do? You can exclude it, you can strike it out. What is the jury system that Mr. Bryan talked so correctly about just about a week ago, when he spoke of this jury system, when he said it was a seal of freedom for free men, in a free state? Who has been excluding the jury for fear it would learn something? Have we? Who has been making the motions to take the jury out of the courtroom? Have we? We want everything. We have to say, on science and religion told and we are ready to submit our theories to the direct and cross examination of the prosecution. We have come in here ready for a battle. We have come in here for this duel. I don't know anything about duelling, your Honor. It is against the law of God; it is against the church; it is against the law of Tennessee, but does the opposition mean by duel that our defendant shall be strapped to a board and that they alone shall carry the sword? Is our only weapon the witnesses who shall testify to the accuracy of our theory? Is our weapon to be taken from us so that the duel will be entirely one-sided? That is not my idea of a duel. Moreover, it isn't going to be a duel. There is never a duel with the truth. The truth always wins and we are not afraid of it. The truth is no coward. The truth does not need the law. The truth does not need the forces of government. The truth does not need Mr. Bryan. The truth is imperishable, eternal and immortal, and needs no human agency to support it.

We are ready to tell the truth as we understand it, and we do not fear all the truth that they can present as facts. We are ready. We are ready. We feel we stand with progress. We feel we stand with science. We feel we stand with intelligence. We feel we stand with fundamental freedom in America. We are not afraid. Where is the fear? We meet it—where is the fear? We defy it; we ask your Honor to admit the evidence as a matter of correct law, as a matter of sound procedure and as a matter of justice to the defense in this case.

The Officer: Order, please. Is the Reverend Dr. Jones or the Reverend Dr. Cartwright in the house? An old resident of Dayton, Mr. Blevins has died, passed away, and his funeral will be this afternoon at 4: 30. Those wishing to attend may go. Pass out quietly.

The Court: Colonel Darrow, did you say you had something you wished to say?

Mr. Darrow: No, I just wanted about that much, to try a little more to specifically answer the question you asked Mr. Malone. I wouldn't think of trespassing or making a speech as I have explained to the Attorney General.

Your question, as understood, it was whether the doctrine of evolution was consistent with the story in Genesis that God created man out of the dust of the earth, whether the doctrine of evolution that he came up from below a long period of time is consistent with it.

What I want to say will not be more than that much. (Indicating) We say that God created man out of the dust of the earth is simply a figure of speech. The same language is used in reference to brutes many times in the scriptures and it doesn't mean, necessarily, that He created him as a boy would roll up a spitball out of dust, out of hand, but Genesis, or the Bible says nothing whatever about the method of creation.

The Court:	The processes?
Mr. Darrow:	It might have been by any other process, that is all.
The Court:	So your theory, your opinion, Colonel, is that God might have created him by a process of growth?
Mr. Darrow:	Yes.
The Court:	Or development?
Mr. Darrow:	Yes.
The Court:	The fact that He created him, did not manufacture him like a carpenter would make a table?
Mr. Darrow:	Yes, that is all; that is what we claim.
The Court:	You recognize God behind the first spark of life?
Mr. Darrow:	You are asking me whether I do?
The Court:	Your theory; no, not you.
Mr. Darrow:	We expect most of our witnesses to take that view. As to me I don't pretend to have any opinion on it.
The Court:	My only concern is that as to your theory of it.
Mr. Darrow:	So far as this question is concerned, we claim there is no conflict because it doesn't mean making man like a carpenter would make him, but that it is perfectly consistent to say that he was made by a process, perfectly consistent with the Bible, not inconsistent with it, that he was made out of the dust of the earth. Animals were made out of the dust of the earth and everything was made out of the dust of the earth and that had nothing to do with the process but simply gives a general statement and there is nothing in the Bible which shows the process.
The Court:	Colonel, let me ask you another question. You have stated your theory. Is it your theory that man and beast had a common origin of life? Does your theory teach that man developed directly from that common origin without first developing into the form of any other animal or that he developed in the one form of life or one physical existence and then passed from that to another form of physical existence, or what is your theory?
Mr. Darrow:	The theory of evolution, as I understand it, and which I believe, it will only take a moment because I have no right to make an

argument. Life commenced probably with very low forms, most likely one-celled animals and probably in the sea or on the border of the land, and sea. That out of that and he was man?

Mr. Darrow: One form of animal life grew out of another, beginning below, variation exists, variations of all kinds. All life varies and we are creating these new variations every day. They are not species, they are variations and as you went on up there would be a variation in animal structures on up to man. That is surely consistent with the story that man was created out of the dust of the earth.

The Court: According to your theory where did man become endowed with reason?

Mr. Darrow: Well, Judge, I don't suppose there is any scientist today but what knows that the lower order of animals have reason.

The Court: It is just in a higher development than man?

Mr. Darrow: No, reason begins way below man.

The Court: I say man has a greater development?

Mr. Darrow: Oh yes, much greater, very much greater, very much greater than any other animal.

The Court: Does your theory of evolution speak at all on the question of immortality?

Mr. Darrow: There are a lot of people who believe in evolution and who believe in the theory of immortality and no doubt many who do not. Evolution as a theory is concerned with the organism of man. Chemistry does not speak of immortality and hasn't anything to do with it. Geology doesn't know anything about it. It is a separate branch of science. I know there are a lot of evolutionists who believe in immortality.

The Court: Those who believe in immortality, where do they—do they also believe that other animals are endowed with immortality?

Mr. Darrow: John Wesley[12] used to believe it; he was an evolutionist in a way. He expected to meet his dog and his horse in the future world. Indians believe it. It has been very common all through the ages, and I don't know, I couldn't say exactly how all evolutionists believe. As to where the idea of immortality came from and as far for me, I am an agnostic on that. I do not claim to know. I have been looking for evidence all my life and never found it.

---

[12]John Wesley (1703–1791), a prominent English religious reformer and preacher

THE MODERN TEMPER
JOSEPH WOOD KRUTCH (1893–1970)

A native of Knoxville, Tennessee, Joseph Wood Krutch graduated from the University of Tennessee and went on for a Ph.D. at Columbia University. He became a drama critic for the periodical The Nation *in 1925. Later, during the Depression, Krutch joined the English faculty at Columbia University where he taught and wrote (nearly a book each year) until the early 1950s, when he resigned his academic position and moved to Arizona.*

In 1929 Krutch's book The Modern Temper *appeared. It offered a penetrating and chilling study of the tensions and conflicts associated with modernity. When first published, the book sparked intense discussion, as it challenged many traditional assumptions about human nature, religion, ethical distinctions, the meaning of history, and the possibility of genuine knowledge. As such, it provides a good statement of the intellectual and spiritual challenges faced by the first "modern" Americans. The following selection is the essay in* Atlantic Monthly *which served as the first chapter of the book two years later.*

1927

It is one of Freud's quaint conceits that the baby in its mother's womb is the happiest of living creatures. Into his consciousness no conflict has yet entered, for he knows no limitations to his desires and the universe is exactly as he wishes it to be. All his needs are satisfied before even he becomes aware of them, and if his awareness is dim, that is but the natural result of a complete harmony   5 between the self and the environment, since, as Spencer pointed out in a remote age, to be omniscient and omnipotent would be to be without any consciousness whatsoever. The discomfort of being born is the first warning which he received that any event can be thrust upon him; it is the first limitation of his omnipotence which he perceives, and he is cast upon the shores of the world   10 wailing his protest against the indignity to which he had been subjected. Years

Joseph Wood Krutch, "The Modern Temper," *Atlantic Monthly* 139 (January–June 1927): 167–75.

pass before he learns to control the expression of enraged surprise which arises within him at every unpleasant fact with which he is confronted, and his parents inspire so to protect him that he will learn only by very slow stages how far is the world from his heart's desire.

5   The cradle is made to imitate as closely as may be the conditions, both physical and spiritual, of the womb. Of its occupant no effort is demanded, and every precaution is taken to anticipate each need before it can arise. If, as the result of any unforeseen circumstance, any unsatisfied desire is born, he need only raise his voice in protest to cause the entire world in so far as he knows it—his
10 nurse or his parents—to rush to his aid. The whole of his physical universe is obedient to his will and he is justified by his experience in believing that his mere volition controls his destiny. Only as he grows older does he become aware that there are wills other than his own or that there are physical circumstances rebellious to any human will. And only after the passage of many years does
15 he become aware of the full extent of his predicament in the midst of a world which is in very few respects what he would wish it to be.

    As a child he is treated as a child, and such treatment implies much more than the physical coddling of which Freud speaks. Not only do those who surround him co-operate more completely than they ever will again to satisfy his
20 wishes in material things, but they encourage him to live in a spiritual world far more satisfactory than their own. He is carefully protected from any knowledge of the cruelties and complexities of life; he is led to suppose that the moral order is simple and clear, that virtue triumphs, and that the world is, as the desires of whole generations of mankind have led them to try to pretend that it
25 is, arranged according to a pattern which would seem reasonable and satisfactory to human sensibilities. He is prevented from realizing how inextricably what men call good and evil are intertwined, how careless is Nature of those values called mercy and justice and righteousness which men have come, in her despite, to value; and he is, besides, encouraged to believe in a vast mythology
30 peopled with figments that range all the way from the Saints to Santa Claus and that represent projections of human wishes which the adult has come to recognize as no more than projections, but which he is willing that the child, for the sake of his own happiness, should believe real. Aware how different is the world which experience reveals from the world which the spirit desires, the
35 mature, as though afraid that reality could not be endured unless the mind had been gradually inured to it, allow the child to become aware of it only by slow stages, and little by little he learns, not only the limitations of his will, but the moral discord of the world. Thus it is, in a very important sense, true that the infant does come trailing clouds of glory from that heaven which his imagina-
40 tion creates, and that as his experience accumulates he sees it fade away into the light of common day.

Now races as well as individuals have their infancy, their adolescence, and their maturity. Experience accumulates not only from year to year but from generation to generation, and in the life of each person it plays a little larger part than it did in the life of his father. As civilization grows older it too has more and more facts thrust upon its consciousness and is compelled to abandon one after another, quite as the child does, certain illusions which have been dear to it. Like the child, it has instinctively assumed that what it would like to be true is true, and it never gives up any such belief until experience in some form compels it to do so. Being, for example, extremely important to itself, it assumes that it is extremely important to the universe also. The earth is the center of all existing things, man is the child and the protégé of those gods who transcend and who will ultimately enable him to transcend all the evil which he has been compelled to recognize. The world and all that it contains were designed for him, and even those things which seem noxious have their usefulness only temporarily hid. Since he knows but little he is free to imagine, and imagination is always the creature of desire.

The world which any consciousness inhabits is a world made up in part of experience and in part of fancy. No experience, and hence no knowledge is complete, but the gaps which lie between the solid fragments are filled in with shadows. Connections, explanations, and reasons are supplied by the imagination, and thus the world gets its patterned completeness from material which is spun out of the desires. But as time goes on and experience accumulates there remains less and less scope for the fancy. The universe becomes more and more what experience has revealed, less and less what imagination has created, and hence, since it was not designed to suit man's needs, less and less what he would have it be. With increasing knowledge his power to manipulate his physical environment increases, but in gaining the knowledge which enables him to do so he so renders insensible the power which in his ignorance he had to mould the universe. The forces of nature obey him, but in learning to master them he has in another sense allowed them to master him. He has exchanged the universe which his desires created, the universe made for man, for the universe of nature of which he is only a part. Like the child growing into manhood, he passes from a world which is fitted to him into a world for which he must fit himself.

If, then, the world of poetry, mythology, and religion represents the world as man would like to have it, while science represents the world as he gradually comes to discover it, we need only compare the two to realize how irreconcilable they appear. For the cozy bowl of the sky arched in a protecting curve above him he must exchange the cold immensities of space, and, for the spiritual order which he has designed, the chaos of nature. God he had loved because God was anthropomorphic, because He was made in man's own image, with purposes and desires which were human and hence understandable. But Nature's purpose, if

purpose she can be said to have, is no purpose of his and is not understandable in his terms. Her desire merely to lie and to propagate in innumerable forms, her ruthless indifference to his values, and the blindness of her irresistible will strike terror to his soul, and he comes in the fullness of his experience to realize that
5 the ends which he proposes to himself—happiness and order and reason—are ends which he must achieve, if he achieve them at all, in her despite. Formerly he had believed in even his darkest moments that the universe was rational if he could only grasp its rationality, but gradually he comes to suspect that rationality is an attribute of himself alone and that there is no reason to suppose that his
10 own life has any more meaning than the life of the humblest insect that crawls from one annihilation to another. Nature, in her blind thirst for life, has filled every possible cranny of the rotting earth with some sort of fantastic creature, and among them man is but one—perhaps the most miserable of all, because he is the only one in whom the instinct of life falters long enough to enable it
15 to ask the question "Why?" As long as life is regarded as having been created, creating may be held to imply a purpose, but merely to have come into being is, in all likelihood, merely to go out of it also.

Fortunately, perhaps, man, like the individual child, was spared in his cradle the knowledge which he could not bear. Illusions have been lost one by one.
20 God, instead of disappearing in an instant, has retreated step by step and sur-rendered gradually his control of the universe. Once he decreed the fall of every sparrow and counted the hairs upon every head; a little later he became merely the original source of the laws of nature, and even today there are thousands who, unable to bear the thought of losing him completely, still fancy that they
25 can distinguish the uncertain outlines of a misty figure. But the role which he plays grows less and less, and man is left more and more alone in a universe to which he is completely alien. His world was once, like the child's world, three quarters myth and poetry. His teleological concepts moulded it into a form which he could appreciate and he gave to it moral laws which would make it
30 meaningful, but step by step the outlines of nature have thrust themselves upon him, and for the dream which he made is substituted a reality devoid of any pattern which he can understand.

In the course of this process innumerable re-adjustments have been made, and always with the effort to disturb as little as possible the myth which is so
35 much more full of human values than the fact which comes in some measure to replace it. Thus, for example, the Copernican theory of astronomy, removing the earth from the centre of the universe and assigning it a very insignificant place among an infinitude of whirling motes, was not merely resisted as a fact, but was, when finally accepted, accepted as far as possible without its implica-
40 tions. Even if taken entirely by itself and without the whole system of facts of

which it is a part, it renders extremely improbable the assumption, fundamental in most human thought, that the universe has man as its centre and is hence understandable in his terms, but this implication was disregarded just as, a little later, the implications of the theory of evolution were similarly disregarded. It is not likely that if man had been aware from the very beginning that his world was a mere detail in the universe, and himself merely one of the innumerable species of living things, he would ever have come to think of himself, as he even now tends to do, as a being whose desires must be somehow satisfiable and whose reason must be matched by some similar reason in nature. But the myth, having been once established, persists long after the assumptions upon which it was made have been destroyed, because, being born of desire, it is far more satisfactory than any fact.

Unfortunately, perhaps, experience does not grow at a constant, but at an accelerated, rate. The Greeks who sought knowledge, not through the study of nature, but through the examination of their own minds, developed a philosophy which was really analogous to myth, because the laws which determined its growth were dictated by human desires, and they discovered few facts capable of disturbing the pattern which they devised. The Middle Ages retreated still further into themselves, but with the Renaissance man began to surrender himself to nature, and the sciences, each nourishing the other, began their iconoclastic march. Three centuries lay between the promulgation of the Copernican theory and the publication of the *Origin of Species*, but in sixty-odd years which have elapsed since that latter event the blows have fallen with a rapidity which left no interval for recovery. The structures which are variously known as mythology, religion, and philosophy, and which are alike in that each has as its functions the interpretation of experience in terms which have human values, have collapsed under the force of successive attacks and shown themselves utterly incapable of assimilating the new store of experience which have been dumped upon the world. With increasing completeness science maps out the pattern of nature, but the latter has no relation to the pattern of human needs and feelings.

Consider, for example, the plight of ethics. Historical criticism having destroyed what used to be called by people of learning and intelligence "Christian Evidences," and biology having shown how unlikely it is that man is the recipient of any transcendental knowledge, there remains no foundation in authority for ideas of right and wrong and if, on the other hand, we turn to the traditions of the human race, anthropology is ready to prove that no consistent human tradition has ever existed. Custom has furnished the only basis which ethics have ever had and there is no conceivable human action which custom has not at one time justified and at another condemned. Standards are imaginary things, and yet it is extremely doubtful if man can live well, either spiritually or physically,

without the belief that they are somehow real. Without them society lapses into anarchy and the individual becomes aware of an intolerable disharmony between himself and the universe. Instinctively and emotionally he is an ethical animal. No known race is so low in the scale of civilization that it has not attributed a
5   moral order to the world, because no known race is so little human as not to suppose a moral order, so innately desirable as to have an inevitable existence. It is man's most fundamental myth, and life seems meaningless to him without it. Yet, as that systematized and cumulative experience which is called science displaces one after another the myths which have been generated by need, it
10   grows more and more likely that he must remain an ethical animal in a universe which contains no ethical element.

Mystical philosophers have sometimes said that they "accepted the universe." They have, that is to say, formed of it some conception which answered the emotional needs of their spirit and which brought them a sense of being in
15   harmony with its aims and processes. They have been aware of no needs which Nature did not seem to supply and of no ideals which she too did not seem to recognize. They have felt themselves one with her because they have had the strength of imagination to make her over in their own image, and it is doubtful if any man can live at peace who does not thus feel himself at home. But as the
20   world assumes the shape which science gives it, it becomes more and more difficult to find such emotional correspondences. Whole realms of human feeling, like the realm of ethics, find no place for themselves in the pattern of nature and generate needs for which no satisfaction is supplied. What man knows is everywhere at war with what he wants.

25   In the course of a few centuries his knowledge, and hence the universe of which he finds himself an inhabitant, have been completely revolutionized, but his instincts and his emotions have remained, relatively at least, unchanged. He is still, as he always was, adjusted to the orderly, purposeful, humanized world which all peoples unburdened by experience have figured to themselves, but
30   that world no longer exists. He has the same sense of dignity to which the myth of his descent from the gods was designed to minister, and the same innate purposefulness which led him to attribute a purpose to Nature, but he can no longer think in terms appropriate to either. The world which his reason and his investigation reveal is a world which his emotions cannot comprehend.

35   Casually he accepts the spiritual iconoclasm of science, and in the detachment of everyday life he learns to play with the cynical wisdom of biology and psychology, which explain away the awe of emotional experience just as earlier science explained away the awe of conventional piety. Yet, under the stress of emotional crises, knowledge is quite incapable of controlling his emotions or of
40   justifying them to himself. In love, he calls upon the illusions of man's grandeur

and dignity to help him accept his emotions, and faced with tragedy he calls upon illusion to dignify his suffering; but lyric flight is checked by the rationality which he has cultivated, and in the world of metabolism and hormones, repressions and complexes, he finds no answer for his needs. He is feeling about love, for example, much as the troubadour felt, but he thinks about it in a very different way. Try as he may, the two halves of his soul can hardly be made to coalesce, and he cannot either feel as his intelligence tells him that he should feel or think as his emotions would have him think, and thus he is reduced to mocking his torn and divided soul. In the grip of passion he cannot, as some romanticist might have done, accept it with a religious trust in the mystery of love, nor yet can he regard it as a psychiatrist, himself quite free from emotion, might suggest—merely as an interesting specimen of psychical botany. Man *qua* thinker may delight in the intricacies of psychology, but man *qua* lover has not learned to feel in its terms; so that, though complexes and ductless glands may serve to explain the feelings of another, one's own still demand all these symbols of the ineffable in which one has long ceased to believe.

Time was when the scientist, the poet, and the philosopher walked hand in hand. In the universe which the one perceived the other found himself comfortably at home. But the world of modern science is one in which the intellect alone can rejoice. The mind leaps, and leaps perhaps with a sort of elation, through the immensities of space, but the spirit, frightened and cold, longs to have once more above its head the inverted bowl beyond which may lie whatever paradise its desires may create. The lover who surrendered himself to the Implacable Aphrodite or who fancied his foot upon the lowest rung of the Platonic ladder of love might retain his self-respect, but one can neither resist nor yield gracefully to a carefully catalogued psychosis. A happy life is a sort of poem, with a poem's elevation and dignity, but emotions cannot be dignified unless they are first respected. They must seem to correspond with, to be justified by, something in the structure of the universe itself; but though it was the function of religion and philosophy to hypostatize some such correspondence, to project a humanity upon Nature, or at least to conceive of a humane force above and beyond her, science finds no justification for such a process and is content instead to show how illusions were born.

The most ardent love of truth, the most resolute determination to follow Nature no matter to what black abyss she may lead, need not blind one to the fact that many of the lost illusions had, to speak the language of science, a survival value. Either individuals or societies whose life is imbued with a cheerful certitude, whose aims are clear, and whose sense of the essential rightness of life is strong, live and struggle with an energy unknown to the skeptical and the pessimistic. Whatever the limitations of their intellects are instruments of

criticism, they possess the physical and emotional vigor which is, unlike critical intelligence, analogous to the processes of nature. They found empires and
conquer wildernesses, and they pour the excess of their energy into works of
art which the intelligence of more sophisticated peoples continues to admire
5   even though it has lost the faith in life which is requisite for the building of a
Chartres or the carving of a Venus de Milo. The one was not erected to a law
of nature or the other designed to celebrate the *libido*, for each presupposed a
sense of human dignity which science nowhere supports.

Thus man seems caught in a dilemma which his intellect has devised. And
10   deliberately managed return to a state of relative ignorance, however desirable
it might be argued to be, is obviously out of the question. We cannot, as the
naive proponents of the various religions, new and old, seem to assume, believe
one thing and forget another merely because we happen to be convinced that
it would be desirable to do so; and it is worth observing that the new psychol-
15   ogy, with its penetrating analysis of the influence of desire upon belief, has
so adequately warned the reason of the tricks which the will can play upon it
that it has greatly decreased the possibility of beneficent delusion and serves
to hold the mind in a steady contemplation of that from which it would fain
escape. Weak and uninstructed intelligences take reform in the monotonous
20   repetition of once living creeds, or are even reduced to the desperate expedient
of going to sleep amid the formulæ of the flabby pseudo-religions in which
the modern world is so prolific. But neither of these classes affords any aid to
the robust but serious mind which is searching for some terms upon which
it may live.

25   And if we are, as by this time we should be, free from any teleological
delusion, if we no longer make the unwarranted assumption that every human problem is somehow of necessity solvable, we must confess it may be that
for the sort of being whom we have described no survival is possible in any
form like that which his soul has now taken. He is a fantastic thing that had
30   developed sensibilities and established values beyond the nature which gave
him birth. He is of all living creatures the one to whom the earth is the least
satisfactory. He has arrived at a point where he can no longer delude himself
as to the extent of his predicament, and should he either become modified
or disappear the earth would continue to spin and the grass to grow as it has
35   always done. Of the thousands of living species the vast majority would be as
unaware of his passing as they are unaware now of his presence, and he would
go as a shadow goes. His arts, his religions, and his civilizations—these are
fair and wonderful things, but they are fair and wonderful to him alone. With
the extinction of his poetry would be extinguished also the only sensibility for
40   which it has any meaning, and there would remain nothing capable of feeling

a loss. Nothing would be left to label the memory of his discontent 'divine,' and those creatures who find in nature no lack would resume their undisputed possession of the earth.

Anthropoid in form some of them might continue to be, and possessed as well of all the human brain that makes possible a cunning adaption to the conditions of physical life. To them nature might yield up subtler secrets than any yet penetrated; their machines might be more wonderful and their bodies more healthy than any yet known—even though there had passed away, not merely all myth and poetry, but the need for them as well. Cured of his transcendental cravings, content with things as they are, accepting the universe as experience had shown it to be, man would be freed of his soul and, like the other animals, either content or at least desirous of nothing which he might not hope ultimately to obtain.

Nor can it be denied that certain adumbrations of this type have before now come into being. Among those of keener intellect there are scientists to whom the test tube and its contents are all-sufficient, and among those of coarser grain, captains of finance and builders of mills, there are those to whom the acquirement of wealth and power seems to constitute a life in which no lack can be perceived. Doubtless they are not new types; doubtless they have always existed; but may they not be the strain from which Nature will select the coming race? Is not their creed the creed of Nature, and are they not bound to triumph over those whose illusions are no longer potent because they are no longer really believed? Certain philosophers, clinging desperately to the ideal of a humanized world, have proposed a retreat into the imagination. Bertrand Russell in his popular essay, *A Free Man's Worship*, Unamuno and Santayana *passim* throughout their works, have argued that the way of salvation lay in a sort of ironic belief, in a determination to act as though one still believed the things which once were really held true. But is not this a desperate expedient, a last refuge likely to appeal only to the leaders of a lost cause? Does it not represent the last, least substantial phase, of fading faith, something which borrows what little substance it seems to have from a reality of the past? If it seems half real to the sons of those who lived in the spiritual world of which it is a shadow, will it not seem, a little further removed, only a faint futility? Surely it has but little to oppose to those who come armed with the certitudes of science and united with, not fleeing from, the nature amid which they live.

And if the dilemma here described is itself a delusion, it is at least as vividly present and as terribly potent as those other delusions which have shaped or deformed the human spirit. There is no significant contemporary writer upon philosophy, ethics, or aesthetics whose speculations do not lead him to it in one form or another, and even the less reflective are aware of it in their own way.

Both our practical morality and our emotional lives are adjusted to a world which no longer exists. In so far as we adhere to a code of conduct, we do so largely because certain habits still persist, not because we can give any logical reason for preferring them, and in so far as we indulge ourselves in the primi-
5   tive emotional satisfactions—romantic love, patriotism, zeal for justice, and so forth—our satisfaction is the result merely of the temporary suspension of our disbelief in the mythology upon which they are founded. Traditionalists in religion are fond of asserting that our moral codes are flimsy because they are rootless; but, true as this is, it is perhaps not so important as the fact that our
10 emotional lives are rootless too.

If the gloomy vision of a dehumanized world which has just been evoked is not to become a reality, some complete re-adjustment must be made, and at least two generations have found themselves unequal to the task. The generation of Thomas Henry Huxley, so busy with destruction as never adequately to
15 realize how much it was destroying, fought with such zeal against frightened conservatives that it never took time to do more than assert with some vehemence that all would be well, and the generation that followed either danced amid the ruins or sought by various compromises to save the remains of a few tottering structures. But neither patches nor evasions will serve. It is not a changed world
20 but a new one in which man must henceforth live if he lives at all, for all his premises have been destroyed and he must proceed to new conclusions. The values which he thought established have been swept away along with the rules by which he thought they might be attained.

To this fact many are not yet awake, but our novels, our poems, and our
25 pictures are enough to reveal that a generation aware of its predicament is at hand. It has awakened to the fact that both the ends which our fathers proposed to themselves and the emotions from which they drew their strength seem irrelevant and remote. With a smile, sad or mocking, according to individual temperament, it regards those works of the past in which were summed up the
30 values of life. The romantic ideal of a world well lost for love and the classic ideal of austere dignity seem equally ridiculous, equally meaningless when referred, not to the temper of the past, but to the temper of the present. The passions which swept through the once major poets no longer awaken any profound response and only in the bleak, torturous complexities of a T. S. Eliot does it
35 find its moods given adequate expression. Here disgust speaks with a robust voice and denunciation is confident, but ecstasy flickering and uncertain, leaps fitfully up only to sink back among the cinders. And if the poet, with his gift of keen perceptions and his power of organization, can achieve only the most momentary and unstable adjustments, what hope can there be for those whose
40 spirit is a less powerful instrument?

And yet it is with such as he, baffled, but content with nothing which plays only upon the surface, that the hope for a still humanized future must rest. No one can tell how many of the old values must go or how new the new will be. Thus, while under the influence of the old mythology the sexual instinct was transformed into romantic love and tribal solidarity into the religion of 5 patriotism, there is nothing in the modern consciousness capable of effecting these transmutations. Neither the one nor the other is capable of being, as it once was, the *raison d'être* of a life or the motif of a poem which is not, strictly speaking, derivative and anachronistic. Each is fading, each becoming as much a shadow as devotion to the cult of purification through self-torture. Either the 10 instincts upon which they are founded will achieve new transformations or they will remain merely instincts, regarded as having no particular emotional significance in a spiritual world which, if it exists at all, will be as different from the spiritual world of, let us say, Robert Browning as that world is different from the world of Cato the Censor. 15

As for this present unhappy time, haunted by ghosts from a dead world and not yet at home in its own, its predicament is not, to return to the comparison with which we began, unlike the predicament of the adolescent who has not yet learned to orient himself without reference to the mythology amid which his childhood was passed. He still seeks in the world of his experience for the 20 values which he had found there, and he is aware only of a vast disharmony. But boys—most of them, at least—grow up, and the world of adult consciousness has always held a relation to myth intimate enough to make re-adjustment possible. The finest spirits have bridged the gulf, have carried over with them something of a child's faith, and only the coarsest have grown into something which was 25 no more than finished animality. Today the gulf is broader, the adjustment more difficult, than ever it was before, and even the possibility of an actual human maturity is problematic. There impends for the human spirit either extinction or a re-adjustment more stupendous than any made before.

Commonwealth Club Address
Franklin D. Roosevelt (1882–1945)
Governor of New York (1929–1932)

The only child of an aristocratic Hudson Valley family, Franklin D. Roosevelt began his political career as an anti-Tammany progressive Democrat in the New York legislature. Woodrow Wilson (r. 1913–1921) appointed him to be Assistant Secretary of the Navy just before World War One began, and he was the Democratic party's nominee for vice president in 1920. He was stricken with polio the following year. Undaunted, he won election as governor of New York in 1928.

Though FDR is usually depicted as a non-ideological "pragmatist" whose New Deal was a series of politically expedient compromises rather than a coherent program, in the Commonwealth Club address he laid out a discernible political agenda of what he called an "economic bill of rights."

Roosevelt shared the conviction of the progressives that twentieth-century American industrial society had outgrown its eighteenth-century Constitution, and their commitment to "change" and "progress" as the new political lodestars. He proposed an alliance between individuals and the central government to curb the power of financial "titans," similar to the way in which strong national governments in Europe broke the power of the aristocracy.

Roosevelt's speech suggests what came to be called the principle of "preferred freedoms"—the idea that property rights were separate from civil rights like free speech or voting, and more properly the objects of government regulation—indeed, that the "real" freedom of the many might depend on the curtailing of the economic freedom.

Assuming that the problem of production has been solved, and that only the problem of distribution remained, Roosevelt proposed to use government to provide for individuals that the economic system had not. Since monopoly capitalism had destroyed equality of opportunity, the countervailing power of the state was needed to secure some degree of equal outcomes in a welfare state or "safety net."

"Text of Governor Roosevelt's Speech at Commonwealth Club, San Francisco," *New York Times* 83 (24 September 1932):6.

*Once elected, FDR moved leftward. He faced challengers on the left, like
Huey Long (1893–1935) and Father Charles Coughlin (1891–1979), who
made stark proposals to redistribute income and wealth. The "second New
Deal"—seen in such provisions as social security, the National Labor Relations
Act, "soak-the-rich" taxes, and public utility divestment plans—responded
to these. Roosevelt aimed most of his rhetoric at his right-wing opponents,
however. The conflict came to a climax when the President proposed to "pack"
the Supreme Court in 1937. The congressional and public reaction to this
scheme effectively brought the New Deal to an end.*

23 September 1932

...I want to speak not of politics but of government. I want to speak not of parties but of universal principles. They are not political except in that larger sense
in which a great American once expressed a definition of politics—that nothing
in all of human life is foreign to the science of politics.

5   I do want to give you, however, a recollection of a long life spent, for a large
part, in public office. Some of my conclusions and observations have been deeply
accentuated in these past few weeks.

I have traveled far—from Albany to the Golden Gate. I have seen many
people, and heard many things, and today, when, in a sense, my journey has
10   reached the half-way mark, I am glad of the opportunity to discuss with you
what it all means to me.

Sometimes, my friends, particularly in years such as these, the hand of dis-
couragement falls upon us. It seems that things are in a rut, fixed, settled, that
the world has grown old and tired and very much out of joint. This is the mood
15   of depression, of dire and weary depression.

But then we look around us in America, and everything tells us that we are
wrong. America is new. It is in the process of change and development. It has the
great potentialities of youth, and particularly is this true of the great West and of
this coast and of California.

20   I would not have you feel that I regard this as in any sense a new community. I
have traveled in many parts of the world, but never have I felt the arresting thought
of the change and development more than here, where the old, mystic East would
seem to be near to us, where the currents of life and thought and commerce of the
whole world meet us. This factor alone is sufficient to cause man to stop and think
25   of the deeper meaning of things when he stands in this community.

But more than that, I appreciate that the membership of this club consists
of men who are thinking in terms beyond the immediate present, beyond their
own immediate tasks, beyond their own individual interests.

I want to invite you, therefore, to consider with me in the large some of the
30   relationships of government and economic life that go deeply into our daily lives,
our happiness, our future and our security.

The issue of government has always been whether individual men and women will have to serve some system of government or economics or whether a system of government and economics exists to serve individual men and women.

This question has persistently dominated the discussion of government for many generations. On questions relating to these things men have differed, and for time immemorial it is probable that honest men will continue to differ.

The final word belongs to no man; yet we can still believe in change and in progress. Democracy, as a dear old friend of mine in Indiana, Meredith Nicholson,[1] has called it, is a quest, a never-ending seeking for better things, and in the seeking for these things and the striving for them there are many roads to follow.

But if we map the course of these roads, we find that there are only two general directions.

When we look about us we are likely to forget how hard people have worked to win the privilege of government.

The growth of the national governments of Europe was a struggle for the development of a centralized force in the nation, strong enough to impose peace upon ruling barons. In many instances the victory of the central government, the creation of a strong central government, was a haven of refuge to the individual. The people preferred the master far away to the exploitation and cruelty of the smaller master near at hand.

But the creators of national government were perforce ruthless men. They were often cruel in their methods, but they did strive steadily toward something that society needed and very much wanted—a strong central State, able to keep the peace, to stamp out civil war, to put the unruly nobleman in his place and to permit the bulk of individuals to live safely.

The man of ruthless force had his place in developing a pioneer country, just as he did in fixing the power of the central government in the development of the nations. Society paid him well for his services and its development. When the development among the nations of Europe, however, had been completed, ambition and ruthlessness, having served its term, tended to overstep their mark.

There came a growing feeling that government was conducted for the benefit of a few who thrived unduly at the expense of all. The people sought a balancing—a limiting force. There came gradually, through town councils, trade guilds, national parliaments, by constitution and by popular participation and control, limitations on arbitrary power.

Another factor that tended to limit the power of those who ruled was the rise of the ethical conception that a ruler bore a responsibility for the welfare of his subjects.

[1]Meredith Nicholson (1866–1947), a prominent American writer and politician

The American colonies were born in this struggle. The American Revolution was a turning point in it. After the Revolution the struggle continued and shaped itself in the public life of the country.

There were those who, because they had seen the confusion which attended
5 the years of war for American independence, surrendered to the belief that popular government was essentially dangerous and essentially unworkable.

They were honest people, my friends, and we cannot deny that their experience had warranted some measure of fear.

The most brilliant, honest, and able exponent of this point of view was
10 Hamilton. He was too impatient of slow-moving methods.

Fundamentally he believed that the safety of the Republic lay in the autocratic strength of its government, that the destiny of individuals was to serve that government and that fundamentally a great and strong group of central institutions, guided by a small group of able and public-spirited citizens, could best direct all
15 government.

But Mr. Jefferson, in the Summer of 1776, after drafting the Declaration of Independence, turned his mind to the same problem and took a different view.

He did not deceive himself with outward forms. Government to him was a means to an end, not an end in itself; it might be either a refuge and a help or a
20 threat and a danger, depending on the circumstances.

We find him carefully analyzing the society for which he was to organize a government:

> We have no paupers—the great mass of our population is of laborers, our
> rich who cannot live without labor, either manual or professional, being
25 > few and of moderate wealth. Most of the laboring class possess property,
> cultivate their own lands, have families and from the demand for their
> labor are enabled to exact from the rich and the competent such prices
> as enable them to feed abundantly, clothe above mere decency, to labor
> moderately and raise their families.

30 These people, he considered, had two sets of rights, those of "personal competency" and those involved in acquiring and possessing property.

By "personal competency" he meant the right of free thinking, freedom of forming and expressing opinions and freedom of personal living, each man according to his own rights.

35 To ensure the first set of rights a government must so order its functions as not to interfere with the individual.

But even Jefferson realized that the exercise of property rights might so interfere with the rights of the individual that the government, without whose assistance the property rights could not exist, must intervene, not to destroy
40 individualism but to protect it.

You are familiar with the great political duel which followed; and how Hamilton and his friends, building toward a dominant centralized power, were at length defeated in the great election of 1800 by Mr. Jefferson's party. Out of that duel came the two parties, Republican and Democratic, as we know them today.

So began, in American political life, the new day, the day of the individual against the system, the day in which individualism was made the great watchword of American life.

The happiest of economic conditions made that day long and splendid. On the western frontier, land was substantially free. No one who did not shirk the task of earning a living was entirely without opportunity to do so. Depressions could, and did, come and go; but they could not alter the fundamental fact that most of the people lived partly by selling their labor and partly by extracting their livelihood from the soil, so that starvation and dislocation were practically impossible.

At the very worst there was always the possibility of climbing into a covered wagon and moving West, where the untilled prairies afforded a haven for men to whom the East did not provide a place.

So great were our natural resources that we could offer this relief not only to our own people, but to the distressed of all the world. We could invite immigration from Europe and welcome it with open arms.

Traditionally, when a depression came a new section of land was opened in the West. And even our temporary misfortune served our manifest destiny.

It was in the middle of the nineteenth century that a new force was released and a new dream created. The force was what is called the industrial revolution, the advance of steam and machinery and the rise of the forerunners of the modern industrial plant.

The dream was the dream of an economic machine, able to raise the standard of living for every one; to bring luxury within the reach of the humblest; to annihilate distance by steam power and later by electricity, and to release every one from the drudgery of the heaviest manual toil.

It was to be expected that this would necessarily affect government. Heretofore, government had merely been called upon to produce conditions within which people could live happily, labor peacefully, and rest secure. Now it was called upon to aid in the consummation of this new dream.

There was, however, a shadow over the dream. To be made real it required use of the talents of men of tremendous will and tremendous ambition, since by no other force could the problems of financing and engineering and new developments be brought to a consummation.

So manifest were the advantages of the machine age, however, that the United States fearlessly, cheerfully, and, I think, rightly accepted the bitter with the sweet.

It was thought that no price was too high to pay for the advantages which we could draw from a finished industrial system.

The history of the last half century is accordingly in large measure a history of a group of financial titans, whose methods were not scrutinized with too much
5   care and who were honored in proportion as they produced the results, irrespective of the means they used.

The financiers who pushed the railroads to the Pacific were always ruthless, often wasteful and frequently corrupt, but they did build railroads and we have them today. It has been estimated that the American investor paid the American
10   railway system more than three times over in the process, but despite this fact the net advantage was to the United States.

As long as we had free land, as long as population was growing by leaps and bounds, as long as our industrial plants were insufficient to supply our own needs, society chose to give the ambitious man free play and unlimited reward, provided
15   only that he produced the economic plant so much desired.

During this period of expansion there was equal opportunity for all and the business of government was not to interfere but to assist in the development of industry.

This was done at the request of businessmen themselves. The tariff was origi-
20   nally imposed for the purpose of "fostering our infant industry," a phrase I think the older among you will remember as a political issue not so long ago.

The railroads were subsidized, sometimes by grants of money, oftener by grants of land. Some of the most valuable oil lands in the United States were granted to assist the financing of the railroad which pushed through the Southwest.

25   A nascent merchant marine was assisted by grants of money, or by mail subsidies, so that our steam shipping might ply the seven seas.

Some of my friends tell me that they do not want the government in business. With this I agree, but I wonder whether they realize the implications of the past.

For while it has been American doctrine that the government must not go
30   into business in competition with private enterprises, still it has been traditional, particularly in Republican administrations, for business urgently to ask the government to put at private disposal all kinds of government assistance.

The same man who tells you that he does not want to see the government interfere in business—and he means it and has plenty of good reasons for saying
35   so—is the first to go to Washington and ask the government for a prohibitory tariff on his product.

When things get just bad enough—as they did two years ago—he will go with equal speed to the United States Government and ask for a loan. And the Reconstruction Finance Corporation is the outcome of it.

40   Each group has sought protection from the government for its own special interests without realizing that the function of government must be to favor no

small group at the expense of its duty to protect the rights of personal freedom and of private property of all its citizens.

In retrospect we can now see that the turn of the tide came with the turn of the century. We were reaching our last frontier; there was no more free land and our industrial combinations had become great uncontrolled and irresponsible 5 units of power within the State.

Clear-sighted men saw with fear the danger that opportunity would no longer be equal; that the growing corporation, like the feudal baron of old, might threaten the economic freedom of individuals to earn a living. In that hour, our anti-trust laws were born. 10

The cry was raised against the great corporations. Theodore Roosevelt, the first great Republican Progressive, fought a presidential campaign on the issue of "trust busting" and talked freely about malefactors of great wealth. If the government had a policy it was rather to turn the clock back, to destroy the large combinations and to return to the time when every man owned his individual small business. 15

This was impossible. Theodore Roosevelt, abandoning the idea of "trust busting," was forced to work out a difference between "good" trusts and "bad" trusts.

The Supreme Court set forth the famous "rule of reason" by which it seems to have meant that a concentration of industrial power was permissible if the method 20 by which it got its power, and the use it made of that power, was reasonable.

Woodrow Wilson, elected in 1912, saw the situation more clearly. Where Jefferson had feared the encroachment of political power on the lives of individuals, Wilson knew that the new power was financial. He saw, in the highly centralized economic system, the despot of the twentieth century, on whom great masses of 25 individuals relied for their safety and their livelihood, and whose irresponsibility and greed (if it were not controlled) would reduce them to starvation and penury.

The concentration of financial power had not proceeded as far in 1912 as it has today; but it had grown far enough for Mr. Wilson to realize fully its implications. 30

It is interesting, now, to read his speeches. What is called "radical" today (and I have reason to know whereof I speak) is mild compared to the campaign of Mr. Wilson. "No man can deny," he said,

> that the lines of endeavor have more and more narrowed and stiffened;
> no man who knows anything about the development of industry in this 35
> country can have failed to observe that the larger kinds of credit are
> more and more difficult to obtain unless you obtain them upon terms
> of uniting your efforts with those who already control the industry of
> the country, and nobody can fail to observe that every man who tries to
> set himself up in competition with any process of manufacture which 40
> has taken place under the control of large combinations of capital will

presently find himself either squeezed out or obliged to sell and allow himself to be absorbed.

Had there been no World War—had Mr. Wilson been able to devote eight years to domestic instead of to international affairs—we might have had a wholly
5   different situation at the present time.

However, the then distant roar of European cannon, growing ever louder, forced him to abandon the study of this issue.

The problem he saw so clearly is left with us as a legacy; and no one of us on either side of the political controversy can deny that it is a matter of grave
10   concern to the government.

A glance at the situation today only too clearly indicates that equality of opportunity as we have known it no longer exists. Our industrial plant is built. The problem just now is whether, under existing conditions, it is not overbuilt.

Our last frontier has long since been reached, and there is practically no more
15   free land. More than half of our people do not live on the farms or on lands and cannot derive a living by cultivating their own property.

There is no safety valve in the form of a Western prairie to which those thrown out of work by the Eastern economic machines can go for a new start. We are not able to invite the immigration from Europe to share our endless plenty. We are
20   now providing a drab living for our own people.

Our system of constantly rising tariffs has at last reacted against us to the point of closing our Canadian frontier on the north, our European markets on the east, many of our Latin-American markets to the south and a goodly proportion of our Pacific markets on the west through the retaliatory tariffs of those countries.
25   It has forced many of our great industrial institutions, who exported their surplus production to such countries, to establish plants in such countries, within the tariff walls.

This has resulted in the reduction of the operation of their American plants and opportunity for employment.
30   Just as freedom to farm has ceased, so also the opportunity in business has narrowed. It still is true that men can start small enterprises, trusting to native shrewdness and ability to keep abreast of competitors; but area after area has been pre-empted altogether by the great corporations, and even in the fields which still have no great concerns the small man starts under a handicap.
35   The unfeeling statistics of the past three decades show that the independent businessman is running a losing race. Perhaps he is forced to the wall; perhaps he cannot command credit; perhaps he is "squeezed out," in Mr. Wilson's words, by highly organized corporate competitors, as your corner grocery man can tell you.

Recently a careful study was made of the concentration of business in the
40   United States.

It showed that our economic life was dominated by some 600-odd corporations who controlled two-thirds of American industry. Ten million small businessmen divided the other third.

More striking still, it appeared that if the process of concentration goes on at the same rate, at the end of another century we shall have all American industry controlled by a dozen corporations, and run by perhaps a hundred men.

Put plainly, we are steering a steady course toward economic oligarchy, if we are not there already.

Clearly, all this calls for a re-appraisal of values.

A mere builder of more industrial plants, a creator of more railroad systems, an organizer of more corporations is as likely to be a danger as a help.

The day of the great promoter or the financial titan, to whom we granted everything if only he would build or develop is over. Our task now is not discovery or exploitation of natural resources or necessarily producing more goods.

It is the soberer, less dramatic business of administering resources and plants already in hand, of seeking to re-establish foreign markets for our surplus production, of meeting the problem of under-consumption, of adjusting production to consumption, of distributing wealth and products more equitably, of adapting existing economic organizations to the service of the people.

The day of enlightened administration has come.

Just as in older times the central government was first a haven of refuge, and then a threat, so now in a closer economic system the central and ambitious financial unit is no longer a servant of national desire but a danger. I would draw the parallel one step farther. We did not think because national government had become a threat in the eighteenth century that therefore we should abandon the principle of national government.

Nor today should we abandon the principle of strong economic units called corporations merely because their power is susceptible of easy abuse.

In other times we dealt with the problem of an unduly ambitious central government. So today we are modifying and controlling our economic units.

As I see it, the task of government in its relation to business is to assist the development of an economic declaration of rights, an economic constitutional order. This is the common task of statesman and businessman. It is the minimum requirement of a more permanently safe order of things.

Happily, the times indicate that to create such an order not only is the proper policy of government but it is the only line of safety for our economic structures as well.

We know, now, that these economic units cannot exist unless prosperity is uniform—that is, unless purchasing power is well distributed throughout every group in the nation.

That is why even the most selfish of corporations for its own interest would be glad to see wages restored and unemployment ended and to bring the Western farmer back to his accustomed level of prosperity and to assure a permanent safety to both groups.

That is why some enlightened industries themselves endeavor to limit the freedom of action of each man and business group within the industry in the common interest of all; why businessmen everywhere are asking a form of organization which will bring the scheme of things into balance, even though it may in some measure qualify the freedom of action of individual units within the business.

The exposition need not further be elaborated. It is brief and incomplete, but you will be able to expand it in terms of your own business or occupation without difficulty.

I think every one who has actually entered the economic struggle—which means every one who was not born to safe wealth—knows in his own experience and his own life that we have now to apply the earlier concepts of American government to the conditions today.

The Declaration of Independence discusses the problem of government in terms of a contract. Government is a relation of give and take—a contract, perforce, if we would follow the thinking out of which it grew.

Under such a contract rulers were accorded power, and the people consented to that power on consideration that they be accorded certain rights.

The task of statesmanship has always been the redefinition of these rights in terms of a changing and growing social order. New conditions impose new requirements upon government and those who conduct government.

I held, for example, in proceedings before me as governor, the purpose of which was the removal of the Sheriff of New York, that under modern conditions it was not enough for a public official merely to evade the legal terms of official wrongdoing. He owed a positive duty as well.

I said, in substance, that if he had acquired large sums of money, he was, when accused, required to explain the sources of such wealth. To that extent this wealth was colored with a public interest.

I said that public servants should, even beyond private citizens, in financial matters be held to a stern and uncompromising rectitude.

I feel that we are coming to a view, through the drift of our legislation and our public thinking in the past quarter century, that private economic power is, to enlarge an old phrase, a public trust as well.

I hold that continued enjoyment of that power by any individual or group must depend upon the fulfillment of that trust. The men who have reached the summit of American business life know this best; happily, many of these urge the binding quality of this greater social contract.

The terms of that contract are as old as the republic and as new as the new economic order.

Every man has a right to life and this means that he has also a right to make a comfortable living. He may by sloth or crime decline to exercise that right, but it may not be denied him. 5

We have no actual famine or dearth; our industrial and agricultural mechanism can produce enough and to spare.

Our government, formal and informal, political and economic, owes to everyone an avenue to possess himself of a portion of that plenty sufficient for his needs through his own work. 10

Every man has a right to his own property, which means a right to be assured to the fullest extent attainable, in the safety of his savings. By no other means can men carry the burdens of those parts of life which in the nature of things afford no chance of labor—childhood, sickness, old age. In all thought of property, this right is paramount; all other property rights must yield to it. 15

If, in accord with this principle, we must restrict the operations of the speculator, the manipulator, even the financier, I believe we must accept the restriction as needful not to hamper individualism but to protect it.

These two requirements must be satisfied, in the main, by the individuals who claim and hold control of the great industrial and financial combinations 20 which dominate so large a part of our industrial life. They have undertaken to be not businessmen but princes—princes of property.

I am not prepared to say that the system which produces them is wrong. I am very clear that they must fearlessly and competently assume the responsibility which go with the power. So many enlightened business men know this that 25 the statement would be little more than a platitude were it not for an added implication.

This implication is, briefly, that the responsible heads of finance and industry, instead of acting each for himself, must work together to achieve the common end. 30

They must, where necessary, sacrifice this or that private advantage, and in reciprocal self-denial must seek a general advantage. It is here that formal government—political government, if you choose—comes in.

Whenever in the pursuit of this objective the lone wolf, the unethical competitor, the reckless promoter, the Ishmael or Insull, whose hand is against every man's, 35 declines to join in achieving an end recognized as being for the public welfare, and threatens to drag the industry back to a state of anarchy, the government may properly be asked to apply restraint.

Likewise, should the group ever use its collective power contrary to the public welfare, the government must be swift to enter and protect the public interest. 40

The government should assume the function of economic regulation only as a last resort, to be tried only when private initiative, inspired by high responsibility, with such assistance and balance as government can give, has finally failed.

As yet there has been no final failure, because there has been no attempt; and I decline to assume that this nation is unable to meet the situation.

The final term of the high contract was for liberty and the pursuit of happiness.

We have learned a great deal of both in the past century. We know that individual liberty and individual happiness mean nothing unless both are ordered in the sense that one man's meat is not another man's poison.

We know that the old "rights of personal competency"—the right to read, to think, to speak, to choose, and live a mode of life—must be respected at all hazards.

We know that liberty to do anything which deprives others of those elemental rights is outside the protection of any compact, and that government in this regard is the maintenance of a balance within which every individual may have a place if he will take it, in which every individual may find safety if he wishes it, in which every individual may attain such power as his ability permits, consistent with his assuming the accompanying responsibility.

All this is a long, slow task. Nothing is more striking than the simple innocence of the men who insist, whenever an object is present, on the prompt production of a patent scheme guaranteed to produce a result.

Human endeavor is not so simple as that. Government includes the art of formulating a policy and using the political technique to attain so much of that policy as will receive general support; persuading, leading, sacrificing, teaching always, because the greatest duty of a statesman is to educate. But in the matters of which I have spoken, we are learning rapidly, in a severe school. The lessons so learned must not be forgotten, even in the mental lethargy of a speculative upturn. We must build toward the time when a major depression cannot occur again; and if this means sacrificing the easy profits of inflationist booms, then let them go; and good riddance.

Faith in America, faith in our tradition of personal responsibility, faith in our institutions, faith in ourselves demand that we recognize the new terms of the old social contract. We shall fulfill them, as we fulfilled the obligation of the apparent utopia which Jefferson imagined for us in 1776, and which Jefferson, Roosevelt, and Wilson sought to bring to realization. We must do so, lest a rising tide of misery, engendered by our common failure, engulf us all. But failure is not an American habit; and in the strength of great hope we must all shoulder our common load.

First Inaugural Address
Franklin D. Roosevelt (1882–1945)
President of the United States (1933–1945)

On 4 March 1933, Franklin Roosevelt took the oath of office as the 32nd president of the United States. The country was mired in the Great Depression, with 25 percent unemployment, and FDR addressed that crisis in his first inaugural address. Roosevelt had a soothing voice that sounded comforting and confident on the radio.

Herbert Hoover, Roosevelt's predecessor, had expanded the federal government through federal price supports for wheat and cotton farmers and subsidies to banks and railroads. He paid for these programs through increasing excise taxes (to six cents a pack on cigarettes, for example) and hiking the income tax on top incomes from 24 to 63 percent. During the presidential campaign of 1932, FDR denounced Hoover as heading "the most reckless and extravagant past that I have been able to discover in the statistical record of any peacetime government anywhere, any time." He pledged to cut "the cost of current federal government operations by 25 percent" if elected president.

4 March 1933

I am certain that my fellow Americans expect that on my induction into the Presidency I will address them with a candor and a decision which the present situation of our nation impels. This is pre-eminently the time to speak the truth, the whole truth, frankly and boldly. Nor need we shrink from honestly facing conditions in our country today. This great nation will endure as it has endured, 5 will revive and will prosper. So, first of all, let me assert my firm belief that the only thing we have to fear is fear itself—nameless, un-reasoning, un-justified terror which paralyzes needed efforts to convert retreat into advance. In every dark hour of our national life a leadership of frankness and vigor has met with that understanding and support of the people themselves which is essential to 10 victory. I am convinced that you will again give that support to leadership in these critical days.

Franklin D. Roosevelt Library, Papers as President, President's Personal File (1933–1945)

In such a spirit on my part and on yours we face our common difficulties. They concern, thank God, only material things. Values have shrunken to fantastic levels; taxes have risen; our ability to pay has fallen; government of all kinds is faced by serious curtailment of income; the means of exchange are frozen in the currents of trade; the withered leaves of industrial enterprise lie on every side; farmers find no markets for their produce; the savings of many years in thousands of families are gone.

More important, a host of unemployed citizens face the grim problem of existence, and an equally great number tell with little return. Only a foolish optimist can deny the dark realities of the moment.

Yet our distress comes from no failure of substance. We are stricken by no plague of locusts. Compared with the perils which our forefathers conquered because they believed and were not afraid, we have still much to be thankful for. Nature still offers her bounty and human efforts have multiplied it. Plenty is at our doorstep, but a generous use of it languishes in the very sight of the supply. Primarily this is because rulers of the exchange of mankind's goods have failed, through their own stubbornness and their own incompetence, have admitted their failure, and abdicated. Practices of the unscrupulous money changers stand indicted in the court of public opinion, rejected by the hearts and minds of men.

True they have tried, but their efforts have been cast in the pattern of an outworn tradition. Faced by failure of credit they have proposed only the lending of more money. Stripped of the lure of profit by which to induce our people to follow their false leadership, they have resorted to exhortations, pleading tearfully for restored confidence. They know only the rules of a generation of self-seekers. They have no vision, and when there is no vision the people perish.

The money changers have fled from their high seats in the temple of our civilization. We may now restore that temple to the ancient truths. The measure of the restoration lies in the extent to which we apply social values more noble than mere monetary profit.

Happiness lies not in the mere possession of money; it lies in the joy of achievement, in the thrill of creative effort. The joy and moral stimulation of work no longer must be forgotten in the mad chase of evanescent profits. These dark days will be worth all they cost us if they teach us that our true destiny is not to be ministered unto but to minister to ourselves and to our fellow men.

Recognition of the falsity of material wealth as the standard of success goes hand in hand with the abandonment of the false belief that public office and high political position are to be valued only by the standards of pride of place and personal profit; and there must be an end to a conduct in banking and in business which too often has given to a sacred trust the likeness of callous and selfish wrongdoing. Small wonder that confidence languishes, for it thrives only on honesty, on honor, on the sacredness of obligations, on faithful protection, on unselfish performance; without them it cannot live.

Restoration calls, however, not for changes in ethics alone. This nation asks for action, and action now. 5

Our greatest primary task is to put people to work. This is no unsolvable problem if we fact it wisely and courageously. It can be accomplished in part by direct recruiting by the Government itself, treating the task as we would treat the emergency of a war, but at the same time, through this employment, accomplishing greatly needed projects to stimulate and reorganize the use of 10 our natural resources.

Hand in hand with this we must frankly recognize the overbalance of population in our industrial centers and, by engaging on a national scale in a redistribution, endeavor to provide a better use of the land for those best fitted for the land. The task can be helped by definite efforts to raise the values of 15 agricultural products and with this the power to purchase the output of our cities. It can be helped by preventing realistically the tragedy of the growing loss through foreclosure of our small homes and our farms. It can be helped by insistence that the Federal, state, and local governments act forthwith on the demand that their cost be drastically reduced. It can be helped by the unifying 20 of relief activities which today are often scattered, uneconomical, and unequal. It can be helped by national planning for and supervision of all forms of trans- portation and of communications and other utilities which have a definitely public character. There are many ways in which it can be helped, but it can never be helped merely by talking about it. We must act and act quickly. 25

Finally, in our progress toward a resumption of work we require two safeguards against a return of the evils of the old order; there must be a strict supervision of all banking and credits and investments; there must be an end to speculation with other people's money, and there must be provision for an adequate but sound currency. 30

These are the lines of attack. I shall presently urge upon a new Congress, in special session, detailed measures for their fulfillment, and I shall seek the immediate assistance of the several states.

Through this program of action we address ourselves to putting our own national house in order and making income balance outgo. Our international 35 trade relations, though vastly important, are in point of time and necessity sec- ondary to the establishment of a sound national economy. I favor as a practical policy the putting of first things first. I shall spare no effort to restore world trade by international economic re-adjustment, but the emergency at home cannot wait on that accomplishment. 40

The basic thought that guides these specific means of national recovery is not narrowly nationalistic. It is the insistence, as a first consideration, upon the interdependence of the various elements in and parts of the United States—a recognition of the old and permanently important manifestation of the American spirit of the pioneer. It is the way to recovery. It is the immediate way. It is the strongest assurance that the recovery will endure.

In the field of world policy I would dedicate this nation to the policy of the good neighbor—the neighbor who resolutely respects himself and, because he does so, respects the rights of others—the neighbor who respects his obligations and respects the sanctity of his agreements in and with a world of neighbors.

If I read the temper of our people correctly, we now realize as we have never realized before our interdependence on each other; that we cannot merely take but we must give as well; that if we are to go forward, we must move as a trained and loyal army willing to sacrifice for the good of a common discipline, because without such discipline no progress is made, no leadership becomes effective. We are, I know, ready and willing to submit our lives and property to such discipline, because it makes possible a leadership which aims at a larger good. This I propose to offer, pledging that the larger purposes will bind upon us all as a sacred obligation with a unity of duty hitherto evoked only in time of armed strife.

With this pledge taken, I assume unhesitatingly the leadership of this great army of our people dedicated to a disciplined attack upon our common problems.

Action in this image and to this end is feasible under the form of government which we have inherited from our ancestors. Our Constitution is so simple and practical that it is possible always to meet extraordinary needs by changes in emphasis and arrangement without loss of essential form. That is why our constitutional system has proved itself the most superbly enduring political mechanism the modern world has produced. It has met every stress of vast expansion of territory, of foreign wars, of bitter internal strife, of world relations.

It is to be hoped that the normal balance of executive and legislative authority may be wholly adequate to meet the unprecedented task before us. But it may be that an unprecedented demand and need for undelayed action may call for temporary departure from that normal balance of public procedure.

I am prepared under my constitutional duty to recommend the measures that a stricken nation in the midst of a stricken world may require. These measures, or such other measures as the Congress may build out of its experience and wisdom, I shall seek, within my constitutional authority, to bring to speedy adoption.

But in the event that the Congress shall fail to take one of these two courses, and in the event that the national emergency is still critical, I shall not evade the clear course of duty that will then confront me. I shall ask the Congress for the one remaining instrument to meet the crisis—broad executive power to wage a war against the emergency, as great as the power that would be given to me   5
if we were in fact invaded by a foreign foe.

For the trust reposed in me I will return the courage and the devotion that befit the time. I can do no less.

We face the arduous days that lie before us in the warm courage of national unity; with the clear consciousness of seeking old and precious moral values;   10
with the clean satisfaction that comes from the stern performance of duty by old and young alike. We aim at the assurance of a rounded and permanent national life.

We do not distrust the future of essential democracy. The people of the United States have not failed. In their need they have registered a mandate that   15
they want direct, vigorous action. They have asked for discipline and direction under leadership. They have made me the present instrument of their wishes. In the spirit of the gift I take it.

In this dedication of a nation we humbly ask the blessing of God. May He protect each and every one of us. May He guide me in the days to come.   20

THE DOMINANT DOGMA
OF THE AGE
WALTER LIPPMANN (1889–1974)

A prolific popular journalist and political philosopher, Walter Lippmann begin his career on the left. He was a student of William James at Harvard, and joined the Socialist Club there. He worked for Lincoln Steffens and George Lum, the Socialist mayor of Schenectady, NY, and was recruited by Herbert Croly to write for the New Republic.

During World War I Lippmann served on a secret commission that advised President Wilson on international affairs and led to the formulation of his Fourteen Points. Lippmann turned against the Versailles Treaty, and helped its Senate opponents to defeat it. Lippmann supported Franklin D. Roosevelt in 1932, but then turned against the New Deal.

Though his political loyalties shifted, Lippmann maintained a consistent concern for individual freedom. In the selection below, he associated the New Deal with the statism and collectivism that seemed to define all the principal ideologies of the 1930s—liberalism as much as fascism and communism. Lippmann ended up supporting John F. Kennedy and Lyndon B. Johnson in the 1960s, but his opposition to the Vietnam War made him a bitter opponent of LBJ and a hero to the New Left.

1938

There will be some fundamental assumptions which adherents of all the various systems within the epoch unconsciously presuppose.... With these assumptions a certain limited number of types of philosophic systems are possible, and this group of systems constitutes the philosophy of the epoch.[1]

In the violent conflicts which now trouble the earth the active contenders believe that since the struggle is so deadly it must be that the issues which divide them are deep. I think they are mistaken. Because parties are bitterly opposed,

---

[1]Alfred North Whitehead, *Science and the Modern World* (Cambridge: Cambridge University Press, 1925), 69.

it does not necessarily follow that they have radically different purposes. The intensity of their antagonism is no measure of the divergence of their views. There has been many a ferocious quarrel among sectarians who worship the same god.

5   Although the partisans who are now fighting for the mastery of the modern world wear shirts of different colors, their weapons are drawn from the same armory, their doctrines are variations of the same theme, and they go forth to battle singing the same tune with slightly different words. Their weapons are the coercive direction of the life and labor of mankind. Their doctrine is that

10   disorder and misery can be overcome only by more and more compulsory organization. Their promise is that through the power of the state men can be made happy.

Throughout the world, in the name of progress, men who call themselves communists, socialists, fascists, nationalists, progressives, and even liberals, are

15   unanimous in holding that government with its instruments of coercion must, by commanding the people how they shall live, direct the course of civilization and fix the shape of things to come. They believe in what Mr. Stuart Chase accurately describes as "the overhead planning and control of economic activity."[2] This is the dogma which all the prevailing dogmas presuppose. This is the

20   mold in which are cast the thought and action of the epoch. No other approach to the regulation of human affairs is seriously considered, or is even conceived as possible. The recently enfranchised masses and the leaders of thought who supply their ideas are almost completely under the spell of this dogma. Only a handful here and there, groups without influence, isolated and disregarded

25   thinkers, continue to challenge it. For the premises of authoritarian collectivism have become the working beliefs, the self-evident assumptions, the unquestioned axioms, not only of all the revolutionary regimes, but of nearly every effort which lays claim to being enlightened, humane, and progressive.

So universal is the dominion of this dogma over the minds of contemporary

30   men that no one is taken seriously as a statesman or a theorist who does not come forward with proposals to magnify the power of public officials and to extend and multiply their intervention in human affairs. Unless he is authoritarian and collectivist, he is a mossback, a reactionary, at best an amiable eccentric swimming hopelessly against the tide. It is a strong tide. Though despotism is

35   no novelty in human affairs, it is probably true that at no time in twenty-five hundred years has any western government claimed for itself a jurisdiction over men's lives comparable with that which is officially attempted in the totalitarian states. No doubt there have been despotisms which were more cruel than those

---

[2]Stuart Chase, *The Economy of Abundance* (New York: Macmillan, 1934), 310.

of Russia, Italy, and Germany. There has been none which was more inclusive. In these ancient centres of civilization, several hundred millions of persons live under what is theoretically the absolute dominion of the dogma that public officials are their masters and that only under official orders may they live, work, and seek their salvation.   5

But it is even more significant that in other lands where men shrink from the ruthless policy of these regimes, it is commonly assumed that the movement of events must be in the same general direction. Nearly everywhere the mark of a progressive is that he relies at last upon the increased power of officials to improve the condition of men. Though the progressives prefer to move gradually   10 and with consideration, by persuading majorities to consent, the only instrument of progress in which they have faith is the coercive agency of government. They can, it would seem, imagine no alternative, nor can they remember how much of what they cherish as progressive has come by emancipation from political dominion, by the limitation of power, by the release of personal energy from   15 authority and collective coercion. For virtually all that now passes for progres- sivism in countries like England and the United States calls for the increasing ascendancy of the state: always the cry is for more officials with more power over more and more of the activities of men.

Yet the assumptions of this whole movement are not so self-evident as they   20 seem. They are, in fact, contrary to the assumptions bred in men by the whole long struggle to extricate conscience, intellect, labor, and personality from the bondage of prerogative, privilege, monopoly, authority. For more than two thousand years, since western men first began to think about the social order, the main preoccupation of political thinking has been to find a law which   25 would be superior to arbitrary power. Men have sought it in custom, in the dictates of reason, in religious revelation, endeavoring always to set up some check upon the exercise of force. This is the meaning of the long debate about Natural Law. This is the meaning of a thousand years of struggle to bring the sovereign under a constitution, to establish for the individual and for voluntary   30 associations of men rights which they can enforce against kings, barons, mag- nates, majorities, and mobs. This is the meaning of the struggle to separate the church from the state, to emancipate conscience, learning, the arts, education, and commerce from the inquisitor, the censor, the monopolist, the policeman, and the hangman.   35

Conceivably the lessons of this history no longer have a meaning for us. Conceivably there has come into the world during this generation some new element which makes it necessary for us to undo the work of emancipation, to retrace the steps men have taken to limit the power of rulers, which compels us to believe that the way of enlightenment in affairs is now to be found by   40

intensifying authority and enlarging its scope. But the burden of proof is upon those who reject the ecumenical tradition of the western world. It is for them to show that their cult of the Providential State is in truth the new revelation they think it is, and that it is not, as a few still believe, the gigantic heresy of
5   an apostate generation.

VIII
AMERICA SINCE
WORLD WAR II

Three salient developments characterized the United States after World War II: the continuation of the New Deal's concentration of power over the social and economic life of the nation in the federal government; the continuation of American involvement in global affairs; and the collapse of traditional moral (especially sexual) standards often characterized as "Victorian."

The New Deal was stalled by 1938, as the public and Congress reacted to President Roosevelt's (r. 1933–1945) attempt to "pack" the Supreme Court, "purge" the Democratic party, and unify control of the administrative state in the president's hands. FDR thus shifted his attention to world affairs, though the war itself (like World War I) had the effect of concentrating power in the central government. In his last annual message to Congress, Roosevelt called for an "economic Bill of Rights" that would guarantee Americans health care, education, housing, and other goods, marking the critical shift from a view of government as protecting the natural rights of individuals to one that provided "entitlements" for them. This mapped out the agenda for all of postwar "liberalism."

In the immediate postwar years, the Truman administration confirmed the New Deal-internationalist commitments of Roosevelt. Though Harry Truman (r. 1945–1953) was unable to advance the "economic Bill of Rights" agenda (which he called the "Fair Deal"), he did prevent the Republicans from rolling back much of it. Truman also made permanent America's postwar role in "containing" communism, through the European Recovery (Marshall) Plan, North Atlantic Treaty Organization (NATO), and especially—after the fall of China to communism in 1950—in committing U.S. troops to the Korean War. These commitments were largely confirmed when Republican Dwight D. Eisenhower (r. 1953–1961) won election in 1952. Eisenhower, like most liberal, east-coast ("Wall Street") Republicans, was committed to preserving the New Deal and internationalism, and helped defeat the more conservative, rural and small-town, Midwestern ("Main Street") wing of the party represented by Robert Taft ("Mr. Republican") (1889–1953) and Joseph McCarthy (1908–1957).

American society underwent a remarkable resurgence of family life in the postwar years—the "baby boom" of 75 million children born between 1946 and 1964. Along with this great demographic expansion (almost unique in the postwar urban-industrial world) went a tremendous expansion in suburbanization, automobiles, television, and especially a separate, independent "youth culture," most visible (or audible) in "rock-and-roll." The decade also saw significant dissent from artistic and intellectual types about the vapid, materialist, consumerist, homogenous "mass culture" of the period, from both left-wing radicals and right-wing traditionalist conservatives and libertarians.

The most important dissent came from black Americans, increasingly assertive of their rights after World War II. The "great migration" of blacks from southern farms into northern and western cities had begun during World War I and continued into the 1970s. Here they broke into industrial jobs, acquired better education, developed their own media and professional organizations, and were able to vote, becoming an important part of the New Deal Democratic coalition. World War II accelerated this process, and when blacks threatened a "March on Washington" in 1941, President Roosevelt issued an executive order prohibiting discrimination in defense employment. Perhaps most important of all, Hitler's racist regime made Americans reconsider the assumption of white supremacy. The Cold War, especially the United States' competition with the Soviets for the support of the colored "Third World," also contributed to changing race relations at home.

The Supreme Court became the leading institution in advancing the interests of blacks and other minority and dissident groups, most importantly in the 1954 decision of *Brown* v. *Board of Education*, which held that racial segregation in public education was unconstitutional. There was almost no desegregation in the decade after *Brown*, as southerners undertook a campaign of "massive resistance." President Eisenhower's use of federal troops to desegregate Central High School in Little Rock, Arkansas, in 1957 was quite atypical. Nevertheless, the Court acquired tremendous moral esteem from liberals. The concurrent Montgomery bus boycott brought Martin Luther King, Jr. (1929–1968) to the fore and led to more decisions against segregation in southern institutions.

Although Eisenhower had campaigned as an aggressive cold warrior (running-mate Richard Nixon [1913–1994]) mocked the Democrats as graduates of "Dean Acheson's cowardly college of communist containment") and promised to "roll back" communism, he actually defused the conflict. He relied on nuclear weapons as the basis for his containment strategy, mostly because they were cheaper than conventional forces. It is most likely that his threat to use nuclear weapons in Korea produced the July 1953 armistice there. He was aided by the 1953 death of Joseph Stalin (*r.* 1924–1953), and the commitment of his successor, Nikita Khrushchev (*r.* 1953–1964), to "peaceful co-existence" with the capitalist world. Eisenhower did not intervene in the 1953 East Berlin uprising or the 1956 Hungarian revolution (in which 30,000 Hungarians died), and he repudiated England and France in their effort to take back the Suez Canal from Egypt in 1956. Perhaps most important, he declined to save northern Vietnam for France in 1954. But in Eisenhower's second term the limits of his Cold War policy caused unrest. In 1957 the Soviets launched *Sputnik*, the first manmade satellite to orbit the earth. In 1959 Fidel Castro overthrew the government of Cuba, and an American U-2 spy plane was shot down over Russia, further embarrassing the administration. In the 1960 presidential election, Democrat John F. Kennedy (1917–1963) won (probably by electoral fraud in Illinois and Texas) a narrow victory over Nixon with a promise to "get the country moving again." JFK was the youngest man ever elected president, the first Roman Catholic, and he took advantage of the new medium of television.

Kennedy shifted America's Cold War policy back to the more aggressive stance that had gotten the U.S. into the Korean War and would get it into Vietnam: his inaugural address promised that the U.S. would "pay *any* price, bear *any* burden, support *any* friend, oppose *any* foe." He hoped to compete with the communists in Third World conflicts by developing a strategy of "flexible response," relying on the expertise of civilian "defense intellectuals" and technocrats like Secretary of Defense Robert McNamara (1916–2009). The administration was especially eager to prove itself after the debacle of attempting to invade Cuba in the April 1961 Bay of Pigs landing and after Kruschev walled off West Berlin later that year. In October 1962 the world was brought to the brink of nuclear war when the U.S. blockaded Cuba after it discovered a Russian attempt to place nuclear missiles there. Kennedy also began to increase the American military role in Vietnam, beyond the limits that Eisenhower had recognized.

Kennedy's domestic program, called the "New Frontier," involved modest expansions of New Deal social and economic programs as well as a significant tax cut to stimulate the economy—the top marginal tax rate was cut from 91 to 70 percent. But the most significant challenge that Kennedy faced was the growing militance of the Civil Rights movement, as black organizations engaged in various protest activities to bring about the end of segregation. In 1963, Martin Luther King, Jr. provoked a brutal southern white repression in Birmingham, awakening the northern public via television images of fire hoses and snarling dogs. Kennedy, heretofore reluctant to antagonize the southern base of the Democratic Party, now called for comprehensive national Civil Rights legislation, the culmination of the "Second Reconstruction." He was assassinated in November, in all probability by Lee Harvey Oswald (1939–1963), a communist angry over the president's tough Cold War and especially anti-Castro policies, acting alone.

Kennedy's successor, Lyndon B. Johnson (r. 1963–1969), intensified the liberalism of both Kennedy's domestic and foreign policies. Erstwhile master of the Senate and a southerner (Texan) himself, Johnson was able to force a strong Civil Rights Act through Congress in 1964 as a monument to his slain predecessor. The act (under Congress' power to regulate interstate commerce) outlawed segregation in all places of public accommodation. It cut off federal funding to any institution that discriminated on the basis of race. It forbade all private employers to discriminate on the basis of race or sex. (Employers who had federal contracts were already under orders to adopt "affirmative action" to recruit minority workers.) The following year, after more violent repression of civil rights marchers in Selma, Congress enacted the Voting Rights Act, establishing federal supervision of elections in the South. These acts went at least as far as fulfilling the intent of the framers of the Reconstruction amendments, and soon went further.

Johnson also oversaw a vast expansion of federal programs in what he called the "Great Society"—the fulfillment of the New Deal agenda. Perhaps the most important was Medicare and Medicaid, providing health insurance for the elderly and indigent. The Elementary and Secondary Education Act began to involve the federal government in schools for the first time, heretofore regarded as a quintessentially state and local affair. (The threat of losing these funds is what finally achieved school desegregation in the South.) One of the most significant but overlooked Great Society programs was the Immigration Reform Act, which did away with the race-biased national-origin quota system of the 1920s. It opened the door to many new, especially Asian and Latin American, immigrants, and through its family-unification provisions resulted in allowing tens of millions of new immigrants (many of them illegal) into the United States. This produced a radical demographic change. Just as the native-born baby boom abated, the U.S. was poised to become a majority non-white nation by the mid-21st century. Other Great Society programs continued into the 1970s, such as federal subsidies for the arts and humanities, workplace health and safety regulations, and environmental protections.

The Supreme Court under Chief Justice Earl Warren (1891–1974) also added to the impact of domestic liberalism in the 1960s. It did so primarily by applying the Bill of Rights (originally limiting only the federal government) to the states, overturning traditional state "police power" to regulate the safety, health, welfare, and morals of the people. The Court forced states to redraw their election districts to comply with a "one person, one vote" standard. It began to construct a "wall of separation" between church and state by outlawing prayer in public schools and many other expressions of religion in public life, using the "establishment" clause of the First Amendment to eclipse its "free exercise" clause. The Court struck down state laws on libel, obscenity, pornography, contraception, and, ultimately, abortion and sodomy. It extended the criminal procedure provisions of the Bill of Rights to the states, expanding the rights of criminal defendants. The Court, and the legal profession more generally, also liberalized the rules of civil lawsuits, making it easier for plaintiffs to sue businesses and state governments.

These decisions fed the rise of a sex and gender revolution in the United States. The development of the oral contraceptive pill in 1960 significantly enabled women to control reproduction and contributed to a further weakening of sexual mores that had been going on since at least the 1920s. Women began to work outside of the home in large numbers, divorce and illegitimacy rates increased, and the nuclear family eroded rapidly.

Johnson decisively expanded the Vietnam War, introducing large numbers of combat troops in 1965. The administration obtained Congress' approval in the Gulf of Tonkin Resolution (1964). While he would not take the steps necessary to win the war (fighting outside of South Vietnam, mostly for fear of Chinese intervention; calling up the national guard reserve; or raising taxes), Johnson was also determined not to lose the war. The result was an ugly war of attrition that ultimately took 58,000 American lives and tore the country apart. In the late 1960s, protest against the Vietnam war, combined with significant riots in black ghettoes and student radicalism on college campuses, as well as a significant spike in crime (the violent crime rate tripled between 1960 and 1980), reflected a "cultural revolution" in the United States.

This cultural war, and the political divisions that arose from it, were rooted in differing religious views—those of "progressives" versus those of the "orthodox." The progressives consisted of mainline Protestants, reformed Jews, many Roman Catholics who followed them, especially after the Vatican II council, as well as Americans who pursued eastern religious traditions, secular humanism, or materialism. Perhaps the most significant of all was the environmental or "green" view, a syncretistic variety of pantheism. Progressives favored radical individualism and personal autonomy, libertarian personal "choice" in all matters, especially sexual matters. They also expressed a "rights conscious" concern for blacks, ethnic minorities, women, the disabled, the young, the elderly, homosexuals, and animals. At the same time, they favored extensive government welfare and regulatory programs. This combination of moral license and economic statism has been called "dependent individualism," an inversion of the Victorian combination of moral self-control and economic liberty. In world affairs, progressives tended to pacifism and world government, and "blamed America first" for the world's problems.

The orthodox coalition consisted of evangelical Protestants, conservative Roman Catholics, and orthodox Jews—groups hostile to one another before the 1960s now saw that what they had in common (traditional Judeo-Christian morals) and defined them against the progressives was more important than their sectarian differences. The legalization of abortion in 1973 especially brought religious conservatives into political action. The orthodox tended to be advocates of American unilateralism in foreign affairs, and ardently anti-communist.

The orthodox were part of a broad, populist reaction against the control of American life by the "new class" of liberal elites. The new class tended to be urban, educated at prestigious universities and professional schools, and controlled the large national media organs (before cable television and the Internet, Americans relied on a few major print newspapers and network television), Hollywood and the arts world, higher education, philanthropic foundations, the mainline churches, and the federal government—particularly the unelected federal courts and bureaucracies. The new class had grown out of the political and economic realignment of the New Deal, depended on public funds, and were hostile to entrepreneurship, and imposed the progressive worldview on ordinary Americans—the white ethnic working class of industrial cities and evangelical whites in the South and West—on such matters as sex education in the schools, busing and other affirmative action programs to benefit blacks, gun control for the law-abiding, and coddling criminals.

Richard Nixon (r. 1969–1974) took advantage of this reaction against the liberal establishment, claiming to speak for the "silent majority." But Nixon was no conservative. The federal government expanded even more under him than under LBJ. Nixon imposed wage and price controls on the American economy, expanded affirmative action, and adopted a foreign policy (détente) that conceded the decline of American power in world affairs before a more aggressive Soviet Union. He was brought down by the Watergate scandal in 1974, and the remainder of the decade was marked by significant declines in American economic strength and world prestige. The domestic and foreign crises of the 1970s brought about a more significant challenge to the liberal establishment in the election of Ronald Reagan (r. 1981–1989) in 1980. While Reagan did not have much success in reducing the size or power of the federal government, he did oversee a significant tax cut and the beginning of a long-term improvement in the U.S. economy. Above all, Reagan revitalized the United States' Cold War policy, challenging the legitimacy of the Soviet Union, which he called an "evil empire." Along with the revival of British conservatism under Margaret Thatcher (r. 1979–1990) and Pope John Paul II's (r. 1978–2005) depiction of the cold war in spiritual terms, the Soviet Union began to lose its grip on its empire.

America First
Charles A. Lindbergh (1902–1974)

The great American foreign policy debate entered a decisive phase with the renewal of war in Europe in 1939. Popular sentiment clearly and overwhelmingly opposed American involvement in the war and was reflected in President Roosevelt's 1940 election campaign promise to American mothers that he would not send their sons into foreign wars. But a series of initiatives to Congress (Lend-Lease, Destroyers for Bases, peacetime conscription) seemed to opponents of intervention to indicate that FDR intended to so align the United States with the European allies as to make war inevitable. Their response was the America First Committee, whose most prominent spokesman was Charles Lindbergh.

Lindbergh was one of the country's great heroes. His solo flight across the Atlantic in 1927 in the Spirit of Saint Louis *made him better-known than perhaps any other single man in the Western world. He became a tireless advocate of air power and military preparedness, although the world knew him better in the 1930s for his stoic response to the tragic kidnapping and murder of his son. Lindbergh's leadership of America First gave it a special power and legitimacy; his speeches packed stadiums across the country. In response, the administration organized the Committee to Defend America by Aiding the Allies, encouraging the debate that ended only with the Japanese attack on Pearl Harbor.*

The following selection is from a speech given at Yankee Stadium. Lindbergh added a practical dimension to the historical and conservative arguments advanced by advocates of American independence since 1899: that a nation cannot fight a war for which it is not prepared and in which there is no compelling national interest.

Charles Lindbergh, "Address" (Chicago: America First Committee, 1941), 1–14.

23 April 1941

There are many viewpoints from which the issues of this war can be argued.
Some are primarily idealistic. Some are primarily practical. One should, I believe,
strive for a balance of both. But, since the subjects that can be covered in a single
5   address are limited, tonight I shall discuss the war from a viewpoint which is
primarily practical. It is not that I believe ideals are unimportant, even among
the realities of war; but if a nation is to survive in a hostile world, its ideals must
be backed by the hard logic of military practicability. If the outcome of war
depended upon ideals alone, this would be a different world than it is today.

10   I know I will be severely criticized by the interventionists in America when
I say we should not enter a war unless we have a reasonable chance of winning.
That, they will claim, is far too materialistic a viewpoint. They will advance
again the same arguments that were used to persuade France to declare war
against Germany in 1939. But I do not believe that our American ideals and our
15   way of life will gain through an unsuccessful war. And I know that the United
States is not prepared to wage war in Europe successfully at this time. We are
no better prepared today than France was when the interventionists in Europe
persuaded her to attack the Siegfried Line.

I have said before and I will say again that I believe it will be a tragedy
20   to the entire world if the British Empire collapses. That is one of the main
reasons why I opposed this war before it was declared and why I have constantly advocated a negotiated peace. I did not feel that England and France
had a reasonable chance of winning. France has now been defeated; and,
despite the propaganda and confusion of recent months, it is now obvious
25   that England is losing the war. I believe this is realized even by the British
government. But they have one last desperate plan remaining. They hope that
they may be able to persuade us to send another American Expeditionary
Force to Europe and to share with England militarily as well as financially
the fiasco of this war.

30   I do not blame England for this hope, or for asking for our assistance. But
we now know that she declared a war under circumstances which led to the
defeat of every nation that sided with her, from Poland to Greece. We know
that in the desperation of war England promised to all these nations armed
assistance that she could not send. We know that she misinformed them, as she
35   has misinformed us, concerning her state of preparation, her military strength,
and the progress of the war.

In time of war, truth is always replaced by propaganda. I do not believe
we should be too quick to criticize the actions of a belligerent nation. There
is always the question whether we, ourselves, would do better under similar
40   circumstances. But we in this country have a right to think of the welfare of

America first, just as the people in England thought first of their own country
when they encouraged the smaller nations of Europe to fight against hopeless
odds. When England asks us to enter this war, she is considering her own future
and that of her Empire. In making our reply, I believe we should consider the
future of the United States and that of the Western Hemisphere.   5

It is not only our right but it is our obligation as American citizens to look
at this war objectively and to weigh our chances for success if we should enter
it. I have attempted to do this, especially from the standpoint of aviation; and
I have been forced to the conclusion that we cannot win this war for England,
regardless of how much assistance we extend.   10

I ask you to look at the map of Europe today and see if you can suggest
any way in which we could win this war if we entered it. Suppose we had a
large army in America, trained and equipped. Where would we send it to fight?
The campaigns of the war show only too clearly how difficult it is to force a
landing, or to maintain an army, on a hostile coast. Suppose we took our Navy   15
from the Pacific and used it to convoy British shipping. That would not win
the war for England. It would, at best, permit her to exist under the constant
bombing of the German air fleet. Suppose we had an air force that we could
send to Europe. Where could it operate? Some of our squadrons might be
based in the British Isles, but it is physically impossible to base enough aircraft   20
in the British Isles alone to equal in strength the aircraft that can be based on
the continent of Europe.

I have asked these questions on the supposition that we had in existence
an army and an air force large enough and well enough equipped to send to
Europe; and that we would dare to remove our Navy from the Pacific. Even on   25
this basis, I do not see how we could invade the continent of Europe successfully
as long as all of that continent and most of Asia is under Axis domination. But
the fact is that none of these suppositions are correct. We have only a one-ocean
Navy. Our army is still untrained and inadequately equipped for foreign war.
Our air force is deplorably lacking in modern fighting planes.   30

When these facts are cited, the interventionists shout that we are defeatists,
that we are undermining the principles of Democracy, and that we are giving
comfort to Germany by talking about our military weakness. But everything
I mention here has been published in our newspapers and in the reports of
congressional hearings in Washington. Our military position is well known to   35
the governments of Europe and Asia. Why, then, should it not be brought to
the attention of our own people?

I say it is the interventionist in America, as it was in England and in
France, who gives comfort to the enemy. I say it is they who are undermining the principles of Democracy when they demand that we take a course to   40

which more than 80 percent of our citizens are opposed. I charge them with being the real defeatists, for their policy has led to the defeat of every country that followed their advice since this war began. There is no better way to give comfort to an enemy than to divide the people of a nation over the issue of
5   foreign war. There is no shorter road to defeat than by entering a war with inadequate preparation. Every nation that has adopted the interventionist policy of depending on some one else for its own defense has met with nothing but defeat and failure.

When history is written, the responsibility for the downfall of the democra-
10 cies of Europe will rest squarely upon the shoulders of the interventionists who led their nations into war, uninformed and unprepared. With their shouts of defeatism and their disdain of reality, they have already sent countless thousands of young men to death in Europe. From the campaign of Poland to that of Greece, their prophecies have been false and their policies have failed. Yet these
15 are the people who are calling us defeatists in America today. And they have led this country, too, to the verge of war.

There are many such interventionists in America, but there are more people among us of a different type. That is why you and I are assembled here tonight. There is a policy open to this nation that will lead to success—a policy that
20 leaves us free to follow our own way of life and to develop our own civiliza-tion. It is not a new and untried idea. It was advocated by Washington. It was incorporated in the Monroe Doctrine. Under its guidance the United States became the greatest nation in the world.

It is based upon the belief that the security of a nation lies in the strength
25 and character of its own people. It recommends the maintenance of armed forces sufficient to defend this hemisphere from attack by any combination of foreign powers. It demands faith in an independent American destiny. This is the policy of the America First Committee today. It is a policy not of isolation but of independence; not of defeat but of courage. It is a policy that led this
30 nation to success during the most trying years of our history, and it is a policy that will lead us to success again.

We have weakened ourselves for many months, and, still worse, we have divided our own people by this dabbling in Europe's wars. While we should have been concentrating on American defense we have been forced to argue
35 over foreign quarrels. We must turn our eyes and our faith back to our own country before it is too late. And when we do this a different vista opens before us. Practically every difficulty we would face in invading Europe becomes an asset to us in defending America. Our enemy, and not we, would then have the problem of transporting millions of troops across the ocean and landing them
40 on a hostile shore. They, and not we, would have to furnish the convoys to

transport guns and trucks and munitions and fuel across 3,000 miles of water. Our battleships and submarines would then be fighting close to their home bases. We would then do the bombing from the air and the torpedoing at sea. And if any part of an enemy convoy should ever pass our Navy and our air force, they would still be faced with the guns of our coast artillery, and behind them, the divisions of our Army.

The United States is better situated from a military standpoint than any other nation in the world. Even in our present condition of unpreparedness no foreign power is in a position to invade us today. If we concentrate on our own defenses, and build the strength that this nation should maintain, no foreign army will ever attempt to land on American shores.

War is not inevitable for this country. Such a claim is defeatism in the true sense. No one can make us fight abroad unless we ourselves are willing to do so. No one will attempt to fight us here if we arm ourselves as a great nation should be armed. Over 100 million people in this nation are opposed to entering the war. If the principles of democracy mean anything at all, that is reason enough for us to stay out. If we are forced into a war against the wishes of an overwhelming majority of our people, we will have proved democracy such a failure at home that there will be little use fighting for it abroad.

The time has come when those of us who believe in an independent American destiny must band together and organize for strength. We have been led toward war by a minority of our people. This minority has power. It has influence. It has a loud voice. But it does not represent the American people.

During the last several years I have travelled over this country from one end to the other. I have talked to many hundreds of men and women, and I have had letters from tens of thousands more who feel the same way as you and I. Most of these people have no influence or power. Most of them have no means of expressing their convictions except by their vote, which has always been against this war. They are the citizens who have had to work too hard at their daily jobs to organize political meetings. Hitherto, they have relied upon their vote to express their feelings; but now they find that it is hardly remembered except in the oratory of a political campaign.

These people, the majority of hard-working American citizens, are with us. They are the true strength of our country. And they are beginning to realize, as you and I, that there are times when we must sacrifice our normal interests in life in order to insure the safety and the welfare of our nation.

Such a time has come. Such a crisis is here. That is why the America First Committee has been formed—to give voice to the people who have no newspaper, or newsreel, or radio station at their command; to the people who must do the paying and the fighting and the dying if this country enters the war.

Whether or not we do enter the war rests upon the shoulders of you in this audience; upon us here on this platform; upon meetings of this kind that are being held by Americans in every section of the United States today. It depends upon the action we take and the courage we show at this time. If you believe

5   in an independent destiny for America, if you believe that this country should not enter the war in Europe, we ask you to join the America First Committee in its stand. We ask you to share our faith in the ability of this nation to defend itself, to develop its own civilization, and to contribute to the progress of mankind in a more constructive and intelligent way than has yet been found

10   by the warring nations of Europe. We need your support, and we need it now. The time to act is here.

STATE OF THE UNION ADDRESS
FRANKLIN D. ROOSEVELT (1882–1945)
PRESIDENT OF THE UNITED STATES (1933–1945)

6 JANUARY 1942

In fulfilling my duty to report upon the state of the Union, I am proud to say to you that the spirit of the American people was never higher than it is today—the Union was never more closely knit together—this country was never more deeply determined to face the solemn tasks before it. The response of the American people has been instantaneous, and it will be sustained until our security is assured. 5

Exactly one year ago today I said to this Congress: "When the dictators are ready to make war upon us, they will not wait for an act of war on our part.... They—not we—will choose the time and the place and the method of their attack." 10

We now know their choice of the time: a peaceful Sunday morning—December 7th, 1941. We know their choice of the place: an outpost—an American outpost in the Pacific. We know their choice of the method: the method of Hitler himself.

Japan's scheme of conquest goes back half a century. It was not merely a 15 policy of seeking living room: it was a plan which included the subjugation of all the peoples in the Far East and in the islands of the Pacific, and the domination of that ocean by Japanese military and naval control of the western coasts of North, Central, and South America.

The development of this ambitious conspiracy was marked by the war 20 against China in 1894; the subsequent occupation of Korea; the war against Russia in 1904; the illegal fortification of the mandated Pacific islands following 1920; the seizure of Manchuria in 1931; and the invasion of China in 1937.

A similar policy of criminal conquest was adopted by Italy. The Fascists first revealed their imperial designs in Libya and Tripoli. In 1935 they seized 25 Abyssinia. Their goal was the domination of all North Africa, Egypt, parts of France, and the entire Mediterranean world.

Franklin D. Roosevelt Library, President's Master Speech File, Box 65, Folder 1490.

But the dreams of empire of the Japanese and Fascist leaders were modest in comparison with the gargantuan aspirations of Hitler and his Nazis. Even before they came to power in 1933, their plans for that conquest had been drawn. Those plans provided for ultimate domination, not of any one section

5   of the world but of the whole earth and all the oceans on it.

When Hitler organized his Berlin-Rome-Tokyo alliance, all these plans of conquest became a single plan. Under this, in addition to her own schemes of conquest, Japan's role was obviously to cut off our supply of weapons of war to Britain, and Russia and China—weapons which increasingly were speeding

10 the day of Hitler's doom. The act of Japan at Pearl Harbor was intended to stun us—to terrify us to such an extent that we would divert our industrial and military strength to the Pacific area, or even to our own continental defense.

The plan has failed in its purpose. We have not been stunned. We have not been terrified or confused. This very reassembling of the Seventy-Seventh

15 Congress today is proof of that; for the mood of quiet, grim resolution which here prevails bodes ill for those who conspired and collaborated to murder world peace. That mood is stronger than any mere desire for revenge. It expresses the will of the American people to make very certain that the world will never so suffer again.

20 Admittedly, we have been faced with hard choices. It was bitter, for example, not to be able to relieve the heroic and historic defenders of Wake Island. It was bitter for us not to be able to land a million men in a thousand ships in the Philippine Islands.

But this adds only to our determination to see to it that the Stars and Stripes

25 will fly again over Wake and Guam. Yes, see to it that the brave people of the Philippines will be rid of Japanese imperialism; and will live in freedom, and security and independence.

Powerful and offensive actions must and will be taken in proper time. The consolidation of the United Nations' total war effort against our com-

30 mon enemies is being achieved. That was and is the purpose of conferences which have been held during the past two weeks in Washington, and Moscow and Chungking. That is the primary objective of the declaration of solidarity signed in Washington on January 1, 1942 by twenty-six nations against the Axis powers.

35 Difficult choices may have to be made in the months to come. We do not shrink from such decisions. We and those united with us will make those decisions with courage and determination.

Plans have been laid here and in the other capitals for coordinated and co-operative action by all the United Nations—military action and economic

40 action. Already we have established, as you know, unified command of land,

sea, and air forces in the southwestern Pacific theatre of war. There will be a continuation of conferences and consultations among military staffs, so that the plans and operations of each will fit into the general strategy designed to crush the enemy. We shall not fight isolated wars—each nation going its own way. These twenty-six nations are united—not in spirit and determination alone,   5 but in the broad conduct of the war in all its phases.

For the first time since the Japanese and the Fascists and the Nazis started along their blood-stained course of conquest they now face the fact that superior forces are assembling against them. Gone forever are the days when the aggressors could attack and destroy them without unity of resistance. We of   10 the United Nations will so dispose our forces that we can strike at the common enemy wherever the greatest damage can be done him.

The militarists of Berlin and Tokyo started this war. But the massed, angered forces of common humanity will finish it.

Destruction of the material and spiritual centers of civilization—this has   15 been and still is the purpose of Hitler and his Italian and Japanese chessmen. They would wreck the power of the British Commonwealth and of Russia and of China and of the Netherlands—and then combine all their forces to achieve their ultimate goal, the conquest of the United States.

They know that victory for us means victory for freedom. They know that   20 victory for us means victory for the institution of democracy—the ideal of the family, the simple principles of common decency and humanity. They know that victory for us means victory for religion.

And they could not tolerate that. The world is too small to provide adequate "living room" for both Hitler and God. In proof of that, the Nazis have now   25 announced their plan for enforcing their new German, pagan religion all over the world—a plan by which the Holy Bible and the Cross of Mercy would be displaced by *Mein Kampf* and the Swastika and the naked sword.

Our own objectives are clear; the objective of smashing the militarism imposed by war lords upon their enslaved peoples—the objective of liberating   30 the subjugated nations—the objective of establishing and securing freedom of speech, freedom of religion, freedom from want, and freedom from fear everywhere in the world.

We shall not stop short of these objectives—nor shall we be satisfied merely to gain them and then call it a day. I know that I speak for the American peo-   35 ple—and I have good reason to believe that I speak also for all the other peoples who fight with us—when I say that this time we are determined not only to win the war, but also to maintain the security of the peace that will follow.

But we know that modern methods of warfare make it a task, not only of shooting and fighting, but an even more urgent one of working and produc-   40

ing. Victory requires the actual weapons of war and the means of transporting them to a dozen points of combat. It will not be sufficient for us and the other United Nations to produce a slightly superior supply of munitions to that of Germany, and Japan, and Italy and the stolen industries in the countries which
5   they have overrun.

The superiority of the United Nations in munitions and ships must be overwhelming—so overwhelming that the Axis nations can never hope to catch up with it. And so, in order to attain this overwhelming superiority the United States must build planes and tanks and guns and ships to the utmost limit of
10   our national capacity. We have the ability and capacity to produce arms not only for our own forces, but also for the armies, navies, and air forces fighting on our side.

And our overwhelming superiority of armament must be adequate to put weapons of war at the proper time into the hands of those men in the conquered
15   nations, who stand ready to seize the first opportunity to revolt against their German and Japanese oppressors, and against the traitors in their own ranks, known by the already infamous name of "Quislings."[1] And I think that it is a fair prophesy to say that as we get guns to the patriots in those lands, they too will fire shots heard "'round the world.'"

20   This production of ours in the United States must be raised far above present levels, even though it will mean the dislocation of the lives and occupations of millions of our own people. We must raise our sights all along the production line. Let no man say it cannot be done. It must be done—and we have undertaken to do it. I have just sent a letter of directive to the appropriate departments
25   and agencies of our government, ordering that immediate steps be taken:

First, to increase our production rate of airplanes so rapidly that in this year, 1942, we shall produce 60,000 planes—10,000, by the way, more than the goal that we set a year and a half ago. This includes 45,000 combat planes—bombers, dive-bombers, pursuit planes. The rate of increase will be maintained and
30   continued so that next year, 1943, we shall produce 125,000 airplanes, including 100,000 combat planes.

Second, to increase our production rate of tanks so rapidly that in this year, 1942, we shall produce 45,000 tanks—and to continue that increase so that next year, 1943, we shall produce 75,000 tanks.

35   Third, to increase our production rate of anti-aircraft guns so rapidly that in this year, 1942, we shall produce 20,000 of them; and to continue that increase so that next year, 1943, we shall produce 35,000 anti-aircraft guns.

---

[1]Vidkun Quisling (1887–1945), leader of Norway's Fascist Party, was appointed Minister-President of Norway by Hitler after his 1940 conquest of that nation.

And fourth, to increase our production rate of merchant ships so rapidly that in this year, 1942, we shall build 6,000,000 deadweight tons as compared with a 1941 completed production of 1,100,000. And finally, we shall continue that increase so that next year, 1943, we shall build 10,000,000 tons of shipping.

These figures and similar figures for a multitude of other implements of war   5
will give the Japanese and the Nazis a little idea of just what they accomplished in the attack at Pearl Harbor. And I rather hope that all these figures which I have given will become common knowledge in Germany and Japan.

Our task is hard—our task is unprecedented—and the time is short. We must strain every existing armament-producing facility to the utmost. We must   10
convert every available plant and tool to war production. That goes all the way from the greatest plants to the smallest—from the huge automobile industry to the village machine shop.

Production for war is based on men and women—the human hands and brains which collectively we call Labor. Our workers stand ready to work long   15
hours; to turn out more in a day's work; to keep the wheels turning and the fires burning twenty-four hours a day, and seven days a week. They realize well that on the speed and efficiency of their work depend the lives of their sons and their brothers and the fighting fronts.

Production for war is based on metals and raw materials—steel, copper,   20
rubber, aluminum, zinc, tin. Greater and greater quantities of them will have to be diverted to war purposes. Civilian use of them will have to be cut further and still further—and, in many cases, completely eliminated.

War costs money. So far, we have hardly even begun to pay for it. We have devoted only 15 percent of our national income to national defense. As will   25
appear in my Budget Message tomorrow, our war program for the coming fiscal year will cost fifty-six billion dollars or, in other words, more than half of the estimated annual national income. That means taxes and bonds and bonds and taxes. It means cutting luxuries and other non-essentials. In a word, it means an "all-out" war by individual effort and family effort in a united country.   30

Only this all-out scale of production will hasten the ultimate all-out victory. Speed will count. Lost ground can always be regained—lost time never. Speed will save lives; speed will save this nation which is in peril; speed will save our freedom and our civilization—and slowness, well it has never been an American characteristic.   35

As the United States goes into its full stride, we must always be on guard, on guard against misconceptions which will arise, some of them naturally, or which will be planted among us by our enemies.

We must guard against complacency. We must not underrate the enemy. He is powerful and cunning—and cruel and ruthless. He will stop at nothing that   40

gives him a chance to kill and to destroy. He has trained his people to believe that their highest perfection is achieved by waging war. For many years he has prepared for this very conflict—planning, and plotting, and training, arming, and fighting. We have already tested defeat. We may suffer further setbacks. We
5   must face the fact of a hard war, a long war, a bloody war, a costly war.

We must, on the other hand, guard against defeatism. That has been one of the chief weapons of Hitler's propaganda machine—used time and again with deadly results. It will not be used successfully on the American people.

We must guard against divisions among ourselves and among all the other
10 United Nations. We must be particularly vigilant against racial discrimination in any of its ugly forms. Hitler will try again to breed mistrust and suspicion between one individual and another, one group and another, one race and another, one government and another. He will try to use the same technique of falsehood and rumor-mongering with which he divided France from Britain.
15 He is trying to do this even now. But he will find a unity, a unity of will and purpose against him, which will persevere until the destruction of all his black designs upon the freedom and people of the world are ended.

We cannot wage this war in a defensive spirit. As our power and our resources are fully mobilized, we shall carry the attack against the enemy—we
20 shall hit him and hit him again wherever and whenever we can reach him. We must keep him far from our shores, for we intend to bring this battle to him on his own home grounds. American armed forces must be used at any place in all the world where it seems advisable to engage the forces of the enemy. In some cases these operations will be defensive, in order to protect key positions. In
25 other causes, these operations will be offensive, in order to strike at the common enemy, with a view to his complete encirclement and eventual total defeat.

American armed forces will operate at many points in the Far East. American armed forces will be on all the oceans—helping to guard the essential communications which are vital to the United Nations. American land and air and
30 sea forces will take stations in the British Isles—which constitute an essential fortress in this great world struggle. American armed forces will help to protect this hemisphere—and also help to protect bases outside this hemisphere, which could be used for an attack on the Americas.

If any of our enemies, from Europe or from Asia, attempt long-range
35 raids by "suicide" squadrons of bombing planes, they will do so only in the hope of terrorizing our people and disrupting our morale. Our people are not afraid of that. We know that we may have to pay a heavy price for freedom. We will pay this price with a will. Whatever the price, it is a thousand times worth it. No matter what our enemies, in their desperation may attempt to do
40 to us—we will say, as the people of London have said, "We can take it." And

what's more—what's more we can give it back—and we will give it back—with compound interest.

When our enemies challenged our country to stand up and fight, they challenged each and every one of us. And each and every one of us has accepted the challenge—for himself and for his nation. 5

There were only some four hundred United States Marines who in the heroic and historic defense of Wake Island inflicted such great losses on the enemy.[2] Some of those men were killed in action; and others are now prisoners of war. When the survivors of that great fight are liberated and restored to their homes, they will learn that a hundred and thirty million of their fellow citizens 10 have been inspired to render their own full share of service and sacrifice. We can well say that our men on the fighting fronts have already proved that Americans today are just as rugged and just as tough as any of the heroes whose exploits we celebrate on the Fourth of July.

Many people ask, "When will this war end"? There is only one answer to 15 that. It will end just as soon as we make it end, by our combined efforts, our combined strength, our combined determination to fight through and work through until the end—the end of militarism in Germany and Italy and Japan. Most certainly we shall not settle for less.

That is the spirit in which discussions have been conducted during the 20 visit of the British Prime Minister to Washington. Mr. Churchill and I understand each other, our motives and our purposes. Together, during the past two weeks, we have faced squarely the major military and economic problems of this greatest world war.

All in our nation have been cheered by Mr. Churchill's visit. We have been 25 deeply stirred by his great message to us. He is welcome in our midst, and we unite in wishing him a safe return to his home. For we are fighting on the same side with the British people, who fought alone for long, terrible months, and withstood the enemy with fortitude and tenacity and skill. We are fighting on the same side with the Russian people who have seen the Nazi hordes swarm 30 up to the very gates of Moscow, and who with almost superhuman will and courage have forced the invaders back into retreat. We are fighting on the same side as the brave people of China—those millions who for four and a half long years have withstood bombs and starvation and have whipped the invaders time and again in spite of the superior Japanese equipment and arms. Yes, we 35 are fighting on the same side as the indomitable Dutch. We are fighting on the

---

[2]In December 1941, the 449-man U.S. garrison on Wake Island withstood a fifteen-day siege by the Japanese before surrendering. The garrison lost 50 men while inflicting more than 2,000 casualties and sinking two Japanese destroyers.

same side as all the other governments in exile, whom Hitler and all his armies
and all his Gestapo have not been able to conquer.

But we of the United Nations are not making all this sacrifice of human
effort and human lives to return to the kind of world we had after the last world
5   war. We are fighting today for security, for progress and for peace, not only for
ourselves, but for all men, not only for one generation but for all generations.
We are fighting to cleanse the world of ancient evils, ancient ills.

Our enemies are guided by brutal cynicism, by unholy contempt for the
human race. We are inspired by a faith that goes back through all the years to
10 the first chapter of the Book of Genesis: "God created man in His own image."
We on our side are striving to be true to that divine heritage. We are fighting,
as our fathers have fought, to uphold the doctrine that all men are equal in the
sight of God. Those on the other side are striving to destroy this deep belief
and to create a world in their own image—a world of tyranny and cruelty and
15 serfdom.

That is the conflict that day and night now pervades our lives. No compromise can end that conflict. There never has been—there never can be—successful
compromise between good and evil. Only—only total victory can reward the
champion of tolerance, and decency, and freedom, and faith.

STATE OF THE UNION ADDRESS
FRANKLIN D. ROOSEVELT (1882–1945)
PRESIDENT OF THE UNITED STATES (1933–1945)

By January 1944, President Roosevelt saw clearly that the United States and its allies were going to defeat the Germans in World War II. Therefore, in this State of the Union address that year, Roosevelt began to plan for a new world order and a new American economic order after the war. Notice, for example, that he promoted "economic security, social security, moral security—in a family of nations."

Toward the end of the address, Roosevelt raised important and powerful questions about rights and obligations.

11 JANUARY 1944

This Nation in the past two years has become an active partner in the world's greatest war against human slavery.

We have joined with like-minded people in order to defend ourselves in a world that has been gravely threatened with gangster rule....

It is our duty now to begin to lay the plans and determine the strategy 5
for the winning of a lasting peace and the establishment of an American standard of living higher than ever before known. We cannot be content, no matter how high that general standard of living may be, if some fraction of our people—whether it be one-third or one-fifth or one-tenth—is ill-fed, ill-clothed, ill-housed, and insecure. 10

This Republic had its beginning, and grew to its present strength, under the protection of certain inalienable political rights—among them the right of free speech, free press, free worship, trial by jury, freedom from unreasonable searches and seizures. They were our rights to life and liberty.

As our Nation has grown in size and stature, however—as our industrial 15
economy expanded—these political rights proved inadequate to assure us equality in the pursuit of happiness.

Samuel Rosenman, ed., *The Public Papers and Addresses of Franklin D. Roosevelt* (New York: Harper, 1950), XIII:40–42.

We have come to a clear realization of the fact that true individual freedom cannot exist without economic security and independence. "Necessitous men are not free men." People who are hungry and out of a job are the stuff of which dictatorships are made.

5 In our day these economic truths have become accepted as self-evident. We have accepted, so to speak, a second Bill of Rights under which a new basis of security and prosperity can be established for all regardless of station, race, or creed.

Among these are:

10 • The right to a useful and remunerative job in the industries or shops or farms or mines of the Nation.

• The right to earn enough to provide adequate food and clothing and recreation;

• The right of every farmer to raise and sell his products at a return which
15 will give him and his family a decent living;

• The right of every businessman, large and small, to trade in an atmosphere of freedom from unfair competition and domination by monopolies at home or abroad;

• The right of every family to a decent home;

20 • The right to adequate medical care and the opportunity to achieve and enjoy good health;

• The right to adequate protection from the economic fears of old age, sickness, accident, and unemployment;

• The right to a good education.

25 All of these rights spell security. And after this war is won we must be prepared to move forward, in the implementation of these rights, to new goals of human happiness and well-being.

America's own rightful place in the world depends in large part upon how fully these and similar rights have been carried into practice for our citizens. For
30 unless there is security here at home there cannot be lasting peace in the world.

One of the great American industrialists of our day—a man who has rendered yeoman service to his country in this crisis—recently emphasized the grave dangers of "rightist reaction" in this Nation. All clear-thinking businessmen share his concern. Indeed, if such reaction should develop—if history were to repeat
35 itself and we were to return to the so-called "normalcy" of the 1920's—then it is certain that even though we shall have conquered our enemies on the battlefields abroad, we shall have yielded to the spirit of Fascism here at home.

I ask the Congress to explore the means for implementing this economic bill of rights—for it is definitely the responsibility of the Congress so to do.

Many of these problems are already before committees of the Congress in the form of proposed legislation. I shall from time to time communicate with the Congress with respect to these and further proposals. In the event that no adequate program of progress is evolved, I am certain that the Nation will be conscious of the fact.

Our fighting men abroad—and their families at home—expect such a program and have the right to insist upon it. It is to their demands that this Government should pay heed rather than to the whining demands of selfish pressure groups who seek to feather their nests while young Americans are dying....

Each and every one of us has a solemn obligation under God to serve this Nation in its most critical hour—to keep this Nation great—to make this Nation greater in a better world.

The Truman Doctrine
Harry S. Truman (1884–1972)
President of the United States (1945–1953)

The "Truman Doctrine" emerged from a speech President Harry S. Truman delivered to the Congress and a nationwide radio audience on March 12, 1947. World War II had ended less than two years earlier, and parts of the world were still engulfed in turmoil. One troubled spot was Greece, where a civil war had been underway between Communist and anti-Communist elements from the moment that the Germans had been driven out. Great Britain had been financing the pro-Western side since 1945, but early in 1947 Foreign Secretary Ernest Bevin informed the Americans that his country could no longer afford such assistance. The prospect was that if the Americans declined to move into the breach, the pro-Communist elements in Greece would likely prevail, thus endangering the survival of freedom in neighboring Turkey as well.

Ostensibly, President Truman was seeking legislative approval of $400 million in assistance for Greece and Turkey to help them maintain their resistance against Communism. As his hearers quickly grasped, however, he was seeking support for a much broader principle as well. Truman won approval of the aid package two months later, and in so doing established a new, comprehensive strategy for post-World War II American foreign policy. One historian has observed that a single sentence of the speech "defined American foreign policy for the next twenty years." It might just as well have been said that Truman, in March 1947, articulated a new understanding of America's duty in foreign affairs for the duration of the Cold War. Undeniably, this speech heralded a more assertive posture for the United States on the world stage than at any earlier time in its history.

12 March 1947

The gravity of the situation which confronts the world today necessitates my appearance before a joint session of the Congress. The foreign policy and the national security of this country are involved.

Harry S. Truman, "Recommendations for Assistance to Greece and Turkey," House of Representatives, 80th Congress, First Session, Document 171 (12 March 1947).

One aspect of the present situation, which I wish to present to you at this time for your consideration and decision, concerns Greece and Turkey.

The United States has received from the Greek Government an urgent appeal for financial and economic assistance. Preliminary reports from the
5   American Economic Mission now in Greece and reports from the American Ambassador in Greece corroborate the statement of the Greek Government that assistance is imperative if Greece is to survive as a free nation....

The British Government has informed us that, owing to its own difficulties can no longer extend financial or economic aid to Turkey. As in the case
10 of Greece, if Turkey is to have the assistance it needs, the United States must supply it. We are the only country able to provide that help.

I am fully aware of the broad implications involved if the United States extends assistance to Greece and Turkey, and I shall discuss these implications with you at this time.
15 One of the primary objectives of the foreign policy of the United States is the creation of conditions in which we and other nations will be able to work out a way of life free from coercion. This was a fundamental issue in the war with Germany and Japan. Our victory was won over countries which sought to impose their will, and their way of life, upon other nations.
20 To ensure the peaceful development of nations, free from coercion, the United States has taken a leading part in establishing the United Nations. The United Nations is designed to make possible lasting freedom and independence for all its members. We shall not realize our objectives, however, unless we are willing to help free peoples to maintain their free institutions
25 and their national integrity against aggressive movements that seek to impose upon them totalitarian regimes. This is no more than a frank recognition that totalitarian regimes imposed on free peoples, by direct or indirect aggression, undermine the foundations of international peace and hence the security of the United States.
30 The peoples of a number of countries of the world have recently had totalitarian regimes forced upon them against their will. The government of the United States has made frequent protests against coercion and intimidation, in violation of the Yalta agreement, in Poland, Rumania and Bulgaria. I must also state that in a number of other countries there have been similar developments.
35 At the present moment in world history nearly every nation must choose between alternative ways of life. The choice is too often not a free one. One way of life is based upon the will of the majority, and is distinguished by free institutions, representative government, free elections, guaranties of individual liberty, freedom of speech and religion, and freedom from political oppression.
40 The second way of life is based upon the will of a minority forcibly imposed

upon the majority. It relies upon terror and oppression, a controlled press and radio, fixed elections, and the suppression of personal freedoms.

I believe that it must be the policy of the United States to support free peoples who are resisting attempted subjugation by armed minorities or by outside pressures. I believe that we must assist free peoples to work out their own destinies in their own way. I believe that our help should be primarily through economic and financial aid which is essential to economic stability and orderly political processes.

The world is not static, and the status quo is not sacred. But we cannot allow changes in the status quo in violation of the Charter of the United Nations by such methods as coercion, or by such subterfuges as political infiltration. In helping free and independent nations to maintain their freedom, the United States will be giving effect to the principles of the Charter of the United Nations.

It is necessary only to glance at a map to realize that the survival and integrity of the Greek nation are of grave importance in a much wider situation. If Greece should fall under the control of an armed minority, the effect upon its neighbor, Turkey, would be immediate and serious. Confusion and disorder might well spread throughout the entire Middle East.

Moreover, the disappearance of Greece as an independent state would have a profound effect upon those countries in Europe whose peoples are struggling against great difficulties to maintain their freedoms and their independence while they repair the damages of war.

It would be an unspeakable tragedy if these countries, which have struggled so long against overwhelming odds, should lose that victory for which they sacrificed so much. Collapse of free institutions and loss of independence would be disastrous not only for them but for the lot of neighboring peoples striving to maintain their freedom and independence.

Should we fail to aid Greece and Turkey in this fateful hour, the effect will be far reaching to the West as well as to the East. We must take immediate and resolute action.

I, therefore, ask the Congress to provide authority for assistance to Greece and Turkey in the amount of $400,000,000 for the period ending June 30, 1948. In requesting these funds, I have taken into consideration the maximum amount of relief assistance which would be furnished to Greece out of the $350,000,000 which I recently requested that the Congress authorize for the prevention of starvation and suffering in countries devastated by the war.

In addition to funds, I ask the Congress to authorize the detail of American civilian and military personnel to Greece and Turkey, at the request of those countries, to assist in the tasks of reconstruction, and for the purpose of supervising the use of such financial and material assistance as may be furnished. I recommend that authority also be provided for the instruction and training of selected Greek and Turkish personnel....

This is a serious course upon which we embark. I would not recommend it except that the alternative is much more serious.

5   The United States contributed $341,000,000,000 toward winning World War II. This is an investment in world freedom and world peace. The assistance that I am recommending for Greece and Turkey amounts to little more than one-tenth of 1 percent of this investment. It is only common sense that we should safeguard this investment and make sure that it was not in vain.

10   The seeds of totalitarian regimes are natured by misery and want. They spread and grow in the evil soil of poverty and strife. They reach their full growth when the hope of a people for a better life has died. We must keep that hope alive.

The free peoples of the world look to us for support in maintaining their 15 freedoms. If we falter in our leadership, we may endanger the peace of the world—and we shall surely endanger the welfare of our own nation. Great responsibilities have been placed upon us by the swift movement of events. I am confident that the Congress will face these responsibilities squarely.

THE SOURCES OF SOVIET CONDUCT
GEORGE F. KENNAN (1904–2005)

George F. Kennan was a career foreign service officer and the chief intel-
lectual advocate of a foreign policy of "realism." Realism counseled the
prudent consideration of American national interests and attention to the
application of limited resources to serve those ends. It warned against the
dangerous moralism and idealism of Wilsonian internationalism, as well
as the danger of volatile and uninformed popular influence on diplomacy
in democratic countries. Kennan's thinking was shaped by Protestant "neo-
orthodoxy," which emphasized the impact of original sin in human society
and thus warned against political perfectionism at home or abroad.

 Explaining that Soviet rulers depended on exaggerating threats from
capitalist powers to justify their own dictatorship, Kennan recommended a
Cold War policy of "containment"—neither submission to Soviet expansion-
ism nor an attempt to roll back communism where it existed. Similar to
the Republican party's strategy against slavery in the 1850s, containment
assumed that the Soviet system would collapse of its own internal patholo-
gies if it were unable to expand. Containment became the basic American
Cold War strategy, but Kennan believed that policymakers distorted it by
an overly broad and militaristic application.

1947

The political personality of Soviet power as we know it today is the product of
ideology and circumstances: ideology inherited by the present Soviet leaders from
the movement in which they had their political origin, and circumstances of the
power which they have now exercised for nearly three decades in Russia....

 It is difficult to summarize the set of ideological concepts with which the 5
Soviet leaders came into power. Marxian ideology, in its Russian-Communist
projection, has always been in process of subtle evolution. The materials on
which it bases itself are extensive and complex. But the outstanding features

X, "The Sources of Soviet Conduct," *Foreign Affairs* 25 (July 1947):566, 568–69, 569, 570, 571–73,
574–75, 576, 580–81, 582. Reprinted by permission of Foreign Affairs. Copyright © 1947 by the
Council on Foreign Relations, Inc. www.Foreign Affairs.com

of Communist thought as it existed in 1916 may perhaps be summarized as follows: (a) that the central factor in the life of man, the fact which determines the character of public life and the "physiognomy of society," is the system by which material goods are produced and exchanged; (b) that the capitalist system
5   of production is a nefarious one which inevitably leads to the exploitation of the working class by the capital-owning class and is incapable of developing adequately the economic resources of society or of distributing fairly the material goods produced by human labor; (c) that capitalism contains the seeds of its own destruction and must, in view of the inability of the capital-owning
10 class to adjust itself to economic change, result eventually and inescapably in a revolutionary transfer of power to the working class; and (d) that imperialism, the final phase of capitalism, leads directly to war and revolution....

The circumstances of the immediate post-Revolution period—the existence in Russia of civil war and foreign intervention, together with the obvious fact that
15 the Communists represented only a tiny minority of the Russian people—made the establishment of dictatorial power a necessity....

...Stalin, and those whom he led in the struggle for succession to Lenin's position of leadership, were not the men to tolerate rival political forces in the sphere of power which they coveted. Their sense of insecurity was too great. Their
20 particular brand of fanaticism, unmodified by any of the Anglo-Saxon traditions of compromise, was too fierce and too jealous to envisage any permanent sharing of power. From the Russian-Asiatic world out of which they had emerged they carried with them a skepticism as to the possibilities of permanent and peaceful coexistence of rival forces. Easily persuaded of their own doctrinaire "rightness,"
25 they insisted on the submission of destruction of all competing power. Outside of the Communist Party, Russian society was to have no rigidity. There were to be no forms of collective human activity or association which would not be dominated by the Party. No other force in Russian society was to be permitted to achieve vitality or integrity. Only the Party was to have structure. All else
30 was to be an amorphous mass.

And within the Party the same principle was to apply. The mass of Party members might go through the motions of election, deliberation, decision and action; but in these motions they were to be animated not by their own individual wills but by the awesome breath of the Party leadership and the
35 overbrooding presence of "the word."...

Now the outstanding circumstance concerning the Soviet régime is that down to the present day this process of political consolidation has never been completed and the men in the Kremlin have continued to be predominantly absorbed with the struggle to secure and make absolute the power which they
40 seized in November 1917. They have endeavored to secure it primarily against forces at home, within Soviet society itself. But they have also endeavored to

secure it against the outside world. For ideology…taught them that the outside world was hostile and that it was their duty eventually to overthrow the political forces beyond their borders….

Now it lies in the nature of the mental world of the Soviet leaders, as well as in the character of their ideology, that no opposition to them can be officially 5 recognized as having any merit or justification whatsoever. Such opposition can flow, in theory, only from the hostile and incorrigible forces of dying capitalism…. [S]ince capitalism no longer existed in Russia and since it could not be admitted that there could be serious or widespread opposition to the Kremlin springing spontaneously from the liberated masses under its authority, it became 10 necessary to justify the retention of the dictatorship by stressing the menace of capitalism abroad….

By the same token, tremendous emphasis has been placed on the original Communist thesis of a basic antagonism between the capitalist and Socialist worlds. It is clear, from many indications, that this emphasis is not founded in reality. The 15 real facts concerning it have been confused by the existence abroad of genuine resentment provoked by Soviet philosophy and tactics and occasionally by the existence of great centers of military power, notably the Nazi régime in Germany and the Japanese government of the late 1930's, which did indeed have aggressive designs against the Soviet Union. But there is ample evidence that the stress laid 20 in Moscow on the menace confronting Soviet society from the world outside its borders is founded not in the realities of foreign antagonism but in the necessity of explaining away the maintenance of dictatorial authority at home….

So much for the historical background. What does it spell in terms of the political personality of Soviet power as we know it today? 25

Of the original ideology, nothing has been officially junked. Belief is maintained in the basic badness of capitalism, in the inevitability of its destruction, in the obligation of the proletariat to assist in that destruction and to take power into its own hands. But stress has come to be laid primarily on those concepts which relate most specifically to the Soviet régime itself: to its position as the 30 sole truly Socialist régime in a dark and misguided world, and the relationships of power within it.

The first of these concepts is that of the innate antagonism between capitalism and Socialism. We have seen how deeply that concept has become imbedded in foundations of Soviet power. It has profound implications for Russia's 35 conduct as a member of international society. It means that there can never be on Moscow's side any sincere assumption of a community of aims between the Soviet Union and powers which are regarded as capitalist. It must invariably be assumed in Moscow that the aims of the capitalist world are antagonistic to the Soviet régime, and therefore to the interests of the peoples it controls. If the 40 Soviet Government occasionally sets its signature to documents which would indicate the contrary, this is to be regarded as a tactical manoeuvre permissible in dealing with the enemy (who is without honor) and should be taken in the spirit of *caveat emptor*. Basically, the antagonism remains. It is postulated. And from it flow many of the phenomena which we find disturbing in the Kremlin's conduct

5   of foreign policy: the secretiveness, the lack of frankness, the duplicity, the wary suspiciousness, and the basic unfriendliness of purpose. These phenomena are there to stay, for the foreseeable future. There can be variations of degree and of emphasis. When there is something the Russians want from us, one or the other of these features of their policy may be thrust temporarily into the background;

10   and when that happens there will always be Americans who will leap forward with gleeful announcements that "the Russians have changed," and some who will even try to take the credit for having brought about such "changes". But we should not be misled by tactical manoeuvres. These characteristics of Soviet policy, like the postulate from which they flow, are basic to the internal nature of

15   Soviet power, and will be with us, whether in the foreground or the background, until the internal nature of Soviet power is changed.

This means that we are going to continue for a long time to find the Russians difficult to deal with. It does not mean that they should be considered as embarked upon a do-or-die program to overthrow our society by a given

20   date. The theory of the inevitability of the eventual fall of capitalism has the fortunate connotation that there is no hurry about it. The forces of progress can take their time in preparing the final *coup de grâce*. Meanwhile, what is vital is that the "Socialist fatherland"—that oasis of power which has been already won for Socialism in the person of the Soviet Union—should be cherished

25   and defended by all good Communists at home and abroad, its fortunes promoted, its enemies badgered and confounded. The promotion of premature, "adventuristic" revolutionary projects abroad which might embarrass Soviet power in any way would be an inexcusable, even a counter-revolutionary act. The cause of Socialism is the support and promotion of Soviet power, as

30   defined in Moscow....

But we have seen the Kremlin is under no ideological compulsion to accomplish its purposes in a hurry. Like the Church, it is dealing in ideological concepts which are of long-term validity, and it can afford to be patient. It has no right to risk the existing achievements of the revolution for the sake of vain

35   baubles of the future. The very teachings of Lenin himself require great caution and flexibility in the pursuit of Communist purposes. Again, these precepts are fortified by the lessons of Russian history: of centuries of obscure battles between nomadic forces over the stretches of a vast unfortified plain. Here caution, circumspection, flexibility and deception are the valuable qualities;

40   and their value finds natural appreciation in the Russian or the oriental mind.

Thus the Kremlin has no compunction about retreating in the face of superior force. And being under the compulsion of no timetable, it does not get panicky under the necessity for such retreat. Its political action is a fluid stream which moves constantly, wherever it is permitted to move, toward a given goal. Its main concern is to make sure that it has filled every nook and cranny available to it   5
in the basin of world power. But if it finds unassailable barriers in its path, it accepts these philosophically and accommodates itself to them. The main thing is that there should always be pressure, unceasing constant pressure, toward the desired goal. There is no trace of any feeling in Soviet psychology that that goal must be reached at any given time.   10

These considerations make Soviet diplomacy at once easier and more difficult to deal with than the diplomacy of individual aggressive leaders like Napoleon and Hitler. On the one hand it is more sensitive to contrary force, more ready to yield on individual sectors of the diplomatic front when that force is felt to be too strong, and thus more rational in the logic and rhetoric of   15
power. On the other hand it cannot be easily defeated or discouraged by a single victory on the part of its opponents. And the patient persistence by which it is animated means that it can be effectively countered not by sporadic acts which represent the momentary whims of democratic opinion but only by intelligent long-range policies on the part of Russia's adversaries—policies no less steady   20
in their purpose, and no less variegated and resourceful in their application, than those of the Soviet Union itself.

In these circumstances it is clear that the main element of any United States policy toward the Soviet Union must be that of a long-term, patient but firm and vigilant containment of Russian expansive tendencies. It is important   25
to note, however, that such a policy has nothing to do with outward histrion-ics: with threats or blustering or superfluous gestures of outward "toughness." While the Kremlin is basically flexible in its reaction to political realities, it is by no means un-amenable to considerations of prestige. Like almost any other government, it can be placed by tactless and threatening gestures in a position   30
where it cannot afford to yield even though this might be dictated by its sense of realism. The Russian leaders are keen judges of human psychology, and as such they are highly conscious that loss of temper and of self-control is never a source of strength in political affairs. They are quick to exploit such evidences of weakness....   35

In the light of the above, it will be clearly seen that the Soviet pressure against the free institutions of the western world is something that can be contained by the adroit and vigilant application of counter-force at a series of constantly shifting geographical and political points, corresponding to the shifts and manoeuvres of Soviet policy, but which cannot be charmed or talked out   40 of existence. The Russians look forward to a duel of infinite duration, and they see that already they have scored great successes....

It is clear that the United States cannot expect in the foreseeable future to enjoy political intimacy with the Soviet régime. It must continue to regard the
5 Soviet Union as a rival, not a partner, in the political arena. It must continue to expect that Soviet policies will reflect no abstract love of peace and stability, no real faith in the possibility of a permanent happy coexistence of the Socialist and capitalist worlds, but rather a cautious, persistent pressure toward the disruption and weakening of all rival influence and rival power.

10 Balanced against this are the facts that Russia, as opposed to the Western world in general, is still by far the weaker party, that Soviet policy is highly flexible, and that Soviet society may well contain deficiencies which will eventually weaken its own total potential. This would of itself warrant the United States entering with reasonable confidence upon a policy of firm containment, designed
15 to confront the Russians with unalterable counter-force at every point where they show signs of encroaching upon the interests of a peaceful and stable world....

It would be an exaggeration to say that American behavior unassisted and alone could exercise a power of life and death over the Communist movement and bring about the early fall of Soviet power in Russia. But the United States
20 has it in its power to increase enormously the strains under which Soviet policy must operate, to force upon the Kremlin a far greater degree of moderation and circumspection than it has had to observe in recent years, and in this way promote tendencies which must eventually find their outlet in either the break-up or the gradual mellowing of Soviet power. For no mystical, Messianic
25 movement—and particularly not that of the Kremlin—can face frustration indefinitely without eventually adjusting itself in one way or another to the logic of that state of affairs.

Thus the decision will really fall in large measure in this country itself. The issue of Soviet-American relations is in essence a test of the over-all worth of
30 the United States as a nation among nations. To avoid destruction the United States need only measure up to its own best traditions and prove itself worthy of preservation as a great nation.

Surely, there was never a fairer test of national quality than this. In the light of these circumstances, the thoughtful observer of Russian-American rela-
35 tions will find no cause for complaint in the Kremlin's challenge to American society. He will rather experience a certain gratitude to a Providence which, by providing the American people with this implacable challenge, has made their entire security as a nation dependent on their pulling themselves together and accepting the responsibilities of moral and political leadership that history
40 plainly intended them to bear.

NSC–68: United States Objectives and Programs for National Security
National Security Council

In the aftermath of the communist takeover of China, the Soviet explosion of an atomic bomb, and the exposure of communist espionage in the United States, President Harry S. Truman (r. 1945–1953) charged his National Security Council to devise a strategy for the Cold War.

The NSC called for strengthening the American and allied position in the world to redress what it perceived a communist advantage in the balance of world power. NSC–68 extended the Truman Doctrine and George F. Kennan's "containment" doctrine to the entire world, and implied an open-ended commitment of U.S. resources; it suggested that the United States could afford to spend 20 percent of its national income on defense.

The strategy of NSC–68 is often referred to as a "symmetrical" response—America should react wherever communists acted, regardless of the proximate threat to vital American national interests and without regard to the costs. It was soon applied to Korea, and would reach its crisis in Vietnam.

14 April 1950

…A continuation of present trends would result in a serious decline in the strength of the free world relative to the Soviet Union and its satellites. This unfavorable trend arises from the inadequacy of current programs and plans rather than from any error in our objectives and aims. These trends lead in the direction of isolation, not by deliberate decision but by lack of the necessary 5
basis for a vigorous initiative in the conflict with the Soviet Union.

Our position as the center of power in the free world places a heavy responsibility upon the United States for leadership. We must organize and enlist the energies and resources of the free world in a positive program for peace which will frustrate the Kremlin design for world domination by creating a situation 10
in the free world to which the Kremlin will be compelled to adjust. Without

NSC–68, *Foreign Relations of the United States, 1950* (Washington, DC: Government Printing Office, 1977), I:254.

such a cooperative effort, led by the United States, we will have to make gradual withdrawals under pressure until we discover one day that we have sacrificed positions of vital interest.

It is imperative that this trend be reversed by a much more rapid and con-
5   certed build-up of the actual strength of both the United States and the other nations of the free world. The analysis shows that this will be costly and will involve significant domestic financial and economic adjustments.

The execution of such a build-up, however, requires that the United States have an affirmative program beyond the solely defensive one of countering
10 the threat posed by the Soviet Union. This program must light the path to peace and order among nations in a system based on freedom and justice, as contemplated in the Charter of the United Nations. Further, it must envisage political and economic measures with which and the military shield behind which the free world can work to frustrate the Kremlin design by the strat-
15 egy of the cold war; for every consideration of devotion to our fundamental values and to our national security demands that we achieve our objectives by the strategy of the cold war, building up our military strength in order that it may not have to be used. The only sure victory lies in the frustration of the Kremlin design by the steady development of the moral and material
20 strength of the free world and its projection into the Soviet world in such a way as to bring about an internal change in the Soviet system. Such a posi-tive program—harmonious with our fundamental national purpose and our objectives—is necessary if we are to regain and retain the initiative and to win and hold the necessary popular support and cooperation in the United States
25 and the rest of the free world.

This program should include a plan for negotiation with the Soviet Union, developed and agreed with our allies and which is consonant with our objec-tives. The United States and its allies, particularly the United Kingdom and France, should always be ready to negotiate with the Soviet Union on terms
30 consistent with our objectives. The present world situation, however, is one which militates against successful negotiations with the Kremlin—for the terms of agreements on important pending issues would reflect present realities and would therefore be unacceptable, if not disastrous, to be United States and the rest of the free world. After a decision and a start on building up the strength of
35 the free world has been made, it might then be desirable for the United States to take an initiative in seeking negotiations in the hope that it might facilitate the process of accommodation by the Kremlin to the new situation. Failing that, the unwillingness of the Kremlin to accept equitable terms or its bad faith in observing them would assist in consolidating popular opinion in the free world
40 in support of the measures necessary to sustain the build-up.

In summary, we must, by means of a rapid and sustained build-up of the political, economic, and military strength of the free world, and by means of an affirmative program intended to wrest the initiative from the Soviet Union, confront it with convincing evidence of the determination and ability of the free world to frustrate the Kremlin design of a world dominated by its will. 5 Such evidence is the only means short of war which eventually may force the Kremlin to abandon its present course of action and to negotiate acceptable agreements on issues of major importance.

The whole success of the proposed program hangs ultimately on recognition by this Government, the American people, and all free peoples, that the 10 cold war is in fact a real war in which the survival of the free world is at stake. Essential prerequisites to success are consultations with Congressional leaders designed to make the program the object of non-partisan legislative support, and a presentation to the public of a full explanation of the facts and implications of the present international situation. The prosecution of the program 15 will require of us all the ingenuity, sacrifice, and unity demanded by the vital importance of the issue and the tenacity to persevere until our national objectives have been attained....

LETTER TO MY CHILDREN
WHITTAKER CHAMBERS (1901–1961)

Communism was not only an issue in foreign policy. As Whittaker Chambers said in his classic autobiography, Witness, *it represented the great spiritual challenge to the West in the twentieth century. Chambers stepped forward as a witness against Alger Hiss in 1948, claiming the former high-ranking State Department official had been a spy for the Soviet Union. Chambers was in a position to know: He revealed that he had served with Hiss as his organizer, contact, and courier. Hiss's trial—for perjury, the statute of limitations having run out on a charge of espionage—was one of the most sensational trials of the century. "Two faiths were on trial," Chambers said. He also insisted later in the book that "At every point religion and politics interlace, and must do so more acutely as the conflict between the two camps of men—those who reject and those who worship God—becomes irrepressible."*

Hiss was convicted, but proclaimed his innocence for five more decades. Chambers died in 1961; only after the end of the Cold War and the release of many American and Soviet documents did the deep truth of Witness *become evident.*

1952

Beloved Children,

I am sitting in the kitchen of the little house at Medfield, our second farm which is cut off by the ridge and a quarter-mile across the fields from our home place, where you are. I am writing a book. In it I am speaking to you. But I am also speaking to the world. To both I owe an accounting.

5

It is a terrible book. It is terrible in what it tells about men. If anything, it is more terrible in what it tells about the world in which you live. It is about what the world calls the Hiss-Chambers Case, or even more simply, the Hiss Case. It is about a spy case. All the props of an espionage case are there—foreign

Whittaker Chambers, *Witness* (Washington, DC: Regnery Publishing, 1952), 3–22. Reprinted by permission of the publisher.

agents, household traitors, stolen documents, microfilm, furtive meetings, secret hideaways, phony names, an informer, investigations, trials, official justice.

But if the Hiss Case were only this, it would not be worth my writing about or your reading about. It would be another fat folder in the sad files of
5   the police, another crime drama in which the props would be mistaken for the play (as many people have consistently mistaken them). It would not be what alone gave it meaning, what the mass of men and women instinctively sensed it to be, often without quite knowing why. It would not be what, at the very beginning, I was moved to call it: "a tragedy of history."

10   For it was more than human tragedy. Much more than Alger Hiss or Whittaker Chambers was on trial in the trials of Alger Hiss. Two faiths were on trial. Human societies, like human beings, live by faith and die when faith dies. At issue in the Hiss Case was the question whether this sick society, which we call Western civilization, could in its extremity still cast up a man whose faith in it
15   was so great that he would voluntarily abandon those things which men hold good, including life, to defend it. At issue was the question whether this man's faith could prevail against a man whose equal faith it was that this society is sick beyond saving, and that mercy itself pleads for its swift extinction and replacement by another. At issue was the question whether, in the desperately divided
20   society, there still remained the will to recognize the issues in time to offset the immense rally of public power to distort and pervert the facts.

At heart, the Great Case was this critical conflict of faiths; that is why it was a great case. On a scale personal enough to be felt by all, but big enough to be symbolic, the two irreconcilable faiths of our time—Communism and
25   Freedom—came to grips in the persons of two conscious and resolute men. Indeed, it would have been hard, in a world still only dimly aware of what the conflict is about, to find two other men who knew so clearly. Both had been schooled in the same view of history (the Marxist view). Both were trained by the same party in the same selfless, semi-soldierly discipline. Neither would
30   nor could yield without betraying, not himself, but his faith; and the different character of these faiths was shown by the different conduct of the two men toward each other throughout the struggle. For, with dark certitude, both knew, almost from the beginning, that the Great Case could end only in the destruction of one or both of the contending figures, just as the history of our times
35   (both men had been taught) can end only in the destruction of one or both of the contending forces.

But this destruction is not the tragedy. The nature of tragedy is itself misunderstood. Part of the world supposes that the tragedy in the Hiss Case lies in the acts of disloyalty revealed. Part believes that the tragedy lies in the fact
40   that an able, intelligent man, Alger Hiss, was cut short in the course of a bril-

liant public career. Some find it tragic that Whittaker Chambers, of his own will, gave up a $30,000-a-year job and a secure future to haunt for the rest of his days the ruins of his life. These are shocking facts, criminal facts, disturbing facts: they are not tragic.

Crime, violence, infamy are not tragedy. Tragedy occurs when a human soul awakes and seeks, in suffering and pain, to free itself from crime, violence, infamy, even at the cost of life. The struggle is the tragedy—not defeat or death. That is why the spectacle of tragedy has always filled men, not with despair, but with a sense of hope and exaltation. That is why this terrible book is also a book of hope. For it is about the struggle of the human soul—of more than one human soul. It is in this sense that the Hiss Case is a tragedy. This is its meaning beyond the headlines, the revelations, the shame and suffering of the people involved. But this tragedy will have been for nothing unless men understand it rightly, and from it the world takes hope and heart to begin its own tragic struggle with the evil that besets it from within and from without, unless it faces the fact that the world, the whole world, is sick unto death and that, among other things, this Case has turned a finger of fierce light into the suddenly opened and reeking body of our time.

My children, as long as you live, the shadow of the Hiss Case will brush you. In every pair of eyes that rests on you, you will see pass, like a cloud passing behind a woods in winter, the memory of your father—dissembled in friendly eyes, lurking in unfriendly eyes. Sometimes you will wonder which is harder to bear: friendly forgiveness or forthright hate. In time, therefore, when the sum of your experience of life gives you authority, you will ask yourselves the question: What was my father?

I will give you an answer: I was a witness. I do not mean a witness for the Government or against Alger Hiss and the others. Nor do I mean the short, squat, solitary figure, trudging through the impersonal halls of public buildings to testify before Congressional committees, grand juries, loyalty boards, courts of law. A man is not primarily a witness *against* something. That is only incidental to the fact that he is a witness *for* something. A witness, in the sense that I am using the word, is a man whose life and faith are so completely one that when the challenge comes to step out and testify for his faith, he does so, disregarding all risks, accepting all consequences.

One day in the great jury room of the Grand Jury of the Southern District of New York, a juror leaned forward slightly and asked me: "Mr. Chambers, what does it mean to be a Communist?" I hesitated for a moment, trying to find the simplest, most direct way to convey the heart of this complex experience to men and women to whom the very fact of the experience was all but incomprehensible. Then I said:

When I was a Communist, I had three heroes. One was a Russian. One was a Pole. One was a German Jew.

The Pole was Felix Djerjinsky.[1] He was ascetic, highly sensitive, intelligent. He was a Communist. After the Russian Revolution, he became head of the Tcheka and organizer of the Red Terror. As a young man, Djerjinsky had been a political prisoner in the Paviak Prison in Warsaw. There he insisted on being given the task of cleaning the latrines of the other prisoners. For he held that the most developed member of any community must take upon himself the lowliest tasks as an example to those who are less developed. That is one thing that it meant to be a Communist.

The German Jew was Eugen Leviné.[2] He was a Communist. During the Bavarian Soviet Republic in 1919, Leviné was the organizer of the Workers and Soldiers Soviets. When the Bavarian Soviet Republic was crushed, Leviné was captured and court-martialed. The court-martial told him: "You are under sentence of death." Leviné answered: "We Communists are always under sentence of death." That is another thing that it meant to be a Communist.

The Russian was not a Communist. He was a pre-Communist revolutionist named Kalyaev.[3] (I should have said Sazonov.) He was arrested for a minor part in the assassination of the Tsarist prime minister, von Plehve.[4] He was sent into Siberian exile to one of the worst prison camps, where the political prisoners were flogged. Kalyaev sought some way to protest this outrage to the world. The means were few, but at last he found a way. In protest against the flogging of other men, Kalyaev drenched himself in kerosene, set himself on fire and burned himself to death. That also is what it meant to be a Communist.

That also is what it means to be a witness.

But a man may also be an involuntary witness. I do not know any way to explain why God's grace touches a man who seems unworthy of it. But neither do I know any other way to explain how a man like myself—tarnished by life, unprepossessing, not brave—could prevail so far against the powers of the world arrayed almost solidly against him, to destroy him and defeat his truth. In this sense, I am an involuntary witness to God's grace and to the fortifying power of faith.

---

[1]Felix Edmundovich Djerjinsky (1877–1926), founder of the Cheka, the first Soviet Secret police, and Commissar for the Interior

[2]Eugen Leviné (1883–1919)

[3]Yegor Sazonov (1879–1910)

[4]Vyacheslav von Plehve (1846–1904), Russian Minister of the Interior (1902–1904)

It was my fate to be in turn a witness to each of the two great faiths of our time. And so we come to the terrible word, Communism. My very dear children, nothing in all these pages will be written so much for you, though it is so unlike anything you would want to read. In nothing shall I be so much a witness, in no way am I so much called upon to fulfill my task, as in trying to make clear to you (and to the world) the true nature of Communism and the source of its power, which was the cause of my ordeal as a man, and remains the historic ordeal of the world in the 20th century. For in this century, within the next decades, will be decided for generations whether all mankind is to become Communist, whether the whole world is to become free, or whether, in the struggle, civilization as we know it is to be completely destroyed or completely changed. It is our fate to live upon that turning point in history.

The world has reached that turning point by the steep stages of a crisis mounting for generations. The turning point is the next to the last step. It was reached in blood, sweat, tears, havoc, and death in World War II. The chief fruit of the First World War was the Russian Revolution and the rise of Communism as a national power. The chief fruit of the Second World War was our arrival at the next to the last step of the crisis with the rise of Communism as a world power. History is likely to say that these were the only decisive results of the world wars.

The last war simplified the balance of political forces in the world by reducing them to two. For the first time, it made the power of the Communist sector of mankind (embodied in the Soviet Union) roughly equal to the power of the free sector of mankind (embodied in the United States). It made the collision of these powers all but inevitable. For the world wars did not end the crisis. They raised its tensions to a new pitch. They raised the crisis to a new stage. All the politics of our time, including the politics of war, will be the politics of this crisis.

Few men are so dull that they do not know that the crisis exists and that it threatens their lives at every point. It is popular to call it a social crisis. It is in fact a total crisis—religious, moral, intellectual, social, political, economic. It is popular to call it a crisis of the Western world. It is in fact a crisis of the whole world. Communism, which claims to be a solution of the crisis, is itself a symptom and an irritant of the crisis.

In part, the crisis results from the impact of science and technology upon mankind which, neither socially nor morally, has caught up with the problems posed by that impact. In part, it is caused by men's efforts to solve those problems. World wars are the military expression of the crisis. World-wide depressions are its economic expression. Universal desperation is its spiritual climate. This is the climate of Communism. Communism in our time can no more be considered apart from the crisis than a fever can be acted upon apart from an infected body.

I see in Communism the focus of the concentrated evil of our time. You will ask: Why, then, do men become Communists? How did it happen that you, our gentle and loved father, were once a Communist? Were you simply stupid? No, I was not stupid. Were you morally depraved? No, I was not morally depraved. Indeed, educated men become Communists chiefly for moral reasons. Did you not know that the crimes and horrors of Communism are inherent in Communism? Yes, I knew that fact. Then why did you become a Communist? It would help more to ask: How did it happen that this movement, once a mere muttering of political outcasts, became this immense force that now contests the mastery of mankind? Even when all the chances and mistakes of history are allowed for, the answer must be: Communism makes some profound appeal to the human mind. You will not find out what it is by calling Communism names. That will not help much to explain why Communism whose horrors, on a scale unparalleled in history, are now public knowledge, still recruits its thousands and holds its millions—among them some of the best minds alive. Look at Klaus Fuchs,[5] standing in the London dock, quiet, doomed, destroyed, and say whether it is possible to answer in that way the simple question: Why?

First, let me try to say what Communism is not. It is not simply a vicious plot hatched by wicked men in a sub-cellar. It is not just the writings of Marx and Lenin, dialectical materialism, the Politburo, the labor theory of value, the theory of the general strike, the Red Army, secret police, labor camps, underground conspiracy, the dictatorship of the proletariat, the technique of the coup d'état. It is not even those chanting, bannered millions that stream periodically, like disorganized armies, through the heart of the world's capitals: Moscow, New York, Tokyo, Paris, Rome. These are expressions of Communism, but they are not what Communism is about.

In the Hiss trials, where Communism was a haunting specter, but which did little or nothing to explain Communism, Communists were assumed to be criminals, pariahs, clandestine men who lead double lives under false names, travel on false passports, deny traditional religion, morality, the sanctity of oaths, preach violence and practice treason. These things are true about Communists, but they are not what Communism is about.

The revolutionary heart of Communism is not the theatrical appeal: "Workers of the world, unite. You have nothing to lose but your chains. You have a world to gain." It is a simple statement of Karl Marx, further simplified for handy use: "Philosophers have explained the world; it is necessary to change the world." Communists are bound together by no secret oath. The tie that binds

---

[5]Klaus Fuchs (1911–1988), a scientist who in 1950 admitted passing American and British atomic research to the Soviets, and was sentenced to 14 years of imprisonment

them across the frontiers of nations, across barriers of language and differences of class and education, in defiance of religion, morality, truth, law, honor, the weaknesses of the body and the irresolutions of the mind, even unto death, is a simple conviction: It is necessary to change the world. Their power, whose nature baffles the rest of the world, because in a large measure the rest of the world has lost that power, is the power to hold convictions and to act on them. It is the same power that moves mountains; it is also an unfailing power to move men. Communists are that part of mankind which has recovered the power to live or die—to bear witness—for its faith. And it is a simple, rational faith that inspires men to live or die for it.

It is not new. It is, in fact, man's second oldest faith. Its promise was whispered in the first days of the Creation under the Tree of the Knowledge of Good and Evil: "Ye shall be as gods." It is the great alternative faith of mankind. Like all great faiths, its force derives from a simple vision. Other ages have had great visions. They have always been different versions of the same vision: the vision of God and man's relationship to God. The Communist vision is the vision of Man without God.

It is the vision of man's mind displacing God as the creative intelligence of the world. It is the vision of man's liberated mind, by the sole force of its rational intelligence, redirecting man's destiny and re-organizing man's life and the world. It is the vision of man, once more the central figure of the Creation, not because God made man in His image, but because man's mind makes him the most intelligent of the animals. Copernicus and his successors displaced man as the central fact of the universe by proving that the earth was not the central star of the universe. Communism restores man to his sovereignty by the simple method of denying God.

The vision is a challenge and implies a threat. It challenges man to prove by his acts that he is the masterwork of the Creation—by making thought and act one. It challenges him to prove it by using the force of his rational mind to end the bloody meaninglessness of man's history—by giving it purpose and a plan. It challenges him to prove it by reducing the meaningless chaos of nature, by imposing on it his rational will to order, abundance, security, peace. It is the vision of materialism. But it threatens, if man's mind is unequal to the problems of man's progress, that he will sink back into savagery (the A and the H bombs have raised the issue in explosive forms), until nature replaces him with a more intelligent form of life.

It is an intensely practical vision. The tools to turn it into reality are at hand—science and technology, whose traditional method, the rigorous exclusion of all supernatural factors in solving problems, has contributed to the intellectual climate in which the vision flourishes, just as they have contributed to the crisis in which Communism thrives. For the vision is shared by millions who are not Communists (they are part of Communism's secret strength). Its first commandment is found, not in the *Communist Manifesto*, but in the first sentence of the physics primer: "All of the progress of mankind to date results from the making of careful measurements." But Communism, for the first time in history, has made this vision the faith of a great modern political movement.

Hence the Communist Party is quite justified in calling itself the most revolutionary party in history. It has posed in practical form the most revolutionary question in history: God or Man? It has taken the logical next step which three hundred years of rationalism hesitated to take, and said what millions of modern minds think, but do not dare or care to say: If man's mind is the decisive force in the world, what need is there for God? Henceforth man's mind is man's fate.

This vision *is* the Communist revolution, which, like all great revolutions, occurs in man's mind before it takes form in man's acts. Insurrection and conspiracy are merely methods of realizing the visions; they are merely part of the politics of Communism. Without its vision, they, like Communism, would have no meaning and could not rally a parcel of pickpockets. Communism does not summon men to crime or to utopia, as its easy critics like to think. On the plane of faith, it summons mankind to turn its vision into practical reality. On the plane of action, it summons men to struggle against the inertia of the past which, embodied in social, political, and economic forms, Communism claims, is blocking the will of mankind to make its next great forward stride. It summons men to overcome the crisis, which, Communism claims, is in effect a crisis of rending frustration, with the world, unable to stand still, but unwilling to go forward along the road that the logic of a technological civilization points out—Communism.

This is Communism's moral sanction, which is twofold. Its vision points the way to the future; its faith labors to turn the future into present reality. It says to every man who joins it: the vision is a practical problem of history; the way to achieve it is a practical problem of politics, which is the present tense of history. Have you the moral strength to take upon yourself the crimes of history so that man at last may close his chronicle of age-old, senseless suffering, and replace it with purpose and a plan? The answer a man makes to this question is the difference between the Communist and those miscellaneous socialists, liberals, fellow travelers, unclassified progressives and men of good will, all of whom share a similar vision, but do not share the faith because they will not take upon themselves the penalties of the faith. The answer is the root of that sense of moral superiority which makes Communists, though caught in crime, berate their opponents with withering self-righteousness.

The Communist vision has a mighty agitator and a mighty propagandist. They are the crisis. The agitator needs no soap box. It speaks insistently to the human mind at the point where desperation lurks. The propagandist writes no Communist gibberish. It speaks insistently to the human mind at the point where man's hope and man's energy fuse to fierceness.

The vision inspires. The crisis impels. The workingman is chiefly moved by the crisis. The educated man is chiefly moved by the vision. The working-man, living upon a mean margin of life, can afford few visions—even practical visions. An educated man, peering from the Harvard Yard, or any college campus upon a world in chaos, finds in the vision the two certainties for which the mind of man tirelessly seeks: a reason to live and a reason to die. No other faith of our time presents them with the same practical intensity. That is why Communism is the central experience of the first half of the 20th century, and may be its final experience—will be, unless the free world, in the agony of its struggle with Communism, overcomes its crisis by discovering, in suffering and pain, a power of faith which will provide man's mind, at the same intensity, with the same two certainties: a reason to live and a reason to die. If it fails, this will be the century of the great social wars. If it succeeds, this will be the century of the great wars of faith.

You will ask: Why, then, do men cease to be Communists? One answer is: Very few do. Thirty years after the Russian Revolution, after the known atrocities, the purges, the revelations, the jolting zig-zags of Communist politics, there is only a handful of ex-Communists in the whole world. By ex-Communists I do not mean those who break with Communism over differences of strategy and tactics (like Trotsky)[6] or organization (like Tito).[7] Those are merely quarrels over a road map by people all of whom are in a hurry to get to the same place.

Nor, by ex-Communists, do I mean those thousands who continually drift into the Communist Party and out again. The turnover is vast. These are the spiritual vagrants of our time whose traditional faith has been leached out in the bland climate of rationalism. They are looking for an intellectual night's lodging. They lack the character for Communist faith because they lack the character for any faith. So they drop away, though Communism keeps its hold on them.

By an ex-Communist, I mean a man who knew clearly why he became a Communist, who served Communism devotedly and knew why he served it, who broke with Communism unconditionally and knew why he broke with it.

---

[6]Leon Trotsky (1879–1940), a leader of the 1917 Russian Revolution. He later fell out with Stalin, was expelled from Russia, and was murdered in exile in 1940.

[7]Josip Broz Tito (1892–1980), Communist leader of Yugoslavia (1945–1980), who broke with Stalin shortly after World War II

Of these there are very few—an index to the power of the vision and the power of the crisis.

History very largely fixes the patterns of force that make men Communists. Hence one Communist conversion sounds much like another—rather imper-
5   sonal and repetitious, awesome and tiresome, like long lines of similar people all stolidly waiting to get in to see the same movie. A man's break with Com-munism is intensely personal. Hence the account of no two breaks is likely to be the same. The reasons that made one Communist break may seem without force to another ex-Communist.

10   It is a fact that a man can join the Communist Party, can be very active in it for years, without completely understanding the nature of Communism or the political methods that follow inevitably from its vision. One day such incomplete Communists discover that the Communist Party is not what they thought it was. They break with it and turn on it with the rage of an honest
15   dupe, a dupe who has given a part of his life to a swindle. Often they forget that it takes two to make a swindle.

Others remain Communists for years, warmed by the light of its vision, firmly closing their eyes to the crimes and horrors inseparable from its practical politics. One day they have to face the facts. They are appalled at what they have
20   abetted. They spend the rest of their days trying to explain, usually without great success, the dark clue to their complicity. As their understanding of Communism was incomplete and led them to a dead end, their understanding of breaking with it is incomplete and leads them to a dead end. It leads to less than Com-munism, which was a vision and a faith. The world outside Communism, the
25   world in crisis, lacks a vision and a faith. There is before these ex-Communists absolutely nothing. Behind them is a threat. For they have, in fact, broken not with the vision, but with the politics of the vision. In the name of reason and intelligence, the vision keeps them firmly in its grip—self-divided, paralyzed, powerless to act against it.

30   Hence the most secret fold of their minds is haunted by a terrifying thought: What if we were wrong? What if our inconstancy is our guilt? That is the fate of those who break without knowing clearly that Communism is wrong because something else is right, because to the challenge: *God or Man?*, they continue to give the answer: *Man*. Their pathos is that not even the Communist ordeal
35   could teach them that man without God is just what Communism said he was: the most intelligent of the animals, that man without God is a beast, never more beastly than when he is most intelligent about his beastliness. "*Er nennt's Vernunft*," says the Devil in Goethe's *Faust*, "*und braucht's allein, nur tierischer als jedes Tier zu sein*"—Man calls it reason and uses it simply to be more beastly
40   than any beast. Not grasping the source of the evil they sincerely hate, such

ex-Communists in general make ineffectual witnesses against it. They are witnesses against something; they have ceased to be witnesses for anything.

Yet there is one experience which most sincere ex-Communists share, whether
or not they go only part way to the end of the question it poses. The daughter of a
former German diplomat in Moscow was trying to explain to me why her father,   5
who, as an enlightened modern man, had been extremely pro-Communist, had
become an implacable anti-Communist. It was hard for her because, as an enlightened modern girl, she shared the Communist vision without being a Communist.
But she loved her father and the irrationality of his defection embarrassed her.
"He was immensely pro-Soviet," she said, "and then—you will laugh at me—but   10
you must not laugh at my father—and then—one night—in Moscow—he heard
screams. That's all. Simply one night he heard screams."

A child of Reason and the twentieth century, she knew that there is a logic
of the mind. She did not know that the soul has a logic that may be more compelling than the mind's. She did not know at all that she had swept away the   15
logic of the mind, the logic of history, the logic of politics, the myth of the 20th
century, with five annihilating words: one night he heard screams.

What Communist has not heard those screams? They come from husbands
torn forever from their wives in midnight arrests. They come, muffled, from the
execution cellars of the secret police, from the torture chambers of the Lubianka,   20
from all the citadels of terror now stretching from Berlin to Canton. They come
from those freight cars loaded with men, women and children, the enemies of
the Communist State, locked in, packed in, left on remote sidings to freeze to
death at night in the Russian winter. They come from minds driven mad by the
horrors of mass starvation ordered and enforced as a policy of the Communist   25
State. They come from the starved skeletons, worked to death, or flogged to
death (as an example to others) in the freezing filth of sub-arctic labor camps.
They come from children whose parents are suddenly, inexplicably, taken away
from them—parents they will never see again.

What Communist has not heard those screams? Execution, says the Com-   30
munist code, is the highest measure of social protection. What man can call
himself a Communist who has not accepted the fact that Terror is an instrument of policy, right if the vision is right, justified by history, enjoined by the
balance of forces in the social wars of this century? Those screams have reached
every Communist's mind. Usually they stop there. What judge willingly dwells   35
upon the man the laws compel him to condemn to death—the laws of nations
or the laws of history?

But one day the Communist really hears those screams. He is going about his
routine party tasks. He is lifting a dripping reel of microfilm from a developing
tank. He is justifying to a Communist fraction in a trade union an extremely   40

unwelcome directive of the Central Committee. He is receiving from a trusted superior an order to go to another country and, in a designated hotel, at a designated hour, meet a man whose name he will never know, but who will give him a package whose contents he will never learn. Suddenly, there closes around
5   that Communist a separating silence, and in that silence he hears screams. He hears them for the first time. For they do not merely reach his mind. They pierce beyond. They pierce to his soul. He says to himself, "Those are not the screams of man in agony." He hears them for the first time because a soul in extremity has communicated with that which alone can hear it—another human soul.
10   Why does the Communist ever hear them? Because in the end there persists in every man, however he may deny it, a scrap of soul. The Communist who suffers this singular experience then says to himself, "What is happening to me? I must be sick." If he does not instantly stifle that scrap of soul, he is lost. If he admits it for a moment, he has admitted that there is something greater than
15   Reason, greater than the logic of mind, of politics, of history, of economics, which alone justifies the vision. If the party senses his weakness, and the party is peculiarly cunning at sensing such weakness, it will humiliate him, degrade him, condemn him, expel him. If it can, it will destroy him. And the party will be right. For he has betrayed that which alone justifies its faith—the vision of
20   Almighty Man. He has brushed the only vision that has force against the vision of Almighty Mind. He stands before the fact of God.
       The Communist Party is familiar with this experience to which its members are sometimes liable in prison, in illness, in indecision. It is recognized frankly as a sickness. There are ways of treating it—if it is confessed. It is when it is not
25   confessed that the party, sensing a subtle crisis, turns upon it savagely. What ex-Communist has not suffered this experience in one form or another, to one degree or another? What he does about it depends on the individual man. That is why no ex-Communist dare answer for his sad fraternity the question: Why do men break with Communism? He can only answer the question: How did
30   you break with Communism? My answer is: Slowly, reluctantly, in agony.
       Yet my break began long before I heard those screams. Perhaps it does for everyone. I do not know how far back it began. Avalanches gather force and crash, unheard, in men as in the mountains. But I date my break from a very casual happening. I was sitting in our apartment on Saint Paul Street in Balti-
35   more. It was shortly before we moved to Alger Hiss' apartment in Washington. My daughter was in her high chair. I was watching her eat. She was the most miraculous thing that had ever happened in my life. I liked to watch her even when she smeared porridge on her face or dropped it meditatively on the floor. My eye came to rest on the delicate convolutions of her ear—those intricate,
40   perfect ears. The thought passed through my mind: "No, those ears were not

created by any chance coming together of atoms in nature (the Communist view). They could have been created only by immense design." The thought was involuntary and unwanted. I crowded it out of my mind. But I never wholly forgot it or the occasion. I had to crowd it out of my mind. If I had completed it, I should have had to say: Design presupposes God. I did not then know that, at that moment, the finger of God was first laid upon my forehead.

One thing most ex-Communists could agree upon: they broke because they wanted to be free. They do not all mean the same thing by "free." Freedom is a need of the soul, and nothing else. It is in striving toward God that the soul strives continually after a condition of freedom. God alone is the inciter and guarantor of freedom. He is the only guarantor. External freedom is only an aspect of interior freedom. Political freedom, as the Western world has known it, is only a political reading of the Bible. Religion and freedom are indivisible. Without freedom the soul dies. Without the soul there is no justification for freedom. Necessity is the only ultimate justification known to the mind. Hence every sincere break with Communism is a religious experience, though the Communist fail to identify its true nature, though he fail to go to the end of the experience. His break is the political expression of the perpetual need of the soul whose first faint stirring he has felt within him, years, months or days before he breaks. A Communist breaks because he must choose at last between irreconcilable opposites—God or Man, Soul or Mind, Freedom or Communism.

Communism is what happens when, in the name of Mind, men free themselves from God. But its view of God, its knowledge of God, its experience of God, is what alone gives character to a society or a nation, and meaning to its destiny. Its culture, the voice of this character, is merely that view, knowledge, experience of God, fixed by its most intense spirits in terms intelligible to the mass of men. There has never been a society or a nation without God. But history is cluttered with the wreckage of nations that became indifferent to God, and died.

The crisis of Communism exists to the degree in which it has failed to free the peoples that it rules from God. Nobody knows this better than the Communist Party of the Soviet Union. The crisis of the Western world exists to the degree in which it is indifferent to God. It exists to the degree in which the Western world actually shares Communism's materialist vision, is so dazzled by the logic of the materialist interpretation of history, politics, and economics that it fails to grasp that, for it, the only possible answer to the Communist challenge: Faith in God or Faith in Man? is the challenge: Faith in God.

Economics is not the central problem of this century. It is a relative problem which can be solved in relative ways. Faith is the central problem of this age. The Western world does not know it, but it already possesses the answer to this problem—but only provided that its faith in God and the freedom He enjoins is as great as Communism's faith in Man.

My dear children, before I close this foreword, I want to recall to you briefly the life that we led in the ten years between the time when I broke with Communism and the time when I began to testify—the things we did, worked for, loved, believed in. For it was that happy life, which, on the human side, in part made it possible for me to do later on the things I had to do, or endure the things that happened to me.

Those were the days of the happy little worries, which then seemed so big. We know now that they were the golden days. They will not come again. In those days, our greatest worry was how to meet the payments on the mortgage, how to get the ploughing done in time, how to get health accreditation for our herd, how to get the hay in before the rain. I sometimes took my vacation in hay harvest so that I could help work the load. You two little children used to trample the load, drive the hay truck in the fields when you could barely reach the foot pedals, or drive the tractor that pulled up the loaded harpoons to the mow. At evening, you would break off to help Mother milk while I went on haying. For we came of age on the farm when we decided not to hire barn help, but to run the herd ourselves as a family.

Often the ovenlike heat in the comb of the barn and the sweet smell of alfalfa made us sick. Sometimes we fell asleep at the supper table from fatigue. But the hard work was good for us; and you knew only the peace of a home governed by a father and mother whose marriage the years (and an earlier suffering which you could not remember) had deepened into the perfect love that enveloped you.

Mother was a slight, overalled figure forever working for you in the house or beside you in the barns and gardens. Papa was a squat, overalled figure, fat but forceful, who taught John, at nine, the man-size glory of driving the tractor; or sat beside Ellen, at the wheel of the truck, an embodiment of security and power, as we drove loads of cattle through the night. On summer Sundays, you sat between Papa and Mama in the Quaker meeting house. Through the open doors, as you tried not to twist and turn in the long silence, you could see the far, blue Maryland hills and hear the redbirds and ground robins in the graveyard behind.

Only Ellen had a vague, troubled recollection of another time and another image of Papa. Then (it was during the years 1938 and 1939), if for any reason she pattered down the hall at night, she would find Papa, with the light on, writing, with a revolver on the table or a gun against the chair. She knew that there were people who wanted to kill Papa and who might try to kidnap her. But a wide sea of sunlight and of time lay between that puzzling recollection and the farm.

The farm was your kingdom, and the world lay far beyond the protecting walls thrown up by work and love. It is true that comic strips were not encouraged, comic books were banned, the radio could be turned on only by permission which was seldom given (or asked), and you saw few movies. But you grew in the presence of eternal wonders. There was the birth of lambs and calves. You remember how once, when I was away and the veterinarian could not come, you saw Mother reach in and turn the calf inside the cow so that it could be born. There was also the death of animals, sometimes violent, sometimes slow and painful—nothing is more constant on a farm than death.

Sometimes, of a spring evening, Papa would hear that distant honking that always makes his scalp tingle, and we would all rush out to see the wild geese, in lines of hundreds, steer up from the southwest, turn over the barn as over a landmark, and head into the north. Or on autumn nights of sudden cold that set the ewes breeding in the orchard, Papa would call you out of the house to stand with him in the now celebrated pumpkin patch and watch the northern lights flicker in electric clouds on the horizon, mount, die down, fade and mount again till they filled the whole northern sky with ghostly light in motion.

Thus, as children, you experienced two of the most important things men ever know—the wonder of life and the wonder of the universe, the wonder of life within the wonder of the universe. More important, you knew them not from books, not from lectures, but simply from living among them. Most important, you knew them with reverence and awe—that reverence and awe that has died out of the modern world and been replaced by man's monkeylike amazement at the cleverness of his own inventive brain.

I have watched greatness touch you in another way. I have seen you sit, uninvited and unforced, listening in complete silence to the third movement of the Ninth Symphony. I thought you understood, as much as children can, when I told you that that music was the moment at which Beethoven finally passed beyond the suffering of his life on earth and reached for the hand of God, as God reaches for the hand of Adam in Michelangelo's vision of the Creation.

And once, in place of a bedtime story, I was reading Shakespeare to John—at his own request, for I never forced such things on you. I came to that passage in which Macbeth, having murdered Duncan, realizes what he has done to his own soul, and asks if all the water in the world can ever wash the blood from his hand, or will it not rather

The multitudinous seas incarnadine?

At that line, John's whole body twitched. I gave great silent thanks to God. For I knew that if, as children, you could thus feel in your souls the reverence and awe for life and the world, which is the ultimate meaning of Beethoven and Shakespeare, as man and woman you could never be satisfied with less. I felt a great faith that sooner or later you would understand what I once told you, not because I expected you to understand it then, but because I hoped that you would remember it later: "True wisdom comes from the overcoming of suffering and sin. All true wisdom is therefore touched with sadness."

5   If all this sounds unduly solemn, you know that our lives were not; that all of us suffer from an incurable itch to puncture false solemnity. In our daily lives, we were fun-loving and gay. For those who have solemnity in their souls generally have enough of it there, and do not need to force it into their faces.

Then, on 3 August 1948, you learned for the first time that your father had
10   once been a Communist, that he had worked in something called "the under-ground," that it was shameful, and that for some reason he was in Washington telling the world about it. While he was in the underground, he testified, he had worked with a number of other Communists. One of them was a man with the odd name of Alger Hiss. Later, Alger Hiss denies the allegation. Thus the Great
15   Case began, and with it our lives were changed forever.

Dear children, one autumn twilight, when you were much smaller, I slipped away from you in play and stood for a moment alone in the apple orchard near the barn. Then I heard your two voices, piping together anxiously, calling to me: "Papa! Papa!" from the harvested cornfield. In the years when I was away
20   five days a week in New York, working to pay for the farm, I used to think of you both before I fell asleep at night. And that is how you almost always came to me—voices of beloved children, calling to me from the gathered fields at dusk.

You called to me once again at night in the same orchard. That was a good
25   many years later. A shadow deeper and more chilling than the autumn evening had closed upon us—I mean the Hiss Case. It was the first year of the Case. We had been doing the evening milking together. For us, one of the few happy results of the Case was that at last I could be home with you most of the time (in life these good things usually come too little or too late). I was washing
30   and disinfecting the cows, and putting on and taking off the milkers. You were stripping after me.

In the quiet, there suddenly swept over my mind a clear realization of our true position—obscure, all but friendless people (some of my great friends had already taken refuge in aloofness; the others I had withdrawn from so as not
35   to involve them in my affairs). Against me was an almost solid line-up of the most powerful groups and men in the country, the bitterly hostile reaction of much of the press, the smiling skepticism of much of the public, the venomous calumnies of the Hiss forces, the all but universal failure to understand the real meaning of the Case or my real purpose. A sense of the enormous futility of
40   my effort, and my own inadequacy, drowned me. I felt a physical cold creep

through me, settle around my heart and freeze any pulse of hope. The sight of your children, guiltless and defenseless, was more than I could bear. I was alone against the world; my longing was to be left completely alone, or not to be at all. It was that death of the will which Communism, with great cunning, always tries to induce in its victims.

I waited until the last cow was stripped and the last can lifted into the cooler. Then I stole into the upper barn and out into the apple orchard. It was a very dark night. The stars were large and cold. This cold was one with the coldness in myself. The lights of the barn, the house and the neighbors' houses were warm in the windows and on the ground; they were not for me. Then I heard Ellen call me in the barn and John called: "Papa!" Still calling, Ellen went down to the house to see if I were there. I heard John opening gates as he went to the calf barn, and he called me there. With all the longing of my love for you, I wanted to answer. But if I answered, I must come back to the living world. I could not do that.

John began to call me in the cow stable, in the milk house. He went into the dark side of the barn (I heard him slide the door back), into the upper barn, where at night he used to be afraid. He stepped outside in the dark, calling: "Papa! Papa!"—then, frantically, on the verge of tears: "Papa!" I walked over to him. I felt that I was making the most terrible surrender I should have to make on earth. "Papa," he cried and threw his arms around me, "don't ever go away." "No," I said, "no, I won't ever go away." Both of us knew that the words "go away" stood for something else, and that I had given him my promise not to kill myself. Later on, as you will see, I was tempted, in my wretchedness, to break that promise.

My children, when you were little, we used sometimes to go for walks in our pine woods. In the open fields, you would run along by yourselves. But you used instinctively to give me your hands as we entered those woods, where it was darker, lonelier, and in the stillness our voices sounded loud and frightening. In this book I am again giving you my hands. I am leading you, not through cool pine woods, but up and up a narrow defile between bare and steep rocks from which in shadow things uncoil and slither away. It will be dark. But, in the end, if I have led you aright, you will make out three crosses, from two of which hang thieves. I will have brought you to Golgotha—the place of skulls. This is the meaning of the journey. Before you understand, I may not be there, my hands may have slipped from yours. It will not matter. For when you understand what you see, you will no longer be children. You will know that life is pain, that each of us hangs always upon the cross of himself. And when you know that this is true of every man, woman and child on earth, you will be wise.

Your Father

The Problem of Tradition
Russell Kirk (1918–1994)

One could argue persuasively that the American conservative intellectual movement owes its very existence to the literary effort and scholarly achievement of Russell Kirk, the Michigan native, occasional Hillsdale College professor, and tireless romantic foe of what he called modern "assembly-line civilization." In the decades following the 1953 appearance of his seminal book, The Conservative Mind, *Kirk resolutely defended social order, mystery, and tradition in the face of the modern world's pressing sins, among which he named utilitarian vocationalism, contemporary egalitarianism, and the illusion of human perfectibility.*

Kirk's career constituted nothing short of what historian George Nash called "a full-scale challenge to modernity." Accordingly, nothing modern, from hyper-athleticized college campuses to four-lane superhighways, escaped Kirk's penetrating critique. But to think of Kirk as a nay-sayer in search of personal fulfillment through denunciation and destruction of the modern world would be deeply mistaken. If Kirk stood against *the errors of the modern project, he stood even more fiercely* for *"the permanent things" which come to us through "tradition." It is important, in this regard, to distinguish between "traditionalism," which is the dead faith of the living, and "tradition," which is the living faith of the dead. While the former is at best a dusty impotent charade, the latter animates the human heart, orders the soul, and ultimately sustains civilizations.*

The word conservative *comes from the Latin* conservare, *which means "to defend, maintain, and preserve." Kirk sought to defend, maintain, and preserve "the permanent things," "tradition," and the eternal "contract" between the dead, living, and yet unborn. As such, his conservatism remained overwhelmingly positive in focus. In a world where so-called "new" things confront Americans daily, we need something unchanging,*

Russell Kirk, *A Program for Conservatives* (Chicago: Henry Regnery Company, 1954), 294–312 [footnotes in original]. Reprinted with the permission of Annette Y. Kirk.

something that is not new, to anchor us, to sustain genuine order, and to
teach us the difference between passing fads and enduring truth. In the
following essay, Kirk defends tradition, arguing that it serves as that anchor
by informing the present with wisdom from the past, and providing the
means by which to transmit that wisdom to our posterity.

1954

When I was a very small boy, I used to lie under an oak on the hillside above the
mill-pond, in the town where I was born, and look beyond the great willows in
the hollow to a curious and handsome house that stood on the opposite slope,
away back from the road, with three or four graceful pines pointing the way to
5   it. This was an octagonal house, its roof crowned with a glass dome—a dignified building, for all its oddity. Well, the county planners have chopped down
the willows and converted the land round about the old mill-pond into what
the traffic-engineers and professional town-planners think a "recreational area"
should look like: a dull sheet of water with some dwarf evergreens to set it off.
10   And the octagon-house was bought by a man with more money than he knew
how to spend, who knocked the house down (it costing him a good deal more
money to dynamite the thick walls of the cellar than ever he had expected, I
am glad to report) and built upon its site a silly "ranch-type" dwelling vaguely
imitated from Californian styles. As Thoreau used to buy all the farms round
15   Walden Pond in his fancy, so I had made myself, often enough, proprietor of
the octagon-house in my mind's eye. But I do not care to look upon the spot
now. The old genius is departed out of the town and the country about it. We
do our best to assimilate every community that retains something of its peculiar
character to the proletarian cosmopolis of modern mass-society.
20   The expectation of change has come to exceed the expectation of continuity
in almost the whole of America, even in the physical environment of the civil
social existence. The annihilation of our traditional architecture and town-pat-
terns, indeed, is only part of a larger revolutionary movement calculated to efface
the Past and establish a new society Utilitarian in its principles, so far as it owns
25   any principles. As Mr. T. S. Eliot observes in his *Notes toward the Definition of*
Culture, we are "destroying our ancient edifices to make ready the ground upon
which the barbarian nomads of the future will encamp in their mechanized cara-
vans." M. Gabriel Marcel, in an essay called "The Concept of Spiritual Heritage,"
published in the quarterly journal *Confluence*, suggests that innumerable men
30   and women no longer desire to be heritors of the ages; they are annoyed and
perplexed at being expected to receive and shelter traditional culture:

> For an ever increasing number of persons, our heritage is no longer
> accepted as such. It is refused, like a legacy that carries with it obliga-
> tions too heavy for the heir to carry. There is the case of the young

Negro communist who furiously protested against an ethnologist's
praise of the African civilization, for this praise seemed in some way to
imprison him in the very traditions which he was trying to thrown off
like a detested yoke. There is the brutal indifference with which in the
New World, particularly in South America, old houses are torn down   5
in order to construct huge buildings without character or dignity, that
are dwellings and nothing more, intended to hold the largest possible
number of people or offices stacked one upon the other. There is the
growing respect for youth and the discredit into which old age has
fallen. The old man is more and more regarded as no longer good for   10
anything—a corollary to the general tendency to regard output as the
only criterion of human value.

A consciousness of our spiritual inheritance, M. Marcel continues, is possible
only in an atmosphere of diffuse gratitude: gratitude not merely to the generations that have preceded us in this life, but gratitude toward the eternal order,   15
and the source of that order, which raises man above the brutes, and makes art
man's nature. *Pietas*, in short, the veneration of man's sacred associations and of
the wisdom of man's ancestors—this spirit survives only in holes and corners of
modern society; and for lack of piety, modern men are bored, impatient, and
ready enough to subvert the civil social state which is the source of their own   20
material prosperity.

Now "the contract of eternal society," that phrase which describes the concept of social obligation presently decaying among us, is the idea which forms
the kernel of Burke's *Reflections*. Society is indeed a contract, Burke says, but
not a contract in any mere historical or commercial sense. It is a partnership   25
between those who are living, those who are dead, and those who are yet to
be born. It is a contract, too, between God and man, "linking the lower with
the higher natures, connecting the visible and invisible worlds, according to a
fixed compact sanctioned by the inviolable oath which holds all physical and
all moral natures, each in their appointed place." We have no right to break   30
this contract of eternal society; and if we do, we are cast out of this world of
love and order into the antagonist world of hate and discord. Burke does not
believe that wisdom began with the eighteenth century. He employs the words
"contract" and "compact" in their most venerable meaning, the bond between
God and man. "I do set my bow in the cloud, and it shall be for a token of a   35
covenant between me and the earth." This is the thirteenth verse of the ninth
chapter of the book of Genesis. This contract, this covenant, is the free promise
of God, and its terms are obeyed by man in gratitude and in fear. Far from being
a grandiloquent transcendence of real meaning, as some of Burke's critics have

protested, Burke's employment of "contract" has the sanction of the Bible, the
Schoolmen, and the whole body of ethical conviction which carries us back to
Job and beyond Job.

5   Burke, then, spoke with the authority of a profound and practical intellect, not merely with the enthusiasm of an accomplished rhetorician, when he
described the great primaeval contract of eternal society; and I believe that our
modern blindness to the reality of this contract, and to the sobriety of Burke's
phrases, has mightily impeded any alleviation of our present discontents, our
maladies of spirit and of the body politic. What Burke illuminates here is the
10 necessity to any high and just civilization of a conscious belief in the value of
continuity: continuity in religious and ethical conviction, continuity in literature and schooling, continuity in political and economic affairs, continuity in
the physical fabric of life. I think we have neglected the principle of continuity to our present grave peril, so that with us, as Aristophanes said of his own
15 generation, "Whirl is king, having overthrown Zeus." Men who do not look
backward to their ancestors, Burke remarks elsewhere, will not look forward
to their posterity.

    If we retain any degree of concern for the future of our race, we need ur-
gently to re-examine the idea of an eternal contract that joins the dead, the living,
20 and those yet unborn. Even if we have lost most of that solicitude for posterity,
still we may need to return to the principle of continuity out of simple anxiety
for self-preservation. We live in a time when the fountains of the great deep are
broken up; half the world has been drowned already, so far as the life of spirit
and liberty and liberal learning is concerned; yet we are complacent, many of
25 us, with Cyrus at the very gates. I think that these ideas of Burke's, rather than
being vestiges of what Paine called "the Quixot age of chivalry nonsense," are
even more pertinent in our time than they were to his own society.

    Burke wrote before the modern proletariat had become a distinct force in
society, although even then its dim lineaments could be discerned in England
30 and France. Yet in passage after passage, with his prophetic gift, Burke touches
upon the terrible question of how men ignorant of tradition, impatient of any
restraint upon appetite, and stripped of true community, may be kept from
indulgence in a leveling envy that would fetch down in ruin the highest achievements of mind and spirit, and kept from releasing that congenital violence in
35 fallen human nature which could reduce to ashes the venerable edifice of the civil
social state. Once most men should forget the principle of continuity, once they
should break the eternal contract, they would be thrown on the meagre resources
of private judgment, having run recklessly through the bank and capital that
is the wisdom of our ancestors. Under this new-fangled system, "laws are to be
40 supported only by their own terrors, and by the concern which each individual

may find in them from his own private speculations, or can spare to them from
his own private interests.... Nothing is left which engages the affections on the
part of the commonwealth. On the principles of this mechanic philosophy, our
institutions can never be embodied, if I may use the expression, in persons; so
as to create in us love, admiration, or attachment. But that sort of reason which   5
banishes the affections is incapable of filling their place."

For, after all, abstract rationality cannot persuade us to observe the contract
of eternal society. It is possible for Reason to persuade us to profit from the
wisdom of our ancestors, true enough, even if pure Reason cannot teach us real
veneration. But simple rationality, guided by self-interest, never can succeed in   10
inducing us to look forward with solicitude to the interests of posterity. Men
who are governed only by an abstract intellectuality will violate their obligations
toward their ancestors by the destruction of tradition and the very monuments
of the past, since we cannot learn veneration from mere logic; and such men will
violate also their obligations toward posterity, for with them immediate appetite   15
always must take precedence over the vague claims of future generations, and
immediate appetites, if indulged without restraint, are insatiable in any society,
however prosperous. Moreover, these men will snap that connection between
the higher and the lower natures which is the sanction of the Eternal Contract,
and thus will expose society to that conflagration of will and appetite which is   20
checked, at length, only by force and a master. When men have repudiated the
divine element in social institutions, then indeed power is everything.

Why, when all is said, do any of us look to the interest of the rising generation, and to the interest of the generations which shall exist in the remote future?
Why do we not exhaust the heritage of the ages, spiritual and material, for our   25
immediate pleasure, and let posterity go hang? So far as simple rationality is
concerned, self-interest can advance no argument against the appetite of present
possessors. Yet within some of us, a voice that is not the demand of self-interest
or pure rationality says that we have no right to give ourselves enjoyment at the
expense of our ancestors' memory and our descendants' prospects. We hold our   30
present advantages only in trust. A profound sentiment informs us of this; yet this
sentiment, however strong, is not ineradicable. In some ages and in some nations,
the consciousness of a sacred continuity has been effaced almost totally. One may
trace in the history of the Roman empire the decay of belief in the contract of
eternal society, so that fewer and fewer men came to sustain greater and greater   35
burdens; the unbought grace of life shrank until only scattered individuals partook
of it—Seneca, Marcus Aurelius, here and there a governor or a scholar to knit
together, by straining his every nerve, the torn fabric of community and spiritual
continuity; until, at length, those men were too few, and the fresh dedication
of Christian faith triumphed too late to redeem the structure of society and the   40

larger part of culture from the ruin that accompanies the indulgence of present appetites in contempt of tradition and futurity.

Respect for the eternal contract is not a mere matter of instinct, then; it is implanted in our consciousness by the experience of the race and by a com-
5 plex process of education. When the disciplines which impart this respect are imperiled by violence or by a passion for novelty, the spiritual bond which joins the generations and links our nature with the divine nature is correspondingly threatened. Mr. Christopher Dawson, in his little book *Understanding Europe*, expresses this better than I can:

10			Indeed the catastrophes of the last thirty years are not only a sign of the bankruptcy of secular humanism, they also go to show that a completely secularized civilization is inhuman in the absolute sense—hostile to human life and irreconcilable with human nature itself. For… the forces of violence and aggressiveness that threaten to destroy our world are the direct result of the starvation and frustration of man's spiritual
15			nature. For a time Western civilization managed to live on the normal tradition of the past, maintained by a kind of sublimated humanitarian idealism. But this was essentially a transitional phenomenon, and as humanism and humanitarianism fade away, we see societies more and more animated by the blind will to power which drives them on to
20			destroy one another and ultimately themselves. Civilization can only be creative and life-giving in the proportion that it is spiritualized. Otherwise the increase of power inevitably increases its power for evil and its destructiveness.

25	For the breaking of the contract of eternal society does not simply obliterate the wisdom of our ancestors: it commonly converts the future into a living death, also, since progress, beneficent change, is the work of men with a sense of continuity, who look forward to posterity out of love for the legacy of their ancestors and the dictates of an authority more than human. The man who truly understands the past does not detest all change; on the contrary, he welcomes
30	change, as the means of renewing society; but he knows how to keep change in a continuous train, so that we will not lose that sense of gratitude which Marcel describes. As Burke puts it, "We must all obey the great law of change. It is the most powerful law of nature, and the means perhaps of its conservation. All we can do, and that human wisdom can do, is to provide that the change shall
35	proceed by insensible degrees. This has all the benefits which may be in change, without any of the inconveniences of mutation."

The outward fabric of our world must alter, as do our forms of society; but to demolish all that is old, out of a mere contempt for the past, is to

impoverish that human faculty which yearns after continuity and things venerable. By such means of measurement as we possess—by such indices as suicide-rate, the incidence of madness and neurosis, the appetites and tastes of the masses, the obliteration of beauty, the increase of crime, the triumph of force over the law of nations—by these signs, it seems clear, all that com-   5
plex of high aspiration and imaginative attainment which makes us civilized men is shrinking to a mere shadow of a shadow. If indeed society is governed by an eternal contract, then we may appeal to the Author of that covenant; but words without thoughts to Heaven never go, and the continuity which pertains directly to society must be repaired by those means which still are   10
within the grasp of man.

This brings us back to my hill above the mill-pond. The eternal contract, the sense of continuity among men, has been made known to succeeding generations, from the dawn of civilization, by the agency of tradition. Tradition is the process of handing on beliefs, not so much through formal schooling,   15
or through books, as through the life of the family and the observances of the church. Until the end of the eighteenth century, no one thought it conceivable that most men could obtain most of their knowledge in any other way than this; and though cheap books and eleemosynary schooling have supplanted to some extent the old functions of traditionary instruction, still tradition remains the   20
principal source of our moral beliefs and our worldly wisdom. Young persons do not acquire in school, to any considerable extent, the sense of continuity and the veneration for the eternal contract which makes possible willing obedience to social order; children acquire this sense from their parents and other elders, and from their gradual introduction to religion, if they obtain any; the   25
process is illative, rather than deliberate. Now let us suppose that parents cease to impart such instruction, or come to regard tradition as superstition; suppose that young people never become acquainted with the church—what happens to tradition? Why, its empire is destroyed, and the young join the crowd of the other-directed whom Mr. David Riesman describes.   30

In a looser sense, by "tradition" we mean all that body of knowledge which is bound up with prescription and prejudice and authority, the accepted beliefs of a people, as distinguished from "scientific" knowledge; and this, too, is greatly weakened in its influence among the rising generation by a growing contempt for any belief that is not founded upon demonstrable "fact." Almost nothing of   35
importance really can be irrefutably demonstrated by finally ascertained "facts"; but the limitations of science are not apprehended by the throng of the quarter-educated who think themselves emancipated from their spiritual heritage. When we confront these people, we are dealing not merely with persons ignorant of tradition, but actively hostile toward it.   40

Now cheap books and free schooling are not the principal reasons for this decay of the influence of tradition. The really decisive factors are the industrialization and urbanization of modern life. Tradition thrives where men follow naturally in the ways of their fathers, and live in the same houses, and
5   experience in their own lives that continuity of existence which assures them that the great things in human nature do not much alter from one generation to another. This is the mood of Ecclesiastes. But the tremendous physical and social changes that have come with the later stages of our industrial growth, and the concentration of population in raw new cities, shake men's confidence
10   that things will be with them as they were with their fathers. The sanction of permanence seems to have been dissolved. Men doubt the validity of their own opinions, founded upon tradition, and hesitate to impart them to their children—indeed, they may thrust all this vast obligation upon the unfortunate school-teacher, and then grow annoyed when the teacher turns out to be inca-
15   pable of bestowing moral certitude, scientific knowledge, and decent manners upon a class of fifty or sixty bewildered and distracted children. Most natural keepers of tradition, in short, abdicate their function when modern life makes them doubt their own virtue.

Though of course I did not understand all this at the time, it was this decay
20   of the force of tradition which was sweeping away the old mill-pond almost before my eyes, as I lay on the hill under my oak. For my part, I still was a tradition-guided boy; but the planners who altered the landscape, presently, were Benthamites confident in the sufficiency of pure rationality, and the man who demolished the octagon-house was an other-directed individual who posi-
25   tively dreaded identification with anything dead and gone, and longed to be associated, however vaguely, with the milieu of Beverly Hills. The Utilitarians and the other-directed people were using up the moral and intellectual capital which had been accumulated by a traditionary society, I came to realize much later; and that process has been in the ascendant, with an increasing velocity,
30   throughout the United States, for more than a generation now.

It cannot continue forever. Our guardians of tradition have been recruited principally, although not wholly, from our farms and small towns; the incertitude of the cities disturbs the equanimity of the tradition-guided man. And our great cities have been swelling at the expense of our country and village population, so
35   that the immense majority of young people today have no direct acquaintance with the old rural verities. Our reservoir of tradition will be drained dry within a very few decades, if we do not deliberately open up once more the springs of tradition. The size of the United States, and the comparative gradualness of industrial development in many regions, until now saved us from a complete
40   exhaustion of tradition, such as Sweden seems to have experienced. At the

beginning of this century, Sweden had seven people in the country for one in the city; now that ratio is precisely inverted; and one may obtain some hint of what the death of tradition means to a people from the fact that the Swedes, previously celebrated for their placidity and old-fashioned heartiness, now have the highest rates of abortion and suicide in the world, dismayed at the thought   5 of bringing life into this world or even of enduring one's own life.[1]

I do not want our traditions to run out, because I do not believe that formal indoctrination, or pure rationality, or simple imitation of our contemporaries, can replace traditions. Traditions are the wisdom of the race; they are the only sure instruments of moral instruction; they have about them a solemnity and a   10 mystery that Dr. Dryasdust the cultural anthropologist never can compensate for; and they teach us the solemn veneration of the eternal contract which cannot be imparted by pure reason. Even our political institutions are sustained principally by tradition, rather than by utilitarian expediency. A people who have exhausted their traditions are starved for imagination and devoid of any   15 general assumptions to give coherence to their life.

Yet I do not say that tradition ought to be our only guide, nor that tradition is always beneficent. There have been ages and societies in which tradition, stifling the creative faculty among men, put an end to variety and change, and so oppressed mankind with the boredom of everlasting worship of the past. In a   20 healthy nation, tradition must be balanced by some strong element of curiosity and individual dissent. Some people who today are conservatives because they protest against the tyranny of neoterism, in another age or nation would be radicals, because they could not endure the tyranny of tradition. It is a question of degree and balance. But I am writing of modern society, especially in the   25 United States; and among us there is not the slightest danger that we shall be crushed beneath the dead weight of tradition; the danger is altogether on the other side. Our modern affliction is the flux of ceaseless change, the repudiation of all enduring values, the agonies of indecision and the social neuroses that come with a questioning of everything in heaven and earth. We are not in the   30 plight of the old Egyptians or Peruvians; it is not prescription which enslaves us, but the lust for innovation. A young novelist, visiting George Santayana in

---

[1]A Scottish friend of mine invites young Swedish connections to his country house every summer, and what interests him most in their behavior is their pleasure at being emancipated from the boredom of the terrestrial paradise called the Third Way. The silent tyranny of democratic conformity, to which they had been always subjected at home, is lifted as soon as they arrive in Fife; at first they are surprised and suspicious, and look about for someone to reprove them for their indulgence of individuality; but once they have grown accustomed to the freedom of a society in which some elements of variety, tradition, and even irrational emotion are not eradicated, they loathe the notion of going home to the superior comforts, the abundant food, and the everlasting monontony of social-democratic Sweden.

his Roman convent in the last year of the philosopher's life, remarked that he
could not endure to live in America, where everything was forever changing and
shifting. Santayana replied, with urbane irony, that he supposed if it were not
for kaleidoscopic change in America, life there would be unbearable. A people
5   infatuated with novelty presently cannot bear to amble along; but the trouble
with this is that the pace becomes vertiginous, and the laws of centrifugal force
begin to operate.

I know that there are people who maintain that nothing is seriously wrong
with life in the United States, and that we need not fret about tradition one way
10   or the other; but I confess, at the risk of being accused of arrogance, that I take
these people for fools, whether they call themselves liberals or conservatives.
They have a fondness for pointing to the comfortable routine of our suburbs
as a demonstration of our mastery over the ancient tragedy of life. Now I am
not one of those critics of society who look upon residence in suburbia a stain
15   worse than the mark of the beast; but neither am I disposed to think that a
commuter's ticket and a lawn-sprinkler are the proofs of national greatness and
personal exaltation. And I am convinced that, if the reservoir of our traditions
is drained dry, there will not be ten thousand tidy little suburbs in America,
very long thereafter; for the suburbs are dependent upon an older order of
20   social organization, as well as upon an intricate modern apparatus of industrial
technology, for their being.

When tradition is dissipated, men do not respond to the old moral injunctions satisfactorily; and our circumstances and national character differing from
Sweden's, I do not think we would experience the comparative good fortune
25   to slip into an equalitarian boredom. The contract of eternal society forgotten, soon every lesser form of contract would lose its sanction. I say, then, that
we need to shake out of their complacency the liberals who are smug in their
conviction of the immortality of Liberal Democratic Folkways in the United
States, and the conservatives who are smug in their conviction of the abiding
30   superiority of the American Standard of Living. Political arrangements, and
economic systems, rest upon the foundation of moral prejudices which find
their expression in tradition.

Men who assail smugness cannot hope to be popular, in any climate of
opinion; so the conservative ought not to expect to be thanked for reminding
35   his age of the contract of eternal society. When he protests against the reduction
of the mass of men to a condition below the dignity of true humanity, he will be
attacked as an enemy of democracy, and ridiculed as a snob—when, in truth, he
is endeavoring to save a democracy of elevation, and to put down the snobbery
of a rootless new managerial elite. Mr. Wyndham Lewis, in *Rude Assignment*,
40   refers to the abuse which many professors and publicists heap upon anyone

who presumes to suggest that there is something wrong with modern minds and hearts: "To keep other people in mental leading-strings, to have *beneath* you a broad mass of humanity to which you (although no intellectual giant) can feel agreeably superior: this petty and disagreeable form of the will-to-power of the average 'smart' man counts for much in the degradation of the Many. And there is no action of this same 'smart' man that is more aggravating than the way in which he will turn upon the critic of the social scene (who has pointed out the degradation of the Many) and accuse him of 'despising the people.'" Nothing is more resented than the truth, and, as Mr. Lewis says, "people have deteriorated. They have neither the will nor common sense of the peasant or guildsman, and are more easily fooled. This can only be a source of concern and regret, to all except 'the leader of men.'"

Wherever human dignity is found, it is the product of a conviction that we are part of some great continuity and essence, which elevates us above the brutes; and wherever popular government is just and free, it is in consequence of a belief that there are standards superior to the interest of the hour and the will of a temporary majority. If these things are forgotten, then indeed the people will become despicable. The conservative, in endeavoring to restore a consciousness among men of the worth of tradition, is not acting in contempt of the masses; he is acting, instead, out of love for them, as human persons, and he is trying to preserve for them such a life as men should lead. The conservative does not believe that learning must be debased "because the people want it," or that a country's aspect must be made hideous "because the people want it," or that literature must vanish before the comic-book "because the people want it." He does not entertain so low an opinion of the people. The proletariat, shorn of tradition and roots, may crave such a degradation; but the conservative hopes to restore the lonely crowd who make up the faceless proletariat to character and individuality once more. And perhaps the first step in that restoration must be a renewed attention to the claims of tradition.

It is possible to revive a sense of traditions among a crowd who have forgotten the whole concept of tradition? The thinking conservative believes so. The work must be slow and subtle; but I suggest here some of the aspects of the undertaking:

(1) A reaffirmation of the truth that lies in tradition. The conservative will contend against the presumption of "intellectuals" who think that all wisdom comes from pure rationality and formal schooling. He will assure men, with Pascal, that the heart has reasons which the reason knows not, and that the immemorial customs and beliefs of a people ordinarily have meaning and value in them, whether or not we can explain them by pure reason.

(2) A defense of the classes and regions in which tradition still is a living force. The conservative will do everything in his power to prevent the further diminution of our rural population; he will recommend decentralization of industry and deconcentration of population; he will seek to keep as many men
5   and women as possible close to the natural and customary world in which tradition flourishes. This will not be an artificial reaction against a natural process of consolidation, for our intensive industrialization and urbanization, from the days of Hamilton to the Korean War, have been deliberate policies, encouraged by state and national governments and by great corporate bodies. If we were
10 to apply half as much energy and thought to the preservation of rural life and the old structure of community as we have put to consolidation, we might be as well balanced in these relationships as is Switzerland.

(3) A humanization of urban life, bringing to the city man a sense of continuity. It is not impossible for urban people to have their traditions, though
15 tradition finds the country more congenial. In America, our towns have thrown all their influence behind a deliberate disruption of old ways and old things, commonly. In an Idaho town, recently, it was proposed that the trees in the public square be chopped down and a parking-lot established there. Someone protested; and a member of the city council, a shopkeeper, was astounded that
20 there should be any objection: "Why, some of those trees are as much as thirty years old!" Whatever had roots and age, in this energumen's view, ought to be extirpated, as anti-progressive. Half the battle for the tradition of townsfolk would be won be a simple change of attitude. The preservation of old houses and neighborhoods, for instance, is a buttress of tradition in general;[2] but most
25 city-planners and traffic-engineers desire to sweep away every vestige of past generations. With the physical past, they abolish the sense of continuity, very commonly. What city-reformers ought to aspire to, rather, is such designs as the Baltimore plan, under which the tax-structure and the regulatory powers of the municipality are employed to bring about the constant repair and improvement
30 of old neighborhoods, not their wholesale destruction.

(4) The returning to family and church and voluntary association of their old responsibilities as transmitters of tradition. The arrogant claim of many educationalists that they have a right to "train the whole child" and to form his character and opinions regardless of the prejudices of his family and his church

---

[2] Perhaps it is worth remarking that the most conservative bodies of citizens in all Italy are the slum-dwellers in the oldest quarters of Rome and Naples, the poorest of the poor, hard haters of all modern social reform. I suspect that there is some unconscious association between their atmosphere of antiquity and their attachment to traditional society. A friend of mine suggests that the same influence may possibly be discerned, in the near future, among the negroes who are moving in to the handsome big houses of the once-fashionable districts of Detroit.

and all the older agencies for education must be denied by the conservative. Parents ought to be encouraged to instruct their children in moral traditions, in the disciplines of private conduct, and in the ways of the world; churches ought to be supported in their endeavors to make religious knowledge the most important part of any educational system. The formal agencies of the state cannot   5
convey to young people, in any satisfactory degree, a sense of continuity and the eternal contract; and we ought to confess this, and restore to other and older agencies the duties which should never have been taken from them. A dismal compulsory salute to the flag, and mumbled collective pledge of allegiance to an abstract state, is a wretched substitute for the feeling of loyalty which grows   10
out of love of family and love of local community.

In the defense of tradition, as with the several other problems I have touched upon in this book, the conservative must not be daunted by the probability that he will be misunderstood by most people, and assaulted by everyone whose material interest seems to be bound up with the continued degradation of the   15
masses. The doctrinaire liberal will call him names, and the unreflecting present possessor of property and power will give him no support. And the conservative must face the fact that he may very well be beaten; unlike the Marxist, the conservative does not profess a fanatic belief in an ultimate inevitable triumph of his cause. But the conservative, despite all this, will not surrender to the   20
contagion of mass-opinion or the temptations of material aggrandizement and power. Convinced that he is a party to the contract of eternal society, he will abide by the sanctity of that contract, and do his appointed part under that compact. His back is to the wall, in our day, so that if he hopes to conserve anything at all, he must make his stand unflinchingly. He is not now defending   25
mere ornaments and details of the civil social existence; he is not arguing simply about the Corn Laws, or the strict interpretation of the Constitution, or the mode of electing senators, or the regulation of wages and hours. All these were important questions in their time, but the modern conservative has Medusa to contend with, and lesser matters shrink to insignificance beside the dilemma   30
of humanity in this century.

The grand question before us is really this: Is life worth living? Are men and women to live as human persons, formed in God's image, with the minds and hearts and individuality of spiritual beings, or are they to become crea-tures less than human, herded by the masters of the total state, debauched by   35
the indulgence of every appetite, deprived of the consolations of religion and tradition and learning and the sense of continuity, drenched in propaganda, aimless amusements, and the flood of sensual triviality which is supplanting the private reason? Are they to be themselves, endowed with personality and

variety and hope, or are they to be the vague faces in the Lonely Crowd, devoid of all the traditional motives to integrity? The radical and the liberal, I think, have failed dismally to show us any road to the redemption of mankind from modern boredom and modern decadence. The conservative is become our guide, whether he likes it or not, and regardless of the will of the crowd. He may not succeed in covering the dry bones of this program with flesh and blood. If he is unequal to the task, the clock will strike, and Faustus will be damned.

Great civilizations do not fall at a single blow. Our civilization has sustained several terrible assaults already, and still it lives; but that does not mean that it can live for ever, or even endure through another generation. Like a neglected old house, a society whose members have forgot the ends of society's being and of their own lives sinks by degrees almost imperceptible toward its ruin. The rain comes in at the broken pane; the dry-rot spreads like the corpse of a tree within the wall; the plaster drops upon the sodden floor; the joists groan with every wind; and the rat, creeping down the stair at midnight, gnaws his dirty way from the desolate kitchen to the mildewed satins of the parlor. We men of the twentieth century have this house only, and no other: the storm outside, in the winter of our discontent, will allow of no idle building of dream-castles; the summer indolence of the age of optimism is long gone by. The conservative, if he knows his own tradition, understands that his appointed part, in the present forlorn state of society, is to save man from fading into a ghost condemned to linger hopeless in a rotten tenement.

BROWN v. BOARD OF EDUCATION

In this landmark decision, the Supreme Court helped initiate a revolution in American race relations (often called the "Second Reconstruction") and signaled the rise of a new kind of liberal activism in the Court led by Chief Justice Earl Warren (r. 1953–1969).

In 1954 the Supreme Court held that segregation in public education was an unconstitutional violation of the Fourteenth Amendment's guarantee of equal protection of the laws. This decision, soon extended to a wider range of public institutions, overturned the Court's precedent in Plessy v. Ferguson *(1896) that segregated institutions were acceptable if equal accommodations were provided. Brown was the capstone to a series of cases going back to 1938 which had desegregated professional schools and universities in the South.*

The Court was aware of the controversy that such a decision would provoke, and so was careful to render a brief, unanimous, and limited decision. In particular, the Court did not hold that all segregation was unconstitutional, let alone that all racial classifications were invalid, as Justice John Marshall Harlan had insisted in his dissent in Plessy. *On the other hand, the Court did not require integration.*

Thus, although the decision has been regarded as a landmark in Supreme Court and civil rights history, and later moral acclamation emboldened the Court to take on other controversial social questions, it was of little immediate effect. Southern schools remained segregated for over another decade, since the Court soon instructed schools to desegregate "with all deliberate speed." The Court survived a number of attempts by southern congressmen and others, alarmed at this extension of national power in the most intimate of local institutions, to curb the jurisdiction of the federal courts. Moreover, the Court was criticized by many supporters

Walter Wyatt, *Cases Adjudged in the Supreme Court at October Term, 1953*, United States Reports 347 (Washington, DC: Government Printing Office, 1954), 483–96.

of desegregation for having based its decision more on intuition or dubious
evidence regarding the sociological and psychological effects of segregation
than on clear and persuasive constitutional principles.

17 MAY 1954

These cases come to us from the states of Kansas, South Carolina, Virginia, and Delaware. They are premised on different facts and different local conditions, but a common legal question justifies their consideration together in this consolidated opinion.

In each of the cases, minors of the Negro race, through their legal represen-
5   tatives, seek the aid of the courts in obtaining admission to the public schools of their community on a non-segregated basis. In each instance, they had been denied admission to schools attended by white children under laws requiring or permitting segregation according to race. This segregation was alleged to deprive the plaintiffs of the equal protection of the laws under the Fourteenth
10 Amendment. In each of the cases other than the Delaware case, a three-judge federal district court denied relief to the plaintiffs on the so-called "separate but equal" doctrine announced by this Court in *Plessy* v. *Ferguson* (163 U.S. 537). Under that doctrine, equality of treatment is accorded when the races are provided substantially equal facilities, even though these facilities be separate.
15 In the Delaware case, the Supreme Court of Delaware adhered to that doctrine, but ordered that the plaintiffs be admitted to the white schools because of their superiority to the Negro schools.

The plaintiffs contend that segregated public schools are not "equal" and cannot be made "equal," and that hence they are deprived of the equal protection
20 of the laws. Because of the obvious importance of the question presented, the Court took jurisdiction. Argument was heard in the 1952 term, and re-argument was heard this term on certain questions propounded by the Court.

Re-argument was largely devoted to the circumstances surrounding the adoption of the Fourteenth Amendment in 1868. It covered exhaustively consid-
25 eration of the Amendment in Congress, ratification by the states, then-existing practices in racial segregation, and the views of proponents and opponents of the Amendment. This discussion and our own investigation convince us that, although these sources cast some light, it is not enough to resolve the problem with which we are faced. At best, they are inconclusive. The most avid propo-
30 nents of the post-War Amendments undoubtedly intended them to remove all legal distinctions among "all persons born or naturalized in the United States." Their opponents, just as certainly, were antagonistic to both the letter and the spirit of the Amendments and wished them to have the most limited effect. What others in Congress and the state legislatures had in mind cannot be determined
35 with any degree of certainty.

An additional reason for the inconclusive nature of the Amendment's history, with respect to segregated schools, is the status of public education at that time. In the South, the movement toward free common schools, supported by general taxation, had not yet taken hold. Education of white children was largely in the hands of private groups. Education of Negroes was almost 5 non-existent, and practically all of the race were illiterate. In fact, any education of Negroes was forbidden by law in some states. Today, in contrast, many Negroes have achieved outstanding success in the arts and sciences as well as in the business and professional world. It is true that public school education at the time of the Amendment had advanced further in the North, but the effect 10 of the Amendment on Northern states was generally ignored in the congressional debates. Even in the North, the conditions of public education did not approximate those existing today. The curriculum was usually rudimentary; un-graded schools were common in rural areas; the school term was but three months a year in many states; and compulsory school attendance was virtually 15 unknown. As a consequence, it is not surprising that there should be so little in the history of the Fourteenth Amendment relating to its intended effect on public education.

In the first cases in this Court construing the Fourteenth Amendment, decided shortly after its adoption, the Court interpreted it as proscribing all 20 state-imposed discriminations against the Negro race. The doctrine of "separate but equal" did not make its appearance in this Court until 1896 in the case of *Plessy* v. *Ferguson, supra*, involving not education but transportation. American courts have since labored with the doctrine for over half a century. In this Court, there have been six cases involving the "separate but equal" doctrine in the field 25 of public education. In *Cumming* v. *County Board of Education* (175 U.S. 528) and *Gong Lum* v. *Rice* (275 U.S. 78), the validity of the doctrine itself was not challenged. In more recent cases, all on the graduate school level, inequality was found in that specific benefits enjoyed by white students were denied to Negro students of the same educational qualifications. *Missouri ex rel. Gaines* v. 30 *Canada* (305 U.S. 337); *Sipuel* v. *Oklahoma* (332 U.S. 631); *Sweatt* v. *Painter* (339 U.S. 629); *McLaurin* v. *Oklahoma State Regents* (339 U.S. 637). In none of these cases was it necessary to re-examine the doctrine to grant relief to the Negro plaintiff. And in *Sweatt* v. *Painter, supra*, the Court expressly reserved decision on the question whether *Plessy* v. *Ferguson* should be held inapplicable 35 to public education.

In the instant cases, that question is directly presented. Here, unlike *Sweatt* v. *Painter*, there are findings below that the Negro and white schools involved have been equalized, or are being equalized, with respect to buildings, curricula, qualifications and salaries of teachers, and other "tangible" factors. Our decision, 40 therefore, cannot turn on merely a comparison of these tangible factors in the Negro and white schools involved in each of the cases. We must look instead to the effect of segregation itself on public education.

5   In approaching this problem, we cannot turn the clock back to 1868 when the Amendment was adopted, or even to 1896, when *Plessy* v. *Ferguson* was written. We must consider public education in the light of its full development and its present place in American life throughout the nation. Only in this way can it be determined if segregation in public schools deprives these plaintiffs of the equal protection of the laws.

10   Today, education is perhaps the most important function of state and local governments. Compulsory school attendance laws and the great expenditures for education both demonstrate our recognition of the importance of education to our democratic society. It is required in the performance of our most basic public responsibilities, even service in the armed forces. It is the very

15   foundation of good citizenship. Today it is a principal instrument in awakening the child to cultural values, in preparing him for later professional training, and in helping him to adjust normally to his environment. In these days, it is doubtful that any child may reasonably be expected to succeed in life if he is denied the opportunity of an education. Such an opportunity, where the

20   state has undertaken to provide it, is a right which must be made available to all on equal terms.

We come then to the question presented: Does segregation of children in public schools solely on the basis of race, even though the physical facilities and other "tangible" factors may be equal, deprive the children of the minority

25   group of equal educational opportunities? We believe that it does.

In *Sweatt* v. *Painter, supra*, in finding that a segregated law school for Negroes could not provide them equal educational opportunities, this Court relied in large part on "those qualities which are incapable of objective measurement but which make for greatness in a law school." In *McLaurin* v. *Oklahoma*

30   *State Regents, supra*, the Court, in requiring that a Negro admitted to a white graduate school be treated like all other students, again resorted to intangible considerations: "...his ability to study, to engage in discussions and exchange views with other students, and, in general, to learn his profession." Such considerations apply with added force to children in grade and high schools. To

35   separate them from others of similar age and qualifications solely because of their race generates a feeling of inferiority as to their status in the community that may affect their hearts and minds in a way unlikely ever to be undone. The effect of this separation on their educational opportunities was well stated by a finding in the Kansas case by a court which nevertheless felt compelled to

40   rule against the Negro plaintiffs:

Segregation of white and colored children in public schools has a detrimental effect upon the colored children. The impact is greater when it has the sanction of the law; for the policy of separating the races is usually interpreted as denoting the inferiority of the negro group. A sense of inferiority affects the motivation of a child to learn. Segregation with the sanction of law, therefore, has a tendency to [retard] the educational and mental development of negro children and to deprive them of some of the benefits they would receive in a racial[ly] integrated school system.

Whatever may have been the extent of psychological knowledge at the time of *Plessy* v. *Ferguson*, this finding is amply supported by modern authority. Any language in *Plessy* v. *Ferguson* contrary to this finding is rejected.

We conclude that in the field of public education the doctrine of "separate but equal" has no place. Separate educational facilities are inherently unequal. Therefore, we hold that the plaintiffs and others similarly situated for whom the actions have been brought are, by reason of the segregation complained of, deprived of the equal protection of the laws guaranteed by the Fourteenth Amendment. This disposition makes unnecessary any discussion whether such segregation also violates the Due Process Clause of the Fourteenth Amendment.

Because these are class actions, because of the wide applicability of this decision, and because of the great variety of local conditions, the formulation of decrees in these cases presents problems of considerable complexity. On re-argument, the consideration of appropriate relief was necessarily subordinated to the primary question—the constitutionality of segregation in public education. We have now announced that such segregation is a denial of the equal protection of the laws. In order that we may have the full assistance of the parties in formulating decrees, the cases will be restored to the docket, and the parties are requested to present further argument on Questions 4 and 5 previously propounded by the Court for the re-argument this term. The Attorney General of the United States is again invited to participate. The Attorneys General of the states requiring or permitting segregation in public education will also be permitted to appear as *amici curiae* upon request to do so by 15 September 1954, and submission of briefs by 1 October 1954.

It is so ordered.

THE SHARON STATEMENT
Young Americans for Freedom

Young Americans for Freedom (YAF) met on the lawn of William F. Buckley's home in Sharon, Connecticut, in 1960 to adopt the "Sharon Statement," drafted originally by M. Stanton Evans. Although not uncontroversial in the conservative movement (in its attempt to "fuse" the individualism of classical liberalism and the more traditional concerns of anti-communists), the statement reflected the uneasy but workable coalition that became the force behind both the Goldwater and Reagan campaigns.

9–11 SEPTEMBER 1960

In this time of moral and political crisis, it is the responsibility of the youth of America to affirm certain eternal truths.

We, as young conservatives, believe:

That foremost among the transcendent values is the individual's use of his God-given free will, whence derives his right to be free from the restrictions   5 of arbitrary force;

That liberty is indivisible, and that political freedom cannot long exist without economic freedom;

That the purposes of government are to protect these freedoms through the preservation of internal order, the provision of national defense, and the   10 administration of justice;

That when government ventures beyond these rightful functions, it accumulates power which tends to diminish order and liberty;

That the Constitution of the United States is the best arrangement yet devised   15 for empowering government to fulfill its proper role, while restraining it from the concentration and abuse of power;

"The Sharon Statement," *National Review* 9 (24 September 1960):173. Reprinted by permission of Young Americans for Freedom.

That the genius of the Constitution—the division of powers—is summed up in the clause which reserves primacy to the several states, or to the people, in those spheres not specifically delegated to the Federal Government;

5   That the market economy, allocating resources by the free play of supply and demand, is the single economic system compatible with the requirements of personal freedom and constitutional government, and that it is at the same time the most productive supplier of human needs;

That when government interferes with the work of the market economy, it tends to reduce the moral and physical strength of the nation; that when it takes
10   from one man to bestow on another, it diminishes the incentive of the first, the integrity of the second, and the moral autonomy of both;

That we will be free only so long as the national sovereignty of the United States is secure; that history shows periods of freedom are rare, and can exist only when free citizens concertedly defend their rights against all enemies;

15   That the forces of international Communism are, at present, the greatest single threat to these liberties;

That the United States should stress victory over, rather than coexistence with, this menace; and

20   That American foreign policy must be judged by this criterion: does it serve the just interests of the United States?

Farewell Address
Dwight D. Eisenhower (1890–1969)
President of the United States (1953–1961)

Dwight David Eisenhower, Allied commander during World War II as well as a two-term American president in the 1950s, understood and feared the increasingly intimate relationship between the state, industry, the university system, and the American military. The Cold War with Soviet Russia seemed to demand all of America's resources. Consequently, the barriers that separated government from the rest of society were breaking down. While Eisenhower believed strongly in combating international communism, he hoped to prevent the breakdown and disintegration of all that was worth defending in the United States. In other words, if the U.S. had to become like the U.S.S.R. to defeat them, a new strategy must be adopted. Events in the 1960s and 1970s—the war in Vietnam and the federal co-option of the universities—proved Eisenhower correct in his dire predictions regarding the military-industrial complex.

17 January 1961

Three days from now, after half a century in the service of our country, I shall lay down the responsibilities of office as, in traditional and solemn ceremony, the authority of the Presidency is vested to my successor.

This evening I come to you with a message of leave-taking and farewell, and to share a few final thoughts with you, my countrymen. 5

Like every other citizen, I wish the new President, and all who will labor with him, Godspeed. I pray that the coming years will be blessed with peace and prosperity for all.

Our people expect their President and the Congress to find essential agreement on issues of great moment, the wise resolution of which will better shape 10 the future of the Nation.

My own relations with the Congress, which began on a remote and tenuous basis when, long ago, a member of the Senate appointed me to West Point, have

Public Papers of the Presidents of the United States, Dwight D. Eisenhower, 1961–1961 (Washington, DC: United States Government Printing Office, 1961), 1035–40.

since ranged to the intimate during the war and immediate post-war period, and, finally, to the mutually interdependent during these past eight years.

In this final relationship, the Congress and the Administration have, on most vital issues, co-operated well, to serve the national good rather than mere
5   partisanship, and so have assured that the business of the Nation should go forward. So, my official relationship with the Congress ends in a feeling, on my part, of gratitude that we have been able to do so much together.

We now stand ten years past the midpoint of a century that has witnessed four major wars among great nations. Three of these involved our own country.
10 Despite these holocausts America is today the strongest, the most influential and most productive nation in the world. Understandably proud of this pre-eminence, we yet realize that America's leadership and prestige depend, not merely upon our unmatched material progress, riches and military strength, but on how we use our power in the interests of world peace and human betterment.

15 Throughout America's adventure in free government, our basic purposes have been to keep the peace; to foster progress in human achievement, and to enhance liberty, dignity and integrity among people and among nations. To strive for less would be unworthy of a free and religious people. Any failure traceable to arrogance, or our lack of comprehension or readiness to sacrifice
20 would inflict upon us grievous hurt both at home and abroad.

Progress toward these noble goals is persistently threatened by the conflict now engulfing the world. It commands our whole attention, absorbs our very beings. We face a hostile ideology—global in scope, atheistic in character, ruthless in purpose, and insidious in method. Unhappily the danger it poses promises
25 to be of indefinite duration. To meet it successfully, there is called for, not so much the emotional and transitory sacrifices of crises, but rather those which enable us to carry forward steadily, surely, and without complaint the burdens of a prolonged and complex struggle—with liberty the stake. Only thus shall we remain, despite every provocation, on our charted course toward permanent
30 peace and human betterment.

Crises there will continue to be. In meeting them, whether foreign or domestic, great or small, there is a recurring temptation to feel that some spectacular and costly action could become the miraculous solution to all current difficulties. A huge increase in newer elements of our defense; development of unrealistic
35 programs to cure every ill in agriculture; a dramatic expansion in basic and applied research—these and many other possibilities, each possibly promising in itself, may be suggested as the only way to the road we wish to travel.

But each proposal must be weighed in the light of a broader consideration: the need to maintain balance in and among national programs—balance be-
40 tween the private and the public economy, balance between cost and hoped for

advantage—balance between the clearly necessary and the comfortably desirable; balance between our essential requirements as a nation and the duties imposed by the nation upon the individual; balance between actions of the moment and the national welfare of the future. Good judgment seeks balance and progress; lack of it eventually finds imbalance and frustration.   5

The record of many decades stands as proof that our people and their government have, in the main, understood these truths and have responded to them well, in the face of stress and threat. But threats, new in kind or degree, constantly arise. I mention two only.

A vital element in keeping the peace is our military establishment. Our   10
arms must be mighty, ready for instant action, so that no potential aggressor may be tempted to risk his own destruction.

Our military organization today bears little relation to that known by any of my predecessors in peacetime, or indeed by the fighting men of World War II or Korea.   15

Until the latest of our world conflicts, the United States had no armaments industry. American makers of plowshares could, with time and as required, make swords as well. But now we can no longer risk emergency improvisation of national defense; we have been compelled to create a permanent armaments industry of vast proportions. Added to this, three and a half million men   20
and women are directly engaged in the defense establishment. We annually spend on military security more than the net income of all United States corporations.

This conjunction of an immense military establishment and a large arms industry is new in the American experience. The total influence—economic,   25
political, even spiritual—is felt in every city, every statehouse, every office of the Federal government. We recognize the imperative need for this development. Yet we must not fail to comprehend its grave implications. Our toil, resources and livelihood are all involved; so is the very structure of our society.

In the councils of government, we must guard against the acquisition of   30
unwarranted influence, whether sought or unsought, by the military-industrial complex. The potential for the disastrous rise of misplaced power exists and will persist.

We must never let the weight of this combination endanger our liberties or democratic processes. We should take nothing for granted. Only an alert and   35
knowledgeable citizenry can compel the proper meshing of the huge industrial and military machinery of defense with our peaceful methods and goals, so that security and liberty may prosper together.

Akin to, and largely responsible for the sweeping changes in our industrial-military posture, has been the technological revolution during recent decades.   40

In this revolution, research has become central; it also becomes more for-malized, complex, and costly. A steadily increasing share is conducted for, by, or at the direction of, the Federal government.

5 Today, the solitary inventor, tinkering in his shop, has been over-shadowed by task forces of scientists in laboratories and testing fields. In the same fashion, the free university, historically the fountainhead of free ideas and scientific dis-covery, has experienced a revolution in the conduct of research. Partly because of the huge costs involved, a government contract becomes virtually a substitute for intellectual curiosity. For every old blackboard there are now hundreds of 10 new electronic computers.

The prospect of domination of the nation's scholars by Federal employment, project allocations, and the power of money is ever present—and is gravely to be regarded.

Yet, in holding scientific research and discovery in respect, as we should, 15 we must also be alert to the equal and opposite danger that public policy could itself become the captive of a scientific-technological elite.

It is the task of statesmanship to mold, to balance, and to integrate these and other forces, new and old, within the principles of our democratic system—ever aiming toward the supreme goals of our free society.

20 Another factor in maintaining balance involves the element of time. As we peer into society's future, we—you and I, and our government—must avoid the impulse to live only for today, plundering, for our own ease and convenience, the precious resources of tomorrow. We cannot mortgage the material assets of our grandchildren without risking the loss also of their political and spiritual 25 heritage. We want democracy to survive for all generations to come, not to become the insolvent phantom of tomorrow.

Down the long lane of the history yet to be written America knows that this world of ours, ever growing smaller, must avoid becoming a community of dreadful fear and hate, and be, instead, a proud confederation of mutual 30 trust and respect.

Such a confederation must be one of equals. The weakest must come to the conference table with the same confidence as do we, protected as we are by our moral, economic, and military strength. That table, though scarred by many past frustrations, cannot be abandoned for the certain agony of the battlefield.

35 Disarmament, with mutual honor and confidence, is a continuing impera-tive. Together we must learn how to compose differences, not with arms, but with intellect and decent purpose. Because this need is so sharp and apparent I confess that I lay down my official responsibilities in this field with a definite sense of disappointment. As one who has witnessed the horror and the linger-40 ing sadness of war—as one who knows that another war could utterly destroy

this civilization which has been so slowly and painfully built over thousands of years—I wish I could say tonight that a lasting peace is in sight.

Happily, I can say that war has been avoided. Steady progress toward our ultimate goal has been made. But, so much remains to be done. As a private citizen, I shall never cease to do what little I can to help the world advance   5
along that road.

So—in this my last good night to you as your President—I thank you for the many opportunities you have given me for public service in war and peace. I trust that in that service you find some things worthy; as for the rest of it, I know you will find ways to improve performance in the future.   10

You and I—my fellow citizens—need to be strong in our faith that all nations, under God, will reach the goal of peace with justice. May we be ever unswerving in devotion to principle, confident but humble with power, diligent in pursuit of the Nation's great goals.

To all the peoples of the world, I once more give expression to America's   15
prayerful and continuing aspiration:

We pray that peoples of all faiths, all races, all nations, may have their great human needs satisfied; that those now denied opportunity shall come to enjoy it to the full; that all who yearn for freedom may experience its spiritual blessings; that those who have freedom will understand, also, its heavy responsibilities;   20
that all who are insensitive to the needs of others will learn charity; that the scourges of poverty, disease and ignorance will be made to disappear from the earth, and that, in the goodness of time, all peoples will come to live together in a peace guaranteed by the binding force of mutual respect and love.

INAUGURAL ADDRESS
JOHN F. KENNEDY (1917–1963)
PRESIDENT OF THE UNITED STATES (1961–1963)

John Fitzgerald Kennedy took office January 20, 1961, after one of the narrowest electoral victories in American history. In looking toward his inauguration, the president-elect told his aides, in the words of James Mac-Gregor Burns, that "he wanted a short, eloquent, non-partisan, optimistic speech that would focus on foreign policy." What he got has become one of the most celebrated inaugural addresses in American history. The speech came in the midst of the Cold War, and it marked the passage of power from one of the oldest presidents, Dwight Eisenhower, to the youngest ever elected. It contained ideas taken from an astonishing collection of people, among them Jean-Jacques Rousseau, Adlai Stevenson, Walter Lippmann, John Kenneth Galbraith, Billy Graham—and, of course, Kennedy himself.

20 JANUARY 1961

We observe today not a victory of party but a celebration of freedom—symbolizing an end as well as a beginning—signifying renewal as well as change. For I have sworn before you and Almighty God the same solemn oath our forebears prescribed nearly a century and three quarters ago.

The world is very different now. For man holds in his mortal hands the 5 power to abolish all forms of human poverty and all forms of human life. And yet the same revolutionary beliefs for which our forebears fought are still at issue around the globe—the belief that the rights of man come not from the generosity of the state but from the hand of God.

We dare not forget today that we are the heirs of the first revolution. Let 10 the word go forth from this time and place, to friend and foe alike, that the torch has been passed to a new generation of Americans—born in this century, tempered by war, disciplined by a hard and bitter peace, proud of our ancient heritage—and unwilling to witness or permit the slow undoing of those human rights to which this nation has always been committed, and to which we are 15 committed today at home and around the world.

Public Papers of the Presidents of the United States, John F. Kennedy, 1961 (Washington, DC: United States Government Printing Office, 1962), 1–3.

Let every nation know, whether it wishes us well or ill, that we shall pay any price, bear any burden, meet any hardship, support any friend, oppose any foe to assure the survival and the success of liberty.

This much we pledge—and more.

5   To those old allies whose cultural and spiritual origins we share, we pledge the loyalty of faithful friends. United, there is little we cannot do in a host of cooperative ventures. Divided, there is little we can do—for we dare not meet a powerful challenge at odds and split asunder.

To those new states whom we welcome to the ranks of the free, we pledge
10 our word that one form of colonial control shall not have passed away merely to be replaced by a far more iron tyranny. We shall not always expect to find them supporting our view. But we shall always hope to find them strongly supporting their own freedom—and to remember that, in the past, those who foolishly sought power by riding the back of the tiger ended up inside.

15 To those peoples in the huts and villages of half the globe struggling to break the bonds of mass misery, we pledge our best efforts to help them help themselves, for whatever period is required—not because the communists may be doing it, not because we seek their votes, but because it is right. If a free society cannot help the many who are poor, it cannot save the few who are rich.

20 To our sister republics south of our border, we offer a special pledge—to convert our good words into good deeds—in a new alliance for progress—to assist free men and free governments in casting off the chains of poverty. But this peaceful revolution of hope cannot become the prey of hostile powers. Let all our neighbors know that we shall join with them to oppose aggression or
25 subversion anywhere in the Americas. And let every other power know that this Hemisphere intends to remain the master of its own house.

To that world assembly of sovereign states, the United Nations, our last best hope in an age where the instruments of war have far outpaced the instruments of peace, we renew our pledge of support—to prevent it from becoming merely
30 a forum for invective—to strength its shield of the new and the weak—and to enlarge the area in which its writ may run.

Finally, to those nations who would make themselves our adversary, we offer not a pledge but a request: that both sides begin anew the quest for peace, before the dark powers of destruction unleashed by science engulf all humanity
35 in planned or accidental self-destruction.

We dare not tempt them with weakness. For only when our arms are sufficient, beyond doubt can we be certain beyond doubt that they will never be employed.

But neither can two great and powerful groups of nations take comfort from
40 our present course—both sides overburdened by the cost of modern weapons,

both rightly alarmed by the steady spread of the deadly atom, yet both racing to alter that uncertain balance of terror that stays the hand of mankind's final war.

So let us begin anew—remembering on both sides that civility is not a sign of weakness, and sincerity is always subject to proof. Let us never negotiate out of fear. But let us never fear to negotiate. 5

Let both sides explore what problems unite us instead of belaboring those problems which divide us.

Let both sides, for the first time, formulate serious and precise proposals for the inspection and control of arms—and bring the absolute power to destroy other nations under the absolute control of all nations. 10

Let both sides seek to invoke the wonders of science instead of its terrors. Together let us explore the stars, conquer the deserts, eradicate disease, tap the ocean depths and encourage the arts and commerce.

Let both sides unite to heed in all corners of the earth the command of Isaiah—to "undo the heavy burdens...(and) let the oppressed go free." 15

And if a beach-head of cooperation may push back the jungle of suspicion, let both sides join in creating a new endeavor, not a new balance of power, but a new world of law, where the strong are just and the weak secure and the peace preserved.

All this will not be finished in the first one hundred days. Nor will it be 20 finished in the first one thousand days, nor in the life of this Administration, nor even perhaps in our lifetime on this planet. But let us begin.

In your hands, my fellow citizens, more than mine, will rest the final success or failure of our course. Since this country was founded, each generation of Americans has been summoned to give testimony to its national loyalty. The graves 25 of young Americans who answered the call to service surround the globe.

Now the trumpet summons us again—not as a call to bear arms, though arms we need—not as a call to battle, though embattled we are—but a call to bear the burden of a long twilight struggle, year in and year out, "rejoicing in hope, patient in tribulation"—a struggle against the common enemies of man: 30 tyranny, poverty, disease and war itself.

Can we forge against these enemies a grand and global alliance, North and South, East and West, that can assure a more fruitful life for all mankind? Will you join in that historic effort?

In the long history of the world, only a few generations have been granted 35 the role of defending freedom in its hour of maximum danger. I do not shrink from this responsibility—I welcome it. I do not believe that any of us would exchange places with any other people or any other generation. The energy, the faith, the devotion which we bring to this endeavor will light our country and all who serve it—and the glow from that fire can truly light the world. 40

And so, my fellow Americans: ask not what your country can do for you—ask what you can do for your country.

My fellow citizens of the world: ask not what America will do for you, but what together we can do for the freedom of man.

5   Finally, whether you are citizens of America or citizens of the world, ask of us here the same high standards of strength and sacrifice which we ask of you. With a good conscience our only sure reward, with history the final judge of our deeds, let us go forth to lead the land we love, asking His blessing and His help, but knowing that here on earth God's work must truly be our own.

THE PORT HURON STATEMENT
STUDENTS FOR A DEMOCRATIC SOCIETY

The Students for a Democratic Society (SDS) drafted their Port Huron statement at the FDR Camp of the United Automobile Workers. Its main author was apparently Tom Hayden, a student at the University of Michigan who had been influenced by the "beat" writers of the 1950s as well as old American radical organizations like the League for Industrial Democracy. It was internally controversial, largely on the question of how anti-communist the organization should be. But SDS was united in calling for a "new left" in American politics, based on "participatory democracy."

YAFers and SDSers clashed on college campuses well into the 1970s. SDS was the more visible organization in the sixties, successfully carrying off protests (mostly related to Vietnam), "teach-ins," and increasingly resorting to direct action. After 1968 it began to fall apart, degenerating into violence. YAF lasted longer and eventually had almost as much impact on college campuses.

PORT HURON, MICHIGAN, 11–15 JUNE 1962

Introduction: Agenda For A Generation

We are people of this generation, bred in at least modest comfort, housed now in universities, looking uncomfortably to the world we inherit.

When we were kids the United States was the wealthiest and strongest country in the world; the only one with the atom bomb, the least scarred by modern war, an initiator of the United Nations that we thought would 5 distribute Western influence throughout the world. Freedom and equality for each individual, government of, by, and for the people—these American values we found good, principles by which we could live as men. Many of us began maturing in complacency.

Students for a Democratic Society, *The Port Huron Statement* (New York, 1964), 3–4, 7–8, 61–63.

As we grew, however, our comfort was penetrated by events too troubling to dismiss. First, the permeating and victimizing fact of human degradation, symbolized by the Southern struggle against racial bigotry, compelled most of us from silence to activism. Second, the enclosing fact of the Cold War, symbolized by the presence of the Bomb, brought awareness that we ourselves, and our friends, and millions of abstract "others" we knew more directly because of our common peril, might die at any time. We might deliberately ignore, or avoid, or fail to feel all other human problems, but not these two, for these were too immediate and crushing in their impact, too challenging in the demand that we as individuals take the responsibility for encounter and resolution.

While these and other problems either directly oppressed us or rankled our consciences and became our own subjective concerns, we began to see complicated and disturbing paradoxes in our surrounding America. The declaration "all men are created equal…" rang hollow before the facts of Negro life in the South and the big cities of the North. The proclaimed peaceful intentions of the United States contradicted its economic and military investments in the Cold War status quo.

We witnessed, and continue to witness, other paradoxes. With nuclear energy whole cities can easily be powered, yet the dominant nation-states seem more likely to unleash destruction greater than that incurred in all wars of human history. Although our own technology is destroying old and creating new forms of social organization, men still tolerate meaningless work and idleness. While two-thirds of mankind suffers undernourishment, our own upper classes revel amidst superfluous abundance. Although world population is expected to double in forty years, the nations still tolerate anarchy as a major principle of international conduct and uncontrolled exploitation governs the sapping of the earth's physical resources. Although mankind desperately needs revolutionary leadership, America rests in national stalemate, its goals ambiguous and tradition-bound instead of informed and clear, its democratic system apathetic and manipulated rather than "of, by, and for the people."…

…We would replace power rooted in possession, privilege, or circumstance by power and uniqueness rooted in love, reflectiveness, reason, and creativity. As a *social system* we seek the establishment of a democracy of individual participation, governed by two central aims:…quality and direction of his life; that society be organized to encourage independence in men and provide the media for their common participation.

In a participatory democracy, the political life would be based in several root principles:

- that decision-making of basic social consequence be carried on by public groupings;
- that politics be seen positively, as the art of collectively creating an acceptable pattern of social relations;
- that politics has the function of bringing people out of isolation and into community, thus being a necessary, though not sufficient, means of finding meaning in personal life;
- that the political order should serve to clarify problems in a way instrumental to their solution; it should provide outlets for the expression of personal grievance and aspiration; opposing views should be organized so as to illuminate choices and facilitate the attainment of goals; channels should be commonly available to relate men to knowledge and to power so that private problems—from bad recreation facilities to personal alienation—are formulated as general issues.

The economic sphere would have as its basis the principles:

- that work should involve incentives worthier than money or survival. It should be educative, not stultifying; creative, not mechanical; self-directed, not manipulated, encouraging independence, a respect for others, a sense of dignity and a willingness to accept social responsibility, since it is this experience that has crucial influence on habits, perceptions and individual ethics;
- that the economic experience is so personally decisive that the individual must share in its full determination;
- that the economy itself is of such social importance that its major resources and means of production should be open to democratic participation and subject to democratic social regulation.

Like the political and economic ones, major social institutions—cultural, educational, rehabilitative, and others—should be generally organized with the well-being and dignity of man as the essential measure of success.

In social change or interchange, we find violence to be abhorrent because it requires generally the transformation of the target, be it a human being or a community of people, into a depersonalized object of hate. It is imperative that the means of violence be abolished and the institutions—local, national, international—that encourage non-violence as a condition of conflict be developed.

These are our central values, in skeletal form. It remains vital to understand their denial or attainment in the context of the modern world....

Social relevance, the accessibility to knowledge, and internal openness—
these together make the university a potential base and agency in a movement
of social change.

1. Any new left in America must be, in large measure, a left with real
   intellectual skills, committed to deliberativeness, honesty, reflection as
   working tools. The university permits the political life to be an adjunct
   to the academic one, and action to be informed by reason.
2. A new left must be distributed in significant social roles throughout the
   country. The universities are distributed in such a manner.
3. A new left must consist of younger people who matured in the post-war
   world, and partially be directed to the recruitment of younger people.
   The university is an obvious beginning point.
4. A new left must include liberals and socialists, the former for their
   relevance, the latter for their sense of thoroughgoing reforms in the
   system. The university is a more sensible place than a political party for
   these two traditions to begin to discuss their differences and look for
   political synthesis.
5. A new left must start controversy across the land, if national policies and
   national apathy are to be reversed. The ideal university is a community
   of controversy, within itself and in its effects on communities beyond.
6. A new left must transform modern complexity into issues that can be
   understood and felt close-up by every human being. It must give form
   to the feelings of helplessness and indifference, so that people may see
   the political, social, and economic sources of their private troubles and
   organize to change society. In a time of supposed prosperity, moral
   complacency, and political manipulation, a new left cannot rely on only
   aching stomachs to be the engine force of social reform. The case for
   change, for alternatives that will involve uncomfortable personal efforts,
   must be argued as never before. The university is a relevant place for all
   of these activities.

But we need not indulge in illusions: the university system cannot complete a movement of ordinary people making demands for a better life. From
its schools and colleges across the nation, a militant left might awaken its allies,
and by beginning the process towards peace, civil rights, and labor struggles,
reinsert theory and idealism where too often reign confusion and political barter.
The power of students and faculty united is not only potential; it has shown its
actuality in the South, and in the reform movements of the North.

The bridge to political power, though, will be built through genuine co-
operation, locally, nationally, and internationally, between a new left of young

people, and an awakening community of allies. In each community we must look within the university and act with confidence that we can be powerful, but we must look outwards to the less exotic but more lasting struggles for justice.

To turn these possibilities into realities will involve national efforts at university reform by an alliance of students and faculty. They must wrest control of the educational process from the administrative bureaucracy. They must make fraternal and functional contact with allies in labor, civil rights, and other liberal forces outside the campus. They must import major public issues into the curriculum—research and teaching on problems of war and peace is an outstanding example. They must make debate and controversy, not dull pedantic cant, the common style for educational life. They must consciously build a base for their assault upon the loci of power.

As students for a democratic society, we are committed to stimulating this kind of social movement, this kind of vision and program in campus and community across the country. If we appear to seek the unattainable, as it has been said, then let it be known that we do so to avoid the unimaginable.

Letter from the Birmingham City Jail
Martin Luther King, Jr. (1929–1968)

Martin Luther King, Jr., grew up in Atlanta, Georgia, the son of a Baptist minister, and attended Morehouse College, Crozer Theological Seminary, and Boston University. He attempted to synthesize the activism of the Social Gospel with the biblical fundamentalism of his upbringing.

In contrast to the patient legal tactics of the NAACP, King brought to the civil rights movement a dynamic, charismatic mix of popular evangelism and avant-garde social psychology.

King's impatience with black and white moderates shows that he had already moved from a more moderate position in the 1955 Montgomery bus boycott, feeling pressure from more militant black power groups that would sweep aside King's spirit of peaceful (but crisis-provoking) protest.

Birmingham was a crisis point for the civil rights movement, as King moved toward "coercive nonviolence" that intended not to convert or persuade the forces of segregation, but to provoke them and show the nation their ugliness. Children from ages six to sixteen were employed, and the first acts of violent protest broke out. But the image of attack dogs and fire hoses turned on civil rights demonstrators became the national image of the Birmingham campaign, one of the set-pieces of the civil rights movement. Birmingham had a decisive impact on the Kennedy administration, forcing it to address the civil rights issue that it had so long avoided for fear of offending southern Democrats in Congress, and to push a civil rights act to end segregation.

16 April 1963

My dear Fellow Clergymen,

While confined here in the Birmingham City Jail, I came across your recent statement calling our present activities "unwise and untimely." Seldom, if ever, do I pause to answer criticism of my work and ideas. If I sought to answer all

Martin Luther King, Jr., *Letter from Birmingham City Jail* (Philadelphia: American Friends Service Committee, 1963), 3–14.

of the criticisms that cross my desk, my secretaries would be engaged in little
else in the course of the day and I would have no time for constructive work.
But since I feel that you are men of genuine goodwill and your criticisms are
sincerely set forth, I would like to answer your statement in what I hope will
5   be patient and reasonable terms.

I think I should give the reason for my being in Birmingham, since you
have been influenced by the argument of "outsiders coming in." I have the honor
of serving as president of the Southern Christian Leadership Conference, an
organization operating in every Southern state with headquarters in Atlanta,
10 Georgia. We have some eighty-five affiliate organizations all across the South—
one being the Alabama Christian Movement for Human Rights. Whenever
necessary and possible we share staff, educational and financial resources with
our affiliates. Several months ago our local affiliate here in Birmingham invited
us to be on call to engage in a nonviolent direct action program if such were
15 deemed necessary. We readily consented and when the hour came we lived up
to our promises. So I am here, along with several members of my staff, because
we were invited here. I am here because I have basic organizational ties here.
Beyond this, I am in Birmingham because injustice is here. Just as the eighth
century prophets left their little villages and carried their "thus saith the Lord"
20 far beyond the boundaries of their home town, and just as the Apostle Paul left
his little village of Tarsus and carried the gospel of Jesus Christ to practically
every hamlet and city of the Greco-Roman world, I too am compelled to carry
the gospel of freedom beyond my particular home town. Like Paul, I must
constantly respond to the Macedonian call for aid.

25 Moreover, I am cognizant of the interrelatedness of all communities and
states. I cannot sit idly by in Atlanta and not be concerned about what happens in
Birmingham. Injustice anywhere is a threat to justice everywhere. We are caught in
an inescapable network of mutuality tied in a single garment of destiny. Whatever
affects one directly affects all indirectly. Never again can we afford to live with the
30 narrow, provincial "outside agitator" idea. Anyone who lives inside the United
States can never be considered an outsider anywhere in this country.

You deplore the demonstrations that are presently taking place in Birmingham. But I am sorry that your statement did not express a similar concern for
the conditions that brought the demonstrations into being. I am sure that each
35 of you would want to go beyond the superficial social analyst who looks merely
at effects, and does not grapple with underlying causes. I would not hesitate
to say that it is unfortunate that so-called demonstrations are taking place in
Birmingham at this time, but I would say in more emphatic terms that it is
even more unfortunate that the white power structure of this city left the Negro
40 community with no other alternative.

In any nonviolent campaign there are four basic steps: (1) collection of the facts to determine whether injustices are alive; (2) negotiation; (3) self-purification; and (4) direct action. We have gone through all of these steps in Birmingham. There can be no gainsaying of the fact that racial injustice engulfs this community. Birmingham is probably the most thoroughly segregated city   5
in the United States. Its ugly record of police brutality is known in every section of this country. Its unjust treatment of Negroes in the courts is a notorious reality. There have been more unsolved bombings of Negro homes and churches in Birmingham than any city in this nation. These are the hard, brutal, and unbelievable facts. On the basis of these conditions Negro leaders sought to   10
negotiate with the city fathers. But the political leaders consistently refused to engage in good faith negotiation.

Then came the opportunity last September to talk with some of the leaders of the economic community. In these negotiating sessions certain promises were made by the merchants—such as the promise to remove the humiliating   15
racial signs from the stores. On the basis of these promises Rev. Shuttlesworth and the leaders of the Alabama Christian Movement for Human Rights agreed to call a moratorium on any type of demonstrations. As the weeks and months unfolded we realized that we were the victims of a broken promise. The signs remained. As in so many experiences of the past we were confronted with blasted   20
hopes, and the dark shadow of a deep disappointment settled upon us. So we had no alternative except that of preparing for direct action, whereby we would present our very bodies as a means of laying our case before the conscience of the local and national community. We were not unmindful of the difficulties involved. So we decided to go through a process of self-purification. We started   25
having workshops on nonviolence and repeatedly asked ourselves the questions, "Are you able to accept blows without retaliating?" "Are you able to endure the ordeals of jail?"

We decided to set our direct action program around the Easter season, realizing that with the exception of Christmas, this was the largest shopping   30
period of the year. Knowing that a strong economic withdrawal program would be the by-product of direct action, we felt that this was the best time to bring pressure on the merchants for the needed changes. Then it occurred to us that the March election was ahead, and so we speedily decided to postpone action until after election day. When we discovered that Mr. Connor was in the run-   35
off, we decided again to postpone action so that the demonstrations could not be used to cloud the issues. At this time we agreed to begin our nonviolent witness the day after the run-off.

This reveals that we did not move irresponsibly into direct action. We, too, wanted to see Mr. Connor defeated; so we went through postponement after   40 postponement to aid in this community need. After this we felt that direct action could be delayed no longer.

You may well ask, "Why direct action? Why sit-ins, marches, etc.? Isn't negotiation a better path?" You are exactly right in your call for negotiation. Indeed, this is the purpose of direct action. Nonviolent direct action seeks to create such a crisis and establish such creative tension that a community that has constantly refused to negotiate is forced to confront the issue. It seeks so to dramatize the issue that it can no longer be ignored. I just referred to the creation of tension as a part of the work of the nonviolent resister. This may sound rather shocking. But I must confess that I am not afraid of the word tension. I have earnestly worked and preached against violent tension, but there is a type of constructive nonviolent tension that is necessary for growth. Just as Socrates felt that it was necessary to create a tension in the mind so that individuals could rise from the bondage of myths and half-truths to the unfettered realm of creative analysis and objective appraisal, we must see the need of having nonviolent gadflies to create the kind of tension in society that will help men rise from the dark depths of prejudice and racism to the majestic heights of understanding and brotherhood. So the purpose of the direct action is to create a situation so crisis-packed that it will inevitably open the door to negotiation. We, therefore, concur with you in your call for negotiation. Too long has our beloved Southland been bogged down in the tragic attempt to live in monologue rather than dialogue.

One of the basic points in your statement is that our acts are untimely. Some have asked, "Why didn't you give the new administration time to act?" The only answer that I can give to this inquiry is that the new administration must be prodded about as much as the outgoing one before it acts. We will be sadly mistaken if we feel that the election of Mr. Boutwell will bring the millennium to Birmingham. While Mr. Boutwell is much more articulate and gentle than Mr. Connor, they are both segregationists dedicated to the task of maintaining the status quo. The hope I see in Mr. Boutwell is that he will be reasonable enough to see the futility of massive resistance to desegregation. But he will not see this without pressure from the devotees of civil rights. My friends, I must say to you that we have not made a single gain in civil rights without determined legal and nonviolent pressure. History is the long and tragic story of the fact that privileged groups seldom give up their privileges voluntarily. Individuals may see the moral light and voluntarily give up their unjust posture; but as Reinhold Niebuhr has reminded us, groups are more immoral than individuals.

We know through painful experience that freedom is never voluntarily given by the oppressor; it must be demanded by the oppressed. Frankly I have never yet engaged in a direct action movement that was "well timed," according to the timetable of those who have not suffered unduly from the disease of segregation. For years now I have heard the word "Wait!" It rings in the ear of every Negro with a piercing familiarity. This "wait" has almost always meant "never." It has been a tranquilizing thalidomide, relieving the emotional stress for a moment, only to give birth to an ill-formed infant of frustration. We must come to see with the distinguished jurist of yesterday that "justice too long delayed is justice denied." We have waited for more than three hundred and forty years for our constitutional and God-given rights. The nations of Asia and Africa are moving with jet-like speed toward the goal of political independence, and we still creep at horse and buggy pace toward the gaining of a cup of coffee at a lunch counter.

I guess it is easy for those who have never felt the stinging darts of segregation to say wait. But when you have seen vicious mobs lynch your mothers and fathers at will and drown your sisters and brothers at whim; when you have seen hate-filled policemen curse, kick, brutalize, and even kill your black brothers and sisters with impunity; when you see the vast majority of your twenty million Negro brothers smothering in an air-tight cage of poverty in the midst of an affluent society; when you suddenly find your tongue twisted and your speech stammering as you seek to explain to your six-year-old daughter why she can't go to the public amusement park that has just been advertised on television, and see tears welling up in her little eyes when she is told that Funtown is closed to colored children, and see the depressing clouds of inferiority begin to form in her little mental sky, and see her begin to distort her little personality by unconsciously developing a bitterness toward white people; when you have to concoct an answer for a five-year-old son asking in agonizing pathos: "Daddy, why do white people treat colored people so mean?"; when you take a cross country drive and find it necessary to sleep night after night in the uncomfortable corners of your automobile because no motel will accept you; when you are humiliated day in and day out by nagging signs reading "white" men and "colored"; when your first name becomes "nigger" and your middle name becomes "boy" (however old you are) and your last name becomes "John," and when your wife and mother are never given the respected title "Mrs."; when you are harried by day and haunted by night by the fact that you are a Negro, living constantly at tip-top stance never quite knowing what to expect next, and plagued with inner fears and outer resentments; when you are forever fighting a degenerating sense of "nobodiness";—then you will understand why we find it difficult to wait. There comes a time when the cup of endurance runs over, and men are no longer willing to be plunged into an abyss of injustice where they experience the bleakness of corroding despair. I hope, sirs, you can understand our legitimate and unavoidable impatience.

You express a great deal of anxiety over our willingness to break laws. This is certainly a legitimate concern. Since we so diligently urge people to obey the Supreme Court's decision of 1954 outlawing segregation in the public schools, it is rather strange and paradoxical to find us consciously breaking laws. One
5   may well ask, "How can you advocate breaking some laws and obeying others?" The answer is found in the fact that there are two types of laws: There are *just* laws and there are *unjust* laws. I would be the first to advocate obeying just laws. One has not only a legal but moral responsibility to obey just laws. Conversely, one has a moral responsibility to dis-obey unjust laws. I would agree with Saint
10 Augustine that "an unjust law is no law at all."

     Now what is the difference between the two? How does one determine when a law is just or unjust? A just law is a manmade code that squares with the moral law or the law of God. An unjust law is a code that is out of harmony with the moral law. To put it in the terms of Saint Thomas Aquinas, an unjust
15 law is a human law that is not rooted in eternal and natural law. Any law that uplifts human personality is just. Any law that degrades human personality is unjust. All segregation statutes are unjust because segregation distorts the soul and damages the personality. It gives the segregator a false sense of superiority and the segregated a false sense of inferiority. To use the words of
20 Martin Buber, the great Jewish philosopher, segregation substitutes an "I-it" relationship for the "I-thou" relationship, and ends up relegating persons to the status of things. So segregation is not only politically, economically, and sociologically unsound, but it is morally wrong and sinful. Paul Tillich has said that sin is separation. Isn't segregation an existential expression of man's tragic
25 separation, an expression of his awful estrangement, his terrible sinfulness? So I can urge men to obey the 1954 decision of the Supreme Court because it is morally right, and I can urge them to disobey segregation ordinances because they are morally wrong.

     Let us turn to a more concrete example of just and unjust laws. An un-
30 just law is a code that a majority inflicts on a minority that is not binding on itself. This is *difference* made legal. On the other hand a just law is a code that a majority compels a minority to follow that it is willing to follow itself. This is *sameness* made legal.

     Let me give another explanation. An unjust law is a code inflicted upon
35 a minority which that minority had no part in enacting or creating because they did not have the unhampered right to vote. Who can say the legislature of Alabama which set up the segregation laws was democratically elected? Throughout the state of Alabama all types of conniving methods are used to prevent Negroes from becoming registered voters and there are some counties without
40 a single Negro registered to vote despite the fact that the Negro constitutes a

majority of the population. Can any law set up in such a state be considered democratically structured?

These are just a few examples of unjust and just laws. There are some instances when a law is just on its fact but unjust in its application. For instance. I was arrested Friday on a charge of parading without a permit. Now there is   5
nothing wrong with an ordinance which requires a permit for a parade, but when the ordinance is used to preserve segregation and to deny citizens the First Amendment privilege of peaceful assembly and peaceful protest, then it becomes unjust.

I hope you can see the distinction I am trying to point out. In no sense   10
do I advocate evading or defying the law as the rabid segregationist would do. This would lead to anarchy. One who breaks an unjust law must do it *openly, lovingly* (not hatefully, as the white mothers did in New Orleans when they were seen on television screaming "nigger, nigger, nigger") and with a willingness to accept the penalty. I submit that an individual who breaks a law that conscience   15
tells him is unjust, and willingly accepts the penalty by staying in jail to arouse the conscience of the community over its injustice, is in reality expressing the very highest respect for law.

Of course there is nothing new about this kind of civil disobedience. It was seen sublimely in the refusal of Shadrach, Meshach, and Abednego to   20
obey the laws of Nebuchadnezzar because a higher moral law was involved. It was practiced superbly by the early Christians who were willing to face hungry lions and the excruciating pain of chopping blocks before submitting to certain unjust laws of the Roman Empire. To a degree academic freedom is a reality today because Socrates practiced civil disobedience.   25

We can never forget that everything Hitler did in Germany was "legal" and everything the Hungarian freedom fighters did in Hungary was "illegal." It was "illegal" to aid and comfort a Jew in Hitler's Germany. But I am sure that, if I had lived in Germany during that time, I would have aided and comforted my Jewish brothers even though it was illegal. If I lived in a communist country   30
today where certain principles dear to the Christian faith are suppressed, I believe I would openly advocate disobeying these anti-religious laws.

I must make two honest confessions to you, my Christian and Jewish brothers. First I must confess that over the last few years I have been gravely disappointed with the white moderate. I have almost reached the regrettable   35
conclusion that the Negroes' great stumbling block in the stride toward freedom is not the White Citizens' "Counciler" or the Ku Klux Klanner, but the white moderate who is more devoted to "order" than to justice; who prefers a negative peace which is the absence of tension to a positive peace which is the presence of justice; who constantly says "I agree with you in the goal you seek, but I   40

can't agree with your methods of direct action"; who paternalistically feels that he can set the time-table for another man's freedom; who lives by the myth of time and who constantly advises the Negro to wait until a "more convenient season." Shallow understanding from people of good will is more frustrating than absolute misunderstanding from people of ill will. Lukewarm acceptance is much more bewildering than outright rejection.

I had hoped that the white moderate would understand that law and order exist for the purpose of establishing justice, and that when they fail to do this they become the dangerously structured dams that block the flow of social progress. I had hoped that the white moderate would understand that the present tension in the South is merely a necessary phase of the transition from an obnoxious negative peace, where the Negro passively accepted his unjust plight, to a substance-filled positive peace, where all men will respect the dignity and worth of human personality. Actually, we who engage in nonviolent direct action are not the creators of tension. We merely bring to the surface the hidden tension that is already alive. We bring it out in the open where it can be seen and dealt with. Like a boil that can never be cured as long as it is covered up but must be opened with all its pus-flowing ugliness to the natural medicines of air and light, injustice must likewise be exposed, with all of the tension its exposing creates, to the light of human conscience and the air of national opinion before it can be cured.

In your statement you asserted that our actions, even though peaceful, must be condemned because they precipitate violence. But can this assertion be logically made? Isn't this like condemning the robbed man because his possession of money precipitated the evil act of robbery? Isn't this like condemning Socrates because his unswerving commitment to truth and his philosophical delvings precipitated the mis-guided popular mind to make him drink the hemlock? Isn't this like condemning Jesus because His unique God consciousness and never-ceasing devotion to His will precipitated the evil act of crucifixion? We must come to see, as federal courts have consistently affirmed, that it is immoral to urge an individual to withdraw his efforts to gain his basic constitutional rights because the quest precipitates violence. Society must protect the robbed and punish the robber.

I had also hoped that the white moderate would reject the myth of time. I received a letter this morning from a white brother in Texas which said: "All Christians know that the colored people will receive equal rights eventually, but is it possible that you are in too great of a religious hurry? It has taken Christianity almost 2000 years to accomplish what it has. The teachings of Christ take time to come to earth." All that is said here grows out of a tragic misconception of time. It is the strangely irrational notion that there is something in the very flow of time that will inevitably cure all ills. Actually time is neutral. It can be used either destructively or constructively. I am coming to feel that the people of ill will have used time much more effectively than the people of good will. We will have to repent in this generation not merely for the vitriolic words and actions of the bad people, but for the appalling silence of the good people. We must come to see that human progress never rolls in on wheels of inevitability. It comes through the tireless efforts and persistent work of men willing to be co-workers with God, and without this hard work time itself becomes an ally of the forces of social stagnation.

We must use time creatively, and forever realize that the time is always ripe to do right. Now is the time to make real the promise of democracy, and transform our pending national elegy into a creative psalm of brotherhood. Now is the time to lift our national policy from the quicksand of racial injustice to the solid rock of human dignity.

You spoke of our activity in Birmingham as extreme. At first I was rather disappointed that fellow clergymen would see my nonviolent efforts as those of the extremist. I started thinking about the fact that I stand in the middle of two opposing forces in the Negro community. One is a force of complacency made up of Negroes who, as a result of long years of oppression, have been so completely drained of self-respect and a sense of "somebodiness" that they had adjusted to segregation, and of a few Negroes in the middle class who, because of a degree of academic and economic security, and because at points they profit by segregation, have unconsciously become insensitive to the problems of the masses. The other force is one of bitterness and hatred and comes perilously close to advocating violence. It is expressed in the various black nationalist groups that are springing up over the nation, the largest and best known being Elijah Muhammad's Muslim movement. This movement is nourished by the contemporary frustration over the continued existence of racial discrimination. It is made up of people who have lost faith in America, who have absolutely repudiated Christianity, and who have concluded that the white man is an incurable "devil." I have tried to stand between these two forces saying that we need not follow the "do-nothingism" of the complacent or the hatred and despair of the black nationalist. There is the more excellent way of love and nonviolent protest. I'm grateful to God that, through the Negro church, the dimension of nonviolence entered our struggle. If this philosophy had not emerged I am convinced that by now many streets of the South would be flowing with floods of blood. And I am further convinced that if our white brothers dismiss us as "rabble rousers" and "outside agitators"—those of us who are working through the channels of nonviolent direct action—and refuse to support our nonviolent efforts, millions of Negroes, out of frustration and despair, will seek solace and security in black nationalist ideologies, a development that will lead inevitably to a frightening racial nightmare.

Oppressed people cannot remain oppressed forever. The urge for freedom will eventually come. This is what has happened to the American Negro. 5 Something within has reminded him of his birthright of freedom; something without has reminded him that he can gain it. Consciously and unconsciously, he has been swept in by what the Germans call the *Zeitgeist*, and with his black brothers of Africa, and his brown and yellow brothers of Asia, South America, and the Caribbean, he is moving with a sense of cosmic urgency toward the 10 promised land of racial justice. Recognizing this vital urge that has engulfed the Negro community, one should readily understand public demonstrations. The Negro has many pent-up resentments and latent frustrations. He has to get them out. So let him march sometime; let him have his prayer pilgrimages to the city hall; understand why he must have sit-ins and freedom rides. 15 If his repressed emotions do not come out in these nonviolent ways, they will come out in ominous expressions of violence. This is not a threat; it is a fact of history. So I have not said to my people, "Get rid of your discontent." But I have tried to say that this normal and healthy discontent can be channeled through the creative outlet of nonviolent direct action. Now this approach is 20 being dismissed as extremist. I must admit that I was initially disappointed in being so categorized.

But as I continued to think about the matter I gradually gained a bit of satisfaction from being considered an extremist. Was not Jesus an extremist in love? "Love your enemies, bless them that curse you, pray for them that 25 despitefully use you." Was not Amos an extremist for justice—"Let justice roll down like waters and righteousness like a mighty stream." Was not Paul an extremist for the gospel of Jesus Christ—"I bear in my body the marks of the Lord Jesus." Was not Martin Luther an extremist—"Here I stand; I can do none other so help me God." Was not John Bunyan an extremist—"I will stay in jail 30 to the end of my days before I make a butchery of my conscience." Was not Abraham Lincoln an extremist—"This nation cannot survive half slave and half free." Was not Thomas Jefferson an extremist—"We hold these truths to be self evident, that all men are created equal." So the question is not whether we will be extremist but what kind of extremist will we be. Will we be extremists for 35 hate or will we be extremists for love? Will we be extremists for the preservation of injustice—or will we be extremists for the cause of justice? In that dramatic scene on Calvary's hill three men were crucified. We must never forget that all three were crucified for the same crime—the crime of extremism. Two were extremists for immorality, and thus fell below their environment. The other, 40 Jesus Christ, was an extremist for love, truth, and goodness, and thereby rose above His environment. So, after all, maybe the South, the nation, and the world are in dire need of creative extremists.

I had hoped that the white moderate would see this. Maybe I was too optimistic. Maybe I expected too much. I guess I should have realized that few members of a race that has oppressed another race can understand or appreciate the deep groans and passionate yearnings of those that have been oppressed, and still fewer have the vision to see that injustice must be rooted out by strong, persistent, and determined action. I am thankful, however, that some of our white brothers have grasped the meaning of this social revolution and committed themselves to it. They are still all too small in quantity, but they are big in quality. Some like Ralph McGill, Lillian Smith, Harry Golden, and James Dabbs have written about our struggle in eloquent, prophetic, and understanding terms. Others have marched with us down nameless streets of the South. They have languished in filthy, roach-infested jails, suffering the abuse and brutality of angry policemen who see them as "dirty nigger lovers." They, unlike so many of their moderate brothers and sisters, have recognized the urgency of the moment and sensed the need for powerful "action" antidotes to combat the disease of segregation.

Let me rush on to mention my other disappointment. I have been so greatly disappointed with the white Church and its leadership. Of course there are some notable exceptions. I am not unmindful of the fact that each of you has taken some significant stands on this issue. I commend you, Reverend Stallings, for your Christian stand on this past Sunday, in welcoming Negroes to your worship service on a nonsegregated basis. I commend the Catholic leaders of this state for integrating Springhill College several years ago.

But despite these notable exceptions I must honestly reiterate that I have been disappointed with the Church. I do not say that as one of those negative critics who can always find something wrong with the Church. I say it as a minister of the gospel, who loves the Church; who was nurtured in its bosom; who has been sustained by its spiritual blessings, and who will remain true to it as long as the cord of life shall lengthen.

I had the strange feeling when I was suddenly catapulted into the leadership of the bus protest in Montgomery several years ago that we would have the support of the white Church. I felt that the white ministers, priests, and rabbis of the South would be some of our strongest allies. Instead, some have been outright opponents, refusing to understand the freedom movement and misrepresenting its leaders; all too many others have been more cautious than courageous and have remained silent behind the anesthetizing security of stained glass windows.

In spite of my shattered dreams of the past, I came to Birmingham with the hope that the white religious leadership of this community would see the justice of our cause and, with deep moral concern, serve as the channel through which our just grievances could get to the power structure. I had hoped that each of you would understand. But again I have been disappointed.

5   I have heard numerous religious leaders of the South call upon their worshippers to comply with a desegregation decision because it is the law, but I have longed to hear white ministers say follow this decree because integration is morally right and the Negro is your brother. In the midst of blatant injustices inflicted upon the Negro, I have watched white churches stand on the sideline and merely mouth pious irrelevancies and sanctimonious trivialities. In the midst

10 of a mighty struggle to rid our nation of racial and economic injustice, I have heard so many ministers say, "Those are social issues with which the Gospel has no real concern," and I have watched so many churches commit themselves to a completely other-worldly religion which made a strange distinction between body and soul, the sacred and the secular.

15 So here we are moving toward the exit of the twentieth century with a religious community largely adjusted to the status quo, standing as a tail light behind other community agencies rather than a headlight leading men to higher levels of justice.

I have travelled the length and breadth of Alabama, Mississippi, and all the

20 other Southern states. On sweltering summer days and crisp autumn mornings I have looked at her beautiful churches with their spires pointing heavenward. I have beheld the impressive outlay of her massive religious education buildings. Over and over again I have found myself asking: "Who worships here? Who is their God? Where were their voices when the lips of Governor Barnett

25 dripped with words of interposition and nullification? Where were they when Governor Wallace gave the clarion call for defiance and hatred? Where were their voices of support when tired, bruised, and weary Negro men and women decided to rise from the dark dungeons of complacency to the bright hills of creative protests?"

30 Yes, these questions are still in my mind. In deep disappointment, I have wept over the laxity of the Church. But be assured that my tears have been tears of love. There can be no deep disappointment where there is not deep love. Yes, I love the Church; I love her sacred walls. How could I do otherwise? I am in the rather unique position of being the son, the grandson, and the

35 great-grandson of preachers. Yes. I see the Church as the body of Christ. But, oh! How we have blemished and scarred that body through social neglect and fear of being nonconformist.

There was a time when the Church was very powerful. It was during that period when the early Christians rejoiced when they were deemed worthy to

40 suffer for what they believed. In those days the Church was not merely a ther-

mometer that recorded the ideas and principles of popular opinion; it was a thermostat that transformed the mores of society. Wherever the early Christians entered a town the power structure got disturbed and immediately sought to convict them for being "disturbers of the peace" and "outside agitators." But they went on with the conviction that they were a "colony of heaven" and had   5
to obey God rather than man. They were small in number but big in commitment. They were too God-intoxicated to be "astronomically intimidated." They brought an end to such ancient evils as infanticide and gladiatorial contest.

Things are different now. The contemporary Church is so often a weak, ineffectual voice with an uncertain sound. It is so often the arch-supporter of   10
the status quo. Far from being disturbed by the presence of the Church, the power structure of the average community is consoled by the Church's silent and often vocal sanction of things as they are.

But the judgment of God is upon the Church as never before. If the Church of today does not recapture the sacrificial spirit of the early Church,   15
it will lost its authentic ring, forfeit the loyalty of millions, and be dismissed as an irrelevant social club with no meaning for the twentieth century. I am meeting young people every day whose disappointment with the Church has risen to outright disgust.

Maybe again I have been too optimistic. Is organized religion too inextri-   20
cably bound to the status quo to save our nation and the world? Maybe I must turn my faith to the inner spiritual Church, the church within the Church, as the true *ecclesia* and the hope of the world. But again I am thankful to God that some noble souls from the ranks of organized religion have broken loose from the paralyzing chains of conformity and joined us as active partners in the   25
struggle for freedom. They have left their secure congregations and walked the streets of Albany, Georgia, with us. They have gone through the highways of the South on torturous rides for freedom. Yes, they have gone to jail with us. Some have been kicked out of their churches and lost the support of their bishops and fellow ministers. But they have gone with the faith that right defeated is   30
stronger than evil triumphant. These men have been the leaven in the lump of the race. Their witness has been the spiritual salt that has preserved the true meaning of the Gospel in these troubled times. They have carved a tunnel of hope through the dark mountain of disappointment.

I hope the Church as a whole will meet the challenge of this decisive   35
hour. But even if the Church does not come to the aid of justice, I have no despair about the future. I have no fear about the outcome of our struggle in Birmingham, even if our motives are presently misunderstood. We will reach the goal of freedom in Birmingham and all over the nation, because the goal of America is freedom. Abused and scorned though we may be, our destiny is   40

tied up with the destiny of America. Before the pilgrims landed at Plymouth, we were here. Before the pen of Jefferson etched across the pages of history the majestic words of the Declaration of Independence, we were here. For more than two centuries our foreparents labored in this country without wages; they
5   made cotton "king"; and they built the homes of their masters in the midst of brutal injustice and shameful humiliation—and yet out of a bottomless vitality the continued to thrive and develop. If the inexpressible cruelties of slavery could not stop us, the opposition we now face will surely fail. We will win our freedom because the sacred heritage of our nation and the eternal will of God
10   are embodied in our echoing demands.

       I must close now. But before closing I am impelled to mention one other point in your statement that troubled me profoundly. You warmly commended the Birmingham police force for keeping "order" and "preventing violence." I don't believe you would have so warmly commended the police force if you had
15   seen its angry violent dogs literally biting six unarmed, nonviolent Negroes. I don't believe you would so quickly commend the policemen if you would observe their ugly and inhuman treatment of Negroes here in the city jail; if you would watch them push and curse old Negro women and young Negro girls; if you would see them slap and kick old Negro men and young Negro
20   boys; if you will observe them, as they did on two occasions, refuse to give us food because we wanted to sing our grace together. I'm sorry that I can't join you in your praise for the police department.

       It is true that they have been rather disciplined in their public handling of the demonstrators. In this sense they have been rather publicly "nonviolent."
25   But for what purpose? To preserve the evil system of segregation. Over the last few years I have consistently preached that nonviolence demands that the means we use must be as pure as the ends we seek. So I have tried to make it clear that it is wrong to use immoral means to attain moral ends. But now I must affirm that it is just as wrong, or even more so, to use moral means to
30   preserve immoral ends. Maybe Mr. Connor and his policemen have been rather publicly nonviolent, as Chief Prichett was in Albany, Georgia, but they have used the moral means of nonviolence to maintain the immoral end of flagrant racial injustice. T. S. Eliot has said that there is no greater treason than to do the right deed for the wrong reason.

35   I wish you had commended the Negro sit-inners and demonstrators of Birmingham for their sublime courage, their willingness to suffer, and their amazing discipline in the midst of the most inhuman provocation. One day the South will recognize its real heroes. They will be the James Merediths, courageously and with a majestic sense of purpose, facing jeering and hostile
40   mobs and the agonizing loneliness that characterizes the life of the pioneer. They

will be old, oppressed, battered Negro women, symbolized in a seventy-two year old woman of Montgomery, Alabama, who rose up with a sense of dignity and with her people decided not to ride the segregated buses, and responded to one who inquired about her tiredness with ungrammatical profundity: "My feets is tired, but my soul is rested." They will be young high school and college students, young ministers of the gospel and a host of the elders, courageously and nonviolently sitting in at lunch counters and willingly going to jail for conscience sake. One day the South will know that when these disinherited children of God sat down at lunch counters they were in reality standing up for the best in the American dream and the most sacred values in our Judeo-Christian heritage, and thus carrying our whole nation back to great wells of democracy which were dug deep by the founding fathers in the formulation of the Constitution and the Declaration of Independence.

Never before have I written a letter this long (or should I say a book?). I'm afraid that it is much too long to take your precious time. I can assure you that it would have been much shorter if I had been writing from a comfortable desk, but what else is there to do when you are alone for days in the dull monotony of a narrow jail cell other than write long letters, think strange thoughts, and pray long prayers?

If I have said anything in this letter that is an over-statement of the truth and is indicative of an unreasonable impatience, I beg you to forgive me. If I have said anything in this letter that is an under-statement of the truth and is indicative of my having a patience that makes me patient with anything less than brotherhood, I beg God to forgive me.

I hope this letter finds you strong in the faith. I also hope that circumstances will soon make it possible for me to meet each of you, not as an integrationist or a civil rights leader, but as a fellow clergyman and a Christian brother. Let us all hope that the dark clouds of racial prejudice will soon pass away and the deep fog of misunderstanding will be lifted from our fear-drenched communities and in some not too distant tomorrow the radiant stars of love and brotherhood will shine over our great nation with all of their scintillating beauty.

Yours for the cause of Peace and Brotherhood.

PEACE WITHOUT CONQUEST
LYNDON B. JOHNSON (1908–1973)
PRESIDENT OF THE UNITED STATES (1963–1969)

President Lyndon B. Johnson's speech explaining the United States' reasons for military intervention in Vietnam shows the extension of the progressive-liberal values to international relations. Based on an assessment of twentieth-century history and of the situation in Southeast Asia that can be regarded as oversimplified but essentially true, Johnson's argument expressed the Wilsonian idealist tradition.

This speech marks the high point of American liberal self-confidence: Johnson implied an open-ended commitment on the part of the United States. He also assumed the North Vietnamese—and everyone in the world—wanted exactly what Americans wanted, and that these desires were best satisfied by New Deal programs like the Tennessee Valley Authority.

7 APRIL 1965

I have come here to review once again with my own people the views of the American Government.

Tonight Americans and Asians are dying for a world where each people may choose its own path to change. This is the principle for which our ancestors fought in the valleys of Pennsylvania. It is the principle for which our sons 5
fight tonight in the jungles of Viet-Nam.

Viet-Nam is far away from this quiet campus. We have no territory there, nor do we seek any. The war is dirty and brutal and difficult. And some 400 young men, born into an America that is bursting with opportunity and promise, have ended their lives on Viet-Nam's steaming soil. 10

Why must we take this painful road? Why must this Nation hazard its ease, and its interest, and its power for the sake of a people so far away?

We fight because we must fight if we are to live in a world where every country can shape its own destiny. And only in such a world will our own freedom be finally secure. This kind of world will never be built by bombs or 15

Public Papers of the Presidents of the United States, Lyndon B. Johnson, 1965 (Washington, DC: United States Government Printing Office, 1966), I:394–99.

bullets. Yet the infirmities of man are such that force must often precede reason, and the waste of war, the works of peace. We wish that this were not so. But we must deal with the world as it is, if it is ever to be as we wish.

The Nature of the Conflict

The world as it is in Asia is not a serene or peaceful place. The first reality is that
5   North Viet-Nam has attacked the independent nation of South Viet-Nam. Its object is total conquest. Of course, some people of South Viet-Nam are participating in attack on their own government. But trained men and supplies, orders and arms, flow in a contrast stream from north to south. This support is the heartbeat of the war.

10   And it is a war of unparalleled brutality. Simple farmers are the targets of assassination and kidnapping. Women and children are strangled in the night because their men are loyal to their government. And helpless villages are ravaged by sneak attacks. Large-scale raids are conducted on towns, and terror strikes in the heart of cities.

15   The confused nature of this conflict cannot mask the fact that it is the new face of an old enemy. Over this war—and all Asia—is another reality: the deepening shadow of Communist China. The rulers in Hanoi are urged on by Peking. This is a regime which has destroyed freedom in Tibet, which has attacked India, and has been condemned by the United Nations for aggression in Korea. It is
20   a nation which is helping the forces of violence in almost every continent. The contest in Viet-Nam is part of a wider pattern of aggressive purposes.

Why Are We in Viet-Nam?

Why are these realities our concern? Why are we in South Viet-Nam? We are there because we have a promise to keep. Since 1954 every American President has offered support to the people of South Viet-Nam. We have helped to build,
25   and we have helped to defend. Thus, over many years, we have made a national pledge to help South Viet-Nam defend its independence.

     And I intend to keep that promise. To dishonor that pledge, to abandon this small and brave nation to its enemies, and to the terror that must follow, would be an unforgivable wrong.

30   We are also there to strengthen world order. Around the globe, from Berlin to Thailand, are people whose well-being rests, in part, on the belief that they can count on us if they are attacked. To leave Viet-Nam to its fate would shake the confidence of all these people in the value of an American commitment and in the value of America's word. The result would be increased unrest and
35   instability, and even wider war.

We are also there because there are great stakes in the balance. Let no one think for a moment that retreat from Viet-Nam would bring an end to conflict. The battle would be renewed in one country and then another. The central lesson of our time is that the appetite of aggression is never satisfied. To withdraw from one battlefield means only to prepare for the next. We must say 5 in southeast Asia—as we did in Europe—in the words of the Bible: "Hitherto shalt thou come, but no further."[1]

There are those who say that all our effort there will be futile—that China's power is such that it is bound to dominate all southeast Asia. But there is no end to that argument until all of the nations of Asia are swallowed up. There 10 are those who wonder why we have a responsibility there. Well, we have it there for the same reason that we have a responsibility for the defense of Europe. World War II was fought in both Europe and Asia, and when it ended we found ourselves with continued responsibility for the defense of freedom.

Our Objective in Viet-Nam

Our objective is the independence of South Viet-Nam, and its freedom 15 from attack. We want nothing for ourselves—only that the people of South Viet-Nam be allowed to guide their own country in their own way. We will do everything necessary to reach that objective. And we will do only what is absolutely necessary.

In recent months attacks on South Viet-Nam were stepped up. Thus, it 20 became necessary for us to increase our response and to make attacks by air. This is not a change of purpose. It is a change in what we believe that purpose requires. We do this in order to slow down aggression. We do this to increase the confidence of the brave people of South Viet-Nam who have bravely borne this brutal battle for so many years with so many casualties. And we do this to convince 25 the leaders of North Viet-Nam—and all who seek to share their conquest—of a very simple fact: We will not be defeated. We will not grow tired. We will not withdraw, either openly or under the cloak of a meaningless agreement.

We know that air attacks alone will not accomplish all of these purposes. But it is our best and prayerful judgment that they are a necessary part of the 30 surest road to peace. We hope that peace will come swiftly. But that is in the hands of others besides ourselves. And we must be prepared for a long continued conflict. It will require patience as well as bravery, the will to endure as well as the will to resist.

I wish it were possible to convince others with words of what we now find 35 it necessary to say with guns and planes: Armed hostility is futile. Our resources

---

[1]Job 38:11

are equal to any challenge. Because we fight for values and we fight for principles, rather than territory or colonies, our patience and our determination are unending.

Once this is clear, then it should also be clear that the only path for reasonable men is the path of peaceful settlement. Such peace demands an independent South Viet-Nam—securely guaranteed and able to shape its own relationships to all others—free from outside interference—tied to no alliance—a military base for no other country. These are the essential of any final settlement. We will never be second in the search for such a peaceful settlement in Viet-Nam.

There may be many ways to this kind of peace: in discussion or negotiation with the governments concerned; in large groups or in small ones; in the reaffirmation of old agreements or their strengthening with new ones. We have stated this position over and over again, fifty times and more, to friend and foe alike. And we remain ready, with this purpose, for unconditional discussions.

And until that bright and necessary day of peace we will try to keep conflict from spreading. We have no desire to see thousands die in battle—Asians or Americans. We have no desire to devastate that which the people of North Viet-Nam have built with toil and sacrifice. We will use our power with restraint and with all the wisdom that we can command. But we will use it.

This war, like most wars, is filled with terrible irony. For what do the people of North Viet-Nam want? They want what their neighbors also desire: food for their hunger; health for their bodies; a chance to learn; progress for their country; and an end to the bondage of material misery. And they would find all these things far more readily in peaceful association with others than in the endless course of battle.

A Co-Operative Effort for Development

These countries of southeast Asia are homes for millions of impoverished people. Each day these people rise at dawn and struggle through until the night to wrestle existence from the soil. They are often wracked by disease, plagued by hunger, and death comes at the early age of 40.

Stability and peace do not come easily in such a land. Neither independence nor human dignity will ever be won, though, by arms alone. It also requires the work of peace. The American people have helped generously in times past in these works. Now there must be a much more massive effort to improve the life of man in that conflict-torn corner of our world.

The first step is for the countries of southeast Asia to associate themselves in a greatly expanded co-operative effort for development. We would hope that North Viet-Nam would take its place in the common effort just as soon as peaceful co-operation is possible.

The United Nations is already actively engaged in development in this area. As far back as 1961 I conferred with our authorities in Viet-Nam in connection with their work there. And I would hope tonight that the Secretary General of the United Nations could use the prestige of his great office, and his deep knowledge of Asia, to initiate, as soon as possible, with the countries of that 5 area, a plan for co-operation in increased development.

For our part I will ask the Congress to join in a billion dollar American investment in this effort as soon as it is underway. And I would hope that all other industrialized countries, including the Soviet Union, will join in this effort to replace despair with hope, and terror with progress. 10

The task is nothing less than to enrich the hopes and the existence of more than a hundred million people. And there is much to be done. The vast Mekong River can provide food and water and power on a scale to dwarf even our own TVA[2]. The wonders of modern medicine can be spread through villages where thousands die every year from lack of care. Schools can be established 15 to train people in the skills that are needed to manage the process of development. And these objectives, and more, are within the reach of a co-operative and determined effort.

I also intend to expand and speed up a program to make available our farm surpluses to assist in feeding and clothing the needy in Asia. We should not allow 20 people to go hungry and wear rags while our own warehouses overflow with an abundance of wheat and corn, rice and cotton. So I will very shortly name a special team of outstanding, patriotic, distinguished Americans to inaugurate our participation in these programs. This team will be headed by Mr. Eugene Black, the very able former President of the World Bank. 25

In areas that are still ripped by conflict, of course development will not be easy. Peace will be necessary for final success. But we cannot and must not wait for peace to begin this job.

The Dream of World Order

This will be a disorderly planet for a long time. In Asia, as elsewhere, the forces of the modern world are shaking old ways and uprooting ancient civilizations. 30 There will be turbulence and struggle and even violence. Great social change—as we see in our own country now—does not always come without conflict.

We must also expect that nations will on occasion be in dispute with us. It may be because we are rich, or powerful; or because we have made some mistakes;

---

[2]Tennessee Valley Authoritiy, a federally owned corporation created in 1933 to provide flood control, electrical power, and economic development across large stretches of rural Tennessee, Kentucky, Alabama, and Mississippi drained by the Tennessee River.

or because they honestly fear our intentions. However, no nation need ever fear that we desire their land, or to impose our will, or to dictate their institutions. But we will always oppose the effort of one nation to conquer another nation. We will do this because our own security is at stake.

5   But there is more to it than that. For our generation has a dream. It is a very old dream. But we have the power and now we have the opportunity to make that dream come true. For centuries nations have struggled among each other. But we dream of a world where disputes are settled by law and reason. And we will try to make it so. For most of history men have hated and killed

10   one another in battle. But we dream of an end to war. And we will try to make it so. For all existence most men have lived in poverty, threatened by hunger. But we dream of a world where all are fed and charged with hope. And we will help to make it so.

The ordinary men and women of North Viet-Nam and South Viet-

15   Nam—of China and India—of Russia and America—are brave people. They are filled with the same proportions of hate and fear, of love and hope. Most of them want the same things for themselves and their families. Most of them do not want their sons to ever die in battle, or to see their homes, or the homes of others, destroyed. Well, this can be their world yet. Man now has the knowl-

20   edge—always before denied—to make this planet serve the real needs of the people who live on it.

I know this will not be easy. I know how difficult it is for reason to guide passion, and love to master hate. The complexities of this world do not bow easily to pure and consistent answers. But the simple truths are there just the same. We must all try to follow them as best we can.

Conclusion
25

We often say how impressive power is. But I do not find it impressive at all. The guns and the bombs, the rockets and the warships, are all symbols of human failure. They are necessary symbols. They protect what we cherish. But they are witness to human folly.

30   A dam built across a great river is impressive. In the countryside where I was born, and where I live, I have seen the night illuminated, and the kitchens warmed, and the homes heated, where once the cheerless night and the cease-less cold held sway. And all this happened because electricity came to our area along the humming wires of the REA[3]. Electrification of the countryside—yes,

35   that, too, is impressive.

---

[3]The federal Rural Electrification Administration was created in 1935 to promote the elec trification of rural areas.

A rich harvest in a hungry land is impressive. The sight of healthy children in a classroom is impressive. These—not mighty arms—are the achievements which the American nation believes to be impressive. And, if we are steadfast, the time may come when all other nations will also find it so.

Every night before I turn out the lights to sleep I ask myself this question: Have I done everything that I can do to unite this country? Have I done everything I can to help unite the world, to try to bring peace and hope to all the peoples of the world? Have I done enough? Ask yourselves that question in your homes—and in this hall tonight. Have we, each of us, all done all we could? Have we done enough?

We may well be living in the time foretold many years ago when it was said, "I call heaven and earth to record this day against you, that I have set before you life and death, blessing and cursing: therefore choose life, that both thou and thy seed may live."[4] This generation of the world must choose: destroy or build, kill or aid, hate or understand. We can do all these things on a scale never dreamed of before.

Well, we will choose life. In so doing we will prevail over the enemies within man, and over the natural enemies of all mankind.

---

[4]Deuteronomy 30:19

THE LIBERAL TWILIGHT
M. STANTON EVANS (1933–)

A conservative activist since his college years at Yale, M. Stanton Evans became an increasingly prominent voice on the Right during the turbulent 1960s. As editor of the Indianapolis News, *a syndicated columnist and radio commentator, author of six books, and later founder of the National Journalism Center in Washington, there was no part of the* Liberal Establishment *(also the title of one of his books) that he did not dissect. By the middle 1970s Evans was convinced that liberal programs (New Deal, Fair Deal, New Frontier, and Great Society versions) had been around long enough that it was time to ask the question, "Do they work?" His answer follows, originally given at a Center for Constructive Alternatives seminar at Hillsdale College.*

1976

In the past four decades, we have seen a dramatic growth in the scope of government power in the United States: a drainage of power upward out of the states into the central government, and within that central government, away from the Congress into the hands of the executive. And, I hasten to stress, not necessarily into the hands of the president, but into the hands of the executive   5
bureaucracy.

As a result, we have established on the banks of the Potomac precisely the kind of unchecked, untethered monolithic power structure that our founding fathers wanted to avoid. This has been done on the basis of a number of arguments and alibis that need examination. One of these is the suggestion that the   10
scope of federal power is not much larger than that which existed forty years ago. As a result of this activity, supposedly, we increase the absolute size of government, but since we are also increasing the productivity of our economy, relatively speaking there isn't that big an increase.

There are lots of ways of looking at that argument, but I think the simplest   15
is to take the spending figures, and trace them down through this period

M. Stanton Evans, "The Liberal Twilight," *Imprimis* 5 (August 1976):1–6.

of four or four and a half decades. If you go back to calendar year 1929, you discover that in that year, the entire outlay of the federal government came to less than $3 billion, $2.6 billion to be exact. If you come forward to fiscal '75, you discover that the outlay of the federal government was about $324 or $326
5   billion. If you round that back down just to $300 billion, you discover that in a span of 46 years, the budget outlays of the federal government increased by 10,000 percent, from $3 billion to $300 billion.

This was a period when the population of the United States was increasing from about 120 million people to perhaps 214 million, an increase of roughly
10   75 percent. So in those terms it is readily apparent that the compulsory sector of our economy, just measuring the federal component of it, has been increasing at a rate much greater than the growth of the economy as a whole.

Now it is true that the increase in spending is measured in dollars devalued by the process of inflation. But it is possible to correct for that and to take the
15   percentage of government spending in terms of gross national product or personal income, and thus to get a constant measure of what is happening to our economy. If we do that, we discover that in 1929 the percent of gross national product consumed by government at all levels was just about 10 percent. Today, it is 37 percent.
20   A single proposal now before Congress, the National Health Insurance Plan of Senator Kennedy, would increase that percentage to 45 percent. If the trend of growth that has prevailed for the past two decades continues simply as it has been with no major additions, by the year 2000 the percent of GNP absorbed by government is going to be 67 percent, according to the estimates
25   of the Office of Management and Budget. In terms of personal income, the story is much the same. In 1930, the percent of personal income consumed by governments at all levels was 15 percent. Today it is 44 percent.

And that, I might stress, is only a threshold measurement. On top of the spending measures, you have layer upon layer of regulatory intervention which
30   itself imposes social costs and economic costs not included in the budget figures. We know, for example, that there are, at various levels of government, 283 different agencies which have some species of superintendence over the activities of American businesses. We know that there are about 150,000 government employees at every level involved in that activity. We know that in the federal
35   government alone there are 63,000 employees involved in that activity.

We know that in paperwork alone, the costs to business and taxpayers amount to about $40 billion a year. We know that there are something like 6,000 different federal forms which have to be filled out by American businesses. President Ford's Council of Economic Advisors has estimated that the additional costs to
40   consumers of various federal regulatory programs is $130 billion a year.

If we compare this level of intervention with the level prevailing in the explicitly collectivist countries, we find there is not much difference. The percent of GNP taken in the Scandanavian countries for social programs is not much higher than the percent which is being taken here. So the assurance that it's all in your mind, it's all relative and isn't really that big, is mistaken. But if that empirical point can be established, one finds other assurances and explanations forthcoming.

One of these is that the burden of guilt for all this spending rests on the military. We experience high taxes and ravaging inflation, allegedly, because we're spending so much money on unneeded military implements and responding to the pressures of the military-industrial complex.

That notion has been sold very effectively in many segments of the national media and by very articulate politicians. But it is totally unsupportable on the empirical record. If you examine the budget figures for the last decade, you discover that the percentage of the federal budget devoted to the military has been falling like a stone. In 1963, 46.9 percent of the federal budget went for defense, almost half. For fiscal '76, it's 27 percent, just a little over a quarter. Even though there has been an absolute dollar increase in outlays for defense, that proportion has fallen steadily because the major spending increases have been for non-defense items, and mostly for welfare.

It's interesting to note the spending history of the Department of Defense as put up against the spending history of the Department of Health, Education, and Welfare. In the two decades, 1952 to 1972, the DOD budget increased by 74 percent, which in constant dollars was not much of an increase at all. In fact, according to the Brookings Institution, that was roughly keeping even in terms of what could be purchased with the dollars.

In that same two decades when Pentagon spending increased by 74 percent, the spending of the Department of HEW increased 4,837 percent, from $1.9 billion to roughly $100 billion. Today, whatever one may think about the Department of Defense, it no longer has a distinction it once did have. That is, it is no longer the largest department of the federal government. Its budge of '76 is about $93 billion. The budget of the Department of HEW is $118 billion. That is where the truly enormous spending increases have occurred—not for defense but for domestic social welfare programs.

If that empirical point can be driven home, one encounters another explanation which also has its plausible aspects. This is the suggestion that even though we are spending all this money on social welfare programs, at least we are helping poor people. We are taking resources from people who don't need them and putting them into the hands of people who do. This is what all the transfer payment programs are about and indeed they have been growing very rapidly.

There is no question that some proportion of this enormous increase in federal spending has gone to help people who are in need. But I would suggest to you that is not the major impact of what has happened. The major impact is something else altogether.

5   Again we face the difficulty of how you quantify these things. I have a formula which I think suggests a kind of answer. It is possible to measure the net increase in social welfare spending over a given span of time. If we do that, we discover that between 1960 and 1971, the total level of expenditure on social welfare programs, broadly defined, increased from $50 billion in 1960 to $171 billion in 1971—about a $120 billion increase.

10   It so happens that, according to the Bureau of the Census, there are about 25 million poor people in the United States, defined as people with an income level of $4,137 or less for a given year, for a family of four. If we take those 25 million poor people and divide them into the $120 billion increase—*not* the whole thing, just the increase—we discover that if we had simply taken that money and given it to the poor people, we could have given each and every one of them an annual stipend of $4,800 a year, which means an income for a family of four of $19,200. That is, we could have made every poor person in America a relatively rich person. But we didn't. Those poor people are still out there.

20   What happened to the money? The answer is that some of it did get into hands of the people who are supposed to get it. But a lot of it didn't. I would say the majority of it went to people who are counseling the poor people, working on their problems, examining the difficulties of the inner city, trying to rescue poor families and devise strategies for getting them out of their doldrums. It went to social workers and counselors and planners, and social engineers and urban renewal experts, and the assistant administrators to the administrative assistants who work for the federal government.

Now it is very interesting to note, if we talk about relative impoverishment and affluence in our society, that the level of income among people who work for the federal government is considerably *higher* than the level of income of people who work for private industry. In 1972 the median income for someone working for the federal government in civilian employment was about $12,700. The corresponding income for someone working in private industry was about $9,000. This means that whenever these programs are adopted, the gross effect, and I use the word in both its senses, is to transfer money from people who are relatively poor—that is, taxpayers—to people who are relatively well off—that is, people who work for the federal government.

It's also interesting to note the two most affluent counties in the United States. What do you think they are? Westchester County, New York? Dupage

County, Illinois? Marin County, California? Orange County, California? No, none of those.

The two richest counties in the United States, according to median family income, are Montgomery County, Maryland, and Fairfax County, Virginia, which happen to be the two bedroom counties for the federal government. That's where the government workers live. The median family income in Montgomery in 1972 was $16,000 plus. In Fairfax, which was not quite so good, it was about $15,700. Every time a program is adopted to enhance the power of the federal government, to cure impoverishment, those are the people who are enriched.

So it seems to me that argument is implausible, although superficially appealing. We simply have not been assuaging poverty by what we're doing. The other justifications are essentially subdivisions of that one. They are contentions that in problem areas throughout our economy, it is necessary to have a federal intervention of some type because the private market economy and the system of voluntary exchange have failed to get the job done.

We need a new health care program, supposedly, because the system of private health care delivery has failed. We need a new spending program to create jobs because the private market economy has failed to provide jobs. We need a new housing program because the private housing construction industry fails to provide new low-income housing. We need environmental constraints, we need energy programs—all allegedly because the system of private exchange doesn't do the job.

It is precisely here, however, that the liberal social philosophy has reached a watershed which even liberal theoreticians have come to recognize as such. If one takes the readouts on all these various programs and all of the difficulties that we allegedly are going to redress by enacting them, two things become apparent.

One is the fact that quite clearly these programs do not solve social problems. They are much more likely to *create* such problems. Second is the fact that in each and every one of these issue categories, you discover that every problem brought forward as a reason for further government intervention is the result of a *prior* intervention. The issue categories in which this is so are worth examining in a bit of detail because they show the phenomenon of self-generating interventions very clearly.

Inflation: We are being told that we have to have various kinds of government action because of rising oil prices or rising food prices. We've seen the enactment of a very complicated system of wage and price controls which obviously failed. We still have price controls in the energy field. We have exhortations on occasion to return to the system of full controls, all of this to cure the problem of inflation.

Well, who creates the problem of inflation? The answer is very plain on the record. Inflation, as I am sure the students of economics here are well aware, is essentially a phenomenon of more dollars chasing fewer goods, or an increasing money supply going after a relatively stable volume of production. That is exactly what has been happening in the United States in recent years. Take a look at what happened to the money supply between '67 and '73, right through the period of controls. The index of industrial production increased only 26 percent. What happened to consumer prices? They were right in between the increase in industrial production and the increase in the money supply, rising by roughly 35 percent. It is very clear on that record, as well as on the theoretical articulation of what causes inflation, that government itself creates the problem government is setting out to cure.

Unemployment: Government wants to cure unemployment through spending programs and job training projects. This is indeed a serious problem. Adolescent unemployment is very high these days; specifically, unemployment among black adolescents has soared to about 40 percent. Now why is black adolescent unemployment that high? What has caused this very serious problem?

The cause of that phenomenon, as it happens, is a "humanitarian" social program called the statutory minimum wage, one of those ideas that sounds great in theory but is not so great in practice. The theory is that we can raise peoples' wages by *fiat*. We simply pass a law saying workers ought to be paid a living wage and it is inhuman to pay less than that wage, making it illegal to go below it.

Unfortunately, it doesn't work that way, because in the final analysis, everybody's wage is paid by the consumer. If a given employee doesn't bring to the job the skills and the education to generate what he or she is being paid, that employee isn't going to get hired, or will be the first to be laid off when the economic crunch arrives. This means that any statutory floor under wages always works to the disadvantage of marginal workers, the people who can least afford further disadvantage because they've already had insufficient education and training.

We see that in our economy precisely in the phenomenon of black adolescent unemployment. In 1954, the federal minimum wage stood at 75 cents an hour. Black adolescent unemployment was 16.5 percent, which was bad enough in itself. By 1968, however, the federal minimum had gone to $1.60 an hour and black adolescent unemployment was 26.5 percent. Now the minimum is $2.10 and it's going to go to $2.20, and black adolescent unemployment is 40 percent.

So in this instance as well the federal government is creating the very problem it allegedly is setting about to cure. The answer to that problem is not further intervention into the market, but to phase out the intervention that we have.

Housing: We're told the private housing construction industry has failed. The record is directly the opposite. In the period since the 1930s, in which the federal government has been involved in housing programs of one sort or another, what has been the result of those programs? There have been many computations made and they all point to the same conclusion. The net impact of federal involvement in the field of housing has been the destruction of over one million units of housing. Now some of that housing, agreed, was unlivable, but much of it was livable, and much of it was destroyed by urban renewal programs which went in to inner cities, obedient to the vision of the planners, and knocked down row after row, unit after unit of livable housing and threw the tenants or the owners of that housing out and packed them into very densely populated neighborhoods elsewhere.

Now while the federal government was creating a net destruction of one million housing units, what was the private construction industry doing? The answer is that it was upgrading American housing in a chronicle of progress, true progress, that is probably unequalled anywhere in the annals of productive enterprise. In 1940, 51 percent of the housing in the United States was rated standard—that is, not in need of major repair, not overcrowded, with indoor plumbing. In the census of 1970 the corresponding figure was over 90 percent.

The same kind of thing is true in the realm of transit, environmental controls, energy, and almost every other issue that is being debated in Washington. The liberal argument has the situation backwards. It is not government that can cure the problems generated by private enterprise, but private enterprise that alleviates and diminishes problems created by government.

There is finally, and perhaps most important of all, another assurance whose failure, in my opinion, indicates that we are entering a period of liberal twilight—a period in which the liberal world view as we have known it beings to fade from vision.

The final assurance is not economic but political and constitutional: that it is possible, on the one hand, to pile up all these powers in the hands of the federal government, eroding the barriers to the exercise of power built into the constitutional system by our founding fathers, and yet maintain our essential freedoms.

What's important, in the liberal view, are human rights or rights of speech and advocacy and political association and religion. These are the core values of a free society, and we guarantee that even though we are doing all of these things to the economy and to the constitutional system, that all these rights are going to survive.

I regret to say that this final assurance is also unjustified, according to an enormous body of evidence that is piling up before us.

To begin with, it is theoretically impractical to reconcile these proposition. If in fact one can control the *economic* elements of a society, then one can control political activity as well. To take a very simple example, if one can control the supply of newsprint, one can control the press. It is interesting to recall that the closest we ever came to seeing a mass shutdown of newspapers in this country was in the fall and winter of 1973 when there were labor problems in Canada and the supply of newsprint was diminished. The result was that newspapers all over the Midwest cut back on the number of pages they could print, and there was a very real fear that they would have to stop publishing altogether. As a result of that particular economic constraint, a number of features and opinion columns were dropped from newspapers—a very clear example of economic factors impinging upon freedom of expression.

But there are other more direct illustrations as well. We know, for example, that there is not freedom of political communication today in a very large segment of the press, namely the electronic media. In that business the basic economic resource, the broadcast frequency, is controlled by the federal government—by the Federal Communications Commission. If you want to operate a commercial broadcasting station, you have to get a license from the FCC and that license is subject to renewal every three years.

If you do not conduct yourself in a manner the FCC considers appropriate, your license can be taken away. There are few instances in which licenses are actually removed but it isn't necessary to have many removed for the point to get across: if you conduct yourself peaceably and don't stir up a lot of fuss and feathers, you probably will get a routine renewal. But if you create problems and become excessively controversial, as has happened in certain cases, then your license can be taken away. Hundreds of thousands, perhaps millions of dollars of revenue, can be lost as a result of that political decision.

Above and beyond this threshold constraint, the Federal Communications Commission has added other very explicit constraints through the fairness and equal time doctrines. The Federal Trade Commission has also gotten into the act with its rulings about commercial content. So the range of debate in commercial broadcasting has been severely constricted, principally because the basic economic resource is in the hands of the government.

During the Watergate controversy, there was a considerable flap when Senator Lowell Weicker of Connecticut, a maverick Republican on the Watergate Committee, came up with a document which allegedly had been drafted by Jeb Stuart Magruder, a functionary with the Committee to Re-Elect the President.

In this memorandum, Magruder spelled out a number of ideas for getting at people in the media who disagreed with the administration. He said things like this: The first thing we do when we get Dean Burch appointed chairman of the FCC is to start monitoring what the networks are doing, and build a case that they are not giving out with balanced programming.

Then we can get the Anti-Trust Division of the Justice Department to take a look at the networks and suggest that there are going to be actions on that score. And then we can get the IRS into the act and start taking a look at the tax situation. There are all kinds of things we can do to intimidate them and back them off a little.

When that came out it caused a tremendous uproar; there was indignation that the Nixon regime was planning to use the powers of government to punish dissenters. It reminded me of a very similar memorandum written back in the early 1960s by a man named Victor Reuther, one of the high officials of the United Auto Workers, addressed to then Attorney General Robert Kennedy. In that memorandum, Victor Reuther spelled out a scenario very similar to that spelled out by Magruder.

Reuther said, in essence, we should take the FCC and the IRS and other agencies of the government and start putting heat on conservative broadcasters creating problems for the Kennedy administration. He very elaborately suggested some of the things that might be done. That advice was acted upon. We know now that this program for inhibiting dissent through the political use of the Federal Communications Commission was pursued very energetically by both the Kennedy and Johnson administrations.

I cite those parallel examples not to say that since it was done under the Kennedy administration and the Johnson administration, therefore it's all right under the Nixon administration—no. Both are wrong. The point is otherwise. That point, it seems to me, is that in neither of these memoranda was it suggested that we needed a single new governmental power to control the media in this country. What was being suggested was that *the power is already here*. We *have* the power. Just take it and use it against the people who disagree with us.

Ultimately the Nixon attempt failed because of Watergate. But nonetheless, the power *was* there and the power is still there. That power has not been dismantled as a result of Watergate. It's all sitting there in Washington, D.C., waiting to be used by somebody who knows how to deploy it in sophisticated fashion.

A second point implicit in what I've been saying is that almost all of these controls are economic in nature. All have to do with controlling some aspect of our economic lives, either through taxation, anti-trust, or the FCC licensing power. By controlling the economy, we control political expression as well.

Alexander Hamilton said a power over a man's subsistence amounts to a power over his will. A very true and very obvious statement. If I could control

the wherewithal of your life, I could control almost everything about you. If I
can control your subsistence and I can control your will, I can certainly control
your voice or pen.

In essence what the liberals have attempted to do, and it has been a heroic
5   enterprise in its way, has been to abandon the premises of a free society, to adopt
the premises of an authoritarian society, and yet to avoid authoritarian result: to
say that we're going to have a collectivized, regimented society and still maintain
our libertarian values. What is happening to us now, in the terminal phase of
that experiment, is a final disintegration of libertarian values. We are beginning
10   to see the indications of an authoritarian state—not simply a regimented state,
but an explicitly authoritarian state—crop up around us.

I think we see this in some very mundane, very ordinary controversies
debated all the time in communities around this country. The issues I pick are
essentially three—busing, sex education, and the population issues.

15   Take a look at those issues. The usual debate on busing, for example, is as
follows. The proponents of the neighborhood school want to preserve their local
neighborhood and autonomy against the people who want to get authentically
integrated schools. All the debate is about "unitary" and "dual" systems and *de
jure* and *de facto* segregation.

20   But if one pursues the busing controversy to its heart, one discovers a totally
different set of issues. If you go back and read the Coleman Report, published
in 1966 by the Department of Health, Education, and Welfare—named for
Professor James Coleman, then of Johns Hopkins, now of Chicago—you find
the rationale for busing spelled out pretty plainly. And it is articulated even
25   further in another document called *Racial Isolation in the Public Schools*, published in 1967.

The Coleman Report in essence was a review of all the factors entering into
public education and the things that resulted from those factors. It found that the
enormous increase in spending for public schools over the past several decades
30   had not resulted in a corresponding increase in learning gains, and in particular
had not produced any diminution in the black-white learning gap which was
observed at the beginning of school and was still observed at the end of school.

The problem as it was perceived by these researchers, and those explaining their research, was that we were sending black kids into these wonderfully
35   appointed, very expensive public schools with all the right facilities and all the
right preparation, and there we were programming into them the good things
they ought to know. But then at the end of their school they were going home
to their ignorant parents, where the good effects of the official programming
were being washed away. They were slipping back into the same culture pattern
40   from which they had originally emerged.

The conclusion drawn from that—to put it in its most brutal, but I think most accurate, form—was that we *had to break the link between the black child and his or her parents*. We had to take that child and get him away from the influence of his parents and immerse him as fully as possible in an artificial environment created by planners who had the proper credentials and the proper   5
expertise and the backing of the state.

Coleman said it very plainly in an article in *The Public Interest* in the summer of 1966.[1] He said that what is needed is a school that begins very early in the day and ends very late in the day, a school that preferably would begin very early in life. We had to replace the home environment by an official environment.   10

Now that's a very interesting idea, and it is particularly interesting when it is proposed in the name of civil rights—to take the black child as an experimental guinea pig in cultural homogenization, and to say that we're going to get that child away from his family and to mold him according to a design desired by official planners.   15

It is this same idea that is apparent beneath the surface in these other controversies. We see it in the sex education debate—and again the superficial level is one thing and the actual level is something else. The superficial, public level is: My kid is being exposed to pornography because they are showing him pictures of frogs copulating. On the other side is the school saying the kids have   20
to learn hygiene and how to avoid getting pregnant, and it's important that we teach them these things.

Again, I'm not downplaying the importance of such issues, but they're not the real issues. The real issues are essentially the same as in the busing controversy. If you push that one far enough, you invariably reach a point where people on   25
the side of the sex education programs say: Look. Let's face it. These parents are too dumb. They don't know what is right for their own kids. They've got all these hang-ups and can't talk to the kids about this. They don't know how to shape them emotionally and physically. We know. We've got the credentials. We studied this. We've got the degrees and we've got the state backing us up.   30

The population question is the ultimate version of this whole controversy. A plausible rhetoric about the "quality of life" would have us suppose that the issue here is *numbers* of people. And, without taking a particular side, that is an issue worth discussing. But it isn't the real issue. The real issue isn't the *number* of people. It's the *kind* of people. Read the literature that has emerged from the   35
abortion and euthanasia movements and examine the meaning of the phrase "quality of life". Sounds good, doesn't it? Everyone wants a better quality of

---

[1]James S. Coleman, "Equal Schools or Equal Students," *The Public Interest* 4 (Summer 1966): 70–75.

life. Well what that means is something rather different. *It means that some lives are better than others*, that there is such a thing as a life that isn't worth living and that it is up to those of us who have the expertise to make the decision as to which lives are worth living and which aren't. And that is the payoff. That is the ultimate phase of this development in which the liberal mindset becomes transformed into something quite the opposite of liberal: in which the libertarian remnants that have persisted through these forty years fall away, and we see the emergence of an authoritarian state.

If one adopts the authoritarian premises, ultimately one is going to emerge with the authoritarian conclusions. The libertarian shell has fallen away, and we're left with the bedrock principles of compulsion and the subjection of human beings to a planning elite.

It doesn't have to be that way and some liberals have turned back in the other direction. It is my hope that those who have become disenchanted with the liberal formula will join with those who have criticized this approach for many years, and that between them they will be able to attack, in an intelligent way, the economic distresses which have afflicted our society and prevent the further erosion of our political system into authoritarian practice.

If such a united front can be, then I think there is some hope that emerging from this liberal twilight will be a more libertarian product than that I have been describing, and that those of us who are concerned for the future of our society can restore it to the ways of freedom intended for it by its founders.

First Inaugural Address
Ronald Reagan (1911–2004)
President of the United States (1981–1989)

A masterful orator, Ronald Reagan moved Americans with his faith in them and their collective history. Taking office at time when the country was experiencing a loss of purpose, a severe economic crisis, and an international debacle in Iran, Reagan's optimism filled Americans with confidence. Or rather, he called on them to find their own confidence and pride. His inaugural address reflected his firmly held beliefs: "I believe we the Americans of today are ready to act worthy of ourselves." Reagan was also the only American president to challenge communism on both moral and military levels. Not content with merely containing Soviet aggression, Reagan wanted to roll it back around the globe.

20 January 1981

To a few of us here today this is a solemn and most momentous occasion, and yet in the history of our nation it is a commonplace occurrence. The orderly transfer of authority as called for in the Constitution routinely takes place, as it has for almost two centuries, and few of us stop to think how unique we really are. In the eyes of many in the world, this every-4-year ceremony we accept as   5
normal is nothing less than a miracle.

Mr. President, I want our fellow citizens to know how much you did to carry on this tradition. By your gracious cooperation in the transition process, you have shown a watching world that we are a united people pledged to maintaining a political system which guarantees individual liberty to a great degree than   10
any other, and I thank you and your people for all your help in maintaining the continuity which is the bulwark of our Republic.

The business of our nation goes forward. These United States are confronted with an economic affliction of great proportions. We suffer from the longest and one of the worst sustained inflations in our national history. It distorts our   15
economic decisions, penalizes thrift, and crushes the struggling young and the

Public Papers of the Presidents of the United States, Ronald Reagan, 1981 (Washington, DC: Government Printing Office, 1982), 1–4.

fixed-income elderly alike. It threatens to shatter the lives of millions of our people.

Idle industries have cast workers into unemployment, human misery, and personal indignity. Those who do work are denied a fair return for their labor
5   by a tax system which penalized successful achievement and keeps us from maintaining full productivity.

But great as our tax burden is, it has not kept pace with public spending. For decades we have piled deficit upon deficit, mortgaging our future and our children's future for the temporary convenience of the present. To continue this
10 long trend is to guarantee tremendous social, cultural, political, and economic upheavals.

You and I, as individuals, can, by borrowing, live beyond our means, but for only a limited period of time. Why, then, should we think that collectively, as a nation, we're not bound by that same limitation? We must act today in order
15 to preserve tomorrow. And let there be no misunderstanding: We are going to begin to act, beginning today.

The economic ills we suffer have come upon us over several decades. They will not go away in days, weeks, or months, but they will go away. They will go away because we as Americans have the capacity now, as we've had in the
20 past, to do whatever needs to be done to preserve this last and greatest bastion of freedom.

In this present crisis, government is not the solution to our problem; government is the problem. From time to time we've been tempted to believe that society has become too complex to be managed by self-rule, that government
25 by an elite group is superior to government for, by, and of the people. Well, if no one among us is capable of governing himself, then who among us has the capacity to govern someone else? All of us together, in and out of government, must bear the burden. The solutions we seek must be equitable, with no one group singled out to pay a higher price.

30 We hear much of special interest groups. Well, our concern must be for a special interest group that has been too long neglected. It knows no sectional boundaries or ethnic and racial divisions, and it crosses political party lines. It is made up of men and women who raise our food, patrol our streets, man our mines and factories, teach our children, keep our homes, and heal us when we're
35 sick—professionals, industrialists, shopkeepers, clerks, cabbies, and truck-drivers. They are, in short, "We the people," this breed called Americans.

Well, this administration's objective will be a healthy, vigorous, growing economy that provides equal opportunities for all Americans, with no barriers born of bigotry or discrimination. Putting America back to work means putting
40 all Americans back to work. Ending inflation means freeing all Americans from

the terror of runaway living costs. All must share in the productive work of this "new beginning," and all must share in the bounty of a revived economy. With the idealism and fair play which are the core of our system and our strength, we can have a strong and prosperous America, at peace with itself and the world.

So, as we begin, let us take inventory. We are a nation that has a govern-   5
ment—not the other way around. And this makes us special among the nations of the Earth. Our government has no power except that granted it by the people. It is time to check and reverse the growth of government, which shows signs of having grown beyond the consent of the governed.

It is my intention to curb the size and influence of the Federal establishment   10
and to demand recognition of the distinction between the powers granted to the Federal Government and those reserved to the states or to the people. All of us need to be reminded that the Federal Government did not create the states; the states created the Federal Government.

Now, so there will be no misunderstanding, it's not my intention to do   15
away with government. It is rather to make it work—work with us, not over us; to stand by our side, not ride on our back. Government can and must provide opportunity, not smother it; foster productivity, not stifle it.

If we look to the answer as to why for so many years we achieved so much, prospered as no other people on Earth, it was because here in this land we   20
unleashed the energy and individual genius of man to a greater extent than has ever been done before. Freedom and the dignity of the individual have been more available and assured here than in any other place on Earth. The price for this freedom at times has been high, but we have never been unwilling to pay that price.   25

It is no coincidence that our present troubles parallel and are proportionate to the intervention and intrusion in our lives that result from unnecessary and excessive growth of government. It is time for us to realize that we're too great a nation to limit ourselves to small dreams. We're not, as some would have us believe, doomed to an inevitable decline. I do not believe in a fate that will   30
fall on us no matter what we do. I do believe in a fate that will fall on us if we do nothing. So, with all the creative energy at our command, let us begin an era of national renewal. Let us renew our determination, our courage, and our strength. And let us renew our faith and our hope.

We have every right to dream heroic dreams. Those who say that we're in   35
a time when there are not heroes, they just don't know where to look. You can see heroes every day going in and out of factory gates. Others, a handful in number, produce enough food to feed all of us and then the world beyond. You meet heroes across a counter, and they're on both sides of that counter. There are entrepreneurs with faith in themselves and faith in an idea who create new   40

jobs, new wealth and opportunity. They're individuals and families whose taxes support the government and whose voluntary gifts support church, charity, culture, art, and education. Their patriotism is quiet, but deep. Their values sustain our national life.

5   Now, I have used the words "they" and "their" in speaking of these heroes. I could say "you" and "your," because I'm addressing the heroes of whom I speak—you, the citizens of this blessed land. Your dreams, your hopes, your goals are going to be the dreams, the hopes, and the goals of this administration, so help me God.

10   We shall reflect the compassion that is so much a part of your makeup. How can we love our country and not love our countrymen; and loving them, reach out a hand when they fall, heal them when they're sick, and provide opportunity to make them self-sufficient so they will be equal in fact and not just in theory?

15   Can we solve the problems confronting us? Well, the answer is an unequivocal and emphatic "yes." To paraphrase Winston Churchill, I did not take the oath I've just taken with the intention of presiding over the dissolution of the world's strongest economy.

In the days ahead I will propose removing the roadblocks that have slowed 20 our economy and reduced productivity. Steps will be taken aimed at restoring the balance between the various levels of government. Progress may be slow, measured in inches and feet, not miles, but we will progress. It is time to reawaken this industrial giant, to get government back within its means, and to lighten our punitive tax burden. And these will be our first priorities, and on 25 these principles there will be no compromise.

On the eve of our struggle for independence a man who might have been one of the greatest among the Founding Fathers, Dr. Joseph Warren, president of the Massachusetts Congress, said to his fellow Americans, "Our country is in danger, but not to be despaired of....On you depend the fortunes of America. 30 You are to decide the important questions upon which rests the happiness and the liberty of millions yet unborn. Act worthy of yourselves."

Well, I believe we, the Americans of today, are ready to act worthy of ourselves, ready to do what must be done to ensure happiness and liberty for ourselves, our children, and our children's children. And as we renew ourselves 35 here in our own land, we will be seen as having greater strength throughout the world. We will again be the exemplar of freedom and a beacon of hope for those who do not now have freedom.

To those neighbors and allies who share our freedom, we will strengthen our historic ties and assure them of our support and firm commitment. We 40 will match loyalty with loyalty. We will strive for mutually beneficial relations.

We will not use our friendship to impose on their sovereignty, for our own sovereignty is not for sale.

As for the enemies of freedom, those who are potential adversaries, they will be reminded that peace is the highest aspiration of the American people. We will negotiate for it, sacrifice for it; we will not surrender for it, now or ever.

Our forbearance should never be misunderstood. Our reluctance for conflict should not be misjudged as a failure of will. When action is required to preserve our national security, we will act. We will maintain sufficient strength to prevail if need be, knowing that if we do so we have the best chance of never having to use that strength.

Above all, we must realize that no arsenal or no weapon in the arsenals of the world is so formidable as the will and moral courage of free men and women. It is a weapon our adversaries in today's world do not have. It is a weapon that we as Americans do have. Let that be understood by those who practice terrorism and prey upon their neighbors.

I'm told that tens of thousands of prayer meetings are being held on this day, and for that I'm deeply grateful. We are a nation under God, and I believe God intended for us to be free. It would be fitting and good, I think, if on each Inaugural Day in future years it should be declared a day of prayer.

This is the first time in our history that this ceremony has been held, as you've been told, on this West Front of the Capitol. Standing here, one faces a magnificent vista, opening up on this city's special beauty and history. At the end of this open mall are those shrines to the giants on whose shoulders we stand.

Directly in front of me, the monument to a monumental man, George Washington, father of our country. A man of humility who came to greatness reluctantly. He led America out of revolutionary victory into infant nationhood. Off to one side, the stately memorial to Thomas Jefferson. The Declaration of Independence flames with his eloquence. And then, beyond the Reflecting Pool, the dignified columns of the Lincoln Memorial. Whoever would understand in his heart the meaning of America will find it in the life of Abraham Lincoln.

Beyond those monuments to heroism is the Potomac River, and on the far shore the sloping hills of Arlington National Cemetery, with its row upon row of simple white markers bearing crosses or Stars of David. They add up to only a tiny fraction of the price that has been paid for our freedom.

Each one of those markers is a monument to the kind of hero I spoke of earlier. Their lives ended in places called Belleau Wood, The Argonne, Omaha Beach, Salerno, and halfway around the world on Guadalcanal, Tarawa, Pork Chop Hill, the Chosin Reservoir, and in a hundred rice paddies and jungles of a place called Vietnam.

Under one such marker lies a young man, Martin Treptow, who left his job in a small town barbershop in 1917 to go to France with the famed Rainbow Division. There, on the western front, he was killed trying to carry a message between battalions under heavy artillery fire.

5   We're told that on his body was found a diary. On the flyleaf under the heading, "My Pledge," he had written these words: "America must win this war. Therefore I will work, I will save, I will sacrifice, I will endure, I will fight cheerfully and do my utmost, as if the issue of the whole struggle depended on me alone."

10   The crisis we are facing today does not require of us the kind of sacrifice that Martin Treptow and so many thousands of others were called upon to make. It does require, however, our best effort and our willingness to believe in ourselves and to believe in our capacity to perform great deeds, to believe that together with God's help we can and will resolve the problems which now
15 confront us.

And after all, why shouldn't we believe that? We are Americans.

God bless you, and thank you.

Speech Before Commons
Ronald Reagan (1911–2004)
President of the United States (1981–1989)

In this speech, delivered before the British Parliament, Reagan spoke of communism in moral terms. The Soviet empire was, he concluded, "evil." Though the American press found this humorous, repressed Eastern Europeans embraced it as a message of hope. Reagan's confidence extended not only to the American people, but it also to those under Soviet rule. When the Berlin Wall came down in 1989 and the Russian Communist party self-destructed in 1991, the average Eastern European gave credit to Reagan's rhetoric and strong posture.

8 June 1982

…We're approaching the end of a bloody century plagued by a terrible political invention—totalitarianism. Optimism comes less easily today, not because democracy is less vigorous, but because democracy's enemies have refined their instruments of repression. Yet optimism is in order, because day by day democracy is proving itself to be a not-at-all-fragile flower. From Stettin on 5
the Baltic to Varna on the Black Sea, the regimes planted by totalitarianism have had more than 30 years to establish their legitimacy. But none—not one regime—has yet been able to risk free elections. Regimes planted by bayonets do not take root.

The strength of the Solidarity movement in Poland demonstrates the truth 10
told in an underground joke in the Soviet Union. It is that the Soviet Union would remain a one-party nation even if an opposition party were permitted, because everyone would join the opposition party. [*Laughter*]….

Historians looking back at our time will note the consistent restraint and peaceful intentions of the West. They will note that it was the democracies who 15
refused to use the threat of their nuclear monopoly in the forties and early fifties for territorial or imperial gain. Had that nuclear monopoly been in the hands

Public Papers of the Presidents of the United States, Ronald Reagan, 1 January–2 July 1982 (Washington, DC: Government Printing Office, 1983), 743, 743–44, 746, 747–48.

of the Communist world, the map of Europe—indeed, the world—would look very different today. And certainly they will note it was not the democracies that invaded Afghanistan or suppressed Polish Solidarity or used chemical and toxin warfare in Afghanistan and Southeast Asia.

5   If history teaches anything it teaches self-delusion in the face of unpleasant facts is folly. We see around us today the marks of our terrible dilemma—predictions of doomsday, anti-nuclear demonstrations, an arms race in which the West must, for its own protection, be an unwilling participant. At the same time we see totalitarian forces in the world who seek subversion and conflict around

10   the globe to further their barbarous assault on the human spirit. What, then, is our course? Must civilization perish in a hail of fiery atoms? Must freedom wither in a quiet, deadening accommodation with totalitarian evil?

Sir Winston Churchill refused to accept the inevitability of war or even that it was imminent. He said, "I do not believe that Soviet Russia desires war. What

15   they desire is the fruits of war and the indefinite expansion of their power and doctrines. But what we have to consider here today while time remains is the permanent prevention of war and the establishment of conditions of freedom and democracy as rapidly as possible in all countries."

Well, this is precisely our mission today: to preserve freedom as well as peace.

20   It may not be easy to see; but I believe we live now at a turning point.

In an ironic sense Karl Marx was right. We are witnessing today a great revolutionary crisis, a crisis where the demands of the economic order are conflicting directly with those of the political order. But the crisis is happening not in the free, non-Marxist West, but in the home of Marxist-Leninism, the Soviet

25   Union. It is the Soviet Union that runs against the tide of history by denying human freedom and human dignity to its citizens. It also is in deep economic difficulty. The rate of growth in the national product has been steadily declining since the fifties and is less than half of what it was then.

The dimensions of this failure are astounding: A country which employs

30   one-fifth of its population in agriculture is unable to feed its own people. Were it not for the private sector, the tiny private sector tolerated in Soviet agriculture, the country might be on the brink of famine. These private plots occupy a bare 3 percent of the arable land but account for nearly one-quarter of Soviet farm output and nearly one-third of meat products and vegetables.

35   Over-centralized, with little or no incentives, year after year the Soviet system pours its best resource into the making of instruments of destruction. The constant shrinkage of economic growth combined with the growth of military production is putting a heavy strain on the Soviet people. What we see here is a political structure that no longer corresponds to its economic base, a society

40   where productive forces are hampered by political ones.

The decay of the Soviet experiment should come as no surprise to us. Wherever the comparisons have been made between free and closed societies—West Germany and East Germany, Austria and Czechoslovakia, Malaysia and Vietnam—it is the democratic countries what are prosperous and responsive to the needs of their people. And one of the simple but overwhelming facts of our time is this: Of all the millions of refugees we've seen in the modern world, their flight is always away from, not toward the Communist world. Today on the NATO line, our military forces face east to prevent a possible invasion. On the other side of the line, the Soviet forces also face east to prevent their people from leaving.

The hard evidence of totalitarian rule has caused in mankind an uprising of the intellect and will. Whether it is the growth of the new schools of economics in America or England or the appearance of the so-called new philosophers in France, there is one unifying thread running through the intellectual work of these groups—rejection of the arbitrary power of the state, the refusal to subordinate the rights of the individual to the super-state, the realization that collectivism stifles all the best human impulses....

As for the Soviet view, Chairman Brezhnev repeatedly has stressed that the competition of ideas and systems must continue and that this is entirely consistent with relaxation of tensions and peace.

Well, we ask only that these systems begin by living up to their own constitutions, abiding by their own laws, and complying with the international obligations they have undertaken. We ask only for a process, a direction, a basic code of decency, not for an instant transformation.

We cannot ignore the fact that even without our encouragement there has been and will continue to be repeated explosions against repression and dictatorships. The Soviet Union itself is not immune to this reality. Any system is inherently unstable that has no peaceful means to legitimize its leaders. In such cases, the very repressiveness of the state ultimately drives people to resist it, if necessary, by force.

While we must be cautious about forcing the pace of change, we must not hesitate to declare our ultimate objectives and to take concrete actions to move toward them. We must be staunch in our conviction that freedom is not the sole prerogative of a lucky few, but the inalienable and universal right of all human beings. So states the United Nations Universal Declaration of Human Rights, which, among other things, guarantees free elections.

The objective I propose is quite simple to state: to foster the infrastructure of democracy, the system of a free press, unions, political parties, universities, which allows a people to choose their own way to develop their own culture, to reconcile their own differences through peaceful means.

This is not cultural imperialism, it is providing the means for genuine self-determination and protection for diversity. Democracy already flourishes in countries with very different cultures and historical experiences. It would be cultural condescension, or worse, to say that any people prefer dictatorship
5   to democracy. Who would voluntarily choose not to have the right to vote, decide to purchase government propaganda handouts instead of independent newspapers, prefer government to worker-controlled unions, opt for land to be owned by the state instead of those who till it, want government repression of religious liberty, a single political party instead of a free choice, a rigid cultural
10 orthodoxy instead of democratic tolerance and diversity?

Since 1917 the Soviet Union has given covert political training and assistance to Marxist-Leninists in many countries. Of course, it also has promoted the use of violence and subversion by these same forces. Over the past several decades, West European and other Social Democrats, Christian Democrats, and
15 leaders have offered open assistance to fraternal, political, and social institutions to bring about peaceful and democratic progress. Appropriately, for a vigorous new democracy, the Federal Republic of Germany's political foundations have become a major force in this effort.

We in America now intend to take additional steps, as many of our allies
20 have already done, toward realizing this same goal. The chairmen and other leaders of the national Republican and Democratic Party organizations are initiating a study with the bipartisan American political foundation to determine how the United States can best contribute as a nation to the global campaign for democracy now gathering force. They will have the co-operation of con-
25 gressional leaders of both parties, along with representatives of business, labor, and other major institutions in our society. I look forward to receiving their recommendations and to working with these institutions and the Congress in the common task of strengthening democracy throughout the world.

It is time that we committed ourselves as a nation—in both the public and
30 private sectors—to assisting democratic development....

...What I am describing now is a plan and a hope for the long term—the march of freedom and democracy which will leave Marxism-Leninism on the ash-heap of history as it has left other tyrannies which stifle the freedom and muzzle the self-expression of the people. And that's why we must continue our
35 efforts to strengthen NATO even as we move forward with our Zero-Option initiative in the negotiations on intermediate-range forces and our proposal for a one-third reduction in strategic ballistic missile warheads.

Our military strength is a prerequisite to peace, but let it be clear we maintain this strength in the hope it will never be used, for the ultimate determinant
40 in the struggle that's now going on in the world will not be bombs and rockets,

but a test of wills and ideas, a trial of spiritual resolve, the values we hold, the beliefs we cherish, the ideals to which we are dedicated.

The British people know that, given strong leadership, time and a little bit of hope, the forces of good ultimately rally and triumph over evil. Here among you is the cradle of self-government, the Mother of Parliaments. Here is the 5 enduring greatness of the British contribution to mankind, the great civilized ideas: individual liberty, representative government, and the rule of law under God.

I've often wondered about the shyness of some of us in the West about standing for these ideals that have done so much to ease the plight of man and 10 the hardships of our imperfect world. This reluctance to use those vast resources at our command reminds me of the elderly lady whose home was bombed in the Blitz. As the rescuers moved about, they found a bottle of brandy she'd stored behind the staircase, which was all that was left standing. And since she was barely conscious, one of the workers pulled the cork to give her a taste of 15 it. She came around immediately and said, "Here now—there now, put it back. That's for emergencies." [*Laughter*]

Well, the emergency is upon us. Let us be shy no longer. Let us go to our strength. Let us offer hope. Let us tell the world that a new age is not only possible but probable. 20

During the dark days of the Second World War, when this island was incandescent with courage, Winston Churchill exclaimed about Britain's adversaries, "What kind of a people do they think we are?" Well, Britain's adversaries found out what extraordinary people the British are. But all the democracies paid a terrible price for allowing the dictators to underestimate us. We dare not make 25 that mistake again. So, let us ask ourselves, "What kind of people do we think we are?" And let us answer, "Free people, worthy of freedom and determined not only to remain so but to help others gain their freedom as well."

Sir Winston led his people to great victory in war and then lost an election just as the fruits of victory were about to be enjoyed. But he left office honorably, 30 and, as it turned out, temporarily, knowing that the liberty of his people was more important than the fate of any single leader. History recalls his greatness in ways no dictator will ever know. And he left us a message of hope for the future, as timely now as when he first uttered it, as opposition leader in the Commons nearly 27 years ago, when he said, "When we look back on all the 35 perils through which we have passed and at the mighty foes that we have laid low and all the dark and deadly designs that we have frustrated, why should we fear for our future? We have," he said, "come safely through the worst."

Well, the task I've set forth will long outlive our own generation. But together, we too have come through the worst. Let us now begin a major effort to 40 secure the best—a crusade for freedom that will engage the faith and fortitude of the next generation. For the sake of peace and justice, let us move toward a world in which all people are at last free to determine their own destiny.

Thank you.

ANTHOLOGIE
DE LA
POÉSIE FRANÇAISE

SUZANNE JULLIARD

ANTHOLOGIE
DE LA
POÉSIE FRANÇAISE

Éditions de Fallois

PARIS

© Éditions de Fallois, 2002
22, rue La Boétie, 75008 Paris

ISBN 2-87706-450-6

À la mémoire de mon père,
Georges Armand Agié

C'est un cri répété par mille sentinelles.

BAUDELAIRE

Car c'est de l'homme qu'il s'agit et de son renouement.
Quelqu'un au monde n'élèvera-t-il la voix ? Témoignage pour l'homme...
Que le Poète se fasse entendre et qu'il dirige le jugement !

SAINT-JOHN PERSE

INTRODUCTION

L'autre langue

La langue de ma mère était le français, celle de mon père la poésie : j'eus donc une enfance bilingue.

J'aurais dû parler aussi le patois aveyronnais ; sa musique m'est familière et c'est lui qui m'a fait aimer d'emblée les troubadours. Mais je n'en sais que des bribes. Son emploi était limité aux échanges entre mon grand-père et ses filles, ma mère et sa sœur, et à quelques dialogues entre ces deux inséparables. Si elles y avaient recours devant moi, c'était toujours pour fonder sur l'autorité d'une sagesse ancestrale les principes qu'elles s'efforçaient de m'inculquer sous forme d'aphorismes. Leur traduction suivait aussitôt, et le double énoncé avait pour effet, au moins à leurs yeux, de rendre chacun d'eux incontestable.

La langue commune ne pouvait être que le français, imposé par mon père et mon oncle. Le premier, fils de paysan, s'il comprenait fort bien la langue habituelle de ses parents, y avait renoncé depuis que l'école l'avait ouvert à un autre mode d'expression. Quant au second, il n'en finissait pas de nous surprendre par les tournures recherchées d'un français littéraire, seul bagage de l'émigré qu'il était. On le lui avait enseigné à Rostov avant la Révolution.

Lorsqu'il était seul, ou distrait au point d'oublier la présence des autres, mon père se mettait à dire des vers. Avec des alexandrins solennels il évoquait la fuite du temps et la fragilité de l'homme, il célébrait l'aurore ou le couchant. Les poètes lui fournissaient mots et rythmes pour décrire le mouvement des planètes et le scintillement des étoiles, sujets de prédilection pour lui que le ciel fascinait. Il récitait comme d'autres chantonnent, à part soi, rêveusement, des poèmes appris sans contrainte, avec une passion d'autodidacte. Il savait des vers par centaines.

Dans la mythique bibliothèque de l'univers que décrit Borgès, mon père avait trouvé ce que cherchent obscurément tant d'infatigables lecteurs : la réponse aux énigmes du monde. Elle lui était apparue dans les œuvres des poètes français.

Écrivait-il lui-même des poèmes ? C'est peu probable. Ceux des autres lui suffisaient. Comme ces croyants pour qui un verset de Bible éclaire chaque circonstance de leur vie, il s'était constitué un livre intérieur inépuisable,

« Et toujours disponible aux rayons de mémoire ».

Les vers que j'écoutais se fondaient en moi en une seule et mystérieuse musique. Vrais « talismans », selon le mot célèbre d'un critique, ils ouvraient à mes yeux des espaces étranges. Très tôt, sans l'avoir voulu, j'en sus quelques-uns. Je les chuchotais pour moi-même, émerveillée. Les tout premiers sont là, intacts dans ma mémoire, et j'entends avec eux la voix qui les disait :

> *L'ombre était sur Babel et l'horreur sur Endor.*
> *On voyait le matin quand l'aube au carquois d'or*
> *Lance aux astres fuyants ses blanches javelines*
> *Des hommes monstrueux assis sur les collines ;*
> *On entendait parler de formidables voix*
> *Et les géants allaient et venaient dans les bois.*

Le commencement en poésie est comme le premier amour, ineffaçable. Je devais plus tard aimer d'autres poètes, et d'autres vers que ceux-là dans l'œuvre de Hugo, mais l'éblouissement originel eut une force initiatique. Le pouvoir que conservent sur moi ces fragments après tant d'années, je ne crois pas qu'il soit lié aux délices des retrouvailles avec le passé, aux résurrections douces-amères des ego anciens. Alors que tant de refrains démodés ou même de vers jadis admirés nous font sourire, et ne nous restent chers que pour la couleur et le parfum des années fugitives qu'ils gardent en eux, les tout premiers poèmes demeurent liés à l'expérience bouleversante d'un autre langage, d'un autre monde.

La poésie était pour mon père une patrie personnelle, un refuge où il s'isolait dans des rêveries sans fin. Il disait des vers comme les Tibétains font tourner leur moulin à prières. Comme eux il créait en lui et autour de lui un espace du divin.

Je l'écoutais. Le rythme régulier, le retour attendu de la rime, les noms inouïs, l'éclat soudain d'une image, rompaient l'ordre terne des jours et m'entraînaient « ad luminis oras » vers ces rivages de lumière dont parle Lucrèce.

J'avais neuf ou dix ans quand il me nomma ses poètes. À ses yeux, Hugo et Baudelaire l'emportaient sur tous les autres. Je ne sais comment il en était venu à les lire. Dans ce choix, assurément, l'école n'était pour rien : il l'avait quittée à quatorze ans pour l'usine. Et leurs œuvres avaient peu de chance d'être enseignées par les Frères des Écoles chrétiennes.

Sa familiarité avec Hugo ne se bornait pas au plaisir des mots ou à l'éblouissement des images. Mais, comme je le compris plus tard, il avait fait sienne la conception du poète mage et prophète, et la vision du salut universel qui s'exprime dans les recueils de l'exil. Il en évoquait pour moi certains aspects, sans didactisme, comme une confidence personnelle, qu'on fait à demi-mot, presque à regret. Devenue adulte je découvris la cohérence de ses propos jadis épars. « Sais-tu, disait-il soudain, que l'œil humain peut voir bien au-delà des apparences. Celui du visionnaire est capable de percevoir ce qui demeurera caché à la plupart des hommes. Il faut en croire Hugo, il en a lui-même fait l'expérience, lorsqu'il écrit :

> *Il n'est point de brouillard, comme il n'est point d'algèbre*
> *Qui résistent au fond des nombres ou des cieux*
> *À la fixité calme et profonde des yeux.* »

D'autres fois il ajoutait : « La surface lisse des choses, leur aspect habituel, nous dérobent une autre réalité qui ne peut échapper au regard du contemplateur ! À travers le poème il nous donne à voir ce qu'il a découvert. Ainsi Baudelaire parle de ce ciel " où son œil voit un trône splendide ". »

Et il s'étonnait aussi de l'indifférence des hommes qui ne cherchent pas à savoir. « Bien des gens, vois-tu, n'ont pas conscience du mystère qui nous cerne de toutes parts. L'animal familier et la plante elle-même ont une vie secrète qui nous échappe. Au poète capable d'entrevoir cet au-delà incombe la mission de le révéler. La plupart d'entre nous cheminent en aveugles à côté de l'abîme. »

Ainsi les routes banales des promenades obligées devenaient chemins d'initiation. Au hasard des rencontres que nous faisions, c'étaient de singulières leçons de choses. Il m'expliquait par exemple pourquoi l'âne hésite à avancer et s'entête dans son refus malgré les cris et les coups, c'est qu'il voit devant lui quelque chose qu'il redoute et qui échappe à nos yeux d'homme. Et il citait le poète à l'appui de ses propos, comme il le faisait aussi en parlant des plantes. S'il se penchait sur elles, ce n'était pas pour herboriser mais pour m'enseigner la pitié. « Vois-tu, disait-il, le chardon ou la ciguë ont leur place dans la création, et même l'araignée que tu crains tant, Hugo, lui, prend leur parti, et il écrit : "J'aime l'araignée et j'aime l'ortie / Parce qu'on les hait..." » La plante comme l'animal souffrent de l'horreur qu'ils nous inspirent, leur univers est celui de l'expiation. »

Souvent nous nous arrêtions pour admirer les arbres : « Regarde leurs bras toujours tendus vers le ciel ! Ils prient comme Moïse durant la bataille, ils implorent sans cesse, Hugo les nomme " ces grands religieux ". »

Nous marchions, j'écoutais, je questionnais parfois. Le monde profane s'abolissait autour de nous. J'entrais dans un espace sacré.

Deux langues

Celle de ma mère, pratique, rationnelle, efficace, m'établissait dans des garde-fous rassurants, les poids et les mesures, les couleurs et les saveurs du quotidien, le prix de chaque chose, la nécessité de l'effort, la beauté de l'ordre.

> *Femmes, je vous le dis, vous rangeriez Dieu même*
> *S'Il venait à passer devant votre maison* [1].

J'ai aimé cette langue, et je lui en sais gré.

---

1. Péguy.

Puis l'autre, essentielle, celle des poètes, celle de mon père, me dévoilait l'envers des choses, ouvrait des brèches lumineuses, substituait l'ailleurs à l'ici-bas et me grisait de mots étranges. Il m'arrivait parfois d'en être dépaysée et comme absente à moi-même, mais le plus souvent je m'accommodais de ces passages de l'un à l'autre univers, et personne ne semblait conscient autour de moi de cet habituel dédoublement.

Vint le temps de l'école. On ne m'y enseigna jamais ce que m'avait appris mon père. Il y eut bien le jour de la récitation où des vers s'ajoutaient à ceux que je savais déjà, mais peu d'entre eux me sont restés : on nous donnait le plus souvent à apprendre une prose rimée assez fade. La Fontaine seul méritait de s'imposer à la mémoire. Les Fables apprises à cette époque-là y sont encore gravées intégralement. Ce peuple d'animaux au comportement humain participait de l'autre réalité entrevue. Ce poète parlait bien une autre langue.

Parfois aussi une image réveillait le souvenir des poèmes de la petite enfance. Elle subsistait seule dans mon souvenir. Ainsi deux vers jamais oubliés, qui couronnent le poème où Richepin décrit le sommeil d'un vagabond :

Comme une mère émue et qui retient son souffle
La Nature se tait pour qu'il dorme longtemps.

L'institutrice ne se doutait pas du pouvoir de ces mots. Ils me confirmaient dans le sentiment que d'invisibles présences nous cernent. Je n'y fis jamais allusion.

Au lycée, quand ce fut l'âge de la littérature, je retrouvai les grands noms familiers et j'en découvris bien d'autres. La récitation, en ce temps-là, occupait une place importante dans l'enseignement du français et l'entraînement de la mémoire permettait d'engranger sans peine de longs poèmes ou des scènes entières du théâtre classique. On nous apprit à fonder notre admiration sur les beautés du texte. Cependant personne devant moi ne me donna le sentiment de parler la langue secrète des poètes. Jamais je n'éprouvai le choc, l'élan intérieur que suscite un vers inconnu jusqu'alors, et qui vient combler en nous une attente encore ignorée.

N'avais-je pas rêvé ? N'était-ce pas seulement un mirage de l'enfance, comme un vert paradis de la parole, que l'on réinvente après avoir perdu à jamais l'âge d'or des commencements ? Et cette langue, à supposer qu'elle existât, pouvait-on la transmettre, alors qu'on l'avait seulement entrevue et jamais possédée ? C'est la question que je me posai, lorsque je dus, à mon tour, enseigner la poésie française.

Enseigner la poésie ?

Une représentation médiévale rend bien compte à mes yeux de la transmission du savoir dans l'enseignement : c'est celle du moulin qu'on désigne sous le nom de « moulin mystique ». On peut en voir un exemple à Vézelay. Le chapiteau représente Moïse versant le grain, tandis que saint Paul recueille la farine ; le moulin figure ici le Christ. La transposition des symboles dans une version laïque en est aisée : le grain ne signifie plus alors la doctrine encore voilée de l'Ancien Testament, mais simplement les connaissances prisonnières des livres et retenues sous l'écorce des pages. Le moulin, dans cette version réductrice, n'est que l'image du professeur et du rôle que joue ici sa sensibilité personnelle. C'est cette dernière, en effet, qui adapte et affine les données que l'élève s'apprête à recevoir. Chaque enseignant apporte à cette tâche ce qu'il sait et surtout ce qu'il est. Rencontres, découvertes, rêveries, lectures, entrent en jeu plus ou moins consciemment dans ce travail de transmutation. Tout l'apport extérieur se métamorphose en un matériau qui reçoit la marque d'une personnalité et d'une voix singulières. Il peut arriver, hélas, que ce travail aboutisse seulement à un bavardage et celui qui parle se borne à être, comme on le dit familièrement, un moulin à paroles. Dans le meilleur des cas, cependant, c'est l'acception la plus noble du terme qui prévaut, celle d'un « moulin de la Parole ». Le passeur parvient alors à communiquer un verbe vivifiant et tel qu'il était seul capable, en cet instant, de le faire advenir.

Enseigner c'est aussi, et peut-être avant tout, transmettre ce que l'on a soi-même reçu. Il se trouve que j'ai beaucoup reçu de mes professeurs de littérature ; je dois ce privilège aux circonstances de la guerre, puis de l'occupation, qui avaient rassemblé et retenu dans mon lycée de province des professeurs remarquables. Ils m'ont fait ce cadeau magnifique : toute la littérature française présentée et portée aux nues. En effet, de la *Cantilène de sainte Eulalie* au *Cantique des colonnes*, aucun des textes que l'on dit majeurs ne fut oublié, et même quelques-uns de ceux que l'on appelle mineurs eurent droit à notre attention. Tous étaient lus et expliqués avec une ferveur contagieuse qui gagnait chaque élève. Nathanaëls enthousiastes, nous savions reconnaître le prix du cadeau qui nous était fait. Ainsi romanciers, auteurs dramatiques, moralistes, mémorialistes, épistoliers nous ont été offerts pour notre plus grand plaisir. Je me suis toujours souvenue de ce parcours, et j'ai souhaité pouvoir m'en inspirer.

Cependant je n'ai jamais eu le sentiment qu'on m'enseignait la poésie. On m'a appris les noms des poètes, leur biographie, les titres de leurs œuvres. Je me suis familiarisée avec les règles de la métrique, et plus tard avec les figures savantes aux noms grecs. J'ai recensé les écoles et lu les manifestes. J'ai eu des éclaircissements sur la doctrine littéraire des uns et les idées philosophiques des autres, mais jamais ne se produisit le miracle espéré, la résurrection, par le contact avec le poème, d'un état poétique comme ceux que j'avais connus jadis, ou peut-être rêvés ?

Aussi le doute s'est insinué : comment pourrai-je jamais moudre ce grain qui m'est venu hors des chemins scolaires en usant des moyens que me donne l'école ? Il ne s'agit évidemment pas de décrier ces moyens et d'aspirer à je ne sais quel verbiage imprécis et fumeux ! Même en poésie les éclaircissements ne sont pas inutiles. Il est regrettable, en effet, d'admirer à contresens par la faute d'une expression obscure, d'un détail historique inconnu ou d'une allusion qui nous échappe, ou encore par la méconnaissance des circonstances de l'œuvre et des modèles qui ont influencé son auteur. Si la poésie se distingue des autres formes littéraires, elle ne peut pour autant se passer des instruments critiques qu'on met en œuvre ailleurs. Rien de pire que ce flou sur lequel Valéry ironise : « Certains ont de la poésie une idée si vague qu'ils prennent ce vague pour l'idée même de la poésie. »

Cependant les erreurs de certains élèves montraient les dangers d'une approche purement technique des poèmes. L'un, croyant bien faire, ramenait ce qui lui paraissait relever d'outrances superflues, dans les sages limites d'une prose intelligible. L'autre, moins besogneux, et par là plus redoutable encore pour le texte, le noyait sous un discours amphigourique et prétentieux. Mais ce qui dominait dans la plupart des explications c'était le rôle de la « musique », le commentaire se limitant alors à un inventaire des effets sonores réels ou imaginaires, qu'offrait le poème. D'où cette confidence un jour : « Le plus beau vers de la langue française, Madame, c'est-à-dire le plus musical, c'est, selon moi, le vers fameux de Mallarmé : Abali babalo [1]... Vous le reconnaîtrez sans doute, j'ai oublié la suite. » Il faut mentionner aussi les ravages de la rigueur scientifique, ou prétendue telle. On se rappelle peut-être la caricature qu'en fait Peter Weir dans son film *Le Cercle des poètes disparus*. Des notes adjugées à chaque œuvre et portées en abscisse et ordonnée engendrent une courbe irrécusable qui permet de classer les poètes anglais par ordre de mérite. Il faudrait encore citer, parmi ces pratiques mortifères, l'exercice qui consiste à faire avouer au poème quelque secret honteux !

Ces excès me désolaient parce que l'élève qui venait à bout du texte de cette manière ne se doutait pas qu'il n'avait à aucun moment écouté le poète, et que l'approche qu'il avait choisie lui interdisait d'avoir accès à une autre dimension du poème.

Cependant je désespérais de trouver moi-même une autre voie, les livres ne m'étant pas d'un plus grand secours que l'enseignement de mes professeurs.

La lumière me vint d'une élève. Il s'agissait ce jour-là de réciter quelques vers de Villon. Une volontaire se proposa pour la *Ballade des pendus*. Il est difficile de rester insensible à ce poème, même s'il n'est que balbutié, mais cette fois, quand le premier vers a résonné dans la classe, quand on a entendu : « Frères humains qui après nous vivez »... c'était dit sur un tel ton, avec un tel accent de douleur, douleur déchirante mais contenue, sans rien de déclamatoire, jaillie du fond de l'âme, et même, à ce qui nous semblait, du fond des âges jusqu'à nous, que tout s'est arrêté. Un silence rare, concentré d'attention et d'émotion a figé l'auditoire. Par le miracle d'une voix juste, la vie et la mort

---

1. « Aboli bibelot d'inanité sonore »...

venaient d'entrer dans la classe pour cet affrontement ultime que le poète anticipe.

Aucune interprétation par la suite n'a égalé celle-là. Pas une qui ait pu me faire oublier le ton d'intensité tragique et de pathétique gouailleur où la voix du poète lui-même s'était fait entendre. Ni l'instant où nous avions communié avec lui dans cette imminence de la mort violente à laquelle nous nous sentions soudain obscurément appelés.

En ce lieu, durant quelques minutes, la poésie venait d'être enseignée. Je n'y étais pour rien.

Me revint en mémoire le conseil de Pierre Clarac, écouté trop distraitement. L'essentiel de l'explication de textes, disait-il en substance, c'est le moment de la relecture à voix haute. La lumière est faite, les difficultés aplanies, *il faut laisser la parole à l'auteur*. Je pris alors conscience de l'utilité de cette règle en général et de son absolue nécessité en poésie, genre littéraire par excellence du « verbe haut ».

La poésie française, au moins pendant dix siècles, est essentiellement orale. Cela semble évident pour l'épopée et pour la fable et ça l'est plus encore pour la poésie lyrique qui fut d'abord chantée ou accompagnée de musique. En perdant ce statut, elle tend à s'appauvrir car la voix du récitant est capable de rendre sensibles des inflexions ou des couleurs que la simple lecture laisse échapper. À travers elle l'œuvre retrouve l'unité que l'explication de détail avait émiettée. Qui n'a éprouvé l'étonnement de découvrir comme pour la première fois un texte connu, du moins que l'on croyait connaître, quand il prend corps, ce corps immatériel et pourtant si sensuel, presque charnel, dont le revêt la voix de l'interprète ?

En somme, enseigner la poésie c'est surtout cela : la donner à entendre. Ce mot prend tout son sens si la lecture à voix haute se refait inlassablement, ou mieux encore, si le poème est appris par cœur. Cependant il ne suffit pas de le savoir à peu près, car passée l'enfance où tout peut être durablement mémorisé, ce qui fut vite appris s'efface aussi assez vite. On ne connaît vraiment un poème qu'à partir du moment où on l'a lu et relu, dans une sorte de rumination lente. L'exercice qu'impose l'apprentissage par cœur, pour être durable, c'est la réitération patiente des mots, cette répétition insistante qui les met en place, à leur juste place.

Ce faisant, certains points obscurs ou dédaignés s'éclairent peu à peu.

Je dirai, en me fondant sur ma propre expérience, qu'il n'y a pas de texte qui ne cède, et cela vaut pour les plus hermétiques, à cette cohabitation complice avec celui qui le redit. Réciter, c'est assimiler, au sens fort. C'est une manière de pratiquer ce que Du Bellay appelle l'innutrition. Le poème livre alors ses secrets, sa richesse, les nuances qui n'étaient pas encore perçues à la première lecture, une musique infiniment plus subtile que celle que l'on prête aux seules allitérations. Puis, à travers cet exercice se fait un autre apprentissage : celui de la langue propre à chaque poète – aucun glossaire ne remplace la familiarité acquise avec cet idiome singulier par le moyen d'une œuvre fréquentée jour après jour –, apprentissage aussi de la voix qui se fait entendre à travers la nôtre, voix unique et inimitable dont nous sommes peu à peu possédés. Enfin, au-delà de toute voix, pressentie et comme goûtée déjà, l'*ur-sprache*, la langue première, royale, universelle, qu'est la poésie elle-même.

Ce que m'avait transmis mon père, je le découvrais enfin. Au moyen des étranges systèmes du monde qu'inventaient les poètes, il m'avait fait entendre leur voix et entrevoir la source inépuisable et profonde d'où elle jaillissait.

Enseigner la poésie c'est d'abord arracher un à un les poèmes à ces linceuls de papier qu'on appelle livres, leur insuffler l'air que nous respirons, leur permettre de retentir. Ils vivent alors et se mêlent à notre vie. Parfois ils nous révèlent à nous-mêmes une part de ce moi profond qui sans eux nous demeurait étrangère.

– En somme il ne s'agit que de cela ? Remettre à l'honneur la récitation !

– Sans doute ! Mais en expliquant ses enjeux, en faisant de cet exercice non plus une performance de la mémoire, mais une ascèse de l'approfondissement, la conquête progressive de langues étranges dont la somme, un jour, nous permettrait, peut-être, de lire l'inconnu en nous et hors de nous.

Un tel choix se fonde sur cet axiome : la poésie est autre chose qu'un jeu subtil ou que l'agencement de sons harmonieux, et elle ne se réduit pas à un savoir-faire, fût-ce le plus savant. Sinon, comment pourrions-nous comprendre le témoignage des rescapés des camps lorsqu'ils évoquent le pouvoir des poèmes qu'ils se remémoraient, devenus pour eux instruments de survie, véritables sésames spirituels ?

Enseigner la poésie, dans cette perspective, c'est se fonder sur la certitude qu'elle garde sur nous le pouvoir qui fut le sien dès l'origine, qu'elle demeure une parole vitale.

La Poésie à deux voix

Le récitant, en se familiarisant avec les mots d'un autre, finit par se les approprier, comme le Turold de la *Chanson de Roland* dont le nom clôt le poème :

> *Ci falt la geste que Turoldus declinet*
> Ici finit la geste dite par Turold.

On doute qu'il en soit l'auteur. Or, s'il n'en est que l'interprète, cette signature n'en est pas moins explicable : le fait d'entrer dans l'intimité des mots donne l'illusion de les inventer.

L'humble diseur se sent poète.

La récitation, exercice à la fois ludique et grave, prend véritablement en charge ces deux fonctions. En s'en tenant à la première il suffirait de faire sonner le vers et rebondir les syllabes comme on le fait, par exemple, dans ce final de Verlaine :

> *Tourbillonnent dans l'extase*
> *D'une lune rose et grise*
> *Et la mandoline jase*
> *Parmi les frissons de brise.*

Mais la seconde entraîne plus loin l'interprète qui épouse alors le mouvement profond du texte, celui-même de sa création. S'il a pu dire les deux premiers quatrains de *L'Ennemi* en se bornant à adopter le ton de la confidence ou de la narration, la rupture de registre qu'introduisent les tercets fait naître en lui des accents différents. Leurs vers semblent issus d'une autre profondeur :

> *Et qui sait si les fleurs nouvelles que je rêve*
> *Trouveront dans ce sol lavé comme une grève*
> *Le mystique aliment qui ferait leur vigueur...*

La voix se transforme involontairement, elle donne à entendre autre chose que l'itinéraire métaphorique d'une vie. À travers elle se fait jour l'inspiration qui soulève ces lignes et qui se manifeste au moment même où Baudelaire se prend à douter de son pouvoir.

Cette dualité de registre est l'écho de la double nature du poète lui-même : ce dernier, de son propre aveu, sent se mêler à sa voix une autre voix, à son souffle, un autre souffle, il appelle cela l'inspiration.

L'inspiration est le dénominateur commun des grandes œuvres, mais la grandeur n'est pas l'apanage obligé des longs poèmes ou de ceux qui traitent de thèmes solennels. On doit considérer comme inspiré, dit Éluard, tout poème qui nous inspire.

Mais comment définir cette source mystérieuse de la création poétique ?

Qu'on lui prête, comme dans l'Antiquité, le visage d'un dieu qui substitue parfois sa voix à celle de l'homme, ou qu'on voie tout simplement en elle une cadence neuve qui impose soudain au poète son rythme propre, matrice de l'œuvre future, il s'agit dans tous les cas d'une dictée dont l'initiative vient d'ailleurs.

On peut tenter d'en modifier le cours en provoquant l'intrusion de la voix étrangère. La Pythie mâchait le laurier pour appeler la transe prophétique et susciter Apollon. À cet effet les poètes inventeront divers « dérèglements des sens » pour mieux capter l'inconnu. Mais quels que soient les cheminements et les visages qu'ils aient prêtés à l'inspiration, ils ont toujours dit leur dépendance à son égard, ou du moins laissé entendre qu'ils n'étaient pas totalement maîtres du jeu. L'un des plus iconoclastes, André Breton, lui-même témoigne de l'universalité de son pouvoir, lorsqu'il reconnaît dans *Le Second Manifeste* : « C'est elle qui a pourvu aux besoins suprêmes d'expression en tous temps et en tous lieux. »

Quelques-uns des plus grands poètes se sont efforcés de rendre compte de la puissance inconnue qui les soumettait à ses caprices.

À la Renaissance où les mythes antiques reprennent vie, Ronsard l'incarne dans les neuf Muses dont il conte l'histoire à sa manière dans ses vers. Tout pouvoir, écrit-il dans l'*Ode à Michel de l'Hospital*, fut d'abord donné aux filles de Zeus et de Mémoire d'instruire les hommes, et surtout parmi eux les « poètes divins ». C'est d'elles que les plus fameux d'entre eux, Musée, Orphée, Hésiode ou Homère ont reçu leur chant. Vinrent des âges plus sombres où leur savoir peu à peu se perdit, au point qu'elles s'éloignèrent de la terre. Voici qu'elles réapparaissent et consentent à séjourner parmi les hommes en ces temps heureux où de nouveaux Mécènes – tels que le dédicataire de l'Ode – aident à la résurrection des Lettres et des Arts. Le règne des Neuf Sœurs est revenu et ceux qu'elles choisissent sont habités « de cette honnête flamme aux peuples non commune » célébrée par Du Bellay. Le poète doit seulement se rendre digne de l'élection dont il est l'objet.

Un autre récit au ton de confidence apparaît deux fois dans l'œuvre de Ronsard et nous touche davantage. Il y relate la rencontre qui fonde sa vocation poétique et, s'il « mythologise » encore, certains accents ne permettent pas de douter de sa sincérité.

Il eut très tôt la faveur des Muses, et l'apparition de l'une d'elles le confirma dans la voie qui l'attirait déjà. Il raconte cet épisode de sa vie avec une insistance particulière au début de *L'Hymne de l'automne* où il décrit d'abord sa quête du frisson sacré :

> *Je n'avais pas quinze ans que les monts et les bois*
> *Et les eaux me plaisaient plus que la cour des rois*
> *Et les noires forêts en feuillage voûtées*
> *Et du bec des oiseaux les roches picotées.*
> *Une vallée, un antre en horreur obscurci,*
> *Un désert effroyable était tout mon souci.*

Ces lieux lui permettent en effet d'entrevoir d'obscures et fugitives présences, de celles qui se dérobent à l'homme ordinaire mais se manifestent aux yeux des humains « fantastiques d'esprit ». L'une des passantes mystérieuses des bois prend la forme de la nymphe Euterpe. Elle lui accorde le don de poésie. Pour cela elle le soumet à un rite baptismal, en le purifiant avec l'eau d'une fontaine « où peu de monde va », c'est-à-dire l'Hippocrène, la source sacrée. Puis elle souffle sur lui. Ainsi vivifié il peut entendre sa prédiction : elle lui promet pour l'avenir une longue survie dans la mémoire des hommes, mais pour le présent l'incompréhension et les moqueries du vulgaire, et, l'inscrivant dans la longue lignée des inspirés, elle ajoute :

> *Mais courage, Ronsard, les plus doctes Poètes,*
> *Les Sibylles, Devins, Augures et Prophètes,*
> *Hués, sifflés, moqués des peuples ont été*
> *Et toutefois, Ronsard, ils disaient vérité.*

Ce récit est déroutant pour le lecteur contemporain. Ces formes de rêverie ne sont plus les nôtres. Cependant l'adolescent qui, de quelque manière, éprouve ces présences et sent cet adoubement est-il si différent de celui qui affirme, trois siècles plus tard : « J'ai embrassé l'Aube d'été » et ajoute triomphal : « En haut de la route, près d'un bois de lauriers, je l'ai entourée de ses voiles amassés, et j'ai senti un peu de son immense corps » [1].

Le dix-neuvième siècle n'a d'ailleurs pas rompu avec les figures antiques. Les Muses sont encore évoquées. Elles peuvent être la présence lumineuse qui exhorte Musset dans *La Nuit de Mai* ou la silhouette fantomatique et blême de *La Muse malade* des *Fleurs du mal*. Au-delà de ces symboles, la doctrine de l'inspiration est présente chez tous les poètes. Baudelaire lui-même, fidèle en cela aux idées de son siècle, peint dans *Bénédiction*, celui qui « par un décret des puissances suprêmes » est élu dès sa naissance. Une phrase de Hugo traduit de façon saisissante le caractère inexplicable de ce don et l'étonnement de celui qui le reçoit, lorsqu'il note : « Il serait singulier et peut-être vrai de dire que l'on est parfois étranger, comme homme, à ce qu'on a écrit comme poète » [2].

Au vingtième siècle Claudel et Saint-John Perse ne sont pas les seuls à parler de l'inspiration mais c'est dans leur œuvre qu'on en trouve la plus étonnante description, et la plus riche.

Le premier reprend à sa façon les figures de la mythologie. Il évoque les Muses, mais ne les sépare pas du souffle de l'Esprit qu'il mêle aux symboles antiques car son œuvre se définit comme « catholique, c'est-à-dire universelle ».

La première des *Cinq Grandes Odes* célèbre « l'entière neuvaine... / Les hautes vierges égales, la rangée des sœurs

---

1. Rimbaud.
2. Article de *La Muse française*, 1824.

éloquentes ». On assiste, dans la deuxième, à la naissance du poème :

Soudain l'Esprit de nouveau, soudain le souffle de nouveau !
Soudain le coup sourd au cœur, soudain le mot donné, soudain le souffle de l'Esprit, le rapt sec, soudain la possession de l'Esprit !

La quatrième dit la puissance créatrice des divinités païennes :

Ah je suis ivre ! Je suis livré au dieu ! j'entends une voix en moi et la mesure qui s'accélère, le mouvement de la joie,
L'ébranlement de la cohorte Olympique, la marche divinement tempérée.

Dans la *Parabole d'Animus et d'Anima*, Claudel illustre sa conception de l'inspiration. En incarnant dans ces deux allégories les domaines distincts de l'intelligence raisonneuse et de la sensibilité créatrice, il souligne la part de mystère inhérente à l'invention poétique : Anima ne chante que lorsque Animus l'a quittée, la solitude lui permet d'être visitée par son « amant divin ». Psyché a besoin des ténèbres pour rencontrer le dieu.

Quant à Saint-John Perse, il s'est expliqué dans le *Discours de Stockholm* sur la nature et la fonction du poète, mais c'est dans son grand poème intitulé *Vents* qu'il le dépeint comme « Homme infesté du songe, homme gagné par l'infection divine » et qu'il définit sa mission :

Son occupation parmi nous : mise en clair des messages. Et la réponse en lui donnée par illumination du cœur.

Avant d'offrir l'une des plus belles définitions jamais proposées du poète :

Ô Poète, ô bilingue, entre toutes choses bisaiguës, et toi-même litige entre toutes choses litigieuses — homme assailli du dieu ! homme parlant dans l'équivoque !... ah ! comme un homme fourvoyé dans une mêlée d'ailes et de ronces, parmi des noces de busaigles.

Ce Janus « lié malgré lui à l'événement historique » échappe ainsi, par la grâce de l'inspiration, à ses propres circonstances, et son assujettissement à la temporalité ne parvient pas à le détourner du versant de l'Être.

La doctrine qui court ainsi d'âge en âge nous conforte dans l'idée que tout grand poème recèle un en-deçà des mots auquel nous pouvons tenter d'accéder à travers lui. Un sens que ne peut pourtant épuiser aucune explication. Verbe premier retranscrit sous une infinité de formes. « Écho redit par mille labyrinthes »[1], transmettant de génération en génération un secret sauvé de l'oubli. On a dit de la poésie qu'elle était une Parole mémorable. Elle l'est en effet, et vaut bien que ses servants en la confiant à leur mémoire en approfondissent le mystère. Cependant je préfère l'appeler une *Parole gardée,* car l'expression rend compte à mes yeux des milliers de poèmes-sentinelles qui veillent sur un trésor dont ils laissent seulement entrevoir l'éclat.

La poésie éclatée ?

Dans le foisonnement des formes et des thèmes, le lecteur a peine à croire qu'on puisse sans méprise regrouper sous le terme général de poésie française tant d'œuvres disparates. Peut-on associer la rigueur du vers et la liberté apparente du poème en prose ? Quel lien imaginer entre l'inspiration familière et mélancolique de Charles d'Orléans et les accents vengeurs d'Agrippa d'Aubigné ? Mais surtout comment faire face à la diversité bigarrée de la poésie au XXe siècle ?

Tant qu'il y eut des poèmes à forme fixe, les conventions d'un même genre établissaient d'un siècle à l'autre une continuité. Le meilleur exemple en est le sonnet, même si les poètes prirent avec lui au fil du temps quelques libertés ; du seizième au dix-neuvième siècle, malgré ses variantes, il entretient l'idée d'un ordre quasi

---

1. Baudelaire.

immuable de la création poétique. De même, les courants littéraires rattachaient entre elles des œuvres qui s'épaulaient et s'éclairaient mutuellement. On voit par exemple que le génie singulier de Nerval n'est pas dissociable du romantisme ou que la doctrine symboliste permet de rapprocher Claudel de Maeterlinck.

Si diverses qu'elles soient, les œuvres des poètes, au moins aux yeux de Boileau, s'ordonnaient et se hiérarchisaient en grands et petits genres, et la qualité de l'inspiration y servait de critère – les premiers, tragédie, épopée, requérant une plus grande puissance créatrice, les seconds une moindre faculté d'invention.

Avec le recul du temps il semble au lecteur du XXIe siècle que *La Franciade* ne porte pas autant la marque du génie de Ronsard que ses sonnets, et il nous apparaît moins essentiel de voir ce que Nerval ou Claudel doivent aux écoles que de caractériser leur génie propre.

Paul Valéry propose un autre code de lecture. Théoricien de la poésie, il réserve ce terme à de précieux et rares fragments, il marque sa distance à l'égard du reste, et de tout long poème en particulier, par là il récuse l'épopée elle-même. Impossible de la considérer en bloc comme poème : ce grand fleuve charrie trop d'épaves. La longueur est, selon lui, le pire ennemi de cette pureté exquise qui définit l'œuvre d'art. La beauté poétique ignore l'étendue, elle n'existe qu'à l'état de fragment, comme ces pépites prisonnières d'un minerai vulgaire. Il faut les en dégager, pour admirer enfin le métal précieux à l'état pur. C'est seulement quand on aura retiré, comme dit un autre poète, « tout ce radium de la pechblende »[1], qu'apparaîtra enfin, arraché à ces milliers de vers, ce corps subtil, ce sublimé, en quoi se reconnaît la poésie véritable.

Cette vision restrictive n'est peut-être pas moins irrecevable que la précédente. Si l'inégalité du matériau poétique à l'intérieur d'un long poème est indiscutable, relève-t-elle pour autant d'une défaillance ou d'une parenthèse du génie ? N'est-il pas plutôt de l'essence même des poèmes d'être faits de temps forts et de reflux ? Desnos, relisant des écrits de lui déjà anciens, note ceci :

« Je ne méconnais point ce qui a vieilli dans les deux premiers

---

1. Aragon.

poèmes. J'y délimite les déserts qui séparent des passages d'une inspiration plus ardente. Mais si une image a jamais excusé un défaut, je les compare à ces espaces vides où le vent se repose, où les oiseaux grands voiliers suspendent leur course. »

Il m'a semblé parfois que l'intrusion du prosaïque dans le cœur du poème n'était pas un appauvrissement mais s'apparentait plutôt à ces collages des peintres où l'élément concret ajouté à la toile renforce l'impression de sa présence au monde, tout en transfigurant l'humble réalité elle-même. Ainsi lorsque la voix du poète, évoquant les jours d'autrefois « radieux et charmants », se brise sur cette exclamation née du sentiment le plus immédiat du malheur : « Et dire qu'elle est morte » [1] !... Par ces mots empruntés à la langue quotidienne, toute la gracieuse évocation du passé bascule dans un jamais plus déchirant, et le poème est transfiguré par la vérité terrible de ce cri.

Cependant à refuser tout classement, toute hiérarchie, l'embarras du lecteur augmente. Déjà grand devant les œuvres du passé, il redouble à propos des poèmes du XXᵉ siècle. L'éclatement des formes y aboutit à une diversité apparemment inépuisable. Il est des poètes fidèles aux rythmes anciens comme Aragon, d'autres retrouvent même l'assonance médiévale et le vers libre des symbolistes comme Supervielle. Des explorateurs de la prose tels que Reverdy voisinent avec les adeptes du verset. Dans ce domaine on ne peut confondre les grandes vagues ondulantes et irrégulières de Claudel et les rythmes majestueux et oraculaires de Saint-John Perse. Ce siècle a vu les lents cheminements litaniques de Péguy et la dérision hachée et violente de Michaux ou l'éclat de silex des aphorismes de Char. *La Chanson du Mal Aimé* oppose sa fluidité et ses méandres à l'immobilité hiératique des *Stèles* de Ségalen. Le seul point commun repérable, à quelques exceptions près, c'est l'abandon de la rime. Dans l'ensemble « ce bijou d'un sou » (ainsi dénoncé par Verlaine qui toutefois n'y renonce jamais lui-même) est tombé en désuétude.

On savait du reste depuis toujours que la rime ne fait pas le poète, et que la poésie se passe d'elle non seulement en d'autres langues, mais même dans les traductions harmonieuses de ces poèmes. Parny au dix-huitième siècle le montre avec les *Chansons*

---

1. Hugo.

Madécasses, et déjà le caractère poétique de la prose de Fénelon dans le *Télémaque* avait frappé ses lecteurs.

Montaigne avait noté au troisième livre des *Essais* : « Mille poètes traînent et languissent à la prosaïque, mais la meilleure prose ancienne (et je la sème céans indifféremment pour vers) reluit partout de la vigueur et hardiesse poétique et représente l'air de sa fureur. » C'est-à-dire donne l'image d'une inspiration véritable.

Pour le lecteur des *Illuminations* plus encore que pour celui du *Spleen de Paris,* cette intuition devient une certitude, l'existence du poème en prose s'impose à lui, dès la fin du XIXe siècle, à l'égal des autres formes reconnues. Sa présence ajoute encore à la difficulté d'embrasser d'un seul regard tout ce que l'on nomme poème.

Où trouver la marque d'une improbable unité ?

Caillois écrivait : « Croire à la poésie, j'imagine que c'est estimer qu'il existe quelque chose de commun entre Homère et Mallarmé. »

Croire à la poésie c'est la concevoir comme une essence qui s'incarne dans ces existences fragmentaires et hétéroclites que sont les poèmes les plus divers. Comme des météorites d'inégale grosseur trouvées sur notre sol peuvent porter témoignage d'une même planète en portant en elles un peu de cette étrangeté radicale qui tient à leur origine, chaque poème inspiré témoigne d'une autre réalité. Faut-il souhaiter que soit isolé l'élément précieux au détriment du reste, prendre ici et là un vers ou une ligne, ailleurs tout un passage, et puis mettre au rebut ce qui semble moins rare ? L'esprit, non plus que l'œil ne peuvent s'éclairer aux seuls feux d'artifice, l'éblouissement ne peut être permanent, les intervalles entre le jaillissement des images et les trouvailles verbales sont la respiration nécessaire du poème, la densité et la force de ces dernières restant la marque de son excellence.

Cependant accepter la diversité, refuser toute hiérarchie ou exclusion n'amène pas à accueillir tous les poèmes avec la même ferveur. Il faut aller d'abord vers ceux qui d'emblée se communiquent à nous, mais savoir que d'autres rencontres nous sont réservées, que d'autres œuvres seront conquises peu à peu, il serait dommage de renoncer trop vite :

> *– Maint joyau dort enseveli*
> *Dans les ténèbres de l'oubli,*
> *Bien loin des pioches et des sondes ;*

> *Mainte fleur épanche à regret*
> *Son parfum doux comme un secret*
> *Dans les solitudes profondes* [1].

On pourrait imaginer une géographie mythique, une sorte de portulan des espaces de la poésie. Paul Bénichou a montré comment le patronage de Narcisse succède à partir de Mallarmé à celui d'Orphée. Comme lui, il me semble que le cartographe de ce territoire y distinguerait plusieurs provinces placées sous le signe de figures mythiques. Une unité se fait jour dans chacune d'elles, unité qui transcende l'éclatement apparent des œuvres et du temps.

Orphée, Prométhée ou Narcisse

« C'est chose légère que le poète, ailée, sacrée ; il n'est pas en état de créer avant d'être inspiré par un dieu, hors de lui, et n'avoir plus sa raison ; tant qu'il garde cette faculté, tout être humain est incapable de faire œuvre poétique et de chanter des oracles. »

Dans *Ion*, le dialogue de Platon où se lit cette définition du poète, Socrate explique que le premier inspiré dans la veine lyrique fut Orphée, et qu'à partir de lui se créent des chaînes d'hommes à qui l'enthousiasme, c'est-à-dire la possession par un dieu, donne, en se transmettant de l'un à l'autre, le pouvoir de composer à leur tour et de prolonger sa lignée.

Orphée est connu six cents ans avant notre ère où déjà le poète lyrique Ibycos de Reghion le nomme « Orphée au nom célèbre ». Simonide de Céos, Pindare, Eschyle témoignent de sa puissance sur la nature. Les détails de sa légende ont pu varier au cours des siècles, mais ses traits essentiels ne changent pas : sa lyre possède toujours le pouvoir de transmettre aux hommes et aux animaux

---

1. Baudelaire.

l'harmonie cosmique. Il communique au poète l'inspiration lyrique, signe de l'intervention divine dans le monde sensible. Le néoplatonisme de la Renaissance accorde une grande place à sa légende, grâce à l'interprétation qu'en donne Marcile Ficin. Ce dernier, dans son commentaire d'*Ion*, enrichit l'image du premier des poètes. Le développement de l'Académie platonicienne, durant la deuxième moitié du quinzième siècle, contribue à répandre dans toute l'Europe sa vision religieuse d'Orphée. L'inventeur de la poésie et de la musique est aussi celui qui apporte aux hommes la « prisca theologia », cette théologie primitive dont Ficin pense qu'elle a préparé la venue du christianisme. L'ivresse poétique, la « fureur », n'est pas seulement le pouvoir de transmettre le message divin, lorsque Orphée la communique à l'homme, elle devient aussi, pour l'âme qui a glissé au monde inférieur, une voie de salut, le moyen par lequel Dieu la fait monter vers lui.

À la lumière de ces traditions, il est permis d'appeler orphique toute expression poétique d'une harmonie entre l'homme et le monde matériel ou spirituel, depuis celle qui naît simplement du jeu avec les mots jusqu'à la plus solennelle célébration. Cette harmonie peut être éprouvée de façon immédiate ou ressentie comme douloureusement absente. Le poète, qu'il se réjouisse de sa présence ou qu'il se lamente sur le désordre qui lui fait obstacle, témoigne à sa manière d'un cosmos idéal. Cette interprétation du mythe donne au terme de lyrisme son sens le plus large. Dans cette acception, en effet, le sujet et le ton du poème se conçoivent comme infiniment variés. La poésie peut peindre les bonheurs simples, les passions ou les malheurs, conter les peines quotidiennes ou les hauts faits des héros, préférer la peinture naïve et idyllique ou les images baroques, ses registres aller du didactique à l'élégiaque, du tragique à l'épique, dans tous les cas, et sous les formes les plus diverses, son chant relève du pouvoir d'Orphée.

On peut ainsi oublier les siècles et les écoles et négliger les distinctions de genre. Il s'agit seulement de considérer comme digne de l'aède fondateur tout poème capable de transmettre l'étincelle qui permet, fût-ce pour un bref instant, un dépassement de ses limites : celles de la raison, mais aussi celles de l'espace et du temps.

Un mot, celui de *charme*, entendu dans son sens le plus fort, peut caractériser toute poésie orphique, car elle envoûte et captive.

En effet, quelque sentiment qu'elle fasse naître en nous – depuis la tendresse jusqu'à l'exaltation – , elle nous devient si proche qu'elle entre dans notre vie et semble avoir partie liée avec elle.

La mythologie grecque déroule aussi la légende de Prométhée. Lui n'est pas poète, même si, au début de la tragédie qui porte son nom, Eschyle lui prête une voix inspirée et puissante :

« Éther divin, vents à l'aile rapide, eaux des fleuves, sourire innombrable des vagues marines, Terre mère des êtres et toi, Soleil, œil qui vois tout, je vous invoque ici : voyez ce qu'un dieu souffre par les dieux. »

Ce n'est pas l'étincelle du verbe que Prométhée a dérobée à la roue du soleil, mais les semences du feu, don qui « s'est révélé pour les hommes un maître de tous les arts, un trésor sans prix ». La légende rapporte qu'il possède aussi un pouvoir de divination. Il peut ainsi révéler à Héraklès le moyen de s'emparer des pommes d'or, et à son fils Deucalion celui d'échapper au déluge. Ces épisodes rattachent plus nettement la figure de ce dieu à la poésie, du moins celle qui se présente comme anticipation et voyance. À la poésie conçue comme une faveur consentie par le dieu à celui qu'il visite, l'exemple de Prométhée substitue l'idée qu'elle peut être une transgression, une violence faite au ciel par l'homme qui lui dérobe ses secrets. Il devient ainsi le héros éponyme de toute la lignée des poètes de la révolte.

Relèvent de cette inspiration de très grandes œuvres comme *Les Tragiques*[1] à la verve violente. Les accents vengeurs des *Ïambes*[2], la véhémence d'*Une saison en enfer*[3], les protestations irritées de Michaux montrent aussi combien cette veine poétique diffère de la précédente. Il y a dans la poésie orphique un acquiescement sinon à l'ordre apparent du monde, du moins à son ordre profond. La poésie prométhéenne dénonce un désordre, refuse l'univers tel qu'il est donné, ou même vise à le détruire. Mais la frontière qui sépare les deux courants passe parfois entre deux œuvres d'un même poète, car *L'Hécatombe à Diane*[1], *La Jeune Tarentine*[2], *Les Illuminations*[3] ou *Magie*[4] sont évidemment du côté d'Orphée.

---

1. Agrippa d'Aubigné. — 2. Chénier. — 3. Rimbaud. — 4. Michaux.

Parfois c'est à l'intérieur d'un même recueil qu'un poème se détache des autres en témoignant d'un autre souffle. Ainsi le cri du poète des *Contemplations* dans le poème intitulé *Ibo* :

> *Pourquoi cacher ces lois profondes ?*
> *Rien n'est muré.*
> *Dans vos flammes et dans vos ondes*
> *Je passerai ;*
>
> *J'irai lire la grande bible ;*
> *J'entrerai nu*
> *Dans le tabernacle terrible*
> *De l'inconnu,*
>
> *Jusqu'au seuil de l'ombre et du vide,*
> *Gouffres ouverts*
> *Que garde la meute livide*
> *Des noirs éclairs,*
>
> *Jusqu'aux portes visionnaires*
> *Du ciel sacré ;*
> *Et, si vous aboyez, tonnerres,*
> *Je rugirai.*

devant une violence qu'il faut prendre au sérieux, comme le souligne Jean Massin, car il s'agit ici, dit-il, « du combat spirituel aussi brutal que la bataille d'hommes dont parle Rimbaud », nous reconnaissons un exemple de la veine prométhéenne qui se manifeste, et avec quelle puissance ! dans *Les Châtiments*.

S'il faut choisir un mot pour caractériser ce versant de la poésie, je propose celui d'*éclat,* comme on dit éclat de voix. Dans de telles œuvres le poète interpelle les hommes, fustige ses ennemis ou lance des anathèmes. Le plus souvent il nous enjoint de prendre parti. C'est qu'en effet il parle ici d'action et non de contemplation rêveuse.

Cette dernière retrouve sa place, mais elle change alors profondément de nature, dans les poèmes que l'on peut rattacher à un troisième mythe, celui de Narcisse. Sa légende est bien connue. Ce très beau jeune homme méprisait l'amour, les jeunes filles dédaignées en demandèrent vengeance au ciel. Un jour donc, en se penchant pour boire, il vit sa propre image affleurer dans l'eau limpide de la source, il en devint éperdument amoureux. Dès lors, insensible au monde, il se laissa mourir, les yeux attachés à son insaisissable reflet.

A priori ce récit ne semble pas concerner la poésie. Pourtant certains poètes fascinés par ce mythe ont vu en lui l'histoire de l'artiste qui contemple sa propre création, et, s'attachant à l'image qu'elle lui renvoie de lui-même, oublie le monde réel autour de lui.

Ce thème est particulièrement présent dans l'œuvre de Valéry où le Narcisse de la *Cantate* qui porte son nom, se définit en disant :

> *Je m'abreuve de moi... L'amour la plus profonde*
> *Vient et revient entre mon âme et l'onde*
> *Dont le miroir divin m'offre le pur retour*
> *De mes charmes vers l'ombre où songe mon amour...*

Plus explicite encore dans un autre poème il s'écrie :

> *Mais moi, Narcisse aimé, je ne suis curieux*
> *Que de ma propre essence ;*
> *Tout autre n'a pour moi qu'un cœur mystérieux.*
> *Tout autre n'est qu'absence.*

Si Paul Bénichou voit dans ce héros la figure dominante de la poésie à la fin du dix-neuvième siècle, ce n'est pas en tant que sujet de prédilection de cette époque, mais parce que Narcisse incarne à ses yeux tout le courant poétique issu de Mallarmé. La poésie n'y a plus d'autre objet que soi et renonce à ce qui la fondait auparavant. Plus de liens. Le poème est désormais un absolu, au sens grammatical, et sans doute aussi alchimique, du terme. Il ne témoigne ni d'un au-delà dont il serait la réfraction terrestre, ni de modèles concrets qui s'offrent à lui. Il n'attend rien d'un souffle venu d'ailleurs. Il se passe de la caution du réel. Il se suffit. Le poète se démet de sa souveraineté non pour donner la parole à une autre voix, mais pour « céder l'initiative aux mots ». À eux d'instaurer un nouvel ordre du langage, de faire advenir un cosmos purement verbal. En les arrachant à la gangue ordinaire du sens immédiat, il les redore d'étrangeté et les fait jouer entre eux. Il attend de cet effort, et de ce hasard, la naissance d'images inouïes.

Parfois le poète se révolte devant

> ...*le pacte dur*
> *De creuser par veillées une fosse nouvelle*
> *Dans le terrain avare et froid de (sa) cervelle* [1].

Mais l'idée très haute qu'il a de la poésie lui impose une ascèse rigoureuse. Pour lui il n'existe pas d'au-delà des mots, le poème est à lui-même sa loi et sa fin. D'où, aussi, son obscurité. L'hermétisme n'est pas ici le fruit d'une volonté délibérée de dérober le sens, comme c'est le cas chez d'autres poètes. Se garder du vulgaire est sans doute nécessaire aux yeux de Mallarmé, mais là n'est pas son but. Le caractère hautain et parfois difficilement accessible de ses poèmes est lié à sa conception d'un statut narcissique de la poésie.

Après lui bien des poètes se réclament de sa doctrine, même s'ils ont renoncé à ce Livre dont rêvait Mallarmé, équivalent verbal du monde, fait de la seule réalité des mots, et qui devait se substituer à lui. Le XXᵉ siècle offre maint exemple de quêtes qui s'inspirent de la sienne.

S'il faut, ici encore, caractériser d'un mot les œuvres qui se rattachent à cette doctrine, je proposerai celui de *scintillation*, car la splendeur des plus beaux poèmes qui répondent à ces exigences, est faite des feux que jettent les mots coupés de leur origine. Nous recevons leur lumière comme nous parvient encore celle des astres morts.

Des trois lignées que l'on vient de distinguer à partir de ces figures de la mythologie découlent des itinéraires de lecture différents. Aucun n'est exclusif, et n'interdit les autres, cependant la préférence spontanée que nous manifestons pour certains poèmes est liée à leur appartenance à l'un de ces territoires. La plupart de ceux qui nous touchent d'emblée se situent à l'intérieur du même domaine délimité par d'invisibles frontières. Les forêts mystérieuses d'Orphée, les sommets prométhéens traversés d'éclairs et le calme miroir des eaux où se penche Narcisse, composent des paysages qu'il est possible d'aimer tour à tour, et l'on peut refuser de choisir. Il est vraisemblable cependant que, sollicité par tous les poèmes rassemblés ici et présentés dans

---

1. Mallarmé.

un ordre chronologique, chaque lecteur s'attachera plus
particulièrement à certains d'entre eux et que, malgré leur
caractère disparate, l'affinité élective qui guide son choix lui fera
pressentir leur commune nature. Il sera clair alors que cette
attirance immédiate ne dépend pas d'une forme, d'une époque ou
d'un style. Elle est plutôt le signe de la reconnaissance instinctive
par chacun de nous d'une contrée poétique qui lui est proche,
d'un milieu originel « au filigrane bleu de l'âme se greffant » [1].

Anthologie pour Robinson

Offrir un tableau exhaustif de la poésie française, à supposer que
ce soit possible, n'est pas le but de cette anthologie. Si l'on s'est
attaché à illustrer chaque période par les œuvres qui semblaient les
plus représentatives, ce n'est pas avec le même nombre de poèmes.
Et s'il allait de soi que tout grand poète figurerait dans ce recueil,
on ne s'est pas cru obligé d'accorder une place égale à chacun
d'eux. Il arrive même que certains autres, moins illustres, en soient
absents. Omissions délibérées, puisqu'il ne s'agit pas ici de
proposer un inventaire rigoureux du domaine poétique français,
mais un ensemble de textes essentiels.
Cependant l'histoire de la poésie en France dans son
déroulement chronologique a été prise en compte. Il a semblé
important par exemple de présenter quelques poèmes des
troubadours. Ces commencements ne sont pas les ébauches de la
poésie à venir, ils ont la perfection d'œuvres d'art savamment
élaborées. On y voit quelques-uns des thèmes qui vont devenir
récurrents chez leurs successeurs et certaines des trouvailles
formelles dont les siècles suivants hériteront. L'obstacle d'une
langue qui rend nécessaire aujourd'hui le recours à une traduction,
n'empêche pas de prendre un réel plaisir à leur lecture. Pour les
époques où la création poétique est moins inventive, quelques
poètes ont été retenus en raison de leur contribution à l'évolution
des formes, ou parce qu'on pressent déjà, à travers eux, les grandes

---

1. Mallarmé.

œuvres à venir. Ils permettent de mesurer la transmutation qui va s'opérer avec les générations suivantes.

Mais pour l'essentiel ce livre est destiné aux Robinsons des îles désertes – ou des îles de solitude qu'on se ménage parfois au milieu du tumulte –, il souhaite leur proposer une bible de survie. Le pain de la poésie dont Baudelaire dit que nous ne pouvons nous passer, peut tenir en un volume, objet au maniement aisé que l'on emporte avec soi. Ce recueil, où l'on s'est affranchi des enthousiasmes de commande mais sans pour autant se priver d'admirer ce qui fut et reste admirable, est moins constitué de gracieux bibelots rimés que d'œuvres fortes. De celles qu'on a éprouvées comme les plus aptes à vaincre la grisaille des jours ou même l'oppression du malheur. Disposer de cette réserve personnelle est un vieux rêve du lecteur de poètes : témoin ces ébauches, les cahiers où l'on recopiait des vers et qui dorment dans la malle aux trésors de l'enfance.

Aussi un critère a prévalu : conserver parmi les poèmes soumis à l'épreuve du temps, du moins à cette mesure humaine du temps qu'est un demi-siècle de lecture, d'abord ceux dont le pouvoir d'enchantement sur ce lecteur ne s'affaiblit pas. C'est dire que ce choix est à la fois sincère et subjectif. Il entraîne naturellement à faire figurer à côté de textes rares (peu cités ou peu accessibles) d'autres textes bien connus et dont chacun croit disposer encore, mais qui, soumis aux caprices de la mémoire, se dérobent au moment où il plaît de les évoquer. Or ces derniers, si l'on a pu se contenter jadis de les apprécier superficiellement, révèlent tout leur prix dans la durée, ils demeurent parmi les plus beaux et peut-être les plus indispensables. Il est clair qu'un tel choix reflète les goûts de celui qui le fait. La fréquentation des grands classiques qu'implique le métier d'enseignant, et aussi l'itinéraire personnel ont influencé la première sélection de poèmes, puis le tri, imposé par les limites d'un seul volume, parmi ceux qui étaient retenus.

Les poètes vivants ne figurent pas dans ce recueil. Si on leur a préféré les poètes disparus, c'est qu'ils n'ont pas encore subi la nécessaire décantation. Ils constituent une terre à découvrir, et le hasard des lectures permet avec eux des rencontres passionnantes, mais leur proximité n'en fait pas encore des compagnons indispensables. D'autres que nous, plus tard, les amèneront au désert.

COMMENCEMENTS

Les poètes des premiers siècles de notre littérature, qu'ils soient de langue d'oc ou de langue d'oïl, ne nous sont plus accessibles sans traduction. Il importe cependant de les évoquer ici succinctement, car ils nous parlent encore malgré l'obstacle de la langue. Chez eux nous reconnaissons les thèmes et les images que leurs successeurs reprendront et développeront, et leur voix est capable de nous émouvoir. Enfin il est aisé de voir, en dépit de la difficulté d'approche, qu'à travers leurs plus beaux poèmes ils ont d'emblée porté la poésie française à un point de perfection.

Au commencement du commencement, au neuvième siècle, apparaît la première œuvre en langue d'oïl qui nous soit parvenue. Et elle est en vers assonancés :

> *Buona pulcella fut Eulalia,*
> *Bel avret corps, bellezour anima.*
> *Voldrent la veintre li Deo inimi...*

Il est plaisant de penser que le premier de nos poèmes est l'éloge d'une jeune fille, « une pucelle à l'âme plus belle encore que le corps, que voulaient vaincre les ennemis de Dieu », et que cette Cantilène à la louange de la jeune fille porte, comme elle, le beau nom d'Eulalie, celle qui parle bien.

La première œuvre poétique d'envergure, celle qui a vraiment valeur inaugurale, est composée aux alentours de 1100, c'est une chanson de geste, *La Chanson de Roland*. Le héros qu'elle célèbre, à la différence des grandes figures de l'Antiquité, ne connaîtra ni la vengeance, ni le retour, ni la gloire de fonder une cité. Il meurt seul, le dernier parmi ses compagnons de l'arrière-garde, dans l'infamie d'une embuscade, apparemment vaincu. Or le poète a fait de cette défaite une victoire, et c'est dans le récit de sa mort que l'épopée culmine et non dans le châtiment ultérieur du coupable. L'assentiment du ciel métamorphose le guerrier mourant en élu. Huit siècles plus tard un autre poète dira : « Heureux ceux qui sont morts d'une mort solennelle » [1].

Roland que l'on croyait mû par l'orgueil et victime de son imprudence lorsqu'il refusait d'appeler au secours a fait seulement la volonté de Dieu. « Le poète veut pour [lui], écrit Jean Dufournet, une mort oratoire, triomphante, exemplaire, presque christique. »

Il meurt sur une hauteur, signe de sa supériorité héroïque, couché sous un pin, symbole d'immortalité. Trois laisses font le récit de ses derniers instants. Tressant ensemble les mêmes motifs, mais avec des déplacements dans l'espace, des variantes dans les termes, et un crescendo final, elles disent la conscience qu'il a de sa fin prochaine, son repentir pour ses péchés et son geste de tendre le gant qui reconnaît en Dieu son seigneur suzerain. Les anges viennent enfin emporter l'âme du héros dont la tête tournée vers l'Espagne souligne qu'il n'a jamais fui.

La réitération de certains mots, leur glissement à des places différentes, font à l'oreille la musique insistante d'un pantoum. On entend sonner les décasyllabes comme un roulement de tambours funèbres jusqu'au moment où le ciel s'ouvre.

---

1. Péguy.

LA CHANSON DE ROLAND

CLXXIV

Ço sent Rollant que la mort le tresprent,
Devers la teste sur le quer li descent.
Desuz un pin i est alet curant,
Sur l'erbe verte s'i est culchet adenz,
Desuz lui met s'espee e l'olifan.
Turnat sa teste vers la paiene gent :
Pur ço l'at fait que il vœlt veirement
Que Carles diet e trestute sa gent,
Li gentilz quens, qu'il fut mort cunquerant.
Cleimet sa culpe e menut e suvent ;
Pur ses pecchez Deu puroffrid lo guant.

CLXXV

Ço sent Rollant de sun tens n'i ad plus.
Devers Espaigne est en un pui agut ;
À l'une main si ad sun piz batud :
« Deus, meie culpe vers les tues vertuz
De mes pecchez, des granz e des menuz,
Que jo ai fait des l'ure que nez fui
Tresqu'a cest jur que ci sui consoüt ! »
Sun destre guant en ad vers Deu tendut :
Angles del ciel i descendent a lui.

CLXXVI

Li quens Rollant se jut desuz un pin ;
Envers Espaigne en ad turnet sun vis.
De plusurs choses a remembrer li prist :
De tantes teres cum li bers cunquist,
De dulce France, des humes de sun lign,

LA CHANSON DE ROLAND

CLXXIV

Roland sent que la mort le pénètre,
Et de la tête vers le cœur lui descend.
Sous un pin il est allé en courant,
Sur l'herbe verte il s'est couché la face au sol.
Il met sous lui son épée et l'olifant.
Il tourne sa tête vers l'armée des païens :
Il fait cela parce qu'il tient absolument
À ce que Charles dise et tous ses gens
Qu'il est mort, le noble comte, en conquérant.
Il bat sa coulpe à petits coups répétés ;
Pour ses péchés à Dieu il offre son gant.

CLXXV

Roland sent que son temps est compté.
Face à l'Espagne il est sur un puy escarpé ;
De l'une de ses mains il bat sa poitrine :
« Mon Dieu, mea culpa, je m'en remets à ta puissance
Pour mes péchés, les grands et les petits,
Que j'ai faits depuis l'heure où je suis né
Jusqu'à ce jour où me voici blessé à mort. »
Il a tendu à Dieu le gant de sa main droite :
Du ciel les anges descendent à lui.

CLXXVI

Le comte Roland s'est couché sous un pin ;
Du côté de l'Espagne il a tourné son visage.
De plusieurs choses il se mit à se souvenir,
De tant de terres qu'il conquit en chevalier,
De douce France, des hommes de son lignage,

De Carlemagne, sun seignor, ki l' nurrit.
Ne pœt muer n'en plurt e ne suspirt.
Mais lui meïsme ne volt mettre en ubli,
Cleimet sa culpe, si priet Deu mercit :
« Veire Patene, ki unkes ne mentis,
Seint Lazaron de mort resurrexis,
E Daniel des leons guaresis,
Guaris de mei l'anme de tuz perilz
Pur les pecchez que en ma vie fis ! »
Sun destre guant a Deu en puroffrit ;
Seint Gabriel de sa main li ad pris.
Desur sun braz teneit le chef enclin ;
Juntes ses mains est alet a sa fin.
Deus li tramist sun angle Cherubin,
E seint Michel de la Mer del Peril ;
Ensembl'od els seint Gabriel i vint.
L'anme del cunte portent en pareïs.

De Charlemagne, son seigneur, qui l'a élevé ;
Il ne peut s'empêcher d'en pleurer et d'en soupirer.
Mais il ne veut s'oublier lui-même,
Il bat sa coulpe, il implore la miséricorde divine :
« Vrai Père, qui jamais ne mentis,
Ressuscitas saint Lazare de la mort,
Et sauvas Daniel des lions,
Sauve mon âme de tous périls
Pour les péchés que je fis en ma vie. »
De sa main droite il a tendu à Dieu son gant ;
Saint Gabriel de sa main l'a reçu.
Sur son bras il gardait la tête penchée ;
Les mains jointes il est allé à sa fin.
Dieu envoya son ange Chérubin
Et saint Michel du Péril de la Mer ;
En même temps qu'eux vint saint Gabriel.
L'âme du comte ils portent en paradis.

XIIe-XIIIe SIÈCLES

XIIᵉ-XIIIᵉ SIÈCLE

Les douzième et treizième siècles sont pour notre littérature l'âge épique par excellence. Ils voient naître les milliers de vers des chansons de geste qui racontent les hauts faits, réels ou imaginaires, de Charlemagne, de Guillaume d'Orange, ou de Huon de Bordeaux. C'est à la même époque que prend naissance et se développe le genre de la poésie lyrique. Des poèmes fleurissent en grand nombre, beaucoup nous sont parvenus, aussi anonymes que les chansons de geste ; parfois nous connaissons seulement le nom de leurs auteurs, quelques-uns sont identifiés. Le lyrisme se développe alors presque simultanément dans le Midi de la France et dans le Nord.

Si le lyrisme du sud, en langue d'oc, influence fortement celui du nord, et non l'inverse, c'est dû pour une grande part à Aliénor d'Aquitaine devenue reine de France. Elle amène à sa suite les troubadours dont elle aimait s'entourer. Celle qui est la petite-fille de l'un des plus illustres d'entre eux, se montre particulièrement sensible à leur chant. Plus tard son mariage avec Henri Plantagenêt élargit encore le domaine d'influence de ses poètes, tandis que ses filles, Marie et Aélis, l'une en Champagne, l'autre à Blois, contribuent au développement de ces échanges et à celui de la poésie du nord, en langue d'oïl.

Les troubadours s'expriment, eux, dans un parler composite où s'entremêlent des éléments venus de chacune des régions qui, du Limousin à la Provence, constituent leur domaine propre. Ils ont développé l'art du *trobar*, c'est-à-dire de l'expression poétique originale, directement accessible comme dans le *trobar plan* ou plus difficile dans le *trobar clus*, poésie fermée fondée sur une recherche volontaire de l'hermétisme. Ils pratiquent aussi le *trobar ric* dont la « richesse » tient au travail d'entrelacement des mots. Il n'y a, en effet, rien de naïvement spontané chez ces artistes du vers. Dante a célébré l'un d'eux, cet Arnaud Daniel qu'Aragon loue aussi pour sa science des sonorités et des rimes. Ces poètes sont en même temps des compositeurs et toutes leurs œuvres sont conçues pour être chantées. Certains les interprètent eux-mêmes, d'autres ont recours à un jongleur qui apprend des vers auprès d'un maître puis le quitte pour un autre. Son répertoire s'étend ainsi, et il l'enrichit encore au contact d'autres musiciens itinérants. Car les jongleurs, comme les troubadours eux-mêmes, voyagent beaucoup et leurs séjours respectifs dans les cours étrangères étendent leur influence en Italie et dans une grande partie de l'Europe.

Le thème dominant du lyrisme médiéval est la peinture de l'amour. Les XIIe et XIIIe siècles conçoivent et peignent particulièrement la *fin'amor*, l'amour parfait, sentiment qui lie le poète à sa *domna* dans un rapport de vassal à suzerain. Cette dame est le plus souvent l'épouse du seigneur du lieu, de haute naissance et inaccessible. La *fin'amor* exige donc le raffinement des mœurs et du décor, et il lui faut l'environnement d'une cour royale ou seigneuriale, d'où le nom qu'on lui donne d'amour courtois. C'est un composé de mystique et d'une sensualité qu'on aurait tort de croire toujours platonique. L'amoureux célèbre parfois les preuves de réciprocité qu'a pu lui donner sa dame. Mais c'est sous sa forme la plus haute et la plus épurée que cet amour apporte la *joy*, qui s'apparente à l'état de grâce, au plein accord avec la divinité, et comble de bonheur celui qui l'atteint.

Quelques poèmes des troubadours

Ils célèbrent la dame, ses beautés et ses mérites, ou se plaignent de ses rigueurs et des souffrances qu'elle inflige à l'amant, ils associent la grâce du printemps à celle de l'amour naissant. C'est par là qu'ils nous touchent et que nous pouvons voir qu'ils inventent pour les siècles à venir les *topoï*, les lieux communs de la poésie amoureuse. Cependant ils ont pratiqué aussi diverses formes de poèmes, les *sirventès*, poèmes satiriques et violents ou le *planh*, déploration funèbre, ceux-là paraissent moins accessibles au lecteur contemporain, ils sont trop liés à des circonstances particulières, alors que leurs chants d'amour, joyeux ou mélancoliques, nous touchent encore.

Qui sont-ils ? Si l'on voit entre leurs œuvres des traits communs, on constate, pour ceux qui nous sont connus, qu'il n'y a entre eux aucune homogénéité sociale. Ils peuvent être nobles et même de très haute lignée comme l'un des plus anciens d'entre eux, Guillaume, ou gueux comme Marcabrun et plus aptes alors à donner un tour satirique et amer à la peinture de l'amour.

On lira ici quelques exemples de *canso* ou chanson d'amour.

Quelques poèmes des trouvères

En lisant les troubadours cités ici, et tant d'autres, comme Cercamon, Bernard de Ventadour, Arnaud Daniel ou Peire Vidal, on prend conscience qu'une commune inspiration les rapproche, alors que les poètes d'oïl offrent une bien plus grande diversité dans leurs écrits.

Les trouvères se distinguent d'abord de ceux qui leur ont si souvent servi de modèles, par la simplicité de l'expression poétique, moins ornée et plus naturelle. Ils ne cherchent ni l'hermétisme, ni l'art savant, et ne pratiquent donc ni le *trobar clus*, ni le *trobar ric*. D'autre part leur registre est plus étendu, tous les tons, du grave au plaisant, se trouvent dans leurs œuvres. On peut y rencontrer l'aveu sans fard d'une déchéance personnelle aussi bien que la description d'un décor printanier, la satire véhémente ou le chuchotement d'une confidence. Chacun de leurs poèmes fortement individualisé témoigne plus de la personnalité de son auteur que de son appartenance à un groupe ou à un courant.

Ils n'ont pas de l'amour courtois la même conception que les poètes du Midi. De sa dame l'amant n'espère rien, car déclarer sa flamme est, à ses yeux, faire outrage à l'élue. Aussi cette poésie passionnée est-elle pudique, et les sentiments qu'elle traduit délicats, presque craintifs. Mais elle donne une très haute idée de l'héroïsme qu'exige d'eux cet amour épuré. Quand pour la langue d'oc le mot « proeza » signifie simplement « valeur » ou « mérite », il désigne ici le courage qui brave la mort en duel ou au combat, et qui affronte les plus redoutables dangers.

On assiste chez eux à la naissance d'un lyrisme qui ne s'accompagne pas de musique, de vers qui ne sont plus chantés. Ainsi *Les Vers de la Mort* composés à la fin du douzième siècle par le moine Hélinand de Froidmont. Cinquante douzains d'octosyllabes à deux rimes, développent une démonstration destinée à ceux de ses amis qui s'attardent encore dans le siècle. Tantôt il s'adresse à la mort elle-même, tantôt il évoque l'étendue de ses pouvoirs, comme dans les fragments cités ici :

Morz, tu abats a un seul tor	Mort, tu abats d'un seul coup
Aussi le roi dedenz sa tour	Aussi bien le roi en sa tour
Com le povre dedenz son toit :	Que le pauvre sous son toit.
Tu erres adès sans sejor	Tu vas toujours sans trêve
Por chacun semondre a son jor	Pour avertir chacun à son heure
De paier Dieu trestot son droit.	De payer à Dieu toute sa dette
Qui paor de mort a jus mise	Qui a vaincu sa peur de la mort
C'est cil qui la mort plus atise,	C'est celui qui excite le plus la mort,
Et vers cui ele ainçois s'adrece.	Et auquel elle s'adresse d'abord.
Cors bien norriz, chars bien alise	Corps bien nourri, chair bien polie
Fait de vers et de feu chemise :	Font chemise de vers et de feu.
Qui plus s'aaise plus se blece.	Plus on en prend à son aise, plus on se blesse..

Le martèlement des deux rimes, les répétitions insistantes viennent à l'appui de ce sermon sur la mort. Et ces strophes ouvrent la voix à un lyrisme funèbre. L'évocation réaliste du corps, que la mort voue à la destruction par les vers et le feu, a des accents dignes de Villon.

Le douzième siècle finissant et le début du siècle suivant voient apparaître de nombreux trouvères. S'il faut choisir, entre tous les plus dignes d'être retenus, Gace Brulé, Thibaud de Champagne et Guillaume de Lorris sont sans doute les plus aptes à donner une idée de leurs talents.

GUILLAUME DE POITIERS

(1071 - 1127)

Le premier poème est composé par Guillaume IX, comte de Poitiers et duc d'Anjou. Nous en possédons d'autres de lui dont l'inspiration est franchement gaillarde, mais il est capable aussi d'exprimer le lyrisme amoureux le plus pur, il le fait même parfois avec une certaine préciosité. On verra ici une expression de la *joy*, la joie qui saisit le poète joyeux (*jauzens* d'aimer. Par la répétition de ce terme dans les cinq premiers sixains il traduit, en une sorte de crescendo, l'exaltation de l'amour, jusqu'à attribuer à sa dame des dons quasi surnaturels. On le voit dans la cinquième strophe où dans une énumération, à la manière des litanies de l'Église, il la loue pour son pouvoir de guérir (*sanar*), de faire périr celui qui est bien portant (*sas morir*), de rendre fou (*enfolezir*), d'enlaidir celui qui était beau (*beutat mudar*), d'avilir le plus noble (*plus cortes vilanejar*) et ennoblir les plus vil (*vilas encortezir*). Les trois dernières strophes sont une demande de réciprocité assortie de promesses, en même temps qu'un aveu de totale allégeance. L'ensemble respecte l'agencement initial des deux rimes en *ar* et *ir* et les huit strophes d'octosyllabes sont fidèles au dessin en a b b a a b. Rien en effet n'est approximatif dans ce poème qui montre une maîtrise parfaite de la forme.

CANSO

Mout jauzens me prenc en amar
Un joy don plus mi vuelh aizir,
E pus en joy vuelh revertir
Ben dey, si puesc, al mielhs anar,
Quar mielhs onra'm, estiers cujar,
Qu'om puesca vezer ni auzir.

Ieu, so sabetz, no'm dey gabar
Ni de grans laus no'm say formir,
Mas si anc nulhs joys poc florir,
Aquest deu sobre totz granar
E part los autres esmerar,
Si cum sol brus jorns esclarzir.

Anc mais no poc hom faissonar
Co's, en voler ni en dezir
Ni en pensar ni en cossir ;
Aitals joys no pot par trobar,
E qui be l volria lauzar
D'un an no y poiri'avenir.

Totz joys li deu humiliar,
Et tota ricors obezir
Mi dons, per son belh aculhir
E per son belh plazent esguar ;
E deu hom mais cent ans durar
Qui'l joy de s'amor pot sazir.

Per son joy pot malautz sanar,
E per sa ira sas morir
E savis hom enfolezir
E belhs hom sa beutat mudar
E'l plus cortes vilanejar
E totz vilas encortezir.

CHANSON

Tout éjoui je ressens en amour
Une joie que je veux éprouver plus vive,
Et puisque à cette joie je veux m'en tenir
Je dois faire tout mon possible
Auprès de la plus belle entre les dames
Que l'on peut voir et entendre.

Vous le savez, je n'ai de quoi me faire valoir
Et ne sais m'envelopper de grands éloges.
Mais si jamais une joie peut fleurir,
Par-dessus toutes celle-là doit donner grain
Et sur les autres l'emporter en éclat
Comme le soleil éclaire un sombre jour.

Jamais homme ne put en imaginer
Une telle, ni en vouloir ni en désir,
Ni en pensée ni en songe ;
Une telle joie ne peut trouver son égale
Et qui s'aviserait de la louer
N'aurait trop d'un an pour y parvenir.

Toute joie lui doit soumission,
Et tout pouvoir obéissance
À ma dame, pour son bel accueil
Et pour son égard si plaisant ;
Et il gagne plus de cent ans de vie
L'homme dont s'empare cette joie d'amour.

Par sa joie peut guérir les malades,
Par sa colère les bien-portants faire mourir,
D'un homme sage faire un fou,
D'un homme beau la beauté changer,
Le plus noble rendre vilain
Et du plus vilain faire un noble.

Pus hom gensor no'n pot trobar
Ni huelhs vezer ni boca dir,
À mos ops la vuelh retenir,
Per lo cor dedins refrescar
E per la carn renovellar,
Que no puesca envellezir.

Si'm vol mi dons s'amor donar,
Pres suy del penr'e del grazir
E del celar e del blandir
E de sos plazers dir e far
E de sos pretz tener en car
E de son laus enavantir.

Ren per autruy non l'aus mandar,
Tal paor ay qu'ades s'azir,
Ni ieu mezeys, tan tem falhir,
No l'aus m'amor fort assemblar ;
Mas elha'm deu mo mielhs triar,
Pus sap qu'ab lieys ai a guerir.

Puisque plus gente on ne peut trouver
Ni voir de ses yeux ni dire de sa bouche,
Près de moi je la veux retenir,
Pour rafraîchir l'intérieur de mon cœur,
Pour rendre jeunesse à ma chair
Et l'empêcher de s'envieillir.

Si ma dame veut m'accorder son amour,
Je suis prêt à le prendre avec reconnaissance,
À le tenir secret et à le choyer,
À ne dire et faire que pour son plaisir,
À tenir grand cas de ce qu'il vaut
Et ses louanges faire retentir.

Je ne lui ai rien fait savoir par autrui
Tant j'ai peur qu'aussitôt elle se fâche,
Et pour moi non plus, tant je crains de faillir,
Je n'ose lui déclarer mon amour ;
Mais c'est elle qui doit choisir au mieux pour moi,
Puisque je sais qu'elle seule me peut guérir.

MARCABRUN

(1ʳᵉ moitié du XIIᵉ siècle)

Sur la vie et la carrière de Marcabrun nous savons peu de choses, sinon qu'il est un enfant trouvé, et qu'il écrit dans la première moitié du douzième siècle. Une quarantaine de ses poèmes ont été conservés dont *Le Chant du lavoir* qu'il a composé en 1137 pour soutenir le roi de Castille dans sa croisade contre les Almohades. C'est le premier chant de croisade connu. Comme les autres troubadours il célèbre la *fin'amor* et se montre fort savant en l'art du *trobar clus*, mais, apparemment misogyne, il lui arrive aussi d'ironiser sur l'amour courtois. Il peut se montrer alors âpre et sarcastique.

Ainsi, à la fin du poème suivant, il parle de lui-même avec l'amertume d'un homme « ques anc non amet neguna, / ni d'autra no fo amats », qui jamais n'en aima aucune, ni d'une autre ne fut aimé. On ne sait s'il s'agit d'une tristesse feinte ou d'une confidence, mais ce ton personnel permet à l'auteur de signer le poème en se nommant.

À entendre la répétition dans chaque strophe de l'injonction qui la sépare en deux parties inégales, on imagine un public qu'il veut soustraire par cette exclamation : « Écoutez ! » au bercement régulier des octosyllabes, afin de mobiliser son attention, public qu'on peut supposer plus rude que celui d'une cour raffinée.

À moins qu'il ne s'agisse là de souligner la sagesse personnelle qui lui vient de son expérience et de faire, d'une manière paradoxale, l'éloge de l'amour, en dénonçant son irrésistible et dangereux pouvoir.

Il est curieux de voir qu'une seule strophe rompt avec le choix de la première rime en *a*, qui prévaut dans les onze autres sixains à deux rimes, et que celle-là précisément, la huitième, est plutôt faite de lieux communs et comme interpolée dans le poème, tandis que la suivante propose d'Amour l'image magnifique d'une cavale que ne maîtrise plus le cavalier.

CANSO

Dirai-vos senes dobtança
d'aquest vèrs la començança ;
Il mot fan de ver semblança ;
    – Escoutatz ! –
qui vers Prœsa balança
semblança fa de malvatz.

Jovents faih e franh e brisa,
et Amors es d'altal guisa
de tots censais a cens prisa,
    – Escoutatz ! –
chascuns en pren sa devisa,
Ja puèls no'n serà coltats.

Amors val com la beluja
que coa'l fuèc en la suja,
ard lo fust e la festuja,
    – Escoutatz ! –
e non sap vas qual part fuja
cel qui del fuèc es gastats.

Dirai-vos d'Amor com signa :
de çal garda, de lai guinha,
çal baisa, de lai rechinha,
    – Escoutatz ! –
plus serà drecha que linha
quand ieu serai sos privats.

Amors solia èsser drecha,
mas era es tòrta e brecha
et a colhida tal decha
    – Escoutatz ! –
lai ont non pòt mòrdre lecha
plus asprament non fai chats.

CHANSON

Je vais vous dire sans retard
De ces vers le commencement ;
Les mots font du vrai l'apparence ;
    – Écoutez ! –
Celui qui devant Prouesse hésite
Prend apparence de méchant.

Jeunesse faillit, se rompt et brise,
Et Amour est d'une autre nature :
Dans tous les cas il a son mot à dire
    – Écoutez ! –
Chacun en prend ce qui l'inspire,
Mais jamais plus n'en sera quitte.

Il en va d'Amour comme de l'étincelle
Qui couve le feu dans la suie,
Brûle la poutre et le faîtage
    – Écoutez ! –
Et il ne sait de quel côté fuir
Celui qui de ce feu est ravagé.

Je vais vous dire les signes d'Amour :
Regarde de çà, guigne de là,
Ici baise, là rechigne
    – Écoutez ! –
Il sera plus droit qu'une ligne
Quand je serai son intime.

Amour avait coutume d'être droit,
Mais il devint tordu et rude
Et chétivement couillu
    – Écoutez ! –
Là où il ne peut mordre il lèche
Plus âprement que ne fait le chat.

Grèu serà mais Amors vera
pòls del mèl trièt la cera,
ans sap si pelar la pera ;
          – Escoutatz ! –
douça'us èr com chants de lera
si sol la coa'lh troncatz.

Ab diables pren barata
qui Faisa Amòr acoata,
no'ih cal qu'autra verga'l bata ;
          – Escoutatz ! –
plus non sent que cel qui's grata
trò que s'es vius escorjats.

Amors es mout de mal avi :
mil òmes a mòrt sens glavi,
Dieu non fetz tan fòrt gramavi,
          – Escoutatz ! –
que tot nèci del plus savi
non faça, si'l ten al laç.

Amors a usatge d'èga
que totjorn vòl qu'òm la sèga
e ditz que no'l darà trèga
          – Escoutatz ! –
mas que puèg de lèga en lèga,
sia dejuns o disnats.

Cujatz-vos qu'ieu non conosca
d'Amor s'es òrba o losca ?
Sos dichs aplana e entosca,
          – Escoutatz ! –
plus suau ponh qu'una mosca
60 mas plus grèu n'es òm sanats,

Jamais Amour ne sera vrai,
Il prend le miel, laisse la cire,
Il sait peler pour lui la poire
        – Écoutez ! –
Et doux sera comme chant de lyre
Si seulement vous lui tranchez la queue.

Au diable il prend sa ruse
Qui s'allie à Fausse-Amour
Et n'a besoin d'autre verge pour le battre
        – Écoutez ! –
Il ne s'en ressent pas plus que qui se gratte
Jusqu'à s'écorcher tout vif.

Amour est de fort mauvais conseil :
Sans glaive il a tué mille hommes,
Dieu n'a fait plus grand sorcier
        – Écoutez ! –
Du plus sage il fait un fol
Dès lors qu'il le tient dans ses lacs.

Amour se conduit comme la cavale
Qui toujours veut qu'on la suive
Et dit qu'il n'y aura pas de trêve
        – Écoutez ! –
Et qui vous traîne de lieue en lieue
Sans déjeuner et sans dîner.

Croyez-vous que je ne sais pas
Si Amour est aveugle ou bigle ?
Ses paroles sont sucre et poison
        – Écoutez ! –
S'il point plus doucement qu'une mouche,
On met soixante fois plus de temps à en guérir.

Qui per sen de femna renha
drechs es que mais il'n avenha,
si com la Letra'ns ensenha ;
      – Escoutatz ! –
malaventura'us en venha
si tuit non vos en gardatz !

Marcabruns, filhs Marcabruna,
fo angenrats en tal luna
qu'el sap d'Amor com degruna,
      – Escoutatz ! –
ques anc non amèt neguna,
ni d'autra non fo amats.

Celui qui se conduit au gré de la femme,
Il est fatal qu'il lui en advienne mal,
Comme l'Écriture nous l'enseigne.
            – Écoutez ! –
Malaventure en vienne à vous tous
Si vous ne vous en gardez pas.

Marcabrun, fils de Marcabrune,
Fut engendré sous telle lune
Qu'il sait d'Amour comme il en va.
            – Écoutez ! –
Jamais il n'aima aucune
Ni d'aucune ne fut aimé.

JAUFRÉ RUDEL

(milieu du XIIᵉ siècle)

Le plus connu sans doute de tous les troubadours est Jaufré Rudel, prince de Blaye, même si on ne sait presque rien de sa vie, sinon la magnifique légende qui court à son sujet et inspira plusieurs écrivains.

Le poème qu'on va lire a suffi à rendre son auteur célèbre et à séduire des générations d'écoliers, car exprimant par là l'une des constantes de la rêverie adolescente, il offre la traduction poétique de la distance qui sépare tout être humain de l'amour idéal. L'infranchissable imaginaire trouve ici son équivalent dans la métaphore spatiale. Lointaine, absente, inaccessible, la femme aimée, qu'on vénère sans l'avoir jamais vue, se trouve sans aucun doute à l'autre bout du monde.

Si l'on en croit la tradition, ce poète fut réellement amoureux d'une princesse de Tripoli dont il connaissait seulement le portrait, et il dut envisager, pour la rejoindre, comme il le dit ici, d'entreprendre un très long voyage « car trop son nostras terras lonh ». On raconte qu'il se croisa et mourut là-bas, « au pays sarrasin », au moment de rencontrer enfin celle qu'il aimait. Ce poème se pare ainsi de l'étrange pressentiment du destin entrevu.

Sans vouloir rien lui ôter de son mystère ou de son prestige, ne peut-on le considérer plutôt comme l'acte de foi d'un pèlerin de l'absolu, dont le but en ces temps de croisade était moins d'atteindre la Terre Sainte, que de témoigner de la sainteté de l'amour ?

Le charme de ce poème tient d'abord à la répétition de la longue et lourde syllabe nasale, *lonh*. Dans cet ensemble de sept strophes comportant chacune sept vers, il revient quatorze fois, ne rimant qu'avec lui-même, et par là isolé et détaché comme un glas qu'on égrène. La disposition interne des septains n'est pas moins remarquable, ils sont construits sur trois rimes (quatre si l'on compte *lonh*) en *ay*, *is*, et *atz*, disposées en a b a b c c d, comme un quatrain à rimes croisées suivi d'un tercet dont la dernière rime isolée reste en suspens, jusqu'à ce que le vers final du septain suivant lui fasse écho. La tierce rime appelle le redoublement du dernier tercet qui referme ainsi la strophe.

Le second attrait de ce poème grave tient aussi à l'évocation du printemps sur laquelle il s'ouvre. Le tableau de l'amant qui s'éveille à l'amour quand le mois de mai l'y invite, se rencontre dans de nombreux poèmes, depuis les *Aubades* anonymes jusqu'au *Roman de la Rose*. Il est l'un des plus gracieux de la poésie médiévale. On le retrouvera au seizième siècle chez Ronsard. Mais ici l'évocation est suivie d'un désespoir : « Si que chans ni flors d'albespis / No-m platz plus que l'yverns gelatz. » Ce refus d'une nature radieuse par un cœur malheureux sera un thème cher aux romantiques.

CANSO

Lanquan li jorn son lonc en may
M'es belhs dous chans d'auzelhs, de lonh,
E quan mi suy partitz de lay
Remembra-m d'un amor de lonh :
Vau de talan embroucx c clis
Si que chans ni flors d'albespis
No-m platz plus que l'yverns gelatz.

Be tenc lo Senhor per veray
Per qu'ieu veirai l'amor de lonh ;
Mas per un ben que m'en eschay
N'ai dos mals, quar tan m'es de lonh.
Ai ! car me fos lai pelegris,
Si que mos fustz e mos tapis
Fos pels sieus belhs huelhs remiratz !

Be-m parra joys quan li querray,
Per amor Dieu, l'alberc de lonh ;
E, s'a lieys platz, alberguarai
Pres de lieys, si be-m suy de lonh ;
Adoncs parra-l parlamens fis,
Quan drutz lonhdas er tan vezis
Qu'ab bels digz jauzira solatz.

Iratz e gauzens m'en partray,
S'ieu ja la vey, l'amor de lonh ;
Mas non sai quoras la veyrai,
Car trop son nostras terras lonh,
Assatz hi a pas e camis,
E per aisso no'n suy devis ;
Mas tot sfa cum a Dieu platz !

CHANSON

Lorsque les jours sont longs en mai
Me plaît un doux chant d'oiseaux lointain,
Et quand je me suis éloigné de là
Il me souvient d'un amour lointain :
Je vais, songeur, morne, tête basse,
Au point que chant ni fleur d'aubépine
Ne me plaisent plus que l'hiver glacé.

Oui, je tiens pour vrai le Seigneur
Grâce auquel je verrai l'amour lointain ;
Mais pour un bien qui m'en échoit
J'en ai deux maux, tant il m'est lointain.
Ah ! Si j'étais là-bas pèlerin,
Pour que mon bâton et mon esclavine [1]
Par ses beaux yeux fussent contemplés !

Grande joie ce me sera de lui demander
Pour l'amour de Dieu le gîte lointain :
Et, s'il lui plaît, je prendrai gîte
Près d'elle, bien que je sois lointain.
Alors viendront les doux entretiens
Quand l'ami lointain sera si voisin
Qu'il fera fête aux beaux propos.

Triste et joyeux je m'en irai,
Si je le vois, l'amour lointain ;
Mais je ne sais quand je le verrai,
Car nos pays sont trop lointains.
Il y a trop de passages et de chemins
Et pour en venir à bout ne suis devin ;
Mais tout soit comme il plaît à Dieu.

---

1. pèlerine.

Ja mais d'amor no-m jauziray
Si no-m jau d'est'amor de lonh,
Que gensor ni melhor no n sai
Ves mulha part, ni pres ni lonh ;
Tant es sos pretz verais e fis
Que lay, el reng dels Sarrazis,
Fos hieu per lieys chaitius clamatz !

Dieus que fetz tot quant ve ni vai
E formet sest'amor de lonh
Mi don poder, que cor ieu n'ai,
Qu'ieu veya sest'amor de lonh,
Verayamen, en tals aizis,
Si que la cambra e-l jardis
Mi resembles tos temps palatz !

Ver ditz qui m'apella lechay
Ni deziron d'amor de lonh,
Car nulhs autres joys tan no-m play
Cum jauzimens d'amor de lonh :
Mas so qu'ieu vuelh m'es atahis,
Qu'enaissi-m fadet mos pairis
Qu'ieu ames e non fos amatz.

Mas so qu'ieu vouill m'es atahis.
Totz sfa mauditz lo pairis
Que-m fadet qu'ieu non fos amatz !

Jamais d'amour je n'aurai joie
Si je n'ai joie de cet amour lointain,
Car de plus gente et de meilleure je n'en connais
En nul endroit, proche ou lointain.
Son prix est si vrai et si sûr
Que là-bas, au pays des Sarrasins,
Puissé-je être appelé captif !

Que Dieu qui fit tout ce qui va et vient
Et fit naître cet amour lointain
Me donne ce pouvoir – comme le veut mon cœur –
De voir cet amour lointain,
Véritablement, en si bonnes conditions
Que la chambre et le jardin
Me semblent un palais sans fin.

Il dit vrai celui qui m'appelle avide
Et désireux d'amour lointain,
Car nulle autre joie ne me plaît autant
Que jouissance d'amour lointain.
Mais ce que je veux m'est refusé,
Car ainsi m'a ensorcelé mon parrain
Que j'aime sans être aimé.

Mais ce que je veux m'est refusé.
Que maudit soit le parrain
Qui m'a jeté le sort de n'être pas aimé !

GACE BRULÉ

(v. 1160 - v. 1213)

Gace Brulé fut admiré par ses contemporains et souvent cité ou imité. Il échappe à l'influence des troubadours avec lesquels il rivalise, quand il peint l'amour avec des accents personnels douloureux. On le voit en particulier lorsqu'il lui arrive de renoncer à ce lieu commun de la poésie amoureuse qu'est l'éveil du printemps, pour lui préférer des saisons jusqu'alors dédaignées. Car chez celui qui fut, dit Jean Frappier, « le plus méditatif des poètes », l'absolue soumission à sa dame :

> *D'Amour ne me puis défendre*
> *Face de moi son plaisir*

et son destin d'amant malheureux, donnent aux poèmes une tonalité sombre qui s'accorde bien avec la mélancolie des fins d'automne. Aussi est-il le premier à choisir ce cadre pour exprimer la tristesse liée à la fatalité d'une passion irrésistible. Quand il dit : « Amer m'estuet », « je suis forcé d'aimer », il se présente aussi comme un homme à qui l'amour trouble l'esprit : « Homme égaré qui ne sait ce qu'il va cherchant. » Et ses poèmes font entendre, de façon insistante, sa plainte qui, au-delà de sa propre histoire, est celle de tous les mal-aimés.

> *Et dites-lui qu'il est né maudit*
> *Lui qui aime toujours et ne sera jamais aimé.*

Quant l'erbe muert, voi la fueille cheoir
Que li venz fait jus des arbres descendre
Dont covient il les dous chanz remanoir
Des oiselez, qui n'i pueënt entendre ;
Lors me covient a Amor mon cuer rendre,
Mes par peché cuidai aillors entendre.

Mout a Amors grant force et grant pooir
Qu'encontre li ne se puet nus desfendre
Fors envios, cui n'en daigne chaloir,
Que hontes est de lor servise prendre
Et qui de li ne vet sa joie atendre
Sachiez de voir que s'onor en iert mendre

Bien puis amer ma dame sens priier,
Mes ce n'est pas Amors qu'a moi apende,
Qu'il n'est pas droiz, ne dire ne le quier,
Que de si haut por moi si bas descende,
Se granz pitiez, qui toute rien amende,
Ne vaint reson en li tant que m'entende.

Amer m'estuet, car jel nel puis lessier,
Ne ja reson ne droiz nel me deffende :
Qu'Amors me puet de grand joie avancier,
Plus que vertuz qui en cest mont s'estende ;
Et s'il li plest que sa valor me vende,
Perduz m'i sui, ne sai qui me rende.

Tant fet Amors sovent vivre et morir
Que je ne sai de mon mal tret que dire :
Quant plus i pens, plus m'estuet esbahir,
Et plu et plus me doble mon martire.
Mais de legier vainquisse peine et ire
Se bel semblant fussent sens escondire.

Quand l'herbe meurt, je vois la feuille choir
Que le vent fait tomber au pied des arbres :
C'est le moment où cessent les doux chants
Des oiselets, on ne saurait les entendre ;
Alors il convient que mon cœur en revienne à Amour,
C'est par péché que je pensais m'occuper ailleurs.

Amour a si grande force et si grand pouvoir
Que contre lui nul ne peut se défendre
Hormis les envieux, dont il ne daigne avoir cure.
Il est honteux de se mettre à leur service
Et qui d'Amour ne veut sa joie attendre
Sachez en vérité que son honneur en sera moindre.

Je puis bien aimer ma dame sans la prier,
Mais ce n'est pas Amour qui dépend de moi.
Car il n'est pas juste, et je ne veux pas prétendre,
Que de si haut pour moi elle descende si bas,
Si grande pitié, qui toute chose rend meilleure,
Ne convainc sa raison de m'entendre.

Il me faut aimer, je n'y puis résister,
Raison ni droit ne me le défendent :
Car Amour de grande joie me peut avantager
Plus que vertu qu'on peut voir en ce monde ;
Et s'il lui plaît que je doive en payer le prix,
Alors je suis perdu, car je n'ai pas de caution.

Amour fait si souvent vivre et mourir
Que de mon mal je ne sais trop quoi dire :
Plus j'y pense, plus il me faut m'étonner
Et ne fait que redoubler mon martyre.
Mais je vaincrais plus facilement peine et colère
Si beau-semblant était sans feintise.

J'aim la meillor que valor puisse élire
Bien ait mes cuers qui tele la désire.

Certes meschins qui por amors empire
N'a en li droit ; por nient en sospire.

J'aime la meilleure au prix de la valeur :
Heureux soit mon cœur qui telle la désire.

Certes un jeune homme qui se rend malade d'amour
N'a aucun droit pour lui, et c'est pour rien qu'il en soupire.

THIBAUD DE CHAMPAGNE

(1201 - 1253)

Le comte Thibaud de Champagne est un trouvère de haut lignage, héritier d'une longue tradition poétique et continuateur de Gace Brulé. Son œuvre est l'une des plus abondantes et des plus variées parmi celles qui nous sont parvenues du XIIIᵉ siècle. Elle comprend des pastourelles et des chansons, des jeux-partis qui correspondent à la *tenso* du Midi, des chansons de croisade, des chansons à la Vierge et des *serventois* qui, comme les *sirventès* d'oc, traitent de sujets historiques ou satiriques.

Lorsqu'on trouve chez lui les grands thèmes de l'amour courtois, qu'il parle de sa fidélité ou de son impatience, qu'il en appelle à la pitié de la dame ou affirme qu'il songe à mourir, ses poèmes sont un témoignage de culture et de talent plus que l'expression de sentiments sincères. Ce qui séduit le lecteur en lui c'est le raffinement de son art et le plaisir manifeste que le poète a de composer.

On voit, dans la chanson suivante, la virtuosité de celui qui choisit le neuvain pour la strophe, l'heptamètre pour le vers, associant les couplets deux par deux par leurs rimes, chaque strophe liant elle-même, sur deux rimes seulement, un quatrain à rimes croisées à un quintil aux rimes embrassées. Le choix de l'impair vaut à ce poème d'être léger malgré sa longueur. La variété des tons qui vont de l'hyperbole à la simplicité (« Si vous plest, si m'ociez » et « je chant et deport / pour moi solacier »), le recours à des images singulières (celle du cerf blanc comme neige, aux tresses d'or), ou la préciosité de la pointe finale : « Mult sont or li mot sanglent / Dont couvient que vos riez », montrent les ressources si diverses de son talent, mais ce qui séduit peut-être encore davantage c'est le surgissement inattendu de l'ironie : « Et se melz m'amez vivant... Mult en seroie plus liez. » Suivant l'expression d'Alexandre Micha : « Il y a du Clément Marot dans ce badinage souriant. »

CHANSON

I

Je me cuidoie partir
D'Amors, mes riens ne me vaut,
Li douz maus du souvenir,
Qui nuit et jor ne m'i faut,
Le jor m'i fet maint assaut,
Et la nuit ne puis dormir,
Ainz plain et pleur et souspir.
Deus ! tant art quant la remir,
Mes bien sai qu'il ne l'en chaut.

II

Nus ne doit Amors traïr
Fors que garçon et ribaut ;
Et, se n'est par son plesir,
Je n'i voi ne bas ne haut ;
Ainz vueil qu'ele me truist baut
Sanz guiler et sanz mentir ;
Mes se je puis consivir
Le cerf, qui tant puet fouir,
Nus n'est joianz a Thiebaut.

III

Li cers est aventureus
Et si est blans conme nois
Et si a les crins andeus
Plus sors que or espanois.
Li cers est en un défois
À l'entrer mult perilleus
Et si est gardez de leus :
Ce sont felon envïeus
Qui trop grievent aus cortois.

CHANSON XVII

I

Je pensais me séparer
D'Amour, mais n'en ai pas la force ;
Les doux maux du souvenir,
Qui nuit et jour ne me manquent,
Le jour me donnent maint assaut
Et la nuit je ne puis dormir,
Mais je me plains, et pleure, et soupire.
Dieu ! je brûle tant quand je la regarde,
Mais je sais bien qu'elle n'en a cure.

II

Nul ne doit Amour trahir
Hormis goujat et ribaud ;
Et en dehors de son bon plaisir
Tout le reste est égal ;
Mais je veux qu'elle me trouve beau
Sans tromper ni mentir ;
En revanche si je puis rattraper
Le cerf, qui si bien peut fuir,`
Nul n'a plus de joie que Thibaud.

III

Le cerf aime l'aventure,
Il est blanc comme neige
Et ses cheveux en tresses
Sont plus blonds qu'or d'Espagne.
Le cerf est dans une réserve
Dont l'entrée est fort périlleuse.
Aussi est-il à l'abri des loups :
Ce sont les traîtres envieux
Qui sont le fléau des amants courtois.

IV

Ainz chevaliers angoisseus
Qui a perdu son hernois,
Ne vile que art li feus
Mesons, vignes, blez et pois,
Ne chacierres qui prent sois,
Ne leus qui est fameilleus
N'est avers moi dolereus,
Que je ne soie de ceus
Qui aiment deseur leur pois.

V

Dame, une riens vous demant :
Cuidiez vous que soit pechiez
D'ocirre son vrai amant ?
Oïl, voir ! bien le sachiez !
S'il vos plest, si m'ocïez,
Que je le vueil et creant,
Et se melz m'amez vivant,
Je le vos di en oiant,
Mult en seroie plus liez.

VI

Dame, ou nule ne se prent,
Mes que vos vueilliez itant
C'un pou i vaille pitiez !

VII

Renaut, Phelippe, Lorent,
Mult sont or li mot sanglent
Dont couvient que vos rïez.

IV

Mais ni chevalier dans le tourment
Qui a perdu son équipement,
Ni village que brûle le feu
Et maisons, vignes, blés et bois,
Ni chasseur qui prend soif,
Ni loup qui meurt de faim
Ne sont plus malheureux que moi,
Car je crains d'être de ceux
Qui aiment contre leur gré.

V

Dame, je ne vous demande qu'une chose :
Pensez-vous que ce soit péché
De tuer celui qui vous aime en vérité ?
Oui, vraiment ! Sachez-le bien !
Si cela vous plaît, alors tuez-moi,
Car je le veux et y consens,
Et si vous me préférez vivant,
Je vous le dis devant témoins,
J'en serai bien plus heureux.

VI

Dame, qui n'a pas de rivale,
Veuillez si peu que ce soit
M'accorder pitié !

VII

Renaud, Philippe, Laurent,
Ils sont maintenant cruels les mots
Qui doivent vous faire sourire.

GUILLAUME DE LORRIS

(v. 1230)

L'Art d'Amors de Guillaume de Lorris est l'œuvre la plus célèbre de la littérature courtoise. La grâce de l'expression vaut à ce code de l'amour parfait un prestige durable : les poètes des siècles suivants, jusqu'à Ronsard lui-même, y trouveront des modèles.

Celui qui parle ici à la première personne chemine gaiement un matin de mai, quand il parvient à un verger clos de murs : c'est l'*hortus conclusus*, ce symbole le plus ancien du Paradis terrestre, et le plus universel. Il va s'efforcer d'y pénétrer et d'y cueillir la Rose qui, entre toutes, l'a séduit. La promenade se fait donc quête amoureuse et ses étapes symboliques sont leçons pour tous les amants.

Ainsi le héros de ce parcours initiatique doit vaincre maint obstacle en la personne de forces mauvaises auxquelles le récit allégorique prête un visage. Mais il est secouru par les servants d'Amour, le dieu qui règne en ce jardin. En effet Jeunesse, Beauté, Courtoisie, Richesse viennent à son aide, et surtout Bel Accueil qui se propose de le conduire enfin jusqu'à la Rose aimée.

Comme on le sait, Guillaume de Lorris n'a pu (ou n'a pas voulu ?) achever son œuvre. Jean de Meung lui donnera une suite de tonalité fort différente. Mais il ne fait pas de doute que l'auteur de la première partie prévoyait un dénouement heureux. La délicatesse de ce préambule, le recours au songe dans lequel s'inscrit toute l'histoire, les couleurs que revêt ce matin de printemps enchanté d'oiseaux, tout contribue à placer le récit sous le signe des contes qui finissent bien. Cependant, et ce n'est pas là le moindre charme de son roman, l'auteur mêle, ainsi que le fera Nerval, à la description d'une nature réinventée qui a pour nous l'attrait des images rêvées, des notations empruntées au réel et qui s'imposent à la mémoire, comme le geste de ce jeune homme qui va « cousant ses manches à videle » avec une aiguille d'argent.

LE ROMAN DE LA ROSE

Ou vintiesme an de mon aage
Ou point qu'Amors prend le paage
Des jones gens, couchiez estoie
Une nuit, si cum ge souloie,
Et me dormoie moult forment ;
Si vi un songe en mon dormant,
Qui moult fu biax et moult me plot.
Mès onques riens ou songe n'ot
Qui avenu trestout ne soit
Si cum li songes devisoit.
Or voil cel songe rimaier,
Por vos cuers plus faire aguissier,
Qu'Amors le me prie et commande ;
Et se nus ne nule demande
Comment ge voil que cilz Rommans
Soit apelez que je commans,
Ce est li Rommanz de la Rose,
Ou l'art d'Amors est tote enclose.
La matire en est bone et nœve ;
Or doint Diex qu'en gré le recœve
Cele por qui ge l'ai empris ;
C'est cele qui tant a de pris
Et tant est digne d'estre amée
Qu'el doit estre Rose clamée.

Avis m'iere qu'il estoit mains
Il a ja bien V. Anz ou mais,
Qu'en may estoie, ce sonjoie,
El tens amoreus, plain de joie,
El tens ou toute rien s'esgaie
Que l'on ne voit boisson ne haie
Qui en may parer ne se vueille
Et covrir de novele fueille
Li bois recuevrent lor verdure,
Qui sont sec tant come hiver dure,

LE ROMAN DE LA ROSE

À la vingtième année de mon âge,
Au moment qu'Amour exige péage
Des jeunes gens, j'étais couché
Une nuit, comme à l'habitude,
Et je dormais profondément,
Lorsque je vis un songe en mon sommeil
Qui était fort beau et fort plaisant.
Or voilà qu'il n'est chose en ce songe
Qui ne soit entièrement advenue
Tout comme le racontait le songe.
Je veux maintenant mettre ce songe en vers
Pour vous réjouir le cœur.
C'est Amour qui m'en prie et m'en donne l'ordre,
Et si tel ou telle demande
Comment je veux que soit appelé
Ce roman que je commence,
C'est le Roman de la Rose
Où l'art d'Amour est tout entier enclos.
La matière en est bonne et nouvelle ;
Dieu accorde que l'agrée
Celle pour qui je l'ai entrepris ;
C'est celle qui a tant de prix
Et qui est si digne d'être aimée
Qu'elle doit être Rose appelée.

Il me semblait que c'était le matin,
Il y a bien cinq ans pour le moins.
Je rêvais que j'étais en mai,
Au temps des amours, rempli de joie,
Au temps où toute chose s'égaye,
Car l'on ne voit buisson ni haie
Qui en mai parer ne se veuille
Et couvrir de nouvelle feuille.
Les bois recouvrent leur verdure,
Eux qui sont secs tant que l'hiver dure.

La terre meïsmes s'orgueille
Por la roses qui la mueille,
Et oublie la povreté
Ou ele a tot hiver esté ;
Lors devient la terre si gobe
Qu'el velt avoir novele robe,
Si set si cointe robe feire
Que de colors i a c. Peire ;
L'erbe et les flors blanches et perses
Et de maintes colors diverses
C'est la robe que je devise,
Por quoi la terre mielz se prise.
Li oisel qui se sont teü
Tant come il ont le froit eü
Et le tens divers et frarin,
Sont en may por le tens serin
Si lié qu'il mostrent en chantant
Qu'en lor cuers a de joie tant
Qu'il lor estuet chanter par force.
Li rosignox lores s'esforce
De chanter et de feire noise ;
Lors se déduit et lors s'envoise
Li papegauz et la Kalandre ;
Lors estuet joines gens entendre
À estre gais et amoureus
Por le tens bel et doucereus.
Mout a dur cuer qui en mai n'aime,
Quant il ot chanter sus la raime
As oisiaus les douz chans piteus.

En icelui tens deliteus
Que toute rien d'amer s'esfroie
Songai une nuit que j'estoie.
Lors m'iere avis en mon dormant
Qu'il iere matin durement ;
De mon lit tantost me levé
Chauçai moi et mes mains lavé ;
Lors très une aiguille d'argent
D'un aguillier mignot et gent,

La terre même tire orgueil
De la rosée qui la mouille
Et oublie la misère
Où elle a été tout l'hiver ;
Alors la terre devient si fière
Qu'elle veut avoir robe nouvelle ;
Elle sait alors se faire robe si belle
Qu'elle a des couleurs par centaines ;
L'herbe et les fleurs blanches et bleues
Et de maintes couleurs diverses,
Voilà la robe dont je parle
Et qui donne à la terre plus haute estime.
Les oiseaux, qui se sont tus
Aussi longtemps qu'ils ont subi le froid
Et le temps changeant et sauvage,
Sont en mai, grâce au temps serein,
Si joyeux qu'ils montrent en chantant
Qu'il y a tant de joie en leur cœur
Qu'il leur faut chanter à toute force.
Le rossignol s'évertue alors
À chanter et mener grand ramage ;
Alors se divertissent et s'amusent
Le perroquet et l'alouette ;
Alors il faut que les jeunes gens pensent
À la gaieté et à l'amour
Puisque le temps est beau et doux.
Il a le cœur bien dur celui qui n'aime en mai
Quand il entend sous la ramée
Les oiseaux pousser leurs doux chants plaintifs.

C'est en ce temps délicieux
Où toute chose est en émoi d'amour
Que j'étais, une nuit, en songe.
Il me semblait en mon sommeil
Qu'il était grand matin.
Je me levai aussitôt de mon lit,
Me chaussai, me lavai les mains ;
Puis je tirai une aiguille d'argent
D'un fin et bel étui,

Si prins l'aguille a enfiler.
Hors de ville oi talant d'aler
Por oïr des oisiaus les sons
Qui chantent dessus les boissons
En icele saison novele.
Cousant mes manches a videle,
M'en vois lors tout sol esbatant
Et les oiseleiz escoutant
Qui de chanter mout s'esjoissoient
Por les vergers qui florissaient.
Jolis, gais et pleins de leesce,
Vers une rivière m'adreice
Que j'oï près d'ilecques bruire,
Car ne me soi aler deduire
Plus bel que sus cele rivière.
D'un tertre qui pres d'ilec iere
Descendait l'eve grant et roide.
Clere estoit l'eve, et aussi froide
Come puis ou come fontaine ;
Si estoit poi maindre de Saine
Mes elle estoit plus espandue.
Onques mes n'avoie veüe
Cele eve qui si bien corroit,
Si m'abelissoit et seoit
À esgarder le leu pleisant.

Et me mis à enfiler l'aiguille.
J'avais envie de sortir de la ville
Pour entendre le concert des oiseaux
Qui chantent au milieu des buissons
En cette saison nouvelle.
Tout en laçant mes manches ajourées,
Je m'en fus tout seul en musardant
Et en écoutant les oiselets
Qui s'égosillaient à chanter
Par les vergers en fleurs.
De bonne humeur, gai et plein de liesse,
Je me dirigeai vers une rivière
Que j'entendais bruire tout près de là.
Je ne pouvais trouver ébat
Plus beau que sur cette rivière.
D'un tertre qui était près de là
Descendait l'eau droit et dru.
Claire était l'eau, et aussi froide
Que celle d'un puits ou d'une fontaine.
Le cours en était moins abondant que la Seine,
Mais il était plus large.
Je n'avais jamais vu
Eau de si belle apparence.
Aussi était-ce enchantement
De regarder ce lieu plaisant.

AUCASSIN ET NICOLETTE

(1ʳᵉ moitié du XIIIᵉ siècle)

Parmi tant de poèmes dont l'auteur nous est resté inconnu, une œuvre a toujours suscité l'admiration, c'est *Aucassin et Nicolette*. Comme le précise l'avant-dernier vers : (« no [notre] cantefable prend fin »), c'est une chantefable, genre dont notre littérature ne nous offre pas d'autre exemple. L'auteur présente ce récit romanesque où alternent laisses et passages de prose comme un divertissement pour « le Viel antif », le vieux bonhomme qu'il est. Ce qui ne nous renseigne guère sur lui, mais on sait que ce surnom est celui du cheval de Roland ! Son goût de la parodie, la caricature d'épisodes obligés des romans d'aventures, les pastiches de Chrétien de Troyes, sont encore des signes de sa malice et de son ironie, ils nous fournissent aussi quelques indications sur le milieu culturel dont il est issu.

Cette chantefable conte une histoire d'amour entre deux jeunes gens que tout sépare. Nicolette n'est qu'une obscure captive rachetée à des Sarrasins, lui est le fils du comte de Beaucaire. Malgré les obstacles, les interdictions du comte et la prison où l'on jette la jeune fille, ils fuient ensemble. Un épisode heureux dans un royaume imaginaire marque un répit dans leurs aventures, puis ils sont de nouveau brutalement séparés. Enfin, après d'innombrables péripéties, Aucassin rentre seul dans son pays et devient comte de Beaucaire, il pleure toujours Nicolette. Celle-ci, bien qu'on ait reconnu en elle la fille du roi de Carthage, s'est enfuie pour rejoindre son ami. Elle lui impose une dernière épreuve. Déguisée en jongleur, le visage noirci, elle lui conte l'histoire de leurs amours. Devant les larmes d'Aucassin, elle se démasque. Et le conte s'arrête, car, dit l'auteur : « N'en sai plu que dire. » Les thèmes dominants sont ici le pouvoir de l'amour qui fait oublier au jeune homme ses devoirs de chevalier ou mépriser insolemment les menaces d'enfer que lui fait son père, mais aussi la supériorité de la femme. C'est elle qui mène le jeu ; à elle les initiatives hardies, évasion, fuite, embarquement, jusqu'au déguisement final. Le mélange du romanesque poétique et d'éléments réalistes ou pittoresques dévolus aux passages contés, la vivacité du récit, l'émotion mêlée d'un sourire, l'humour de l'auteur, confèrent à cette œuvre un charme inaltéré à travers les siècles.

I

Qui vauroit bons vers oïr
del deport du viel antif
de deus biax enfans petits,
Nicholete et Aucassins,
des grans paines qu'il soufri
et des proueces qu'il fist
por s'amie o le cler vis ?
Dox est li cans, biax li dis
et cortois et bien asis.
Nus hom n'est si esbahis,
tant dolans ni entrepris,
de grant mal amaladis,
se il l'oit, ne soit garis
et de joie resbaudis,
tant par est douce.

V

or se cante

Nicole est en prison mise
en une canbre vautie
ki faite est par grant devisse,
panturee a miramie.
À la fenestre marbrine
la s'apoia la mescine.
Ele avoit blonde la crigne
et bien faite la sorcille,
la face clere et traitice :
ainc plus bele ne veïstes.
Esgarda par le gaudine
et vit la rose espanie
et les oisax qui s'ecrient,
dont se clama orphenine:

I

Qui aimerait entendre de bons vers
– Divertissement du grand âge –
Sur deux beaux jeunes gens,
Nicolette et Aucassin,
Sur les grandes peines qu'il souffrit
Et les prouesses qu'il accomplit
Pour son amie au clair visage ?
Le chant est doux, beau le récit,
Courtois et bien composé :
Personne n'est si abattu,
Si affligé, si mal en point
Si gravement atteint
Qu'il ne soit guéri à l'ouïr
Et de joie ragaillardi,
Tant cette histoire est douce.

V

chanté

Nicole est mise en prison
Dans une chambre voûtée
Qui est faite avec grand art,
Couverte de merveilleuses fresques.
À la fenêtre de marbre
S'appuya la jeune fille ;
Elle avait les cheveux blonds
Et bien dessinés les sourcils,
Le visage clair et bien fait.
Jamais vous n'en vîtes de plus beau.
Elle regarda dans le parc
Et vit la rose épanouie
Et les oiseaux qui chantent.
Alors elle se sentit abandonnée :

« Ai mi ! lasse moi, caitive !
por coi sui en prison misse ?
Aucassins, damoisiax sire,
ja sui jou li vostre amie
et vos ne me haés mie !
Por vos sui en prison misse
en ceste canbre vautie
u je trai molt male vie ;
mais, par Diu le fil Marie,
longement n'i serai mie,
se jel puis far. »

VII

or se cante

Aucasins s'en est tornés
molt dolans et abosmés :
De s'amie o le vis cler
nus ne le puet conforter
ne nul bon consel doner.
Vers le palais est alés,
il en monta les degrés,
en une canbre est entrés,
si comença a plorer
et grant dol a demener
et s'amie a regreter :
« Nicolete, biax esters,
biax venir et biax alers,
biax deduis et dous parlers,
biax borders et biax jouers,
biax baisiers, biax acolers,
por vos sui si adolés
et si malement menés
que je n'en cuit vis aler,
suer, douce amie. »

« Hélas ! Malheureuse que je suis, captive !
Pourquoi m'a-t-on mise en prison ?
Aucassin, jeune seigneur,
Certes je suis votre amie
Et vous ne me haïssez pas !
C'est pour vous que je suis en prison
Dans cette chambre voûtée
Où je mène une vie misérable ;
Mais par Dieu, le fils de Marie,
Je n'y resterai pas longtemps,
Si j'en viens à mes fins. »

VII
chanté

Aucassin s'en est retourné
Tout en peine et abattu.
De son amie au clair visage
Nul ne peut le consoler
Ni lui donner un bon conseil.
Il est allé vers le palais,
Il en a monté l'escalier,
En une chambre il est entré,
Et là il s'est mis à pleurer,
À mener grand deuil
Et son amie regretter :
« Nicolette, belle au repos,
Belle dans l'aller et le venir,
Belle au jeu et douce en paroles,
Belle dans la taquinerie gentille,
Belle en vos baisers, belle en vos étreintes,
À cause de vous je suis si affligé
Et si cruellement traité
Que je crois que j'en mourrai,
Ma sœur, ma douce amie. »

XXV

or se cante

« Estoilete, je te voi,
que la lune trait a soi.
Nicolete est aveuc toi,
m'amïete o le blont poil.
Je quid Dix le veut avoir
por la lu [mier] e de s [oir]
[que par li plus bele soit.
Douce suer, com me plairoit
se monter pooie droit,]
que que fust du recaoir,
que fuisse lassus o toi !
Ja te baiseroie estroit.
Se j'estoie fix a roi,
s'afferriés vos bien a moi,
suer, douce amie. »

XXV
chanté

Petite étoile, je te vois,
Que la lune attire à soi.
Nicolette est avec toi,
Ma petite amie aux cheveux blonds.
Je crois que Dieu veut l'avoir
Pour que la lumière du soir
Par elle soit plus belle.
Douce sœur, comme je serais heureux
Si je pouvais monter tout droit,
Au risque de retomber,
Pourvu que je sois là-haut avec toi.
Je t'embrasserais tendrement.
Même si j'étais fils de roi,
Vous me conviendriez parfaitement,
Ma sœur, ma douce amie. »

RUTEBEUF

(v. 1230 - v. 1283)

Un grand poète clôt cette période du Moyen Âge, c'est Rutebeuf, que l'on situe approximativement entre les années 30 et les années 80 du treizième siècle. Son inspiration est variée ; il compose des poèmes religieux aussi bien que satiriques et son œuvre comprend des poèmes de commande et d'autres qu'anime une inspiration personnelle. Il a visiblement le savoir d'un clerc et se montre sensible aux débats de son temps ainsi qu'aux événements contemporains. Mais la précarité de sa condition de jongleur lui vaut l'expérience de la misère et ne laisse pas de place chez lui à l'esthétique et l'éthique courtoises. C'est pourquoi il sort des conventions et des modèles sur lesquels le génie ou le talent des poètes médiévaux s'est plu à broder à l'infini. Il fait entendre une voix différente.

Dans les *Poèmes de l'infortune* dont on lira ici un passage, on peut voir, comme l'écrit Jean Dufournet, « une vertigineuse litanie toujours recommencée » de la pauvreté ou du malheur. S'agit-il d'un ressassement quasi morbide ou de l'exploitation quelque peu cynique d'une veine susceptible d'attendrir les riches protecteurs dont il dépend ? Il est difficile de le dire. Quoi qu'il en soit, ces thèmes confèrent à l'œuvre une unité que renforce le recours fréquent à l'auto-dérision et à une sorte d'humour désespéré. Lorsqu'il s'accuse d'être responsable de ses malheurs, il semble sincère, puisqu'il le fait encore dans la confession inquiète de la *Repentance*. Cet examen de conscience n'est pas sans rappeler l'*Examen de Minuit* de Baudelaire :

Nous avons, pour plaire à la brute,
Digne vassale des Démons
Insulté ce que nous aimons
Et flatté ce qui nous rebute

lorsque Rutebeuf avoue :

J'ai fet rimes et s'ai chanté
Sors les uns por aus autres plaire
Dont Anemis m'a enchanté.

LA GRIESCHE D'YVER

Contre le tens qu'arbre desfueille,
Qu'il ne remaint en branche fueille
  Qui n'aut a terre,
Por povreté qui moi aterre,
Qui de toutes pars me muet guerre,
  Contre l'yver,
Dont moult me sont changié li ver,
Mon dit commence trop diver
  De povre estoire.
Povre sens et povre memoire
M'a Diex doné, li rois de gloire,
  Et povre rente,
Et froit au cul quant bise vente :
Li vens me vient, li vens m'esvente
  Et trop sovent
Plusors foies sent le vent.
Bien le m'ot griesche en covent
  Quanques me livre :
Bien me paie, bien me delivre,
Contre le sout me rent la livre
  De grant poverte.
Povretez est sor moi reverte :
Toz jors m'en est la porte ouverte,
  Toz jors i sui
Ne nule foiz ne m'en eschui.
Par pluie moil, par chaut essui :
  Ci a riche homme !
Je ne dorm que le premier somme.
De mon avoir ne sai la somme,
  Qu'il n'i a point.
Diex me fet le tens si a point :
Noire mousche en esté me point,
  En yver blanche.

LE GUIGNON D'HIVER

Au temps où l'arbre s'effeuille,
Qu'il ne reste sur branche feuille
        Qui n'aille à terre,
Sous le coup de pauvreté qui me met à terre,
Qui de tous côtés me fait la guerre,
        Au temps d'hiver
Qui donne un autre ton à mes vers,
Je commence mon dit inconsistant
        Vu sa pauvre substance.
Pauvre sens et pauvre mémoire
M'a donnés Dieu, le roi de gloire,
        Et pauvre rente,
Et froid au cul quand bise vente :
Le vent me vient dessus, le vent m'évente
        Et trop souvent
À maintes reprises je sens le vent.
Grièche [1] m'avait bien promis
        Tout ce qu'elle me livre
Elle me paie bien, s'acquitte bien,
Pour un sou me rend une livre
        De grande pauvreté.
Pauvreté est sur moi revenue :
Toujours sa porte m'est ouverte,
        Toujours j'y suis
Et jamais ne m'en esquive.
Mouillé s'il pleut, au sec s'il fait chaud :
        Voyez ma richesse !
Je ne dors que le premier sommeil.
De mon avoir j'ignore la somme :
        Car je n'en ai point.
Dieu me donne saison bien à point :
En été me pique la mouche noire,
        En hiver c'est la blanche.

_____

1. malheur.

Issi sui com l'osiere franche
Ou com li oisiaus seur la branche :
    En esté chante,
En yver plor et me gaimante,
Et me desfuel ausi com l'ente
    Au premier giel.
En moi n'a ne venin ne fiel :
Il ne me remaint rien souz ciel.
    Tout va sa voie.

Je suis comme l'osier sauvage
Ou comme l'oiseau sur la branche :
 En été je chante,
En hiver je pleure et me lamente,
Et me dépouille comme arbre greffé
 Au premier gel.
Il n'y a en moi ni venin ni fiel :
Il ne me reste rien sous le ciel :
 Tout est dans l'ordre.

LA COMPLAINTE DE RUTEBEUF

. . . .
Le mal ne sevent seul venir ;
Tout ce m'estoit a avenir,
    S'est avenu.
Que sont mi ami devenu
Que j'avoie si pres tenu
    Et tant amé ?
Je cuit qu'il sont trop cler semé ;
Il ne furent pas bien femé,
    Si sont failli.
Itel ami m'ont mal bailli,
C'onques, tant com Diex m'assailli
    En maint coste,
N'en vu un seul en mon osté.
Je cuit le vens les m'a osté,
    L'amor est morte :
Ce sont ami que vens enporte,
Et il ventoit devant ma porte,
    Ses emporta,
C'onques nus ne m'en conforta
Ne du sien riens ne m'aporta.
    Ice m'aprent
Qui auques a, privé le prent ;
Més cil trop a tart se repent
    Qui trop a mis
De son avoir por fere amis,
Qu'il nes trueve entiers ne demis
    A lui secorre.
Or lerai donc Fortune corre
Si entendrai a moi rescorre
    Se jel puis fere.

LA COMPLAINTE DE RUTEBEUF

. . . .
Un malheur ne vient jamais seul :
Tout cela devait m'arriver,
   Et c'est arrivé.
Que sont mes amis devenus,
Que j'avais si près tenus
   Et tant aimés ?
Je crois qu'ils sont trop clairsemés ;
Ils n'ont pas été assez fumés,
   Aussi les voilà disparus.
De tels amis m'ont mal traité,
Car jamais, tant que Dieu me frappa
   De maints côtés,
Je n'en vis un seul en ma maison.
Le vent, je crois, me les a enlevés,
   L'amitié est morte.
Ce sont amis que vent emporte,
Le vent soufflait devant ma porte
   Et il les emporta.
Car jamais aucun ne me réconforta
Ni ne m'a fait le moindre don.
   J'en retiens
Que le peu qu'on a un ami le prend ;
Et il se repent trop tard
   Celui qui a trop mis
De son bien pour gagner des amis,
Car il n'en trouve pas la moitié d'un
   Pour lui porter secours.
Maintenant je laisserai donc courir la Fortune
Je m'appliquerai à me porter secours à moi-même
   Si j'en suis capable.

XIVe-XVe SIÈCLES

La poésie des XIVe et XVe siècles est dominée par l'art de ceux que l'on nomme les Rhétoriqueurs. Ce sont des poètes conscients des règles de l'art poétique, et soucieux de les respecter, voire de les multiplier. Ils élisent et développent les genres à forme fixe qui existaient mais qu'ils pratiquent avec une rigueur nouvelle.

Ainsi le rondeau, dont on peut penser que l'origine est folklorique (la chanson enfantine et ses refrains), devient à cette époque un poème aux règles assez strictes. Il est d'abord apparu dans le nord de la France sous sa forme la plus simple : il est fait de strophes de quatre vers dont les deux derniers sont chaque fois identiques. Puis il évolue vers le modèle qui domine dans l'œuvre de Charles d'Orléans : en tête des trois quatrains qui le composent se trouvent obligatoirement les deux vers du refrain, ils deviennent le troisième et quatrième vers du deuxième quatrain, puis seul le premier d'entre eux réapparaît à la fin de la troisième strophe où il vient fermer la ronde et déguiser le quatrain en quintil.

De même le virelai, déjà connu, prend chez les Rhétoriqueurs la forme régulière d'un poème cyclique dont la base est constituée de cinq couplets. Ceux-ci commencent par le refrain sur deux rimes, lui-même est composé le plus souvent de cinq vers. Puis viennent deux tercets, l'un ouvert, l'autre fermé, dont les rimes sont conformes aux précédentes. Ensuite une quatrième strophe reproduit exactement la composition et les rimes de la première, avec un texte différent. Enfin le refrain initial clôt le cycle. Cet agencement est reproduit autant de fois qu'il plaît au poète, cependant le refrain de ce « lai qui vire » n'apparaît plus, après le premier énoncé, qu'à la fin de chaque cycle et non plus au début.

Quant à la ballade qu'ils ont tous pratiquée, elle est faite de strophes qui s'achèvent sur un même refrain. Elle naît du huitain sur trois rimes tel que le pratique Guillaume de Machaut : la répétition du dernier vers dans chacune des strophes constitue sa forme primitive. Elle devient ensuite un poème de trois strophes que vient clore une clausule de quatre vers. L'usage se répand de faire de ces quatre vers un « envoi », c'est-à-dire une adresse à un destinataire, généralement un prince, et pour cela les quatre vers commencent par un vocatif, Prince, Sire, Seigneur...

Une forme plus noble encore, celle de la grande ballade, offre trois strophes de dix vers et un quintil final rimant sur quatre rimes comme dans l'épitaphe de Villon.

À ce souci d'un code poétique des formes s'ajoute celui d'une maîtrise des mots qui amène ces poètes à des jeux subtils avec le langage. Pour ceux d'entre eux qu'on nomme les grands Rhétoriqueurs, ces subtilités sont, plutôt qu'un jeu, un effort plus ou moins conscient pour conquérir un savoir nouveau. Paul Zumthor en donne l'interprétation suivante : « Au sein d'un monde princier qui faisait profession d'immutabilité et où toute existence spontanément tournait en spectacle, les rhétoriqueurs tentèrent de faire, du langage même, dans la matérialité de ses structures propres (sonores, lexicales, rythmiques), le seul spectacle vrai et le seul acteur... c'est à rien de moins qu'à la déconstruction du discours poétique traditionnel (aussi contraignant que les rites de la Cour) qu'humblement ils travaillaient. »

Cependant, cette anthologie n'a rien retenu d'œuvre de ces poètes. On ne lira pas ici Meschinot, Molinet, Robertet, Lemaire, Saint Gelays, Cretin pour ne citer que les plus célèbres d'entre eux. Ces mal aimés de notre littérature, même si l'on tend à leur rendre justice, déroutent souvent le lecteur par leur formalisme, et les performances verbales ou rythmiques de leurs œuvres étonnent plus qu'elles ne séduisent. Du XIVe siècle (et du XVe auquel tous appartiennent), on n'a retenu que quelques poètes dont l'œuvre est pour nous plus « sensible au cœur ». Aucun d'eux pourtant n'est tout à fait étranger à la « rhétorique », c'est-à-dire à la conviction que des lois régissent l'art de poésie, qu'on ne peut se passer d'elles et qu'il convient de les connaître et de les observer. Les plus grands d'entre eux n'ont pas dédaigné même les jeux poétiques les plus formels dont les contraintes arbitraires, loin d'entraver leur lyrisme personnel, leur paraissaient propres à le stimuler.

EUSTACHE DESCHAMPS

(v. 1340 - v. 1407)

Il est à la fois le poète le plus prolixe du Moyen Âge (il composa plus de 80 000 vers) et le théoricien auquel on doit le premier traité de poétique et l'un des plus importants : *L'Art de dictier*. Il y décrit en prose ce que doit être la poésie : recherche du mot rare et de la rime difficile, définissant ainsi l'art des Rhétoriqueurs, et il pourrait être considéré comme le premier d'entre eux, s'il ne donnait déjà ce titre au très grand musicien et poète dont il est le disciple, Guillaume de Machaut. Sans être musicien lui-même il pratique les mêmes formes que son maître, le rondeau, le virelai et surtout la ballade, mais ses œuvres ne semblent pas faites pour être chantées.

Une part importante de celles-ci est consacrée à des sujets de circonstance. Il y peint la cour à laquelle l'attache sa fonction d' « écuyer et huissier d'armes du Roi ». Il y évoque les pays qu'il a pu voir durant ses voyages :

> *Quand j'ai la terre et mer avironnée*
> *Et visité en chacune partie*
> *Jérusalem, Égypte et Galilée,*
> *Alexandrie, Damas et la Syrie*
> *Babylone, Le Caire et Tartarie...*
> *Valent trop mieux ce que les Français ont :*
> *Rien ne se peut comparer à Paris.*

Il se fait aussi l'écho des grands événements de son temps, mais ne dédaigne pas de parler des soucis quotidiens avec une verve moqueuse et une vision pessimiste de l'homme. Ce qui le caractérise c'est le recours constant à une sagesse pratique tirée de l'expérience. On le voit dans ses *Ballades de moralités*. S'il est capable aussi de célébrer les exploits de Du Guesclin ou faire son éloge funèbre avec lyrisme, sa poésie marque presque toujours une nette rupture avec l'inspiration aristocratique qui prévalait avant lui.

Les poèmes retenus ici montrent, pour le premier d'entre eux, qu'éloquence rhétorique et inspiration peuvent se conjuguer, pour le suivant que le poète sait donner au lieu commun du memento mori une résonance personnelle. Enfin la fable citée témoigne de ses qualités de fabuliste et de sa malice goguenarde.

Adieu printemps, adieu jeune saison,
Que tous déduiz[1] sont dus à créature.
Adieu Amours, adieu noble maison,
Pleine jadis de fleurs et de verdure.
Adieu été, automne qui peu dure :
Hiver me vient, c'est-à-dire vieillesse,
Pour ce, triste, te dis adieu, Jeunesse.

De printemps puis faire comparaison
Jusqu'à seize ans que notre enfance dure,
Que les biens sont à petit d'achoison[2]
Pour leur tendreur[3] mis en déconfiture ;
Si sommes-nous : par un peu de froidure
Peu de meschief[4] en cet âge nous blesse,
Pour ce, triste, te dis adieu, Jeunesse.

Été nourrit et croît selon raison
Vignes et blés et tous biens de nature ;
Lors croît aussi et prend des forces l'hom(me) :
Autres XVI ans l'a Jeunesse en sa cure.
Les biens requeult automne si figure[5]
Par les XVI ans ; d'autant l'hiver m'oppresse,
Pour ce, triste, te dis adieu, Jeunesse.

---

1. plaisirs. — 2. à la moindre occasion. — 3. fragilité. — 4. le plus petit désagrément. — 5. l'automne récolte ces biens et représente aussi seize années.

Puissant défaillant de puissance [1],
Sage où il n'y a point de sens,
Vaillant qui manque de vaillance,
Orgueilleux d'orgueil défaillant [2],
Riche de richesses faillant [3],
Qui dois par nature pourrir.
Corps corrompable et corrumpant [4],
Avise qu'il te faut mourir.

Au naître cries la pesance [5]
Du monde, et si n'es innocent :
Toi et ta mort tantôt commence ;
Ton âge est bref et pesant
Qui ne peut passer LX ans,
Et encore est-ce au mieux venir,
Et les plusieurs meurent enfants :
Avise qu'il te faut mourir.

Certaineté [6] n'as en science,
Tu n'es en force permanent,
En seigneurie, en éloquence,
En richesse : ce n'est que vent
Du monde qui est décevant ;
Tantôt te fait la mort finir.
Où est Olivier et Roland ?
Avise qu'il te faut mourir.

Envoi

Prince, qui fait bien dès l'enfance
Sans mal et sans s'enorgueillir,
Sage est, qui à la fin pense :
Avise qu'il te faut mourir.

---

1. à qui la puissance manque. — 2. manquant. — 3. privé. — 4. corruptible et corrompu. — 5. le fardeau. — 6. certitude.

LE CHAT ET LA SOURIS

Je trouve qu'entre les souris
Eut un merveilleux parlement [1]
Contre les chats leurs ennemis
À veoir [2] manière comment
Elles vécussent sûrement
Sans demeurer en tel débat [3] ;
L'une dit alors en arguant [4] :
« Qui pendra la sonnette au chat ? »

Ce conseil fut conclu et pris ;
Lors se partent communément [5].
Une souris du plat pays
Les rencontre, et va demandant
Qu'on a fait [6]. Lors vont répondant
Que leurs ennemis seront mat [7].
Sonnette auront au cou pendant :
« Qui pendra la sonnette au chat ? »

– C'est le plus fort [8], dit un rat gris.
Elle demande sagement
Par qui sera ce fait fourni [9].
Lors s'en va chacune excusant :
Il n'y eut point d'exécutant,
S'en va leur besogne de plat [10].
Bien fut dit, mais au demeurant,
« Qui pendra la sonnette au chat ? »

Envoi

Prince, on conseille bien souvent,
Mais on peut dire, comme le rat,
Du conseil qui sa fin ne prend :
« Qui pendra la sonnette au chat ? »

---

1. délibération. — 2. voir. — 3. difficulté. — 4. en raisonnant. — 5. se séparent. — 6. ce qu'on a fait. — 7. vaincus. — 8. c'est le point délicat. — 9. accompli. — 10. leur entreprise tombe à plat.

CHRISTINE DE PISAN

(1361-v. 1430)

On peut l'évoquer avec le mot de Nerval : elle est
« l'inconsolée », à cause du plus célèbre de ses poèmes, véritable
litanie de la solitude. Très jeune elle a perdu un mari qu'elle
aimait et sa mélancolie se devine même lorsqu'elle parvient à
dissimuler sa tristesse et à s'exprimer sur un ton de gaieté
apparente. S'il lui arrive de parler de l'amour, il ne s'agit que d'un
jeu d'esprit. Elle s'en explique à propos du recueil des *Cent
Ballades* :

> *Aucuns gens pourraient méjuger*
> *Pour ce sur moi que je fais dits d'amour.*
> . . . .
> *Mais d'Amour je n'ai tourment*
> *Joie ni deuil.*

La diversité de ses talents poétiques et son savoir d'érudite lui
permettent de composer dans les formes les plus diverses, des
plus légères, telles que les lais, virelais ou rondeaux, jusqu'aux
plus graves. C'est son *Épître au Dieu d'Amour* qui ouvre la
controverse qu'on voit se développer autour du *Roman de la Rose*.
Elle y interviendra à plusieurs reprises pour prendre la défense
des femmes. Mais elle sait aussi, malgré sa gravité naturelle,
inventer de ces *Jeux à vendre* dont la règle oblige chaque
partenaire à lancer à tour de rôle le nom d'une fleur ou d'un objet
sur lequel l'autre doit répondre par un compliment ou une
épigramme rimée. Elle excelle dans ce divertissement d'une grâce

toute naïve et on lui doit soixante-dix de ces poèmes. C'est tous ces dons qui lui valent la faveur dont elle jouit auprès de très puissants protecteurs comme le duc de Berry ou la reine Isabelle de Bavière. Elle est sans doute la première femme de lettres à vivre de sa plume grâce à la générosité de ceux auxquels elle dédie ses œuvres.

Seulette suis et seulette veux être,
Seulette m'a mon doux ami laissée,
Seulette suis, sans compagnon ni maître,
Seulette suis, dolente et courroucée,
Seulette suis en langueur mesaisée [1],
Seulette suis, plus que nulle égarée [2],
Seulette suis, sans ami demeurée.

Seulette suis à huis ou à fenêtre,
Seulette suis en un anglet muciée [3],
Seulette suis pour moi de pleurs repaître,
Seulette suis, dolente ou apaisée ;
Seulette suis, rien n'est qui tant me siée [4]
Seulette suis, en ma chambre enserrée,
Seulette suis, sans ami demeurée.

Seulette suis partout et en tout estre [5],
Seulette suis, ou je voise ou je siée [6],
Seulette suis plus qu'autre rien terrestre [7],
Seulette suis, de chacun délaissée,
Seulette suis, durement abaissée,
Seulette suis, souvent toute éplorée,
Seulette suis, sans ami demeurée.

Envoi

Prince, or est ma douleur commencée :
Seulette suis, de tout deuil menacée,
Seulette suis plus teinte que morée [8],
Seulette suis sans ami demeurée.

---

1. mal à l'aise. — 2. perdue. — 3. cachée. — 4. déplaît. — 5. endroit. —
6. que j'aille ou que je sois assise. — 7. plus qu'autre chose au monde. —
8. plus sombre qu'une tenture noire.

Je ne sais comment je dure,
Car mon dolent cœur fond d'ire [1]
Et plaindre n'ose, ni dire
Ma douloureuse aventure,

Ma dolente vie obscure.
Rien fors la mort ne désire.
Je ne sais comment je dure.

Et me faut, par couverture,
Chanter quand mon cœur soupire ;
Et faire semblant de rire.
Mais Dieu sait ce que j'endure ;
Je ne sais comment je dure.

---

1. colère. Ici, plutôt irritation.

JEUX À VENDRE

Je vous vends la passerose.
– Belle, dire ne vous ose
Comment Amour vers vous me tire,
Si l'apercevez tout sans dire.

Je vous vends la feuille tremblant.
– Maint faux amants, par leur semblant
Font grand mensonge sembler voire [1],
Si ne doit-on mie tout croire.

Je vous vends la turterelle.
– Seulette et toute à part elle
Sans per [2] s'envole égarée ;
Ainsi suis-je demeurée
Dont jamais n'aurai joie
Pour nulle chose que j'ois.

Je vous vends le songe amoureux,
Qui fait joyeux ou douloureux
Être celui qui l'a songé.
– Ma dame, le songe que j'ai
Fait la nuit, ferez être voir [3],
Si je puis votre amour avoir.

---

1. vérité. — 2. sans compagnon. — 3. être vrai.

ALAIN CHARTIER

(1385-1430)

La Belle Dame sans merci est une longue narration en vers. On y voit le poète chevaucher tristement : il pense à la maîtresse que la mort lui a ravie. Il lui faut sans doute renoncer désormais à célébrer l'amour. (« Désormais est temps de moi taire / Car de dire je suis lassé. ») Cependant une rencontre imprévue va l'amener à témoigner encore sur l'amour, mais d'une autre façon, ce sera pour dire la faiblesse de son pouvoir. Dans le lieu où il fait étape, se déroule une fête. Bien des couples joyeux s'y rencontrent, mais le poète s'intéresse surtout à un homme dont la tristesse fait pressentir qu'il doit être un amant malheureux. Il va, bien malgré lui, l'entendre se plaindre à sa dame de l'indifférence qu'elle lui manifeste. La scène a lieu dans le jardin où le poète s'est réfugié. Une treille le dissimule aux regards, il devient l'acteur invisible et le témoin involontaire de ce débat entre l'indifférence et l'amour. La belle est inflexible et répond par des railleries aux propos de l'amant. Tout galant est à ses yeux infidèle et vantard, c'est-à-dire capable de perdre de réputation celle qu'il prétend aimer.

Le poète qui rapporte leurs propos conclut en donnant des conseils aux amoureux.

Si ce poème connaît une célébrité immédiate, ce n'est ni à la forme choisie qu'il le doit (le huitain d'octosyllabes n'innove pas), ni peut-être à la grâce constante de ses cent strophes. S'il est souvent cité et imité en son temps et jusqu'au seizième siècle, et souvent critiqué aussi, c'est pour avoir osé proposer l'image d'une femme cruelle et insensible, si contraire aux conventions établies.

LA BELLE DAME SANS MERCI

. . . .

I

Naguère, chevauchant, pensois
Comme homme triste et douloureux,
Au deuil où il faut que je sois
Le plus dolent des amoureux,
Puisque, par son dard rigoureux,
La mort me toulit [1] ma maîtresse
Et me laissa seul, langoureux,
En la conduite de Tristesse.

II

Si disais : « Il faut que je cesse
De ditter et de rimoyer [2]
Et que j'abandonne et délaisse
Le rire pour le larmoyer.
Là me faut le temps employer,
Car plus n'ai sentiment ni aise,
Soit d'écrire soit d'envoyer
Chose qu'à moi n'à d'autre plaise. »

V

« Désormais est temps de moi taire
Car de dire je suis lassé,
Je veux laisser aux autres faire,
Leur temps est, le mien est passé,
Fortune a le forcier cassé [3]
Où j'épargnoie ma richesse
Et le bien que j'ai amassé
Au meilleur temps de ma jeunesse. »

---

1. m'enleva. — 2. de composer et de rimer. — 3. coffre.

VI

« Amour a gouverné mon sens,
Si faute y a, Dieu me pardonne.
Si j'ai bien fait, plus ne m'en sens,
Cela ne me toult'[1] ne me donne
Car au trépas de la très bonne
Tout mon bien fait se trépassa.
La mort m'assit illec[2] la borne
Qu'onques puis mon cuer ne passa. »

XCV

L'amant

« Puisque de grâce tout seul mot
De votre rigoureux cœur n'yst[3],
J'appelle devant Dieu qui m'ot[4]
De vo durté qui me honnist[5]
Et me plains qu'il ne parfornist[6]
Pitié qu'en vous il oublia,
Ou que ma vie ne finist[7]
Que si tôt mis en oubli a. »

XCVI

La Dame

« Mon cœur et moi ne vous feismes[8]
Onc rien dont plaindre vos doyez[9].
Rien ne vous nuit fors vous meismes[10].
De vous même juge soyez.
Une fois pour toutes croyez
Que vous demourrez escondit[11].
De tant redire m'ennuyez,
Car je vous en ai assez dit. »

---

1. prive. — 2. la mort a posé là... — 3. ne sort. — 4. m'entend. — 5. de votre dureté qui me raille. — 6. qu'il n'ait pas mis en vous. — 7. n'ait pas fini. — 8. fimes. — 9. deviez. — 10. sinon vous-même. — 11. que vous resterez éconduit.

XCVII

L'Acteur

Adonc le dolent se leva
À part de la fête et pleurant.
À peu [1] que son cœur ne creva
Comme a homme qui va mourant.
Et dit : « Mort, viens à moi courant
Ains que mon sens se décognoisse [2],
Et m'abrège le demourant [3]
De ma vie pleine d'angoisse. »

XCVIII

Depuis je ne sus qu'il devint
Ni de quel part se transporta.
Mais à sa dame n'en souvint
Qui aux danses se déporta.
Et depuis on me rapporta
Qu'il avait ses cheveux déroups [4]
Et que tant se déconforta
Qu'il en était mort de courroux.

C

Et vous, dames et demoiselles,
En qui honneur naît et s'assemble,
Ne soyez mie si cruelles,
Chacune ni toutes ensemble.
Que ja nulle de vous ressemble
Celle que m'oyez nommer ci
Qu'on appellera, ce me semble,
La Belle Dame sans merci.

---

1. il s'en fallut de peu. — 2. avant que je retrouve mes sens. — 3. le reste.
4. qu'il s'était arraché les cheveux.

CHARLES D'ORLÉANS

(1394-1465)

La grâce naturelle de Charles d'Orléans inaugure une veine poétique qui court dans notre littérature de Marot à La Fontaine, traverse les chansons de Musset, brille parfois chez Apollinaire et s'épanouit dans l'œuvre de Supervielle. Mais peut-être n'aura-t-elle plus jamais cette couleur d'enfance préservée, cette qualité d'un chant qui paraît spontané, tant la science poétique certaine de son auteur s'efface sous la naïveté à peine feinte. On dirait d'une source vive sans cesse jaillissante, capable d'enchanter le malheur, pourtant réel, de cette existence captive.

Ni l'infortune ni l'exil n'appellent les accents tragiques. Le soupir plutôt que les larmes, la plainte plutôt que le cri, et toujours l'humour, cette élégance du désespoir. La transposition allégorique chère à son siècle fait du voyage de la vie, pour Charles d'Orléans, un long cheminement dans la « Forêt d'ennuyeuse Tristesse », ou la remontée de fleuves qui opposent leurs vents contraires à la Nef de Fortune sur laquelle est embarqué malgré lui le voyageur. Or le charme de sa langue opère ce prodige : loin d'élever entre ce destin et nous la barrière d'une abstraction froide, l'allégorie estompe la confidence sans l'abolir et l'histoire personnelle s'universalise.

Un mot éclaire toute l'œuvre du poète, celui de mélancolie qu'il écrit, selon l'usage médiéval, Mérencolie, ce qui insinue obscurément en nous l'idée qu'il en est, non seulement comme il le dit « l'écolier », mais encore le fils exemplaire et prédestiné.

RONDEAUX
XXX

Les fourriers d'Été sont venus
Pour appareiller son logis,
Et ont fait tendre ses tapis
De fleurs et verdure tissus.

En étendant tapis velus,
De vert herbe par le pays,
Les fourriers d'Été sont venus,
Pour appareiller son logis.

Cœur d'ennui piéça [1] morfondus,
Dieu merci, sont sains et jolis ;
Allez-vous en, prenez pays [2],
Hiver, vous ne demeurez plus !
Les fourriers d'Été sont venus !

XXXI

Le Temps a laissé son manteau
De vent, de froidure et de pluie,
Et s'est vêtu de broderie
De soleil luisant, clair et beau.

Il n'y a bête ni oiseau
Qu'en son jargon ne chante ou crie :
« Le Temps a laissé son manteau
De vent, de froidure et de pluie. »

Rivière, fontaine et ruisseau
Portent en livrée jolie
Gouttes d'argent d'orfèvrerie.
Chacun s'habille de nouveau [3] :
Le Temps a laissé son manteau.

1. depuis longtemps. — 2. prenez le large. — 3. de neuf.

XXXVIII

Quand j'ai ouï le tambourin
Sonner pour s'en aller au mai [1],
En mon lit n'en ai fait effray [2]
Ni levé mon chef du coussin.

En disant : « Il est trop matin.
Un peu je me rendormirai »,
Quand j'ai ouï le tambourin
Sonner pour s'en aller au mai.

Jeunes gens partent [3] leur butin !
De Nonchaloir m'acointerai [4].
À lui je m'abutinerai [5] ;
Trouvé l'ai plus prochain voisin
Quand j'ai ouï le tambourin

LII

Allons nous ébattre,
Mon cœur, vous et moi !
Laissons, à part soi,
Souci se combattre.

Toujours veut débattre,
Et jamais n'est coi [6] :
Allons nous ébattre,
Mon cœur, vous et moi !

On vous devrait battre,
Et montrer au doigt,
Si dessous sa loi
Vous laissez abattre.
Allons nous ébattre
Mon cœur, vous et moi !

---

1. s'en aller cueillir le muguet. — 2. mouvement. — 3. partagent. — 4. je ferai d'Insouciance ma compagnie. — 5. je partagerai mon butin. — 6. tranquille.

CCXXV

En la forêt de Longue Attente,
Par vent de Fortune Dolente,
Tant y vois abattu de bois
Que, sur ma foi, je n'y connois
À présent ni voie, ni sente.

Piéça [1] y pris joyeuse rente ;
Jeunesse la payait contente.
Or n'y ai qui vaille une noix,
En la forêt de Longue Attente.

Vieillesse dit, qui me tourmente :
Pour toi n'y a pesson [2], ni vente,
Comme tu as eu autrefois ;
Passés sont tes jours, ans et mois ;
Souffize toi et te contente [3],
En la forêt de Longue Attente.

CCCXXX

Petit mercier, petit panier !
Pourtant si je n'ai marchandise
Qui soit du tout [4] à votre guise,
Ne blâmez pour ce mon métier !

Je gagne denier à denier ;
C'est loin du trésor de Venise,
Petit mercier, petit panier !
Pourtant si je n'ai marchandise...

Et tandis qu'il est jour ouvrier [5],
Le temps perd quand à vous devise ;
Je vais parfaire mon emprise [6]
Et parmi les rues crier :
Petit mercier, petit panier !

---

1. Il y a longtemps. — 2. tu n'as plus de prix (*pesson* : petite monnaie). —
3. satisfais-toi et contente-toi. — 4. tout à fait. — 5. ouvrable. — 6. entreprise.

CCCXCVII

Écolier de Mérencolie [1],
Des verges de Souci battu,
Je suis à l'étude tenu,
Dans les derniers jours de ma vie.

Si j'ai ennui, n'en doutez mie,
Quand me sens vieillard devenu,
Écolier de Mérencolie,
Des verges de Souci battu !

Pitié convient que pour moi prie
Qui me trouve tout éperdu ;
Mon temps je perds et ai perdu,
Comme rassoté en folie,
Écolier de Mérencolie.

---

1. Mélancolie.

BALLADES

LXXXII

Nouvelles ont couru en France
Par maints lieux que j'étais mort,
Dont avaient peu de déplaisance
Aucuns qui me hayent[1] à tort ;
Autres en ont eu déconfort,
Qui m'aiment de loyal vouloir,
Comme mes bons et vrais amis.
Si fais à toutes gens savoir
Qu'encore est vive la souris !

Je n'ai eu ni mal ni grevance[2],
Dieu merci, mais suis sain et fort,
Et passe temps en espérance
Que paix, qui trop longuement dort,
S'éveillera, et par accord
À tous fera liesse avoir.
Pour ce, de Dieu soient maudits
Ceux qui sont dolents de v(e)oir
Qu'encore est vive la souris !

Jeunesse sur moi a puissance,
Mais Vieillesse fait son effort
De m'avoir en sa gouvernance ;
À présent faillira son sort.
Je suis assez loin de son port,
De pleurer veux garder mon hoir[3] ;
Loué soit Dieu de Paradis,
Qui m'a donné force et pouvoir
Qu'encore est vive la souris !

Nul ne porte pour moi le noir ;
On vend meilleur marché drap gris !
Or tienne chacun pour tout voir[4]
Qu'encore est vive la souris !

---

1. haïssent. — 2. peine. — 3. héritier. — 4. très vrai.

LX

Quand Souvenir me ramentait [1]
La grand beauté dont était pleine
Celle que mon cœur appelait
Sa seule Dame souveraine,
De tous biens la vraie fontaine,
Qui est morte nouvellement,
Je dis, en pleurant tendrement :
Ce monde n'est que chose vaine !

Au vieux temps, grand renom courait
De Créseide, Yseult, Hélène
Et maintes autres qu'on nommait
Parfaites en beauté hautaine.
Mais, au derrain [2], en son domaine
La mort les prit piteusement [3]
Par quoi puis v(e)oir clairement :
Ce monde n'est que chose vaine

La Mort a voulu et voudrait,
Bien le connais, mettre sa peine
De détruire, s'elle pouvait,
Liesse et Plaisance Mondaine,
Quand tant de belles dames mène
Hors du monde ; car vra(ye)ment
Sans elles, à mon jugement,
Ce monde n'est que chose vaine !

Amour, pour vérité certaine,
Mort vous guerrie fellement [4] ;
Si n'y trouvez amendement,
Ce monde n'est que chose vaine !

---

1. me rappelait. — 2. au dernier, pour finir. — 3. avec compassion. —
4. vous combat de façon déloyale.

LXXV

En regardant vers le pays de France,
Un jour m'advint, à Douvres sur la mer,
Qu'il me souvint de la douce plaisance
Que souloye [1] au dit pays trouver.
Si commençai de cœur à soupirer,
Combien certes que grand bien me faisoit
De voir France que mon cœur aimer doit.

Je m'avisai que c'était non savance [2]
De tels soupirs dedans mon cœur garder,
Vu que je vois que la voie commence
De bonne paix, qui tous biens peut donner ;
Pour ce tournai en confort mon penser,
Mais non pourtant mon cœur ne se lassoit
De voir France que mon cœur aimer doit.

Alors chargeai en la nef d'Espérance
Tous mes souhaits, en leur priant d'aller
Outre la mer, sans faire demeurance [3],
Et à France de me recommander.
Or nous doint Dieu bonne paix sans tarder !
Adonc aurai loisir, mais qu'ainsi soit,
De voir France que mon cœur aimer doit.

Paix est trésor qu'on ne peut trop louer.
Je hais guerre, point ne la dois priser ;
Destourbé [4] m'a longtemps, soit tort ou droit,
De voir France que mon cœur aimer doit.

---

1. j'avais coutume. — 2. manque de sagesse. — 3. sans tarder. — 4. empêché.

CXVII

Écolier de Mérencolie,
À l'étude je suis venu,
Lettres de mondaine clergie [1]
Épelant à tout un fêtu [2],
Et moult fort m'y trouve éperdu.
Lire n'écrire, ne sais mie,
Des verges de Souci battu
Dans les derniers jours de ma vie.

Piéça [3], en jeunesse fleurie,
Quand de vif entendement fus,
J'eusse appris en heure et demie
Plus qu'à présent ; tant ai vécu
Que d'engin je me sens vaincu [4] ;
On me dût bien, sans flatterie,
Châtier, dépouillé tout nu,
Dans les derniers jours de ma vie.

Que voulez-vous que je vous die ?
Je suis pour un ânier tenu
Banni de bonne compagnie
Et de Nonchaloir retenu
Pour le servir. Il est conclu !
Qui voudra, pour moi étudie :
Trop tard, je m'y suis entendu,
Dans les derniers jours de ma vie.

Si j'ai mon temps mal dépendu,
Fait l'ai par conseil de Folie ;
Je m'en sens et m'en suis sentu [5]
Dans les derniers jours de ma vie.

---

1. savoir. Les lettres de textes profanes. — 2. mot à mot : Épelant au bout d'une paille. — 3. jadis. — 4. que je sens mon esprit vaincu. — 5. autre forme pour *senti*.

FRANÇOIS VILLON

(1431- ?)

Deux fois dans sa vie, à quelques années d'intervalle, Villon dicte ses dernières volontés, d'abord dans les quarante strophes du *Lais*, puis dans le long poème du *Testament*. Ces deux pseudo-recueils de dernières volontés nous font passer, dans un mouvement qui leur est commun, de l'examen de conscience et du retour sur soi, à la liste des legs imaginaires attribués à des destinataires bien réels. Le ton de douleur et parfois de rage dominant dans la première partie fait place à la dérision et à la gaieté vengeresse dans la seconde. Ces dons d'un homme qui, de son propre aveu, ne possède rien, lui permettent de louer ses amis, et surtout de régler ses comptes avec ses ennemis. C'est pourquoi, à la difficulté d'une langue qui mêle aux expressions populaires et aux termes familiers des références de clerc, s'ajoute alors celle d'allusions difficiles à déchiffrer : comment deviner, par exemple, sans un savant commentaire, que les trois orphelins bénéficiaires de ses largesses apparentes, désignent clairement pour ses contemporains trois usuriers rapaces et détestés de tous.

Malgré ces obstacles, Villon s'impose à nous comme un très grand poète. La tapisserie du *Testament*, en particulier, est le miroir de la puissance d'invention poétique de son auteur, déroulant, au milieu de ses huitains, des ballades, rondeaux et chansons avec une diversité d'inspiration qui permet le passage de l'invective à la plainte, de l'anecdote à la méditation.

Villon est aussi pour le lecteur une voix extraordinairement proche parce qu'elle abolit les barrières en se fondant sur une fraternité irrécusable entre les hommes, celle qui naît de leur commun destin de mort. Ils sont, à ses yeux, comme lui des condamnés « de droit commun ». À l'insistance de cette voix s'ajoute le pouvoir de suggestion d'un poète qui fait surgir, par le jeu de l'énumération et du rythme, la vision d'une danse macabre mêlant âges et conditions, ou qui peint l'horreur de soi chez la femme que la vieillesse défigure. Il est celui qui fait entendre à jamais l'appel à la pitié des pendus sans visage. Seul enfin il a le pouvoir de glisser de la description atroce de l'agonie à l'évocation mélancolique et gracieuse des Dames du temps jadis. Son génie est d'avoir su, en partant de la réalité sordide de sa vie, hausser celle-ci jusqu'à la transmutation en œuvre d'art. Il est le premier poète alchimiste qui puisse dire au monde avant Baudelaire : « Tu m'as donné ta boue, et j'en ai fait de l'or. »

LE LAIS

I

L'an quatre cent cinquante et six,
Je, François Villon, écolier,
Considérant, de sens rassis,
Le frein [1] aux dents, franc au collier [2],
Qu'on doit ses œuvres conseillier [3],
Comme Végèce le raconte,
Sage romain, grand conseillier,
Ou autrement on se mécompte [4]...

II

En ce temps que j'ai dit devant,
Sur le Noël, morte saison,
Que les loups se vivent de vent
Et qu'on se tient en sa maison,
Pour le frimas, près du tison,
Me vint un vouloir de briser
La très amoureuse prison [5]
Qui souloit [6] mon cœur débriser.

VI

Pour obvier à ces dangers,
Mon mieux est, je crois, de partir,
Adieu ! Je m'en vais à Angers ;
Puis qu'elle ne me veut impartir [7]
Sa grâce, ne la me départir [8]
Par elle meurs, les membres sains ;
Au fort [9], je suis amant martyr
Du nombre des amoureux saints.

---

1. mors. — 2. plein d'ardeur. — 3. examiner ce qu'on doit faire. — 4. on s'expose à des mécomptes. — 5. rompre la prison d'amour. — 6. avait l'habitude. — 7. accorder sa faveur. — 8. ni m'en donner un peu. — 9. bref.

VIII

Et puisque départir me faut,
Et du retour ne suis certain,
– Je ne suis homme sans défaut
Ne qu'autre [1] d'acier ne d'étain ;
Vivre aux humains est incertain,
Et après mort n'y a relais ;
Je m'en vais en pays lointain –
Si établis ce présent lais [2].

IX

Premièrement, ou nom du Père,
Du Fils et du Saint Esprit,
Et de sa glorieuse Mère,
Par qui grâce [3] rien ne périt,
Je laisse, de par Dieu, mon bruit [4]
À maître Guillaume Villon,
Qui en l'honneur de son nom bruit,
Mes tentes et mon pavillon [5].

X

Item, à celle que j'ai dit,
Qui si durement m'a chassé
Que je suis de joie interdit
Et de tout plaisir déchassé,
Je laisse mon cœur enchassé,
Pâle, piteux [6], mort et transi :
Elle m'a ce mal pourchassé [7]
Mais Dieu lui en fasse merci !

---

1. pas plus qu'un autre. — 2. cette pièce poétique contenant des legs. —
3. par la grâce de qui. — 4. renom. — 5. grande tente. — 6. digne de pitié. —
7. procuré, apporté

LE TESTAMENT

I

En l'an trentième de mon âge
Que toutes mes hontes j'eus bues,
Ne du tout fol, ne du tout sage,
Non obstant[1] maintes peines eues,
Lesquelles j'ai toutes reçues
Sous la main Thibaut d'Aussigny...
S'évêque il est, signant[2] les rues,
Qu'il soit le mien je le regny[3] !

II

Mon seigneur n'est ne mon évêque ;
Sous lui ne tiens, s'il n'est en friche[4] ;
Foi ne lui dois n'hommage avecque ;
Je ne suis son serf ne sa biche[5].
Pu[6] m'a d'une petite miche
Et de froide eau tout un été.
Large ou étroit[7], mout me fut chiche :
Tel lui soit Dieu qu'il m'a été.

III

Et s'aucun[8] me voulait reprendre
Et dire que je le maudis,
Non fais[9], si bien le sait comprendre,
En rien de lui je ne médis.
Voici tout le mal que je dis :
S'il m'a été miséricors,
Jésus, le roi de paradis,
Tel lui soit à l'âme et au corps !

---

1. malgré. — 2. bénissant. — 3. renie. — 4. je ne tiens rien de lui qui ne soit en friche. — 5. jeu de mots : son mignon. — 6. nourri. — 7. qu'il soit généreux ou avare. — 8. quelqu'un. —9. je ne le fais pas.

XXII

Je plains le temps de ma jeunesse
Auquel j'ai plus qu'autre galé [1]
Jusqu'à l'entrée de vieillesse
Qui son partement [2] m'a celé.
Il ne s'en est a pied allé
N'a cheval, hélas ! comment don ?
Soudainement s'en est volé
Et ne m'a laissé quelque don.

XXIII

Allé s'en est, et je demeure,
Pauvre de sens et de savoir,
Triste, pâli, plus noir que meure [3],
Qui n'ai n'écus rente n'avoir ;
Des miens le mendre [4], je dis voir,
De me désavouer s'avance [5],
Oubliant naturel devoir
Par faute d'un peu de chevance [6].

XXVI

Bien sais, si j'eusse étudié
Au temps de ma jeunesse folle,
Et à bonnes mœurs dédié,
J'eusse maison et couche molle.
Mais quoi ? je fuyoie l'école,
Comme fait le mauvais enfant.
En écrivant cette parole
À peu que le cœur ne me fend.

---

1. fait le galant. — 2. départ. — 3. mûre. — 4. la moindre. — 5. va jusqu'à.
— 6. argent.

XXXIX

Je congnois que pauvres et riches,
Sages et fous, prêtres et lais [1],
Nobles, vilains [2], larges et chiches,
Petits et grands, et beaux et laids,
Dames à rebrassés collets [3],
De quelconque condition,
Portant atours et bourrelets [4],
Mort saisit sans exception.

XL

Et meure ou Paris ou Hélène,
Quiconque meurt, meurt à douleur :
Celui qui perd vent [5] et haleine,
Son fiel se crève sur son cœur,
Puis sue, Dieu sait quel sueur,
Et qui de ses maux si l'allège ?
Car enfant n'a, frère ne sœur
Qui lors vousït être son pleige [6].

XLI

La mort le fait frémir, pâlir,
Le nez courber, les veines tendre,
Le col enfler, lâcher, mollir,
Jointes [7], et nerfs croître et étendre.
Corps féminin, qui tant es tendre,
Poli, souef [8], si précieux,
Te faudra-il ces maux attendre ?
Oui, ou tout vif aller aux cieux.

---

1. laïcs. — 2. paysans. — 3. cols relevés. — 4. coiffures étagées. —
5. souffle. — 6. veuille lui servir de garant. — 7. articulations. — 8. suave.

BALLADE DES DAMES DU TEMPS JADIS

Dites-moi où, n [1] en quel pays
Est Flora la belle Romaine,
Archipiades ne Thaïs
Qui fut sa cousine germaine ;
Écho, parlant quand bruit on mène
Dessus rivière ou sur étang,
Qui beauté ot [2] trop plus qu'humaine ?
Mais où sont les neiges d'antan ?

Où est la très sage Héloïs,
Pour qui fut châtré et puis moine
Pierre Esbaillart à Saint-Denis ?
Pour son amour eut cette essoine [3],
Semblablement, où est la reine
Qui commanda que Buridan
Fût jeté en un sac en Seine ?
Mais où sont les neiges d'antan ?

La roine Blanche comme un lis
Qui chantoit à voix de seraine,
Berthe au grand pied, Bietrix, Aliz,
Haramburgis qui tint le Maine,
Et Jeanne, la bonne Lorraine,
Qu'Anglois brûlèrent à Rouen ;
Où sont-ils [4], où, Vierge souveraine ?
Mais où sont les neiges d'antan ?

Prince, n'enquerrez de semaine
Où elles sont, ne de cet an,
Qu'à ce refrain ne vous remaine [5] :
Mais où sont les neiges d'antan ?

_____

1. et. — 2. eut. — 3. épreuve, peine. — 4. elles. — 5. ramène

LES REGRETS DE LA BELLE HËAUMIÈRE

XLVII

Avis m'est que j'oi [1] regretter
La Belle qui fut hëaumière [2],
Soi jeune fille souhaiter
Et parler en telle manière :
« Ha ! vieillesse félonne et fière [3],
Pourquoi m'as si tôt abattue !
Qui me tient, qui, que ne me fière [4].
Et qu'à ce coup je ne me tue ?

XLVIII

« Tolu m'as ma haute franchise [5]
Que beauté m'avait ordonné [6]
Sur clercs, marchands et gens d'Église :
Car lors il n'étoit homme né
Qui tout le sien [7] ne m'eût donné,
Quoiqu'il en fût des repentailles,
Mais que [8] lui eusse abandonné
Ce que refusent truandailles [9].

XLIX

« À maint homme l'ai refusé,
Qui [10] n'étoit à moi grand sagesse,
Pour l'amour d'un garçon rusé,
Auquel j'en fis grande largesse.
À qui que je fisse finesse [11],
Par m'âme, je l'aimoie bien !
Or ne me faisoit que rudesse,
Et ne m'aimoit que pour le mien [12].

---

1. entends. — 2. qui vend des casques. — 3. cruelle. — 4. que je ne me frappe ? — 5. tu m'as ôté le pouvoir. — 6. donnée. — 7. tout son bien. — 8. à condition. — 9. ce que refusent aujourd'hui les truands. — 10. ce qui. — 11. si j'ai menti aux autres. — 12. pour mon argent.

LI

« Or est-il mort, passé trente ans,
Et je remains [1] vieille, chenue.
Quand je pense, lasse ! au bon temps,
Que me regarde toute nue,
Quelle suis, quelle devenue,
Et je me vois si très changée,
Pauvre, sèche, maigre, menue,
Je suis presque toute enragée.

LII

« Qu'est devenu ce front poli,
Ces cheveux blonds, sourcils voutis [2],
Grand entrœil, ce regard joli,
Dont prenoie les plus subtils ;
Ce beau nez droit, grand ne petiz
Ces petites jointes oreilles,
Menton fourchu [3], clair vis traitis [4],
Et ces belles lèvres vermeilles ?

LVI

« Ainsi le bon temps regrettons
Entre nous, pauvres vieilles sottes,
Assises bas, à croupetons,
Tout en un tas comme pelotes,
À petit feu de chenevottes [5],
Tôt allumées, tôt éteintes...
Et jadis fûmes si mignottes !
Ainsi en prend [6] à maints et maintes. »

---

1. reste. — 2. arqués. — 3. à fossette. — 4. beau visage fin. — 5. de chanvre.
— 6. c'est ce qui arrive.

LXIX

Ainsi m'ont Amours abusé
Et pourmené de l'huis au pêle [1].
Je crois qu'homme n'est si rusé,
Fût fin comme argent de coupelle [2],
Qui n'y laissât linge, drapelle [3],
Mais qu'il fût ainsi manié [4]
Comme moi, qui partout m'appelle
L'amant remis [5] et renié.

LXX

Je renie Amours et dépite [6]
Et défie à feu et à sang.
Mort par elles me précipite [7],
Et ne leur en chaut pas d'un blanc [8].
Ma vielle ai mis sous le banc [9] ;
Amants je ne suivrai jamais :
Se jadis je fus de leur rang [10],
Je déclare que n'en suis mais [11].

LXXI

Car j'ai mis le plumail au vent [12],
Or le suive qui a attente [13].
De ce me tais dorénavant,
Poursuivre je veuil mon entente [14].
Et s'aucun m'interroge ou tente [15]
Comment d'Amour j'ose médire,
Cette parole le contente :
Qui meurt, a ses lois [16] de tout dire.

---

1. verrou. — 2. argent très fin. — 3. vêtement. — 4. malmené. —
5. congédié. — 6. méprise. — 7. fait tomber. — 8. cela leur est égal. — 9. j'ai
mis ma vielle sous le banc, c'est-à-dire j'ai renoncé. — 10. nombre. —
11. plus. — 12. j'ai abandonné la partie. — 13. qui a de l'espoir. — 14. projet.
— 15. cherche à savoir. — 16. le droit.

LXXXIV

Ou nom de Dieu, comme j'ai dit,
Et de sa glorieuse Mère,
Sans péché soit parfait ce dit [1]
Par moi, plus maigre que chimère.
Se je n'ai eu fièvre éphémère,
Ce m'a fait divine clémence,
Mais d'autre deuil et peine amère
Je me tais, et ainsi commence.

LXXXV

Premier, je doue [2] de ma pauvre âme
La glorieuse Trinité,
Et la commande [3] à Notre Dame,
Chambre de la divinité,
Priant toute la charité
Des dignes neuf Ordres [4] des Cieux
Que par eux soit ce don porté
Devant le Trône précieux.

LXXXVI

Item, mon corps j'ordonne et laisse
À notre grand mère la terre ;
Les vers n'y trouveront grand graisse,
Trop lui a fait faim dure guerre.
Or lui soit délivré grand erre [5] :
De terre vint, en terre tourne ;
Toute chose, se par trop n'erre [6],
Volontiers en son lieu retourne.

---

1. soit achevé ce Testament. — 2. je fais don. — 3. recommande. —
4. allusion à la hiérarchie des anges. — 5. rapidement. — 6. s'égare.

RONDEAU

Mort, j'appelle de ta rigueur,
Qui m'as ma maîtresse ravie,
Et n'es pas encore assouvie
Se tu ne me tiens en langueur :

Onc puis n'eus force ne vigueur ;
Mais que te nuisoit-elle en vie,
   Mort ?

Deux étions et n'avions qu'un cœur ;
S'il [1] est mort, force est que dévie [2],
Voire, ou que je vive sans vie
Comme les images, par cœur [3],
   Mort !

---

1. si elle. — 2. cesse de vivre. — 3. par la mémoire ou en apparence.

ÉPITAPHE ET RONDEAU

CI GÎT ET DORT EN CE SOLIER[1],
QU'AMOUR OCCIT DE SON RAILLON[2],
UN PAUVRE PETIT ÉCOLIER
QUI FUT NOMMÉ FRANÇOIS VILLON.
ONCQUES DE TERRE N'EUT SILLON.
IL DONNA TOUT, CHACUN LE SAIT :
TABLES, TRÉTEAUX, PAIN, CORBILLON.
POUR DIEU, DITES-EN CE VERSET :

REPOS ÉTERNEL, DONNE A CIL[3],
SIRE, ET CLARTÉ PERPÉTUELLE,
QUI VAILLANT PLAT NI ÉCUELLE[4]
N'OT ONCQUES, N'UN BRIN DE PERSIL.

IL FUT RÉS[5], CHEF, BARBE ET SOURCIL,
COMME UN NAVET QU'ON RET[6] OU PÈLE.
REPOS ÉTERNEL DONNE A CIL.

RIGUEUR LE TRANSMIT EN EXIL
ET LUI FRAPPA AU CUL LA PELLE,
NONOBSTANT QU'IL DÎT : « J'EN APPELLE ! »
QUI N'EST PAS TERME TROP SUBTIL.
REPOS ÉTERNEL DONNE A CIL.

---

1. en ce grenier. — 2. sa flèche. — 3. celui-là. — 4. la valeur d'un plat ou d'une écuelle. — 5. rasé. — 6. rase.

L'ÉPITAPHE DE VILLON
EN FORME DE BALLADE

Frères humains, qui après nous vivez,
N'ayez les cœurs contre nous endurcis,
Car, se pitié de nous pauvres avez,
Dieu en aura plus tôt de vous mercis.
Vous nous voyez ci attachés cinq, six :
Quant de la chair, que trop avons nourrie,
Elle est piéça [1] devorée [2] et pourrie,
Et nous, les os, devenons cendre et poudre [3].
De notre mal personne ne s'en rie ;
Mais priez Dieu que tous nous veuille absoudre !

Se frères vous clamons, pas n'en devez
Avoir dédain, quoique fûmes occis
Par justice. Toutefois, vous savez
Que tous hommes n'ont pas bon sens rassis ;
Excusez-nous, puisque sommes transis [4],
Envers le fils de la Vierge Marie :
Que sa grâce ne soit pour nous tarie,
Nous préservant de l'infernale foudre.
Nous sommes morts, âme ne nous harie [5],
Mais priez Dieu que tous nous veuille absoudre !

La pluie nous a débués [6] et lavés,
Et le soleil desséchés et noircis ;
Pies, corbeaux, nous ont les yeux cavés [7]
Et arraché la barbe et les sourcils.
Jamais nul temps nous ne sommes assis ;
Puis çà, puis là, comme le vent varie,
À son plaisir sans cesser nous charrie,
Plus becquetés d'oiseaux que dés à coudre.
Ne soyez donc de notre confrérie ;
Mais priez Dieu que tous nous veuille absoudre !

---

1. depuis longtemps. — 2. détruite. — 3. poussière. — 4. trépassés. —
5. que personne ne nous moleste. — 6. lessivés. — 7. creusés.

Prince-Jésus, qui sur tous a maîtrie,
Garde qu'Enfer n'ait de nous seigneurie :
À lui n'ayons que faire ne que soudre [1].
Hommes, ici n'a point de moquerie ;
Mais priez Dieu que tous nous veuille absoudre !

Les textes de François Villon reproduits ici sont extraits de *Poésies* de François Villon, éd. établie, présentée et annotée par Jean Dufournet © Gallimard.

1. ni à payer.

XVIᵉ SIÈCLE

Certains des poètes de cette époque qui s'inscrivent parmi les plus grands de notre littérature, comme Ronsard ou d'Aubigné, donnent la mesure d'un siècle qui fut, entre tous, un siècle de poésie. Il faudra attendre trois cents ans pour revoir pareille effervescence créatrice parmi les poètes, et un tel sentiment de la dignité de leur art. En renouvelant leurs modèles, en s'attachant à des formes neuves mais surtout en prenant conscience de leur pouvoir, ils ont conféré à la poésie un nouveau statut, elle se voit investie des plus hautes missions, elle participe à tous les grands mouvements d'idées contemporaines et en acquiert une importance et une dimension singulières.

En apparence, cependant, si l'on se réfère à la condition faite au poète dans la société, il semble que rien n'ait changé. Comme auparavant, chacun d'eux doit être attaché à la personne et à la cour d'un grand seigneur. C'est l'unique moyen d'obtenir les bénéfices et les pensions qui permettront de s'affranchir des soucis matériels. Les *Épîtres au Roi* de Marot, malgré leur ton rieur, témoignent assez de cette dépendance. Et le service des grands peut brider plus étroitement encore le poète, lorsqu'il se voit chargé d'affaires diplomatiques ou financières étrangères à sa vocation et qui laissent peu de temps aux Muses. Du Bellay, depuis son exil romain, envie son ami resté à la cour de France où, quelles que soient ses obligations, il a, du moins, l'occasion et le temps de composer des vers :

> *Tu courtises les rois, et d'un plus heureux son*
> *Chantant l'heur de Henri qui son siècle décore,*
> *Tu t'honores toi-même, et celui qui honore*
> *L'honneur que tu lui fais par ta docte chanson.*

La rançon littéraire de cette situation, ce sont les poèmes de circonstance et les panégyriques des princes qu'il est de règle de composer à chaque occasion. On en a de très nombreux exemples. Il n'est pas jusqu'aux poèmes d'amour qui ne soient parfois inspirés par la nécessité de servir de secrétaire au prince amoureux. Cependant le génie des poètes est capable de leur donner un ton personnel et de faire croire que le cœur s'exprime quand le talent seul tient la plume. Mais cette sujétion leur pèse, on les entend regretter leur liberté et se plaindre comme le fait Ronsard dans sa *Complainte contre Fortune* :

> *Avant que d'être à vous, je vivais sans émoi*
> . . . .
> *Et depuis, mon esprit, comme il soulait, ne peut*
> *Se ranger à l'étude, et ma plume fertile,*
> *Faute de l'exercer, se moisit inutile.*

On sait ce qu'était pour eux cette « étude » : elle consistait d'abord à se mettre à l'école des poètes du passé. Marot avait encore les Rhétoriqueurs pour modèles, même s'il subit plus tard l'influence de l'humanisme. Pour la génération suivante, l'originalité consiste à rompre avec les poètes français qui l'ont précédée et à s'attacher uniquement aux Anciens et aux Italiens. Il ne s'agit pas de les imiter servilement, mais de se nourrir d'eux au point de les assimiler entièrement et de refaire, à partir de là, une œuvre originale. C'est la doctrine de l'innutrition, telle que l'expose Du Bellay, en 1549, dans *La Deffence et Illustration de la Langue Françoyse*. Plusieurs arts poétiques avaient paru avant ce dernier, en particulier celui de Thomas Sébillet auquel Du Bellay répond. Son traité, fruit d'une réflexion collective, est d'abord consacré à des considérations sur la langue française qu'il faut « amplifier par l'imitation des anciens auteurs »... puis il souligne la nécessité du travail pour qui veut faire œuvre poétique durable :

« Qui veut voler par les mains et les bouches des hommes, doit longuement demeurer en sa chambre »... Il condamne ensuite les genres anciens « comme rondeaux, ballades, virelais, chants royaux... et autres telles épiceries qui corrompent le goût de notre langue » pour prôner l'épigramme, l'élégie, l'ode et « ces beaux sonnets, non moins docte que plaisante invention italienne » et aussi l'églogue, et il enjoint encore au poète de « restituer en leur ancienne dignité les anciennes comédies et tragédies ».

On voit à quel point la rupture avec le Moyen Âge est consommée, au moins théoriquement. Le groupe d'amis qui prendra le nom de Pléiade va s'efforcer de se conformer en tous points à un programme si ambitieux qu'il sonne comme un défi de ces poètes aux autres et à eux-mêmes.

Ce qui vaut à la poésie une place nouvelle c'est donc le lien qu'elle entretient avec l'Humanisme, ce mouvement de redécouverte des textes de l'Antiquité. Elle va aussi avoir partie liée avec l'autre courant qui caractérise le siècle : l'Évangélisme (qui deviendra la Réforme). Tous deux prônent un retour aux origines. Pour le premier il s'agit de retrouver la poésie et la pensée antique, pour le second de revenir aux textes fondateurs du christianisme. Scève, Du Bartas, et surtout d'Aubigné témoignent de l'importance pour les poètes de ce retour à la Bible, mais on trouve des marques de cette influence chez la plupart des poètes de ce siècle.

Ce retour aux textes se fait en France par l'intermédiaire de l'humanisme italien. Les Italiens ont, les premiers, approfondi la connaissance de l'Antiquité, et leur pratique des textes anciens au XVᵉ siècle exerce une influence essentielle sur la Renaissance française. Même si les écrits de Ficin ou de Pic de la Mirandole ne sont connus, le plus souvent, qu'à travers des œuvres intermédiaires, le commentaire de Platon et des néoplatoniciens par le premier, les interprétations allégoriques du second se reflètent dans les idées et les images de la poésie française au siècle suivant.

À Maurice Scève et, plus encore, aux hommes de la Pléiade, ils ont révélé que la poésie est connaissance. La « fureur » de l'inspiration élève l'homme au-dessus de lui-même, lui permettant ainsi de communiquer avec Dieu et avec la Nature. Et Pontus de Tyard qui expose la théorie des « Quatre Fureurs », nomme les degrés successifs de cette montée initiatique vers le savoir universel, auquel aspire l'humaniste. Il faut souligner que la connaissance poétique, si elle n'emprunte pas les voies de la raison, vise cependant les mêmes objets que la science. D'où le *Microcosme* de Scève et les efforts de poésie « scientifique » de Ronsard.

D'où surtout l'idée que la poésie est capable d'assumer l'univers et de donner sens à la vie humaine. Car le savoir, en élevant l'âme vers le divin, restaure en elle sa dignité originelle. L'enthousiasme pour les lettres antiques nourrit la foi en l'homme. On le juge perfectible et l'on est sûr qu'enrichi de tout le savoir légué par l'Antiquité il deviendra capable de conquérir des domaines sans cesse plus vastes.

Les poètes portés par cet élan s'efforcent, chacun à sa manière, de le traduire. Les plus inspirés d'entre eux ont recours aux mythes. Ils mêlent, dans une synthèse qui peut surprendre, les grandes légendes antiques aux dogmes du christianisme, comme l'ont fait les Italiens du Quattrocento. Leur vision du cosmos s'exprime en images plus qu'en théories. La description des forces qui régissent l'univers aboutit à une vision animiste où l'exposé scientifique est heureusement sacrifié à l'expression poétique.

La grandeur des poètes de la Pléiade est d'avoir joint à ces hautes aspirations la sensualité la plus terrestre qui soit, d'avoir aimé les plaisirs humains et chanté avec délice la beauté de la vie simple. Si la Nature, au sens le plus ample du terme, est leur objet, le sont aussi le « petit village », la fontaine « jasarde », « les ombrages verts ». Et ces réunions où la « joyeuse troupe » festoie en récitant des vers. Et les grandes orgies de lecture :

> *Je veux lire en trois jours l'*Iliade *d'Homère*
> *Et pour ce, Corydon, ferme bien l'huis sur moi...*

Le corps n'a pas moins de dignité à leurs yeux que l'esprit et tous les plaisirs de la vie méritent d'être loués. Chacun d'eux, au moins dans sa jeunesse, aurait pu dire comme Montaigne : « Tout bon ! Il a fait tout bon ! »

C'est pourquoi ils nous laissent d'abord l'impression d'avoir été les maîtres de la poésie amoureuse. Ils ont, dans un premier temps, célébré la femme en l'idéalisant, à la manière de Pétrarque et de ses disciples, mais ils ont aussi donné de l'amour une peinture plus charnelle dans des poèmes où le trouble et la sensualité du poète se communiquent au lecteur, même si une certaine distance rêveuse et parfois ironique en permet une traduction voilée. La grâce de l'expression, la parfaite maîtrise du rythme, ainsi que le jeu des images et des sons contribuent à créer l'émotion. Un point de perfection poétique insurpassable semble parfois atteint dans quelques-uns de leurs sonnets.

Les querelles religieuses de ce siècle, puis les guerres de religion qui déchirent le pays, donnent l'occasion aux poètes qui y sont mêlés, indirectement comme Ronsard, ou en participant aux combats comme d'Aubigné, de faire preuve d'une verve satirique puissante. *Les Discours* où Ronsard s'inspire de Virgile et de l'Arioste, et dans lesquels la personnification et l'allégorie lui permettent parfois d'échapper au didactisme de son propos, ne sont sans doute pas la partie la plus accessible de son œuvre, mais en donnant pour la première fois une forme poétique à la controverse politique et à la polémique, il ouvre à la poésie un nouveau domaine.

D'Aubigné trouve pour *Les Tragiques* une adéquation parfaite entre son sujet et les images qu'il met en œuvre car il les puise dans l'Ancien Testament qui lui est familier. Sa verve polémique, son engagement militant directement rattachés à la veine prophétique de la Bible, donnent au récit d'événements contemporains une ampleur épique inégalable. Tout imprégné de la langue des *Psaumes* qu'il lit dans le texte hébreu, il a le don d'imiter le style biblique jusque dans ses tournures.

La conception ambitieuse de la poésie, la conjonction d'un renouveau intellectuel de très grande envergure et de talents exceptionnels qui mirent en œuvre ce projet poétique au moyen des idées nouvelles, suffiraient à forcer l'admiration. S'y ajoute la séduction d'une langue, qui, moins déroutante pour nous que celle du Moyen Âge, nous charme d'emblée par sa force expressive. Son art de faire voisiner les termes familiers et les vocables les plus savants empruntés à l'Antiquité, cette exubérance bigarrée si savoureuse – que condamneront plus tard les rigoureux théoriciens –, le rythme enfin, capable de suspendre un ample développement rhétorique par l'abrupt d'un raccourci inattendu, sont la cause la plus immédiate du plaisir qu'on éprouve à la lire et surtout à la dire à voix haute.

CLÉMENT MAROT

(1496-1544)

L'œuvre de Marot s'inscrit d'abord dans la continuité de ses prédécesseurs immédiats ou lointains, mais il sait n'être pas écrasé par cet héritage qu'il vénère. En l'assumant, il le modifie et l'infléchit à sa manière. Il a appris des poètes Jean Marot, son père, ou Jean Lemaire de Belges, les artifices de la Grande Rhétorique, entre autres les vers équivoqués et les rimes concaténées ou senées, mais il plie ce savoir à sa guise et s'en amuse avec une virtuosité iconoclaste : témoin cette ballade *Du Jour de Noël* :

> *Or est Noël venu son petit trac.*
> *Sus donc aux champs, Bergères de respec :*
> *Prenons chascun Panetière et Bissac,*
> *Flûte, Flageol, Cornemuse, et rebec :*
> *Ores n'est pas temps de clorre le bec,*
> *Chantons, sautons, et dansons ric à ric :*
> *Puis allons voir l'Enfant au pauvre nic...*

Fidèle aussi à la tradition médiévale, en particulier à Villon dont il se fait l'éditeur, il se coule avec facilité dans les formes existantes, mais se montre également grand novateur, puisqu'il introduit en France des formes nouvelles comme l'épigramme, l'épître, l'élégie, l'églogue et même le sonnet. Composant le premier blason du corps féminin, il ouvre la voie à une foule d'imitateurs. Surtout il offre, aux poètes lyriques à venir, les modèles si divers des strophes qu'il crée pour traduire les Psaumes de David.

La diversité des tons n'est pas moins étonnante chez lui que celle des genres : il peut être élégiaque ou burlesque, exprimer la passion ou fustiger un ennemi. Ce qui fond, en une seule, toutes ces voix, c'est cet « élégant badinage » loué par Boileau, ce tour primesautier et naturel qu'il donne à ses vers, effet de la parfaite maîtrise de son art, au moins autant que de son heureux tempérament. La justesse du trait subtil et prompt, le sourire complice, et, par-dessus tout, la simplicité de l'expression et l'authenticité du sentiment, firent de lui le poète le plus lu et admiré de ses contemporains. Les critiques de la Pléiade, qui visaient surtout ses imitateurs, lui valurent, un temps, un injuste décri, mais le lecteur d'aujourd'hui peut éprouver, même s'il n'a pas eu le bonheur d'apprendre dès l'enfance, à Cahors-en-Quercy, ville natale du poète, à goûter cette œuvre, qu'il y a un charme de Marot, toujours renouvelé, auquel La Fontaine était sensible, et qu'il est bien, suivant le mot d'Étienne Dolet, ce « poète de facilité et de grâce tant singulière que toujours laisse un désir de soi ».

ÉPÎTRE À SON AMI LION

Je ne t'écris de l'amour vaine, et folle,
Tu vois assez, s'elle sert, ou affolle :
Je ne t'écris ne d'Armes, ne de Guerre,
Tu vois, qui peut bien, ou mal y acquerre :
Je ne t'écris de Fortune puissante,
Tu vois assez, s'elle est ferme, ou glissante :
Je ne t'écris d'abus trop abusant,
Tu en sais prou, et si n'en vas usant :
Je ne t'écris de Dieu, ne sa puissance,
C'est à lui seul t'en donner connaissance :
Je ne t'écris des Dames de Paris,
Tu en sais plus que leurs propres Maris :
Je ne t'écris, qui est rude, ou affable,
Mais je te veux dire une belle fable :
C'est assavoir du Lion, et du Rat.
Cettui Lion plus fort qu'un vieux Verrat,
Vit une fois, que le Rat ne savait
Sortir d'un lieu, pour autant qu'il avait
Mangé le lard, et la chair toute crue :
Mais ce Lion (qui jamais ne fut Grue)
Trouva moyen, et manière, et matière
D'ongles, et dents, de rompre la ratière :
Dont maître rat échappe vitement :
Puis mit à terre un genou gentement,
Et en ostant son bonnet de la tête,
A mercié mille fois la grand Bête :
Jurant le dieu des Souris, et des Rats,
Qu'il luy rendrait. Maintenant tu verras
Le bon du conte. Il advint d'aventure,
Que le Lion pour chercher sa pâture,
Saillit dehors sa caverne, et son siège ;
Dont (par malheur) se trouva pris au piège,
Et fut lié contre un ferme poteau.
Adonc le Rat, sans serpe, ne couteau,
Y arriva joyeux, et ébaudi,
Et du Lion (pour vrai) ne s'est gaudi :
Mais dépita Chats, Chates, et Chatons,

Et prisa fort Rats, Rates, et Ratons,
Dont il avait trouvé temps favorable
Pour secourir le Lion secourable :
Auquel a dit : tais-toi Lion lié,
Par moi seras maintenant délié :
Tu le vaux bien, car le cœur joli as.
Bien y parut, quand tu me délias.
Secouru m'as fort Lionneusement,
Ors secouru seras Rateusement.
Lors le Lion ses deux grands yeux vêtit,
Et vers le Rat les tourna un petit,
En lui disant, ô pauvre verminière,
Tu n'as sur toi instrument, ne manière,
Tu n'as couteau, serpe, ne serpillon,
Qui sut couper corde, ne cordillon,
Pour me jeter de cette étroite voie.
Va te cacher, que le Chat ne te voie.
Sire Lion (dit le fils de Souris)
De ton propos (certes) je me souris :
J'ai des couteaux assez, ne te soucie,
De bel os blanc plus tranchant qu'une Scie :
Leur gaine c'est ma gencive, et ma bouche :
Bien couperont la corde, qui te touche
De si très près : car j'y mettrai bon ordre.
Lors Sire Rat va commencer à mordre
Ce gros lien : vrai est qu'il y songea
Assez long temps : mais il le vous rongea
Souvent et tant, qu'à la parfin tout rompt :
Et le Lion de s'en aller fut prompt,
Disant en soi : nul plaisir (en effet)
Ne se perd point, quelque part où soit fait.
Voilà le compte en termes rimassez :
Il est bien long : mais il est vieil assez,
Témoin Ésope, et plus d'un million.
Or viens me voir, pour faire le Lion :
Et je mettrai peine, sens, et étude
D'être le Rat, exempt d'ingratitude :
J'entends, si Dieu te donne autant d'affaire,
Qu'au grand Lion : ce qu'il ne veuille faire.

L'Adolescence Clementine, Épitres

DE SA GRAND AMIE

Dedans Paris Ville jolie
Un jour passant mélancolie
Je pris alliance nouvelle
À la plus gaie Damoiselle,
Qui soit d'ici en Italie.

D'honnêteté elle est saisie,
Et crois (selon ma fantaisie)
Qu'il n'en est guère de plus belle
    Dedans Paris.

Je ne la vous nommerai mie,
Si non que c'est ma grand Amie ;
Car l'alliance se fit telle,
Par un doux baiser que j'eus d'elle,
Sans penser aucune infamie,
    Dedans Paris.

Rondeaux, **XXXIX**

DE L'AMOUR DU SIÈCLE ANTIQUE

Au bon vieux temps un train d'Amour régnait,
Qui sans grand art et dons se démenait,
Si qu'un bouquet donné d'Amour profonde,
C'était donné toute la Terre ronde,
Car seulement au cœur on se prenait.

Et si par cas à jouir on venait,
Savez-vous bien comme on s'entretenait ?
Vingt ans, trente ans : cela durait un Monde
         Au bon vieux temps.

Or est perdu ce qu'Amour ordonnait,
Rien que pleurs feints, rien que changes on n'oit.
Qui voudra donc qu'à aimer je me fonde,
Il faut premier que l'Amour on refonde,
Et qu'on la mène ainsi qu'on la menait
         Au bon vieux temps.

Rondeaux, LXII

AU ROI

On dit bien vrai, la mauvaise Fortune
Ne vient jamais, qu'elle n'en apporte une,
Ou deux, ou trois avecques elle (Sire).
Votre cœur noble en saurait bien que dire :
Et moi chétif, qui ne suis Roi, ne rien
L'ai éprouvé. Et vous compterai bien,
Si vous voulez, comment vint la besogne.
J'avais un jour un Valet de Gascogne,
Gourmant, Ivrogne, et assuré Menteur,
Pipeur, Larron, Jureur, Blasphémateur,
Sentant la Hart de cent pas à la ronde,
Au demeurant le meilleur fils du Monde,
Prisé, loué, fort estimé des filles
Par les Bourdeaux, et beau Joueur de Quilles.
Ce vénérable Hillot fut averti
De quelque argent, que m'aviez départi,
Et que ma Bourse avait grosse apostume :
Si se leva plus tôt que de coutume,
Et me va prendre en tapinois icelle :
Puis la vous mit très bien sous son Aisselle,
Argent et tout (cela se doit entendre),
Et ne croi point, que ce fut pour la rendre,
Car oncques puis n'en ai ouï parler.
Bref, le Vilain ne s'en voulut aller
Pour si petit : mais encor il me happe
Saye, et Bonnet, Chausses, Pourpoint, et Cape :
De mes Habits (en effet) il pilla
Tous les plus beaux : et puis s'en habilla
Si justement, qu'à le voir ainsi être,
Vous l'eussiez pris (en plein jour) pour son Maître.
Finablement, de ma Chambre il s'en va
Droit à l'étable, où deux Chevaux trouva :
Laisse le pire, et sur le meilleur monte,
Pique, et s'en va. Pour abréger le conte,
Soyez certain, qu'au partir dudit lieu

N'oublia rien, fors à me dire Adieu.
Ainsi s'en va chatouilleux de la gorge
Ledit Valet, monté comme un saint George :
Et vous laissa Monsieur dormir son saoul :
Qui au réveil n'eut su finer d'un sou.
Ce Monsieur là (Sire) c'était moi même :
Qui sans mentir fus au Matin bien blème,
Quand je me vis sans honnête vêture,
Et fort fâché de perdre ma monture :
Mais de l'argent, que vous m'aviez donné,
Je ne fus point de le perdre étonné,
Car votre argent (très débonnaire Prince)
Sans point de faute est sujet à la pince.
Bien tôt après ceste fortune là,
Une autre pire encores se mêla
De m'assaillir, et chacun jour m'assaut,
Me menaçant de me donner le saut,
Et de ce saut m'envoyer à l'envers,
Rimer sous terre, et y faire des Vers.
C'est une lourde, et longue maladie
De trois bons mois, qui m'a toute élourdie
La pauvre tête, et ne veut terminer,
Ains me contraint d'apprendre à cheminer.
Tant affaibli m'a d'étrange manière,
Et si m'a fait la cuisse héronnière,
L'estomac sec, le Ventre plat, et vague :
Quand tout est dit, aussi mauvaise bague
(Ou peu s'en faut) que femme de Paris,
Sauve l'honneur d'elles, et leurs Maris.
Que dirai plus ? au misérable corps
(Dont je vous parle) il n'est demeuré fors
Le pauvre esprit, qui lamente, et soupire,
Et en pleurant tâche à vous faire rire.
Et pour autant (Sire) que suis à vous,
De trois jours l'un viennent tâter mon pouls
Messieurs Braillon, le Coq, Akaquia,
Pour me garder d'aller jusque à quia.
Tout consulté ont remis au Printemps
Ma guérison : mais à ce que j'entends,

Si je ne puis au Printemps arriver,
Je suis taillé de mourir en Hiver,
Et en danger (si en Hiver je meurs)
De ne voir pas les premiers Raisins mûrs.
Voilà comment depuis neuf mois en çà
Je suis traité. Or ce que me laissa
Mon Larronneau (long temps a) l'ai vendu,
Et en Sirops, et Juleps dépendu :
Ce néanmoins ce que je vous en mande,
N'est pour vous faire ou requête, ou demande :
Je ne veux point tant de gens ressembler,
Qui n'ont souci autre que d'assembler.
Tant qu'ils vivront, ils demanderont eux,
Mais je commence à devenir honteux,
Et ne veux plus à vos dons m'arrêter.
Je ne dis pas, si voulez rien prêter,
Que ne le prenne. Il n'est point de Prêteur
(S'il veut prêter) qui ne fasse un Debteur.
Et savez-vous (Sire) comment je paye ?
Nul ne le sait, si premier ne l'essaye.
Vous me devrez (si je puis) de retour :
Et vous ferai encores un bon tour,
À celle fin qu'il n'y ait faute nulle,
Je vous ferai une belle Cedulle,
À vous payer (sans usure il s'entend)
Quand on verra tout le Monde content :
Ou (si voulez) à payer ce sera,
Quand votre Loz, et Renom cessera.
Et si sentez, que sois faible de reins
Pour vous payer, les Deux Princes Lorrains
Me plegeront. Je les pense si fermes,
Qu'ils ne faudront pour moi à l'un des termes.
Je sais assez, que vous n'avez pas peur
Que je m'enfuie, ou que je sois trompeur :
Mais il fait bon assurer ce qu'on prête.
Bref, votre paye (ainsi que je l'arrête)
Est aussi sûre, advenant mon trépas,
Comme advenant, que je ne meure pas.
Avisez donc, si vous avez désir

De rien prêter, vous me ferez plaisir :
Car puis un peu, j'ai bâti à Clément,
Là où j'ai fait un grand desboursement :
Et à Marot, qui est un peu plus loin :
Tout tombera, qui n'en aura le soin.
Voilà le point principal de ma Lettre.
Vous savez tout, il n'y faut plus rien mettre :
Rien mettre, las ! Certes, et si ferai,
En ce faisant, mon style j'enflerai,
Disant, ô Roi amoureux des neufs Muses,
Roi, en qui sont leurs sciences infuses,
Roi, plus que Mars, d'honneur environné,
Roi, le plus Roi, qui fut onc couronné,
Dieu tout puissant te doint (pour t'étrenner)
Les quatre coins du Monde gouverner,
Tant pour le bien de la ronde Machine,
Que pour autant que sur tous en es digne.

La Suite de l'Adolescence, Épitres

L'ADIEU ENVOYÉ AUX DAMES DE COUR,
AU MOIS D'OCTOBRE MIL CINQ CENT TRENTE SEPT

Adieu la Cour, adieu les Dames,
Adieu les filles, et les femmes,
Adieu vous dis, pour quelque temps,
Adieu vos plaisants passetemps,
Adieu le bal, adieu la danse,
Adieu mesure, adieu cadence,
Tambourins, Hautbois, et Violons,
Puisqu'à la guerre nous allons.
Adieu donc les belles, adieu,
Adieu Cupido votre Dieu,
Adieu ses flèches, et flambeaux,
Adieu vos serviteurs tant beaux,
Tant polis, et tant damerets ;
Ô comment vous les traiterez
Ceux, qui vous servent à cette heure !
Or adieu quiconque demeure,
Adieu Jacquais [1], et le valet,
Adieu la torche, et le mulet,
Adieu Monsieur, qui se retire,
Navré de l'amoureux martyre,
Qui la nuit sans dormir sera,
Mais en ses amours pensera.
Adieu le bon jour du matin,
Et le blanc, et le dur Tétin
De la belle, qui n'est pas prête :
Adieu un autre, qui s'enquète
S'il est jour ou non là dedans :
Adieu les signes évidents,
Que l'un est trop mieux retenu,
Que l'autre n'est le bien venu :
Adieu, qui n'est aimé de nulle,

---

1. synonyme de laquais.

Et ne sert que tenir la Mule.
Adieu fêtes, adieu banquets.
Adieu devises, et caquets,
Où plus y a de beau langage
Que de serviette d'ouvrage :
Et moins de vraie affection,
Que de dissimulation.
Adieu les regards gracieux,
Messagers des cœurs soucieux :
Adieu les profondes pensées,
Satisfaites, ou offensées :
Adieu les harmonieux sons
De rondeaux, dizains, et chansons :
Adieu piteux département,
Adieu regrets, adieu tourment,
Adieu la lettre, adieu le page,
Adieu la Cour, et l'équipage :
Adieu l'amitié si loyale,
Qu'on la pourrait dire Royale,
Étant gardée en ferme Foi
Par ferme cœur digne de Roi :
. . . .
Or adieu m'amie, la dernière,
En vertus, et beauté première :
Je vous prie me rendre à présent
Le cœur, dont je vous fis présent,
Pour en la guerre, où il faut être,
En faire service à mon maître.
Or quand de vous se souviendra,
L'aiguillon d'honneur l'époindra
Aux armes, et vertueux fait.
Et s'il en sortait quelque effet
Digne d'une louange entière,
Vous en seriez seule héritière.
De votre cœur, donc vous souvienne.
Car si Dieu veut, que je revienne,
Je le rendrai en ce beau lieu.
Or je fais fin à mon adieu.

Les Épitres, **XXIII**

DU DÉPART DE S'AMIE

Elle s'en va de moi la mieux aimée,
Elle s'en va (certes) et si demeure
Dedans mon cœur tellement imprimée,
Qu'elle y sera jusques à ce qu'il meure.
Voise où vouldra, d'elle mon cœur s'assure :
Et s'assurant n'est mélancolieux :
Mais l'œil veut mal à l'espace des lieux,
De rendre ainsi sa liesse lointaine :
Or Adieu donc le plaisir de mes yeux,
Et de mon cœur l'assurance certaine.

Les Épigrammes,
Premier Livre, **XXIII**

DU LIEUTENANT CRIMINEL DE PARIS,
ET DE SAMBLANÇAY

Lors que Maillart Juge d'Enfer menait
À Montfaulcon Samblançay l'âme rendre,
À votre avis, lequel des deux tenait
Meilleur maintien ? Pour le vous faire entendre,
Maillart semblait homme qui mort va prendre :
Et Samblançay fut si ferme vieillard,
Que l'on cuidait (pour vrai) qu'il menât pendre
À Montfaulcon le Lieutenant Maillart.

Les Épigrammes,
Premier Livre, XLIII

HUICTAIN

Plus ne suis ce que j'ai été,
Et ne le saurais jamais être.
Mon beau printemps et mon été,
Ont fait le saut par la fenêtre.
Amour, tu as été mon maître,
Je t'ai servi sur tous les Dieux.
Ô, si je pouvais deux fois naître,
Comme je te servirais mieux !

Les Épigrammes,
Troisième Livre, LIII

MAURICE SCÈVE

(1500-1563 ?)

Délie Objet de plus haute vertu

Pour la première fois en France, un poète consacre tout un recueil de vers à une seule femme, à l'exemple des *canzioneri* italiens. Pétrarquisme et néo-platonisme dominent alors la pensée humaniste. Scève emprunte au premier le jeu précieux des métaphores obligées, toutes les larmes et les flammes qui disent la douleur de l'absence ou celle plus cruelle encore de l'indifférence. Le platonisme, lui, ouvre une voie à l'amour pur, capable de transcender la souffrance et de sublimer le désir. Cette vision confère à l'œuvre gravité et profondeur, et l'écriture savante, la perfection recherchée dans la clôture de la strophe, et les obscurités qui en découlent, ne relèvent pas d'un jeu ou d'une ascèse pure, elles disent aussi les étapes d'un cheminement spirituel. Le poète a réellement aimé Pernette du Guillet mariée à un autre. Sa jalousie éclate parfois, comme impossible à contenir, en termes fort clairs :

> *Ha, lui indigne, il la tient, il la touche*
> *Elle le souffre...*

Mais la raison étouffe en lui les « silentes clameurs » et lui fait peu à peu concevoir la vraie nature de l'amour, capable en séparant l'âme du corps, de communiquer à celle-ci une joie ineffable, une vie plus intense et, par là, de vaincre le temps et la mort.

Aussi les 449 dizains qui composent la *Délie* relèvent-ils d'une double lecture : chacun d'eux doit être déchiffré comme une unité autonome, puisque le sens y est enclos, mais il faut aussi l'appréhender en fonction de sa place dans l'ensemble de l'œuvre : tous appartiennent à un cosmos qui s'ordonne autour de l'unique étoile, Délie, divinité à la fois terrestre, souterraine et céleste.

L'esprit naturellement abstrait de Scève, marqué par sa formation scolastique et savante, et visiblement épris de symbolique des nombres, ouvre même la voie à une lecture ésotérique de son œuvre, comme le souligne Albert-Marie Schmidt, et confère à celle-ci une ampleur poétique inconnue des pétrarquistes.

La *Délie* n'est pas d'accès facile, et chaque strophe ne se donne pas d'emblée, mais le lecteur, entraîné par le rythme suggestif du dizain et la force de certaines images, est finalement amené à se passionner pour ce combat sans fin de l'amour refusé et pourtant triomphant.

DÉLIE

XII

Ce lien d'or, rais de toi, mon Soleil,
Qui par le bras t'asservit Âme et vie,
Détient si fort avec la vue l'œil,
Que ma pensée il t'a toute ravie,
Me démontrant, certes, qu'il me convie
À me stiller [1] tout sous ton habitude.
    Heureux service en libre servitude,
Tu m'apprends donc être trop plus de gloire,
Souffrir pour une en sa mansuétude,
Que d'avoir eu de toute autre victoire.

XXII

Comme Hecaté tu me feras errer
Et vif et mort cent ans parmi les Ombres ;
Comme Diane au Ciel me resserrer,
D'où descendis en ces mortels encombres ;
Comme régnante aux infernales ombres
Amoindriras ou accroîtras mes peines.
    Mais comme Lune infuse dans mes veines
Celle tu fus, es, et seras DÉLIE,
Qu'Amour a jointe à mes pensées vaines
Si fort que Mort jamais ne l'en délie.

---

1. conformer.

XLIX

Tant je l'aimai qu'en elle encor je vis :
Et tant la vis que, malgré moi, je l'aime.
Le sens et l'âme y furent tant ravis,
Que par l'Œil faut que le cœur la désaime.
    Est-il possible en ce degré suprême
Que fermeté son oultrepas [1] révoque ?
    Tant fut la flamme en nous deux réciproque
Que mon feu luit, quand le sien clair m'appert.
Mourant le sien, le mien tôt se suffoque,
Et ainsi elle, en se perdant, me perd.

LI

Si grand beauté, mais bien si grand merveille,
Qui à Phébus offusque sa clarté,
Soit que je sois présent ou écarté,
De sorte l'âme en sa lueur m'éveille,
Qu'il m'est avis en dormant que je veille,
Et qu'en son jour un espoir je prévois,
Qui, de bien bref, sans délai ou renvois,
M'éclaircira mes pensées funèbres.
    Mais, quand sa face en son Midi je vois,
À tous clarté, et à moi rend ténèbres.

---

1. *oultrepas* : perfection.

LXXIX

L'Aube éteignait Étoiles à foison,
Tirant le jour des régions infimes,
Quand Apollo montant sur l'Horizon
Des monts cornus dorait les hautes cimes.
Lors du profond des ténébreux Abîmes,
Où mon penser par ses fâcheux ennuis
Me fait souvent percer les longues nuits,
Je révoquai à moi l'âme ravie.
Qui, desséchant mes larmoyants conduits,
Me fit clair voir le Soleil de ma vie.

XCVI

Te voyant rire avecques si grand grâce,
Ce doux souris me donne espoir de vie,
Et la douceur de cette tienne face
Me promet mieux de ce dont j'ai envie.
    Mais la froideur de ton cœur me convie
À désespoir, mon dessein dissipant.
Puis ton parler, du Miel participant,
Me remet sus le désir qui me mord.
    Par quoi tu peux, mon bien anticipant,
En un moment me donner vie et mort.

CLXI

Seul avec moi, elle avec sa partie ;
Moi en ma peine, elle en sa molle couche.
Couvert d'ennui je me vautre en l'Ortie,
Et elle nue entre ses bras se couche.
　　　Hà – lui indigne – il la tient, il la touche,
Elle le souffre ; et, comme moins robuste,
Viole amour par ce lien injuste
Que droit humain, et non divin, a fait.
　　　Ô sainte loi à tous, fors à moi, juste,
Tu me punis pour elle avoir méfait !

CXCVI

Tes doigts tirant non le doux son des cordes,
Mais des hauts cieux l'Angélique harmonie,
Tiennent encor en telle symphonie,
Et tellement les oreilles concordes,
Que paix et guerre ensemble tu accordes
En ce concent [1], que lors je concevois.
　　　Car du plaisir, qu'avecques toi j'avais,
Comme le vent se joue avec la flamme,
L'esprit divin de ta céleste voix
Soudain m'éteint et plus soudain m'enflamme.

---

1. harmonie.

CCXXVIII

Tout en esprit ravi sur la beauté,
De notre siècle et honneur et merveille,
Celant en soi la douce cruauté,
Qui en mon mal si plaisamment m'éveille,
Je songe et vois, et voyant m'émerveille
De ses doux ris et élégantes mœurs.
     Les admirant, si doucement je meurs,
Que plus profond à y penser je r'entre :
Et, y pensant, mes silentes [1] clameurs
Se font ouïr et des Cieux et du Centre.

CCLXII

Je vais cherchant les lieux plus solitaires,
De désespoir et d'horreur habités,
Pour de mes maux les rendre secrétaires,
Maux de tout bien, certes, déshérités,
Qui de me nuire, et autrui usités,
Font encor peur, même à la solitude,
Sentant ma vie en telle inquiétude,
Que plus fuyant, et de nuit et de jour,
Ses beaux yeux saints, plus loin de servitude
À mon penser sont ici doux séjour.

---

1. silencieuses.

CCLXIV

La Mort pourra m'ôter et temps et heur(e),
Voire encendrir [1] la mienne arse [2] dépouille :
Mais qu'elle fasse en fin que je ne veuille
Te désirer, encor que mon feu meure ?
Si grand pouvoir en elle ne demeure.
    Tes fiers dédains, toute ta froide essence,
Ne feront point, me niant ta présence,
Qu'en mon penser audacieux ne vive,
Qui, malgré Mort, et malgré toute absence,
Te représente à moi trop plus que vive.

CCCVII

Plus je la vois, plus j'adore sa face,
Miroir meurtrier de ma vie mourante ;
Et n'est plaisir qu'à mes yeux elle fasse,
Qu'il ne leur soit une joie courante,
Comme qui est de leur mal ignorante,
Et qui puis vient en deuil se convertir.
    Car du profond du Cœur me fait sortir
Deux grands ruisseaux, procédant d'une veine,
Qui ne se peut tarir ne [3] divertir,
Pour être vive et sourgeante [4] fontaine.

---

1. réduire en cendres. — 2. brûlée. — 3. ni. — 4. jaillissante.

PERNETTE DU GUILLET

(v. 1520-1545)

Si elle avait vécu plus longtemps, Pernette du Guillet aurait sans doute regroupé et ordonné ces *Rymes* éparses – épigrammes, chansons, « coq à l'âne » et autres – qui nous ont été transmises dans le désordre où elles furent trouvées après sa mort. Telles quelles elles s'apparentent à un journal de sa rencontre avec Scève où elle consigne, en vers, ses réflexions sur leur « parfaite amitié », et, pourrait-on dire, son étonnement sans fin devant un amour qui éclaire et oriente sa vie.

Elle y exprime avec grâce sa certitude d'être indigne d'une telle passion, affirmation tempérée par l'assurance de son pouvoir sur le poète dont elle loue le génie. Elle l'appelle « mon Jour » car de lui elle attend pour elle-même illumination intellectuelle et progrès spirituel. Ne doit-il pas en effet lui communiquer un peu de son immense savoir, puisqu'elle lui appartient tout entière, du moins en esprit car elle persiste à se refuser à lui.

Ce témoignage sur l'univers mental et affectif d'une très jeune femme de la Renaissance nous est précieux, même si cette dernière n'a pas le talent d'une autre Lyonnaise célèbre. Surtout il y a quelque chose de touchant dans l'évocation d'un destin dont le cours fut modifié et enrichi par un dialogue amoureux devenu pour nous (quelles qu'aient pu être les faveurs accordées à cet amant prestigieux) un exemple de la puissance édifiante de l'amour platonique.

RYMES

La nuit était pour moi si très obscure
Que Terre, et Ciel elle m'obscurcissait,
Tant qu'à Midi de discerner figure
N'avais pouvoir – qui fort me marrissait :
Mais quand je vis que l'aube apparaissait
En couleurs mille et diverse, et sereine,
Je me trouvai de liesse si pleine –
Voyant déjà la clarté à la ronde –
Que commençai louer à voix hautaine
Celui qui fit pour moi ce Jour au Monde.

Esprit céleste, et des Dieux transformé
En corps mortel transmis en ce bas Monde,
À Apollo peux être conformé
Pour la vertu, dont es la source, et l'onde.
Ton éloquence, avecques ta faconde,
Et haut savoir, auquel tu es appris,
Démontre assez le bien en toi compris :
Car en douceur ta plume tant fluante
A mérité d'emporter gloire, et prix,
Voyant ta veine en haut style affluante.

Comme le corps ne permet point de voir
À son esprit, ni savoir sa puissance :
Ainsi l'erreur, qui tant me fait avoir
Devant les yeux le bandeau d'ignorance,
Ne m'a permis d'avoir la connaissance
De celui là que, pour près le chercher,
Les Dieux avaient voulu le m'approcher :
Mais si haut bien ne m'a su apparaître.
Par quoi à droit l'on me peut reprocher,
Que plus l'ai vu, et moins l'ai su connaître.

LOUISE LABÉ

(v. 1524-1566)

Vingt-trois sonnets ont rendu Louise Labé à jamais célèbre.
C'est que leur auteur ne se contente pas de variations sur des
thèmes empruntés. Instruite autant que pouvait l'être une femme
intelligente de la Renaissance formée par les meilleurs maîtres, elle
lit dans leur langue les poètes néo-latins et italiens, et les interprète
en s'accompagnant du luth, mais cette « innutrition » pour
reprendre le mot de Du Bellay, si elle lui permet d'assimiler tout
l'héritage de Pétrarque, ne fait pas obstacle à des accents très
personnels. Sa sincérité dans l'expression de la passion, une
véhémence amoureuse impudique et si peu usitée en son temps de
la part d'une femme, lui valurent alors les blâmes et parfois même
les injures des censeurs, mais les inscrivent dans notre mémoire de
manière ineffaçable.

Nous connaissons le destinataire de ces vers : c'est le poète
Olivier de Magny. Aussi, loin de voir seulement dans le premier
sonnet cité un jeu poétique et une habile réplique du modèle
italien (« *O passi sparsi ! o pensier vaghi et pronti* »), il faut le lire
comme un aveu enflammé. On pourra en juger plus loin par le
parfait écho que lui renvoie le sonnet symétrique de Magny. Par ce
procédé il se désigne lui-même clairement comme l'amant de la
Belle Cordière, et marque la réciprocité de leur passion.

SONNETS

I

Ô beaux yeux bruns, ô regards détournés,
Ô chauds soupirs, ô larmes épandues,
Ô noires nuits vainement attendues,
Ô jours luisants vainement retournés :

Ô tristes plaintes, ô désirs obstinés,
Ô temps perdus, ô peines dépendues,
Ô mille morts en mille rets tendues,
Ô pires maux contre moi destinés :

Ô ris, ô front, cheveux, bras, mains et doigts :
Ô luth plaintif, viole, archet et voix :
Tant de flambeaux pour ardre une femelle !

De toi me plains, que, tant de feux portant,
En tant d'endroits d'iceux mon cœur tâtant,
N'en est sur toi volé quelque étincelle.

XI

Luth, compagnon de ma calamité,
De mes soupirs témoin irréprochable,
De mes ennuis contrôleur véritable,
Tu as souvent avec moi lamenté :

Et tant le pleur piteux t'a molesté,
Que, commençant quelque son délectable,
Tu le rendais tout soudain lamentable,
Feignant le ton que plein avait chanté.

Et si te veux efforcer au contraire,
Tu te détends, et si me contrains taire :
Mais, me voyant tendrement soupirer,

Donnant faveur à ma tant triste plainte,
En mes ennuis me plaire suis contrainte,
Et d'un doux mal douce fin espérer.

XII

Oh, si j'étais en ce beau sein ravie
De celui là pour lequel vais mourant :
Si avec lui vivre le demeurant
De mes courts jours ne m'empêchait envie :

Si m'accolant me disait : chère Amie,
Contentons nous l'un l'autre, s'assurant
Que jà tempête, Euripe, ne Courant
Ne nous pourra desjoindre en notre vie :

Si, de mes bras le tenant accolé,
Comme du Lierre est l'arbre encercelé,
La mort venait, de mon aise envieuse,

Lors que souef[1] plus il me baiserait,
Et mon esprit sur ses lèvres fuirait,
Bien je mourrais, plus que vivante, heureuse.

---

1. doucement.

XIII

Tant que mes yeux pourront larmes épandre
À l'heur passé avec toi regretter :
Et qu'aux sanglots et soupirs résister
Pourra ma voix, et un peu faire entendre :

Tant que ma main pourra les cordes tendre
Du mignard Luth, pour tes grâces chanter :
Tant que l'esprit se voudra contenter
De ne vouloir rien fors que toi comprendre :

Je ne souhaitte encore point mourir.
Mais quand mes yeux je sentirai tarir,
Ma voix cassée, et ma main impuissante,

Et mon esprit en ce mortel séjour
Ne pouvant plus montrer signe d'amante :
Prierai la Mort noircir mon plus clair jour.

XIV

Pour le retour du Soleil honorer,
Le Zéphir l'air serein lui appareille,
Et du sommeil l'eau et la terre éveille,
Qui les gardait, l'une de murmurer

En doux coulant, l'autre de se parer
De mainte fleur de couleur non pareille.
Jà les oiseaux ès arbres font merveille
Et aux passants font l'ennui modérer :

Les Nymphes jà en mille jeux s'ébattent
Au clair de Lune, et, dansant, l'herbe abattent :
Veux tu, Zéphir, de ton heur me donner,

Et que par toi toute me renouvelle ?
Fais mon Soleil devers moi retourner,
Et tu verras s'il ne me rend plus belle.

XXIII

Ne reprenez, Dames, si j'ai aimé,
Si j'ai senti mille torches ardentes,
Mille travaux, mille douleurs mordantes.
Si, en pleurant, j'ai mon temps consumé,

Las ! que mon nom n'en soit par vous blâmé.
Si j'ai failli, les peines sont présentes,
N'aigrissez point leurs pointes violentes :
Mais estimez qu'Amour, à point nommé,

Sans votre ardeur d'un Vulcain excuser,
Sans la beauté d'Adonis accuser,
Pourra, s'il veut, plus vous rendre amoureuses,

En ayant moins que moi d'occasion,
Et plus d'étrange et forte passion.
Et gardez vous d'être plus malheureuses !

OLIVIER DE MAGNY

(v. 1529-1561)

Il fut l'ami des poètes de la Pléiade, et son nom est cité par Du Bellay dont il partagea l'exil romain. *Les Souspirs* sont un mélange de poésies amoureuses et satiriques, le poète y fait souvent allusion à des événements de la vie romaine, mais la comparaison avec *Les Regrets* permet de mesurer tout ce qui le sépare de Du Bellay.

Il ne prend pas de distance vis-à-vis de ses modèles et il ressasse les thèmes des poètes pétrarquisants sans faire entendre une voix originale. L'amour qu'il célèbre dans ses vers n'est pas seulement celui que lui inspira Louise Labé, et pour tout dire ses « souspirs » nous semblent, pour la plupart, assez conventionnels ! Certains cependant retiennent notre attention et ne sont pas sans charme. Ainsi ceux que l'on va lire. Il est vrai que le modèle est ici Pétrarque lui-même, aussi le poète parvient à exprimer avec grâce, dans l'un la douleur d'aimer, dans l'autre la victoire espérée de l'amour, en dépit des obstacles, selon la figure rhétorique de l'« adynaton », c'est-à-dire le jeu sur l'impossible.

Ô beaux yeux bruns, ô regards détournés,
Ô chauds soupirs, ô larmes épandues,
Ô noires nuits vainement attendues,
Ô jours luisants vainement retournés :

Ô tristes plaintes, ô désirs obstinés,
Ô temps perdu, ô peines dépendues,
Ô mille morts en mille rets tendues,
Ô pires maux contre moi destinés :

Ô pas épars, ô trop ardente flamme,
Ô douce erreur, ô pensers de mon âme,
Qui çà, qui là, me tournez nuit et jour,

Ô vous mes yeux, non plus yeux mais fontaines,
Ô dieux, ô cieux, et personnes humaines,
Soyez pour dieu témoins de mon amour.

Les Souspirs, **IV**

SONNET

Âpre cœur, et sauvage, et fière volonté,
En tant douce, et tant humble, angélique figure,
Si vos grandes rigueurs plus longuement j'endure,
Vous aurez peu d'honneur de m'avoir surmonté.

Soit l'automne, ou l'hiver, le printemps, ou l'été,
Ou soit-il jour luisant, ou soit-il nuit obscure,
Je me plains en tout temps de ma rude avanture,
De ma dame et d'amour sans cesse tourmenté.

L'espoir seul me fait vivre, et me fait souvenir
Que j'ai vu maintes fois par épreuve advenir,
Que l'eau par trait de temps les grands marbres entame

Et qu'il n'est point de cœur si dur ne si cruel,
Qu'on ne puisse amollir d'un pleur continuel,
Ni de si froid vouloir qui parfois ne s'enflamme.

DU BELLAY

(1522-1560)

Les thèmes dominants de son œuvre nous amènent souvent à le lire comme un lointain avant-coureur des romantiques. Le leitmotiv de la plainte élégiaque peut faire croire, en effet, que le poète laisse parler son cœur. N'appelle-t-il pas *Les Regrets* ses « papiers journaux » ou ses « commentaires » ? Mais l'imitation des anciens et les modèles italiens tiennent une très grande place chez l'auteur de *La Deffence et Illustration*, il n'eut sans doute pas écrit *Les Regrets* si Ovide ne lui avait fourni la caution des *Tristes*. Il faut donc voir en lui un poète qui, à la différence des romantiques, souhaite moins parler de sa souffrance que lui conférer un caractère universel en l'inscrivant dans des formes reconnues. Cependant la tristesse qui domine dans les recueils rapportés d'Italie est bien réelle. Ses premières œuvres, *Le Chant*, puis *La Complainte du désespéré*, traduisent déjà ses dispositions naturelles à la mélancolie. Mais son désarroi d'humaniste devant le spectacle que lui offrent à Rome ces « poudreux tombeaux », seuls vestiges de la grandeur passée, la méditation qu'il fait naître sur le caractère périssable de toute entreprise humaine, fût-ce la plus prestigieuse, sa déception personnelle devant les fonctions d'intendant – si peu faites pour lui – qui lui sont assignées, le mépris que lui inspirent les basses intrigues de la cour romaine, vont nourrir son désespoir et parfois sa colère. Il craint en outre d'avoir sacrifié à la chimère d'un avenir matériellement assuré, tout son pouvoir d'invention poétique. Nous voyons cependant que c'est dans ses vers les plus inspirés qu'il se plaint d'avoir perdu l'inspiration !

On lira d'abord ici l'un des sonnets les plus connus de *L'Olive*.

S'il y reprend un thème déjà présent dans la *Délie*, c'est lui qui inaugure vraiment toute la lignée des « Belles Matineuses », aucune n'aura autant de grâce à peindre l'apparition de la jeune fille dont la beauté éclipse celle de l'Aurore. Viennent ensuite *Les Antiquités* qui montrent le poète fasciné par les ruines et prolongeant sa méditation funèbre par une vision symbolique reçue en songe. *Les Regrets* enfin disent la nostalgie du pays natal et la douleur de l'exil. En eux on peut voir quelques-uns des plus beaux vers-talismans de la langue française.

Déjà la nuit en son parc amassait
Un grand troupeau d'étoiles vagabondes,
Et pour entrer aux cavernes profondes,
Fuyant le jour, ses noirs chevaux chassait.

Déjà le ciel aux Indes rougissait,
Et l'Aube encor de ses tresses tant blondes
Faisant grêler mille perlettes rondes,
De ses trésors les prés enrichissait.

Quand d'occident, comme une étoile vive,
Je vis sortir dessus ta verte rive,
Ô fleuve mien ! une Nymphe en riant.

Alors voyant cette nouvelle Aurore,
Le jour honteux d'un double teint colore
Et l'Angevin et l'Indique orient.

L'Olive, **LXXXIII**

Nouveau venu, qui cherches Rome en Rome
Et rien de Rome en Rome n'aperçois,
Ces vieux palais, ces vieux arcs que tu vois,
Et ces vieux murs, c'est ce que Rome on nomme.

Vois quel orgueil, quelle ruine : et comme
Celle qui mit le monde sous ses lois,
Pour dompter tout, se dompta quelquefois,
Et devint proie au temps, qui tout consomme.

Rome de Rome est le seul monument,
Et Rome Rome a vaincu seulement,
Le Tibre seul, qui vers la mer s'enfuit,

Reste de Rome. Ô mondaine inconstance !
Ce qui est ferme, est par le temps détruit,
Et ce qui fuit, au temps fait résistance.

Les Antiquités de Rome, III

Telle que dans son char la Bérécynthienne
Couronnée de tours, et joyeuse d'avoir
Enfanté tant de Dieux, telle se faisait voir
En ses jours plus heureux cette ville ancienne :

Cette ville qui fut, plus que la Phrygienne,
Foisonnante en enfants, et de qui le pouvoir
Fut le pouvoir du monde, et ne se peut revoir,
Pareille à sa grandeur, grandeur, sinon la sienne.

Rome seule pouvait à Rome ressembler,
Rome seule pouvait Rome faire trembler :
Aussi n'avait permis l'ordonnance fatale

Qu'autre pouvoir humain, tant fût audacieux,
Se vantât d'égaler celle qui fit égale
Sa puissance à la terre et son courage aux cieux.

Les Antiquités de Rome, VI

Comme on passe en été le torrent sans danger,
Qui soulait en hiver être roi de la plaine,
Et ravir par les champs d'une fuite hautaine
L'espoir du laboureur et l'espoir du berger ;

Comme on voit les couards animaux outrager
Le courageux lion gisant dessus l'arène,
Ensanglanter leurs dents, et d'une audace vaine
Provoquer l'ennemi qui ne se peut venger ;

Et comme devant Troie on vit des Grecs encor
Braver les moins vaillants autour du corps d'Hector :
Ainsi ceux qui jadis soulaient, à tête basse,

Du triomphe Romain la gloire accompagner,
Sur ces poudreux tombeaux exercent leur audace,
Et osent les vaincus les vainqueurs dédaigner.

Les Antiquités de Rome, XIV

Ayant tant de malheurs gémi profondément,
Je vis une Cité quasi semblable à celle
Que vit le messager de la bonne nouvelle,
Mais bâti sur le sable était son fondement.

Il semblait que son chef touchât au firmament,
Et sa forme n'était moins superbe que belle :
Digne, s'il en fut onc, digne d'être immortelle,
Si rien dessous le ciel se fondait fermement.

J'étais émerveillé de voir si bel ouvrage,
Quand du côté du Nord vint le cruel orage,
Qui soufflant la fureur de son cœur dépité

Sur tout ce qui s'oppose encontre sa venue,
Renversa sur le champ, d'une poudreuse nue,
Les faibles fondements de la grande Cité.

Songe, **XII**

Ceux qui sont amoureux, leurs amours chanteront,
Ceux qui aiment l'honneur, chanteront de la gloire,
Ceux qui sont près du Roi publiront sa victoire,
Ceux qui sont courtisans, leurs faveurs vanteront,

Ceux qui aiment les arts, les sciences diront,
Ceux qui sont vertueux, pour tels se feront croire,
Ceux qui aiment le vin, deviseront de boire,
Ceux qui sont de loisir, de fables écriront,

Ceux qui sont médisants, se plairont à médire,
Ceux qui sont moins fâcheux, diront des mots pour rire,
Ceux qui sont plus vaillants, vanteront leur valeur,

Ceux qui se plaisent trop, chanteront leur louange,
Ceux qui veulent flatter, feront d'un diable un ange,
Moi qui suis malheureux, je plaindrai mon malheur.

Les Regrets, V

Las, où est maintenant ce mépris de Fortune ?
Où est ce cœur vainqueur de toute adversité,
Cet honnête désir de l'immortalité,
Et cette honnête flamme au peuple non commune ?

Où sont ces doux plaisirs, qu'au soir, sous la nuit brune,
Les Muses me donnaient, alors qu'en liberté,
Dessus le vert tapis d'un rivage écarté,
Je les menais danser aux rayons de la Lune ?

Maintenant la Fortune est maîtresse de moi,
Et mon cœur, qui soulait être maître de soi,
Est serf de mille maux et regrets qui m'ennuyent.

De la postérité je n'ai plus de souci,
Cette divine ardeur, je ne l'ai plus aussi,
Et les Muses, de moi, comme étranges, s'enfuyent.

Les Regrets, VI

France, mère des arts, des armes et des lois,
Tu m'as nourri long temps du lait de ta mamelle :
Ores, comme un agneau qui sa nourrice appelle,
Je remplis de ton nom les antres et les bois.

Si tu m'as pour enfant avoué quelquefois,
Que ne me réponds-tu maintenant, ô cruelle ?
France, France, réponds à ma triste querelle.
Mais nul, sinon Écho, ne répond à ma voix.

Entre les loups cruels j'erre parmi la plaine ;
Je sens venir l'hiver, de qui la froide haleine
D'une tremblante horreur fait hérisser ma peau.

Las, tes autres agneaux n'ont faute de pâture,
Ils ne craignent le loup, le vent, ni la froidure :
Si ne suis-je pourtant le pire du troupeau.

Les Regrets, IX

Cependant que Magny suit son grand Avanson,
Panjas son Cardinal, et moi le mien encore,
Et que l'espoir flatteur, qui nos beaux ans dévore,
Appâte nos désirs d'un friand hameçon,

Tu courtises les Rois, et d'un plus heureux son
Chantant l'heur de Henri, qui son siècle décore,
Tu t'honores toi-même, et celui qui honore
L'honneur que tu lui fais par ta docte chanson.

Las, et nous cependant nous consumons notre âge
Sur le bord inconnu d'un étrange rivage,
Où le malheur nous fait ces tristes vers chanter :

Comme on voit quelquefois, quand la mort les appelle,
Arrangés flanc à flanc parmi l'herbe nouvelle,
Bien loin sur un étang trois cygnes lamenter.

Les Regrets, **XVI**

Heureux qui, comme Ulysse, a fait un beau voyage ;
Ou comme celui-là qui conquit la toison,
Et puis est retourné, plein d'usage et raison,
Vivre entre ses parents le reste de son âge !

Quand reverrai-je, hélas, de mon petit village
Fumer la cheminée, et en quelle saison
Reverrai-je le clos de ma pauvre maison,
Qui m'est une province, et beaucoup davantage ?

Plus me plaît le séjour qu'ont bâti mes aïeux,
Que des palais Romains le front audacieux :
Plus que le marbre dur me plaît l'ardoise fine,

Plus mon Loire Gaulois que le Tibre Latin,
Plus mon petit Liré que le mont Palatin,
Et plus que l'air marin la douceur Angevine.

Les Regrets, **XXXI**

Et je pensais aussi ce que pensait Ulysse,
Qu'il n'était rien plus doux que voir encor un jour
Fumer sa cheminée, et après long séjour
Se retrouver au sein de sa terre nourrice.

Je me réjouissais d'être échappé au vice,
Aux Circés d'Italie, aux Sirènes d'amour,
Et d'avoir rapporté en France à mon retour
L'honneur que l'on s'acquiert d'un fidèle service.

Las, mais après l'ennui de si longue saison,
Mille soucis mordants je trouve en ma maison,
Qui me rongent le cœur sans espoir d'allégeance.

Adieu donques, Dorat, je suis encor Romain,
Si l'arc que les neuf Sœurs te mirent en la main
Tu ne me prête ici, pour faire ma vengeance.

Les Regrets, CXXX

RONSARD

(1524-1585)

Les poèmes sur le Vendômois sont l'une des clefs de l'œuvre de
Ronsard : la fraîcheur des fontaines « jazardes », les berceaux
d'ombre au bord des ruisseaux, refuge à l'heure de la canicule, les
épaisses forêts aux grottes profondes où il se plaît à frissonner,
dessinent son paysage de prédilection, et comme le miroir de son
âme. S'il se distingue d'autres poètes qui ont célébré leur pays
natal, c'est qu'il a, à propos du sien, les accents d'un paysan qui
parle de sa terre, il l'aime d'un amour charnel. Le même rapport
au réel colore les sonnets dédiés à Cassandre, Marie, Hélène ou à
d'autres belles inconnues. Certes, il reste tributaire des modèles
italiens, mais il s'en distingue par un accent nouveau, le trouble
qu'il décrit a réellement été éprouvé par lui, sa sensualité donne
une force inhabituelle à l'expression codée du sentiment, et rompt
avec la mièvrerie convenue des protestations amoureuses. Ce qui
s'offre à nos yeux, ce n'est plus une image idéale, mais, par le jeu
d'un détail concret, un visage et un corps désirables. Et si le poète
associe à l'émoi amoureux la grâce d'un sourire, ou l'ironie légère
qui en estompe l'expression directe, il atteint la perfection. C'est
ce qu'il recherche, et qui lui fait sans cesse retoucher ses poèmes
au fil des éditions successives. Car il ne lui suffit pas d'être l'élu des
Muses, il ne s'arrête pas à leurs dons mais entreprend de savantes
études auprès de Dorat qui lui enseigne l'art des vers. Il peut alors
enrichir la langue de mots qu'il crée ou qu'il retrouve, et aborder,
avec cet instrument perfectionné, tous les genres, de l'élégiaque à
l'épique, tous les tons aussi, qui vont dans son œuvre du badinage
des *Folastries* à la véhémence polémique des *Discours*, ou à la veine

tragique des derniers vers. Il sait aussi bien s'adonner aux formes
brèves, comme le sonnet ou la chanson, que dérouler les grands
Hymnes solennels imités de Pindare. Cette puissance créatrice lui
valut, comme on sait, le titre de « prince des poètes », et justifie
pleinement la réplique orgueilleuse qu'il fit à ses détracteurs :

Vous êtes tous issus de la grandeur de moi.

Une beauté de quinze ans enfantine,
Un or frisé de maint crêpe anelet,
Un front de rose, un teint damoiselet,
Un ris qui l'âme aux Astres achemine ;

Une vertu de telle beauté digne,
Un col de neige, une gorge de lait,
Un cœur jà mûr en un sein verdelet,
En Dame humaine une beauté divine ;

Un œil puissant de faire jours les nuits,
Une main douce à forcer les ennuis,
Qui tient ma vie en ses doigts enfermée ;

Avec un chant découpé doucement
Or' d'un souris, or' d'un gémissement,
De tels sorciers ma raison fut charmée.

Le Premier Livre des Amours,
Les Amours de Cassandre, **XVIII**

Comme un chevreuil, quand le printemps détruit
Du froid hiver la poignante gelée,
Pour mieux brouter la feuille emmiellée,
Hors de son bois avec l'Aube s'enfuit,

Et seul, et sûr, loin de chiens et de bruit,
Or' sur un mont, or' dans une vallée,
Or' près d'une onde à l'écart recelée,
Libre, folâtre où son pied le conduit,

De rets ne d'arc sa liberté n'a crainte
Sinon alors que sa vie est atteinte
D'un trait meurtrier empourpré de son sang.

Ainsi j'allai sans espoir de dommage,
Le jour qu'un œil sur l'avril de mon âge
Tira d'un coup mille traits en mon flanc.

Le Premier Livre des Amours,
Les Amours de Cassandre, **LIX**

Quand ces beaux yeux jugeront que je meure,
Avant mes jours me bannissant là bas,
Et que la Parque aura porté mes pas
À l'autre bord de la rive meilleure,

Antres et prés, et vous forêts, à l'heure,
Pleurant mon mal, ne me dédaignez pas ;
Ains donnez-moi, sous l'ombre de vos bras,
Une éternelle et paisible demeure.

Puisse avenir qu'un poète amoureux,
Ayant pitié de mon sort malheureux,
Dans un cyprès note cet épigramme :

Ci dessous gît un amant vandômois,
Que la douleur tua dedans ce bois
Pour aimer trop les beaux yeux de sa dame.

Le Premier Livre des Amours,
Les Amours de Cassandre, LXII

Ciel, air et vents, plains et monts découverts,
Tertres vineux et forêts verdoyantes,
Rivages tors et sources ondoyantes,
Taillis rasés et vous bocages verts,

Antres moussus à demi-front ouverts,
Prés, boutons, fleurs et herbes rousoyantes,
Vallons bossus et plages blondoyantes,
Et vous rochers, les hôtes de mes vers,

Puisqu'au partir, rongé de soin et d'ire,
À ce bel œil adieu je n'ai su dire,
Qui près et loin me détient en émoi,

Je vous supplie, Ciel, air, vents, monts et plaines,
Taillis, forêts, rivages et fontaines,
Antres, prés, fleurs, dites-le lui pour moi.

Le Premier Livre des Amours,
Les Amours de Cassandre, **LXVI**

Amour, que j'aime à baiser les beaux yeux
De ma maîtresse, et à tordre en ma bouche
De ses cheveux l'or fin qui s'escarmouche
Dessus son front astré comme les cieux !

C'est à mon gré le meilleur de son mieux
Que son bel œil, qui jusqu'au cœur me touche,
Dont le beau nœud d'un Scythe plus farouche
Rendrait le cœur courtois et gracieux.

Son beau poil d'or, et ses sourcils encore
De leurs beautés font vergogner l'Aurore,
Quand au matin elle embellit le jour.

Dedans son œil une vertu demeure,
Qui va jurant par les flèches d'Amour
De me guérir ; mais je ne m'en asseure.

Le Premier Livre des Amours,
Les Amours de Cassandre, **CCXVI**

Marie, vous avez la joue aussi vermeille
Qu'une rose de mai, vous avez les cheveux
Entre bruns et châtains, frisés de mille nœuds,
Gentement tortillés tout autour de l'oreille.

Quand vous étiez petite, une mignarde abeille
Sur vos lèvres forma son nectar savoureux,
Amour laissa ses traits en vos yeux rigoureux,
Pithon vous fit la voix à nulle autre pareille.

Vous avez les tétins comme deux monts de lait,
Qui pommellent ainsi qu'au printemps nouvelet
Pommellent deux boutons que leur chasse environne.

De Junon sont vos bras, des Grâces votre sein,
Vous avez de l'Aurore et le front et la main,
Mais vous avez le cœur d'une fière Lionne.

Le Second Livre des Amours,
Les Amours de Marie, II

Marie, qui voudrait votre nom retourner,
Il trouverait aimer : aimez-moi donc, Marie,
Votre nom de nature à l'amour vous convie :
À qui trahit Nature il ne faut pardonner.

S'il vous plaît votre cœur pour gage me donner,
Je vous offre le mien : ainsi de cette vie
Nous prendrons les plaisirs, et jamais autre envie
Ne me pourra l'esprit d'une autre emprisonner.

Il faut aimer, maîtresse, au monde quelque chose.
Celui qui n'aime point, malheureux se propose
Une vie d'un Scythe, et ses jours veut passer

Sans goûter la douceur, des douceurs la meilleure.
Rien n'est doux sans Vénus et sans son fils : à l'heure
Que je n'aimerai plus, puissé-je trépasser !

Le Second Livre des Amours,
Les Amours de Marie, IX

Marie, levez-vous, ma jeune paresseuse :
Jà la gaie alouette au ciel a fredonné,
Et jà le rossignol doucement jargonné,
Dessus l'épine assis, sa complainte amoureuse.

Sus ! debout ! allons voir l'herbelette perleuse,
Et votre beau rosier de boutons couronné,
Et vos œillets mignons auxquels aviez donné,
Hier au soir, de l'eau d'une main si songeuse.

Harsoir en vous couchant vous jurâtes vos yeux
D'être plus-tôt que moi ce matin éveillée ;
Mais le dormir de l'aube, aux filles gracieux,

Vous tient d'un doux sommeil encor les yeux sillée.
Çà ! çà ! que je les baise et votre beau tétin
Cent fois, pour vous apprendre à vous lever matin.

Le Second Livre des Amours,
Les Amours de Marie, XIX

Quand ravi je me pais de votre belle face,
Je vois dedans vos yeux je ne sais quoi de blanc,
Je ne sais quoi de noir, qui m'émeut tout le sang,
Et qui jusques au cœur de veine en veine passe.

Je vois dedans Amour qui va changeant de place,
Ores bas, ores haut, toujours me regardant,
Et son arc contre moi coup sur coup débandant.
Si je faux, ma raison, que veux-tu que je fasse ?

Tant s'en faut que je sois alors maître de moi,
Que je nierais les Dieux, et trahirais mon Roi,
Je vendrais mon pays, je meurtrirais mon père,

Telle rage me tient après que j'ai tâté
À longs traits amoureux de la poison amère
Qui sort de ces beaux yeux dont je suis enchanté !

Le Second Livre des Amours,
Les Amours de Marie, XL

Marie, tout ainsi que vous m'avez tourné
Ma raison qui de libre est maintenant servile,
Ainsi m'avez tourné mon grave premier style,
Qui pour chanter si bas n'était point ordonné.

Au moins si vous m'aviez pour ma perte donné
Congé de manier votre cuisse gentille,
Ou bien si vous étiez à mes désirs facile,
Je n'eusse regretté mon style abandonné.

Las ! ce qui plus me deult, c'est que n'êtes contente
De voir que ma Muse est si basse et si rampante,
Qui soulait apporter aux Français un effroi.

Mais votre peu d'amour ma loyauté tourmente,
Et sans aucun espoir d'une meilleure attente,
Toujours vous me liez et triomphez de moi.

Le Second Livre des Amours,
Les Amours de Marie, LX

ÉLÉGIE À MARIE

. . . .

Ô ma belle Maîtresse, hé ! que je voudrais bien
Qu'amour nous eût conjoints d'un semblable lien,
Et qu'après nos trépas, dans nos fosses ombreuses,
Nous fussions la chanson des bouches amoureuses !
Que ceux de Vendômois dissent tous d'un accord,
Visitant le tombeau sous qui je serais mort :
« Notre Ronsard, quittant son Loir et sa Gastine.
À Bourgueil fut épris d'une belle Angevine » ;
Et que les Angevins dissent tous d'une voix :
« Notre belle Marie aimait un Vendômois :
Les deux n'avaient qu'un cœur, et l'amour mutuelle
Qu'on ne voit plus ici leur fut perpétuelle ;
Siècle vraiment heureux, siècle d'or estimé,
Où toujours l'amoureux se voyait contre-aimé. »
Puisse arriver après l'espace d'un long âge,
Qu'un esprit vienne à bas, sous le mignard ombrage
Des Myrtes, me conter que les âges n'ont peu
Effacer la clarté qui luit de notre feu ;
Mais que de voix en voix, de parole en parole,
Notre gentille ardeur par la jeunesse vole,
Et qu'on apprend par cœur les vers et les chansons
Qu'Amour chanta pour vous en diverses façons...

Le Second Livre des Amours,
Les Amours de Marie

CHANSON

. . . .
Je voudrais, au bruit de l'eau
     D'un ruisseau,
Déplier ses tresses blondes,
Frisant en autant de nœuds
     Ses cheveux,
Que je verrais friser d'ondes.

Je voudrais, pour la tenir,
     Devenir
Dieu de ces forêts désertes,
La baisant autant de fois
     Qu'en un bois
Il y a de feuilles vertes.

Hà ! maîtresse, mon souci,
     Viens ici.
Viens contempler la verdure !
Les fleurs de mon amitié
     Ont pitié,
Et seule tu n'en as cure.

Au moins lève un peu tes yeux
     Gracieux,
Et vois ces deux colombelles,
Qui font naturellement,
     Doucement,
L'amour du bec et des ailes ;

Et nous, sous ombre d'honneur,
     Le bon-heur
Trahissons par une crainte :
Les oiseaux sont plus heureux
     Amoureux,
Qui font l'amour sans contrainte.

Toutefois ne perdons pas
     Nos ébats
Pour ces lois tant rigoureuses ;
Mais si tu m'en crois, vivons,
     Et suivons
Les colombes amoureuses.

Pour effacer mon émoi,
     Baise moi,
Rebaise moi, ma Déesse !
Ne laissons passer en vain
     Si soudain
Les ans de notre jeunesse.

Le Second Livre des Amours,
Les Amours de Marie

SUR LA MORT DE MARIE

Comme on voit sur la branche au mois de mai la rose,
En sa belle jeunesse, en sa première fleur,
Rendre le ciel jaloux de sa vive couleur,
Quand l'Aube de ses pleurs au point du jour l'arrose ;

La grâce dans sa feuille, et l'amour se repose,
Embaumant les jardins et les arbres d'odeur ;
Mais, battue ou de pluie ou d'excessive ardeur,
Languissante, elle meurt, feuille à feuille déclose.

Ainsi en ta première et jeune nouveauté,
Quand la Terre et le Ciel honoraient ta beauté,
La Parque t'a tuée, et cendre tu reposes.

Pour obsèques reçois mes larmes et mes pleurs,
Ce vase plein de lait, ce panier plein de fleurs,
Afin que vif et mort ton corps ne soit que roses.

Le Second Livre des Amours,
Les Amours de Marie, II, 4

Te regardant assise auprès de ta cousine,
Belle comme une Aurore, et toi comme un Soleil,
Je pensai voir deux fleurs d'un même teint pareil,
Croissantes en beauté, l'une à l'autre voisine.

La chaste, sainte, belle et unique Angevine,
Vite comme un éclair sur moi jeta son œil.
Toi, comme paresseuse et pleine de sommeil,
D'un seul petit regard tu ne m'estimas digne.

Tu t'entretenais seule, au visage abaissé,
Pensive toute à toi, n'aimant rien que toi-même,
Dédaignant un chacun d'un sourcil ramassé,

Comme une qui ne veut qu'on la cherche ou qu'on l'aime.
J'eus peur de ton silence, et m'en allai tout blême,
Craignant que mon salut n'eût ton œil offensé.

Sonnets pour Hélène,
Premier Livre, XVI

Vous me dîtes, Maîtresse, étant à la fenêtre,
Regardant vers Mont-martre et les champs d'alentour :
La solitaire vie, et le désert séjour
Valent mieux que la Cour, je voudrais bien y être.

À l'heure mon esprit de mes sens serait maître,
En jeûne et oraison je passerais le jour,
Je défierais les traits et les flammes d'Amour ;
Ce cruel de mon sang ne pourrait se repaître,

Quand je vous répondis : Vous trompez de penser
Qu'un feu ne soit pas feu pour se couvrir de cendre,
Sur les cloîtres sacrés la flamme on voit passer.

Amour dans les déserts comme aux villes s'engendre,
Contre un Dieu si puissant, qui les Dieux peut forcer,
Jeûnes ni oraisons ne se peuvent défendre.

Sonnets pour Hélène,
Premier Livre, **XXXVI**

Afin qu'à tout jamais de siècle en siècle vive
La parfaite amitié que Ronsard vous portait,
Comme votre beauté la raison lui ôtait,
Comme vous enchaînez sa liberté captive ;

Afin que d'âge en âge à nos neveux arrive
Que toute dans mon sang votre figure était,
Et que rien sinon vous mon cœur ne souhaitait,
Je vous fais un présent de cette Sempervive.

Elle vit longuement en sa jeune verdeur ;
Long temps après la mort je vous ferai revivre,
Tant peut le docte soin d'un gentil serviteur,

Qui veut en vous servant toutes vertus ensuivre.
Vous vivrez, croyez-moi, comme Laure en grandeur,
Au moins tant que vivront les plumes et le livre.

Sonnets pour Hélène,
Second Livre, II

Je plante en ta faveur cet arbre de Cybèle,
Ce pin, où tes honneurs se liront tous les jours :
J'ai gravé sur le tronc nos noms et nos amours,
Qui croîtront à l'envi de l'écorce nouvelle.

Faunes qui habitez ma terre paternelle,
Qui menez sur le Loir vos danses et vos tours,
Favorisez la plante et lui donnez secours,
Que l'Été ne la brûle, et l'Hiver ne la gèle.

Pasteur, qui conduiras en ce lieu ton troupeau,
Flageolant une Églogue en ton tuyau d'aveine,
Attache tous les ans à cet arbre un tableau,

Qui témoigne aux passants mes amours et ma peine ;
Puis l'arrosant de lait et du sang d'un agneau,
Dis : « Ce pin est sacré, c'est la plante d'Hélène. »

Sonnets pour Hélène,
Second Livre, VIII

Quand je pense à ce jour où, près d'une fontaine,
Dans le jardin royal ravi de ta douceur,
Amour te découvrit les secrets de mon cœur,
Et de combien de maux j'avais mon âme pleine,

Je me pâme de joie, et sens de veine en veine
Couler ce souvenir, qui me donne vigueur,
M'aiguise le penser, me chasse la langueur,
Pour espérer un jour une fin à ma peine.

Mes sens de toutes parts se trouvèrent contents,
Mes yeux en regardant la fleur de ton Printemps,
L'oreille en t'écoutant, et sans cette compagne

Qui toujours nos propos tranchait par le milieu,
D'aise au Ciel je volais, et me faisais un Dieu ;
Mais toujours le plaisir de douleur s'accompagne.

Sonnets pour Hélène,
Second Livre, **XIII**

Vous triomphez de moi, et pour ce je vous donne
Ce lierre qui coule et se glisse à l'entour
Des arbres et des murs, lesquels tour dessus tour,
Plis dessus plis il serre, embrasse et environne.

À vous de ce lierre appartient la Couronne,
Je voudrais, comme il fait, et de nuit et de jour,
Me plier contre vous, et languissant d'amour,
D'un nœud ferme enlacer vostre belle colonne.

Ne viendra point le temps que dessous les rameaux,
Au matin où l'Aurore éveille toutes choses,
En un Ciel bien tranquille, au caquet des oiseaux,

Je vous puisse baiser à lèvres demi-closes,
Et vous conter mon mal, et de mes bras jumeaux
Embrasser à souhait votre ivoire et vos roses ?

Sonnets pour Hélène,
Second Livre, **XXIX**

Quand vous serez bien vieille, au soir, à la chandelle,
Assise auprès du feu, dévidant et filant,
Direz, chantant mes vers, en vous émerveillant :
« Ronsard me célébrait du temps que j'étais belle. »

Lors, vous n'aurez servante, oyant telle nouvelle,
Déjà sous le labeur à demi sommeillant,
Qui au bruit de mon nom ne s'aille réveillant,
Bénissant votre nom de louange immortelle.

Je serai sous la terre, et fantôme sans os
Par les ombres myrteux je prendrai mon repos ;
Vous serez au foyer une vieille accroupie,

Regrettant mon amour et votre fier dédain,
Vivez, si m'en croyez, n'attendez à demain :
Cueillez dès aujourd'hui les roses de la vie.

Sonnets pour Hélène,
Second Livre, XLIII

Genèvres hérissés, et vous, houx épineux,
L'un hôte des déserts, et l'autre d'un bocage,
Lierre, le tapis d'un bel antre sauvage,
Sources qui bouillonnez d'un surgeon sablonneux ;

Pigeons, qui vous baisez d'un baiser savoureux,
Tourtres qui lamentez d'un éternel veuvage,
Rossignols ramagers, qui d'un plaisant langage
Nuit et jour rechantez vos versets amoureux ;

Vous à la gorge rouge, étrangère Arondelle,
Si vous voyez aller ma Nymphe en ce Printemps
Pour cueillir des bouquets par cette herbe nouvelle,

Dites lui, pour néant que sa grâce j'attends,
Et que pour ne souffrir le mal que j'ai pour elle,
J'ai mieux aimé mourir que languir si long temps.

Sonnets pour Hélène,
Second Livre, **XLIV**

Le soir qu'Amour vous fit en la salle descendre
Pour danser d'artifice un beau ballet d'Amour,
Vos yeux, bien qu'il fût nuit, ramenèrent le jour,
Tant ils surent d'éclairs par la place répandre.

Le ballet fut divin, qui se soulait reprendre,
Se rompre, se refaire, et tour dessus retour
Se mêler, s'écarter, se tourner à l'entour,
Contre-imitant le cours du fleuve de Méandre.

Ores il était rond, ores long, or' étroit,
Or' en pointe, en triangle en la façon qu'on voit
L'escadron de la Grue évitant la froidure.

Je faux, tu ne dansais, mais ton pied voletait
Sur le haut de la terre ; aussi ton corps s'était
Transformé pour ce soir en divine nature.

Sonnets pour Hélène,
Second Livre, **XLIX**

Je vous envoie un bouquet que ma main
Vient de trier de ces fleurs épanies :
Qui ne les eût à ce vêpre cueillies,
Chutes à terre elles fussent demain.

Cela vous soit un exemple certain
Que vos beautés, bien qu'elles soient fleuries,
En peu temps cherront toutes flétries,
Et, comme fleurs, périront tout soudain.

Le temps s'en va, le temps s'en va, ma Dame,
Las ! le temps non, mais nous nous en allons,
Et tôt serons étendus sous la lame,

Et des amours, desquelles nous parlons,
Quand serons morts, n'en sera plus nouvelle :
Pour ce aimez moi, cependant qu'êtes belle.

Continuation des Amours (1555)

L'an se rajeunissait en sa verte jouvence,
Quand je m'épris de vous, ma Sinope cruelle ;
Seize ans était la fleur de votre âge nouvelle,
Et votre teint sentait encore son enfance.

Vous aviez d'une infante encor la contenance,
La parole, et les pas ; votre bouche était belle,
Votre front et vos mains dignes d'une Immortelle,
Et votre œil, qui me fait trépasser quand j'y pense.

Amour, qui ce jour là si grandes beautés vit,
Dans un marbre, en mon cœur, d'un trait les écrivit ;
Et si pour le jourd'hui vos beautés si parfaites

Ne sont comme autrefois, je n'en suis moins ravi,
Car je n'ai pas égard à cela que vous êtes,
Mais au doux souvenir des beautés que je vis.

Continuation des Amours (1560)

À SA MAÎTRESSE

Mignonne, allons voir si la rose
Qui ce matin avait déclose
Sa robe de pourpre au Soleil,
A point perdu cette vesprée
Les plis de sa robe pourprée,
Et son teint au vôtre pareil.

Las ! voyez comme en peu d'espace,
Mignonne, elle a dessus la place
Las ! las ! ses beautés laissé choir !
Ô vraiment marâtre Nature,
Puis qu'une telle fleur ne dure
Que du matin jusques au soir !

Donc, si vous me croyez, mignonne,
Tandis que votre âge fleuronne
En sa plus verte nouveauté,
Cueillez, cueillez votre jeunesse :
Comme à cette fleur, la vieillesse
Fera ternir votre beauté.

Les Odes, Premier Livre, XVII

Ô Fontaine Bellerie,
Belle fontaine chérie
De nos Nymphes, quand ton eau
Les cache au creux de ta source,
Fuyantes le Satyreau,
Qui les pourchasse à la course
Jusqu'au bord de ton ruisseau,

Tu es la Nymphe éternelle
De ma terre paternelle ;
Pour ce en ce pré verdelet
Vois ton Poète qui t'orne
D'un petit chevreau de lait,
À qui l'une et l'autre corne
Sortent du front nouvelet.

L'Été je dors ou repose
Sur ton herbe, où je compose,
Caché sous tes saules verts,
Je ne sais quoi, qui ta gloire
Enverra par l'univers,
Commandant à la Mémoire
Que tu vives par mes vers.

L'ardeur de la Canicule
Ton vert rivage ne brûle,
Tellement qu'en toutes parts
Ton ombre est épaisse et drue
Aux pasteurs venant des parcs,
Aux bœufs las de la charrue,
Et au bestial épars.

Iô ! tu seras sans cesse
Des fontaines la princesse,
Moi célébrant le conduit

Du rocher percé, qui darde
Avec un enroué bruit
L'eau de ta source jasarde
Qui trépillante se suit.

Les Odes, Second Livre, **IX**

À LA FORÊT DE GASTINE

Couché sous tes ombrages verts,
 Gastine, je te chante
Autant que les Grecs par leurs vers
 La forêt d'Érymanthe.

Car, malin, celer je ne puis
 À la race future
De combien obligé je suis
 À ta belle verdure :

Toi, qui sous l'abri de tes bois
 Ravi d'esprit m'amuses ;
Toi, qui fais qu'à toutes les fois
 Me répondent les Muses ;

Toi, par qui de ce méchant soin
 Tout franc je me délivre,
Lors qu'en toi je me perds bien loin,
 Parlant avec un livre.

Tes bocages soient toujours pleins
 D'amoureuses brigades,
De Satyres et de Sylvains,
 La crainte des Naiades.

En toi habite désormais
 Des Muses le collège,
Et ton bois ne sente jamais
 La flamme sacrilège.

Les Odes, Second Livre, XV

J'ai l'esprit tout ennuyé
D'avoir trop étudié
Les Phénomènes d'Arate :
Il est temps que je m'ébatte,
Et que j'aille aux champs jouer.
Bons Dieux ! qui voudrait louer
Ceux qui collés sur un livre
N'ont jamais souci de vivre ?

Que nous sert l'étudier,
Sinon de nous ennuyer ?
Et soin dessus soin accroître
À nous, qui serons peut-être
Ou ce matin ou ce soir
Victime de l'Orque noir ?
De l'Orque qui ne pardonne,
Tant il est fier, à personne.

Corydon, marche devant,
Sache où le bon vin se vend,
Fais rafraîchir la bouteille,
Cherche une ombrageuse treille
Pour sous elle me coucher :
Ne m'achète point de chair,
Car tant soit-elle friande,
L'Été je hais la viande.

Achète des abricots,
Des pompons, des artichauds,
Des fraises, et de la crème :
C'est en Été ce que j'aime,
Quand sur le bord d'un ruisseau
Je la mange au bruit de l'eau,
Étendu sur le rivage,
Ou dans un antre sauvage.

Ores que je suis dispos,
Je veux rire sans repos,
De peur que la maladie
Un de ces jours ne me die :
« Je t'ai maintenant vaincu,
Meurs, galant, c'est trop vécu. »

Les Odes. Second Livre, XVIII

DE L'ÉLECTION DE SON SÉPULCRE

Antres, et vous, fontaines,
De ces roches hautaines
Qui tombez contre-bas
    D'un glissant pas,

Et vous, forêts et ondes
Par ces prés vagabondes,
Et vous, rives et bois,
    Oyez ma voix.

Quand le Ciel et mon heure
Jugeront que je meure,
Ravi du beau séjour
    Du commun jour,

Je défends qu'on ne rompe
Le marbre, pour la pompe
De vouloir mon tombeau
    Bâtir plus beau ;

Mais bien je veux qu'un arbre
M'ombrage en lieu d'un marbre,
Arbre qui soit couvert
    Toujours de vert.

De moi puisse la terre
Engendrer un lierre,
M'embrassant en maint tour
    Tout à l'entour,

Et la vigne tortisse
Mon sépulcre embellisse,
Faisant de toutes parts
    Un ombre épars.

Là viendront chaque année
À ma fête ordonnée
Avecques leurs troupeaux
Les pastoureaux ;

Puis ayant fait l'office
De leur beau sacrifice,
Parlant à l'île ainsi
Diront ceci :

« Que tu es renommée
D'être tombeau nommée
D'un de qui l'univers
Chante les vers ! »

Les Odes, Quatrième Livre, IV

Quand je suis vingt ou trente mois
Sans retourner en Vendômois,
Plein de pensées vagabondes,
Plein d'un remords et d'un souci,
Aux rochers je me plains ainsi,
Aux bois, aux antres et aux ondes.

Rochers, bien que soyez âgés
De trois mil ans, vous ne changez
Jamais ni d'état ni de forme ;
Mais toujours ma jeunesse fuit,
Et la vieillesse qui me suit,
De jeune en vieillard me transforme.

Bois, bien que perdiez tous les ans
En l'hiver vos cheveux plaisants,
L'an d'après qui se renouvelle,
Renouvelle aussi votre chef ;
Mais le mien ne peut derechef
R'avoir sa perruque nouvelle.

Antres, je me suis vu chez vous
Avoir jadis verts les genous,
Le corps habile, et la main bonne ;
Mais ores j'ai le corps plus dur,
Et les genoux, que n'est le mur
Qui froidement vous environne.

Ondes, sans fin vous promenez
Et vous menez et ramenez
Vos flots d'un cours qui ne séjourne ;
Et moi sans faire long séjour
Je m'en vais, de nuit et de jour,
Au lieu d'où plus on ne retourne.

Si est-ce que je ne voudrais
Avoir été rocher ou bois,
Pour avoir la peau plus épaisse,
Et vaincre le temps emplumé ;
Car ainsi dur je n'eusse aimé
Toi qui m'as fait vieillir, Maîtresse.

Les Odes, Quatrième Livre, **X**

HYMNE DE LA MORT

. . . .
Que ta puissance, ô Mort, est grande et admirable !
Rien au monde par toi ne se dit perdurable ;
Mais, tout ainsi que l'onde aval des ruisseaux fuit
Le pressant coulement de l'autre qui la suit,
Ainsi le temps se coule, et le présent fait place
Au futur importun, qui les talons lui trace.
Ce qui fut, se refait ; tout coule, comme une eau,
Et rien dessous le Ciel ne se voit de nouveau,
Mais la forme se change en une autre nouvelle,
Et ce changement-là, vivre, au monde s'appelle,
Et Mourir, quand la forme en une autre s'en-va.
Ainsi, avec Vénus, la Nature trouva
Moyen de r'animer, par longs et divers changes,
La matière restant, tout cela que tu manges ;
Mais notre âme immortelle est toujours en un lieu,
Au change non sujette, assise auprès de Dieu,
Citoyenne à jamais de la ville éthérée
Qu'elle avait si long temps en ce corps désirée.
Je te salue, heureuse et profitable Mort,
Des extrêmes douleurs médecin et confort.
Quand mon heure viendra, Déesse, je te prie,
Ne me laisse longtemps languir en maladie,
Tourmenté dans un lit, mais puisqu'il faut mourir,
Donne-moi que soudain je te puisse encourir,
Ou pour l'honneur de Dieu, ou pour servir mon Prince,
Navré d'une grand' plaie au bord de ma province.

Ah ! longues Nuits d'hiver, de ma vie bourrelles,
Donnez-moi patience, et me laissez dormir !
Votre nom seulement et suer et frémir
Me fait par tout le corps, tant vous m'êtes cruelles.

Le sommeil tant soit peu n'évente de ses ailes
Mes yeux toujours ouverts, et ne puis affermir
Paupière sur paupière, et ne fais que gémir,
Souffrant comme Ixion des peines éternelles.

Vieille ombre de la terre, ainçois l'ombre d'Enfer,
Tu m'as ouvert les yeux d'une chaîne de fer,
Me consumant au lit, navré de mille pointes ;

Pour chasser mes douleurs amène moi la Mort.
Hà ! Mort, le port commun, des hommes le confort,
Viens enterrer mes maux, je t'en prie à mains jointes !

Les Derniers Vers, IV

Il faut laisser maisons et vergers et jardins,
Vaisselles et vaisseaux que l'artisan burine,
Et chanter son obsèque en la façon du Cygne,
Qui chante son trépas sur les bords Méandrins.

C'est fait, j'ai dévidé le cours de mes destins ;
J'ai vécu, j'ai rendu mon nom assez insigne,
Ma plume vole au Ciel pour être quelque signe,
Loin des appas mondains, qui trompent les plus fins.

Heureux qui ne fut onc, plus heureux qui retourne
En rien comme il était, plus heureux qui séjourne,
D'homme, fait nouvel ange, auprès de Jésus-Christ,

Laissant pourrir çà-bas sa dépouille de boue,
Dont le Sort, la Fortune, et le Destin se joue,
Franc des liens du corps pour n'être qu'un esprit.

Les Derniers Vers, VI

À SON ÂME

Amelette Ronsardelette,
Mignonnelette, doucelette,
Très-chère hôtesse de mon corps,
Tu descends là-bas, faiblelette,
Pâle, maigrelette, seulette,
Dans le froid royaume des morts ;
Toutefois simple, sans remords
De meurtre, poison, ou rancune,
Méprisant faveurs et trésors,
Tant enviés par la commune.
Passant, j'ai dit : suis ta fortune,
Ne trouble mon repos, je dors.

GUILLAUME DE SALUSTE DU BARTAS

(1544-1590)

Très admirée de son vivant, souvent rééditée et commentée, son œuvre fut traduite en latin et en diverses langues, et lue en Italie, en Angleterre ou en Allemagne. Puis elle tomba dans un oubli que Goethe déplorait en disant son admiration pour l'auteur de *La Semaine*. Le dix-neuvième siècle l'exhume et s'intéresse à lui, comme le fait par exemple Nerval en l'accueillant parmi ses *Poètes du 16ᵉ siècle* et en l'invoquant dans un sonnet :

> *Ô Seigneur Du Bartas, je suis de ton lignage*
> *Moi qui soude mon vers à ton vers d'autrefois...*

Le propos de *La Semaine ou la Création de l'univers* est de retracer les étapes de la naissance du monde en suivant le texte de la *Genèse* et l'ordre des sept jours dans *La Première Semaine*, et de consacrer la *Seconde* aux grands épisodes de l'histoire de l'homme. Mais Du Bartas n'eut pas le temps d'achever cette dernière. Ce long récit poétique du commencement du monde s'inscrit dans la lignée du *Microcosme* de Scève ou des *Hymnes* de Ronsard, l'intention apologétique y est dominante. Si les cieux, suivant l'adage connu, disent la gloire de Dieu, le poète qui raconte leur origine en exaltant la toute-puissance du Créateur, contribue aussi à sa louange et remplit sa mission qui est l'édification des hommes.

À ce didactisme religieux s'ajoute la volonté encyclopédique d'embrasser dans ses vers toute la science de son temps ; ce qu'il fait sans en adopter cependant les plus récentes acquisitions.

Fidèle à l'héritage du Moyen Âge, il s'en tient au système de Ptolémée et à une conception fixiste de l'univers.

Vouloir dire ce Tout, par essence indicible, et prétendre donner à voir l'inimaginable, c'est faire preuve d'un bel optimisme. Du Bartas ne doute pas d'y parvenir, l'inspiration aidant, en prenant dans la réalité quotidienne concrète les comparaisons capables de traduire l'ineffable, et en enrichissant son outil verbal de mots qu'il forge à son usage. D'où la prolifération d'images familières, la lourdeur de certaines descriptions, l'incongruité, parfois, des métaphores et l'abus d'adjectifs composés. Sainte-Beuve a quelque raison de trouver chez lui « du trivial et du pédantesque », et le lecteur de se décourager. Cependant certains passages s'imposent à sa mémoire, soit parce que la Bible ou Ronsard y ont guidé de plus près la main du poète, soit parce que ce dernier retrouve alors, de lui-même, la voie du pur lyrisme baroque.

FIN DU MONDE

Un jour de comble-en-fond les rochers crouleront,
Les monts plus sourcilleux de peur se dissoudront,
Le Ciel se crèvera, les plus basses campagnes,
Boursouflées, croîtront en superbes montagnes ;
Les fleuves tariront, et si dans quelque étang
Reste encor quelque flot, ce ne sera que sang ;
La mer deviendra flamme, et les sèches baleines,
Horribles, mugleront sur les cuites arènes ;
En son midi plus clair le jour s'épaissira,
Le ciel d'un fer rouillé sa face voilera.
Sur les astres plus clairs courra le bleu Neptune,
Phoebus s'emparera du noir char de la lune ;
Les étoiles cherront. Le désordre, la nuit,
La frayeur, le trépas, la tempête, le bruit,
Entreront en quartier ; et l'ire vengeresse
Du Juge criminel, qui jà déjà nous presse,
Ne fera de ce Tout qu'un bûcher flamboyant,
Comme il n'en fit jadis qu'un marais ondoyant.

La Première Semaine, Le Premier Jour

ÉLOGE À LA TERRE

Je te salue, ô terre, ô terre porte-grains,
Porte-or, porte-santé, porte-habits, porte-humains,
Porte-fruits, porte-tours, alme, belle, immobile,
Patiente, diverse, odorante, fertile,
Vêtue d'un manteau tout damassé de fleurs,
Passementé de flots, bigarré de couleurs.
Je te salue, ô cœur, racine basse, ronde,
Pied du grand animal qu'on appelle le monde,
Chaste épouse du ciel, assuré fondement
Des étages divers d'un si grand bâtiment.
Je te salue, ô sœur, mère, nourrice, hôtesse
Du roi des animaux. Tout, ô grande princesse,
Vit en faveur de toi. Tant de cieux tournoyants
Portent, pour t'éclairer, leurs astres flamboyants.
Le feu, pour t'échauffer, sur les flottantes nues
Tient ses pures ardeurs en arcade étendues.
L'air, pour te rafraîchir, se plaît d'être secous
Or d'un âpre Borée, or d'un zéphire doux.
L'eau, pour te détremper, de mers, fleuves, fontaines,
Entrelace ton corps tout ainsi que des veines.

La Première Semaine, Le Troisième Jour

PHILIPPE DESPORTES

(1546-1606)

On a peine à croire, en lisant les sonnets et les chansons de Desportes, que tant de fadeur précieuse ait pu, un temps, faire illusion et laisser croire à ses contemporains que Ronsard avait un successeur en la personne de ce poète. La belle aisance avec laquelle il répète jusqu'à satiété les mêmes plaintes et les mêmes soupirs, illustre assez bien la formule railleuse de Boileau sur les désespoirs versifiés du poète qui va

> *Pour quelque Iris en l'air faire le langoureux,*
> *Lui prodiguer les noms de Soleil et d'Aurore,*
> *Et toujours bien mangeant mourir par métaphore.*

Pourtant ce rimeur, au milieu de poèmes d'une élégante vacuité, a trouvé parfois le moyen, grâce à une comparaison empruntée à la mythologie, de se dépasser lui-même, en donnant à ses vers et à la pointe finale du sonnet un relief et un éclat inattendus.

Icare est chut ici, le jeune audacieux,
Qui pour voler au Ciel eut assez de courage :
Ici tomba son corps dégarni de plumage,
Laissant tous braves cœurs de sa chute envieux.

Ô bien-heureux travail d'un esprit glorieux,
Qui tire un si grand gain d'un si petit dommage !
Ô bien-heureux malheur plein de tant d'avantage,
Qu'il rende le vaincu des ans victorieux !

Un chemin si nouveau n'étonna sa jeunesse,
Le pouvoir lui faillit mais non la hardiesse,
Il eut pour le brûler des astres le plus beau.

Il mourut poursuivant une haute aventure,
Le ciel fut son désir, la Mer sa sépulture :
Est-il plus beau dessein, ou plus riche tombeau ?

Les Amours d'Hippolyte, I

Je ressemble en aimant au valeureux Persée,
Que sa belle entreprise a fait si glorieux,
Ayant d'un vol nouveau pris la route des dieux,
Et sur tous les mortels sa poursuite haussée.

Emporté tout ainsi par ma haute pensée,
Je vole aventureux aux soleils de vos yeux
Et vois mille beautés qui m'élèvent aux cieux,
Et me font oublier toute peine passée.

Mais hélas ! je n'ai pas le bouclier renommé,
Dont contre tous périls Vulcain l'avait armé,
Par lequel sans danger il put voir la Gorgonne :

Au contraire à l'instant que je m'ose approcher
De ma belle Méduse, inhumaine et félonne,
Un trait de ses regards me transforme en rocher.

Les Amours d'Hippolyte, **XLI**

AGRIPPA D'AUBIGNÉ

(1552-1630)

On l'a comparé à Hugo : tous deux prosateurs et poètes, ils ont en commun la verve satirique et l'imagination épique. Mais pour d'Aubigné la reconnaissance de son génie ne vint que longtemps après sa mort. Il la doit à la puissance de son inspiration, à la fois orphique et prométhéenne. Dans les cent poèmes offerts à Diane Salviati, le lyrisme domine. *L'Hécatombe à Diane* est le tableau de son « amoureuse rage », il le peint aux couleurs les plus violentes du style baroque :

> *Quand du sort inhumain les tenailles flambantes*
> *Du milieu de mon corps tirent cruellement*
> *Mon cœur qui bat encor...*

Pour dire sa souffrance d'amoureux déçu, il emprunte même parfois son langage à la guerre qu'il connaît bien :

> *Je suis le champ sanglant où la fureur hostile*
> *Vomit le meurtre rouge et la scytique horreur*
> *Qui saccage le sang richesse de mon cœur...*

Pourtant on le voit aussi rêver, sous les ombrages de Talcy, d'un jardin idyllique où Diane régnerait, et exalter sa beauté ; sa manière, alors, rappelle celle de Ronsard. L'originalité de cette œuvre est dans le contraste entre cette veine gracieuse et les accents déchirants de son désespoir, l'amour y acquiert une dimension tragique.

Plus que les sonnets de *L'Hécatombe*, ou les Stances et les Odes qui composent avec eux le recueil du *Printemps*, ce qui fait la gloire du poète, c'est le souffle épique qui anime son grand poème en sept Chants, *Les Tragiques*. Près de dix mille vers pour dire d'abord les *Misères* d'un pays que ravage la guerre civile, et stigmatiser dans *Les Princes* et *La Chambre dorée* la responsabilité des rois ou des grands et celle des juges. Les deux livres suivants, *Les Feux* et *Les Fers*, racontent les supplices et les combats des réformés pour la foi. Vient enfin, dans *Vengeances* et *Jugement*, le rétablissement de la justice des hommes et de celle de Dieu. À l'origine de cet immense édifice poétique, selon d'Aubigné, l'extase qu'il relate dans *Les Fers* : grièvement blessé, il a senti son esprit se détacher du corps et, transporté dans les « régions pures » par « l'Ange consolant [ses] amères blessures », il a pu contempler ce qu'il va décrire. Même si la rédaction des *Tragiques* ne fut entreprise qu'assez longtemps après, leur caractère visionnaire et leur dimension spirituelle rendent plausible cette naissance du poème. Le merveilleux chrétien y domine en effet, et le ciel et la terre y sont mis en scène dans un style apocalyptique. Nourri de Bible jusque dans son écriture aux tournures hébraïques, le poète n'emprunte pas seulement au Livre des images et des récits, mais les accents mêmes des prophètes avec leurs imprécations et leurs rappels des exigences divines. Aussi en se faisant l'historien des guerres de religion, dont il fut l'acteur et le témoin partisan, il confère aux événements qu'il relate une grandeur mythique. Militant de la cause protestante, il retrace à grands traits les combats et les souffrances des siens et fustige les catholiques ; à ses yeux les persécutés s'identifient au peuple d'Israël, et il témoigne de sa foi inébranlable dans le triomphe final pour redonner l'espoir à ceux de son parti que découragent les conversions ou les reniements dans leurs rangs. Il mêle aussi aux références à l'Ancien et au Nouveau Testament, les mythes antiques et les épisodes fameux de l'histoire romaine. À l'ampleur des matériaux ainsi mis en œuvre, s'ajoute le flamboiement d'une langue où l'outrance baroque du vocabulaire et des images, la passion de l'antithèse, le recours fréquent à l'allégorie, font, sans répit, violence au lecteur. Ce dernier ne peut qu'être sensible à la beauté de certains passages, mais il doit également s'efforcer d'épouser le mouvement puissant qui porte le poème tout entier, depuis la description initiale des épreuves ici-bas, jusqu'à la lumière éblouissante du Jugement dernier.

L'HÉCATOMBE À DIANE

Je sens bannir ma peur et le mal que j'endure [1],
Couché au doux abri d'un myrthe et d'un cyprès,
Qui de leurs verts rameaux s'accolant près à près
Encourtinent la fleur qui mon chevet azure !

Oyant virer au fil d'un musicien murmure
Milles nymphes d'argent, qui de leurs flots secrets
Bebrouillent en riant les perles dans les prés,
Et font les diamants rouler à l'aventure.

Ce bosquet de verbrun qui cette onde obscurcit,
D'échos harmonieux et de chants retentit.
Ô séjour amiable ! ô repos précieux !

Ô giron, doux support au chef qui se tourmente !
Ô mes yeux bien heureux éclairés de ses yeux !
Heureux qui meurt ici, et mourant ne lamente !

Le Printemps, **XIX**

---

1. Le premier vers du second tercet éclaire le sonnet : la tête du poète repose sur les genoux de sa maîtresse.

MISÈRES

. . . .
Je n'écris plus les feux d'un amour inconnu,
Mais, par l'affliction plus sage devenu,
J'entreprends bien plus haut, car j'apprends à ma plume
Un autre feu, auquel la France se consume.
Ces ruisselets d'argent, que les Grecs nous feignaient,
Où leurs poètes vains buvaient et se baignaient,
Ne courent plus ici : mais les ondes si claires,
Qui eurent les saphirs et les perles contraires,
Sont rouges de nos morts ; le doux bruit de leurs flots,
Leur murmure plaisant heurte contre des os.
Telle est en écrivant ma non-commune image :
Autre fureur qu'amour reluit en mon visage ;
Sous un inique Mars, parmi les durs labeurs
Qui gâtent le papier et l'encre de sueurs,
Au lieu de Thessalie aux mignardes vallées
Nous avortons ces chants au milieu des armées,
En délassant nos bras de crasse tout rouillés
Qui n'osent s'éloigner des brassards dépouillés.
Le luth que j'accordais avec mes chansonnettes
Est ores étouffé de l'éclat des trompettes ;
Ici le sang n'est feint, le meurtre n'y défaut,
La mort joue elle-même en ce triste échafaud,
Le Juge criminel tourne et emplit son urne.
D'ici la botte en jambe, et non pas le cothurne,
J'appelle Melpomène en sa vive fureur,
Au lieu de l'Hippocrène éveillant cette Sœur
Des tombeaux rafraîchis, dont il faut qu'elle sorte,
Échevelée, affreuse, et bramant en la sorte
Que fait la biche après le faon qu'elle a perdu.
Que la bouche lui saigne, et son front éperdu
Fasse noircir du ciel les voûtes éloignées,
Qu'elle éparpille en l'air de son sang deux poignées
Quand, épuisant ses flancs de redoublés sanglots,
De sa voix enrouée elle bruira ces mots :

« Ô France désolée ! ô terre sanguinaire,
Non pas terre, mais cendre ! ô mère, si c'est mère
Que trahir ses enfans aux douceurs de son sein
Et quand on les meurtrit les serrer de sa main !
Tu leur donnes la vie, et dessous ta mamelle
S'émeut des obstinés la sanglante querelle ;
Sur ton pis blanchissant ta race se débat,
Là le fruit de ton flanc fait le champ du combat. »

Je veux peindre la France une mère affligée,
Qui est entre ses bras de deux enfants chargée.
Le plus fort, orgueilleux, empoigne les deux bouts
Des tétins nourriciers ; puis, à force de coups
D'ongles, de poings, de pieds, il brise le partage
Dont nature donnait à son besson l'usage ;
Ce voleur acharné, cet Esau malheureux
Fait dégât du doux lait qui doit nourrir les deux,
Si que, pour arracher à son frère la vie,
Il méprise la sienne et n'en a plus d'envie.
Mais son Jacob, pressé d'avoir jeûné meshui,
Ayant dompté longtemps en son cœur son ennui,
À la fin se défend, et sa juste colère
Rend à l'autre un combat dont le champ est la mère.
Ni les soupirs ardents, les pitoyables cris,
Ni les pleurs réchauffés ne calment leurs esprits ;
Mais leur rage les guide et leur poison les trouble,
Si bien que leur courroux par leurs coups se redouble.
Leur conflit se r'allume et fait si furieux
Que d'un gauche malheur ils se crèvent les yeux.
Cette femme éplorée, en sa douleur plus forte,
Succombe à la douleur, mi-vivante, mi-morte ;
Elle voit les mutins tous déchirés, sanglants,
Qui, ainsi que du cœur, des mains se vont cherchant.
Quand, pressant à son sein d'un amour maternelle
Celui qui a le droit et la juste querelle,
Elle veut le sauver, l'autre qui n'est pas las
Viole en poursuivant l'asile de ses bras.
Adonc se perd le lait, le suc de sa poitrine ;

Puis, aux derniers abois de sa proche ruine,
Elle dit : « Vous avez, félons, ensanglanté
Le sein qui vous nourrit et qui vous a porté ;
Or vivez de venin, sanglante géniture,
Je n'ai plus que du sang pour votre nourriture. »

Les Tragiques

JUGEMENT

. . . .

Mais quoi ! c'est trop chanté, il faut tourner les yeux
Éblouis de rayons dans le chemin des cieux.
C'est fait, Dieu vient régner, de toute prophétie
Se voit la période à ce point accomplie.
La terre ouvre son sein, du ventre des tombeaux
Naissent des enterrés les visages nouveaux :
Du pré, du bois, du champ, presque de toutes places
Sortent les corps nouveaux et les nouvelles faces.
Ici les fondemens des châteaux rehaussés
Par les ressuscitants promptement sont percés ;
Ici un arbre sent des bras de sa racine
Grouiller un chef vivant, sortir une poitrine ;
Là l'eau trouble bouillonne, et puis s'éparpillant
Sent en soi des cheveux et un chef s'éveillant.
Comme un nageur venant du profond de son plonge,
Tous sortent de la mort comme l'on sort d'un songe.
Les corps par les tyrans autrefois déchirés
Se sont en un moment en leurs corps asserrés,
Bien qu'un bras ait vogué par la mer écumeuse
De l'Afrique brûlée en Thulé froiduleuse.
Les cendres des brûlés volent de toutes parts ;
Les brins, plus tôt unis qu'ils ne furent épars,
Viennent à leur poteau, en cette heureuse place,
Riants au ciel riant d'une agréable audace.
Le curieux s'enquiert si le vieux et l'enfant
Tels qu'ils sont jouiront de l'état triomphant,
Leurs corps n'étant parfaits, ou défaits en vieillesse ?
Sur quoi la plus hardie ou plus haute sagesse
Ose présupposer que la perfection
Veut en l'âge parfait son élévation,
Et la marquent au point des trente-trois années
Qui étaient en Jésus closes et terminées
Quand il quitta la terre et changea, glorieux,
La croix et le sépulcre au tribunal des cieux.

Venons de cette douce et pieuse pensée
À celle qui nous est aux saints écrits laissée.
Voici le Fils de l'homme et du grand Dieu le Fils,
Le voici arrivé à son terme préfix.
Déjà l'air retentit et la trompette sonne,
Le bon prend assurance et le méchant s'étonne.
Les vivants sont saisis d'un feu de mouvement,
Ils sentent mort et vie en un prompt changement,
En une période ils sentent leurs extrêmes ;
Ils ne se trouvent plus eux-mêmes comme eux-mêmes,
Une autre volonté et un autre savoir
Leur arrache des yeux le plaisir de se voir,
Le ciel ravit leurs yeux : des yeux premiers l'usage
N'eût pu du nouveau ciel porter le beau visage.
L'autre ciel, l'autre terre ont cependant fui,
Tout ce qui fut mortel se perd évanoui,
Les fleuves sont séchés, la grand mer se dérobe,
Il fallait que la terre allât changer de robe.
Montagnes, vous sentez douleurs d'enfantements ;
Vous fuyez comme agneaux, ô simples éléments !
Cachez-vous, changez-vous ; rien mortel ne supporte
Le front de l'Éternel ni sa voix rude et forte.
Dieu paraît : le nuage entre lui et nos yeux
S'est tiré à l'écart, il s'est armé de feux ;
Le ciel neuf retentit du son de ses louanges ;
L'air n'est plus que rayons tant il est semé d'Anges,
Tout l'air n'est qu'un soleil ; le soleil radieux
N'est qu'une noire nuit au regard de ses yeux,
Car il brûle le feu, au soleil il éclaire,
Le centre n'a plus d'ombre et ne fuit sa lumière.
Un grand Ange s'écrie à toutes nations :
« Venez répondre ici de toutes actions,
L'Éternel veut juger. » Toutes âmes venues
Font leurs sièges en rond en la voûte des nues,
Et là les Chérubins ont au milieu planté
Un trône rayonnant de sainte majesté.
Il n'en sort que merveille et qu'ardente lumière,
Le soleil n'est pas fait d'une étoffe si claire ;
L'amas de tous vivants en attend justement

La désolation ou le contentement.
Les bons du Saint Esprit sentent le témoignage,
L'aise leur saute au cœur et s'épand au visage :
Car s'ils doivent beaucoup, Dieu leur en a fait don ;
Ils sont vêtus de blanc et lavés de pardon.

Les Tragiques

MARC PAPILLON DE LASPHRISE

(1555-1606)

Le recueil des *Premières Œuvres poétiques du Capitaine Lasphrise*, paraît en 1597. Après Ronsard et Desportes un poète célèbre la jeune fille aimée. Sa première inspiratrice se nomme Théophile, c'est une novice qu'il ne parviendra pas à détourner de sa vocation. La seconde est Noémie, elle répond à son amour et les vers qu'il lui consacre évoquent joyeusement, et parfois même crûment, la réciprocité de leur passion.

Longtemps oublié, ou même tout à fait ignoré, le poète est redécouvert au XXe siècle grâce à Verdun L. Saulnier qui écrit à son propos dans son *Dictionnaire des Lettres françaises* : « ...à dire son expérience sensuelle, il sut mettre une variété, une abondance, une sensibilité, qui font de lui, avec un excellent métier du vers, l'un des poètes les plus attachants de notre Renaissance. »

Le titre d'un article d'A.M. Schmidt sur Lasphrise : *L'eros baroque*, caractérise la fougue, l'éloquence imagée, et le réalisme sans fard qui le distingue de ses prédécesseurs, aucun risque de le confondre avec eux, même s'ils ont des modèles littéraires communs. C'est avec un accent tout à fait personnel de jubilation, et sans recourir aux euphémismes que Marc Papillon parle des plaisirs de l'amour tels qu'il les a goûtés.

Je l'œilladais mi-nue, échevelée,
Par un pertuis dérobé finement,
Mon cœur battait d'un tel débattement,
Qu'on m'eût jugé comme en peur déréglée.

Or j'étais plein d'une ardeur enflammée,
Ore de glace en ce frissonnement.
Je fus ravi d'un doux contentement,
Tant que ma vie en fut toute pâmée.

Là folâtrait le beau Soleil joyeux,
Avec un vent – Zéphyre gracieux –
Parmi l'or blond de sa tresse ondoyante,

Qui haut volante ombrageait ses genoux.
Que de beautés ! mais le destin jaloux
Ne me permit de voir ma chère attente.

L'Amour passionnée de Noémie, XXXV

JEAN DE SPONDE

(1557-1595)

Il est, avec d'Aubigné, à l'origine de la poésie religieuse qui va se développer au XVIIᵉ siècle. Ses sonnets sont l'équivalent littéraire des vanités où la mort, sous la forme d'un crâne, est le point de convergence du tableau. Chez Sponde tout s'ordonne autour de l'idée du néant de la vie humaine, et ses variations sur ce thème, loin de lasser le lecteur, l'impressionnent par leur force et leur insistance. Ce poète humaniste, traducteur d'Homère, est aussi un lecteur passionné de la Bible, en particulier des *Psaumes* sur lesquels il publie des *Méditations*. Leur lecture, dit-il en substance dans une de ses lettres, lui a communiqué la « fureur poétique » qui décida de sa vocation. Esprit profondément religieux, dont la foi et la culture théologique nourrissent l'inspiration, il offre l'image insolite du poète-prédicateur. Rien de péjoratif ne doit s'entendre sous ce vocable car le foisonnement baroque des images colore l'argumentation, et crée un univers singulier qui s'impose à la mémoire.

Mais si [1] faut-il mourir, et la vie orgueilleuse,
Qui brave de la mort, sentira ses fureurs,
Les Soleils hâleront ces journalières fleurs,
Et le temps crèvera cette ampoule venteuse.

Ce beau flambeau, qui lance une flamme fumeuse,
Sur le vert de la cire éteindra ses ardeurs,
L'huile de ce Tableau ternira ses couleurs
Et ces flots se rompront à la rive écumeuse.

J'ai vu ces clairs éclairs passer devant mes yeux,
Et le tonnerre encor qui gronde dans les Cieux,
Où d'une ou d'autre part éclatera l'orage.

J'ai vu fondre la neige, et ces torrents tarir,
Ces lions rugissants je les ai vus sans rage,
Vivez, hommes, vivez, mais si faut-il mourir.

---

1. pourtant

Qui sont, qui sont ceux là, dont le cœur idolâtre
Se jette aux pieds du Monde, et flatte ses honneurs ?
Et qui sont ces valets, et qui sont ces Seigneurs ?
Et ces Âmes d'Ébène, et ces Faces d'Albâtre ?

Ces masques déguisés, dont la troupe folâtre
S'amuse à caresser je ne sais quels donneurs
De fumées de Cour, et ces entrepreneurs
De vaincre encor le Ciel qu'ils ne peuvent combattre ?

Qui sont ces louvoyeurs qui s'éloignent du Port,
Hommagers à la Vie, et félons à la Mort,
Dont l'étoile est leur Bien, le vent leur fantaisie ?

Je vogue en même mer, et craindrais de périr,
Si ce n'est que je sais que cette même vie
N'est rien que le fanal qui me guide au mourir ?

XVIIᵉ SIÈCLE

Ce siècle compte de nombreux poètes. On ne peut cependant le considérer comme un siècle de poésie comme l'était si manifestement le précédent. La poésie que l'on nommera raisonnable, celle qui raconte, analyse, persuade et s'adresse par conséquent à l'intelligence plutôt qu'à la sensibilité, y est dominante. Tandis que celle qui émeut ou fascine et dont l'emprise sur nous reste mystérieuse, s'efface ici au profit de la première. Le souci d'exacte adéquation du mot et de l'idée, la volonté de faire du poète un artisan toujours conscient de son art et capable de conserver sur lui une entière maîtrise, éclipse les conceptions ambitieuses de la Renaissance. Le poète s'attache désormais au moins autant à convaincre qu'à charmer.

Ce qui caractérise encore l'époque c'est un foisonnement de versificateurs habiles. Tout homme cultivé se plaît à rimer : des épigrammes, des impromptus, de piquantes épîtres, ou encore des sonnets comme celui d'Oronte, creux mais fort bien tournés. Ces jeux passent pour de la poésie aux yeux des « beaux esprits ». Les salons préfèrent en effet les « petits vers doux, tendres et langoureux » raillés par Alceste, et raffolent en particulier des madrigaux. Un exemple des joutes ingénieuses auxquelles on se complaît alors, est donné par la « guerre des sonnets » qui oppose, à des années d'intervalle, *L'Uranie* de Voiture au *Job* de Benserade. On peut penser que la manie de rimer met en péril « l'art de poésie », au sens que Ronsard donnait à ce terme, et que ces créations éphémères détournent leurs inventeurs de plus nobles projets. Cependant les grands poètes, s'ils ne dédaignent pas de prendre part à ces amusements, parviennent aussi, dans cet aimable concert de lettrés, à faire entendre une tout autre voix.

Si les premières années du siècle étaient encore dominées par Desportes, sa renommée peu à peu estompée cède tout à fait devant les critiques de Malherbe. Lui se démarque avec autorité de ses prédécesseurs. Il se pose en contempteur de la profusion verbale de la Renaissance et de ses archaïsmes, mais aussi des fadeurs maniéristes de Desportes. Il rejette les outrances du style baroque qui prévaut alors et qui était le sien dans ses premiers écrits, pour faire entendre une exigence nouvelle : celle de la rigueur dans l'expression. À ses yeux la poésie elle-même doit obéir aux lois qu'impose la raison. Il soumet la création dans le domaine des lettres à la toute-puissance d'un esprit capable de construire un univers équilibré et harmonieux dont il donne l'exemple dans son œuvre. Il fonde une nouvelle esthétique où les prosateurs paraissent a priori mieux placés que les poètes pour donner la mesure de leur talent. Cependant Malherbe lui-même cède parfois à un lyrisme moins strictement contrôlé, et sa rigueur laisse alors surgir des vers où l'inspiration prend le pas sur la raison, mais c'est par la rupture qu'il instaure avec le siècle précédent qu'il va influencer durablement le sien, et fonder un classicisme auquel, bien au-delà de ses disciples immédiats, la plupart des poètes qui lui succèdent adhéreront. S'il est difficile de croire que de telles exigences n'aient pas bridé la création poétique, quelques grands poètes montrent pourtant que le génie est capable de transcender les règles en s'y soumettant.

Ainsi en est-il de Racine et de La Fontaine. Les tragédies du premier sont l'un des plus parfaits exemples de cette mystérieuse alliance de la lucidité et de l'obscur. Les lois contraignantes qui régissent le théâtre classique l'obligent à une densité de l'expression où vérité humaine et beauté poétique s'unissent étroitement. C'est sans doute dans les tragédies de ce siècle que l'on entend les vers les plus admirables.

Quant aux *Fables*, elles sont la grande œuvre poétique du classicisme. Elles permettent de goûter à la fois une forme parfaite et des accents très personnels. La Fontaine y mêle, de façon harmonieuse, ce qu'il emprunte aux anciens qu'il admire et ce que lui ont enseigné les plus doués de ses prédécesseurs, c'est-à-dire Théophile et Tristan. Il a pu voir chez eux la grâce dans l'évocation de la nature, la diversité des tons, la liberté de la confidence, la transfiguration du réel par la fantaisie, l'art de traduire son rêve intérieur mais rien qui l'obligeât à renier les canons du classicisme.

En effet Théophile, par exemple, malgré ses affirmations d'indépendance (« je ne défère guère aux exemples et me déplais surtout en l'imitation d'autrui »), en dépit des préciosités de son style ou d'images qui relèvent d'une esthétique baroque, ne renonce jamais à la clarté ni aux règles. Si son individualisme, sa sensibilité, la recherche d'une expression sincère et personnelle, font de lui un « moderne », il n'en est pas moins fidèle à la réforme de Malherbe qu'il admire et dont il est peut-être le plus pur héritier.

On ne peut reprocher à cette époque d'avoir dédaigné aucune des principales formes d'expression poétique, car les poètes si habiles aux « petits genres » s'essaient aux plus nobles. Ils pratiquent l'Ode pour louer les princes ou célébrer les hauts faits et s'efforcent de continuer l'épopée, comme Ronsard avant eux, avec ces « poèmes héroïques », pour lesquels ils s'inspirent du Tasse autant que de l'Antiquité. De même la diversité des registres ne connaît aucun resserrement, et depuis la poésie religieuse jusqu'aux grivoiseries du *Parnasse satyrique*, il y a place pour tous les tons, du plaisant au sévère, du grave au burlesque.

Malgré cette abondance, et tant de poètes honorables dont les noms ne pouvaient tous figurer dans une anthologie, malgré le talent ou le génie de ceux qui sont cités, malgré la diversité des styles baroque, précieux ou classique que l'on peut voir tour à tour dominer ou se fondre, le lecteur mesure à quel point la ferveur de la Renaissance est retombée. Il a le sentiment d'un manque. La poésie a renoncé aux grandes ambitions qui portaient les poètes au-delà d'eux-mêmes. Il semble bien que les périodes les plus fécondes pour elle sont au contraire celles où prévaut une conception quasi sacrée de sa nature et de sa place dans la société.

JEAN BERTAUT

(1552-1611)

Il forme, avec Desportes et Du Perron, la triade désignée par leurs contemporains sous le nom de « poètes du Louvre ». Ils travaillent, en effet, aux ordres de la Cour, d'où une production de vers de circonstance dont la froideur nous rebute souvent. Ronsard appréciait Jean Bertaut, mais lui reprochait de manquer un peu de l'enthousiasme qui, seul, fait les grands poètes. Cependant on peut être sensible chez lui à la noblesse d'un style qui annonce Malherbe.

S'il publie encore en 1602 un recueil de poèmes d'amour, c'est sous le couvert de l'anonymat, car sa fonction de premier aumônier de la Reine, depuis 1600, et plus tard celle d'évêque, lui imposent de privilégier la poésie d'inspiration religieuse.

Dans l'extrait du *Cantique de la Vierge Marie* qu'on va lire, ce qui retient notre attention c'est peut-être moins la facture déjà classique des vers que la progression à la fois lente et exultante des strophes aux enchaînements martelés et répétitifs, ce pèlerinage du verbe qui trouvera son accomplissement chez Péguy.

CANTIQUE DE LA VIERGE MARIE

Quand au dernier sommeil la Vierge eut clos les yeux,
Les Anges qui veillaient autour de leur maîtresse,
Élevèrent son corps en la gloire des Cieux,
Et les Cieux furent pleins de nouvelle allégresse.

Les plus hauts Séraphins à son avénement
Sortaient au devant d'elle et lui cédaient la place,
Se sentant tout ravis d'aise et d'étonnement
De pouvoir contempler la splendeur de sa face.

Dessus les Cieux des Cieux elle va paraissant,
Les flambeaux étoilés lui servent de couronne :
La Lune est sous ses pieds en forme de Croissant,
Et comme un vêtement le Soleil l'environne.

. . . .

C'est l'astre lumineux qui jamais ne s'éteint,
Où comme en un miroir tout le ciel se contemple ;
Le luisant tabernacle et le lieu pur et saint
Où Dieu même a voulu se consacrer un temple.

C'est le palais royal tout rempli de clarté,
Plus pur et transparent que le ciel qui l'enserre,
C'est le beau Paradis vers l'Orient planté,
Les délices du ciel et l'espoir de la terre.

C'est cette myrrhe et fleur et ce baume odorant
Qui rend de sa senteur nos âmes consolées ;
C'est ce Jardin reclus suavement fleurant :
C'est la Rose des champs et le Lys des vallées ;

C'est le rameau qui garde en tout temps sa couleur,
La branche de Jessé, la tige pure et sainte,
Qui rapporte son fruit et ne perd point sa fleur,
Qui demeure pucelle et qui se voit enceinte.

C'est l'Aube du matin qui produit le Soleil
Tout couvert de rayons et de flammes ardentes,
L'Astre des navigants, le Phare non-pareil
Qui la nuit leur éclaire au milieu des tourmentes.

Étoile de la mer, notre seul réconfort,
Sauve-nous des rochers, du vent et du naufrage,
Aide-nous de tes vœux pour nous conduire au port,
Et nous montre ton Fils sur le bord du rivage.

JACQUES DU PERRON

(1556-1618)

L'histoire voit surtout en lui l'homme d'Église et l'homme d'État. Réformé converti, devenu évêque, c'est lui qui obtient de Rome la réconciliation d'Henri IV, avant de devenir archevêque de Sens, puis cardinal en 1604, et d'entrer au Conseil de Régence. Pour l'histoire littéraire, il est avec Desportes et Bertaut le principal représentant de la poésie dans la première décennie du siècle, même s'il quitte « l'amusement des vers » dès 1595. À sa mort, l'un de ses contemporains dira que les Muses ont perdu leur Apollon. Nous ne pouvons souscrire à cet éloge, mais il faut savoir gré à ce poète d'avoir, en usant de son autorité, introduit Malherbe à la cour et favorisé sa carrière poétique. Il avait de réelles affinités, comme le souligne Antoine Adam, avec le style qu'allait faire triompher ce dernier, et il était, dit encore le critique, un malherbien avant Malherbe.

À ses paraphrases des psaumes ou ses poèmes religieux, on peut préférer la poésie profane, en particulier son *Temple de l'inconstance*, prélude aux ironies d'Hylas, l'un des héros de *L'Astrée*, moins cynique cependant, et surtout plus imagé grâce à l'invention baroque qui inspire cette parodie des temples de Cupidon ; on peut y voir, comme dans le texte suivant, l'image mouvante du moi que la nature renvoie au rêveur en le faisant douter de lui-même et du monde.

Au bord tristement doux des eaux je me retire,
Et vois couler ensemble, et les eaux, et mes jours,
Je m'y vois sec et pâle, et si j'aime toujours
Leur rêveuse mollesse où ma peine se mire.

Au plus secret des bois je conte mon martyre,
Je pleure mon martyre en chantant mes amours,
Et si j'aime les bois, et les bois les plus sourds,
Quand j'ai jeté mes cris, me les viennent redire.

Dame dont les beautés me possèdent si fort
Qu'étant absent de vous je n'aime que la mort,
Les eaux en votre absence, et les bois me consolent.

Je vois dedans les eaux, j'entends dedans les bois,
L'image de mon teint, et celle de ma voix,
Toutes peintes de morts qui nagent, et qui volent.

MALHERBE

(1555-1628)

Il ne séduit pas d'abord, et même il serait peut-être vrai de dire qu'il déplaît. Du reste, lui ne cherche pas à charmer le lecteur – dans des poèmes de circonstance ou de commande pour la plupart d'entre eux – en ayant recours à des tours inattendus, à des bonheurs d'expression ou des métaphores originales. Il veut une langue claire, une construction solide, une progression logique. En somme, des exigences de prosateur. Cela lui vaut la faveur de Boileau et celle de Ponge. Le premier approuve en lui le censeur des obscurités savantes de Ronsard, et des afféteries de Desportes, venu « enfin » introduire l'ordre et la raison dans un domaine où elles faisaient si visiblement défaut.

Le second le nomme le Père des lettres françaises, car il possède à ses yeux le secret de la langue, comme d'un alliage inconnu, et il a pu, selon lui, donner « une perfection absolue à la Parole ».

Malgré ces cautions, pour apprécier aujourd'hui cette œuvre, il est nécessaire de surmonter d'abord l'irritation que l'on ressent devant la fatuité du personnage, lorsqu'il promet l'éternité à ses écrits, et se range lui-même au nombre des « trois ou quatre seulement » capables de tresser aux rois d'impérissables couronnes. Il faut aussi oublier que cet artisan laborieux et lent d'une œuvre peu abondante a claironné son mépris de gentilhomme et de guerrier pour les poètes inspirés et le métier de poète en général. On peut alors convenir avec impartialité que ses architectures verbales, monuments classiques avant l'heure, en imposent par leur noblesse. Il n'est pas impossible cependant que l'on préfère les *Larmes de Saint Pierre*, long poème à l'esthétique encore marquée par le goût du temps pour la redondance et l'emphase, et qu'il a renié, à d'autres plus tardifs, exemples de ce classicisme que Ponge propose de définir comme « la corde la plus tendue du baroque ».

Enfin il ne sera pas inutile, pour que s'ouvrent sur cette œuvre d'autres horizons, d'avoir en mémoire la confidence de Baudelaire :

« Je connais un poète d'une nature toujours orageuse et vibrante, qu'un vers de Malherbe, symétrique et carré de mélodie, jette dans de longues extases. »

LES LARMES DE SAINT PIERRE

. . . .

Que je porte d'envie à la troupe innocente
De ceux qui, massacrés d'une main violente,
Virent dès le matin leur beau jour accourci !
Le fer qui les tua leur donna cette grâce
Que, si de faire bien ils n'eurent pas l'espace,
Ils n'eurent pas le temps de faire mal aussi.

De ces jeunes guerriers la flotte vagabonde
Allait courre fortune aux orages du monde,
Et déjà pour voguer abandonnait le bord,
Quand l'aguet d'un pirate arrêta le voyage ;
Mais leur sort fut si bon, que d'un même naufrage
Ils se virent sous l'onde, et se virent au port.

Ce furent de beaux lis qui, mieux que la nature,
Mêlant à leur blancheur l'incarnate peinture
Que tira de leur sein le couteau criminel,
Devant que d'un hiver la tempête et l'orage
À leur teint délicat pussent faire dommage,
S'en allèrent fleurir au printemps éternel.

Ces enfants bienheureux (créatures parfaites,
Sans l'imperfection de leurs bouches muettes)
Ayant Dieu dans le cœur ne le purent louer :
Mais leur sang leur en fut un témoin véritable,
Et moi, pouvant parler, j'ai parlé, misérable,
Pour lui faire vergogne et le désavouer.

. . . .

DESSEIN DE QUITTER UNE DAME
QUI NE LE CONTENTAIT QUE DE PROMESSE

Beauté, mon beau souci, de qui l'âme incertaine
A comme l'Océan son flux et son reflux :
Pensez de vous résoudre à soulager ma peine,
Ou je me vais résoudre à ne la souffrir plus.

Vos yeux ont des appas que j'aime et que je prise,
Et qui peuvent beaucoup dessus ma liberté :
Mais pour me retenir, s'ils font cas de ma prise,
Il leur faut de l'amour autant que de beauté.

Quand je pense être au point que cela s'accomplisse,
Quelque excuse toujours en empêche l'effet :
C'est la toile sans fin de la femme d'Ulysse,
Dont l'ouvrage du soir au matin se défait.

Madame, avisez-y, vous perdez votre gloire
De me l'avoir promis et vous rire de moi,
S'il ne vous en souvient vous manquez de mémoire,
Et s'il vous en souvient vous n'avez point de foi.

J'avais toujours fait compte, aimant chose si haute,
De ne m'en séparer qu'avecque le trépas,
S'il arrive autrement ce sera votre faute,
De faire des serments et ne les tenir pas.

CONSOLATION À MONSIEUR DU PÉRIER,
GENTILHOMME D'AIX-EN-PROVENCE,
SUR LA MORT DE SA FILLE

Ta douleur, Du Périer, sera donc éternelle,
        Et les tristes discours
Que te met en l'esprit l'amitié paternelle
        L'augmenteront toujours ?

Le malheur de ta fille au tombeau descendue
        Par un commun trépas,
Est-ce quelque dédale, où ta raison perdue
        Ne se retrouve pas ?

Je sais de quels appas son enfance était pleine,
        Et n'ai pas entrepris,
Injurieux ami, de soulager ta peine
        Avecque son mépris.

Mais elle était du monde, où les plus belles choses
        Ont le pire destin,
Et rose elle a vécu ce que vivent les roses,
        L'espace d'un matin.

Puis quand ainsi serait, que selon ta prière
        Elle aurait obtenu
D'avoir en cheveux blancs terminé sa carrière,
        Qu'en fût-il advenu ?

Penses-tu que, plus vieille, en la maison céleste
        Elle eût eu plus d'accueil ?
Ou qu'elle eût moins senti la poussière funeste
        Et les vers du cercueil ?

Non, non, mon Du Périer, aussitôt que la Parque
        Ôte l'âme du corps,
L'âge s'évanouit au-deçà de la barque
        Et ne suit point les morts.

Tithon n'a plus les ans qui le firent cigale,
       Et Pluton, aujourd'hui,
Sans égard du passé, les mérites égale
       D'Archémore et de lui.

Ne te lasse donc plus d'inutiles complaintes ;
       Mais, sage à l'avenir,
Aime une ombre comme ombre, et de cendres éteintes
       Éteins le souvenir.

C'est bien, je le confesse, une juste coutume,
       Que le cœur affligé,
Par le canal des yeux vidant son amertume,
       Cherche d'être allégé.

Même, quand il advient que la tombe sépare
       Ce que Nature a joint,
Celui qui ne s'émeut a l'âme d'un Barbare,
       Ou n'en a du tout point.

Mais d'être inconsolable, et dedans sa mémoire
       Enfermer un ennui,
N'est-ce pas se haïr pour acquérir la gloire
       De bien aimer autrui ?

. . . .

La Mort a des rigueurs à nulle autre pareilles :
       On a beau la prier,
La cruelle qu'elle est se bouche les oreilles,
       Et nous laisse crier.

Le pauvre en sa cabane, où le chaume le couvre,
       Est sujet à ses lois,
Et la garde qui veille aux barrières du Louvre
       N'en défend point nos rois.

De murmurer contre elle, et perdre patience,
       Il est mal à propos :
Vouloir ce que Dieu veut est la seule science
       Qui nous met en repos.

STANCES

Paraphrase d'une partie du Psaume CXLV

N'espérons plus, mon âme, aux promesses du monde :
Sa lumière est un verre, et sa faveur une onde,
Que toujours quelque vent empêche de calmer ;
Quittons ces vanités, lassons-nous de les suivre :
      C'est Dieu qui nous fait vivre,
      C'est Dieu qu'il faut aimer.

En vain, pour satisfaire à nos lâches envies,
Nous passons près des rois tout le temps de nos vies,
À souffrir des mépris et ployer les genoux ;
Ce qu'ils peuvent n'est rien : ils sont comme nous sommes,
      Véritablement hommes,
      Et meurent comme nous.

Ont-ils rendu l'esprit, ce n'est plus que poussière
Que cette majesté si pompeuse et si fière,
Dont l'éclat orgueilleux étonne l'univers ;
Et dans ces grands tombeaux où leurs âmes hautaines
      Font encore les vaines,
      Ils sont mangés des vers.

Là se perdent ces noms de maîtres de la terre,
D'arbitres de la paix, de foudres de la guerre :
Comme ils n'ont plus de sceptre, ils n'ont plus de flatteurs,
Et tombent avecque eux d'une chute commune
      Tous ceux que leur fortune
      Faisait leurs serviteurs.

HONORÉ D'URFÉ

(1567 -1625)

Il ne fut pas un grand poète, et même Malherbe, si l'on en croit Segrais, fit tout ce qu'il put, mais en vain, pour le dissuader d'écrire des vers. Cependant ses contemporains ont tout aimé en lui, ses poèmes autant que sa prose. Boileau en donne la raison : « Ses vers, pour méchants qu'ils étaient, ne laissèrent pas de passer, en faveur de l'art avec lequel il les mit en œuvre. »

On peut penser, en effet, qu'ils bénéficièrent de l'engouement extraordinaire de tout le siècle pour *L'Astrée* ; enchâssés dans le roman ils se paraient d'une séduction qu'ils ne méritaient pas tous, car réduits à eux-mêmes, loin des aventures de Céladon, de Silvanire, de Sireine et de tant d'autres héros amoureux, ils ne sont plus, au moins pour la plupart d'entre eux, que des variations conventionnelles sur des thèmes connus.

Cependant quelques vers nous touchent encore par leur grâce surannée ; et surtout nous sommes charmés par l'insolence et l'ironie du volage Hylas. En célébrant l'infidélité joyeuse, il rompt avec la veine éplorée de la poésie amoureuse et nous venge de tant de plaintes ressassées d'amants inconsolables mais diserts qui n'en finissent jamais de mourir d'amour.

SONNET DE CÉLADON

SUR UNE ATTENTE

Ô moments paresseux traînés si lentement !
Ô jours longs à venir, longs à clore vos heures,
Qui vous tient endormis en vos tristes demeures ?
Vous souliez autrefois couler si vivement.

Ô Ciel, qui traînes tout avec ton roulement
Et qui des autres Cieux les cadences mesures,
Dis-moi : qu'ai-je commis ? et par quelles injures
T'ai-je fait alentir ton léger mouvement ?

Moments, vous êtes jours, jours, vous êtes années,
Qui de vos pas de plomb n'êtes jamais bornées,
Que les siècles plus longs vous n'alliez égalant :

Pénélope, de nuit, défaisait sa journée ;
Je crois que le Soleil va ses pas rappelant
Pour prolonger le tour et ma peine obstinée.

STANCES D'HYLAS

DE SON HUMEUR INCONSTANTE

Je le confesse bien, Philis est assez belle
    Pour brûler qui le veut ;
Mais que, pour tout cela, je ne sois que pour elle,
    Certes il ne se peut.

Lorsqu'elle me surprit, mon humeur en fut cause,
    Et non pas sa beauté ;
Ores qu'elle me perd, ce n'est pour autre chose
    Que pour ma volonté.

J'honore sa vertu, j'estime son mérite
    Et tout ce qu'elle fait ;
Mais veut-elle savoir d'où vient que je la quitte ?
    C'est parce qu'il me plaît.

Chacun doit préférer, au moins s'il est bien sage,
    Son propre bien à tous ;
Je vous aime, il est vrai, je m'aime davantage :
    Si faites-vous bien, vous.

Bergers, si dans vos cœurs ne régnait la feintise,
    Vous en diriez autant ;
Mais j'aime beaucoup mieux conserver ma franchise
    Et me dire inconstant.

Qu'elle n'accuse donc sa beauté d'impuissance,
    Ni moi d'être léger ;
Je change, il est certain ; mais c'est grande prudence
    De savoir bien changer.

Pour être sage aussi, qu'elle en fasse de même :
    Égale en soit la loi ;
Que s'il faut, par destin, que la pauvrette m'aime,
    Qu'elle m'aime sans moi !

JEAN-BAPTISTE CHASSIGNET

(1570-1635)

La démarche de ce poète peu connu n'est pas sans rappeler celle de Sponde. Comme ce dernier, Chassignet est fasciné par la mort. Il consacre, à 24 ans, un recueil de 444 sonnets au seul thème du mépris de la vie ; ce sera le titre de l'ouvrage. Sa volonté d'obliger le lecteur à fixer, comme lui, les yeux sur sa fin prochaine, son désir de l'épouvanter par un *memento mori* plus cruel que *La Charogne* de Baudelaire, ont quelque chose de pascalien. On croit entendre certains accents de terreur des *Pensées* : « ..j'entre en effroi comme un homme qu'on aurait porté tout endormi dans une île déserte et effroyable... » C'est un regard de cette nature que le poète jette sur la condition humaine. L'abondance baroque des images, la tension soutenue qu'imprime à la strophe le recours à l'enjambement, la force démonstrative des allitérations, nous rendent sensibles – au moins pour un temps – à l'imminence de la menace qu'il nous montre pesant sur nous.

LE MÉPRIS DE LA VIE...

LXXIX

Nos corps aggravantés sous le poids des tombeaux,
Quand du clairon bruyant la clameur résonnante
Élancera le feu sur la terre flambante,
Purifiant du ciel les étonnés flambeaux,

Du cercueil oublieux ressortiront plus beaux,
Comme on voit par les champs la palme verdoyante
Malgré le faix pesant plus belle et fleurissante
Contre le ciel ouvert, relever ses rameaux.

Lors nous serons ravis, autant que le pilote
Qui dormant en la nef quand douteuse elle flotte,
Se voit au réveiller dans le môle arrivé.

Et jouissant là haut d'une paix éternelle,
Le corps ne sera plus à son âme rebelle,
Ni l'esprit de son corps si longuement privé.

CXXV

Mortel, pense quel est dessous la couverture
D'un charnier mortuaire un corps mangé de vers,
Décharné, dénervé, où les os découverts,
Dépoulpés, dénoués, délaissent leur jointure ;

Ici l'une des mains tombe en la pourriture,
Les yeux d'autre côté détournés à l'envers
Se distillent en glaire, et les muscles divers
Servent aux vers goulus d'ordinaire pâture ;

Le ventre déchiré cornant de puanteur
Infecte l'air voisin de mauvaise senteur,
Et le nez mi-rongé difforme le visage ;

Puis, connaissant l'état de la fragilité,
Fonde en DIEU seulement, estimant vanité
Tout ce qui ne te rend plus savant et plus sage.

MATHURIN RÉGNIER

(1573 -1613)

La satire que Régnier élève à la dignité d'un genre littéraire n'a que peu de rapport avec l'abondante production du même nom qui foisonne au début du XVIIᵉ siècle. Ces recueils de *Muses gaillardes* ou autres *Délices satiriques* comportent pas mal de poèmes pornographiques qui ne sont sans doute pas étrangers à leur succès. Toutefois d'autres vers, moins sulfureux, plaisent aussi et l'on goûte par-dessus tout la liberté de langage et le réalisme de ces recueils. De façon assez surprenante ils sont tolérés jusqu'en 1623, année de la condamnation du *Parnasse des poètes satiriques*, dont les auteurs, réels ou supposés, sont poursuivis. Ce qui vaut au poète Théophile de Viau son incarcération.

Régnier, auteur de *Satires*, a d'autres ambitions. Il s'inscrit dans la lignée de Marot et du Ronsard des *Folastries*, et surtout se veut le continuateur des Anciens qu'il vénère. S'il écarte l'octosyllabe, c'est pour leur ressembler, l'alexandrin étant le rythme le plus proche de l'hexamètre latin. Horace et Ovide sont ses modèles. S'il lui arrive parfois de pétrarquiser à la manière de son oncle, le poète Philippe Desportes, il ne met pas son ambition dans cette poésie légère, mais la place tout entière dans la satire qu'il élève jusqu'à la poésie morale. À travers ses thèmes favoris, la folie humaine, l'incohérence de la raison, le hasard de nos destinées, on sent que Montaigne est son maître. C'est à lui et à Rabelais qu'il doit sa langue savoureuse et drue aux archaïsmes recherchés. Très apprécié de ses contemporains, il suscita des imitateurs, aucun ne fut digne de lui jusqu'à Boileau.

SATIRE V

Pères des siècles vieux, exemples de la vie,
Dignes d'être admirés d'une honorable envie,
(Si quelque beau désir vivait encor en nous)
Nous voyant de là-haut, pères, qu'en dites vous ?
Jadis, de votre temps, la vertu simple et pure,
Sans fard, sans fiction, imitait sa nature,
Austère en ses façons, sévère en ses propos,
Qui dans un labeur juste égayait son repos ;
D'hommes vous faisant dieux, vous paissait d'ambroisie
Et donnait place au ciel à votre fantaisie.
La lampe de son front partout vous éclairait,
Et de toutes frayeurs vos esprits assurait ;
Et, sans penser aux biens où le vulgaire pense,
Elle était votre prix et votre récompense ;
Où la nôtre aujourd'hui, qu'on révère ici-bas,
Va la nuit dans le bal et danse les cinq pas,
Se parfume, se frise, et des façons nouvelles
Veut avoir par le fard du nom entre les belles ;
Fait crever les courtaux [1] en chassant aux forêts ;
Court le faquin, la bague [2], escrime des fleurets,
Monte un cheval de bois, fait dessus des pommades [3],
Talonne le genet et le dresse aux passades,
Chante des airs nouveaux, invente des ballets,
Sait écrire et porter les vers et les poulets ;
A l'œil toujours au guet pour des tours de souplesse,
Glose sur les habits et sur la gentillesse,
Se plaît à l'entretien, commente les bons mots,
Et met à même prix les sages et les sots.
Et ce qui plus encor m'empoisonne de rage,

---

1. Cheval auquel on a coupé la queue et les oreilles. — 2. Le faquin et la bague : jeux de manège. Le faquin est un mannequin qu'il s'agit de frapper avec sa lance. La bague est l'anneau suspendu où le cavalier doit passer sa lance. — 3. Voltiges au-dessus du pommeau de la selle.

Est quand un charlatan relève son langage,
Et, de coquin faisant le Prince revêtu,
Bâtit un Paranymphe [1] à sa belle vertu,
Et qu'il n'est crocheteur ni courtaut de boutique
Qui n'estime à vertu l'art où sa main s'applique,
Et qui, paraphrasant sa gloire et son renom,
Entre les vertueux ne veuille avoir du nom.

---

1. Nom grec du discours en faveur du candidat prononcé dans les facultés de médecine et de théologie.

STANCES

Quand sur moi je jette les yeux,
À trente ans me voyant tout vieux,
Mon cœur de frayeur diminue ;
Étant vieilli dans un moment,
Je ne puis dire seulement
Que ma jeunesse est devenue.

Du berceau courant au cercueil,
Le jour se dérobe à mon œil,
Mes sens troublés s'évanouissent.
Les hommes sont comme des fleurs,
Qui naissent et vivent en pleurs,
Et d'heure en heure se fanissent.

Leur âge, à l'instant écoulé,
Comme un trait qui s'est envolé,
Ne laisse après soi nulle marque ;
Et leur nom, si fameux ici,
Si-tôt qu'ils sont morts, meurt aussi,
Du pauvre autant que du monarque.

Naguère vert, sain et puissant,
Comme un aubépin florissant,
Mon printemps était délectable.
Les plaisirs logeaient en mon sein ;
Et lors était tout mon dessein
Du jeu d'amour et de la table.

Mais, las ! mon sort est bien tourné ;
Mon âge en un rien s'est borné ;
Faible languit mon espérance ;
En une nuit, à mon malheur,
De la joie et de la douleur
J'ai bien appris la différence !

La douleur aux traits vénéneux,
Comme d'un habit épineux,
Me ceint d'une horrible torture ;
Mes beaux jours sont changés en nuits,
Et mon cœur, tout flétri d'ennuis,
N'attend plus que la sépulture.

Enivré de cent maux divers,
Je chancelle et vais de travers,
Tant mon âme en regorge pleine ;
J'en ai l'esprit tout hébété,
Et, si peu qui m'en est resté,
Encor me fait-il de la peine.

La mémoire du temps passé,
Que j'ai follement dépensé,
Épand du fiel en mes ulcères ;
Si peu que j'ai de jugement
Semble animer mon sentiment,
Me rendant plus vif aux misères.

ÉPITAPHE DE RÉGNIER

J'ai vécu sans nul pensement,
Me laissant aller doucement
À la bonne loi naturelle ;
Et si m'étonne fort pourquoi
La mort daigna songer à moi,
Qui n'ai daigné penser à elle.

FRANCOIS MAYNARD

(1582-1646)

Malherbe eut des disciples qu'il appelait ses « écoliers ».
Maynard fut l'un d'eux. On voit bien en le lisant ce qu'il doit à son
maître en poésie, le goût du vers aux contours nets, celui de
l'expression claire, fruit d'un long travail de polissage, le refus du
détour et de la pointe. Ce dernier trait aurait dû le détourner du
genre de l'épigramme qu'il affectionnait. Sur ce point il n'écouta
pas les conseils de Malherbe qui le jugeait, non sans raison,
dépourvu de cette force incisive qui fait les satiriques. Il restait
néanmoins aux yeux de ce dernier « celui qui faisait les meilleurs
vers ». On voit dans certaines odes élégiaques combien l'éloge
est justifié à cause de la douceur de vers, qu'on pourrait dire
lamartinienne, douceur très étrangère à la rudesse de son modèle.

On peut admirer aussi, dans les faux sonnets, la liberté de ce
classique vis-à-vis des règles traditionnelles du genre : les quatorze
vers rompent avec l'ordre habituel des rimes et leur symétrie dans
les quatrains. On en compte sept, au lieu des cinq du sonnet
régulier. Le dialogue avec son âme n'a pas la majesté biblique
de celui qui s'exprimera dans *La Vigne et la Maison*[1], mais
l'alternance de l'alexandrin et du décasyllabe en font une
méditation lyrique assez touchante.

---

1. Lamartine.

IV

Mon âme, il faut partir. Ma vigueur est passée,
Mon dernier jour est dessus l'horizon.
Tu crains ta liberté. Quoi ? n'es-tu pas lassée
D'avoir souffert soixante ans de prison ?

Tes désordres sont grands, tes vertus sont petites ;
Parmi tes maux on trouve peu de bien.
Mais si le bon Jésus te donne ses mérites,
Espère tout et n'appréhende rien.

Mon âme, repens-toi d'avoir aimé le monde,
Et de mes yeux fais la source d'une onde
Qui touche de pitié le Monarque des rois.

Que tu serais courageuse et ravie,
Si j'avais soupiré durant toute ma vie
Dans le désert, sous l'ombre de la Croix !

V

Déserts où j'ai vécu dans un calme si doux,
Pins qui d'un si beau vert couvrez mon ermitage,
La cour depuis un an me sépare de vous,
Mais elle ne saurait m'arrêter davantage.

La vertu la plus nette y fait des ennemis ;
Les palais y sont pleins d'orgueil et d'ignorance ;
Je suis las d'y souffrir, et honteux d'avoir mis
Dans ma tête chenue une vaine espérance.

Ridicule abusé, je cherche du soutien
Au pays de la fraude, où l'on ne trouve rien
Que des pièges dorés et des malheurs célèbres.

Je me veux dérober aux injures du sort ;
Et sous l'aimable horreur de vos belles ténèbres,
Donner toute mon âme aux pensers de la mort.

RACAN

(1589-1670)

Il fut le disciple préféré de Malherbe, « celui qui avait le plus de force » à ses yeux ; toutefois il lui reprochait ses « trop grandes licences », car il ne montrait pas assez de rigueur dans son style. Racan, lui, manifesta toute sa vie pour son maître une grande admiration et une affection filiale.

Ce qui le rendit célèbre ce sont ses *Bergeries*. Cette pastorale, qui n'est pas la première du genre en France, fit date et fut très imitée. Certaines préciosités ont beaucoup vieilli et on pardonne moins à l'un de ses héros, Tisimandre, ses flots de larmes (« Les pleurs que mes yeux ont versés / Ont fait dans ces déserts de nouvelles rivières ») qu'à Pyrrhus les feux qui le brûlent ! Ces outrances ne doivent pas cependant nous priver du charme d'autres passages où se manifeste le talent de Racan à peindre la vie champêtre. Ses bergers, moins enrubannés que ceux d'Honoré d'Urfé, évoquent leurs travaux et leurs plaisirs simples sur un ton de vérité assez touchant. Ce réalisme tempéré se voit encore dans les *Stances* à Tircis dont quelques accents annoncent La Fontaine, qui fera, lui aussi, dans des termes voisins, l'éloge de la solitude. On a souvent rapproché ces deux poètes, sans doute à cause d'une paresse et d'une indolence qu'ils ont en commun et dont ils se vantent, mais surtout parce qu'ils sont l'un et l'autre des poète nés.

STANCES

Tircis, il faut penser à faire la retraite,
La course de nos jours est plus qu'à demi faite ;
L'âge insensiblement nous conduit à la mort.
Nous avons assez vu sur la mer de ce monde
Errer au gré des flots notre nef vagabonde,
Il est temps de jouir des délices du port.

Le bien de la fortune est un bien périssable,
Quand on bâtit sur elle, on bâtit sur le sable ;
Plus on est élevé, plus on court de dangers ;
Les grands pins sont en butte aux coups de la tempête,
Et la rage des vents brise plutôt le faîte
Des maisons de nos rois, que des toits des bergers.

Ô bienheureux celui qui peut de sa mémoire
Effacer pour jamais ce vain espoir de gloire,
Dont l'inutile soin traverse nos plaisirs,
Et qui, loin retiré de la foule importune,
Vivant dans sa maison content de sa fortune,
A selon son pouvoir mesuré ses désirs.

Il laboure le champ que labourait son père,
Il ne s'informe point de ce qu'on délibère
Dans ces graves conseils d'affaires accablés ;
Il voit sans intérêt la mer grosse d'orages,
Et n'observe des vents les sinistres présages
Que pour le soin qu'il a du salut de ses blés.

Roi de ses passions, il a ce qu'il désire ;
Son fertile domaine est son petit empire,
Sa cabane est son Louvre et son Fontainebleau ;
Ses champs et ses jardins sont autant de provinces ;
Et, sans porter envie à la pompe des princes,
Se contente chez lui de les voir en tableau.

Il voit de toutes parts combler d'heur sa famille,
La javelle à plein poing tomber sous la faucille,
Le vendangeur ployer sous le faix des paniers ;
Et semble qu'à l'envi les fertiles montagnes,
Les humides vallons et les grasses campagnes
S'efforcent à remplir sa cave et ses greniers.

Il suit aucunes fois un cerf par les foulées
Dans ces vieilles forêts du peuple reculées,
Et qui même du jour ignorent le flambeau ;
Aucunes fois des chiens il suit les voix confuses,
Et voit enfin le lièvre, après toutes ses ruses,
Du lieu de sa naissance en faire son tombeau.

Tantôt il se promène au long de ces fontaines
De qui les petits flots font luire dans les plaines
L'argent de leurs ruisseaux parmi l'or des moissons ;
Tantôt il se repose avecque les bergères
Sur des lits naturels de mousse et de fougères
Qui n'ont autres rideaux que l'ombre des buissons.

Il soupire en repos l'ennui de sa vieillesse
Dans ce même foyer où sa tendre jeunesse
A vu dans le berceau ses bras emmaillotés.
Il tient par les moissons registre des années,
Et voit, de temps en temps, leurs courses enchaînées
Vieillir avecque lui les bois qu'il a plantés.

Il ne va point fouiller aux terres inconnues,
À la merci des vents et des ondes chenues,
Ce que nature avare a caché de trésors,
Et ne recherche point pour honorer sa vie
De plus illustre mort ni plus digne d'envie
Que de mourir au lit où ses pères sont morts.

Il contemple du port les insolentes rages
Des vents de la faveur, auteurs de nos orages,
Allumer des mutins les desseins factieux ;
Et voit en un clin d'œil, par un contraire échange,
L'un déchiré du peuple au milieu de la fange,
Et l'autre à même temps élevé dans les cieux.

S'il ne possède point ces maisons magnifiques,
Ces tours, ces chapiteaux, ces superbes portiques,
Où la magnificence étale ses attraits,
Il jouit des beautés qu'ont les saisons nouvelles,
Il voit de la verdure et des fleurs naturelles
Qu'en ces riches lambris l'on ne voit qu'en portraits.

Crois-moi, retirons-nous hors de la multitude,
Et vivons désormais loin de la servitude
De ces palais dorés où tout le monde accourt,
Sous un chêne élevé les arbrisseaux s'ennuient,
Et devant le soleil tous les astres s'enfuient,
De peur d'être obligés de lui faire la cour.

Après qu'on a suivi sans aucune assurance
Cette vaine faveur qui nous paît d'espérance,
L'envie en un moment tous nos desseins détruit ;
Ce n'est qu'une fumée, il n'est rien de si frêle,
Sa plus belle moisson est sujette à la grêle,
Et souvent elle n'a que des fleurs pour du fruit.

Agréables déserts, séjour de l'innocence,
Où loin des vanités, de la magnificence,
Commence mon repos et finit mon tourment,
Vallons, fleuves, rochers, plaisante solitude,
Si vous fûtes témoins de mon inquiétude,
Soyez-le désormais de mon contentement.

THÉOPHILE DE VIAU

(1590-1626)

Il est sans doute le premier grand lyrique du XVIIᵉ siècle. Ses
odes consacrées à des descriptions de la nature, son sujet de
prédilection, montrent bien l'originalité de son inspiration. Un
paysage émeut tous ses sens et il parvient à traduire en un seul vers
l'impression qu'il reçoit du toucher, de la vue et de l'ouïe, lorsqu'il
parle, par exemple, d'« un froid et ténébreux silence ». La
sensualité qui lui fait appréhender voluptueusement le monde
autour de lui se marque aussi dans la personnification discrète des
éléments du paysage, ainsi « l'amoureuse violence » des vents, ou
les « fontaines violentes » mêlent à la réalité concrète de l'air ou de
l'eau la force contenue du désir. La délicatesse et la subtilité de
certaines notations, le trait descriptif, proche de l'art de l'esquisse
plus que du dessin achevé, font penser à Verlaine. Comme lui,
Théophile de Viau excelle à peindre l'eau et les reflets fugitifs
qui l'animent. L'incertain des heures crépusculaires colore ses
tableaux du matin ou du soir d'une imprécision suggestive. Ce
sont des instantanés où l'intuition d'un secret des choses se mêle
à leur peinture.

Il a dit de lui-même : « J'écris confusément », faisant entendre
par là que c'est au gré de son humeur ou de sa fantaisie. On est
loin de Malherbe ! – on le lui a d'ailleurs reproché – cependant il
n'ignore pas son enseignement, et à sa suite il proscrit de son
œuvre l'imitation servile des anciens et toute surcharge savante qui
alourdit le poème. Mais il n'appartient à aucune école, même si ses
premiers vers évoquent quelquefois Ronsard, ou si ailleurs, comme
dans la fantasque Ode XLIX, il peut être qualifié de baroque.

Théophile Gautier qui l'admirait a vu en lui un avant-coureur du romantisme. Nous, nous sommes plutôt frappés par ce qu'il y a en lui d'irréductible aux autres, et même de moderne.

Sa dernière œuvre, qu'il achèvera en prison, célèbre le domaine de Chantilly où il trouve refuge un temps contre ses persécuteurs. Sous le nom de Sylvie il y fait l'éloge de celle qui l'accueille, la duchesse de Montmorency. Les odes qui composent le recueil offrent des passages qui témoignent de sa maîtrise, de son art de mêler, sur un ton familier et comme naturellement, les figures mythologiques à la description, et de sa science de peintre qui fait de la nature la traduction imagée de ses états d'âme.

CONTRE L'HIVER

Plein de colère et de raison,
Contre toi, barbare saison,
Je prépare une rude guerre,
Malgré les lois de l'univers,
Qui de la glace des hivers
Chassent les flammes du tonnerre,
Aujourd'hui l'ire de mes vers
Des foudres contre toi desserre.

. . . .

Tous nos arbres sont dépouillés,
Nos promenoirs sont tout mouillés,
L'émail de notre beau parterre
A perdu ses vives couleurs,
La gelée a tué les fleurs,
L'air est malade d'un caterre ¹,
Et l'œil du ciel noyé de pleurs
Ne sait plus regarder la terre.

La nacelle, attendant le flux
Des ondes qui ne courent plus,
Oisive au port est retenue ;
La tortue et les limaçons
Jeûnent perclus sous les glaçons ;
L'oiseau sur une branche nue
Attend pour dire ses chansons
Que la feuille soit revenue.

Le héron, quand il veut pêcher,
Trouvant l'eau toute de rocher,
Se paît du vent et de sa plume ;
Il se cache dans les roseaux
Et contemple, au bord des ruisseaux,
La bise contre sa coutume
Souffler la neige sur les eaux
Où bouillait autrefois l'écume.

_____

1. catarrhe.

Les poissons dorment assurés,
D'un mur de glace remparés,
Francs de tous les dangers du monde,
Fors que de toi tant seulement,
Qui restreins leur moite élément
Jusqu'à la goutte plus profonde,
Et les laisses sans mouvement,
Enchassés en l'argent de l'onde.

Édition de 1623

LE MATIN

L'Aurore sur le front du jour
Sème l'azur, l'or et l'ivoire,
Et le Soleil, lassé de boire,
Commence son oblique tour.

Ses chevaux, au sortir de l'onde,
De flamme et de clarté couverts,
La bouche et les naseaux ouverts,
Ronflent la lumière du monde.

La lune fuit devant nos yeux ;
La nuit a retiré ses voiles ;
Peu à peu le front des étoiles
S'unit à la couleur des cieux.

. . . .

Une confuse violence
Trouble le calme de la nuit,
Et la lumière avec le bruit
Dissipe l'ombre et le silence.

Alidor cherche à son réveil
L'ombre d'Iris qu'il a baisée,
Et pleure en son âme abusée
La fuite d'un si doux sommeil.

Les bêtes sont dans leur tanière,
Qui tremblent de voir le soleil ;
L'homme, remis par le sommeil,
Reprend son œuvre coutumière.

Le forgeron est au fourneau :
Ois comme le charbon s'allume !
Le fer rouge, dessus l'enclume,
Étincelle sous le marteau.

Cette chandelle semble morte,
Le jour la fait évanouir ;
Le Soleil vient nous éblouir :
Vois qu'il passe au travers la porte.

Il est jour : levons-nous, Philis ;
Allons à notre jardinage
Voir s'il est, comme ton visage,
Semé de roses et de lis.

Édition de 1623

LA SOLITUDE

Dans ce val solitaire et sombre,
Le cerf qui brame au bruit de l'eau,
Penchant ses yeux dans un ruisseau,
S'amuse à regarder son ombre.

De cette source une Naïade
Tous les soirs ouvre le portal
De sa demeure de cristal
Et nous chante une sérénade.

Les Nymphes, que la chasse attire
À l'ombrage de ces forêts,
Cherchent les cabinets secrets
Loin de l'embûche du Satyre.

Jadis au pied de ce grand chêne,
Presque aussi vieux que le soleil,
Bacchus, l'Amour et le Sommeil
Firent la fosse de Silène.

Un froid et ténébreux silence
Dort à l'ombre de ces ormeaux,
Et les vents battent les rameaux
D'une amoureuse violence.

L'esprit plus retenu s'engage
Au plaisir de ce doux séjour,
Où Philomèle nuit et jour
Renouvelle un piteux langage.

. . . .

Corinne, je te prie, approche ;
Couchons-nous sur ce tapis vert ;
Et pour être mieux à couvert
Entrons au creux de cette roche.

. . . .

D'un air plein d'amoureuse flamme,
Aux accents de ta douce voix,
Je vois les fleuves et les bois
S'embraser comme a fait mon âme.

Si tu mouilles tes doigts d'ivoire
Dans le cristal de ce ruisseau,
Le Dieu qui loge dans cette eau
Aimera s'il en ose boire.

Présente-lui ta face nue,
Tes yeux avecque l'eau riront,
Et dans ce miroir écriront
Que Vénus est ici venue.

Si bien elle y sera dépeinte,
Les Faunes s'en enflammeront,
Et de tes yeux qu'ils aimeront,
Ne sauront découvrir la feinte.

Entends ce Dieu qui te convie
À passer dans son élément,
Ois qu'il soupire bellement
Sa liberté déjà ravie.

Trouble-lui cette fantaisie,
Détourne-toi de ce miroir,
Tu le mettras au désespoir
Et m'ôteras la jalousie.

Vois-tu ce tronc et cette pierre ?
Je crois qu'ils prennent garde à nous,
Et mon amour devient jaloux
De ce myrte et de ce lierre.

Sus, ma Corinne, que je cueille
Tes baisers du matin au soir !
Vois comment pour nous faire asseoir
Ce myrte a laissé choir sa feuille.

Ois le pinson et la linotte
Sur la branche de ce rosier,
Vois branler leur petit gosier,
Ois comme ils ont changé de note.

Approche, approche, ma Dryade !
Ici murmureront les eaux,
Ici les amoureux oiseaux
Chanteront une sérénade.

Prête-moi ton sein pour y boire
Des odeurs qui m'embaumeront ;
Ainsi mes sens se pâmeront
Dans les lacs de tes bras d'ivoire.

Je baignerai mes mains folâtres
Dans les ondes de tes cheveux,
Et ta beauté prendra les vœux
De mes œillades idolâtres.

Ne crains rien, Cupidon nous garde.
Mon petit ange, es-tu pas mien ?
Ah ! Je vois que tu m'aimes bien :
Tu rougis quand je te regarde.

Dieux ! que cette façon timide
Est puissante sur mes esprits !
Renaud ne fut pas mieux épris
Par les charmes de son Armide.

Ma Corinne, que je t'embrasse !
Personne ne nous voit qu'Amour ;
Vois que même les yeux du jour
Ne trouvent point ici de place.

Les vents qui ne se peuvent taire
Ne peuvent écouter aussi,
Et ce que nous ferons ici
Leur est un inconnu mystère.

Édition de 1623

ODE

Un corbeau devant moi croasse,
Une ombre offusque mes regards,
Deux belettes et deux renards
Traversent l'endroit où je passe,
Les pieds faillent à mon cheval,
Mon laquais tombe du haut mal,
J'entends craqueter le tonnerre,
Un esprit se présente à moi,
J'ois Charon qui m'appelle à soi,
Je vois le centre de la terre.

Ce ruisseau remonte en sa source,
Un bœuf gravit sur un clocher,
Le sang coule de ce rocher,
Un aspic s'accouple d'une ourse,
Sur le haut d'une vieille tour
Un serpent déchire un vautour,
Le feu brûle dedans la glace,
Le soleil est devenu noir,
Je vois la lune qui va choir,
Cet arbre est sorti de sa place.

Édition de 1623

SONNET

Au moins ai-je songé que je vous ai baisée,
Et bien que tout l'amour ne s'en soit pas allé,
Ce feu qui dans mes sens a doucement coulé,
Rend en quelque façon ma flamme rapaisée.

Après ce doux effort mon âme reposée
Peut rire du plaisir qu'elle vous a volé,
Et de tant de refus à demi consolé,
Je trouve désormais ma guérison aisée.

Mes sens déjà remis commencent à dormir,
Le sommeil qui deux nuits m'avait laissé gémir,
Enfin dedans mes yeux vous fait quitter la place.

Et quoiqu'il soit si froid au jugement de tous,
Il a rompu pour moi son naturel de glace,
Et s'est montré plus chaud et plus humain que vous.

Édition de 1623

SONNET

D'un sommeil plus tranquille à mes amours rêvant,
J'éveille avant le jour mes yeux et ma pensée,
Et cette longue nuit si durement passée,
Je me trouve étonné de quoi je suis vivant.

Demi désespéré je jure en me levant
D'arracher cet objet à mon âme insensée,
Et soudain de ses vœux ma raison offensée
Se dédit et me laisse aussi fol que devant.

Je sais bien que la mort suit de près ma folie,
Mais je vois tant d'appas en ma mélancolie
Que mon esprit ne peut souffrir sa guérison.

Chacun à son plaisir doit gouverner son âme,
Mithridate autrefois a vécu de poison,
Les Lestrygons de sang, et moi je vis de flamme.

Édition de 1623

LA MAISON DE SYLVIE

Dans ce parc un vallon secret
Tout voilé de ramages sombres,
Où le Soleil est si discret
Qu'il n'y force jamais les ombres,
Presse d'un cours si diligent
Les flots de deux ruisseaux d'argent
Et donne une fraîcheur si vive
À tous les objets d'alentour,
Que même les martyrs d'amour
Y trouvent leur douleur captive.

Un étang dort là tout auprès,
Où ces fontaines violentes
Courent et font du bruit exprès
Pour éveiller ses vagues lentes.
Lui d'un maintien majestueux
Reçoit l'abord impétueux
De ces Naïades vagabondes,
Qui dedans ce large vaisseau
Confondent leur petit ruisseau
Et ne discernent plus ses ondes.

. . . .

Zéphyr en chasse les chaleurs,
Rien que les cygnes n'y repaissent,
On n'y trouve rien sous les fleurs
Que la fraîcheur dont elles naissent.
Le gazon garde quelquefois
Le bandeau, l'arc et le carquois
De mille Amours qui se dépouillent
À l'ombrage de ses roseaux
Et dans l'humidité des eaux
Trempent leurs jeunes corps qui bouillent.

L'étang leur prête sa fraîcheur,
La Naïade leur verse à boire,
Toute l'eau prend de leur blancheur
L'éclat d'une couleur d'ivoire.
On voit là ces nageurs ardents
Dans les ondes qu'ils vont fendant
Faire la guerre aux Néréides,
Qui devant leur teint mieux uni
Cachent leur visage terni
Et leur front tout coupé de rides.

Or ensemble, ores dispersés,
Ils brillent dans ce crêpe sombre,
Et sous les flots qu'ils ont percés
Laissent évanouir leur ombre.
Parfois dans une claire nuit,
Qui du feu de leurs yeux reluit
Sans aucun ombrage des nues,
Diane quitte son berger
Et s'en va là-dedans nager
Avecque ses étoiles nues.

Les ondes qui leur font l'amour
Se refrisent sur leurs épaules
Et font danser tout alentour
L'ombre des roseaux et des saules.
Le dieu de l'eau tout furieux
Haussé pour regarder leurs yeux
Et leur poil qui flotte sur l'onde,
Du premier qu'il voit approcher
Pense voir ce jeune cocher
Qui fit jadis brûler le monde.

Et ce pauvre amant langoureux
Dont le feu toujours se rallume
Et de qui les soins amoureux
Ont fait ainsi blanchir la plume,
Ce beau cygne à qui Phaéton

Laissa ce lamentable ton
Témoin d'une amitié si sainte,
Sur le dos son aile élevant
Met ses voiles blanches au vent
Pour chercher l'objet de sa plainte.

Ainsi pour flatter son ennui
Il demande au dieu Mélicerte
Si chaque dieu n'est pas celui
Dont il soupire tant la perte,
Et contemplant de tous côtés
La semblance de leurs beautés,
Il sent renouveler sa flamme,
Errant avec de faux plaisirs
Sur les traces des vieux désirs
Que conserve encore son âme.

. . . .

Édition de 1623

SAINT-AMANT

(1594-1651)

Parmi les poètes du XVIIᵉ siècle que Gautier choisit de remettre à l'honneur, et qu'il nomme *Les Grotesques*, s'il en est un qui justifie ce titre, c'est bien Saint-Amant. Sa truculence, la verdeur de sa langue, héritière de Rabelais et de Régnier, son goût pour la caricature et l'emphase relèvent de ce terme ou de celui de burlesque. Ailleurs, cependant, on peut parfois le qualifier de précieux, car il cultive l'art des *concetti* venu d'Italie avec le Cavalier Marin. Ses contemporains l'ont admiré pour l'originalité de son esprit, pour sa culture qui s'étendait aux sciences, pour son expérience de voyageur au long cours et la diversité de ses talents poétiques. Il s'essaye en effet à différents genres – avec des bonheurs inégaux – depuis l'ode bachique ou l'épigramme jusqu'au poème héroïque. C'est dans ce dernier qu'il convainc le moins. Et Boileau ironise :

> *N'imitez pas ce fou qui, décrivant les mers*
> *Et peignant au milieu de leurs flots entrouverts*
> *L'Hébreu sauvé du joug de ses injustes maîtres,*
> *Met, pour les voir passer, les poissons aux fenêtres.*

Le Moïse sauvé, visé dans ces vers, fut trop souvent pour son auteur l'occasion de donner libre cours à son imagination, à son goût pour le pittoresque, et surtout à sa verve intarissable. Il est vrai que l'œuvre est inégale et parfois lassante, mais dans quelques passages un souffle épique soulève le poète et la réussite, alors, est incontestable. Mais on préfère le plus souvent à cette grande machine, la brièveté efficace des portraits qu'il campe dans les sonnets, à la manière flamande, ou la gouaille satirique du *Poète crotté*, dans la lignée de Rutebeuf et de Villon, ou encore ses étonnantes *Visions* consacrées aux apparitions et aux cauchemars qui hantent ses nuits. Son intérêt, insolite à l'époque, pour les fantômes, les châteaux ruinés, et les squelettes pendus, apparaît ailleurs, en particulier dans *La Solitude*, son chef-d'œuvre. En introduisant ainsi le fantastique dans une retraite champêtre qu'il situe, de manière inhabituelle, sur le rivage de la mer, il rompt avec les conventions descriptives du temps. L'esthétique baroque le porte à accentuer les contrastes entre les aspects sereins du site et sa face sauvage, contrastes encore soulignés par les alliances de mots (ainsi le vers : « Que je trouve doux le ravage »...), ce qui ajoute à la séduction d'un poème qui fut souvent imité. On comprend en le lisant que Saint-Amant ait pu fasciner les romantiques à la fois par sa manière et par ses thèmes.

LA SOLITUDE

À Alcidon

Ô que j'aime la solitude !
Que ces lieux sacrés à la nuit,
Éloignés du monde et du bruit,
Plaisent à mon inquiétude !
Mon Dieu ! que mes yeux sont contents
De voir ces bois, qui se trouvèrent
À la nativité du temps,
Et que tous les siècles révèrent,
Être encore aussi beaux et verts
Qu'aux premiers jours de l'univers !

Un gai zéphire les caresse
D'un mouvement doux et flatteur.
Rien que leur extrême hauteur
Ne fait remarquer leur vieillesse.
Jadis Pan et ses demi-dieux
Y vinrent chercher du refuge,
Quand Jupiter ouvrit les cieux
Pour nous envoyer le déluge,
Et, se sauvant sur leurs rameaux,
À peine virent-ils les eaux.

Que sur cette épine fleurie,
Dont le printemps est amoureux,
Philomèle, au chant langoureux,
Entretient bien ma rêverie !
Que je prends de plaisir à voir
Ces monts pendant en précipices,
Qui, pour les coups du désespoir,
Sont aux malheureux si propices,
Quand la cruauté de leur sort
Les force à rechercher la mort !

Que je trouve doux le ravage
De ces fiers torrents vagabonds,
Qui se précipitent par bonds
Dans ce vallon vert et sauvage !
Puis, glissant sous les arbrisseaux,
Ainsi que des serpents sur l'herbe,
Se changent en plaisants ruisseaux,
Où quelque naïade superbe
Règne, comme en son lit natal,
Dessus un trône de cristal !

Que j'aime ce marais paisible !
Il est tout bordé d'aliziers,
D'aulnes, de saules et d'osiers,
À qui le fer n'est point nuisible.
Les nymphes, y cherchant le frais,
S'y viennent fournir de quenouilles,
De pipeaux, de joncs et de glais ;
Où l'on voit sauter les grenouilles,
Qui de frayeur s'y vont cacher
Sitôt qu'on veut s'en approcher.

Là, cent mille oiseaux aquatiques
Vivent, sans craindre, en leur repos,
Le giboyeur fin et dispos,
Avec ses mortelles pratiques.
L'un, tout joyeux d'un si beau jour,
S'amuse à becqueter sa plume ;
L'autre alentit le feu d'amour
Qui dans l'eau même se consume,
Et prennent tous innocemment
Leur plaisir en cet élément.

Jamais l'été ni la froidure
N'ont vu passer dessus cette eau
Nulle charrette ni bateau,
Depuis que l'un et l'autre dure ;
Jamais voyageur altéré

N'y fit servir sa main de tasse ;
Jamais chevreuil désespéré
N'y finit sa vie à la chasse ;
Et jamais le traître hameçon
N'en fit sortir aucun poisson.

Que j'aime à voir la décadence
De ces vieux châteaux ruinés,
Contre qui les ans mutinés
Ont déployé leur insolence !
Les sorciers y font leur sabbat ;
Les démons follets s'y retirent,
Qui d'un malicieux ébat
Trompent nos sens et nous martyrent ;
Là se nichent en mille trous
Les couleuvres et les hiboux.

L'orfraie, avec ses cris funèbres,
Mortels augures des destins,
Fait rire et danser les lutins
Dans ces lieux remplis de ténèbres.
Sous un chevron de bois maudit
Y branle le squelette horrible
D'un pauvre amant qui se pendit
Pour une bergère insensible,
Qui d'un seul regard de pitié
Ne daigna voir son amitié.

Aussi le Ciel, juge équitable,
Qui maintient les lois en vigueur,
Prononça contre sa rigueur
Une sentence épouvantable :
Autour de ces vieux ossements
Son ombre, aux peines condamnée,
Lamente en longs gémissements
Sa malheureuse destinée,
Ayant, pour croître son effroi,
Toujours son crime devant soi.

. . . .

LES VISIONS

À Damon

Le cœur plein d'amertume et l'âme ensevelie
Dans la plus sombre humeur de la mélancolie,
Damon, je te décris mes travaux intestins,
Où tu verras l'effort des plus cruels destins
Qui troublèrent jamais un pauvre misérable,
À qui le seul trépas doit être désirable.
Un grand chien maigre et noir, se traînant lentement,
Accompagné d'horreur et d'épouvantement,
S'en vient toutes les nuits hurler devant ma porte,
Redoublant ses abois d'une effroyable sorte.
Mes voisins, éperdus à ce triste réveil,
N'osent ni ne sauraient rappeler le sommeil ;
Et chacun, le prenant pour un sinistre augure,
Dit avec des soupirs tout ce qu'il s'en figure.
Moi, qu'un sort rigoureux outrage à tout propos,
Et qui ne puis goûter ni plaisir ni repos,
Les cheveux hérissés, j'entre en des rêveries
De contes de sorciers, de sabbats, de furies ;
J'erre dans les enfers, je rôde dans les cieux ;
L'âme de mon aïeul se présente à mes yeux ;
Ce fantôme léger, coiffé d'un vieux suaire,
Et tristement vêtu d'un long drap mortuaire,
À pas affreux et lents s'approche de mon lit ;
Mon sang en est glacé, mon visage en pâlit,
De frayeur mon bonnet sur mes cheveux se dresse,
Je sens sur l'estomac un fardeau qui m'oppresse.
Je voudrais bien crier, mais je l'essaye en vain :
Il me ferme la bouche avec sa froide main ;
Puis d'une voix plaintive en l'air évanouie,
Murmurant certains mots funestes à l'ouïe,
Me prédit mes malheurs, et longtemps sans ciller,
Me contemple debout contre mon oreiller.

. . . .

LE POÈTE CROTTÉ

Ville où j'ai tant traîné mes guêtres
Que j'en dois mieux savoir les êtres
Qu'un rat ne fait de son grenier,
Je te chante l'adieu dernier.
Adieu doncques, Paris sur Seine,
Seine, rivière humide et pleine,
A Sanitas nommée ainsi,
Comme dit quelque auteur chanci [1],
Adieu Paris, cité superbe,
Paris sans pair, rare proverbe !
Qui montre, en cachant mille appas,
Que Vaugirard ne te vaut pas,
Adieu Pont-Neuf, sous qui l'eau passe
Si ce n'est quand hiver la glace,
Car, adonc ne bougeant d'un point,
Elle est ferme, et ne passe point.
Adieu, roi de bronze ou de cuivre,
Qu'à pied l'on peut aisément suivre,
Quoi que vous soyez à cheval,
Sans aller par mont ni par val ;
Adieu, belle place Dauphine,
Où l'éloquence se raffine
Par ces bateleurs, ces marmots,
De qui j'ai pris tant de beaux mots
Pour fabriquer mes épigrammes.
Bon mots qui, plus pointus que lames,
Font qu'on ne peut, sans se piquer,
En torche-culs les appliquer.
Adieu, grande et fameuse Grève,
Hélas ! de te quitter je crève.

---

1. vieilli ou ranci.

SONNETS

I

Assis sur un fagot, une pipe à la main,
Tristement accoudé contre une cheminée,
Les yeux fixés vers terre, et l'âme mutinée,
Je songe aux cruautés de mon sort inhumain.

L'espoir, qui me remet du jour au lendemain,
Essaie à gagner temps sur ma peine obstinée,
Et, me venant promettre une autre destinée,
Me fait monter plus haut qu'un empereur romain.

Mais à peine cette herbe est-elle mise en cendre,
Qu'en mon premier état, il me convient descendre,
Et passer mes ennuis à redire souvent :

Non, je ne trouve point beaucoup de différence
De prendre du tabac à vivre d'espérance,
Car l'un n'est que fumée, et l'autre n'est que vent.

II

LE PARESSEUX

Accablé de paresse et de mélancolie,
Je rêve dans un lit où je suis fagoté
Comme un lièvre sans os qui dort dans un pâté,
Ou comme un Don Quichotte en sa morne folie.

Là, sans me soucier des guerres d'Italie,
Du comte Palatin, ni de sa royauté,
Je consacre un bel hymne à cette oisiveté
Où mon âme en langueur est comme ensevelie.

Je trouve ce plaisir si doux et si charmant,
Que je crois que les biens me viendront en dormant,
Puisque je vois déjà s'en enfler ma bedaine,

Et hais tant le travail que, les yeux entrouverts,
Une main hors des draps, cher Baudoin, à peine
Ai-je pu me résoudre à t'écrire ces vers.

LES GOINFRES

Coucher trois dans un drap, sans feu ni sans chandelle,
Au profond de l'hiver, dans la salle aux fagots
Où les chats, ruminant le langage des Goths,
Nous éclairent sans cesse en roulant la prunelle ;

Hausser notre chevet avec une escabelle,
Être deux ans à jeun comme les escargots,
Rêver en grimaçant ainsi que les magots
Qui, bâillant au soleil, se grattent sous l'aisselle ;

Mettre au lieu d'un bonnet la coiffe d'un chapeau,
Prendre pour se couvrir la frise d'un manteau,
Dont le dessus servit à nous doubler la panse ;

Puis souffrir cent brocards d'un vieux hôte irrité
Qui peut fournir à peine à la moindre dépense,
C'est ce qu'engendre enfin la prodigalité.

VINCENT VOITURE

(1597-1648)

À l'Hôtel de Rambouillet on le surnomme : *El rey chiquito*, ironie sur sa petite taille, mais aussi reconnaissance du pouvoir qu'il y exerce. C'est un homme spirituel et inventif qui s'amuse à rimer sans jamais se prendre au sérieux. Qu'il propose de remettre à la mode une forme un peu oubliée comme le rondeau, ou certains mots désuets du vieux français, ou encore les rythmes des chansons populaires, c'est toujours dans le seul but de divertir Arthénice et ses amis en leur offrant des jeux nouveaux. Dans la société galante et policée qui compose le célèbre salon, on voit certains des esprits les plus remarquables du temps côtoyer l'aristocratie. Pour y être admis la roture n'est pas un obstacle, du moins si l'on sait, comme Voiture, faire preuve de talent. Ce mélange permet aux uns d'échapper au pédantisme en se formant au goût de la cour, et aux autres de se soustraire pour un temps aux rites codifiés de la vie mondaine.

Rimailleur, comme disait Marot qu'il admire et s'efforce d'imiter, plutôt que grand poète, Voiture joue un rôle indéniable dans l'histoire de la poésie française, parce qu'il contribue à développer le courant précieux qui imprégnera les écrivains de ce siècle. Mêlant désinvolture et raffinement, il affranchit la langue poétique de la gravité démonstrative héritée de Malherbe et aussi des formes exténuées du pétrarquisme qui l'encombraient encore.

Le sonnet sur l'amour d'Uranie, parfait exemple de préciosité, fut le prétexte de la fameuse querelle entre les partisans du poète et ceux de Benserade. À côté de lui on lira le début d'une chanson au ton badin qui témoigne de la fantaisie et de la malice du personnage, celle qui fit le succès de ses épîtres en prose ; on verra aussi l'un de ces rondeaux qu'il chérissait, et une « Belle Matineuse » imitée de l'italien Annibale Caro (on pourra la comparer avec celle de Du Bellay ou celle de Tristan). Le choix de ces poèmes se justifie dans une anthologie surtout parce qu'ils sont une étape significative de la formation du goût du Grand Siècle, et les prémices de la langue qui va triompher dans l'œuvre de La Fontaine et celle de Racine.

Il faut finir mes jours en l'amour d'Uranie :
L'absence ni le temps ne m'en sauraient guérir,
Et je ne vois plus rien qui me pût secourir,
Ni qui sût rappeler ma liberté bannie.

Dès longtemps je connais sa rigueur infinie ;
Mais, pensant aux beautés pour qui je dois périr,
Je bénis mon martyre, et content de mourir,
Je n'ose murmurer contre sa tyrannie.

Quelquefois ma raison, par de faibles discours,
M'incite à la révolte et me promet secours ;
Mais, lorsqu'à mon besoin je me veux servir d'elle,

Après beaucoup de peine et d'efforts impuissants,
Elle dit qu'Uranie est seule aimable et belle,
Et m'y rengage plus que ne font tous mes sens.

Les demoiselles de ce temps
Ont depuis peu beaucoup d'amants ;
On dit qu'il n'en manque à personne,
    L'année est bonne.

Nous avons vu les ans passés
Que les galants étaient glacés ;
Mais maintenant tout en foisonne,
    L'année est bonne.

Le temps n'est pas bien loin encor
Qu'ils se vendaient au poids de l'or,
Et pour le présent on les donne,
    L'année est bonne.

Le soleil de nous rapproché
Rend le monde plus échauffé ;
L'amour règne, le sang bouillonne,
    L'année est bonne.

Des portes du matin l'amante de Céphale
Ses roses épandait dans le milieu des airs,
Et jetait sur les cieux nouvellement ouverts
Ces traits d'or et d'azur qu'en naissant elle étale,

Quand la Nymphe divine, à mon repos fatale,
Apparut, et brilla de tant d'attraits divers,
Qu'il semblait qu'elle seule éclairait l'univers
Et remplissait de feux la rive orientale.

Le Soleil, se hâtant pour la gloire des cieux,
Vint opposer sa flamme à l'éclat de ses yeux,
Et prit tous les rayons dont l'Olympe se dore.

L'onde, la terre et l'air s'allumaient à l'entour ;
Mais auprès de Philis on le prit pour l'Aurore,
Et l'on crut que Philis était l'Astre du jour.

FRANÇOIS L'HERMITE *dit* TRISTAN

(1601-1655)

Tristan est un solitaire : il n'appartient ni au groupe des disciples attardés de Malherbe, ni à celui des Académiciens et il n'entre pas dans le clan choisi des hôtes de la marquise de Rambouillet. Est-ce pour cela qu'il tombe assez vite dans l'oubli, malgré la célébrité que lui valent d'abord ses œuvres ? Dans son *Art poétique* Boileau l'ignore, et après lui les deux siècles suivants. On ne le redécouvre qu'au début du XXᵉ où Debussy met en musique quelques strophes de son premier recueil, celui qui lui valut son nom de plume, *Les Amours de Tristan*. Auteur prolifique d'une œuvre variée, il raconte en la romançant sa jeunesse errante et aventureuse dans *Le Page disgracié* et fait jouer plusieurs tragédies. En 1636, sa *Marianne* est applaudie à l'égal du *Cid*. En tant que poète lyrique il publie des recueils qui peuvent être rattachés à deux modèles, celui que lui offre le Cavalier Marin, et celui tout proche de Théophile. Comme Marin, Tristan se plaît à célébrer la beauté dans sa réalité sensuelle et à la traduire par des images que renouvelle une trouvaille subtile ou un détour inattendu : il importe de surprendre ; ainsi, pour évoquer la blancheur des mains l'image ordinaire de la neige glisse vers une autre, plus insolite, qui dira moins la couleur que la perfection quasi irréelle et menacée :

> *Fais-moi boire au creux de tes mains*
> *Si l'eau n'en dissout point la neige.*

Cette tension vers les *concetti* n'échappe pas toujours aux excès précieux et nous n'admirons pas forcément chez le poète ce qui séduisait le plus ses contemporains.

On mesure l'influence de Théophile sur lui dans *Le Promenoir des deux amants*. On voit ce qu'il doit à *La Solitude*. Tristan est, lui aussi, sensible à la beauté de la nature et entretient avec elle une sorte de proximité complice. Il aime composer « sous un arbre bien couvert / Étendu sur le gazon vert / En une rêveuse posture ». L'eau qui court sous les ombrages le séduit plus que tout au monde – on songe à Ronsard – mais lui l'aime pour son pouvoir de doter la réalité d'un double impalpable, ce reflet qui amène à penser qu'elle n'est rien d'autre elle-même que « les songes de l'eau qui sommeille ».

LE PROMENOIR DES DEUX AMANTS

Auprès de cette Grotte sombre
Où l'on respire un air si doux,
L'onde lutte avec les cailloux,
Et la lumière avecque l'ombre.

Ces flots lassés de l'exercice
Qu'ils ont fait dessus ce gravier,
Se reposent dans ce Vivier
Où mourut autrefois Narcisse.

C'est un des miroirs où le Faune
Vient voir si son teint cramoisi,
Depuis que l'Amour l'a saisi,
Ne serait point devenu jaune.

L'ombre de cette fleur vermeille
Et celle de ces joncs pendants
Paraissent être là-dedans
Les songes de l'eau qui sommeille.

Les plus aimables influences
Qui rajeunissent l'univers
Ont relevé ces tapis verts
De fleurs de toutes les nuances.

Dans ce Bois, ni dans ces montagnes
Jamais Chasseur ne vint encor :
Si quelqu'un y sonne du Cor,
C'est Diane avec ses compagnes.

Ce vieux chêne a des marques saintes ;
Sans doute qui le couperait,
Le sang chaud en découlerait
Et l'arbre pousserait des plaintes.

Ce Rossignol mélancolique
Du souvenir de son malheur,
Tâche de charmer sa douleur
Mettant son Histoire en musique.

Il reprend sa note première
Pour chanter d'un art sans pareil
Sous ce rameau que le Soleil
A doré d'un trait de lumière.

Sur ce frêne deux Tourterelles
S'entretiennent de leurs tourments,
Et font les doux appointemens
De leurs amoureuses querelles.

Un jour Vénus avec Anchise
Parmi ses forts s'allait perdant
Et deux Amours, en l'attendant,
Disputaient pour une Cerise.

Dans toutes ces routes divines
Les Nymphes dansent aux chansons,
Et donnent la grâce aux buissons
De porter des fleurs sans épines.

Jamais les vents ni le Tonnerre
N'ont troublé la paix de ces lieux ;
Et la complaisance des Cieux
Y sourit toujours à la Terre.

Crois mon conseil, chère Climène,
Pour laisser arriver le soir,
Je te prie, allons nous asseoir
Sur le bord de cette fontaine.

. . . .

Je tremble en voyant ton visage
Flotter avecque mes désirs,
Tant j'ai de peur que mes soupirs
Ne lui fassent faire naufrage.

De crainte de cette aventure,
Ne commets pas si librement
À cet infidèle Élément
Tous les trésors de la Nature.

Veux-tu par un doux privilège
Me mettre au-dessus des humains ?
Fais-moi boire au creux de tes mains
Si l'eau n'en dissout point la neige.

.. . .

IMITATION D'ANNIBAL CARO

L'Amante de Céphale entr'ouvrait la barrière
Par où le dieu du jour monte sur l'horizon ;
Et, pour illuminer la plus belle saison,
Déjà ce clair flambeau commençait sa carrière,

Quand la Nymphe qui tient mon âme prisonnière
Et de qui les appas sont sans comparaison,
En un pompeux habit sortant de sa maison,
À cet astre brillant opposa sa lumière.

Le soleil s'arrêtant devant cette beauté
Se trouva tout confus de voir que sa clarté
Cédait au vif éclat de l'objet que j'adore ;

Et, tandis que de honte il était tout vermeil,
En versant quelques pleurs, il passa pour l'aurore,
Et Philis en riant passa pour le soleil.

PIERRE CORNEILLE

(1606-1684)

Tout l'effort de Corneille, après les critiques des doctes sur *Le Cid*, vise à l'unité de ses pièces de théâtre, à leur construction, à l'enchaînement et à la progression de l'action. La beauté des vers n'est pas gratuite, elle est au service de cette architecture savante. C'est par elle que le poète imprime aux monologues narratifs, aux affrontements verbaux des protagonistes, aux dialogues des amants en forme de chant alterné, le caractère sublime qui convient à l'univers héroïque, et certains vers, ciselés et concis comme des sentences latines, inscrivent en abrégé dans la mémoire la vision du monde de leur auteur, la conception de la liberté et de la gloire qui lui est propre.

Aussi, vouloir, en une « promenade anthologique », comme disait Jean Schlumberger, isoler pour notre plaisir certains passages de cette œuvre peut sembler arbitraire ou même aller à contre-courant du mouvement d'ensemble qui les porte. Et pourtant c'est bien dans son théâtre que se manifeste pleinement le génie poétique de Corneille ! plus que dans les petits poèmes, d'ailleurs charmants, qu'il compose à la manière de son temps, plus que dans sa traduction des *Psaumes*, bien qu'il y montre sa science de la strophe lyrique.

Dans son théâtre sa Muse est d'abord baroque, comme on l'est au début de son siècle. On le voit dans les délires de Matamore, ou plus tard, dans la faconde du Menteur et la fantaisie irrésistible de ses romans improvisés. Hors de la comédie, son inspiration est plus proche des exigences du classicisme naissant. Il y a souvent recours au style épique où il excelle, témoin le récit du Cid ou le plaidoyer de Nicomède. Le héros semble seul, mais il apparaît soudain épaulé par une foule invisible, qui, derrière lui, épouse sa cause et le suit. C'est la condition même de l'épopée. Sa verve satirique éclate dans les imprécations de Camille et la veine lyrique est manifeste dans les Stances de Rodrigue ou celles de Polyeucte. Enfin les plaintes de Bérénice et surtout, dans sa dernière tragédie, celles de Suréna, plus émouvantes encore par leur caractère testamentaire, ont une grâce dans l'expression qui fait de Corneille, dans ces vers, comme son rival, un poète élégiaque.

LE CID

ACTE I – *Scène VI*

DON RODRIGUE

Percé jusques au fond du cœur
D'une atteinte imprévue aussi bien que mortelle,
Misérable vengeur d'une juste querelle
Et malheureux objet d'une injuste rigueur,
Je demeure immobile, et mon âme abattue
Cède au coup qui me tue.
Si près de voir mon feu récompensé,
Ô Dieu, l'étrange peine !
En cet affront mon père est l'offensé,
Et l'offenseur le père de Chimène !

Que je sens de rudes combats !
Contre mon propre honneur mon amour s'intéresse :
Il faut venger un père, et perdre une maîtresse ;
L'un m'anime le cœur, l'autre retient mon bras.
Réduit au triste choix ou de trahir ma flamme
Ou de vivre en infâme,
Des deux côtés mon mal est infini.
Ô Dieu, l'étrange peine !
Faut-il laisser un affront impuni ?
Faut-il punir le père de Chimène ?

Père, maîtresse, honneur, amour,
Noble et dure contrainte, aimable tyrannie,
Tous mes plaisirs sont morts, ou ma gloire ternie.
L'un me rend malheureux, l'autre indigne du jour.
Cher et cruel espoir d'une âme généreuse,
Mais ensemble amoureuse,
Digne ennemi de mon plus grand bonheur,
Fer qui causes ma peine,
M'es-tu donné pour venger mon honneur ?
M'es-tu donné pour perdre ma Chimène ?

Il vaut mieux courir au trépas.
Je dois à ma maîtresse aussi bien qu'à mon père,
J'attire en me vengeant sa haine et sa colère,
J'attire ses mépris en ne me vengeant pas.
À mon plus doux espoir l'un me rend infidèle
  Et l'autre indigne d'elle.
 Mon mal augmente à le vouloir guérir,
  Tout redouble ma peine.
 Allons, mon âme, et puisqu'il faut mourir,
Mourons du moins sans offenser Chimène.

  Mourir sans tirer ma raison !
Rechercher un trépas si mortel à ma gloire !
Endurer que l'Espagne impute à ma mémoire
D'avoir mal soutenu l'honneur de ma maison !
Respecter un amour dont mon âme égarée
  Voit la perte assurée !
 N'écoutons plus ce penser suborneur
  Qui ne sert qu'à ma peine.
 Allons, mon bras, sauvons du moins l'honneur,
Puisqu'après tout il faut perdre Chimène.

  Oui, mon esprit s'était déçu.
Je dois tout à mon père avant qu'à ma maîtresse :
Que je meure au combat ou meure de tristesse,
Je rendrai mon sang pur comme je l'ai reçu.
Je m'accuse déjà de trop de négligence :
  Courons à la vengeance ;
 Et tout honteux d'avoir tant balancé,
  Ne soyons plus en peine,
 Puisqu'aujourd'hui mon père est l'offensé,
Si l'offenseur est père de Chimène.

LE CID

Acte IV – *Scène III*

DON RODRIGUE

Sous moi donc cette troupe s'avance
Et porte sur le front une mâle assurance.
Nous partîmes cinq cents, mais par un prompt renfort
Nous nous vîmes trois mille en arrivant au port,
Tant à nous voir marcher avec un tel visage
Les plus épouvantés reprenaient leur courage !
J'en cache les deux tiers, aussitôt qu'arrivés,
Dans le fond des vaisseaux qui lors furent trouvés ;
Le reste, dont le nombre augmentait à toute heure,
Brûlant d'impatience autour de moi demeure,
Se couche contre terre, et sans faire aucun bruit,
Passe une bonne part d'une si belle nuit.
Par mon commandement la garde en fait de même
Et, se tenant cachée, aide à mon stratagème,
Et je feins hardiment d'avoir reçu de vous
L'ordre qu'on me voit suivre et que je donne à tous.
Cette obscure clarté qui tombe des étoiles
Enfin avec le flux nous fait voir trente voiles ;
L'onde s'enfle dessous et d'un commun effort
Les Mores et la mer montent jusques au port.
On les laisse passer, tout leur paraît tranquille :
Point de soldats au port, point aux murs de la ville.
Notre profond silence abusant leurs esprits,
Ils n'osent plus douter de nous avoir surpris ;
Ils abordent sans peur, ils ancrent, ils descendent
Et courent se livrer aux mains qui les attendent.
Nous nous levons alors et tous en même temps
Poussons jusques au ciel mille cris éclatants.
Les nôtres, à ces cris, de nos vaisseaux répondent ;
Ils paraissent armés, les Mores se confondent,
L'épouvante les prend à demi descendus ;
Avant que de combattre, ils s'estiment perdus.
Ils couraient au pillage et rencontrent la guerre ;
Nous les pressons sur l'eau, nous les pressons sur terre

Et nous faisons courir des ruisseaux de leur sang,
Avant qu'aucun résiste ou reprenne son rang.
Mais bientôt, malgré nous, leurs princes les rallient ;
Leur courage renaît et leurs terreurs s'oublient :
La honte de mourir sans avoir combattu
Arrête leur désordre et leur rend leur vertu.
Contre nous de pied ferme ils tirent leurs alfanges,
De notre sang au leur font d'horribles mélanges
Et la terre et le fleuve et leur flotte et le port
Sont des champs de carnage où triomphe la mort.
    Ô combien d'actions, combien d'exploits célèbres
Sont demeurés sans gloire au milieu des ténèbres,
Où chacun, seul témoin des grands coups qu'il donnait,
Ne pouvait discerner où le sort inclinait !
J'allais de tous côtés encourager les nôtres,
Faire avancer les uns, et soutenir les autres,
Ranger ceux qui venaient, les pousser à leur tour
Et ne l'ai pu savoir jusques au point du jour.
Mais enfin sa clarté montre notre avantage :
Le More voit sa perte et perd soudain courage
Et voyant un renfort qui nous vient secourir,
L'ardeur de vaincre cède à la peur de mourir.
Ils gagnent leurs vaisseaux, ils en coupent les câbles,
Poussent jusques aux cieux des cris épouvantables,
Font retraite en tumulte, et sans considérer
Si leurs rois avec eux peuvent se retirer.
Pour souffrir ce devoir leur frayeur est trop forte :
Le flux les apporta, le reflux les remporte,
Cependant que leurs rois, engagés parmi nous
Et quelque peu des leurs, tous percés de nos coups,
Disputent vaillamment et vendent bien leur vie.
À se rendre moi-même en vain je les convie :
Le cimeterre au poing ils ne m'écoutent pas,
Mais voyant à leurs pieds tomber tous leurs soldats
Et que seuls désormais en vain ils se défendent,
Ils demandent le chef : je me nomme, ils se rendent.
Je vous les envoyai tous deux en même temps
Et le combat cessa faute de combattants.

POLYEUCTE

ACTE IV – *Scène II*

POLYEUCTE
(Les gardes se retirent aux coins du théâtre.)

Source délicieuse, en misères féconde,
Que voulez-vous de moi, flatteuses voluptés ?
Honteux attachements de la chair et du monde,
Que ne me quittez-vous, quand je vous ai quittés ?
Allez, honneurs, plaisirs, qui me livrez la guerre :
    Toute votre félicité,
    Sujette à l'instabilité,
    En moins de rien tombe par terre ;
    Et comme elle a l'éclat du verre,
    Elle en a la fragilité.

Ainsi n'espérez pas qu'après vous je soupire :
Vous étalez en vain vos charmes impuissants ;
Vous me montrez en vain par tout ce vaste empire
Les ennemis de Dieu pompeux et florissants.
Il étale à son tour des revers équitables
    Par qui les grands sont confondus ;
    Et les glaives qu'il tient pendus
    Sur les plus fortunés coupables
    Sont d'autant plus inévitables
    Que leurs coups sont moins attendus.

Tigre altéré de sang, Décie impitoyable,
Ce Dieu t'a trop longtemps abandonné les siens ;
De ton heureux destin vois la suite effroyable :
Le Scythe va venger la Perse et les chrétiens ;
Encore un peu plus outre, et ton heure est venue ;
    Rien ne t'en saurait garantir ;
    Et la foudre qui va partir,
    Toute prête à crever la nue,
    Ne peut plus être retenue
    Par l'attente du repentir.

Que cependant Félix m'immole à ta colère ;
Qu'un rival plus puissant éblouisse ses yeux ;
Qu'aux dépens de ma vie il s'en fasse beau-père,
Et qu'à titre d'esclave il commande en ces lieux :
Je consens, ou plutôt j'aspire à ma ruine.
     Monde, pour moi tu n'as plus rien :
     Je porte en un cœur tout chrétien
     Une flamme toute divine ;
     Et je ne regarde Pauline
     Que comme un obstacle à mon bien.

Saintes douceurs du ciel, adorables idées,
Vous remplissez un cœur qui vous peut recevoir ;
De vos sacrés attraits les âmes possédées
Ne conçoivent plus rien qui les puisse émouvoir.
Vous promettez beaucoup, et donnez davantage :
     Vos biens ne sont point inconstants ;
     Et l'heureux trépas que j'attends
     Ne vous sert que d'un doux passage
     Pour nous introduire au partage
     Qui nous rend à jamais contents.

C'est vous, ô feu divin que rien ne peut éteindre,
Qui m'allez faire voir Pauline sans la craindre.
Je la vois ; mais mon cœur, d'un saint zèle enflammé,
N'en goûte plus l'appas dont il était charmé ;
Et mes yeux, éclairés des célestes lumières,
Ne trouvent plus aux siens leurs grâces coutumières.

POLYEUCTE

ACTE IV – *Scène III*

PAULINE

Cruel, car il est temps que ma douleur éclate,
Et qu'un juste reproche accable une âme ingrate,
Est-ce là ce beau feu ? sont-ce là tes serments ?
Témoignes-tu pour moi les moindres sentiments ?
Je ne te parlais point de l'état déplorable
Où ta mort va laisser ta femme inconsolable ;
Je croyais que l'amour t'en parlerait assez,
Et je ne voulais pas de sentiments forcés ;
Mais cette amour si ferme et si bien méritée
Que tu m'avais promise, et que je t'ai portée,
Quand tu me veux quitter, quand tu me fais mourir,
Te peut-elle arracher une larme, un soupir ?
Tu me quittes, ingrat, et le fais avec joie ;
Tu ne la caches pas, tu veux que je la voie ;
Et ton cœur, insensible à ces tristes appas,
Se figure un bonheur où je ne serai pas !
C'est donc là le dégoût qu'apporte l'hyménée ?
Je te suis odieuse après m'être donnée ?

POLYEUCTE

Hélas !

PAULINE

            Que cet hélas a de peine à sortir !
Encor s'il commençait un heureux repentir,
Que tout forcé qu'il est, j'y trouverais de charmes !
Mais courage, il s'émeut, je vois couler des larmes.

POLYEUCTE

J'en verse, et plût à Dieu qu'à force d'en verser
Ce cœur trop endurci se pût enfin percer !
Le déplorable état où je vous abandonne
Est bien digne des pleurs que mon amour vous donne ;
Et si l'on peut au ciel sentir quelques douleurs,

J'y pleurerai pour vous l'excès de vos malheurs ;
Mais si, dans ce séjour de gloire et de lumière,
Ce Dieu tout juste et bon peut souffrir ma prière,
S'il y daigne écouter un conjugal amour,
Sur votre aveuglement il répandra le jour.
Seigneur, de vos bontés il faut que je l'obtienne :
Elle a trop de vertus pour n'être pas chrétienne ;
Avec trop de mérite il vous plut la former,
Pour ne vous pas connaître et ne vous pas aimer,
Pour vivre des enfers esclave infortunée,
Et sous leur triste joug mourir comme elle est née.

PAULINE

Que dis-tu, malheureux ? Qu'oses-tu souhaiter ?

POLYEUCTE

Ce que de tout mon sang je voudrais acheter.

PAULINE

Que plutôt...

POLYEUCTE

C'est en vain qu'on se met en défense :
Ce Dieu touche les cœurs lorsque moins on y pense.
Ce bienheureux moment n'est pas encor venu ;
Il viendra, mais le temps ne m'en est pas connu.

PAULINE

Quittez cette chimère, et m'aimez.

POLYEUCTE

Je vous aime,
Beaucoup moins que mon Dieu, mais bien plus que moi-même.

PAULINE

Au nom de cet amour ne m'abandonnez pas,

POLYEUCTE

Au nom de cet amour, daignez suivre mes pas.

PAULINE

C'est peu de me quitter, tu veux donc me séduire ?

POLYEUCTE

C'est peu d'aller au Ciel, je vous y veux conduire.

PAULINE

Imaginations !

POLYEUCTE

Célestes vérités !

PAULINE

Étrange aveuglement !

POLYEUCTE

Éternelles clartés !

PAULINE

Tu préfères la mort à l'amour de Pauline !

POLYEUCTE

Vous préférez le monde à la bonté divine !

PAULINE

Va, cruel, va mourir : tu ne m'aimas jamais.

POLYEUCTE

Vivez heureuse au monde, et me laissez en paix.

TITE ET BÉRÉNICE

ACTE V – *Scène IV*

BÉRÉNICE

Laissez-moi la douceur de languir en ces lieux,
D'y soupirer pour vous, d'y mourir à vos yeux.
C'en sera bientôt fait, ma douleur est trop vive
Pour y tenir longtemps votre attente captive,
Et si je tarde trop à mourir de douleur,
J'irai loin de vos yeux terminer mon malheur.
Mais laissez-m'en choisir la funeste journée,
Et du moins jusque-là, Seigneur, pas d'hyménée.
Pour votre ambitieuse avez-vous tant d'amour
Que vous ne le puissiez différer d'un seul jour ?
Pouvez-vous refuser à ma douleur profonde...

TITE

Hélas ! que voulez-vous que la mienne réponde,
Et que puis-je résoudre alors que vous parlez,
Moi qui ne puis vouloir que ce que vous voulez ?
Vous parlez de languir, de mourir à ma vue,
Mais, ô Dieux ! songez-vous que chaque mot me tue,
Et porte dans mon cœur de si sensibles coups
Qu'il ne m'en faut plus qu'un pour mourir avant vous ?
De ceux qui m'ont percé souffrez que je soupire.
Pourquoi partir, Madame, et pourquoi me le dire ?
Ah ! si vous vous forcez d'abandonner ces lieux,
Ne m'assassinez pas de vos cruels adieux.
Je vous suivrais, Madame, et flatté de l'idée
D'oser mourir à Rome, et revivre en Judée,
Pour aller de mes feux vous demander le fruit,
Je quitterais l'Empire et tout ce qui leur nuit.

BÉRÉNICE

Daigne me préserver le ciel...

TITE

       De quoi, Madame ?

BÉRÉNICE

De voir tant de faiblesse en une si grande âme !
Si j'avais droit par là de vous moins estimer,
Je cesserais peut-être aussi de vous aimer.

SURÉNA

ACTE I – *Scène III*

SURÉNA

Que tout meure avec moi, Madame. Que m'importe
Qui foule après ma mort la terre qui me porte ?
Sentiront-ils percer par un éclat nouveau,
Ces illustres aïeux, la nuit de leur tombeau ?
Respireront-ils l'air où les feront revivre
Ces neveux qui peut-être auront peine à les suivre,
Peut-être ne feront que les déshonorer,
Et n'en auront le sang que pour dégénérer ?
Quand nous avons perdu le jour qui nous éclaire,
Cette sorte de vie est bien imaginaire,
Et le moindre moment d'un bonheur souhaité
Vaut mieux qu'une si froide et vaine éternité.

ISAAC DE BENSERADE

(1613-1691)

Voiture a pu voir en lui un rival et s'inquiéter, un temps, de son succès auprès de la marquise de Rambouillet. Capable d'être lui aussi un amuseur, il acquiert vite le ton de la nouvelle galanterie, mais la poésie de salon l'occupe moins que le théâtre auquel il se consacre surtout. Ses tragédies sont jouées avec succès.

Cependant son nom reste attaché aussi au sonnet de Job. Une coterie se constitue, celle des « Jobelins », pour soutenir que ce sonnet l'emporte sur celui d'Uranie composé quelque vingt ans plus tôt par Voiture, et que défendent les « Uranistes ». On connaît maints jugements formulés par les doctes que l'on consulta à ce propos. Corneille évita, avec élégance, de trancher :

> *Deux sonnets partagent la ville,*
> *Deux sonnets partagent la Cour,*
> *Et semblent vouloir à leur tour*
> *Rallumer la guerre civile.*
>
> . . . .
>
> *Chacun en parle hautement*
> *Suivant son petit jugement,*
> *Et, s'il faut y mêler le nôtre,*
>
> *L'un est sans doute mieux rêvé.*
> *Mieux conduit et mieux achevé ;*
> *Mais je voudrais avoir fait l'autre.*

Cette querelle amuse encore parfois les écoliers.

SUR JOB

Job, de mille tourments atteint,
Vous rendra sa douleur connue ;
Et raisonnablement il craint
Que vous n'en soyez point émue.

Vous verrez sa misère nue :
Il s'est lui-même ici dépeint ;
Accoutumez-vous à la vue
D'un homme qui souffre et se plaint.

Bien qu'il eût d'extrêmes souffrances,
On voit aller des patiences
Plus loin que la sienne n'alla.

S'il souffrit des maux incroyables,
Il s'en plaignit, il en parla ;
J'en connais de plus misérables.

JEAN DE LA FONTAINE

(1621-1695)

Il est pour nous si exclusivement le fabuliste, ou pour mieux dire, le « fablier », pareil au « poêmier », l'arbre à poèmes de Paul Fort, que nous oublions ses autres œuvres, et cependant elles valent d'être lues, en particulier celle que commente et admire Valéry. Elle relate les amours d'Adonis et de Vénus, la chasse où le jeune homme trouve la mort, et le désespoir de la déesse. La mythologie n'y est pas alourdie d'allusions savantes, mais, ornementale et familière, elle s'inscrit dans la lignée du poème héroïque, du moins celle qui est issue d'Ovide. Le vers par sa fluidité et son élégance (« Jours devenus moments, moments filés de soie »…) suppose de la part de l'auteur tant de métier déjà, qu'il permet à Valéry de récuser la réputation de nonchalance que l'on fait au poète. « L'art et la pureté si soutenus, dit-il, excluent à mon regard toute paresse et toute bonhomie. » Et il souligne que c'est la discipline poétique à laquelle La Fontaine s'astreint en composant les six cents vers d'*Adonis*, qui lui permet de se jouer plus tard des difficultés du vers aux mètres et aux rythmes variés.

C'est à la fin du Premier Recueil des Fables que le poète confie à ses lecteurs ce que sera son prochain ouvrage, en disant : « Revenons à Psyché. » La rédaction de cette œuvre singulière s'étend en effet sur une assez longue période car l'ambition de son auteur ne se borne pas simplement au conte. Certes *L'Âne d'or* lui fournit une trame et Francesco Colona dans *Le Songe de Poliphile* en enrichit les données d'une dimension symbolique. Mais il s'agit de créer un genre inédit et de trouver un ton nouveau. Le récit des épreuves de cette mortelle aimée et punie par un dieu se présente sous la forme d'une lecture, faite à haute voix par son auteur, au cours d'une promenade dans les jardins de Versailles. Poliphile – entendons La Fontaine – soumet au jugement de ses trois amis le « récit poétique » qu'il vient de composer. Il y passe librement de la prose aux vers et l'on peut s'étonner ici de sa virtuosité de prosateur-poète : il a su inventer une langue assez souple pour permettre une alternance qui se fait sans dissonance ni rupture de ton. Interrompant assez souvent la lecture par leurs commentaires, se querellant même parfois, les amis vont ajouter aux registres imbriqués de l'imaginaire du conte et de la réalité du décor une composante insolite, celle de la réflexion critique et du débat théorique.

L'*Hymne à la volupté* sert de conclusion aux *Amours de Psyché et de Cupidon*, les quatre amis l'approuvent sans réserve, puis s'éloignent dans l'éclatante lumière d'un soleil couchant qui donne à cette œuvre un final de ballet de cour.

La fable, elle aussi, est un genre nouveau et composite, car si elle a sa source dans les modèles du passé auxquels le poète rend hommage, elle offre une synthèse absolument unique en mêlant l'anecdote, qui l'apparente aux contes, aux commentaires et interventions de l'auteur dont l'ironie les rattache à la satire, qu'ils soient une attaque directe : « Je définis la Cour un pays... », ou voilée d'une feinte objectivité : « Le désir peut loger chez une précieuse. » Cette intrusion prend parfois la forme d'une confidence qui donne à la fable une ampleur lyrique. Tous ces éléments sont fondus ensemble par le génie poétique de La Fontaine qui colore chacune d'elles de sa vision originale. À ces subtils entrelacs s'ajoute la plupart du temps la morale. Ici simple constat sur le monde comme il va – et Rousseau s'en offusque –, ailleurs leçon de prudence ou encore critique indignée et éloquente, dans tous les cas le fabuliste la croit capable, comme il l'écrit à propos d'Ésope, de « répandre insensiblement dans les âmes les semences de la vertu ». La richesse et la diversité de ce savant assemblage permet tous les jeux avec la langue. En mêlant de vieux mots du français aux tournures précieuses de son temps, ou la trivialité du réel au raffinement lyrique, le poète réussit à unir dans les fables la naïve espièglerie de Marot aux traits d'esprit de Voiture, et peut se réclamer à la fois de Rabelais et de Théophile.

C'est cette diversité de tons que la transmutation poétique fond en une seule musique, qui rend La Fontaine, entre tous les poètes français, le plus difficile à dire, et qui, cependant, se passe le moins d'être dit. La voix fait surgir ce que le regard laisse échapper, elle oblige à prendre parti. Pierre Clarac l'a montré avec humour en particulier à propos de la confession du lion :

> *Même il m'est arrivé de manger*
> *Le berger.*

On ne sait trop, dit-il en substance, si ces trois syllabes s'efforcent d'escamoter le forfait en étouffant l'aveu, se réduisant alors à un chuchotement, si elles l'assument au contraire en se détachant avec netteté, ou si, par l'écho d'un rythme ternaire et dansant, elles ne le réduisent pas à la confidence amusée et désinvolte d'un grand seigneur. L'interprète devra choisir.

ADONIS

. . . .
Tout ce qui naît de doux en l'amoureux empire,
Quand d'une égale ardeur l'un pour l'autre on soupire
Et que, de la contrainte ayant banni les lois,
On se peut assurer au silence des bois,
Jours devenus moments, moments filés de soie,
Agréables soupirs, pleurs enfants de la joie,
Vœux, serments et regards, transports, ravissements,
Mélange dont se fait le bonheur des amants,
Tout par ce couple heureux fut lors mis en usage.
Tantôt ils choisissaient l'épaisseur d'un ombrage :
Là sous les chênes vieux où leurs chiffres gravés
Se sont avec les troncs accrus et conservés,
Mollement étendus ils consumaient les heures,
Sans avoir pour témoins en ces sombres demeures
Que les chantres des bois, pour confidents qu'Amour,
Qui seul guidait leurs pas en cet heureux séjour.
Tantôt sur des tapis d'herbe tendre et sacrée
Adonis s'endormait auprès de Cythérée,
Dont les yeux, enivrés par des charmes puissants,
Attachaient au héros leurs regards languissants.
Bien souvent ils chantaient les douceurs de leurs peines ;
Et quelquefois assis sur le bord des fontaines,
Tandis que cent cailloux, luttant à chaque bond,
Suivaient les longs replis du cristal vagabond,
« Voyez, disait Vénus, ces ruisseaux et leur course,
Ainsi jamais le temps ne remonte à sa source :
Vainement pour les dieux il fuit d'un pas léger ;
Mais vous autres mortels le devez ménager,
Consacrant à l'Amour la saison la plus belle. »
Souvent, pour divertir leur ardeur mutuelle,
Ils dansaient aux chansons, de Nymphes entourés.
Combien de fois la lune a leurs pas éclairés,
Et, couvrant de ses rais l'émail d'une prairie,
Les a vus à l'envi fouler l'herbe fleurie !
. . . .

LES AMOURS DE PSYCHÉ ET DE CUPIDON

Que nos plaisirs passés augmentent nos supplices !
Qu'il est dur d'éprouver, après tant de délices,
    Les cruautés du Sort !
Fallait-il être heureuse avant qu'être coupable ?
Et si de me haïr, Amour, tu fus capable,
    Pourquoi m'aimer d'abord ?

Que ne punissais-tu mon crime par avance !
Il est bien temps d'ôter à mes yeux ta présence,
    Quand tu luis dans mon cœur !
Encor si j'ignorais la moitié de tes charmes !
Mais je les ai tous vus : j'ai vu toutes les armes
    Qui te rendent vainqueur.

J'ai vu la beauté même et les grâces dormantes.
Un doux ressouvenir de cent choses charmantes
    Me suit dans les déserts.
L'image de ces biens rend mes maux cent fois pires.
Ma mémoire me dit : « Quoi ! Psyché, tu respires,
    Après ce que tu perds ? »

Cependant il faut vivre ; Amour m'a fait défense
D'attenter sur des jours qu'il tient en sa puissance,
    Tout malheureux qu'ils sont.
Le cruel veut, hélas ! que mes mains soient captives.
Je n'ose me soustraire aux peines excessives
    Que mes remords me font.

C'est ainsi qu'en un bois Psyché contait aux arbres
Sa douleur, dont l'excès faisait fendre les marbres
    Habitants de ces lieux.
Rochers, qui l'écoutiez avec quelque tendresse,
Souvenez-vous des pleurs qu'au fort de sa tristesse
    Ont versés ses beaux yeux.

HYMNE À LA VOLUPTÉ

Ô douce Volupté, sans qui, dès notre enfance,
Le vivre et le mourir nous deviendraient égaux ;
Aimant universel de tous les animaux,
Que tu sais attirer avecque violence !
        Par toi tout se meut ici-bas.
        C'est pour toi, c'est pour tes appas,
        Que nous courons après la peine :
        Il n'est soldat, ni capitaine,
Ni ministre d'État, ni prince, ni sujet,
        Qui ne t'ait pour unique objet.
Nous autres nourrissons, si pour fruit de nos veilles
Un bruit délicieux ne charmait nos oreilles,
Si nous ne nous sentions chatouillés de ce son,
        Ferions-nous un mot de chanson ?
Ce qu'on appelle gloire en termes magnifiques,
Ce qui servait de prix dans les jeux olympiques,
N'est que toi proprement, divine Volupté.
Et le plaisir des sens n'est-il de rien compté ?
        Pour quoi sont faits les dons de Flore,
        Le soleil couchant et l'Aurore,
        Pomone et ses mets délicats,
        Bacchus, l'âme des bons repas,
        Les forêts, les eaux, les prairies,
        Mères des douces rêveries ?
Pour quoi tant de beaux arts, qui tous sont tes enfants ?
Mais pour quoi les Chloris aux appas triomphants,
        Que pour maintenir ton commerce ?
J'entends innocemment : sur son propre désir
        Quelque rigueur que l'on exerce,
        Encore y prend-on du plaisir.
Volupté, Volupté, qui fus jadis maîtresse
        Du plus bel esprit de la Grèce,
Ne me dédaigne pas, viens-t'en loger chez moi ;
        Tu n'y seras pas sans emploi.
J'aime le jeu, l'amour, les livres, la musique,

La ville et la campagne, enfin tout ; il n'est rien
            Qui ne me soit souverain bien,
Jusqu'au sombre plaisir d'un cœur mélancolique.
Viens donc ; et de ce bien, ô douce Volupté,
Veux-tu savoir au vrai la mesure certaine ?
Il m'en faut tout au moins un siècle bien compté ;
            Car trente ans, ce n'est pas la peine.

Les Amours de Psyché et de Cupidon

LA MORT ET LE BÛCHERON

Un pauvre bûcheron tout couvert de ramée,
Sous le faix du fagot aussi bien que des ans
Gémissant et courbé marchait à pas pesants,
Et tâchait de gagner sa chaumine enfumée.
Enfin, n'en pouvant plus d'effort et de douleur,
Il met bas son fagot, il songe à son malheur.
Quel plaisir a-t-il eu depuis qu'il est au monde ?
En est-il un plus pauvre en la machine ronde ?
Point de pain quelquefois, et jamais de repos :
Sa femme, ses enfants, les soldats, les impôts,
     Le créancier et la corvée
Lui font d'un malheureux la peinture achevée.
Il appelle la Mort, elle vient sans tarder,
     Lui demande ce qu'il faut faire.
     « C'est, dit-il, afin de m'aider
À recharger ce bois ; tu ne tarderas guère. »

     Le trépas vient tout guérir ;
     Mais ne bougeons d'où nous sommes.
     Plutôt souffrir que mourir,
     C'est la devise des hommes.

Fables, Livre I

LE CHÊNE ET LE ROSEAU

Le chêne un jour dit au roseau :
« Vous avez bien sujet d'accuser la Nature :
Un roitelet pour vous est un pesant fardeau.
Le moindre vent qui d'aventure
Fait rider la face de l'eau.
Vous oblige à baisser la tête :
Cependant que mon front, au Caucase pareil,
Non content d'arrêter les rayons du soleil,
Brave l'effort de la tempête.
Tout vous est aquilon, tout me semble zéphir.
Encor si vous naissiez à l'abri du feuillage
Dont je couvre le voisinage,
Vous n'auriez pas tant à souffrir :
Je vous défendrais de l'orage ;
Mais vous naissez le plus souvent
Sur les humides bords des royaumes du vent.
La Nature envers vous me semble bien injuste.
– Votre compassion, lui répondit l'arbuste,
Part d'un bon naturel ; mais quittez ce souci.
Les vents me sont moins qu'à vous redoutables.
Je plie, et ne romps pas. Vous avez jusqu'ici
Contre leurs coups épouvantables
Résisté sans courber le dos ;
Mais attendons la fin. » Comme il disait ces mots,
Du bout de l'horizon accourt avec furie
Le plus terrible des enfants
Que le Nord eût porté jusque-là dans ses flancs.
L'arbre tient bon ; le roseau plie.
Le vent redouble ses efforts,
Et fait si bien qu'il déracine
Celui de qui la tête au ciel était voisine,
Et dont les pieds touchaient à l'Empire des morts.

Fables, Livre I

LE LIÈVRE ET LES GRENOUILLES

Un lièvre en son gîte songeait
(Car que faire en un gîte, à moins que l'on ne songe ?) ;
Dans un profond ennui ce lièvre se plongeait :
Cet animal est triste, et la crainte le ronge.
    « Les gens de naturel peureux
    Sont, disait-il, bien malheureux ;
Ils ne sauraient manger morceau qui leur profite.
Jamais un plaisir pur, toujours assauts divers.
Voilà comme je vis : cette crainte maudite
M'empêche de dormir, sinon les yeux ouverts.
Corrigez-vous, dira quelque sage cervelle.
    Et la peur se corrige-t-elle ?
    Je crois même qu'en bonne foi
    Les hommes ont peur comme moi. »
    Ainsi raisonnait notre lièvre
    Et cependant faisait le guet.
    Il était douteux, inquiet :
Un souffle, une ombre, un rien, tout lui donnait la fièvre.
    Le mélancolique animal,
    En rêvant à cette matière,
Entend un léger bruit : ce lui fut un signal
    Pour s'enfuir devers sa tanière.
Il s'en alla passer sur le bord d'un étang.
Grenouilles aussitôt de sauter dans les ondes,
Grenouilles de rentrer en leurs grottes profondes.
    « Oh ! dit-il, j'en fais faire autant
    Qu'on m'en fait faire ! Ma présence
Effraye aussi les gens, je mets l'alarme au camp !
    Et d'où me vient cette vaillance ?
Comment ! des animaux qui tremblent devant moi !
    Je suis donc un foudre de guerre ?
Il n'est, je le vois bien, si poltron sur la terre
Qui ne puisse trouver un plus poltron que soi. »

Fables, Livre II

LE COCHET, LE CHAT ET LE SOURICEAU

Un souriceau tout jeune, et qui n'avait rien vu,
          Fut presque pris au dépourvu.
Voici comme il conta l'aventure à sa mère :
« J'avais franchi les monts qui bornent cet État,
          Et trottais comme un jeune rat
          Qui cherche à se donner carrière,
Lorsque deux animaux m'ont arrêté les yeux :
          L'un doux, bénin et gracieux,
Et l'autre turbulent, et plein d'inquiétude.
          Il a la voix perçante et rude,
          Sur la tête un morceau de chair,
Une sorte de bras dont il s'élève en l'air
          Comme pour prendre sa volée,
          La queue en panache étalée. »
Or c'était un cochet dont notre souriceau
          Fit à sa mère le tableau,
Comme d'un animal venu de l'Amérique.
« Il se battait, dit-il, les flancs avec ses bras,
          Faisant tel bruit et tel fracas,
Que moi, qui grâce aux dieux de courage me pique,
          En ai pris la fuite de peur,
          Le maudissant de très bon cœur.
          Sans lui j'aurais fait connaissance
Avec cet animal qui m'a semblé si doux.
          Il est velouté comme nous,
     Marqueté, longue queue, une humble contenance,
Un modeste regard, et pourtant l'œil luisant.
          Je le crois fort sympathisant
Avec Messieurs les Rats ; car il a des oreilles
          En figure aux nôtres pareilles.
Je l'allais aborder, quand d'un son plein d'éclat
          L'autre m'a fait prendre la fuite.
– Mon fils, dit la souris, ce doucet est un chat,
          Qui sous son minois hypocrite
          Contre toute ta parenté

D'un malin vouloir est porté.
L'autre animal tout au contraire,
Bien éloigné de nous mal faire,
Servira quelque jour peut-être à nos repas.
Quant au chat, c'est sur nous qu'il fonde sa cuisine,

Garde-toi, tant que tu vivras,
De juger des gens sur la mine. »

Fables, Livre VI

LA JEUNE VEUVE

La perte d'un époux ne va point sans soupirs.
On fait beaucoup de bruit, et puis on se console.
Sur les ailes du Temps la tristesse s'envole ;
   Le Temps ramène les plaisirs.
    Entre la veuve d'une année
    Et la veuve d'une journée
La différence est grande : on ne croirait jamais
    Que ce fût la même personne.
L'une fait fuir les gens, et l'autre a mille attraits.
Aux soupirs vrais ou faux celle-là s'abandonne ;
C'est toujours même note et pareil entretien :
    On dit qu'on est inconsolable ;
    On le dit, mais il n'en est rien,
    Comme on verra par cette fable,
    Ou plutôt par la vérité,

    L'époux d'une jeune beauté
Partait pour l'autre monde. À ses côtés sa femme
Lui criait : « Attends-moi, je te suis ; et mon âme,
Aussi bien que la tienne, est prête à s'envoler. »
    Le mari fait seul le voyage.
La belle avait un père, homme prudent et sage :
    Il laissa le torrent couler.
    À la fin, pour la consoler,
« Ma fille, lui dit-il, c'est trop verser de larmes :
Qu'a besoin le défunt que vous noyiez vos charmes ?
Puisqu'il est des vivants, ne songez plus aux morts.
    Je ne dis pas que tout à l'heure
    Une condition meilleure
    Change en des noces ces transports ;
Mais, après certain temps, souffrez qu'on vous propose
Un époux beau, bien fait, jeune, et tout autre chose
    Que le défunt. – Ah ! dit-elle aussitôt,
    Un cloître est l'époux qu'il me faut. »
Le père lui laissa digérer sa disgrâce.

Un mois de la sorte se passe.
L'autre mois on l'emploie à changer tous les jours
Quelque chose à l'habit, au linge, à la coiffure.
Le deuil enfin sert de parure,
En attendant d'autres atours.
Toute la bande des Amours
Revient au colombier ; les jeux, les ris, la danse,
Ont aussi leur tour à la fin.
On se plonge soir et matin
Dans la fontaine de Jouvence.
Le père ne craint plus ce défunt tant chéri ;
Mais comme il ne parlait de rien à notre belle :
« Où donc est le jeune mari
Que vous m'avez promis ? » dit-elle.

Fables, Livre VI

LES ANIMAUX MALADES DE LA PESTE

Un mal qui répand la terreur,
Mal que le Ciel en sa fureur
Inventa pour punir les crimes de la terre,
La peste (puisqu'il faut l'appeler par son nom),
Capable d'enrichir en un jour l'Achéron,
Faisait aux animaux la guerre.
Ils ne mouraient pas tous, mais tous étaient frappés :
On n'en voyait point d'occupés
À chercher le soutien d'une mourante vie ;
Nul mets n'excitait leur envie ;
Ni loups ni renards n'épiaient
La douce et l'innocente proie.
Les tourterelles se fuyaient :
Plus d'amour, partant plus de joie.
Le lion tint conseil, et dit : « Mes chers amis,
Je crois que le Ciel a permis
Pour nos péchés cette infortune ;
Que le plus coupable de nous
Se sacrifie aux traits du céleste courroux,
Peut-être il obtiendra la guérison commune.
L'histoire nous apprend qu'en de tels accidents
On fait de pareils dévouements :
Ne nous flattons donc point ; voyons sans indulgence
L'état de notre conscience.
Pour moi, satisfaisant mes appétits gloutons
J'ai dévoré force moutons.
Que m'avaient-ils fait ? Nulle offense :
Même il m'est arrivé quelquefois de manger
Le berger.
Je me dévouerai donc, s'il le faut ; mais je pense
Qu'il est bon que chacun s'accuse ainsi que moi :
Car on doit souhaiter selon toute justice
Que le plus coupable périsse.
– Sire, dit le renard, vous êtes trop bon roi ;
Vos scrupules font voir trop de délicatesse.

Eh bien ! manger moutons, canaille, sotte espèce,
Est-ce un péché ? Non, non. Vous leur fîtes, Seigneur,
    En les croquant beaucoup d'honneur.
    Et quant au berger l'on peut dire
    Qu'il était digne de tous maux,
Étant de ces gens-là qui sur les animaux
    Se font un chimérique empire. »
Ainsi dit le renard, et flatteurs d'applaudir.
    On n'osa trop approfondir
Du tigre, ni de l'ours, ni des autres puissances,
    Les moins pardonnables offenses.
Tous les gens querelleurs, jusqu'aux simples mâtins,
Au dire de chacun, étaient de petits saints.
L'âne vint à son tour et dit : « J'ai souvenance
    Qu'en un pré de moines passant,
La faim, l'occasion, l'herbe tendre, et je pense
    Quelque diable aussi me poussant,
Je tondis de ce pré la largeur de ma langue.
Je n'en avais nul droit, puisqu'il faut parler net. »
À ces mots on cria haro sur le baudet.
Un loup quelque peu clerc prouva par sa harangue
Qu'il fallait dévouer ce maudit animal,
Ce pelé, ce galeux, d'où venait tout le mal.
Sa peccadille fut jugée un cas pendable.
Manger l'herbe d'autrui ! quel crime abominable !
    Rien que la mort n'était capable
D'expier son forfait : on le lui fit bien voir.
Selon que vous serez puissant ou misérable,
Les jugements de cour vous rendront blanc ou noir.

Fables, Livre VII

LE HÉRON

Un jour, sur ses longs pieds, allait je ne sais où
Le héron au long bec emmanché d'un long cou :
        Il côtoyait une rivière.
L'onde était transparente ainsi qu'aux plus beaux jours ;
Ma commère la carpe y faisait mille tours
        Avec le brochet son compère.
Le héron en eût fait aisément son profit :
Tous approchaient du bord, l'oiseau n'avait qu'à prendre ;
        Mais il crut mieux faire d'attendre
        Qu'il eût un peu plus d'appétit :
Il vivait de régime, et mangeait à ses heures.
Après quelques moments l'appétit vint : l'oiseau
        S'approchant du bord vit sur l'eau
Des tanches qui sortaient du fond de ces demeures.
Le mets ne lui plut pas : il s'attendait à mieux,
        Et montrait un goût dédaigneux
        Comme le rat du bon Horace.
« Moi, des tanches ? dit-il, moi héron que je fasse
Une si pauvre chère ? Et pour qui me prend-on ? »
La tanche rebutée il trouva du goujon.
« Du goujon ? c'est bien là le dîner d'un héron !
J'ouvrirais pour si peu le bec ! aux dieux ne plaise ! »
Il l'ouvrit pour bien moins : tout alla de façon
        Qu'il ne vit plus aucun poisson.
La faim le prit ; il fut tout heureux et tout aise
        De rencontrer un limaçon.

        Ne soyons pas si difficiles :
Les plus accommodants, ce sont les plus habiles :
On hasarde de perdre en voulant trop gagner.
        Gardez-vous de rien dédaigner.

Fables, Livre VII

LE SAVETIER ET LE FINANCIER

Un savetier chantait du matin jusqu'au soir :
          C'était merveilles de le voir,
Merveilles de l'ouïr ; il faisait des passages,
          Plus content qu'aucun des Sept Sages.
Son voisin au contraire, étant tout cousu d'or,
          Chantait peu, dormait moins encor.
          C'était un homme de finance.
Si sur le point du jour parfois il sommeillait,
Le savetier alors en chantant l'éveillait,
          Et le financier se plaignait
          Que les soins de la Providence
N'eussent pas au marché fait vendre le dormir,
          Comme le manger et le boire.
          En son hôtel il fait venir
Le chanteur, et lui dit : « Or çà, sire Grégoire,
Que gagnez-vous par an ? – Par an ? Ma foi, Monsieur,
          Dit avec un ton de rieur
Le gaillard savetier, ce n'est point ma manière
De compter de la sorte ; et je n'entasse guère
          Un jour sur l'autre : il suffit qu'à la fin
          J'attrape le bout de l'année :
          Chaque jour amène son pain.
– Eh bien ! que gagnez-vous, dites-moi, par journée ?
– Tantôt plus, tantôt moins : le mal est que toujours,
(Et sans cela nos gains seraient assez honnêtes),
Le mal est que dans l'an s'entremêlent des jours
          Qu'il faut chômer : on nous ruine en fêtes.
          L'une fait tort à l'autre, et monsieur le curé
De quelque nouveau saint charge toujours son prône. »
          Le financier riant de sa naïveté
Lui dit : « Je vous veux mettre aujourd'hui sur le trône.
Prenez ces cent écus : gardez-les avec soin,
          Pour vous en servir au besoin. »
Le savetier crut voir tout l'argent que la terre
          Avait depuis plus de cent ans

Produit pour l'usage des gens.
Il retourne chez lui : dans sa cave il enserre
L'argent et sa joie à la fois.
Plus de chant ; il perdit la voix
Du moment qu'il gagna ce qui cause nos peines.
Le sommeil quitta son logis ;
Il eut pour hôtes les soucis,
Les soupçons, les alarmes vaines.
Tout le jour il avait l'œil au guet ; et la nuit,
Si quelque chat faisait du bruit,
Le chat prenait l'argent. À la fin le pauvre homme
S'en courut chez celui qu'il ne réveillait plus :
« Rendez-moi, lui dit-il, mes chansons et mon somme,
Et reprenez vos cent écus. »

Fables, Livre VIII

L'OURS ET L'AMATEUR DES JARDINS

Certain ours montagnard, ours à demi léché,
Confiné par le Sort dans un bois solitaire,
Nouveau Bellérophon, vivait seul et caché.
Il fût devenu fou : la raison d'ordinaire
N'habite pas longtemps chez les gens séquestrés.
Il est bon de parler, et meilleur de se taire ;
Mais tous deux sont mauvais alors qu'ils sont outrés.
            Nul animal n'avait affaire
            Dans les lieux que l'ours habitait ;
            Si bien que tout ours qu'il était
Il vint à s'ennuyer de cette triste vie.
Pendant qu'il se livrait à la mélancolie,
            Non loin de là certain vieillard
            S'ennuyait aussi de sa part.
Il aimait les jardins, était prêtre de Flore,
            Il l'était de Pomone encore :
Ces deux emplois sont beaux ; mais je voudrais parmi
            Quelque doux et discret ami.
Les jardins parlent peu, si ce n'est dans mon livre ;
            De façon que, lassé de vivre
Avec des gens muets, notre homme un beau matin
Va chercher compagnie, et se met en campagne.
            L'ours porté d'un même dessein
            Venait de quitter sa montagne :
            Tous deux, par un cas surprenant,
            Se rencontrent en un tournant.
L'homme eut peur : mais comment esquiver ? et que faire ?
Se tirer en Gascon d'une semblable affaire
Est le mieux : il sut donc dissimuler sa peur.
            L'ours, très mauvais complimenteur,
Lui dit : « Viens-t'en me voir. » L'autre reprit : « Seigneur,
Vous voyez mon logis ; si vous me vouliez faire
Tant d'honneur que d'y prendre un champêtre repas,
J'ai des fruits, j'ai du lait : ce n'est peut-être pas
De Nosseigneurs les Ours le manger ordinaire ;

Mais j'offre ce que j'ai. » L'ours l'accepte ; et d'aller.
Les voilà bons amis avant que d'arriver
Arrivés, les voilà se trouvant bien ensemble ;
      Et bien qu'on soit à ce qu'il semble
      Beaucoup mieux seul qu'avec des sots,
Comme l'ours en un jour ne disait pas deux mots,
L'homme pouvait sans bruit vaquer à son ouvrage.
L'ours allait à la chasse, apportait du gibier,
      Faisait son principal métier
D'être bon émoucheur, écartait du visage
De son ami dormant ce parasite ailé
      Que nous avons mouche appelé.
Un jour que le vieillard dormait d'un profond somme,
Sur le bout de son nez une allant se placer
Mit l'ours au désespoir ; il eut beau la chasser :
« Je t'attraperai bien, dit-il. Et voici comme. »
Aussitôt fait que dit : le fidèle émoucheur
Vous empoigne un pavé, le lance avec roideur,
Casse la tête à l'homme en écrasant la mouche,
Et non moins bon archer que mauvais raisonneur,
Roide mort étendu sur la place il le couche.

Rien n'est si dangereux qu'un ignorant ami ;
      Mieux vaudrait un sage ennemi.

Fables, Livre VIII

LES OBSÈQUES DE LA LIONNE

La femme du lion mourut :
Aussitôt chacun accourut
Pour s'acquitter envers le prince
De certains compliments de consolation,
Qui sont surcroît d'affliction.
Il fit avertir sa province
Que les obsèques se feraient
Un tel jour, en tel lieu : ses prévôts y seraient
Pour régler la cérémonie,
Et pour placer la compagnie.
Jugez si chacun s'y trouva.
Le prince aux cris s'abandonna,
Et tout son antre en résonna :
Les lions n'ont point d'autre temple.
On entendit à son exemple
Rugir en leurs patois messieurs les courtisans.
Je définis la cour un pays où les gens
Tristes, gais, prêts à tout, à tout indifférents,
Sont ce qu'il plaît au prince, ou, s'ils ne peuvent l'être,
Tâchent au moins de le paraître,
Peuple caméléon, peuple singe du maître,
On dirait qu'un esprit anime mille corps ;
C'est bien là que les gens sont de simples ressorts.
Pour revenir à notre affaire
Le cerf ne pleura point. Comment eût-il pu faire ?
Cette mort le vengeait : la reine avait jadis
Étranglé sa femme et son fils.
Bref, il ne pleura point. Un flatteur l'alla dire,
Et soutint qu'il l'avait vu rire.
La colère du roi, comme dit Salomon,
Est terrible, et surtout celle du roi lion ;
Mais ce cerf n'avait pas accoutumé de lire.
Le monarque lui dit : « Chétif hôte des bois,
Tu ris ! tu ne suis pas ces gémissantes voix !
Nous n'appliquerons point sur tes membres profanes

Nos sacrés ongles. Venez, loups,
Vengez la reine, immolez tous
Ce traître à ses augustes mânes. »
Le cerf reprit alors : « Sire, le temps de pleurs
Est passé ; la douleur est ici superflue.
Votre digne moitié, couchée entre des fleurs,
Tout près d'ici m'est apparue ;
Et je l'ai d'abord reconnue.
« Ami, m'a-t-elle dit, garde que ce convoi,
Quand je vais chez les dieux, ne t'oblige à des larmes.
Aux champs Élysiens j'ai goûté mille charmes,
Conversant avec ceux qui sont saints comme moi.
Laisse agir quelque temps le désespoir du roi.
J'y prends plaisir. » À peine on eut ouï la chose,
Qu'on se mit à crier : « Miracle ! Apothéose ! »
Le cerf eut un présent, bien loin d'être puni.

Amusez les rois par des songes,
Flattez-les, payez-les d'agréables mensonges :
Quelque indignation dont leur cœur soit rempli,
Ils goberont l'appât, vous serez leur ami.

Fables, Livre VIII

LES DEUX PIGEONS

Deux pigeons s'aimaient d'amour tendre.
L'un d'eux s'ennuyant au logis
Fut assez fou pour entreprendre
Un voyage en lointain pays.
L'autre lui dit : « Qu'allez-vous faire ?
Voulez-vous quitter votre frère ?
L'absence est le plus grand des maux :
Non pas pour vous, cruel. Au moins que les travaux,
Les dangers, les soins du voyage,
Changent un peu votre courage.
Encor si la saison s'avançait davantage !
Attendez les zéphirs. Qui vous presse ? Un corbeau
Tout à l'heure annonçait malheur à quelque oiseau.
Je ne songerai plus que rencontre funeste,
Que faucons, que réseaux. « Hélas ! dirai-je, il pleut :
Mon frère a-t-il tout ce qu'il veut,
Bon soupé, bon gîte, et le reste ? »
Ce discours ébranla le cœur
De notre imprudent voyageur ;
Mais le désir de voir et l'humeur inquiète
L'emportèrent enfin. Il dit : « Ne pleurez point :
Trois jours au plus rendront mon âme satisfaite ;
Je reviendrai dans peu conter de point en point
Mes aventures à mon frère.
Je le désennuierai : quiconque ne voit guère
N'a guère à dire aussi. Mon voyage dépeint
Vous sera d'un plaisir extrême.
Je dirai : « J'étais là ; telle chose m'avint » ;
Vous y croirez être vous-même. »
À ces mots en pleurant ils se dirent adieu.
Le voyageur s'éloigne ; et voilà qu'un nuage
L'oblige de chercher retraite en quelque lieu.
Un seul arbre s'offrit, tel encor que l'orage
Maltraita le pigeon en dépit du feuillage.
L'air devenu serein, il part tout morfondu,

Sèche du mieux qu'il peut son corps chargé de pluie,
Dans un champ à l'écart voit du blé répandu,
Voit un pigeon auprès : cela lui donne envie ;
Il y vole, il est pris : ce blé couvrait d'un lacs
   Les menteurs et traîtres appas.
Le lacs était usé ! si bien que de son aile,
De ses pieds, de son bec, l'oiseau le rompt enfin.
Quelque plume y périt ; et le pis du destin
Fut qu'un certain vautour à la serre cruelle
Vit notre malheureux, qui, traînant la ficelle
Et les morceaux du lacs qui l'avait attrapé,
   Semblait un forçat échappé.
Le vautour s'en allait le lier, quand des nues
Fond à son tour un aigle aux ailes étendues.
Le pigeon profita du conflit des voleurs,
S'envola, s'abattit auprès d'une masure,
   Crut, pour ce coup, que ses malheurs
   Finiraient par cette aventure ;
Mais un fripon d'enfant, cet âge est sans pitié,
Prit sa fronde et, du coup, tua plus d'à moitié
   La volatile malheureuse,
  Qui, maudissant sa curiosité,
   Traînant l'aile et tirant le piè,
   Demi-morte et demi-boiteuse,
   Droit au logis s'en retourna.
   Que bien, que mal, elle arriva
   Sans autre aventure fâcheuse.
Voilà nos gens rejoints ; et je laisse à juger
De combien de plaisirs ils payèrent leurs peines.

Amants, heureux amants, voulez-vous voyager ?
   Que ce soit aux rives prochaines ;
Soyez-vous l'un à l'autre un monde toujours beau,
   Toujours divers, toujours nouveau ;
Tenez-vous lieu de tout, comptez pour rien le reste.
J'ai quelquefois aimé : je n'aurais pas alors
   Contre le Louvre et ses trésors,
Contre le firmament et sa voûte céleste,
   Changé les bois, changé les lieux

Honorés par les pas, éclairés par les yeux
    De l'aimable et jeune bergère
    Pour qui, sous le fils de Cythère.
Je servis, engagé par mes premiers serments.
Hélas ! quand reviendront de semblables moments ?
Faut-il que tant d'objets si doux et si charmants
Me laissent vivre au gré de mon âme inquiète ?
Ah ! si mon cœur osait encor se renflammer !
Ne sentirai-je plus de charme qui m'arrête ?
    Ai-je passé le temps d'aimer ?

Fables, Livre IX

LE SONGE D'UN HABITANT DU MOGOL

Jadis certain Mogol vit en songe un vizir
Aux champs Élysiens possesseur d'un plaisir
Aussi pur qu'infini, tant en prix qu'en durée ;
Le même songeur vit en une autre contrée
   Un ermite entouré de feux,
Qui touchait de pitié même les malheureux.
Le cas parut étrange, et contre l'ordinaire :
Minos en ces deux morts semblait s'être mépris.
Le dormeur s'éveilla, tant il en fut surpris.
Dans ce songe pourtant soupçonnant du mystère,
   Il se fit expliquer l'affaire.
L'interprète lui dit : « Ne vous étonnez point ;
Votre songe a du sens ; et, si j'ai sur ce point
   Acquis tant soit peu d'habitude,
C'est un avis des dieux. Pendant l'humain séjour,
Ce vizir quelquefois cherchait la solitude ;
Cet ermite aux vizirs allait faire sa cour. »

Si j'osais ajouter au mot de l'interprète,
J'inspirerais ici l'amour de la retraite :
Elle offre à ses amants des biens sans embarras,
Biens purs, présents du Ciel, qui naissent sous les pas.
Solitude où je trouve une douceur secrète,
Lieux que j'aimai toujours, ne pourrai-je jamais,
Loin du monde et du bruit, goûter l'ombre et le frais ?
Oh ! qui m'arrêtera sous vos sombres asiles !
Quand pourront les neuf Sœurs, loin des cours et des villes,
M'occuper tout entier, et m'apprendre des cieux
Les divers mouvements inconnus à nos yeux,
Les noms et les vertus de ces clartés errantes
Par qui sont nos destins et nos mœurs différentes !
Que si je ne suis né pour de si grands projets,
Du moins que les ruisseaux m'offrent de doux objets !
Que je peigne en mes vers quelque rive fleurie !
La Parque à filets d'or n'ourdira point ma vie ;

Je ne dormirai point sous de riches lambris :
Mais voit-on que le somme en perde de son prix ?
En est-il moins profond, et moins plein de délices ?
Je lui voue au désert de nouveaux sacrifices.
Quand le moment viendra d'aller trouver les morts,
J'aurai vécu sans soins, et mourrai sans remords.

Fables, Livre XI

MOLIÈRE

(1622-1673)

Le génie de Molière est dans la vision qu'il a du monde et dans sa mise en œuvre théâtrale, et non dans ses vers. Cependant nombre d'entre eux sont gravés en nous depuis toujours. Très tôt il fut notre fournisseur d'injures nobles pour altercations lycéennes : « Mon Dieu ! que votre esprit est d'un étage bas »... ou encore : « C'est un fort méchant plat que [ta] sotte personne. »

La forme aphoristique de bien des assertions rimées aidait à les engranger sans peine. Puis la volonté de s'approprier tout ce qu'il dévoilait d'une réalité encore peu familière encourageait à apprendre des tirades entières, celles où il peignait la casuistique insinuante de Tartuffe ou l'idéal en pantoufles de Chrysale, et tant de passages encore où il dénonce le mensonge des apparences. Mais on pouvait aussi redire sans fin, simplement pour en rire, les trouvailles cocasses où il fait jouer la logique de l'absurde :

Je ne sais ce que c'est, Monsieur, mais il me semble
Qu'Agnès et le corps mort s'en sont allés ensemble !

Malgré cela nous avons peine à voir en lui un poète au même titre que les auteurs tragiques de son siècle. C'est que le plaisir de la comédie, lue ou représentée, est rarement désintéressé. Proche du réel, celle-ci n'instaure pas entre son objet et le lecteur ou spectateur la distance nécessaire à la contemplation rêveuse que requiert la poésie. Cependant *Amphitryon* ou *Le Misanthrope* échappent la plupart du temps à cette critique. La fantaisie de l'un, qui rappelle Marot ou La Fontaine, libère Molière du poids du réel.

La tension douloureuse de l'autre, chaque fois que l'expression maladroite de la passion accentue le ridicule d'Alceste, en même temps que sa sincérité, face à l'insensible Célimène, permet à l'auteur de prêter à son héros certains accents proches du lyrisme.

LE MISANTHROPE

ACTE IV – *Scène III*

ALCESTE

Ah ! traîtresse ! mon faible est étrange pour vous !
Vous me trompez sans doute avec des mots si doux ;
Mais il n'importe, il faut suivre ma destinée :
À votre foi mon âme est toute abandonnée ;
Je veux voir jusqu'au bout quel sera votre cœur,
Et si de me trahir il aura la noirceur.

CÉLIMÈNE

Non, vous ne m'aimez point comme il faut que l'on aime.

ALCESTE

Ah ! rien n'est comparable à mon amour extrême ;
Et dans l'ardeur qu'il a de se montrer à tous,
Il va jusqu'à former des souhaits contre vous.
Oui, je voudrais qu'aucun ne vous trouvât aimable,
Que vous fussiez réduite en un sort misérable,
Que le Ciel, en naissant, ne vous eût donné rien,
Que vous n'eussiez ni rang, ni naissance, ni bien,
Afin que de mon cœur l'éclatant sacrifice
Vous pût d'un pareil sort réparer l'injustice,
Et que j'eusse la joie et la gloire, en ce jour,
De vous voir tenir tout des mains de mon amour.

CÉLIMÈNE

C'est me vouloir du bien d'une étrange manière !
Me préserve le Ciel que vous ayez matière… !

AMPHITRYON

PROLOGUE

Mercure, sur un nuage ; la Nuit, dans un char traîné dans l'air par deux chevaux.

MERCURE

Tout beau ! charmante Nuit, daignez vous arrêter.
Il est certain secours que de vous on désire ;
  Et j'ai deux mots à vous dire
  De la part de Jupiter.

LA NUIT

 Ah ! Ah ! c'est vous, seigneur Mercure !
Qui vous eût deviné, là, dans cette posture ?

MERCURE

Ma foi, me trouvant las, pour ne pouvoir fournir
Aux différents emplois où Jupiter m'engage,
Je me suis doucement assis sur ce nuage,
  Pour vous attendre venir.

LA NUIT

Vous vous moquez, Mercure, et vous n'y songez pas :
Sied-il bien à des dieux de dire qu'ils sont las ?

MERCURE

Les dieux sont-ils de fer ?

LA NUIT

    Non ; mais il faut sans cesse
Garder le *decorum* de la divinité.
Il est de certains mots dont l'usage rabaisse
  Cette sublime qualité,
  Et que, pour leur indignité,
  Il est bon qu'aux hommes on laisse.

MERCURE

À votre aise vous en parlez,
Et vous avez, la belle, une chaise roulante
Où, par deux bons chevaux, en dame nonchalante,
Vous vous faites traîner partout où vous voulez.
    Mais de moi ce n'est pas de même :
Et je ne puis vouloir, dans mon destin fatal,
    Aux poètes assez de mal
    De leur impertinence extrême,
    D'avoir, par une injuste loi
    Dont on veut maintenir l'usage,
    À chaque dieu, dans son emploi,
    Donné quelque allure en partage,
    Et de me laisser à pied, moi,
    Comme un messager de village ;
Moi qui suis, comme on sait, en terre et dans les cieux,
Le fameux messager du souverain des dieux ;
    Et qui, sans rien exagérer,
    Par tous les emplois qu'il me donne,
    Aurais besoin, plus que personne,
    D'avoir de quoi me voiturer.

LA NUIT

Que voulez-vous faire à cela ?
Les poètes font à leur guise.
Ce n'est pas la seule sottise
Qu'on voit faire à ces messieurs-là.
Mais contre eux toutefois votre âme à tort s'irrite,
Et vos ailes aux pieds sont un don de leurs soins.

MERCURE

Oui ; mais, pour aller plus vite,
Est-ce qu'on s'en lasse moins ?

NICOLAS BOILEAU

(1636-1711)

Les poètes de son temps sont ses cibles préférées. Et d'abord le plus honoré d'entre eux, le mieux nanti, Chapelain, dispensateur des pensions royales.

> *Il se tue à rimer ! que n'écrit-il en prose ?*

Les autres, moins connus, qu'il nomme dans une lettre « la racaille poétique », ne sont pas épargnés, témoin cette esquisse de la Satire III :

> *Il est vrai que Quinault est un esprit profond,*
> *A repris certain fat, qu'à sa mine discrète*
> *Et son maintien jaloux, j'ai reconnu poète.*

Surtout il est sans indulgence pour certains de ceux qui l'ont précédé. Ni Ronsard, ni Théophile ne trouvent grâce à ses yeux. De façon générale, il pourrait dire, à la manière de Teste [1] : « Le lyrisme n'est pas mon fort. »

Celui qu'il admire entre tous les modernes, c'est Malherbe, il en donne la raison, moins convaincante qu'il ne croit, du moins à nos yeux : n'est-ce pas lui, dit-il, qui

> *Fit sentir dans les vers une juste cadence :*
> *D'un mot mis à sa place enseigna le pouvoir*
> *Et réduisit la Muse aux règles du devoir.*

---

1. Monsieur Teste (personnage de Valéry) : « La bêtise n'est pas mon fort. »

Lui-même, rimeur scrupuleux, homme d'esprit, censeur des lettres françaises, est-il vraiment poète ? On peut en douter, car s'il est bien un satirique comme Régnier, c'est avec une mesure jusque dans la raillerie et la pointe, qui exclut la truculence ou la violence de l'invective inspirée.

Alors pourquoi le citer ici ? D'abord parce qu'il hante nos mémoires, on l'enseignait beaucoup, jadis, aux écoliers. Et aussi pour nous avoir appris très tôt que dans ce monde, contrairement au mot de La Bruyère, on peut, ne fût-ce qu'en rimant, tirer vengeance des fats et des sots. Surtout, enfin, parce qu'il laisse entrevoir, malgré l'instrument désincarné de la langue classique et la prosodie corsetée qu'impose son époque, qu'il n'ignorait pas

> *...ces violents transports*
> *Qui d'un esprit divin font mouvoir les ressorts*

et qu'il proclame au début de son *Art poétique* la primauté de l'inspiration et de l'élection pour celui qui veut « de l'art des vers atteindre la hauteur ». Et puis nous trouvons parfois chez lui un trait qui semble avoir échappé à sa vigilance, tel que celui-ci :

> *On voit sous les lauriers haleter les Orphées.*

ÉPÎTRE X

À mes vers

.   .   .   .

Que si mêmes un jour le Lecteur gracieux
Amorcé par mon nom, sur vous tourne les yeux.
Pour m'en récompenser, mes Vers, avec usure,
De votre Auteur alors faites-lui la peinture :
Et sur tout prenez soin d'effacer bien les traits
Dont tant de peintres faux ont flétri mes portraits.
Déposez hardiment qu'au fond cet Homme horrible,
Ce Censeur qu'ils ont peint si noir, et si terrible,
Fut un esprit doux, simple, ami de l'équité,
Qui cherchant dans ses vers la seule vérité,
Fit, sans être malin, ses plus grandes malices,
Et qu'enfin sa candeur seule a fait tous ses vices.
Dites que harcelé par les plus vils rimeurs,
Jamais, blessant leurs vers, il n'effleura leurs mœurs :
Libre dans ses discours, mais pourtant toujours sage,
Assez faible de corps, assez doux de visage,
Ni petit ni trop grand, très-peu voluptueux,
Ami de la vertu plutôt que vertueux.
Que si quelqu'un, mes Vers, alors vous importune
Pour savoir mes parents, ma vie et ma fortune,
Contez lui qu'allié d'assez hauts magistrats,
Fils d'un père greffier, né d'aïeux avocats,
Dès le berceau perdant une fort jeune mère,
Réduit seize ans après à pleurer mon vieux père,
J'allai d'un pas hardi, par moi-même guidé,
Et de mon seul génie en marchant secondé,
Studieux amateur et de Perse, et d'Horace,
Assez près de Régnier m'asseoir sur le Parnasse ;
Que par un coup du sort au grand jour amené,
Et des bords du Permesse à la Cour entraîné,
Je sus, prenant l'essor par des routes nouvelles,
Élever assez haut mes poétiques ailes ;
Que ce Roi dont le nom fait trembler tant de rois
Voulut bien que ma main crayonnât ses exploits ;

Que plus d'un Grand m'aima jusques à la tendresse ;
Que ma vue à Colbert inspirait l'allégresse ;
Qu'aujourd'hui même encor, de deux sens affaibli,
Retiré de la Cour, et non mis en oubli,
Plus d'un héros, épris des fruits de mon étude,
Vient quelquefois chez moi goûter la solitude.
. . . .

ÉPÎTRE XI

À mon jardinier

Laborieux valet du plus commode maître,
Qui pour te rendre heureux ici-bas pouvait naître,
Antoine, gouverneur de mon jardin d'Auteuil,
Qui diriges chez moi l'if, et le chèvrefeuil,
Et sur mes espaliers, industrieux génie,
Sais si bien exercer l'art de la Quintinie,
Oh ! que de mon esprit triste et mal ordonné,
Ainsi que de ce champ par toi si bien orné,
Ne puis-je faire ôter les ronces, les épines,
Et des défauts sans nombre arracher les racines !
Mais parle : raisonnons. Quand, du matin au soir,
Chez moi poussant la bêche, ou portant l'arrosoir,
Tu fais d'un sable aride une terre fertile,
Et rends tout mon jardin à tes lois si docile ;
Que dis-tu de m'y voir rêveur, capricieux,
Tantôt baissant le front, tantôt levant les yeux,
De paroles dans l'air par élans envolées
Effrayer les oiseaux perchés dans mes allées ?
Ne soupçonnes-tu point qu'agité du démon,
Ainsi que ce cousin des quatre fils Aymon,
Dont tu lis quelquefois la merveilleuse histoire,
Je rumine en marchant quelque endroit du grimoire ?
Mais non : Tu te souviens qu'au village on t'a dit
Que ton maître est nommé pour coucher par écrit
Les faits d'un Roi plus grand en sagesse, en vaillance,
Que Charlemagne aidé des douze Pairs de France.
Tu crois qu'il y travaille, et qu'au long de ce mur
Peut-être en ce moment il prend Mons, et Namur.
Que penserais-tu donc, si l'on t'allait apprendre
Que ce grand chroniqueur des gestes d'Alexandre
Aujourd'hui méditant un projet tout nouveau,
S'agite, se démène, et s'use le cerveau,
Pour te faire à toi-même en rimes insensées
Un bizarre portrait de ses folles pensées ?
« Mon maître, dirais-tu, passe pour un docteur,

Et parle quelquefois mieux qu'un prédicateur.
Sous ces arbres pourtant, de si vaines sornettes
Il n'irait point troubler la paix de ces fauvettes,
S'il lui fallait toujours, comme moi, s'exercer,
Labourer, couper, tondre, aplanir, palisser,
Et, dans l'eau de ces puits sans relâche tirée,
De ce sable étancher la soif démesurée. »
Antoine, de nous deux tu crois donc, je le vois,
Que le plus occupé dans ce jardin, c'est toi ?
Oh ! que tu changerais d'avis, et de langage,
Si deux jours seulement, libre du jardinage,
Tout à coup devenu poète et bel-esprit,
Tu t'allais engager à polir un écrit
Qui dît, sans s'avilir, les plus petites choses
Fît des plus secs chardons des œillets et des roses ;
Et sût même au discours de la rusticité
Donner de l'élégance et de la dignité
. . . .
Bientôt de ce travail revenu sec et pâle,
Et le teint plus jauni que de vingt ans de hâle
Tu dirais, reprenant ta pelle et ton râteau :
« J'aime mieux mettre encor cent arpents au niveau,
Que d'aller follement, égaré dans les nues,
Me lasser à chercher des visions cornues,
Et, pour lier des mots si mal s'entr'accordants,
Prendre dans ce jardin la lune avec les dents. »
. . . .

JEAN RACINE

(1639-1699)

Les admirateurs passionnés de Racine savent que l'on peut, comme Aurélien [1], rêver indéfiniment sur un seul vers de lui :

Je demeurai longtemps errant dans Césarée...

ou s'émouvoir à la manière de l'élève interrogée sur le poète qui répondit avec une ferveur touchante : « Ce que je préfère en lui ? c'est ce que dit Bérénice :

J'aimais, Seigneur, j'aimais, je voulais être aimée... »

La mémoire ne privilégie pas dans cette œuvre des sentences qui imposeraient la force et la densité de leur sens – son théâtre n'en comporte guère –, mais certains vers qui éveillent en nous un écho intérieur, ils s'évasent dans l'âme comme un cercle sur l'eau.

On ne sait d'abord d'où vient leur pouvoir tant l'alliage qui les compose est fait de matériaux ordinaires, et cela jusque dans les moments les plus tragiques : l'extrême douleur se dit chez Racine avec un extrême dénuement du langage :

Dans un mois, dans un an comment souffrirons-nous,
Seigneur, que tant de mers me séparent de vous...

---

1. Personnage d'Aragon.

Le sortilège de leur séduction est moins mystérieux quand la mythologie ajoute au texte la couleur de noms prestigieux. Ces derniers se mêlent cependant de façon si naturelle à la langue très pure du poète, et l'univers auquel ils appartiennent lui est si familier, qu'ils n'apparaissent jamais comme des ornements factices ou superflus. Ils ne sont pas introduits pour leur valeur pittoresque, mais parce qu'ils portent en eux un peu de cette essence du tragique grec que Racine restaure sur la scène française. Pour la première fois, en effet, depuis le début du siècle, on n'y assiste plus aux conflits d'intrigues ou de grands intérêts qui l'occupaient jusqu'alors, le style noble s'y voit aboli et la déclamation laisse la place au chant. Ce qui domine dans le théâtre de Racine, dès *Andromaque* et jusque dans les pièces historiques, ce sont les plaintes déchirantes d'êtres indécis ou torturés. Et jamais l'auteur ne se substitue à ses personnages en s'abandonnant à des morceaux d'éloquence, ce sont eux qui parlent, et leur parole en même temps les révèle à eux-mêmes et aux autres et les enchaîne plus étroitement à leur destin. Dans les paroxysmes de fureur ou d'angoisse, si leur voix s'élève, ce n'est pas par un effet oratoire, mais parce qu'une action plus tendue entraîne cette tension plus grande en eux. Rien de superflu ou d'ostentatoire ne se mêle à leurs propos. On trouve dans ce théâtre, souligne Thierry Maulnier, « une coïncidence exacte de la pensée et de l'expression ».

Il est probable que son pouvoir sur nous est lié à cette adéquation de l'être et du langage, mais il vient aussi de la qualité du chant qui s'y fait entendre. Une science, qui semble innée, du rythme, du poids des syllabes, de la coloration que peuvent donner au vers certaines voyelles sonores, mais aussi une pratique de l'atténuation de l'expression, cet « effet de sourdine » que Leo Spitzer a mis en lumière, entrent dans l'alchimie du verbe chez Racine. Au-delà, ce qui fait de lui un grand poète, c'est la continuité d'une inspiration élégiaque qui semble inépuisable, comme si, même célèbre et fêté par tous, il conservait en lui enfouie une inconsolable douleur.

ANDROMAQUE

Acte III – *Scène IV*

ANDROMAQUE

Où fuyez-vous, Madame ?
N'est-ce point à vos yeux un spectacle assez doux
Que la veuve d'Hector pleurante à vos genoux ?
Je ne viens point ici, par de jalouses larmes,
Vous envier un cœur qui se rend à vos charmes.
Par une main cruelle, hélas ! j'ai vu percer
Le seul où mes regards prétendaient s'adresser.
Ma flamme par Hector fut jadis allumée ;
Avec lui dans la tombe elle s'est enfermée.
Mais il me reste un fils. Vous saurez quelque jour,
Madame, pour un fils jusqu'où va notre amour ;
Mais vous ne saurez pas, du moins je le souhaite,
En quel trouble mortel son intérêt nous jette,
Lorsque de tant de biens qui pouvaient nous flatter,
C'est le seul qui nous reste, et qu'on veut nous l'ôter.
Hélas ! lorsque, lassés de dix ans de misère,
Les Troyens en courroux menaçaient votre mère,
J'ai su de mon Hector lui procurer l'appui.
Vous pouvez sur Pyrrhus ce que j'ai pu sur lui.
Que craint-on d'un enfant qui survit à sa perte ?
Laissez-moi le cacher en quelque île déserte.
Sur les soins de sa mère on peut s'en assurer,
Et mon fils avec moi n'apprendra qu'à pleurer.

ANDROMAQUE

Acte III – *Scène VI*

ANDROMAQUE, à *Pyrrhus*

Seigneur, voyez l'état où vous me réduisez.
J'ai vu mon père mort, et nos murs embrasés ;
J'ai vu trancher les jours de ma famille entière,
Et mon époux sanglant traîné sur la poussière,
Son fils, seul avec moi, réservé pour les fers.
Mais que ne peut un fils ! Je respire, je sers.
J'ai fait plus : je me suis quelquefois consolée
Qu'ici, plutôt qu'ailleurs, le sort m'eût exilée ;
Qu'heureux dans son malheur, le fils de tant de rois,
Puisqu'il devait servir, fût tombé sous vos lois.
J'ai cru que sa prison deviendrait son asile.
Jadis Priam soumis fut respecté d'Achille :
J'attendais de son fils encor plus de bonté.
Pardonne, cher Hector, à ma crédulité !
Je n'ai pu soupçonner ton ennemi d'un crime :
Malgré lui-même enfin je l'ai cru magnanime.
Ah ! s'il l'était assez pour nous laisser du moins
Au tombeau qu'à ta cendre ont élevé mes soins,
Et que, finissant là sa haine et nos misères,
Il ne séparât point des dépouilles si chères !

ANDROMAQUE

Acte III – *Scène VIII*

CÉPHISE

Ainsi le veut son fils, que les Grecs vous ravissent.
Pensez-vous qu'après tout ses mânes en rougissent,
Qu'il méprisât, Madame, un roi victorieux
Qui vous fait remonter au rang de vos aïeux,
Qui foule aux pieds pour vous vos vainqueurs en colère,
Qui ne se souvient plus qu'Achille était son père,
Qui dément ses exploits, et les rend superflus ?

ANDROMAQUE

Dois-je les oublier, s'il ne s'en souvient plus ?
Dois-je oublier Hector privé de funérailles,
Et traîné sans honneur autour de nos murailles ?
Dois-je oublier son père à mes pieds renversé,
Ensanglantant l'autel qu'il tenait embrassé ?
Songe, songe, Céphise, à cette nuit cruelle
Qui fut pour tout un peuple une nuit éternelle.
Figure-toi Pyrrhus, les yeux étincelants,
Entrant à la lueur de nos palais brûlants,
Sur tous mes frères morts se faisant un passage,
Et, de sang tout couvert, échauffant le carnage.
Songe aux cris des vainqueurs, songe aux cris des mourants,
Dans la flamme étouffés, sous le fer expirants.
Peins-toi dans ces horreurs Andromaque éperdue :
Voilà comme Pyrrhus vint s'offrir à ma vue ;
Voilà par quels exploits il sut se couronner ;
Enfin voilà l'époux que tu me veux donner.
Non, je ne serai point complice de ses crimes ;
Qu'il nous prenne, s'il veut, pour dernières victimes.
Tous mes ressentiments lui seraient asservis !

ANDROMAQUE

Acte IV – *Scène V*

HERMIONE

Je ne t'ai point aimé, cruel ! Qu'ai-je donc fait ?
J'ai dédaigné pour toi les vœux de tous nos princes ;
Je t'ai cherché moi-même au fond de tes provinces ;
J'y suis encor, malgré tes infidélités,
Et malgré tous mes Grecs honteux de mes bontés.
Je leur ai commandé de cacher mon injure ;
J'attendais en secret le retour d'un parjure ;
J'ai cru que tôt ou tard, à ton devoir rendu,
Tu me rapporterais un cœur qui m'était dû.
Je t'aimais inconstant, qu'aurais-je fait fidèle ?
Et même en ce moment où ta bouche cruelle
Vient si tranquillement m'annoncer le trépas,
Ingrat, je doute encor si je ne t'aime pas.
Mais, Seigneur, s'il le faut, si le ciel en colère
Réserve à d'autres yeux la gloire de vous plaire,
Achevez votre hymen, j'y consens ; mais du moins
Ne forcez pas mes yeux d'en être les témoins.
Pour la dernière fois je vous parle peut-être.
Différez-le d'un jour, demain vous serez maître...
Vous ne répondez point ! Perfide, je le vois.
Tu comptes les moments que tu perds avec moi !
Ton cœur, impatient de revoir ta Troyenne,
Ne souffre qu'à regret qu'une autre t'entretienne.
Tu lui parles du cœur, tu la cherches des yeux.
Je ne te retiens plus, sauve-toi de ces lieux :
Va lui jurer la foi que tu m'avais jurée ;
Va profaner des dieux la majesté sacrée.
Ces dieux, ces justes dieux n'auront pas oublié
Que les mêmes serments avec moi t'ont lié.
Porte aux pieds des autels ce cœur qui m'abandonne :
Va, cours ; mais crains encor d'y trouver Hermione.

BÉRÉNICE

ACTE I – *Scène IV*

ANTIOCHUS

Je me suis tu cinq ans,
Madame, et vais encor me taire plus longtemps.
De mon heureux rival j'accompagnai les armes ;
J'espérai de verser mon sang après mes larmes,
Ou qu'au moins, jusqu'à vous porté par mille exploits,
Mon nom pourrait parler, au défaut de ma voix.
Le Ciel sembla promettre une fin à ma peine :
Vous pleurâtes ma mort, hélas ! trop peu certaine.
Inutiles périls ! Quelle était mon erreur !
La valeur de Titus surpassait ma fureur.
Il faut qu'à sa vertu mon estime réponde.
Quoique attendu, Madame, à l'empire du monde,
Chéri de l'univers, enfin aimé de vous,
Il semblait à lui seul appeler tous les coups,
Tandis que, sans espoir, haï, lassé de vivre,
Son malheureux rival ne semblait que le suivre.
Je vois que votre cœur m'applaudit en secret ;
Je vois que l'on m'écoute avec moins de regret,
Et que, trop attentive à ce récit funeste,
En faveur de Titus vous pardonnez le reste.
Enfin, après un siège aussi cruel que lent,
Il dompta les mutins, reste pâle et sanglant
Des flammes, de la faim, des fureurs intestines,
Et laissa leurs remparts cachés sous leurs ruines.
Rome vous vit, Madame, arriver avec lui.
Dans l'Orient désert quel devint mon ennui !
Je demeurai longtemps errant dans Césarée,
Lieux charmants où mon cœur vous avait adorée.
Je vous redemandais à vos tristes États ;
Je cherchais en pleurant les traces de vos pas.
Mais enfin, succombant à ma mélancolie,
Mon désespoir tourna mes pas vers l'Italie.
Le sort m'y réservait le dernier de ses coups :
Titus en m'embrassant m'amena devant vous.

Un voile d'amitié vous trompa l'un et l'autre,
Et mon amour devint le confident du vôtre.
Mais toujours quelque espoir flattait mes déplaisirs :
Rome, Vespasien traversaient vos soupirs ;
Après tant de combats Titus cédait peut-être.
Vespasien est mort, et Titus est le maître.
Que ne fuyais-je alors ! J'ai voulu quelques jours
De son nouvel empire examiner le cours.
Mon sort est accompli ; votre gloire s'apprête.
Assez d'autres, sans moi, témoins de cette fête,
À vos heureux transports viendront joindre les leurs ;
Pour moi, qui ne pourrais y mêler que des pleurs,
D'un inutile amour trop constante victime,
Heureux dans mes malheurs d'en avoir pu sans crime
Conter toute l'histoire aux yeux qui les ont faits,
Je pars, plus amoureux que je ne fus jamais.

                    BÉRÉNICE
Seigneur, je n'ai pas cru que, dans une journée
Qui doit avec César unir ma destinée,
Il fût quelque mortel qui pût impunément
Se venir à mes yeux déclarer mon amant.
Mais de mon amitié mon silence est un gage :
J'oublie en sa faveur un discours qui m'outrage.
Je n'en ai point troublé le cours injurieux.
Je fais plus : à regret je reçois vos adieux.
Le Ciel sait qu'au milieu des honneurs qu'il m'envoie,
Je n'attendais que vous pour témoin de ma joie.
Avec tout l'univers j'honorais vos vertus ;
Titus vous chérissait, vous admiriez Titus.
Cent fois je me suis fait une douceur extrême
D'entretenir Titus dans un autre lui-même.

                    ANTIOCHUS
Et c'est ce que je fuis. J'évite, mais trop tard,
Ces cruels entretiens où je n'ai point de part.
Je fuis Titus ; je fuis ce nom qui m'inquiète,
Ce nom qu'à tous moments votre bouche répète.
Que vous dirai-je enfin ? je fuis des yeux distraits,

Qui, me voyant toujours, ne me voyaient jamais.
Adieu. Je vais, le cœur trop plein de votre image,
Attendre, en vous aimant, la mort pour mon partage.
Surtout ne craignez point qu'une aveugle douleur
Remplisse l'univers du bruit de mon malheur.
Madame, le seul bruit d'une mort que j'implore
Vous fera souvenir que je vivais encore.
Adieu.

BÉRÉNICE

ACTE IV – *Scène V*

BÉRÉNICE

Hé bien, régnez, cruel, contentez votre gloire :
Je ne dispute plus. J'attendais, pour vous croire,
Que cette même bouche, après mille serments
D'un amour qui devait unir tous nos moments,
Cette bouche, à mes yeux s'avouant infidèle,
M'ordonnât elle-même une absence éternelle.
Moi-même j'ai voulu vous entendre en ce lieu.
Je n'écoute plus rien ; et, pour jamais, adieu...
Pour jamais ! Ah ! Seigneur ! songez-vous en vous-même
Combien ce mot cruel est affreux quand on aime ?
Dans un mois, dans un an, comment souffrirons-nous,
Seigneur, que tant de mers me séparent de vous ;
Que le jour recommence, et que le jour finisse,
Sans que jamais Titus puisse voir Bérénice,
Sans que, de tout le jour, je puisse voir Titus ?
Mais quelle est mon erreur, et que de soins perdus !
L'ingrat, de mon départ consolé par avance,
Daignera-t-il compter les jours de mon absence ?
Ces jours si longs pour moi lui sembleront trop courts.

BÉRÉNICE

Acte V – *Scène VII*

BÉRÉNICE, *se levant*

Arrêtez, arrêtez ! Princes trop généreux,
En quelle extrémité me jetez-vous tous deux !
Soit que je vous regarde, ou que je l'envisage,
Partout du désespoir je rencontre l'image.
Je ne vois que des pleurs, et je n'entends parler
Que de trouble, d'horreurs, de sang prêt à couler.

À Titus,

Mon cœur vous est connu, Seigneur, et je puis dire
Qu'on ne l'a jamais vu soupirer pour l'empire.
La grandeur des Romains, la pourpre des Césars,
N'ont point, vous le savez, attiré mes regards.
J'aimais, Seigneur, j'aimais, je voulais être aimée.
Ce jour, je l'avouerai, je me suis alarmée :
J'ai cru que votre amour allait finir son cours.
Je connais mon erreur, et vous m'aimez toujours.
Votre cœur s'est troublé, j'ai vu couler vos larmes :
Bérénice, Seigneur, ne vaut point tant d'alarmes,
Ni que par votre amour l'univers malheureux,
Dans le temps que Titus attire tous ses vœux
Et que de vos vertus il goûte les prémices,
Se voie en un moment enlever ses délices.
Je crois, depuis cinq ans jusqu'à ce dernier jour,
Vous avoir assuré d'un véritable amour.
Ce n'est pas tout : je veux, en ce moment funeste,
Par un dernier effort couronner tout le reste :
Je vivrai, je suivrai vos ordres absolus.
Adieu, Seigneur, régnez : je ne vous verrai plus.

À Antiochus.

Prince, après cet adieu, vous jugez bien vous-même
Que je ne consens pas de quitter ce que j'aime
Pour aller loin de Rome écouter d'autres vœux.
Vivez, et faites-vous un effort généreux.
Sur Titus et sur moi réglez votre conduite :
Je l'aime, je le fuis ; Titus m'aime, il me quitte ;

Portez loin de mes yeux vos soupirs et vos fers.
Adieu. Servons tous trois d'exemple à l'univers
De l'amour la plus tendre et la plus malheureuse
Dont il puisse garder l'histoire douloureuse.
Tout est prêt : on m'attend. Ne suivez point mes pas.

À Titus.

Pour la dernière fois, adieu, Seigneur.

ANTIOCHUS

Hélas !

PHÈDRE

ACTE I – *Scène III*

ŒNONE

Quoi ! de quelques remords êtes-vous déchirée ?
Quel crime a pu produire un trouble si pressant ?
Vos mains n'ont point trempé dans le sang innocent.

PHÈDRE

Grâces au Ciel, mes mains ne sont point criminelles.
Plût aux dieux que mon cœur fût innocent comme elles !

ŒNONE

Et quel affreux projet avez-vous enfanté
Dont votre cœur encor doive être épouvanté ?

PHÈDRE

Je t'en ai dit assez : épargne-moi le reste.
Je meurs, pour ne point faire un aveu si funeste.

ŒNONE

Mourez donc, et gardez un silence inhumain ;
Mais pour fermer vos yeux cherchez une autre main.
Quoiqu'il vous reste à peine une faible lumière,
Mon âme chez les morts descendra la première ;
Mille chemins ouverts y conduisent toujours,
Et ma juste douleur choisira les plus courts.
Cruelle ! quand ma foi vous a-t-elle déçue ?
Songez-vous qu'en naissant mes bras vous ont reçue ?
Mon pays, mes enfants, pour vous j'ai tout quitté.
Réserviez-vous ce prix à ma fidélité ?

PHÈDRE

Quel fruit espères-tu de tant de violence ?
Tu frémiras d'horreur si je romps le silence.

ŒNONE

Et que me direz-vous qui ne cède, grands dieux,
À l'horreur de vous voir expirer à mes yeux ?

PHÈDRE

Quand tu sauras mon crime et le sort qui m'accable,
Je n'en mourrai pas moins : j'en mourrai plus coupable.

ŒNONE

Madame, au nom des pleurs que j'ai pour vous versés,
Par vos faibles genoux que je tiens embrassés,
Délivrez mon esprit de ce funeste doute.

PHÈDRE

Tu le veux : lève-toi.

ŒNONE

Parlez : je vous écoute.

PHÈDRE

Ciel ! que lui vais-je dire ? et par où commencer ?

ŒNONE

Par de vaines frayeurs cessez de m'offenser.

PHÈDRE

Ô haine de Vénus ! ô fatale colère !
Dans quels égarements l'amour jeta ma mère !

ŒNONE

Oublions-les, Madame ; et qu'à tout l'avenir
Un silence éternel cache ce souvenir.

PHÈDRE

Ariane, ma sœur, de quel amour blessée
Vous mourûtes aux bords où vous fûtes laissée !

ŒNONE

Que faites-vous, Madame ? et quel mortel ennui
Contre tout votre sang vous anime aujourd'hui ?

PHÈDRE

Puisque Vénus le veut, de ce sang déplorable
Je péris la dernière et la plus misérable.

PHÈDRE

ACTE II – *Scène II.* Hippolyte. Aricie

HIPPOLYTE

Vous voyez devant vous un prince déplorable,
D'un téméraire orgueil exemple mémorable.
Moi qui, contre l'amour fièrement révolté,
Aux fers de ses captifs ai longtemps insulté ;
Qui, des faibles mortels déplorant les naufrages,
Pensais toujours du bord contempler les orages ;
Asservi maintenant sous la commune loi,
Par quel trouble me vois-je emporté loin de moi !
Un moment a vaincu mon audace imprudente :
Cette âme si superbe est enfin dépendante.
Depuis près de six mois, honteux, désespéré,
Portant partout le trait dont je suis déchiré,
Contre vous, contre moi, vainement je m'éprouve :
Présente, je vous fuis ; absente, je vous trouve ;
Dans le fond des forêts votre image me suit ;
La lumière du jour, les ombres de la nuit,
Tout retrace à mes yeux les charmes que j'évite ;
Tout vous livre à l'envi le rebelle Hippolyte.
Moi-même, pour tout fruit de mes soins superflus,
Maintenant je me cherche, et ne me trouve plus ;
Mon arc, mes javelots, mon char, tout m'importune ;
Je ne me souviens plus des leçons de Neptune ;
Mes seuls gémissements font retentir les bois,
Et mes coursiers oisifs ont oublié ma voix.
Peut-être le récit d'un amour si sauvage
Vous fait, en m'écoutant, rougir de votre ouvrage ?
D'un cœur qui s'offre à vous quel farouche entretien !
Quel étrange captif pour un si beau lien !
Mais l'offrande à vos yeux en doit être plus chère :
Songez que je vous parle une langue étrangère ;
Et ne rejetez pas des vœux mal exprimés,
Qu'Hippolyte sans vous n'aurait jamais formés.

PHÈDRE

ACTE II – *Scène V*

HIPPOLYTE

Madame, il n'est pas temps de vous troubler encore.
Peut-être votre époux voit encore le jour ;
Le Ciel peut à nos pleurs accorder son retour.
Neptune le protège, et ce dieu tutélaire
Ne sera pas en vain imploré par mon père.

PHÈDRE

On ne voit point deux fois le rivage des morts,
Seigneur. Puisque Thésée a vu les sombres bords,
En vain vous espérez qu'un dieu vous le renvoie ;
Et l'avare Achéron ne lâche point sa proie.
Que dis-je ? il n'est point mort, puisqu'il respire en vous ;
Toujours devant mes yeux je crois voir mon époux ;
Je le vois, je lui parle ; et mon cœur... Je m'égare,
Seigneur, ma folle ardeur malgré moi se déclare.

HIPPOLYTE

Je vois de votre amour l'effet prodigieux :
Tout mort qu'il est, Thésée est présent à vos yeux ;
Toujours de son amour votre âme est embrasée.

PHÈDRE

Oui, Prince, je languis, je brûle pour Thésée :
Je l'aime, non point tel que l'ont vu les enfers,
Volage adorateur de mille objets divers,
Qui va du dieu des morts déshonorer la couche ;
Mais fidèle, mais fier, et même un peu farouche,
Charmant, jeune, traînant tous les cœurs après soi,
Tel qu'on dépeint nos dieux, ou tel que je vous vois.
Il avait votre port, vos yeux, votre langage ;
Cette noble pudeur colorait son visage
Lorsque de notre Crète il traversa les flots,
Digne sujet des vœux des filles de Minos.
Que faisiez-vous alors ? pourquoi, sans Hippolyte,

Des héros de la Grèce assembla-t-il l'élite ?
Pourquoi, trop jeune encor, ne pûtes-vous alors
Entrer dans le vaisseau qui le mit sur nos bords ?
Par vous aurait péri le monstre de la Crète,
Malgré tous les détours de sa vaste retraite :
Pour en développer l'embarras incertain,
Ma sœur du fil fatal eût armé votre main.
Mais non ; dans ce dessein je l'aurais devancée ;
L'amour m'en eût d'abord inspiré la pensée :
C'est moi, Prince, c'est moi dont l'utile secours
Vous eût du labyrinthe enseigné les détours.
Que de soins m'eût coûtés cette tête charmante !
Un fil n'eût point assez rassuré votre amante :
Compagne du péril qu'il vous fallait chercher,
Moi-même devant vous j'aurais voulu marcher ;
Et Phèdre au labyrinthe avec vous descendue
Se serait avec vous retrouvée, ou perdue.

XVIIIᵉ SIÈCLE

Il foisonne en rimeurs, laborieux ou prolixes, qui prennent leur prose rimée pour de la poésie. Du reste cette époque tient l'art des vers en suspicion. Ce que traduit, par exemple, Montesquieu dans *Les Lettres persanes* : « Le lendemain il me mena dans un autre cabinet : Ce sont ici les poètes, dit-il, c'est-à-dire ces auteurs dont le métier est de mettre des entraves au bon sens et d'accabler la raison sous les agréments comme on ensevelissait autrefois les femmes sous leurs parures et leurs ornements. »

Rivarol est plus sévère encore dans son *Discours sur l'universalité de la langue française* : « On ne dit rien en vers qu'on ne puisse exprimer aussi bien dans notre prose et cela n'est pas toujours réciproque. Le prosateur tient plus étroitement sa pensée et la conduit par le plus court chemin ; tandis que le versificateur laisse flotter les rênes et va où la rime le pousse... que de faiblesse ne cache pas l'art des vers ! La prose accuse le nu de la pensée ; il n'est pas permis d'être faible avec elle. »

Malgré le peu de crédit qui est fait à leur art, on rencontre cependant quelques personnalités qui méritent le nom de poètes. Mais, à l'exception de Chénier, il n'y a pas de grand poète parmi eux. Et lui ne sera connu que plus tard.

Ceux qui semblent s'élever au-dessus du médiocre sont peu nombreux. Encore devons-nous pour les lire chercher en eux un écho de l'ancienne grandeur classique, ou, mieux encore, les prémices du siècle suivant, comme un frémissement de ce qui va naître, les signes avant-coureurs d'une saison fertile.

JEAN-BAPTISTE ROUSSEAU

(1671-1741)

Ses contemporains le nomment « le prince des poètes ». Ce titre glorieux nous étonne, sauf si nous comparons ses œuvres à celles de tous les rimeurs fades ou lourdement didactiques de son temps. Nous devons reconnaître que dans un siècle qui se contente de peu en matière de vers, son aspiration au grand lyrisme fait de lui un poète véritable.

Dans sa jeunesse, l'amitié et les conseils de Boileau l'aident à acquérir une parfaite maîtrise dans l'art poétique. Influencé par son exemple, et d'ailleurs doué pour cela, il se consacre d'abord à la satire et à l'épigramme. Sa verve cruelle lui fait des ennemis et lui vaudra l'exil. C'est alors qu'il compose son œuvre lyrique. Ses Odes majestueuses et froides, dans lesquelles il met peu de lui-même, sont admirées de tous ; de son vivant déjà on les fait apprendre aux écoliers. La plupart d'entre elles ne retiennent guère notre attention, leur caractère impersonnel nous rebute. Nous nous demandons ce que voyait en elles le dix-neuvième siècle qui les lisait encore et même les imitait parfois. Cette interrogation nous amène à y chercher les signes avant-coureurs d'une autre inspiration.

Ainsi dans l'Ode citée ici, il nous semble percevoir des accents lamartiniens. La première strophe, qui mêle au lamento solennel du psalmiste une plainte plus personnelle, trouve un écho dans le début de *La Vigne et la maison*. Plus loin ce sont les mots et les rimes chères à Hugo :

> *Mon âme est dans les ténèbres...*
> *Écoutez mes cris funèbres...*

En réalité Jean-Baptiste Rousseau n'est pas un poète tourné vers l'avenir, mais vers le passé. Il rejette son temps et dénonce, avec les accents du Qohélet, la vanité des efforts de l'homme pour acquérir science ou sagesse. Ses admonestations, dans le second poème, montrent combien il est proche du Grand Siècle et de ses prédicateurs. On peut alors être sensible à la perfection formelle de vers « carrés » que n'eût pas désavoués Malherbe, et à l'austère grandeur du memento mori qu'ils font entendre.

ODE

J'ai vu mes tristes journées
Décliner vers leur penchant ;
Au midi de mes années,
Je touchais à mon couchant :
La Mort, déployant ses ailes,
Couvrait d'ombres éternelles
La clarté dont je jouis ;
Et, dans cette nuit funeste,
Je cherchais en vain le reste
De mes jours évanouis.

Grand Dieu, votre main réclame
Les dons que j'en ai reçus ;
Elle vient couper la trame
Des jours qu'elle m'a tissus :
Mon dernier soleil se lève ;
Et votre souffle m'enlève
De la terre des vivants,
Comme la feuille séchée,
Qui, de sa tige arrachée,
Devient le jouet des vents.

Comme un lion plein de rage,
Le mal a brisé mes os ;
Le tombeau m'ouvre un passage
Dans ses lugubres cachots.
Victime faible et tremblante,
À cette image sanglante
Je soupire nuit et jour ;
Et, dans ma crainte mortelle,
Je suis comme l'hirondelle
Sous les griffes du vautour.

Ainsi, de cris et d'alarmes,
Mon mal semblait se nourrir ;
Et mes yeux, noyés de larmes,
Étaient lassés de s'ouvrir.
Je disais à la Nuit sombre :
Ô Nuit, tu vas dans ton ombre
M'ensevelir pour toujours !
Je redisais à l'Aurore :
Le jour que tu fais éclore
Est le dernier de mes jours !

Mon âme est dans les ténèbres,
Mes sens sont glacés d'effroi :
Écoutez mes cris funèbres,
Dieu juste, répondez-moi.
Mais enfin sa main propice
A comblé le précipice
Qui s'entr'ouvrait sous mes pas :
Son secours me fortifie,
Et me fait trouver la vie
Dans les horreurs du trépas.

SUR L'AVEUGLEMENT DES HOMMES DU SIÈCLE

Qu'aux accents de ma voix la terre se réveille !
Rois, soyez attentifs ; peuples, ouvrez l'oreille !
Que l'univers se taise, et m'écoute parler !
Mes chants vont seconder les efforts de ma lyre :
L'Esprit saint me pénètre, il m'échauffe, et m'inspire
Les grandes vérités que je vais révéler.

L'homme en sa propre force a mis sa confiance ;
Ivre de ses grandeurs et de son opulence,
L'éclat de sa fortune enfle sa vanité.
Mais, ô moment terrible ! ô jour épouvantable,
Où la mort saisira ce fortuné coupable
Tout chargé des liens de son iniquité !

Que deviendront alors, répondez, grands du monde,
Que deviendront ces biens où votre espoir se fonde
Et dont vous étalez l'orgueilleuse moisson ?
Sujets, amis, parents, tout deviendra stérile,
Et, dans ce jour fatal, l'homme à l'homme inutile
Ne paiera point à Dieu le prix de sa rançon.

Vous avez vu tomber les plus illustres têtes,
Et vous pourriez encore, insensés que vous êtes,
Ignorer le tribut que l'on doit à la mort !
Non, non, tout doit franchir ce terrible passage :
Le riche et l'indigent, l'imprudent et le sage,
Sujets à même loi, subissent même sort.

D'avides étrangers, transportés d'allégresse,
Engloutissent déjà toute cette richesse,
Ces terres, ces palais, de vos noms anoblis.
Et que vous reste-t-il en ces moments suprêmes ?
Un sépulcre funèbre, où vos noms, où vous-mêmes
Dans l'éternelle nuit serez ensevelis.

Les hommes, éblouis de leurs honneurs frivoles,
Et de leurs vains flatteurs écoutant les paroles,
Ont de ces vérités perdu le souvenir.
Pareils aux animaux farouches et stupides,
Les lois de leur instinct sont leurs uniques guides,
Et pour eux le présent paraît sans avenir.

Un précipice affreux devant eux se présente,
Mais toujours leur raison, soumise et complaisante,
Au-devant de leurs yeux met un voile imposteur.
Sous leurs pas cependant s'ouvrent les noirs abîmes,
Où la cruelle mort, les prenant pour victimes,
Frappe ces vils troupeaux dont elle est le pasteur.

Là s'anéantiront ces titres magnifiques,
Ce pouvoir usurpé, ces ressorts politiques,
Dont le juste autrefois sentit le poids fatal.
Ce qui fit leur bonheur deviendra leur torture ;
Et Dieu, de sa justice apaisant le murmure,
Livrera ces méchants au pouvoir infernal.

Justes, ne craignez point le vain pouvoir des hommes ;
Quelque élevés qu'ils soient, ils sont ce que nous sommes.
Si vous êtes mortels, ils le sont comme vous.
Nous avons beau vanter nos grandeurs passagères,
Il faut mêler sa cendre aux cendres de ses pères,
Et c'est le même Dieu qui nous jugera tous.

VOLTAIRE

(1694-1778)

Voltaire a pratiqué tous les genres poétiques de l'épopée à l'épigramme et triomphé dans la tragédie. Cependant son génie est ailleurs, et si les œuvres en vers occupent une assez grande place dans les écrits de cet habile rimeur, nous ne pensons pas d'abord à lui comme à un poète. C'est qu'à ses yeux la poésie doit servir, au même titre que la prose, au combat philosophique. On le voit rarement renoncer à démontrer, persifler ou pourfendre. Certes les poèmes amoureux échappent à cette fonction utilitaire et ne manquent pas de charme avec leurs accents de tendresse vraie ou feinte, et de mélancolie élégante, mais ils ne sont pas vraiment originaux. On peut leur préférer *Le Mondain* qui s'inscrit dans la lignée libertine et satirique du siècle précédent tout en traitant un sujet inédit. Ici encore l'auteur défend une thèse, celle de la supériorité de la civilisation sur l'état de nature, mais sa fantaisie iconoclaste, sa verve épicurienne, son enthousiasme, font oublier la démonstration et goûter la liberté du ton.

LE MONDAIN

Regrettera qui veut le bon vieux temps,
Et l'âge d'or, et le règne d'Astrée,
Et les beaux jours de Saturne et de Rhée,
Et le jardin de nos premiers parents ;
Moi je rends grâce à la nature sage
Qui, pour mon bien, m'a fait naître en cet âge
Tant décrié par nos tristes frondeurs :
Ce temps profane est tout fait pour mes mœurs.
J'aime le luxe, et même la mollesse,
Tous les plaisirs, les arts de toute espèce,
La propreté, le goût, les ornements :
Tout honnête homme a de tels sentiments.
Il est bien doux pour mon cœur très immonde
De voir ici l'abondance à la ronde,
Mère des arts et des heureux travaux,
Nous apporter, de sa source féconde,
Et des besoins et des plaisirs nouveaux.
L'or de la terre et les trésors de l'onde,
Leurs habitants et les peuples de l'air,
Tout sert au luxe, aux plaisirs de ce monde.
Ô le bon temps que ce siècle de fer !
. . . .
Quand la nature était dans son enfance,
Nos bons aïeux vivaient dans l'ignorance,
Ne connaissant ni le *tien* ni le *mien*.
Qu'auraient-ils pu connaître ? ils n'avaient rien ;
Ils étaient nus : et c'est chose très claire
Que qui n'a rien n'a nul partage à faire.
Sobres étaient. Ah ! je le crois encor :
Martialo n'est point du siècle d'or.
D'un bon vin frais ou la mousse ou la sève
Ne gratta point le triste gosier d'Ève ;
La soie et l'or ne brillaient point chez eux.
Admirez-vous pour cela nos aïeux ?
Il leur manquait l'industrie et l'aisance :

Est-ce vertu ? c'était pure ignorance.
Quel idiot, s'il avait eu pour lors
Quelque bon lit, aurait couché dehors ?
Mon cher Adam, mon gourmand, mon bon père,
Que faisais-tu dans les jardins d'Éden ?
Travaillais-tu pour ce sot genre humain ?
Caressais-tu madame Ève, ma mère ?
Avouez-moi que vous aviez tous deux
Les ongles longs, un peu noirs et crasseux,
La chevelure un peu mal ordonnée,
Le teint bruni, la peau bise et tannée.
Sans propreté l'amour le plus heureux
N'est plus amour, c'est un besoin honteux.
Bientôt lassés de leur belle aventure,
Dessous un chêne ils soupent galamment
Avec de l'eau, du millet, et du gland :
Le repas fait, ils dorment sur la dure :
Voilà l'état de la pure nature.
Or maintenant voulez-vous, mes amis,
Savoir un peu, dans nos jours tant maudits,
Soit à Paris, soit dans Londres, ou dans Rome,
Quel est le train des jours d'un honnête homme ?
Entrez chez lui : la foule des beaux-arts,
Enfants du goût, se montre à vos regards.
De mille mains l'éclatante industrie
De ces dehors orna la symétrie.
L'heureux pinceau, le superbe dessin
Du doux Corrège et du savant Poussin
Sont encadrés dans l'or d'une bordure ;
C'est Bouchardon qui fit cette figure,
Et cet argent fut poli par Germain.
Des Gobelins l'aiguille et la teinture
Dans ces tapis surpassent la peinture.
Tous ces objets sont vingt fois répétés
Dans des trumeaux tout brillants de clartés.
De ce salon je vois par la fenêtre,
Dans des jardins, des myrtes en berceaux ;
Je vois jaillir les bondissantes eaux.
Mais du logis j'entends sortir le maître.

. . . .
Il faut se rendre à ce palais magique
Où les beaux vers, la danse, la musique,
L'art de tromper les yeux par les couleurs,
L'art plus heureux de séduire les cœurs,
De cent plaisirs font un plaisir unique.
Il va siffler quelque opéra nouveau,
Ou, malgré lui, court admirer Rameau.
Allons souper. Que ces brillants services,
Que ces ragoûts ont pour moi de délices !
Qu'un cuisinier est un mortel divin !
Chloris, Églé, me versent de leur main
D'un vin d'Aï dont la mousse pressée,
De la bouteille avec force élancée,
Comme un éclair fait voler le bouchon ;
Il part, on rit ; il frappe le plafond.
De ce vin frais l'écume pétillante
De nos Français est l'image brillante.
Le lendemain donne d'autres désirs,
D'autres soupers, et de nouveaux plaisirs.
Or maintenant, monsieur du Télémaque,
Vantez-nous bien votre petite Ithaque,
Votre Salente, et vos murs malheureux,
Où vos Crétois, tristement vertueux,
Pauvres d'effet, et riches d'abstinence,
Manquent de tout pour avoir l'abondance :
J'admire fort votre style flatteur,
Et votre prose, encor qu'un peu traînante ;
Mais, mon ami, je consens de grand cœur
D'être fessé dans vos murs de Salente,
Si je vais là pour chercher mon bonheur.
Et vous, jardin de ce premier bonhomme,
Jardin fameux par le diable et la pomme,
C'est bien en vain que, par l'orgueil séduits,
Huet, Calmet, dans leur savante audace,
Du paradis ont recherché la place :
Le paradis terrestre est où je suis.

ÉCOUCHARD-LEBRUN

(1729-1807)

C'est un autre Rousseau, mais lui, dans la deuxième moitié du siècle, met tout son art au service de son époque, jusque dans sa période révolutionnaire. Il se fait d'abord connaître par une Ode pindarique sur la ruine de Lisbonne, ce poème, ainsi que ses fréquentes références au poète grec qu'il prend pour modèle, lui valent le surnom de Lebrun-Pindare, honneur qui nous semble démesuré, mais que son orgueil accepte aisément. Il ne doute pas, en effet, de pouvoir égaler celui dont il imite les éloges solennels en célébrant ce que son époque lui offre de grand. C'est ainsi qu'il loue les conquêtes de l'homme sur la nature, le génie de Buffon, ou le courage des marins du *Vengeur*.

Dans ses Odes triomphales, il a plus souvent recours aux procédés de la rhétorique, reprises oratoires, parallèles, invocations, qu'aux mouvements du pur lyrisme. Cependant sa quête de la grandeur engendre parfois une démesure dans l'expression et une outrance baroque qui séduisent.

L'Ode sur l'enthousiasme, l'une des plus souvent citées parmi les quelque 150 odes qu'il a écrites, même si l'on juge pesant l'appareil mythologique qu'il déploie, et naïvement présomptueuse l'image de lui et de son talent qu'il y propose, parvient à donner du génie poétique et de sa puissance souveraine une idée que ne renieront pas les romantiques.

ODE SUR L'ENTHOUSIASME

Aigle qui ravis les Pindares
Jusqu'au trône enflammé des dieux,
Enthousiasme, tu m'égares
À travers l'abîme des cieux.
Ce vil globe à mes yeux s'abaisse ;
Mes yeux s'épurent, et je laisse
Cette fange, empire des rois :
Déjà, sous mon regard immense,
Les astres roulent en silence,
L'Olympe tressaille à ma voix.

Ô muse, dans l'ombre infernale
Ton fils plongea ses pas vivants :
Moi, sur les ailes de Dédale,
Je franchis la route des vents.
« Il est beau, mais il est funeste
De tenter la voûte céleste. »
Arrête, importune raison !
Je vole, je devance Icare,
Dussé-je à quelque mer barbare
Laisser mes ailes et mon nom.

Que la colombe d'Amathonte
S'épouvante au feu des éclairs ;
Le noble oiseau qui les affronte
Prouve seul qu'il est roi des airs.
Je brûle du feu qui l'anime :
Jamais un front pusillanime
N'a ceint des lauriers immortels.
L'audace enfante les trophées.
Qu'importe la mort aux Orphées,
Si leurs tombeaux sont des autels ?

Ô génie ! ô vainqueur des âges,
Toi qui sors brillant du tombeau,
Sous de mystérieux nuages,
Souvent tu caches ton berceau.
C'est dans la solitude et l'ombre
Que ta gloire muette et sombre
Prépare ses jours éclatants :
L'œil profane qui vit ta source
Ne se doutait pas que ta course
Dût franchir la borne des temps.

Tel on voit, dans l'empire aride
Des fils basanés de Memnon,
Le Nil, de son berceau liquide
S'échapper sans gloire et sans nom.
Du haut des rocs ses flots jaillissent,
Et quelque temps s'ensevelissent
Parmi des gouffres ignorés ;
Mais tout à coup à la lumière
Il renaît pour Memphis entière ;
Et ses flots en sont adorés...

ANTOINE-LÉONARD THOMAS

(1732-1785)

Il peut sembler superflu de tirer de l'oubli ce poète académicien. Sa pratique de l'éloge des grands hommes qui lui inspira ensuite un *Essai sur les éloges*, ou l'élaboration de longs poèmes en plusieurs chants tels que *Le Tzar Pierre*, sont très éloignées de nos préférences en matière poétique. Mais il a composé une *Ode sur le Temps* dont un vers, ou plutôt un hémistiche, va enchanter les siècles suivants dès que le magicien de l'harmonie poétique s'en sera emparé. De cette transmutation, l'Ode tout entière tire une aura qui nous amène à la lire avec un réel plaisir.

ODE SUR LE TEMPS

. . . .
Trop aveugles humains, quelle erreur vous enivre !
Vous n'avez qu'un instant pour penser et pour vivre,
Et cet instant qui fuit est pour vous un fardeau !
Avare de ses biens, prodigue de son être,
   Dès qu'il peut se connaître,
L'homme appelle la mort et creuse son tombeau.

L'un, courbé sous cent ans, est mort dès sa naissance ;
L'autre engage à prix d'or sa vénale existence ;
Celui-ci la tourmente à de pénibles jeux ;
Le riche se délivre, au prix de sa fortune,
   Du Temps qui l'importune ;
C'est en ne vivant pas que l'on croit vivre heureux.

Abjurez, ô mortels, cette erreur insensée !
L'homme vit par son âme, et l'âme est la pensée.
C'est elle qui pour vous doit mesurer le Temps !
Cultivez la sagesse ; apprenez l'art suprême
   De vivre avec soi-même ;
Vous pourrez sans effroi compter tous vos instants.

Si je devais un jour pour de viles richesses
Vendre ma liberté, descendre à des bassesses,
Si mon cœur par mes sens devait être amolli,
Ô Temps ! je te dirais : « Préviens ma dernière heure,
   Hâte-toi, que je meure ;
J'aime mieux n'être pas que de vivre avili. »

Mais si de la vertu les généreuses flammes
Peuvent de mes écrits passer dans quelques âmes ;
Si je peux d'un ami soulager les douleurs ;
S'il est des malheureux dont l'obscure innocence
   Languisse sans défense,
Et dont ma faible main doive essuyer les pleurs,

Ô Temps, suspends ton vol, respecte ma jeunesse ;
Que ma mère, longtemps témoin de ma tendresse,
Reçoive mes tributs de respect et d'amour ;
Et vous, Gloire, Vertu, déesses immortelles,
              Que vos brillantes ailes
Sur mes cheveux blanchis se reposent un jour.

CHARLES-LOUIS DE MALFILÂTRE

(1733-1767)

C'est en choisissant la voie la plus ambitieuse, celle de la poésie scientifique, à l'exemple de Lucrèce, que Malfilâtre se fait connaître et devient célèbre à vingt-six ans en publiant l'ode qu'il intitule : *Le Soleil fixe au milieu des planètes.* On l'admire d'avoir su expliquer le système de Copernic avec une clarté qui n'exclut pas la grâce de l'expression. Mais parmi ses œuvres ultérieures, aucune n'aura le même accueil et ne semblera à ses contemporains tenir les promesses de cet éclatant début. Comme eux nous préférons ce premier poème, car les autres, s'ils ne manquent pas d'élégance, sont affadis par une certaine mièvrerie. Au dix-neuvième siècle son nom est encore connu, mais c'est moins pour ses vers que pour son destin de poète mort jeune, oublié de tous et misérable, il offre ainsi aux romantiques une figure émouvante de la malédiction du génie.

LE SOLEIL FIXE AU MILIEU DES PLANÈTES

L'homme a dit : « Les cieux m'environnent,
Les cieux ne roulent que pour moi ;
De ces astres qui me couronnent
La nature me fit le roi :
Pour moi seul le soleil se lève,
Pour moi seul le soleil achève
Son cercle éclatant dans les airs ;
Et je vois, souverain tranquille,
Sur son poids la terre immobile
Au centre de cet univers. »

Fier mortel, bannis ces fantômes,
Sur toi-même jette un coup d'œil.
Que sommes-nous, faibles atomes,
Pour porter si loin notre orgueil ?
Insensés ! nous parlons en maîtres,
Nous qui dans l'océan des êtres
Nageons tristement confondus,
Nous dont l'existence légère,
Pareille à l'ombre passagère,
Commence, paraît, et n'est plus !

Mais quelles routes immortelles
Uranie entrouvre à mes yeux !
Déesse, est-ce toi qui m'appelles
Aux voûtes brillantes des cieux ?
Je te suis... Mon âme agrandie,
S'élançant d'une aile hardie,
De la terre a quitté les bords :
De ton flambeau la clarté pure
Me guide au temple où la nature
Cache ses augustes trésors.

Grand Dieu ! quel sublime spectacle
Confond mes sens, glace ma voix !...
Où suis-je ? Quel nouveau miracle
De l'Olympe a changé les lois ?
Au loin, dans l'étendue immense,
Je contemple seul, en silence,
La marche du grand univers ;
Dans un tourbillon de l'espace
Mon œil surpris voit sur leur trace
Retourner les orbes divers.

Portés du couchant à l'aurore
Par un mouvement éternel,
Sur leur axe ils tournent encore
Dans les vastes plaines du ciel.
Quelle intelligence secrète
Règle en son cours chaque planète
Par d'imperceptibles ressorts ?
Le soleil est-il le génie
Qui fait avec tant d'harmonie
Circuler les célestes corps ?

. . . .

Je te salue, âme du monde,
Sacré Soleil, astre de feu,
De tous les dons source féconde,
Soleil, image de mon Dieu !
Aux globes qui, dans leur carrière,
Rendent hommage à ta lumière,
Annonce-le par ta splendeur :
Règne à jamais sur ses ouvrages,
Triomphe, entretiens tous les âges
De son éternelle grandeur.

NICOLAS-GERMAIN LÉONARD

(1744-1793)

Le thème du retour n'est pas nouveau dans la poésie française. Des exilés tels que Charles d'Orléans ou Du Bellay – l'un captif, retenu malgré lui, l'autre consentant mais déçu – ont dit la douceur de la terre natale retrouvée. L'originalité de Léonard, que sa veine mélancolique et tendre inscrit dans leur lignée, est de mettre l'accent sur ce que Baudelaire nomme « l'amer savoir qu'on tire du voyage ». Né à la Guadeloupe et venu très tôt en France, il choisit de revoir le lieu de sa naissance et de s'y fixer. Puis après plusieurs traversées, désenchanté, il décide de se réfugier définitivement en France à Romainville, comme on le voit dans le poème qui suit. Pourtant, en vrai voyageur, (« ... mais les vrais voyageurs sont ceux-là seuls qui partent / Pour partir »...) il allait embarquer une fois encore quand la mort l'en empêche. Le final de ce poème, écrit un an à peine auparavant, semble plein de pressentiments funèbres. Lorsque, dans ses vers testamentaires (« J'ai perdu ma force et ma vie »...), Musset écrit : « Le seul bien qui me reste au monde / Est d'avoir quelquefois pleuré », il se souvient de la tristesse de Léonard :

> *...Et le dernier bien qui me reste*
> *Est-il la douceur de pleurer ?*

AU BOIS DE ROMAINVILLE

. . . .

J'ai vu le monde et ses misères :
Je suis las de les parcourir.
C'est dans ces ombres tutélaires,
C'est ici que je veux mourir !

Je graverai sur quelque hêtre :
« Adieu, fortune, adieu, projets !
Adieu, rocher qui m'as vu naître,
Je renonce à vous pour jamais. »

Que je puisse cacher ma vie
Sous les feuilles d'un arbrisseau,
Comme le frêle vermisseau
Qu'enferme une tige fleurie !

Si l'enfant qui porte un bandeau
Voulait embellir mon asile,
Ô bocage de Romainville !
Couronne de fleurs ton berceau.

Et si, sans bruit et sans escorte,
L'amitié venait sur ses pas
Frapper doucement à ma porte,
Laisse-la voler dans mes bras.

Amours, Plaisirs, troupe céleste,
Ne pourrai-je vous attirer,
Et le dernier bien qui me reste
Est-il la douceur de pleurer ?

Mais, hélas ! le temps qui m'entraîne
Va tout changer autour de moi :
Déjà mon cœur que rien n'enchaîne
Ne sent que tristesse et qu'effroi !...

Ils viendront ces jours de ténèbres
Où la vieillesse aux doigts pesants,
Couvrira de voiles funèbres
Les images de mon printemps.

Ce bois même, avec tous ses charmes,
Je dois peut-être l'oublier ;
Et le temps que j'ai beau prier
Me ravira jusqu'à mes larmes.

NICOLAS GILBERT

(1750-1780)

Ce poète eut très tôt le pressentiment de l'échec. Dans l'un de ses premiers poèmes, *Le Poète malheureux*, il parle déjà de lui-même au passé, comme un homme dont le destin douloureux est achevé :

> *Savez-vous quel trésor eût satisfait mon cœur ?*
> *La gloire : mais la gloire est rebelle au malheur.*

Son pessimisme s'étend à l'univers qu'il nomme « le Temple de l'injustice » car la vertu y est toujours « victime du dédain ».

> *Et les pâles talents couchés sur des grabats*
> *Y veillent consumés par la faim qui les presse.*

Le destin de Malfilâtre illustre à ses yeux cette injustice des hommes, et le vers souvent cité : « La faim mit au tombeau Malfilâtre ignoré », est moins l'expression de la compassion qu'un moyen de dresser un réquisitoire contre un siècle impitoyable envers les vrais talents mais plein d'indulgence pour les flatteurs et les intrigants. De ce siècle il fustige les fausses gloires et les faux grands hommes, c'est-à-dire, selon lui, les encyclopédistes et les philosophes des Lumières. Son mépris n'en épargne aucun :

> *Saint Lambert noble auteur dont la muse pédante*
> *Fait des vers fort vantés par Voltaire qu'il vante*
> *Et ce vain Beaumarchais...*
> *Et ce lourd Diderot...*
> *Et ce froid d'Alembert...*

Et tant d'autres encore dont le public épris
Connaît beaucoup les noms et fort peu les écrits.

À côté du satirique mordant, il y a en lui un élégiaque et un lyrique. Sa mort prématurée ne lui laissa pas le temps de donner toute sa mesure dans ces domaines. Cependant la grâce surannée de ses poèmes amoureux, où il fait de la nature le décor de ses plaisirs ou le témoin de ses peines, ne manque pas de charme. Et la dernière de ses Odes, « composée huit jours avant sa mort », témoigne de son talent. Son rythme ample et la noblesse du ton s'accordent avec la sincérité de cette déploration résignée. L'image du banquet, dans un vers que la postérité a retenu, vient sans doute de La Fontaine, et à travers lui d'Horace ou de Lucrèce, mais ce « pavillon du ciel », tente céleste dressée au-dessus de l'homme, est neuf, peut-être à l'origine de l'image splendide de Baudelaire (« Cheveux bleus, pavillon de ténèbres tendu / Vous me rendez l'azur du ciel... ») Et Vigny s'est souvenu de cette Ode en idéalisant le destin de Gilbert dans *Stello*, pour en faire la figure exemplaire du poète maudit.

L'AMANT DÉSESPÉRÉ

Forêts solitaires et sombres,
Je viens, dévoré de douleurs,
Sous vos majestueuses ombres,
Du repos qui me fuit respirer les douceurs.
Recherchez, vains mortels, le tumulte des villes ;
Ce qui charme vos yeux aux miens est en horreur.
Ce silence imposant, ces lugubres asiles,
Voilà ce qui peut plaire au trouble de mon cœur,
Arbres, répondez-moi !... Cachez-vous ma Sylvie ?
Sylvie, ô ma Sylvie !... Elle ne m'entend pas,
Tyrans de ces forêts, me l'auriez-vous ravie ?
Hélas ! je cherche en vain la trace de ses pas.
Ô feuillages chéris, voluptueux feuillages,
        Combien de fois vos noirs ombrages
Nous ont aux yeux jaloux l'un et l'autre voilés,
Et que ces doux instants se sont vite écoulés !
Toi qui me répétais les chants de ma Sylvie,
Quand, seule, elle vantait les douceurs de sa vie,
L'entends-tu ? parle, écho ; dis, me la rendra-t-on ?
        Hélas ! il semble qu'il dit non...
Mais quel son a frappé mon oreille éperdue ?
Peut-être est-ce un soupir de ma divinité,
        Qui dit à mon cœur agité :
        Viens, elle te sera rendue...
C'est elle ! ô doux retour ! hâtons-nous d'approcher.
J'entends ses pieds fouler les feuilles gémissantes ;
Mais non... c'est ce ruisseau qui va contre un rocher
Briser, en murmurant, ses ondes blanchissantes.
Ce ruisseau murmurer ?... Il gémit sur mon sort...
Ces arbres attristants et voués à la mort,
        Qui couronnent ces rives,
Ces sapins, ces cyprès, leur morne majesté,
Ces bois silencieux, leur vaste obscurité,
Tout semble prendre part à mes douleurs plaintives.
Ah ! revînt-elle encore, il ne sera plus temps.

Ses yeux, au lieu de moi, retrouveront ma cendre,
Et les pleurs que sur elle on la verra répandre,
Ses regrets douloureux, ses longs gémissements,
Viendront au tombeau même éveiller mes tourments.

ODE IMITÉE DE PLUSIEURS PSAUMES
ET COMPOSÉE PAR L'AUTEUR
HUIT JOURS AVANT SA MORT

. . . .
Soyez béni, mon Dieu, vous qui daignez me rendre
      L'innocence et son noble orgueil ;
Vous qui, pour protéger le repos de ma cendre,
      Veillerez près de mon cercueil.

Au banquet de la vie, infortuné convive,
      J'apparus un jour, et je meurs.
Je meurs ; et, sur ma tombe où lentement j'arrive,
      Nul ne viendra verser des pleurs.

Salut, champs que j'aimais ! et vous, douce verdure !
      Et vous, riant exil des bois !
Ciel, pavillon de l'homme, admirable nature,
      Salut pour la dernière fois !

Ah ! puissent voir longtemps votre beauté sacrée
      Tant d'amis sourds à mes adieux !
Qu'ils meurent pleins de jours ! que leur mort soit pleurée !
      Qu'un ami leur ferme les yeux !

ÉVARISTE DE PARNY

(1783-1814)

L'histoire littéraire voit en lui l'inventeur du poème en prose. Lorsqu'il publie ses *Chansons madécasses* en 1787, il n'est pourtant pas le premier à faire connaître en France, à travers une traduction non rimée, des poèmes écrits dans d'autres langues. D'ailleurs, au-delà des modèles que lui a fournis l'île Bourbon où il est né, il s'inspire aussi, assez largement, de sources européennes, en particulier des poèmes d'Ossian, connus chez nous depuis 1760. Ce qui a dû l'encourager à proposer au public ces douze chansons, c'est l'accueil enthousiaste qui est fait à cette forme nouvelle de poésie. On croit y trouver, loin des entraves de la rime et des règles contraignantes, loin aussi des conventions du sentiment, l'expression vraie de la passion amoureuse, et celle de la nature dans sa pureté originelle. Cependant il ne se contente pas de céder au goût du temps, il innove. En s'écartant de la prose ordinaire ou même poétique, il invente des modes d'expression que retiendront ses successeurs. Pour faire de chaque poème un système clos, il a recours ici à la strophe unique où la répétition de certains motifs (invocation, tour syntaxique) donne au lecteur le sentiment d'une architecture concertée ; là ce sont des couplets séparés dont le premier et le dernier se rejoignent par le retour du même thème. L'utilisation du refrain à la fin de chaque strophe, suivant le modèle des chansons populaires, est sans doute l'un des procédés les plus efficaces pour donner l'impression d'unité, impression à laquelle contribuent également l'exotisme du décor et le ton de volupté tendre qui caractérisent chacune des douze *Chansons madécasses*. Toutes ces trouvailles fondent un genre nouveau.

Mais Parny est célèbre dès 1778 pour avoir chanté ses amours dans les formes traditionnelles. Voltaire l'appelle Tibulle. Ses *Poésies érotiques*, nous dirions plutôt amoureuses, inspirées par sa propre histoire, disent la naissance et les jeux de l'amour, son rêve d'une solitude où s'abolissent les contraintes sociales. Plus tard, il complète ce livre par un recueil d'élégies où il tente de consoler son inconsolable cœur de la rupture définitive avec la jeune fille qu'il aimait. Il tire, de sa douleur réelle et d'un sentiment de la nature qui lui est propre, des accents qui nous touchent encore.

PROJET DE SOLITUDE

Fuyons ces tristes lieux, ô maîtresse adorée !
Nous perdons en espoir la moitié de nos jours,
Et la crainte importune y trouble nos amours.
Non loin de ce rivage est une île ignorée,
Interdite aux vaisseaux, et d'écueils entourée.
Un zéphyr éternel y rafraîchit les airs.
Libre et nouvelle encor, la prodigue nature
Embellit de ses dons ce point de l'univers :
Des ruisseaux argentés roulent sur la verdure,
Et vont en serpentant se perdre au sein des mers.
Une main favorable y reproduit sans cesse
L'ananas parfumé des plus douces odeurs ;
Et l'oranger touffu, courbé sous sa richesse,
Se couvre en même temps et de fruits et de fleurs.
Que nous faut-il de plus ? Cette île fortunée
Semble par la nature aux amants destinée.
L'océan la resserre, et deux fois en un jour
De cet asile étroit on achève le tour.
Là, je ne craindrai plus un père inexorable ;
C'est là qu'en liberté tu pourras être aimable,
Et couronner l'amant qui t'a donné son cœur.
Vous coulerez alors, mes paisibles journées,
Par les nœuds du plaisir l'une à l'autre enchaînées :
Laissez-moi peu de gloire et beaucoup de bonheur.
Viens : la nuit est obscure et le ciel sans nuage ;
D'un éternel adieu saluons ce rivage,
Où par toi seule encor mes pas sont retenus.
Je vois à l'horizon l'étoile de Vénus :
Vénus dirigera notre course incertaine.
Éole exprès pour nous vient d'enchaîner les vents ;
Sur les flots aplanis Zéphyre souffle à peine ;
Viens : l'Amour jusqu'au port conduira deux amants.

ÉLÉGIES

I

D'un long sommeil j'ai goûté la douceur ;
Sous un ciel pur, qu'elle embellit encore,
À mon réveil j'ai vu briller l'aurore ;
Le dieu du jour la suit avec lenteur.
Moment heureux ! la nature est tranquille ;
Zéphyre dort sur la fleur immobile ;
L'air plus serein a repris sa fraîcheur,
Et le silence habite mon asile.
Mais quoi ! le calme est aussi dans mon cœur !
Je ne vois plus la triste et chère image
Qui s'offrait seule à ce cœur tourmenté ;
Et la raison, par sa douce clarté,
De mes ennuis dissipe le nuage.
Toi, que ma voix implorait chaque jour,
Tranquillité, si longtemps attendue,
Des cieux enfin te voilà descendue,
Pour remplacer l'impitoyable amour.
J'allais périr ; au milieu de l'orage
Un sûr abri me sauve du naufrage ;
De l'aquilon j'ai trompé la fureur ;
Et je contemple, assis sur le rivage,
Des flots grondants la vaste profondeur.
Fatal objet, dont j'adorais les charmes,
À ton oubli je vais m'accoutumer.
Je t'obéis enfin ; sois sans alarmes ;
Je sens pour toi mon âme se fermer.
Je pleure encor ; mais j'ai cessé d'aimer.
Et mon bonheur fait seul couler mes larmes.

VI

Tandis qu'avec mes pleurs la plainte et les regrets
    Coulent de mon âme attendrie,
    J'avance, et de nouveaux objets
    Interrompent ma rêverie.
Je vois naître à mes pieds ces ruisseaux différents
Qui, changés tout à coup en rapides torrents,
Traversent à grand bruit les ravines profondes,
Roulent avec leurs flots le ravage et l'horreur,
Fondent sur le rivage, et vont avec fureur
Dans l'océan troublé précipiter leurs ondes.
Je vois des rocs noircis, dont le front orgueilleux
    S'élève et va frapper les cieux.
    Le temps a gravé sur leurs cimes
    L'empreinte de la vétusté.
    Mon œil rapidement porté
De torrents en torrents, d'abîmes en abîmes,
      S'arrête épouvanté.
Ô nature ! qu'ici je ressens ton empire !
J'aime de ce désert la sauvage âpreté ;
De tes travaux hardis j'aime la majesté ;
Oui, ton horreur me plaît ; je frissonne et j'admire.

Dans ce séjour tranquille, aux regards des humains
Que ne puis-je cacher le reste de ma vie !
Que ne puis-je du moins y laisser mes chagrins !
Je venais oublier l'ingrate qui m'oublie,
Et ma bouche indiscrète a prononcé son nom ;
Je l'ai redit cent fois, et l'écho solitaire
De ma voix douloureuse a prolongé le son ;
    Ma main l'a gravé sur la pierre ;
    Au mien il est entrelacé.
Un jour, le voyageur, sous la mousse légère,
    De ces noms connus à Cythère
    Verra quelque reste effacé.
Soudain il s'écriera : « Son amour fut extrême ;
Il chanta sa maîtresse au fond de ces déserts.
    Pleurons sur ses malheurs et relisons les vers
    Qu'il soupira dans ce lieu même. »

IX

Que le bonheur arrive lentement !
Que le bonheur s'éloigne avec vitesse !
Durant le cours de ma triste jeunesse,
Si j'ai vécu, ce ne fut qu'un moment.
Je suis puni de ce moment d'ivresse.
L'espoir qui trompe a toujours sa douceur,
Et dans nos maux du moins il nous console ;
Mais loin de moi l'illusion s'envole,
Et l'espérance est morte dans mon cœur.
Ce cœur, hélas ! que le chagrin dévore,
Ce cœur malade et surchargé d'ennui,
Dans le passé veut ressaisir encore
De son bonheur la fugitive aurore,
Et tous les biens qu'il n'a plus aujourd'hui ;
Mais du présent l'image trop fidèle
Me suit toujours dans ces rêves trompeurs,
Et sans pitié la vérité cruelle
Vient m'avertir de répandre des pleurs.
J'ai tout perdu ; délire, jouissance,
Transports brûlants, paisible volupté,
Douces erreurs, consolante espérance,
J'ai tout perdu ; l'amour seul est resté.

CHANSONS MADÉCASSES

XII

Nahandove, ô belle Nahandove ! l'oiseau nocturne a commencé ses cris, la pleine lune brille sur ma tête, et la rosée naissante humecte mes cheveux. Voici l'heure : qui peut t'arrêter, Nahandove, ô belle Nahandove ? Le lit de feuilles est préparé ; je l'ai parsemé de fleurs et d'herbes odoriférantes, il est digne de tes charmes, Nahandove, ô belle Nahandove !

Elle vient. J'ai reconnu la respiration précipitée que donne une marche rapide ; j'entends le froissement de la pagne qui l'enveloppe : c'est elle, c'est Nahandove, la belle Nahandove !

Reprends haleine, ma jeune amie ; repose-toi sur mes genoux. Que ton regard est enchanteur ! que le mouvement de ton sein est vif et délicieux sous la main qui le presse ! Tu souris, Nahandove, ô belle Nahandove !

Tes baisers pénètrent jusqu'à l'âme ; tes caresses brûlent tous mes sens : arrête, ou je vais mourir. Meurt-on de volupté, Nahandove, ô belle Nahandove ?

Le plaisir passe comme un éclair ; ta douce haleine s'affaiblit, tes yeux humides se referment, ta tête se penche mollement, et tes transports s'éteignent dans la langueur. Jamais tu ne fus si belle, Nahandove, ô belle Nahandove !

Que le sommeil est délicieux dans les bras d'une maîtresse ! moins délicieux pourtant que le réveil. Tu pars, et je vais languir dans les regrets et les désirs ; je languirai jusqu'au soir ; tu reviendras ce soir, Nahandove, ô belle Nahandove !

JEAN-PIERRE CLARIS DE FLORIAN

(1755-1794)

Il est le plus célèbre des fabulistes français après La Fontaine, qui eut pourtant de nombreux émules en son temps et durant tout le dix-huitième siècle. Il est aussi le moins indigne de son modèle. Ses fables paraissent en 1792, après avoir circulé dans des cercles privilégiés ; quelques-unes sont encore recueillies après sa mort. S'il a les mêmes sources que son prédécesseur, comme il le dit dans sa préface (mais il puise aussi chez tel fabuliste anglais ou allemand ou chez le poète espagnol Iriarte), il ne s'intéresse qu'aux sujets inédits, ceux que La Fontaine n'a pas abordés. Une grande sensibilité, des élans du cœur propres au siècle de J. J. Rousseau, l'amènent parfois à privilégier la morale ou la méditation au détriment de l'anecdote. La fable y gagne en émotion ce qu'elle perd en pittoresque ; on peut le regretter. Ses histoires, de façon générale, n'ont pas la saveur et le relief de celles de La Fontaine. Mais il ne manque pas de verve pour stigmatiser les vices et quand il s'en prend à la sottise, qu'il raille le dindon ou le riche, on croit entendre Beaumarchais ; et parfois même Voltaire quand il donne à ses traits la concision de l'épigramme :

> *Sans vice et sans travail je voudrais m'enrichir.*
> *Eh bien ! sois un simple imbécile,*
> *J'en ai vu beaucoup réussir.*

Ses contemporains reprochaient à ses bergeries de manquer de loup !

Et il est vrai qu'en le lisant on l'imagine assez volontiers sous l'apparence débonnaire du « bon fermier » auquel il fait dire :

Mon livre est la nature,
Et mon unique précepteur
C'est mon cœur.

Si la part de son œuvre qui compte pour nous ce sont ses fables, il faut rappeler que c'est son roman de *Galatée* qui le rendit célèbre, puis une idylle pastorale : *Estelle et Némorin* et que, s'il est connu même de ceux qui ignorent son nom, il le doit à un poème qu'on n'a pu s'empêcher de citer, ce *Plaisir d'amour* que l'on fredonne depuis deux siècles.

LA FABLE ET LA VÉRITÉ

La Vérité toute nue
Sortit un jour de son puits.
Ses attraits par le temps étaient un peu détruits,
        Jeunes et vieux fuyaient sa vue.
La pauvre Vérité restait là morfondue,
Sans trouver un asile où pouvoir habiter.
        À ses yeux vient se présenter
        La Fable richement vêtue,
        Portant plumes et diamants,
        La plupart faux, mais très brillants.
        « Eh ! vous voilà ! bonjour, dit-elle ;
Que faites-vous ici seule sur un chemin ? »
La Vérité répond : « Vous le voyez, je gèle ;
        Aux passants je demande en vain
        De me donner une retraite ;
Je leur fais peur à tous. Hélas ! je le vois bien,
        Vieille femme n'obtient plus rien.
        – Vous êtes pourtant ma cadette,
        Dit la Fable, et, sans vanité,
        Partout je suis fort bien reçue.
        Mais aussi, dame Vérité,
        Pourquoi vous montrer toute nue ?
Cela n'est pas adroit. Tenez, arrangeons-nous ;
        Qu'un même intérêt nous rassemble :
Venez sous mon manteau, nous marcherons ensemble.
        Chez le sage, à cause de vous,
        Je ne serai point rebutée ;
        À cause de moi, chez les fous
        Vous ne serez point maltraitée.
Servant par ce moyen chacun selon son goût,
Grâce à votre raison et grâce à ma folie,
        Vous verrez, ma sœur, que partout
        Nous passerons de compagnie. »

LES SERINS ET LE CHARDONNERET

Un amateur d'oiseaux avait, en grand secret,
  Parmi les œufs d'une serine
  Glissé l'œuf d'un chardonneret.
La mère des serins, bien plus tendre que fine,
Ne s'en aperçut point, et couva comme sien
  Cet œuf qui dans peu vint à bien.
Le petit étranger, sorti de sa coquille,
Des deux époux trompés reçoit les tendres soins,
  Par eux traité ni plus ni moins
  Que s'il était de la famille.
Couché dans le duvet, il dort le long du jour
À côté des serins dont il se croit le frère,
  Reçoit la becquée à son tour,
Et repose la nuit sous l'aile de la mère.
Chaque oisillon grandit, et, devenant oiseau,
  D'un brillant plumage s'habille ;
Le chardonneret seul ne devient point jonquille,
Et ne s'en croit pas moins des serins le plus beau.
  Ses frères pensent de même :
Douce erreur qui toujours fait voir l'objet qu'on aime
  Ressemblant à nous trait pour trait !
Jaloux de son bonheur, un vieux chardonneret
Vient lui dire : « Il est temps enfin de vous connaître ;
Ceux pour qui vous avez de si doux sentiments
  Ne sont point du tout vos parents.
C'est d'un chardonneret que le sort vous fit naître,
Vous ne fûtes jamais serin : regardez-vous,
Vous avez le corps fauve et la tête écarlate,
Le bec… – Oui, dit l'oiseau, j'ai ce qu'il vous plaira,
  Mais je n'ai point une âme ingrate,
  Et mon cœur toujours chérira
  Ceux qui soignèrent mon enfance.
Si mon plumage au leur ne ressemble pas bien,
  J'en suis fâché ; mais leur cœur et le mien
  Ont une grande ressemblance.

Vous prétendez prouver que je ne leur suis rien,
   Leurs soins me prouvent le contraire :
   Rien n'est vrai comme ce qu'on sent.
   Pour un oiseau reconnaissant
   Un bienfaiteur est plus qu'un père. »

LE SINGE QUI MONTRE LA LANTERNE MAGIQUE

Messieurs les beaux esprits, dont la prose et les vers
Sont d'un style pompeux et toujours admirable,
Mais que l'on n'entend point, écoutez cette fable,
    Et tâchez de devenir clairs.

Un homme qui montrait la lanterne magique
    Avait un singe dont les tours
    Attiraient chez lui grand concours.
Jacqueau, c'était son nom, sur la corde élastique
    Dansait et voltigeait au mieux,
    Puis faisait le saut périlleux,
Et puis sur un cordon, sans que rien le soutienne,
    Le corps droit, fixe, d'aplomb,
    Notre Jacqueau fait tout du long
    L'exercice à la prussienne.
Un jour qu'au cabaret son maître était resté,
    (C'était, je pense, un jour de fête),
    Notre singe en liberté
    Veut faire un coup de sa tête.
Il s'en va rassembler les divers animaux
    Qu'il peut rencontrer dans la ville :
    Chiens, chats, poulets, dindons, pourceaux,
    Arrivent bientôt à la file.
« Entrez, entrez, Messieurs, criait notre Jacqueau ;
C'est ici, c'est ici qu'un spectacle nouveau
Vous charmera gratis. Oui, Messieurs, à la porte
On ne prend point d'argent, je fais tout pour l'honneur. »
    À ces mots, chaque spectateur
    Va se placer, et l'on apporte
La lanterne magique ; on ferme les volets ;
    Et, par un discours fait exprès,
    Jacqueau prépare l'auditoire.
    Ce morceau vraiment oratoire
    Fit bâiller ; mais on applaudit.
Content de son succès, notre singe saisit

Un verre peint qu'il met dans sa lanterne.
    Il sait comment on le gouverne,
Et crie en le poussant : « Est-il rien de pareil ?
    Messieurs, vous voyez le soleil,
    Ses rayons et toute sa gloire.
Voici présentement la lune ; et puis l'histoire
    D'Adam, d'Ève et des animaux...
    Voyez, messieurs, comme ils sont beaux !
    Voyez la naissance du monde ;
Voyez... » Les spectateurs, dans une nuit profonde,
Écarquillaient leurs yeux et ne pouvaient rien voir :
    L'appartement, le mur, tout était noir.
« Ma foi, disait un chat, de toutes les merveilles
    Dont il étourdit nos oreilles,
    Le fait est que je ne vois rien.
    – Ni moi non plus, disait un chien.
– Moi, disait un dindon, je vois bien quelque chose,
    Mais je ne sais pour quelle cause
    Je ne distingue pas très bien. »
Pendant tous ces discours, le Cicéron moderne
Parlait éloquemment et ne se lassait point.
    Il n'avait oublié qu'un point :
    C'était d'éclairer sa lanterne.

LE VOYAGE

Partir avant le jour, à tâtons, sans voir goutte,
Sans songer seulement à demander sa route ;
Aller de chute en chute, et, se traînant ainsi,
Faire un tiers du chemin jusqu'à près de midi ;
Voir sur sa tête alors s'amasser les nuages,
Dans un sable mouvant précipiter ses pas,
Courir, en essuyant orages sur orages,
Vers un but incertain où l'on n'arrive pas ;
Détrompé vers le soir, chercher une retraite,
Arriver haletant, se coucher, s'endormir :
On appelle cela naître, vivre, et mourir.
            La volonté de Dieu soit faite !

PLAISIR D'AMOUR

Plaisir d'amour ne dure qu'un moment,
Chagrin d'amour dure toute la vie.

J'ai tout quitté pour l'ingrate Sylvie,
Elle me quitte et prend un autre amant...

Plaisir d'amour ne dure qu'un moment
Chagrin d'amour dure toute la vie.

Tant que cette eau coulera doucement
Vers ce ruisseau qui borde la prairie,
Je t'aimerai, me répétait Sylvie ;
L'eau coule encore, elle a changé pourtant

Plaisir d'amour ne dure qu'un moment,
Chagrin d'amour dure toute la vie.

ANDRÉ CHÉNIER

(1762-1794)

« Un vers d'André Chénier chantait dans ma mémoire. »

La citation est de Musset, mais pourrait être attribuée à chacun des poètes romantiques : tous ont entendu ce chant.

La publication posthume de l'œuvre de Chénier, quasi inconnue jusque-là date de 1819, un an avant *Les Méditations*. Aux yeux de tous il est clair qu'elle ouvre à la poésie une voie ignorée ou du moins oubliée. « C'était, écrira plus tard Lamartine, une corde nouvelle, une corde trempée de sang et de larmes, que la mort avait ajoutée à la lyre moderne. » Pour Hugo qui fait très tôt l'éloge de Chénier dans *La Muse française*, son souvenir est constamment présent, comme l'attestent les vers mis en exergue à plusieurs de ses poèmes, la pièce des *Contemplations* qui lui est dédiée, ainsi que l'une des *Idylles* de *La Légende*.

Cependant ce poète si prisé au dix-neuvième siècle n'a pas rompu avec le sien : son goût de l'Antiquité rejoint celui d'une époque qui, avec Lebrun-Pindare, le peintre David ou l'auteur du *Voyage du jeune Anacharsis*, l'abbé Barthélemy, se passionnait pour la Grèce. En prenant l'*Anthologie grecque* ou les poètes latins comme source d'inspiration, Chénier s'inscrit dans ce mouvement. On peut alors se demander comment ce choix du passé a pu séduire les romantiques si épris de nouveauté et de rupture. Sans doute son destin tragique les fascine, mais leur admiration durable repose sur la reconnaissance de son génie. Ils découvrent en lui une imitation qui n'est jamais plagiat mais « innutrition ». Il sait réinventer la lumière grecque et traduire avec les mots la pureté d'une attitude ou la grâce d'un mouvement qu'ont fixées le marbre ou la peinture. Son art rend vivant tout ce qu'il touche. Sa science innée du vers lui permet d'échapper aux pièges de la prose versifiée, il le déroule en usant de toutes les libertés syntaxiques qui lui sont propres, telles que l'inversion, et de toutes les ressources de l'image. Il change l'équilibre du vers en le fragmentant par des rejets et des coupes insolites, sa langue en acquiert une souplesse et une musicalité exquises.

Il a rêvé, quelques fragments en témoignent, d'un grand poème à la manière de Lucrèce, où il mettrait tout son art au service des temps modernes, (« Sur des pensers nouveaux faisons des vers antiques »). Sa courte vie ne lui a pas permis de mener à bien ce projet, non plus que d'achever les esquisses de poèmes qu'on trouva dans ses papiers. La séduction que son œuvre exerce sur nous tient peut-être aussi à ce caractère inaccompli, marque de la mort qui l'éternise. Les *Ïambes* vengeurs que lui inspire l'échafaud, révèlent une véhémence et une force qui l'égalent à d'Aubigné et à Hugo.

NÉÆRE

Tel qu'à sa mort, pour la dernière fois,
Un beau cygne soupire, et de sa douce voix,
De sa voix qui bientôt lui doit être ravie,
Chante, avant de partir, ses adieux à la vie :
Ainsi, les yeux remplis de langueur et de mort,
Pâle, elle ouvrit la bouche en un dernier effort.
« Ô vous, du Sébéthus Naïades vagabondes,
Coupez sur mon tombeau vos chevelures blondes.
Adieu, mon Clinias ; moi, celle qui te plus,
Moi, celle qui t'aimai, que tu ne verras plus.
Ô cieux, ô terre, ô mer, prés, montagnes, rivages,
Fleurs, bois mélodieux, vallons, grottes sauvages,
Rappelez-lui souvent, rappelez-lui toujours
Néære tout son bien, Néære ses amours,
Cette Néære, hélas ! qu'il nommait sa Néære ;
Qui pour lui criminelle abandonna sa mère ;
Qui pour lui fugitive, errant de lieux en lieux,
Aux regards des humains n'osa lever les yeux.
Oh ! soit que l'astre pur des deux frères d'Hélène
Calme sous ton vaisseau la vague ionienne ;
Soit qu'aux bords de Paestum, sous ta soigneuse main,
Les roses deux fois l'an couronnent ton jardin,
Au coucher du soleil, si ton âme attendrie
Tombe en une muette et molle rêverie,
Alors, mon Clinias, appelle, appelle-moi.
Je viendrai, Clinias, je volerai vers toi.
Mon âme vagabonde, à travers le feuillage,
Frémira. Sur les vents ou sur quelque nuage
Tu la verras descendre, ou du sein de la mer,
S'élevant comme un songe, étinceler dans l'air ;
Et ma voix, toujours tendre et doucement plaintive,
Caresser en fuyant ton oreille attentive. »

Bucoliques

LES COLOMBES

Que les deux beaux oiseaux, les colombes fidèles,
Se baisent. Pour s'aimer les Dieux les firent belles.
Sous leur tête mobile, un cou blanc, délicat,
Se plie, et de la neige effacerait l'éclat.
Leur voix est pure et tendre, et leur âme innocente,
Leurs yeux doux et sereins, leur bouche caressante.

Bucoliques

LA JEUNE TARENTINE

Pleurez, doux alcyons ! ô vous, oiseaux sacrés,
Oiseaux chers à Thétis, doux alcyons, pleurez !
Elle a vécu, Myrto, la jeune Tarentine !
Un vaisseau la portait aux bords de Camarine.
Là, l'hymen, les chansons, les flûtes, lentement
Devaient la reconduire au seuil de son amant.
Une clef vigilante a, pour cette journée,
Dans le cèdre enfermé sa robe d'hyménée,
Et l'or dont au festin ses bras seront parés,
Et pour ses blonds cheveux les parfums préparés.
Mais, seule sur la proue, invoquant les étoiles,
Le vent impétueux qui soufflait dans les voiles
L'enveloppe. Étonnée, et loin des matelots,
Elle crie, elle tombe, elle est au sein des flots.

Elle est au sein des flots, la jeune Tarentine !
Son beau corps a roulé sous la vague marine.
Thétis, les yeux en pleurs, dans le creux d'un rocher,
Aux monstres dévorants eut soin de le cacher.
Par ses ordres bientôt les belles Néréides
L'élèvent au-dessus des demeures humides,
Le portent au rivage, et dans ce monument
L'ont, au cap du Zéphyr, déposé mollement.
Puis de loin, à grands cris appelant leurs compagnes,
Et les Nymphes des bois, des sources, des montagnes,
Toutes, frappant leur sein, et traînant un long deuil,
Répétèrent : « Hélas ! » autour de son cercueil.
Hélas ! chez ton amant tu n'es point ramenée.
Tu n'as point revêtu ta robe d'hyménée.
L'or autour de tes bras n'a point serré de nœuds.
Les doux parfums n'ont point coulé sur tes cheveux.

Bucoliques

ÉPILOGUE

Voilà ce que chantait aux Naïades prochaines
Ma Muse jeune et fraîche, amante des fontaines,
Assise au fond d'un antre aux Nymphes consacré,
D'acanthe et d'aubépine et de lierre entouré.
L'Amour, qui l'écoutait caché dans le feuillage,
Sortit, la salua Sirène du bocage.
Ses blonds cheveux flottants par lui furent pressés,
D'hyacinthe et de myrte en couronne tressés :
« Car ta voix, lui dit-il, est douce à mon oreille,
Comme le doux cytise à la mielleuse abeille. »

Bucoliques

LA MORT D'HERCULE

Œta, mont ennobli par cette nuit ardente,
Quand l'infidèle époux d'une épouse imprudente
Reçut de son amour un présent trop jaloux,
Victime du Centaure immolé par ses coups.
Il brise tes forêts. Ta cime épaisse et sombre
En un bûcher immense amoncelle sans nombre
Les sapins résineux que son bras a ployés.
Il y porte la flamme. Il monte ; sous ses pieds
Étend du vieux lion la dépouille héroïque,
Et l'œil au ciel, la main sur sa massue antique,
Attend sa récompense et l'heure d'être un dieu.
Le vent souffle et mugit. Le bûcher tout en feu
Brille autour du héros ; et la flamme rapide
Porte aux palais divins l'âme du grand Alcide !

Bucoliques

L'ASTRONOMIE

. . . .

Salut, ô belle nuit, étincelante et sombre,
Consacrée au repos. Ô silence de l'ombre
Qui n'entends que la voix de mes vers, et les cris
De la rive aréneuse où se brise Thétis.
Muse, Muse nocturne, apporte-moi ma lyre.
Comme un fier météore, en ton brûlant délire,
Lance-toi dans l'espace ; et pour franchir les airs,
Prends les ailes des vents, les ailes des éclairs,
Les bonds de la comète aux longs cheveux de flamme.
Mes vers impatients élancés de mon âme
Veulent parler aux Dieux, et volent où reluit
L'enthousiasme errant, fils de la belle nuit.
Accours, grande nature, ô mère du génie.
Accours, reine du monde, éternelle Uranie,
Soit que tes pas divins sur l'astre du Lion
Ou sur les triples feux du superbe Orion
Marchent, ou soit qu'au loin, fugitive emportée,
Tu suives les détours de la voie argentée,
Soleils amoncelés dans le céleste azur
Où le peuple a cru voir les traces d'un lait pur ;
Descends, non, porte-moi sur ta route brûlante ;
Que je m'élève au ciel comme une flamme ardente.
Déjà ce corps pesant se détache de moi.
Adieu, tombeau de chair, je ne suis plus à toi.
Terre, fuis sous mes pas. L'éther où le ciel nage
M'aspire. Je parcours l'océan sans rivage.
Plus de nuit. Je n'ai plus, d'un globe opaque et dur
Entre le jour et moi, l'impénétrable mur.
Plus de nuit, et mon œil et se perd et se mêle
Dans les torrents profonds de lumière éternelle.
Me voici sur les feux que le langage humain
Nomme Cassiopée et l'Ourse et le Dauphin.
Maintenant la Couronne autour de moi s'embrase.
Ici l'Aigle et le Cygne et la Lyre et Pégase.

Et voici que plus loin le Serpent tortueux
Noue autour de mes pas ses anneaux lumineux.
Féconde immensité, les esprits magnanimes
Aiment à se plonger dans tes vivants abîmes ;
Abîmes de clartés, où, libre de ses fers,
L'homme siège au conseil qui créa l'univers ;
Où l'âme remontant à sa grande origine
Sent qu'elle est une part de l'essence divine.

FANNY

4

Fanny, l'heureux mortel qui près de toi respire
Sait, à te voir parler et rougir et sourire,
De quels hôtes divins le ciel est habité.
La grâce, la candeur, la naïve innocence
      Ont, depuis ton enfance,
De tout ce qui peut plaire enrichi ta beauté.

Sur tes traits, où ton âme imprime sa noblesse,
Elles ont su mêler aux roses de jeunesse
Ces roses de pudeur, charmes plus séduisants ;
Et remplir tes regards, tes lèvres, ton langage,
      De ce miel dont le sage
Cherche lui-même en vain à défendre ses sens.

Oh ! que n'ai-je moi seul tout l'éclat et la gloire
Que donnent les talents, la beauté, la victoire,
Pour fixer sur moi seul ta pensée et tes yeux !
Que, loin de moi, ton cœur fût plein de ma présence,
      Comme, dans ton absence,
Ton aspect bien-aimé m'est présent en tous lieux !

Je pense : elle était là. Tous disaient : « Qu'elle est belle ! »
Tels furent ses regards, sa démarche fut telle,
Et tels ses vêtements, sa voix et ses discours.
Sur ce gazon assise, et dominant la plaine,
      Des méandres de Seine,
Rêveuse, elle suivait les obliques détours.

Ainsi dans les forêts j'erre avec ton image :
Ainsi le jeune faon, dans son désert sauvage,
D'un plomb volant percé, précipite ses pas.
Il emporte en fuyant sa mortelle blessure ;
      Couché près d'une eau pure,
Palpitant, hors d'haleine, il attend le trépas.

Les Amours

LA JEUNE CAPTIVE

« L'épi naissant mûrit de la faux respecté ;
Sans crainte du pressoir, le pampre tout l'été
      Boit les doux présents de l'aurore ;
Et moi, comme lui belle, et jeune comme lui,
Quoi que l'heure présente ait de trouble et d'ennui,
      Je ne veux point mourir encore.

Qu'un stoïque aux yeux secs vole embrasser la mort :
Moi je pleure et j'espère. Au noir souffle du nord
      Je plie et relève ma tête.
S'il est des jours amers, il en est de si doux !
Hélas ! quel miel jamais n'a laissé de dégoûts ?
      Quelle mer n'a point de tempête ?

L'illusion féconde habite dans mon sein.
D'une prison sur moi les murs pèsent en vain,
      J'ai les ailes de l'espérance.
Échappée aux réseaux de l'oiseleur cruel,
Plus vive, plus heureuse, aux campagnes du ciel
      Philomèle chante et s'élance.

Est-ce à moi de mourir ? Tranquille je m'endors
Et tranquille je veille ; et ma veille aux remords
      Ni mon sommeil ne sont en proie.
Ma bienvenue au jour me rit dans tous les yeux ;
Sur des fronts abattus, mon aspect dans ces lieux
      Ranime presque de la joie.

Mon beau voyage encore est si loin de sa fin !
Je pars, et des ormeaux qui bordent le chemin
      J'ai passé les premiers à peine.
Au banquet de la vie à peine commencé,
Un instant seulement mes lèvres ont pressé
      La coupe en mes mains encor pleine.

Je ne suis qu'au printemps. Je veux voir la moisson,
Et comme le soleil, de saison en saison,
      Je veux achever mon année.
Brillante sur ma tige et l'honneur du jardin,
Je n'ai vu luire encor que les feux du matin ;
      Je veux achever ma journée.

Ô mort ! tu peux attendre ; éloigne, éloigne-toi ;
Va consoler les cœurs que la honte, l'effroi,
      Le pâle désespoir dévore.
Pour moi Palès encore a des asiles verts,
Les Amours des baisers, les Muses des concerts.
      Je ne veux point mourir encore. »

Ainsi, triste et captif, ma lyre toutefois
S'éveillait, écoutant ces plaintes, cette voix,
      Ces vœux d'une jeune captive ;
Et secouant le faix de mes jours languissants,
Aux douces lois des vers je pliai les accents
      De sa bouche aimable et naïve.

Ces chants, de ma prison témoins harmonieux,
Feront à quelque amant des loisirs studieux
      Chercher quelle fut cette belle.
La grâce décorait son front et ses discours,
Et, comme elle, craindront de voir finir leurs jours
      Ceux qui les passeront près d'elle.

Odes, VII

ODE

STROPHE I

Ô mon esprit, au sein des cieux,
Loin de tes noirs chagrins, une ardente allégresse
Te transporte au banquet des Dieux,
Lorsque ta haine vengeresse,
Rallumée à l'aspect et du meurtre et du sang,
Ouvre de ton carquois l'inépuisable flanc.
De là vole aux méchants ta flèche redoutée,
D'un fiel vertueux humectée,
Qu'au défaut de la foudre, esclave du plus fort,
Sur tous ces pontifes du crime,
Par qui la France, aveugle et stupide victime,
Palpite et se débat contre une longue mort,
Lance ta fureur magnanime.

ANTISTROPHE I

Tu crois, d'un éternel flambeau
Éclairant les forfaits d'une horde ennemie,
Défendre à la nuit du tombeau
D'ensevelir leur infamie.
Déjà tu penses voir, des bouts de l'univers,
Sur la foi de ma lyre, au nom de ces pervers,
Frémir l'horreur publique ; et d'honneur et de gloire
Fleurir ma tombe et ta mémoire ;
Comme autrefois tes Grecs accouraient à des jeux,
Quand l'amoureux fleuve d'Élide
Eut de traîtres punis vu triompher Alcide ;
Ou quand l'arc pythien d'un reptile fangeux
Eut purgé les champs de Phocide.

ÉPODE I

Vain espoir ! inutile soin !
Ramper est des humains l'ambition commune ;
    C'est leur plaisir, c'est leur besoin.
Voir fatigue leurs yeux ; juger les importune ;
    Ils laissent juger la Fortune,
Qui fait juste celui qu'elle fait tout-puissant ;
Ce n'est point la vertu, c'est la seule victoire
    Qui donne et l'honneur et la gloire :
Teint du sang des vaincus, tout glaive est innocent.

Odes, **IV**

ÏAMBES

IX

Comme un dernier rayon, comme un dernier zéphyre
　　　　　Animent la fin d'un beau jour,
Au pied de l'échafaud j'essaye encor ma lyre.
　　　　　Peut-être est-ce bientôt mon tour.
Peut-être avant que l'heure en cercle promenée
　　　　　Ait posé sur l'émail brillant,
Dans les soixante pas où sa route est bornée,
　　　　　Son pied sonore et vigilant,
Le sommeil du tombeau pressera ma paupière.
　　　　　Avant que de ses deux moitiés
Ce vers que je commence ait atteint la dernière,
　　　　　Peut-être en ces murs effrayés
Le messager de mort, noir recruteur des ombres,
　　　　　Escorté d'infâmes soldats,
Ébranlant de mon nom ces longs corridors sombres,
　　　　　Où seul dans la foule à grands pas
J'erre, aiguisant ces dards persécuteurs du crime,
　　　　　Du juste trop faibles soutiens,
Sur mes lèvres soudain va suspendre la rime ;
　　　　　Et chargeant mes bras de liens,
Me traîner, amassant en foule à mon passage
　　　　　Mes tristes compagnons reclus,
Qui me connaissaient tous avant l'affreux message,
　　　　　Mais qui ne me connaissent plus.
Eh bien ! j'ai trop vécu. Quelle franchise auguste,
　　　　　De mâle constance et d'honneur,
Quels exemples sacrés, doux à l'âme du juste,
　　　　　Pour lui quelle ombre de bonheur,
Quelle Thémis terrible aux têtes criminelles,
　　　　　Quels pleurs d'une noble pitié,
Des antiques bienfaits quels souvenirs fidèles,
　　　　　Quels beaux échanges d'amitié,
Font digne de regrets l'habitacle des hommes ?
　　　　　La peur fugitive est leur dieu,
La bassesse, la feinte. Ah ! lâches que nous sommes

Tous, oui, tous. Adieu, terre, adieu.
Vienne, vienne la mort ! – Que la mort me délivre !
Ainsi donc mon cœur abattu
Cède au poids de ses maux ? Non, non. Puissé-je vivre !
Ma vie importe à la vertu.
Car l'honnête homme enfin, victime de l'outrage,
Dans les cachots, près du cercueil,
Relève plus altiers son front et son langage,
Brillants d'un généreux orgueil.
S'il est écrit aux cieux que jamais une épée
N'étincellera dans mes mains,
Dans l'encre et l'amertume une autre arme trempée
Peut encor servir les humains.
Justice, Vérité, si ma main, si ma bouche,
Si mes pensers les plus secrets
Ne froncèrent jamais votre sourcil farouche,
Et si les infâmes progrès,
Si la risée atroce, ou, plus atroce injure,
L'encens de hideux scélérats
Ont pénétré vos cœurs d'une longue blessure ;
Sauvez-moi. Conservez un bras
Qui lance votre foudre, un amant qui vous venge.
Mourir sans vider mon carquois !
Sans percer, sans fouler, sans pétrir dans leur fange
Ces bourreaux barbouilleurs de lois !
Ces vers cadavéreux de la France asservie,
Égorgée ! Ô mon cher trésor,
Ô ma plume ! fiel, bile, horreur, dieux de ma vie !
Par vous seuls je respire encor :
Comme la poix brûlante agitée en ses veines
Ressuscite un flambeau mourant,
Je souffre ; mais je vis. Par vous, loin de mes peines,
D'espérance un vaste torrent
Me transporte. Sans vous, comme un poison livide,
L'invisible dent du chagrin,
Mes amis opprimés, du menteur homicide
Les succès, le sceptre d'airain,
Des bons proscrits par lui la mort ou la ruine,
L'opprobre de subir sa loi,

Tout eût tari ma vie ; ou contre ma poitrine
   Dirigé mon poignard. Mais quoi !
Nul ne resterait donc pour attendrir l'histoire
   Sur tant de justes massacrés ?
Pour consoler leurs fils, leurs veuves, leur mémoire ?
   Pour que des brigands abhorrés
Frémissent aux portraits noirs de leur ressemblance ?
   Pour descendre jusqu'aux enfers
Nouer le triple fouet, le fouet de la vengeance
   Déjà levé sur ces pervers ?
Pour cracher sur leurs noms, pour chanter leur supplice ?
   Allons, étouffe tes clameurs ;
Souffre, ô cœur gros de haine, affamé de justice.
   Toi, Vertu, pleure si je meurs.

XIXe SIÈCLE

C'est pour la poésie un temps d'extraordinaire floraison. De grands créateurs, et même parmi eux des géants comme Hugo, y occupent presque sans discontinuité l'espace littéraire. On assiste à un incessant jaillissement d'œuvres majeures.

Aucune époque, depuis celle de la Renaissance qui a vu les poètes lyonnais et ceux de la Pléiade, n'a donné cette impression de puissant renouveau poétique. Entre-temps, cependant, de vrais poètes sont apparus, mais malgré leur présence, la poésie elle-même, comme un fleuve enfoui dont les résurgences sporadiques ne suffisent pas à dessiner le cours, a semblé un secret perdu. Et soudain de nouvelles sources d'inspiration sont trouvées, de nouveaux territoires ouverts, bientôt un autre langage s'instaure.

La conscience de l'individualité irréductible du moi, et la volonté de sincérité poussée jusqu'à l'impudeur, sont l'un des premiers fondements de cette mutation. L'intrusion du sentiment en littérature, préparée par des prosateurs tels que Rousseau ou Bernardin de Saint-Pierre, joue en effet un rôle essentiel dans la rupture avec le passé. Désormais le cœur, ce cœur « trop sensible », se fait entendre sans détour. Confidences ou aveux, récits d'une crise passagère ou expression d'une douleur inconsolable, échappent à la raison, cette mesure universelle, et traduisent une expérience unique. L'homme qui parle est seul, et le moi s'expose nu. La sincérité du ton, ses accents passionnés rendent bien pâle, tout à coup, la plainte des élégiaques du siècle précédent, atténuée et comme figée dans le carcan des conventions. D'ailleurs le poète ne s'en tient pas à l'expression de ses tourments, il s'efforce de trouver à travers eux un sens à sa destinée, et d'y voir les étapes spirituelles de son histoire qui est avant tout « l'histoire d'une âme »[1]. Le lien qui s'établit entre poésie et religion est, en effet, l'autre aspect fondamental de la poésie au XIXᵉ siècle. La restauration des institutions et des dogmes n'est sans doute pas étrangère à cette redécouverte, ou l'influence du *Génie du christianisme*, mais le poète, qui emprunte à la Bible ses figures et ses récits, n'est pas le porte-parole d'une révélation déjà élaborée qui lui serait extérieure : l'inspiration lui permet de se passer de l'entremise des religions établies. Comme le prophète biblique il est l'interprète du divin, capable d'assumer ce que Paul Bénichou appelle un « sacerdoce laïque », et de donner aux hommes une réponse à leurs interrogations, un enseignement du mystère.

À ses anciens domaines la poésie annexe d'autres contrées. Même les plus familiers d'entre eux apparaissent dans une autre perspective. Ainsi la Nature n'est plus seulement un décor qui séduit l'œil et les sens, ou la figure tutélaire de la Terre-mère. Soit qu'il se fonde en elle dans une sorte de miraculeuse symbiose où s'abolit la conscience de son être propre, soit qu'il prenne, de par sa présence « triste et superbe », la mesure de sa finitude et de la soif d'infini qui l'habite, le poète, qu'il l'aime ou qu'il la craigne, se sent en proie à une puissance qui l'arrache à ses limites et l'égare parfois jusqu'au vertige.

Le rêve, comme l'a montré Albert Béguin, est la grande conquête du romantisme. Le poète franchit désormais les « portes d'ivoire ou de corne »[2] qui séparent le monde des vivants de l'obscur au-delà, et glisse de la contemplation rêveuse aux visions. De cette transgression du réel naissent des images inouïes que le siècle suivant s'attachera encore à inventorier. Dès maintenant elles font du poète un voyant.

Le souci d'innover dans la langue elle-même surgit très tôt. Si Hugo revendique l'honneur d'avoir le premier rompu avec les vocables fanés et les convenances désuètes, « le bonnet rouge » qu'il a mis « au vieux dictionnaire » devient au fil du siècle de plus en plus éclatant. Il s'agit moins alors de libérer la langue que d'en créer une nouvelle, séparée de l'autre, et donc, au sens propre, sacrée.

---

1. Hugo. — 2. Nerval.

Le plus grand enrichissement apporté par ce siècle dans l'expression poétique, ce n'est sans doute ni la pratique de rythmes nouveaux, ni le développement du poème en prose, ni celui du vers libre, mais plutôt le statut royal accordé à la métaphore. Figure poétique essentielle, elle a toujours été un ornement recherché, mais la théorie des correspondances fait d'elle tout autre chose : elle est désormais le lien entre le visible et l'invisible. Elle ne se fonde plus sur la trouvaille gratuite ou l'approximation ingénieuse ; liant deux réalités distinctes, elle témoigne d'un ordre caché, elle est la traduction nécessaire de l'unité pressentie.

La conscience de leur nouveau pouvoir va progressivement amener les poètes à se sentir responsables des autres hommes. D'où chez beaucoup d'entre eux la volonté d'épouser les combats ou les rêves de progrès de leur temps, d'être, comme le dit en substance Vigny, ceux qui lisent la route du navire dans les étoiles. À cette idée du poète civilisateur quelques-uns opposent une conception marmoréenne de l'art qui n'aurait d'autre fin que lui-même. Leur débat, s'il remet en cause la place du poète et de son œuvre dans la cité, n'en est pas moins fondé sur une vision de la poésie qui leur est commune : pour tous elle est la langue des dieux.

MARCELINE DESBORDES-VALMORE

(1786-1859)

C'est la voix d'une femme qui ouvre le siècle. Son premier recueil de vers paraît un an avant *Les Méditations*. Isolée, ne se réclamant d'aucun modèle, Marceline Desbordes-Valmore est très vite reconnue et admirée. Elle le doit d'abord à sa sincérité qui émeut. Car elle n'est pas savante comme celles qui l'ont précédée dans ce domaine, elle n'écoute que son cœur. Pourtant on croit parfois entendre en la lisant, quand elle se plaint de sa solitude et de son malheur, les accents douloureux de Christine de Pisan, et lorsqu'elle s'adresse à l'homme qu'elle aime et qui s'éloigne, ceux de l'ardente Louise Labé.

Elle écrit d'instinct, « d'une plume fougueuse et inconsciente », selon les mots de Baudelaire dans l'article élogieux qu'il lui consacre. S'il est séduit par une œuvre si étrangère à sa propre conception de l'art, et dont il n'ignore, dit-il, ni les défauts ni les négligences de forme, c'est qu'il y rencontre des passages dont la force soudaine « l'enlève irrésistiblement au fond du ciel poétique ». Hugo est sans doute l'un des premiers à avoir apporté sa caution de poète et de critique à cette œuvre dans laquelle il perçoit « les trouées profondes faites à l'improviste dans le cœur, les explosions magiques de la passion ».

À cause de l'intensité affective qu'elle confère au verbe poétique, pour la musicalité de certains de ses poèmes – son sens inné de l'harmonie se marque particulièrement dans l'usage qu'elle fait avant Verlaine du rythme impair –, et surtout parce que son inspiration est de nature « essentiellement rêveuse », comme le dit encore Hugo, les poètes de son temps se devaient d'accueillir parmi eux cette romantique avant la lettre.

S'IL L'AVAIT SU

S'il avait su quelle âme il a blessée,
Larmes du cœur, s'il avait pu vous voir,
Ah ! si ce cœur, trop plein de sa pensée,
De l'exprimer eût gardé le pouvoir,
Changer ainsi n'eût pas été possible ;
Fier de nourrir l'espoir qu'il a déçu,
À tant d'amour il eût été sensible,
            S'il avait su.

S'il avait su tout ce qu'on peut attendre
D'une âme simple, ardente et sans détour,
Il eût voulu la mienne pour l'entendre,
Comme il l'inspire, il eût connu l'amour.
Mes yeux baissés recelaient cette flamme ;
Dans leur pudeur n'a-t-il rien aperçu ?
Un tel secret valait toute son âme,
            S'il l'avait su.

Si j'avais su, moi-même, à quel empire
On s'abandonne en regardant ses yeux,
Sans le chercher comme l'air qu'on respire,
J'aurais porté mes jours sous d'autres cieux.
Il est trop tard pour renouer ma vie,
Ma vie était un doux espoir déçu.
Diras-tu pas, toi qui me l'as ravie,
            Si j'avais su !

MA CHAMBRE

Ma demeure est haute,
Donnant sur les cieux ;
La lune en est l'hôte,
Pâle et sérieux :
En bas que l'on sonne,
Qu'importe aujourd'hui ?
Ce n'est plus personne,
Quand ce n'est pas lui !

Aux autres cachée,
Je brode mes fleurs ;
Sans être fâchée,
Mon âme est en pleurs :
Le ciel bleu sans voiles,
Je le vois d'ici ;
Je vois les étoiles :
Mais l'orage aussi !

Vis-à-vis la mienne
Une chaise attend :
Elle fut la sienne,
La nôtre un instant :
D'un ruban signée,
Cette chaise est là,
Toute résignée,
Comme me voilà !

LA JEUNE FILLE ET LE RAMIER

Les rumeurs du jardin disent qu'il va pleuvoir.
Tout tressaille averti de la prochaine ondée :
Et toi qui ne lis plus sur ton livre accoudée,
Plains-tu l'absent aimé qui ne pourra te voir ?

Là-bas, pliant son aile et mouillé sous l'ombrage,
Banni de l'horizon qu'il n'atteint que des yeux,
Appelant sa compagne et regardant les cieux,
Un ramier, comme toi, soupire de l'orage.

Laissez pleuvoir, ô cœurs solitaires et doux !
Sous l'orage qui passe il renaît tant de choses.
Le soleil sans la pluie ouvrirait-il les roses ?
Amants, vous attendez, de quoi vous plaignez-vous ?

LES ROSES DE SAADI

J'ai voulu ce matin te rapporter des roses ;
Mais j'en avais tant pris dans mes ceintures closes
Que les nœuds trop serrés n'ont pu les contenir.

Les nœuds ont éclaté. Les roses envolées
Dans le vent, à la mer s'en sont toutes allées.
Elles ont suivi l'eau pour ne plus revenir.

La vague en a paru rouge et comme enflammée.
Ce soir, ma robe encore en est toute embaumée...
Respires-en sur moi l'odorant souvenir.

ALPHONSE DE LAMARTINE

(1790-1869)

La nouveauté des *Méditations poétiques*, qui marquent l'avènement du romantisme en poésie, paraît moins évidente au lecteur d'aujourd'hui qu'au public ébloui de 1820. Le recours à un vocabulaire usé par deux siècles de classicisme, et à une prosodie traditionnelle, semble inscrire le poète dans la lignée de ses prédécesseurs et révéler une continuité plutôt qu'une rupture. C'est dans le titre qu'il faut chercher l'originalité réelle de ce livre : plus que l'indication d'un contenu, il est l'annonce d'une forme poétique nouvelle qui mêle les genres connus et estompe les distinctions traditionnelles. On passe désormais, sans rupture de ton, à l'intérieur d'un même poème, du registre de la confidence personnelle à celui du grand lyrisme, de la plainte élégiaque à la réflexion philosophique la plus large. D'où peut-être le reproche fait assez souvent au poète d'être imprécis et flou. Il en conviendra lui-même plus tard, « la langue vague et indéterminée de la poésie se prête mal à la rigueur des termes que doit préciser la métaphysique ». La poésie ne peut renoncer pour autant à prendre en charge « les vastes et profonds sujets », ni cesser d'être, comme il le souhaite, « de la raison chantée ». Elle doit donc se tourner vers la langue qui lui est propre, c'est-à-dire le chant. Ce « chant intérieur qu'on appelle poésie », le poète peut l'écouter en lui, il sourd des profondeurs, il est comme l'écho de la langue des origines

Où chaque verbe était la chose avec l'image.

Dans les *Harmonies poétiques et religieuses*, Lamartine donne la mesure de son génie lyrique en liant cette musique personnelle aux grands thèmes religieux. Il avait auparavant associé, de manière tout à fait inusitée, amour divin et passion humaine, mais ici il semble avoir pleinement entendu la leçon de Chateaubriand qui mettait en lumière dans *Le Génie du christianisme* la puissance poétique de la religion du Christ. Son inspiration en acquiert une singulière ampleur. C'est alors qu'il prend peu à peu conscience de sa mission parmi les hommes. Il est le premier parmi les poètes de sa génération à concevoir son rôle comme celui d'un guide spirituel. Penseur en qui la connaissance des fins dernières de l'homme se conjugue avec celle de la réalité humaine terrestre, il a pour tâche d'éclairer ses semblables. C'est ce qu'il projette de faire lorsqu'il conçoit la grande fresque des *Visions*. Une illumination lui en a suggéré le dessein : ce sera l'épopée religieuse de l'humanité peinte à travers les réincarnations successives d'un même héros. Ce dernier montrera, de la chute initiale au rachat final, la valeur rédemptrice de la souffrance. Certes Lamartine ne pourra mener ce projet à son terme, mais les deux grands poèmes qui en constituent l'ébauche magnifique témoignent de son ambition et de sa puissance créatrice : ce sont *Jocelyn*, roman du sacrifice, qui se déroule à l'époque de la Révolution française, et *La Chute d'un ange*, épopée de l'expiation, histoire du commencement des temps.

Ce souci du destin des hommes, qu'il nomme « l'élargissement de son cœur », lui inspire d'autres œuvres, notamment son *Ode sur les Révolutions* par laquelle il invite les peuples à la poursuite du progrès, ou sa *Lettre à Félix Guillemardet*, véritable examen de son itinéraire personnel qui relate la métamorphose de sa poésie, ouverte désormais à un lyrisme plus large :

> *Frère, le temps n'est plus où j'écoutais mon âme*
> *Se plaindre et soupirer comme une faible femme...*
> *L'âme d'un seul ouverte aux plaintes de la foule*
> *A gémi toutes les douleurs.*

Pour lui mission spirituelle et action politique sont peu à peu conçues comme indissociables, aussi s'engage-t-il dès 1830 dans l'arène politique. Après l'avoir porté au sommet, 1848 met fin à

sa carrière. Il devra désormais renoncer à toute charge publique.
La fin de sa vie est assez amère ; mais ni l'échec, ni les deuils, ni
les travaux forcés littéraires qui l'accablent, n'ont jamais tari sa
veine poétique. Il compose peu avant sa mort l'un de ses plus
beaux poèmes, *La Vigne et la maison*. La richesse de ce destin, la
complexité de cette personnalité à facettes sont assez fascinantes,
moins cependant que sa science du vers fluide et mélodieux, dont
on cherche en vain comment il naît sous sa plume. Le chant
qui lui est propre semble jaillir d'une source qui nous demeure
cachée.

L'ISOLEMENT

Souvent sur la montagne, à l'ombre du vieux chêne,
Au coucher du soleil, tristement je m'assieds ;
Je promène au hasard mes regards sur la plaine,
Dont le tableau changeant se déroule à mes pieds.

Ici, gronde le fleuve aux vagues écumantes,
Il serpente, et s'enfonce en un lointain obscur ;
Là, le lac immobile étend ses eaux dormantes
Où l'étoile du soir se lève dans l'azur.

Au sommet de ces monts couronnés de bois sombres,
Le crépuscule encor jette un dernier rayon,
Et le char vaporeux de la reine des ombres
Monte, et blanchit déjà les bords de l'horizon.

Cependant, s'élançant de la flèche gothique,
Un son religieux se répand dans les airs,
Le voyageur s'arrête, et la cloche rustique
Aux derniers bruits du jour mêle de saints concerts.

Mais à ces doux tableaux mon âme indifférente
N'éprouve devant eux ni charme, ni transports,
Je contemple la terre, ainsi qu'une ombre errante :
Le soleil des vivants n'échauffe plus les morts.

De colline en colline en vain portant ma vue,
Du sud à l'aquilon, de l'aurore au couchant,
Je parcours tous les points de l'immense étendue,
Et je dis : Nulle part le bonheur ne m'attend.

Que me font ces vallons, ces palais, ces chaumières ?
Vains objets dont pour moi le charme est envolé ;
Fleuves, rochers, forêts, solitudes si chères,
Un seul être vous manque, et tout est dépeuplé.

Que le tour du soleil ou commence ou s'achève,
D'un œil indifférent je le suis dans son cours ;
En un ciel sombre ou pur qu'il se couche ou se lève,
Qu'importe le soleil ? je n'attends rien des jours.

Quand je pourrais le suivre en sa vaste carrière,
Mes yeux verraient partout le vide et les déserts ;
Je ne désire rien de tout ce qu'il éclaire,
Je ne demande rien à l'immense univers.

Mais peut-être au delà des bornes de sa sphère,
Lieux où le vrai soleil éclaire d'autres cieux,
Si je pouvais laisser ma dépouille à la terre,
Ce que j'ai tant rêvé paraîtrait à mes yeux ?

Là, je m'enivrerais à la source où j'aspire,
Là, je retrouverais et l'espoir et l'amour,
Et ce bien idéal que toute âme désire,
Et qui n'a pas de nom au terrestre séjour !

Que ne puis-je, porté sur le char de l'aurore,
Vague objet de mes vœux, m'élancer jusqu'à toi,
Sur la terre d'exil pourquoi resté-je encore ?
Il n'est rien de commun entre la terre et moi.

Quand la feuille des bois tombe dans la prairie,
Le vent du soir s'élève et l'arrache aux vallons ;
Et moi, je suis semblable à la feuille flétrie :
Emportez-moi comme elle, orageux aquilons !

Les Méditations poétiques

LE VALLON

Mon cœur, lassé de tout, même de l'espérance,
N'ira plus de ses vœux importuner le sort ;
Prêtez-moi seulement, vallons de mon enfance,
Un asile d'un jour pour attendre la mort.

Voici l'étroit sentier de l'obscure vallée :
Du flanc de ces coteaux pendent des bois épais
Qui, courbant sur mon front leur ombre entremêlée,
Me couvrent tout entier de silence et de paix.

Là, deux ruisseaux cachés sous des ponts de verdure
Tracent en serpentant les contours du vallon ;
Ils mêlent un moment leur onde et leur murmure,
Et non loin de leur source ils se perdent sans nom.

La source de mes jours comme eux s'est écoulée,
Elle a passé sans bruit, sans nom, et sans retour :
Mais leur onde est limpide, et mon âme troublée
N'aura pas réfléchi les clartés d'un beau jour.

La fraîcheur de leurs lits, l'ombre qui les couronne,
M'enchaînent tout le jour sur les bords des ruisseaux ;
Comme un enfant bercé par un chant monotone,
Mon âme s'assoupit au murmure des eaux.

Ah ! c'est là qu'entouré d'un rempart de verdure,
D'un horizon borné qui suffit à mes yeux,
J'aime à fixer mes pas, et, seul dans la nature,
À n'entendre que l'onde, à ne voir que les cieux.

J'ai trop vu, trop senti, trop aimé dans ma vie,
Je viens chercher vivant le calme du Léthé ;
Beaux lieux, soyez pour moi ces bords où l'on oublie :
L'oubli seul désormais est ma félicité.

Mon cœur est en repos, mon âme est en silence !
Le bruit lointain du monde expire en arrivant,
Comme un son éloigné qu'affaiblit la distance,
À l'oreille incertaine apporté par le vent.

D'ici je vois la vie, à travers un nuage,
S'évanouir pour moi dans l'ombre du passé ;
L'amour seul est resté ; comme une grande image
Survit seule au réveil dans un songe effacé.

Repose-toi, mon âme, en ce dernier asile,
Ainsi qu'un voyageur, qui, le cœur plein d'espoir,
S'assied avant d'entrer aux portes de la ville,
Et respire un moment l'air embaumé du soir.

Comme lui, de nos pieds secouons la poussière ;
L'homme par ce chemin ne repasse jamais :
Comme lui, respirons au bout de la carrière
Ce calme avant-coureur de l'éternelle paix.

Tes jours, sombres et courts comme des jours d'automne,
Déclinent comme l'ombre au penchant des coteaux ;
L'amitié te trahit, la pitié t'abandonne,
Et, seule, tu descends le sentier des tombeaux.

Mais la nature est là qui t'invite et qui t'aime ;
Plonge-toi dans son sein qu'elle t'ouvre toujours ;
Quand tout change pour toi, la nature est la même,
Et le même soleil se lève sur tes jours.

De lumière et d'ombrage elle t'entoure encore ;
Détache ton amour des faux biens que tu perds ;
Adore ici l'écho qu'adorait Pythagore,
Prête avec lui l'oreille aux célestes concerts.

Suis le jour dans le ciel, suis l'ombre sur la terre,
Dans les plaines de l'air vole avec l'aquilon,
Avec les doux rayons de l'astre du mystère
Glisse à travers les bois dans l'ombre du vallon.

Dieu, pour le concevoir, a fait l'intelligence ;
Sous la nature enfin découvre son auteur !
Une voix à l'esprit parle dans son silence,
Qui n'a pas entendu cette voix dans son cœur ?

Les Méditations poétiques

LE LAC

Ainsi, toujours poussés vers de nouveaux rivages,
Dans la nuit éternelle emportés sans retour,
Ne pourrons-nous jamais sur l'océan des âges
         Jeter l'ancre un seul jour ?

Ô lac ! l'année à peine a fini sa carrière,
Et près des flots chéris qu'elle devait revoir,
Regarde ! je viens seul m'asseoir sur cette pierre
         Où tu la vis s'asseoir !

Tu mugissais ainsi sous ces roches profondes,
Ainsi tu te brisais sur leurs flancs déchirés,
Ainsi le vent jetait l'écume de tes ondes
         Sur ses pieds adorés.

Un soir, t'en souvient-il ? nous voguions en silence ;
On n'entendait au loin, sur l'onde et sous les cieux,
Que le bruit des rameurs qui frappaient en cadence
         Tes flots harmonieux.

Tout à coup des accents inconnus à la terre
Du rivage charmé frappèrent les échos :
Le flot fut attentif, et la voix qui m'est chère
         Laissa tomber ces mots :

« Ô temps ! suspends ton vol, et vous, heures propices !
         Suspendez votre cours :
Laissez-nous savourer les rapides délices
         Des plus beaux de nos jours !

Assez de malheureux ici-bas vous implorent,
         Coulez, coulez pour eux ;
Prenez avec leurs jours les soins qui les dévorent,
         Oubliez les heureux.

Mais je demande en vain quelques moments encore,
        Le temps m'échappe et fuit ;
Je dis à cette nuit : Sois plus lente ; et l'aurore
        Va dissiper la nuit.

Aimons donc, aimons donc ! de l'heure fugitive,
        Hâtons-nous, jouissons !
L'homme n'a point de port, le temps n'a point de rive ;
        Il coule, et nous passons ! »

Temps jaloux, se peut-il que ces moments d'ivresse,
Où l'amour à longs flots nous verse le bonheur,
S'envolent loin de nous de la même vitesse
        Que les jours de malheur ?

Eh quoi ! n'en pourrons-nous fixer au moins la trace ?
Quoi ! passés pour jamais ! quoi ! tout entiers perdus !
Ce temps qui les donna, ce temps qui les efface,
        Ne nous les rendra plus !

Éternité, néant, passé, sombres abîmes,
Que faites-vous des jours que vous engloutissez ?
Parlez : nous rendrez-vous ces extases sublimes
        Que vous nous ravissez ?

Ô lac ! rochers muets ! grottes ! forêt obscure !
Vous, que le temps épargne ou qu'il peut rajeunir,
Gardez de cette nuit, gardez, belle nature,
        Au moins le souvenir !

Qu'il soit dans ton repos, qu'il soit dans tes orages,
Beau lac, et dans l'aspect de tes riants coteaux,
Et dans ces noirs sapins, et dans ces rocs sauvages
        Qui pendent sur tes eaux.

Qu'il soit dans le zéphyr qui frémit et qui passe,
Dans les bruits de tes bords par tes bords répétés,
Dans l'astre au front d'argent qui blanchit ta surface
    De ses molles clartés.

Que le vent qui gémit, le roseau qui soupire,
Que les parfums légers de ton air embaumé,
Que tout ce qu'on entend, l'on voit ou l'on respire,
    Tout dise : Ils ont aimé !

Les Méditations poétiques

L'AUTOMNE

Salut ! bois couronnés d'un reste de verdure !
Feuillages jaunissants sur les gazons épars !
Salut, derniers beaux jours ! le deuil de la nature
Convient à la douleur et plaît à mes regards !

Je suis d'un pas rêveur le sentier solitaire,
J'aime à revoir encor, pour la dernière fois,
Ce soleil pâlissant, dont la faible lumière
Perce à peine à mes pieds l'obscurité des bois !

Oui, dans ces jours d'automne où la nature expire,
À ses regards voilés, je trouve plus d'attraits,
C'est l'adieu d'un ami, c'est le dernier sourire
Des lèvres que la mort va fermer pour jamais !

Ainsi, prêt à quitter l'horizon de la vie,
Pleurant de mes longs jours l'espoir évanoui,
Je me retourne encore, et d'un regard d'envie
Je contemple ses biens dont je n'ai pas joui !

Terre, soleil, vallons, belle et douce nature,
Je vous dois une larme aux bords de mon tombeau ;
L'air est si parfumé ! la lumière est si pure !
Aux regards d'un mourant le soleil est si beau !

Je voudrais maintenant vider jusqu'à la lie
Ce calice mêlé de nectar et de fiel !
Au fond de cette coupe où je buvais la vie,
Peut-être restait-il une goutte de miel ?

Peut-être l'avenir me gardait-il encore
Un retour de bonheur dont l'espoir est perdu ?
Peut-être dans la foule, une âme que j'ignore
Aurait compris mon âme, et m'aurait répondu ?...

La fleur tombe en livrant ses parfums au zéphire ;
À la vie, au soleil, ce sont là ses adieux ;
Moi, je meurs ; et mon âme, au moment qu'elle expire,
S'exhale comme un son triste et mélodieux.

Les Méditations poétiques

LA TRISTESSE

L'âme triste est pareille
Au doux ciel de la nuit,
Quand l'astre qui sommeille
De la voûte vermeille
A fait tomber le bruit ;

Plus pure et plus sonore,
On y voit sur ses pas
Mille étoiles éclore,
Qu'à l'éclatante aurore
On n'y soupçonnait pas !

Des îles de lumière
Plus brillante qu'ici,
Et des mondes derrière,
Et des flots de poussière
Qui sont mondes aussi !

On entend dans l'espace
Les chœurs mystérieux
Ou du ciel qui rend grâce,
Ou de l'ange qui passe,
Ou de l'homme pieux !

Et pures étincelles
De nos âmes de feu,
Les prières mortelles
Sur leurs brûlantes ailes
Nous soulèvent un peu !

Tristesse qui m'inonde,
Coule donc de mes yeux,
Coule comme cette onde
Où la terre féconde
Voit un présent des cieux !

Et n'accuse point l'heure
Qui te ramène à Dieu !
Soit qu'il naisse ou qu'il meure,
Il faut que l'homme pleure
Ou l'exil, ou l'adieu !

Harmonies poétiques et religieuses

JOCELYN

. . . .
Quand j'eus seul devant Dieu pleuré toutes mes larmes,
Je voulus sur ces lieux si pleins de tristes charmes,
Attacher un regard avant que de mourir,
Et je passai le soir à les tous parcourir.
Oh ! qu'en peu de saisons les étés et les glaces
Avaient fait du vallon évanouir nos traces !
Et que sur ces sentiers si connus de mes pieds,
La terre en peu de jours nous avait oubliés !
La végétation, comme une mer de plantes,
Avait tout recouvert de ses vagues grimpantes,
La liane et la ronce entravaient chaque pas ;
L'herbe que je foulais ne me connaissait pas ;
Le lac, déjà souillé par les feuilles tombées,
Les rejetait partout de ses vagues plombées ;
Rien ne se reflétait dans son miroir terni,
Et son écume morte aux bords avait jauni ;
Des chênes qui couvraient l'antre de leurs racines,
Deux, hélas ! n'étaient plus que de mornes ruines,
Leurs troncs couchés à terre étaient noirs et pourris,
Les lézards de leurs cœurs s'étaient déjà nourris ;
Un seul encor debout, mais tronqué par l'orage,
Étendait vers la grotte un long bras sans feuillage,
Comme ces noirs poteaux qu'on plante avec la main
Pour surmonter la neige et marquer un chemin ;
Ah ! je connaissais trop cette fatale route ;
Mes genoux fléchissants m'entraînaient vers la voûte ;
J'y marchais pas à pas sur des monceaux mouvants
De feuillages d'automne entassés par les vents...

2e époque

LA VIGNE ET LA MAISON

PSALMODIES DE L'ÂME
DIALOGUE ENTRE MON ÂME ET MOI

MOI

Quel fardeau te pèse, ô mon âme !
Sur ce vieux lit des jours par l'ennui retourné,
Comme un fruit de douleurs qui pèse aux flancs de femme
Impatient de naître et pleurant d'être né ?
La nuit tombe, ô mon âme ! un peu de veille encore !
Ce coucher d'un soleil est d'un autre l'aurore.
Vois comme avec tes sens s'écroule ta prison !
Vois comme aux premiers vents de la précoce automne
Sur les bords de l'étang où le roseau frissonne,
S'envole brin à brin le duvet du chardon !
Vois comme de mon front la couronne est fragile !
Vois comme cet oiseau dont le nid est la tuile
Nous suit pour emporter à son frileux asile
Nos cheveux blancs pareils à la toison que file
La vieille femme assise au seuil de sa maison !

Dans un lointain qui fuit ma jeunesse recule,
Ma sève refroidie avec lenteur circule,
L'arbre quitte sa feuille et va nouer son fruit :
Ne presse pas ces jours qu'un autre doigt calcule,
Bénis plutôt ce Dieu qui place un crépuscule
Entre les bruits du soir et la paix de la nuit !
Moi qui par des concerts saluai ta naissance,
Moi qui te réveillai neuve à cette existence
Avec des chants de fête et des chants d'espérance,
Moi qui fis de ton cœur chanter chaque soupir,
Veux-tu que, remontant ma harpe qui sommeille,
Comme un David assis près d'un Saül qui veille,
     Je chante encor pour t'assoupir ?

L'ÂME

Non ! Depuis qu'en ces lieux le temps m'oublia seule,
La terre m'apparaît vieille comme une aïeule
Qui pleure ses enfants sous ses robes de deuil.
Je n'aime des longs jours que l'heure des ténèbres,

Je n'écoute des chants que ces strophes funèbres
Que sanglote le prêtre en menant un cercueil.

MOI

Pourtant le soir qui tombe a des langueurs sereines
Que la fin donne à tout, aux bonheurs comme aux peines ;
Le linceul même est tiède au cœur enseveli :
On a vidé ses yeux de ses dernières larmes,
L'âme à son désespoir trouve de tristes charmes,
Et des bonheurs perdus se sauve dans l'oubli.
Cette heure a pour nos sens des impressions douces
Comme des pas muets qui marchent sur des mousses :
C'est l'amère douceur du baiser des adieux.
De l'air plus transparent le cristal est limpide,
Des mots vaporisés l'azur vague et liquide
          S'y fond avec l'azur des cieux.

Je ne sais quel lointain y baigne toute chose,
Ainsi que le regard l'oreille s'y repose,
On entend dans l'éther glisser le moindre vol ;
C'est le pied de l'oiseau sur le rameau qui penche,
Ou la chute d'un fruit détaché de la branche
          Qui tombe du poids sur le sol.
. . . .
Viens, reconnais la place où ta vie était neuve,
N'as-tu point de douceur, dis-moi, pauvre âme veuve,
À remuer ici la cendre des jours morts ?
À revoir ton arbuste et ta demeure vide,
Comme l'insecte ailé revoit sa chrysalide,
          Balayure qui fut son corps ?
. . . .

L'ÂME

Que me fait le coteau, le toit, la vigne aride ?
Que me ferait le ciel, si le ciel était vide ?
Je ne vois en ces lieux que ceux qui n'y sont pas !
Pourquoi ramènes-tu mes regrets sur leur trace ?
Des bonheurs disparus se rappeler la place,
C'est rouvrir des cercueils pour revoir des trépas !
. . . .

II

Efface ce séjour, ô Dieu ! de ma paupière,
Ou rends-le-moi semblable à celui d'autrefois,
Quand la maison vibrait comme un grand cœur de pierre
De tous ces cœurs joyeux qui battaient sous ses toits.

À l'heure où la rosée au soleil s'évapore
Tous ces volets fermés s'ouvraient à sa chaleur,
Pour y laisser entrer, avec la tiède aurore,
Les nocturnes parfums de nos vignes en fleur.

On eût dit que ces murs respiraient comme un être
Des pampres réjouis la jeune exhalaison ;
La vie apparaissait rose, à chaque fenêtre,
Sous les beaux traits d'enfants nichés dans la maison.
. . . .

III

Puis ces bruits d'année en année
Baissèrent d'une vie, hélas ! et d'une voix,
Un fenêtre en deuil, à l'ombre condamnée,
Se ferma sous le bord des toits.

Printemps après printemps de belles fiancées
Suivirent de chers ravisseurs,
Et, par la mère en pleurs sur le seuil embrassées,
Partirent en baisant leurs sœurs.

Puis sortit un matin pour le champ où l'on pleure
Le cercueil tardif de l'aïeul,
Puis un autre, et puis deux, et puis dans la demeure
Un vieillard morne resta seul !

Puis la maison glissa sur la pente rapide
Où le temps entasse les jours ;
Puis la porte à jamais se ferma sur le vide,
Et l'ortie envahit les cours !...
. . . .

Cours familier de littérature

VIGNY

(1797-1863)

C'est lui qui donne du sacerdoce du poète la vision la plus pessimiste. La Renaissance prédisait à l'élu incompréhension ou moquerie, Vigny peint la solitude radicale du génie, privé de son droit d'être un homme au milieu des autres. Le silence de Dieu au jardin des Oliviers, à travers la déréliction du Christ, dit clairement qu'il ne faut rien attendre d'une improbable divinité et que seule la raideur stoïcienne, la sombre fierté du loup que cernent les chasseurs et qui meurt « sans jeter un cri », peut répondre au malheur de la condition humaine. Cette hauteur de ton n'exclut pas la grâce exquise de l'expression, et la beauté des images, dans cette œuvre essentiellement symbolique, donne à chaque poème une ampleur souveraine. Chacune de ces œuvres, renvoyant à autre chose qu'elle-même, se présente comme la partie visible d'une réalité morale ou spirituelle qui peut être atteinte à travers elle. L'Écriture Sainte, et la tradition chrétienne en général, fournissent au poète nombre de sujets qui se prêtent à cet élargissement. Peu soucieux du dogme, le poète agnostique interprète librement ses modèles et fait de Moïse, que saint Augustin nomme « le plus modeste des humains », la figure orgueilleuse et quasi maudite du poète-prophète.

Cependant Vigny ne rompt pas avec l'humanitarisme religieux de son siècle, il rêve d'un salut universel et d'un avènement futur du règne de l'Esprit Pur auquel tout poète doit œuvrer, même s'il est certain de ne pas le voir advenir de son vivant. En effet sa mission a un caractère christique, elle implique le sacrifice de soi. Un jour viendra où, par la voie du Beau poétique, les hommes, grâce à lui, accéderont au Bien.

L'espoir d'un paradis terrestre possible s'exprime dans le long poème de *La Maison du berger* qui est sans doute son chef-d'œuvre. Il y invite Éva, figure rêvée, à partir avec lui des « cités serviles », vers les bois et les champs. Là se trouve pour eux un refuge sûr, non par la grâce d'une Nature dont le poète connaît trop bien l'indifférence hautaine qu'il redoute, mais par le miracle de cette présence aimée à ses côtés. À travers elle il peut contempler les paysages splendides, embrasser par la pensée les temps anciens et à venir, et se regarder lui-même « au miroir d'une autre âme ». La pauvreté de la maison du berger, que sa mobilité rend libre de toute attache, ainsi que la mélancolie de ses occupants, évoquent plutôt une ascèse de vie qu'un bonheur humain, mais il semble qu'il y ait une parfaite consonance entre cet univers imaginaire et l'âme du poète car c'est l'œuvre qui lui inspire ses plus beaux vers, et certains d'entre eux, notamment dans la dernière strophe, figurent parmi les plus parfaits de la langue française.

LA MAISON DU BERGER

LETTRE À ÉVA

I

Si ton cœur, gémissant du poids de notre vie,
Se traîne et se débat comme un aigle blessé,
Portant comme le sien, sur son aile asservie,
Tout un monde fatal, écrasant et glacé ;
S'il ne bat qu'en saignant par sa plaie immortelle,
S'il ne voit plus l'amour, son étoile fidèle,
Éclairer pour lui seul l'horizon effacé ;

Si ton âme enchaînée, ainsi que l'est mon âme,
Lasse de son boulet et de son pain amer,
Sur sa galère en deuil laisse tomber la rame,
Penche sa tête pâle et pleure sur la mer,
Et, cherchant dans les flots une route inconnue,
Y voit, en frissonnant, sur son épaule nue
La lettre sociale écrite avec le fer ;

Si ton corps, frémissant des passions secrètes,
S'indigne des regards, timide et palpitant ;
S'il cherche à sa beauté de profondes retraites
Pour la mieux dérober au profane insultant ;
Si ta lèvre se sèche au poison des mensonges,
Si ton beau front rougit de passer dans les songes
D'un impur inconnu qui te voit et t'entend :

Pars courageusement, laisse toutes les villes ;
Ne ternis plus tes pieds aux poudres du chemin ;
Du haut de nos pensers vois les cités serviles
Comme les rocs fatals de l'esclavage humain.
Les grands bois et les champs sont de vastes asiles,
Libres comme la mer autour des sombres îles.
Marche à travers les champs une fleur à la main.

La Nature t'attend dans un silence austère ;
L'herbe élève à tes pieds son nuage des soirs,
Et le soupir d'adieu du soleil à la terre
Balance les beaux lys comme des encensoirs.
La forêt a voilé ses colonnes profondes,
La montagne se cache, et sur les pâles ondes
Le saule a suspendu ses chastes reposoirs.

Le crépuscule ami s'endort dans la vallée
Sur l'herbe d'émeraude et sur l'or du gazon,
Sous les timides joncs de la source isolée
Et sous le bois rêveur qui tremble à l'horizon,
Se balance en fuyant dans les grappes sauvages,
Jette son manteau gris sur le bord des rivages,
Et des fleurs de la nuit entrouvre la prison.

Il est sur ma montagne une épaisse bruyère
Où les pas du chasseur ont peine à se plonger,
Qui plus haut que nos fronts lève sa tête altière,
Et garde dans la nuit le pâtre et l'étranger.
Viens y cacher l'amour et ta divine faute ;
Si l'herbe est agitée ou n'est pas assez haute,
J'y roulerai pour toi la Maison du Berger.

Elle va doucement avec ses quatre roues,
Son toit n'est pas plus haut que ton front et tes yeux ;
La couleur du corail et celle de tes joues
Teignent le char nocturne et ses muets essieux.
Le seuil est parfumé, l'alcôve est large et sombre,
Et là, parmi les fleurs, nous trouverons dans l'ombre,
Pour nos cheveux unis, un lit silencieux.

Je verrai, si tu veux, les pays de la neige,
Ceux où l'astre amoureux dévore et resplendit,
Ceux que heurtent les vents, ceux que la neige assiège,
Ceux où le pôle obscur sous sa glace est maudit.
Nous suivrons du hasard la course vagabonde.
Que m'importe le jour ? que m'importe le monde ?
Je dirai qu'ils sont beaux quand tes yeux l'auront dit.
. . . .

II

Poésie ! ô trésor ! perle de la pensée !
Les tumultes du cœur, comme ceux de la mer,
Ne sauraient empêcher ta robe nuancée
D'amasser les couleurs qui doivent te former.
Mais sitôt qu'il te voit briller sur un front mâle,
Troublé de ta lueur mystérieuse et pâle,
Le vulgaire effrayé commence à blasphémer.

Le pur enthousiasme est craint des faibles âmes
Qui ne sauraient porter son ardeur et son poids.
Pourquoi le fuir ? – La vie est double dans les flammes.
D'autres flambeaux divins nous brûlent quelquefois :
C'est le Soleil du ciel, c'est l'Amour, c'est la Vie ;
Mais qui de les éteindre a jamais eu l'envie ?
Tout en les maudissant, on les chérit tous trois.

La Muse a mérité les insolents sourires
Et les soupçons moqueurs qu'éveille son aspect.
Dès que son œil chercha le regard des satyres,
Sa parole trembla, son serment fut suspect,
Il lui fut interdit d'enseigner la sagesse.
Au passant du chemin elle criait : « Largesse ! »
Le passant lui donna sans crainte et sans respect.

Ah ! fille sans pudeur, fille du saint Orphée,
Que n'as-tu conservé ta belle gravité !
Tu n'irais pas ainsi, d'une voix étouffée,
Chanter aux carrefours impurs de la cité ;
Tu n'aurais pas collé sur le coin de ta bouche
Le coquet madrigal, piquant comme une mouche,
Et, près de ton œil bleu, l'équivoque effronté.

Tu tombas dès l'enfance et, dans la folle Grèce,
Un vieillard, t'enivrant de son baiser jaloux,
Releva le premier ta robe de prêtresse,
Et parmi les garçons t'assit sur ses genoux.
De ce baiser mordant ton front porte la trace ;
Tu chantas en buvant dans les banquets d'Horace
Et Voltaire à la cour te traîna devant nous.

Vestale aux feux éteints ! les hommes les plus graves
Ne posent qu'à demi ta couronne à leur front ;
Ils se croient arrêtés, marchant dans tes entraves,
Et n'être que poète est pour eux un affront.
Ils jettent leurs pensers aux vents de la tribune,
Et ces vents, aveuglés comme l'est la Fortune,
Les rouleront comme elle et les emporteront.

Ils sont fiers et hautains dans leur fausse attitude,
Mais le sol tremble aux pieds de ces tribuns romains.
Leurs discours passagers flattent avec étude
La foule qui les presse et qui leur bat des mains ;
Toujours renouvelé sous ses étroits portiques,
Ce parterre ne jette aux acteurs politiques
Que des fleurs sans parfums, souvent sans lendemains.

Ils ont pour horizon leur salle de spectacle ;
La chambre où ces élus donnent leurs faux combats
Jette en vain, dans son temple, un incertain oracle,
Le peuple entend de loin le bruit de leurs débats ;
Mais il regarde encore le jeu des assemblées
De l'œil dont ses enfants et ses femmes troublées
Voient le terrible essai des vapeurs aux cent bras.

L'ombrageux paysan gronde à voir qu'on dételle,
Et que pour le scrutin on quitte le labour.
Cependant le dédain de la chose immortelle
Tient jusqu'au fond du cœur quelque avocat d'un jour.
Lui qui doute de l'âme, il croit à ses paroles.
Poésie, il se rit de tes graves symboles,
Ô toi des vrais penseurs impérissable amour !

Comment se garderaient les profondes pensées
Sans rassembler leurs feux dans ton diamant pur
Qui conserve si bien leurs splendeurs condensées ?
Ce fin miroir solide, étincelant et dur,
Reste des nations mortes, durable pierre
Qu'on trouve sous ses pieds lorsque dans la poussière
On cherche les cités sans en voir un seul mur.

Diamant sans rival, que tes feux illuminent
Les pas lents et tardifs de l'humaine Raison !
Il faut, pour voir de loin les peuples qui cheminent,
Que le Berger t'enchâsse au toit de sa Maison.
Le jour n'est pas levé. – Nous en sommes encore
Au premier rayon blanc qui précède l'aurore
Et dessine la terre aux bords de l'horizon.

Les peuples tout enfants à peine se découvrent
Par-dessus les buissons nés pendant leur sommeil,
Et leur main, à travers les ronces qu'ils entrouvrent,
Met aux coups mutuels le premier appareil.
La barbarie encor tient nos pieds dans sa gaîne.
Le marbre des vieux temps jusqu'aux reins nous enchaîne,
Et tout homme énergique au dieu Terme est pareil.

Mais notre esprit rapide en mouvements abonde :
Ouvrons tout l'arsenal de ses puissants ressorts.
L'Invisible est réel. Les âmes ont leur monde
Où sont accumulés d'impalpables trésors.
Le Seigneur contient tout dans ses deux bras immenses,
Son Verbe est le séjour de nos intelligences,
Comme ici-bas l'espace est celui de nos corps.

III

Éva, qui donc es-tu ? Sais-tu bien ta nature ?
Sais-tu quel est ici ton but et ton devoir ?
Sais-tu que, pour punir l'homme, sa créature,
D'avoir porté la main sur l'arbre du savoir,
Dieu permit qu'avant tout, de l'amour de soi-même
En tout temps, à tout âge, il fît son bien suprême,
Tourmenté de s'aimer, tourmenté de se voir ?

Mais si Dieu près de lui t'a voulu mettre, ô femme !
Compagne délicate ! Éva ! sais-tu pourquoi ?
C'est pour qu'il se regarde au miroir d'une autre âme,
Qu'il entende ce chant qui ne vient que de toi :
– L'enthousiasme pur dans une voix suave.
C'est afin que tu sois son juge et son esclave
Et règnes sur sa vie en vivant sous sa loi.

Ta parole joyeuse a des mots despotiques ;
Tes yeux sont si puissants, ton aspect est si fort,
Que les rois d'Orient ont dit dans leurs cantiques
Ton regard redoutable à l'égal de la mort ;
Chacun cherche à fléchir tes jugements rapides...
– Mais ton cœur, qui dément tes formes intrépides,
Cède sans coup férir aux rudesses du sort.

Ta pensée a des bonds comme ceux des gazelles,
Mais ne saurait marcher sans guide et sans appui.
Le sol meurtrit ses pieds, l'air fatigue ses ailes,
Son œil se ferme au jour dès que le jour a lui ;
Parfois sur les hauts lieux d'un seul élan posée,
Troublée au bruit des vents, ta mobile pensée
Ne peut seule y veiller sans crainte et sans ennui.

Mais aussi tu n'as rien de nos lâches prudences,
Ton cœur vibre et résonne au cri de l'opprimé,
Comme dans une église aux austères silences
L'orgue entend un soupir et soupire alarmé.
Tes paroles de feu meuvent les multitudes,
Tes pleurs lavent l'injure et les ingratitudes,
Tu pousses par le bras l'homme... Il se lève armé.

C'est à toi qu'il convient d'ouïr les grandes plaintes
Que l'humanité triste exhale sourdement.
Quand le cœur est gonflé d'indignations saintes,
L'air des cités l'étouffe à chaque battement.
Mais de loin les soupirs des tourmentes civiles,
S'unissant au-dessus du charbon noir des villes,
Ne forment qu'un grand mot qu'on entend clairement.

Viens donc ! le ciel pour moi n'est plus qu'une auréole
Qui t'entoure d'azur, t'éclaire et te défend ;
La montagne est ton temple et le bois sa coupole,
L'oiseau n'est sur la fleur balancé par le vent,
Et la fleur ne parfume et l'oiseau ne soupire
Que pour mieux enchanter l'air que ton sein respire ;
La terre est le tapis de tes beaux pieds d'enfant.

Éva, j'aimerai tout dans les choses créées,
Je les contemplerai dans ton regard rêveur
Qui partout répandra ses flammes colorées,
Son repos gracieux, sa magique saveur :
Sur mon cœur déchiré viens poser ta main pure,
Ne me laisse jamais seul avec la Nature,
Car je la connais trop pour n'en pas avoir peur.

Elle me dit : « Je suis l'impassible théâtre
Que ne peut remuer le pied de ses acteurs ;
Mes marches d'émeraude et mes parvis d'albâtre,
Mes colonnes de marbre ont les dieux pour sculpteurs.
Je n'entends ni vos cris ni vos soupirs ; à peine
Je sens passer sur moi la comédie humaine
Qui cherche en vain au ciel ses muets spectateurs,

Je roule avec dédain, sans voir et sans entendre,
À côté des fourmis les populations ;
Je ne distingue pas leur terrier de leur cendre,
J'ignore en les portant les noms des nations.
On me dit une mère et je suis une tombe.
Mon hiver prend vos morts comme son hécatombe,
Mon printemps ne sent pas vos adorations.

Avant vous, j'étais belle et toujours parfumée,
J'abandonnais au vent mes cheveux tout entiers,
Je suivais dans les cieux ma route accoutumée
Sur l'axe harmonieux des divins balanciers.
Après vous, traversant l'espace où tout s'élance,
J'irai seule et sereine, en un chaste silence
Je fendrai l'air du front et de mes seins altiers. »

C'est là ce que me dit sa voix triste et superbe,
Et dans mon cœur alors je la hais, et je vois
Notre sang dans son onde et nos morts sous son herbe
Nourrissant de leurs sucs la racine des bois.
Et je dis à mes yeux qui lui trouvaient des charmes :
« Ailleurs tous vos regards, ailleurs toutes vos larmes,
Aimez ce que jamais on ne verra deux fois. »

Oh ! qui verra deux fois ta grâce et ta tendresse,
Ange doux et plaintif qui parle en soupirant ?
Qui naîtra comme toi portant une caresse
Dans chaque éclair tombé de ton regard mourant,
Dans les balancements de ta tête penchée,
Dans ta taille dolente et mollement couchée
Et dans ton pur sourire amoureux et souffrant ?

Vivez, froide Nature, et revivez sans cesse
Sous nos pieds, sur nos fronts, puisque c'est votre loi ;
Vivez, et dédaignez, si vous êtes déesse,
L'Homme, humble passager, qui dut vous être un Roi ;
Plus que tout votre règne et que ses splendeurs vaines
J'aime la majesté des souffrances humaines :
Vous ne recevrez pas un cri d'amour de moi.

Mais toi, ne veux-tu pas, voyageuse indolente,
Rêver sur mon épaule, en y posant ton front ?
Viens du paisible seuil de la maison roulante
Voir ceux qui sont passés et ceux qui passeront.
Tous les tableaux humains qu'un Esprit pur m'apporte
S'animeront pour toi, quand devant notre porte
Les grands pays muets longuement s'étendront.

Nous marcherons ainsi, ne laissant que notre ombre
Sur cette terre ingrate où les morts ont passé ;
Nous nous parlerons d'eux à l'heure où tout est sombre,
Où tu te plais à suivre un chemin effacé,
À rêver, appuyée aux branches incertaines,
Pleurant, comme Diane au bord de ses fontaines,
Ton amour taciturne et toujours menacé.

LA MORT DU LOUP

I

Les nuages couraient sur la lune enflammée
Comme sur l'incendie on voit fuir la fumée,
Et les bois étaient noirs jusques à l'horizon.
– Nous marchions, sans parler, dans l'humide gazon,
Dans la bruyère épaisse et dans les hautes brandes,
Lorsque, sous des sapins pareils à ceux des Landes,
Nous avons aperçu les grands ongles marqués
Par les loups voyageurs que nous avions traqués.
Nous avons écouté, retenant notre haleine
Et le pas suspendu. – Ni le bois ni la plaine
Ne poussaient un soupir dans les airs ; seulement
La girouette en deuil criait au firmament ;
Car le vent, élevé bien au-dessus des terres,
N'effleurait de ses pieds que les tours solitaires,
Et les chênes d'en bas, contre les rocs penchés,
Sur leurs coudes semblaient endormis et couchés.
– Rien ne bruissait donc, lorsque, baissant la tête,
Le plus vieux des chasseurs qui s'étaient mis en quête
A regardé le sable en s'y couchant ; bientôt,
Lui que jamais ici l'on ne vit en défaut,
A déclaré tout bas que ces marques récentes
Annonçaient la démarche et les griffes puissantes
De deux grands loups-cerviers et de deux louveteaux.
Nous avons tous alors préparé nos couteaux
Et, cachant nos fusils et leurs lueurs trop blanches,
Nous allions, pas à pas, en écartant les branches.
Trois s'arrêtent, et moi, cherchant ce qu'ils voyaient,
J'aperçois tout à coup deux yeux qui flamboyaient,
Et je vois au delà quatre formes légères
Qui dansaient sous la lune au milieu des bruyères,
Comme font chaque jour, à grand bruit, sous nos yeux,
Quand le maître revient, les lévriers joyeux.
Leur forme était semblable et semblable la danse ;

Mais les enfants du Loup se jouaient en silence,
Sachant bien qu'à deux pas, ne dormant qu'à demi,
Se couche dans ses murs l'homme, leur ennemi.
Le père était debout, et plus loin, contre un arbre,
Sa Louve reposait comme celle de marbre
Qu'adoraient les Romains, et dont les flancs velus
Couvaient les demi-dieux Rémus et Romulus.
Le Loup vient et s'assied, les deux jambes dressées
Par leurs ongles crochus dans le sable enfoncées.
Il s'est jugé perdu, puisqu'il était surpris,
Sa retraite coupée et tous ses chemins pris ;
Alors il a saisi, dans sa gueule brûlante,
Du chien le plus hardi la gorge pantelante
Et n'a pas desserré ses mâchoires de fer,
Malgré nos coups de feu qui traversaient sa chair
Et nos couteaux aigus qui, comme des tenailles,
Se croisaient en plongeant dans ses larges entrailles,
Jusqu'au dernier moment où le chien étranglé,
Mort longtemps avant lui, sous ses pieds a roulé.
Le Loup le quitte alors et puis il nous regarde.
Les couteaux lui restaient au flanc jusqu'à la garde,
Le clouaient au gazon tout baigné dans son sang ;
Nos fusils l'entouraient en sinistre croissant.
– Il nous regarde encore, ensuite il se recouche
Tout en léchant le sang répandu sur sa bouche,
Et, sans daigner savoir comment il a péri,
Refermant ses grands yeux, meurt sans jeter un cri.

II

J'ai reposé mon front sur mon fusil sans poudre,
Me prenant à penser, et n'ai pu me résoudre
À poursuivre sa Louve et ses fils qui, tous trois,
Avaient voulu l'attendre, et, comme je le crois,
Sans ses deux louveteaux la belle et sombre veuve
Ne l'eût pas laissé seul subir la grande épreuve ;
Mais son devoir était de les sauver, afin
De pouvoir leur apprendre à bien souffrir la faim,

À ne jamais entrer dans le pacte des villes
Que l'homme a fait avec les animaux serviles
Qui chassent devant lui, pour avoir le coucher,
Les premiers possesseurs du bois et du rocher.

III

Hélas ! ai-je pensé, malgré ce grand nom d'Hommes,
Que j'ai honte de nous, débiles que nous sommes !
Comment on doit quitter la vie et tous ses maux,
C'est vous qui le savez, sublimes animaux !
À voir ce que l'on fut sur terre et ce qu'on laisse,
Seul le silence est grand ; tout le reste est faiblesse.
– Ah ! je t'ai bien compris, sauvage voyageur,
Et ton dernier regard m'est allé jusqu'au cœur !
Il disait : « Si tu peux, fais que ton âme arrive,
À force de rester studieuse et pensive,
Jusqu'à ce haut degré de stoïque fierté
Où, naissant dans les bois, j'ai tout d'abord monté.
Gémir, pleurer, prier est également lâche.
Fais énergiquement ta longue et lourde tâche
Dans la voie où le Sort a voulu t'appeler.
Puis après, comme moi, souffre et meurs sans parler. »

Écrit au château du M***, 1843

LE MONT DES OLIVIERS

III

Ainsi le divin Fils parlait au divin Père.
Il se prosterne encore, il attend, il espère...
Mais il renonce et dit : « Que votre volonté
Soit faite et non la mienne, et pour l'Éternité ! »
Une terreur profonde, une angoisse infinie
Redoublent sa torture et sa lente agonie.
Il regarde longtemps, longtemps cherche sans voir.
Comme un marbre de deuil tout le ciel était noir ;
La Terre sans clartés, sans astre et sans aurore,
Et sans clartés de l'âme ainsi qu'elle est encore,
Frémissait. – Dans le bois il entendit des pas,
Et puis il vit rôder la torche de Judas.

LE SILENCE

S'il est vrai qu'au Jardin sacré des Écritures,
Le Fils de l'homme ait dit ce qu'on voit rapporté ;
Muet, aveugle et sourd au cri des créatures,
Si le Ciel nous laissa comme un monde avorté,
Le juste opposera le dédain à l'absence
Et ne répondra plus que par un froid silence
Au silence éternel de la Divinité.

2 avril 1862

VICTOR HUGO

(1802-1885)

Comment évoquer le génie poétique de Victor Hugo ? Peut-être par une image. Celle d'un arbre immense ombrageant tout son siècle, déployé dans le ciel comme le chêne de la fable, avec des frondaisons bruissantes de mots et de chants, et dont les racines s'enfoncent « dans la profondeur noire », jusqu'au royaume des morts. Le tronc noueux et puissant, figurant ici son courage dans les luttes et les deuils, et une fermeté que la tempête de l'exil ne put ébranler, peut aussi suggérer sa présence passionnée au monde, à toute forme de vie, fût-ce la plus humble, et le jaillissement inextinguible de la sève.

Dans les milliers de pages de ses poèmes culminent les divers courants de son époque. Ceux du romantisme pittoresque, intimiste, humanitaire ou prophétique y trouvent leur expression la plus magistrale et aussi la plus durable, car on les entend encore dans sa voix longtemps après qu'ils se sont tus autour de lui. Toutes les cordes de la lyre, depuis le murmure de la confidence jusqu'à l'âpre véhémence de la satire, résonnent dans cette œuvre. Hugo utilise en se jouant les multiples ressources du vers et imprime au poème, à sa guise, aussi bien le rythme saccadé du galop que le large déroulement de la vague. Quant à ses sujets, il les prend indifféremment dans la réalité familière, la nature ou l'histoire. Son œil, à l'acuité légendaire, est capable de saisir le détail, de cerner les contours de l'objet, mais, comme le montrent aussi ses dessins, le contemplateur succède souvent en lui au « regardeur », et suscite alors l'apparition fantastique. Il a, depuis longtemps en effet, découvert la voie qui fait accéder aux visions.

Ce n'est pas celle du « dérèglement des sens », mais la pente insensible qui le conduit de la simple rêverie où s'estompent les choses vues, au basculement dans l'au-delà des apparences.

La prodigieuse diversité de ses registres n'empêche pas de reconnaître en chacun d'eux, du croquis à la fresque, le même Hugo. Partout, à des degrés divers, on retrouve des mots et des rimes, des énumérations et des antithèses où l'on croirait qu'il se parodie. Sa voix, dit Gaëtan Picon, « ne s'écarte jamais d'elle-même ». C'est toujours le déferlement de la parole, le jaillissement d'une poésie ininterrompue, comme une mer montante du langage à laquelle il s'abandonnerait :

« Les mots heurtent le front comme l'eau le récif. »

Le retour, de plus en plus obsédant à partir de l'exil, de « formidable » rimant avec « insondable », ou de « funèbre » annonçant « ténèbre », les longs alignements énumératifs, un système d'oppositions binaires où la pensée semble captive, sont autant de traits qui découragent le lecteur épris du rare et du précieux, et qui ont valu bien des sarcasmes au poète. Mais il ne conçoit pas de renoncer à des modes d'expression qui peuvent passer pour des approximations ou des faiblesses, tant cette monotonie répétitive est pour lui consubstantielle à la poésie et nécessaire à sa mission. L'habile arrangeur de vers qu'il savait être cède la place désormais au prophète porteur de révélations. Son devoir est de communiquer aux hommes les secrets qu'il a pénétrés. Peindre le combat du Bien et du Mal, qui est aussi celui de la lumière et de l'ombre, c'est-à-dire de l'esprit et de la matière, voilà sa tâche. Expliquer que notre monde est celui de l'expiation, et donc éclairer d'un jour nouveau la souffrance des hommes. Car toute vie paie le prix des fautes d'une vie antérieure. Par là chacune d'elles peut se racheter et remonter sur l'échelle invisible qui relie les profondeurs au sommet divin. Certains seront, à cause de leurs crimes, ravalés pour un temps au rang de l'animalité ou plus bas encore, mais, à la fin des temps, tous, jusqu'à Satan lui-même, obtiendront le pardon divin. Il n'y a pas d'enfer éternel, toutes les créatures un jour « s'étoileront ».

Dans l'attente de ce salut universel, le contemplateur porte sur toutes choses, sans exclusive, un regard de pitié. Il sait que « tout vit, tout est plein d'âmes ». D'où ces vers surprenants :

> *J'aime l'araignée et j'aime l'ortie*
> *Parce qu'on les hait...*

Car cette étrange cosmogonie anime ou sous-tend la plupart de ses poèmes, c'est elle qui nous vaut tant de formes et d'idées récurrentes jusqu'au vertige.

On a souvent rapproché la vision du monde de Hugo de théologies ou de théosophies auxquelles, en effet, elle s'apparente. Le poète connaissait probablement les idées de Ballanche et sa *Palingénésie*, mais il n'a pas conçu un système ou froidement élaboré une théorie à partir de modèles existants, même si ces derniers se sont mêlés à ses rêveries visionnaires. Cela a surgi en lui, comme jaillissant de façon incontrôlable, dans le tête-à-tête harassant qu'il entretient avec les forces obscures. Il en mesure le danger, la menace de la folie est constamment présente à son esprit. Il n'en poursuit pas moins sa quête. Comme le lui rappellent les tables tournantes, entre l'aveuglement de l'ignorance et l'obscurité du mystère, nous n'avons que le choix du noir.

Pourquoi cette voix étrangère qui le dépossède de sa propre voix s'est-elle frayée un chemin à travers lui ? Il l'ignore. Son destin lui demeure une énigme. On le dit obsédé de soi, jouant sans cesse avec des « EGO HUGO » au graphisme démesuré, on peut voir là plutôt une question insistante sur son identité, et sa fascination terrifiée devant une élection inexplicable. Car il dit aussi la déperdition étrange de son être propre, la dilution du moi réduit à n'être que le trait d'union entre ce monde et un ailleurs insondable :

> *Moi qu'on nomme le poète,*
> *Je suis dans la nuit muette*
> *L'escalier mystérieux.*
> *Je suis l'escalier Ténèbres ;*
> *Dans mes spirales funèbres*
> *L'ombre ouvre ses vagues yeux.*

Parfois il attribue son destin à l'étrange similitude qu'il perçoit entre le cosmos en creux, sorte de Babel inversée, qui nous enserre et la caverne obscure de son crâne :

> *J'interroge l'abîme étant moi-même gouffre.*

Il entretient avec l'univers, et surtout le ciel nocturne ou l'océan, ses témoins privilégiés, ce que Pierre Albouy appelle « une intimité épouvantée ». Mais il ne se dérobe pas à sa tâche, il est « l'homme-devoir » qui œuvre aussi à cette amélioration terrestre de la condition humaine que le Progrès rendra possible, au triomphe de la justice ici-bas, à l'avènement d'une République universelle, à la naissance des États-Unis d'Europe.

Sa conception de la fonction du poète, quelle qu'en soit la grandeur, nous toucherait moins si elle n'avait porté en elle un puissant moteur de création mythologique, comme on le voit dans *La Légende des siècles* ou dans les grands poèmes inachevés de *Dieu* ou de *La Fin de Satan* ; et si elle n'avait suscité les métaphores splendides dont son œuvre foisonne. S'il faut n'en citer qu'une, on choisira celle que Borgès aimait entre toutes :

L'hydre Univers tordant son corps écaillé d'astres.

LE PAS D'ARMES DU ROI JEAN

Çà, qu'on selle,
Écuyer,
Mon fidèle
Destrier.
Mon cœur ploie
Sous la joie,
Quand je broie
L'étrier.

Par saint-Gille,
Viens-nous-en,
Mon agile
Alezan ;
Viens, écoute,
Par la route,
Voir la joute
Du roi Jean.

. . . .

Nous qui sommes,
De par Dieu,
Gentilshommes
De haut lieu,
Il faut faire
Bruit sur terre,
Et la guerre
N'est qu'un jeu.

Ma vieille âme
Enrageait ;
Car ma lame,
Que rongeait
Cette rouille
Qui la souille,
En quenouille
Se changeait.

Cette ville,
Aux longs cris,
Qui profile
Son front gris,
Des toits frêles,
Cent tourelles,
Clochers grêles,
C'est Paris !

Quelle foule,
Par mon sceau !
Qui s'écoule
En ruisseau,
Et se rue,
Incongrue,
Par la rue
Saint-Marceau.

Notre-Dame !
Que c'est beau !
Sur mon âme
De corbeau,
Voudrais être
Clerc ou prêtre
Pour y mettre
Mon tombeau !

. . . .

On commence.
Le beffroi !
Coups de lance,
Cris d'effroi !
On se forge,
On s'égorge,
Par saint-George !
Par le roi !

La cohue,
Flot de fer,
Frappe, hue,
Remplit l'air,
Et, profonde,
Tourne et gronde,
Comme une onde
Sur la mer.

Dans la plaine
Un éclair
Se promène
Vaste et clair ;
Quels mélanges !
Sang et franges !
Plaisirs d'anges !
Bruit d'enfer !

. . . .

Dans l'orage,
Lys courbé,
Un beau page
Est tombé.
Il se pâme,
Il rend l'âme ;
Il réclame
Un abbé.

La fanfare
Aux sons d'or,
Qui t'effare,
Sonne encore
Pour sa chute ;
Triste lutte
De la flûte
Et du cor !

. . . .

Çà, mon frère,
Viens, rentrons
Dans notre aire
De barons.
Va plus vite,
Car au gîte
Qui t'invite,
Trouverons,

Toi, l'avoine
Du matin,
Moi, le moine
Augustin,
Ce saint homme
Suivant Rome,
Qui m'assomme
De latin,

Et rédige
En romain
Tout prodige
De ma main,
Qu'à ma charge
Il émarge
Sur un large
Parchemin.

Un vrai sire
Châtelain
Laisse écrire
Le vilain ;
Sa main digne,
Quand il signe,
Égratigne
Le vélin.

24-26 juin 1828

Odes et Ballades, Ballade Douzième

LES DJINNS

E como i gru van cantando lor lai
Facendo in aer di se lunga riga,
Cosi vid'io venir traendo guai
Ombre portate dalla detta briga.

                              DANTE

Et comme les grues qui font dans l'air de
longues files vont chantant leur plainte, ainsi
je vis venir traînant des gémissements les
ombres emportées par cette tempête.

Murs, ville,
Et port,
Asile
De mort,
Mer grise
Où brise,
La brise,
Tout dort.

Dans la plaine
Naît un bruit.
C'est l'haleine
De la nuit.
Elle brame
Comme une âme
Qu'une flamme
Toujours suit !

La voix plus haute
Semble un grelot. –
D'un nain qui saute
C'est le galop.
Il fuit, s'élance,
Puis en cadence
Sur un pied danse
Au bout d'un flot.

La rumeur approche,
L'écho la redit.
C'est comme la cloche
D'un couvent maudit ; –
Comme un bruit de foule,
Qui tonne et qui roule,
Et tantôt s'écroule,
Et tantôt grandit.

Dieu ! la voix sépulcrale
Des Djinns !... Quel bruit ils font !
Fuyons sous la spirale
De l'escalier profond.
Déjà s'éteint ma lampe,
Et l'ombre de la rampe,
Qui le long du mur rampe,
Monte jusqu'au plafond.

C'est l'essaim des Djinns qui passe,
Et tourbillonne en sifflant !
Les ifs, que leur vol fracasse,
Craquent comme un pin brûlant.
Leur troupeau, lourd et rapide,
Volant dans l'espace vide,
Semble un nuage livide
Qui porte un éclair au flanc.

Ils sont tout près ! – Tenons fermée
Cette salle, où nous les narguons.
Quel bruit dehors ! Hideuse armée
De vampires et de dragons !
La poutre du toit descellée
Ploie ainsi qu'une herbe mouillée,
Et la vieille porte rouillée
Tremble, à déraciner ses gonds !

Cris de l'enfer ! voix qui hurle et qui pleure !
L'horrible essaim, poussé par l'aquilon,
Sans doute, ô ciel ! s'abat sur ma demeure.
Le mur fléchit sous le noir bataillon.
La maison crie et chancelle penchée,
Et l'on dirait que, du sol arrachée,
Ainsi qu'il chasse une feuille séchée,
Le vent la roule avec leur tourbillon !

Prophète ! si ta main me sauve
De ces impurs démons des soirs,
J'irai prosterner mon front chauve
Devant tes sacrés encensoirs !
Fais que sur ces portes fidèles
Meure leur souffle d'étincelles,
Et qu'en vain l'ongle de leurs ailes
Grince et crie à ces vitraux noirs !

Ils sont passés ! – Leur cohorte
S'envole, et fuit, et leurs pieds
Cessent de battre ma porte
De leurs coups multipliés.
L'air est plein d'un bruit de chaînes,
Et dans les forêts prochaines
Frissonnent tous les grands chênes,
Sous leur vol de feu pliés !

De leurs ailes lointaines
Le battement décroît,
Si confus dans les plaines,
Si faible, que l'on croit
Ouïr la sauterelle
Crier d'une voix grêle,
Ou pétiller la grêle,
Sur le plomb d'un vieux toit.

D'étranges syllabes
Nous viennent encor ; –
Ainsi, des arabes
Quand sonne le cor,
Un chant sur la grève
Par instants s'élève,
Et l'enfant qui rêve
Fait des rêves d'or.

Les Djinns funèbres,
Fils du trépas,
Dans les ténèbres
Pressent leurs pas ;
Leur essaim gronde :
Ainsi, profonde,
Murmure une onde
Qu'on ne voit pas.

Ce bruit vague
Qui s'endort,
C'est la vague
Sur le bord ;
C'est la plainte,
Presque éteinte,
D'une sainte
Pour un mort.

On doute
La nuit...
J'écoute : –
Tout fuit,
Tout passe ;
L'espace
Efface
Le bruit.

28 août 1828

Les Orientales

EXTASE

Et j'entendis une grande voix.

APOCALYPSE

J'étais seul près des flots, par une nuit d'étoiles.
Pas un nuage aux cieux, sur les mers pas de voiles.
Mes yeux plongeaient plus loin que le monde réel.
Et les bois, et les monts, et toute la nature,
Semblaient interroger dans un confus murmure
   Les flots des mers, les feux du ciel.

Et les étoiles d'or, légions infinies,
À voix haute, à voix basse, avec mille harmonies,
Disaient, en inclinant leurs couronnes de feu ;
Et les flots bleus, que rien ne gouverne et n'arrête,
Disaient, en recourbant l'écume de leur crête :
   – C'est le Seigneur, le Seigneur Dieu !

25 novembre 1828

Les Orientales

SOLEILS COUCHANTS

Merveilleux tableaux que la vue découvre à la pensée.

CH. NODIER

I

J'aime les soirs sereins et beaux, j'aime les soirs,
Soit qu'ils dorent le front des antiques manoirs
    Ensevelis dans les feuillages ;
Soit que la brume au loin s'allonge en bancs de feu ;
Soit que mille rayons brisent dans un ciel bleu
    À des archipels de nuages.

Oh ! regardez le ciel ! cent nuages mouvants,
Amoncelés là-haut sous le souffle des vents,
    Groupent leurs formes inconnues ;
Sous leurs flots par moments flamboie un pâle éclair,
Comme si tout à coup quelque géant de l'air
    Tirait son glaive dans les nues.

Le soleil, à travers leurs ombres, brille encor ;
Tantôt fait, à l'égal des larges dômes d'or,
    Luire le toit d'une chaumière ;
Ou dispute aux brouillards les vagues horizons ;
Ou découpe, en tombant sur les sombres gazons,
    Comme de grands lacs de lumière.

Puis voilà qu'on croit voir, dans le ciel balayé,
Pendre un grand crocodile au dos large et rayé,
    Aux trois rangs de dents acérées ;
Sous son ventre plombé glisse un rayon du soir ;
Cent nuages ardents luisent sous son flanc noir
    Comme des écailles dorées.

Puis se dresse un palais. Puis l'air tremble, et tout fuit.
L'édifice effrayant des nuages détruit
        S'écroule en ruines pressées ;
Il jonche au loin le ciel, et ses cônes vermeils
Pendent, la pointe en bas, sur nos têtes, pareils
        À des montagnes renversées.

Ces nuages de plomb, d'or, de cuivre, de fer,
Où l'ouragan, la trombe, et la foudre, et l'enfer
        Dorment avec de sourds murmures,
C'est Dieu qui les suspend en foule aux cieux profonds,
Comme un guerrier qui pend aux poutres des plafonds
        Ses retentissantes armures.

Tout s'en va ! Le soleil, d'en haut précipité,
Comme un globe d'airain qui, rouge, est rejeté
        Dans les fournaises remuées,
En tombant sur leurs flots que son choc désunit
Fait en flocons de feu jaillir jusqu'au zénith
        L'ardente écume des nuées.

Oh ! contemplez le ciel ! et dès qu'a fui le jour,
En tout temps, en tout lieu, d'un ineffable amour,
        Regardez à travers ses voiles ;
Un mystère est au fond de leur grave beauté,
L'hiver, quand ils sont noirs comme un linceul, l'été,
        Quand la nuit les brode d'étoiles.

                    Novembre 1828

V

Quelquefois, sous les plis des nuages trompeurs,
Loin dans l'air, à travers les brèches des vapeurs
        Par le vent du soir remuées,
Derrière les derniers brouillards, plus loin encor,
Apparaissent soudain les mille étages d'or
        D'un édifice de nuées !

Et l'œil épouvanté, par-delà tous nos cieux,
Sur une île de l'air au vol audacieux,
      Dans l'éther libre aventurée,
L'œil croit voir jusqu'au ciel monter, monter toujours,
Avec ses escaliers, ses ponts, ses grandes tours,
      Quelque Babel démesurée !

Septembre 1828

VI

Le soleil s'est couché ce soir dans les nuées.
Demain viendra l'orage, et le soir, et la nuit ;
Puis l'aube, et ses clartés de vapeurs obstruées ;
Puis les nuits, puis les jours, pas du temps qui s'enfuit !

Tous ces jours passeront ; ils passeront en foule
Sur la face des mers, sur la face des monts,
Sur les fleuves d'argent, sur les forêts où roule
Comme un hymne confus des morts que nous aimons.

Et la face des eaux, et le front des montagnes,
Ridés et non vieillis, et les bois toujours verts
S'iront rajeunissant ; le fleuve des campagnes
Prendra sans cesse aux monts le flot qu'il donne aux mers.

Mais moi, sous chaque jour courbant plus bas ma tête,
Je passe, et, refroidi sous ce soleil joyeux,
Je m'en irai bientôt, au milieu de la fête,
Sans que rien manque au monde immense et radieux !

22 avril 1829

Les Feuilles d'automne

TRISTESSE D'OLYMPIO

Les champs n'étaient point noirs, les cieux n'étaient pas mornes ;
Non, le jour rayonnait dans un azur sans bornes
       Sur la terre étendu,
L'air était plein d'encens et les prés de verdures
Quand il revit ces lieux où par tant de blessures
       Son cœur s'est répandu.

L'automne souriait ; les coteaux vers la plaine
Penchaient leurs bois charmants qui jaunissaient à peine ;
       Le ciel était doré ;
Et les oiseaux, tournés vers celui que tout nomme,
Disant peut-être à Dieu quelque chose de l'homme,
       Chantaient leur chant sacré.

Il voulut tout revoir, l'étang près de la source,
La masure où l'aumône avait vidé leur bourse,
       Le vieux frêne plié,
Les retraites d'amour au fond des bois perdues,
L'arbre où dans les baisers leurs âmes confondues
       Avaient tout oublié.

Il chercha le jardin, la maison isolée,
La grille d'où l'œil plonge en une oblique allée,
       Les vergers en talus.
Pâle, il marchait. – Au bruit de son pas grave et sombre,
Il voyait à chaque arbre, hélas ! se dresser l'ombre
       Des jours qui ne sont plus.

Il entendait frémir dans la forêt qu'il aime
Ce doux vent qui, faisant tout vibrer en nous-même,
       Y réveille l'amour,
Et, remuant le chêne ou balançant la rose,
Semble l'âme de tout qui va sur chaque chose
       Se poser tour à tour.

Les feuilles qui gisaient dans le bois solitaire,
S'efforçant sous ses pas de s'élever de terre,
          Couraient dans le jardin ;
Ainsi, parfois, quand l'âme est triste, nos pensées
S'envolent un moment sur leurs ailes blessées,
          Puis retombent soudain.

Il contempla longtemps les formes magnifiques
Que la nature prend dans les champs pacifiques ;
          Il rêva jusqu'au soir ;
Tout le jour il erra le long de la ravine,
Admirant tour à tour le ciel, face divine,
          Le lac, divin miroir.

Hélas ! se rappelant ses douces aventures,
Regardant, sans entrer, par-dessus les clôtures,
          Ainsi qu'un paria,
Il erra tout le jour. Vers l'heure où la nuit tombe,
Il se sentit le cœur triste comme une tombe,
          Alors il s'écria :

– « Ô douleur ! j'ai voulu, moi dont l'âme est troublée,
Savoir si l'urne encor conservait la liqueur,
Et voir ce qu'avait fait cette heureuse vallée
De tout ce que j'avais laissé là de mon cœur !

Que peu de temps suffit pour changer toutes choses !
Nature au front serein, comme vous oubliez !
Et comme vous brisez dans vos métamorphoses
Les fils mystérieux où nos cœurs sont liés !

Nos chambres de feuillage en halliers sont changées !
L'arbre où fut notre chiffre est mort ou renversé ;
Nos roses dans l'enclos ont été ravagées
Par les petits enfants qui sautent le fossé.

Un mur clôt la fontaine où, par l'heure échauffée,
Folâtre, elle buvait en descendant des bois ;
Elle prenait de l'eau dans sa main, douce fée,
Et laissait retomber des perles de ses doigts !

On a pavé la route âpre et mal aplanie,
Où, dans le sable pur se dessinant si bien,
Et de sa petitesse étalant l'ironie,
Son pied charmant semblait rire à côté du mien.

La borne du chemin, qui vit des jours sans nombre,
Où jadis pour m'attendre elle aimait à s'asseoir,
S'est usée en heurtant, lorsque la route est sombre,
Les grands chars gémissants qui reviennent le soir.

La forêt ici manque et là s'est agrandie.
De tout ce qui fut nous presque rien n'est vivant ;
Et, comme un tas de cendre éteinte et refroidie,
L'amas des souvenirs se disperse à tout vent !

N'existons-nous donc plus ? Avons-nous eu notre heure ?
Rien ne la rendra-t-il à nos cris superflus ?
L'air joue avec la branche au moment où je pleure ;
Ma maison me regarde et ne me connaît plus.

D'autres vont maintenant passer où nous passâmes.
Nous y sommes venus, d'autres vont y venir ;
Et le songe qu'avaient ébauché nos deux âmes,
Ils le continueront sans pouvoir le finir !

Car personne ici-bas ne termine et n'achève ;
Les pires des humains sont comme les meilleurs ;
Nous nous réveillons tous au même endroit du rêve.
Tout commence en ce monde et tout finit ailleurs.

Oui, d'autres à leur tour viendront, couples sans tache,
Puiser dans cet asile heureux, calme, enchanté,
Tout ce que la nature à l'amour qui se cache
Mêle de rêverie et de solennité !

D'autres auront nos champs, nos sentiers, nos retraites,
Ton bois, ma bien aimée, est à des inconnus.
D'autres femmes viendront, baigneuses indiscrètes,
Troubler le flot sacré qu'ont touché tes pieds nus.

Quoi donc ! c'est vainement qu'ici nous nous aimâmes !
Rien ne nous restera de ces coteaux fleuris
Où nous fondions notre être en y mêlant nos flammes !
L'impassible nature a déjà tout repris.

Oh ! dites-moi, ravins, frais ruisseaux, treilles mûres,
Rameaux chargés de nids, grottes, forêts, buissons,
Est-ce que vous ferez pour d'autres vos murmures ?
Est-ce que vous direz à d'autres vos chansons ?

Nous vous comprenions tant ! doux, attentifs, austères,
Tous nos échos s'ouvraient si bien à votre voix !
Et nous prêtions si bien, sans troubler vos mystères,
L'oreille aux mots profonds que vous dites parfois !

Répondez, vallon pur, répondez, solitude,
Ô nature abritée en ce désert si beau,
Lorsque nous dormirons tous deux dans l'attitude
Que donne aux morts pensifs la forme du tombeau ;

Est-ce que vous serez à ce point insensible
De nous savoir couchés, morts avec nos amours,
Et de continuer votre fête paisible,
Et de toujours sourire et de chanter toujours ?

Est-ce que, nous sentant errer dans vos retraites,
Fantômes reconnus par vos monts et vos bois,
Vous ne nous direz pas de ces choses secrètes
Qu'on dit en revoyant des amis d'autrefois ?

Est-ce que vous pourrez, sans tristesse et sans plainte,
Voir nos ombres flotter où marchèrent nos pas,
Et la voir m'entraîner, dans une morne étreinte,
Vers quelque source en pleurs qui sanglote tout bas ?

Et s'il est quelque part, dans l'ombre où rien ne veille,
Deux amants sous vos fleurs abritant leurs transports,
Ne leur irez-vous pas murmurer à l'oreille :
— Vous qui vivez, donnez une pensée aux morts !

Dieu nous prête un moment les prés et les fontaines,
Les grands bois frissonnants, les rocs profonds et sourds,
Et les cieux azurés et les lacs et les plaines,
Pour y mettre nos cœurs, nos rêves, nos amours ;

Puis il nous les retire. Il souffle notre flamme ;
Il plonge dans la nuit l'antre où nous rayonnons ;
Et dit à la vallée, où s'imprima notre âme,
D'effacer notre trace et d'oublier nos noms.

« Eh bien ! oubliez-nous, maison, jardin, ombrages !
Herbe, use notre seuil ! ronce, cache nos pas !
Chantez, oiseaux ! ruisseaux, coulez ! croissez, feuillages !
Ceux que vous oubliez ne vous oublieront pas.

Car vous êtes pour nous l'ombre de l'amour même !
Vous êtes l'oasis qu'on rencontre en chemin !
Vous êtes, ô vallon, la retraite suprême
Où nous avons pleuré nous tenant par la main !

Toutes les passions s'éloignent avec l'âge,
L'une emportant son masque et l'autre son couteau,
Comme un essaim chantant d'histrions en voyage
Dont le groupe décroît derrière le coteau.

Mais toi, rien ne t'efface, amour ! toi qui nous charmes,
Toi qui, torche ou flambeau, luis dans notre brouillard !
Tu nous tiens par la joie, et surtout par les larmes.
Jeune homme on te maudit, on t'adore vieillard.

Dans ces jours où la tête au poids des ans s'incline,
Où l'homme, sans projets, sans but, sans visions,
Sent qu'il n'est déjà plus qu'une tombe en ruine
Où gisent ses vertus et ses illusions ;

Quand notre âme en rêvant descend dans nos entrailles,
Comptant dans notre cœur, qu'enfin la glace atteint,
Comme on compte les morts sur un champ de batailles,
Chaque douleur tombée et chaque songe éteint,

Comme quelqu'un qui cherche en tenant une lampe,
Loin des objets réels, loin du monde rieur,
Elle arrive à pas lents par une obscure rampe
Jusqu'au fond désolé du gouffre intérieur ;

Et là, dans cette nuit qu'aucun rayon n'étoile,
L'âme, en un repli sombre où tout semble finir,
Sent quelque chose encor palpiter sous un voile... –
C'est toi qui dors dans l'ombre, ô sacré souvenir ! »

21 octobre 1837

Les Rayons et les ombres, **XXXIV**

Puisque le juste est dans l'abîme,
Puisqu'on donne le sceptre au crime,
Puisque tous les droits sont trahis,
Puisque les plus fiers restent mornes,
Puisqu'on affiche au coin des bornes
Le déshonneur de mon pays ;

Ô République de nos pères,
Grand Panthéon plein de lumières,
Dôme d'or dans le libre azur,
Temple des ombres immortelles,
Puisqu'on vient avec des échelles
Coller l'empire sur ton mur ;

Puisque toute âme est affaiblie,
Puisqu'on rampe, puisqu'on oublie
Le vrai, le pur, le grand, le beau,
Les yeux indignés de l'histoire,
L'honneur, la loi, le droit, la gloire,
Et ceux qui sont dans le tombeau ;

Je t'aime, exil ! douleur, je t'aime !
Tristesse, sois mon diadème !
Je t'aime, altière pauvreté !
J'aime ma porte aux vents battue.
J'aime le deuil, grave statue
Qui vient s'asseoir à mon côté.

J'aime le malheur qui m'éprouve,
Et cette ombre où je vous retrouve,
Ô vous à qui mon cœur sourit,
Dignité, foi, vertu voilée,
Toi, liberté, fière exilée,
Et toi, dévouement, grand proscrit !

J'aime cette île solitaire,
Jersey, que la libre Angleterre
Couvre de son vieux pavillon,
L'eau noire, par moments accrue,
Le navire, errante charrue,
Le flot, mystérieux sillon.

J'aime ta mouette, ô mer profonde,
Qui secoue en perles ton onde
Sur son aile aux fauves couleurs,
Plonge dans les lames géantes,
Et sort de ces gueules béantes
Comme l'âme sort des douleurs.

J'aime la roche solennelle
D'où j'entends la plainte éternelle,
Sans trêve comme le remords,
Toujours renaissant dans les ombres,
Des vagues sur les écueils sombres,
Des mères sur leurs enfants morts.

10 décembre. Jersey

Les Châtiments,
Livre Deuxième, V

CHANSON

Nous nous promenions parmi les décombres
          À Rozel-Tower,
Et nous écoutions les paroles sombres
          Que disait la mer.

L'énorme océan, – car nous entendîmes
          Ses vagues chansons, –
Disait : « Paraissez, vérités sublimes
          Et bleus horizons !

Le monde captif, sans lois et sans règles,
          Est aux oppresseurs ;
Volez dans les cieux, ailes des grands aigles,
          Esprits des penseurs !

Naissez, levez-vous sur les flots sonores,
          Sur les flots vermeils,
Faites dans la nuit poindre vos aurores,
          Peuples et soleils !

Vous, – laissez passer la foudre et la brume,
          Les vents et les cris,
Affrontez l'orage, affrontez l'écume,
          Rochers et proscrits ! »

Jersey, 5 août 1853

Les Châtiments,
Livre Sixième, VI

Sonnez, sonnez toujours, clairons de la pensée.

Quand Josué rêveur, la tête aux cieux dressée,
Suivi des siens, marchait, et, prophète irrité,
Sonnait de la trompette autour de la cité,
Au premier tour qu'il fit, le roi se mit à rire ;
Au second tour, riant toujours, il lui fit dire :
« Crois-tu donc renverser ma ville avec du vent ? »
À la troisième fois l'arche allait en avant,
Puis les trompettes, puis toute l'armée en marche,
Et les petits enfants venaient cracher sur l'arche,
Et, soufflant dans leur trompe, imitaient le clairon ;
Au quatrième tour, bravant les fils d'Aaron,
Entre les vieux créneaux tout brunis par la rouille,
Les femmes s'asseyaient en filant leur quenouille,
Et se moquaient, jetant des pierres aux hébreux ;
À la cinquième fois, sur ces murs ténébreux,
Aveugles et boiteux vinrent, et leurs huées
Raillaient le noir clairon sonnant sous les nuées ;
À la sixième fois, sur sa tour de granit
Si haute qu'au sommet l'aigle faisait son nid,
Si dure que l'éclair l'eût en vain foudroyée,
Le roi revint, riant à gorge déployée,
Et cria : « Ces hébreux sont bons musiciens ! »
Autour du roi joyeux riaient tous les anciens
Qui le soir sont assis au temple, et délibèrent.

À la septième fois, les murailles tombèrent.

19 mars 1853. Jersey

Les Châtiments,
Livre Septième, I

Elle était déchaussée, elle était décoiffée,
Assise, les pieds nus, parmi les joncs penchants ;
Moi qui passais par là, je crus voir une fée,
Et je lui dis : Veux-tu t'en venir dans les champs ?

Elle me regarda de ce regard suprême
Qui reste à la beauté quand nous en triomphons,
Et je lui dis : Veux-tu, c'est le mois où l'on aime,
Veux-tu nous en aller sous les arbres profonds ?

Elle essuya ses pieds à l'herbe de la rive ;
Elle me regarda pour la seconde fois,
Et la belle folâtre alors devint pensive.
Oh ! comme les oiseaux chantaient au fond des bois !

Comme l'eau caressait doucement le rivage !
Je vis venir à moi, dans les grands roseaux verts,
La belle fille heureuse, effarée et sauvage,
Ses cheveux dans ses yeux, et riant au travers.

                              Mont-l'Am., juin 183.

                              Les Contemplations,
                              Livre Premier, **XXI**

Quand nous habitions tous ensemble
Sur nos collines d'autrefois,
Où l'eau court, où le buisson tremble,
Dans la maison qui touche aux bois,

Elle avait dix ans, et moi trente ;
J'étais pour elle l'univers.
Oh ! comme l'herbe est odorante
Sous les arbres profonds et verts !

Elle faisait mon sort prospère,
Mon travail léger, mon ciel bleu.
Lorsqu'elle me disait : Mon père,
Tout mon cœur s'écriait : Mon Dieu !

À travers mes songes sans nombre,
J'écoutais son parler joyeux,
Et mon front s'éclairait dans l'ombre
À la lumière de ses yeux.

Elle avait l'air d'une princesse
Quand je la tenais par la main ;
Elle cherchait des fleurs sans cesse
Et des pauvres dans le chemin.

Elle donnait comme on dérobe,
En se cachant aux yeux de tous.
Oh ! la belle petite robe
Qu'elle avait, vous rappelez-vous ?

Le soir, auprès de ma bougie,
Elle jasait à petit bruit,
Tandis qu'à la vitre rougie
Heurtaient les papillons de nuit.

Les anges se miraient en elle.
Que son bonjour était charmant !
Le ciel mettait dans sa prunelle
Ce regard qui jamais ne ment.

Oh ! je l'avais, si jeune encore,
Vue apparaître en mon destin !
C'était l'enfant de mon aurore,
Et mon étoile du matin !

Quand la lune claire et sereine
Brillait aux cieux, dans ces beaux mois,
Comme nous allions dans la plaine !
Comme nous courions dans les bois !

Puis, vers la lumière isolée
Étoilant le logis obscur,
Nous revenions par la vallée
En tournant le coin du vieux mur ;

Nous revenions, cœurs pleins de flamme,
En parlant des splendeurs du ciel.
Je composais cette jeune âme
Comme l'abeille fait son miel.

Doux ange aux candides pensées,
Elle était gaie en arrivant... –
Toutes ces choses sont passées
Comme l'ombre et comme le vent !

Villequier, 4 septembre 1844

Les Contemplations,
Livre Quatrième, VI

VENI, VIDI, VIXI

J'ai bien assez vécu, puisque dans mes douleurs
Je marche sans trouver de bras qui me secourent,
Puisque je ris à peine aux enfants qui m'entourent,
Puisque je ne suis plus réjoui par les fleurs ;

Puisqu'au printemps, quand Dieu met la nature en fête,
J'assiste, esprit sans joie, à ce splendide amour ;
Puisque je suis à l'heure où l'homme fuit le jour,
Hélas ! et sent de tout la tristesse secrète ;

Puisque l'espoir serein dans mon âme est vaincu ;
Puisqu'en cette saison des parfums et des roses,
Ô ma fille ! j'aspire à l'ombre où tu reposes,
Puisque mon cœur est mort, j'ai bien assez vécu.

Je n'ai pas refusé ma tâche sur la terre.
Mon sillon ? Le voilà. Ma gerbe ? La voici.
J'ai vécu souriant, toujours plus adouci,
Debout, mais incliné du côté du mystère.

J'ai fait ce que j'ai pu ; j'ai servi, j'ai veillé,
Et j'ai vu bien souvent qu'on riait de ma peine.
Je me suis étonné d'être un objet de haine,
Ayant beaucoup souffert et beaucoup travaillé.

Dans ce bagne terrestre où ne s'ouvre aucune aile,
Sans me plaindre, saignant, et tombant sur les mains,
Morne, épuisé, raillé par les forçats humains,
J'ai porté mon chaînon de la chaîne éternelle.

Maintenant, mon regard ne s'ouvre qu'à demi ;
Je ne me tourne plus même quand on me nomme ;
Je suis plein de stupeur et d'ennui, comme un homme
Qui se lève avant l'aube et qui n'a pas dormi.

Je ne daigne plus même, en ma sombre paresse,
Répondre à l'envieux dont la bouche me nuit.
Ô Seigneur ! ouvrez-moi les portes de la nuit,
Afin que je m'en aille et que je disparaisse !

Avril 1848

Les Contemplations,
Livre Quatrième, XIII

Demain, dès l'aube, à l'heure où blanchit la campagne,
Je partirai. Vois-tu, je sais que tu m'attends.
J'irai par la forêt, j'irai par la montagne.
Je ne puis demeurer loin de toi plus longtemps.

Je marcherai les yeux fixés sur mes pensées,
Sans rien voir au dehors, sans entendre aucun bruit,
Seul, inconnu, le dos courbé, les mains croisées,
Triste, et le jour pour moi sera comme la nuit.

Je ne regarderai ni l'or du soir qui tombe,
Ni les voiles au loin descendant vers Harfleur,
Et quand j'arriverai, je mettrai sur ta tombe
Un bouquet de houx vert et de bruyère en fleur.

3 septembre 1847

Les Contemplations,
Livre Quatrième, **XIV**

À VILLEQUIER

Maintenant que Paris, ses pavés et ses marbres,
Et sa brume et ses toits sont bien loin de mes yeux ;
Maintenant que je suis sous les branches des arbres,
Et que je puis songer à la beauté des cieux ;

Maintenant que du deuil qui m'a fait l'âme obscure
Je sors, pâle et vainqueur,
Et que je sens la paix de la grande nature
Qui m'entre dans le cœur ;

Maintenant que je puis, assis au bord des ondes,
Ému par ce superbe et tranquille horizon,
Examiner en moi les vérités profondes
Et regarder les fleurs qui sont dans le gazon ;

Maintenant, ô mon Dieu ! que j'ai ce calme sombre
De pouvoir désormais
Voir de mes yeux la pierre où je sais que dans l'ombre
Elle dort pour jamais ;

Maintenant qu'attendri par ces divins spectacles,
Plaines, forêts, rochers, vallons, fleuve argenté,
Voyant ma petitesse et voyant vos miracles,
Je reprends ma raison devant l'immensité ;

Je viens à vous, Seigneur, père auquel il faut croire ;
Je vous porte, apaisé,
Les morceaux de ce cœur tout plein de votre gloire
Que vous avez brisé ;

Je viens à vous, Seigneur ! confessant que vous êtes
Bon, clément, indulgent et doux, ô Dieu vivant !
Je conviens que vous seul savez ce que vous faites,
Et que l'homme n'est rien qu'un jonc qui tremble au vent ;

Je dis que le tombeau qui sur les morts se ferme
        Ouvre le firmament ;
Et que ce qu'ici-bas nous prenons pour le terme
        Est le commencement ;

Je conviens à genoux que vous seul, père auguste,
Possédez l'infini, le réel, l'absolu ;
Je conviens qu'il est bon, je conviens qu'il est juste
Que mon cœur ait saigné, puisque Dieu l'a voulu !

Je ne résiste plus à tout ce qui m'arrive
        Par votre volonté.
L'âme de deuils en deuils, l'homme de rive en rive,
        Roule à l'éternité.

Nous ne voyons jamais qu'un seul côté des choses ;
L'autre plonge en la nuit d'un mystère effrayant.
L'homme subit le joug sans connaître les causes.
Tout ce qu'il voit est court, inutile et fuyant.

Vous faites revenir toujours la solitude
        Autour de tous ses pas.
Vous n'avez pas voulu qu'il eût la certitude
        Ni la joie ici-bas !

Dès qu'il possède un bien, le sort le lui retire.
Rien ne lui fut donné, dans ses rapides jours,
Pour qu'il s'en puisse faire une demeure, et dire :
C'est ici ma maison, mon champ et mes amours !

Il doit voir peu de temps tout ce que ses yeux voient ;
        Il vieillit sans soutiens.
Puisque ces choses sont, c'est qu'il faut qu'elles soient ;
        J'en conviens, j'en conviens !

Le monde est sombre, ô Dieu ! l'immuable harmonie
Se compose des pleurs aussi bien que des chants ;
L'homme n'est qu'un atome en cette ombre infinie,
Nuit où montent les bons, où tombent les méchants.

Je sais que vous avez bien autre chose à faire
              Que de nous plaindre tous,
Et qu'un enfant qui meurt, désespoir de sa mère,
              Ne vous fait rien, à vous !

Je sais que le fruit tombe au vent qui le secoue,
Que l'oiseau perd sa plume et la fleur son parfum ;
Que la création est une grande roue
Qui ne peut se mouvoir sans écraser quelqu'un ;

Les mois, les jours, les flots des mers, les yeux qui pleurent,
              Passent sous le ciel bleu ;
Il faut que l'herbe pousse et que les enfants meurent ;
              Je le sais, ô mon Dieu !

Dans vos cieux, au-delà de la sphère des nues,
Au fond de cet azur immobile et dormant,
Peut-être faites-vous des choses inconnues
Où la douleur de l'homme entre comme élément.

Peut-être est-il utile à vos desseins sans nombre
              Que des êtres charmants
S'en aillent, emportés par le tourbillon sombre
              Des noirs événements.

Nos destins ténébreux vont sous des lois immenses
Que rien ne déconcerte et que rien n'attendrit.
Vous ne pouvez avoir de subites clémences
Qui dérangent le monde, ô Dieu, tranquille esprit !

Je vous supplie, ô Dieu ! de regarder mon âme,
              Et de considérer
Qu'humble comme un enfant et doux comme une femme,
              Je viens vous adorer !

Considérez encor que j'avais, dès l'aurore,
Travaillé, combattu, pensé, marché, lutté,
Expliquant la nature à l'homme qui l'ignore,
Éclairant toute chose avec votre clarté ;

Que j'avais, affrontant la haine et la colère,
    Fait ma tâche ici-bas,
Que je ne pouvais pas m'attendre à ce salaire,
    Que je ne pouvais pas

Prévoir que, vous aussi, sur ma tête qui ploie
Vous appesantiriez votre bras triomphant,
Et que, vous qui voyiez comme j'ai peu de joie,
Vous me reprendriez si vite mon enfant !

Qu'une âme ainsi frappée à se plaindre est sujette,
    Que j'ai pu blasphémer,
Et vous jeter mes cris comme un enfant qui jette
    Une pierre à la mer !

Considérez qu'on doute, ô mon Dieu ! quand on souffre,
Que l'œil qui pleure trop finit par s'aveugler,
Qu'un être que son deuil plonge au plus noir du gouffre,
Quand il ne vous voit plus, ne peut vous contempler,

Et qu'il ne se peut pas que l'homme, lorsqu'il sombre
    Dans les afflictions,
Ait présente à l'esprit la sérénité sombre
    Des constellations !

Aujourd'hui, moi qui fus faible comme une mère,
Je me courbe à vos pieds devant vos cieux ouverts.
Je me sens éclairé dans ma douleur amère
Par un meilleur regard jeté sur l'univers.

Seigneur, je reconnais que l'homme est en délire
    S'il ose murmurer ;
Je cesse d'accuser, je cesse de maudire,
    Mais laissez-moi pleurer !

Hélas ! laissez les pleurs couler de ma paupière,
Puisque vous avez fait les hommes pour cela !
Laissez-moi me pencher sur cette froide pierre
Et dire à mon enfant : Sens-tu que je suis là ?

Laissez-moi lui parler, incliné sur ses restes,
    Le soir, quand tout se tait,
Comme si, dans sa nuit rouvrant ses yeux célestes,
    Cet ange m'écoutait !

Hélas ! vers le passé tournant un œil d'envie,
Sans que rien ici-bas puisse m'en consoler,
Je regarde toujours ce moment de ma vie
Où je l'ai vue ouvrir son aile et s'envoler !

Je verrai cet instant jusqu'à ce que je meure,
    L'instant, pleurs superflus !
Où je criai : L'enfant que j'avais tout à l'heure,
    Quoi donc ! je ne l'ai plus !

Ne vous irritez pas que je sois de la sorte,
Ô mon Dieu ! cette plaie a si longtemps saigné !
L'angoisse dans mon âme est toujours la plus forte,
Et mon cœur est soumis, mais n'est pas résigné.

Ne vous irritez pas ! fronts que le deuil réclame,
    Mortels sujets aux pleurs,
Il nous est malaisé de retirer notre âme
    De ces grandes douleurs.

Voyez-vous, nos enfants nous sont bien nécessaires,
Seigneur ; quand on a vu dans sa vie, un matin,
Au milieu des ennuis, des peines, des misères,
Et de l'ombre que fait sur nous notre destin,

Apparaître un enfant, tête chère et sacrée,
    Petit être joyeux,
Si beau, qu'on a cru voir s'ouvrir à son entrée
    Une porte des cieux ;

Quand on a vu, seize ans, de cet autre soi-même
Croître la grâce aimable et la douce raison,
Lorsqu'on a reconnu que cet enfant qu'on aime
Fait le jour dans notre âme et dans notre maison,

Que c'est la seule joie ici-bas qui persiste
    De tout ce qu'on rêva,
Considérez que c'est une chose bien triste
    De le voir qui s'en va !

Villequier, 4 septembre 1847
(24 octobre 1846)

Les Contemplations,
Livre Quatrième, XV

PAROLES SUR LA DUNE

Maintenant que mon temps décroît comme un flambeau,
    Que mes tâches sont terminées ;
Maintenant que voici que je touche au tombeau
    Par les deuils et par les années,

Et qu'au fond de ce ciel que mon essor rêva,
    Je vois fuir, vers l'ombre entraînées,
Comme le tourbillon du passé qui s'en va,
    Tant de belles heures sonnées ;

Maintenant que je dis : – Un jour, nous triomphons ;
    Le lendemain, tout est mensonge ! –
Je suis triste, et je marche au bord des flots profonds,
    Courbé comme celui qui songe.

Je regarde, au-dessus du mont et du vallon,
    Et des mers sans fin remuées,
S'envoler, sous le bec du vautour aquilon,
    Toute la toison des nuées ;

J'entends le vent dans l'air, la mer sur le récif,
    L'homme liant la gerbe mûre ;
J'écoute, et je confronte en mon esprit pensif
    Ce qui parle à ce qui murmure ;

Et je reste parfois couché sans me lever
    Sur l'herbe rare de la dune,
Jusqu'à l'heure où l'on voit apparaître et rêver
    Les yeux sinistres de la lune.

Elle monte, elle jette un long rayon dormant
    À l'espace, au mystère, au gouffre ;
Et nous nous regardons tous les deux fixement,
    Elle qui brille et moi qui souffre.

Où donc s'en sont allés mes jours évanouis ?
    Est-il quelqu'un qui me connaisse ?
Ai-je encor quelque chose en mes yeux éblouis,
    De la clarté de ma jeunesse ?

Tout s'est-il envolé ? Je suis seul, je suis las ;
    J'appelle sans qu'on me réponde ;
Ô vents ! ô flots ! ne suis-je aussi qu'un souffle, hélas !
    Hélas ! ne suis-je aussi qu'une onde ?

Ne verrai-je plus rien de tout ce que j'aimais ?
    Au dedans de moi le soir tombe.
Ô terre, dont la brume efface les sommets,
    Suis-je le spectre, et toi la tombe ?

Ai-je donc vidé tout, vie, amour, joie, espoir ?
    J'attends, je demande, j'implore ;
Je penche tour à tour mes urnes pour avoir
    De chacune une goutte encore !

Comme le souvenir est voisin du remord !
    Comme à pleurer tout nous ramène !
Et que je te sens froide en te touchant, ô mort,
    Noir verrou de la porte humaine !

Et je pense, écoutant gémir le vent amer,
    Et l'onde aux plis infranchissables ;
L'été rit, et l'on voit sur le bord de la mer
    Fleurir le chardon bleu des sables.

5 août 1854, anniversaire de mon arrivée à Jersey

Les Contemplations,
Livre Cinquième, XIII

PASTEURS ET TROUPEAUX

Le vallon où je vais tous les jours est charmant,
Serein, abandonné, seul sous le firmament,
Plein de ronces en fleurs ; c'est un sourire triste.
Il vous fait oublier que quelque chose existe,
Et, sans le bruit des champs remplis de travailleurs,
On ne saurait plus là si quelqu'un vit ailleurs.
Là, l'ombre fait l'amour ; l'idylle naturelle
Rit ; le bouvreuil avec le verdier s'y querelle,
Et la fauvette y met de travers son bonnet ;
C'est tantôt l'aubépine et tantôt le genêt ;
De noirs granits bourrus, puis des mousses riantes ;
Car Dieu fait un poème avec des variantes ;
Comme le vieil Homère, il rabâche parfois,
Mais c'est avec les fleurs, les monts, l'onde et les bois !
Une petite mare est là, ridant sa face,
Prenant des airs de flot pour la fourmi qui passe,
Ironie étalée au milieu du gazon,
Qu'ignore l'océan grondant à l'horizon.
J'y rencontre parfois sur la roche hideuse
Un doux être ; quinze ans, yeux bleus, pieds nus, gardeuse
De chèvres, habitant, au fond d'un ravin noir,
Un vieux chaume croulant qui s'étoile le soir ;
Ses sœurs sont au logis et filent leur quenouille ;
Elle essuie aux roseaux ses pieds que l'étang mouille ;
Chèvres, brebis, béliers, paissent ; quand, sombre esprit,
J'apparais, le pauvre ange a peur, et me sourit ;
Et moi, je la salue, elle étant l'innocence.
Ses agneaux, dans le pré plein de fleurs qui l'encense,
Bondissent, et chacun, au soleil s'empourprant,
Laisse aux buissons, à qui la bise le reprend,
Un peu de sa toison, comme un flocon d'écume.
Je passe ; enfant, troupeau, s'effacent dans la brume ;
Le crépuscule étend sur les longs sillons gris
Ses ailes de fantôme et de chauve-souris ;
J'entends encore au loin dans la plaine ouvrière

Chanter derrière moi la douce chevrière ;
Et, là-bas, devant moi, le vieux gardien pensif
De l'écume, du flot, de l'algue, du récif,
Et des vagues sans trêve et sans fin remuées,
Le pâtre promontoire au chapeau de nuées,
S'accoude et rêve au bruit de tous les infinis,
Et, dans l'ascension des nuages bénis,
Regarde se lever la lune triomphale,
Pendant que l'ombre tremble, et que l'âpre rafale
Disperse à tous les vents avec son souffle amer
La laine des moutons sinistres de la mer.

Jersey, Grouville, avril 1855

Les Contemplations,
Livre Cinquième, XXIII

BOOZ ENDORMI

Booz s'était couché de fatigue accablé ;
Il avait tout le jour travaillé dans son aire ;
Puis avait fait son lit à sa place ordinaire ;
Booz dormait auprès des boisseaux pleins de blé.

Ce vieillard possédait des champs de blés et d'orge ;
Il était, quoique riche, à la justice enclin ;
Il n'avait pas de fange en l'eau de son moulin ;
Il n'avait pas d'enfer dans le feu de sa forge.

Sa barbe était d'argent comme un ruisseau d'avril.
Sa gerbe n'était point avare ni haineuse ;
Quand il voyait passer quelque pauvre glaneuse :
« Laissez tomber exprès des épis », disait-il.

Cet homme marchait pur loin des sentiers obliques,
Vêtu de probité candide et de lin blanc ;
Et, toujours du côté des pauvres ruisselant,
Ses sacs de grains semblaient des fontaines publiques.

Booz était bon maître et fidèle parent ;
Il était généreux, quoiqu'il fût économe ;
Les femmes regardaient Booz plus qu'un jeune homme,
Car le jeune homme est beau, mais le vieillard est grand.

Le vieillard, qui revient vers la source première,
Entre aux jours éternels et sort des jours changeants ;
Et l'on voit de la flamme aux yeux des jeunes gens,
Mais dans l'œil du vieillard on voit de la lumière.

★

Donc, Booz dans la nuit dormait parmi les siens.
Près des meules, qu'on eût prises pour des décombres,
Les moissonneurs couchés faisaient des groupes sombres ;
Et ceci se passait dans des temps très-anciens.

Les tribus d'Israël avaient pour chef un juge ;
La terre, où l'homme errait sous la tente, inquiet
Des empreintes de pieds de géants qu'il voyait,
Était mouillée encore et molle du déluge.

★

Comme dormait Jacob, comme dormait Judith,
Booz, les yeux fermés, gisait sous la feuillée ;
Or, la porte du ciel s'étant entrebâillée
Au-dessus de sa tête, un songe en descendit.

Et ce songe était tel, que Booz vit un chêne
Qui, sorti de son ventre, allait jusqu'au ciel bleu ;
Une race y montait comme une longue chaîne ;
Un roi chantait en bas, en haut mourait un Dieu.

Et Booz murmurait avec la voix de l'âme :
« Comment se pourrait-il que de moi ceci vînt ?
Le chiffre de mes ans a passé quatre-vingt,
Et je n'ai pas de fils, et je n'ai plus de femme.

Voilà longtemps que celle avec qui j'ai dormi,
Ô Seigneur ! a quitté ma couche pour la vôtre ;
Et nous sommes encor tout mêlés l'un à l'autre,
Elle à demi vivante et moi mort à demi.

Une race naîtrait de moi ! Comment le croire ?
Comment se pourrait-il que j'eusse des enfants ?
Quand on est jeune, on a des matins triomphants ;
Le jour sort de la nuit comme d'une victoire ;

Mais vieux, on tremble ainsi qu'à l'hiver le bouleau ;
Je suis veuf, je suis seul, et sur moi le soir tombe,
Et je courbe, ô mon Dieu ! mon âme vers la tombe,
Comme un bœuf ayant soif penche son front vers l'eau. »

Ainsi parlait Booz dans le rêve et l'extase,
Tournant vers Dieu ses yeux par le sommeil noyés ;
Le cèdre ne sent pas une rose à sa base,
Et lui ne sentait pas une femme à ses pieds.

★

Pendant qu'il sommeillait, Ruth, une moabite,
S'était couchée aux pieds de Booz, le sein nu,
Espérant on ne sait quel rayon inconnu,
Quand viendrait du réveil la lumière subite.

Booz ne savait point qu'une femme était là,
Et Ruth ne savait point ce que Dieu voulait d'elle.
Un frais parfum sortait des touffes d'asphodèle ;
Les souffles de la nuit flottaient sur Galgala.

L'ombre était nuptiale, auguste et solennelle ;
Les anges y volaient sans doute obscurément,
Car on voyait passer dans la nuit, par moment,
Quelque chose de bleu qui paraissait une aile.

La respiration de Booz qui dormait
Se mêlait au bruit sourd des ruisseaux sur la mousse.
On était dans le mois où la nature est douce,
Les collines ayant des lys sur leur sommet.

Ruth songeait et Booz dormait ; l'herbe était noire ;
Les grelots des troupeaux palpitaient vaguement ;
Une immense bonté tombait du firmament ;
C'était l'heure tranquille où les lions vont boire.

Tout reposait dans Ur et dans Jérimadeth ;
Les astres émaillaient le ciel profond et sombre ;
Le croissant fin et clair parmi ces fleurs de l'ombre
Brillait à l'occident, et Ruth se demandait,

Immobile, ouvrant l'œil à moitié sous ses voiles,
Quel dieu, quel moissonneur de l'éternel été,
Avait, en s'en allant, négligemment jeté
Cette faucille d'or dans le champ des étoiles.

1er mai 1859

La Légende des siècles, II, VI

AYMERILLOT

. . . .
Voilà comme parlaient tous ces fiers batailleurs
Pendant que les torrents mugissaient sous les chênes.

L'empereur fit le tour de tous ses capitaines ;
Il appela les plus hardis, les plus fougueux,
Eudes, duc de Bourgogne, Albert de Périgueux,
Samo, que la légende aujourd'hui divinise,
Garin, qui, se trouvant un beau jour à Venise,
Emporta sur son dos le lion de Saint-Marc,
Ernaut de Bauléande, Ogier de Danemark,
Roger enfin, grande âme au péril toujours prête.

Ils refusèrent tous.

                    Alors, levant la tête,
Se dressant tout debout sur ses grand étriers,
Tirant sa large épée aux éclairs meurtriers,
Avec un âpre accent plein de sourdes huées,
Pâle, effrayant, pareil à l'aigle des nuées,
Terrassant du regard son camp épouvanté,
L'invincible empereur s'écria : « Lâcheté !
Ô comtes palatins tombés dans ces vallées,
Ô géants qu'on voyait debout dans les mêlées,
Devant qui Satan même aurait crié merci,
Olivier et Roland, que n'êtes-vous ici !
Si vous étiez vivants, vous prendriez Narbonne,
Paladins ! vous, du moins, votre épée était bonne,
Votre cœur était haut, vous ne marchandiez pas !
Vous alliez en avant sans compter tous vos pas !
Ô compagnons couchés dans la tombe profonde,
Si vous étiez vivants, nous prendrions le monde !
Grand Dieu ! que voulez-vous que je fasse à présent ?
Mes yeux cherchent en vain un brave au cœur puissant,
Et vont, tout effrayés de nos immenses tâches,

De ceux-là qui sont morts à ceux-ci qui sont lâches !
Je ne sais point comment on porte des affronts !
Je les jette à mes pieds, je n'en veux pas ! – Barons,
Vous qui m'avez suivi jusqu'à cette montagne,
Normands, Lorrains, marquis des marches d'Allemagne,
Poitevins, Bourguignons, gens du pays Pisan,
Bretons, Picards, Flamands, Français, allez-vous-en !

. . . .

Ainsi Charle de France appelé Charlemagne,
Exarque de Ravenne, empereur d'Allemagne,
Parlait dans la montagne avec sa grande voix ;
Et les pâtres lointains, épars au fond des bois,
Croyaient en l'entendant que c'était le tonnerre.

Les barons consternés fixaient leurs yeux à terre.
Soudain, comme chacun demeurait interdit,
Un jeune homme bien fait sortit des rangs, et dit :

« Que monsieur saint Denis garde le roi de France ! »

L'empereur fut surpris de ce ton d'assurance.

Il regarda celui qui s'avançait, et vit,
Comme le roi Saül lorsque apparut David,
Une espèce d'enfant au teint rose, aux mains blanches,
Que d'abord les soudards dont l'estoc bat les hanches
Prirent pour une fille habillée en garçon,
Doux, frêle, confiant, serein, sans écusson
Et sans panache, ayant, sous ses habits de serge,
L'air grave d'un gendarme et l'œil froid d'une vierge.

« Toi, que veux-tu, dit Charles, et qu'est-ce qui t'émeut ?

– Je viens vous demander ce dont pas un ne veut :
L'honneur d'être, ô mon roi, si Dieu ne m'abandonne,
L'homme dont on dira : « C'est lui qui prit Narbonne. »

L'enfant parlait ainsi d'un air de loyauté,
Regardant tout le monde avec simplicité.

Le Gantois, dont le front se relevait très vite,
Se mit à rire, et dit aux reîtres de sa suite :
« Hé ! c'est Aymerillot, le petit compagnon.

– Aymerillot, reprit le roi, dis-nous ton nom.

– Aymery. Je suis pauvre autant qu'un pauvre moine ;
J'ai vingt ans, je n'ai point de paille et point d'avoine,
Je sais lire en latin, et je suis bachelier.
Voilà tout, sire. Il plut au sort de m'oublier
Lorsqu'il distribua les fiefs héréditaires.
Deux liards couvriraient fort bien toutes mes terres,
Mais tout le grand ciel bleu n'emplirait pas mon cœur.
J'entrerai dans Narbonne et je serai vainqueur.
Après, je châtierai les railleurs, s'il en reste. »

Charle, plus rayonnant que l'archange céleste,
S'écria :
            « Tu seras, pour ce propos hautain,
Aymery de Narbonne et comte palatin,
Et l'on te parlera d'une façon civile.
Va, fils ! »
            Le lendemain Aymery prit la ville.

La Légende des siècles, X, III

LA ROSE DE L'INFANTE

Elle est toute petite ; une duègne la garde.
Elle tient à la main une rose et regarde.
Quoi ? que regarde-t-elle ? Elle ne sait pas. L'eau ;
Un bassin qu'assombrit le pin et le bouleau ;
Ce qu'elle a devant elle ; un cygne aux ailes blanches,
Le bercement des flots sous la chanson des branches,
Et le profond jardin rayonnant et fleuri.
Tout ce bel ange a l'air dans la neige pétri.
On voit un grand palais comme au fond d'une gloire,
Un parc, de clairs viviers où les biches vont boire,
Et des paons étoilés sous les bois chevelus.
L'innocence est sur elle une blancheur de plus ;
Toutes ses grâces font comme un faisceau qui tremble.
Autour de cette enfant l'herbe est splendide et semble
Pleine de vrais rubis et de diamants fins ;
Un jet de saphirs sort des bouches des dauphins.
Elle se tient au bord de l'eau ; sa fleur l'occupe ;
Sa basquine est en point de Gênes ; sur sa jupe
Une arabesque, errant dans les plis du satin,
Suit les mille détours d'un fil d'or florentin.
La rose épanouie et toute grande ouverte,
Sortant du frais bouton comme d'une urne verte,
Charge la petitesse exquise de sa main ;
Quand l'enfant, allongeant ses lèvres de carmin,
Fronce, en la respirant, sa riante narine,
La magnifique fleur, royale et purpurine,
Cache plus qu'à demi ce visage charmant ;
Si bien que l'œil hésite, et qu'on ne sait comment
Distinguer de la fleur ce bel enfant qui joue,
Et si l'on voit la rose ou si l'on voit la joue.

. . . .

Pendant que l'enfant rit, cette fleur à la main,
Dans le vaste palais catholique romain
Dont chaque ogive semble au soleil une mitre,
Quelqu'un de formidable est derrière la vitre …

. . . .

C'est lui ; l'homme en qui vit et tremble le royaume.
Si quelqu'un pouvait voir dans l'œil de ce fantôme
Debout en ce moment l'épaule contre un mur,
Ce qu'on apercevrait dans cet abîme obscur,
Ce n'est pas l'humble enfant, le jardin, l'eau moirée
Reflétant le ciel d'or d'une claire soirée,
Les bosquets, les oiseaux se becquetant entre eux,
Non : au fond de cet œil comme l'onde vitreux,
Sous ce fatal sourcil qui dérobe à la sonde
Cette prunelle autant que l'océan profonde,
Ce qu'on distinguerait, c'est, mirage mouvant,
Tout un vol de vaisseaux en fuite dans le vent,
Et dans l'écume, au pli des vagues, sous l'étoile,
L'immense tremblement d'une flotte à la voile,
Et, là-bas, sous la brume, une île, un blanc rocher,
Écoutant sur les flots ces tonnerres marcher.

. . . .

Morne en son noir pourpoint, la toison d'or au cou,
On dirait du destin la froide sentinelle ;
Son immobilité commande ; sa prunelle
Luit comme un soupirail de caverne ; son doigt
Semble, ébauchant un geste obscur que nul ne voit,
Donner un ordre à l'ombre et vaguement l'écrire.
Chose inouïe ! il vient de grincer un sourire.
Un sourire insondable, impénétrable, amer.
C'est que la vision de son armée en mer
Grandit de plus en plus dans sa sombre pensée ;
C'est qu'il la voit voguer par son dessein poussée,
Comme s'il était là, planant sous le zénith ;
Tout est bien ; l'océan docile s'aplanit ;
L'armada lui fait peur comme au déluge l'arche ;
La flotte se déploie en bon ordre de marche,
Et, les vaisseaux gardant les espaces fixés,
Échiquier de tillacs, de ponts, de mâts dressés,
Ondule sur les eaux comme une immense claie.
Ces vaisseaux sont sacrés ; les flots leur font la haie ;
Les courants, pour aider ces nefs à débarquer,
Ont leur besogne à faire et n'y sauraient manquer ;

Autour d'elles la vague avec amour déferle,
L'écueil se change en port, l'écume tombe en perle.
. . . .
Les voiles font un vaste et sourd battement d'ailes ;
L'eau gronde, et tout ce groupe énorme vogue, fuit,
Et s'enfle et roule avec un prodigieux bruit.
Et le lugubre roi sourit de voir groupées
Sur quatre cents vaisseaux quatre-vingt mille épées.
. . . .
Cependant, sur le bord du bassin, en silence,
L'infante tient toujours sa rose gravement,
Et, doux ange aux yeux bleus, la baise par moment.
Soudain un souffle d'air, une de ces haleines
Que le soir frémissant jette à travers les plaines,
Tumultueux zéphyr effleurant l'horizon,
Trouble l'eau, fait frémir les joncs, met un frisson
Dans les lointains massifs de myrte et d'asphodèle,
Vient jusqu'au bel enfant tranquille, et, d'un coup d'aile,
Rapide, et secouant même l'arbre voisin,
Effeuille brusquement la fleur dans le bassin.
Et l'infante n'a plus dans la main qu'une épine.
Elle se penche, et voit sur l'eau cette ruine ;
Elle ne comprend pas ; qu'est-ce donc ? Elle a peur ;
Et la voilà qui cherche au ciel avec stupeur
Cette brise qui n'a pas craint de lui déplaire.
Que faire ? Le bassin semble plein de colère ;
Lui, si clair tout à l'heure, il est noir maintenant ;
Il a des vagues ; c'est une mer bouillonnant ;
Toute la pauvre rose est éparse sur l'onde ;
Ses cent feuilles, que noie et roule l'eau profonde,
Tournoyant, naufrageant, s'en vont de tous côtés
Sur mille petits flots par la brise irrités ;
On croit voir dans un gouffre une flotte qui sombre.
« – Madame, dit la duègne avec sa face d'ombre
À la petite fille étonnée et rêvant,
Tout sur terre appartient aux princes, hors le vent. »

23 mai 1859

La Légende des siècles, XXVI

LA TROMPETTE DU JUGEMENT

Je vis dans la nuée un clairon monstrueux.

Et ce clairon semblait, au seuil profond des cieux,
Calme, attendre le souffle immense de l'archange.

Ce qui jamais ne meurt, ce qui jamais ne change,
L'entourait. À travers un frisson, on sentait
Que ce buccin fatal, qui rêve et qui se tait,
Quelque part, dans l'endroit où l'on crée, où l'on sème,
Avait été forgé par quelqu'un de suprême
Avec de l'équité condensée en airain.
Il était là, lugubre, effroyable, serein.
Il gisait sur la brume insondable qui tremble,
Hors du monde, au delà de tout ce qui ressemble
À la forme de quoi que ce soit.

                                    Il vivait.

Il semblait un réveil songeant près d'un chevet.

Oh ! quelle nuit ! là, rien n'a de contour ni d'âge ;
Et le nuage est spectre, et le spectre est nuage.

                          ★

Et c'était le clairon de l'abîme.

                                    Une voix
Un jour en sortira qu'on entendra sept fois.
En attendant, glacé, mais écoutant, il pense ;
Couvant le châtiment, couvant la récompense ;
Et toute l'épouvante éparse au ciel est sœur
De cet impénétrable et morne avertisseur.
Je le considérais dans les vapeurs funèbres
Comme on verrait se taire un coq dans les ténèbres.

Pas un murmure autour du clairon souverain.
Et la terre sentait le froid de son airain,
Quoique, là, d'aucun monde on ne vît les frontières.

Et l'immobilité de tous les cimetières,
Et le sommeil de tous les tombeaux, et la paix
De tous les morts couchés dans la fosse, étaient faits
Du silence inouï qu'il avait dans la bouche ;
Ce lourd silence était pour l'affreux mort farouche
L'impossibilité de faire faire un pli
Au suaire cousu sur son front par l'oubli.
Ce silence tenait en suspens l'anathème :
On comprenait que tant que ce clairon suprême
Se tairait, le sépulcre, obscur, roidi, béant,
Garderait l'attitude horrible du néant,
Que la momie aurait toujours sa bandelette,
Que l'homme irait tombant du cadavre au squelette,
Et que ce fier banquet radieux, ce festin
Que les vivants gloutons appellent le destin,
Toute la joie errante en tourbillons de fêtes,
Toutes les passions de la chair satisfaites,
Gloire, orgueil, les héros ivres, les tyrans soûls,
Continueraient d'avoir pour but et pour dessous
La pourriture, orgie offerte aux vers convives ;
Mais qu'à l'heure où soudain, dans l'espace sans rives,
Cette trompette vaste et sombre sonnerait,
On verrait, comme un tas d'oiseaux d'une forêt,
Toutes les âmes, cygne, aigle, éperviers, colombes,
Frémissantes, sortir du tremblement des tombes,
Et tous les spectres faire un bruit de grandes eaux,
Et se dresser, et prendre à la hâte leurs os,
Tandis qu'au fond, au fond du gouffre, au fond du rêve,
Blanchissant l'absolu, comme un jour qui se lève,
Le front mystérieux du juge apparaîtrait !
Ce clairon avait l'air de savoir le secret

. . . .

Quand le monde atteindra son but, quand les instants,
Les jours, les mois, les ans, auront rempli le temps,

Quand tombera du ciel l'heure immense et nocturne,
Cette goutte qui doit faire déborder l'urne,
Alors, dans le silence horrible, un rayon blanc,
Long, pâle, glissera, formidable et tremblant,
Sur ces haltes de nuit qu'on nomme cimetières ;
Les tentes frémiront, quoiqu'elles soient des pierres,
Dans tous ces sombres camps endormis ; et, sortant
Tout à coup de la brume où l'univers l'attend,
Ce clairon, au-dessus des êtres et des choses,
Au-dessus des forfaits et des apothéoses,
Des ombres et des os, des esprits et des corps,
Sonnera la diane effrayante des morts.

La Légende des siècles, LX

NOVEMBRE

I

DU HAUT DE LA MURAILLE DE PARIS
À LA NUIT TOMBANTE

L'occident était blanc, l'orient était noir,
Comme si quelque bras sorti des ossuaires
Dressait un catafalque aux colonnes du soir,
Et sur le firmament déployait deux suaires.

Et la nuit se fermait ainsi qu'une prison.
L'oiseau mêlait sa plainte au frisson de la plante.
J'allais. Quand je levai mes yeux vers l'horizon,
Le couchant n'était plus qu'une lame sanglante.

Cela faisait penser à quelque grand duel
D'un monstre contre un dieu, tous deux de même taille ;
Et l'on eût dit l'épée effrayante du ciel
Rouge et tombée à terre après une bataille.

L'Année terrible

LE CRUCIFIX

« Ils se sont partagé le manteau, mais la robe
N'ayant pas de couture, ils l'ont jouée aux dés. »

« De six à neuf, les monts furent d'ombre inondés ;
Toute la terre fut couverte de ténèbres ;
Comme si quelque main eût ployé ses vertèbres,
Il baissa tout à coup la tête, et dans ses yeux
Lugubres apparut la profondeur des cieux ;
Et, poussant un grand cri, Jésus expira. L'ombre
Monta, fumée infâme, aux étoiles sans nombre ;
Dans le temple, les bœufs d'airain firent un pas,
Le voile se fendit en deux, du haut en bas.
Hors des murs, il se fit un gouffre où se dressèrent
Tous ces êtres sur qui les rochers se resserrent
Et que la vaste fange inconnue enfouit ;
Et tout devint si noir que tout s'évanouit ;
Les sépulcres, s'ouvrant subitement, restèrent
Béants, montrant leur cave où les taupes déterrent
Les squelettes couchés dans les draps en lambeaux ;
Des morts blêmes, étant sortis de leurs tombeaux,
Furent vus par plusieurs personnes dans la ville. »

*

Dix-huit cents ans ont pu s'écouler sans que l'homme,
Autour duquel mouraient Byzance, Athène et Rome,
Et passait Charlemagne et montait Mahomet,
Ait quitté du regard cette croix, ce sommet,
Cette blancheur sanglante, et ces lueurs divines
Sous l'entrelacement monstrueux des épines ;
Et sans qu'il ait cessé d'entendre un seul moment
L'immense cri jeté dans le noir firmament
Et lisible à jamais sur ce sombre registre,
Et le déchirement du grand voile sinistre,
Et dans l'obscurité consciente, au-dessus

De ce gibet où pend l'être appelé Jésus,
Au-dessus des songeurs étudiant les bibles,
Le sanglot effrayant des bouches invisibles.

★

La flagellation du Christ n'est pas finie.
Tout ce qu'il a souffert dans sa lente agonie,
Au mont des Oliviers et dans les carrefours,
Sous la croix, sur la croix, il le souffre toujours.
Après le Golgotha, Jésus, ouvrant son aile,
A beau s'être envolé dans l'aurore éternelle ;
Il a beau resplendir, superbe et gracieux,
Dans la tranquillité sidérale des cieux,
Dans la gloire, parmi les archanges solaires,
Au-dessus des douleurs, au-dessus des colères,
Au-dessus du nuage âpre et confus des jours ;
Chaque fois que sur terre et dans nos temples sourds
Et dans nos vils palais, des docteurs et des scribes
Versent sur l'innocent leurs lâches diatribes,
Chaque fois que celui qui doit enseigner, ment,
Chaque fois que d'un traître il jaillit un serment,
Chaque fois que le juge, après une prière,
Jette au peuple ce mot : Justice ! et, par derrière,
Tend une main hideuse à l'or mystérieux,
Chaque fois que le prêtre, époussetant ses dieux,
Chante au crime hosanna, bat des mains aux désastres,
Et dit : gloire à César ! – là-haut, parmi les astres,
Dans l'azur qu'aucun souffle orageux ne corrompt,
Christ frémissant essuie un crachat sur son front.

★

Ainsi mourut Jésus ; et les peuples depuis,
Atterrés, ont senti que l'Inconnu lui-même
Leur était apparu dans cet Homme Suprême,
Et que son évangile était pareil au ciel.
Le Golgotha, funeste et pestilentiel,
Leur semble la tumeur difforme de l'abîme ;

Fauve, il se dresse au fond mystérieux du crime ;
Et le plus blême éclair du gouffre est sur ce lieu
Où la religion, sinistre, tua Dieu.

La Fin de Satan, III

LES VOIX DU SEUIL

(Et je vis au-dessus de ma tête un point noir)

Et ce point prit bientôt la forme d'un suaire.

Ses plis vagues jetaient une odeur d'ossuaire ;
Et sous le drap hideux et livide on sentait
Un de ces êtres noirs sur qui la nuit se tait.
C'était de ce linceul qu'était sorti le rire
Qui m'avait par trois fois troublé jusqu'au délire.
Sans que l'être le dit, je le compris. Mon sang
Se glaça ; je frémis.

　　　　　　　　L'être parla :

　　　　　　　　　　　　　　　　　– Passant,
Écoute. Tu n'as vu jusqu'ici que des songes,
Que de vagues lueurs flottant sur des mensonges,
Que les aspects confus qui passent dans les vents
Ou tremblent dans la nuit pour vous autres vivants.
Mais maintenant veux-tu d'une volonté forte
Entrer dans l'infini, quelle que soit la porte ?
Ce que l'homme endormi peut savoir, tu le sais.
Mais, esprit, trouves-tu que ce n'est pas assez ?
Ton regard, d'ombre en ombre et d'étage en étage,
A vu plus d'horizon... – en veux-tu davantage ?
Veux-tu, perçant le morne et ténébreux réseau,
T'envoler dans le vrai comme un sinistre oiseau ?
Veux-tu derrière toi laisser tous les décombres,
Temps, espace, et, hagard, sortir des branches sombres
Veux-tu, réponds, aller plus loin qu'Amos n'alla,
Et plus avant qu'Esdras et qu'Élie, au delà
Des prophètes pensifs et des blancs cénobites,
Percer l'ombre, emporté par des ailes subites ?
Ô semeur du sillon nébuleux, laboureur
Perdu dans la fumée horrible de l'erreur,

Front où s'abat l'essaim tumultueux des rêves,
Doutes, systèmes vains, effrois, luttes sans trêves,
Te plaît-il de savoir comment s'évanouit
En adoration toute cette âpre nuit ?
Veux-tu, flèche tremblante, atteindre enfin la cible ?
Veux-tu toucher le but, regarder l'invisible,
L'innommé, l'idéal, le réel, l'inouï ;
Comprendre, déchiffrer, lire ? être un ébloui ?
Veux-tu planer plus haut que la sombre nature ?
Veux-tu dans la lumière inconcevable et pure
Ouvrir tes yeux, par l'ombre affreuse appesantis ?
Le veux-tu ? Réponds.

                    – Oui ! – criai-je.

                              Et je sentis
Que la création tremblait comme une toile ;
Alors, levant un bras et, d'un pan de son voile,
Couvrant tous les objets terrestres disparus,
Il me toucha le front du doigt, et je mourus.

                                        Dieu, II

À THÉOPHILE GAUTIER

Ami, poète, esprit, tu fuis notre nuit noire.
Tu sors de nos rumeurs pour entrer dans la gloire,
Et désormais ton nom rayonne aux purs sommets.
Moi qui t'ai connu jeune et beau, moi qui t'aimais,
Moi qui, plus d'une fois, dans nos altiers coups d'aile,
Éperdu, m'appuyais sur ton âme fidèle,
Moi, blanchi par les jours sur ma tête neigeant,
Je me souviens des temps écoulés, et songeant
À ce jeune passé qui vit nos deux aurores,
À la lutte, à l'orage, aux arènes sonores,
À l'art nouveau qui s'offre, au peuple criant : oui,
J'écoute ce grand vent sublime évanoui.

. . . .

Lorsqu'un vivant nous quitte, ému, je le contemple ;
Car entrer dans la mort, c'est entrer dans le temple ;
Et, quand un homme meurt, je vois distinctement
Dans son ascension mon propre avènement.
Ami, je sens du sort la sombre plénitude ;
J'ai commencé la mort par de la solitude,
Je vois mon profond soir vaguement s'étoiler ;
Voici l'heure où je vais aussi, moi, m'en aller.
Mon fil, trop long, frissonne et touche presque au glaive ;
Le vent qui t'emporta doucement me soulève,
Et je vais suivre ceux qui m'aimaient, moi, banni.
Leur œil fixe m'attire au fond de l'infini.
J'y cours. Ne fermez pas la porte funéraire.

Passons, car c'est la loi ; nul ne peut s'y soustraire ;
Tout penche, et ce grand siècle avec tous ses rayons
Entre en cette ombre immense où pâles nous fuyons.
Oh ! quel farouche bruit font dans le crépuscule
Les chênes qu'on abat pour le bûcher d'Hercule !
Les chevaux de la Mort se mettent à hennir
Et sont joyeux, car l'âge éclatant va finir ;
Ce siècle altier, qui sut dompter le vent contraire,

Expire... – Ô Gautier ! toi, leur égal et leur frère,
Tu pars après Dumas, Lamartine et Musset.
L'onde antique est tarie où l'on rajeunissait ;
Comme il n'est plus de Styx, il n'est plus de Jouvence.
Le dur faucheur avec sa large lame avance
Pensif et pas à pas vers le reste du blé ;
C'est mon tour ; et la nuit emplit mon œil troublé
Qui, devinant, hélas, l'avenir des colombes,
Pleure sur des berceaux et sourit à des tombes.

Hauteville-House, 2 novembre 1872. Jour des Morts

Toute la lyre, **IV, XXVI**

AUGUSTE BARBIER

(1805-1882)

Son recueil des *Ïambes* le rend immédiatement célèbre lorsqu'il paraît en 1831. Le titre et le mètre choisi dans la plupart des poèmes – alexandrin et octosyllabes alternés – viennent de Chénier, mais le choix des sujets et la violence du ton lui appartiennent en propre, qu'il décrive *L'Idole*, entendez Napoléon, ou *La Cuve*, c'est-à-dire Paris, ou qu'il fustige dans *La Curée* les profiteurs de la révolution de Juillet, héritiers dégénérés des hommes de 89, il le fait toujours avec la même sincérité véhémente. La brutalité de certains traits, le réalisme des descriptions, l'emploi de mots crus valent à cette œuvre d'être perçue comme proche par le grand public. L'auteur avait voulu ce vers « rude et grossier », ce sont ses propres termes, et accepté d'être honni :

> *De tous les charlatans qui donnent de la voix*
> *Les marchands de pathos et les faiseurs d'emphase*
> *Et tous les baladins qui dansent sur la phrase.*

Toute son œuvre semble dire, comme La Bruyère : « Faut-il opter ? Je ne balance pas : je suis peuple. » On peut l'aimer pour cela.

LA CURÉE

Oh ! lorsqu'un lourd soleil chauffait les grandes dalles
      Des ponts et de nos quais déserts,
Que les cloches hurlaient, que la grêle des balles
      Sifflait et pleuvait par les airs ;
Que dans Paris entier, comme la mer qui monte,
      Le peuple soulevé grondait,
Et qu'au lugubre accent des vieux canons de fonte
      La Marseillaise répondait,
Certes, on ne voyait pas, comme au jour où nous sommes,
      Tant d'uniformes à la fois :
C'était sous des haillons que battaient les cœurs d'hommes,
      C'étaient alors de sales doigts
Qui chargeaient les mousquets et renvoyaient la foudre ;
      C'était la bouche aux vils jurons
Qui mâchait la cartouche, et qui, noire de poudre,
      Criait aux citoyens : Mourons !
. . . .
Mais, ô honte ! Paris, si beau dans sa colère,
      Paris, si plein de majesté
Dans ce jour de tempête où le vent populaire
      Déracina la royauté ;
Paris, si magnifique avec ses funérailles,
      Ses débris d'hommes, ses tombeaux,
Ses chemins dépavés et ses pans de murailles
      Troués comme de vieux drapeaux ;
Paris, cette cité de lauriers toute ceinte,
      Dont le monde entier est jaloux,
Que les peuples émus appellent tous la sainte,
      Et qu'ils ne nomment qu'à genoux,
Paris n'est maintenant qu'une sentine impure,
      Un égout sordide et boueux,
Où mille noirs courants de limon et d'ordure
      Viennent traîner leurs flots honteux ;
Un taudis regorgeant de faquins sans courage,
      D'effrontés coureurs de salons,

Qui vont de porte en porte, et d'étage en étage,
 Gueusant quelques bouts de galons ;
Une halle cynique aux clameurs insolentes,
 Où chacun cherche à déchirer
Un misérable coin des guenilles sanglantes
 Du pouvoir qui vient d'expirer.

ALOYSIUS BERTRAND

(1807-1841)

Louis Bertrand meurt dans la misère et quasi inconnu, bien que certains de ses poèmes aient paru dans des revues, et qu'il les ait lus parfois chez ses compagnons du cénacle romantique. David d'Angers, fidèle à leur amitié, fait paraître après sa mort un recueil que les libraires refusaient de son vivant.

Sainte-Beuve avait noté « l'exquise curiosité pittoresque du vocabulaire » de l'un des poèmes, et c'est, en effet, au courant du romantisme pittoresque qu'il faut rattacher cette œuvre. Elle en a les principaux traits, passion pour le Moyen Âge, prédilection pour le fantastique, et recours fréquent au grotesque comme chez la plupart des « petits romantiques ». Le parti pris médiéval, souligné par l'adoption d'une version de son prénom propre à cette époque, est manifeste dans le vocabulaire de ce *Gaspard de la nuit* où lansquenets, pertuisanes, carolus et ducats colorent le poème. L'invention de Scarbo, gnome malfaisant et moqueur, prompt à torturer le pauvre dormeur, relève du fantastique, et d'autres inventions, comme celle du fou « un œil à la lune et l'autre – crevé ! », mêlent à la poésie du clair de lune la trivialité d'un portrait caricatural.

Mais ce pittoresque, explicitement revendiqué par le sous-titre : « Fantaisies à la manière de Rembrandt et de Callot », qui n'est pas sans rappeler Nodier et, naturellement, Hoffmann, emprunte aussi à ces modèles une vision onirique de la réalité. Le personnage qui s'exprime dans les poèmes est un rêveur « lunatique » comme certains des héros de ces deux conteurs, et le décor qu'il évoque mêle au pittoresque des éléments issus du rêve, ouvrant ainsi d'autres espaces.

Aloysius Bertrand est le véritable inventeur du poème en prose. S'il s'est souvenu, comme c'est vraisemblable, des *Chansons madécasses* de Parny, c'est-à-dire de courtes unités de prose poétique auxquelles un refrain ajoute le charme d'une chanson, il rompt tout à fait avec les facilités que fournissaient le prétexte d'une traduction et l'exotisme du sujet. Il se fixe des règles, il impose une mesure à ses versets, il s'en tient, la plupart du temps, pour ses ballades à six couplets (cinq ou sept plus rarement), il arrive à créer une musique répétitive et insistante à l'aide de constructions symétriques, il y a chez lui la rapidité du trait qui enserre une image en quelques mots, le sens de la valeur imitative des sons, et du graphisme du poème, comme le montre l'utilisation des tirets, et les blancs ménagés entre les couplets. Tous ces éléments donnent à ses compositions un vrai pouvoir suggestif, c'est-à-dire une valeur poétique indéniable.

Baudelaire lui a rendu hommage, comme on sait, dans la dédicace du *Spleen de Paris* à Arsène Houssaye, en avouant qu'après avoir feuilleté le recueil d'Aloysius Bertrand « pour la vingtième fois au moins... l'idée [lui] est venue de tenter quelque chose d'analogue ». Mallarmé l'admirait, et André Breton le considère comme un surréaliste dans le passé. Ces illustres cautions ne sont plus nécessaires, pour voir, après un siècle et demi de développement et d'extension du poème en prose, qu'il avait d'emblée trouvé dans ce domaine l'une des formes les plus incontestables et les plus séduisantes.

LA CHAMBRE GOTHIQUE

« Nox et solitudo plenae sunt diabolo. »
LES PÈRES DE L'ÉGLISE
La nuit, ma chambre est pleine de diables.

« Oh ! la terre, – murmurai-je à la nuit, – est un calice embaumé dont le pistil et les étamines sont la lune et les étoiles ! »

Et les yeux lourds de sommeil, je fermai la fenêtre qu'incrusta la croix du calvaire, noire dans la jaune auréole des vitraux.

★

Encore, – si ce n'était à minuit, – l'heure blasonnée de dragons et de diables ! – que le gnome qui se soûle de l'huile de ma lampe !

Si ce n'était que la nourrice qui berce avec un chant monotone, dans la cuirasse de mon père, un petit enfant mort-né !

Si ce n'était que le squelette du lansquenet emprisonné dans la boiserie, et heurtant du front, du coude et du genou !

Si ce n'était que mon aïeul qui descend en pied de son cadre vermoulu, et trempe son gantelet dans l'eau bénite du bénitier !

Mais c'est Scarbo qui me mord au cou, et qui, pour cautériser ma blessure sanglante, y plonge son doigt de fer rougi à la fournaise !

V

LE CLAIR DE LUNE

> Réveillez-vous, gens qui dormez,
> Et priez pour les trépassés.
> LE CRI DU CRIEUR DE NUIT

Oh ! qu'il est doux, quand l'heure tremble au clocher, la nuit, de regarder la lune qui a le nez fait comme un carolus d'or !

*

Deux ladres se lamentaient sous ma fenêtre, un chien hurlait dans le carrefour, et le grillon de mon foyer vaticinait tout bas.

Mais bientôt mon oreille n'interrogea plus qu'un silence profond. Les lépreux étaient rentrés dans leurs chenils, aux coups de Jacquemart qui battait sa femme.

Le chien avait enfilé une venelle, devant les pertuisanes du guet enrouillé par la pluie et morfondu par la bise.

Et le grillon s'était endormi, dès que la dernière bluette avait éteint sa dernière lueur dans la cendre de la cheminée.

Et moi, il me semblait, – tant la fièvre est incohérente ! – que la lune, grimant sa face, me tirait la langue comme un pendu !

II

SCARBO

« Mon Dieu, accordez-moi, à l'heure de ma
mort, les prières d'un prêtre, un linceul de toile,
une bière de sapin et un lieu sec. »
LES PATENÔTRES DE M. LE MARÉCHAL

« Que tu meures absous ou damné, – marmottait Scarbo cette
nuit à mon oreille, – tu auras pour linceul une toile d'araignée, et
j'ensevelirai l'araignée avec toi !

– Oh ! que du moins j'aie pour linceul, lui répondais-je, les yeux
rouges d'avoir tant pleuré, – une feuille du tremble dans laquelle
me bercera l'haleine du lac.

– Non ! – ricanait le nain railleur, – tu serais la pâture de
l'escarbot qui chasse, le soir, aux moucherons aveuglés par le soleil
couchant !

– Aimes-tu donc mieux, – lui répliquais-je larmoyant toujours, –
aimes-tu donc mieux que je sois sucé d'une tarentule à la trompe
d'éléphant ?

– Eh bien, – ajouta-t-il, – console-toi, tu auras pour linceul les
bandelettes tachetées d'or d'une peau de serpent, dont je
t'emmailloterai comme une momie.

Et de la crypte ténébreuse de Saint-Bénigne, où je te coucherai
debout contre la muraille, tu entendras à loisir les petits enfants
pleurer dans les limbes. »

FÉLIX ARVERS

(1806-1850)

C'est un poète mineur dont la postérité n'a retenu qu'un seul poème. La plupart des anthologies l'ignorent et les manuels l'oublient. Quand ces derniers consentent à évoquer « le célèbre sonnet d'Arvers », ils ne citent que la première ligne du *Secret*, et si négligemment parfois qu'une inversion des termes en fausse le rythme.

Il fut, en son temps, accueilli avec enthousiasme. Mérimée se plaint d'avoir dû en subir la lecture trois fois en une semaine. S'il est alors tellement apprécié, on peut penser que la curiosité y est pour quelque chose, et qu'on s'efforce d'identifier la mystérieuse destinataire. Mais lorsque le nom qui fut avancé le plus souvent, celui de Marie Nodier, n'évoque plus rien pour le lecteur, comment expliquer cet engouement durable ?

Les écoliers de naguère savaient par cœur ce sonnet, et se le transmettaient, d'une génération à l'autre, oralement, puisqu'il ne figurait pas non plus dans leur bible d'alors, le manuel Braunschvig de littérature. Il vaut donc la peine qu'on s'attarde sur les raisons possibles d'un tel succès.

Les lieux communs de la poésie amoureuse, surgissement foudroyant d'un amour éternel, malheur « d'aimer et n'être pas aimé », ont sans doute moins d'importance ici que la nature tout à fait insolite de l'interdit qui pèse sur l'aveu, c'est, chez la jeune femme, l'ignorance de la passion qu'elle inspire. Ni la cruauté ni l'éloignement ni la mort, autres thèmes habituels, simplement l'irréprochable candeur d'une vie prise dans le réseau ordinaire des jours. Celle qui ne devine pas l'amour, comment pourrait-elle l'entendre ?

Les lecteurs émus que nous étions, oscillaient entre l'espoir vague que l'aveu indirect du sonnet ait pu jadis briser le secret, atteindre enfin la femme aimée, et le vœu plus profond qu'il n'en ait rien été, car la pérennité du malheur, nous le savions, est le garant de celle de l'amour.

UN SECRET

Mon âme a son secret, ma vie a son mystère ;
Un amour éternel en un instant conçu :
Le mal est sans espoir, aussi j'ai dû le taire,
Et celle qui l'a fait n'en a jamais rien su.

Hélas ! j'aurai passé près d'elle inaperçu,
Toujours à ses côtés, et pourtant solitaire,
Et j'aurai jusqu'au bout fait mon temps sur la terre.
N'osant rien demander et n'ayant rien reçu.

Pour elle, quoique Dieu l'ait faite douce et tendre,
Elle ira son chemin, distraite, et sans entendre
Ce murmure d'amour élevé sur ses pas ;

À l'austère devoir pieusement fidèle,
Elle dira, lisant ces vers tout remplis d'elle :
« Quelle est donc cette femme ? » et ne comprendra pas.

GÉRARD DE NERVAL

(1808-1855)

« Parmi les poètes modernes et les grands esprits du XIXᵉ siècle, il n'en est aucun qui ait moins que lui le style orgueilleux des demi-dieux », écrit à son sujet Albert Béguin. Si les domaines du rêve sont, plus qu'à d'autres, familiers à Nerval, puisque les crises de démence nourrissent aussi, chez lui, l'imaginaire, s'il rapporte de ses descentes aux enfers des figures et des récits étonnants, il ne se donne pas pour autant le statut de grand inspiré. Sa modestie ordinaire, la discrétion et l'humour avec lesquels il évoque les terribles crises qui lui valent plusieurs hospitalisations douloureuses, font sans doute de lui le plus humble et l'un des plus attachants de nos écrivains.

Et cependant, à l'instar des troubadours, il réinvente le *trobar clus*, cette forme de poésie dont le sens se dérobe, mais qui séduit par l'agencement d'images et de sons dont on ignore le secret. *Les Chimères* vont apparaître aux yeux des symbolistes, puis des surréalistes, comme une avancée poétique essentielle vers les chemins nouveaux de la poésie. On a essayé d'en déchiffrer les différents sonnets à l'aide des grilles les plus diverses. La critique a pu voir dans plusieurs des images d'*El Desdichado* la réplique de celles du tarot, ou retrouver des points de convergence entre l'alchimie et certaines formules mystérieuses de Nerval. Ses lectures érudites, sa curiosité vis-à-vis de toutes les doctrines illuministes du siècle précédent, justifiaient ces tentatives d'explication. Cependant les essais d'interprétation ne sont pas parvenus jusqu'à présent à rendre compte du pouvoir de ces poèmes sur le lecteur, pas plus qu'à l'affaiblir : leur force d'envoûtement et leur mystère demeurent.

D'autres écrits témoignent que Nerval fut aussi un jeune romantique épris de pittoresque et de couleur, voyageur passionné, attentif à tout ce que le monde offre de curiosités et de légendes ; mais de toutes les contrées visitées aucune n'avait pour lui le pouvoir d'enchantement de son cher Valois où il recueille, à la manière d'Arnim et Brentano, les vieilles chansons qui passent à ses yeux pour d'authentiques chansons populaires, et où il situe le récit poétique de *Sylvie*. On a longtemps considéré ce texte comme une idylle gracieuse à la manière de Gessner, et comme une forme de poésie du terroir. Proust en a fait une autre lecture « ...aux antipodes des claires et faciles aquarelles », et il affirme : « Cette histoire que vous appelez la peinture naïve, c'est le rêve d'un rêve. » Nerval y retrouve la fluidité d'une prose poétique dont Rousseau et « l'Enchanteur »[1] avaient donné le modèle :

« Je suis entré au bal de Loisy à cette heure mélancolique et douce encore où les lumières pâlissent et tremblent aux approches du jour »...

Aurélia paraît d'emblée se rattacher à la même veine que *Les Chimères*, il en a fourni lui-même la clef : « Je résolus de fixer le rêve et d'en connaître le secret », dit-il dans les dernières lignes de ce récit où il relate ses délires et ses visions merveilleuses. Il le conclut en ces termes : « Je compare cette série d'épreuves que j'ai traversées à ce qui, pour les anciens, représentait l'idée d'une descente aux enfers. »

Ce qui appartient à Gérard de Nerval et, sans doute, à nul autre avant lui, c'est la fonction particulière qu'il assigne à l'écriture poétique. C'est ce que souligne Albert Béguin : « L'œuvre, chez Nerval, est le lieu même où se décide le Destin. La phrase, le mot se chargent d'une mission immense... ils deviennent l'instrument à l'aide duquel Nerval a résolu de " forcer les portes mystiques " qui nous séparent du monde visible. Il joue autre chose que son talent et son intelligence, quelque chose que l'on peut appeler son salut. »

---

1. Chateaubriand.

EL DESDICHADO

Je suis le ténébreux, – le veuf, – l'inconsolé,
Le prince d'Aquitaine à la tour abolie :
Ma seule *étoile* est morte, – et mon luth constellé
Porte le *soleil* noir de la *Mélancolie*.

Dans la nuit du tombeau, toi qui m'as consolé,
Rends-moi le Pausilippe et la mer d'Italie,
La *fleur* qui plaisait tant à mon cœur désolé,
Et la treille où le pampre à la rose s'allie.

Suis-je Amour ou Phébus ?... Lusignan ou Biron ?
Mon front est rouge encor du baiser de la reine ;
J'ai rêvé dans la grotte où nage la sirène...

Et j'ai deux fois vainqueur traversé l'Achéron :
Modulant tour à tour sur la lyre d'Orphée
Les soupirs de la sainte et les cris de la fée.

Les Chimères

MYRTHO

Je pense à toi, Myrtho, divine enchanteresse,
Au Pausilippe altier, de mille feux brillant,
À ton front inondé des clartés d'Orient,
Aux raisins noirs mêlés avec l'or de ta tresse.

C'est dans ta coupe aussi que j'avais bu l'ivresse,
Et dans l'éclair furtif de ton œil souriant,
Quand aux pieds d'Iacchus on me voyait priant,
Car la Muse m'a fait l'un des fils de la Grèce.

Je sais pourquoi là-bas le volcan s'est rouvert…
C'est qu'hier tu l'avais touché d'un pied agile,
Et de cendres soudain l'horizon s'est couvert.

Depuis qu'un duc normand brisa tes dieux d'argile,
Toujours, sous les rameaux du laurier de Virgile,
Le pâle hortensia s'unit au myrte vert !

Les Chimères

DELFICA

La connais-tu, Dafné, cette ancienne romance,
Au pied du sycomore, ou sous les lauriers blancs,
Sous l'olivier, le myrte, ou les saules tremblants,
Cette chanson d'amour qui toujours recommence ?...

Reconnais-tu le TEMPLE au péristyle immense,
Et les citrons amers où s'imprimaient tes dents,
Et la grotte, fatale aux hôtes imprudents,
Où du dragon vaincu dort l'antique semence ?...

Ils reviendront, ces Dieux que tu pleures toujours !
Le temps va ramener l'ordre des anciens jours ;
La terre a tressailli d'un souffle prophétique...

Cependant la sibylle au visage latin
Est endormie encor sous l'arc de Constantin
– Et rien n'a dérangé le sévère portique.

Les Chimères

ARTÉMIS

La Treizième revient... C'est encor la première ;
Et c'est toujours la seule, – ou c'est le seul moment ;
Car es-tu reine, ô toi ! la première ou dernière ?
Es-tu roi, toi le seul ou le dernier amant ?...

Aimez qui vous aima du berceau dans la bière ;
Celle que j'aimai seul m'aime encor tendrement :
C'est la mort – ou la morte... Ô délice ! ô tourment !
La rose qu'elle tient, c'est la *Rose trémière*.

Sainte napolitaine aux mains pleines de feux,
Rose au cœur violet, fleur de sainte Gudule :
As-tu trouvé ta croix dans le désert des cieux ?

Roses blanches, tombez ! vous insultez nos dieux,
Tombez, fantômes blancs, de votre ciel qui brûle :
– La sainte de l'abîme est plus sainte à mes yeux !

Les Chimères

VERS DORÉS

> Eh quoi ! tout est sensible !
> PYTHAGORE.

Homme, libre penseur ! te crois-tu seul pensant
Dans ce monde où la vie éclate en toute chose ?
Des forces que tu tiens ta liberté dispose,
Mais de tous tes conseils l'univers est absent.

Respecte dans la bête un esprit agissant :
Chaque fleur est une âme à la Nature éclose ;
Un mystère d'amour dans le métal repose ;
« Tout est sensible ! » Et tout sur ton être est puissant.

Crains, dans le mur aveugle, un regard qui t'épie :
À la matière même un verbe est attaché...
Ne la fais pas servir à quelque usage impie !

Souvent dans l'être obscur habite un Dieu caché ;
Et comme un œil naissant couvert par ses paupières,
Un pur esprit s'accroît sous l'écorce des pierres !

Les Chimères

FANTAISIE

Il est un air pour qui je donnerais
Tout Rossini, tout Mozart et tout Weber,
Un air très vieux, languissant et funèbre,
Qui pour moi seul a des charmes secrets !

Or, chaque fois que je viens à l'entendre,
De deux cents ans mon âme rajeunit...
C'est sous Louis treize ; et je crois voir s'étendre
Un coteau vert, que le couchant jaunit,

Puis un château de brique à coins de pierre,
Aux vitraux teints de rougeâtres couleurs,
Ceint de grands parcs, avec une rivière
Baignant ses pieds, qui coule entre des fleurs ;

Puis une dame, à sa haute fenêtre,
Blonde aux yeux noirs, en ses habits anciens,
Que, dans une autre existence peut-être,
J'ai déjà vue... et dont je me souviens !

Odelettes

UNE ALLÉE DU LUXEMBOURG

Elle a passé, la jeune fille
Vive et preste comme un oiseau :
À la main une fleur qui brille,
À la bouche un refrain nouveau.

C'est peut-être la seule au monde
Dont le cœur au mien répondrait,
Qui venant dans ma nuit profonde
D'un seul regard l'éclaircirait !

Mais non, – ma jeunesse est finie...
Adieu, doux rayon qui m'as lui, –
Parfum, jeune fille, harmonie...
Le bonheur passait, – il a fui !

Odelettes

NI BONJOUR NI BONSOIR

Sur un air grec.

Νὴ καλιμέρα, νὴ ὥρα καλί.

Le matin n'est plus ! le soir pas encore !
Pourtant de nos yeux l'éclair a pâli.

Νὴ καλιμέρα, νὴ ὥρα καλί.

Mais le soir vermeil ressemble à l'aurore,
Et la nuit plus tard amène l'oubli !

Odelettes

ÉPITAPHE

Il a vécu tantôt gai comme un sansonnet,
Tour à tour amoureux insoucieux et tendre,
Tantôt sombre et rêveur comme un triste Clitandre.
Un jour il entendit qu'à sa porte on sonnait.

C'était la Mort ! Alors il la pria d'attendre
Qu'il eût posé le point à son dernier sonnet ;
Et puis sans s'émouvoir, il s'en alla s'étendre
Au fond du coffre froid où son corps frissonnait.

Il était paresseux, à ce que dit l'histoire,
Il laissait trop sécher l'encre dans l'écritoire.
Il voulait tout savoir mais il n'a rien connu.

Et quand vint le moment où, las de cette vie,
Un soir d'hiver, enfin l'âme lui fut ravie,
Il s'en alla disant : « Pourquoi suis-je venu ? »

Odelettes

ALFRED DE MUSSET

(1810-1857)

« Le romantisme, c'est l'étoile qui pleure, c'est le vent qui vagit, c'est la nuit qui frissonne, l'oiseau qui vole et la fleur qui embaume ; c'est le jet inespéré, l'extase alanguie, la citerne sous les palmiers, et l'espoir vermeil et ses mille amours, l'ange et la perle, la robe blanche des saules ; ô la belle chose, monsieur ! C'est l'infini et l'étoilé, le chaud, le rompu, le désenivré... le diamétral, le pyramidal, l'oriental, le nu à vif, l'étreint, l'embrassé, le tourbillonnant ; quelle science nouvelle ! » Voilà la définition enthousiaste donnée à Dupuis et son ami Cotonet qui l'interrogent sur ce terme mystérieux, par le clerc d'avoué poète de La Ferté-sous-Jouarre !

Et voilà aussi Musset lui-même, railleur, fantaisiste, iconoclaste, rassemblant sous la plume de ces deux enquêteurs dépourvus d'humour, toutes les définitions que ce mot protéiforme a pu connaître depuis qu'il est à la mode, un Musset ironique à la manière du XVIIIᵉ siècle prompt à souligner les dérives de la raison, l'auteur de comédies où l'on croit entendre Marivaux (et parfois Shakespeare). Lui, qui incarne pourtant, aux yeux de ses contemporains, la forme la plus sensible et la plus pathétique du lyrisme amoureux de ce siècle, et leur semble, depuis la parution des *Nuits*, le poète romantique par excellence.

Ces dialogues lyriques, expression de l'amour trahi, et de la douleur, sont un ensemble de quatre grands poèmes. La forme à deux voix, soulignée par le choix de métriques différentes, leur est commune, et le rapport que le poète établit entre eux et les saisons, les relie étroitement, ainsi que leur titre. Il n'est pas indifférent que Musset leur ait donné ce cadre nocturne cher aux romantiques allemands. La Nuit est l'espace privilégié de la plongée intérieure. Dans *La Nuit de Mai* citée ici, comme dans celle d'Août et d'Octobre, les protagonistes sont le poète, amer et meurtri, et la Muse qui l'incite à chanter. On pourrait voir, avec Claudel, dans cette incarnation féminine du chant, l'intervention d'Anima, l'inspiratrice, sans laquelle Animus ne peut accéder à sa propre voix. Cependant le poète n'est pas prêt encore à écouter en lui la montée de l'inspiration et *La Nuit de Décembre* est le théâtre d'une autre confrontation, celle du moi et de son double, « sorte de caricature tragique de l'être qui avait jadis vécu » selon les termes de Georges Poulet, plutôt que figure allégorique de la Solitude comme le dit le poète. Ombre de sa vie, ombre de ses songes, l'apparition matérialise l'impossible unité, le déchirement intérieur.

On peut aimer les chansons légères et tendres où le poète excelle et que nous citons, ou le pittoresque de *Venise* et le badinage de la *Ballade à la lune*, sans, rejeter pour autant, comme on a parfois tenté de le faire depuis que l'on a cru bon de railler « les pleureurs à nacelles », cette œuvre majeure où la poésie devient l'instrument privilégié d'une exploration de l'inconscient et qui permet à Musset de donner la mesure de son incontestable génie poétique.

VENISE

Dans Venise la rouge,
Pas un bateau qui bouge,
Pas un pêcheur dans l'eau,
    Pas un falot.

Seul, assis à la grève,
Le grand lion soulève,
Sur l'horizon serein,
    Son pied d'airain.

Autour de lui, par groupes,
Navires et chaloupes,
Pareils à des hérons
    Couchés en ronds,

Dorment sur l'eau qui fume,
Et croisent dans la brume,
En légers tourbillons,
    Leurs pavillons.

La lune qui s'efface
Couvre son front qui passe
D'un nuage étoilé
    Demi-voilé.

Ainsi, la dame abbesse
De Sainte-Croix rabaisse
Sa cape aux larges plis
    Sur son surplis.

Et les palais antiques,
Et les graves portiques,
Et les blancs escaliers
    Des chevaliers,

Et les ponts, et les rues,
Et les mornes statues,
Et le golfe mouvant
    Qui tremble au vent,

Tout se tait, fors les gardes
Aux longues hallebardes,
Qui veillent aux créneaux
    Des arsenaux.

— Ah ! maintenant plus d'une
Attend, au clair de lune,
Quelque jeune muguet,
    L'oreille au guet.

Pour le bal qu'on prépare,
Plus d'une qui se pare,
Met devant son miroir
    Le masque noir.

Sur sa couche embaumée,
La Vanina pâmée
Presse encor son amant,
    En s'endormant ;

Et Narcissa, la folle,
Au fond de sa gondole,
S'oublie en un festin
    Jusqu'au matin.

Et qui, dans l'Italie,
N'a son grain de folie ?
Qui ne garde aux amours
    Ses plus beaux jours ?

Laissons la vieille horloge,
Au palais du vieux doge,
Lui compter de ses nuits
    Les longs ennuis.

Comptons plutôt, ma belle,
Sur ta bouche rebelle
Tant de baisers donnés...
    Ou pardonnés.

Comptons plutôt tes charmes,
Comptons les douces larmes,
Qu'à nos yeux a coûté
    La volupté.

BALLADE À LA LUNE

C'était, dans la nuit brune,
Sur le clocher jauni,
        La lune,
Comme un point sur un i.

Lune, quel esprit sombre
Promène au bout d'un fil,
        Dans l'ombre,
Ta face et ton profil ?

Es-tu l'œil du ciel borgne ?
Quel chérubin cafard
        Nous lorgne
Sous ton masque blafard ?

N'es-tu rien qu'une boule ?
Qu'un grand faucheux bien gras
        Qui roule
Sans pattes et sans bras ?

Es-tu, je t'en soupçonne,
Le vieux cadran de fer
        Qui sonne
L'heure aux damnés d'enfer ?

Sur ton front qui voyage
Ce soir ont-ils compté
        Quel âge
A leur éternité ?

Est-ce un ver qui te ronge
Quand ton disque noirci
        S'allonge
En croissant rétréci ?

Qui t'avait éborgnée
L'autre nuit ? T'étais-tu
    Cognée
À quelque arbre pointu ?

Car tu vins, pâle et morne,
Coller sur mes carreaux
    Ta corne,
À travers les barreaux.

Va, lune moribonde,
Le beau corps de Phœbé
    La blonde
Dans la mer est tombé.

Tu n'en es que la face,
Et déjà, tout ridé,
    S'efface
Ton front dépossédé.

Rends-nous la chasseresse
Blanche, au sein virginal,
    Qui presse
Quelque cerf matinal !

Oh ! sous le vert platane
Sous les frais coudriers,
    Diane,
Et ses grands lévriers !

Le chevreau noir qui doute,
Pendu sur un rocher,
    L'écoute,
L'écoute s'approcher.

Et, suivant leurs curées,
Par les vaux, par les blés,
    Les prées,
Ses chiens s'en sont allés.

Oh ! le soir, dans la brise,
Phœbé, sœur d'Apollo,
          Surprise
À l'ombre, un pied dans l'eau !

Phœbé qui, la nuit close,
Aux lèvres d'un berger
          Se pose,
Comme un oiseau léger.

Lune, en notre mémoire,
De tes belles amours
          L'histoire
T'embellira toujours.

Et toujours rajeunie,
Tu seras du passant
          Bénie,
Pleine lune ou croissant.

T'aimera le vieux pâtre,
Seul, tandis qu'à ton front
          D'albâtre
Ses dogues aboieront.

T'aimera le pilote
Dans son grand bâtiment,
          Qui flotte,
Sous le clair firmament !

Et la fillette preste
Qui passe le buisson,
          Pied leste,
En chantant sa chanson.

Comme un ours à la chaîne,
Toujours sous tes yeux bleus
          Se traîne
L'Océan monstrueux.

Et qu'il vente ou qu'il neige,
Moi-même, chaque soir,
  Que fais-je,
Venant ici m'asseoir ?

Je viens voir à la brune,
Sur le clocher jauni,
  La lune
Comme un point sur un i.

TRISTESSE

J'ai perdu ma force et ma vie,
Et mes amis et ma gaieté ;
J'ai perdu jusqu'à la fierté
Qui faisait croire à mon génie.

Quand j'ai connu la Vérité,
J'ai cru que c'était une amie ;
Quand je l'ai comprise et sentie,
J'en étais déjà dégoûté.

Et pourtant elle est éternelle,
Et ceux qui se sont passés d'elle
Ici-bas ont tout ignoré.

Dieu parle, il faut qu'on lui réponde.
Le seul bien qui me reste au monde
Est d'avoir quelquefois pleuré.

1840

CHANSON

J'ai dit à mon cœur, à mon faible cœur :
N'est-ce point assez d'aimer sa maîtresse ?
Et ne vois-tu pas que changer sans cesse,
C'est perdre en désirs le temps du bonheur ?

Il m'a répondu : Ce n'est point assez,
Ce n'est point assez d'aimer sa maîtresse ;
Et ne vois-tu pas que changer sans cesse
Nous rend doux et chers les plaisirs passés ?

J'ai dit à mon cœur, à mon faible cœur :
N'est-ce point assez de tant de tristesse ?
Et ne vois-tu pas que changer sans cesse,
C'est à chaque pas trouver la douleur ?

Il m'a répondu : Ce n'est point assez,
Ce n'est point assez de tant de tristesse ;
Et ne vois-tu pas que changer sans cesse
Nous rend doux et chers les chagrins passés ?

1831

CHANSON

À Saint-Blaise, à la Zuecca,
Vous étiez, vous étiez bien aise
À Saint-Blaise.
À Saint-Blaise, à la Zuecca,
Nous étions bien là.

Mais de vous en souvenir
Prendrez-vous la peine ?
Mais de vous en souvenir
Et d'y revenir,

À Saint-Blaise, à la Zuecca,
Dans les prés fleuris cueillir la verveine,
À Saint-Blaise, à la Zuecca,
Vivre et mourir là !

1835

CHANSON DE BARBERINE

Beau chevalier qui partez pour la guerre,
    Qu'allez-vous faire
    Si loin d'ici ?
Voyez-vous pas que la nuit est profonde,
    Et que le monde
    N'est que souci ?

Vous qui croyez qu'une amour délaissée
    De la pensée
    S'enfuit ainsi,
Hélas ! hélas ! chercheurs de renommée,
    Votre fumée
    S'envole aussi.

Beau chevalier qui partez pour la guerre,
    Qu'allez-vous faire
    Si loin de nous ?
J'en vais pleurer, moi qui me laissais dire
    Que mon sourire
    Était si doux.

1836

À NINON

Si je vous le disais pourtant, que je vous aime,
Qui sait, brune aux yeux bleus, ce que vous en diriez ?
L'amour, vous le savez, cause une peine extrême ;
C'est un mal sans pitié que vous plaignez vous-même ;
Peut-être cependant que vous m'en puniriez.

Si je vous le disais, que six mois de silence
Cachent de longs tourments et des vœux insensés :
Ninon, vous êtes fine, et votre insouciance
Se plaît, comme une fée, à deviner d'avance ;
Vous me répondriez peut-être : je le sais.

Si je vous le disais, qu'une douce folie
A fait de moi votre ombre, et m'attache à vos pas :
Un petit air de doute et de mélancolie,
Vous le savez, Ninon, vous rend bien plus jolie ;
Peut-être diriez-vous que vous n'y croyez pas,

Si je vous le disais, que j'emporte dans l'âme
Jusques aux moindres mots de nos propos du soir :
Un regard offensé, vous le savez, madame,
Change deux yeux d'azur en deux éclairs de flamme ;
Vous me défendriez peut-être de vous voir.

Si je vous le disais, que chaque nuit je veille,
Que chaque jour je pleure et je prie à genoux ;
Ninon, quand vous riez, vous savez qu'une abeille
Prendrait pour une fleur votre bouche vermeille ;
Si je vous le disais, peut-être en ririez-vous.

Mais vous n'en saurez rien. — Je viens, sans rien en dire,
M'asseoir sous votre lampe et causer avec vous ;
Votre voix, je l'entends ; votre air, je le respire ;
Et vous pouvez douter, deviner et sourire,
Vos yeux ne verront pas de quoi m'être moins doux.

. . . .

J'aime, et je sais répondre avec indifférence ;
J'aime, et rien ne le dit ; j'aime, et seul je le sais ;
Et mon secret m'est cher, et chère ma souffrance ;
Et j'ai fait le serment d'aimer sans espérance,
Mais non pas sans bonheur ; – je vous vois, c'est assez.

Non, je n'étais pas né pour ce bonheur suprême,
De mourir dans vos bras et de vivre à vos pieds.
Tout me le prouve, hélas ! jusqu'à ma douleur même...
Si je vous le disais pourtant, que je vous aime,
Qui sait, brune aux yeux bleus, ce que vous en diriez ?

1837

LA NUIT DE MAI

LA MUSE

. . . .

Poète, prends ton luth ; c'est moi ton immortelle,
Qui t'ai vu cette nuit triste et silencieux,
Et qui, comme un oiseau que sa couvée appelle,
Pour pleurer avec toi descends du haut des cieux.
Viens, tu souffres, ami. Quelque ennui solitaire
Te ronge, quelque chose a gémi dans ton cœur ;
Quelque amour t'est venu, comme on en voit sur terre,
Une ombre de plaisir, un semblant de bonheur.
Viens, chantons devant Dieu ; chantons dans tes pensées,
Dans tes plaisirs perdus, dans tes peines passées ;
Partons dans un baiser pour un monde inconnu.
Éveillons au hasard les échos de ta vie,
Parlons-nous de bonheur, de gloire, et de folie,
Et que ce soit un rêve, et le premier venu.
Inventons quelque part des lieux où l'on oublie ;
Partons, nous sommes seuls, l'univers est à nous.
Voici la verte Écosse et la brune Italie,
Et la Grèce, ma mère, où le miel est si doux,
Argos, et Ptéléon, ville des hécatombes,
Et Messa la divine, agréable aux colombes,
Et le front chevelu du Pélion changeant.
Et le bleu Titarèse, et le golfe d'argent
Qui montre dans ses eaux, où le cygne se mire,
La blanche Oloossone à la blanche Camyre.
Dis-moi, quel songe d'or nos chants vont-ils bercer ?
D'où vont venir les pleurs que nous allons verser ?
Ce matin, quand le jour a frappé ta paupière,
Quel séraphin pensif, courbé sur ton chevet,
Secouait des lilas dans sa robe légère,
Et te contait tout bas les amours qu'il rêvait ?
Chanterons-nous l'espoir, la tristesse ou la joie ?
Tremperons-nous de sang les bataillons d'acier ?

Suspendrons-nous l'amant sur l'échelle de soie ?
Jetterons-nous au vent l'écume du coursier ?

. . . .

Prends ton luth ! prends ton luth ! je ne peux plus me taire ;
Mon aile me soulève au souffle du printemps.
Le vent va m'emporter ; je vais quitter la terre.
Une larme de toi ! Dieu m'écoute ; il est temps.

                                                      1835

LA NUIT DE DÉCEMBRE

LE POÈTE

Du temps que j'étais écolier,
Je restais un soir à veiller
Dans notre salle solitaire.
Devant ma table vint s'asseoir
Un pauvre enfant vêtu de noir,
Qui me ressemblait comme un frère.

Son visage était triste et beau :
À la lueur de mon flambeau,
Dans mon livre ouvert il vint lire.
Il pencha son front sur sa main,
Et resta jusqu'au lendemain,
Pensif, avec un doux sourire.

Comme j'allais avoir quinze ans
Je marchais un jour, à pas lents,
Dans un bois, sur une bruyère.
Au pied d'un arbre vint s'asseoir
Un jeune homme vêtu de noir,
Qui me ressemblait comme un frère.

Je lui demandai mon chemin ;
Il tenait un luth d'une main,
De l'autre un bouquet d'églantine.
Il me fit un salut d'ami,
Et, se détournant à demi,
Me montra du doigt la colline.

À l'âge où l'on croit à l'amour,
J'étais seul dans ma chambre un jour,
Pleurant ma première misère.
Au coin de mon feu vint s'asseoir
Un étranger vêtu de noir,
Qui me ressemblait comme un frère.

Il était morne et soucieux ;
D'une main il montrait les cieux,
Et de l'autre il tenait un glaive.
De ma peine il semblait souffrir,
Mais il ne poussa qu'un soupir,
Et s'évanouit comme un rêve.

À l'âge où l'on est libertin,
Pour boire un toast en un festin,
Un jour je soulevai mon verre.
En face de moi vint s'asseoir
Un convive vêtu de noir,
Qui me ressemblait comme un frère.

. . . .

Un an après, il était nuit ;
J'étais à genoux près du lit
Où venait de mourir mon père.
Au chevet du lit vint s'asseoir
Un orphelin vêtu de noir,
Qui me ressemblait comme un frère.

Ses yeux étaient noyés de pleurs ;
Comme les anges de douleurs,
Il était couronné d'épine ;
Son luth à terre était gisant,
Sa pourpre de couleur de sang,
Et son glaive dans sa poitrine.

Je m'en suis si bien souvenu,
Que je l'ai toujours reconnu
À tous les instants de ma vie.
C'est une étrange vision,
Et cependant, ange ou démon,
J'ai vu partout cette ombre amie.

. . . .

Qui donc es-tu, spectre de ma jeunesse,
    Pèlerin que rien n'a lassé ?
Dis-moi pourquoi je te trouve sans cesse
    Assis dans l'ombre où j'ai passé.

Qui donc es-tu, visiteur solitaire,
   Hôte assidu de mes douleurs ?
Qu'as-tu donc fait pour me suivre sur terre ?
Qui donc es-tu, qui donc es-tu, mon frère,
   Qui n'apparais qu'au jour des pleurs ?

LA VISION

– Ami, notre père est le tien.
Je ne suis ni l'ange gardien,
Ni le mauvais destin des hommes.
Ceux que j'aime, je ne sais pas
De quel côté s'en vont leurs pas
Sur ce peu de fange où nous sommes.

Je ne suis ni dieu ni démon,
Et tu m'as nommé par mon nom
Quand tu m'as appelé ton frère ;
Où tu vas, j'y serai toujours,
Jusques au dernier de tes jours,
Où j'irai m'asseoir sur ta pierre.

Le ciel m'a confié ton cœur.
Quand tu seras dans la douleur,
Viens à moi sans inquiétude.
Je te suivrai sur le chemin :
Mais je ne puis toucher ta main,
Ami, je suis la Solitude.

1835

THÉOPHILE GAUTIER

(1811-1872)

Si on a gardé de l'enfance le souvenir de certains conciliabules d'hirondelles pleins de charme, si, adulte, on a retenu la formule de Baudelaire parlant de lui comme du « parfait magicien ès lettres », on ne le relit pas sans quelque déception, ni sans éprouver le sentiment que la plupart de ses poèmes tournent court. En choisissant d'exclure le lyrisme et de brider l'enthousiasme, Théophile Gautier a fait, presque de chacun d'eux, l'objet poétique dont il rêvait, un fragment de réalité détaché de son auteur, parfaitement ciselé et impersonnel, mais qui nous reste assez étranger.

Sa démarche, qui consiste à privilégier la forme, annonce la génération des années 50 et rompt déjà clairement avec les ambitions des poètes précédents. Artisan scrupuleux du vers, tenant de ce qu'on a appelé « l'art pour l'art », il n'aspire plus à être le prophète qui guide les peuples, mais ne se reconnaît d'autre mission que la poursuite passionnée de la perfection formelle. Cependant la filiation entre sa démarche et le romantisme n'est pas douteuse. Toute une poétique de la description est issue des *Orientales*, c'est à elle que se rattachent les premiers poèmes de Gautier par sa recherche du pittoresque et de la couleur, mais peu à peu s'opère en lui ce que Paul Bénichou appelle « la mue pessimiste du romantisme français » : à l'hédonisme gracieux de certaines pièces succède la préoccupation exclusive du beau, un esthétisme fondé sur une vision pessimiste de la société et de l'homme, et selon laquelle, face à leur décadence, l'art reste le seul refuge, la seule valeur.

Gautier n'en demeurera pas moins durant toute sa vie l'ami fidèle et l'admirateur de Hugo dont il proclame, même pendant l'exil, la souveraineté incontestable :

> *Seule la poésie incarnée en Hugo*
> *Ne nous a pas déçus, et de palmes divines*
> *Vers l'avenir tournée ombrage nos ruines.*

On lira ici, à côté du poème sans doute le plus célèbre de Gautier, et qui a valeur de manifeste, deux de ses *Fantaisies d'hiver* proches de Musset, et qui semblent aussi annoncer Verlaine ou Laforgue ainsi que *L'Impassible*, sonnet aux accents parnassiens que n'aurait pas renié Baudelaire. On le voit par ces rapprochements, l'œuvre de Gautier nous retient moins pour elle-même que par sa place au carrefour des grandes avenues poétiques de son siècle.

L'ART

Oui, l'œuvre sort plus belle
D'une forme au travail
    Rebelle,
Vers, marbre, onyx, émail.

Point de contraintes fausses !
Mais que pour marcher droit
    Tu chausses,
Muse, un cothurne étroit !

Fi du rythme commode
Comme un soulier trop grand,
    Du mode
Que tout pied quitte et prend !

Statuaire, repousse
L'argile que pétrit
    Le pouce,
Quand flotte ailleurs l'esprit ;

Lutte avec le carrare,
Avec le paros dur
    Et rare,
Gardiens du contour pur ;

Emprunte à Syracuse
Son bronze où fermement
    S'accuse
Le trait fier et charmant ;

D'une main délicate
Poursuis dans un filon
    D'agate
Le profil d'Apollon.

Peintre, fuis l'aquarelle,
Et fixe la couleur
    Trop frêle
Au four de l'émailleur ;

Fais les sirènes bleues,
Tordant de cent façons
    Leurs queues,
Les monstres des blasons ;

Dans son nimbe trilobe
La Vierge et son Jésus,
    Le globe
Avec la croix dessus.

Tout passe. – L'art robuste
Seul a l'éternité :
    Le buste
Survit à la cité.

Et la médaille austère
Que trouve un laboureur
    Sous terre
Révèle un empereur.

Les dieux eux-mêmes meurent.
Mais les vers souverains
    Demeurent
Plus forts que les airains.

Sculpte, lime, cisèle ;
Que ton rêve flottant
    Se scelle
Dans le bloc résistant !

FANTAISIES D'HIVER

I

Le nez rouge, la face blême,
Sur un pupitre de glaçons,
L'Hiver exécute son thème
Dans le quatuor des saisons.

Il chante d'une voix peu sûre
Des airs vieillots et chevrotants ;
Son pied glacé bat la mesure
Et la semelle en même temps ;

Et comme Hændel, dont la perruque
Perdait sa farine en tremblant,
Il fait envoler de sa nuque
La neige qui la poudre à blanc.

II

Dans le bassin des Tuileries,
Le cygne s'est pris en nageant,
Et les arbres, comme aux féeries,
Sont en filigrane d'argent.

Les vases ont des fleurs de givre,
Sous la charmille aux blancs réseaux ;
Et sur la neige on voit se suivre
Les pas étoilés des oiseaux.

Au piédestal où, court-vêtue,
Vénus coudoyait Phocion,
L'Hiver a posé pour statue
La Frileuse de Clodion.

L'IMPASSIBLE

La Satiété dort au fond de vos grands yeux ;
En eux plus de désirs, plus d'amour, plus d'envie ;
Ils ont bu la lumière, ils ont tari la vie,
Comme une mer profonde où s'absorbent les cieux.

Sous leur bleu sombre on lit le vaste ennui des Dieux,
Pour qui toute chimère est d'avance assouvie,
Et qui, sachant l'effet dont la cause est suivie,
Mélangent au présent l'avenir déjà vieux.

L'infini s'est fondu dans vos larges prunelles,
Et devant ce miroir qui ne réfléchit rien
L'amour découragé s'assoit, fermant ses ailes,

Vous, cependant, avec un calme olympien,
Comme la Mnémosyne à son socle accoudée,
Vous poursuivez, rêveuse, une impossible idée.

TERZA RIMA

Quand Michel-Ange eut peint la chapelle Sixtine,
Et que de l'échafaud, sublime et radieux,
Il fut redescendu dans la cité latine,

Il ne pouvait baisser ni les bras ni les yeux.
Ses pieds ne savaient pas comment marcher sur terre ;
Il avait oublié le monde dans les cieux.

Trois grands mois il garda cette attitude austère,
On l'eût pris pour un ange en extase devant
Le saint triangle d'or, au moment du mystère

Frère, voilà pourquoi les poètes, souvent,
Buttent à chaque pas sur les chemins du monde ;
Les yeux fichés au ciel, ils s'en vont en rêvant.

Les anges secouant leur chevelure blonde,
Penchent leur front sur eux et leur tendent les bras,
Et les veulent baiser avec leur bouche ronde.

Eux marchent au hasard et font mille faux pas ;
Ils cognent les passants, se jettent sous les roues,
Ou tombent dans des puits qu'ils n'aperçoivent pas.

Que leur font les passants, les pierres et les boues ?
Ils cherchent dans le jour le rêve de leurs nuits,
Et le feu du désir leur empourpre les joues.

Ils ne comprennent rien aux terrestres ennuis,
Et, quand ils ont fini leur chapelle Sixtine,
Ils sortent rayonnants de leurs obscurs réduits.

Un auguste reflet de leur œuvre divine
S'attache à leur personne et leur dore le front,
Et le ciel qu'ils ont vu, dans leurs yeux se devine.

Les nuits suivront les jours et se succéderont,
Avant que leurs regards et leurs bras ne s'abaissent ;
Et leurs pieds, de longtemps, ne se raffermiront.

Tous nos palais sous eux s'éteignent et s'affaissent ;
Leur âme, à la coupole où leur œuvre reluit,
Revole, et ce ne sont que leurs corps qu'ils nous laissent.

Notre jour leur paraît plus sombre que la nuit ;
Leur œil cherche toujours le ciel bleu de la fresque,
Et le tableau quitté les tourmente et les suit.

Comme Buonarotti, le peintre gigantesque,
Ils ne peuvent plus voir que les choses d'en haut,
Et que le ciel de marbre où leur front touche presque.

Sublime aveuglement ? magnifique défaut !

LECONTE DE LISLE

(1818-1894)

L'impassibilité apparente de l'écrivain n'est pas chez lui, comme c'est le cas, par exemple, pour Flaubert, l'effet d'un romantisme contrarié et d'une victoire sur soi-même. Aucune trace dans ses écrits d'une œuvre de jeunesse où s'épancherait son cœur. Ses choix philosophiques et politiques sont antérieurs à sa vocation poétique et ses convictions scientistes ont été déterminantes dans son parti pris de réalisme descriptif et dans sa recherche d'une perfection formelle au service de la vérité. Au premier nous devons cette justesse dans l'observation qui fait de lui un grand poète animalier. La seconde fonde sa prédilection pour les sujets « barbares » et « antiques », à travers lesquels il s'efforce d'être fidèle à l'histoire et de prendre en compte les connaissances de la science contemporaine sur les civilisations du passé. C'est ce qui l'amène à redonner aux noms anciens leurs rugueuses sonorités originelles, à tenter de restituer aux héros leur véritable visage, et aux époques lointaines qu'il évoque, leur couleur authentique. Son génie, essentiellement épique, le porte à entreprendre de longues fresques mythologiques ou historiques qui ne manquent pas de grandeur. Cependant elles ne séduisent pas toujours le lecteur à cause d'une raideur hautaine qui est la constante de l'œuvre. Le stoïcisme majestueux qui s'y exprime rappelle parfois Vigny et laisse entrevoir une âme douloureuse. En réalité, bien qu'il ait violemment récusé l'expression des sentiments personnels (« Il y a, écrit-il dans la préface des *Poèmes antiques*, dans l'aveu public des angoisses du cœur et de ses voluptés non moins amères, une vanité et une profanation gratuites »), il parle néanmoins de soi dans certains de ses poèmes : ainsi ses évocations de paysages exotiques, grâce aux souvenirs de son île natale, ne valent pas seulement par leur pittoresque, on y devine parfois une confidence voilée. Surtout l'œuvre entière est traversée par l'expression du sentiment tragique de l'existence. Dans cette vision pessimiste l'implication personnelle du poète ne fait pas de doute, et le cri de révolte de ses héros devant le malheur de la condition humaine, est bien le sien. Les passages que soulève un souffle puissant, les grands mythes auxquels il redonne vie et les symboles qu'il attache aux paysages ou aux animaux qu'il décrit, montrent assez que l'idéologue en lui n'a pas fait taire le poète.

QAÏN

En la trentième année, au siècle de l'épreuve.
Étant captif parmi les cavaliers d'Assur,
Thogorma, le Voyant, fils d'Élam, fils de Thur,
Eut ce rêve, couché dans les roseaux du fleuve,
À l'heure où le soleil blanchit l'herbe et le mur.

Depuis que le Chasseur Iahvèh, qui terrasse
Les forts et de leur chair nourrit l'aigle et le chien,
Avait lié son peuple au joug assyrien,
Tous, se rasant les poils du crâne et de la face,
Stupides, s'étaient tus et n'entendaient plus rien.

Ployés sous le fardeau des misères accrues,
Dans la faim, dans la soif, dans l'épouvante assis,
Ils revoyaient leurs murs écroulés et noircis,
Et, comme aux crocs publics pendent les viandes crues,
Leurs princes aux gibets des Rois incirconcis,

Le pied de l'infidèle appuyé sur la nuque
Des vaillants, le saint temple où priaient les aïeux
Souillé, vide, fumant, effondré par les pieux,
Et les vierges en pleurs sous le fouet de l'eunuque
Et le sombre Iahvèh muet au fond des cieux.

Or, laissant, ce jour-là, près des mornes aïeules
Et des enfants couchés dans les nattes de cuir,
Les femmes aux yeux noirs de sa tribu gémir,
Le fils d'Élam, meurtri par la sangle des meules,
Le long du grand Khobar se coucha pour dormir.

Les bandes d'étalons, par la plaine inondée
De lumière, gisaient sous le dattier roussi,
Et les taureaux, et les dromadaires aussi,
Avec les chameliers d'Iran et de Khaldée.
Thogorma, le Voyant, eut ce rêve. Voici :

C'était un soir des temps. Par monceaux, les nuées,
Émergeant de la cuve ardente de la mer,
Tantôt, comme des blocs d'airain, pendaient dans l'air,
Tantôt, d'un tourbillon véhément remuées,
Hurlantes, s'écroulaient en un immense éclair.

. . . .

Thogorma dans ses yeux vit monter des murailles
De fer d'où s'enroulaient des spirales de tours
Et de palais cerclés d'airain sur des blocs lourds ;
Ruche énorme, géhenne aux lugubres entrailles
Où s'engouffraient les Forts, princes des anciens jours.

Ils s'en venaient de la montagne et de la plaine,
Du fond des sombres bois et du désert sans fin,
Plus massifs que le cèdre et plus hauts que le pin,
Suants, échevelés, soufflant leur rude haleine
Avec leur bouche épaisse et rouge, et pleins de faim.

C'est ainsi qu'ils rentraient, l'ours velu des cavernes
À l'épaule, ou le cerf, ou le lion sanglant.
Et les femmes marchaient, géantes, d'un pas lent,
Sous les vases d'airain qu'emplit l'eau des citernes,
Graves, et les bras nus, et les mains sur le flanc.

Elles allaient, dardant leurs prunelles superbes,
Les seins droits, le col haut, dans la sérénité
Terrible de la force et de la liberté,
Et posant tour à tour dans la ronce et les herbes
Leurs pieds fermes et blancs avec tranquillité.

Puis, quand tout, foule et bruit et poussière mouvante,
Eut disparu dans l'orbe immense des remparts,
L'abîme de la nuit laissa de toutes parts
Suinter la terreur vague et sourdre l'épouvante
En un rauque soupir sous le ciel morne épars.

Et le Voyant sentit le poil de sa peau rude
Se hérisser tout droit en face de cela,
Car il connut, dans son esprit, que c'était là
La Ville de l'angoisse et de la solitude,
Sépulcre de Qaïn au pays d'Hévila ;

. . . .

LES HURLEURS

Le soleil dans les flots avait noyé ses flammes,
La ville s'endormait aux pieds des monts brumeux.
Sur de grands rocs lavés d'un nuage écumeux
La mer sombre en grondant versait ses hautes lames.

La nuit multipliait ce long gémissement.
Nul astre ne luisait dans l'immensité nue ;
Seule, la lune pâle, en écartant la nue,
Comme une morne lampe oscillait tristement.

Monde muet, marqué d'un signe de colère,
Débris d'un globe mort au hasard dispersé,
Elle laissait tomber de son orbe glacé
Un reflet sépulcral sur l'océan polaire.

Sans borne, assise au Nord, sous les cieux étouffants,
L'Afrique, s'abritant d'ombre épaisse et de brume,
Affamait ses lions dans le sable qui fume,
Et couchait près des lacs ses troupeaux d'éléphants.

Mais sur la plage aride, aux odeurs insalubres,
Parmi les ossements de bœufs et de chevaux,
De maigres chiens, épais, allongeant leurs museaux,
Se lamentaient, poussant des hurlements lugubres.

La queue en cercle sous leurs ventres palpitants,
L'œil dilaté, tremblant sur leurs pattes fébriles,
Accroupis çà et là, tous hurlaient, immobiles,
Et d'un frisson rapide agités par instants.

L'écume de la mer collait sur leurs échines
De longs poils qui laissaient les vertèbres saillir ;
Et, quand les flots par bonds les venaient assaillir,
Leurs dents blanches claquaient sous leurs rouges babines.

Devant la lune errante aux livides clartés,
Quelle angoisse inconnue, au bord des noires ondes,
Faisait pleurer une âme en vos formes immondes ?
Pourquoi gémissiez-vous, spectres épouvantés ?

Je ne sais ; mais, ô chiens qui hurliez sur les plages,
Après tant de soleils qui ne reviendront plus,
J'entends toujours, du fond de mon passé confus,
Le cri désespéré de vos douleurs sauvages !

LE MANCHY

Sous un nuage frais de claire mousseline,
    Tous les dimanches au matin,
Tu venais à la ville en manchy de rotin,
    Par les rampes de la colline.

La cloche de l'église alertement tintait ;
    Le vent de mer berçait les cannes ;
Comme une grêle d'or, aux pointes des savanes,
    Le feu du soleil crépitait.

Le bracelet aux poings, l'anneau sur la cheville,
    Et le mouchoir jaune aux chignons,
Deux Telingas portaient, assidus compagnons,
    Ton lit aux nattes de Manille.

Ployant leur jarret maigre et nerveux, et chantant,
    Souples dans leurs tuniques blanches,
Le bambou sur l'épaule et les mains sur les hanches,
    Ils allaient le long de l'Étang.

Le long de la chaussée et des varangues basses
    Où les vieux créoles fumaient,
Par les groupes joyeux des Noirs, ils s'animaient
    Au bruit des bobres Madécasses.

Dans l'air léger flottait l'odeur des tamarins ;
    Sur les houles illuminées,
Au large, les oiseaux, en d'immenses traînées,
    Plongeaient dans les brouillards marins.

Et tandis que ton pied, sorti de la babouche,
    Pendait, rose, au bord du manchy,
À l'ombre des Bois-Noirs touffus et du letchi
    Aux fruits moins pourprés que ta bouche ;

Tandis qu'un papillon, les deux ailes en fleur,
    Teinté d'azur et d'écarlate,
Se posait par instants sur ta peau délicate
    En y laissant de sa couleur ;

On voyait, au travers du rideau de batiste,
    Tes boucles dorer l'oreiller,
Et, sous leurs cils mi-clos, feignant de sommeiller,
    Tes beaux yeux de sombre améthyste.

Tu t'en venais ainsi, par ces matins si doux,
    De la montagne à la grand-messe,
Dans ta grâce naïve et ta rose jeunesse,
    Au pas rythmé de tes Hindous.

Maintenant, dans le sable aride de nos grèves,
    Sous les chiendents, au bruit des mers,
Tu reposes parmi les morts qui me sont chers,
    Ô charme de mes premiers rêves !

Poèmes barbares

CHARLES BAUDELAIRE

(1821-1867)

Au poète impeccable
Au parfait magicien ès lettres...

Ce double éloge décerné à Théophile Gautier, dédicataire des *Fleurs du mal*, nous éclaire d'abord sur son auteur, car c'est bien sa conception de la poésie et de la fonction du poète que Baudelaire condense dans ces lignes. Un vers au moins le confirme, celui qu'il destinait à l'épilogue inachevé de ce recueil, et dans lequel il s'attribue, en des termes très proches, le mérite d'avoir fait son livre : « Comme un parfait chimiste et comme une âme sainte. »

Alchimiste ou magicien parfait, le poète est d'abord à ses yeux détenteur d'un secret, celui du grand-œuvre qui permet la conversion du métal vil en métal noble. Aussi peut-il dire à la ville qui fut toujours pour lui source d'inspiration : « Tu m'as donné ta boue et j'en ai fait de l'or. » Il doit être encore, et ce n'est pas moins essentiel, l' « âme sainte », le « poète impeccable » qui veille à ne pas trahir sa vocation spirituelle. Ce n'est possible que lorsque son vers, détaché de toute fonction utilitaire, de toute complaisance à des fins trop immédiates, devient pour lui le moyen d'opérer la transmutation souhaitée, et de sublimer le trivial. Il lui faut aussi pour cela le don de déceler, sous la matérialité des choses visibles, le sens allégorique qu'elles recèlent. Bien des pièges lui sont tendus dans cette voie ! Le « Mauvais Moine », de *Spleen et idéal* ou encore le théologien satanique du « Châtiment de l'orgueil » le montrent assez. Chez l'un, paresse et désespoir entravent la quête spirituelle, tandis que le vertige du pouvoir aveugle le second et le condamne à la damnation. Si le spleen est le gouffre où s'engloutit la volonté, l'idéal, cette seconde postulation de l'homme, comporte aussi un danger : le rêve trop ambitieux de l'artiste peut l'égarer et le perdre. Mais surtout un impitoyable ennemi lui barre la route, c'est le Temps, « Noir assassin de la Vie et de l'Art ». La grandeur de l'artiste tient à la lutte qu'il mène pour son œuvre, à l'ascèse de la création, car il sacrifie sa vie, en acceptant de n'être, cependant, qu'un phare brièvement allumé dans les ténèbres humaines ou le cri d'une sentinelle vigilante au pays de la mort. Témoignant de la dignité de l'homme, il n'a pas accès aux « rivages de lumière » mais son inlassable effort pour y parvenir est son honneur :

> *Car c'est vraiment, Seigneur, le meilleur témoignage*
> *Que nous puissions donner de notre dignité*
> *Que cet ardent sanglot qui roule d'âge en âge*
> *Et vient mourir au bord de votre éternité !*

Baudelaire ne rompt pas avec le romantisme, il conserve la plupart de ses thèmes mais il a renoncé à cette forme de lyrisme où le poète, dans le long déroulement de ses vers, comme enchanté de sa propre voix, semblait être porté par elle au-delà de lui-même. Sa poétique est toute de concentration. Brièveté et recherche de perfection formelle lui sont essentielles, il n'y a plus de place chez lui pour le déferlement de strophes éloquentes, c'est la mise en œuvre, par un patient travail sur les mots et les sons, d'une « sorcellerie évocatoire » concertée, qui permet la vision d'une autre réalité. C'est pourquoi, lorsqu'il reprend des sujets tels que la malédiction du poète, la mélancolie ou le désir d'espaces inconnus, si souvent présents dans les œuvres de ses prédécesseurs immédiats, le sentiment de familiarité du lecteur se dissipe très vite, car sa manière neuve de les traiter leur confère une sorte d'étrangeté. On le voit, par exemple, avec le *Chant d'automne* où le poète, en évoquant le choc des bûches « sur le pavé des cours », donne à la réalité la plus ordinaire une valeur métaphorique, et traduit en elle l'angoisse de l'esprit envahi par un pressentiment de mort. Ce dépassement des apparences par leur interprétation, cet univers où tout devient allégorie lui permet d'échapper à une esthétique purement réaliste malgré sa prédilection évidente pour les choses vues des « tableaux parisiens » et pour l'outrance baroque dans la description que manifeste, par exemple, « une Charogne », ou l'ex-voto « À une Madone ». Et cependant la réalité sensible est indispensable à l'artiste, c'est elle la grande pourvoyeuse d'images, et il peut puiser indéfiniment dans la vie quotidienne des hommes, comme dans une autre « forêt de symboles ».

Dans les principes esthétiques qu'il a posés à travers ses *Salons* ou ses textes de critique littéraire et musicale, il affirme, en effet, que deux éléments entrent dans la composition du Beau, l'un éternel, hors du temps, l'autre circonstanciel, qui varie avec chaque époque. C'est de cette conception que découle le principe de « modernité » essentiel à ses yeux : le présent immédiat offre à chaque génération un réservoir inouï de suggestions inexploitées. D'où la fécondité poétique de la ville qui propose au passant des architectures changeantes et des scènes insolites dont l'interprétation fait naître autant d'allégories.

La différence la plus significative entre la doctrine romantique et la vision du Beau chez Baudelaire, c'est le refus par ce dernier de toute esthétique qui se fonderait sur la nature ou sur le naturel. Attitude qui inspirera plus tard au mouvement symboliste son antinaturalisme. Cependant si l'on voit dans le célèbre sonnet des *Correspondances* le texte clef de la poétique de l'allégorie, on peut s'étonner d'y trouver la Nature sacralisée. La contradiction n'est qu'apparente : ce que la Nature offre à l'homme c'est un dépassement du sensible et non la contemplation de sa beauté. Dans la tradition de l'Antiquité, le temple est la projection terrestre de l'espace que les prêtres tracent dans le ciel. La Nature, écho d'une autre réalité, ne se propose pas à l'artiste comme modèle, elle n'est que l'intermédiaire qui lui permet de retrouver le monde idéal dont elle est la réplique, grâce aux symboles qu'elle présente à ses yeux. S'il est vrai que Baudelaire n'invente pas la théorie de l'unité cachée du monde d'en haut et du monde d'en bas, non plus que cette autre unité, on pourrait dire horizontale, qui relie secrètement les composantes de nos sensations, lorsqu'il enchâsse, dans l'espace étroit d'un sonnet, les traditions qu'il recueille, il leur donne, sous cette forme resserrée, l'autorité d'un code sacré sur lequel se fonde la quête spirituelle du poète.

Ainsi la métaphore, figure poétique par excellence, quelque

singulière qu'elle soit, n'est que la traduction, à chaque fois nouvelle, du lien secret qui unit les êtres et les choses. Dans le poème, les rythmes et la composition des strophes tendent aussi à exprimer cette unité. D'ailleurs, au-delà des formes existantes, le poète rêve encore « le miracle d'une prose poétique, musicale, sans rythme et sans rime, assez souple et assez heurtée pour s'adapter aux mouvements lyriques de l'âme, aux ondulations de la rêverie, aux soubresauts de la conscience », celle même qu'il expérimente dans les *Petits Poèmes en prose*. Car l'homme en cheminant à travers les symboles « qui l'observent avec des regards familiers », prend conscience de son appartenance à cet univers et du pouvoir qui lui est donné d'interpréter son être même, jusque dans la conscience de son extrême misère, pour en faire jaillir le sens caché, et transfigurer le sol aride par l'épanouissement des « fleurs nouvelles ».

CORRESPONDANCES

La Nature est un temple où de vivants piliers
Laissent parfois sortir de confuses paroles ;
L'homme y passe à travers des forêts de symboles
Qui l'observent avec des regards familiers.

Comme de longs échos qui de loin se confondent
Dans une ténébreuse et profonde unité,
Vaste comme la nuit et comme la clarté,
Les parfums, les couleurs et les sons se répondent.

Il est des parfums frais comme des chairs d'enfants,
Doux comme les hautbois, verts comme les prairies,
– Et d'autres, corrompus, riches et triomphants,

Ayant l'expansion des choses infinies,
Comme l'ambre, le musc, le benjoin et l'encens,
Qui chantent les transports de l'esprit et des sens.

Les Fleurs du mal,
Spleen et idéal, IV

L'ENNEMI

Ma jeunesse ne fut qu'un ténébreux orage,
Traversé çà et là par de brillants soleils ;
Le tonnerre et la pluie ont fait un tel ravage,
Qu'il reste en mon jardin bien peu de fruits vermeils.

Voilà que j'ai touché l'automne des idées,
Et qu'il faut employer la pelle et les râteaux
Pour rassembler à neuf les terres inondées,
Où l'eau creuse des trous grands comme des tombeaux.

Et qui sait si les fleurs nouvelles que je rêve
Trouveront dans ce sol lavé comme une grève
Le mystique aliment qui ferait leur vigueur ?

– Ô douleur ! ô douleur ! Le Temps mange la vie,
Et l'obscur Ennemi qui nous ronge le cœur
Du sang que nous perdons croît et se fortifie !

Les Fleurs du mal,
Spleen et idéal, X

LA VIE ANTÉRIEURE

J'ai longtemps habité sous de vastes portiques
Que les soleils marins teignaient de mille feux,
Et que leurs grands piliers, droits et majestueux,
Rendaient pareils, le soir, aux grottes basaltiques.

Les houles, en roulant les images des cieux,
Mêlaient d'une façon solennelle et mystique
Les tout-puissants accords de leur riche musique
Aux couleurs du couchant reflété par mes yeux.

C'est là que j'ai vécu dans les voluptés calmes,
Au milieu de l'azur, des vagues, des splendeurs
Et des esclaves nus, tout imprégnés d'odeurs,

Qui me rafraîchissaient le front avec des palmes,
Et dont l'unique soin était d'approfondir
Le secret douloureux qui me faisait languir.

Les Fleurs du mal,
Spleen et idéal, XII

LA BEAUTÉ

Je suis belle, ô mortels ! comme un rêve de pierre,
Et mon sein, où chacun s'est meurtri tour à tour,
Est fait pour inspirer au poète un amour
Éternel et muet ainsi que la matière.

Je trône dans l'azur comme un sphinx incompris ;
J'unis un cœur de neige à la blancheur des cygnes ;
Je hais le mouvement qui déplace les lignes,
Et jamais je ne pleure et jamais je ne ris.

Les poëtes, devant mes grandes attitudes,
Que j'ai l'air d'emprunter aux plus fiers monuments,
Consumeront leurs jours en d'austères études ;

Car j'ai, pour fasciner ces dociles amants,
De purs miroirs qui font toutes choses plus belles :
Mes yeux, mes larges yeux aux clartés éternelles !

Les Fleurs du mal,
Spleen et idéal, XVII

PARFUM EXOTIQUE

Quand, les deux yeux fermés, en un soir chaud d'automne,
Je respire l'odeur de ton sein chaleureux,
Je vois se dérouler des rivages heureux
Qu'éblouissent les feux d'un soleil monotone ;

Une île paresseuse où la nature donne
Des arbres singuliers et des fruits savoureux ;
Des hommes dont le corps est mince et vigoureux,
Et des femmes dont l'œil par sa franchise étonne.

Guidé par ton odeur vers de charmants climats,
Je vois un port rempli de voiles et de mâts
Encor tout fatigués par la vague marine,

Pendant que le parfum des verts tamariniers,
Qui circule dans l'air et m'enfle la narine,
Se mêle dans mon âme au chant des mariniers.

Les Fleurs du mal,
Spleen et idéal, XXII

LA CHEVELURE

Ô toison, moutonnant jusque sur l'encolure !
Ô boucles ! Ô parfum chargé de nonchaloir !
Extase ! Pour peupler ce soir l'alcôve obscure
Des souvenirs dormant dans cette chevelure,
Je la veux agiter dans l'air comme un mouchoir !

La langoureuse Asie et la brûlante Afrique,
Tout un monde lointain, absent, presque défunt,
Vit dans tes profondeurs, forêt aromatique !
Comme d'autres esprits voguent sur la musique,
Le mien, ô mon amour ! nage sur ton parfum.

J'irai là-bas où l'arbre et l'homme, pleins de sève,
Se pâment longuement sous l'ardeur des climats ;
Fortes tresses, soyez la houle qui m'enlève !
Tu contiens, mer d'ébène, un éblouissant rêve
De voiles, de rameurs, de flammes et de mâts :

Un port retentissant où mon âme peut boire
À grands flots le parfum, le son et la couleur ;
Où les vaisseaux, glissant dans l'or et dans la moire,
Ouvrent leurs vastes bras pour embrasser la gloire
D'un ciel pur où frémit l'éternelle chaleur.

Je plongerai ma tête amoureuse d'ivresse
Dans ce noir océan où l'autre est enfermé ;
Et mon esprit subtil que le roulis caresse
Saura vous retrouver, ô féconde paresse !
Infinis bercements du loisir embaumé !

Cheveux bleus, pavillon de ténèbres tendues,
Vous me rendez l'azur du ciel immense et rond ;
Sur les bords duvetés de vos mèches tordues
Je m'enivre ardemment des senteurs confondues
De l'huile de coco, du musc et du goudron.

Longtemps ! toujours ! ma main dans ta crinière lourde
Sèmera le rubis, la perle et le saphir,
Afin qu'à mon désir tu ne sois jamais sourde !
N'es-tu pas l'oasis où je rêve, et la gourde
Où je hume à longs traits le vin du souvenir ?

Les Fleurs du mal,
Spleen et idéal, **XXIII**

LE BALCON

Mère des souvenirs, maîtresse des maîtresses,
Ô toi, tous mes plaisirs ! ô toi, tous mes devoirs !
Tu te rappelleras la beauté des caresses,
La douceur du foyer et le charme des soirs,
Mère des souvenirs, maîtresse des maîtresses !

Les soirs illuminés par l'ardeur du charbon,
Et les soirs au balcon, voilés de vapeurs roses.
Que ton sein m'était doux ! que ton cœur m'était bon !
Nous avons dit souvent d'impérissables choses
Les soirs illuminés par l'ardeur du charbon.

Que les soleils sont beaux dans les chaudes soirées !
Que l'espace est profond ! que le cœur est puissant !
En me penchant vers toi, reine des adorées,
Je croyais respirer le parfum de ton sang.
Que les soleils sont beaux dans les chaudes soirées !

La nuit s'épaississait ainsi qu'une cloison,
Et mes yeux dans le noir devinaient tes prunelles,
Et je buvais ton souffle, ô douceur ! ô poison !
Et tes pieds s'endormaient dans mes mains fraternelles.
La nuit s'épaississait ainsi qu'une cloison.

Je sais l'art d'évoquer les minutes heureuses,
Et revis mon passé blotti dans tes genoux.
Car à quoi bon chercher tes beautés langoureuses
Ailleurs qu'en ton cher corps et qu'en ton cœur si doux ?
Je sais l'art d'évoquer les minutes heureuses !

Ces serments, ces parfums, ces baisers infinis,
Renaîtront-ils d'un gouffre interdit à nos sondes,
Comme montent au ciel les soleils rajeunis
Après s'être lavés au fond des mers profondes ?
– Ô serments ! ô parfums ! ô baisers infinis !

Les Fleurs du mal, Spleen et idéal, **XXXVI**

HARMONIE DU SOIR

Voici venir les temps où vibrant sur sa tige
Chaque fleur s'évapore ainsi qu'un encensoir ;
Les sons et les parfums tournent dans l'air du soir ;
Valse mélancolique et langoureux vertige !

Chaque fleur s'évapore ainsi qu'un encensoir ;
Le violon frémit comme un cœur qu'on afflige ;
Valse mélancolique et langoureux vertige !
Le ciel est triste et beau comme un grand reposoir.

Le violon frémit comme un cœur qu'on afflige,
Un cœur tendre, qui hait le néant vaste et noir !
Le ciel est triste et beau comme un grand reposoir ;
Le soleil s'est noyé dans son sang qui se fige.

Un cœur tendre, qui hait le néant vaste et noir,
Du passé lumineux recueille tout vestige !
Le soleil s'est noyé dans son sang qui se fige...
Ton souvenir en moi luit comme un ostensoir !

Les Fleurs du mal,
Spleen et idéal, XLVII

L'INVITATION AU VOYAGE

Mon enfant, ma sœur,
Songe à la douceur
D'aller là-bas vivre ensemble !
Aimer à loisir,
Aimer et mourir
Au pays qui te ressemble !
Les soleils mouillés
De ces ciels brouillés
Pour mon esprit ont les charmes
Si mystérieux
De tes traîtres yeux,
Brillant à travers leurs larmes.

Là, tout n'est qu'ordre et beauté,
Luxe, calme et volupté.

Des meubles luisants,
Polis par les ans,
Décoreraient notre chambre ;
Les plus rares fleurs
Mêlant leurs odeurs
Aux vagues senteurs de l'ambre,
Les riches plafonds,
Les miroirs profonds,
La splendeur orientale,
Tout y parlerait
À l'âme en secret
Sa douce langue natale.

Là, tout n'est qu'ordre et beauté,
Luxe, calme et volupté.

Vois sur ces canaux
Dormir ces vaisseaux
Dont l'humeur est vagabonde ;
C'est pour assouvir
Ton moindre désir
Qu'ils viennent du bout du monde.
– Les soleils couchants
Revêtent les champs,
Les canaux, la ville entière,
D'hyacinthe et d'or ;
Le monde s'endort
Dans une chaude lumière.

Là, tout n'est qu'ordre et beauté,
Luxe, calme et volupté.

Les Fleurs du mal,
Spleen et idéal, LIII

CHANT D'AUTOMNE

Bientôt nous plongerons dans les froides ténèbres ;
Adieu, vive clarté de nos étés trop courts !
J'entends déjà tomber avec des chocs funèbres
Le bois retentissant sur le pavé des cours.

Tout l'hiver va rentrer dans mon être : colère,
Haine, frissons, horreur, labeur dur et forcé,
Et, comme le soleil dans son enfer polaire,
Mon cœur ne sera plus qu'un bloc rouge et glacé.

J'écoute en frémissant chaque bûche qui tombe ;
L'échafaud qu'on bâtit n'a pas d'écho plus sourd.
Mon esprit est pareil à la tour qui succombe
Sous les coups du bélier infatigable et lourd.

Il me semble, bercé par ce choc monotone,
Qu'on cloue en grande hâte un cercueil quelque part.
Pour qui ? – C'était hier l'été ; voici l'automne !
Ce bruit mystérieux sonne comme un départ.

Les Fleurs du mal,
Spleen et idéal, LVI

MŒSTA ET ERRABUNDA

Dis-moi, ton cœur parfois s'envole-t-il, Agathe,
Loin du noir océan de l'immonde cité,
Vers un autre océan où la splendeur éclate,
Bleu, clair, profond, ainsi que la virginité ?
Dis-moi, ton cœur parfois s'envole-t-il, Agathe ?

La mer, la vaste mer, console nos labeurs !
Quel démon a doté la mer, rauque chanteuse
Qu'accompagne l'immense orgue des vents grondeurs,
De cette fonction sublime de berceuse ?
La mer, la vaste mer, console nos labeurs !

Emporte-moi, wagon ! enlève-moi, frégate !
Loin ! loin ! ici la boue est faite de nos pleurs !
– Est-il vrai que parfois le triste cœur d'Agathe
Dise : Loin des remords, des crimes, des douleurs,
Emporte-moi, wagon, enlève-moi, frégate ?

Comme vous êtes loin, paradis parfumé,
Où sous un clair azur tout n'est qu'amour et joie,
Où tout ce que l'on aime est digne d'être aimé,
Où dans la volupté pure le cœur se noie !
Comme vous êtes loin, paradis parfumé !

Mais le vert paradis des amours enfantines,
Les courses, les chansons, les baisers, les bouquets,
Les violons vibrant derrière les collines,
Avec les brocs de vin, le soir, dans les bosquets,
– Mais le vert paradis des amours enfantines,

L'innocent paradis, plein de plaisirs furtifs,
Est-il déjà plus loin que l'Inde et que la Chine ?
Peut-on le rappeler avec des cris plaintifs,
Et l'animer encor d'une voix argentine,
L'innocent paradis plein de plaisirs furtifs ?

Les Fleurs du mal, Spleen et idéal, LXII

SPLEEN

J'ai plus de souvenirs que si j'avais mille ans.

Un gros meuble à tiroirs encombré de bilans,
De vers, de billets doux, de procès, de romances,
Avec de lourds cheveux roulés dans des quittances,
Cache moins de secrets que mon triste cerveau.
C'est une pyramide, un immense caveau,
Qui contient plus de morts que la fosse commune.
— Je suis un cimetière abhorré de la lune,
Où, comme des remords, se traînent de longs vers
Qui s'acharnent toujours sur mes morts les plus chers.
Je suis un vieux boudoir plein de roses fanées,
Où gît tout un fouillis de modes surannées,
Où les pastels plaintifs et les pâles Boucher,
Seuls, respirent l'odeur d'un flacon débouché.

Rien n'égale en longueur les boiteuses journées,
Quand sous les lourds flocons des neigeuses années
L'ennui, fruit de la morne incuriosité,
Prend les proportions de l'immortalité.
— Désormais tu n'es plus, ô matière vivante !
Qu'un granit entouré d'une vague épouvante,
Assoupi dans le fond d'un Sahara brumeux ;
Un vieux sphinx ignoré du monde insoucieux,
Oublié sur la carte, et dont l'humeur farouche
Ne chante qu'aux rayons du soleil qui se couche.

Les Fleurs du mal,
Spleen et idéal, **LXXVI**

SPLEEN

Je suis comme le roi d'un pays pluvieux,
Riche, mais impuissant, jeune et pourtant très vieux,
Qui, de ses précepteurs méprisant les courbettes,
S'ennuie avec ses chiens comme avec d'autre bêtes.
Rien ne peut l'égayer, ni gibier, ni faucon,
Ni son peuple mourant en face du balcon.
Du bouffon favori la grotesque ballade
Ne distrait plus le front de ce cruel malade ;
Son lit fleurdelisé se transforme en tombeau,
Et les dames d'atour, pour qui tout prince est beau,
Ne savent plus trouver d'impudique toilette
Pour tirer un souris de ce jeune squelette.
Le savant qui lui fait de l'or n'a jamais pu
De son être extirper l'élément corrompu,
Et dans ces bains de sang qui des Romains nous viennent,
Et dont sur leurs vieux jours les puissants se souviennent,
Il n'a su réchauffer ce cadavre hébété
Où coule au lieu de sang l'eau verte du Léthé.

Les Fleurs du mal,
Spleen et idéal, LXXVII

SPLEEN

Quand le ciel bas et lourd pèse comme un couvercle
Sur l'esprit gémissant en proie aux longs ennuis,
Et que de l'horizon embrassant tout le cercle
Il nous verse un jour noir plus triste que les nuits ;

Quand la terre est changée en un cachot humide,
Où l'Espérance, comme une chauve-souris,
S'en va battant les murs de son aile timide
Et se cognant la tête à des plafonds pourris ;

Quand la pluie étalant ses immenses traînées
D'une vaste prison imite les barreaux,
Et qu'un peuple muet d'infâmes araignées
Vient tendre ses filets au fond de nos cerveaux,

Des cloches tout à coup sautent avec furie
Et lancent vers le ciel un affreux hurlement,
Ainsi que des esprits errants et sans patrie
Qui se mettent à geindre opiniâtrement.

– Et de longs corbillards, sans tambours ni musique,
Défilent lentement dans mon âme ; l'Espoir,
Vaincu, pleure, et l'Angoisse atroce, despotique,
Sur mon crâne incliné plante son drapeau noir.

Les Fleurs du mal,
Spleen et idéal, **LXXVIII**

PAYSAGE

Je veux, pour composer chastement mes églogues,
Coucher auprès du ciel, comme les astrologues,
Et, voisin des clochers, écouter en rêvant
Leurs hymnes solennels emportés par le vent.
Les deux mains au menton, du haut de ma mansarde,
Je verrai l'atelier qui chante et qui bavarde ;
Les tuyaux, les clochers, ces mâts de la cité,
Et les grands ciels qui font rêver d'éternité.

Il est doux, à travers les brumes, de voir naître
L'étoile dans l'azur, la lampe à la fenêtre,
Les fleuves de charbon monter au firmament
Et la lune verser son pâle enchantement.
Je verrai les printemps, les étés, les automnes ;
Et quand viendra l'hiver aux neiges monotones,
Je fermerai partout portières et volets
Pour bâtir dans la nuit mes féeriques palais.
Alors je rêverai des horizons bleuâtres,
Des jardins, des jets d'eau pleurant dans les albâtres,
Des baisers, des oiseaux chantant soir et matin,
Et tout ce que l'Idylle a de plus enfantin.
L'Émeute, tempêtant vainement à ma vitre,
Ne fera plus lever le front de mon pupitre ;
Car je serai plongé dans cette volupté
D'évoquer le Printemps avec ma volonté,
De tirer un soleil de mon cœur, et de faire
De mes pensers brûlants une tiède atmosphère.

Les Fleurs du mal,
Tableaux parisiens, LXXXVI

À UNE PASSANTE

La rue assourdissante autour de moi hurlait.
Longue, mince, en grand deuil, douleur majestueuse,
Une femme passa, d'une main fastueuse
Soulevant, balançant le feston et l'ourlet ;

Agile et noble, avec sa jambe de statue.
Moi, je buvais, crispé comme un extravagant,
Dans son œil, ciel livide où germe l'ouragan,
La douceur qui fascine et le plaisir qui tue.

Un éclair... puis la nuit ! – Fugitive beauté
Dont le regard m'a fait soudainement renaître,
Ne te verrai-je plus que dans l'éternité ?

Ailleurs, bien loin d'ici ! trop tard ! *jamais* peut-être !
Car j'ignore où tu fuis, tu ne sais où je vais,
Ô toi que j'eusse aimée, ô toi qui le savais !

Les Fleurs du mal,
Tableaux parisiens, XCIII

LA MORT DES AMANTS

Nous aurons des lits pleins d'odeurs légères,
Des divans profonds comme des tombeaux,
Et d'étranges fleurs sur des étagères,
Écloses pour nous sous des cieux plus beaux.

Usant à l'envi leurs chaleurs dernières,
Nos deux cœurs seront deux vastes flambeaux,
Qui réfléchiront leurs doubles lumières
Dans nos deux esprits, ces miroirs jumeaux.

Un soir fait de rose et de bleu mystique,
Nous échangerons un éclair unique,
Comme un long sanglot, tout chargé d'adieux ;

Et plus tard un Ange, entrouvrant les portes,
Viendra ranimer, fidèle et joyeux,
Les miroirs ternis et les flammes mortes.

Les Fleurs du mal,
La Mort, **CXXI**

LE VOYAGE

À Maxime Du Camp

I

Pour l'enfant, amoureux de cartes et d'estampes,
L'univers est égal à son vaste appétit.
Ah ! que le monde est grand à la clarté des lampes !
Aux yeux du souvenir que le monde est petit !

Un matin nous partons, le cerveau plein de flamme,
Le cœur gros de rancune et de désirs amers,
Et nous allons, suivant le rythme de la lame,
Berçant notre infini sur le fini des mers :

Les uns, joyeux de fuir une patrie infâme ;
D'autres, l'horreur de leurs berceaux, et quelques-uns,
Astrologues noyés dans les yeux d'une femme,
La Circé tyrannique aux dangereux parfums.

Pour n'être pas changés en bêtes, ils s'enivrent
D'espace et de lumière et de cieux embrasés ;
La glace qui les mord, les soleils qui les cuivrent,
Effacent lentement la marque des baisers.

Mais les vrais voyageurs sont ceux-là seuls qui partent
Pour partir ; cœurs légers, semblables aux ballons,
De leur fatalité jamais ils ne s'écartent,
Et, sans savoir pourquoi, disent toujours : Allons !

Ceux-là dont les désirs ont la forme des nues,
Et qui rêvent, ainsi qu'un conscrit le canon,
De vastes voluptés, changeantes, inconnues,
Et dont l'esprit humain n'a jamais su le nom !

II

Nous imitons, horreur ! la toupie et la boule
Dans leur valse et leurs bonds ; même dans nos sommeils
La Curiosité nous tourmente et nous roule,
Comme un Ange cruel qui fouette des soleils.

Singulière fortune où le but se déplace,
Et, n'étant nulle part, peut être n'importe où !
Où l'Homme, dont jamais l'espérance n'est lasse,
Pour trouver le repos court toujours comme un fou !

Notre âme est un trois-mâts cherchant son Icarie ;
Une voix retentit sur le pont : « Ouvre l'œil ! »
Une voix de la hune, ardente et folle, crie :
« Amour... gloire... bonheur ! » Enfer ! c'est un écueil !

Chaque îlot signalé par l'homme de vigie
Est un Eldorado promis par le Destin ;
L'Imagination qui dresse son orgie
Ne trouve qu'un récif aux clartés du matin.

Ô le pauvre amoureux des pays chimériques !
Faut-il le mettre aux fers, le jeter à la mer,
Ce matelot ivrogne, inventeur d'Amériques
Dont le mirage rend le gouffre plus amer ?

Tel le vieux vagabond, piétinant dans la boue,
Rêve, le nez en l'air, de brillants paradis ;
Son œil ensorcelé découvre une Capoue
Partout où la chandelle illumine un taudis.

III

Étonnants voyageurs ! quelles nobles histoires
Nous lisons dans vos yeux profonds comme les mers !
Montrez-nous les écrins de vos riches mémoires,
Ces bijoux merveilleux, faits d'astres et d'éthers.

Nous voulons voyager sans vapeur et sans voile !
Faites, pour égayer l'ennui de nos prisons,
Passer sur nos esprits, tendus comme une toile,
Vos souvenirs avec leurs cadres d'horizons.

Dites, qu'avez-vous vu ?

IV

                         « Nous avons vu des astres
Et des flots ; nous avons vu des sables aussi ;
Et, malgré bien des chocs et d'imprévus désastres,
Nous nous sommes souvent ennuyés, comme ici.

La gloire du soleil sur la mer violette,
La gloire des cités dans le soleil couchant,
Allumaient dans nos cœurs une ardeur inquiète
De plonger dans un ciel au reflet alléchant.

Les plus riches cités, les plus grands paysages,
Jamais ne contenaient l'attrait mystérieux
De ceux que le hasard fait avec les nuages.
Et toujours le désir nous rendait soucieux !

– La jouissance ajoute au désir de la force.
Désir, vieil arbre à qui le plaisir sert d'engrais,
Cependant que grossit et durcit ton écorce,
Tes branches veulent voir le soleil de plus près !

Grandiras-tu toujours, grand arbre plus vivace
Que le cyprès ? – Pourtant nous avons, avec soin,
Cueilli quelques croquis pour votre album vorace,
Frères qui trouvez beau tout ce qui vient de loin !

Nous avons salué des idoles à trompe ;
Des trônes constellés de joyaux lumineux ;
Des palais ouvragés dont la féerique pompe
Serait pour vos banquiers un rêve ruineux ;

Des costumes qui sont pour les yeux une ivresse ;
Des femmes dont les dents et les ongles sont teints,
Et des jongleurs savants que le serpent caresse. »

V

Et puis, et puis encore ?

VI

« Ô cerveaux enfantins !

Pour ne pas oublier la chose capitale,
Nous avons vu partout, et sans l'avoir cherché,
Du haut jusques en bas de l'échelle fatale,
Le spectacle ennuyeux de l'immortel péché :

La femme, esclave vile, orgueilleuse et stupide,
Sans rire s'adorant et s'aimant sans dégoût ;
L'homme, tyran goulu, paillard, dur et cupide,
Esclave de l'esclave et ruisseau dans l'égout ;

Le bourreau qui jouit, le martyr qui sanglote ;
La fête qu'assaisonne et parfume le sang ;
Le poison du pouvoir énervant le despote,
Et le peuple amoureux du fouet abrutissant ;

Plusieurs religions semblables à la nôtre,
Toutes escaladant le ciel ; la Sainteté,
Comme en un lit de plume un délicat se vautre,
Dans les clous et le crin cherchant la volupté ;

L'Humanité bavarde, ivre de son génie,
Et, folle maintenant comme elle était jadis,
Criant à Dieu, dans sa furibonde agonie :
« Ô mon semblable, ô mon maître, je te maudis ! »

Et les moins sots, hardis amants de la Démence,
Fuyant le grand troupeau parqué par le Destin
Et se réfugiant dans l'opium immense
– Tel est du globe entier l'éternel bulletin. »

VII

Amer savoir, celui qu'on tire du voyage !
Le monde, monotone et petit, aujourd'hui,
Hier, demain, toujours, nous fait voir notre image :
Une oasis d'horreur dans un désert d'ennui !

Faut-il partir ? rester ? Si tu peux rester, reste ;
Pars, s'il le faut. L'un court, et l'autre se tapit
Pour tromper l'ennemi vigilant et funeste,
Le Temps ! Il est, hélas ! des coureurs sans répit,

Comme le Juif errant et comme les apôtres,
À qui rien ne suffit, ni wagon ni vaisseau,
Pour fuir ce rétiaire infâme ; il en est d'autres
Qui savent le tuer sans quitter leur berceau.

Lorsque enfin il mettra le pied sur notre échine,
Nous pourrons espérer et crier : En avant !
De même qu'autrefois nous partions pour la Chine,
Les yeux fixés au large et les cheveux au vent,

Nous nous embarquerons sur la mer des Ténèbres
Avec le cœur joyeux d'un jeune passager.
Entendez-vous ces voix, charmantes et funèbres,
Qui chantent : « Par ici ! vous qui voulez manger

Le Lotus parfumé ! c'est ici qu'on vendange
Les fruits miraculeux dont votre cœur a faim ;
Venez vous enivrer de la douceur étrange
De cette après-midi qui n'a jamais de fin » ?

À l'accent familier nous devinons le spectre ;
Nos Pylades là-bas tendent leurs bras vers nous.
« Pour rafraîchir ton cœur nage vers ton Électre ! »
Dit celle dont jadis nous baisions les genoux.

VIII

Ô Mort, vieux capitaine, il est temps ! levons l'ancre !
Ce pays nous ennuie, ô Mort ! Appareillons !
Si le ciel et la mer sont noirs comme de l'encre,
Nos cœurs que tu connais sont remplis de rayons !

Verse-nous ton poison pour qu'il nous réconforte !
Nous voulons, tant ce feu nous brûle le cerveau,
Plonger au fond du gouffre, Enfer ou Ciel, qu'importe ?
Au fond de l'Inconnu pour trouver du *nouveau* !

Les Fleurs du mal,
La Mort, CXXVI

RECUEILLEMENT

Sois sage, ô ma Douleur, et tiens-toi plus tranquille.
Tu réclamais le Soir ; il descend ; le voici :
Une atmosphère obscure enveloppe la ville,
Aux uns portant la paix, aux autres le souci.

Pendant que des mortels la multitude vile,
Sous le fouet du Plaisir, ce bourreau sans merci,
Va cueillir des remords dans la fête servile,
Ma Douleur, donne-moi la main ; viens par ici,

Loin d'eux. Vois se pencher les défuntes Années,
Sur les balcons du ciel, en robes surannées ;
Surgir du fond des eaux le Regret souriant ;

Le Soleil moribond s'endormir sous une arche,
Et, comme un long linceul traînant à l'Orient,
Entends, ma chère, entends la douce Nuit qui marche.

Nouvelles Fleurs du mal, VII

LES BIENFAITS DE LA LUNE

La Lune, qui est le caprice même, regarda par la fenêtre, pendant que tu dormais dans ton berceau, et se dit : « Cette enfant me plaît. »

Et elle descendit moelleusement son escalier de nuages, et passa sans bruit à travers les vitres. Puis elle s'étendit sur toi avec la tendresse souple d'une mère, et elle déposa ses couleurs sur ta face. Tes prunelles en sont restées vertes, et tes joues extraordinairement pâles. C'est en contemplant cette visiteuse que tes yeux se sont si bizarrement agrandis ; et elle t'a si tendrement serrée à la gorge que tu en as gardé pour toujours l'envie de pleurer.

Cependant, dans l'expansion de sa joie, la Lune remplissait toute la chambre, comme une atmosphère phosphorique ; comme un poison lumineux ; et toute cette lumière vivante pensait et disait : « Tu subiras éternellement l'influence de mon baiser. Tu seras belle à ma manière. Tu aimeras ce que j'aime et ce qui m'aime : l'eau, les nuages, le silence et la nuit ; la mer immense et verte ; l'eau informe et multiforme ; le lieu où tu ne seras pas ; l'amant que tu ne connaîtras pas ; les fleurs monstrueuses ; les parfums qui font délirer ; les chats qui se pâment sur les pianos, et qui gémissent comme les femmes, d'une voix rauque et douce !

« Et tu seras aimée de mes amants, courtisée par mes courtisans. Tu seras la reine des hommes aux yeux verts, dont j'ai serré aussi la gorge dans mes caresses nocturnes ; de ceux-là qui aiment la mer, la mer immense, tumultueuse et verte, l'eau informe et multiforme, le lieu où ils ne sont pas, la femme qu'ils ne connaissent pas, les fleurs sinistres qui ressemblent aux encensoirs d'une religion inconnue, les parfums qui troublent la volonté, et les animaux sauvages et voluptueux qui sont les emblèmes de leur folie. »

Et c'est pour cela, maudite chère enfant gâtée, que je suis maintenant couché à tes pieds, cherchant dans toute ta personne le reflet de la redoutable Divinité, de la fatidique marraine, de la nourrice empoisonneuse de tous les *lunatiques*.

LE PORT

Un port est un séjour charmant pour une âme fatiguée des luttes de la vie. L'ampleur du ciel, l'architecture mobile des nuages, les colorations changeantes de la mer, le scintillement des phares, sont un prisme merveilleusement propre à amuser les yeux sans jamais les lasser. Les formes élancées des navires, au gréement compliqué, auxquels la houle imprime des oscillations harmonieuses, servent à entretenir dans l'âme le goût du rythme et de la beauté. Et puis, surtout, il y a une sorte de plaisir mystérieux et aristocratique pour celui qui n'a plus ni curiosité ni ambition, à contempler, couché dans le belvédère ou accoudé sur le môle, tous ces mouvements de ceux qui partent et de ceux qui reviennent, de ceux qui ont encore la force de vouloir, le désir de voyager ou de s'enrichir.

Le Spleen de Paris, XLI

THÉODORE DE BANVILLE

(1823-1891)

Le poète est chose légère, si l'on en croit Platon, et chose ailée.
À sa manière, le clown bondissant du *Saut du Tremplin* le dit aussi.
Capable d'échapper à toutes les entraves terrestres, il incarne le
rêve de celui qui aspire seulement aux étoiles. Chez ce poète-là
aucune ambition de transmettre un savoir ou de guider les
peuples. L'art pour l'art est son unique propos. Toutefois, pour
Banville, la doctrine de Gautier dont il est le disciple, se nuance
d'humour et de désinvolture, ce qui n'est pas incompatible avec le
souci de la perfection. On lui doit le chapitre le plus court de
tous les arts poétiques connus, celui qui a pour titre « Licences
poétiques » et qui consiste en ces mots : « Il n'y en a pas. » Acrobate
du vers, il se joue des difficultés et s'amuse aux formes anciennes
du rondel ou de la ballade. Sous l'apparent badinage se fait jour
une conception exigeante du métier du poète, et ses débuts ont
semblé à ses contemporains pleins de promesses. Mais la suite,
souvent, les a déçus : c'est qu'il n'a jamais envisagé, semble-t-il, de
se mesurer aux plus grands.

Quand il écrit dans son *Petit traité de Poésie française* : « En fait
de vers, bien lire Hugo, c'est tout apprendre », on a le sentiment
que pour lui, comme pour Gautier, la présence de ce modèle fut
écrasante et l'empêcha peut-être de donner pleinement la mesure
de son génie propre. Cependant certains de ses sonnets, en
particulier ceux des *Princesses* – on lira ici *Hérodiade* – ne sont pas
inférieurs aux meilleurs des Parnassiens dont il est proche, tandis
que le mélange d'ironie et de sentimentalité qui domine souvent
dans ses poèmes, ouvre la voie aux Décadents. Mais il est difficile

de le rattacher à l'un ou l'autre des courants de la fin du siècle, on peut aussi bien souligner l'influence sur lui des poètes du passé ou de ses prédécesseurs immédiats que noter ses affinités avec Baudelaire, car il loue, comme lui, la poésie d'être « le seul art complet nécessaire et qui contienne tous les autres, comme elle préexiste à tous les autres », et croit que « dès qu'un groupe d'hommes est réuni, la Poésie lui est révélée d'une manière extra-humaine et surnaturelle, sans quoi il ne pourrait pas vivre ». La gravité de ces professions de foi ne doit pas faire oublier que le trait dominant chez lui est la fantaisie, elle lui a valu d'être comparé à Heine. Et le charme de son œuvre tient à sa grâce malicieuse, à cette sorte d'apesanteur qui la caractérise.

BALLADE DES PENDUS

Sur ses larges bras étendus,
La forêt où s'éveille Flore,
A des chapelets de pendus
Que le matin caresse et dore.
Ce bois sombre, où le chêne arbore
Des grappes de fruits inouïs
Même chez le Turc et le More,
C'est le verger du roi Louis.

Tous ces pauvres gens morfondus,
Roulant des pensers qu'on ignore,
Dans les tourbillons éperdus
Voltigent, palpitant encore.
Le soleil levant les dévore.
Regardez-les, cieux éblouis,
Danser dans les feux de l'aurore.
C'est le verger du roi Louis.

Ces pendus, du diable entendus,
Appellent des pendus encore.
Tandis qu'aux cieux, d'azur tendus,
Où semble luire un météore,
La rosée en l'air s'évapore,
Un essaim d'oiseaux réjouis
Par dessus leur tête picore.
C'est le verger du roi Louis.

Envoi

Prince, il est un bois que décore
Un tas de pendus, enfouis
Dans le doux feuillage sonore.
C'est le verger du roi Louis !

LA LUNE

Avec ses caprices, la Lune
Est comme une frivole amante ;
Elle sourit et se lamente,
Elle fuit et vous importune.

La nuit, suivez-la sur la dune,
Elle vous raille et vous tourmente ;
Avec ses caprices, la Lune
Est comme une frivole amante.

Et souvent elle se met une
Nuée en manière de mante ;
Elle est absurde, elle est charmante ;
Il faut adorer sans rancune,
Avec ses caprices, la Lune.

Rondels

LE THÉ

Miss Ellen, versez-moi le Thé
Dans la belle tasse chinoise,
Où des poissons d'or cherchent noise
Au monstre rose épouvanté.

J'aime la folle cruauté
Des chimères qu'on apprivoise :
Miss Ellen, versez-moi le Thé
Dans la belle tasse chinoise.

Là sous un ciel rouge irrité,
Une dame fière et sournoise
Montre en ses longs yeux de turquoise
L'extase et la naïveté :
Miss Ellen, versez-moi le Thé.

Rondels

LE SAUT DU TREMPLIN

Clown admirable, en vérité !
Je crois que la postérité,
Dont sans cesse l'horizon bouge,
Le reverra, sa plaie au flanc.
Il était barbouillé de blanc,
De jaune, de vert et de rouge.

Même jusqu'à Madagascar
Son nom était parvenu, car
C'était selon tous les principes
Qu'après les cercles de papier,
Sans jamais les estropier
Il traversait le rond des pipes.

De la pesanteur affranchi,
Sans y voir clair il eût franchi
Les escaliers de Piranèse.
La lumière qui le frappait
Faisait resplendir son toupet
Comme un brasier dans la fournaise.

Il s'élevait à des hauteurs
Telles, que les autres sauteurs
Se consumaient en luttes vaines.
Ils le trouvaient décourageant,
Et murmuraient : « Quel vif-argent
Ce démon a-t-il dans les veines ? »

Tout le peuple criait : « Bravo ! »
Mais lui, par un effort nouveau,
Semblait roidir sa jambe nue,
Et, sans que l'on sût avec qui,
Cet émule de la Saqui
Parlait bas en langue inconnue.

C'était avec son cher tremplin.
Il lui disait : « Théâtre, plein
D'inspiration fantastique,
Tremplin qui tressailles d'émoi
Quand je prends un élan, fais-moi
Bondir plus haut, planche élastique !

Frêle machine aux reins puissants,
Fais-moi bondir, moi qui me sens
Plus agile que les panthères,
Si haut que je ne puisse voir
Avec leur cruel habit noir
Ces épiciers et ces notaires !

Par quelque prodige pompeux,
Fais-moi monter, si tu le peux,
Jusqu'à ces sommets où, sans règles,
Embrouillant les cheveux vermeils
Des planètes et des soleils,
Se croisent la foudre et les aigles.

Jusqu'à ces éthers pleins de bruit,
Où, mêlant dans l'affreuse nuit
Leurs haleines exténuées,
Les autans ivres de courroux
Dorment, échevelés et fous,
Sur les seins pâles des nuées.

Plus haut encor, jusqu'au ciel pur !
Jusqu'à ce lapis dont l'azur
Couvre notre prison mouvante !
Jusqu'à ces rouges Orients
Où marchent des Dieux flamboyants,
Fous de colère et d'épouvante.

Plus loin ! plus haut ! je vois encor
Des boursiers à lunettes d'or,
Des critiques, des demoiselles

Et des réalistes en feu.
Plus haut ! plus loin ! de l'air ! du bleu !
Des ailes ! des ailes ! des ailes ! »

Enfin, de son vil échafaud,
Le clown sauta si haut, si haut,
Qu'il creva le plafond de toiles
Au son du cor et du tambour,
Et, le cœur dévoré d'amour,
Alla rouler dans les étoiles.

Odes funambulesques

HÉRODIADE

Ses yeux sont transparents comme l'eau du Jourdain.
Elle a de lourds colliers et des pendants d'oreilles ;
Elle est plus douce à voir que le raisin des treilles,
Et la rose des bois a peur de son dédain.

Elle rit et folâtre avec un air badin,
Laissant de sa jeunesse éclater les merveilles.
Sa lèvre est écarlate, et ses dents sont pareilles,
Pour la blancheur, aux lys orgueilleux du jardin.

Voyez-la, voyez-la venir, la jeune reine !
Un petit page noir tient sa robe qui traîne
En flots voluptueux le long du corridor.

Sur ses doigts le rubis, le saphir, l'améthyste
Font resplendir leurs feux charmants : dans un plat d'or
Elle porte le chef sanglant de Jean-Baptiste.

Odes funambulesques

CHARLES CROS

(1842-1888)

« Un véritable inventeur, celui-là », écrit à son propos André Breton. Il l'est assurément, puisqu'on lui doit le paléophone, appelé plus tard phonographe (qu'il met au point un an avant Edison), et les premières épreuves photographiques positives en couleur. Autant qu'au physicien et au chimiste génial, l'admiration de Breton va au poète, pour sa liberté de ton, sa désinvolture de jeune homme doué, son humour et la manière dont il joue avec les idées neuves qui fleurissent alors dans le domaine de l'art.

Charles Cros est, pendant un temps, l'ami de Rimbaud et Verlaine, et on le voit dans tous les groupes aux noms provocants qui ont en commun l'habitude de tourner en dérision les autres et eux-mêmes. On le rencontre chez les « Hydropathes », puis il devient le président du nouveau groupe des « Zutistes », ce dernier succédant au « Cercle zutique » qu'il fréquentait avec ses frères. Dès la création du Chat Noir, ce cabaret qui regroupe de nombreux artistes, il s'y produit sur la scène. Mais s'il participe de cette forme de sensibilité qui vaut aux poètes des années 80, l'épithète péjorative de « décadents », dénomination qu'ils adoptent et dont ils se glorifient, il n'appartient vraiment lui-même à aucune école. Héritier des Parnassiens, admirateur de Baudelaire, lecteur attentif et curieux de toutes les productions contemporaines, il n'a pas de doctrine propre, et l'on trouve dans Le Coffret de Santal, le seul recueil de poèmes publié de son vivant, ainsi que dans Le Collier de griffes, paru après sa mort, une grande diversité d'inspirations et de manières. Toutes les formes poétiques anciennes l'attirent, il recherche des strophes originales et des effets de rythme. Il excelle dans le triolet, et cultive aussi bien la chanson que la ballade ou le sonnet. Ce qui est sa marque propre, c'est sa spontanéité et sa fantaisie, et s'il s'inscrit par là dans la lignée de Marot, La Fontaine ou Musset il a, plus qu'eux, le goût de l'insolite et du pastiche. Ce qui lui a valu une célébrité immédiate, c'est la drôlerie inattendue de son poème intitulé « le Hareng saur » dont le final narquois ravit son auditoire :

> *J'ai composé cette histoire – simple, simple, simple,*
> *Pour mettre en fureur les gens – graves, graves, graves,*
> *Et amuser les enfants – petits, petits, petits.*

Le public le connaît aussi pour les monologues destinés au théâtre, qu'il compose à l'intention de Coquelin, ressuscitant un genre à peu près oublié depuis le Moyen Âge. Cela fera de lui « le premier des monologuistes », titre glorieux, décerné, il est vrai, par le journal *Le Chat Noir*, en un temps où il a peu de concurrents. La cocasserie de ces textes annonce parfois les surréalistes.

Si Verlaine lui consacre un article des « Hommes d'aujourd'hui », Charles Cros n'en est pas moins, de son vivant, assez méconnu comme poète. Il s'en est plaint un jour en disant : « Physicien, chimiste, philosophe et poète, je suis depuis longtemps condamné à n'être que l'humoriste titubant de *Pituite* et du *Hareng saur*. »

Son œuvre poétique, si elle ne se limite pas à ces jeux verbaux, est assez disparate, mais, à côté de poèmes qui semblent écrits au gré des circonstances et où il cède parfois à la facilité, d'autres ont des accents de révolte qui sonnent juste, beaucoup masquent d'un sourire une détresse réelle. Surtout quelques traits dans l'œuvre et la vie de ce « Vrai sauvage égaré dans la ville de pierre » évoquent pour nous Rimbaud.

LE BUT

À Henri Ghys

Le long des peupliers je marche, le front nu,
Poitrine au vent, les yeux flagellés par la pluie.
Je m'avance hagard vers le but inconnu.

Le printemps a des fleurs dont le parfum m'ennuie,
L'été promet, l'automne offre ses fruits, d'aspects
Irritants ; l'hiver blanc, même, est sali de suie.

Que les corbeaux, trouant mon ventre de leurs becs,
Mangent mon foie, où sont tant de colères folles,
Que l'air et le soleil blanchissent mes os secs,

Et, surtout, que le vent emporte mes paroles !

CONCLUSION

À Maurice Rollinat

J'ai rêvé les amours divins,
L'ivresse des bras et des vins,
L'or, l'argent, les royaumes vains,

Moi, dix-huit ans, Elle, seize ans.
Parmi les sentiers amusants
Nous irions sur nos alezans.

Il est loin le temps des aveux
Naïfs, des téméraires vœux !
Je n'ai d'argent qu'en mes cheveux.

Les âmes dont j'aurais besoin
Et les étoiles sont trop loin.
Je vais mourir soûl, dans un coin.

PLAINTE

Vrai sauvage égaré dans la ville de pierre,
À la clarté du gaz je végète et je meurs.
Mais vous vous y plaisez, et vos regards charmeurs
M'attirent à la mort, parisienne fière.

Je rêve de passer ma vie en quelque coin
Sous les bois verts ou sur les monts aromatiques,
En Orient, ou bien près du pôle, très loin,
Loin des journaux, de la cohue et des boutiques.

Mais vous aimez la foule et les éclats de voix,
Le bal de l'Opéra, le gaz et la réclame.
Moi, j'oublie, à vous voir, les rochers et les bois,
Je me tue à vouloir me civiliser l'âme.

Je vous ennuie à vous le dire si souvent :
Je mourrai, papillon brûlé, si cela dure…
Vous feriez bien pourtant, vos cheveux noirs au vent,
En clair peignoir ruché, sur un fond de verdure !

AVENIR

Les coquelicots noirs et les bleuets fanés
Dans le foin capiteux qui réjouit l'étable,
La lettre jaunie où mon aïeul respectable
À mon aïeule fit des serments surannés,

La tabatière où mon grand-oncle a mis le nez,
Le trictrac incrusté sur la petite table
Me ravissent. Ainsi dans un temps supputable
Mes vers vous raviront, vous qui n'êtes pas nés.

Or, je suis très vivant. Le vent qui vient m'envoie
Une odeur d'aubépine en fleur et de lilas,
Le bruit de mes baisers couvre le bruit des glas.

Ô lecteurs à venir, qui vivez dans la joie
Des seize ans, des lilas et des premiers baisers,
Vos amours font jouir mes os décomposés.

STÉPHANE MALLARMÉ

(1842-1898)

Mallarmé introduit une rupture dans l'histoire de la poésie. Pour la première fois sans doute celle-ci ne se propose plus d'autre fin qu'elle-même : « Le sujet de l'œuvre est la Beauté, et le sujet apparent n'est qu'un prétexte pour aller vers elle. »

Ses premiers poèmes, à l'inspiration baudelairienne ou parnassienne, ne laissent pas encore deviner le retournement qui se prépare. Mais de Baudelaire encore, et de Poe, ses modèles, il retient la leçon essentielle : l'intelligence critique doit accompagner toute création, la concevoir et en contrôler l'élaboration. C'est pour lui le point de départ d'une réflexion qu'il va mener jusqu'à ses conséquences ultimes, faisant de l'intellect le seul véritable maître d'œuvre. Du choix du matériau verbal à son organisation dans le poème, rien ne doit échapper à son emprise. Cette exigence l'amène à rejeter tout lyrisme, fût-il mesuré, en qui il ne voit qu'illusion. Le poète est désormais cet ouvrier conscient et volontaire qui cisèle le vers à son gré en s'efforçant d'arracher les mots à la gangue de l'habitude, et de rendre le poème autonome en le libérant de tout lien avec le monde extérieur : « À quoi bon la merveille de transposer un fait de nature en sa presque disparition vibratoire selon le jeu de la parole, cependant ; si ce n'est pour qu'en émane, sans la gêne d'un proche ou concret rappel, la notion pure. » Cette conception exigeante et neuve de la poésie et du métier poétique fait de lui, pour toute une génération, comme l'écrit Claudel, « un professeur d'attention ». Dans la seconde partie de sa vie, quand le roman de Huysmans, *À rebours*, l'a fait connaître, se regroupent autour de lui, dans son salon, admirateurs et amis, le cercle choisi des fameux mardis. Il est pour eux le Maître : ils recueillent ses propos et savourent les poèmes qu'il leur lit. Cela n'empêche pas le poète de douter et de ne voir là qu'une ébauche et la traduction imparfaite de ce qu'il tente d'écrire. Il voudrait des vers « teintés seulement d'absolu » et aimerait créer à cette fin « une langue immaculée ». Éprouvé depuis toujours par des crises de doute et d'angoisse, il se sent chaque fois frappé d'une stérilité qu'il croit définitive. Sa correspondance témoigne de ces agonies spirituelles. La hantise de la feuille blanche est sans doute à l'origine des silences qu'il introduit sous forme d'espaces entre les lignes du poème, comme on le voit dans *Un coup de dés*.

Peu à peu s'élabore cependant une œuvre à l'originalité incontestable où l'usage insolite qu'il fait des mots, la puissance de suggestion des images, le tour énigmatique et oraculaire du vers fascinent certains lecteurs, tandis que d'autres récusent un art dont l'hermétisme précieux écarte le profane par un jeu qui leur semble gratuit. Cet hermétisme pourtant ne relève pas d'une volonté délibérée de surprendre ou de dérober le sens. En comparant Mallarmé à quelques-uns de ses prédécesseurs on comprend mieux à quel point son art est différent. Chez Scève, par exemple, le dizain refermé sur soi offre au lecteur lettré de son temps la récompense d'un sens dont l'auteur est le garant. À l'humaniste de découvrir les liens que tisse chaque strophe entre l'aimée, l'amant et le monde, et de goûter l'ingéniosité du chiffre qui les dissimule. Chez Nerval, rêveur éveillé, l'obscurité tient à la part nocturne de son être. Figures de la nuit, personnages de légende, souvenirs recomposés et fantaisie d'un syncrétisme personnel disparate, font des *Chimères* le miroir voilé du poète lui-même.

Mallarmé, quant à lui, n'est pas comme l'auteur de *Délie* un inventeur de savantes énigmes, et pas davantage un romantique interrogeant ses propres gouffres. Son travail sur les mots vise à faire jaillir d'eux une réalité inconnue qui ne leur préexiste pas. Ceux-ci, qu'ils soient familiers mais détournés de leur usage habituel, ou choisis pour leur rareté, construisent ensemble un univers clos sur lui-même qui se suffit. Privé du signifié, le jeu verbal n'est pas pour autant gratuit. Tout un réseau d'échos internes, fait d'allitérations insistantes ou des liens fortuits que tissent entre elles les images inattendues, donne au poème sa densité et son éclat. Mallarmé recherche cet effet de miroir où les mots peuvent « s'allumer de feux réciproques ». Pour cela il dédaigne l'appui de la voix humaine qui prolonge et amplifie le vocable. L'idéal de la poésie est ici, pour la première fois, de se passer de l'intonation pour ne rechercher que l'effet visuel. Ce n'est pas d'un interprète que le poème tient une part de son pouvoir, mais du seul agencement interne du vers par lequel le poète-diamantaire provoque la scintillation du texte. Celui qui souhaitait « la disparition élocutoire du poète » s'efface devant l'objet précieux qu'il a façonné.

Le terme de précieux s'impose à la lecture de talismans verbaux récurrents, ces glaces, grottes, lustres, miroirs ou mandores, et ces violes encore, aux mains de séraphins, dont les imitateurs du poète abuseront parfois, « sans oublier », dit Claudel citant le texte d'Igitur, « dans sa vacuité transparente cette goutte de Néant qui manque à la mer ». Il convient en effet d'ajouter à la liste l'illustre « aboli bibelot », le ptyx singulier.

Pourtant il ne s'agit pas ici d'un excès de raffinement ornemental comme il en existe ailleurs, mais de moyens qui s'imposent au poète pour dissiper le réel et n'en laisser subsister qu'une impalpable quintessence. On peut voir les états successifs de cette alchimie lorsque le poète a conservé différentes versions d'un même thème, Le Pitre châtié en offrirait un exemple, comme le sonnet en x.

Ainsi il s'agit bien d'une révolution poétique, même si les formes anciennes, sonnet ou alexandrin, demeurent inchangées. Narcisse se substitue à Orphée. L'objet du poème n'est plus de célébrer l'homme ou le monde, mais de se refermer sur sa propre contemplation. Ce choix ne résulte pas d'une trouvaille ingénieuse ou d'une volonté d'étonner, il est l'aboutissement d'un long cheminement intérieur. En s'efforçant de « penser sa pensée », de la libérer de ses entraves, d'atteindre l'Absolu, le poète a voulu se dépouiller de son individualité. Il a atteint son but, il en a la certitude et l'annonce à son ami Cazalis : « Je suis maintenant impersonnel. »

L'absolu, « le moi projeté absolu », c'est cette disparition de toute détermination individuelle.

« Cet absolu, écrit Guy Michaud [1], c'est dans une totale élimination de tout... l'abstraction totale d'où tout relatif est exclu, c'est le Rien, c'est le Néant. »

L'œuvre qui se fonde sur un tel cheminement personnel, et sur cette expérience extrême est donc marquée d'un sceau de gravité, et Valéry qualifie de « mystique sans Dieu » l'homme qui dut affronter ce vertige. On peut récuser l'expression, contradictoire dans les termes, et préférer nommer Mallarmé l'ascète héroïque du verbe. Ceux-là mêmes qui demeurent insensibles à ses vers doivent rendre hommage à la hardiesse de son entreprise et dire de lui comme d'un autre Icare :

Il mourut poursuivant une haute aventure
. . . .
Est-il plus beau dessein ou plus riche tombeau.

---

1. Guy Michaud, *Message poétique du symbolisme*, Nizet, 1966.

APPARITION

La lune s'attristait. Des séraphins en pleurs
Rêvant, l'archet aux doigts dans le calme des fleurs
Vaporeuses, tiraient de mourantes violes
De blancs sanglots glissant sur l'azur des corolles
– C'était le jour béni de ton premier baiser.
Ma songerie aimant à me martyriser
S'enivrait savamment du parfum de tristesse
Que même sans regret et sans déboire laisse
La cueillaison d'un Rêve au cœur qui l'a cueilli.
J'errais donc, l'œil rivé sur le pavé vieilli
Quand avec du soleil aux cheveux, dans la rue
Et dans le soir, tu m'es en riant apparue
Et j'ai cru voir la fée au chapeau de clarté
Qui jadis sur mes beaux sommeils d'enfant gâté
Passait, laissant toujours de ses mains mal fermées
Neiger de blancs bouquets d'étoiles parfumées.

Las de l'amer repos où ma paresse offense
Une gloire pour qui jadis j'ai fui l'enfance
Adorable des bois de roses sous l'azur
Naturel, et plus las sept fois du pacte dur
De creuser par veillée une fosse nouvelle
Dans le terrain avare et froid de ma cervelle,
Fossoyeur sans pitié pour la stérilité,
– Que dire à cette Aurore, ô Rêves, visité
Par les roses, quand, peur de ses roses livides,
Le vaste cimetière unira les trous vides ? –
Je veux délaisser l'Art vorace d'un pays
Cruel, et, souriant aux reproches vieillis
Que me font mes amis, le passé, le génie,
Et ma lampe qui sait pourtant mon agonie,
Imiter le Chinois au cœur limpide et fin
De qui l'extase pure est de peindre la fin
Sur ses tasses de neige à la lune ravie
D'une bizarre fleur qui parfume sa vie
Transparente, la fleur qu'il a sentie, enfant,
Au filigrane bleu de l'âme se greffant.
Et, la mort telle avec le seul rêve du sage,
Serein, je vais choisir un jeune paysage
Que je peindrais encore sur les tasses, distrait.
Une ligne d'azur mince et pâle serait
Un lac, parmi le ciel de porcelaine nue,
Un clair croissant perdu par une blanche nue
Trempe sa corne calme en la glace des eaux,
Non loin de trois grands cils d'émeraude, roseaux.

BRISE MARINE

La chair est triste, hélas ! et j'ai lu tous les livres.
Fuir ! là-bas fuir ! Je sens que des oiseaux sont ivres
D'être parmi l'écume inconnue et les cieux !
Rien, ni les vieux jardins reflétés par les yeux
Ne retiendra ce cœur qui dans la mer se trempe
Ô nuits ! ni la clarté déserte de ma lampe
Sur le vide papier que la blancheur défend.
Et ni la jeune femme allaitant son enfant.
Je partirai ! Steamer balançant ta mâture,
Lève l'ancre pour une exotique nature !
Un Ennui, désolé par les cruels espoirs,
Croit encore à l'adieu suprême des mouchoirs !
Et, peut-être, les mâts, invitant les orages
Sont-ils de ceux qu'un vent penche sur les naufrages
Perdus, sans mâts, sans mâts, ni fertiles îlots...
Mais, ô mon cœur, entends le chant des matelots !

CANTIQUE DE SAINT JEAN

Le soleil que sa halte
Surnaturelle exalte
Aussitôt redescend
    Incandescent

Je sens comme aux vertèbres
S'éployer des ténèbres
Toutes dans un frisson
    À l'unisson

Et ma tête surgie
Solitaire vigie
Dans les vols triomphaux
    De cette faux

Comme rupture franche
Plutôt refoule ou tranche
Les anciens désaccords
    Avec le corps

Qu'elle de jeûnes ivre
S'opiniâtre à suivre
En quelque bond hagard
    Son pur regard

Là-haut où la froidure
Éternelle n'endure
Que vous le surpassiez
    Tous ô glaciers

Mais selon un baptême
Illuminée au même
Principe qui m'élut
    Penche un salut.

SAINTE

À la fenêtre recélant
Le santal vieux qui se dédore
De sa viole étincelant
Jadis avec flûte ou mandore,

Est la Sainte pâle, étalant
Le livre vieux qui se déplie
Du Magnificat ruisselant
Jadis selon vêpre et complie :

À ce vitrage d'ostensoir
Que frôle une harpe par l'Ange
Formée avec son vol du soir
Pour la délicate phalange

Du doigt que, sans le vieux santal
Ni le vieux livre, elle balance
Sur le plumage instrumental,
Musicienne du silence.

ÉVENTAIL

de Madame Mallarmé

Avec comme pour langage
Rien qu'un battement aux cieux
Le futur vers se dégage
Du logis très précieux

Aile tout bas la courrière
Cet éventail si c'est lui
Le même par qui derrière
Toi quelque miroir a lui

Limpide (où va redescendre
Pourchassée en chaque grain
Un peu d'invisible cendre
Seule à me rendre chagrin)

Toujours tel il apparaisse
Entre tes mains sans paresse.

AUTRE ÉVENTAIL

de Mademoiselle Mallarmé

Ô rêveuse, pour que je plonge
Au pur délice sans chemin,
Sache, par un subtil mensonge,
Garder mon aile dans ta main.

Une fraîcheur de crépuscule
Te vient à chaque battement
Dont le coup prisonnier recule
L'horizon délicatement.

Vertige ! voici que frissonne
L'espace comme un grand baiser
Qui, fou de naître pour personne,
Ne peut jaillir ni s'apaiser.

Sens-tu le paradis farouche
Ainsi qu'un rire enseveli
Se couler du coin de ta bouche
Au fond de l'unanime pli !

Le sceptre des rivages roses
Stagnants sur les soirs d'or, ce l'est,
Ce blanc vol fermé que tu poses
Contre le feu d'un bracelet.

PLUSIEURS SONNETS

II

Le vierge, le vivace et le bel aujourd'hui
Va-t-il nous déchirer avec un coup d'aile ivre
Ce lac dur oublié que hante sous le givre
Le transparent glacier des vols qui n'ont pas fui !

Un cygne d'autrefois se souvient que c'est lui
Magnifique mais qui sans espoir se délivre
Pour n'avoir pas chanté la région où vivre
Quand du stérile hiver a resplendi l'ennui.

Tout son col secouera cette blanche agonie
Par l'espace infligé à l'oiseau qui le nie,
Mais non l'horreur du sol où le plumage est pris.

Fantôme qu'à ce lieu son pur éclat assigne,
Il s'immobilise au songe froid de mépris
Que vêt parmi l'exil inutile le Cygne.

IV

Ses purs ongles très-haut dédiant leur onyx,
L'Angoisse, ce minuit, soutient, lampadophore,
Maint rêve vespéral brûlé par le Phénix
Que ne recueille pas de cinéraire amphore

Sur les crédences, au salon vide : nul ptyx,
Aboli bibelot d'inanité sonore,
(Car le Maître est allé puiser des pleurs au Styx
Avec ce seul objet dont le Néant s'honore.)

Mais proche la croisée au nord vacante, un or
Agonise selon peut-être le décor
Des licornes ruant du feu contre une nixe,

Elle, défunte nue en le miroir, encor
Que, dans l'oubli fermé par le cadre, se fixe
De scintillations sitôt le septuor.

LE TOMBEAU D'EDGAR POE

Tel qu'en Lui-même enfin l'éternité le change,
Le Poëte suscite avec un glaive nu
Son siècle épouvanté de n'avoir pas connu
Que la mort triomphait dans cette voix étrange !

Eux, comme un vil sursaut d'hydre oyant jadis l'ange
Donner un sens plus pur aux mots de la tribu
Proclamèrent très haut le sortilège bu
Dans le flot sans honneur de quelque noir mélange.

Du sol et de la nue hostiles, ô grief !
Si notre idée avec ne sculpte un bas-relief
Dont la tombe de Poe éblouissante s'orne,

Calme bloc ici-bas chu d'un désastre obscur
Que ce granit du moins montre à jamais sa borne
Aux noirs vols du Blasphème épars dans le futur.

JOSÉ MARIA DE HEREDIA

(1842-1905)

On le dit passé de mode, c'est ne pas tenir compte de son extraordinaire prestige auprès des lycéens. Sollicités sur leurs préférences en matière de poésie, même s'ils connaissent très peu de poèmes par cœur, ils citent avec enthousiasme ses vers les plus célèbres. L'enfance des peuples aime l'épopée, il en va de même pour celle de l'homme. Toutefois la plupart des poèmes épiques exigent, pour être retenus, un effort de mémoire dont bien peu sont capables ; car la nature, essentiellement narrative, de cette forme de poésie, appelle les longues séquences d'alexandrins, c'est d'ordinaire la prolixité qui la caractérise. Aussi Hugo, génie épique s'il en est, n'a presque jamais eu recours à la brièveté corsetée du sonnet. Or c'est dans la clôture stricte de ce dernier que José Maria de Heredia enferme ses épopées, les couleurs violentes de leur décor et leurs héros à la stature surhumaine. D'où le plaisir de ses jeunes lecteurs, d'où le reproche fait par d'autres, aux quatorze vers ainsi lestés, de grandiloquence ou d'amplification du trait et d'effets trop appuyés, en particulier dans le final solennel qui scelle presque tous ses sonnets. Cependant on peut y voir plutôt la nécessaire réduction à l'essentiel que requiert l'art du graveur de médailles. Jadis, nos professeurs, empruntant au poète l'un de ses vers pour caractériser sa manière, louaient en lui l'habile sculpteur d' « Un combat de Titans au pommeau d'une dague ».

Disciple de Leconte de Lisle, il est le représentant le plus tardif mais aussi le plus incontestable du Parnasse. Son maître laisse parfois entendre des accents de désespoir personnel, et prend ainsi quelques libertés avec l'impassibilité qu'il prône. Mais dans

Les Trophées, ce livre si longtemps travaillé et peaufiné, l'auteur ne se montre pas (même si le lecteur attentif croit deviner la sensualité, la fougue et l'« espagnolisme » de son caractère). En outre le choix d'un moule quasi unique pour ce recueil, puisque 118 sonnets en constituent l'essentiel, répond pleinement à l'exigence de perfection à travers « une forme / Au travail rebelle » qui constitue l'un des dogmes des Parnassiens.

Avant même la parution, en 1893, de son unique livre, Heredia est déjà célèbre, grâce aux nombreux sonnets qu'il a publiés dans diverses revues, ainsi qu'au prestige de son salon fréquenté notamment par de jeunes poètes. Parmi eux Henri de Régnier. Symboliste, grand admirateur de son hôte dont il devient le gendre, il compare *Les Trophées* aux *Bucoliques* d'André Chénier, chacune de ces œuvres faisant, selon lui, le lien entre deux écoles, l'une du classicisme au romantisme, et l'autre du Parnasse au Symbolisme. Parallèle intéressant mais difficile à justifier au premier abord, sauf à évoquer un éloge de complaisance. On ne peut cependant contester que les circonstances de leur parution justifient le rapprochement : elles sont, l'une et l'autre, publiées très tard, quand les tenants des courants auxquels elles se rattachent ont déjà cédé la place à des générations qui n'ont plus le même code esthétique. De plus toutes les deux disent la fascination de leur auteur pour l'Antiquité qu'ils réinterprètent ; mais, alors que Chénier le fait avec une sensibilité très personnelle, en laissant deviner son propre cœur, et enthousiasme par là le romantisme naissant, l'auteur des *Trophées* a recours à l'Histoire en érudit soucieux d'exactitude, et ses poèmes sont d'une parfaite objectivité. On doit pourtant reconnaître que ces derniers ne tirent pas leur pouvoir de suggestion de la science de l'auteur ou de son apparente neutralité, mais de ses images. Celle sur laquelle se referme le sonnet, en particulier, se déploie bien au-delà du contexte, elle dépasse l'objet qu'elle peint, et le poème qui semble clos s'ouvre au moyen du symbole à une autre vision du réel. Certes le symbole a toujours existé en poésie, et l'on pourrait par exemple, comparer à cet égard, le final d'*Antoine et Cléopâtre* à celui de *La Rose de l'Infante*. Toutefois son emploi récurrent dans les sonnets d'Heredia est sans doute ce qui permet de voir un rapport entre *Les Trophées* et le mouvement symboliste car Régnier donne lui-même de ce courant la définition qui suit :

« Jusqu'ici le symbole ne surgissait qu'instinctivement dans
les œuvres d'art, en dehors de tout parti pris, parce qu'en effet
on sentait qu'il ne peut pas y avoir d'œuvre d'art véritable
sans symbole... [maintenant] on fait du symbole la condition
essentielle de l'art. »

LA TREBBIA

L'aube d'un jour sinistre a blanchi les hauteurs.
Le camp s'éveille. En bas roule et gronde le fleuve
Où l'escadron léger des Numides s'abreuve.
Partout sonne l'appel clair des buccinateurs.

Car malgré Scipion, les augures menteurs,
La Trebbia débordée, et qu'il vente et qu'il pleuve,
Sempronius consul, fier de sa gloire neuve,
A fait lever la hache et marcher les licteurs.

Rougissant le ciel noir de flamboiements lugubres,
À l'horizon, brûlaient les villages Insubres ;
On entendait au loin barrir un éléphant.

Et là-bas, sous le pont, adossé contre une arche,
Hannibal écoutait, pensif et triomphant,
Le piétinement sourd des légions en marche.

Les Trophées

SOIR DE BATAILLE

Le choc avait été très rude. Les tribuns
Et les centurions, ralliant les cohortes,
Humaient encor, dans l'air où vibraient leurs voix fortes,
La chaleur du carnage et ses âcres parfums

D'un œil morne, comptant leurs compagnons défunts,
Les soldats regardaient, comme des feuilles mortes,
Au loin tourbillonner les archers de Phraortes ;
Et la sueur coulait de leurs visages bruns.

C'est alors qu'apparut, tout hérissé de flèches,
Rouge du flux vermeil de ses blessures fraîches,
Sous la pourpre flottante et l'airain rutilant,

Au fracas des buccins qui sonnaient leur fanfare,
Superbe, maîtrisant son cheval qui s'effare,
Sur le ciel enflammé, l'Imperator sanglant.

Les Trophées

ANTOINE ET CLÉOPÂTRE

Tous deux ils regardaient, de la haute terrasse,
L'Égypte s'endormir sous un ciel étouffant
Et le Fleuve, à travers le Delta noir qu'il fend,
Vers Bubaste ou Saïs rouler son onde grasse.

Et le Romain sentait sous la lourde cuirasse,
Soldat captif berçant le sommeil d'un enfant,
Ployer et défaillir sur son cœur triomphant
Le corps voluptueux que son étreinte embrasse.

Tournant sa tête pâle entre ses cheveux bruns
Vers celui qu'enivraient d'invincibles parfums,
Elle tendit sa bouche et ses prunelles claires ;

Et sur elle courbé, l'ardent Imperator
Vit dans ses larges yeux étoilés de points d'or
Toute une mer immense où fuyaient des galères.

Les Trophées

LES CONQUÉRANTS

Comme un vol de gerfauts hors du charnier natal,
Fatigués de porter leurs misères hautaines,
De Palos de Moguer routiers et capitaines
Partaient, ivres d'un rêve héroïque et brutal.

Ils allaient conquérir le fabuleux métal
Que Cipango mûrit dans ses mines lointaines,
Et les vents alizés inclinaient leurs antennes
Aux bords mystérieux du monde occidental.

Chaque soir, espérant des lendemains épiques,
L'azur phosphorescent de la mer des Tropiques
Enchantait leur sommeil d'un mirage doré ;

Ou, penchés à l'avant des blanches caravelles,
Ils regardaient monter en un ciel ignoré
Du fond de l'Océan des étoiles nouvelles.

Les Trophées

PAUL VERLAINE

(1844-1896)

L'originalité de Verlaine ne se fonde pas sur une rupture avec ses prédécesseurs : il ne ménage pas son admiration aux grands romantiques et compose un éloge de Marceline Desbordes-Valmore que Rimbaud lui fait découvrir et dont il imite les rythmes. Loin de se poser en novateur, il emprunte le titre de son premier recueil à Baudelaire qui écrivait : « Jette ce livre saturnien / Orgiaque et mélancolique. » Cette filiation revendiquée n'empêche pas, dans le même temps, l'évident parti pris descriptif, à la manière de Leconte de Lisle, d'un certain nombre de poèmes.

Dans quelques autres cependant se marque déjà son génie propre. Disparaissent alors les constructions oratoires ou les descriptions structurées, et le contenu narratif s'estompe. Place est faite d'abord au chant. Le poète maîtrise l'harmonie du vers comme personne sans doute avant lui ne l'avait fait. Le poème tend désormais à n'être, comme il le dit, « qu'un frisson d'eau sur de la mousse ». Or la mutation qu'il opère alors, semble sans commune mesure avec les moyens énumérés dans son célèbre *Art poétique*. On l'y entend récuser la rime, mais quelque liberté qu'il prenne à son égard, il ne renonce jamais à ce « bijou d'un sou ». Il enjoint au destinataire de préférer l'impair, lui-même y excelle, mais les rythmes pairs n'en restent pas moins dominants dans son œuvre. Aussi ces conseils au poète Charles Morice, sous la plume d'un autre poète qui a toujours refusé, lui, les théories et les écoles, ne font pas de ces strophes l'exposé d'une doctrine élaborée, et n'expliquent guère le miracle de son art. Et si le terme de « chanson grise » convient à la « fadeur » d'un univers en demi-

teintes tel que l'a décrit Jean-Pierre Richard, il faut chercher
ailleurs que dans ce poème ce qui fonde la nouveauté et la
singularité de son génie poétique.

« Verlaine, écrit Octave Nadal, introduit dans la finitude et les
équilibres du mètre accoutumé... les figures les plus complexes et
les plus imprévisibles du mouvement, en remontant à la source
jaillissante des vocables. » Il choisit ses mots en fonction de leur
valeur musicale. L'écho des consonnes et des voyelles récurrentes
ne vise pas à abolir le sens, mais seulement à le rendre
approximatif ; le poème est fait d'abord pour l'oreille ; les
allitérations et les analogies de sons qui se répondent et prolongent
le vers au-delà de lui-même, substituent à l'énoncé clair la
suggestion. Déplacement ou hésitation de la césure, atténuation
discrète de la rime par les enjambements ou les rejets, contribuent
aussi à cette mutation. Mais surtout, le jeu avec l'e muet en est
sans doute l'instrument le plus efficace. En introduisant un silence
il suspend le vers ; la voyelle quasi inaudible trouble secrètement
l'équilibre du mètre pair et le libère de son martèlement cadencé :
il lui substitue une sorte de faux pas permanent, comme un
gracieux trébuchement des syllabes. L'accentuation même du vers
surprend en se faisant entendre là où on ne l'attendait pas. Le
danger de monotonie de la rime est ainsi écarté, elle n'est plus
qu'un repère discret dans la fluidité continue de sons harmonieux.

Les thèmes favoris de Verlaine portent aussi sa marque
propre : même s'il les emprunte à Baudelaire, il les transforme
profondément. Ainsi pour le spleen : le vague à l'âme verlainien ne
lui ressemble qu'en apparence. Lorsque le poète écrit : « Il pleure
dans mon cœur / Comme il pleut sur la ville »... il peint un état
assez neutre, quasi impersonnel, et fort étranger au désespoir
métaphysique du spleen. Atteinte de cette inexplicable langueur,
l'âme semble s'y diluer dans une absence à soi-même, elle n'est
pas déchirée, mais atone.

C'est surtout lorsque Verlaine a recours aux symboles que la
distance prise par rapport à son modèle est manifeste, les soleils
couchants, les « ondes blêmes » ou le rossignol, sont de simples
miroirs du moi, rien ne se fonde ici sur l'idée de l'universelle unité.
Si les parfums, les couleurs et les sons se répondent, ils ne sont
nullement le signe sensible d'une totalité intelligible, les sensations
valent en elles-mêmes et ne permettent aucun transfert vers une

réalité spirituelle. « Le symbolisme ? comprends pas »... répondait-il ironiquement à l'enquête de Jules Huré sur la poésie contemporaine, et il ajoutait : « ça doit être un mot allemand... » Pourtant des équivalences s'établissent entre la nature et le poète qui la regarde. L'âme peut être vue comme un « paysage choisi », et ce dernier revêtir la couleur d'un état d'âme. Cette fusion donne à l'objet extérieur la consistance poreuse du moi et permet au poète de substituer un monde fait d'impressions plus que de couleurs au tableau pittoresque du réel. En conjuguant ainsi les données des sens et les dispositions intérieures rêveuses le poème s'accroît d'une sorte de halo mystérieux que sa musique prolonge en nous indéfiniment.

Que doit cette magie à la rencontre de Rimbaud ? Sans doute l'audace dans la recherche de rythmes nouveaux, et l'emploi insolite de l'hendécasyllabe, mais Verlaine ne va pas plus loin dans l'invention d'une langue. Peut-être aussi la confiance dans la richesse illimitée du rêve, mais il ne tente pas de le provoquer et, toujours docile à l'envahissement de la rêverie, il ne se fait pas l'artisan des savants cauchemars. Son propos n'est pas de « changer la vie », tout au plus, pour lui-même, de changer sa vie, comme il le fait, un temps, après le retour à la foi qui s'exprime dans *Sagesse*.

Il reste pour nous essentiellement l'auteur des *Fêtes galantes*, à la grâce surannée et moqueuse, et de ces *Romances sans paroles* dont le titre évoque à la fois la chanson populaire et naïve qu'une science subtile, et sans doute innée, du vers lui a permis de recréer, et les ritournelles qui s'imposent à la mémoire. Il est l'artisan inégalé de ce « sfumato verbal », cette vaporisation ou dilution des mots, dans des vers dont l'écoute requiert moins l'attention lucide que le glissement insensible de la conscience vers les « espaces du dedans ».

APRÈS TROIS ANS

Ayant poussé la porte étroite qui chancelle,
Je me suis promené dans le petit jardin
Qu'éclairait doucement le soleil du matin,
Pailletant chaque fleur d'une humide étincelle.

Rien n'a changé. J'ai tout revu : l'humble tonnelle
De vigne folle avec les chaises de rotin...
Le jet d'eau fait toujours son murmure argentin
Et le vieux tremble sa plainte sempiternelle.

Les roses comme avant palpitent ; comme avant,
Les grands lys orgueilleux se balancent au vent.
Chaque alouette qui va et vient m'est connue.

Même j'ai retrouvé debout la Velléda,
Dont le plâtre s'écaille au bout de l'avenue,
– Grêle, parmi l'odeur fade du réséda.

Poèmes saturniens

MON RÊVE FAMILIER

Je fais souvent ce rêve étrange et pénétrant
D'une femme inconnue, et que j'aime, et qui m'aime,
Et qui n'est, chaque fois, ni tout à fait la même
Ni tout à fait une autre, et m'aime et me comprend.

Car elle me comprend, et mon cœur, transparent
Pour elle seule, hélas ! cesse d'être un problème
Pour elle seule, et les moiteurs de mon front blême,
Elle seule les sait rafraîchir, en pleurant.

Est-elle brune, blonde ou rousse ? – Je l'ignore.
Son nom ? Je me souviens qu'il est doux et sonore
Comme ceux des aimés que la Vie exila.

Son regard est pareil au regard des statues,
Et, pour sa voix, lointaine, et calme, et grave, elle a
L'inflexion des voix chères qui se sont tues.

Poèmes saturniens

EFFET DE NUIT

La nuit. La pluie. Un ciel blafard que déchiquette
De flèches et de tours à jour la silhouette
D'une ville gothique éteinte au lointain gris.
La plaine. Un gibet plein de pendus rabougris
Secoués par le bec avide des corneilles
Et dansant dans l'air noir des gigues nonpareilles,
Tandis que leurs pieds sont la pâture des loups.
Quelques buissons d'épine épars, et quelques houx
Dressant l'horreur de leur feuillage à droite, à gauche,
Sur le fuligineux fouillis d'un fond d'ébauche.
Et puis, autour de trois livides prisonniers
Qui vont pieds nus, un gros de hauts pertuisaniers
En marche, et leurs fers droits, comme des fers de herse,
Luisent à contre-sens des lances de l'averse.

Poèmes saturniens

SOLEILS COUCHANTS

Une aube affaiblie
Verse par les champs
La mélancolie
Des soleils couchants.
La mélancolie
Berce de doux chants
Mon cœur qui s'oublie
Aux soleils couchants.
Et d'étranges rêves,
Comme des soleils
Couchants sur les grèves,
Fantômes vermeils,
Défilent sans trêves,
Défilent, pareils
À des grands soleils
Couchants sur les grèves.

Poèmes saturniens

CHANSON D'AUTOMNE

Les sanglots longs
        Des violons
De l'automne
Blessent mon cœur
D'une langueur
        Monotone.

Tout suffocant
Et blême, quand
        Sonne l'heure,
Je me souviens
Des jours anciens
        Et je pleure ;

Et je m'en vais
Au vent mauvais
        Qui m'emporte
Deçà, delà,
Pareil à la
        Feuille morte.

Poèmes saturniens

CLAIR DE LUNE

Votre âme est un paysage choisi
Que vont charmant masques et bergamasques
Jouant du luth et dansant et quasi
Tristes sous leurs déguisements fantasques.

Tout en chantant sur le mode mineur
L'amour vainqueur et la vie opportune,
Ils n'ont pas l'air de croire à leur bonheur
Et leur chanson se mêle au clair de lune,

Au calme clair de lune triste et beau,
Qui fait rêver les oiseaux dans les arbres
Et sangloter d'extase les jets d'eau,
Les grands jets d'eau sveltes parmi les marbres.

Fêtes galantes

PANTOMIME

Pierrot qui n'a rien d'un Clitandre
Vide un flacon sans plus attendre,
Et, pratique, entame un pâté.

Cassandre, au fond de l'avenue,
Verse une larme méconnue
Sur son neveu déshérité.

Ce faquin d'Arlequin combine
L'enlèvement de Colombine
Et pirouette quatre fois.

Colombine rêve, surprise
De sentir un cœur dans la brise
Et d'entendre en son cœur des voix.

Fêtes galantes

SUR L'HERBE

– L'abbé divague. – Et toi, marquis,
Tu mets de travers ta perruque.
– Ce vieux vin de Chypre est exquis
Moins, Camargo, que votre nuque.

– Ma flamme... – Do, mi, sol, la, si.
– L'abbé, ta noirceur se dévoile.
– Que je meure, mesdames, si
Je ne vous décroche une étoile !

– Je voudrais être petit chien !
– Embrassons nos bergères, l'une
Après l'autre. – Messieurs, eh bien ?
– Do, mi, sol. – Hé ! bonsoir, la Lune !

Fêtes galantes

À LA PROMENADE

Le ciel si pâle et les arbres si grêles
Semblent sourire à nos costumes clairs
Qui vont flottant légers avec des airs
De nonchalance et des mouvements d'ailes

Et le vent doux ride l'humble bassin,
Et la lueur du soleil qu'atténue
L'ombre des bas tilleuls de l'avenue
Nous parvient bleue et mourante à dessein.

Trompeurs exquis et coquettes charmantes,
Cœurs tendres, mais affranchis du serment,
Nous devisons délicieusement,
Et les amants lutinent les amantes,

De qui la main imperceptible sait
Parfois donner un soufflet, qu'on échange
Contre un baiser sur l'extrême phalange
Du petit doigt, et comme la chose est

Immensément excessive et farouche,
On est puni par un regard très sec,
Lequel contraste, au demeurant, avec
La moue assez clémente de la bouche.

Fêtes galantes

LES INGÉNUS

Les hauts talons luttaient avec les longues jupes,
En sorte que, selon le terrain et le vent,
Parfois luisaient des bas de jambes, trop souvent
Interceptés ! – et nous aimions ce jeu de dupes.

Parfois aussi le dard d'un insecte jaloux
Inquiétait le col des belles sous les branches,
Et c'était des éclairs soudains de nuques blanches,
Et ce régal comblait nos jeunes yeux de fous.

Le soir tombait, un soir équivoque d'automne :
Les belles, se pendant rêveuses à nos bras,
Dirent alors des mots si spécieux, tout bas,
Que notre âme, depuis ce temps, tremble et s'étonne.

Fêtes galantes

EN BATEAU

L'étoile du berger tremblote
Dans l'eau plus noire, et le pilote
Cherche un briquet dans sa culotte.

C'est l'instant, Messieurs, ou jamais,
D'être audacieux, et je mets
Mes deux mains partout désormais !

Le chevalier Atys, qui gratte
Sa guitare, à Chloris l'ingrate
Lance une œillade scélérate.

L'abbé confesse bas Églé,
Et ce vicomte déréglé
Des champs donne à son cœur la clé.

Cependant la lune se lève
Et l'esquif en sa course brève
File gaiement sur l'eau qui rêve.

Fêtes galantes

COLOMBINE

Léandre le sot,
Pierrot qui d'un saut
      De puce
Franchit le buisson,
Cassandre sous son
      Capuce,

Arlequin aussi,
Cet aigrefin si
      Fantasque
Aux costumes fous,
Ses yeux luisants sous
      Son masque,

— Do, mi, sol, mi, fa, —
Tout ce monde va,
      Rit, chante
Et danse devant
Une belle enfant
      Méchante

Dont les yeux pervers
Comme les yeux verts
      Des chattes
Gardent ses appas
Et disent : « À bas
      Les pattes ! »

— Eux ils vont toujours ! —
Fatidique cours
      Des astres,
Oh ! dis-moi vers quels
Mornes ou cruels
      Désastres

L'implacable enfant,
Preste et relevant
     Ses jupes,
La rose au chapeau,
Conduit son troupeau
     De dupes ?

Fêtes galantes

COLLOQUE SENTIMENTAL

Dans le vieux parc solitaire et glacé,
Deux formes ont tout à l'heure passé.

Leurs yeux sont morts et leurs lèvres sont molles,
Et l'on entend à peine leurs paroles.

Dans le vieux parc solitaire et glacé
Deux spectres ont évoqué le passé.

– Te souvient-il de notre extase ancienne ?
– Pourquoi voulez-vous donc qu'il m'en souvienne ?

– Ton cœur bat-il toujours à mon seul nom ?
Toujours vois-tu mon âme en rêve ? – Non.

– Ah ! les beaux jours de bonheur indicible
Où nous joignions nos bouches ! – C'est possible.

– Qu'il était bleu, le ciel, et grand, l'espoir !
– L'espoir a fui, vaincu, vers le ciel noir.

Tels ils marchaient dans les avoines folles,
Et la nuit seule entendit leurs paroles.

Fêtes galantes

La lune blanche
Luit dans les bois ;
De chaque branche
Part une voix
Sous la ramée...

Ô bien-aimée.

L'étang reflète,
Profond miroir,
La silhouette
Du saule noir
Où le vent pleure...

Rêvons, c'est l'heure.

Un vaste et tendre
Apaisement
Semble descendre
Du firmament
Que l'astre irise...

C'est l'heure exquise.

La Bonne Chanson, VI

J'ai presque peur, en vérité,
Tant je sens ma vie enlacée
À la radieuse pensée
Qui m'a pris l'âme l'autre été,

Tant votre image, à jamais chère,
Habite en ce cœur tout à vous,
Mon cœur uniquement jaloux
De vous aimer et de vous plaire ;

Et je tremble, pardonnez-moi
D'aussi franchement vous le dire,
À penser qu'un mot, un sourire
De vous est désormais ma loi,

Et qu'il vous suffirait d'un geste,
D'une parole ou d'un clin d'œil,
Pour mettre tout mon être en deuil
De son illusion céleste.

Mais plutôt je ne veux vous voir,
L'avenir dût-il m'être sombre
Et fécond en peines sans nombre,
Qu'à travers un immense espoir,

Plongé dans ce bonheur suprême
De me dire encore et toujours,
En dépit des mornes retours,
Que je vous aime, que je t'aime !

La Bonne Chanson, XV

Il pleut doucement sur la ville.

Arthur Rimbaud

Il pleure dans mon cœur
Comme il pleut sur la ville,
Quelle est cette langueur
Qui pénètre mon cœur ?

Ô bruit doux de la pluie
Par terre et sur les toits !
Pour un cœur qui s'ennuie
Ô le chant de la pluie !

Il pleure sans raison
Dans ce cœur qui s'écœure.
Quoi ! nulle trahison ?
Ce deuil est sans raison.

C'est bien la pire peine
De ne savoir pourquoi,
Sans amour et sans haine,
Mon cœur a tant de peine !

Romances sans paroles, III

Ô triste, triste était mon âme
À cause, à cause d'une femme.

Je ne me suis pas consolé
Bien que mon cœur s'en soit allé,

Bien que mon cœur, bien que mon âme
Eussent fui loin de cette femme.

Je ne me suis pas consolé,
Bien que mon cœur s'en soit allé.

Et mon cœur, mon cœur trop sensible
Dit à mon âme : Est-il possible,

Est-il possible, – le fût-il, –
Ce fier exil, ce triste exil ?

Mon âme dit à mon cœur : Sais-je
Moi-même, que nous veut ce piège

D'êtres présents bien qu'exilés,
Encore que loin en allés ?

Romances sans paroles, VII

*Le rossignol qui du haut d'une
branche se regarde dedans, croit
être tombé dans la rivière. Il est au
sommet d'un chêne et toutefois il a
peur de se noyer.*

CYRANO DE BERGERAC

L'ombre des arbres dans la rivière embrumée
    Meurt comme de la fumée,
Tandis qu'en l'air, parmi les ramures réelles,
    Se plaignent les tourterelles.

Combien, ô voyageur, ce paysage blême
    Te mira blême toi-même,
Et que tristes pleuraient dans les hautes feuillées
    Tes espérances noyées !

Mai-Juin 1872

Romances sans paroles, IX

GREEN

Voici des fruits, des fleurs, des feuilles et des branches,
Et puis voici mon cœur, qui ne bat que pour vous.
Ne le déchirez pas avec vos deux mains blanches
Et qu'à vos yeux si beaux l'humble présent soit doux.

J'arrive tout couvert encore de rosée
Que le vent du matin vient glacer à mon front.
Souffrez que ma fatigue, à vos pieds reposée,
Rêve des chers instants qui la délasseront.

Sur votre jeune sein laissez rouler ma tête
Toute sonore encor de vos derniers baisers ;
Laissez-la s'apaiser de la bonne tempête,
Et que je dorme un peu puisque vous reposez.

Romances sans paroles

Bon chevalier masqué qui chevauche en silence,
Le malheur a percé mon vieux cœur de sa lance.

Le sang de mon vieux cœur n'a fait qu'un jet vermeil
Puis s'est évaporé sur les fleurs, au soleil.

L'ombre éteignit mes yeux, un cri vint à ma bouche
Et mon vieux cœur est mort dans un frisson farouche.

Alors le chevalier Malheur s'est rapproché,
Il a mis pied à terre et sa main m'a touché.

Son doigt ganté de fer entra dans ma blessure
Tandis qu'il attestait sa loi d'une voix dure.

Et voici qu'au contact glacé du doigt de fer
Un cœur me renaissait, tout un cœur pur et fier.

Et voici que, fervent d'une candeur divine,
Tout un cœur jeune et bon battit dans ma poitrine.

Or, je restais tremblant, ivre, incrédule un peu,
Comme un homme qui voit des visions de Dieu.

Mais le bon chevalier, remonté sur sa bête,
En s'éloignant me fit un signe de la tête

Et me cria (j'entends *encore* cette voix) :
« Au moins, prudence ! Car c'est bon pour une fois. »

Sagesse, I, I

Écoutez la chanson bien douce
Qui ne pleure que pour vous plaire.
Elle est discrète, elle est légère :
Un frisson d'eau sur de la mousse !

La voix vous fut connue (et chère ?)
Mais à présent elle est voilée
Comme une veuve désolée,
Pourtant comme elle encore fière,

Et dans les longs plis de son voile
Qui palpite aux brises d'automne,
Cache et montre au cœur qui s'étonne
La vérité comme une étoile.

Elle dit, la voix reconnue,
Que la bonté c'est notre vie,
Que de la haine et de l'envie
Rien ne reste, la mort venue.

Elle parle aussi de la gloire
D'être simple sans plus attendre,
Et de noces d'or et du tendre
Bonheur d'une paix sans victoire.

Accueillez la voix qui persiste
Dans son naïf épithalame.
Allez, rien n'est meilleur à l'âme
Que de faire une âme moins triste !

Elle est *en peine et de passage*,
L'âme qui souffre sans colère,
Et comme sa morale est claire !...
Écoutez la chanson bien sage.

Sagesse, I, XVI

Gaspard Hauser chante :

Je suis venu, calme orphelin,
Riche de mes seuls yeux tranquilles,
Vers les hommes des grandes villes :
Ils ne m'ont pas trouvé malin.

À vingt ans un trouble nouveau,
Sous le nom d'amoureuses flammes,
M'a fait trouver belles les femmes :
Elles ne m'ont pas trouvé beau.

Bien que sans patrie et sans roi
Et très brave ne l'étant guère,
J'ai voulu mourir à la guerre :
La mort n'a pas voulu de moi.

Suis-je né trop tôt ou trop tard ?
Qu'est-ce que je fais en ce monde ?
Ô vous tous, ma peine est profonde :
Priez pour le pauvre Gaspard !

Sagesse, III, IV

Un grand sommeil noir
Tombe sur ma vie :
Dormez, tout espoir,
Dormez, toute envie !

Je ne vois plus rien,
Je perds la mémoire
Du mal et du bien...
Ô la triste histoire !

Je suis un berceau
Qu'une main balance
Au creux d'un caveau :
Silence ! silence !

Sagesse, III, V

Le ciel est, par-dessus le toit,
        Si bleu, si calme !
Un arbre, par-dessus le toit,
        Berce sa palme.

La cloche, dans le ciel qu'on voit
        Doucement tinte.
Un oiseau sur l'arbre qu'on voit
        Chante sa plainte.

Mon Dieu, mon Dieu, la vie est là,
        Simple et tranquille.
Cette paisible rumeur-là
        Vient de la ville.

— Qu'as-tu fait, ô toi que voilà
        Pleurant sans cesse,
Dis, qu'as-tu fait, toi que voilà,
        De ta jeunesse ?

Sagesse, III, VI

Le son du cor s'afflige vers les bois
D'une douleur on veut croire orpheline
Qui vient mourir au bas de la colline
Parmi la bise errant en courts abois.

L'âme du loup pleure dans cette voix
Qui monte avec le soleil qui décline
D'une agonie on veut croire câline
Et qui ravit et qui navre à la fois.

Pour faire mieux cette plainte assoupie
La neige tombe à longs traits de charpie
À travers le couchant sanguinolent,

Et l'air a l'air d'être un soupir d'automne,
Tant il fait doux par ce soir monotone
Où se dorlote un paysage lent.

Sagesse, III, IX

ART POÉTIQUE

À Charles Morice

De la musique avant toute chose,
Et pour cela préfère l'Impair
Plus vague et plus soluble dans l'air,
Sans rien en lui qui pèse ou qui pose.

Il faut aussi que tu n'ailles point
Choisir tes mots sans quelque méprise :
Rien de plus cher que la chanson grise
Où l'Indécis au Précis se joint.

C'est des beaux yeux derrière des voiles,
C'est le grand jour tremblant de midi,
C'est, par un ciel d'automne attiédi,
Le bleu fouillis des claires étoiles !

Car nous voulons la Nuance encor,
Pas la Couleur, rien que la nuance !
Oh ! la nuance seule fiance
Le rêve au rêve et la flûte au cor !

Fuis du plus loin la Pointe assassine,
L'Esprit cruel et le Rire impur,
Qui font pleurer les yeux de l'Azur,
Et tout cet ail de basse cuisine !

Prends l'éloquence et tords-lui son cou !
Tu feras bien, en train d'énergie,
De rendre un peu la Rime assagie,
Si l'on n'y veille, elle ira jusqu'où ?

Ô qui dira les torts de la Rime !
Quel enfant sourd ou quel nègre fou
Nous a forgé ce bijou d'un sou
Qui sonne creux et faux sous la lime ?

De la musique encore et toujours !
Que ton vers soit la chose envolée
Qu'on sent qui fuit d'une âme en allée
Vers d'autres cieux à d'autres amours.

Que ton vers soit la bonne aventure
Éparse au vent crispé du matin
Qui va fleurant la menthe et le thym...
Et tout le reste est littérature.

Jadis et naguère

TRISTAN CORBIÈRE

(1845-1875)

Ce prénom qu'il a préféré à son nom de baptême, pour sa connotation romantique, apparaît plutôt à nos yeux comme la préfiguration d'une vie marquée par l'échec et la douleur, et c'est à juste titre que Verlaine lui consacre le premier de ses articles sur les « Poètes maudits ». Ses voisins bretons le surnommeront l'An-Ankou, c'est-à-dire le spectre de la mort, tant son aspect physique annonce la maladie et le désespoir. Sa santé ne lui permettra jamais de réaliser son rêve d'être marin à l'instar de ce père dont le modèle l'écrase. Une laideur peut-être réelle, mais que son horreur de soi amplifie et qu'il rappelle avec insistance, lui laisse peu de chances d'être aimé. C'est pourquoi il se peint lui-même férocement, il cherche la provocation dans ses poèmes comme dans sa vie. Ici il se déguise et multiplie les canulars, là il veut surprendre et choquer. On dirait qu'il s'agit pour lui d'abord de déplaire. Plus question de dire au lecteur « Insensé qui crois que je ne suis pas toi », pas même de lui murmurer « Hypocrite lecteur, mon semblable, mon frère ! », il lui faut souligner sa différence et se proclamer avec rage : « Trop Soi pour se pouvoir souffrir. » Son unique recueil : *Les Amours jaunes* – dont le titre signifie sans doute que l'on peut aimer par défaut comme l'on rit par dépit –, séduit par cette violence vengeresse déployée contre soi-même et jusqu'alors inédite en poésie, car si on lui trouve des prédécesseurs dans l'auto-dérision, celle-ci se fonde chez lui moins sur une complaisance que sur un désespoir profond. Il retient aussi l'attention par son refus des conventions du vers harmonieux et de l'expression rhétorique de la passion. On lui doit, par son recours constant à un déferlement baroque d'images saugrenues, à un vers volontairement rompu, désarticulé au point de sembler parfois bancal, d'avoir introduit dans le langage poétique une rupture dont les surréalistes se souviendront. Sa *Litanie du sommeil* les séduit parce qu'elle leur semble préfigurer l'écriture automatique, par le jeu d'associations d'images insolites, cet onirisme verbal que souligne le rythme. La longue succession d'invocations ponctuées de points d'exclamation, qui marque l'importance attachée par le poète à l'organisation typographique du poème, leur apparaît comme une innovation essentielle. Mais si Tristan Corbière peut passer pour l'un de leurs précurseurs, en « faisant, comme l'écrit Henri Lemaitre, de l'arythmie formelle le signe d'une correspondante arythmie spirituelle », il se rattache aussi au symbolisme naissant dont la doctrine posera un rapport nécessaire entre le langage et l'idée, entre la matière du poème et son univers spirituel.

LE CRAPAUD

Un chant dans une nuit sans air...
– La lune plaque en métal clair
Les découpures du vert sombre.

... Un chant ; comme un écho, tout vif
Enterré, là, sous le massif...
– Ça se tait : Viens, c'est là, dans l'ombre...

– Un crapaud ! – Pourquoi cette peur,
Près de moi, ton soldat fidèle !
Vois-le, poète tondu, sans aile,
Rossignol de la boue... – Horreur ! –

– Il chante. – Horreur ! ! – Horreur pourquoi ?
Vois-tu pas son œil de lumière...
Non : il s'en va, froid, sous sa pierre.

. . . .

Bonsoir – ce crapaud-là c'est moi.

Le soir, 20 juillet

LA FIN

Oh ! combien de marins, combien de capitaines
Qui sont partis joyeux pour des courses lointaines
Dans ce morne horizon se sont évanouis !...
. . . .
Combien de patrons morts avec leurs équipages !
L'Océan de leur vie a pris toutes les pages,
Et, d'un souffle, il a tout dispersé sur les flots.
Nul ne saura leur fin dans l'abîme plongée...
. . . .
Nul ne saura leurs noms, pas même l'humble pierre,
Dans l'étroit cimetière où l'écho nous répond,
Pas même un saule vert qui s'effeuille à l'automne,
Pas même la chanson plaintive et monotone
D'un aveugle qui chante à l'angle d'un vieux pont.

V. HUGO, *Oceano nox*

Eh bien, tous ces marins – matelots, capitaines,
Dans leur grand Océan à jamais engloutis,
Partis insoucieux pour leurs courses lointaines,
Sont morts – absolument comme ils étaient partis.

Allons ! c'est leur métier ; ils sont morts dans leurs bottes
Leur *boujaron* [1] au cœur, tout vifs dans leurs capotes...
– *Morts...* Merci : la *Camarde* a pas le pied marin ; –
Qu'elle couche avec vous : c'est votre bonne femme...
– Eux, allons donc : Entiers ! enlevés par la lame !
     Ou perdus dans un grain...

Un grain... est-ce la mort, ça ? La basse voilure
Battant à travers l'eau ! – Ça se dit *encombrer*...
Un coup de mer plombé, puis la haute mâture
Fouettant les flots ras – et ça se dit *sombrer*.

---

1. ration d'eau-de-vie.

– Sombrer. – Sondez ce mot. Votre *mort* est bien pâle
Et pas grand'chose à bord, sous la lourde rafale...
Pas grand'chose devant le grand sourire amer
Du matelot qui lutte. – Allons donc, de la place ! –
Vieux fantôme éventé, la Mort change de face :
          La Mer !...

Noyés ? – Eh allons donc ! Les *noyés* sont d'eau douce.
– Coulés ! corps et biens ! Et, jusqu'au petit mousse,
Le défi dans les yeux, dans les dents le juron !
À l'écume crachant une chique râlée,
Buvant sans hauts-de-cœur *la grand'tasse salée*...
     – Comme ils ont bu leur boujaron. –

– Pas de fond de six pieds, ni rats de cimetière :
Eux ils vont aux requins ! L'âme d'un matelot,
Au lieu de suinter dans vos pommes de terre,
      Respire à chaque flot.

– Voyez à l'horizon se soulever la houle ;
      On dirait le ventre amoureux
D'une fille de joie en rut, à moitié soûle...
      Ils sont là ! – La houle a du creux. –

– Écoutez, écoutez la tourmente qui beugle !...
C'est leur anniversaire – Il revient bien souvent. –
Ô poète, gardez pour vous vos chants d'aveugle ;
– Eux : le *De profundis* que vous corne le vent.

... Qu'ils roulent infinis dans les espaces vierges !...
      Qu'ils roulent verts et nus,
Sans clous et sans sapin, sans couvercle, sans cierges !...
– Laissez-les donc rouler, *terriens* parvenus !

                 À bord. – 11 février

MIRLITON

Dors d'amour, méchant ferreur de cigales !
Dans le chiendent qui te couvrira
La cigale aussi pour toi chantera,
Joyeuse, avec ses petites cymbales.

La rosée aura des pleurs matinales ;
Et le muguet blanc fait un joli drap...
Dors d'amour, méchant ferreur de cigales !

Pleureuses en troupeau passeront les rafales...

La Muse camarde ici posera,
Sur ta bouche noire encore elle aura
Ces rimes qui vont aux moelles des pâles...
Dors d'amour, méchant ferreur de cigales.

PETIT MORT POUR RIRE

Va vite, léger peigneur de comètes !
Les herbes au vent seront tes cheveux ;
De ton œil béant jailliront les feux
Follets, prisonniers dans les pauvres têtes...

Les fleurs de tombeau qu'on nomme Amourettes
Foisonneront plein ton rire terreux...
Et les myosotis, ces fleurs d'oubliettes...

Ne fais pas le lourd : cercueils de poètes
Pour les croque-morts sont de simples jeux,
Boîtes à violon qui sonnent le creux...
Ils te croiront mort – les bourgeois sont bêtes –
Va vite, léger peigneur de comètes !

MAURICE ROLLINAT

(1846-1906)

C'est un singulier personnage : musicien, acteur et poète, il chante dans les cabarets des poèmes de Baudelaire qu'il a lui-même mis en musique. Sa voix, ses gestes fascinent un public hétéroclite, où l'on note la présence de musiciens tels que Gounod ou Massenet, et celle d'écrivains les plus divers auxquels se mêle parfois Victor Hugo lui-même. Un témoin affirme que « le prestige sur ses auditoires de hasard était immédiat, total, vainqueur... il était dû à un art indiscutable ».

Poète, il a d'abord publié *Les Brandes*, volume de vers où il peint le paysage et les gens du Berry, sa terre natale ; il s'y montre particulièrement sensible aux aspects fantastiques et sauvages des brandes. Lorsqu'il monte à Paris, et se produit aux Hydropathes ou au Chat Noir, s'il choisit d'y interpréter Baudelaire, c'est à cause d'affinités profondes qui le portent vers ce poète et vers Edgar Poe. Toute la part macabre ou hallucinée qu'il voit en eux, va passer dans son deuxième recueil : *Les Névroses*. Chacune des parties de cette œuvre (*Les Âmes, Les Luxures, Les Refuges, Les Spectres, Les Ténèbres, De profundis*) atteste de cette influence.

En effet il n'y a guère d'innovation, par rapport aux *Fleurs du mal*, dans les thèmes qu'il traite, et surtout il ne crée pas une langue poétique qui lui serait propre. Aussi, après l'accueil triomphal que l'on fait d'abord à son livre, quand on s'avise de cette indéniable proximité avec son modèle, elle lui est reprochée, et on se met alors à l'accuser d'insincérité et à le traiter de cabot. Pourtant Barbey d'Aurevilly l'avait encensé, écrivant que « l'auteur de ces poésies a inventé pour elles une musique qui fait ouvrir des ailes de feu à ses vers et qui enlève fougueusement, comme un hippogriffe, ses auditeurs fanatisés... », et ceux qui l'ont bien connu ont toujours cru à la réalité de ses angoisses. Mais ses détracteurs l'emportent, ses livres tombent dans l'oubli.

Pour le lecteur d'aujourd'hui qui ne peut être influencé ni par l'accompagnement de la musique et du geste, ni surtout par le spectacle du visage halluciné de l'auteur-interprète, dont les témoins assurent qu'il suffisait à communiquer une véritable angoisse à son auditoire, que vaut cette œuvre ?

Elle est d'abord un témoignage précieux sur l'époque, qui voit paraître, un an après *Les Névroses*, en 1884, le célèbre *À rebours* de Huysmans, et découvre, l'année suivante, *Les Déliquescences d'Adoré Floupette*, la plus célèbre des parodies du « décadentisme ». Cependant, au-delà de sa valeur documentaire, elle peut encore nous toucher, car à travers un mimétisme qui emprunte au modèle ses thèmes et ses mots, (ici l'innutrition chère à la Pléiade semble avoir confisqué au poète sa parole propre), Rollinat traduit un drame intérieur irrécusable et exprime avec force un désespoir qu'on ne peut mettre en doute.

L'ANGE GARDIEN

Archange féminin dont le bel œil, sans trêve,
Miroite en s'embrumant comme un soleil navré,
Apaise le chagrin de mon cœur enfiévré,
Reine de la douceur, du silence et du rêve.

Inspire-moi l'effort qui fait qu'on se relève,
Enseigne le courage à mon corps éploré,
Sauve-moi de l'ennui qui me rend effaré,
Et fourbis mon espoir rouillé comme un vieux glaive.

Rallume à ta gaîté mon pauvre rire éteint ;
Use en moi le vieil homme, et puis, soir et matin,
Laisse-moi t'adorer comme il convient aux anges !

Laisse-moi t'adorer loin du monde moqueur,
Au bercement plaintif de tes regards étranges,
Zéphyrs bleus charriant les parfums de ton cœur !

Poème mis en musique

LA PLUIE

Lorsque la pluie, ainsi qu'un immense écheveau
Brouillant à l'infini ses longs fils d'eau glacée,
Tombe d'un ciel funèbre et noir comme un caveau
Sur Paris, la Babel hurlante et convulsée,

J'abandonne mon gîte, et sur les ponts de fer,
Sur le macadam, sur les pavés, sur l'asphalte,
Laissant mouiller mon crâne où crépite un enfer,
Je marche à pas fiévreux sans jamais faire halte.

La pluie infiltre en moi des rêves obsédants
Qui me font patauger lentement dans les boues,
Et je m'en vais, rôdeur morne, la pipe aux dents,
Sans cesse éclaboussé par des milliers de roues.

Cette pluie est pour moi le spleen de l'inconnu :
Voilà pourquoi j'ai soif de ces larmes fluettes
Qui sur Paris, le monstre au sanglot continu,
Tombent obliquement lugubres, et muettes.

L'éternel coudoiement des piétons effacés
Ne me révolte plus, tant mes pensés fermentent :
À peine si j'entends les amis rencontrés
Bourdonner d'un air vrai leurs paroles qui mentent.

Mes yeux sont si perdus, si morts et si glacés,
Que dans le va-et-vient des ombres libertines,
Je ne regarde pas sous les jupons troussés
Le gai sautillement des fringantes bottines.

En ruminant tout haut des poèmes de fiel,
J'affronte sans les voir la flaque et la gouttière ;
Et mêlant ma tristesse à la douleur du ciel,
Je marche dans Paris comme en un cimetière.

Et parmi la cohue impure des démons,
Dans le grand labyrinthe, au hasard et sans guide,
Je m'enfonce, et j'aspire alors à pleins poumons
L'affreuse humidité de ce brouillard liquide.

Je suis tout à la pluie ! À son charme assassin,
Les vers dans mon cerveau ruissellent comme une onde :
Car pour moi, le sondeur du triste et du malsain,
C'est de la poésie atroce qui m'inonde.

JEAN RICHEPIN

(1849-1926)

Il est presque oublié aujourd'hui ce normalien iconoclaste, pourtant son histoire se dit encore Rue d'Ulm. Histoire ou légende ? Ce qui est certain c'est qu'il fut expulsé de l'École, (chose rare), mais on ne sait plus de quel forfait il s'était rendu coupable. Puis il y fut réintégré ; mais est-ce bien, comme on le rapporte, pour avoir ouvert, juste en face, une boutique ambulante de frites ou de marrons dont l'enseigne précisait : « Jean Richepin, ancien élève de l'École Normale Supérieure » ? Ce récit a le mérite de souligner le penchant précoce à l'ironie et au non-conformisme, qui déterminera ses choix littéraires. Il est de la lignée des bohèmes romantiques, ceux qui, suivant la formule bien connue, « buvaient l'eau des mers dans le crâne des morts ». Son goût du scandale se manifeste d'abord par son comportement provocateur, puis il va apparaître dans ses livres. Le titre de son premier recueil, *La Chanson des gueux*, indique clairement qu'il choisit d'emblée de célébrer les hommes que la société rejette. Le poème liminaire s'inspire de Villon, et s'il ne va pas jusqu'au jargon des Coquillards, il fait preuve d'une invention verbale assez cocasse. Les aspects volontairement choquants de cette œuvre valurent quelques ennuis à son auteur (une amende et même un mois de prison), mais il y a parfois chez lui, à côté d'une agressivité trop systématique, une vraie tendresse pour les déshérités.

BALLADE DU ROI DES GUEUX

Venez à moi, claquepatins,
Loqueteux, joueurs de musettes,
Clampins, loupeurs, voyous, catins,
Et marmousets, et marmousettes,
Tas de traîne-cul-les-housettes,
Race d'indépendants fougueux !
Je suis du pays dont vous êtes :
Le poète est le Roi des Gueux.

Vous que la bise des matins,
Que la pluie aux âpres sagettes,
Que les gendarmes, les mâtins,
Les coups, les fièvres, les disettes
Prennent toujours pour amusettes,
Vous dont l'habit mince et fongueux,
Paraît fait de vieilles gazettes,
Le poète est le Roi des Gueux.

Vous que le chaud soleil a teints,
Hurlubiers dont les peaux bisettes,
Ressemblent à l'or des gratins,
Gouges au front plein de frisettes,
Momignards nus sans chemisettes,
Vieux à l'œil cave, au nez rugueux,
Au menton en casse-noisettes,
Le poète est le Roi des Gueux.

ENVOI

Ô Gueux, mes sujets, mes sujettes,
Je serai votre maître queux.
Tu vivras, monde qui végètes !
Le poète est le Roi des Gueux.

LE CHEMIN CREUX

Le long d'un chemin creux que nul arbre n'égaie,
Un grand champ de blé mûr, plein de soleil, s'endort,
Et le haut du talus, couronné d'une haie,
Est comme un ruban vert qui tient des cheveux d'or.

De la haie au chemin tombe une pente herbeuse
Que la taupe soulève en sommets inégaux,
Et que les grillons noirs à la chanson verbeuse
Font pétiller de leurs monotones échos.

Passe un insecte bleu vibrant dans la lumière,
Et le lézard s'éveille et file, étincelant,
Et près des flaques d'eau qui luisent dans l'ornière
La grenouille coasse un chant rauque et râlant.

Ce chemin est très loin du bourg et des grand'routes,
Comme il est mal commode on ne s'y risque pas.
Et du matin au soir les heures passent toutes
Sans qu'on voie un visage ou qu'on entende un pas.

C'est là, le front couvert par une épine blanche,
Au murmure endormeur des champs silencieux,
Sous cette urne de paix dont la liqueur s'épanche
Comme un vin de soleil dans le saphir des cieux,

C'est là que vient le gueux, en bête poursuivie,
Parmi l'âcre senteur des herbes et des blés,
Baigner son corps poudreux, et rajeunir sa vie
Dans le repos brûlant de ses sens accablés.

Et quand il dort, le noir vagabond, le maroufle
Aux souliers éculés, aux haillons dégoûtants,
Comme une mère émue et qui retient son souffle,
La nature se tait pour qu'il dorme longtemps.

GERMAIN NOUVEAU

(1851-1920)

Il est l'ami de Verlaine et de Rimbaud qu'il suit en Angleterre. Durant ses années de bohème il écrit, mais sans jamais se soucier du sort de ses poèmes, ni surtout de faire carrière en littérature. L'un de ses recueils de vers, qui paraît d'ailleurs à son insu, est signé de son pseudonyme d'Humilis. Ce choix dit assez clairement combien il se sent étranger aux gens de lettres. Quant à l'ensemble de ses œuvres poétiques, elles ne seront publiées qu'en 1963, aussi reste-t-il longtemps ignoré du grand public.

Il exerce d'abord divers métiers, puis, après quelques années de relative stabilité, une crise de démence lui vaut un internement d'un an à Bicêtre. On songe au destin de Nerval. Comme lui, au sortir de l'asile, il voyage, mais c'est une errance apparemment sans but à travers l'Europe et jusqu'en Algérie. Son dénuement est total, il note dans *Le Calepin du mendiant* :

> *Sans amis, sans parents, sans emploi, sans fortune*
> *Je n'ai que la prison pour y passer la nuit*
> *Je n'ai rien à manger que du gâteau mal cuit*
> *Et rien pour me vêtir que déjeuners de lune...*

Cependant il n'est pas un chemineau ordinaire, car à son retour d'Angleterre, il a été brusquement touché par la grâce dans la maison où habita saint Benoît-Joseph Labre. Sa conversion a fait de lui un vagabond mystique. C'est alors qu'il écrit *La Doctrine de l'amour*, il y célèbre *L'Amour de l'amour* :

Aimez l'antique amour du règne de Saturne,
Aimez le dieu charmant, aimez le dieu caché,
Qui suspendait, ainsi qu'un papillon nocturne,
Un baiser invisible aux lèvres de Psyché !

Car c'est lui dont la terre appelle encore la flamme,
Lui dont la caravane humaine allait rêvant,
Et qui, triste d'errer, cherchant toujours une âme,
Gémissait dans la lyre et pleurait dans le vent.

Il revient ; le voici : son aurore éternelle
A frémi comme un monde au ventre de la nuit,
C'est le commencement des rumeurs de son aile ;
Il veille sur le sage, et la vierge le suit...

Épris de Dieu, épris aussi des femmes, il écrit ensuite *Les Valentines*, volume consacré à célébrer une passion tout humaine dont on ignore si elle fut réelle ou rêvée.

La misère de ses dernières années semble reproduire celle de Benoît-Joseph Labre, qui voulut se faire gueux parmi les gueux. Il meurt dans un dénuement total, mendiant anonyme sous un porche d'église. Ses écrits ne sont pas moins anticonformistes que son christianisme : la bizarrerie de certains poèmes bouffons où affleure la folie n'empêche pas que d'autres, dans leur lenteur solennelle, relèvent du lyrisme le plus grave. Par les premiers Germain Nouveau reste proche des décadents, mais les seconds annoncent Péguy. Quelque insolite, cependant, qu'apparaisse son œuvre, elle est moins étonnante que le caractère d'un poète en qui se mêlent candeur naïve et sensualité, humilité vraie et délire. Son comportement insolite d'écrivain indifférent au sort de ses écrits, son invraisemblable existence entre ascèse et divagations, font de lui une des personnalités les plus singulières de notre littérature.

AUX SAINTS

Si tous les matins de nos fêtes,
Nous chantions tous avec amour
Sur les harpes de nos prophètes,
Je ne serais pas dans la cour.

Si nous récitions nos prières
Dans le crépuscule du soir
Avec des lèvres régulières,
Avant d'allumer les lumières,
Je ne serais pas au chauffoir.

Si les yeux remplis de beaux songes,
Nous demandions, quand vient le jour,
Au ciel qui voit tous nos mensonges
L'humble foi du pêcheur d'éponges,
Je ne serais pas dans la cour.

Et quand la lampe s'est éteinte,
Si nous sentions sur nos lits noirs
La caresse d'une aile sainte,
Attendant que l'Angélus tinte,
Je ne serais pas au dortoir.

Si l'homme s'oubliait lui-même
Pour ses frères, comme un retour
Des bienfaits du Seigneur qui l'aime,
Qui le marque de son Saint-Chrême,
Je ne serais pas dans la cour.

Et si nous, les fous de Bicêtre,
Nous avions fait notre devoir,
Le devoir dicté par son prêtre,
Nous serions au parloir peut-être,
Ce ne serait pas ce parloir.

Sans le diable qui nous malmène,
Nul, avec les yeux de son corps,
N'aurait vu ma figure humaine
Dans la cour où je me promène
Et dans le dortoir où je dors.

LE CORPS ET L'ÂME

Dieu fit votre corps noble et votre âme charmante.
Le corps sort de la terre et l'âme aspire aux cieux ;
L'un est un amoureux et l'autre est une amante.

Dans la paix d'un jardin vaste et délicieux,
Dieu souffla dans un peu de boue un peu de flamme,
Et le corps s'en alla sur ses pieds gracieux.

Et ce souffle enchantait le corps, et c'était l'âme
Qui, mêlée à l'amour des bêtes et des bois,
Chez l'homme adorait Dieu que contemplait la femme.

L'âme rit dans les yeux et vole avec la voix,
Et l'âme ne meurt pas, mais le corps ressuscite,
Sortant du limon noir une seconde fois.

Une flèche est légère et les éclairs vont vite,
Mais le mystérieux élan de l'âme est tel
Que l'ange qui veut bien lutter contre elle, hésite.

Dieu fit suave et beau votre corps immortel :
Les jambes sont les deux colonnes de ce temple,
Les genoux sont la chaise et le buste est l'autel.

Et la ligne du torse à son sommet plus ample,
Comme aux flancs purs du vase antique, rêve et court
Dans l'ordre harmonieux dont la lyre est l'exemple.

Pendant qu'un hymne à Dieu dans un battement court,
Comme au cœur de la lyre, une éternelle phrase
Chante aux cordes du cœur mélodieux et sourd.

Des épaules planant comme les bords du vase,
La tête émerge et c'est une adorable fleur
Noyée en une longue et lumineuse extase.

Si l'âme est un oiseau, le corps est l'oiseleur,
Le regard brûle au fond des yeux qui sont des lampes,
Où chaque larme douce est l'huile de douleur.

. . . .

Ni les béliers frisés ni les plumes de cygne,
Ni la crinière en feu des crieurs de la faim
N'effacent ta splendeur, ô chevelure insigne

Faite avec l'azur noir de la nuit, ou l'or fin
De l'aurore, et sur qui nage un parfum farouche,
Où la femme endort l'homme en une mer sans fin.

. . . .

La grâce de votre âme éclôt dans la parole,
Et l'autre dans le geste, aimant les frais essors,
Au vêtement léger comme une âme qui vole.

Sachez aimer votre âme en aimant votre corps ;
Cherchez l'eau musicale aux bains de marbre pâle,
Et l'onde du génie au cœur des hommes forts.

Mêlez vos membres lourds de fatigue, où le hâle
De la vie imprima son baiser furieux
Au gémissement frais que la Naïade exhale ;

Afin qu'au jour prochain votre corps glorieux,
Plus léger que celui des Mercures fidèles,
Monte à travers l'azur du ciel victorieux.

Dans l'onde du génie, aux sources sûres d'elles,
Plongez votre âme à nu, comme les bons nageurs,
Pour qu'elle en sorte avec la foi donneuse d'ailes.

Dans la nuit vers une aube aux divines rougeurs,
Marchez par le sentier de la bonne habitude,
Soyez de patients et graves voyageurs.

Que cette jeune sœur charmante de l'étude
Et du travail tranquille et gai, la Chasteté,
Parfume vos discours et votre solitude.

La pâture de l'âme est toute vérité ;
Le corps content de peu, cueille une nourriture
Dans le baiser mystique où règne la beauté.

Puisque Dieu répandit l'homme dans la nature,
Sachez l'aimer en vous, et d'abord soyez doux
À vous-mêmes, et doux à toute créature.

Si vous ne vous aimez en Dieu, vous aimez-vous ?

ARTHUR RIMBAUD

(1854-1891)

On connaît en poésie d'autres enfants prodiges, aucun ne
s'inscrit d'emblée, comme Rimbaud, dans la lignée prométhéenne :
la violence du verbe exige d'ordinaire l'amertume d'une expérience
de la vie ou l'engagement militant. La révolte précoce de ce
Prométhée-adolescent est d'un autre ordre, elle n'est pas liée à des
circonstances particulières mais à sa nature, il affirme pour l'avoir
éprouvé par lui-même : « Le poète est vraiment voleur de feu. » Si
le débraillé et les outrances de langage à la manière des « petits
romantiques », ces poètes turbulents qui se plaisaient à scandaliser
« les épiciers et les notaires », et à fronder l'ordre bourgeois, ne sont
pas sans quelque rapport avec ses premiers poèmes – on conçoit
que ces tapages aient pu séduire un très jeune garçon –, il ne cède
pas longtemps au simple goût de la provocation. Lorsqu'il écrit
qu'il « s'agit de se faire l'âme monstrueuse », il se propose tout autre
chose, il veut œuvrer d'abord contre lui-même et pour lui seul. Il a
fait sien le vœu de celui qu'il nomme « le roi des poètes, un vrai
dieu », et tente donc, comme le rêvait Baudelaire de

Plonger dans l'inconnu, pour trouver du nouveau.

Pour cela il ne suffit pas d'être né poète. Confiant en ses dons
naturels (« je me suis reconnu poète », dit-il aussi), il lui reste à se
faire voyant. Or il tient pour certain que les visions peuvent être
provoquées, c'est affaire d'audace et de volonté lucide : « Le Poète se
fait voyant par un long, immense et raisonné dérèglement de tous les
sens. » Il sait le prix qu'il faut payer pour parvenir, car le poète s' « il
épuise en lui tous les poisons » devient « entre tous le grand malade,

le grand criminel, le grand maudit ». Mais il doit en assumer le risque et accepter aussi l'éventualité de l'échec. Son effort, même inabouti, marquera du moins une étape dans la conquête de la nouvelle réalité, après quoi « viendront d'autres horribles travailleurs » pour dépasser « les horizons où l'autre s'est affaissé ».

Cependant Rimbaud ne croit pas la réussite impossible, puisqu'il en connaît les moyens, alors, parfois, dans un élan d'enthousiasme, il se juge digne de la « promesse surhumaine faite à notre corps et à notre âme créée » et il exulte, comme dans *Matinée d'ivresse*, en proclamant : « Nous t'affirmons, méthode ! » D'ailleurs le poète, même s'il échoue dans sa quête, ne devient-il pas « le suprême Savant » ? « Et quand, affolé, il finirait par perdre l'intelligence de ses visions, il les a vues ! »

On a peine à croire que la conception de la poésie qui s'exprime à travers ces formules saisissantes soient le fait d'un jeune homme de 17 ans. Pourtant c'est dans la célèbre lettre à son ami Demeny, dite du Voyant, ou dans celle à Izambard son professeur, qui datent de mai 71, qu'on peut les lire. C'est là aussi qu'il annonce son désir de rompre avec une poésie qu'il juge exsangue car elle se contente d'une paraphrase des apparences en usant de procédés ressassés, là qu'il dit encore la nécessité d'abolir les liens habituels avec le monde, ce qui exige d'abord à ses yeux de « s'encrapuler ». Cette transgression est le préalable nécessaire à toute création. C'est seulement après ce dépaysement radical que le poète pourra enfin proférer une parole inouïe, inaugurale.

Or tenter de dire l'inexprimable exige d'autres mots : « Les inventions d'inconnu réclament des formes nouvelles. » Il rêve d'une langue qui sera « de l'âme pour l'âme, résumant tout, parfums, sons, couleurs, de la pensée accrochant la pensée et tirant ». Le sonnet des *Voyelles* en est une première approche, mais, comme il le montre dans *Alchimie du verbe*, d'autres voies s'offrent à lui : « Je me flattai d'inventer un verbe poétique accessible, un jour ou l'autre, à tous les sens... Ce fut d'abord une étude. J'écrivais des silences, des nuits, je notais l'inexprimable. Je fixais des vertiges. » L'usage qu'il fait des images est l'un des aspects les plus révélateurs de la mutation qu'il opère dans l'expression poétique. C'est surtout à travers elles, en effet, que surgit pour nous le monde nouveau de ses visions. Ces images juxtaposées, sans cohérence apparente, semblables à des éclairs lumineux qui dévoileraient dans l'ombre des pans discontinus d'une autre réalité, ont le pouvoir de communiquer au lecteur les vertiges et les bondissements qu'elles traduisent, les hallucinations que procurèrent au poète « dérèglements » et poisons.

Avant d'être, comme il l'écrit, « rendu au sol, et la réalité rugueuse à étreindre », durant les trois années qui précèdent son départ pour le Harar et le long silence de l'exil volontaire, il compose des poèmes rimés ou en prose dont le lyrisme échevelé, les couleurs brutales, l'étrangeté vont imposer aux lecteurs des *Illuminations*, et, près de dix ans plus tard, à ceux d'*Une saison en enfer*, le sentiment de l'originalité sans précédent de cet univers poétique. Dans le premier de ces recueils – mais on n'est pas certain de son antériorité dans la vie de Rimbaud, même si elle semble probable – les enluminures vives comme des images populaires mêlent aux figures naïves de l'enfance, des spectacles, des paysages et des confidences où s'expriment le plus souvent l'orgueil et la jubilation ; « j'ai seul la clef de cette parade sauvage », avec le sentiment d'un pouvoir souverain sur les choses et les êtres, mais parfois aussi une angoisse : « J'attends de devenir un très méchant fou. »

Une saison en enfer, découverte longtemps après que Rimbaud l'eut lui-même publiée, est essentielle à la connaissance de ses années de création poétique et de la manière dont il les a vécues. Le prélude retrace les étapes de sa vie, depuis le temps du « festin » (sans aucun doute une figure de l'enfance heureuse), jusqu'à la damnation inévitable, malgré le désir de « rechercher la clef du festin ancien ». À travers les dix poèmes en prose de longueur inégale qui composent le recueil on entend les cris, les blasphèmes, la moquerie grinçante, et, sous diverses formes, cette plainte récurrente « Alors, – oh ! – chère pauvre âme, l'éternité serait-elle pas perdue pour nous ! »

De ce dialogue avec soi-même, récit autobiographique et bilan, avec ses formules étrangement prophétiques quand on connaît son histoire ultérieure : « Je reviendrai... la peau sombre, l'œil furieux... Les femmes soignent ces féroces infirmes retour des pays chauds. » On retient, au-delà de la violence des mots, et du vertige de la folie magnifiquement traduit, l'idée qu'il impose avec force : « Le combat spirituel est aussi brutal que la bataille d'hommes. »

SENSATION

Par les soirs bleus d'été, j'irai dans les sentiers,
Picoté par les blés, fouler l'herbe menue :
Rêveur, j'en sentirai la fraîcheur à mes pieds.
Je laisserai le vent baigner ma tête nue.

Je ne parlerai pas, je ne penserai rien :
Mais l'amour infini me montera dans l'âme,
Et j'irai loin, bien loin, comme un bohémien,
Par la Nature, – heureux comme avec une femme.

Mars 1870

MA BOHÈME

(Fantaisie)

Je m'en allais, les poings dans mes poches crevées ;
Mon paletot aussi devenait idéal ;
J'allais sous le ciel, Muse ! et j'étais ton féal ;
Oh ! là ! là ! que d'amours splendides j'ai rêvées !

Mon unique culotte avait un large trou.
– Petit-Poucet rêveur, j'égrenais dans ma course
Des rimes. Mon auberge était à la Grande-Ourse.
– Mes étoiles au ciel avaient un doux frou-frou

Et je les écoutais, assis au bord des routes,
Ces bons soirs de septembre où je sentais des gouttes
De rosée à mon front, comme un vin de vigueur ;

Où, rimant au milieu des ombres fantastiques,
Comme des lyres, je tirais les élastiques
De mes souliers blessés, un pied près de mon cœur !

TÊTE DE FAUNE

Dans la feuillée, écrin vert taché d'or,
Dans la feuillée incertaine et fleurie
De fleurs splendides où le baiser dort,
Vif et crevant l'exquise broderie,

Un faune effaré montre ses deux yeux
Et mord les fleurs rouges de ses dents blanches
Brunie et sanglante ainsi qu'un vin vieux
Sa lèvre éclate en rires sous les branches.

Et quand il a fui — tel qu'un écureuil —
Son rire tremble encore à chaque feuille
Et l'on voit épeuré par un bouvreuil
Le Baiser d'or du Bois, qui se recueille.

LES POÈTES DE SEPT ANS

Et la Mère, fermant le livre du devoir,
S'en allait satisfaite et très fière, sans voir,
Dans les yeux bleus et sous le front plein d'éminences,
L'âme de son enfant livrée aux répugnances.

Tout le jour il suait d'obéissance ; très
Intelligent ; pourtant des tics noirs, quelques traits
Semblaient prouver en lui d'âcres hypocrisies.
Dans l'ombre des couloirs aux tentures moisies,
En passant il tirait la langue, les deux poings
À l'aine, et dans ses yeux fermés voyait des points.
Une porte s'ouvrait sur le soir : à la lampe
On le voyait, là-haut, qui râlait sur la rampe,
Sous un golfe de jour pendant du toit. L'été
Surtout, vaincu, stupide, il était entêté
À se renfermer dans la fraîcheur des latrines :
Il pensait là, tranquille et livrant ses narines.

Quand, lavé des odeurs du jour, le jardinet
Derrière la maison, en hiver, s'illunait,
Gisant au pied d'un mur, enterré dans la marne
Et pour des visions écrasant son œil darne,
Il écoutait grouiller les galeux espaliers.
Pitié ! Ces enfants seuls étaient ses familiers
Qui, chétifs, fronts nus, œil déteignant sur la joue,
Cachant de maigres doigts jaunes et noirs de boue
Sous des habits puant la foire et tout vieillots,
Conversaient avec la douceur des idiots !
Et si, l'ayant surpris à des pitiés immondes,
Sa mère s'effrayait ; les tendresses, profondes,
De l'enfant se jetaient sur cet étonnement.
C'était bon. Elle avait le bleu regard, – qui ment !

À sept ans, il faisait des romans, sur la vie
Du grand désert, où luit la Liberté ravie,

Forêts, soleils, rives, savanes ! – Il s'aidait
De journaux illustrés où, rouge, il regardait
Des Espagnoles rire et des Italiennes.
Quand venait, l'œil brun, folle, en robes d'indiennes,
– Huit ans, – la fille des ouvriers d'à côté,
La petite brutale, et qu'elle avait sauté,
Dans un coin, sur son dos, en secouant ses tresses,
Et qu'il était sous elle, il lui mordait les fesses,
Car elle ne portait jamais de pantalons ;
– Et, par elle meurtri des poings et des talons,
Remportait les saveurs de sa peau dans sa chambre.

Il craignait les blafards dimanches de décembre,
Où, pommadé, sur un guéridon d'acajou,
Il lisait une Bible à la tranche vert-chou ;
Des rêves l'oppressaient chaque nuit dans l'alcôve.
Il n'aimait pas Dieu ; mais les hommes, qu'au soir fauve,
Noirs, en blouse, il voyait rentrer dans le faubourg
Où les crieurs, en trois roulements de tambour,
Font autour des édits rire et gronder les foules.
– Il rêvait la prairie amoureuse, où des houles
Lumineuses, parfums sains, pubescences d'or
Font leur remuement calme et prennent leur essor !

Et comme il savourait surtout les sombres choses,
Quand, dans la chambre nue aux persiennes closes,
Haute et bleue, âcrement prise d'humidité,
Il lisait son roman sans cesse médité,
Plein de lourds ciels ocreux et de forêts noyées,
De fleurs de chair aux bois sidérals déployées,
Vertige, écroulements, déroutes et pitié !
– Tandis que se faisait la rumeur du quartier,
En bas, – seul, et couché sur des pièces de toile
Écrue, et pressentant violemment la voile !

26 mai 1871

LE CŒUR DU PITRE

Mon triste cœur bave à la poupe,
Mon cœur est plein de caporal :
Ils y lancent des jets de soupe,
Mon triste cœur bave à la poupe :
Sous les quolibets de la troupe
Qui pousse un rire général,
Mon triste cœur bave à la poupe,
Mon cœur est plein de caporal !

Ithyphalliques et pioupiesques
Leurs insultes l'ont dépravé !
À la vesprée ils font des fresques
Ithyphalliques et pioupiesques.
Ô flots abracadabrantesques,
Prenez mon cœur, qu'il soit sauvé :
Ithyphalliques et pioupiesques
Leurs insultes l'ont dépravé !

Quand ils auront tari leurs chiques,
Comment agir, ô cœur volé ?
Ce seront des refrains bachiques
Quand ils auront tari leurs chiques
J'aurai des sursauts stomachiques
Si mon cœur triste est ravalé :
Quand ils auront tari leurs chiques,
Comment agir, ô cœur volé ?

VOYELLES

A noir, E blanc, I rouge, U vert, O bleu : voyelles,
Je dirai quelque jour vos naissances latentes :
A, noir corset velu des mouches éclatantes
Qui bombinent autour des puanteurs cruelles,

Golfes d'ombres ; E, candeurs des vapeurs et des tentes,
Lances des glaciers fiers, rois blancs, frissons d'ombelles ;
I, pourpres, sang craché, rire des lèvres belles
Dans la colère ou les ivresses pénitentes ;

U, cycles, vibrements divins des mers virides,
Paix des pâtis semés d'animaux, paix des rides
Que l'alchimie imprime aux grands fronts studieux ;

O, suprême Clairon plein des strideurs étranges,
Silences traversés des Mondes et des Anges :
– O l'Oméga, rayon violet de Ses Yeux !

LE BATEAU IVRE

Comme je descendais des Fleuves impassibles,
Je ne me sentis plus guidé par les haleurs :
Des Peaux-Rouges criards les avaient pris pour cibles
Les ayant cloués nus aux poteaux de couleurs.

J'étais insoucieux de tous les équipages,
Porteur de blés flamands ou de cotons anglais.
Quand avec mes haleurs ont fini ces tapages
Les Fleuves m'ont laissé descendre où je voulais.

Dans les clapotements furieux des marées,
Moi, l'autre hiver, plus sourd que les cerveaux d'enfants,
Je courus ! Et les Péninsules démarrées
N'ont pas subi tohu-bohus plus triomphants.

La tempête a béni mes éveils maritimes.
Plus léger qu'un bouchon j'ai dansé sur les flots
Qu'on appelle rouleurs éternels de victimes,
Dix nuits, sans regretter l'œil niais des falots !

Plus douce qu'aux enfants la chair des pommes sures,
L'eau verte pénétra ma coque de sapin
Et des taches de vins bleus et des vomissures
Me lava, dispersant gouvernail et grappin.

Et dès lors, je me suis baigné dans le Poème
De la Mer, infusé d'astres, et lactescent,
Dévorant les azurs verts ; où, flottaison blême
Et ravie, un noyé pensif parfois descend ;

Où, teignant tout à coup les bleuités, délires
Et rythmes lents sous les rutilements du jour,
Plus fortes que l'alcool, plus vastes que nos lyres,
Fermentent les rousseurs amères de l'amour !

Je sais les cieux crevant en éclairs, et les trombes
Et les ressacs et les courants : je sais le soir,
L'Aube exaltée ainsi qu'un peuple de colombes,
Et j'ai vu quelquefois ce que l'homme a cru voir !

J'ai vu le soleil bas, taché d'horreurs mystiques,
Illuminant de longs figements violets,
Pareils à des acteurs de drames très-antiques
Les flots roulant au loin leurs frissons de volets !

J'ai rêvé la nuit verte aux neiges éblouies,
Baiser montant aux yeux des mers avec lenteurs,
La circulation des sèves inouïes,
Et l'éveil jaune et bleu des phosphores chanteurs !

J'ai suivi, des mois pleins, pareille aux vacheries
Hystériques, la houle à l'assaut des récifs,
Sans songer que les pieds lumineux des Maries
Pussent forcer le mufle aux Océans poussifs !

J'ai heurté, savez-vous, d'incroyables Florides
Mêlant aux fleurs des yeux de panthères à peaux
D'hommes ! Des arcs-en-ciel tendus comme des brides
Sous l'horizon des mers, à de glauques troupeaux !

J'ai vu fermenter les marais énormes, nasses
Où pourrit dans les joncs tout un Léviathan !
Des écroulements d'eaux au milieu des bonaces,
Et les lointains vers les gouffres cataractant !

Glaciers, soleils d'argent, flots nacreux, cieux de braises !
Échouages hideux au fond des golfes bruns
Où les serpents géants dévorés des punaises
Choient, des arbres tordus, avec de noirs parfums !

J'aurais voulu montrer aux enfants ces dorades
Du flot bleu, ces poissons d'or, ces poissons chantants.
– Des écumes de fleurs ont bercé mes dérades
Et d'ineffables vents m'ont ailé par instants.

Parfois, martyr lassé des pôles et des zones,
La mer dont le sanglot faisait mon roulis doux
Montait vers moi ses fleurs d'ombre aux ventouses jaunes
Et je restais, ainsi qu'une femme à genoux...

Presque île, ballottant sur mes bords les querelles
Et les fientes d'oiseaux clabaudeurs aux yeux blonds.
Et je voguais, lorsqu'à travers mes liens frêles
Des noyés descendaient dormir, à reculons !

Or moi, bateau perdu sous les cheveux des anses,
Jeté par l'ouragan dans l'éther sans oiseau,
Moi dont les Monitors et les voiliers des Hanses
N'auraient pas repêché la carcasse ivre d'eau ;

Libre, fumant, monté de brumes violettes,
Moi qui trouais le ciel rougeoyant comme un mur
Qui porte, confiture exquise aux bons poètes,
Des lichens de soleil et des morves d'azur,

Qui courais, taché de lunules électriques,
Planche folle, escorté des hippocampes noirs,
Quand les juillets faisaient crouler à coups de triques
Les cieux ultramarins aux ardents entonnoirs ;

Moi qui tremblais, sentant geindre à cinquante lieues
Le rut des Béhémots et les Maelströms épais,
Fileur éternel des immobilités bleues,
Je regrette l'Europe aux anciens parapets !

J'ai vu des archipels sidéraux ! et des îles
Dont les cieux délirants sont ouverts au vogueur :
– Est-ce en ces nuits sans fond que tu dors et t'exiles,
Million d'oiseaux d'or, ô future Vigueur ? –

Mais, vrai, j'ai trop pleuré ! Les Aubes sont navrantes.
Toute lune est atroce et tout soleil amer :
L'âcre amour m'a gonflé de torpeurs enivrantes.
Ô que ma quille éclate ! Ô que j'aille à la mer !

Si je désire une eau d'Europe, c'est la flache
Noire et froide où vers le crépuscule embaumé
Un enfant accroupi plein de tristesses, lâche
Un bateau frêle comme un papillon de mai.

Je ne puis plus, baigné de vos langueurs, ô lames,
Enlever leur sillage aux porteurs de cotons,
Ni traverser l'orgueil des drapeaux et des flammes,
Ni nager sous les yeux horribles des pontons.

CHANSON DE LA PLUS HAUTE TOUR

Oisive jeunesse
À tout asservie,
Par délicatesse
J'ai perdu ma vie.
Ah ! Que le temps vienne
Où les cœurs s'éprennent.

Je me suis dit : laisse,
Et qu'on ne te voie :
Et sans la promesse
De plus hautes joies.
Que rien ne t'arrête
Auguste retraite.

J'ai tant fait patience
Qu'à jamais j'oublie ;
Craintes et souffrances
Aux cieux sont parties.
Et la soif malsaine
Obscurcit mes veines.

Ainsi la Prairie
À l'oubli livrée,
Grandie, et fleurie
D'encens et d'ivraies
Au bourdon farouche
De cent sales mouches.

Ah ! Mille veuvages
De la si pauvre âme
Qui n'a que l'image
De la Notre-Dame !
Est-ce que l'on prie
La Vierge Marie ?

Oisive jeunesse
À tout asservie
Par délicatesse
J'ai perdu ma vie.
Ah ! Que le temps vienne
Où les cœurs s'éprennent !

Mai 1872

L'ÉTERNITÉ

Elle est retrouvée.
Quoi ? – L'Éternité.
C'est la mer allée
Avec le soleil.

Âmes sentinelle,
Murmurons l'aveu
De la nuit si nulle
Et du jour en feu.

Des humains suffrages,
Des communs élans
Là tu te dégages
Et voles selon.

Puisque de vous seules,
Braises de satin,
Le Devoir s'exhale
Sans qu'on dise : enfin.

Là pas d'espérance,
Nul orietur.
Science avec patience,
Le supplice est sûr.

Elle est retrouvée.
Quoi ? – l'Éternité.
C'est la mer allée.
Avec le soleil.

Mai 1872

DÉLIRES

II
ALCHIMIE DU VERBE

À moi. L'histoire d'une de mes folies.

Depuis longtemps je me vantais de posséder tous les paysages possibles, et trouvais dérisoires les célébrités de la peinture et de la poésie moderne.

J'aimais les peintures idiotes, dessus de portes, décors, toiles de saltimbanques, enseignes, enluminures populaires ; la littérature démodée, latin d'église, livres érotiques sans orthographe, romans de nos aïeules ; contes de fées, petits livres de l'enfance, opéras vieux, refrains niais, rythmes naïfs.

Je rêvais croisades, voyages de découvertes dont on n'a pas de relations, républiques sans histoires, guerres de religion étouffées, révolutions de mœurs, déplacements de races et de continents : je croyais à tous les enchantements.

J'inventai la couleur des voyelles ! – *A* noir, *E* blanc, *I* rouge, *O* bleu, *U* vert. – Je réglai la forme et le mouvement de chaque consonne, et, avec des rythmes instinctifs, je me flattai d'inventer un verbe poétique accessible, un jour ou l'autre, à tous les sens. Je réservais la traduction.

Ce fut d'abord une étude. J'écrivais des silences, des nuits, je notais l'inexprimable. Je fixais des vertiges.

————

Loin des oiseaux, des troupeaux, des villageoises,
Que buvais-je, à genoux dans cette bruyère
Entourée de tendres bois de noisetiers,
Dans un brouillard d'après-midi tiède et vert ?

Que pouvais-je boire dans cette jeune Oise,
– Ormeaux sans voix, gazon sans fleurs, ciel couvert !
Boire à ces gourdes jaunes, loin de ma case
Chérie ? Quelque liqueur d'or qui fait suer.

Je faisais une louche enseigne d'auberge.
– Un orage vint chasser le ciel. Au soir
L'eau des bois se perdait sur les sables vierges,
Le vent de Dieu jetait des glaçons aux mares ;

Pleurant, je voyais de l'or – et ne pus boire. –

———

. . . .

Je devins un opéra fabuleux : je vis que tous les êtres ont une fatalité de bonheur ; l'action n'est pas la vie, mais une façon de gâcher quelque force, un énervement. La morale est la faiblesse de la cervelle.

À chaque être, plusieurs *autres* vies me semblaient dues. Ce monsieur ne sait ce qu'il fait : il est un ange. Cette famille est une nichée de chiens. Devant plusieurs hommes, je causai tout haut avec un moment d'une de leurs autres vies – Ainsi, j'ai aimé un porc.

Aucun des sophismes de la folie, – la folie qu'on enferme, – n'a été oublié par moi : je pourrais les redire tous, je tiens le système.

Ma santé fut menacée. La terreur venait. Je tombais dans des sommeils de plusieurs jours, et, levé, je continuais les rêves les plus tristes. J'étais mûr pour le trépas, et par une route de dangers ma faiblesse me menait aux confins du monde et de la Cimmérie, patrie de l'ombre et des tourbillons.

Je dus voyager, distraire les enchantements assemblés sur mon cerveau. Sur la mer, que j'aimais comme si elle eût dû me laver d'une souillure, je voyais se lever la croix consolatrice. J'avais été damné par l'arc-en-ciel. Le Bonheur était ma fatalité, mon remords, mon ver : ma vie serait toujours trop immense pour être dévouée à la force et à la beauté.

Le Bonheur ! Sa dent, douce à la mort, m'avertissait au chant du coq, –*ad matutinum*, au *Christus venit*, – dans les plus sombres villes :

Ô saisons, ô châteaux !
Quelle âme est sans défauts ?

J'ai fait la magique étude
Du bonheur, qu'aucun n'élude.

Salut à lui, chaque fois
Que chante le coq gaulois.

Ah ! je n'aurai plus d'envie :
Il s'est chargé de ma vie.

Ce charme a pris âme et corps
Et dispersé les efforts.

Ô saisons, ô châteaux !

L'heure de sa fuite, hélas !
Sera l'heure du trépas.

Ô saisons, ô châteaux !

————

Cela s'est passé. Je sais aujourd'hui saluer la beauté.

Une saison en enfer

MATIN

N'eus-je pas *une fois* une jeunesse aimable, héroïque, fabuleuse, à écrire sur des feuilles d'or, – trop de chance ! Par quel crime, par quelle erreur, ai-je mérité ma faiblesse actuelle ? Vous qui prétendez que des bêtes poussent des sanglots de chagrin, que des malades désespèrent, que des morts rêvent mal, tâchez de raconter ma chute et mon sommeil. Moi, je ne puis pas plus m'expliquer que le mendiant avec ses continuels *Pater* et *Ave Maria*. *Je ne sais plus parler !*

Pourtant, aujourd'hui, je crois avoir fini la relation de mon enfer. C'était bien l'enfer ; l'ancien, celui dont le fils de l'homme ouvrit les portes.

Du même désert, à la même nuit, toujours mes yeux las se réveillent à l'étoile d'argent, toujours, sans que s'émeuvent les Rois de la vie, les trois mages, le cœur, l'âme, l'esprit. Quand irons-nous, par delà les grèves et les monts, saluer la naissance du travail nouveau, la sagesse nouvelle, la fuite des tyrans et des démons, la fin de la superstition, adorer – les premiers ! – Noël sur la terre !

Le chant des cieux, la marche des peuples ! Esclaves, ne maudissons pas la vie.

Une saison en enfer

ADIEU

. . . .

  – Quelquefois je vois au ciel des plages sans fin couvertes de blanches nations en joie. Un grand vaisseau d'or, au-dessus de moi, agite ses pavillons multicolores sous les brises du matin. J'ai créé toutes les fêtes, tous les triomphes, tous les drames. J'ai essayé d'inventer de nouvelles fleurs, de nouveaux astres, de nouvelles chairs, de nouvelles langues. J'ai cru acquérir des pouvoirs surnaturels. Eh bien ! je dois enterrer mon imagination et mes souvenirs ! Une belle gloire d'artiste et de conteur emportée !

  Moi ! moi qui me suis dit mage ou ange, dispensé de toute morale, je suis rendu au sol, avec un devoir à chercher, et la réalité rugueuse à étreindre ! Paysan !

  Suis-je trompé ? la charité serait-elle sœur de la mort, pour moi ?

  Enfin, je demanderai pardon pour m'être nourri de mensonge. Et allons.

  Mais pas une main amie ! et où puiser le secours ?

––––––––––

  Oui, l'heure nouvelle est au moins très sévère.

  Car je puis dire que la victoire m'est acquise : les grincements de dents, les sifflements de feu, les soupirs empestés se modèrent. Tous les souvenirs immondes s'effacent. Mes derniers regrets détalent, – des jalousies pour les mendiants, les brigands, les amis de la mort, les arriérés de toutes sortes. – Damnés, si je me vengeais !

  Il faut être absolument moderne.

  Point de cantiques : tenir le pas gagné. Dure nuit ! le sang séché fume sur ma face, et je n'ai rien derrière moi, que cet horrible arbrisseau !... Le combat spirituel est aussi brutal que la bataille d'hommes ; mais la vision de la justice est le plaisir de Dieu seul.

  Cependant, c'est la veille. Recevons tous les influx de vigueur et de tendresse réelle. Et à l'aurore, armés d'une ardente patience, nous entrerons aux splendides villes.

  Que parlais-je de main amie ! Un bel avantage, c'est que je puis rire des vieilles amours mensongères, et frapper de honte ces couples menteurs, – j'ai vu l'enfer des femmes là-bas ; – et il me sera loisible de *posséder la vérité dans une âme et un corps.*

Avril-août, 1873

Une saison en enfer

ENFANCE

. . . .

III

Au bois il y a un oiseau, son chant vous arrête et vous fait rougir.

Il y a une horloge qui ne sonne pas.

Il y a une fondrière avec un nid de bêtes blanches.

Il y a une cathédrale qui descend et un lac qui monte.

Il y a une petite voiture abandonnée dans le taillis, ou qui descend le sentier en courant, enrubannée.

Il y a une troupe de petits comédiens en costumes, aperçus sur la route à travers la lisière du bois.

Il y a enfin, quand l'on a faim et soif, quelqu'un qui vous chasse.

IV

Je suis le saint, en prière sur la terrasse, – comme les bêtes pacifiques paissent jusqu'à la mer de Palestine.

Je suis le savant au fauteuil sombre. Les branches et la pluie se jettent à la croisée de la bibliothèque.

Je suis le piéton de la grand'route par les bois nains ; la rumeur des écluses couvre mes pas. Je vois longtemps la mélancolique lessive d'or du couchant.

Je serais bien l'enfant abandonné sur la jetée partie à la haute mer, le petit valet suivant l'allée dont le front touche le ciel.

Les sentiers sont âpres. Les monticules se couvrent de genêts. L'air est immobile. Que les oiseaux et les sources sont loin ! Ce ne peut être que la fin du monde, en avançant.

. . . .

Illuminations

MATINÉE D'IVRESSE

Ô *mon* Bien ! Ô *mon* Beau ! Fanfare atroce où je ne trébuche point ! Chevalet féerique ! Hourra pour l'œuvre inouïe et pour le corps merveilleux, pour la première fois ! Cela commença sous les rires des enfants, cela finira par eux. Ce poison va rester dans toutes nos veines même quand, la fanfare tournant, nous serons rendus à l'ancienne inharmonie. Ô maintenant nous si digne de ces tortures ! rassemblons fervemment cette promesse surhumaine faite à notre corps et à notre âme créés : cette promesse, cette démence ! L'élégance, la science, la violence ! On nous a promis d'enterrer dans l'ombre l'arbre du bien et du mal, de déporter les honnêtetés tyranniques, afin que nous amenions notre très pur amour. Cela commença par quelques dégoûts et cela finit, – ne pouvant nous saisir sur-le-champ de cette éternité, – cela finit par une débandade de parfums.

Rire des enfants, discrétion des esclaves, austérité des vierges, horreur des figures et des objets d'ici, sacrés soyez-vous par le souvenir de cette veille. Cela commençait par toute la rustrerie, voici que cela finit par des anges de flamme et de glace.

Petite veille d'ivresse, sainte ! quand ce ne serait que pour le masque dont tu nous as gratifié. Nous t'affirmons, méthode ! Nous n'oublions pas que tu as glorifié hier chacun de nos âges. Nous avons foi au poison. Nous savons donner notre vie tout entière tous les jours.

Voici le temps des *Assassins*.

Illuminations

AUBE

J'ai embrassé l'aube d'été.

Rien ne bougeait encore au front des palais. L'eau était morte. Les camps d'ombres ne quittaient pas la route du bois. J'ai marché, réveillant les haleines vives et tièdes, et les pierreries regardèrent, et les ailes se levèrent sans bruit.

La première entreprise fut, dans le sentier déjà empli de frais et blêmes éclats, une fleur qui me dit son nom.

Je ris au wasserfall blond qui s'échevela à travers les sapins : à la cime argentée je reconnus la déesse.

Alors je levai un à un les voiles. Dans l'allée, en agitant les bras. Par la plaine, où je l'ai dénoncée au coq. À la grand'ville elle fuyait parmi les clochers et les dômes, et courant comme un mendiant sur les quais de marbre, je la chassais.

En haut de la route, près d'un bois de lauriers, je l'ai entourée avec ses voiles amassés ; et j'ai senti un peu son immense corps. L'aube et l'enfant tombèrent au bas du bois.

Au réveil il était midi.

Illuminations

NOCTURNE VULGAIRE

Un souffle ouvre des brèches opéradiques dans les cloisons, – brouille le pivotement des toits rongés, – disperse les limites des foyers, – éclipse les croisées. – Le long de la vigne, m'étant appuyé du pied à une gargouille, – je suis descendu dans ce carrosse dont l'époque est assez indiquée par les glaces convexes, les panneaux bombés et les sophas contournés. Corbillard de mon sommeil, isolé, maison de berger de ma niaiserie, le véhicule vire sur le gazon de la grande route effacée : et dans un défaut en haut de la glace de droite tournoient les blêmes figures lunaires, feuilles, seins ; – Un vert et un bleu très foncés envahissent l'image. Dételage aux environs d'une tache de gravier.

– Ici va-t-on siffler pour l'orage, et les Sodomes – et les Solymes, – et les bêtes féroces et les armées,

– (Postillons et bêtes de songe reprendront-ils sous les plus suffocantes futaies, pour m'enfoncer jusqu'aux yeux dans la source de soie)

– Et nous envoyer, fouettés à travers les eaux clapotantes et les boissons répandues, rouler sur l'aboi des dogues...

– Un souffle disperse les limites du foyer.

Illuminations

MARINE

Les chars d'argent et de cuivre –
Les proues d'acier et d'argent –
Battent l'écume, –
Soulèvent les souches des ronces.
Les courants de la lande,
Et les ornières immenses du reflux,
Filent circulairement vers l'est,
Vers les piliers de la forêt, –
Vers les fûts de la jetée,
Dont l'angle est heurté par des tourbillons de lumière.

Illuminations

FIN DE SIÈCLE : LE SYMBOLISME

« Enfin je lui demandais : "Et la poésie ?"... – "Mon cher me dit-il, tu arrives de province ; tu n'es pas à la hauteur. Ne te désole pas, nous te formerons." – "Ainsi le Parnasse..." – "Oh la vieille histoire !" – "La poésie rustique..." – "Bonne pour les Félibres !" – "Et le naturalisme ?" – "Hum, hum ! Pas de rêve, pas d'au-delà..." J'étais devenu inquiet ; sans réfléchir, je m'écriai : "Mais enfin que reste-t-il donc ?" Il me regarda fixement et d'une voix grave qui tremblait un peu, il prononça :"Il reste le Symbole." »

Ce dialogue des retrouvailles entre Adoré Floupette, poète parisien bien que né à Lons-le-Saulnier, et son ami pharmacien, Marius Tapora, fraîchement débarqué de leur patrie commune, est retranscrit par ce dernier dans sa préface au recueil de vers d'Adoré Floupette : *Les Déliquescences*.

Cette joyeuse parodie nous éclaire sur la jeune école poétique. Les noms cocasses dissimulent des personnalités repérables : le Grec Catapatidès est sans doute Moréas et l'illustre Bleucoton pourrait bien être Verlaine. Nous y découvrons les lieux de rencontre favoris des poètes (ainsi le « Panier fleuri », vraisemblablement La Closerie des Lilas) et les thèmes de leurs discussions ne sont pas choisis au hasard : on y vante la décadence, le macabre, le mystique et le satanique, et l'on affirme qu'« À la délicieuse corruption, au détraquement exquis de l'âme contemporaine, une suave névrose de langue devrait correspondre ». Les vers qui composent le recueil sont des pastiches assez drôles et lorsque, à la fin d'un repas, Adoré veut bien réciter « La Mort de la Pénultième », ce qui ne manque pas de plonger ses hôtes dans la stupeur, l'allusion narquoise à Mallarmé est transparente.

Tout pastiche suppose une certaine célébrité de son modèle ; en effet, lorsque paraissent les *Déliquescences*, en 1883, dans *Lutèce*, il y a déjà deux ans que dans la même revue, Verlaine a présenté Corbière, Rimbaud et Mallarmé, et qu'on a pu lire *Les Névroses* de Maurice Rollinat. À cette époque se développe un nouveau mal du siècle. Cette fois ce ne sont plus les ferveurs retombées de l'Empire, ou l'horreur du bourgeois louis-philippard, qui vont provoquer cette crise, mais le rejet de l'idée de progrès, du scientisme, et du naturalisme dans l'art qui en est le corollaire ; l'espoir qu'avaient entretenu ces mots s'est effondré. Toute une civilisation matérialiste a écrasé l'individu, le privant de cette intériorité qui faisait sa force, étouffant sa sensibilité. C'est au nom de la part profonde et mystérieuse de l'être, de la nécessité de la laisser venir au jour, que s'exprime le nouveau courant poétique.

Ce qui distingue cette génération de poètes des précédentes, c'est le rejet de la nature. Pour ceux qui durent à Verlaine d'être appelés « les Décadents » (« Je suis l'empire à la fin de la décadence ») il n'est d'autre refuge pour l'homme que le culte du Beau, celui qu'il est seul capable de créer ou d'élire. L'artifice est toujours préférable au naturel ; Des Esseintes, le héros de Huysmans, en donne maint exemple : c'est ainsi qu'il rassemble dans sa serre des plantes exotiques et vénéneuses aux formes étranges, à l'exclusion de toute fleur familière. Le culte du rare, de l'excentrique, le rejet du commun et du vulgaire, le raffinement aristocratique vont engendrer « les solitaires et bizarres névroses » que décrit alors Paul Bourget, et dont le héros de *À Rebours* donne un parfait exemple. Le maître et le modèle de ces poètes est Baudelaire ; en outre la lecture du philosophe allemand Schopenhauer apporte à leur mal de vivre et à leur spleen un fondement métaphysique. Aussi les poètes romantiques sont dédaignés, à l'exception peut-être de Hugo que Floupette nomme cependant avec quelque condescendance « un burgrave ». On admire en Leconte de Lisle son pessimisme désespéré, mais on déclare la guerre au Parnasse : il ne peut plus être question de réprimer ses sentiments, ses désirs ou ses rêves, il faut au contraire faire place, comme le dit Guy Michaud, « aux émotions indéfinissables, aux sensations exacerbées, aux rêves que commandent les désirs refoulés ».

Les Décadents, comme les Jeunes Romantiques avant eux, sont issus de la bohème littéraire. Dès les années 70, revues éphémères et cercles littéraires se multiplient ; Verlaine, Rimbaud, Cros, ont fréquenté celui des Zutistes ou des Hydropathes et le cabaret du Chat Noir. Parmi les poètes que l'on rattache à la « décadence » Jules Laforgne est sans doute le plus doué. Il a lu les *Amours jaunes* de Corbière et pratique comme ce dernier l'ironie sur soi. Il sait exprimer, sur un ton badin et de manière fantaisiste, un désespoir réel lié à l'impossibilité d'accepter l'absurdité de sa présence au monde.

Les symbolistes sont les héritiers des décadents (et quelques-uns d'entre eux furent de l'une et l'autre école). Ils s'en distinguent cependant et d'abord de manière tout extérieure, par une imagerie différente. L'univers symboliste est imprégné de figures et de décors wagnériens. Le soleil y fait reluire casques et armures des héros médiévaux et de languissantes princesses y sont captives, le goût des légendes et des coffres gothiques semble faire renaître la période « troubadour » du début du siècle, mais ici ce n'est plus la passion de l'histoire et d'une période antérieure au règne de la raison classique qui triomphe ; c'est, au-delà d'un décor jugé propice à éveiller la rêverie, la mise en œuvre de symboles capables de traduire un inconscient collectif. La poésie décadente percevait et tentait d'exprimer le mystère d'une âme, la quête des symbolistes vise à atteindre, à l'aide de symboles universels, une Vérité cachée derrière les apparences, cet Absolu où tendait Mallarmé, mais qui, pour eux du moins, ressemble assez aux Idées platoniciennes. René Ghil, dans le *Traité du Verbe*, le dit en ces termes :

« L'Idée, qui seule importe, en la Vie est éparse.

« Aux ordinaires et mille visions (pour elles-mêmes à négliger) où l'Immortelle se dissémine, le logique et méditant poète les lignes saintes ravisse, desquelles il composera la vision seule digne d'intérêt : le réel et suggestif SYMBOLE d'où, palpitante pour le rêve, en son intégrité nue se lèvera l'idée prime et dernière, ou Vérité. »

Les moyens mis en œuvre par les poètes de cette école tendent à rendre compte de l'unité de l'univers telle que la révèle la théorie des correspondances. Le recours aux théosophes, à l'occultisme, aux traditions de l'hindouisme, les confirme dans leur certitude qu'il existe une analogie entre réalité spirituelle et réalité matérielle, et que l'inspiré peut atteindre à cette unité primordiale dont Baudelaire avait donné la clef. Le rôle du symbolisme est, selon eux, de proposer de vastes synthèses, et si l'on peut douter que le déploiement d'un décor féerique, le recours aux chevaliers et aux princesses prisonnières, la présence obsédante des licornes et des cygnes puisse en quelque manière y contribuer, même s'ils sont la traduction imagée de nos inconscients, il faut lire ce qu'écrivait Charles Morice dans *La Littérature de tout à l'heure* :

« Dans cette acception du Beau n'est œuvre d'art que celle qui précisément commence où elle semblerait finir, celle dont le symbolisme est comme une porte vibrante dont les gonds harmonieux font tressaillir l'âme dans toute son humanité béante au Mystère... celle qui révèle... Car la forme, dans l'œuvre ainsi parfaite et idéale, n'est que l'appât offert à la séduction sensuelle pour que soient apaisés, endormis dans une ivresse délicieuse, les sens enchantés de *reconnaître les lignes et les sons primitifs*... Ainsi entendu l'Art n'est pas que le révélateur de l'Infini : il est au Poète un moyen même d'y pénétrer. »

D'une conception aussi haute de la poésie, de cette volonté d'entrevoir l'universelle harmonie, naît la nécessité d'un langage musical. Les poètes doivent, écrit Mallarmé, « reprendre à la Musique leur bien ». De là une préférence de la poésie symboliste pour les rythmes irréguliers, les libertés syntaxiques, de là les obscurités, fruits d'une recherche sur le langage, d'un effort pour tirer des mots leur musique propre encore inconnue.

« Considéré en sa splendeur nue et magique, le mot s'élève à la puissance élémentale d'une note, d'une couleur, d'un claveau de voûte. Le vers se manifeste comme un accord permettant l'introduction de deux modes, où l'épithète mystérieuse et sacrée, miroir des souterraines suggestions, est comme un accompagnement prononcé en sourdine », écrit Valéry dans une lettre à Mallarmé citée par Henri Mondor.

Les poètes de cette fin de siècle ne furent pas tous dignes des hautes conceptions qu'ils professaient ou qu'on exprimait à leur propos, et il y eut sans doute alors moins d'œuvres marquantes que d'exposés théoriques. Mais celles de Claudel ou de Valéry, pour ne citer que les noms les plus illustres, montrent que les ambitions du symbolisme, quelque démesurées ou confuses qu'elles aient paru, n'étaient pas de pures chimères et pouvaient se voir un jour réalisées.

ÉMILE VERHAEREN

(1855-1916)

On a pu voir en lui le Walt Whitman européen. Rapprochement qui figure en particulier dans le livre que lui consacre Stefan Zweig. Le comparant au poète américain, « ce prophète de tout art vigoureux et sincère fondé sur la réalité », il écrit ceci : « Verhaeren a tenté de représenter toute notre époque dans son expression physique et intellectuelle. Son lyrisme est le symbole de l'Europe à la fin du siècle précédent et dans son état actuel. C'est une encyclopédie poétique de notre temps, d'où se dégage l'atmosphère spirituelle de notre monde au tournant du vingtième siècle. »

Un tel éloge se fonde sur la nature propre du lyrisme dans une œuvre où le poète ne se borne pas à traduire sa ferveur personnelle, mais où il peint la réalité du monde moderne, s'efforce d'en déchiffrer le sens afin de préparer l'avenir car, dans ses années de maturité, son propos est de prendre en charge les luttes et les souffrances des hommes de son temps.

> *J'aime la violente et terrible atmosphère*
> *Où tout esprit se meut, en notre temps, sur terre*
> *Et les essais et les combats et les labeurs*
> *D'autant plus téméraires*
> *Qu'ils n'ont pour feux qui les éclairent*
> *Que des lueurs.*

Cependant on a pu ne voir en lui, à ses débuts, qu'un poète régional attaché à célébrer sa terre natale. Dans *Les Flamandes*,

son premier recueil, il se veut proche du naturalisme et s'efforce
d'imiter la manière des peintres de son pays :

> *Vous conceviez, maîtres vantés,*
> *Avec de larges opulences,*
> *Avec de rouges violences,*
> *Les corps charnus de vos beautés...*

Il retrouve ces thèmes, près de vingt ans plus tard, lorsqu'il chante
sa terre natale dans *Toute la Flandre,* avec une inspiration plus
large et dans une langue véhémente et forte qui ne doit plus rien
aux maîtres de jadis.

Très tôt il a rejoint le groupe de poètes qui collaborent à
La Jeune Belgique, revue de la renaissance littéraire belge
d'expression française. Son deuxième livre, *Les Moines,* montre
qu'il adhère au credo parnassien, mais quelques traits, déjà,
peuvent être qualifiés de symbolistes. On le voit souvent à Paris, il
y fréquente Huysmans et René Ghil et prend part aux débats et
aux recherches de la nouvelle école. Dans un texte de 1887, où il
s'efforce, comme il le dit, « d'éclaircir quelque peu le brouillard
ambiant », il distingue le Symbolisme actuel du Symbolisme
grec, et note que, tandis que ce dernier était « la concrétion de
l'abstrait » (ainsi Vénus incarne l'amour ou Minerve la sagesse),
celui d'aujourd'hui « sollicite vers l'abstraction du concret », c'est
pourquoi il voit dans le symbole « un sublimé de perceptions et de
sensations » qui, préférant la suggestion à la démonstration, « ruine
toute contingence, tout fait, tout détail ». Ces caractéristiques font
de lui « la plus haute expression d'art et la plus spiritualiste qui
soit ».

Mais l'itinéraire poétique de Verhaeren, s'il est marqué par le
symbolisme, reste très personnel. Son œuvre renouant avec
l'inspiration épique, se distingue de toutes les productions de ses
contemporains par son caractère oratoire. Rythmée par le retour
de refrains, ou de sonorités semblables, qui, se répondant d'une
strophe à l'autre, donnent à ses poèmes une unité rhapsodique,
elle est faite pour être dite à haute voix, et même déclamée. Dès les
recueils de la « Trilogie noire » (*Les Soirs, Les Débâcles, Les
Flambeaux noirs*), il utilise le vers libre qui épouse le tempo des
élans intérieurs et lie son écriture à son souffle.

Il y a aussi chez lui une démesure naturelle et une puissance créatrice qui font penser à Hugo. Il les met au service d'un monde dont il veut cerner la réalité la plus brutale. Il peint alors dans *Les Campagnes hallucinées* ou *Les Villes tentaculaires*, la misère et le dur travail des hommes. C'est son réalisme visionnaire, lorsqu'il évoque le monde industriel et urbain, qui donne à ses poèmes leur valeur de témoignage inspiré sur l'évolution de la société de son temps. Dans ses poèmes, les cités, pareilles à des êtres humains, ont, comme eux, leurs grandeurs et leurs vices. Plus tard il célébrera le travail ou la solidarité universelle, et surtout la force des hommes, sainte à ses yeux, puisque c'est par elle qu'ils impriment leur marque sur le monde. Il est le premier à donner une traduction poétique aux aspects de la ville qui semblaient le moins faits pour être chantés, par là il appartient déjà au siècle suivant où Unanimisme et Futurisme développeront ce thème. C'est lui qui a imposé la vision de la cité « tentaculaire », en inventant ce mot qui montre bien, comme l'explique son biographe, comment « avec ses bras de pieuvre elle aspire à elle sans discernement toutes les forces de l'univers qui l'environne ». Les poètes qui parleront de la ville après Verhaeren ne reprendront pas toujours son hymne aux temps modernes, aux usines, aux quais, à la foule, et n'adhéreront pas forcément à la vision qu'il en propose, mais il leur aura montré qu'on peut trouver dans les plus triviales réalités, celles que le temps n'a pas encore poétisées, la voie, comme le dit encore Zweig, d'une « découverte lyrique » du monde, et adhérer, comme il leur en donnait l'exemple « à la beauté nouvelle enclose dans les choses nouvelles ».

SOIR RELIGIEUX

L'averse a sabré l'air de ses lames de grêle,
Et voici que le ciel luit comme un parvis bleu,
Et que c'est l'heure où meurt à l'occident, le feu
Où l'argent de la nuit à l'or du jour se mêle.

À l'horizon, plus rien ne passe, si ce n'est
Une allée invaincue et géante de chênes,
Se prolongeant là-bas jusqu'aux fermes prochaines,
Le long des champs en friche et des coins de genêt.

Ces arbres vont – ainsi des moines mortuaires
Qui s'en iraient, le cœur assombri par les soirs,
Comme jadis partaient les longs pénitents noirs
Pèleriner au loin vers d'anciens sanctuaires.

Et la route montant et tout à coup s'ouvrant
Sur le couchant rougi comme un plant de pivoines,
À voir ces arbres nus, à voir passer ces moines,
On dirait qu'ils s'en vont, ensemble, et tous en rang,

Vers leur Dieu dont l'azur d'étoiles s'ensemence ;
Et les astres, brillant là-haut sur leur chemin,
Semblent les feux de grands cierges, tenus en main,
Dont on n'aperçoit pas monter la tige immense.

Les Moines, 1885

LE MOULIN

Le moulin tourne au fond du soir, très lentement,
Sur un ciel de tristesse et de mélancolie,
Il tourne et tourne, et sa voile, couleur de lie,
Est triste et faible et lourde et lasse, infiniment.

Depuis l'aube, ses bras, comme des bras de plainte,
Se sont tendus et sont tombés ; et les voici
Qui retombent encor, là-bas, dans l'air noirci
Et le silence entier de la nature éteinte.

Un jour souffrant d'hiver sur les hameaux s'endort,
Les nuages sont las de leurs voyages sombres,
Et le long des taillis qui ramassent leurs ombres,
Les ornières s'en vont vers un horizon mort.

Sous un ourlet de sol, quelques huttes de hêtre
Très misérablement sont assises en rond ;
Une lampe de cuivre est pendue au plafond
Et patine de feu le mur et la fenêtre.

Et dans la plaine immense et le vide dormeur
Elles fixent – les très souffreteuses bicoques ! –
Avec les pauvres yeux, de leurs carreaux en loques,
Le vieux moulin qui tourne et, las, qui tourne et meurt.

Les Soirs, 1887

UN MATIN

Dès le matin, par mes grand'routes coutumières
            Qui traversent champs et vergers,
            Je suis parti clair et léger,
Le corps enveloppé de vent et de lumière.

Je vais, je ne sais où. Je vais, je suis heureux ;
            C'est fête et joie en ma poitrine ;
            Que m'importent droits et doctrines,
Le caillou sonne et luit sous mes talons poudreux ;

Je marche avec l'orgueil d'aimer l'air et la terre,
            D'être immense et d'être fou
            Et de mêler le monde et tout
À cet enivrement de vie élémentaire.

Oh ! les pas voyageurs et clairs des anciens dieux !
            Je m'enfouis dans l'herbe sombre
            Où les chênes versent leurs ombres
Et je baise les fleurs sur leurs bouches de feu.

Les bras fluides et doux des rivières m'accueillent ;
            Je me repose et je repars
            Avec mon guide, le hasard,
Par des sentiers sous bois dont je mâche les feuilles.

Il me semble jusqu'à ce jour n'avoir vécu
            Que pour mourir et non pour vivre :
            Oh ! quels tombeaux creusent les livres
Et que de fronts armés y descendent vaincus !

Dites, est-il vrai qu'hier il existât des choses,
            Et que des yeux quotidiens
            Aient regardé, avant les miens,
Se pavoiser les fruits et s'exalter les roses !

Pour la première fois, je vois les vents vermeils
     Briller dans la mer des branchages,
     Mon âme humaine n'a point d'âge ;
Tout est jeune, tout est nouveau sous le soleil.

J'aime mes yeux, mes bras, mes mains, ma chair, mon torse
     Et mes cheveux amples et blonds
     Et je voudrais, par mes poumons,
Boire l'espace entier pour en gonfler ma force.

Oh ! ces marches à travers bois, plaines, fossés,
     Où l'être chante et pleure et crie
     Et se dépense avec furie
Et s'enivre de soi ainsi qu'un insensé !

Les Forces tumultueuses, 1902

LES TOURS AU BORD DE LA MER

Veuves debout au long des mers,
Les tours de Lisweghe et de Furnes
Pleurent, aux vents des vieux hivers
Et des automnes taciturnes.

Elles règnent sur le pays,
Depuis quels jours, depuis quels âges,
Depuis quels temps évanouis
Avec les brumes de leurs plages ?

Jadis, on allumait des feux
Sur leur sommet, dans le soir sombre ;
Et le marin fixait ses yeux
Vers ce flambeau tendu par l'ombre.

Quand la guerre battait l'Escaut
De son tumulte militaire,
Les tours semblaient darder là-haut,
La rage en flamme de la terre.

Quand on tuait de ferme en bouge,
Pêle-mêle vieux et petits,
Les tours jetaient leurs gestes rouges
En suppliques, vers l'infini.

Depuis,
La guerre,
Au bruit roulant de ses tonnerres,
Crispe, sous d'autres cieux, son poing ensanglanté ;
Et d'autres blocs et d'autres phares,
Armés de grands yeux d'or et de cristaux bizarres,
Jettent, vers d'autres flots, de plus nettes clartés.

Mais vous êtes, quand même
Debout encor, au long des mers,

Debout, dans l'ombre et dans l'hiver,
Sans couronne, sans diadème,
Sans feux épars sur vos fronts lourds ;
Et vous demeurez là, seules au vent nocturne,
Oh ! vous, les tours, les tours gigantesques, les tours
De Nieuport, de Lisweghe et de Furnes.

Sur les villes et les hameaux flamands,
Au-dessus des maisons vieilles et basses,
Vous carrez votre masse,
Tragiquement ;
Et ceux qui vont, au soir tombant, le long des grèves,
À voir votre grandeur et votre deuil,
Sentent toujours, comme un afflux d'orgueil,
Battre leur rêve :
Et leur cœur chante, et leur cœur pleure, et leur cœur bout
D'être jaillis du même sol que vous.

Flandre tenace au cœur ; Flandre des aïeux morts,
Avec la terre aimée entre leurs dents ardentes ;
Pays de fruste orgueil ou de rage mordante,
Dès qu'on barre ta vie ou qu'on touche à ton sort ;
Pays de labours verts autour de blancs villages ;
Pays de poings boudeurs et de fronts redoutés ;

Pays de patiente et sourde volonté ;
Pays de fête rouge ou de pâle silence ;
Clos de tranquillité ou champs de violence,
Tu te dardes dans tes beffrois ou dans tes tours,
Comme en un cri géant vers l'inconnu des jours !
Chaque brique, chaque moellon ou chaque pierre,
Renferme un peu de ta douleur héréditaire
Ou de ta joie éparse aux âges de grandeur ;
Tours de longs deuils passés ou beffrois de splendeur,
Vous êtes des témoins dont nul ne se délivre :
Votre ombre est là, sur mes pensers et sur mes livres,
Sur mes gestes nouant ma vie avec sa mort.
Ô que mon cœur toujours reste avec vous d'accord !
Qu'il puise en vous l'orgueil et la fermeté haute,

Tours debout près des flots, tours debout près des côtes,
Et que tous ceux qui s'en viennent des pays clairs
Que brûle le soleil, à l'autre bout des mers,
Sachent, rien qu'en longeant nos grèves taciturnes,
Rien qu'en posant le pied sur notre sol glacé,
Quel vieux peuple rugueux vous leur symbolisez
Vous, les tours de Nieuport, de Lisweghe et de Furnes !

Toute la Flandre, 1904

L'ARBRE

Tout seul,
Que le berce l'été, que l'agite l'hiver,
Que son tronc soit givré ou son branchage vert,
Toujours, au long des jours de tendresse ou de haine,
Il impose sa vie énorme et souveraine
Aux plaines.

Il voit les mêmes champs depuis cent et cent ans
Et les mêmes labours et les mêmes semailles ;
Les yeux aujourd'hui morts, les yeux
Des aïeules et des aïeux
Ont regardé, maille après maille,
Se nouer son écorce et ses rudes rameaux.
Il présidait tranquille et fort à leurs travaux ;
Son pied velu leur ménageait un lit de mousse ;
Il abritait leur sieste à l'heure de midi
Et son ombre fut douce
À ceux de leurs enfants qui s'aimèrent jadis.

Dès le matin, dans les villages,
D'après qu'il chante ou pleure, on augure du temps ;
Il est dans le secret des violents nuages
Et du soleil qui boude aux horizons latents ;
Il est tout le passé debout sur les champs tristes,
Mais quels que soient les souvenirs
Qui, dans son bois, persistent,
Dès que janvier vient de finir
Et que la sève, en son vieux tronc, s'épanche,
Avec tous ses bourgeons, avec toutes ses branches,
– Lèvres folles et bras tordus –
Il jette un cri immensément tendu
Vers l'avenir.

. . . .

En octobre, quand l'or triomphe en son feuillage,
Mes pas larges encor, quoique lourds et lassés,
Souvent ont dirigé leur long pèlerinage
Vers cet arbre d'automne et de vent traversé.
Comme un géant brasier de feuilles et de flammes,
Il se dressait, superbement, sous le ciel bleu,
Il semblait habité par un million d'âmes
Qui doucement chantaient en son branchage creux.
J'allais vers lui les yeux emplis par la lumière,
Je le touchais, avec mes doigts, avec mes mains,
Je le sentais bouger jusqu'au fond de la terre
D'après un mouvement énorme et surhumain ;
Et j'appuyais sur lui ma poitrine brutale,
Avec un tel amour, une telle ferveur,
Que son rythme profond et sa force totale
Passaient en moi et pénétraient jusqu'à mon cœur.

Alors, j'étais mêlé à sa belle vie ample ;
Je me sentais puissant comme un de ses rameaux ;
Il se plantait, dans la splendeur, comme un exemple ;
J'aimais plus ardemment le sol, les bois, les eaux,
La plaine immense et nue où les nuages passent ;
J'étais armé de fermeté contre le sort,
Mes bras auraient voulu tenir en eux l'espace ;
Mes muscles et mes nerfs rendaient léger mon corps
Et je criais : « La force est sainte,
Il faut que l'homme imprime son empreinte
Tranquillement, sur ses desseins hardis :
Elle est celle qui tient les clefs des paradis
Et dont le large poing en fait tourner les portes. »
Et je baisais le tronc noueux, éperdument,
Et quand le soir se détachait du firmament,
Je me perdais, dans la campagne morte,
Marchant droit devant moi, vers n'importe où,
Avec des cris jaillis du fond de mon cœur fou.

Multiple Splendeur, 1906

JEAN MORÉAS

(1856-1910)

Le premier volume de vers que publie Jean Moréas, en 1881, après avoir fait paraître de nombreux poèmes dans *Lutèce* ou dans le *Chat Noir*, semble retrouver les thèmes du romantisme, en particulier son goût du Moyen Âge, et aussi, en évoquant le Remords ou le Spleen, s'inspirer directement de Baudelaire. Rien de très nouveau en cela, si ce n'est un vocabulaire recherché. Les pierres précieuses, béryl, chrysoprase, améthyste, chargent les vers, comme elles le font pour la tortue de Des Esseintes. Les plantes aux pouvoirs magiques, le népenthès et le lotus d'or ou les floraisons palustres, composent un décor que l'on va bientôt qualifier de décadent. Cependant Moréas récuse l'épithète et se proclame symboliste. À lire les recueils suivants, *Les Cantilènes* et *Le Pèlerin passionné*, on hésite sur la pertinence de ce terme. S'il y a bien là des langueurs proches de la couleur de mélancolie répandue à profusion dans leurs vers par ceux qui se réclament du symbole, on ne perçoit à aucun moment chez Moréas ce sens du mystère et cette religiosité qui, diffuse ou profonde, est commune aux poètes de sa génération nourris de philosophie orientale ou de théosophie. Néanmoins Moréas suscite la manifestation publique qui aura, pour un temps, le prestige d'une nouvelle bataille d'Hernani, autour de son livre, *Le Pèlerin passionné*. Sont conviés à un banquet tous les poètes qui se réclament, de près ou de loin, d'une forme nouvelle de poésie, ainsi que quelques critiques. Présidée par Mallarmé, la réunion, dont son initiateur avait sans doute souhaité qu'elle s'ordonnât autour de son livre, prend une autre ampleur et devient une célébration du Symbolisme tout entier : le « Banquet du Pèlerin passionné » confère à ce mouvement l'éclat qui le fait connaître du grand public En 1886 Moréas donne au *Figaro littéraire* un Manifeste qui a le ton d'autorité d'un texte fondateur. Le poète y décrit les évolutions successives de la poésie, dont le nouveau courant est le nécessaire aboutissement, et souligne que la dénomination de Symbolisme, déjà utilisée par certains, peut être à bon droit maintenue ; il désigne les grands précurseurs, Baudelaire, Mallarmé, Verlaine, y ajoutant aussi Banville, puis décrit les perspectives qui s'ouvrent à la poésie nouvelle : « vêtir l'Idée d'une forme sensible » car l'Idée « ne doit point se priver des somptueuses simarres des analogies extérieures ». Pour cela « il faut au symbolisme un style archétype et complexe : d'impollués vocables, la période qui s'arc-boute alternant avec la période aux défaillances ondulées, les pléonasmes significatifs », et pour le rythme il préconise « l'ancienne métrique avivée ; un désordre savamment ordonné ; la rime illucescente et martelée comme un bouclier d'or et d'airain auprès de la rime aux fluidités absconses... »

Malgré ce ton de conviction et d'autorité, et ce goût du langage précieux, Moréas ne reste pas longtemps attaché aux principes qu'il a lui-même énoncés. En 1891 il fonde l' « école romane », la poésie devant, selon lui, retrouver la tradition classique. Il sera peu suivi, mais cet effort vers la simplicité nous vaut les six livres des *Stances* où se rencontrent la plupart des poèmes qui nous touchent encore.

TES MAINS

Tes mains semblant sortir d'une tapisserie
Très ancienne où l'argent à l'or brun se marie,
Où parmi les fouillis bizarres des ramages
Se bossue en relief le contour des images,
Me parlent de beaux rapts et de royale orgie,
Et de tournois de preux dont j'ai la nostalgie.

Tes mains à l'ongle rose et tranchant comme un bec
Durent pincer jadis la harpe et le rebec,
Sous le dais incrusté du portique ogival
Ouvrant ses treillis d'or à la fraîcheur du val,
Et, pleines d'onction, rougir leurs fins anneaux
De chrysoprase dans le sang des huguenots.

Tes mains aux doigts pâlis semblent des mains de sainte
Par Giotto rêvée et pieusement peinte
En un coin très obscur de quelque basilique
Pleine de chapes d'or, de cierges, de reliques
Où je voudrais dormir tel qu'un évêque mort,
Dans un tombeau sculpté, sans crainte et sans remords.

Les Syrtes

ACCALMIE

Ô mer immense, mer aux rumeurs monotones,
Tu berças doucement mes rêves printaniers ;
Ô mer immense, mer perfide aux mariniers,
Sois clémente aux douleurs sages de mes automnes.

Vague qui viens avec des murmures câlins
Te coucher sur la dune où pousse l'herbe amère,
Berce, berce mon cœur comme un enfant sa mère,
Fais le repu d'azur et d'effluves salins.

Loin des villes, je veux sur les falaises mornes
Secouer la torpeur de mes obsessions,
– Et mes pensers, pareils aux calmes alcyons,
Monteront à travers l'immensité sans bornes.

Les Syrtes

Je vous revois toujours, immobiles cyprès
 Dans la lumière dure,
Découpés sur l'azur, au bord des flots, auprès
 D'une blanche clôture :

Je garde aussi les morts ; elle a votre couleur,
 Mon âme, sombre abîme.
Mais je m'élance hors la Parque et le malheur,
 Pareil à votre cime.

Stances

ALBERT SAMAIN

(1858-1900)

Il est le plus accessible des poètes de sa génération, à cause de sa fidélité aux rythmes traditionnels malgré la vogue contemporaine du vers libre, et surtout pour l'usage qu'il fait du symbole. Les siens n'étant jamais voilés, chacun peut les entendre et interpréter ses métaphores. Il semble évident aussi à ses lecteurs que la tonalité mélancolique de cette œuvre ne relève pas d'un parti pris esthétique, mais d'une nécessité intérieure : reflétant une constante de sa personnalité, elle en est la dominante. On se rappelle comment ses vers les plus connus traduisent en une image empruntée à Vélasquez, la nature singulière du spleen qui l'accable, ce calme désespoir où le temps se fige :

> *Mon âme est une infante en robe de parade*
> *Dont l'exil se reflète, éternel et royal,*
> *Aux grands miroirs déserts d'un vieil Escurial,*
> *Ainsi qu'une galère oubliée en la rade...*

On peut voir dans chacun de ses recueils, *Au jardin de l'Infante, Aux flancs du vase, Le Chariot d'or,* comment la référence discrète à Baudelaire et Verlaine, ses véritables maîtres, se marie chez lui à une manière toute parnassienne de privilégier la couleur d'un détail. Quant au maniérisme délicat de l'expression, il est la marque de son appartenance au courant décadent. Cette confluence de styles, si elle ne fait pas de lui un écrivain vraiment original, a du moins le mérite de se fondre harmonieusement. La souplesse d'une langue très musicale y contribue ainsi que l'élégance nonchalante du poète qui chante le « monotone effort de vivre ». L'évocation nostalgique d'un passé prestigieux, ou celle d'un paysage intérieur aux pâleurs délicates, la prédominance du thème de l'eau : « L'eau musicale et triste est la sœur de son rêve », et la teinte crépusculaire dont il se plaît à voiler le réel, donne encore à cette œuvre un charme et une grâce incontestables.

Mes pas ont suscité les prestiges enfuis.
Ô psyché de vieux saxe où le Passé se mire...
C'est ici que la reine, en écoutant *Zémire*,
Rêveuse, s'éventait dans la tiédeur des nuits.

Ô visions : paniers, poudre et mouches ; et puis,
Léger comme un parfum, joli comme un sourire,
C'est cet air vieille France ici que tout respire ;
Et toujours cette odeur pénétrante des buis...

Mais ce qui prend mon cœur d'une étreinte infinie,
Aux rayons d'un long soir dorant son agonie,
C'est ce Grand-Trianon solitaire et royal,

Et son perron désert où l'automne, si douce,
Laisse pendre, en rêvant, sa chevelure rousse
Sur l'eau divinement triste du grand canal.

                                        Le Chariot d'or, III

RETRAITE

Remonte, lent rameur, le cours de tes années,
Et, les yeux clos, suspends ta rame par endroits...
La brise qui s'élève aux jardins d'autrefois
Courbe suavement les âmes inclinées.

Cherche en ton cœur, loin des grand'routes calcinées,
L'enclos plein d'herbe épaisse et verte où sont les croix.
Écoutes-y l'air triste où reviennent les voix,
Et baise au cœur tes petites mortes fanées.

Songe à tels yeux poignants dans la fuite du jour.
Les heures, que toucha l'ongle d'or de l'amour,
À jamais sous l'archet chantent mélodieuses.

Lapidaire secret des soirs quotidiens,
Taille tes souvenirs en pierres précieuses,
Et fais-en pour tes doigts des bijoux anciens.

Le Chariot d'or

WATTEAU

Au-dessus des grands bois profonds
L'étoile du berger s'allume...
Groupes sur l'herbe dans la brume...
Pizzicati des violons...
Entre les mains, les mains s'attardent ;
Le ciel où les amants regardent
Laisse un reflet rose dans l'eau ;
Et dans la clairière indécise,
Que la nuit proche idéalise,
Passe entre Estelle et Cydalise
L'ombre amoureuse de Watteau.

Watteau, peintre idéal de la *Fête jolie*,
Ton art léger fut tendre et doux comme un soupir,
Et tu donnas une âme inconnue au Désir
En l'asseyant aux pieds de la Mélancolie.

Tes bergers fins avaient la canne d'or au doigt ;
Tes bergères, non sans quelques façons hautaines,
Promenaient, sous l'ombrage où chantaient les fontaines,
Leurs robes qu'effilait derrière un grand pli droit...

Dans l'air bleuâtre et tiède agonisaient les roses ;
Les cœurs s'ouvraient dans l'ombre au jardin apaisé,
Et les lèvres, prenant aux lèvres le baiser,
Fiançaient l'amour triste à la douceur des choses.

Les Pèlerins s'en vont au Pays idéal...
La galère dorée abandonne la rive ;
Et l'amante à la proue écoute au loin, pensive,
Une flûte mourir, dans le soir de cristal...

Oh ! partir avec eux par un soir de mystère,
Ô maître, vivre un soir dans ton rêve enchanté !
La mer est rose... Il souffle une brise d'été,
Et quand la nef aborde au rivage argenté,
La lune doucement se lève sur Cythère.

L'éventail balancé sans trêve
Au rythme intime des aveux
Fait, chaque fois qu'il se soulève,
S'envoler au front des cheveux.
L'ombre est suave... Tout repose.
Agnès sourit ; Léandre pose
Sa viole sur son manteau ;
Et sur les robes parfumées,
Et sur les mains des Bien-Aimées,
Flotte, au long des molles ramées,
L'âme divine de Watteau.

Le Chariot d'or

JULES LAFORGUE

(1860-1887)

Lorsque Laforgue, pour justifier son recours à un poème d'introduction qui semble étranger au contexte des *Complaintes*, écrit à ses amis : « Je tiens à dire... qu'avant d'être dilettante et pierrot, j'ai séjourné dans le Cosmique », il faut voir là plus qu'une boutade. Il a d'abord rêvé, en effet, de peindre le malheur de la condition humaine, et le statut précaire de notre planète menacée de disparaître un jour. Il n'achève pas la grande fresque projetée qui devait s'intituler *Le Sanglot de la terre*, mais à travers les poèmes qu'il conserve et seront imprimés dans cet état fragmentaire, on prend la mesure du pessimisme et de l'angoisse qui l'habitent. Ses modèles sont alors Baudelaire, comme on le voit dans ses Spleens ; ou bien les Parnassiens, et parfois Hugo : en témoigne la très belle *Marche funèbre pour la mort de la terre* :

> *Ô convoi solennel des soleils magnifiques,*
> *Nouez et dénouez vos vastes masses d'or,*
> *Doucement, tristement, sur de graves musiques*
> *Menez le deuil très-lent de votre sœur qui dort.*

S'il s'exhorte, non sans ironie, à adopter une impassibilité résignée : « Sirote chaque jour ta tasse de néant », la terreur manifeste que l'absurdité de notre condition, et le caractère périssable de la terre elle-même, suscitent en lui, n'est pas sans évoquer Pascal (« Qu'est-ce qu'un homme dans l'infini ? ») :

Comme nous sommes seuls, pourtant, sur notre terre
Avec notre infini, nos misères, nos dieux,
Abandonnés de tout, sans amour et sans père,
Seuls dans l'affolement universel des Cieux !

Or ce poète épris de métaphysique, lecteur de Schopenhauer, puis de Hegel, durant les années passées en Allemagne, où il découvre aussi l'inconscient à travers Hartmann, va s'éloigner de sa première veine poétique grave, et trouver dans la dérision une nouvelle manière de peindre l'absurdité du monde. Il est désormais « En deuil d'un Moi-le Magnifique / Lançant de front les cent pur-sang, / De ses vingt ans tout hennissants... » Et il choisit de dire sa difficulté d'être, dans une forme populaire, aux tournures naïves, à travers *Les Complaintes*, avec un humour qui s'efforce de masquer son lyrisme naturel, mais qui laisse deviner sa fragilité. Toutes ses évocations de l'enfance et de la province, sont, malgré leur ton léger, pleines de nostalgie et d'une amertume qui est la constante de son œuvre. Ces poèmes traduisent la défiance, ou même la peur de la femme, l'obsession de la mort imminente et un incurable sentiment de solitude : « Le cœur crève soudain d'un immense abandon. »

On peut rattacher ce recueil et les suivants à l'école des Décadents, mais la culture philosophique de l'auteur, sa lucidité intellectuelle, la distance narquoise qu'il garde vis-à-vis de lui-même, et plus que tout, sa conscience tragique, le distinguent de tous les autres. S'il les connaît et les fréquente, s'il sait fort bien se moquer, en les parodiant, des vocables et des procédés stylistiques qui leur sont chers, il préfère à la préciosité des termes rares et obscurs qu'ils affectionnent, la cocasserie de mots fort clairs qu'il invente. Dans son œuvre en effet, on « s'aubade » ou on « s'engrandeuille », on a le don de « s'ubiquiter », on attend, en vain, le jour où « feu-d'artificeront » les allégresses « hosannahles », et si l'on peut y éprouver les « voluptés », les humeurs « exilescentes » l'emportent, en attendant les « dies iraemissibles », et rien jamais ne s'y console de l' « Éternullité. »

Un deuxième recueil paraît les premiers jours de 86, six mois à peine après le précédent, c'est *L'Imitation de Notre-Dame la Lune*. La métaphysique resurgit et se mêle à l'ironie. (« Ô radeau du Nihil aux quais seuls de nos nuits !... et surtout, quelle leçon de calme !

/ Tout à l'air émané d'un même acte de foi / Au Néant quotidien sans comment ni pourquoi ! »)

Pierrot, déjà présent dans *Les Complaintes*, et qui occupe ici une place importante, c'est sans aucun doute Laforgue lui-même, ce « viveur lunaire », à qui l'astre mort offre l'image de son ennui et de son néant. Grâce au rythme et aux sonorités de ces poèmes qui rappellent Verlaine, ces vers constamment bridés par l'ironie, conservent leur pouvoir de séduction lyrique et sous la figure dérisoire du pantin rêveur laissent reconnaître l'essence même du poète, cet exilé définitif.

Il lui reste moins de deux ans à vivre, il travaille à « un livre enfin de bonne foi », mais il n'achève pas ces *Fleurs de bonne volonté*, dont le titre fait écho à celui de Baudelaire. Elles paraissent après sa mort, dans une édition réservée aux seuls souscripteurs (ils sont cinquante-huit), édition dont Émile Dujardin et Félix Fénéon se sont chargés ; elles y seront regroupées avec *Le Concile féerique* et les *Derniers Vers* où pour la première fois le poète a recours au vers libre. En lisant :

> *Blocus sentimental ! Messageries du Levant !...*
> *Oh, tombée de la pluie ! Oh ! tombée de la nuit,*
> *Oh ! le vent !...*
> *La Toussaint, la Noël et la Nouvelle Année*
> *Oh ! dans les bruines, toutes mes cheminées !...*
> *D'usines.*

on croit entendre Apollinaire, et l'on sent que la page du siècle se tourne. Car la diffusion si limitée de cette œuvre, la brièveté de cette vie, n'ont pas empêché Laforgue d'occuper une place essentielle. À lui aussi on aurait pu dire qu'il avait « créé un frisson nouveau ».

Les « fantaisistes » comme Toulet, et des poètes aussi originaux que Max Jacob, Apollinaire ou Desnos se souviendront de lui. Dans la lignée des poètes de la dérision de soi et de l'autodénigrement, lignée jamais éteinte depuis Rutebeuf, il est « l'héautontimorouménos » le plus sincère, le plus tragique, le plus inspiré.

COMPLAINTE
DE LA LUNE EN PROVINCE

Ah ! la belle pleine Lune,
Grosse comme une fortune !

La retraite sonne au loin,
Un passant, monsieur l'adjoint ;

Un clavecin joue en face,
Un chat traverse la place :

La province qui s'endort !
Plaquant un dernier accord,

Le piano clôt sa fenêtre.
Quelle heure peut-il bien être ?

Calme Lune, quel exil !
Faut-il dire : ainsi soit-il ?

Lune, ô dilettante Lune,
À tous les climats commune,

Tu vis hier le Missouri,
Et les remparts de Paris,

Les fiords bleus de la Norvège,
Les pôles, les mers, que sais-je ?

Lune heureuse ! ainsi tu vois,
À cette heure, le convoi

De son voyage de noce !
Ils sont partis pour l'Écosse.

Quel panneau, si, cet hiver,
Elle eût pris au mot mes vers !

Lune, vagabonde Lune,
Faisons cause et mœurs communes ?

Ô riches nuits ! je me meurs,
La province dans le cœur !

Et la lune a, bonne vieille,
Du coton dans les oreilles.

Les Complaintes

COMPLAINTE

DU PAUVRE JEUNE HOMME

Sur l'air populaire :
« Quand le bonhomm' revint du bois. »

Quand ce jeune homm' rentra chez lui,
Quand ce jeune homm' rentra chez lui ;
Il prit à deux mains son vieux crâne,
Qui de science était un puits !
      Crâne,
        Riche crâne,
Entends-tu la Folie qui plane ?
Et qui demande le cordon,
Digue dondaine, digue dondaine,
Et qui demande le cordon,
Digue dondaine, digue dondon ?

Quand ce jeune homm' rentra chez lui,
Quand ce jeune homm' rentra chez lui ;
Il entendit de tristes gammes,
Qu'un piano pleurait dans la nuit !
      Gammes,
        Vieilles gammes,
Ensemble, enfants, nous vous cherchâmes ;
Son mari m'a fermé sa maison,
Digue dondaine, digue dondaine,
Son mari m'a fermé sa maison,
Digue dondaine, digue dondon !

Quand ce jeune homm' rentra chez lui,
Quand ce jeune homm' rentra chez lui ;
Il mit le nez dans sa belle âme,
Où fermentaient des tas d'ennuis !
      Âme,
        Ma belle âme,
Leur huile est trop sal' pour ta flamme !
Puis, nuit partout ! lors, à quoi bon ?
Digue dondaine, digue dondaine,

Puis, nuit partout ! lors, à quoi bon ?
Digue dondaine, digue dondon !

Quand ce jeune homm' rentra chez lui,
Quand ce jeune homm' rentra chez lui ;
Il vit que sa charmante femme,
Avait déménagé sans lui !
        Dame,
          Notre-Dame,
Je n'aurai pas un mot de blâme !
Mais t'aurais pu m' laisser l' charbon
Digue dondaine, digue dondaine,
Mais t'aurais pu m' laisser l' charbon,
Digue dondaine, digue dondon.

Lors, ce jeune homme aux tels ennuis,
Lors, ce jeune homme aux tels ennuis ;
Alla décrocher une lame,
Qu'on lui avait fait cadeau avec l'étui !
        Lame,
          Fine lame,
Soyez plus droite que la femme !
Et vous, mon Dieu, pardon ! pardon !
Digue dondaine, digue dondaine,
Et vous, mon Dieu, pardon ! pardon !
Digue dondaine, digue dondon !

Quand les croq' morts vinrent chez lui,
Quand les croq' morts vinrent chez lui ;
Ils virent qu' c'était un' belle âme,
Comme on n'en fait plus aujourd'hui !
        Âme,
          Dors, belle âme !
Quand on est mort c'est pour de bon,
Digue dondaine, digue dondaine,
Quand on est mort c'est pour de bon,
Digue dondaine, digue dondon !

Les Complaintes

COMPLAINTE

DES DÉBATS MÉLANCOLIQUES ET LITTÉRAIRES

> *On peut encore aimer, mais confier toute*
> *son âme est un bonheur qu'on ne retrouvera*
> *plus.*
>
> CORINNE OU L'ITALIE

Le long d'un ciel crépusculâtre,
Une cloche angéluse en paix
L'air exilescent et marâtre
Qui ne pardonnera jamais.

Paissant des débris de vaisselle,
Là-bas, au talus des remparts,
Se profile une haridelle
Convalescente ; il se fait tard.

Qui m'aima jamais ? Je m'entête
Sur ce refrain bien impuissant,
Sans songer que je suis bien bête
De me faire du mauvais sang.

Je possède un propre physique,
Un cœur d'enfant bien élevé,
Et pour un cerveau magnifique
Le mien n'est pas mal, vous savez !

Eh bien, ayant pleuré l'Histoire,
J'ai voulu vivre un brin heureux ;
C'était trop demander, faut croire ;
J'avais l'air de parler hébreux.

Ah ! tiens, mon cœur, de grâce, laisse !
Lorsque j'y songe, en vérité,
J'en ai des sueurs de faiblesse,
À choir dans la malpropreté.

Le cœur me piaffe de génie
Éperdument pourtant, mon Dieu !
Et si quelqu'une veut ma vie,
Moi je ne demande pas mieux !

Eh va, pauvre âme véhémente !
Plonge, être, en leurs Jourdains blasés,
Deux frictions de vie courante
T'auront bien vite exorcisé.

Hélas, qui peut m'en répondre !
Tenez, peut-être savez-vous
Ce que c'est qu'une âme hypocondre ?
J'en suis une dans les prix doux.

Ô Hélène, j'erre en ma chambre ;
Et tandis que tu prends le thé,
Là-bas, dans l'or d'un fier septembre,
Je frissonne de tous mes membres,
En m'inquiétant de ta santé.

Tandis que, d'un autre côté...

Les Complaintes

Je ne suis qu'un viveur lunaire
Qui fait des ronds dans les bassins,
Et cela, sans autre dessein
Que devenir un légendaire.

Retroussant d'un air de défi
Mes manches de mandarin pâle,
J'arrondis ma bouche et – j'exhale
Des conseils doux de Crucifix.

Ah ! oui, devenir légendaire,
Au seuil des siècles charlatans !
Mais où sont les Lunes d'antan ?
Et que Dieu n'est-il à refaire ?

L'Imitation de Notre-Dame la Lune,
Locutions des Pierrots, XVI

CHARLES VAN LERBERGHE

(1861-1907)

Il est, comme Maeterlinck son compatriote, auteur dramatique
et poète. Son premier recueil de vers, *Solyane*, mais surtout les
suivants, *Entrevisions* et *La Chanson d'Ève*, œuvres de sa maturité,
font de lui l'un des plus représentatifs parmi les écrivains belges
de la seconde génération symboliste. Cependant l'influence du
réalisme et du Parnasse reste vive en Belgique, même durant cette
période, et Guy Michaud le montre en citant un propos de Van
Lerberghe, tiré de sa correspondance : « Tous mes poèmes, comme
l'ont dit Maeterlinck et d'autres, sont des tableaux. Ma *Chanson
d'Ève* est peinte autant que chantée. » Ce caractère pictural est
manifeste, lorsque, s'inspirant d'une scène de l'Évangile souvent
reproduite par les peintres, il décrit la fin de l'averse dans l'un de
ses poèmes les plus connus : « Puis vient le soleil qui essuie / De
ses cheveux d'or, / Les pieds de la pluie. »

Son goût de la description est également évident si l'on se
reporte aux poèmes qui suivent, toutefois leur résonance
fondamentale demeure symboliste à cause d'une constante aura
de mystère. Mais on n'y trouve pas « le parfum de tristesse » si
caractéristique des poètes de cette école. Le modèle du *Cantique
des Cantiques*, explicitement évoqué, est sans doute la source de
l'exultation qui les porte, mais la grâce de l'expression, la liberté
de la forme, appartiennent au poète et le pouvoir d'évocation
de certains vers où l'on croit entendre Valéry. « Toute ceinte
d'étreintes sombres / Je plonge en des vagues de feu. »

DANS LA NYMPHÉE

Quoique tes yeux ne la voient pas,
Sache, en ton âme, qu'elle est là,
Comme autrefois, divine et blanche.

Sur ce bord reposent ses mains.
Sa tête est entre ces jasmins ;
Là, ses pieds effleurent les branches.

Elle sommeille en ces rameaux.
Ses lèvres et ses yeux sont clos,
Et sa bouche à peine respire.

Parfois, la nuit, dans un éclair
Elle apparaît les yeux ouverts,
Et l'éclair dans ses yeux se mire.

Un bref éblouissement bleu
La découvre en ses longs cheveux ;
Elle s'éveille, elle se lève.

Et tout un jardin ébloui
S'illumine au fond de la nuit,
Dans le rapide éclair d'un rêve.

Entrevisions, 1898

LE JARDIN CLOS

Hortus conclusus, fons signatus,
Canticum Canticorum

Fulcite me floribus

Il m'est cher, Amour, le bandeau
Qui me tient les paupières closes ;
Il pèse comme un doux fardeau
De soleil sur de faibles roses.

Si j'avance, l'étrange chose !
Je parais marcher sur des eaux ;
Mes pieds trop lourds où je les pose,
S'enfoncent comme en des anneaux.

Qui donc a délié dans l'ombre
Le faix d'or de mes longs cheveux ?
Toute ceinte d'étreintes sombres,
Je plonge en des vagues de feu.

Mes lèvres où mon âme chante,
Toute d'extase et de baiser,
S'ouvrent comme une fleur ardente
Au-dessus d'un fleuve embrasé.

★

Dormio et cor meum vigilat

Sur mes seins mes mains endormies,
Lasses des jeux et des fuseaux,
Mes blanches mains, mes mains amies,
Semblent dormir au fond des eaux.

Loin des peines tristes et vaines,
En ce trône de ma beauté,
Calmes, douces et frêles reines,
Mes mains songent de royauté.

Et, seule dans mes tresses blondes
Et mes yeux clos, comme jadis
Je suis l'enfant qui tient des mondes,
Et la vierge qui tient des lys.

★

Ne suscitetis quoadusque velit

Que lui chanterons-nous, tandis qu'elle s'éveille ?
        Voyez, les paupières baissées,
        Comme elle songe en souriant.
Comment accorderons-nous nos voix à ses pensées ?

De quel nom d'amour lui nommerons-nous
        Ce qui l'entoure ;
        De quel nom d'amour saluerons-nous
Notre jeune sœur, en ce jour ?

Nous ne dirons rien, mais autour d'elle rangées,
        Comme les images de sa pensée,
        Avec des lys entre nos doigts
        Nous nous tiendrons immobiles.

La Chanson d'Ève, 1901

SAINT-POL-ROUX

(1861-1940)

Ce pseudonyme n'est pas, pour Pierre-Paul-Roux, le masque qui dissimule une identité, mais un moyen de mettre en lumière une métamorphose intérieure. Une force spirituelle l'a fait poète, par elle il prend conscience de la mission qui lui incombe, c'est-à-dire la recherche « de la Beauté parmi la Vérité » ; or, « la Beauté étant la forme de Dieu, il appert que la chercher induit à chercher Dieu ». Il est clair pour lui que « le rôle du poète consiste... en ceci : réaliser Dieu. », et que la poésie c'est « Dieu manifesté dans l'humain... tout le chaos informulé du monde, rendu clair par le médiateur qu'est le poète ».

Ce sont là, en effet, les termes de sa réponse à l'enquête de Jules Huret, et c'est ainsi qu'il définit le nouveau courant poétique. Pour le désigner il préfère l'appellation d'« idéo-réalisme » à celle de symbolisme, mais il le nommera ensuite « Magnificisme ». Lui-même se désigne comme le premier de ce mouvement, d'autres le rejoindront, mais nul ne mérite mieux l'épithète qu'il accole désormais à son nom, et qui fait de lui Saint-Pol-Roux le Magnifique. À l'intention de ceux qui s'engagent dans la même voie, il a cette formule qui sonne comme un orgueilleux défi : « Poètes, haussons nos âmes par dessus les horizons et que nos vœux appareillent pour l'Infini ! »

Le symbolisme tel qu'il le conçoit est avant tout un instrument de connaissance. S'il le choisit, en se détournant d'une réalité dont la reproduction lui semble vaine, ce n'est pas pour fonder sa parole sur une absence au monde comme chez Mallarmé, mais bien pour accéder à la vision d'un réel au-delà des apparences, cette surréalité que Breton et quelques autres entreprendront à leur tour de faire advenir. C'est, en effet, grâce aux possibilités infinies du symbole, qu'il croit le langage capable d'explorer ces régions où ne peut accéder la seule raison humaine. C'est pourquoi son œuvre représente la forme la plus extrême de ce courant, celle dans laquelle les composantes religieuses sont dominantes. À des éléments de la doctrine chrétienne librement réinterprétée par le poète, se mêle un composé d'ésotérisme et d'occultisme puisé dans l'enseignement de Joseph Péladan. Car Saint-Pol-Roux est l'un des premiers membres de La Rose-Croix du Temple, cette société secrète créée à l'initiative de celui qui se fait appeler le « Sâr » Péladan. Le but de ce dernier est de fonder une esthétique nouvelle qui donnerait à la démarche de l'artiste un caractère sacré, et de rassembler à cette fin quelques élus « capables de concentrer leur effort de lumière sur le plan artistique ».

Le poète qui prend assez vite ses distances vis-à-vis de ce groupe, conserve cependant de cette Rose-Croix esthétique les plus hautes ambitions. Il se voue à la poésie comme d'autres à la vie religieuse, tâchant d'incarner, aussi bien dans ses actes que dans ses œuvres, les exigences spirituelles qui sont les siennes. Qu'il choisisse la Bretagne, lors d'un voyage impromptu, pour s'y installer définitivement (« Je sentais que mon destin m'y conduisait, que je n'avais plus le droit de partir »), qu'il donne à ses enfants leurs noms de Cœcilian, Loredan, Magnus et Divine, ou qu'il mène une vie retirée dans son manoir de Camaret, tout contribue à faire de lui, de son vivant, un personnage de légende hors du siècle. Mais la rançon de cet effacement volontaire loin de Paris, est l'oubli dans lequel il tombe peu à peu. Du moins de la part du grand public, car un certain nombre de disciples continuent à encenser l'homme et son œuvre et les surréalistes lui manifestent leur admiration. À leurs yeux le Magnifique est un annonciateur, et sa démarche leur semble le trait d'union entre le symbolisme et leur mouvement. André Breton lui dédie *Clair de Terre*. Il s'en suit un regain d'intérêt pour les écrits et la personne du patriarche de Camaret. Quelques admirateurs font le pèlerinage vers le manoir de Cœcilian et le tiennent pour un Maître. À la fin de sa vie ses malheurs personnels et la perte irrémédiable de ses écrits encore inédits dans l'incendie criminel de sa maison ajoutent une aura tragique à ce destin hors du commun.

Si cette œuvre retient aujourd'hui encore l'attention, c'est d'abord par la place privilégiée qu'elle occupe entre deux siècles et le témoignage qu'elle fournit sur les ambitions de la poésie à cette époque. Ainsi par exemple *Seul et la flamme* emprunte à Victor Hugo l'épopée des origines, ou le poème barbare à Leconte de Lisle, et les transforme en une Genèse métaphysique singulière. Mais au-delà de son intérêt historique, c'est surtout par le foisonnement de métaphores surprenantes qu'elle séduit, et par le plaisir évident que prend à les multiplier un inventeur à la verve inépuisable. Enfin, si l'on néglige les présupposés théoriques, désormais datés, qui fondent la démarche du poète, c'est la modernité de certains de ses poèmes en prose qui nous frappe. Par la densité mystérieuse et imagée de leur langue, ils font déjà pressentir René Char.

SOIR DE BREBIS

La tache de sang dépoint à l'horizon de ci.

La goutte de lait point à l'horizon de là.

Homme simple qui s'éparpille dans la flûte et dont la prudence a la forme d'un chien noir, le pâtre descend l'adolescence du coteau.

Le suivent ses brebis, avec deux pampres pour oreilles et deux grappes pour mamelles, le suivent ses brebis, ambulantes vignes.

Si pur le troupeau ! que, ce soir estival, il semble neiger vers la plaine enfantinement.

Ces menus écrins de vie ont, là-haut, brouté les cassolettes, et redescendent pleines.

Mes Désirs aussi, stimulés par la flûte de l'Espoir et le chien de la Foi, montèrent ce matin le coteau du Mystère ; et s'en furent plus hauts que les brebis de mon hameau, les brebis de mon âme.

Mais parmi la prairie de jacinthes, l'odorante étoile incendia les dents avides qui voulaient dégrafer son corsage fertile.

C'est pourquoi mon troupeau subtil, à l'heure d'angélus, rentre en moi-même, les flancs désespérés. Les brebis sont au bercail, et l'homme simple va dormir entre sa flûte et son chien noir.

Les Reposoirs de la procession

MAURICE MAETERLINCK

(1862-1949)

Maurice Maeterlinck est issu, comme Verhaeren, du groupe de poètes belges d'expression française qui se regroupaient autour de la revue *La Jeune Belgique*. Mais si tous deux ont en commun leur adhésion à l'idéal symboliste, ils évoluent de façon différente. Maeterlinck poursuit toute sa vie, à travers poésie et théâtre, la quête des virtualités du symbole. Ce dernier n'est pas seulement à ses yeux la traduction de l'Idée, au sens platonicien du terme, mais il y voit surtout un instrument nécessaire à l'homme pour la connaissance de ses profondeurs. Il privilégie donc « le symbole inconscient », celui qui surgit dans l'esprit du poète comme pour lui dévoiler ses propres mystères. Des images jaillissent ainsi involontairement, liées à des états d'âme. Ce qu'elles amènent à la lumière, paysages secrets, personnages ou spectacles insolites, constitue un monde d'associations qui n'ont rien d'arbitraire : elles font apparaître une réalité essentielle, cachée derrière les apparences, et que l'on peut bien appeler déjà *surréalité*.

Son premier livre de poèmes, *Serres chaudes*, paraît en 1889, six ans plus tard il publie les *Douze Chansons*. L'originalité de ces recueils est incontestable, le lecteur se trouve soudain immergé, comme sous une cloche de verre (image chère au poète), dans l'azur opalescent d'une contrée onirique. Le retour obsédant des mêmes termes, la couleur bleue, la transparence du cristal, l'éclairage lunaire, l'immobilité et le silence contribuent à créer la magie de ces serres intérieures où de « grandes végétations », lys immobiles, roseaux ou nénuphars dormant sur « l'eau très lente », composent des paysages pareils à ceux que l'on voit en rêve.

Le théâtre de Maeterlinck, plus encore que son œuvre poétique, fit de lui le représentant, illustre entre tous, de l'école symboliste, mais il n'y a pas de hiatus entre ses deux formes d'écriture : les inventions du dramaturge participent de la même inspiration que ses poèmes, en particulier ceux des *Douze Chansons*. Dans ces dernières le poète recrée l'univers légendaire des princesses et des fées : et les sept filles d'Orlamonde

> *Les sept filles d'Orlamonde,*
> *Quand la fée fut morte,*
> *Les sept filles d'Orlamonde*
> *Ont cherché les portes*
>
> *Ont allumé leurs sept lampes*
> *Ont ouvert les tours*
> *Ont ouvert quatre cent salles*
> *Sans trouver le jour...*

ou les trois sœurs

> *Les trois sœurs ont voulu mourir*
> *Elles ont mis leur couronne d'or*
> *Et sont allées chercher leur mort...*

éveillent chez le lecteur par la vertu des nombres ou des noms, par la simplicité d'une narration allusive et leur vocabulaire emprunté au conte, toute une part de lui-même enfouie depuis l'enfance.

Ceux qui s'en tiendraient à une lecture superficielle de ces poèmes, pourraient y voir une certaine mièvrerie, et sourire de ce spleen élégant aux langueurs diaphanes. Leur style « fin de siècle » peut paraître désuet, cependant des générations successives de poètes y furent immédiatement sensibles et l'œuvre poétique de Maeterlinck, après s'être imposée à ses contemporains, a influencé Apollinaire ou Éluard. Ils se sont efforcés de retrouver la grâce d'une écriture qui ne semble qu'effleurer ce qu'elle touche, alors qu'elle explore et révèle l'obscur mais en masquant son propos sous la trompeuse apparence de la limpidité.

SERRE D'ENNUI

Ô cet ennui bleu dans le cœur !
Avec la vision meilleure,
Dans le clair de lune qui pleure,
De mes rêves bleus de langueur !

Cet ennui bleu comme la serre,
Où l'on voit closes à travers
Les vitrages profonds et verts,
Couvertes de lune et de verre,

Les grandes végétations
Dont l'oubli nocturne s'allonge,
Immobilement comme un songe,
Sur les roses des passions ;

Où de l'eau très lente s'élève,
En mêlant la lune et le ciel
En un sanglot glauque éternel,
Monotonement comme un rêve.

FEUILLAGE DU CŒUR

Sous la cloche de cristal bleu
De mes lasses mélancolies,
Mes vagues douleurs abolies
S'immobilisent peu à peu :

Végétations de symboles,
Nénuphars mornes des plaisirs,
Palmes lentes de mes désirs,
Mousses froides, lianes molles.

Seul, un lys érige d'entre eux,
Pâle et rigidement débile,
Son ascension immobile
Sur les feuillages douloureux,

Et dans les lueurs qu'il épanche
Comme une lune, peu à peu,
Élève vers le cristal bleu
Sa mystique prière blanche.

VERRE ARDENT

Je regarde d'anciennes heures,
Sous le verre ardent des regrets ;
Et du fond bleu de leurs secrets
Émergent des flores meilleures.

Ô ce verre sur mes désirs !
Mes désirs à travers mon âme !
Et l'herbe morte qu'elle enflamme
En approchant des souvenirs !

Je l'élève sur mes pensées,
Et je vois éclore au milieu
De la fuite du cristal bleu,
Les feuilles des douleurs passées.

Jusqu'à l'éloignement des soirs
Morts si longtemps en ma mémoire,
Qu'ils troublent de leur lente moire
L'âme verte d'autres espoirs.

ET S'IL REVENAIT UN JOUR

Et s'il revenait un jour
Que faut-il lui dire ?
– Dites-lui qu'on l'attendit
Jusqu'à s'en mourir...

Et s'il m'interroge encore
Sans me reconnaître ?
– Parlez-lui comme une sœur,
Il souffre peut-être...

Et s'il demande où vous êtes
Que faut-il répondre ?
– Donnez-lui mon anneau d'or
Sans rien lui répondre...

Et s'il veut savoir pourquoi
La salle est déserte ?
– Montrez-lui la lampe éteinte
Et la porte ouverte...

Et s'il m'interroge alors
Sur la dernière heure ?
– Dites-lui que j'ai souri
De peur qu'il ne pleure...

FRANCIS VIELÉ-GRIFFIN

(1864-1937)

Il est l'un des tenants les plus convaincus du vers libre. Il justifie son choix, en expliquant que la forme fixe ne doit plus passer pour le moule nécessaire à l'expression poétique, puisque ce qui a toujours été pour le poète le fondement essentiel de sa parole c'est son rythme intérieur, il se soumettra désormais à sa loi, plutôt qu'à la contrainte de règles qui lui sont imposées du dehors. Cependant cette liberté vis-à-vis de la prosodie traditionnelle n'entraîne pas chez lui de véritables audaces, et l'on entend encore, sous son vers « libéré », affleurer les cadences anciennes. Un trait fait sa singularité à l'intérieur de la mouvance symboliste : à la différence de tous les poètes spleeniques ses contemporains, reclus dans des décors précieux ou prisonniers de leurs « serres chaudes », il est un homme épris de la nature et capable d'exprimer sa joie.

Aussi échappe-t-il à la névrose de cette fin de siècle. De même, s'il est l'admirateur passionné et le disciple de Mallarmé auquel il dédie après sa mort l'hommage d'un long poème :

> . . . .
> *Je pense à vous sans douleur solennelle,*
> *Maître, vous vivez*
> *De cette vie plus haute et immortelle,*
> *De cette vie invectivée,*
> *La vie de ceux qui procréèrent leur âme*
> *Et naquirent de leur volonté,*
> *Invulnérables au rire infâme,*
> *Joyeux d'avoir vu la Beauté...*

il n'y a pas d'obscurité dans son œuvre, mais « son vers, dit André Breton admiratif, est le plus ensoleillé de l'époque, le plus fluide ».

CES HEURES-LÀ

Ces heures-là nous furent bonnes,
Comme des sœurs apitoyées ;
Heures douces et monotones,
Pâles et de brumes noyées,
Avec leurs pâles voiles de nonnes.

Ne valaient-ils donc pas nos rires,
Ces sourires sans amertumes
Vers le lourd passé dont nous fûmes ?
Ah ! chère, il est des heures pires
Que ces heures aux voiles de brumes.

Elles passaient en souriant
– Comme des nonnes vont priant –
De lueurs opalines baignées,
Les douces heures résignées.

Va, nos âmes sont encor sœurs
Des heures de l'automne grises,
Dont la pénombre dans nos cœurs
Estompait les vieilles méprises
Et nous ne voyions plus nos pleurs.

Joies

II

J'ai choisi l'automne attendri
Et cette heure des ombres longues ;
Je cueille une rose flétrie ;
On marche et les feuilles tombent.

J'ai choisi ce tournant de route
D'où le ciel est plus loin dans le soir ;
Tout est si calme ! on écoute
Des rires au fond de la mémoire...

J'ai choisi ce soir d'automne
– Je suis si lâche si tu souris –
Si j'hésite et me retourne
Je ne reverrai que la nuit.

XVII

On part... et l'automne morose
Que l'on croise au tournant du chemin
Flétrit d'un souffle les roses
Qu'on emportait dans la main ;

On part, et la pluie éployée
Comme une aile, vous frôle la joue :
La pluie banale a noyé
Tes larmes et les mêle à la boue.

On part vers l'aventure neuve ;
Hier est là en sa jeune beauté
Qui sourit sous son voile de veuve ;
On part – et l'on pourrait rester...

Les Partenza

HENRI DE RÉGNIER

(1864-1936)

On a pu voir en lui, après sa période parnassienne, le représentant le plus incontestable du symbolisme. Et c'est, en effet, à son expérience de l'écriture symbolique, autant qu'à sa connaissance approfondie de la démarche de Mallarmé, qu'il doit de pouvoir expliquer, avec une clarté dont on lui sait gré, ce qu'est le Symbole :

« Le poète cherchera moins à dire qu'à suggérer. Le lecteur aura moins à comprendre qu'à deviner. La poésie... ne chante plus, elle incante. De vocale, si l'on peut dire, elle devient musicale... Ce désir, d'être plus suggestive que péremptoire, est, je le crois bien, l'invention capitale de la poésie d'aujourd'hui... Cela explique ce qu'elle a acquis de vague, d'incertain, et de mystérieux. Le Symbole est le couronnement d'une série d'opérations intellectuelles qui commencent au mot même, passent par l'image et la métamorphose, comprennent l'emblème et l'allégorie. Il est la plus parfaite, et la plus complète figuration de l'Idée... »

Cependant, Guy Michaud, qui cite le texte d'où sont extraites ces lignes dans son *Message poétique du Symbolisme*, montre aussi comment Henri de Régnier, « à mi-chemin entre le symbolisme intellectuel d'un Mallarmé et l'impressionnisme affectif d'un Verlaine », glisse peu à peu vers un néoclassicisme. L'influence de Heredia, dont il devient le gendre n'est sans doute pas étrangère à cette évolution. Néanmoins il reste fidèle, jusque dans ses œuvres tardives, à l'emploi du vers libre : il est au premier rang de ceux qui ont contribué à l'imposer ; il continue à l'utiliser dans certains de ses poèmes, aussi bien que l'alexandrin régulier ailleurs, passant de l'un à l'autre avec une maîtrise égale, sans rompre l'harmonie de l'ensemble.

De même son œuvre, malgré ces évolutions successives, conserve, du premier au dernier recueil, une réelle unité. Celle-ci tient d'abord à son art d'esthète raffiné, à la perfection formelle de sa langue poétique et à la musicalité du vers, elle est due aussi à la permanence de thèmes qui sont liés aux constantes de son être : nostalgie du passé, sentiment mélancolique de la fuite du temps si « furtif », conscience des plus subtiles nuances du cœur. Ces leitmotive laissent deviner sa nature sensuelle et rêveuse, mais, comme il garde toujours à son propre égard la distance que lui impose une aristocratique réserve, il ne livre rien de son âme qui ne soit voilé sous des images ou des mythes réinventés.

L'ALLUSION À NARCISSE

Un enfant vint mourir, les lèvres sur tes eaux,
Fontaine ! de s'y voir au visage trop beau
Du transparent portrait auquel il fut crédule...
Les flûtes des bergers chantaient au crépuscule ;
Une fille cueillait des roses et pleura ;
Un homme qui marchait au loin se sentit las.
L'ombre vint. Les oiseaux volaient sur la prairie ;
Dans les vergers, les fruits d'une branche mûrie
Tombèrent, un à un, dans l'herbe déjà noire,
Et, dans la source claire où j'avais voulu boire,
Je m'entrevis comme quelqu'un qui s'apparaît.
Était-ce qu'à cette heure, en toi-même, mourait
D'avoir voulu poser ses lèvres sur les siennes
L'adolescent aimé des miroirs, ô Fontaine ?

Les Jeux rustiques et divins,
Anthruce

ODELETTE I

Un petit roseau m'a suffi
Pour faire frémir l'herbe haute
Et tout le pré
Et les doux saules
Et le ruisseau qui chante aussi ;
Un petit roseau m'a suffi
À faire chanter la forêt.

Ceux qui passent l'ont entendu
Au fond du soir, en leurs pensées,
Dans le silence et dans le vent,
Clair ou perdu,
Proche ou lointain...
Ceux qui passent en leurs pensées,
En écoutant, au fond d'eux-mêmes
L'entendront encore et l'entendent
Toujours qui chante.

Il m'a suffi
De ce petit roseau cueilli
À la fontaine où vint l'Amour
Mirer, un jour,
Sa face grave
Et qui pleurait,
Pour faire pleurer ceux qui passent
Et trembler l'herbe et frémir l'eau ;
Et j'ai, du souffle d'un roseau,
Fait chanter toute la forêt.

Les Jeux rustiques et divins,
La Corbeille des heures

L'INVISIBLE PRÉSENCE

Le temps furtif vient, tourne et rôde
Invisible autour de nos vies
Et l'on entend glisser sa robe
Sur le sable et sur les orties.

Il nous signale sa présence
Minutieuse et souveraine
Par un taret dans la crédence,
Par une moire en la fontaine,

Un craquement, une fêlure.
Rouille qui mord, bloc qui s'effrite,
Doigt qui laisse à la place mûre
L'empreinte où le fruit pourrit vite ;

Il ne lui faut pour qu'on l'entende
Passer au fond de nos pensées
Ni la pendule où se distendent
Les aiguilles désenlacées,

Ni l'inflexible voix de bronze
Du campanile ou des horloges,
Ni l'heure qui sonne dans l'ombre,
Ni l'angélus qui sonne à l'aube ;

Jamais il n'est plus dans nos vies
Qu'imperceptible et taciturne,
Quand il effeuille en l'eau pâlie
Les pétales du clair de lune.

Les Jeux rustiques et divins,
La Corbeille des heures

PAUL-JEAN TOULET

(1867-1920)

C'est un virtuose qui joue à composer des *Contrerimes*. Ce nom souligne le parti pris formel auquel il s'astreint dans l'agencement de ses vers, puisque, transgressant les règles de la versification traditionnelle, il substitue un schéma de rimes masculines et féminines embrassées, sur le modèle ABBA, à l'alternance des genres qui est de règle depuis le XVIᵉ siècle. Le caractère ludique de ses courts poèmes, et le ton de désinvolture et d'ironie de la plupart d'entre eux, font que nul ne mérite plus que lui l'épithète de « fantaisiste ». La tradition du badinage, toujours représentée en France depuis Marot, est encore vivante chez les romantiques, mais, au tournant du siècle, un certain nombre de poètes groupés autour de Toulet, font de la fantaisie une école, ce qui est assez inattendu ! Pour cela ils ont leurs raisons : ils veulent marquer leur rupture avec le symbolisme et, loin des rêveries mystiques et des figures obscures où se sont complus leurs aînés, renouer avec une célébration de la vie sous ses aspects les plus familiers et le faire dans un langage simple. Cette légèreté apparente se teinte le plus souvent de mélancolie, même si celle-ci se dissimule sous un sourire, et l'humour de Toulet est un humour triste, mais lui ne connaît pas le rire grinçant et la douleur déchirante d'un Laforgue, ou son refus du lyrisme. Car le choix de sujets ténus, liés aux circonstances, n'exclut des poèmes ni le chant ni leur pouvoir d'envoûtement. C'est pourquoi ce poète mineur, apparemment peu soucieux de laisser une œuvre et dont *Les Contrerimes*, les *Chansons* et les *Coples*, qu'il publie au hasard des revues, paraissent seulement après sa mort en un mince recueil de vers, occupe cependant une place privilégiée. En effet on ne peut lire ses strophes malicieuses et musicales ou ses aphorismes poétiques sans s'approprier quelques-uns de ses vers, sans adjoindre à ses propres fantômes, les « trois châtes de Provence », ces jeunes filles au pas dansant, ou « la dame aux yeux d'aventure ». Et l'on continue à entendre celui qui disait : « Prends garde à la douceur des choses. »

LES CONTRERIMES

IX

Nocturne

Ô mer, toi que je sens frémir
À travers la nuit creuse,
Comme le sein d'une amoureuse
Qui ne peut pas dormir ;

Le vent lourd frappe la falaise...
Quoi ! si le chant moqueur
D'une sirène est dans mon cœur –
Ô cœur, divin malaise.

Quoi, plus de larmes, ni d'avoir
Personne qui vous plaigne...
Tout bas, comme d'un flanc qui saigne,
Il s'est mis à pleuvoir.

X

Fô a dit...

« Ce tapis que nous tissons comme
    Le ver dans son linceul
Dont on ne voit que l'envers seul
    C'est le destin de l'homme.

Mais peut-être qu'à d'autres yeux,
    L'autre côté déploie
Le rêve, et les fleurs, et la joie
    D'un dessein merveilleux. »

Tel Fô, que l'or noir des tisanes
    Enivre, ou bien ses vers,
Chante, et s'en va tout de travers
    Entre deux courtisanes.

LVII

Dans la rue-des-Deux-Décadis
Brillait en devanture
Un citron plus beau que nature
Ou même au Paradis ;

Et tel qu'en mûrissait la terre
Où mes premiers printemps
Ombrageaient leurs jours inconstants
Sous ton arbre, ô Cythère.

Dans la rue-des-Deux-Décadis
Passa dans sa voiture
Une dame aux yeux d'aventure
Le long des murs verdis.

LVIII

C'était sur un chemin crayeux
Trois châtes de Provence
Qui s'en allaient d'un pas qui danse
Le soleil dans les yeux.

Une enseigne, au bord de la route,
– Azur et jaune d'œuf, –
Annonçait : Vin de Châteauneuf,
Tonnelles, Casse-croûte.

Et, tandis que les suit trois fois
Leur ombre violette,
Noir pastou, sous la gloriette,
Toi, tu t'en fous : tu bois...

C'était trois châtes de Provence,
Des oliviers poudreux,
Et le mistral brûlant aux yeux
Dans un azur immense.

LXX

La vie vaine n'est qu'une image
    Que l'ombre sur le mur,
Pourtant l'hiéroglyphe obscur
    Qu'y trace ton passage

M'enchante, et ton rire pareil
    Au vif éclat des armes ;
Et jusqu'à ces menteuses larmes
    Qui miraient le soleil.

Mourir non plus n'est ombre vaine
    La nuit, quand tu as peur,
N'écoute pas battre ton cœur :
    C'est une étrange peine.

CHANSONS

I

ROMANCES SANS MUSIQUE

En Arles

Dans Arle, où sont les Aliscams,
Quand l'ombre est rouge, sous les roses,
Et clair le temps,

Prends garde à la douceur des choses.
Lorsque tu sens battre sans cause
Ton cœur trop lourd ;

Et que se taisent les colombes :
Parle tout bas, si c'est d'amour,
Au bord des tombes.

COPLES

XVIII

Brouillard de l'opium tout trempé d'indolence,
Robe d'or suspendue aux jardins du silence.

LIII

Voici que j'ai touché les confins de mon âge.
Tandis que mes désirs sèchent sous le ciel nu,
Le temps passe et m'emporte à l'abyme inconnu,
Comme un grand fleuve noir, où s'engourdit la nage.

LXIII

Dessous le flamboyant qui couvre l'herbe nue
D'un dôme violet, où je vous vois encor
Fraîche comme l'eau vive en un brûlant décor,
Jeanne aux yeux ténébreux, qu'êtes-vous devenue ?

LXV

Ne crains pas que le Temps sache les cieux briser ;
Ni qu'en ses mains varient les fleurs ou les Empires.
Rien ne change. Le même lys tu le respires
Qu'autrefois Cléopâtre, – et le même baiser.

XXe SIÈCLE

Pour avoir une vue panoramique du siècle que l'on vient de quitter, il faudrait prendre en compte les nombreux poètes vivants. Certains d'entre eux sont reconnus et généralement admirés. D'autres commencent à se faire entendre. Quelques œuvres semblent ouvrir des perspectives nouvelles. Cependant, avant que le temps ait opéré une nécessaire décantation, comment faire le tri qu'imposent évidemment les limites d'un seul volume, sinon de manière arbitraire ? Qui peut dire si ce qui semble digne d'être retenu aujourd'hui subsistera demain ? Une anthologie des années vingt, présentant les poètes qui comptaient alors, mettait sur un pied d'égalité ceux qui demeurent à nos yeux les grands noms du Parnasse et beaucoup d'autres dont la notoriété passagère pouvait faire illusion, mais qui sont, depuis, tombés dans un oubli que justifie leur lecture ! On pourrait, pourtant, prendre le risque d'une approche au moins partielle de ces contemporains immédiats, si le projet de cette anthologie n'était de thésauriser plutôt que d'explorer. Pour les œuvres les plus récentes, faute de cette patine que confère aux poèmes du passé leur permanence dans la mémoire des générations successives, l'adhésion du lecteur est plus hésitante et souvent moins enthousiaste. Le tableau qui suit se limite donc volontairement aux poètes disparus. Leurs œuvres, quel qu'en soit le volume ou l'éclat particulier, s'auréolent de leur insertion dans un temps révolu, et de cet achèvement que scelle la mort du poète. Aussi ne prétend-on proposer ici autre chose qu'une esquisse fragmentaire de la poésie du XXᵉ siècle.

Celle-ci peut sembler d'abord, comme ce fut toujours le cas, l'héritière de ce qui l'a précédée. C'est assez clair avant la Première Guerre mondiale. Si, à quelques exceptions près, les poètes renoncent très tôt aux écoles et aux manifestes qui fleurissaient auparavant, ils en utilisent encore certains acquis sans les remettre réellement en question. Ainsi le Symbolisme marque de façon durable l'écriture poétique de ce siècle qui en retient le vers libre, même si elle en offre les versions les plus disparates. Surtout, les poètes paraissent plus que jamais conscients de l'importance du symbole comme moyen d'accéder à une réalité cachée, ils s'efforcent, chacun à sa manière, d'en approfondir les pouvoirs.

On peut encore apercevoir chez eux les traces d'un legs antérieur : le Surréalisme, (qui apparaît à partir de 1924, date du Premier Manifeste), renoue en effet avec le Romantisme dont il est un superbe avatar, même s'il fait un choix dans les territoires de ce prédécesseur pour n'en conserver et magnifier que la part nocturne ou l'aspect prophétique. On voit aussi parfois resurgir des signes d'appartenance à une tradition plus ancienne. L'un se réclame des troubadours ou choisit pour célébrer la femme aimée de se placer dans la lignée d'un Ronsard. Tel autre renoue, bien au-delà de l'école récente des fantaisistes, avec le badinage de Marot ou de Musset. L'épopée est réinventée, la chanson perdure, qu'elle soit complainte à la manière d'un Rutebeuf ou compromis naïf entre fable et comptine. Il en est qui se refusent à abandonner la prosodie classique et font une large place à l'octosyllabe ou à l'alexandrin. Le lecteur n'est donc pas sans repères. Et pourtant il va souffrir désormais d'un étrange dépaysement : le sol de certitudes sur lequel il cheminait jusqu'alors, passant d'un poète à l'autre – comme lorsqu'on change progressivement de paysage, en percevant à la fois l'unité de l'ensemble et la configuration particulière de chaque contrée –, s'est soudain fissuré : il lui est souvent impossible de trouver d'emblée un lien, même ténu, entre des œuvres aussi disparates que celle de Péguy et de Michaux, de Claudel et de Reverdy, ou encore de Supervielle et de Saint-John Perse. Et il ne s'agit plus ici seulement d'une diversité des genres, d'une différence de tonalité, mais plutôt de l'impossibilité de ramener aucune de ces grandes œuvres à des schémas qui leur seraient communs. On pouvait jadis hésiter un instant sur l'attribution de certains vers à l'un ou l'autre des principaux romantiques, étudier dans un même chapitre leurs conceptions de la poésie ou leurs engagements respectifs dans la bataille des idées. La possibilité de tels parallèles a désormais à peu près disparu. Si la Résistance a vu de grands poètes s'engager, dans un même combat, au risque de leur vie, et mettre leur plume au service de leur lutte, à la Libération leur destin poétique les sépare et leur génie propre, au-delà des recueils militants, ne permet guère de les regrouper. Quel rapport, par exemple, entre l'œuvre de Char dans sa maturité et celle d'Éluard ? Mais déjà la Première Guerre mondiale avait précipité cet éclatement. La contestation radicale de Dada, en rejetant les valeurs traditionnelles, a mis en cause, dès 1916, le lien implicitement admis entre raison et langage. Dada proclame qu'un monde vient de finir, qu'il faut prendre acte de sa mort de toutes les manières possibles, et d'abord en inventant un mode de création poétique sans aucun lien avec le passé. Si l'on peut penser que ce mouvement doit son prestige durable à sa volonté affichée de faire table rase et à ses excès plus qu'à ses écrits, on ne peut nier qu'il eut alors un rôle décisif. Le Surréalisme, même s'il se sépare de lui avec éclat, prolonge sa démarche en choisissant de rompre avec la « littérature ». Lui-même, cependant, ne renonce pas complètement au passé, il se reconnaît des ancêtres, non les romantiques auxquels il fait songer, mais les chantres d'une révolte radicale, Rimbaud et Lautréamont en particulier. Surtout il s'efforce d'élaborer une doctrine, de constituer un groupe, d'inventer une méthode. Cependant ce qui prévaut aux yeux du public, c'est un sentiment de nouveauté absolue, et la certitude que dorénavant le poète est libre comme il ne l'a jamais été, au point de pouvoir aller jusqu'au renoncement à l'écriture au profit d'une aventure personnelle. S'impose aussi l'idée que tout objet verbal peut mériter d'être considéré comme poème s'il est présenté comme tel ; le poète n'a de compte à rendre à personne sur ce point car la poésie réside avant tout dans l'ivresse du langage dégagé de toute contrainte. Ceux qui mesurent très tôt la part d'illusion et parfois de supercherie que peut entraîner la systématisation de cette doctrine, ne sont guère entendus (on songe par exemple à l'attitude critique d'un Caillois devant le recours trop facile à l'irrationnel). Chaque poète écrira donc sans la caution d'un modèle ou d'un principe directeur. La poésie se fait plus que jamais quête singulière, conquête d'un pouvoir, cheminement à l'issue incertaine, exploration à haut risque. Le poète qui peut se vouloir, en même temps, philosophe ou moraliste, n'est plus attaché à des formes spécifiques et ne conçoit pas de hiérarchie entre les différents modes d'expression poétique, au point que les pages qu'il propose se présentent souvent comme des hybrides inattendus, par exemple en mêlant aphorisme et verset ou encore en faisant alterner prose poétique et poème. Ces « objets poétiques » ont la particularité de n'être plus bridés par l'exigence d'un sens sinon univoque du moins circonscrit. Ils offrent à la guise de l'interprète toutes les dérives possibles des lectures arbitraires.

Les plus grands poètes imposent cependant, comme ce fut toujours le cas, la cohérence d'une vision unique. Et si la force et l'originalité de celle-ci engendre pour chacun un nouveau cosmos verbal, si le lecteur se voit obligé d'apprendre une langue nouvelle pour entrer dans leur univers, la fréquentation assidue de chaque œuvre en donne peu à peu la clef. Pour les autres, les sensibilités individuelles seront plus ou moins accordées ou fermées à tel d'entre eux. Ce qu'ils ont de commun c'est sans doute, directement ou non, ce qu'ils ont appris des surréalistes. Ces derniers, par leur application passionnée à l'exploration de nouveaux domaines et de nouveaux moyens, par leur foi aux possibilités infinies de l'homme dans cette entreprise, ont ouvert un chemin même à ceux de leurs successeurs qui se sentent les plus étrangers à leur mouvement.

Il est clair que la poésie a changé de statut, même s'il subsiste dans les œuvres citées ici bien des aspects connus, encore que renouvelés, des thèmes anciens. Le parti pris de l'exotisme ou celui du quotidien, l'exaltation des villes comme la célébration de la terre, la gouaille populaire et l'esprit d'enfance retrouvé, l'humour, la fantaisie, l'absurde y ont toujours leur place, mais s'y expriment sous des formes inattendues, et surtout dans une perspective et avec des ambitions différentes. Certes on croit encore reconnaître des veines poétiques traditionnelles, par exemple, en écoutant Apollinaire, Desnos ou Cadou, celle qui fait du poète le chantre de l'amour unique. Cependant l'essentiel pour ce siècle, ce qui, surtout dans sa deuxième moitié, a fait éclater cette cohésion et individualisé à l'extrême chacune des grandes œuvres, c'est le rang auquel la poésie se trouve désormais placée. Non plus un art parmi d'autres, même si les poètes sont attentifs comme jamais aux recherches des peintres ou des musiciens, mais l'instrument par excellence d'un dépassement, d'une invention. Cet « ailleurs » qu'annonçait Rimbaud est le but recherché ; la plupart rêvent de trouver un chemin personnel inouï vers ce qui fut la visée des anciens alchimistes : la conquête de l'absolu.

FRANCIS JAMMES

(1868-1938)

Si Virgile habitait la douce Parthénope,
Francis Jammes, poète anxieux, misanthrope
Qui dois ton franc génie à la douleur, tu vis
Dans Orthez,...

écrit Charles Guérin au début de l'hommage adressé au poète
après leur rencontre, et il le conclut par ce voeu :

Et qu'en lien touffu le laurier vert se noue
Du rossignol d'Orthez au cygne de Mantoue.

L'éclat d'un tel éloge, bien antérieur à la parution des *Géorgiques*
chrétiennes qui pourraient justifier la comparaison avec Virgile,
montre la séduction qu'exercent sur ce visiteur, et plus tard sur
tant d'autres, le charme mystérieux de la demeure provinciale,
l'homme et la chaleur de son accueil, et surtout la rare qualité du
dialogue qui s'établit avec lui : (« Je m'en venais vers toi depuis
longtemps, ô Jammes / Et je t'ai trouvé tel que je t'avais rêvé... »).
Leur amitié les amène à publier ensemble le recueil de vers qui les
fait connaître.

Bien des admirateurs feront le pèlerinage d'Orthez, et le poète, à
qui l'un de ses premiers ouvrages a valu des lettres flatteuses signées
de Mallarmé, de Gide et d'Henri de Régnier, va se lier avec quelques-
unes des personnalités les plus marquantes de son temps, qui lui
prodigueront conseils et marques d'estime. Quand paraissent après
sa mort les volumes contenant sa correspondance, on peut voir qu'il

a beaucoup conversé avec Colette, Albert Samain, Valery Larbaud, ou Gide et que, tout en ayant un statut marginal au regard du microcosme parisien, il est en rapport avec toute une pléiade d'écrivains de premier plan dans l'histoire littéraire de ce tournant du siècle. Au nombre de ses interlocuteurs illustres, il faut avant tout mentionner celui qui, à un certain moment, va jouer un rôle essentiel dans sa vie, c'est-à-dire Claudel, dont les réflexions et les encouragements l'aident à renouer avec la foi de son enfance.

Dès 1897 Francis Jammes s'affirme, avec une certaine audace, et non sans ironie, dans un Manifeste. Ce dernier, succédant pourtant à beaucoup d'autres, connaît un vif succès. En effet, après le « vers-libriste », le « romanisme », le « magnificisme » (et la liste est loin d'être exhaustive !), qui ont tour à tour affirmé leurs principes, il propose, lui, le « jammisme » dont il est, et pour cause, l'unique représentant. Avec une grande simplicité dans les termes employés, il présente ses choix en matière de poésie. Les écoles sont vaines, dit-il en substance, il n'existe qu'un système valable, la peinture du vrai, car « toutes choses sont bonnes à décrire lorsqu'elles sont naturelles, aussi bien un thyrse qu'une paire de bas », aucun sujet ne peut donc être privilégié, et la joie de vivre mérite d'être célébrée au moins autant que l'angoisse de la mort. D'ailleurs le choix du poète ne peut dépendre d'un décret extérieur, il n'obéit qu'à une seule règle : être lui-même. Il conclut en invitant tous ceux qui, comme lui, ne souhaitent point former d'école littéraire, à envoyer leur adhésion à « Orthez, Basses-Pyrénées, rue Saint-Pierre ». Le ton léger et plaisant séduit ses lecteurs, sa rupture avec le langage chiffré et obscur lui vaut nombre d'adeptes ; le « jammisme » ne tarde pas à s'imposer. Il est clair dès ce moment, et surtout quand paraît l'année suivante *De l'angélus de l'aube à l'angélus du soir*, que l'art de Francis Jammes est en marge de tous les courants existants, même si on tente de rattacher ce poète de la campagne et des paysages pyrénéens au « naturisme » surgi à la même époque. Chez lui, la peinture de la vie paysanne et des humbles est éclairée par un sentiment religieux quasi originel, plus païen que chrétien, et le style traduit fidèlement son attitude naïve en face des choses et des êtres. S'il pouvait être rattaché, dans ses tout premiers vers, au symbolisme et même au décadentisme, très tôt la voie de la sincérité et l'expression directe de ses sentiments l'en éloignent. Il dira : « Pour être vrai, j'ai parlé comme un enfant. » Pourtant il n'ignore ni la mélancolie ni le désespoir, il lui arrive, comme à ses contemporains, de peindre l'ennui ou la nostalgie du passé, mais même lorsqu'il aborde ces thèmes, il ne ressemble à aucun d'entre eux, tant il parvient à se dépouiller de toute littérature. Il trouve, en particulier pour parler des bêtes dont l'humilité s'accorde à la sienne, des accents franciscains. Il est aussi le poète des jeunes filles, il parle, avec une grâce inimitable, de celles, à peine entrevues, qui l'ont inspiré, comme la couseuse à la fenêtre dont il se souvient longtemps ; de celles qu'il a aimées, Mamoure ou Mine, et d'autres encore, mi-inventées, mi-réelles, dont les noms surannés, liés dans une même strophe, ont un charme incantatoire :

> *Clara d'Ellébeuse, Éléonore Derval,*
> *Victoire d'Étremont, Laure de la Vallée,*
> *Lia Fauchereuse, Blanche de Percival,*
> *Rose de Liméreuil et Sylvie Laboulaye.*

Ce qui domine dans son œuvre, et cela même avant son retour au christianisme, c'est l'expression d'une spiritualité, la vision intérieure d'un homme en harmonie avec le monde créé. On aime en lui la transparence de l'âme, qui sait traduire de manière sincère et savoureuse sa sensualité et ses rêves amoureux aussi bien que son ingénuité première, et ce lyrisme spontané qui joue avec le vers libre. Cependant certains ont cru devoir distinguer dans ses écrits, entre une première manière, celle qui vient d'être décrite, et une autre, moins séduisante, apparue après sa conversion, c'est-à-dire au moment où il choisit de consacrer ses vers à la louange divine, et, faisant succéder l'alexandrin ancien à la forme prosodique nouvelle, renoue avec une tradition classique. Ceux-là ont pu, comme le fait Arland, railler « les cantiques de patronage » ou dire méchamment avec Anna de Noailles : « Je préférais sa rosée à son eau bénite. » Mais la candeur de ce cœur d'enfant qui se manifeste jusque dans ses derniers *Quatrains* ne mérite pas cette sévérité, et Jammes est bien resté jusqu'au bout, suivant le mot de Gide, cet « accident heureux de notre littérature », c'est-à-dire celui chez qui les « bons sentiments » n'ont jamais contrevenu aux exigences de l'art.

Avec ton parapluie bleu et tes brebis sales,
avec tes vêtements qui sentent le fromage,
tu t'en vas vers le ciel du coteau, appuyé
sur ton bâton de houx, de chêne ou de néflier.
Tu suis le chien au poil dur et l'âne portant
les bidons ternes sur son dos saillant.
Tu passeras devant les forgerons des villages,
puis tu regagneras la balsamique montagne
où ton troupeau paîtra comme des buissons blancs.
Là, des vapeurs cachent les pics en se traînant.
Là, volent des vautours au col pelé et s'allument
des fumées rouges dans des brumes nocturnes.
Là, tu regarderas avec tranquillité,
l'esprit de Dieu planer sur cette immensité.

1897

De l'angélus de l'aube à l'angélus du soir
© Mercure de France, 1898

J'aime dans le temps Clara d'Ellébeuse,
l'écolière des anciens pensionnats,
qui allait, les soirs chauds, sous les tilleuls
lire les *magazines* d'autrefois.

Je n'aime qu'elle, et je sens sur mon cœur
la lumière bleue de sa gorge blanche.
Où est-elle ? où était donc ce bonheur ?
Dans sa chambre claire il entrait des branches.

Elle n'est peut-être pas encore morte
– ou peut-être que nous l'étions tous deux.
La grande cour avait des feuilles mortes
dans le vent froid des fins d'Été très vieux.

Te souviens-tu de ces plumes de paon,
dans un grand vase, auprès de coquillages ?...
on apprenait qu'on avait fait naufrage,
on appelait Terre-Neuve : *le Banc.*

Viens, viens, ma chère Clara d'Ellébeuse :
aimons-nous encore si tu existes.
Le vieux jardin a de vieilles tulipes.
Viens toute nue, ô Clara d'Ellébeuse.

De l'angélus de l'aube à l'angélus du soir
© Mercure de France, 1898

JE FUS À HAMBOURG...

. . . .
Comme toi, Robinson, j'essuyai des tempêtes
et, comme toi, j'ai vu au-dessus de ma tête
la mer verser au ciel des flots couleur de plomb.
Et l'amour furieux qui balayait le pont
me jetait à genoux et sifflait. Crusoë !
Crusoë ! L'océan et l'amour sont pareils :
À l'un et l'autre il faut de desséchants soleils
qui creusent notre cœur ainsi qu'une coquille ;
il faut que les agrès grincent comme des filles,
et que la passion soit cette noire mer
qui monte et nous emplit avec son bruit amer. [...]

Maintenant, comme toi, ô Crusoë ! je pense
qu'il est bon de rêver de cela dans sa chambre.
Ma cafetière bout comme un roman anglais.
J'ai des lettres d'amour que j'entends murmurer
ainsi que murmurait l'Océan Pacifique
où tu avais conduit ton âme magnifique.
Repartirai-je un jour ? Je ne l'affirme pas.
J'eusse voulu pourtant encor nouer mes bras
à la blanche bouée que nous nommons la femme,
et revenir rieur parmi les hautes lames.
Tous les oiseaux de Mars me conseillent d'aimer.
Ce matin, au réveil, leurs chants neufs s'essayaient.
Un moineau insistait beaucoup. Que vais-je faire ?
Petits oiseaux, ô rouges-gorges de mon cœur,
je ne pourrais vous suivre ou, du moins, j'en ai peur.
Les buissons sont trop verts. Je vous attristerais...
Il faut laisser tomber l'ombre sur la forêt.

Clairières dans le ciel
© Mercure de France, 1901

ÉLÉGIE X

Quand mon cœur sera mort d'aimer : sur le penchant
du coteau où les renards font leurs terriers,
à l'endroit où l'on trouve des tulipes sauvages,
que deux jeunes gens aillent par quelque jour d'Été.
Qu'ils se reposent au pied du chêne, là où les vents,
toute l'année, font se pencher les herbes fines.
Quand mon cœur sera mort d'aimer : ô jeune fille
qui suivras ce jeune homme, essoufflée et charmante,
pense à mon âme qui, en proie aux noires luttes,
cherchait sur ce coteau raclé par les grands vents
une âme d'eau d'azur qui ne la blessât plus.
Dis-toi, ô jeune fille, dis-toi : Il était fou,
pareil aux amoureux bergers de Cervantès
paissant leurs chevreaux blancs sur la paix des pelouses...
Ils délaissaient les vieilles bourgades enfumées
où Quittéria, peut-être, avait meurtri leurs cœurs.
Dis-toi : Il fut pareil à ces malheureux pâtres
qui essayaient, en vain, couchés aux belles fleurs,
de chanter leurs chagrins en soufflant dans des outres.

II

Quand mon cœur sera mort d'aimer, enviez-le.
Il passa comme un saut de truite au torrent bleu.
Il passa comme le filement d'une étoile.
Il passa comme le parfum du chèvrefeuille.
Quand mon cœur sera mort n'allez pas le chercher...
Je vous en prie : laissez-le bien dormir tranquille
sous l'yeuse où, au matin, le rouge-gorge crie
des cantiques sans fin à la Vierge Marie.

Le Deuil des primevères
© Mercure de France, 1901

PRIÈRE POUR ALLER AU PARADIS AVEC LES ÂNES

Lorsqu'il faudra aller vers vous, ô mon Dieu, faites
que ce soit par un jour où la campagne en fête
poudroiera. Je désire, ainsi que je fis ici-bas,
choisir un chemin pour aller, comme il me plaira,
au Paradis, où sont en plein jour les étoiles.
Je prendrai mon bâton et sur la grande route
j'irai, et je dirai aux ânes, mes amis :
Je suis Francis Jammes et je vais au Paradis,
car il n'y a pas d'enfer au pays du Bon-Dieu.
Je leur dirai : Venez, doux amis du ciel bleu,
pauvres bêtes chéries qui, d'un brusque mouvement d'oreille,
chassez les mouches plates, les coups et les abeilles...

Que je vous apparaisse au milieu de ces bêtes
que j'aime tant parce qu'elles baissent la tête
doucement, et s'arrêtent en joignant leurs petits pieds
d'une façon bien douce et qui vous fait pitié.
J'arriverai suivi de leurs milliers d'oreilles,
suivi de ceux qui portèrent au flanc des corbeilles,
de ceux traînant des voitures de saltimbanques
ou des voitures de plumeaux et de fer-blanc,
de ceux qui ont au dos des bidons bossués,
des ânesses pleines comme des outres, aux pas cassés,
de ceux à qui l'on met de petits pantalons
à cause des plaies bleues et suintantes que font
les mouches entêtées qui s'y groupent en ronds.
Mon Dieu, faites qu'avec ces ânes je vous vienne.
Faites que dans la paix, des anges nous conduisent
vers des ruisseaux touffus où tremblent des cerises
lisses comme la chair qui rit des jeunes filles,
et faites que, penché dans ce séjour des âmes,
sur vos divines eaux, je sois pareil aux ânes
qui mireront leur humble et douce pauvreté
à la limpidité de l'amour éternel.

Le Deuil des primevères
© Mercure de France, 1901

PRIÈRE POUR LOUER DIEU

La torpeur de midi. Une cigale éclate
dans le pin. Le figuier seul semble épais et frais
dans le brasillement de l'azur écarlate.
Je suis seul avec vous, mon Dieu, car tout se tait
sous les jardins profonds, tristes et villageois.
Les noirs poiriers luisants, à forme d'encensoir,
dorment au long des buis qui courent en guirlandes
auprès des graviers blancs comme de Saintes-Tables.
Quelques humbles labiées donnent une odeur sainte
à celui qui médite assis près des ricins.
Mon Dieu, j'aurais, jadis, ici, rêvé d'amour,
mais l'amour ne bat plus dans mon sang inutile,
et c'est en vain qu'un banc de bois noir démoli
demeure là parmi les feuillages des lys.
Je n'y mènerai pas d'amie tendre et heureuse
pour reposer mon front sur son épaule creuse.
Il ne me reste plus, mon Dieu, que la douleur
et la persuasion que je ne suis rien
que l'écho inconscient de mon âme légère
comme une effeuillaison de grappe de bruyère.
J'ai lu et j'ai souri. J'ai écrit, j'ai souri.
J'ai pensé, j'ai souri, pleuré et j'ai aussi
souri, sachant le monde impossible au bonheur,
et j'ai pleuré parfois quand j'ai voulu sourire.

Mon Dieu, calmez mon cœur, calmez mon pauvre cœur,
et faites qu'en ce jour d'été où la torpeur
s'étend comme de l'eau sur les choses égales,
j'aie le courage encore, comme cette cigale
dont éclate le cri dans le sommeil du pin,
de vous louer, mon Dieu, modestement et bien.

Le Deuil des primevères
© Mercure de France, 1901

PAUL CLAUDEL

(1868-1955)

Je chanterai le grand poëme de l'homme soustrait au hasard !...
Je le ferai avec un poëme qui ne sera plus l'aventure d'Ulysse
parmi les Lestrygons et les Cyclopes, mais la connaissance de la Terre,
Le grand poëme de l'homme enfin par delà les causes secondes
réconcilié aux forces éternelles,
La grande Voie triomphale au travers de la Terre réconciliée pour
que l'homme soustrait au hasard s'y avance !

On songe, en lisant ces versets exultants de la quatrième des
Grandes Odes, au regret exprimé par Chateaubriand, lorsqu'il
écrivait cent ans plus tôt, dans le *Génie du christianisme* : « Il est
certain que les poètes n'ont pas su tirer du merveilleux chrétien
tout ce qu'il peut fournir aux Muses », car il a fallu tout un siècle
pour qu'un poète lie étroitement Écriture sainte et poésie. Certes
la Bible était devenue entre-temps une mine poétique. Elle offrait
aux écrivains sujets et personnages, leurs écrits s'enrichissaient
des références allusives ou explicites qu'ils lui empruntaient. La
méditation sur Job ou sur le Christ, et plus encore la rêverie sur
les Anges déchus, semblaient avoir suffisamment « fourni aux
Muses ». Mais voici que surgit un poète qui ne se contente plus
d'une théologie ornementale ou des effusions d'un cœur
christianisé, mais fonde sa vision sur une lecture canonique des
textes et se veut catholique, à tous les sens du terme, mais d'abord
au sens d'universel. C'est à travers le prisme de la foi qu'il
déchiffre le monde, c'est elle qui anime son œuvre radicalement
neuve.

Sa définition de l'entreprise poétique ne rompt pas avec celle de ses prédécesseurs, mais son point de vue la renouvelle entièrement : la Création étant, selon lui, un immense poème métaphorique, le travail du poète qui s'efforce de le lire et de le traduire avec ses propres métaphores, n'a plus rien d'arbitraire ou de gratuit. En cela il se montre d'abord l'héritier de l'école symboliste, et, à travers elle, de Baudelaire, mais son théocentrisme donne une dimension nouvelle à la doctrine des Correspondances, étant donné que « par le symbole on va réellement et substantiellement à Dieu ». Derrière les symboles, en effet, c'est Dieu lui-même que l'on découvre, garant du sens, et de la cohésion dans l'univers de ce qui semblait fortuit et disparate, puisque « les choses ne sont point comme les pièces d'une machine, mais comme les éléments en travail inépuisable d'un dessin toujours nouveau ».

Ses biographes ont retracé le chemin qui l'a mené à ces certitudes.

Il y eut d'abord Rimbaud. La lecture des *Illuminations* en 1886 lui apporte, suivant ses propres termes, « la révélation du surnaturel ». Il écrit à Jacques Rivière : « Rimbaud a été l'influence capitale que j'ai subie. D'autres... ont été mes maîtres et m'ont révélé les secrets de mon art. Mais Rimbaud a eu une action que j'appellerai séminale et paternelle... » Un cri du poète, en particulier, l'a soudain délivré des fausses apparences et des simulacres : « Nous ne sommes pas au monde ! » Il n'en finira jamais de retentir en lui comme un appel décisif. Cette même année, il se convertit. Il a raconté son chemin de Damas, le foudroiement à Notre-Dame, mais il lui faudra quatre ans encore pour que s'accomplisse pleinement la mutation intérieure. La lecture de l'Écriture, et celle de saint Thomas d'Aquin fourniront à la foi retrouvée sa base théologique.

Il y eut aussi Mallarmé. Admis aux fameux mardis, Claudel écoute et se tait. Quelque admiration que lui inspire le Maître, il retient surtout de lui son questionnement de l'univers, mais les réponses qu'il propose le laissent insatisfait. Il dira un jour que le poète qui voulait laisser l'initiative aux mots eût mieux fait de la laisser au Verbe. S'il cherche, comme lui, « l'ensemble des rapports existants dans tout », ce n'est pas pour aboutir au « Livre », et pour substituer aux choses visibles « leur équation typologique », leur équivalent verbal définitif, car s'il est évident, pour lui comme pour Mallarmé, qu'il faut dépasser l'ordre des apparences, il ne s'agit pas de renier et de rejeter ces dernières. Le monde matériel est digne d'admiration, d'abord pour sa beauté délectable et parce qu'il est porteur de sens, dès lors que nous le regardons à la lumière de l'esprit dont il ne peut être séparé. Nous sommes loin ici de tout manichéisme ! Citant l'adage latin suivant lequel nous devons être entraînés de l'amour des choses visibles à celui des invisibles, Claudel souligne qu'il faut dire aussi que « de l'amour et de la connaissance des choses invisibles nous sommes induits à l'amour et à la connaissance des choses visibles ». Car la richesse du réel c'est le lien qui unit les divers aspects du monde créé. « Tout devient par rapport à Dieu », écrit-il dans un texte cité par Guy Michaud, « tout ce qui se passe est promu à la dignité d'expression, tout ce qui se passe est promu à la dignité de signification ». Or le poète est plus apte que le savant à appréhender cet aspect de la réalité : chez ce dernier prévaut « l'affirmation générale et absolue qui crée en les définissant les individus abstraits », tandis qu'il est donné au poète de comprendre « que chaque chose ne subsiste pas sur elle seule, mais dans un rapport infini avec toutes les autres ». Aussi lui incombe-t-il de traduire les liens tissés entre les objets, et par là de rendre compte de « la syntaxe de l'univers ». Mais la réalité qu'il observe n'est pas figée, elle lui apparaît en un perpétuel mouvement, et « ce mouvement n'est pas un état momentané de la matière… il est son acte permanent et le suppôt même de son existence ». Il découvre donc que le monde est en enfantement perpétuel. La vision qui en résulte est source de joie :

Et je compris l'harmonie des choses dans leur accord et dans leur succession ;
Et enfin, ayant fait la grande découverte, dans l'intelligence de l'unité et la distinction de la différence, je trouvai le ravissement.

Ce qu'exprime le personnage de Cœuvre dans ces versets de *La Ville*, Claudel en développe l'explication dans son *Art poétique*, où il pose les fondements de sa propre théorie de la connaissance. Pour lui, connaître c'est exister en même temps, c'est-à-dire « co-naître ». Le poète devra rendre compte de ce réseau de présences simultanées (« toute la nature ensemble est occupée à naître ») et du mouvement qui anime d'une « vibration fondamentale » toute créature « prise entre la fuite de son origine et la résistance que lui oppose la forme ». Or, pour épouser cette dynamique de la création, il ne peut s'en tenir à des métaphores statiques, mais il doit inventer sans cesse des rapprochements neufs, révélateurs du poème divin en cours de création. Le rythme même participe à cette transcription, et la forme nouvelle du verset répond à cette nécessité en se déployant sur le modèle du souffle vital, des pulsations du cœur et des modulations de la voix.

Les Cinq Grandes Odes sont l'illustration triomphale de cette conception originale de la poésie, mais c'est dans le drame que le poète trouve la forme la plus adéquate à son lyrisme personnel et à la fonction qu'il assigne au poème. Là où le théâtre symboliste avait tenté de rendre visibles les symboles, par le recours à des figures de conte ou à de transparentes allégories, lui parvient à donner chair et vie à des personnages qui, en signifiant leur propre histoire, laissent apparaître aussi, au-delà d'eux-mêmes, le mystérieux canevas spirituel sur lequel se dessinent leurs destins.

Personne avant Claudel n'avait accordé une telle place au poète parmi les hommes : s'il demeure le *vates*, cet interprète du divin qu'il fut dès l'origine, et si on le voit, toujours attentif au monde qui l'entoure, en rendre compte et en exalter la beauté, il devient aussi le créateur conscient qui, au moyen des mots, se fait l'auxiliaire efficace du Verbe, le témoin actif de cet Ouvrier toujours à l'œuvre dans sa Création, de ce Dieu dont il révèle aux hommes la présence, ce poète enfin à qui il incombe, dit-il, de « recevoir l'être et de restituer l'éternel ».

TÊTE D'OR

2ᵉ version

Première partie

Ô Arbre, accueille-moi ! C'est tout seul que je suis sorti de la protection de tes branches, et maintenant c'est tout seul que je m'en reviens vers toi, ô mon père immobile !

Reprends-moi donc sous ton ombrage, ô fils de la Terre ! Ô bois, à cette heure de détresse ! Ô murmurant, fais-moi part

De ce mot que je suis dont je sens en moi l'horrible effort !

Pour toi, tu n'es qu'un effort continuel, le tirement assidu de ton corps hors de la matière inanimée.

Comme tu tètes, vieillard, la terre,

Enfonçant, écartant de tous côtés tes racines fortes et subtiles !

Et le ciel, comme tu y tiens ! comme tu te bandes tout entier

À son aspiration dans une feuille immense, Forme de Feu !

La terre inépuisable dans l'étreinte de toutes les racines de ton être

Et le ciel infini avec le soleil, avec les astres dans le mouvement de l'Année,

Où tu t'attaches avec cette bouche, faite de tous tes bras, avec le bouquet de ton corps, le saisissant de tout cela en toi qui respire,

La terre et le ciel tout entiers, il les faut pour que tu te tiennes droit !

De même, que je me tienne droit ! Que je ne perde pas mon âme ! Cette sève essentielle, cette humidité intérieure de moi-même, cette effervescence

Dont le sujet est cette personne que je suis, que je ne la perde pas en une vaine touffe d'herbe et de fleurs !

Que je grandisse dans mon unité ! Que je demeure unique et droit !

Mais ce n'est point vous dont je viens aujourd'hui écouter la rumeur,

Ô branches maintenant nues parmi l'air opaque et nébuleux !

Mais je veux vous interroger, profondes racines, et ce fonds original de la terre où vous vous nourrissez.

Tête d'or

© Mercure de France, 1901

LE SOULIER DE SATIN
1re version
Troisième journée, scène XIII

Le Vice-Roi. – Officiers, compagnons d'armes, hommes assemblés ici qui respirez vaguement autour de moi dans l'obscurité,

Et qui tous avez entendu parler de la lettre à Rodrigue et de ce long désir entre cette femme et moi qui est un proverbe depuis dix ans entre les deux Mondes,

Regardez-la, comme ceux-là qui de leurs yeux maintenant fermés ont pu regarder Cléopâtre, ou Hélène, ou Didon, ou Marie d'Écosse,

Et toutes celles qui ont été envoyées sur la terre pour la ruine des Empires et des Capitaines et pour la perte de beaucoup de villes et de bateaux.

L'amour a achevé son œuvre sur toi, ma bien-aimée, et le rire sur ton visage a été remplacé par la douleur et l'or pour te couronner par la couleur mystérieuse de la neige.

Mais cela en toi qui autrefois m'a fait cette promesse, sous cette forme maintenant rapprochée de la disparition,

N'a pas cessé un moment de ne pas être ailleurs.

Cette promesse entre ton âme et la mienne par qui le temps un moment a été interrompu,

Cette promesse que tu m'as faite, cet engagement que tu as pris, ce devoir envers moi que tu as assumé,

Elle est telle que la mort aucunement

Envers moi n'est pas propre à t'en libérer,

Et que si tu ne la tiens pas mon âme au fond de l'Enfer pour l'éternité t'accusera devant le trône de Dieu.

Meurs puisque tu le veux, je te le permets ! Va en paix, retire pour toujours de moi le pied de ta présence adorée !

Consomme l'absence !

La joie d'un être est-elle pas dans sa perfection ? et si notre perfection est d'être nous-mêmes, cette personne exactement que le destin nous a donnée à remplir,

D'où vient cette profonde exultation comme le prisonnier qui dans le mur entend la sape au travail qui le désagrège, quand le trait de la mort dans notre côté s'est enfoncé en vibrant ?

Ainsi la vue de cet Ange pour moi qui fut comme le trait de la mort ! Ah ! cela prend du temps de mourir et la vie la plus longue n'est pas de trop pour apprendre à correspondre à ce patient appel !

Une blessure à mon côté comme la flamme peu à peu qui tire toute l'huile de la lampe !

Et si la perfection de l'œil n'est pas dans sa propre géométrie mais dans la lumière qu'il voit et chaque objet qu'il montre

Et la perfection de la main non pas dans ses doigts mais dans l'ouvrage qu'elle génère,

Pourquoi aussi la perfection de notre être et de notre noyau substantiel serait-elle toujours associée à l'opacité et à la résistance,

Et non pas l'adoration et le désir et la préférence d'autre chose et de livrer sa lie pour de l'or et de céder son temps pour l'éternité et de se présenter à la transparence et de se fendre enfin et de s'ouvrir enfin dans un état de dissolution ineffable ?

De ce déliement, de cette délivrance mystique nous savons que nous sommes par nous-mêmes incapables et de là ce pouvoir sur nous de la femme pareil à celui de la Grâce.

Le Soulier de satin
© Éditions Gallimard

LES MUSES

. . . .

Je vous ai reconnu, ô conseil complet des neuf Nymphes intérieures !

Phrase mère ! engin profond du langage et peloton des femmes vivantes !

Présence créatrice ! Rien ne naîtrait si vous n'étiez neuf !

Voici soudain, quand le poète nouveau comblé de l'explosion intelligible,

La clameur noire de toute la vie nouée par le nombril dans la commotion de la base,

S'ouvre, l'accès

Faisant sauter la clôture, le souffle de lui-même

Violentant les mâchoires coupantes,

Le frémissant Novénaire avec un cri !

Maintenant il ne peut plus se taire ! L'interrogation sortie de lui-même, comme du chanvre

Aux femmes de journée, il l'a confiée pour toujours

Au savant chœur de l'inextinguible Écho !

. . . .

Pour toi, Mnémosyne, ces premiers vers, et la déflagration de l'Ode soudaine !

Ainsi subitement du milieu de la nuit que mon poëme de tous côtés frappe comme l'éclat de la foudre trifourchue !

Et nul ne peut prévoir où soudain elle fera fumer le soleil,

Chêne, ou mât de navire, ou l'humble cheminée, liquéfiant le pot comme un astre !

Ô mon âme impatiente ! nous n'établirons aucun chantier ! nous ne pousserons, nous ne roulerons aucune trirème

Jusqu'à une grande Méditerranée de vers horizontaux,

Pleine d'îles, praticable aux marchands, entourée par les ports de tous les peuples !

Nous avons une affaire plus laborieuse à concerter

Que ton retour, patient Ulysse !

Toute route perdue ! sans relâche pourchassé et secouru

Par les dieux chauds sur la piste, sans que tu voies rien d'eux
que parfois
   La nuit un rayon d'or sur la Voile, et dans la splendeur du matin,
un moment,
      Une face radieuse aux yeux bleus, une tête couronnée de persil,
Jusqu'à ce jour que tu restas seul !
   Quel combat soutenaient la mère et l'enfant, dans Ithaque là-
bas,
      Cependant que tu reprisais ton vêtement, cependant que tu
interrogeais les Ombres,
      Jusque la longue barque Phéacienne te ramenât, accablé d'un
sommeil profond !
   Et toi aussi, bien que ce soit amer,
      Il me faut enfin délaisser les bords de ton poëme, ô Énée, entre
les deux mondes l'étendue de ses eaux pontificales !
      Quel calme s'est fait dans le milieu des siècles, cependant qu'en
arrière la patrie et Didon brûlent fabuleusement !
      Tu succombes à la main ramifère ! tu tombes, Palinure, et ta
main ne retient plus le gouvernail.
      Et d'abord on ne voyait que leur miroir infini, mais soudain sous
la propagation de l'immense sillage,
      Elles s'animent et le monde entier se peint sur l'étoffe magique.
      Car voici que par le grand clair de lune
      Le Tibre entend venir la nef chargée de la fortune de Rome
      Mais maintenant, quittant le niveau de la mer liquide,
      Ô rimeur Florentin ! nous ne te suivrons point, pas après pas,
dans ton investigation,
      Descendant, montant jusqu'au ciel, descendant jusque dans
l'Enfer,
      Comme celui qui assurant un pied sur le sol logique avance
l'autre en une ferme enjambée.
      Et comme quand en automne on marche dans des flaques de
petits oiseaux,
      Les ombres et les images par tourbillons s'élèvent sous ton pas
suscitateur !
      Rien de tout cela ! toute route à suivre nous ennuie ! toute
échelle à escalader !
      Ô mon âme ! le poème n'est point fait de ces lettres que je
plante comme des clous, mais du blanc qui reste sur le papier.

Ô mon âme ! il ne faut concerter aucun plan ! ô mon âme sauvage, il faut nous tenir libres et prêts,

Comme les immenses bandes fragiles d'hirondelles quand sans voix retentit l'appel automnal !

Ô mon âme impatiente, pareille à l'aigle sans art ! comment ferions-nous pour ajuster aucun vers ? à l'aigle qui ne sait pas faire son nid même ?

Que mon vers ne soit rien d'esclave ! mais tel que l'aigle marin qui s'est jeté sur un grand poisson,

Et l'on ne voit rien qu'un éclatant tourbillon d'ailes et l'éclaboussement de l'écume !

Mais vous ne m'abandonnerez point, ô Muses modératrices.

. . . .

Ô mon amie sur le navire ! (Car l'année qui fut celle-là

Quand je commençai à voir le feuillage se décomposer et l'incendie du monde prendre,

Pour échapper aux saisons le soir frais me parut une aurore, l'automne le printemps d'une lumière plus fixe,

Je le suivis comme une armée qui se retire en brûlant tout derrière elle. Toujours

Plus avant, jusqu'au cœur de la mer luisante !)

Ô mon amie ! car le monde n'était plus là

Pour nous assigner notre place dans la combinaison de son mouvement multiplié,

Mais décollés de la terre, nous étions seuls l'un avec l'autre,

Habitants de cette noire miette mouvante, noyés,

Perdus dans le pur Espace, là où le sol même est lumière.

Et chaque soir, à l'arrière, à la place où nous avions laissé le rivage, vers l'Ouest,

Nous allions retrouver la même conflagration

Nourrie de tout le présent bondé, la Troie du monde réel en flammes !

Et moi, comme la mèche allumée d'une mine sous la terre, ce feu secret qui me ronge,

Ne finira-t-il point par flamber dans le vent ? qui contiendra la grande flamme humaine ?

Toi-même, amie, tes grands cheveux blonds dans le vent de la mer,

Tu n'as pas su les tenir bien serrés sur ta tête ; ils s'effondrent ! les lourds anneaux

Roulent sur tes épaules, la grande chose joconde

S'enlève, tout part dans le clair de la lune !

Et les étoiles ne sont-elles point pareilles à des têtes d'épingles luisantes ? et tout l'édifice du monde ne fait-il pas une splendeur aussi fragile

Qu'une royale chevelure de femme prête à crouler sous le peigne !

Ô mon amie ! ô Muse dans le vent de la mer ! ô idée chevelue à la proue !

Ô grief ! ô revendication !

Érato ! tu me regardes, et je lis une résolution dans tes yeux !

Je lis une réponse, je lis une question dans tes yeux ! Une réponse et une question dans tes yeux !

Le hourra qui prend en toi de toutes parts comme de l'or, comme du feu dans le fourrage !

Une réponse dans tes yeux ! Une réponse et une question dans tes yeux.

Paris, 1900.
Foutchéou, 1904.

Les Cinq Grandes Odes
© Éditions Gallimard

L'ESPRIT ET L'EAU

Après le long silence fumant,
Après le grand silence civil de maints jours tout fumant de
rumeurs et de fumées,
Haleine de la terre en culture et ramage des grandes villes dorées,
Soudain l'Esprit de nouveau, soudain le souffle de nouveau,
Soudain le coup sourd au cœur, soudain le mot donné, soudain
le souffle de l'Esprit, le rapt sec, soudain la possession de l'Esprit !
Comme quand dans le ciel plein de nuit avant que ne claque le
premier feu de foudre,
Soudain le vent de Zeus, dans un tourbillon plein de pailles et
de poussières avec la lessive de tout le village !

Mon Dieu, qui au commencement avez séparé les eaux
supérieures des eaux inférieures,
Et qui de nouveau avez séparé de ces eaux humides que je dis,
L'aride, comme un enfant divisé de l'abondant corps maternel,
La terre bien chauffante, tendre-feuillante et nourrie du lait de
la pluie,
Et qui dans le temps de la douleur comme au jour de la création
saisissez dans votre main toute-puissante
L'argile humaine et l'esprit de tous côtés vous gicle entre les
doigts,
De nouveau après les longues routes terrestres,
Voici l'Ode, voici que cette grande Ode nouvelle vous est
présente,
Non point comme une chose qui commence, mais peu à peu
comme la mer qui était là,
La mer de toutes les paroles humaines avec la surface en divers
endroits
Reconnue par un souffle sous le brouillard et par l'œil de la
matrone Lune !

Les Cinq Grandes Odes
© Éditions Gallimard

LA MUSE QUI EST LA GRÂCE

Encore ! encore la mer qui revient me rechercher comme une barque,

La mer encore qui retourne vers moi à la marée de syzygie et me lève et remue de mon ber comme une galère allégée,

Comme une barque qui ne tient plus qu'à sa corde, et qui danse furieusement, et qui tape, et qui saque, et qui fonce, et qui encense, et qui culbute, le nez à son piquet,

Comme le grand pur-sang que l'on tient aux naseaux et qui tangue sous le poids de l'amazone qui bondit sur lui de côté et qui saisit brutalement les rênes avec un rire éclatant !

Encore la nuit qui revient me rechercher,

Comme la mer qui atteint sa plénitude en silence à cette heure qui joint à l'Océan les ports humains pleins de navires attendants et qui décolle la porte et le batardeau !

Encore le départ, encore la communication établie, encore la porte qui s'ouvre !

Ah, je suis las de ce personnage que je fais entre les hommes ! Voici la nuit ! Encore la fenêtre qui s'ouvre !

Et je suis comme la jeune fille à la fenêtre du beau château blanc, dans le clair de lune,

Qui entend, le cœur bondissant, ce bienheureux sifflement sous les arbres et le bruit de deux chevaux qui s'agitent,

Et elle ne regrette point la maison, mais elle est comme un petit tigre qui se ramasse, et tout son cœur est comme soulevé par l'amour de la vie et par la grande force comique !

Hors de moi la nuit, et en moi la fusée de la force nocturne, et le vin de la Gloire, et le mal de ce cœur trop plein !

Si le vigneron n'entre pas impunément dans la cuve,

Croirez-vous que je sois puissant à fouler ma grande vendange de paroles,

Sans que les fumées m'en montent au cerveau !

Ah, ce soir est à moi ! ah, cette grande nuit est à moi ! tout le gouffre de la nuit comme la salle illuminée pour la jeune fille à son premier bal !

Elle ne fait que de commencer ! il sera temps de dormir un autre jour !

Ah, je suis ivre ! ah, je suis livré au dieu ! j'entends une voix en moi et la mesure qui s'accélère, le mouvement de la joie,

L'ébranlement de la cohorte Olympique, la marche divinement tempérée !

Que m'importent tous les hommes à présent ! Ce n'est pas pour eux que je suis fait, mais pour le

Transport de cette mesure sacrée !

Ô le cri de la trompette bouchée ! ô le coup sourd sur la tonne orgiaque !

Que m'importe aucun d'eux ? Ce rythme seul ! Qu'ils me suivent ou non ? Que n'importe qu'ils m'entendent ou pas ?

Voici le dépliement de la grande Aile poétique !

Que me parlez-vous de la musique ? laissez-moi seulement mettre mes sandales d'or !

Je n'ai pas besoin de tout cet attirail qu'il lui faut. Je ne demande pas que vous vous bouchiez les yeux.

Les mots que j'emploie,

Ce sont les mots de tous les jours, et ce ne sont point les mêmes !

Vous ne trouverez point de rimes dans mes vers ni aucun sortilège. Ce sont vos phrases mêmes. Pas aucune de vos phrases que je ne sache reprendre !

Ces fleurs sont vos fleurs et vous dites que vous ne les reconnaissez pas.

Et ces pieds sont vos pieds, mais voici que je marche sur la mer et que je foule les eaux de la mer en triomphe !

Les Cinq Grandes Odes
© Éditions Gallimard

ANDRÉ GIDE

(1869-1951)

Gide a renié ses premiers vers, les *Poésies d'André Walter,* tout imprégnées de symbolisme. Il donne, quelques années plus tard, avec *Les Nourritures terrestres,* un récit autobiographique dont certaines pages ont la forme et le rythme de poèmes en prose. L'ouvrage passe inaperçu lors de sa parution mais il devient la bible de la génération suivante, avant de retomber dans un demi-oubli.

Le livre se présente, écrit Gide dans la préface de 1927, comme « un manuel d'évasion, de délivrance... » L'auteur y transmet à son disciple, Nathanaël, l'enseignement qu'il a lui-même reçu de Ménalque... L'avertissement précise que maître et disciple sont imaginaires. Seules les « nourritures terrestres » ne doivent rien à la fiction, s'attacher à les décrire c'est privilégier le réel. Pour une époque surtout attentive aux symboles, l'éloge passionné de la sensualité que suppose ce choix apparaît comme audacieux et neuf : « Nathanaël, j'aimerais te donner une joie que ne t'aurait donnée encore aucun autre. » Cette joie ne peut se trouver dans les livres, c'est le monde qui l'offre à qui veut la saisir. Inépuisable réserve de délices, il les propose à chaque instant à l'homme capable d'entretenir en lui la soif et l'attente, à celui qui osera dire comme l'auteur : « J'ai porté hardiment ma main sur chaque chose et me suis cru des droits sur chaque objet de mes désirs. »

Prôner une liberté que ne limite aucun interdit et un état d'incessante disponibilité aux plaisirs rencontrés, enseigner par l'exemple un hédonisme sans frein (« J'espère bien avoir connu toutes les passions et tous les vices, au moins les ai-je favorisés ») risquait de choquer. C'est ce que voulait Gide qui célébrait ainsi sa rupture avec l'austère morale qu'on lui avait inculquée, désormais il pouvait écrire : « Nathanaël, je ne crois plus au péché. » Plus tard il devait ouvertement assumer la liberté sexuelle dont il faisait alors dans ces pages la confidence voilée.

Ce qui retient le lecteur d'aujourd'hui, à qui le propos du livre peut paraître suranné, c'est l'élan lyrique des plus belles pages, la « ferveur » poétique qu'elles ont le pouvoir de communiquer.

Nathanaël, je t'enseignerai la ferveur.

Nos actes s'attachent à nous comme sa lueur au phosphore. Ils nous consument, il est vrai, mais ils nous font notre splendeur.

Et si notre âme a valu quelque chose, c'est qu'elle a brûlé plus ardemment que quelques autres.

Je vous ai vus, grands champs baignés de la blancheur de l'aube ; lacs bleus, je me suis baigné dans vos flots – et que chaque caresse de l'air riant m'ait fait sourire, voilà ce que je ne me lasserai pas de te redire, Nathanaël. Je t'enseignerai la ferveur.

Si j'avais su des choses plus belles, c'est celles-là que je t'aurais dites – celles-là, certes, et non pas d'autres.

Tu ne m'as pas enseigné la sagesse, Ménalque.
Pas la sagesse, mais l'amour.

Les Nourritures terrestres, Livre I, 1
© Éditions Gallimard

PIERRE LOUŸS

(1870-1925)

C'est un érudit et un précieux. Sa connaissance de la littérature grecque et de l'Antiquité classique le rendent assez proche des parnassiens. D'ailleurs il admire Leconte de Lisle ainsi que Heredia. Il épousera l'une des filles de ce dernier. Mais avant même de devenir le gendre du poète, il fréquente les cercles symbolistes et reçoit dans sa garçonnière des artistes, peintres, poètes, sculpteurs ou musiciens comme Debussy, tous conscients qu'existe une correspondance entre les arts, tous, à des degrés divers, passionnés de symboles. Il a fait connaître Mallarmé au jeune Valéry avec qui il se lie d'amitié, Gide les rejoint bientôt. Ensemble ils demandent au Maître son patronage pour *La Conque*, la revue à tirage limité qu'ils viennent de fonder et dont ils veulent faire la tribune des idées nouvelles, ils publient là leurs premiers vers. Plus tard Pierre Louÿs réunit les siens dans un volume qui paraît en 1893, sous le titre d'*Astarté*. La même année il traduit les *Poésies* de Méléagre et peu après les *Scènes de la vie des courtisanes* de Lucien. Mais ce qui va le rendre célèbre, c'est, en 1894, un recueil de courts poèmes en prose : *Les Chansons de Bilitis*. Bien qu'il les présente comme l'œuvre retrouvée d'une poétesse grecque contemporaine de Sappho, dont il serait le traducteur, c'est à sa seule imagination que l'on doit la gracieuse figure de Bilitis, qui « le jour où elle cessa d'être aimée... cessa d'écrire », et les presque deux cents poèmes qu'il lui attribue. À travers eux se dessine l'enfance pastorale de son héroïne, puis sa venue à Lesbos et ses amours avec la très jeune Mnasidika, enfin son destin de courtisane consacrée au service du culte d'Aphrodite, et les trois épitaphes destinées à son tombeau. La grâce de ce récit fragmenté en petits tableaux, le pittoresque des détails précis empruntés à la vie quotidienne des Grecs, l'art avec lequel le poète redonne vie à l'idylle antique, suffisent à justifier un succès auquel l'érotisme léger de ces pages ajouta, à l'époque de leur parution, un léger parfum de scandale.

On pourra lire ici à côté d'une chanson prise dans ce recueil, plutôt que les strophes à la facture classique de *Pervigilium Mortis*, son dernier recueil de vers, souvent cité, un poème de jeunesse qui montre l'influence probable de Verlaine sur le jeune poète, dont témoignent le mépris de la rime et la préférence pour « l'impair ».

Je chanterai des vers de onze syllabes,
De grands vers murmurés, des vers rouge et or,
Comme je les entends battre à mon oreille ;
Je chanterai la strophe éparse et distraite,
Bouclée au dernier mot par l'appel du cor.

J'ouvrirai sans effort le carcan des rimes,
Ô muse ! qui serra ta gorge longtemps !
– On entendra briller le chant des sourires. –
Tu quitteras pour moi les voiles antiques,
Idole vénérée aux seins éclatants.

Je chanterai le rythme, *unique harmonie,*
Souffle vivant du vers, chant mystérieux,
– On entendra bondir les voix sanglotantes –
Et j'oserai scander l'homme et la nature
Aux battements du cœur, aux sanglots des yeux.

Je dirai pour moi seul la douceur d'écrire
Et je posséderai mon rêve en rêvant ;
– On entendra frémir des odeurs de femme –
Je dirai les frissons amoureux qui passent
Et laissent le poète au soleil levant.

1889

Les Chansons de Bilitis
© Éditions Albin Michel

DERNIÈRE ÉPITAPHE

Sous les feuilles noires des lauriers, sous les fleurs amoureuses des roses, c'est ici que je suis couchée, moi qui sus tresser le vers au vers, et faire fleurir le baiser.

J'ai grandi sur la terre des nymphes ; j'ai vécu dans l'île des amies ; je suis morte dans l'île de Kypris. C'est pourquoi mon nom est illustre et ma stèle frottée d'huile.

Ne me pleure pas, toi qui t'arrêtes ; on m'a fait de belles funérailles : les pleureuses se sont arraché les joues ; on a couché dans ma tombe mes miroirs et mes colliers.

Et maintenant, sur les pâles prairies d'asphodèles, je me promène, ombre impalpable, et le souvenir de ma vie terrestre est la joie de ma vie souterraine.

Les Chansons de Bilitis
© Éditions Albin Michel

PAUL VALÉRY

(1871-1945)

Ce qui fait la singularité de son œuvre poétique, c'est qu'en dépit de son importance, elle n'occupe pas une place majeure dans l'ensemble de ses écrits, et même si nous plaçons très haut Valéry, il n'est jamais poète à la manière de Hugo, Claudel ou Aragon qui le demeurent jusque dans la masse de leurs écrits en prose : lui, au contraire, semble ne l'avoir été que par accident, et presque à regret, tant la réflexion sur l'acte créateur l'emportait dans son esprit sur la création elle-même. Et pourtant il n'y a pas non plus dans sa vie ce renoncement définitif à la poésie, observé chez tant d'écrivains qui ont commencé en écrivant des vers, puis, passée leur jeunesse, en sont venus à d'autres modes d'écriture. Il a quarante-six ans lorsqu'il compose cette œuvre majeure qu'est *La Jeune Parque*, et plus de cinquante ans lorsque paraît *Charmes*.

Très tôt, on l'a vu, quelques vers de lui avaient été publiés dans *La Conque*, mais en 1892, au cours d'un crise morale, il choisit de renoncer à cet excès de sensibilité qu'engendre le commerce des arts et décide de privilégier désormais la démarche de connaissance, et d'abord celle que l'on peut exercer sur soi. De l'examen intérieur permanent qu'il entreprend alors, naîtront les deux cent cinquante quatre *Cahiers* publiés après sa mort, qu'il remplira jour après jour, sa vie durant, et cette crise engendre aussi *Monsieur Teste*, ce personnage qu'on est tenté d'identifier au poète. Il est clair en effet, bien que Valéry refuse de lui être assimilé, qu'il s'est donné là un double caricatural, auquel il prête sa passion de l'introspection et la volonté qui est la sienne d'arriver à une maîtrise parfaite de l'intellect.

Lorsque ses amis l'invitent en 1917 à regrouper ses premiers vers en un volume, le désir lui vient de les compléter à l'aide d'un « exercice » poétique qui donne naissance à *La Jeune Parque*. Il compose ensuite le long poème du *Cimetière marin*, sans doute son chef-d'œuvre, livre enfin au public, la même année, dans *L'Album de vers anciens*, ses poèmes de jeunesse jusqu'alors dispersés dans des revues, puis, en 1922, le recueil de *Charmes*.

Les vers de Valéry, des plus obscurs aux plus immédiatement accessibles, apparaissent, autant que ses *Dialogues* et ses pages de critique littéraire, comme les moments d'une pensée qui réfléchit sur soi et sur l'acte créateur. Si on les lit dans l'ordre où ils furent écrits, *L'Album* témoigne encore de l'influence directe du symbolisme sur l'auteur, comme on le voit dans *Le Bois dormant* lorsqu'il peint « la princesse, dans un palais de rose pure »... Surtout les réminiscences mallarméennes y affleurent, ainsi de ces Vaines Danseuses...

> *Troupe divine et douce errante sous les nues*
> *Qu'effleure ou crée un clair de lune... Les voici*
> *Mélodieuses fuir dans le bois éclairci...*

autour d'elles le décor « de mourantes roses » et « l'eau frêle où dort le pur oubli » recréent l'univers précieux des « bois de roses sous l'azur / Naturel... » chers à « l'enfance adorable » du Maître. Mais l'originalité poétique de Valéry se manifeste ensuite pleinement par l'intellectualisation des symboles. S'il n'a pas renié l'esthétique de perfection et de recherche formelle héritée de Mallarmé, il la met au service, non de l'improbable « Livre », mais d'une exploration de ses domaines intérieurs et à travers eux de l'énigme de l'esprit humain. Et sa recherche l'amène à doter ses poèmes d'une rigoureuse architecture interne, même si celle-ci ne se révèle que progressivement. La critique a montré comment les vingt-quatre strophes du *Cimetière marin*, sous le déroulement d'une méditation qui semble procéder librement par associations d'idées, suit un plan strict en six parties de quatre sixains chacune, consacrées successivement à la mer, au poète, au cimetière, aux morts puis à la philosophie de la mort et à celle de la vie, et comment dans chacune de ces parties trois figures essentielles incarnent les trois pôles de la pensée, le soleil correspondant ici à l'être absolu, la mer à l'être relatif, et le cimetière au non-être. Même si d'autres lectures sont possibles, ce qu'il faut retenir de chacune d'elles c'est qu'elles proposent toujours de voir dans ce poème une parfaite maîtrise de la pensée. Le poète ne se laisse pas emporter, il conduit sa méditation. Son lyrisme est volontairement contenu. Celui qui notait dans *Variété* : « Notre poésie ignore et même redoute tout l'épique et le pathétique de l'intellect » ou qui exprimait ce regret : « Nous n'avons point encore chez nous de poète de la connaissance » a tenté d'être ce poète et, prenant conscience, comme le souligne Émilie Noulet dans son étude sur Valéry, que l'intelligence dans l'exercice normal de sa force ne révèle que peu de choses de ses mécanismes et s'efface devant les idées qu'elle produit, s'est attaché à l'épier dans ses états limites c'est-à-dire dans sa faiblesse ou dans sa toute-puissance : au réveil quand elle n'est pas sur ses gardes, comme dans *Aurore*, ou à son point pur comme dans *Le Cimetière marin*. D'où l'obscurité de certains poèmes, moins réellement obscurs que difficiles, à cause de l'abstraction de leur sujet. Ce qui retient d'abord en eux, malgré l'obstacle du sens, c'est ce qu'Émilie Noulet appelle joliment « le velouté de l'abstraction », car dans ses vers il sait unir la sensation à l'idée, et l'emploi précis des mots n'exclut jamais chez lui la recherche de l'effet musical qu'il tire de leur sonorité. Son œuvre poétique illustre parfaitement la célèbre définition qu'il propose de la poésie, et qui est si proche de l'idéal classique :

« La véritable condition d'un véritable poète est ce qu'il y a de plus distinct de l'état de rêve. Je n'y vois que recherches volontaires, assouplissement des pensées, consentement de l'âme à des gênes exquises, et le triomphe perpétuel du sacrifice. »

LA FILEUSE

Lilia..., neque nent

Assise, la fileuse au bleu de la croisée
Où le jardin mélodieux se dodeline ;
Le rouet ancien qui ronfle l'a grisée.

Lasse, ayant bu l'azur, de filer la câline
Chevelure, à ses doigts si faibles évasive,
Elle songe, et sa tête petite s'incline.

Un arbuste et l'air pur font une source vive
Qui, suspendue au jour, délicieuse arrose
De ses pertes de fleurs le jardin de l'oisive.

Une tige, où le vent vagabond se repose,
Courbe le salut vain de sa grâce étoilée,
Dédiant magnifique, au vieux rouet, sa rose.

Mais la dormeuse file une laine isolée ;
Mystérieusement l'ombre frêle se tresse
Au fil de ses doigts longs et qui dorment, filée.

Le songe se dévide avec une paresse
Angélique, et sans cesse, au doux fuseau crédule,
La chevelure ondule au gré de la caresse...

Derrière tant de fleurs, l'azur se dissimule,
Fileuse de feuillage et de lumière ceinte :
Tout le ciel vert se meurt. Le dernier arbre brûle.

Ta sœur, la grande rose où sourit une sainte,
Parfume ton front vague au vent de son haleine
Innocente, et tu crois languir... Tu es éteinte

Au bleu de la croisée où tu filais la laine.

Album de vers anciens
© Éditions Gallimard

FRAGMENTS DU NARCISSE

I

Cur aliquid vidi ?

Que tu brilles enfin, terme pur de ma course !

Ce soir, comme d'un cerf, la fuite vers la source
Ne cesse qu'il ne tombe au milieu des roseaux,
Ma soif me vient abattre au bord même des eaux.
Mais, pour désaltérer cette amour curieuse,
Je ne troublerai pas l'onde mystérieuse :
Nymphes ! si vous m'aimez, il faut toujours dormir !
La moindre âme dans l'air vous fait toutes frémir ;
Même, dans sa faiblesse, aux ombres échappée,
Si la feuille éperdue effleure la napée,
Elle suffit à rompre un univers dormant...
. . . .
Rêvez, rêvez de moi !... Sans vous, belles fontaines,
Ma beauté, ma douleur, me seraient incertaines.
Je chercherais en vain ce que j'ai de plus cher,
Sa tendresse confuse étonnerait ma chair,
Et mes tristes regards, ignorants de mes charmes,
À d'autres que moi-même adresseraient leurs larmes...
. . . .
Heureux vos corps fondus, Eaux planes et profondes !
Je suis seul !... Si les Dieux, les échos et les ondes
Et si tant de soupirs permettent qu'on le soit !
Seul !... mais encor celui qui s'approche de soi
Quand il s'approche aux bords que bénit ce feuillage...
Des cimes, l'air déjà cesse le pur pillage ;
La voix des sources change, et me parle du soir ;
Un grand calme m'écoute, où j'écoute l'espoir.
J'entends l'herbe des nuits croître dans l'ombre sainte,
Et la lune perfide élève son miroir
Jusque dans les secrets de la fontaine éteinte...
Jusque dans les secrets que je crains de savoir,
Jusque dans le repli de l'amour de soi-même,
Rien ne peut échapper au silence du soir...
La nuit vient sur ma chair lui souffler que je l'aime.

Sa voix fraîche à mes vœux tremble de consentir ;
À peine, dans la brise, elle semble mentir,
Tant le frémissement de son temple tacite
Conspire au spacieux silence d'un tel site.

Ô douceur de survivre à la force du jour,
Quand elle se retire enfin rose d'amour,
Encore un peu brûlante, et lasse, mais comblée,
Et de tant de trésors tendrement accablée
Par de tels souvenirs qu'ils empourprent sa mort,
Et qu'ils la font heureuse agenouiller dans l'or,
Puis s'étendre, se fondre, et perdre sa vendange,
Et s'éteindre en un songe en qui le soir se change.
    Quelle perte en soi-même offre un si calme lieu !
L'âme, jusqu'à périr, s'y penche pour un Dieu
Qu'elle demande à l'onde, onde déserte, et digne
Sur son lustre, du lisse effacement d'un cygne...
. . . .

II

Fontaine, ma fontaine, eau froidement présente,
Douce aux purs animaux, aux humains complaisante
Qui d'eux-mêmes tentés suivent au fond la mort,
Tout est songe pour toi, Sœur tranquille du Sort !
À peine en souvenir change-t-il un présage,
Que pareille sans cesse à son fuyant visage,
Sitôt de ton sommeil les cieux te sont ravis !
Mais si pure tu sois des êtres que tu vis,
Onde, sur qui les ans passent comme les nues,
Que de choses pourtant doivent t'être connues,
Astres, roses, saisons, les corps et leurs amours !
    Claire, mais si profonde, une nymphe toujours
Effleurée, et vivant de tout ce qui l'approche,
Nourrit quelque sagesse à l'abri de sa roche,
À l'ombre de ce jour qu'elle peint sous les bois.
Elle sait à jamais les choses d'une fois...

Ô présence pensive, eau calme qui recueilles
Tout un sombre trésor de fables et de feuilles,
L'oiseau mort, le fruit mûr, lentement descendus,
Et les rares lueurs des clairs anneaux perdus.
Tu consommes en toi leur perte solennelle ;
Mais, sur la pureté de ta face éternelle,
L'amour passe et périt...

Charmes

LE CIMETIÈRE MARIN

Μή, φίλα ψυχά, βίον ἀθάνατον
σπεῦδε, ταν δ'ἔμπρακτον ἄντλεῖ
μαχανάν.   PINDARE, *Pythiques III*

Ce toit tranquille, où marchent des colombes,
Entre les pins palpite, entre les tombes ;
Midi le juste y compose de feux
La mer, la mer, toujours recommencée !
Ô récompense après une pensée
Qu'un long regard sur le calme des dieux !

Quel pur travail de fins éclairs consume
Maint diamant d'imperceptible écume,
Et quelle paix semble se concevoir !
Quand sur l'abîme un soleil se repose,
Ouvrages purs d'une éternelle cause,
Le Temps scintille et le Songe est savoir.

Stable trésor, temple simple à Minerve,
Masse de calme, et visible réserve,
Eau sourcilleuse, Œil qui gardes en toi
Tant de sommeil sous un voile de flamme,
Ô mon silence !... Édifice dans l'âme,
Mais comble d'or aux mille tuiles, Toit !

Temple du Temps, qu'un seul soupir résume,
À ce point pur je monte et m'accoutume,
Tout entouré de mon regard marin ;
Et comme aux dieux mon offrande suprême,
La scintillation sereine sème
Sur l'altitude un dédain souverain.

Comme le fruit se fond en jouissance,
Comme en délice il change son absence
Dans une bouche où sa forme se meurt,

Je hume ici ma future fumée,
Et le ciel chante à l'âme consumée
Le changement des rives en rumeur.

Beau ciel, vrai ciel, regarde-moi qui change !
Après tant d'orgueil, après tant d'étrange
Oisiveté, mais pleine de pouvoir,
Je m'abandonne à ce brillant espace,
Sur les maisons des morts mon ombre passe
Qui m'apprivoise à son frêle mouvoir.

L'âme exposée aux torches du solstice,
Je te soutiens, admirable justice
De la lumière aux armes sans pitié !
Je te rends pure à ta place première :
Regarde-toi !... Mais rendre la lumière
Suppose d'ombre une morne moitié.

Ô pour moi seul, à moi seul, en moi-même,
Auprès d'un cœur, aux sources du poème,
Entre le vide et l'événement pur,
J'attends l'écho de ma grandeur interne,
Amère, sombre et sonore citerne,
Sonnant dans l'âme un creux toujours futur !

Sais-tu, fausse captive des feuillages,
Golfe mangeur de ces maigres grillages,
Sur mes yeux clos, secrets éblouissants,
Quel corps me traîne à sa fin paresseuse,
Quel front l'attire à cette terre osseuse ?
Une étincelle y pense à mes absents.

Fermé, sacré, plein d'un feu sans matière,
Fragment terrestre offert à la lumière,
Ce lieu me plaît, dominé de flambeaux,
Composé d'or, de pierre et d'arbres sombres,
Où tant de marbre est tremblant sur tant d'ombres ;
La mer fidèle y dort sur mes tombeaux !

Chienne splendide, écarte l'idolâtre !
Quand solitaire au sourire de pâtre,
Je pais longtemps, moutons mystérieux,
Le blanc troupeau de mes tranquilles tombes,
Éloignes-en les prudentes colombes,
Les songes vains, les anges curieux !

Ici venu, l'avenir est paresse.
L'insecte net gratte la sécheresse ;
Tout est brûlé, défait, reçu dans l'air
À je ne sais quelle sévère essence...
La vie est vaste, étant ivre d'absence,
Et l'amertume est douce, et l'esprit clair.

Les morts cachés sont bien dans cette terre
Qui les réchauffe et sèche leur mystère.
Midi là-haut, Midi sans mouvement
En soi se pense et convient à soi-même...
Tête complète et parfait diadème,
Je suis en toi le secret changement.

Tu n'as que moi pour contenir tes craintes !
Mes repentirs, mes doutes, mes contraintes
Sont le défaut de ton grand diamant...
Mais dans leur nuit toute lourde de marbres,
Un peuple vague aux racines des arbres
À pris déjà ton parti lentement.

Ils ont fondu dans une absence épaisse,
L'argile rouge a bu la blanche espèce,
Le don de vivre a passé dans les fleurs !
Où sont des morts les phrases familières,
L'art personnel, les âmes singulières ?
La larve file où se formaient des pleurs.

Les cris aigus des filles chatouillées,
Les yeux, les dents, les paupières mouillées,
Le sein charmant qui joue avec le feu,

Le sang qui brille aux lèvres qui se rendent,
Les derniers dons, les doigts qui les défendent,
Tout va sous terre et rentre dans le jeu !

Et vous, grande âme, espérez-vous un songe
Qui n'aura plus ces couleurs de mensonge
Qu'aux yeux de chair l'onde et l'or font ici ?
Chanterez-vous quand serez vaporeuse ?
Allez ! Tout fuit ! Ma présence est poreuse,
La sainte impatience meurt aussi !

Maigre immortalité noire et dorée,
Consolatrice affreusement laurée,
Qui de la mort fais un sein maternel,
Le beau mensonge et la pieuse ruse !
Qui ne connaît, et qui ne les refuse,
Ce crâne vide et ce rire éternel !

Pères profonds, têtes inhabitées,
Qui sous le poids de tant de pelletées,
Êtes la terre et confondez nos pas,
Le vrai rongeur, le ver irréfutable
N'est point pour vous qui dormez sous la table,
Il vit de vie, il ne me quitte pas !

Amour, peut-être, ou de moi-même haine ?
Sa dent secrète est de moi si prochaine
Que tous les noms lui peuvent convenir !
Qu'importe ! Il voit, il veut, il songe, il touche !
Ma chair lui plaît, et jusque sur ma couche,
À ce vivant je vis d'appartenir !

Zénon ! Cruel Zénon ! Zénon d'Élée !
M'as-tu percé de cette flèche ailée
Qui vibre, vole, et qui ne vole pas !
Le son m'enfante et la flèche me tue !
Ah ! le soleil… Quelle ombre de tortue
Pour l'âme, Achille immobile à grands pas !

Non, non !... Debout ! Dans l'ère successive !
Brisez, mon corps, cette forme pensive !
Buvez, mon sein, la naissance du vent !
Une fraîcheur, de la mer exhalée,
Me rend mon âme... Ô puissance salée !
Courons à l'onde en rejaillir vivant !

Oui ! Grande mer de délires douée,
Peau de panthère et chlamyde trouée
De mille et mille idoles du soleil,
Hydre absolue, ivre de ta chair bleue,
Qui te remords l'étincelante queue
Dans un tumulte au silence pareil,

Le vent se lève !... il faut tenter de vivre !
L'air immense ouvre et referme mon livre,
La vague en poudre ose jaillir des rocs !
Envolez-vous, pages tout éblouies !
Rompez, vagues ! Rompez d'eaux réjouies
Ce toit tranquille où picoraient des focs !

Charmes
© Éditions Gallimard

PAUL FORT

(1872-1960)

Voici l'invention du poème en prose... versifié. Plus
sérieusement voici un poète qui joue à dissimuler, sous une prose
continue ou répartie en versets, des rimes et des rythmes
traditionnels. Libre au lecteur de s'en tenir aux apparences ou
de restituer le mètre caché. Dans ce dernier cas, il lui suffira de
pratiquer quelques élisions propres à la langue parlée : « la ceris'
commence à rougir » ou « je ne me lass' point d'admirer », et s'il dit
le poème à voix haute, il n'aura aucune peine à mettre en évidence
alexandrins ou octosyllabes dissimulés.

Pourquoi ce jeu ? Sans doute parce qu'une langue qui semble
simplement parlée convient mieux au ton de familiarité qui
caractérise l'œuvre de Paul Fort. Rien de solennel ou de guindé
dans des poèmes qui célèbrent la vie quotidienne, les villages
aimés, les joies et les peines de petites gens. Ce qui n'exclut pas,
comme on peut le voir ici, la veine goguenarde et l'humour
souriant.

On risque d'oublier devant cette simplicité si naturelle que le
poète fut aussi l'un des défenseurs du symbolisme, proche de
Pierre Louÿs et de Gide, et qu'il a fondé le théâtre de l'Art pour
faire connaître les drames peu joués qui relevaient de cette
esthétique, ceux de Maeterlinck en particulier, et aussi ceux qu'il
écrivit lui-même.

Il reste cependant avant tout l'auteur prolixe – une cinquantaine
de volumes de ballades publiées en un demi-siècle – qui donne
parfois l'impression d'une trop grande facilité. Abondance et
spontanéité le distinguent de ses contemporains plus soucieux de

« gênes exquises ». Lui ignore l'orgueil de la tour d'ivoire, le mépris
des mots ordinaires. Il est le « poémier » qu'il a décrit, cet arbre qui
donne des poèmes comme d'autres donnent des fruits, ou encore
ce vieux chêne rempli d'oiseaux auquel le comparait l'un de ses
amis. Car il fait entendre sa voix avec la naïveté de ceux qui
chantent sans avoir appris et qui aiment chanter. Quelques-uns de
ses poèmes, peut-être trop ressassés, comme *Si toutes les filles du
monde* ou *Le bonheur est dans le pré*, risquent de faire oublier le
charme secret de beaucoup d'autres, et le succès de quelques
ballades ne suffit pas à rendre justice à la qualité de son lyrisme
souriant et tendre.

LES BALEINES

Du temps qu'on allait encore aux baleines, si loin qu' ça faisait, mat'lot, pleurer nos belles, y avait sur chaque route un Jésus en croix, y avait des marquis couverts de dentelles, y avait la Sainte-Vierge et y avait le Roi !

Du temps qu'on allait encore aux baleines, si loin qu' ça faisait, mat'lot, pleurer nos belles, y avait des marins qui avaient la foi, et des grands seigneurs qui crachaient sur elle, y avait la Sainte-Vierge et y avait le Roi !

Eh bien, à présent, tout le monde est content, c'est pas pour dire, mat'lot, mais on est content !... y a plus d'grands seigneurs ni d' Jésus qui tiennent, y a la république et y a l' président, et y a plus d' baleines !

Ballades françaises
© Flammarion

VILLANELLE DE LA VOIX PERDUE

Où sont les jours de Taillebois, ses nuits couleur de crépuscule,
la jeune fille qui pour moi chantait sous un rayon de lune,

Où sont-ils, ces tendres appels du rossignol vers tout le ciel
étoilé, mais où donc est-elle, la jeune fille qui pour moi

chantait sous un rayon de lune, où donc la brune ou blonde
belle qui faisait taire les appels que le rossignol jette au ciel

étoilé, mais où donc est-elle la charmeuse de Taillebois, la
Jeunesse à l'orée du bois, – la jeune fille qui pour moi

chantait sous un rayon de lune, chantait la Vie au clair de lune ?

Ballades françaises
© Flammarion

LE BEAU TEMPS

La cerise commence à rougir, mon cœur à n'avoir plus de peine, et les lavandières à rire le long de l'Oise et de la Seine.

Assis, à l'ombre du village, je ne me lasse point d'admirer, d'ici au fond du paysage, l'herbe à lapin aux fleurs dorées.

Sur un mur frissonnant de lierres, avec leurs couronnes aux bras, les croix de fer du cimetière font une ronde tout là-bas.

Est-il bien utile d'agir ? Entre mes doigts fleure une rose. La cerise commence à rougir. Ah ! Phébus, laissons faire aux choses

et se coiffer d'autres villages, comme de gais bonnets pointus, ces villages près des nuages dans les bleus lointains confondus.

Ballades françaises
© Flammarion

CHARLES PÉGUY

(1873-1914)

Depuis Baudelaire, les poètes pensent qu'ils sont des étrangers sur cette terre et que leur patrie est ailleurs. Si quelques voix se font entendre au tournant du siècle, qui semblent prendre leur parti de cet exil et chantent les joies quotidiennes et l'humble vie humaine, celles-ci témoignent encore, de façon indirecte, d'une réalité supérieure et lointaine qui en est la source, et ne sont pas en rupture avec le symbolisme dominant.

L'œuvre poétique de Péguy s'inscrit dans un tout autre registre, sa différence est manifeste dès son premier poème, *Jeanne d'Arc*. C'est un drame en trois pièces dédié « ... à toutes celles et à tous ceux qui seront morts pour tâcher de porter remède au mal universel... morts de leur mort humaine pour l'établissement de la République socialiste universelle ». Cet idéal n'a pas de peine à se transformer après sa conversion en une conscience aiguë du lien essentiel qui unit le charnel et le spirituel. Jamais il ne sépare la nature et la grâce, et il fait de la réalité visible, non plus l'écho affaibli d'une patrie idéale, mais notre point d'attache décisif et le véritable lieu de notre salut : pour lui, contrairement à Rimbaud, nous sommes au monde ! Écrivain chrétien, il place désormais la figure du Christ, Verbe fait chair, au centre de la Création, et voit dans la croix dressée entre ciel et terre, le signe incontestable du rattachement des hommes à Dieu. Tous ses écrits de poète témoignent de cette présence de l'Esprit au cœur même de l'humanité, miracle permanent et défi à la raison ordinaire. Tous pourraient en cela mériter le titre de « mystère » qu'il donne à trois d'entre eux, *Le Mystère de la charité de Jeanne d'Arc, Le Porche du mystère de la deuxième vertu* et *Le Mystère des saints Innocents*. Partout en effet, il unit à la peinture historique de l'aventure humaine la vision de sa dimension sacrée. D'où sa fascination pour la figure de Jeanne d'Arc à laquelle il consacre aussi la longue suite de sonnets, de tierces rimes, et de quatrains qui constituent *La Tapisserie de sainte Geneviève et de Jeanne d'Arc*. La geste héroïque de la jeune fille de Domrémy est à ses yeux l'une des preuves les plus évidentes de la présence permanente du divin au milieu des hommes.

La place prépondérante de l'alexandrin régulier dans son œuvre ne doit pas faire oublier qu'il eut d'abord recours au vers libre et surtout qu'il fut un lyrique, comme en témoignent les *Quatrains*, cette méditation élégiaque aux accents déchirants. Si le vers de douze syllabes s'impose à lui dans les *Tapisseries* et pour les mille neuf cent onze strophes d'*Ève*, c'est que leur rythme appuyé convient bien au caractère volontairement répétitif de ces longs poèmes. Il les conçoit en effet sur le modèle des litanies : ils en ont la lenteur insistante ; leur sourd piétinement reproduit la marche patiente des processions, scandée par les invocations réitérées aux saints intercesseurs. Ses vers ont l'humilité de ce monde charnel dont ils disent la pesanteur mais avec une force poétique capable de le magnifier.

Ce parti pris du poète implique la nécessité de dire ses vers à haute voix. C'est alors que l'interprète docile au texte, porté par le bercement et l'enchaînement des strophes, peut acquiescer à la vision de l'auteur, à sa foi en l'aventure humaine capable d'opérer la transfiguration spirituelle de l'Histoire. Car après tant de révoltes romantiques ou de désespoirs fin de siècle, voici, et ce n'est pas la moindre originalité de Péguy, une poésie de l'assentiment et de la louange.

Sa tentative la plus audacieuse à cet égard, et celle qui fut la moins comprise, c'est le poème d'*Ève*. La mère du genre humain incarne aussi pour lui l'humanité tout entière qui se souvient du paradis perdu. Mais après l'évocation de son exil originel, et l'annonce du Jugement dernier, il se tourne vers l'histoire des hommes. Et le rappel du salut obtenu par la croix du Christ, ouvre alors une tout autre perspective, le temps humain n'est plus désormais un temps de déchéance mais dans son mouvement ascendant « il est occupé, comme l'écrit Albert Béguin, à faire l'éternité ». À la fin du poème, dit en substance le critique, les figures de Geneviève et de Jeanne donnent de cette espérance l'exemple le plus humble et le plus extraordinaire. Elles permettent de risquer cette affirmation étonnante : « Dieu lui-même a besoin de l'œuvre du temps. »

Les passages les plus célèbres d'*Ève* – après les premières strophes où le climat de la grâce est restitué dans le jardin d'Éden pareil à un jardin à la française – sont l'évocation de la résurrection des morts qui mêle à des accents d'épouvante des descriptions idylliques, et surtout la prière sur ceux qui sont tombés au champ d'honneur, prière à laquelle la mort du poète au combat, deux ans plus tard, confère une valeur prophétique.

La vision qu'il propose ici de l'Histoire, l'immense pitié pour la détresse des hommes qui s'exprime dans ces strophes, la résurgence du thème de la mort sous des formes différentes dans chacune des parties du poème, tout contribue à faire d'*Ève* une œuvre originale et puissante qui peut être comparée aux plus grandes. Ainsi, par exemple, d'Aubigné et Hugo ont eux aussi évoqué la résurrection et le jugement, le premier en décrivant, avec la puissance du visionnaire et l'effervescence baroque de l'expression, l'extraordinaire poussée des corps qui échappent à leur prison souterraine, le second en s'arrêtant fasciné devant l'orbite béante du clairon de l'Apocalypse, et opposant, en une démarche antithétique de l'imaginaire, à l'attente immobile de la multitude infinie des gisants, l'immensité déserte du ciel, pour faire, de ce vide même, la figure inversée d'une inconcevable Présence.

Péguy choisit de faire des ressuscités les pèlerins d'un ultime pèlerinage, cheminant tous ensemble, de leur pas d'autrefois, vers le tribunal du dernier verdict, riches du souvenir de ce que fut leur vie, et confiants, malgré leurs fautes, en la clémence du Juge. Assez étrangères au modèle apocalyptique, ses images naissent ici du patient tissage des mots. Avec le retour d'expressions presque semblables qu'un détail seul suffit à modifier, par variations successives sur un même thème et dans une langue souvent proche de la prose qui mêle simplicité et solennité, il fait surgir l'impressionnant tableau de cette foule en marche. On peut mesurer à la force de l'émotion que suscitent chez le récitant l'alliance du sacré et du familier le plus proche, et ce recours au merveilleux chrétien dans la vision du destin collectif de l'humanité, qu'il est bien, au même titre que ses prédécesseurs, un grand poète épique.

JEANNE

Un long silence.

Adieu, Meuse endormeuse et douce à mon enfance,
Qui demeures aux prés, où tu coules tout bas.
  Meuse, adieu : j'ai déjà commencé ma partance
En des pays nouveaux où tu ne coules pas.

  Voici que je m'en vais en des pays nouveaux :
Je ferai la bataille et passerai les fleuves ;
Je m'en vais m'essayer à de nouveaux travaux,
Je m'en vais commencer là-bas les tâches neuves.

  Et pendant ce temps-là, Meuse ignorante et douce,
Tu couleras toujours, passante accoutumée,
Dans la vallée heureuse où l'herbe vive pousse,

Ô Meuse inépuisable et que j'avais aimée.

Un silence.

  Tu couleras toujours dans l'heureuse vallée ;
Où tu coulais hier, tu couleras demain.
Tu ne sauras jamais la bergère en allée,
Qui s'amusait, enfant, à creuser de sa main
Des canaux dans la terre, – à jamais écroulés.

  La bergère s'en va, délaissant les moutons,
Et la fileuse va, délaissant les fuseaux.
Voici que je m'en vais loin de tes bonnes eaux,
Voici que je m'en vais bien loin de nos maisons.

  Meuse qui ne sais rien de la souffrance humaine,
Ô Meuse inaltérable et douce à toute enfance,
Ô toi qui ne sais pas l'émoi de la partance,
Toi qui passes toujours et qui ne pars jamais,

Ô toi qui ne sais rien de nos mensonges faux,

Ô Meuse inaltérable, ô Meuse que j'aimais,

Un silence.

Quand reviendrai-je ici filer encor la laine ?
Quand verrai-je tes flots qui passent par chez nous ?
Quand nous reverrons-nous ? et nous reverrons-nous ?

Meuse que j'aime encore, ô ma Meuse que j'aime.

Jeanne d'Arc
© Éditions Gallimard

LE PORCHE DU MYSTÈRE DE LA DEUXIÈME VERTU

. . . .
Nuit tu es une belle invention
De ma sagesse.
Nuit ô ma fille la Nuit ô ma fille silencieuse
Au puits de Rébecca, au puits de la Samaritaine
C'est toi qui puises l'eau la plus profonde
Dans le puits le plus profond
Ô nuit qui berces toutes les créatures
Dans un sommeil réparateur.
Ô nuit qui laves toutes les blessures
Dans la seule eau fraîche et dans la seule eau profonde
Au puits de Rébecca tirée du puits le plus profond.
Amie des enfants, amie et sœur de la jeune Espérance
Ô nuit qui panses toutes les blessures
Au puits de la Samaritaine toi qui tires du puits le plus profond
La prière la plus profonde.
Ô nuit, ô ma fille la Nuit, toi qui sais te taire, ô ma fille au beau
   manteau.
Toi qui verses le repos et l'oubli. Toi qui verses le baume, et le
   silence, et l'ombre
Ô ma Nuit étoilée je t'ai créée la première.
Toi qui endors, toi qui ensevelis déjà dans une Ombre éternelle
Toutes mes créatures
Les plus inquiètes, le cheval fougueux, la fourmi laborieuse,
Et l'homme ce monstre d'inquiétude.
Nuit qui réussis à endormir l'homme
Ce puits d'inquiétude.
À lui seul plus inquiet que toute la création ensemble.
L'homme, ce puits d'inquiétude.
Comme tu endors l'eau du puits.
. . . .
Ô ma fille *étincelante et sombre* je te salue
Toi qui répares, toi qui nourris, toi qui reposes
Ô silence de l'ombre
Un tel silence régnait avant la création de l'inquiétude.

Avant le commencement du règne de l'inquiétude.
Un tel silence régnera, mais un silence de lumière
Quand toute cette inquiétude sera consommée,
Quand toute cette inquiétude sera épuisée.
Quand ils auront tiré toute l'eau du puits.
Après la consommation, après l'épuisement de toute cette
    inquiétude
D'homme.
. . . .

© Éditions Gallimard

CHÂTEAUX DE LOIRE

Le long du coteau courbe et des nobles vallées
Les châteaux sont semés comme des reposoirs,
Et dans la majesté des matins et des soirs
La Loire et ses vassaux s'en vont par ces allées.

Cent vingt châteaux lui font une suite courtoise,
Plus nombreux, plus nerveux, plus fins que des palais.
Ils ont nom Valençay, Saint-Aignan et Langeais,
Chenonceaux et Chambord, Azay, le Lude, Amboise.

Et moi j'en connais un dans les châteaux de Loire
Qui s'élève plus haut que le château de Blois,
Plus haut que la terrasse où les derniers Valois
Regardaient le soleil se coucher dans sa gloire.

La moulure est plus fine et l'arceau plus léger.
La dentelle de pierre est plus dure et plus grave.
La décence et l'honneur et la mort qui s'y grave
Ont inscrit leur histoire au cœur de ce verger.

Et c'est le souvenir qu'a laissé sur ces bords
Une enfant qui menait son cheval vers le fleuve.
Son âme était récente et sa cotte était neuve.
Innocente elle allait vers le plus grand des sorts.

Car celle qui venait du pays tourangeau,
C'était la même enfant qui quelques jours plus tard,
Gouvernant d'un seul mot le rustre et le soudard,
Descendait devers Meung ou montait vers Jargeau.

LA BALLADE DU CŒUR QUI A TANT BATTU

. . . .
Cœur dur comme une tour,
        Ô cœur de pierre,
Donjon de jour en jour
        Vêtu de lierre.

Cœur tu as fait ton jeu
        Au tapis vert,
Tu as jeté ton feu
        Au vent d'hiver.

Cœur dur comme une tour
        Rectangulaire,
Voici monter le jour
        Quadrangulaire.

De tous liens lié
        À cette terre,
Ô cœur humilié,
        Cœur solitaire.

Cœur qui as tant crevé
        De pleurs secrets,
Buveur inabreuvé,
        Cendre et regrets.

Cœur tant de fois baigné
        Dans la lumière,
Et tant de fois noyé,
        Source première.

Pris dans ta capitale,
        Et dans ton lit,
Prince en terre natale
        Enseveli...
. . . .

PRÉSENTATION DE PARIS À NOTRE DAME

Étoile de la mer voici la lourde nef
Où nous ramons tout nuds sous vos commandements ;
Voici notre détresse et nos désarmements ;
Voici le quai du Louvre, et l'écluse, et le bief.

Voici notre appareil et voici notre chef.
C'est un gars de chez nous qui siffle par moments.
Il n'a pas son pareil pour les gouvernements.
Il a la tête dure et le geste un peu bref.

Reine qui vous levez sur tous les océans,
Vous penserez à nous quand nous serons au large.
Aujourd'hui c'est le jour d'embarquer notre charge.
Voici l'énorme grue et les longs meuglements.

S'il fallait le charger de nos pauvres vertus,
Ce vaisseau s'en irait vers votre auguste seuil
Plus creux que la noisette après que l'écureuil
L'a laissé retomber de ses ongles pointus.

Nuls ballots n'entreraient par les panneaux béants,
Et nous arriverions dans la mer de sargasse
Traînant cette inutile et grotesque carcasse
Et les Anglais diraient : Ils n'ont rien mis dedans.

Mais nous saurons l'emplir et nous vous le jurons.
Il sera le plus beau dans cet illustre port.
La cargaison ira jusque sur le plat-bord.
Et quand il sera plein nous le couronnerons.

Nous n'y chargerons pas notre pauvre maïs,
Mais de l'or et du blé que nous emporterons.
Et il tiendra la mer : car nous le chargerons
Du poids de nos péchés payés par votre fils.

La Tapisserie de Notre-Dame © Gallimard

PRÉSENTATION DE LA BEAUCE
À NOTRE DAME DE CHARTRES

Étoile de la mer voici la lourde nappe
Et la profonde houle et l'océan des blés
Et la mouvante écume et nos greniers comblés,
Voici votre regard sur cette immense chape

Et voici votre voix sur cette lourde plaine
Et nos amis absents et nos cœurs dépeuplés,
Voici le long de nous nos poings désassemblés
Et notre lassitude et notre force pleine.

Étoile du matin, inaccessible reine,
Voici que nous marchons vers votre illustre cour,
Et voici le plateau de notre pauvre amour,
Et voici l'océan de notre immense peine.

Un sanglot rôde et court par-delà l'horizon.
À peine quelques toits font comme un archipel.
Du vieux clocher retombe une sorte d'appel.
L'épaisse église semble une basse maison.

Ainsi nous naviguons vers votre cathédrale.
De loin en loin surnage un chapelet de meules,
Rondes comme des tours, opulentes et seules
Comme un rang de châteaux sur la barque amirale.

Deux mille ans de labeur ont fait de cette terre
Un réservoir sans fin pour les âges nouveaux.
Mille ans de votre grâce ont fait de ces travaux
Un reposoir sans fin pour l'âme solitaire.

· · · · · · · · · · · · · · · · · · · ·

Un homme de chez nous, de la glèbe féconde
À fait jaillir ici d'un seul enlèvement,
Et d'une seule source et d'un seul portement,
Vers votre assomption la flèche unique au monde.

Tour de David voici votre tour beauceronne.
C'est l'épi le plus dur qui soit jamais monté
Vers un ciel de clémence et de sérénité,
Et le plus beau fleuron dedans votre couronne.

Un homme de chez nous a fait ici jaillir,
Depuis le ras du sol jusqu'au pied de la croix,
Plus haut que tous les saints, plus haut que tous les rois
La flèche irréprochable et qui ne peut faillir.

. . . .

Quand on nous aura mis dans une étroite fosse,
Quand on aura sur nous dit l'absoute et la messe,
Veuillez vous rappeler, reine de la promesse,
Le long cheminement que nous faisons en Beauce.

Quand nous aurons quitté ce sac et cette corde,
Quand nous aurons tremblé nos derniers tremblements,
Quand nous aurons raclé nos derniers raclements,
Veuillez vous rappeler votre miséricorde.

Nous ne demandons rien, refuge du pécheur,
Que la dernière place en votre Purgatoire,
Pour pleurer longuement notre tragique histoire,
Et contempler de loin votre jeune splendeur.

La Tapisserie de Notre-Dame
© Éditions Gallimard

ÈVE

Fideli Fidelis

Jésus parle.

– Ô mère ensevelie hors du premier jardin,
Vous n'avez plus connu ce climat de la grâce,
Et la vasque et la source et la haute terrasse,
Et le premier soleil sur le premier matin.

Et les bondissements de la biche et du daim
Nouant et dénouant leur course fraternelle
Et courant et sautant et s'arrêtant soudain
Pour mieux commémorer leur vigueur éternelle,

Et pour bien mesurer leur force originelle
Et pour poser leurs pas sur ces moelleux tapis,
Et ces deux beaux coureurs sur soi-même tapis
Afin de saluer leur lenteur solennelle.

Et les ravissements de la jeune gazelle
Laçant et délaçant sa course vagabonde,
Galopant et trottant et suspendant sa ronde
Afin de saluer sa race intemporelle.

Et les dépassements du bouc et du chevreuil
Mêlant et démêlant leur course audacieuse
Et dressés tout à coup sur quelque immense seuil
Afin de saluer la terre spacieuse.

Et tous ces filateurs et toutes ces fileuses
Mêlant et démêlant l'écheveau de leur course,
Et dans le sable d'or des vagues nébuleuses
Sept clous articulés découpaient la Grande Ourse.

. . . .

Et Dieu lui-même jeune ensemble qu'éternel
Se reposait penché sur sa création.
Et l'amour filial et l'amour paternel
Se nourrissaient d'hommage et de libation.

Et Dieu lui-même juste ensemble qu'éternel
Avait pesé le monde au gré de sa balance.
Et il considérait d'un regard paternel
L'homme de son image et de sa ressemblance.

. . . .

Vous n'avez plus connu que le temps dans le lieu.
Vous n'avez plus connu la jeunesse du monde,
Et cette paix du cœur plus lourde et plus profonde
Que l'énorme Océan sous le regard de Dieu.

Vous n'avez plus connu que des biens périssables,
Et la succession et le vieillissement.
Et la procession des maux ineffaçables.
Et le regard voilé d'un appauvrissement.

. . . .

Et je vous aime tant, mère de notre mère,
Vous avez tant pleuré les larmes de vos yeux.
Vous avez tant levé vers de plus pauvres cieux
Un regard inventé pour une autre lumière.

. . . .

Et moi je vous salue ô la première femme
Et la plus malheureuse et la plus décevante
Et la plus immobile et la plus émouvante,
Aïeule aux longs cheveux, mère de Notre Dame.

. . . .

Femme, vous m'entendez : quand les âmes des morts
S'en reviendront chercher dans les vieilles paroisses,
Après tant de bataille et parmi tant d'angoisses,
Le peu qui restera de leurs malheureux corps ;

. . . .

Quand on n'entendra plus que le sourd craquement
D'un monde qui s'abat comme un échafaudage,
Quand le globe sera comme un baraquement
Plein de désuétude et de dévergondage ;

. . . .

Et quand se lèveront dans les champs d'épandage
Tant de martyrs jetés dans les égouts de Rome,
Et quand se lèvera dans le cœur de tout homme
Le long ressouvenir de son vagabondage ;

Et quand sur le parvis des hautes cathédrales
Les peuples libérés des vastes nécropoles,
Dans Paris et dans Reims et dans les métropoles
Transporteront l'horreur des chambres sépulcrales ;

. . . .

Quand l'homme relevé du plus ancien tombeau
Écartera la pierre et le vase d'oubli,
Quand le plus vieil aveugle et l'homme enseveli
Rallumera l'éclair du plus ancien flambeau ;

. . . .

Quand l'homme reviendra dans son premier village
Chercher son ancien corps parmi ses compagnons
Dans ce modeste enclos où nous accompagnons
Les morts de la paroisse et ceux du voisinage ;

Quand il reconnaîtra ceux de son parentage
Modestement couchés à l'ombre de l'église,
Quand il retrouvera sous le jaune cytise
Les dix-huit pieds carrés qui faisaient son partage ;

. . . .

Quand les ressuscités s'en iront par les bourgs,
Encor tout ébaubis et cherchant leur chemin,
Et les yeux éblouis et se tenant la main,
Et reconnaissant mal ces tours et ces détours

Des sentiers qui menaient leur candide jeunesse,
Encor tout ébahis que ce jour soit venu,
Encor tout assaillis du regret revenu,
Et reconnaissant mal, avant que l'aube naisse,

Ces sentiers qui menaient leur enfance première,
Encor tout démolis d'être ainsi revenus,
Et reconnaissant mal ces corps pauvres et nus,
Et reconnaissant mal cette vieille chaumière

Et ces sentiers fleuris qui menaient leur tendresse,
Et les anciens lilas dans les vieilles venelles,
Et la rose et l'œillet et tant de fleurs charnelles,
Avant que de monter jusqu'aux fleurs de hautesse ;

. . . .

Quand vos enfants perdus, aïeule utilitaire,
Chemineront le long de leurs anciens amours,
Et le long des soucis qui ramenaient toujours
En un centre de peine en un point de la terre

Les longs égarements d'un cœur délibéré,
Quand ils reconnaîtront les antiques serments,
Quand ils retrouveront les antiques tourments,
La poudre et le débris d'un cœur dilacéré ;

. . . .

Aïeule du lépreux et du grand sénéchal,
Saurez-vous retrouver dans cet encombrement,
Pourrez-vous allumer dans cet égarement
Pour éclairer leurs pas quelque pauvre fanal,

Et quand ils passeront sous la vieille poterne,
Aurez-vous retrouvé pour ces gamins des rues,
Et pour ces vétérans et ces jeunes recrues,
Pour éclairer leurs pas quelque vieille lanterne ;

Aurez-vous retrouvé dans vos forces décrues
Le peu qu'il en fallait pour mener cette troupe
Et pour mener ce deuil et pour mener ce groupe
Dans le raccordement des routes disparues.

. . . .

– Heureux ceux qui sont morts pour la terre charnelle,
Mais pourvu que ce fût dans une juste guerre.
Heureux ceux qui sont morts pour quatre coins de terre.
Heureux ceux qui sont morts d'une mort solennelle.

Heureux ceux qui sont morts dans les grandes batailles,
Couchés dessus le sol à la face de Dieu.
Heureux ceux qui sont morts sur un dernier haut lieu,
Parmi tout l'appareil des grandes funérailles.

Heureux ceux qui sont morts pour des cités charnelles.
Car elles sont le corps de la cité de Dieu.
Heureux ceux qui sont morts pour leur âtre et leur feu,
Et les pauvres honneurs des maisons paternelles.

Car elles sont l'image et le commencement
Et le corps et l'essai de la maison de Dieu.
Heureux ceux qui sont morts dans cet embrassement,
Dans l'étreinte d'honneur et le terrestre aveu.

. . . .

Heureux ceux qui sont morts, car ils sont retournés
Dans ce premier terroir d'où Dieu les révoqua,
Et dans ce reposoir d'où Dieu les convoqua.
Heureux les grands vaincus, les rois dépossédés.

. . . .

Heureux ceux qui sont morts, car ils sont retournés
Dans ce premier terreau nourri de leur dépouille,
Dans ce premier caveau, dans la tourbe et la houille.
Heureux les grands vaincus, les rois désabusés.

– Heureux les grands vainqueurs. Paix aux hommes de guerre.
Qu'ils soient ensevelis dans un dernier silence.
Que Dieu mette avec eux dans la juste balance
Un peu de ce terreau d'ordure et de poussière.

Que Dieu mette avec eux dans le juste plateau
Ce qu'ils ont tant aimé, quelques grammes de terre.
Un peu de cette vigne, un peu de ce coteau,
Un peu de ce ravin sauvage et solitaire.

. . . .

Mère voici vos fils qui se sont tant battus.
Qu'ils ne soient pas pesés comme Dieu pèse un ange.
Que Dieu mette avec eux un peu de cette fange
Qu'ils étaient en principe et sont redevenus.

. . . .

Mère voici vos fils et leur immense armée.
Qu'ils ne soient pas jugés sur leur seule misère.
Que Dieu mette avec eux un peu de cette terre
Qui les a tant perdus et qu'ils ont tant aimée.

.. . .

28 décembre 1911

CHARLES GUÉRIN

(1873-1907)

On devine en lisant ses premiers vers, publiés sous l'anagramme de Heirclas Rügen, où vont les préférences de ce débutant. D'ailleurs, dès 1894, il manifeste son attachement au symbolisme en dédiant à Rodenbach *Les Joies Grises*, signées de son nom et par cet aveu dans l'un des poèmes : « Or je suis rongé par de bizarres névroses. » L'année suivante *Le Sang des crépuscules* vaut au jeune poète une lettre élogieuse de Mallarmé.

« ... Habitude du mètre ou les complexités et fluidité aussi, en la pensée rien que de sûr parmi votre invention ; même, une des toutes premières fois, l'assonance y suffisant à marquer le vers, comme coloration, apparaît dans son feu plus ou presque plus précieuse que la rime... »

Cependant il se détache progressivement de sa première manière et se montre de plus en plus soucieux de perfection formelle, sensible en cela à l'exemple donné par Heredia. Une rencontre décisive dans son évolution est celle de Jammes comme l'atteste la deuxième partie du *Cœur solitaire* ; c'est Jammes qui l'aide à renoncer, selon ses propres termes, aux « perversités » et aux « mots subtils ». Il rêve alors, dit-il, de réaliser l'impossible unité entre les deux courants poétiques dominants, et d'être le « poète absolu », c'est-à-dire celui en qui fusionneraient ce qu'il nomme l'école des Coloristes et celle des « Nuancistes », la première regroupant tous les peintres du monde extérieur, l'autre tous les analystes du moi, autrement dit Parnasse et Symbolisme. À supposer la chose réalisable, il n'aura pas le temps d'y parvenir ni même celui de le tenter. Et pourtant il laisse une œuvre véritable, et d'une inspiration très personnelle malgré les diverses influences subies. Le ton de tristesse et de mélancolie qui en assure l'unité n'est pas une concession à l'air du temps, il traduit les tourments réels d'un être que déchirent les exigences contradictoires du désir amoureux et d'une obsession de pureté héritée de son éducation chrétienne. On le sent constamment hanté par la mort, par un sentiment déchirant de solitude que même l'amour ne parvient pas à vaincre, par l'angoisse d'avoir dilapidé sa vie :

> *On se retourne, un soir, sur la route suivie ;*
> *Il fait froid, la nuit tombe, on est seul... Pauvre vie*
> *Qu'on n'a pas dévouée au service de Dieu !*

Insatisfait de lui-même comme homme, il l'est aussi dans son œuvre, et il regrette dans *L'Homme intérieur*, son dernier recueil, l'inspiration d'autrefois (« Une veine de poésie / Tout ingénue avec des airs / De ruisseau bleu qui balbutie ») en se demandant avec tristesse : « Pourquoi ne suis-je pas ainsi / Resté naïvement poète ? » Il l'est resté pourtant, on ne peut en douter, durant toute sa trop courte vie et certains vers témoignent qu'il aurait pu égaler les plus grands, comme ce cri du *Semeur de cendres* :

> *Nuit d'ombre, nuit tragique, ô nuit désespérée !*

ÉPITAPHE POUR LUI-MÊME

Il fut le très subtil musicien des vents
Qui se plaignent en de nocturnes symphonies ;
Il nota le murmure des herbes jaunies
Entre les pavés gris des cours d'anciens couvents.

Il trouva sur la viole des dévots servants
Pour ses maîtresses des tendresses infinies ;
Il égrena les ineffables litanies
Où s'alanguissent tous les amoureux fervents.

Un soir, la chair brisée aux voluptés divines,
Il détourna du ciel son front fleuri d'épines,
Et se coucha, les pieds meurtris et le cœur las.

Ô toi qui dégoûté du rire et de la lutte
Odieuse, vibras aux sanglots de sa flûte,
Poète, ralentis le pas : cy dort Heirclas.

Joies grises

LA VOIX DU SOIR

La voix du soir est sainte et forte,
Lourde de songes et de parfums,
Et son flot d'ombre me rapporte
La cendre des espoirs défunts.

J'ai dit à l'amour qu'il s'en aille,
Et son pas d'aube, je l'écoute
Qui dans la gaieté des sonnailles
S'étouffe au tournant de la route.

La douceur de ce soir témoigne
De la bonté calme des choses.
Je voudrais vivre ! qu'on éloigne
Le vin où macèrent les roses,

Qu'on éloigne les mots subtils,
Les rythmes triples en tiare,
Les stylets stellés de béryls
Et les simarres d'or barbares.

Je suis las des perversités,
Je voudrais que mon âme lasse
Redevienne enfant des cités
Où le lys règne sur les places,

Que mon âme d'ombre délaisse
Les jardins de ronces haineuses,
Et laisse l'orgueil pour l'humblesse
Et redevienne lumineuse.

Le ciel est tendu d'améthyste,
Et maints péchés sont déliés...
Je songe un livre de pitié
Pour les âmes simples et tristes.

Le Sang des crépuscules

ANNA DE NOAILLES

(1876-1933)

Son premier recueil, *Le Cœur innombrable*, connaît un immense
succès. Elle-même est fêtée, adulée et devient la plus connue de
toutes les femmes poètes de ce début de siècle, mais cinquante ans
plus tard elle est déjà presque oubliée. Cependant son lyrisme ne
se confond avec aucun autre parce qu'elle mêle à une expression
des passions proche du romantisme, un chant personnel singulier.
En célébrant la beauté du monde, et sa communion sensuelle avec
la nature, elle dit inlassablement la saveur du réel et sa passion
pour la vie. Saisons, odeurs, jardins, ombres et lumières des
paysages, tout lui est occasion d'éblouissement. Sa vision païenne
de la terre, ce panthéisme diffus qui personnifie et divinise les
forces telluriques, se traduit dans des images qui parlent aux cinq
sens et dans des rythmes que sous-tend une constante ferveur.
Mais elle sait aussi, lorsqu'elle prend conscience de la fragilité de
ce bonheur et de la mort si proche, faire entendre des accents
stoïciens. Ils donnent à certains poèmes, en particulier à ceux des
derniers recueils, une gravité émouvante. S'y ajoute l'exigence,
toujours plus forte au fil des années, de rigueur formelle. Ses vers
en acquièrent une perfection classique et une sorte
d'intemporalité.

OFFRANDE À LA NATURE

Nature au cœur profond sur qui les cieux reposent,
Nul n'aura comme moi si chaudement aimé
La lumière des jours et la douceur des choses,
L'eau luisante et la terre où la vie a germé.

La forêt, les étangs et les plaines fécondes
Ont plus touché mes yeux que les regards humains,
Je me suis appuyée à la beauté du monde
Et j'ai tenu l'odeur des saisons dans mes mains.

J'ai porté vos soleils ainsi qu'une couronne
Sur mon front plein d'orgueil et de simplicité,
Mes jeux ont égalé les travaux de l'automne
Et j'ai pleuré d'amour aux bras de vos étés...

. . . .

Je vous tiens toute vive entre mes bras, Nature.
Ah ! faut-il que mes yeux s'emplissent d'ombre un jour,
Et que j'aille au pays sans vent et sans verdure
Que ne visitent pas la lumière et l'amour.

Le Cœur innombrable

IL FERA LONGTEMPS CLAIR CE SOIR

Il fera longtemps clair ce soir, les jours allongent.
La rumeur du jour vif se disperse et s'enfuit,
Et les arbres, surpris de ne pas voir la nuit,
Demeurent éveillés dans le soir blanc, et songent...

Les marronniers, sur l'air plein d'or et de lourdeur,
Répandent leurs parfums et semblent les étendre ;
On n'ose pas marcher ni remuer l'air tendre
De peur de déranger le sommeil des odeurs.

De lointains roulements arrivent de la ville...
La poussière qu'un peu de brise soulevait,
Quittant l'arbre mouvant et las qu'elle revêt,
Redescend doucement sur les chemins tranquilles ;

Nous avons tous les jours l'habitude de voir
Cette route si simple et si souvent suivie,
Et pourtant quelque chose est changé dans la vie ;
Nous n'aurons plus jamais notre âme de ce soir...

Les Éblouissements

MAX JACOB

(1876-1944)

Cocasserie et mysticisme s'allient étrangement chez Max Jacob. Peu de poètes eurent au même degré cet esprit d'enfance qui lui fait écrire des contes naïfs, de nombreux poèmes d'une verve populaire, et toujours assembler les mots en regardant ce qui peut en jaillir. Il essaye les techniques les plus diverses pour percer le secret des choses que dérobe aux yeux leur fréquentation habituelle. La mystification, les parodies, les rapprochements burlesques constituent pour lui les modalités saugrenues d'une recherche plus sérieuse comme le suggère l'un de ses recueils qu'il intitule *Le Laboratoire central*. Mais cet esprit original, d'abord passionné d'occultisme et de Kabbale, se convertit au christianisme après avoir vu, comme il le rapporte, le Christ lui apparaître. Dès lors il va, sa vie durant, exprimer sa ferveur religieuse sincère dans des œuvres où cependant il ne renonce ni à sa fantaisie naturelle ni à son humour. S'il déconcerte souvent le lecteur, c'est parce qu'il se montre sérieux dans la bouffonnerie, et apparemment iconoclaste ou irrévérencieux dans la démarche spirituelle, sans qu'on puisse pour autant mettre en doute sa sincérité. À l'intention de ceux qui ironisent sur sa conversion il fait paraître *La Défense de Tartuffe*, endossant par là le nom dont on l'affuble, et s'efforçant de témoigner de sa foi, comme le suggère le sous-titre : « Extases, remords, visions, prières, poèmes et méditations d'un Juif converti. »

Son apport à la poésie est important. Il rompt vraiment avec le symbolisme et ouvre le siècle à un esprit nouveau. Dans la préface du *Cornet à dés*, après avoir raconté qu'il composait déjà des poèmes en prose quand il était enfant, il ajoute : « ... quand il a été avéré que j'étais parmi les poètes [et cité dans le fameux "après-midi des poètes", conférence faite par Apollinaire... en 1907...] je me suis appliqué à saisir en moi, de toutes manières, les données de l'inconscient : mots en liberté, associations hasardeuses des idées, rêves de la nuit et du jour, hallucinations, etc. » Son amitié avec Picasso qui sera son parrain lors de son baptême, ou encore avec Derain puis Modigliani et de nombreux écrivains ou poètes, fait de lui un artiste attentif aux recherches esthétiques de ses contemporains et capable en plus d'un point de les devancer. Les surréalistes vont apprendre de lui à laisser l'initiative au hasard et à explorer les ressources de l'inconscient. Il va formuler dans son *Art poétique* des règles clés comme celle-ci : « La poésie moderne saute toutes les explications. »

Cependant ce naïf jongleur n'ignore pas la souffrance d'une mauvaise conscience : « Je pleure et le démon dit : "Comédien tu triches, / En trésor d'amour ton cœur n'est pas si riche." »

Ni l'attrait du péché :

> *Quand Dieu nous tire par en haut*
> *Il nous vient des monstres nouveaux,*
> *Car le démon n'est jamais loin*
> *Et guette bien par quelque coin.*

Et surtout il dissimule, sous l'apparente fantaisie de son inspiration et son jeu avec les mots, une angoisse et une peur de la mort qui pour être voilées n'en sont pas moins réelles et auxquelles sa fin au camp de Drancy confère rétrospectivement une valeur prémonitoire.

VILLONELLE

Dis-moi quelle fut la chanson
Que chantaient les belles sirènes
Pour faire pencher des trirèmes
Les Grecs qui lâchaient l'aviron.

Achille qui prit Troie, dit-on,
Dans un cheval bourré de son
Achille fut grand capitaine
Or, il fut pris par des chansons
Que chantaient des vierges hellènes
Dis-moi, Vénus, je t'en supplie
Ce qu'était cette mélodie.

Un prisonnier dans sa prison
En fit une en Tripolitaine
Et si belle que sans rançon
On le rendit à sa marraine
Qui pleurait contre la cloison.

Nausicaa à la fontaine
Pénélope en tissant la laine
Zeuxis peignant sur les maisons
Ont chanté la faridondaine !...
Et les chansons des échansons ?

Échos d'échos des longues plaines
Et les chansons des émigrants !
Où sont les refrains d'autres temps
Que l'on a chantés tant et tant ?
Où sont les filles aux belles dents
Qui l'amour par les chants retiennent ?
Et mes chansons ? qu'il m'en souvienne !

Le Laboratoire central
© Éditions Gallimard

PASSÉ ET PRÉSENT

Poète et ténor
L'oriflamme au nord
Je chante la mort.

Poète et tambour
Natif de Colliour
Je chante l'amour.

Poète et marin
Versez-moi du vin
Versez ! versez ! Je divulgue
Le secret des algues.

Poète et chrétien
Le Christ est mon bien
Je ne dis plus rien.

Le Laboratoire central
© Éditions Gallimard

LA TERRE

Envolez-moi au-dessus des chandelles noires de la terre.
Au-dessus des cornes venimeuses de la terre.
Il n'y a de paix qu'au-dessus des serpents de la terre.
La terre est une grande bouche souillée :
ses hoquets, ses rires à gorge déployée
sa toux, son haleine, ses ronflements quand elle dort
me triturent l'âme. Attirez-moi dehors !
Secouez-moi, empoignez-moi, et toi Terre chasse-moi.
Surnaturel, je me cramponne à ton drapeau de soie !
que le grand vent me coule dans tes plis qui ondoient.
Je craque de discordes militaires avec moi-même
je me suis comme une poulie, une voiture de dilemmes
et je ne pourrai dormir que dans vos évidences.
Je vous envie, phénix, faisan doré, condors.
Donnez-moi une couverture volante qui me porte
au-dessus du tonnerre, dehors au cristal de vos portes.

Ballades, Sacrifice impérial,
© Éditions Gallimard

AMOUR DU PROCHAIN

à Jean Rousselot

Qui a vu le crapaud traverser une rue ? C'est un tout petit homme : une poupée n'est pas plus minuscule. Il se traîne sur les genoux : il a honte, on dirait... ? Non ! Il est rhumatisant. Une jambe reste en arrière, il la ramène ! Où va-t-il ainsi ? Il sort de l'égout, pauvre clown. Personne n'a remarqué ce crapaud dans la rue. Jadis personne ne me remarquait dans la rue, maintenant les enfants se moquent de mon étoile jaune. Heureux crapaud ! tu n'as pas l'étoile jaune.

Derniers Poèmes
© Éditions Gallimard

O. V. DE L. MILOSZ

(1877-1939)

Le terme de nostalgie s'impose au lecteur de Milosz, il caractérise l'univers personnel du poète.

Nostalgie du pays de ses premières années, la Lituanie, terre de ses ancêtres, mais aussi d'une autre contrée, le territoire magique de l'enfance recréé par l'imagination, celui dont il ne parvint jamais à se détacher tout à fait, et à qui il est redevable de sa mélancolie, de son goût du silence et de la solitude :

> *Soyez la bienvenue, vous qui venez à ma rencontre*
> *Dans l'écho de mes propres pas, du fond du corridor*
> *   obscur et froid du temps.*
> *Soyez la bienvenue, solitude, ma mère...*

Son premier recueil, *Le Poème des décadences*, indique par son titre que l'auteur n'échappe pas au mal du siècle symboliste, cependant le recours à des refrains naïfs, les répétitions insistantes, une manière de laisser parfois le poème en suspens et comme inachevé, donnent déjà un tour très personnel à certains d'entre eux. Avec *Les Sept Solitudes* l'originalité de Milosz apparaît pleinement. Son art consiste, quel que soit son propos, à donner l'impression d'une « musique entendue dans un demi-sommeil ». Une récurrence de décors de brume et de pluie, l'effacement du moment présent sous le poids d'un passé vaguement entrevu mais qui s'impose à la conscience, tout contribue à créer une impression d'étrangeté. Elle ne naît pas d'un exotique dépaysement mais plutôt de l'inexplicable familiarité éprouvée parfois devant les images inconnues qui naissent du sommeil. Cette œuvre est en effet d'essence onirique.

On rapporte qu'Oscar Wilde s'est écrié un jour : « Voici Moréas-le-poète et Milosz-la-poésie. » Le mot met l'accent sur un trait essentiel : Milosz est moins un savant faiseur de poèmes qu'un homme habité par ses songes dont la traduction naturelle est la poésie. S'il est sensible à certaines influences, en particulier à celle des romantiques allemands ou de Byron, car la passion et le désordre romantiques le séduisent plus que les formes classiques, et si sa vaste culture lui permet de s'alimenter à bien des sources littéraires françaises et étrangères, aucune ne le marque au point de le détourner des voies personnelles de son inspiration. Très tôt cet élégiaque associe la méditation philosophique et les recherches ésotériques à la création poétique. Sa connaissance des traditions occultistes, et les études hébraïques qu'il mène pour lire et interpréter la Bible – et notamment l'Apocalypse – vont imprégner ses poèmes. Ainsi dans *La Confession de Lemuel*, ce double de lui-même, il adresse *Le Cantique de la Connaissance* « à ceux que la prière a conduits à la méditation sur l'origine du langage ». Il leur explique comment le pouvoir de nommer les objets sensibles nous vient de la connaissance des archétypes, et comment les hommes qui sont impuissants à s'élever jusqu'à eux... « ont imaginé, dans la nuit de leur ignorance, un monde intermédiaire, flottant et stérile, le monde des symboles ». Il est lui-même homme de prière et de méditation, et, de manière peu conforme au dogme, il associe à la foi retrouvée, les doctrines théosophiques anciennes ou récentes. Mais même ses œuvres les plus difficiles gardent encore les traits propres de son chant, l'harmonie, l'éclat du verbe.

Si *Miguel Manara*, ce drame qui relate la conversion et le repentir du Dom Juan historique, est toujours interprété au théâtre, son œuvre poétique est beaucoup moins connue. Le caractère déconcertant de certains de ses poèmes peut expliquer le silence qui s'est fait autour d'eux, mais surtout Milosz fut un poète peu soucieux d'être publié, et il choisit, après avoir mené une carrière de diplomate français au service de la Lituanie, une retraite et une solitude qui contribuèrent à son oubli. Et même s'il est peu à peu redécouvert, il demeure encore de nos jours un grand poète méconnu.

BRUMES

Je suis un grand jardin de novembre, un jardin éploré
Où grelottent les abandonnés du vieux faubourg ;
Où la couleur misérable des brumes dit : Toujours !
Où le battement des fontaines est le mot : Jamais...
– Autour d'un buste ridicule qui médite,
(Marie, tu dors, ton moulin va trop vite).
Tourne la ronde des désespoirs du vieux faubourg.

Entendez-vous la ronde qui pleure, dans le jardin noyé
De brume aveugle, au fond du vieux faubourg ?
Pauvres amitiés mortes, burlesques amours oubliées,
Ô vous les mensonges d'un soir, ô vous les illusions d'un jour,
Autour du buste ridicule qui médite,
(Marie, tu dors, ton moulin va trop vite),
Venez danser la ronde noire du vieux faubourg.

La brume a tout mangé, rien n'est gai, rien n'irrite,
Le rêve est aussi creux que la réalité.
Mais dans le parc où vous avez connu l'été
La ronde, la ronde immense tourne, tourne toujours,
Amis que l'on remplace, amantes que l'on quitte...
(Marie, tu dors, ton moulin va trop vite...)

Je suis un grand jardin de novembre, au fond d'un vieux faubourg.

Poésies I, Le Poème des décadences
© Éditions André Silvaire

DANS UN PAYS D'ENFANCE...

Dans un pays d'enfance retrouvée en larmes,
Dans une ville de battements de cœur morts,
(De battements d'essor tout un berceur vacarme,
De battements d'ailes des oiseaux de la mort,
De clapotis d'ailes noires sur l'eau de mort).
Dans un passé hors du temps, malade de charme,
Les chers yeux de deuil de l'amour brûlent encore
D'un doux feu de minéral roux, d'un triste charme ;
Dans un pays d'enfance retrouvée en larmes...
– Mais le jour pleut sur le vide de tout.

Pourquoi m'as-tu souri dans la vieille lumière
Et pourquoi, et comment m'avez-vous reconnu
Étrange fille aux archangéliques paupières,
Aux riantes, bleuies, soupirantes paupières,
Lierre de nuit d'été sur la lune des pierres ;
Et pourquoi et comment, n'ayant jamais connu
Ni mon visage, ni mon deuil, ni la misère
Des jours, m'as-tu si soudainement reconnu
Tiède, musicale, brumeuse, pâle, chère,
Pour qui mourir dans la nuit grande de tes paupières ?
– Mais le jour pleut sur le vide de tout.

Quels mots, quelles musiques terriblement vieilles
Frissonnent en moi de ta présence irréelle,
Sombre colombe des jours loin, tiède, belle,
Quelles musiques en écho dans le sommeil ?
Sous quels feuillages de solitude très vieille,
Dans quel silence, quelle mélodie ou quelle
Voix d'enfant malade vous retrouver, ô belle,
Ô chaste, ô musique entendue dans le sommeil ?
– Mais le jour pleut sur le vide de tout.

Poésies I, Les Sept Solitudes
© Éditions André Silvaire

L'ANNÉE…

L'année était du temps des souvenirs,
Le mois était de la lune des roses,
Les cœurs étaient de ceux qu'un rien console.

Près de la mer, des chants doux à mourir,
Dans le crépuscule aux paupières closes ;
Et puis, que sais-je ? Tambourins, paroles.

Cris de danse qui ne devaient finir,
Touchant désir adolescent qui n'ose
Et meurt en finale de barcarolle.

– T'en souvient-il, souvient-il, Souvenir ?
Au mois vague de la lune des roses.
Mais rien n'est resté de ce qui console.

Est-ce pour dormir, est-ce pour mourir
Que sur mes genoux ta tête repose
Avec la langueur de ses roses folles ?

L'ombre descend, la lune va mûrir.
La vie est riche de si douces choses,
Pleurs pour les yeux, rosée pour les corolles.

Oui, vivre est presque aussi doux que dormir…
Poisons tièdes pris à petites doses
Et poèmes pleins de charmants symboles.

Ô passé ! pourquoi fallut-il mourir ?
Ô présent ! pourquoi ces heures moroses,
Bouffon qui prends au sérieux ton rôle !

– L'année était du temps des souvenirs,
Le mois était de la lune des roses,
Les cœurs étaient de ceux qu'un rien console.

Mais tôt ou tard cela devait finir
De la très vieille fin de toutes choses
Et ce n'est ni triste, vraiment, ni drôle.

Des os vont jaunir d'abord, puis verdir
Dans le froid moisi des ténèbres closes,
– Fin des actes et fin des paraboles.

Et le reste ne vaut pas une obole.

Poésies I, Les Sept Solitudes
© Éditions André Silvaire

ET SURTOUT QUE...

– Et surtout que Demain n'apprenne pas où je suis –
Les bois, les bois sont pleins de baies noires –
Ta voix est comme un son de lune dans le vieux puits
Où l'écho, l'écho de juin vient boire.

Et que nul ne prononce mon nom là-bas, en rêve,
Les temps, les temps sont bien accomplis –
Comme un tout petit arbre souffrant de prime sève
Est ta blancheur en robe sans pli.

Et que les ronces se referment derrière nous,
Car j'ai peur, car j'ai peur du retour.
Les grandes fleurs blanches caressent tes doux genoux
Et l'ombre, et l'ombre est pâle d'amour.

Et ne dis pas à l'eau de la forêt qui je suis ;
Mon nom, mon nom est tellement mort.
Tes yeux ont la couleur des jeunes pluies,
Des jeunes pluies sur l'étang qui dort.

Et ne raconte rien au vent du vieux cimetière.
Il pourrait m'ordonner de le suivre.
Ta chevelure sent l'été, la lune et la terre.
Il faut vivre, vivre, rien que vivre...

Poésies I, Les Sept Solitudes
© Éditions André Silvaire

TOUS LES MORTS SONT IVRES...

Tous les morts sont ivres de pluie vieille et sale
Au cimetière étrange de Lofoten.
L'horloge du dégel tictaque lointaine
Au cœur des cercueils pauvres de Lofoten.

Et grâce aux trous creusés par le noir printemps
Les corbeaux sont gras de froide chair humaine ;
Et grâce au maigre vent à la voix d'enfant
Le sommeil est doux aux morts de Lofoten.

Je ne verrai très probablement jamais
Ni la mer ni les tombes de Lofoten
Et pourtant c'est en moi comme si j'aimais
Ce lointain coin de terre et toute sa peine.

Vous disparus, vous suicidés, vous lointaines
Au cimetière étranger de Lofoten
– Le nom sonne à mon oreille étrange et doux,
Vraiment, dites-moi, dormez-vous, dormez-vous ?

– Tu pourrais me conter des choses plus drôles
Beau claret dont ma coupe d'argent est pleine,
Des histoires plus charmantes ou moins folles ;
Laisse-moi tranquille avec ton Lofoten.

Il fait bon. Dans le foyer doucement traîne
La voix du plus mélancolique des mois.
– Ah ! les morts, y compris ceux de Lofoten –
Les morts, les morts sont au fond moins morts que moi.

Poésies I, Les Sept Solitudes
© Éditions André Silvaire

VICTOR SEGALEN

(1878-1919)

Le premier recueil de poèmes de Segalen, le seul qui parut de son vivant, *Stèles*, peut dérouter plus d'un lecteur : personne en effet n'avait eu recours avant lui à cette forme d'expression poétique, à cet « art lapidaire », comme il l'écrit à Claudel à qui le recueil est dédié. Il en a trouvé le modèle en Chine dans ces « monuments restreints à une table de pierre, haut dressée, portant une inscription ». L'image de stabilité qu'elles offrent au passant le fascine. Évoquant leur lointaine origine, il rappelle dans sa préface leur utilité primitive, appuis de bois percés qui servaient à descendre le mort dans la fosse et qu'on prit l'habitude d'orner d'inscriptions, ils gardent ensuite seulement leur fonction commémorative. Plus tard le nom de stèle désigne le poteau où l'on attache la victime rituelle, il permet aussi, au moyen de l'ombre qu'il jette, de mesurer « le moment du soleil ». Les caractères chinois gravés sur ces monuments, « devenus pensée de la pierre dont ils prennent le grain », ne sont pas faits pour informer le passant : « Ils dédaignent d'être lus. Ils ne réclament point la voix ou la musique... Ils n'expriment pas ; ils signifient ; ils sont. » Ces précisions éclairent le projet du poète qui est de conserver à la Stèle écrite certains des traits de celle de pierre.

L'introduction à l'édition critique de cette œuvre par Henry Bouillier met en lumière la pleine conscience qu'a le poète d'inventer ainsi un monde d'expression original, sa volonté de faire de la Stèle « un jour de connaissance au fond de soi », l'astre qui projetait sa lumière sur le monument de pierre devenant ici tout intérieur, le poème est alors le moyen pour son auteur d'accéder à son propre mystère. D'ailleurs, lorsqu'il explique le sens des directions adoptées par les Stèles (face au Midi pour celles qui portent des décrets, face au nord les Stèles amicales, vers l'ouest les guerrières et du côté de l'orient les amoureuses), il accorde une importance particulière à quelques autres, celles du Milieu, « le lieu par excellence », région mystérieuse. « Segalen, dit son commentateur, traduit ici sa nostalgie presque mystique de la Connaissance suprême. »

Cette entreprise exige une écriture particulière. Pour faire écho au graphisme hiératique des idéogrammes chinois, la langue poétique doit avoir recours à toutes les formes possibles de sobriété suggestive, éviter la narration, les enchaînements explicatifs, la désignation claire. D'où le tour souvent mystérieux des *Stèles*, leur forme aphoristique et la solennité de certaines d'entre elles. D'où aussi la nécessité pour le lecteur de s'arrêter, comme le fit le voyageur-poète pour leurs modèles, de se pencher longuement sur chacune d'elles, de les envisager jusqu'au point d'en être peu à peu pénétré. Enfin leur exotisme, dû au foisonnement d'allusions aux coutumes et à la civilisation chinoise, s'il est d'abord déroutant, contribue aussi peu à peu à la fascination qu'elles exercent sur nous.

Grand voyageur et sinologue, Victor Segalen laisse encore, outre des nouvelles et les récits de ses missions archéologiques, des *Odes* et un poème intitulé *Thibet*

> *Puissé-je moi scander à coups de reins dans ta grandeur*
> *Cet hymne mouvant, ce don farouche,*
> *Tribut d'essor escaladant à Toi des pays le plus haut !*
> *– Mon cœur, qu'il en batte chaque mot.*

L'importance que le poète attache au mot, porteur inépuisable du sens à venir, on la perçoit à travers chaque poème. Il note pour lui-même : « Aphorisme préféré : les mots ont une valeur supérieure aux choses représentées. » Cette phrase citée par Henry Bouillier nous éclaire sur son art poétique.

Segalen est bien un héritier du symbolisme par son projet de quête intérieure, proche de l'idéal mallarméen, par le pouvoir qu'il attribue au verbe poétique, mais ces rapprochements n'atténuent en rien la singularité irréductible de son œuvre.

MON AMANTE A LES VERTUS DE L'EAU

Mon amante a les vertus de l'eau : un sourire clair, des gestes
   coulants, une voix pure et chantant goutte à goutte.
Et quand parfois, — malgré moi — du feu passe dans mon regard,
   elle sait comment on l'attise en frémissant : eau jetée sur les
   charbons rouges.

★

Mon eau vive, la voici répandue, toute, sur la terre !
Elle glisse, elle me fuit ; – et j'ai soif, et je cours après elle.
De mes mains je fais une coupe. De mes deux mains je l'étanche
   avec ivresse, je l'étreins, je la porte à mes lèvres :
Et j'avale une poignée de boue.

Stèles orientées

PERDRE LE MIDI QUOTIDIEN

Perdre le Midi quotidien ; traverser des cours, des arches, des
   ponts ; tenter les chemins bifurqués ; m'essouffler aux marches,
   aux rampes, aux escalades ;
Éviter la stèle précise ; contourner les murs usuels ; trébucher
   ingénument parmi ces rochers factices ; sauter ce ravin ;
   m'attarder en ce jardin ; revenir parfois en arrière,
Et par un lacis réversible égarer enfin le quadruple sens des Points
   du Ciel.

                              ★

Tout cela, – amis, parents, familiers et femmes, – tout cela, pour
   tromper aussi vos chères poursuites ; pour oublier quel coin de
   l'horizon carré vous recèle,
Quel sentier vous ramène, quelle amitié vous guide, quelles bontés
   menacent, quels transports vont éclater.

                              ★

Mais, perçant la porte en forme de cercle parfait ; débouchant
   ailleurs : (au beau milieu du lac en forme de cercle parfait, cet
   abri fermé, circulaire, au beau milieu du lac, et de tout,)
Tout confondre, de l'orient d'amour à l'occident héroïque, du
   midi face au Prince au nord trop amical, – pour atteindre
   l'autre, le cinquième, centre et Milieu
Qui est moi.

Stèles du Milieu

GUILLAUME APOLLINAIRE

(1880-1918)

Son poème intitulé *Chantre* est le plus court de la langue française, il se compose d'un seul vers :

Et l'unique cordeau des trompettes marines

dont tous les termes sont clairs mais le sens assez énigmatique. Cela pourrait bien tenir lieu pour le poète, comme le suggère Jean Pommier, de manifeste narquois, d'art poétique minimal, de manière de dire : « Paulo minora canamus. » L'instrument évoqué, déjà élu par Monsieur Jourdain, voit ici son unique corde réduite encore à l'état rustique de cordeau. *Alcools*, cependant, comme toute grande œuvre poétique, semble devoir plutôt sa naissance à la lyre. Mais Apollinaire se veut différent et il est vrai que des poèmes tels que *Zone* ou *L'Émigrant de Landor Road* ouvrent une voie nouvelle. Ce n'est pas l'emploi du vers libre, déjà admis, qui fait leur originalité, mais l'introduction, au milieu des thèmes éternels de la mélancolie ou de l'errance, de réalités du monde moderne dont les matériaux n'ont pas encore reçu la patine du temps (« Tour Eiffel », « hangars de Port Aviation », « belles sténo-dactylographes »), bizarreries renforcées par l'emploi d'images insolites et d'expressions inhabituelles, comme le célèbre « Soleil cou coupé ». D'ailleurs l'étonnement du lecteur n'est pas moins grand lorsque les mots et le rythme lui sont familiers. Sa surprise naît alors de brusques ruptures de ton, de changements apparents de sujet, de parenthèses inattendues et surtout de longues digressions où le poète semble divaguer. On peut en donner un exemple significatif avec la lettre des cosaques zaporogues, cette réponse au Sultan que sa verdeur rend incongrue parmi les vers nostalgiques de la *Chanson du mal-aimé*. Autre contraste frappant, celui qui oppose une langue familière et parlée à ces termes rares qu'Apollinaire affectionne. Ce qui permet de voir en lui aussi bien un poète à la portée de tous (« Comment faire pour être heureux / Comme un petit enfant candide ? »), qu'un érudit dont le vocabulaire requiert un dictionnaire (« Mort d'immortels argyraspides »). Cependant, même égaré, le lecteur que captive la succession des images, et l'harmonie des vers, demeure sous le charme. L'absence de ponctuation contribue à cet effet d'entraînement du poème qui semble fait d'une seule coulée. On sait qu'Apollinaire, au moment où il corrigeait les épreuves de son livre, prit la décision de supprimer tous les repères ordinaires du discours. Son vers y gagne une fluidité mélodieuse, parfois aussi une ambiguïté qui entraîne « quelque méprise » comme le souhaitait Verlaine, mais jamais au point de le rendre irrémédiablement obscur. En matière de rime, sa liberté est grande : rimes riches, rimes approximatives ou assonances (adore et morts, étoiles et mâle, citronniers et saigné), simple répétition d'un mot ou même suppression de tout écho en fin de vers, tout lui est bon.

L'homme est aussi déroutant que son œuvre. La culture étendue et disparate que lui vaut son insatiable curiosité de lecteur, sous-tend la diversité de l'inspiration. Si la découverte du Moyen Âge a surtout nourri son roman, *L'Enchanteur pourrissant,* et si sa familiarité avec « l'enfer » de la Bibliothèque Nationale a fourni à ses éditeurs plusieurs écrits érotiques qui n'ajoutent rien à sa gloire mais lui apportèrent quelque argent, ces lectures laissent aussi des traces dans les poèmes : ainsi certains commentateurs voient un symbole phallique dans chacune des « Sept épées de mélancolie ». Un autre de ses centres d'intérêt est l'occultisme, et, chez lui comme chez Nerval, la lecture de théosophes et de traités ésotériques a certainement alimenté la rêverie. Mais c'est surtout sa connaissance des poètes qui l'ont précédé qui imprègne ses poèmes. Aussi a-t-on fait de lui successivement un décadent, un symboliste, ou même un romantique attardé ; on peut également souligner ses affinités avec les baroques, et noter que plus d'une fois, par le ton de confidence mi-ironique, mi-désespéré, il fait songer à Villon. Cela ne l'empêche nullement d'être original et parfois intemporel.

Sa passion pour l'art, l'amitié qui le lie à de grands artistes tels que Picasso, Derain, Braque, Delaunay, l'intelligence qu'il a de leurs recherches, ont une influence indirecte sur ses poèmes car il y puise l'idée d'une nécessaire rupture dans les formes et dans la manière de peindre, qu'il étend ensuite aux autres arts. Il réunit, dans le volume des *Peintres cubistes*, les articles qu'il a consacrés à des œuvres majeures à nos yeux, mais totalement incomprises ou ignorées au moment où il s'enthousiasmait pour elles. Ses qualités de critique d'art contemporain (c'est d'abord par là qu'il est connu du public), comme le « lancement » du douanier Rousseau, même si l'événement ressemblait à un jeu, ou l'invention du terme de surréalisme, témoignent de son ouverture d'esprit, de sa facilité à accueillir les idées nouvelles.

À la croisée de tant de courants divers, qui est donc Apollinaire ? Cette question sans réponse il se l'est posée à lui-même :

> *Un jour*
> *Un jour je m'attendais moi-même*
> *Je me disais Guillaume il est temps que tu viennes*
> *Pour que je sache enfin celui-là que je suis...*

On peut considérer *Alcools* et *Calligrammes* comme ses œuvres poétiques majeures, mais *Les Poèmes à Lou* ou *Le Guetteur mélancolique*, plus inégaux, comportent également de très beaux poèmes.

La diversité d'inspiration du recueil de 1913, dont le titre évoque les sources multiples d'ivresse que la vie offre au poète, associe des souvenirs rêvés ou réels à des tableaux pittoresques. Ainsi le lyrisme des *Rhénanes* mêle aux allusions à sa passion pour Annie Playden les légendes du Rhin, et des croquis de paysages ou de figures pittoresques. *La Chanson du mal-aimé*, dans le récit d'une errance à la recherche de l'amour perdu, utilise aussi bien les mythes et légendes de l'Antiquité que des détails d'histoire contemporaine ; la description de Londres ou de Paris s'y juxtapose aux associations d'idées que tisse une conscience égarée dans le labyrinthe de sa mémoire. Toutefois le retour de refrains estompe les contrastes et unifie le poème. D'ailleurs une lecture attentive repère, sous le délire apparent, le jeu des symétries, des échos, des oppositions qui le structurent. Ces procédés se retrouvent aussi dans *Zone*, ou *L'Émigrant de Landor Road*, qui se présentent cependant comme des œuvres d'avant-garde par leur vocabulaire ou leurs images insolites. D'autres poèmes relèvent au contraire d'une conception plus traditionnelle de l'écriture poétique, comme *Le Pont Mirabeau* à la fluidité verlainienne, ou les quatrains classiques des *Rhénanes*.

La liberté et la fantaisie d'Apollinaire apparaissent encore dans *Calligrammes* publié en 1918. Ici c'est la disposition typographique de certains poèmes qui les métamorphose en illustration graphique de leur propre thème. Toutefois il n'est pas l'inventeur de ces idéogrammes, Rabelais a proposé un jeu du même ordre avec la *Dive Bouteille*, et lui-même avait des modèles. Ces formes gracieuses, qui ont fait la célébrité du recueil, n'en constituent pas l'essentiel, parmi ces « Poèmes de la paix et de la guerre » comme le précise le sous-titre, on peut encore retenir ceux où il peint sa vie la plus immédiate :

> *Je me suis engagé sous le plus beau des cieux*
> *Dans Nice la marine au nom victorieux*
> *Perdu parmi les 900 conducteurs anonymes*
> *Je suis un charretier du neuf charroi de Nîmes*
> *L'Amour dit reste ici, mais là-bas les obus*
> *Épousent ardemment et sans cesse les buts,*

d'autres où se mêlent souvenirs proches et lointains, (« L'olive du temps / Souvenirs qui n'en faites qu'un »), et quelques-uns où il s'adresse à lui-même :

> *Ulysse que de jours pour rentrer dans Ithaque*
> *Couche-toi sur la paille et songe un beau remords*
> *Qui pur effet de l'art soit aphrodisiaque…*

On y voit encore des lettres à ses amis ou à la femme aimée. Les épîtres amoureuses fourniront d'autres livres, et d'abord celui des *Poèmes à Lou*. Autant de poèmes que l'on voudrait pouvoir citer pour essayer de découvrir la mystérieuse alchimie qui fait de lui un poète inoubliable !

Le disparate des œuvres évoquées ne permet guère de parler à son propos d'une vision poétique unifiante. Ses vers semblent surgis capricieusement, au gré des circonstances, et coulent avec une merveilleuse facilité. Or, malgré cette bigarrure, ils sont reconnaissables à leur musique et leur tonalité particulière. Ils nous hantent, nous les fredonnons intérieurement, ils se mêlent à notre vie avec une instance magique. Sans doute Apollinaire a-t-il su, mieux que d'autres, écouter le chant spontané et secret d'Anima. Les refrains « talismaniques » de *La Chanson du mal-aimé*, les aphorismes parfaits comme : « Les souvenirs sont cors de chasse / Dont meurt le bruit parmi le vent », la grâce exquise de strophes telles que celle de l'*Adieu* :

> *J'ai cueilli ce brin de bruyère*
> *L'automne est morte souviens-t'en*
> *Nous ne nous verrons plus sur terre*
> *Odeur du temps brin de bruyère*
> *Et souviens-toi que je t'attends*

sont le signe du caractère orphique, du lyrisme essentiel de cette poésie.

Apollinaire est bien ce « Chantre » capable de traduire la mystérieuse voix qu'il évoque en disant : « J'entends mourir et remourir un chant lointain. »

LE PONT MIRABEAU

Sous le pont Mirabeau coule la Seine
              Et nos amours
          Faut-il qu'il m'en souvienne
La joie venait toujours après la peine

              Vienne la nuit sonne l'heure
              Les jours s'en vont je demeure

Les mains dans les mains restons face à face
              Tandis que sous
          Le pont de nos bras passe
Des éternels regards l'onde si lasse

              Vienne la nuit sonne l'heure
              Les jours s'en vont je demeure

L'amour s'en va comme cette eau courante
              L'amour s'en va
          Comme la vie est lente
Et comme l'Espérance est violente

              Vienne la nuit sonne l'heure
              Les jours s'en vont je demeure

Passent les jours et passent les semaines
              Ni temps passé
          Ni les amours reviennent
Sous le pont Mirabeau coule la Seine

              Vienne la nuit sonne l'heure
              Les jours s'en vont je demeure

Alcools

LA CHANSON DU MAL-AIMÉ

À Paul Léautaud

Et je chantais cette romance
En 1903 sans savoir
Que mon amour à la semblance
Du beau Phénix s'il meurt un soir
Le matin voit sa renaissance.

Un soir de demi-brume à Londres
Un voyou qui ressemblait à
Mon amour vint à ma rencontre
Et le regard qu'il me jeta
Me fit baisser les yeux de honte

Je suivis ce mauvais garçon
Qui sifflotait mains dans les poches
Nous semblions entre les maisons
Onde ouverte de la mer Rouge
Lui les Hébreux moi Pharaon

Que tombent ces vagues de briques
Si tu ne fus pas bien aimée
Je suis le souverain d'Égypte
Sa sœur-épouse son armée
Si tu n'es pas l'amour unique

Au tournant d'une rue brûlant
De tous les feux de ses façades
Plaies du brouillard sanguinolent
Où se lamentaient les façades
Une femme lui ressemblant

C'était son regard d'inhumaine
La cicatrice à son cou nu
Sortit saoule d'une taverne
Au moment où je reconnus
La fausseté de l'amour même

Lorsqu'il fut de retour enfin
Dans sa patrie le sage Ulysse
Son vieux chien de lui se souvint
Près d'un tapis de haute lisse
Sa femme attendait qu'il revînt

L'époux royal de Sacontale
Las de vaincre se réjouit
Quand il la retrouva plus pâle
D'attente et d'amour yeux pâlis
Caressant sa gazelle mâle

J'ai pensé à ces rois heureux
Lorsque le faux amour et celle
Dont je suis encore amoureux
Heurtant leurs ombres infidèles
Me rendirent si malheureux

Regrets sur quoi l'enfer se fonde
Qu'un ciel d'oubli s'ouvre à mes vœux
Pour son baiser les rois du monde
Seraient morts les pauvres fameux
Pour elle eussent vendu leur ombre

J'ai hiverné dans mon passé
Revienne le soleil de Pâques
Pour chauffer un cœur plus glacé
Que les quarante de Sébaste
Moins que ma vie martyrisés

Mon beau navire ô ma mémoire
Avons-nous assez navigué
Dans une onde mauvaise à boire
Avons-nous assez divagué
De la belle aube au triste soir

Adieux faux amour confondu
Avec la femme qui s'éloigne
Avec celle que j'ai perdue
L'année dernière en Allemagne
Et que je ne reverrai plus

Voie lactée ô sœur lumineuse
Des blancs ruisseaux de Chanaan
Et des corps blancs des amoureuses
Nageurs morts suivrons-nous d'ahan
Ton cours vers d'autres nébuleuses

Je me souviens d'une autre année
C'était l'aube d'un jour d'avril
J'ai chanté ma joie bien-aimée
Chanté l'amour à voix virile
Au moment d'amour de l'année

AUBADE CHANTÉE À LÆTARE UN AN PASSÉ

C'est le printemps viens-t'en Pâquette
Te promener au bois joli
Les poules dans la cour caquètent
L'aube au ciel fait de roses plis
L'amour chemine à ta conquête

Mars et Vénus sont revenus
Ils s'embrassent à bouches folles
Devant des sites ingénus
Où sous les roses qui feuillolent
De beaux dieux roses dansent nus

Viens ma tendresse est la régente
De la floraison qui paraît
La nature est belle et touchante
Pan sifflote dans la forêt
Les grenouilles humides chantent

Beaucoup de ces dieux ont péri
C'est sur eux que pleurent les saules
Le grand Pan l'amour Jésus-Christ
Sont bien morts et les chats miaulent
Dans la cour je pleure à Paris

Moi qui sais des lais pour les reines
Les complaintes de mes années
Des hymnes d'esclave aux murènes
La romance du mal-aimé
Et des chansons pour les sirènes

L'amour est mort j'en suis tremblant
J'adore de belles idoles
Les souvenirs lui ressemblant
Comme la femme de Mausole
Je reste fidèle et dolent

Je suis fidèle comme un dogue
Au maître le lierre au tronc
Et les Cosaques Zaporogues
Ivrognes pieux et larrons
Aux steppes et au décalogue

Portez comme un joug le Croissant
Qu'interrogent les astrologues
Je suis le Sultan tout-puissant
  Ô mes Cosaques Zaporogues
Votre Seigneur éblouissant

Devenez mes sujets fidèles
Leur avait écrit le Sultan
Ils rirent à cette nouvelle
Et répondirent à l'instant
À la lueur d'une chandelle

RÉPONSE DES COSAQUES ZAPOROGUES
AU SULTAN DE CONSTANTINOPLE

Plus criminel que Barrabas
Cornu comme les mauvais anges
Quel Belzébuth es-tu là-bas
Nourri d'immondice et de fange
Nous n'irons pas à tes sabbats

Poisson pourri de Salonique
Long collier des sommeils affreux
D'yeux arrachés à coup de pique
Ta mère fit un pet foireux
Et tu naquis de sa colique

Bourreau de Podolie Amant
Des plaies des ulcères des croûtes
Groin de cochon cul de jument
Tes richesses garde-les toutes
Pour payer tes médicaments

Voie lactée ô sœur lumineuse
Des blancs ruisseaux de Chanaan
Et des corps blancs des amoureuses
Nageurs morts suivrons-nous d'ahan
Ton cours vers d'autres nébuleuses

Regret des yeux de la putain
Et belle comme une panthère
Amour vos baisers florentins
Avaient une saveur amère
Qui a rebuté nos destins

Ses regards laissaient une traîne
D'étoiles dans les soirs tremblants
Dans ses yeux nageaient les sirènes
Et nos baisers mordus sanglants
Faisaient pleurer nos fées marraines

Mais en vérité je l'attends
Avec mon cœur avec mon âme
Et sur le pont des Reviens-t'en
Si jamais revient cette femme
Je lui dirai Je suis content

Mon cœur et ma tête se vident
Tout le ciel s'écoule par eux
Ô mes tonneaux des Danaïdes
Comment faire pour être heureux
Comme un petit enfant candide

Je ne veux jamais l'oublier
Ma colombe ma blanche rade
Ô marguerite exfoliée
Mon île au loin ma Désirade
Ma rose mon giroflier

Les satyres et les pyraustes
Les égypans les feux follets
Et les destins damnés ou faustes
La corde au cou comme à Calais
Sur ma douleur quel holocauste

Douleur qui doubles les destins
La licorne et le capricorne
Mon âme et mon corps incertain
Te fuient ô bûcher divin qu'ornent
Des astres des fleurs du matin

Malheur dieu pâle aux yeux d'ivoire
Tes prêtres fous t'ont-ils paré
Tes victimes en robe noire
Ont-elles vainement pleuré
Malheur dieu qu'il ne faut pas croire

Et toi qui me suis en rampant
Dieu de mes dieux morts en automne
Tu mesures combien d'empans
J'ai droit que la terre me donne
Ô mon ombre ô mon vieux serpent

Au soleil parce que tu l'aimes
Je t'ai menée souviens-t'en bien
Ténébreuse épouse que j'aime
Tu es à moi en n'étant rien
Ô mon ombre en deuil de moi-même

L'hiver est mort tout enneigé
On a brûlé les ruches blanches
Dans les jardins et les vergers
Les oiseaux chantent sur les branches
Le printemps clair l'avril léger

Mort d'immortels argyraspides
La neige aux boucliers d'argent
Fuit les dendrophores livides
Du printemps cher aux pauvres gens
Qui resourient les yeux humides

Et moi j'ai le cœur aussi gros
Qu'un cul de dame damascène
Ô mon amour je t'aimais trop
Et maintenant j'ai trop de peine
Les sept épées hors du fourreau

Sept épées de mélancolie
Sans morfil ô claires douleurs
Sont dans mon cœur et la folie
Veut raisonner pour mon malheur
Comment voulez-vous que j'oublie

LES SEPT ÉPÉES

La première est toute d'argent
Et son nom tremblant c'est Pâline
Sa lame un ciel d'hiver neigeant
Son destin sanglant gibeline
Vulcain mourut en la forgeant

La seconde nommée Noubosse
Est un bel arc-en-ciel joyeux
Les dieux s'en servent à leurs noces
Elle a tué trente Bé-Rieux
Et fut douée par Carabosse

La troisième bleu féminin
N'en est pas moins un chibriape
Appelé Lul de Faltenin
Et que porte sur une nappe
L'Hermès Ernest devenu nain

La quatrième Malourène
Est un fleuve vert et doré
C'est le soir quand les riveraines
Y baignent leurs corps adorés
Et des chants de rameurs s'y traînent

La cinquième Sainte-Fabeau
C'est la plus belle des quenouilles
C'est un cyprès sur un tombeau
Où les quatre vents s'agenouillent
Et chaque nuit c'est un flambeau

La sixième métal de gloire
C'est l'ami aux si douces mains
Dont chaque matin nous sépare
Adieu voilà votre chemin
Les coqs s'épuisaient en fanfares

Et la septième s'exténue
Une femme une rose morte
Merci que le dernier venu
Sur mon amour ferme la porte
Je ne vous ai jamais connue

Voie lactée ô sœur lumineuse
Des blancs ruisseaux de Chanaan
Et des corps blancs des amoureuses
Nageurs morts suivrons-nous d'ahan
Ton cours vers d'autres nébuleuses

Les démons du hasard selon
Le chant du firmament nous mènent
À sons perdus leurs violons
Font danser notre race humaine
Sur la descente à reculons

Destins destins impénétrables
Rois secoués par la folie
Et ces grelottantes étoiles
De fausses femmes dans vos lits
Aux déserts que l'histoire accable

Luitpold le vieux prince régent
Tuteur de deux royautés folles
Sanglote-t-il en y songeant
Quand vacillent les lucioles
Mouches dorées de la Saint-Jean

Près d'un château sans châtelaine
La barque aux barcarols chantants
Sur un lac blanc et sous l'haleine
Des vents qui tremblent au printemps
Voguait cygne mourant sirène

Un jour le roi dans l'eau d'argent
Se noya puis la bouche ouverte
Il s'en revint en surnageant
Sur la rive dormir inerte
Face tournée au ciel changeant

Juin ton soleil ardente lyre
Brûle mes doigts endoloris
Triste et mélodieux délire
J'erre à travers mon beau Paris
Sans avoir le cœur d'y mourir

Les dimanches s'y éternisent
Et les orgues de Barbarie
Y sanglotent dans les cours grises
Les fleurs aux balcons de Paris
Penchent comme la tour de Pise

Soirs de Paris ivres du gin
Flambant de l'électricité
Les tramways feux verts sur l'échine
Musiquent au long des portées
De rails leur folie de machines

Les cafés gonflés de fumée
Crient tout l'amour de leurs tziganes
De tous leurs siphons enrhumés
De leurs garçons vêtus d'un pagne
Vers toi toi que j'ai tant aimée

Moi qui sais des lais pour les reines
Les complaintes de mes années
Des hymnes d'esclave aux murènes
La romance du mal-aimé
Et des chansons pour les sirènes

Alcools
© Éditions Gallimard

CLOTILDE

L'anémone et l'ancolie
Ont poussé dans le jardin
Où dort la mélancolie
Entre l'amour et le dédain

Il y vient aussi nos ombres
Que la nuit dissipera
Le soleil qui les rend sombres
Avec elles disparaîtra

Les déités des eaux vives
Laissent couler leurs cheveux
Passe il faut que tu poursuives
Cette belle ombre que tu veux

Alcools
© Éditions Gallimard

LE VOYAGEUR

À Fernand Fleuret

Ouvrez-moi cette porte où je frappe en pleurant

La vie est variable aussi bien que l'Euripe

Tu regardais un banc de nuages descendre
Avec le paquebot orphelin vers les fièvres futures
Et de tous ces regrets de tous ces repentirs
   Te souviens-tu

Vagues poissons arqués fleurs surmarines
Une nuit c'était la mer
Et les fleuves s'y répandaient

Je m'en souviens je m'en souviens encore

Un soir je descendis dans une auberge triste
Auprès de Luxembourg
Dans le fond de la salle il s'envolait un Christ
Quelqu'un avait un furet
Un autre un hérisson
L'on jouait aux cartes
Et toi tu m'avais oublié

Te souviens-tu du long orphelinat des gares
Nous traversâmes des villes qui tout le jour tournaient
Et vomissaient la nuit le soleil des journées

Ô matelots ô femmes sombres et vous mes compagnons
   Souvenez-vous-en

Deux matelots qui ne s'étaient jamais quittés
Deux matelots qui ne s'étaient jamais parlé
Le plus jeune en mourant tomba sur le côté

   Ô vous chers compagnons
Sonneries électriques des gares chant des moissonneuses
Traîneau d'un boucher régiment des rues sans nombre

Cavalerie des ponts nuits livides de l'alcool
Les villes que j'ai vues vivaient comme des folles

Te souviens-tu des banlieues et du troupeau plaintif
des paysages

Les cyprès projetaient sous la lune leurs ombres
J'écoutais cette nuit au déclin de l'été
Un oiseau langoureux et toujours irrité
Et le bruit éternel d'un fleuve large et sombre

Mais tandis que mourants roulaient vers l'estuaire
Tous les regards tous les regards de tous les yeux
Les bords étaient déserts herbus silencieux
Et la montagne à l'autre rive était très claire

Alors sans bruit sans qu'on pût voir rien de vivant
Contre le mont passèrent des ombres vivaces
De profil ou soudain tournant leurs vagues faces
Et tenant l'ombre de leurs lances en avant

Les ombres contre le mont perpendiculaire
Grandissaient ou parfois s'abaissaient brusquement
Et ces ombres barbues pleuraient humainement
En glissant pas à pas sur la montagne claire

Qui donc reconnais-tu sur ces vieilles photographies
Te souviens-tu du jour où une abeille tomba dans le feu
C'était tu t'en souviens à la fin de l'été

Deux matelots qui ne s'étaient jamais quittés
L'aîné portait au cou une chaîne de fer
Le plus jeune mettait ses cheveux blonds en tresse

Ouvrez-moi cette porte où je frappe en pleurant

La vie est variable aussi bien que l'Euripe

Alcools
© Éditions Gallimard

MARIE

Vous y dansiez petite fille
Y danserez-vous mère-grand
C'est la maclotte qui sautille
Toutes les cloches sonneront
Quand donc reviendrez-vous Marie

Les masques sont silencieux
Et la musique est si lointaine
Qu'elle semble venir des cieux
Oui je veux vous aimer mais vous aimer à peine
Et mon mal est délicieux

Les brebis s'en vont dans la neige
Flocons de laine et ceux d'argent
Des soldats passent et que n'ai-je
Un cœur à moi ce cœur changeant
Changeant et puis encor que sais-je

Sais-je où s'en iront tes cheveux
Crépus comme mer qui moutonne
Sais-je où s'en iront tes cheveux
Et tes mains feuilles de l'automne
Que jonchent aussi nos aveux

Je passais au bord de la Seine
Un livre ancien sous le bras
Le fleuve est pareil à ma peine
Il s'écoule et ne tarit pas
Quand donc finira la semaine

Alcools
© Éditions Gallimard

SALOMÉ

Pour que sourie encore une fois Jean-Baptiste
Sire je danserais mieux que les séraphins
Ma mère dites-moi pourquoi vous êtes triste
En robe de comtesse à côté du Dauphin

Mon cœur battait battait très fort à sa parole
Quand je dansais dans le fenouil en écoutant
Et je brodais des lys sur une banderole
Destinée à flotter au bout de son bâton

Et pour qui voulez-vous qu'à présent je la brode
Son bâton refleurit sur les bords du Jourdain
Et tous les lys quand vos soldats ô roi Hérode
L'emmenèrent se sont flétris dans mon jardin

Venez tous avec moi là-bas sous les quinconces
     Ne pleure pas ô joli fou du roi
Prends cette tête au lieu de ta marotte et danse
N'y touchez pas son front ma mère est déjà froid

Sire marchez devant trabants marchez derrière
Nous creuserons un trou et l'y enterrerons
Nous planterons des fleurs et danserons en rond
Jusqu'à l'heure où j'aurai perdu ma jarretière
     Le roi sa tabatière
     L'infante son rosaire
     Le curé son bréviaire

Alcools
© Éditions Gallimard

NUIT RHÉNANE

Mon verre est plein d'un vin trembleur comme une flamme
Écoutez la chanson lente d'un batelier
Qui raconte avoir vu sous la lune sept femmes
Tordre leurs cheveux verts et longs jusqu'à leurs pieds

Debout chantez plus haut en dansant une ronde
Que je n'entende plus le chant du batelier
Et mettez près de moi toutes les filles blondes
Au regard immobile aux nattes repliées

Le Rhin le Rhin est ivre où les vignes se mirent
Tout l'or des nuits tombe en tremblant s'y refléter
La voix chante toujours à en râle-mourir
Ces fées aux cheveux verts qui incantent l'été

Mon verre s'est brisé comme un éclat de rire

Alcools, Rhénanes
© Éditions Gallimard

MAI

Le mai le joli mai en barque sur le Rhin
Des dames regardaient du haut de la montagne
Vous êtes si jolies mais la barque s'éloigne
Qui donc a fait pleurer les saules riverains

Or des vergers fleuris se figeaient en arrière
Les pétales tombés des cerisiers de mai
Sont les ongles de celle que j'ai tant aimée
Les pétales flétris sont comme ses paupières

Sur le chemin du bord du fleuve lentement
Un ours un singe un chien menés par des tziganes
Suivaient une roulotte traînée par un âne
Tandis que s'éloignait dans les vignes rhénanes
Sur un fifre lointain un air de régiment

Le mai le joli mai a paré les ruines
De lierre de vigne vierge et de rosiers
Le vent du Rhin secoue sur le bord les osiers
Et les roseaux jaseurs et les fleurs nues des vignes

Alcools, Rhénanes
© Éditions Gallimard

LA LORELEY

À Jean Sève

À Bacharach il y avait une sorcière blonde
Qui laissait mourir d'amour tous les hommes à la ronde

Devant son tribunal l'évêque la fit citer
D'avance il l'absolvit à cause de sa beauté

Ô belle Loreley aux yeux pleins de pierreries
De quel magicien tiens-tu ta sorcellerie

Je suis lasse de vivre et mes yeux sont maudits
Ceux qui m'ont regardée évêque en ont péri

Mes yeux ce sont des flammes et non des pierreries
Jetez jetez aux flammes cette sorcellerie

Je flambe dans ces flammes ô belle Loreley
Qu'un autre te condamne tu m'as ensorcelé

Évêque vous riez Priez plutôt pour moi la Vierge
Faites-moi donc mourir et que Dieu vous protège

Mon amant est parti pour un pays lointain
Faites-moi donc mourir puisque je n'aime rien

Mon cœur me fait si mal il faut bien que je meure
Si je me regardais il faudrait que j'en meure

Mon cœur me fait si mal depuis qu'il n'est plus là
Mon cœur me fit si mal du jour où il s'en alla

L'évêque fit venir trois chevaliers avec leurs lances
Menez jusqu'au couvent cette femme en démence

Va-t'en Lore en folie va Lore aux yeux tremblants
Tu seras une nonne vêtue de noir et blanc

Puis ils s'en allèrent sur la route tous les quatre
La Loreley les implorait et ses yeux brillaient comme des astres

Chevaliers laissez-moi monter sur ce rocher si haut
Pour voir une fois encore mon beau château

Pour me mirer une fois encore dans le fleuve
Puis j'irai au couvent des vierges et des veuves

Là-haut le vent tordait ses cheveux déroulés
Les chevaliers criaient Loreley Loreley

Tout là-bas sur le Rhin s'en vient une nacelle
Et mon amant s'y tient il m'a vue il m'appelle

Mon cœur devient si doux c'est mon amant qui vient
Elle se penche alors et tombe dans le Rhin

Pour avoir vu dans l'eau la belle Loreley
Ses yeux couleur du Rhin ses cheveux de soleil

Alcools, Rhénanes
© Éditions Gallimard

À LA SANTÉ

I

Avant d'entrer dans ma cellule
Il a fallu me mettre nu
Et quelle voix sinistre ulule
Guillaume qu'es-tu devenu

Le Lazare entrant dans la tombe
Au lieu d'en sortir comme il fit
Adieu adieu chantante ronde
Ô mes années ô jeunes filles

II

Non je ne me sens plus là
       Moi-même
Je suis le quinze de la
       Onzième

Le soleil filtre à travers
       Les vitres
Ses rayons font sur mes vers
       Les pitres

Et dansent sur le papier
       J'écoute
Quelqu'un qui frappe du pied
       La voûte

Alcools
© Éditions Gallimard

CORS DE CHASSE

Notre histoire est noble et tragique
Comme le masque d'un tyran
Nul drame hasardeux ou magique
Aucun détail indifférent
Ne rend notre amour pathétique

Et Thomas de Quincey buvant
L'opium poison doux et chaste
À sa pauvre Anne allait rêvant
Passons passons puisque tout passe
Je me retournerai souvent

Les souvenirs sont cors de chasse
Dont meurt le bruit parmi le vent

Alcools
© Éditions Gallimard

VALERY LARBAUD

(1881-1957)

Valery Larbaud se fait d'abord connaître par une traduction de
La Chanson du vieux marin de Coleridge. Avec Joyce, dont il est
l'ami, il travaille aussi à la révision de la version française d'*Ulysse*,
il est également l'introducteur en France de plusieurs poètes
étrangers, dont l'Américain Walt Whitman. Dans le même temps,
il compose des poèmes, mais il préfère les attribuer à un
personnage de fiction, un double avec lequel on ne peut tout à fait
le confondre, bien qu'il lui prête ses goûts, ses mœurs de riche
dilettante et de grand voyageur. Son héros, le jeune milliardaire
A. O. Barnabooth, parcourt l'Europe dont plusieurs langues lui
sont familières, et, de palace en train de luxe, visite différents pays,
se délecte du mouvement incessant de sa vie, et note ses
impressions, tout en esquissant de lui-même un portrait fait de
confidences et d'interrogations, à la fois complaisant et critique.
Ses *Poésies* et son *Journal intime* qui en sont le registre, sont
publiés, en même temps que le conte du *Pauvre Chemisier*, sous le
titre général d'*Œuvres complètes d'A. O. Barnabooth*.

Pourquoi ce déguisement ? C. L. Philippe, dans une lettre à
Larbaud, suggère que c'est sans doute l'invention romanesque
qui a rendu possible la création poétique : « Peut-être est-ce
Barnabooth qui vous a donné l'idée de chanter ces choses, mais la
matière en était si belle que vous les avez chantées pour vous-
même... Vous avez créé Barnabooth parce que vous le conteniez...
il vous faut, mon cher ami, accepter maintenant votre livre comme
il est. » Marcel Arland qui cite ces lignes dans sa préface à l'édition
de La Pléiade, explique cette distance par le plaisir qu'aurait eu

Larbaud à écrire sans contrainte tout en n'ayant pas à assumer les imperfections qui pouvaient en résulter. On peut penser plutôt que l'altérité de Barnabooth (tant il est vrai que « je est un autre »), fut pour l'auteur l'indispensable révélateur d'une singulière présence qui le hantait. Dans le poème intitulé *Ma Muse*, il s'interroge :

> *Je suis agi par les lois invincibles du rythme,*
> *Je ne les comprends pas moi-même : elles sont là,*
> *Ô Diane, Apollon, grands dieux neurasthéniques*
> *Et farouches, est-ce vous qui me dictez ces accents,*
> *Ou n'est-ce qu'une illusion, quelque chose*
> *De moi-même purement – un borborygme ?*

À travers l'humour sur soi qui est une constante de son œuvre, perce l'étonnement sur ce qu'il nomme ailleurs par dérision « la bête lyrique qui bondit dans mon sein ! » Le ton de sarcasme, l'emphase caricaturale, les juxtapositions cocasses (« éclairs du génie ; agitation / De la digestion qui se fait ;... ») appartiennent depuis toujours au registre des fantaisistes dont la lignée se prolonge à travers les siècles et finit même par donner son nom à une école. L'originalité de Barnabooth est de les mêler à la peinture des régions lointaines qu'il visite. La littérature de l'exotisme se présente le plus souvent chez les autres, avec le sérieux du témoignage, la jubilation de la découverte ou la gravité du désenchantement. Or, qu'il célèbre l'Europe d'Elseneur à Leuconoë, et de Kharkov à Naples, qu'il évoque une jeune mendiante d'Andalousie ou de Trafalgar Square, ou bien le spectacle d'un port contemplé depuis le navire à travers « le hublot rond et clair, découpant la nuit », ou encore les paysages que déroule l'Orient-Express « entre Wirballen et Pskow », ce jeune homme iconoclaste ne cesse jamais de se moquer de lui-même, de railler sa soif de voyage et de dénoncer le désir quasi satanique de possession du monde qui le meut :

> *Oh ! tout savoir, toutes les langues !*
> *Avoir lu tous les livres et tous les commentaires :*
> *... et dominer le monde,*
> *Par la science, de la coulisse, comme on tiendrait*
> *Dans un seul poing les ficelles de ces pantins multicolores.*

Sentir qu'on est si haut qu'on est pris de vertige,
Comme si quelqu'un vous murmurait les mots.
« Je te donnerai tout cela » sur la montagne.

Cependant il arrive aussi à cet insatiable voyageur de souffrir de cet éternel exil. Mais après une halte, il repart, car son cœur de vagabond réclame « la trépidation des trains et des navires, / Et une angoisse sans bonheur sans cesse alimentée ».

On ne trouve pas vraiment de modèle à la poésie de Larbaud, même s'il a aimé, et peut-être parfois imité, les cartes postales rimées et moqueuses du poète H. J. M. Levet dont il préfaça l'édition. La poésie exotique des Parnassiens ne fait pas de place au voyage lui-même. Avant eux c'est à la prose que les romantiques confiaient leurs impressions des lointains, réservant aux vers le croquis pittoresque, le dessin pris sur le vif et parfois imaginaire où s'immobilise un fragment d'espace. Baudelaire, le premier, a dit l'allégresse des départs et les promesses qu'offre le monde au « vaste appétit » du voyageur, mais en soulignant la vanité de cette fuite hors de soi et l'amer savoir qu'on en retire. Si Barnabooth n'est pas étranger à ce spleen, le voyage n'en demeure pas moins pour lui à chaque moment cette « porte ouverte sur l'immensité charmante / De la Terre... » une porte qui ne doit jamais être refermée. Larbaud étend ainsi le domaine de la poésie à des thèmes nouveaux, d'autres poètes le suivront dans cette voie. Aucun d'eux n'aura le ton d'élégante et spirituelle désinvolture qui le caractérise.

ODE

Prête-moi ton grand bruit, ta grande allure si douce,
Ton glissement nocturne à travers l'Europe illuminée,
Ô train de luxe ! et l'angoissante musique
Qui bruit le long de tes couloirs de cuir doré,
Tandis que derrière les portes laquées, aux loquets de cuivre lourd,
Dorment les millionnaires.
Je parcours en chantonnant tes couloirs
Et je suis ta course vers Vienne et Budapesth,
Mêlant ma voix à tes cent mille voix,
Ô Harmonika-Zug !

J'ai senti pour la première fois toute la douceur de vivre,
Dans une cabine du Nord-Express, entre Wirballen et Pskow.
On glissait à travers des prairies où des bergers,
Au pied de groupes de grands arbres pareils à des collines,
Étaient vêtus de peaux de moutons crues et sales...
(Huit heures du matin en automne, et la belle cantatrice
Aux yeux violets chantait dans la cabine à côté.)
Et vous, grandes places à travers lesquelles j'ai vu passer la Sibérie
    et les monts du Samnium,
La Castille âpre et sans fleurs, et la mer de Marmara sous une
    pluie tiède !

Prêtez-moi, ô Orient-Express, Sud-Brenner-Bahn, prêtez-moi
Vos miraculeux bruits sourds et
Vos vibrantes voix de chanterelle ;
Prêtez-moi la respiration légère et facile
Des locomotives hautes et minces, aux mouvements
Si aisés, les locomotives des rapides,
Précédant sans effort quatre wagons jaunes à lettres d'or
Dans les solitudes montagnardes de la Serbie,
Et, plus loin, à travers la Bulgarie pleine de roses...

Ah ! il faut que ces bruits et que ce mouvement
Entrent dans mes poèmes et disent
Pour moi ma vie indicible, ma vie
D'enfant qui ne veut rien savoir, sinon
Espérer éternellement des choses vagues.

Les Poésies d'A. O. Barnabooth © Éditions Gallimard

L'ANCIENNE GARE DE CAHORS

Voyageuse ! ô cosmopolite ! à présent
Désaffectée, rangée, retirée des affaires.
Un peu en retrait de la voie,
Vieille et rose au milieu des miracles du matin,
Avec ta marquise inutile
Tu étends au soleil des collines ton quai vide
(Ce quai qu'autrefois balayait
La robe d'air tourbillonnant des grands express)
Ton quai silencieux au bord d'une prairie,
Avec les portes toujours fermées de tes salles d'attente,
Dont la chaleur de l'été craquèle les volets...
Ô gare qui as vu tant d'adieux,
Tant de départs et tant de retours,
Gare, ô double porte ouverte sur l'immensité charmante
De la Terre, où quelque part doit se trouver la joie de Dieu
Comme une chose inattendue, éblouissante ;
Désormais tu reposes et tu goûtes les saisons
Qui reviennent portant la brise ou le soleil, et tes pierres
Connaissent l'éclair froid des lézards ; et le chatouillement
Des doigts légers du vent dans l'herbe où sont les rails
Rouges et rugueux de rouille,
Est ton seul visiteur.
L'ébranlement des trains ne te caresse plus :
Ils passent loin de toi sans s'arrêter sur ta pelouse,
Et te laissent à ta paix bucolique, ô gare enfin tranquille
Au cœur frais de la France.

Les Poésies d'A. O. Barnabooth
© Éditions Gallimard

MATIN DE NOVEMBRE PRÈS D'ABINGDON

Les collines dans le brouillard, sous le ciel de cendre bleue
Comme elles sont hautes et belles !
Ô jour simple, mêlé de brume et de soleil !

Marcher dans l'air froid, à travers ces jardins,
Le long de cette Tamise qui me fait songer aux vers de Samain,
Marcher sur la terre de nouveau inconnue, toute changée,
Et pareille au pays des fées, ce matin d'arrière-automne...
Ô nature voilée, mystérieux paysages, vous ressemblez
Aux blocs des maisons géantes et aux avenues brumeuses de la
    ville,
Vous avez l'imprécis grandiose des horizons urbains.

Les Poésies d'A. O. Barnabooth
© Éditions Gallimard

CATHERINE POZZI

(1882-1937)

L'œuvre poétique de Catherine Pozzi tient en une mince plaquette de vers. Il n'importe, la découverte de ces strophes qui semblent surgies d'un autre temps donne au lecteur l'émotion que fait naître la vue d'une belle amphore remontée des profondeurs. Par leur métrique et leur vocabulaire ces poèmes évoquent la Renaissance. La très haute conception de l'amour qui s'y exprime semble nourrie du néoplatonisme cher à l'École lyonnaise et on croit parfois entendre la voix ardente de Louise Labé à qui un poème intitulé *Nyx* est d'ailleurs dédié.

L'influence de Paul Valéry, dont Catherine Pozzi fut l'admiratrice et l'amie passionnée, est également évidente dans cette œuvre. On en voit la marque en particulier dans *Maya* dont certains vers semblent extraits de *Charmes* ; celui qui clôt le poème, « Singulier soleil de calme couronné », peut en fournir un exemple : le recours à une alliance de l'abstrait et du concret, à la recherche d'effet sonore par la répétition des sifflantes et des sons durs, et à la diérèse classique, sont des procédés fréquents chez Valéry.

Cependant ces vers ont un accent personnel qui les fait échapper à leurs modèles. Au-delà de la recherche exigeante de perfection formelle et de concentration de l'idée, ce qui frappe dans ces poèmes plus abstraits que métaphoriques, c'est l'intensité pathétique de la passion et parfois du désespoir.

AVE

Très haut amour, s'il se peut que je meure
Sans avoir su d'où je vous possédais,
En quel soleil était votre demeure
En quel passé votre temps, en quelle heure
Je vous aimais,

Très haut amour qui passez la mémoire,
Feu sans foyer dont j'ai fait tout mon jour,
En quel destin vous traciez mon histoire,
En quel sommeil se voyait votre gloire,
Ô mon séjour...

Quand je serai pour moi-même perdue
Et divisée à l'abîme infini,
Infiniment, quand je serai rompue,
Quand le présent dont je suis revêtue
Aura trahi,

Par l'univers en mille corps brisée,
De mille instants non rassemblés encor,
De cendre aux cieux jusqu'au néant vannée,
Vous referez pour une étrange année
Un seul trésor

Vous referez mon nom et mon image
De mille corps emportés par le jour,
Vive unité sans nom et sans visage,
Cœur de l'esprit, ô centre du mirage
Très haut amour.

MARIE-NOËL

(1883-1967)

Il y a de nombreuses demeures dans la Maison de poésie, comme dans celle du Père, Marie Noël a reçu en partage la plus humble et la plus cachée, à l'image de sa vie toute de discrétion et de prière. Même si un prix de l'Académie française vint à la fin couronner son œuvre, on peut dire qu'elle vécut presque ignorée de ses contemporains durant de longues années, ou parfois dédaignée pour des poèmes trop vite qualifiés de poèmes « d'eau bénite ».

Elle écrit le premier d'entre eux en 1908, elle a vingt-cinq ans, et son premier recueil, *Les Chansons et les heures*, publié à compte d'auteur, paraît en 1921. Elle a d'abord composé des musiques : « J'ai commencé par chercher des paroles pour mes airs... il m'arriva de ne plus trouver que des paroles. »

Voici les termes qu'elle emploie pour parler de l'inspiration :

> *Les chansons que je fais, qu'est-ce qui les a faites ?...*
>
> *Souvent il m'en arrive une au plus noir de moi...*
> *Je ne sais pas comment, je ne sais pas pourquoi*
> *C'est cette folle au lieu de cent que je souhaite.*

Tous ses poèmes semblent en effet appeler une musique, les mots et les rythmes de la chanson viennent spontanément sous sa plume, mais elle pratique aussi les formes anciennes du rondeau ou de la villanelle et elle n'ignore pas le poème en prose. Sous l'apparente simplicité des sujets et du vocabulaire, un sens très sûr de la langue poétique se fait jour. La sienne est la traduction d'une intériorité dont la richesse est sans rapport avec l'effacement d'une vie pauvre en événements, occupée aux travaux quotidiens ou à des œuvres charitables. On aurait tort, dit en substance Henri Gouhier dans sa préface au recueil de 1921, de voir en elle une de ces vieilles filles des *Scènes de la vie de province*, ou une pieuse demoiselle dont la vie se limite aux activités de sa paroisse et aux visites de Monsieur le Doyen.

Le père de Marie, Louis Rouget (Noël est un pseudonyme), professeur agrégé de philosophie et incroyant, veille à la formation intellectuelle de sa fille. Il choisit pour ses études le collège puis le lycée d'Auxerre, et non un pensionnat pour jeunes filles, il lui fait aimer les tragiques grecs et les philosophes. Sa curiosité de lectrice est très grande ; elle découvre les grands mystiques et recopie des citations de leurs œuvres, elle en relève aussi dans Goethe, Rilke, Milosz, Mauriac ou Julien Green. Dans ses dernières années, dit encore Henri Gouhier, devenue presque aveugle, elle se fait lire des vers d'Aragon.

Elle laisse publier à la fin de sa vie ses *Notes intimes*. Ce n'est pas un journal au sens habituel du terme, car le quotidien y est constamment transfiguré par la méditation spirituelle ; on y trouve notamment la relation de deux crises intérieures où sa foi a vacillé et où elle a fait l'expérience des ténèbres intérieures :

« Dieu écroulé. Trois jours durant, trois nuits, j'essayais de le reconstruire... Trois jours durant, combat désespéré, vaine sueur pour ressusciter, pour sauver Dieu. Agonie, obsession... » C'est le récit de la première d'entre elles, « L'Enfer des trois jours » ; sept ans plus tard, elle désignera la suivante sous le titre de « L'Enfer des sept semaines ». Les mystiques connaissent ces nuits de la foi, et l'expérience dont témoignent ces épreuves terribles interdit de voir en Marie Noël on ne sait quelle fade dévote. La mort d'un enfant de douze ans, son jeune frère, plus tard le spectacle terrible de l'agonie de blessés de guerre, l'ont affrontée au scandale de la mort et elle n'a jamais cessé d'entendre, à travers le *Livre de Job*, comme elle le dit, « l'inconsolable cri de l'homme ». Sa simplicité, la volontaire humilité de son inspiration ne sont pas le fruit d'une vie paisible bercée d'illusions réconfortantes, mais sa manière propre de traduire ce qu'elle appelle « le chant de l'âme ». La limpidité de la rivière n'en exclut pas la profondeur, et l'on peut percevoir à travers ses strophes transparentes quelque chose du mystère des êtres et de l'amour, la trace d'une ineffable présence.

PRIÈRE

Mon Dieu, source sans fond de la douceur humaine,
Je laisse en m'endormant couler mon cœur en Vous
Comme un vase tombé dans l'eau de la fontaine
Et que Vous remplissez de Vous-même sans nous.

En Vous demain matin je reviendrai le prendre
Plein de l'amour qu'il faut pour la journée. Ô Dieu,
Il n'en tient guère, hélas ! Vous avez beau répandre
Vos flots en lui, jamais il n'en garde qu'un peu.

Mais renouvelez-moi sans fin ce peu d'eau vive,
Donnez-le-moi dès l'aube, au pied du jour ardu
Et redonnez-le-moi lorsque le soir arrive,
Avant le soir, Seigneur, car je l'aurai perdu.

Ô Vous de qui le jour reçoit le jour sans trêve,
Par qui l'herbe qui pousse est poussée en la nuit,
Qui sans cesse ajoutez à l'arbre qui s'élève
L'invisible hauteur qui dans l'air le conduit,

Donnez à mon cœur faible et de pauvres limites,
Mon cœur à si grand peine aimant et fraternel,
Dieu patient des œuvres lentes et petites,
Donnez à chaque instant mon amour éternel.

Les Chants de la merci
© Éditions Gallimard

RETRAITE

Quand viendra le soir au bout des années
Où, l'épaule basse et les yeux rougis,
Je ne serai plus, traînante et fanée,
Qu'une vieille en trop qui vague au logis ;

Quand la maison mienne à qui je fus douce
Ne me fera plus ni place, ni part ;
Quand le feu qui prend, le jardin qui pousse,
Tous ingrats, tiendront mes mains à l'écart ;

Quand j'aurai perdu ma dernière aiguille
Et ne pourrai plus rien qu'aimer tout bas,
Rien que gêner peu mes petites-filles,
Mes belles enfants qui ne m'aiment pas ;

Alors j'ouvrirai la porte à voix basse
Comme une pauvresse à jamais qui sort
Pour aller jeter au chemin qui passe
Le bout déchiré de son mauvais sort.

Alors, quand le jour hésite et décline,
Comme une étrangère à jamais qui part
À jamais... alors, comme une orpheline
Dont le cri n'a plus d'abri nulle part,

Je m'en irai seule avec mon pauvre âge
Qui n'a plus ni chant, ni charme, ni fleur,
Je m'en irai seule à la mort sauvage,
Sans faire alentour ni bruit, ni malheur.

J'irai retrouver le pré seul au monde
Où je traversais, petite, un bonheur
Que nul autre pré ne sut à la ronde,
Le champ oublié de tous les faneurs ;

Le champ égaré depuis mon enfance
Que les bois au fond de leur secret noir
Ont si loin serré dans un grand silence
Que nul sentier clair n'a su le revoir.

Là se tient la fleur qui n'est pas sortie
Pour d'autres que moi de mon prime temps.
Peut-être en ce champ, derrière l'ortie,
Que l'oiseau de l'aube à mi-ciel m'attend ?...

J'entrerai dedans sans bouquet ni gerbe,
La fleur et l'oiseau perdus y seront.
Je m'enfermerai dans ma chambre d'herbe...
Ce que j'y viens faire, eux seuls le sauront.

Comme un qui se dit sa dernière messe,
Alors, en ce champ pris d'une pâleur,
Je commencerai d'une voix qui baisse
À me chanter l'air qui brise le cœur.

Là je pleurerai mes petites belles
À qui leurs beaux ans dorés font la cour ;
Là pour les quitter sans qu'on me rappelle,
Je les aimerai de dernier amour.

Là je pleurerai pour finir de vivre...
Une tourterelle au soleil couchant
Gémira longtemps sans qu'on la délivre.
Le jour fleur à fleur sortira du champ.

Pas à pas le temps faible qui persiste
À battre en mon cœur sans savoir pourquoi
Sortira du monde... Et les feuilles tristes
Qui meurent le soir tomberont sur moi.

Chants d'arrière-saison

CRÉPUSCULE

L'heure viendra... l'heure vient... elle est venue
Où je serai l'étrangère en ma maison,
Où j'aurai sous le front une ombre inconnue
Qui cache ma raison aux autres raisons.

Ils diront que j'ai perdu ma lumière
Parce que je vois ce que nul œil n'atteint :
La lueur d'avant mon aube la première
Et d'après mon soir le dernier qui s'éteint.

Ils diront que j'ai perdu ma présence
Parce qu'attentive aux présages épars
Qui m'appellent de derrière ma naissance,
J'entends s'ouvrir les demeures d'autre part.

Ils diront que ma bouche devient folle
Et que les mots n'y savent plus ce qu'ils font
Parce qu'au bord du jour pâle, mes paroles
Sortent d'un silence insolite et profond.

Ils diront que je retombe au bas âge
Qui n'a pas encore appris la vérité
Des ans clairs et leur sagesse de passage,
Parce que je retourne à l'Éternité.

Chants d'arrière-saison

L'ÎLE

Solitude au vent, ô sans pays, mon Île
Que les barques de loin entourent d'élans
Et d'appels sous l'essor gris des goëlands,
Mon Île, mon lieu sans port, ni quai, ni ville,

Mon Île où s'élance en secret la montagne
La plus haute que Dieu heurte du talon
Et repousse... Ô Seule entre les aquilons
Qui n'as que la mer farouche pour compagne.

Temps où se plaint l'air en éternels préludes,
Mon Île où l'Amour me héla sur le bord
D'un chemin de cieux qui descendait à mort,
Espace où les vols se brisent, Solitude,

Solitude, Aire en émoi de Cœur immense
Qui sans cesse jette au large ses oiseaux,
Sans cesse au-dessus d'infranchissables eaux,
Sans cesse les perd, sans cesse recommence

Désolation royale, terre folle
Que berce l'abîme entre ses bras massifs,
Mon Île, tu tiens un Silence captif
Qu'interroge en vain la houle des paroles.

Chants des temps irréels

JULES SUPERVIELLE

(1884-1960)

Dans l'un de ses premiers recueils, *Les Poèmes de l'humour triste*, dont le ton rappelle celui de Laforgue, Supervielle sollicite notre indulgence pour le poète :

> *Soyez bons pour le Poète,*
> *Le plus doux des animaux,*
> *Nous prêtant son cœur sa tête,*
> *Incorporant tous nos maux,*
> *Il se fait notre jumeau...*

Ce ton de dérision affectueuse est sa marque personnelle ; on le retrouve jusque dans les œuvres plus ambitieuses, ainsi *La Fable du monde* qui réinvente la Genèse et fait intervenir le Créateur, nous présente un « Dieu très atténué », celui auquel le poète adresse sa « Prière à l'inconnu » :

> *Je voudrais, mon Dieu sans visage et peut-être sans espérance,*
> *Attirer ton attention, parmi tant de ciels, vagabonde,*
> *Sur les hommes qui n'ont plus de repos sur la planète...*

Car le poète choisit toujours de parler à mi-voix, sans jamais hausser le ton, il a toujours l'air, dit Albert Béguin, « de ne jamais insister sur rien, de s'en tenir à ce qu'on pourrait appeler la surface profonde du monde »...) mais sa discrétion, l'humilité voulue de la parole poétique n'excluent ni l'expression de la douleur ni celle de l'angoisse, simplement le parti pris de simplicité et la musique des mots exorcisent le malheur, s'attachent à le rendre moins lourd.

Supervielle n'appartient à aucun des mouvements littéraires du siècle. Comme Michaux dont il fut l'ami, il reste en marge de tous les courants, et il côtoie les surréalistes sans être des leurs. Si son univers intérieur qui mêle rêve et réalité est assez proche de la surréalité dont ils se réclament, il n'y a aucun hermétisme dans ses poèmes, ils tendent au contraire « à ce que le surnaturel devienne naturel et coule de source (ou en ait l'air) » et à « faire en sorte que l'ineffable nous devienne familier tout en gardant ses racines fabuleuses ». C'est ce qu'il écrit dans des pages de réflexion sur la poésie qu'il intitule modestement : *En songeant à un art poétique.* Il ne s'agit pas pour moi, dit-il en substance, de refermer le poème sur un secret, mais de faire sortir de l'ombre tout ce qui peut en être soustrait. Et il ajoute en des termes dépourvus de toute prétention : « Je me donne l'illusion de seconder l'obscur dans sa montée vers la lumière. »

Ses écrits, qu'on lise son théâtre, ses contes ou ses poèmes, rendent tous un son semblable. Tous témoignent de l'originalité de sa vision et de l'authenticité de sa vocation de poète. Cette unité vient aussi de la présence de thèmes récurrents qui lui sont essentiels. Le premier, celui de l'espace, lui est presque imposé par son histoire personnelle. Il y associe l'océan qu'il a traversé tant de fois pour quitter ou rejoindre l'Uruguay sa terre natale, et la prairie des grandes chevauchées qui donne son surnom à Guanamiru : *l'Homme de la Pampa*, un « Hors venu », comme lui. L'espace de la nuit, devient par la suite le lieu privilégié d'aventures tout intérieures. Ce thème est l'un des plus révélateurs de son imaginaire personnel. Comme l'écrit encore Albert Béguin : « Supervielle poète de la Nuit. Poète des deux nuits, plutôt, "nuit du dehors, nuit du dedans" et son geste, sa magie propre est de rassembler ces ombres de la vie secrète tapie en nous, et ces autres ombres, celles des ténèbres sensibles. »

> *Nuit en moi, nuit au dehors,*
> *Elles risquent leurs étoiles,*
> *Les mêlant sans le savoir.*
> *Et je fais force de rames*
> *Entre ces nuits coutumières,*
> *Puis je m'arrête et regarde.*
> *Comme je me vois de loin !*

C'est parce que le corps du poète, et son cœur fragile, ce « Mineur obscur dont on entend les coups de pioche », ne sont pas fermés au monde extérieur, mais perméables à des allées et venues d'étoiles ou de créatures diverses, qu'ils deviennent le lieu des échanges et des métamorphoses, cette incessante féerie par laquelle le monde s'immisce dans un être poreux à toutes les présences. De cette disposition très particulière Supervielle témoigne avec simplicité : « Quand je vais à la campagne le paysage me devient presque tout de suite intérieur par je ne sais quel glissement du dehors vers le dedans, j'avance comme dans mon propre monde mental. » Cette connivence naturelle avec toute chose créée favorise le surgissement en lui de ces « amis inconnus », poisson, antilope ou oiseau, jaillis de son esprit et qui s'en détachent soudain, « Ce cheval qui s'élance est parti de mes yeux ». Il les a accueillis « plein de déférence et de songe », comme il laisse s'approcher de lui, l'envahir peu à peu, les « voix qui perdirent visage », ces âmes veuves de leur corps. N'est-il pas en effet plus apte que quiconque à entendre leurs voix, lui « le moins sûr de la grande assemblée » des vivants. Puis il les regarde s'éloigner, emportant un peu de sa force, un peu de sa vie.

Supervielle, et c'est là un autre aspect essentiel de sa personnalité poétique, a une vision du temps et de la mort assez insolite. L'enfance, qu'on peut croire irrémédiablement perdue, parle encore à travers sa voix d'adulte, elle est là, vivante, inchangée. Des défunts, connus ou inconnus, l'entourent, le serrent de près, si fraternels, si pareils à lui. Quant à l'âme, lorsqu'elle veille auprès du corps endormi dont elle a craint un instant d'être délogée, elle semble avoir la claire vision anticipée de sa propre mort. Voici ce qu'elle en dit :

> *Il n'est plus grande douleur*
> *Que ne pas pouvoir souffrir*
> *Et que l'âme soit sans gîte*
> *Devant des portes fermées.*
> *Un jour je serai privée*
> *De ce grand corps près de moi.*

Il est enfin le poète du silence et de la solitude :

C'est la couleuvre du silence
Qui vient dans ma chambre et s'allonge
Elle contourne l'encrier
Puis se glissant jusqu'à mon lit,
S'enroule autour de mon cœur même...,

et qui prévient son lecteur du poème *Toujours sans titre.*

Et vous pensiez avoir longtemps écrit,
Il n'en resta que cette page blanche
Où nul ne lit, où chacun pense lire,
Et qui se donne à force de silence.

Il est difficile, en effet, de lire ce poète sans entrer dans son univers. On pourrait même glisser avec lui dans une rêverie dont ce familier du songe tâche de se garder : « La poésie vient chez moi d'un rêve toujours latent. Ce rêve j'aime à le diriger, sauf les jours d'inspiration où j'ai l'impression qu'il se dirige tout seul. Je n'aime pas le rêve qui s'en va à la dérive (j'allais dire à la dérêve)... je n'aime l'étrange que s'il est acclimaté, amené à la température humaine. » Il n'impose rien. Cependant sa pudeur, son humanité, la simplicité voulue de ses poèmes, sa liberté prosodique – tout lui est bon du vers régulier à la prose rythmée –, et surtout une sorte d'innocence miraculeuse font de son lecteur un complice émerveillé.

LA SPHÈRE

Roulé dans tes senteurs, belle terre tourneuse,
Je suis enveloppé d'émigrants souvenirs,
Et mon cœur délivré des attaches peureuses
Se propage, gorgé d'aise et de devenir.

Sous l'émerveillement des sources et des grottes
Je me fais un printemps de villes et de monts
Et je passe de l'alouette au goémon,
Comme sur une flûte on va de note en note.

J'azure, fluvial, les gazons de mes jours,
Je narre le neigeux leurre de la Montagne
Aux collines venant à mes pieds de velours
Tandis que les hameaux dévalent des campagnes.

Et comme un éclatant abrégé des saisons,
Mon cœur découvre en soi tropiques et banquises
Voyageant d'île en cap et de port en surprise
Il démêle un intime écheveau d'horizons.

Gravitations
© Éditions Gallimard

LE MATIN DU MONDE

À Victor Llona

Alentour naissaient mille bruits
Mais si pleins encor de silence
Que l'oreille croyait ouïr
Le chant de sa propre innocence.

Tout vivait en se regardant,
Miroir était le voisinage
Où chaque chose allait rêvant
À l'éclosion de son âge.

Les palmiers trouvant une forme
Où balancer leur plaisir pur
Appelaient de loin les oiseaux
Pour leur montrer des dentelures.

Un cheval blanc découvrait l'homme
Qui s'avançait à petit bruit,
Avec la Terre autour de lui
Tournant pour son cœur astrologue.

Le cheval bougeait les naseaux
Puis hennissait comme en plein ciel
Et tout entouré d'irréel
S'abandonnait à son galop.

Dans la rue, des enfants, des femmes,
À de beaux nuages pareils,
S'assemblaient pour chercher leur âme
Et passaient de l'ombre au soleil.

Mille coqs traçaient de leurs chants
Les frontières de la campagne
Mais les vagues de l'océan
Hésitaient entre vingt rivages.

L'heure était si riche en rameurs,
En nageuses phosphorescentes
Que les étoiles oublièrent
Leurs reflets dans les eaux parlantes.

Gravitations
© Éditions Gallimard

LES CHEVAUX DU TEMPS

Quand les chevaux du Temps s'arrêtent à ma porte
J'hésite un peu toujours à les regarder boire
Puisque c'est de mon sang qu'ils étanchent leur soif.
Ils tournent vers ma face un œil reconnaissant
Pendant que leurs longs traits m'emplissent de faiblesse
Et me laissent si las, si seul et décevant
Qu'une nuit passagère envahit mes paupières
Et qu'il me faut soudain refaire en moi des forces
Pour qu'un jour où viendrait l'attelage assoiffé
Je puisse encore vivre et les désaltérer.

Les Amis inconnus
© Éditions Gallimard

LE POMMIER

À force de mourir et de n'en dire rien
Vous aviez fait un jour jaillir, sans y songer,
Un grand pommier en fleurs au milieu de l'hiver
Et des oiseaux gardaient de leurs becs inconnus
L'arbre non saisonnier, comme en plein mois de mai,
Et des enfants joyeux de soleil et de brume
Faisaient la ronde autour, à vivre résolus.
Ils étaient les témoins de sa vitalité.
Et l'arbre de donner ses fruits sans en souffrir
Comme un arbre ordinaire, et, sous un ciel de neige,
De passer vos espoirs de toute sa hauteur.
Et son humilité se voyait de tout près.
Oui, craintive, souvent, vous vous en approchiez.

Les Amis inconnus
© Éditions Gallimard

Le monde est plein de voix qui perdirent visage
Et tournent nuit et jour pour en demander un.
Je leur dis : « Parlez-moi de façon familière
Car c'est moi le moins sûr de la grande assemblée.
– N'allez pas comparer notre sort et le vôtre »,
Me répond une voix, « je m'appelais un tel,
Je ne sais plus mon nom, je n'ai plus de cervelle
Et ne puis disposer que de celle des autres.
Laissez-moi m'appuyer un peu sur vos pensées.
C'est beaucoup d'approcher une oreille vivante
Pour quelqu'un comme moi qui ne suis presque plus.
Croyez ce que j'en dis, je ne suis plus qu'un mort,
Je veux dire quelqu'un qui pèse ses paroles. »

Les Amis inconnus
© Éditions Gallimard

UN POÈTE

Je ne vais pas toujours seul au fond de moi-même
Et j'entraîne avec moi plus d'un être vivant.
Ceux qui seront entrés dans mes froides cavernes
Sont-ils sûrs d'en sortir même pour un moment ?
J'entasse dans ma nuit, comme un vaisseau qui sombre,
Pêle-mêle, les passagers et les marins,
Et j'éteins la lumière aux yeux, dans les cabines,
Je me fais des amis des grandes profondeurs.

Les Amis inconnus
© Éditions Gallimard

Attendre que la Nuit, toujours reconnaissable
À sa grande altitude où n'atteint pas le vent,
           Mais le malheur des hommes,
Vienne allumer ses feux intimes et tremblants
Et dépose sans bruit ses barques de pêcheurs,
Ses lanternes de bord que le ciel a bercées,
Ses filets étoilés dans notre âme élargie,
Attendre qu'elle trouve en nous sa confidente
Grâce à mille reflets et secrets mouvements
Et qu'elle nous attire à ses mains de fourrure,
Nous les enfants perdus maltraités par le jour
           Et la grande lumière,
Ramassés par la Nuit poreuse et pénétrante,
Plus sûre qu'un lit sûr sous un toit familier,
C'est l'abri murmurant qui nous tient compagnie,
C'est la couche où poser la tête qui déjà
           Commence à graviter,
À s'étoiler en nous, à trouver son chemin.

Les Amis inconnus
© Éditions Gallimard

DIEU CRÉE LA FEMME

Pense aux plages, pense à la mer,
Au lisse du ciel, aux nuages,
À tout cela devenant chair
Et dans le meilleur de son âge,
Pense aux tendres bêtes des bois,
Pense à leur peur sur tes épaules,
Aux sources que tu ne peux voir
Et dont le murmure t'isole,
Pense à tes plus profonds soupirs,
Ils deviendront un seul désir,
À ce dont tu chéris l'image,
Tu l'aimeras bien davantage.
Ce qui était beaucoup trop loin
Pour le parfum ou le reproche,
Tu vas voir comme il se rapproche
Se faisant femme jusqu'au lien,
Ce dont rêvaient tes yeux, ta bouche,
Tu vas voir comme tu le touches.
Elle aura des mains comme toi
Et pourtant combien différentes,
Elle aura des yeux comme toi
Et pourtant rien ne leur ressemble.
Elle ne te sera jamais
Complètement familière,
Tu voudras la renouveler
De mille confuses manières.
Voilà, tu peux te retourner
C'est la femme que je te donne
Mais c'est à toi de la nommer,
Elle approche de ta personne.

La Fable du monde
© Éditions Gallimard

Quand dorment les soleils sous nos humbles manteaux
Dans l'univers obscur qui forme notre corps,
Les nerfs qui voient en nous ce que nos yeux ignorent
Nous précèdent au fond de notre chair plus lente,
Ils peuplent nos lointains de leurs herbes luisantes
Arrachant à la chair de tremblantes aurores.

C'est le monde où l'espace est fait de notre sang ;
Des oiseaux teints de rouge et toujours renaissants
Ont du mal à voler près du cœur qui les mène
Et ne peuvent s'en éloigner qu'en périssant,
Car c'est en nous que sont les plus cruelles plaines
Où l'on périt de soif près de fausses fontaines.

Et nous allons ainsi, parmi les autres hommes,
Les uns parlant parfois à l'oreille des autres.

La Fable du monde
© Éditions Gallimard

« Beau monstre de la nuit, palpitant de ténèbres,
Vous montrez un museau humide d'outre-ciel,
Vous approchez de moi, vous me tendez la patte
Et vous la retirez comme pris d'un soupçon.
Pourtant je suis l'ami de vos gestes obscurs,
Mes yeux touchent le fond de vos sourdes fourrures.
Ne verrez-vous en moi un frère ténébreux
Dans ce monde où je suis bourgeois de l'autre monde,
Gardant par devers moi ma plus claire chanson.
Allez, je sais aussi les affres du silence
Avec mon cœur hâtif, usé de patience,
Qui frappe sans réponse aux portes de la mort.
– Mais la mort te répond par des intermittences
Quand ton cœur effrayé se cogne à la cloison,
Et tu n'es que d'un monde où l'on craint de mourir. »
Et les yeux dans les yeux, à petits reculons,
Le monstre s'éloigna dans l'ombre téméraire,
Et le ciel comme à l'ordinaire s'étoila.

La Fable du monde
© Éditions Gallimard

FRANCIS CARCO

(1886-1958)

Il a d'abord chanté la province où « les vergers sont remplis d'abeilles » et le décor familier :

> *Rien n'a changé : la maison blanche est toujours là,*
> *Mais la rouille a rongé les gonds et la serrure ...*
> *On n'entend plus bouger le cœur de la maison*
> *Qui se meurt de tristesse et de long abandon*
> *Parmi l'effeuillaison nostalgique des roses.*

Malgré la grâce de ces premiers vers où l'on décèle l'influence de Jammes et quelques traces aussi d'un symbolisme finissant, Carco n'a pas encore trouvé sa voie. Son originalité se manifeste lorsqu'il prend conscience, avec le groupe des Fantaisistes, d'un nouvel état d'esprit qui s'accommode mal des formes poétiques cultivées par la génération précédente. Ses amis et lui pensent alors qu'il faut en finir avec la préciosité, les recherches savantes et le verbe aristocratique, et renoncer aussi aux enflures de l'éloquence. « C'était, écrira plus tard le poète, une réaction profonde de la sensibilité contre de vieux clichés, des procédés usés jusqu'à la corde et un incroyable charabia. » Tous souhaitent donc composer, à l'exemple de Toulet, des pièces courtes où domine le décor, la sensation, et où l'on s'efforce dans un langage simple de faire affleurer l'indicible, en s'inspirant aussi des rythmes et de la grâce nonchalante de Verlaine.

Cependant ce qui est la marque propre de Carco dans ce groupe, c'est qu'il se fait le chantre des rues de Paris, en particulier de Montmartre, son quartier, dont les figures familières vont désormais peupler ses poèmes. Il trouve, pour évoquer les filles des rues et les voyous, une langue simple, une musique proche de la chanson populaire où la nostalgie et la tendresse amoureuse transfigurent la réalité sordide à la manière d'Apollinaire.

> *Cependant tu n'étais qu'une fille des rues,*
> *Qu'une innocente prostituée,*
> *Comme celle qui apparut,*
> *Dans le quartier de Whitechapel,*
> *Un soir, à Thomas de Quincey...*

On croit parfois entendre son modèle dans la fluidité naturelle du vers, et la tristesse du thème :...

> *Je marche seul comme autrefois,*
> *Et ton ombre couleur de pluie,*
> *Que le vent chasse à chaque pas,*
> *Ton ombre se perd dans la nuit*
> *Mais je la sens tout près de moi.*

La tristesse est l'une des dominantes de cette œuvre. Carco semble avoir une prédilection pour la pluie et la brume où se projette son inguérissable mélancolie. Mais il sait aussi célébrer ses amis vivants ou morts, à l'égard desquels sa fidélité est sans faille, et il enchâsse leurs noms dans ses vers ; il associe à ces évocations les poètes dont il se sent proche et dont il suit les traces, ceux qui ont avant lui déambulé dans Paris. Et c'est surtout le poète-chanteur de rues qui reste dans nos mémoires, car ces rues n'étaient pas pour lui un simple décor, le moyen d'un pittoresque facile, mais l'objet d'une étrange fascination. Ses vers en acquièrent un charme particulier. Il a témoigné aussi dans ses poèmes en prose du pouvoir de la ville sur son être :

> *Il existe dans Paris des lieux dont les forces mystérieuses agissent si*
> *puissamment sur moi que je ne puis m'y dérober... on dirait qu'un*
> *autre moi-même n'aura jamais fini d'errer à la poursuite de je ne sais*
> *quelles équivoques révélations.*

POÈME TRISTE

Mes amours pourrissent sous terre,
Où la pluie filtre doucement
Pour leur rappeler le mystère
De ce bruit d'eau que nous aimions...

Et le vent qui chassait les feuilles
Mortes déjà de l'autre année,
Qui les chassait dans les allées,
Qui les chassait, feuille après feuille,
Ou toutes ensemble envolées...

Le vent agite les feuillages...
Ce n'est pas un grand vent d'orage
Mais une voix qui se plaindrait
D'appeler, à bout de courage,
Ses tristes amours enterrées.

VERLAINIEN

Un arbre tremble sous le vent.
Les volets claquent.
Comme il a plu, l'eau fait des flaques.

Des feuilles volent sous le vent
      Qui les disperse
Et, brusquement, il pleut à verse.

Le jour décroît.
Sur l'horizon qui diminue,
Je vois la silhouette nue
D'un clocher mince avec sa croix.

Dans le silence,
J'entends la cloche d'un couvent.
Elle s'élève, elle s'élance
Et puis retombe avec le vent.

Un arbre que le vent traverse
      Geint doucement,
Comme une floue et molle averse
Qui s'enfle et tombe à tout moment.

Du vieil amour mélancolique
      Que j'ai pour toi,
Restera-t-il que la musique
Monotone de cette voix ?...

À L'AMITIÉ
(Fragments)

Emporte-moi dans ton délire,
Muse errante aux yeux clignotants,
Qui vaticines et prétends :
« *Mon bout de crayon, c'est ma lyre !*
Mais je n'ai plus de papier blanc. »
Tu me diras tes soirs d'ivresse,
Tes nuits de gloire, tes succès,
Villon, Nerval, Rimbaud, Musset,
Et, sous tes grands airs de pauvresse,
Je devinerai la détresse
De ton vieux cœur sombre et blessé.

Tu me raconteras Verlaine,
Son absinthe au petit matin
Dans ce bar des Grands-Augustins
D'où l'on voyait couler la Seine ;
Moustache en croc et cheveux teints,
Moréas, fier de son monocle,
Qui pérorait du haut d'un socle,
Pour un chœur d'antiques catins ;
Tu me raconteras Corbière
Tenant la toile, en matelot ;
Et Laforgue, les pieds dans l'eau,
Avec son gibus en arrière,
Son air lunaire et rigolo,
D'un rigolo à la manière
Falote d'un Pierrot falot,
Avant de mourir poitrinaire...

Un chien nous suit en gémissant,
On dirait presque un chien d'aveugle.
Sur la Seine un remorqueur beugle...
Mais quels sont ces autres passants
Qui vont piteux, honteux, grotesques
Et qui, sur le pavé glissant,

Enchevêtrent une arabesque
À la fois navrante et burlesque,
À contre-cœur, à contresens ?

Regarde, ce sont des artistes !
Ils s'en allaient le long des quais
Et le vent les entre-choquait
Tout en arrachant les feuillets
De leurs livres dépareillés
Dans les boîtes des bouquinistes.

« Ils ont tous été mes amants,
Dit la Muse en levant la tête
Eux aussi, se croyaient poètes
Et ils l'étaient à leurs vingt ans ! »

MORTEFONTAINE
(Fragments)

C'est le pays de Gérard de Nerval,
Avec ses bois, ses sources, ses prairies,
Ses horizons chargés de rêverie
Où le cerf brame et fait, de val en val,
Comme un caillou ricoche au clair de lune,
Sur l'eau qui dort, retentir tantôt l'une,
Tantôt l'autre des voix que l'écho multiplie.

Comme aux beaux jours de l'aimable Sylvie,
Près des étangs se tenant par la main,
On voit tourner, sous la paix des feuillages,
Telles qu'hier et telles que demain,
Les jeunes sœurs de ces fillettes sages
Qui sont, hélas ! mortes depuis longtemps
Sans qu'on en ait oublié les visages
Ni les yeux purs ni les jeux innocents.

On tire encore à l'arc dans le village :
Mortefontaine, est-il un nom plus doux ?
Mais on entend gémir la tourterelle
Au lent refrain que chante la plus belle :
« Beau chevalier, quand nous reviendrez-vous ? »

. . . .

Peut-être suis-je, après bien des années,
Le chevalier qui n'est pas revenu
Ou ce garçon qui, dans ses randonnées,
Surgissait brusquement du fond de l'avenue
Puis, sans un mot, passait et s'éloignait.

Ni toi ni moi n'en saurons davantage.
Pourquoi faut-il que nous ne puissions pas
Lever le voile et capter le message
Ou définir, dans le parfum des seringas,
La cause, ô mon amour, de ces vagabondages
Qui toujours en secret guidaient vers toi mes pas !

Je me souviens de la bohème,
De mes amours de ce temps-là !
Ô mes amours, j'ai trop de peine
Quand refleurissent les lilas...
Qu'est-ce que c'est que cette antienne ?
Qu'est-ce que c'est que cet air-là ?
Ô mes amours, j'ai trop de peine...
Le temps n'est plus de la bohème.
Au diable soient tous les lilas !
Il pleut dans le petit jour blême.
Il pleut, nous n'irons plus au bois.
Toutes les amours sont les mêmes,
Les morts ne ressuscitent pas.

Un vieil orgue, comme autrefois,
Moud, essoufflé « la Marjolaine ».
Ô mes amours de ce temps-là,
Jamais les mortes ne reviennent.
Elles dorment sous les lilas
Où les oiseaux chantent ma peine,
Sous les lilas qu'on a mis là...
Les jours s'en vont et les semaines :
Ô mes amours, priez pour moi...

SAINT-JOHN PERSE

(1887-1975)

Le lecteur de Saint-John Perse est arrêté par un premier obstacle, celui de la langue. Comme le souligne Claude Roy : « La phrase se parsème de vocables très rares, dont la bizarrerie n'est engendrée souvent que par nos ignorances. » Il est clair, par exemple, que « les plantes à siliques », « le fruit noir de l'amibe » ou « la sapotille », tout comme « les gomphrènes » ou « les acalyphes », sont plus connus du botaniste que du profane, et les termes de « ciliées de ris », de « guis » ou de « dalot », surtout familiers aux gens de mer. Par bien d'autres aspects cette œuvre est d'accès difficile. Dans l'étude qu'il consacre à la syntaxe si particulière du poète et à son vocabulaire, Caillois en fait le constat. Mais à ses yeux le recours aux termes rares et la rupture délibérée avec l'usage ordinaire de la langue n'ont rien de gratuit, non plus d'ailleurs que ses allusions parfois obscures à des civilisations lointaines. Tous ces partis pris sont nécessaires au poète, garant du sens, pour rendre compte de sa vision. Jamais en effet il ne cède « l'initiative aux mots ». S'en tenir à une approximation hâtive de l'expression ou à une fonction purement décorative du langage lui est impossible, comme le montre le soin méticuleux avec lequel il revoit, en parfait bilingue, la traduction anglaise de ses poèmes, et propose à son interlocuteur des variantes plus aptes, pense-t-il, à rendre les nuances du texte.

La forme qu'il adopte, celle du verset, est moins étrangère à la versification classique qu'il n'y paraît. À la différence de Claudel, Perse ne rompt jamais totalement avec les mesures habituelles du vers, mais lorsque viennent de se succéder hexamètres et alexandrins facilement décelables, un passage de prose poétique rompt soudain l'enchaînement trop régulier et libère le verset de tous les rythmes anciens. On peut cependant convenir avec Caillois que « le compte des syllabes, le parallélisme des formules, la distribution des sonorités, les métagrammes ou rimes accessoires contraignent l'auteur qui se sert d'une pareille prose à plus de servitudes que la métrique classique n'en imposa jamais à un versificateur ».

Celui qui s'est progressivement familiarisé avec cet idiome singulier peut découvrir l'ampleur majestueuse de l'œuvre. Une grande voix solennelle y redonne à la poésie sa dimension sacrée. Mais elle édifie un temple où les dieux sont absents.

Le « poème de la solitude dans l'action » qu'est *Anabase*, suggère par ce titre, à la fois la remontée vers les terres lointaines, – et l'on songe à celle des Grecs même si l'auteur récuse ce rapprochement –, et l'effort du cavalier qui se remet en selle prêt à reprendre le combat pour s'adjuger de nouveaux territoires, et surtout prendre possession de soi. « C'est, dit le poète, une "expédition vers l'intérieur" avec une signification à la fois géographique et spirituelle. »

Quelques années plus tôt il a composé et publié *Éloges*, il y peint le paradis de l'enfance et, à travers l'évocation de Crusoé revenu dans sa patrie, l'amertume de l'exil londonien. Le recueil suivant, *La Gloire des Rois*, avec les figures hiératiques de la Reine et du Prince, joint au dépaysement de l'exotisme un symbolisme assez mystérieux des personnages et des coutumes. Cependant c'est avec *Anabase* que Perse donne toute la mesure de son génie poétique. Sa parution suscite un concert d'éloges : Valéry, Gide, Jammes, Rilke, Hugo von Hoffmannstahl, Ungaretti, ou Eliot disent leur admiration. Valery Larbaud écrit alors : « La langue de la poésie française est entre ses mains comme un cheval de grande race dont il utilise les qualités mais qu'il oblige à marcher à une allure nouvelle et qui contrarie ses habitudes. »

À travers les quatre grands poèmes suivants s'exprime encore, sous une autre forme, la transhumance de l'âme et du verbe. Le dernier d'entre eux, *Vents*, dit avec une particulière éloquence le renouvellement de l'être qu'opère la puissance régénératrice « de très grandes forces en croissance sur toutes pistes de ce monde... » Elles seules sont capables d'enseigner « ce chant très pur où nul n'a connaissance » et dont le poète témoigne. C'est là, en effet, que Perse décrit sous forme métaphorique l'éveil de la conscience poétique. Les images qui surgissent dans ces livres détournent parfois le lecteur du dessein qui anime l'ensemble, tant elles offrent de prise au rêve : ainsi dès les premières lignes de *Pluies*, cette vision :

Le banyan de la pluie prend ses assises sur la Ville,
Un polypier hâtif monte à ses noces de corail dans tout ce lait d'eau vive...

ou encore celle-ci dans *Neiges* :

Il neigeait, et voici, nous en dirons merveilles : l'aube muette dans sa plume, comme une grande chouette fabuleuse en proie aux souffles de l'esprit, enflait son corps de dahlia blanc.

Amers paraît dix ans plus tard. C'est sans doute son œuvre majeure. Ses versets déploient la vision poétique originale que l'on pressentait auparavant. À travers le titre (les amers sont les repères visuels offerts au navigateur), la Mer est désignée comme pivot de ce grand poème dont l'objet essentiel est la marche de l'humanité vers son destin. Une lettre de Saint-John Perse est particulièrement explicite à cet égard :

« Et c'est la Mer que j'ai choisie, symboliquement comme miroir offert à ce destin – comme lieu de convergence et de rayonnement, vrai " lieu géométrique " et table d'orientation, en même temps que réservoir de forces éternelles pour l'accomplissement et le dépassement de l'homme cet insatiable migrateur. »

La parole humaine vouée jusqu'alors aux « choses de la Ville », éloquence, prière ou théâtre, va connaître enfin une dilatation dont la Mer est le signe. La fête incessante du rivage assailli de vagues offre l'image et la promesse d'une vie renouvelée. La Mer, mesure des rêves les plus audacieux, prophète de grandeur pour l'homme, fait écho en lui à son impatience des limites. Comme on le voit clairement ici, la conscience qu'a le poète « du drame de l'homme à la recherche du sacré » fonde chez lui la démarche poétique. Celle-ci consiste à proposer à la conscience individuelle, et à l'humanité tout entière, l'alliance avec les grandes forces élémentaires comme moyen de vivifier l'humain. La distribution du poème en Invocation, Strophe, Chœur, Dédicace, le rattache à la dramaturgie antique ; le souffle lyrique qui le porte l'apparente à l'Ode pindarique et à son inspiration religieuse. Car il s'agit, comme le montre une étude critique pénétrante (Henriette Levillain, *Le Rituel poétique de Saint-John Perse*, Idées Gallimard, 1977), d'instaurer un rituel. Déjà esquissé dans les œuvres précédentes, celui-ci se déploie enfin pleinement : l'homme, au moyen du contact avec les éléments, et particulièrement dans sa marche vers la mer, peut reprendre conscience de son origine sacrée ; à travers le *processionnal initiatique* que déroule le poème, la révélation ne vient pas d'en haut mais consiste pour lui en un dévoilement progressif de son secret intérieur.

La réflexion critique accompagne ici la création comme chez Baudelaire ou Mallarmé. La correspondance du poète, et surtout les deux textes majeurs que sont le *Discours de Stockholm*, à l'occasion de la remise du prix Nobel, et *L'Hommage à Dante*, pour le septième centenaire de sa naissance, nous apprennent ce que fut son propre cheminement spirituel, et la place, éminente à ses yeux, qu'occupe la poésie dans l'aventure humaine. Le très haut registre où se situe son œuvre permet d'appliquer à Saint-John Perse ce qu'il dit lui-même à propos de *La Divine Comédie* : « Toute poétique est une ontologie. »

LE LIVRE

Et quelle plainte alors sur la bouche de l'âtre, un soir de longues pluies en marche vers la ville, remuait dans ton cœur l'obscure naissance du langage :

« …D'un exil lumineux – et plus lointain déjà que l'orage qui roule – comment garder les voies, ô mon Seigneur ! que vous m'aviez livrées ?

« … Ne me laisserez-vous que cette confusion du soir – après que vous m'ayez, un si long jour, nourri du sel de votre solitude,

« témoin de vos silences, de votre ombre et de vos grands éclats de voix ? »

– Ainsi tu te plaignais, dans la confusion du soir.

Mais sous l'obscure croisée, devant le pan de mur d'en face, lorsque tu n'avais pu ressusciter l'éblouissement perdu,

alors, ouvrant le Livre,

tu promenais un doigt usé entre les prophéties, puis le regard fixé au large, tu attendais l'instant du départ, le lever du grand vent qui te descellerait d'un coup, comme un typhon, divisant les nuées devant l'attente de tes yeux.

Éloges
© Éditions Gallimard

CHANSON

Il naissait un poulain sous les feuilles de bronze. Un homme mit des baies amères dans nos mains. Étranger. Qui passait. Et voici qu'il est bruit d'autres provinces à mon gré... « Je vous salue, ma fille, sous le plus grand des arbres de l'année. »

★

Car le soleil entre au Lion et l'Étranger a mis son doigt dans la bouche des morts. Étranger. Qui riait. Et nous parle d'une herbe. Ah ! tant de souffles aux provinces ! Qu'il est d'aisance dans nos voies ! que la trompette m'est délice, et la plume savante au scandale de l'aile !... « Mon âme, grande fille, vous aviez vos façons qui ne sont pas les nôtres. »

★

Il naquit un poulain sous les feuilles de bronze. Un homme mit ces baies amères dans nos mains. Étranger. Qui passait. Et voici d'un grand bruit dans un arbre de bronze. Bitume et roses, don du chant ! Tonnerre et flûtes dans les chambres ! Ah ! tant d'aisance dans nos voies, ah ! tant d'histoires à l'année, et l'Étranger à ses façons par les chemins de toute la terre !... « Je vous salue, ma fille, sous la plus belle robe de l'année. »

Anabase
© Éditions Gallimard

Nous n'habiterons pas toujours ces terres jaunes, notre délice...

L'Été plus vaste que l'Empire suspend aux tables de l'espace plusieurs étages de climats. La terre vaste sur son aire roule à pleins bords sa braise pâle sous les cendres.

– Couleur de soufre, de miel, couleur de choses immortelles, toute la terre aux herbes s'allumant aux pailles de l'autre hiver – et de l'éponge verte d'un seul arbre le ciel tire son suc violet.

Un lieu de pierres à mica ! Pas une graine pure dans les barbes du vent. Et la lumière comme une huile.

– De la fissure des paupières au fil des cimes m'unissant, je sais la pierre tachée d'ouïes, les essaims du silence aux ruches de lumière ; et mon cœur prend souci d'une famille d'acridiens...

Chamelles douces sous la tonte, cousues de mauves cicatrices, que les collines s'acheminent sous les données du ciel agraire – qu'elles cheminent en silence sur les incandescences pâles de la plaine ; et s'agenouillent à la fin, dans la fumée des songes, là où les peuples s'abolissent aux poudres mortes de la terre.

Ce sont de grandes lignes calmes qui s'en vont à des bleuissements de vignes improbables. La terre en plus d'un point mûrit les violettes de l'orage ; et ces fumées de sable qui s'élèvent au lieu des fleuves morts, comme des pans de siècles en voyage...

À voix plus basse pour les morts, à voix plus basse dans le jour. Tant de douceur au cœur de l'homme, se peut-il qu'elle faille à trouver sa mesure ?... « Je vous parle, mon âme ! – mon âme tout enténébrée d'un parfum de cheval ! » Et quelques grands oiseaux de terre, naviguant en Ouest, sont de bons mimes de nos oiseaux de mer.

À l'orient du ciel si pâle, comme un lieu saint scellé des linges de l'aveugle, des nuées calmes se disposent, où tournent les cancers du camphre et de la corne... Fumées qu'un souffle nous dispute ! la terre tout attente en ses barbes d'insectes, la terre enfante des merveilles !...

Et à midi, quand l'arbre jujubier fait éclater l'assise des tombeaux, l'homme clôt ses paupières et rafraîchit sa nuque dans les âges... Cavaleries du songe au lieu des poudres mortes, ô routes vaines qu'échevèle un souffle jusqu'à nous ! où trouver, où trouver les guerriers qui garderont les fleuves dans leurs noces ? Au bruit des grandes eaux en marche sur la terre, tout le sel de la terre tressaille dans les songes. Et soudain, ah ! soudain que nous veulent ces voix ? Levez un peuple de miroirs sur l'ossuaire des fleuves, qu'ils interjettent appel dans la suite des siècles ! Levez des pierres à ma gloire, levez des pierres au silence, et à la garde de ces lieux les cavaleries de bronze vert sur de vastes chaussées !...

(L'ombre d'un grand oiseau me passe sur la face.)

Anabase

Telle est l'instance extrême où le Poète a témoigné.

En ce point extrême de l'attente, que nul ne songe à regagner les chambres.

« Enchantement du jour à sa naissance... Le vin nouveau n'est pas plus vrai, le lin nouveau n'est pas plus frais...

« Quel est ce goût d'airelle, sur ma lèvre d'étranger, qui m'est chose nouvelle et m'est chose étrangère ?...

« À moins qu'il ne se hâte, en perdra trace mon poème... Et vous aviez si peu de temps pour naître à cet instant... »

(Ainsi quand l'Officiant s'avance pour les cérémonies de l'aube, guidé de marche en marche et assisté de toutes parts contre le doute – la tête glabre et les mains nues, et jusqu'à l'ongle, sans défaut – c'est un très prompt message qu'émet aux premiers feux du jour la feuille aromatique de son être.)

Et le Poète aussi est avec nous, sur la chaussée des hommes de son temps.

Allant le train de notre temps, allant le train de ce grand vent.

Son occupation parmi nous : mise en clair des messages. Et la réponse en lui donnée par illumination du cœur.

Non point l'écrit, mais la chose même. Prise en son vif et dans son tout.

Conservation non des copies, mais des originaux. Et l'écriture du poète suit le procès-verbal.

(Et ne l'ai-je pas dit ? les écritures aussi évolueront. – Lieu du propos : toutes grèves de ce monde.)

« Tu te révéleras, chiffre perdu !... Que trop d'attente n'aille énerver

« L'usage de notre ouïe ! nulle impureté souiller le seuil de la vision !... »

Et le Poète encore est avec nous, parmi les hommes de son temps, habité de son mal...

Comme celui qui a dormi dans le lit d'une stigmatisée, et il en est tout entaché,

Comme celui qui a marché dans une libation renversée, et il en est comme souillé,

Homme infesté du songe, homme gagné par l'infection divine,

Non point de ceux qui cherchent l'ébriété dans les vapeurs du chanvre, comme un Scythe,

Ni l'intoxication de quelque plante solanée – belladone ou jusquiame,

De ceux qui prisent la graine ronde d'Ologhi mangée par l'homme d'Amazonie,

Yaghé, liane du pauvre, qui fait surgir l'envers des choses – ou la plante Pî-lu,

Mais attentif à sa lucidité, jaloux de son autorité, et tenant clair au vent le plein midi de sa vision :

« Le cri ! le cri perçant du dieu ! qu'il nous saisisse en pleine foule, non dans les chambres,

« Et par la foule propagé qu'il soit en nous répercuté jusqu'aux limites de la perception...

« Une aube peinte sur les murs, muqueuse en quête de son fruit, ne saurait nous distraire d'une telle adjuration ! »

Et le Poète encore est parmi nous... Cette heure peut-être la dernière, cette minute même, cet instant !... Et nous avons si peu de temps pour naître à cet instant !

« ... Et à cette pointe extrême de l'attente, où la promesse elle-même se fait souffle.

« Vous feriez mieux vous-même de tenir votre souffle... Et le Voyant n'aura-t-il pas sa chance ? l'Écoutant sa réponse ?... »

Poète encore parmi nous... Cette heure peut-être la dernière... cette minute même !... cet instant !

– « Le cri ! le cri perçant du dieu sur nous ! »

Vents, III.6
© Éditions Gallimard

INVOCATION

I

Et vous, Mers, qui lisiez dans de plus vastes songes, nous
laisserez-vous un soir aux rostres de la Ville, parmi la pierre
publique et les pampres de bronze ?
Plus large, ô foule, notre audience sur ce versant d'un âge sans
déclin : la Mer, immense et verte comme une aube à l'orient des
hommes,
La Mer en fête sur ses marches comme une ode de pierre : vigile
et fête à nos frontières, murmure et fête à hauteur d'hommes – la
Mer elle-même notre veille, comme une promulgation divine...

L'odeur funèbre de la rose n'assiégera plus les grilles du
tombeau ; l'heure vivante dans les palmes ne taira plus son âme
d'étrangère... Amères, nos lèvres de vivants le furent-elles jamais ?
J'ai vu sourire aux feux du large la grande chose fériée : la Mer
en fête de nos songes, comme une Pâque d'herbe verte et comme
fête que l'on fête,
Toute la Mer en fête des confins, sous sa fauconnerie de nuées
blanches, comme domaine de franchise et comme terre de
mainmorte, comme province d'herbe folle et qui fut jouée aux
dés...

Inonde, ô brise, ma naissance ! Et ma faveur s'en aille au cirque
de plus vastes pupilles !... Les sagaies de Midi vibrent aux portes
de la joie. Les tambours du néant cèdent aux fifres de lumière. Et
l'Océan, de toutes parts, foulant son poids de roses mortes,
Sur nos terrasses de calcium lève sa tête de Tétrarque !

Amers
© Éditions Gallimard

PIERRE-JEAN JOUVE

(1887-1976)

L'évolution de son œuvre épouse son itinéraire intérieur. S'il renie ses premiers écrits marqués par l'unanimisme, c'est qu'après sa conversion il les sent étrangers à son être profond. Cependant le catholicisme ne lui apporte pas une réponse ou un apaisement, il y puise l'exigence d'une interrogation incessante sur son être. Or les lumières de la foi, non plus que sa connaissance de Freud et de la psychanalyse, ne lui permettent de surmonter les démons qu'il découvre dans son inconscient. Dans l'avant-propos du recueil *Sueur de sang* qu'il intitule *Inconscient, spiritualité et catastrophe*, il écrit : « Nous avons connaissance à présent de milliers de mondes à l'intérieur du monde de l'homme... L'homme moderne a découvert l'inconscient et sa structure ; il y a vu l'impulsion de l'éros et l'impulsion de la mort nouées ensemble, et la face du monde de la Faute, je veux dire du monde de l'homme, en est définitivement changée. » Il regarde avec horreur ce « conflit insoluble » entre la détermination animale de l'être humain et son aspiration au spirituel. Sa vie lui apparaît comme le terrain d'un combat toujours recommencé entre les exigences de la chair et celles de l'esprit, et pour lui toute pulsion sexuelle s'identifie d'abord au péché. D'où l'étrangeté apparente de certains de ses poèmes pour qui en ignore l'enjeu véritable. Les images violentes du sang, du crachat, de la tache, traduisent sa vision du corps humain comme souillure. Mais ce dernier lui inspire, en même temps que le dégoût, une irrésistible fascination, car de la libido même, si elle est capable de se transcender, peut naître le salut. La peinture qu'il fait de ces combats, quoique proche de celle de

Baudelaire, tend moins à extraire les fleurs de ce mal qu'à chercher, par le moyen de la poésie, la voie de la délivrance et du salut. « Nous devons donc, poètes, produire cette " sueur de sang " qu'est l'élévation à des substances si profondes ou si élevées, qui dérivent de la pauvre, de la belle puissance érotique humaine. » Les symboles auxquels il a recours sont souvent obscurs, certains, comme celui du cerf, plusieurs fois présent dans ses poèmes, s'éclairent par leur contexte de légendes : on sait que cet animal apparut un jour, les bois surmontés d'une croix, à un chasseur assoiffé de carnage qui se convertit et devint saint Hubert. De la même manière il est donné à l'homme en proie au mal et au péché de s'arracher à ce désordre. Le verbe poétique par son pouvoir de porter à la lumière les inextricables nœuds où l'inconscient mêle instinct de mort et énergie spirituelle, est comme le Cerf, une manifestation de la grâce.

TOUTE POÉSIE EST À DIEU. Sans cette ambition d'ange
Et cette humilité d'archange et l'engendrement humain
Des accords des nombres du temps et du secret de lumière,
Le vers ne serait que le jeu des osselets de la mort.

Les poèmes qui rendent compte de cette aventure personnelle ne font pas de concession aux modèles traditionnels ou aux écoles. Ce poète est un solitaire, et s'il s'efforce de clarifier l'obscur, c'est d'abord pour lui-même plus que pour autrui ; aussi sa lecture exige-t-elle, le plus souvent, une approche patiente et réitérée, mais ce qui contribue à la séduction de cette œuvre distante, c'est son lyrisme, de plus en plus ample au fil des recueils, ainsi que la vision tragique de la condition humaine qui l'anime.

CIEL

Ciel vaste ciel sans ride poids ou souffle
Signe et demeure du remous ô temple unanime et bleu
Contemple énorme coupe aveugle néant heureux
Celui qui dans la pierre est ici-bas et souffre

De ses chagrins comme des sirènes de la mer
Séduit – voyant ton infini hautain inaccessible
Infini ou absurde auquel il est amer
Son angoisse visant le seul bleu d'une cible

Ciel matière de Dieu ! symbole plus qu'éther.

Diadème, III
© Mercure de France, 1966

ADIEU

II

De longues lignes de tristesse et de brouillard
Ouvrent de tous côtés cette plaine sans fin
Où les monts s'évaporent puis reprennent
À des hauteurs que ne touche plus le regard :
Là où nous sommes arrivés, donne ta main,

Puis aux saules plus écroulés que nos silences
À l'herbe de l'été que détruisent tes pieds
Dis un mot sans raison profère un vrai poème,
Laisse que je caresse enfin tes cheveux morts
Car la mort vient roulant pour nous ses tambours loin,

Laisse que je retouche entièrement ton corps
Dans son vallon ou plage extrême fleur du temps
Que je plie un genou devant ta brune erreur
Ta beauté ton parfum défunt près du départ
Adorant ton défaut ton vice et ton caprice
Adorant ton abîme noir sans firmament.

Laisse ô déjà perdue, et que je te bénisse
Pour tous les maux par où tu m'as appris l'amour
Par tous les mots en quoi tu m'as appris le chant.

Diadème, III
© Mercure de France, 1966

BLAISE CENDRARS

(1887-1961)

« Je suis en route
« J'ai toujours été en route, écrit-il dans *La Prose du Transsibérien et de la petite Jehanne de France*,
   « J'ai passé mon enfance dans les jardins suspendus de Babylone
   « Et l'école buissonnière, dans les gares devant les trains en partance... »

Son écriture épouse le cours tumultueux de sa vie. Il invente un rythme nouveau, une langue capable de supprimer toutes les composantes qui ralentissent l'expression de l'immédiat. Ainsi la ponctuation disparaît presque totalement de son premier poème, publié en 1912, *Pâques à New York* (ce procédé est repris par Apollinaire qui corrige en ce sens, sur épreuves, le recueil d'*Alcools* l'année suivante). Mais c'est surtout sa manière de juxtaposer les images, imitant le défilé rapide des paysages aux vitres des trains, qui donne à ses poèmes une sorte de pulsation haletante. Il conçoit la transcription verbale de la réalité à la manière du reporter-photographe qu'il fut aussi, la livrant telle qu'elle s'offre à lui dans sa rugosité chaotique au fil des contrées traversées ; puis il mêle à ces instantanés objectifs des notations personnelles : récit de rencontres réelles ou fictives, associations d'idées, souvenirs qui s'offrent soudain à la mémoire, images simultanées du monde et du rêve. Aussi est-il, autant que le témoin de ce qu'il a réellement découvert, l'inventeur, à la manière de Nerval, d'une géographie magique.

Le grand poème suivant, *La Prose du Transsibérien*, ouvre à la

poésie de nouveaux domaines. Auparavant déjà, Larbaud a
modifié et enrichi le thème, cher aux romantiques, de l'ailleurs
auquel on aspire, ces « espaces d'une autre vie », ce « N'importe où
hors du monde » où l'on pourra enfin se perdre. Il l'a fait par le
truchement de Barnabooth, son double. Le voyage devient pour ce
milliardaire cosmopolite le moyen de s'approprier l'Europe,
d'enrichir sa sensibilité de dilettante nonchalant et voluptueux
de mille impressions nouvelles. Cendrars, lui, privilégie l'aventure,
c'est elle qui impose le poème, et l'écriture nouvelle. Rien ici de
prémédité. Ce que d'autres attendent de l'inspiration ou de la
drogue, Cendrars le reçoit du hasard qui agit sur l'esprit comme
un stimulant. La transe poétique se traduit alors en un tempo
qui mime les soubresauts irréguliers des trains aussi bien que
leur rapide glissement. En cela il est déjà surréaliste, même s'il
n'appartint jamais à ce groupe. Il montre, avant les autres, que tout
peut devenir poésie, que chaque objet qui s'offre à la conscience
lorsqu'elle s'abandonne à l'imprévu peut être le matériau d'une
transmutation lyrique.

La première édition de *La Prose du Transsibérien*, illustrée par
Sonia Delaunay, se présentait sous la forme d'un long dépliant.
Les couleurs débordant sur les caractères du texte contribuaient
avec la disposition typographique, elle-même insolite, à faire de
cette œuvre un objet-poème tout à fait nouveau. Il n'est pas
indifférent en effet que ce poète ait été l'ami des peintres de son
temps, Delaunay, Picasso, Braque, Gris, Chagall, Picabia, Léger,
Modigliani. Ce compagnonnage l'a incité à rechercher avec eux
des formes d'expression qui rompent avec la tradition. Mais le
modernisme de Cendrars précède et préfigure les tentatives du
cubisme.

Pourtant ce précurseur n'a jamais vraiment exploité ses
découvertes, son métier, selon lui, n'étant pas d'écrire mais de
vivre et de se laisser éblouir par la beauté du monde. L'écriture, il
le dit en substance, lui apparaît surtout comme une abdication,
car elle immobilise, et par là elle est un obstacle à l'aventure, à
l'émerveillement sans cesse renouvelé du voyage. Cette attitude lui
confère un statut particulier : poète, mais jamais homme de lettres,
il séduit par sa liberté.

PROSE DU TRANSSIBÉRIEN
ET DE LA PETITE JEHANNE DE FRANCE

Dédiée aux musiciens.

En ce temps-là j'étais en mon adolescence
J'avais à peine seize ans et je ne me souvenais déjà plus de mon
    enfance
J'étais à 16 000 lieues du lieu de ma naissance
J'étais à Moscou, dans la ville des mille et trois clochers et des sept
    gares
Et je n'avais pas assez des sept gares et des mille et trois tours
Car mon adolescence était si ardente et si folle
Que mon cœur, tour à tour, brûlait comme le temple d'Éphèse ou
    comme la Place Rouge de Moscou.
Quand le soleil se couche.
Et mes yeux éclairaient des voies anciennes.
Et j'étais déjà si mauvais poète
Que je ne savais pas aller jusqu'au bout.

Le Kremlin était comme un immense gâteau tartare
Croustillé d'or,
Avec les grandes amandes des cathédrales toutes blanches
Et l'or mielleux des cloches...
Un vieux moine me lisait la légende de Novgorod
J'avais soif
Et je déchiffrais des caractères cunéiformes
Puis, tout à coup, les pigeons du Saint-Esprit s'envolaient sur la
    place
Et mes mains s'envolaient aussi, avec des bruissements d'albatros
Et ceci, c'était les dernières réminiscences du dernier jour
Du tout dernier voyage
Et de la mer.
. . . .
Tous les visages entrevus dans les gares
Toutes les horloges
L'heure de Paris l'heure de Berlin l'heure de Saint-Pétersbourg et
    l'heure de toutes les gares

Et, à Oufa, le visage ensanglanté du canonnier
Et le cadran bêtement lumineux de Grodno
Et l'avance perpétuelle du train
Tous les matins ont met les montres à l'heure
Le train avance et le soleil retarde
Rien n'y fait, j'entends les cloches sonores
Le gros bourdon de Notre-Dame
La cloche aigrelette du Louvre qui sonna la Barthélemy
Les carillons rouillés de Bruges-la-Morte
Les sonneries électriques de la bibliothèque de New York
Les campanes de Venise
Et les cloches de Moscou, l'horloge de la Porte-Rouge qui me
    comptait les heures quand j'étais dans un bureau
Et mes souvenirs
Le train tonne sur les plaques tournantes
Le train roule
Un gramophone grasseye une marche tzigane
Et le monde, comme l'horloge du quartier juif de Prague, tourne
    éperdument à rebours.

. . . .

À partir d'Irkoutsk le voyage devint beaucoup trop lent
Beaucoup trop long
Nous étions dans le premier train qui contournait le lac Baïkal
On avait orné la locomotive de drapeaux et de lampions
Et nous avions quitté la gare aux accents tristes de l'hymne au
    Tzar.
Si j'étais peintre je déverserais beaucoup de rouge, beaucoup de
    jaune sur la fin de ce voyage
Car je crois bien que nous étions tous un peu fous
Et qu'un délire immense ensanglantait les faces énervées de mes
    compagnons de voyage
Comme nous approchions de la Mongolie
Qui ronflait comme un incendie.
Le train avait ralenti son allure
Et je percevais dans le grincement perpétuel des roues
Les accents fous et les sanglots
D'une éternelle liturgie

J'ai vu
J'ai vu les trains silencieux les trains noirs qui revenaient de
    l'Extrême-Orient et qui passaient en fantômes
Et mon œil, comme le fanal d'arrière, court encore derrière ces
    trains
À Talga 100 000 blessés agonisaient faute de soins
J'ai visité les hôpitaux de Krasnoïarsk
Et à Khilok nous avons croisé un long convoi de soldats fous
J'ai vu dans les lazarets des plaies béantes des blessures qui
    saignaient à pleines orgues
Et les membres amputés dansaient autour ou s'envolaient dans
    l'air rauque
L'incendie était sur toutes les faces dans tous les cœurs
Des doigts idiots tambourinaient sur toutes les vitres
Et sous la pression de la peur les regards crevaient comme des
    abcès
Dans toutes les gares on brûlait tous les wagons
Et j'ai vu
J'ai vu des trains de 60 locomotives qui s'enfuyaient à toute vapeur
    pourchassées par les horizons en rut et des bandes de corbeaux
    qui s'envolaient désespérément après
Disparaître
Dans la direction de Port-Arthur.
...

JEAN COCTEAU

(1889-1963)

La poésie ne représente qu'une partie de ses écrits : il compose aussi des essais, des récits, des pièces de théâtre ou des scénarios. On peut dire de lui comme. La Fontaine de l'un de ses personnages « Diversité c'est sa devise ». L'impression d'élégance et de grâce qui se dégage de son œuvre, sa déconcertante facilité à aborder tous ces genres, ainsi que son goût du jeu, lui ont parfois valu une réputation d'écrivain léger et superficiel. D'ailleurs lui-même s'est plu à entretenir sa légende de « *Prince frivole* » (titre de l'un de ses recueils). Si l'on y regarde de plus près, on doit plutôt admirer son génie protéiforme et sa curiosité constamment attentive aux nouveautés de son siècle. En effet lorsqu'il s'intéresse aux recherches des peintres (comme en témoigne son *Ode à Picasso* en 1919), aux modes d'expression qu'offre le cinéma, ou aux inventions chorégraphiques de Diaghilev, ce n'est jamais en simple dilettante. Sa passion pour ces moyens d'expression si divers fait de lui alternativement un dessinateur, un cinéaste ou le créateur d'arguments de ballets, doté d'un réel talent dans chacun de ces domaines. Ils témoignent tous de sa personnalité de poète, et l'on passe de l'un à l'autre en reconnaissant dans leur style la composante onirique qui est sa marque propre.

Pour traduire son univers intérieur il a recours aux mythes grecs d'Orphée ou du Sphinx qu'il enrichit de significations inédites, ou encore aux légendes médiévales. Il mêle quotidien et surréalité dans une féerie de miroirs et de masques. Sa volonté de surprendre est manifeste, mais loin d'être gratuite elle se veut opératoire : il faut faire accéder le profane à un monde d'enchantement dont l'auteur a la clef, en redonnant son pouvoir magique à la parole, et permettre ainsi à chacun d'entrevoir l'au-delà qu'elle révèle, comme par exemple ces messagers célestes, présences terribles qui nous cernent, tel l'ange Heurtebise, persécuteur attitré de l'âme du poète.

Si l'on se réfère aux conceptions esthétiques de Cocteau, on voit, à travers les divers textes regroupés par lui sous le titre de *Poésie critique*, que, même s'il a, brièvement, participé au dadaïsme, il demeure libre vis-à-vis des différents courants poétiques de son temps, et marque sa préférence pour le classicisme de la forme et du sens. On a d'ailleurs la surprise de constater que ce fantaisiste né choisit délibérément pour ses vers une prosodie traditionnelle. Aussi, malgré la liberté inventive de son inspiration, n'hésite-t-il pas à affirmer que « la poésie c'est l'exactitude ». Ce n'est pas le seul paradoxe d'un poète pour qui la vérité a partie liée avec le mensonge, et la pure gratuité du jeu avec la quête de l'essentiel.

J'ai, pour tromper du temps la mal-sonnante horloge,
    Chanté de vingt façons.
Ainsi de l'habitude évitai-je l'éloge,
    Et les nobles glaçons.

C'est peu que l'habitude une gloire couronne
    Lorsqu'elle a vieux le chef ;
Il faut qu'un long amour souvent le cœur étonne
    À force d'être bref.

Alors, jeune toujours, libre de récompenses,
    Et son livre à la main,
On devine les yeux, les manœuvres, les danses,
    Qui formeront demain.

Voilà pourquoi la mort également m'effraye,
    Et me fait les yeux doux ;
C'est qu'une grande voix murmure à mon oreille :
    Pense à mon rendez-vous ;

Laisse partir ces gens, laisse fermer la porte,
    Laisse perdre le vin,
Laisse mettre au sépulcre une dépouille morte ;
    Je suis ton nom divin.

Plain-Chant, I
© Jean Cocteau

Je veux tout oublier, et cet ange cornu
Comme le vieux Moïse,
Qui de moi se sachant le visage inconnu
À coups de front me brise.

Mêlons dans notre lit nos jambes et nos bras,
D'un si tendre mélange,
Que ne puisse, voulant m'arracher de mes draps,
S'y reconnaître l'ange.

Formons étroitement, en haut de ce tortil,
D'un baiser, une rose ;
Et l'ange, à ce baiser parfumé, puisse-t-il,
Avoir l'âme déclose.

Le cœur indifférent à ce que je serai,
Aux gloires du poème,
Je vivrai, libre enfin, par toi seule serré,
Et te serrant de même,

Alors profondément devenus à nous deux
Une seule machine
À maints têtes et bras, ainsi que sont les dieux
Dans les temples de Chine.

Plain-Chant, II
© Jean Cocteau

Je n'aime pas dormir quand ta figure habite,
        La nuit, contre mon cou ;
Car je pense à la mort laquelle vient si vite
        Nous endormir beaucoup.

Je mourrai, tu vivras et c'est ce qui m'éveille !
        Est-il une autre peur ?
Un jour ne plus entendre auprès de mon oreille
        Ton haleine et ton cœur.

Quoi, ce timide oiseau, replié par le songe
        Déserterait son nid,
Son nid d'où notre corps à deux têtes s'allonge
        Par quatre pieds fini.

Puisse durer toujours une si grande joie
        Qui cesse le matin,
Et dont l'ange chargé de construire ma voie
        Allège mon destin.

Léger, je suis léger sous cette tête lourde
        Qui semble de mon bloc,
Et reste en mon abri, muette, aveugle, sourde,
        Malgré le chant du coq.

Cette tête coupée, allée en d'autres mondes,
        Où règne une autre loi,
Plongeant dans le sommeil des racines profondes
        Loin de moi, près de moi.

Ah ! je voudrais, gardant ton profil sur ma gorge,
        Par ta bouche qui dort
Entendre de tes seins la délicate forge
        Souffler jusqu'à ma mort.

                                Plain-Chant, II

Mauvaise compagne, espèce de morte,
        De quels corridors,
De quels corridors pousses-tu la porte,
        Dès que tu t'endors ?

Je te vois quitter ta figure close,
        Bien fermée à clé,
Ne laissant ici plus la moindre chose,
        Que ton chef bouclé.

Je baise ta joue et serre tes membres,
        Mais tu sors de toi,
Sans faire de bruit, comme d'une chambre,
        On sort par le toit.

Plain-Chant, II
© Jean Cocteau

Rien ne m'effraye plus que la fausse accalmie
        D'un visage qui dort ;
Ton rêve est une Égypte et toi c'est la momie
        Avec son masque d'or.

Où ton regard va-t-il sous cette riche empreinte.
        D'une reine qui meurt,
Lorsque la nuit d'amour t'a défaite et repeinte
        Comme un noir embaumeur ?

Abandonne, ô ma reine, ô mon canard sauvage,
        Les siècles et les mers ;
Reviens flotter dessus, regagne ton visage
        Qui s'enfonce à l'envers.

                            Plain-Chant, II
                            © Jean Cocteau

PAR LUI-MÊME

I

Accidents du mystère et fautes de calculs
Célestes, j'ai profité d'eux, je l'avoue.
Toute ma poésie est là : Je décalque
L'invisible (invisible à vous).
J'ai dit : « Inutile de crier, haut les mains ! »
Au crime déguisé en costume inhumain ;
J'ai donné le contour à des charmes informes ;
Des ruses de la mort la trahison m'informe ;
J'ai fait voir, en versant mon encre bleue en eux,
Des fantômes soudain devenus arbres bleus.

Dire que l'entreprise est simple ou sans danger
Serait fou. Déranger les anges !
Découvrir le hasard apprenant à tricher
Et des statues en train d'essayer de marcher.
Sur le belvédère des villes que l'on voit
Vides, et d'où l'on ne distingue plus que les voix
Des coqs, les écoles, les trompes d'automobile
(Ces bruits étant les seuls qui montent d'une ville),
J'ai entendu descendre des faubourgs du ciel,
Étonnantes rumeurs, cris d'une autre Marseille.

Opéra

PIERRE REVERDY

(1889-1960)

*L'image est une création pure de l'esprit.
Elle ne peut naître d'une comparaison mais du rapprochement
de deux réalités plus ou moins éloignées. Plus les rapports des deux
réalités rapprochées seront lointains et justes, plus l'image sera forte –
plus elle aura de puissance émotive et de réalité poétique...*

Ce texte date de 1917. Sept ans plus tard, Breton le cite et le
commente dans le *Manifeste du Surréalisme*, « ces mots, quoique
sibyllins pour le profane, étaient de très forts révélateurs et je les
méditai longtemps ». Entre-temps Reverdy, dont on connaissait
déjà les *Poèmes en prose* et *La Lucarne ovale*, a publié plusieurs
autres recueils *(Les Ardoises du toit, Les Jockeys camouflés, La
Guitare endormie, Cœur de chêne, Étoiles peintes, Cravates de
chanvre)*, le plus souvent illustrés par ses amis peintres. Leurs
recherches lui inspirent le désir d'inventer comme eux des formes
d'expression inédites, un équivalent poétique du langage pictural.
Dès cette époque, il fait paraître un texte sur Picasso, plus tard sur
Matisse ou Braque. S'il est d'abord poète, il s'efforce aussi de
mettre au clair ses intuitions et ses théories sur la poésie. On a pu
les lire, comme Breton lui-même, dans *Nord Sud*, la revue qu'il a
fondée. Par la suite il les regroupe dans plusieurs ouvrages. Le plus
important d'entre eux est sans doute *Le Gant de crin*. Il compose
également un « roman », c'est du moins le nom qu'il donne à son
premier récit poétique en 1917 : *Le Voleur de Talan*. La « Dédicace
Préface » qui l'introduit en fait plutôt un poème :

> *L'Arme qui lui perça le flanc*
> *Sa plume*
> *Et le sang qui coulait noir*
> *de l'encre...*

Il s'agit d'une autobiographie transposée dont l'aspect onirique séduit Dada, puis les surréalistes. Ces derniers s'inspirent aussi des trouvailles formelles du poète. Pour tous il est « l'initiateur ». Cependant lui-même, influencé dans un premier temps par Apollinaire ou Max Jacob, ne fera partie d'aucun groupe, ne se réclamera d'aucun modèle. Rien de plus étranger à sa démarche que les techniques d'écriture automatique prônées autour de lui. Son exploration des ressources de la poésie se veut essentiellement consciente et volontaire. Elle exige du poète une ascèse, au sens plein du terme. Aussi choisit-il l'exil de la province, loin de l'agitation parisienne, des querelles et des modes, pour mieux se consacrer à sa propre quête poétique et spirituelle. Il se retire près de l'abbaye de Solesmes, abandonnant de manière quasi définitive la capitale et tous ses amis. Lorsqu'il perd à nouveau la foi de son enfance qu'il avait cru retrouver, il n'en demeure pas moins dans sa retraite, à poursuivre obstinément la même recherche patiente.

Ce qui frappe le lecteur de Reverdy, c'est l'absence de complaisance à soi-même et à autrui, la sincérité du ton et l'authenticité de la démarche. La rigueur de son style le montre : il vise à l'essentiel. Nul souci de joliesse dans des poèmes où le thème du désespoir et du dénuement sont si souvent présents. Le poète est aux prises avec un réel dont il sent qu'il se dérobe, et aussi avec l'univers du rêve qu'il s'agit d'inventorier sans céder à la facilité. Dans le combat qu'il mène alors, l'image, victoire sur l'insaisissable, surgit comme un objet singulier, médiateur entre la surface des choses et leur profondeur entrevue. On est frappé par le contraste entre sa densité et la simplicité apparente des moyens mis en œuvre pour la faire advenir. En effet, les mots sont familiers, et comme la disposition typographique des vers écartelés sur la blancheur de la page, même si elle est insolite, ne constitue pas un obstacle, chaque ligne du poème paraît accessible. Pourtant le sens d'ensemble se dérobe à la première approche. Sans jamais se vouloir hermétique, cette œuvre secrète, qui récuse toute facilité, ne se donne que lentement. Cependant le lecteur, percevant la tension tragique qui la sous-tend, se convainc qu'il vaut la peine d'y entrer pas à pas, en une patiente initiation, afin d'entendre un poète qui a joué sa vie dans la conquête du verbe poétique.

SUR LE TALUS

Le soir couchant ferme une porte
Nous sommes au bord du chemin
Dans l'ombre
    près du ruisseau où tout se tient

Si c'est encore une lumière
      La ligne part à l'infini

L'eau monte comme une poussière

      Le silence ferme la nuit

Plupart du temps
© Flammarion

UN HOMME FINI

Le soir, il promène, à travers la pluie et le danger nocturne, son ombre informe et tout ce qui l'a fait amer.

À la première rencontre, il tremble – où se réfugier contre le désespoir ?

Une foule rôde dans le vent qui torture les branches, et le Maître du ciel le suit d'un œil terrible.

Une enseigne grince – la peur. Une porte bouge et le volet d'en haut claque contre le mur ; il court et les ailes qui emportaient l'ange noir l'abandonnent.

Et puis, dans les couloirs sans fin, dans les champs désolés de la nuit, dans les limites sombres où se heurte l'esprit, les voix imprévues traversent les cloisons, les idées mal bâties chancellent, les cloches de la mort équivoque résonnent.

Main-d'œuvre, La Balle au bond
© Mercure de France, 1949

CHEMIN TOURNANT

Il y a un terrible gris de poussière dans le temps
Un vent du sud avec de fortes ailes
Les échos sourds de l'eau dans le soir chavirant
Et dans la nuit mouillée qui jaillit du tournant
      Des voies rugueuses qui se plaignent
Un goût de cendre sur la langue
Un bruit d'orgue dans les sentiers
Le navire du cœur qui tangue
Tous les désastres du métier

Quand les feux du désert s'éteignent un à un
Quand les yeux sont mouillés comme des brins d'herbe
Quand la rosée descend les pieds nus sur les feuilles
Le matin à peine levé
Il y a quelqu'un qui cherche
Une adresse perdue dans le chemin caché
Les astres dérouillés et les fleurs dégringolent
À travers les branches cassées
Et le ruisseau obscur essuie ses lèvres molles à peine décollées
Quand le pas du marcheur sur le cadran qui compte
      Règle le mouvement et pousse l'horizon
Tous les cris sont passés tous les temps se rencontrent
Et moi je marche au ciel les yeux dans les rayons
Il y a du bruit pour rien et des noms dans ma tête
Des visages vivants
      Tout ce qui s'est passé au monde
Et cette fête
   Où j'ai perdu mon temps

Main-d'œuvre, Sources du vent
© Mercure de France, 1949

JOUR ÉCLATANT

Un mouvement de bras
        Comme un battement d'ailes
Le vent qui se déploie
        Et la voix qui appelle
Dans le silence épais
        qu'aucun souffle ne ride
Les larmes du matin et les doigts de la rive
        L'eau qui coule au dehors
L'ornière suit le pas
        Le soleil se déroule
        Et le ciel ne tient pas
L'arbre du carrefour se penche et interroge
La voiture qui roule enfonce l'horizon
Tous les murs au retour sèchent contre le vent
Et le chemin perdu se cache sous le pont
        Quand la forêt remue
        Et que la nuit s'envole
Entre les branches mortes où la fumée s'endort
L'œil fermé au couchant
        La dernière étincelle
Sur le fil bleu du ciel
        le cri d'une hirondelle

Main-d'œuvre, Sources du vent
© Mercure de France, 1949

LE CŒUR ÉCARTELÉ

Il se ménage tellement
Il a si peur des couvertures
Les couvertures bleues du ciel
Et les oreillers de nuages
Il est mal couvert par sa foi
Il craint tant les pas de travers
Et les rues taillées dans la glace
Il est trop petit pour l'hiver
Il a tellement peur du froid
Il est transparent dans sa glace
Il est si vague qu'il se perd
Le temps le roule sous ses vagues
Parfois son sang coule à l'envers
Et ses larmes tachent le linge
Sa main cueille les arbres verts
Et les bouquets d'algues des plages
Sa foi est un buisson d'épines
Ses mains saignent contre son cœur
Ses yeux ont perdu la lumière
Et ses pieds traînent sur la mer
Comme les bras morts des pieuvres
Il est perdu dans l'univers
Il se heurte contre les villes
Contre lui-même et ses travers
Priez donc pour que le Seigneur
Efface jusqu'au souvenir
De lui-même dans sa mémoire

Main-d'œuvre, Ferraille
© Mercure de France, 1949

PAUL ÉLUARD

(1895-1952)

Il y a au moins deux manières de le lire. La première, qui s'impose d'évidence, consiste à privilégier dans l'œuvre tout ce qui témoigne des engagements poétiques et politiques de l'auteur. On note donc qu'il est unanimiste dans ses premiers recueils, mais que, prenant assez tôt ses distances avec cette conception de la poésie, il devient, suivant l'expression cocasse de Ponge, ce « jeune coq dada volant dans les plumes de la vieille poule unanimiste qui l'avait couvé ». On voit qu'après avoir été l'un des membres les plus en vue de Dada aux côtés de Tzara, il participe aux premières publications des surréalistes et coopère au développement du mouvement et à ses actions spectaculaires. Ainsi en 1930 il signe avec Breton et Char *Ralentir travaux*, puis avec Breton seul *L'Immaculée Conception*. Le fait qu'il n'ait jamais encouru les foudres de celui qu'on nomme « le pape du surréalisme », prompt, comme on sait, à fulminer des exclusions, et qu'il n'ait jamais pris au moins explicitement de distances avec lui, témoigne de la sincérité et de la permanence de ses choix. Son écriture a beau afficher une autonomie de plus en plus grande à mesure que paraissent de nouveaux recueils, il ne renie jamais la composante onirique de toute création héritée du surréalisme : elle reste consubstantielle à sa propre conception de la poésie.

L'engagement politique occupe, lui aussi, une place essentielle dans son parcours. Une première adhésion au communisme dans sa jeunesse, puis sa participation active à la Résistance et son adhésion réfléchie et définitive au parti communiste, influencent en lui le poète, non seulement dans *Poésie et vérité* en 42, ou dans les *Poèmes politiques* en 48, mais dans l'ensemble d'une œuvre où il va constamment s'efforcer de passer, suivant l'expression d'Aragon qui préface ce dernier recueil, « de l'horizon d'un homme à l'horizon de tous ».

Sans nier l'importance de ces influences et de ces choix, la critique a pu souligner à quel point Éluard échappe par son lyrisme naturel aux circonstances de son écriture. Dix ans après sa mort, dans le numéro d'*Europe* qui lui était consacré, Henri Meschonnic intitulait un article : « Éluard poète classique » et voyait en lui « le mainteneur d'une continuité de la poésie française ». Ce qui justifie ce point de vue c'est en particulier la place faite au thème de l'amour chez un poète qui a célébré avec ferveur, comme Ronsard, les femmes qu'il a aimées. Celle qui lui inspire ses plus beaux poèmes c'est d'abord Gala (mariés en 17, ils se séparent en 1930), puis Nush dont la mort en 46 le plonge dans un désespoir profond, et enfin Dominique rencontrée lors d'un voyage au Mexique trois ans plus tard. Certes les surréalistes ont tous chanté « l'amour fou », mais le terme a pour chacun d'eux une acception différente. « Il n'y a pas un amour surréaliste, dit encore ce critique. L'amour d'Aragon n'a pas l'inquiétude de Desnos, l'amour d'Éluard n'a pas le pressentiment métaphysique de Breton. C'est chez Éluard la force élémentaire... » En effet l'amour le rend sensible à la saveur du réel, il l'initie à la beauté de toute chose car la femme aimée, en abolissant pour lui les frontières qui le séparent du réel, le lui rend soudain accessible. L'étrangeté du monde est apprivoisée à travers une présence et surtout un regard. L'érotisme prévaut dans la célébration du corps et des jeux des amants mais il n'exclut jamais la perfection d'un sentiment amoureux qui semble hors du temps, et comme issu du chant des troubadours. On peut d'ailleurs voir dans la publication, en 1951, d'une *Anthologie vivante de la poésie du passé* qu'il travaillait à rassembler depuis longtemps, la marque d'une volonté d'assumer l'héritage et de souligner la continuité entre sa poésie et celle qui l'a précédée. Il n'a jamais renoncé aux formes anciennes, au mètre régulier, l'alexandrin en particulier subsiste dans divers poèmes. On a parlé de sa préciosité. Il lui arrive en effet de pratiquer l'art des blasons et de renouer avec l'expression métaphorique du sentiment amoureux. Mais ce qui domine dans ses plus beaux poèmes c'est un lyrisme très pur qui s'accommode, comme chez

Racine, de la langue commune et des mots ordinaires. Même s'il apparaît aujourd'hui qu'il s'est quelque peu fourvoyé dans les engagement par lesquels il aspirait à prendre place « parmi / Les constructeurs d'un vivant édifice / La foule immense où l'homme est un ami », cette ambition généreuse l'a conduit « à élargir son âme aux plaintes de la foule », comme l'avait souhaité Lamartine au siècle précédent, et l'évolution de son œuvre devenue au fil des ans plus ample, plus humaine, plus universelle a fait d'elle l'une de celles que ce siècle a préférées.

POUR VIVRE ICI

Je fis un feu, l'azur m'ayant abandonné,
Un feu pour être son ami,
Un feu pour m'introduire dans la nuit d'hiver,
Un feu pour vivre mieux.

Je lui donnai ce que le jour m'avait donné :
Les forêts, les buissons, les champs de blé, les vignes,
Les nids et leurs oiseaux, les maisons et leurs clés,
Les insectes, les fleurs, les fourrures, les fêtes.

Je vécus au seul bruit des flammes crépitantes,
Au seul parfum de leur chaleur ;
J'étais comme un bateau coulant dans l'eau fermée,
Comme un mort je n'avais qu'un unique élément.

1918

Le Livre ouvert, I, 1938-1940
© Éditions Gallimard

La courbe de tes yeux fait le tour de mon cœur,
Un rond de danse et de douceur,
Auréole du temps, berceau nocturne et sûr,
Et si je ne sais plus tout ce que j'ai vécu
C'est que tes yeux ne m'ont pas toujours vu.

Feuilles de jour et mousse de rosée,
Roseaux du vent, sourires parfumés,
Ailes couvrant le monde de lumière,
Bateaux chargés du ciel et de la mer,
Chasseurs des bruits et sources des couleurs,

Parfums éclos d'une couvée d'aurores
Qui gît toujours sur la paille des astres,
Comme le jour dépend de l'innocence
Le monde entier dépend de tes yeux purs
Et tout mon sang coule dans leurs regards.

1923

Capitale de la douleur
© Éditions Gallimard

L'AMOUREUSE

Elle est debout sur mes paupières
Et ses cheveux sont dans les miens,
Elle a la forme de mes mains,
Elle a la couleur de mes yeux,
Elle s'engloutit dans mon ombre
Comme une pierre sur le ciel.

Elle a toujours les yeux ouverts
Et ne me laisse pas dormir.
Ses rêves en pleine lumière
Font s'évaporer les soleils,
Me font rire, pleurer et rire,
Parler sans avoir rien à dire.

Mourir de ne pas mourir
© Éditions Gallimard

Le front aux vitres comme font les veilleurs de chagrin
Ciel dont j'ai dépassé la nuit
Plaines toute petites dans mes mains ouvertes
Dans leur double horizon inerte indifférent
Le front aux vitres comme font les veilleurs de chagrin
Je te cherche par delà l'attente
Par delà moi-même
Et je ne sais plus tant je t'aime
Lequel de nous deux est absent.

L'Amour, la poésie
© Éditions Gallimard

Pour qu'un seul baiser la retienne
Pour que l'entoure le plaisir,
Comme un été blanc bleu et blanc
Pour qu'il lui soit règle d'or pur
Pour que sa gorge bouge douce
Sous la chaleur tirant la chair
Vers une caresse infinie
Pour qu'elle soit comme la plaine
Nue et visible de partout
Pour qu'elle soit comme une pluie
Miraculeuse sans nuage
Comme une pluie entre deux feux
Comme une larme entre deux rires
Pour qu'elle soit neige bénie
Sous l'aile tiède d'un oiseau
Lorsque le sang coule plus vite
Dans les veines d'un vent nouveau
Pour que ses paupières ouvertes
Approfondissent la lumière
Parfum total à son image
Pour que sa bouche et le silence
Intelligibles se comprennent
Pour que ses mains posent leur paume
Sur chaque tête qui s'éveille
Pour que les lignes de ses mains
Se continuent dans d'autres mains
Distances à passer le temps

Je fortifierai mon délire

Poésie ininterrompue
© Éditions Gallimard

ANDRÉ BRETON

(1896-1966)

Figure essentielle de l'histoire de la poésie au xxe siècle, théoricien en même temps que poète, André Breton élabore une doctrine dont l'ambition est d'étendre le champ de la poésie à toute activité humaine, bien plus que de produire des poèmes. S'il n'a pas inventé le terme de surréalisme qui apparaît pour la première fois dans la préface des *Mamelles de Tirésias*, la pièce d'Apollinaire, en 1917, c'est lui qui, dans le *Manifeste du surréalisme*, en donne la première définition : « Automatisme psychique pur par lequel on se propose d'exprimer, soit verbalement, soit par écrit, soit de toute autre manière, le fonctionnement réel de la pensée. Dictée de la pensée, en l'absence de tout contrôle exercé par la raison, en dehors de toute préoccupation esthétique ou morale. »

Il appartient à la génération de jeunes gens révoltés par la guerre qui trouvent d'abord, dans le mouvement lancé à Zurich par Tzara, l'expression de leur refus violent de la société et la dérision de l'art tel que le concevaient leurs aînés. Dans un premier temps, Breton milite donc pour Dada mais il s'en détache et détourne peu à peu au profit du surréalisme naissant les tenants de ce mouvement iconoclaste.

Son parcours personnel éclaire les choix décisifs qu'il fait dès cette époque. La rencontre de Jacques Vaché à l'hôpital de Nantes, où il est affecté comme médecin pendant la guerre, est déterminante. Cet esthète anticonformiste et provocateur lui fournit le modèle du personnage surréaliste par excellence. « Sans lui, écrit Breton, j'aurais peut-être été un poète ; il a déjoué en moi ce complot de forces qui mène à se croire quelque chose d'aussi absurde qu'une vocation. » Les recherches de Freud sur l'inconscient le passionnent ; il s'agira pour lui et ses amis d'en explorer les richesses. En poésie, s'il a d'abord admiré Mallarmé et composé ses premiers poèmes en le prenant pour modèle, il s'en détache et c'est Rimbaud qui lui ouvre la voie d'une poésie intégrale, c'est-à-dire capable de transformer la vie tout entière. La découverte de Lautréamont entre aussi pour une grande part dans l'élaboration de sa doctrine poétique. Il signe avec Soupault le premier texte surréaliste : *Les Champs magnétiques* en 1920. Avec ce dernier et Aragon il a fondé la revue *Littérature* au titre délibérément paradoxal car, suivant l'expression de Caillois, « ce fut toujours l'équivoque du mouvement surréaliste de faire partie de la littérature et, en même temps, de se présenter comme une mise en question de cette même littérature ».

C'est dans la seconde série de cette revue, à partir de 1922, que paraissent les comptes rendus de rêves et de jeux sur le langage. L'écriture automatique, celle qui naît sous la plume sans le contrôle de la raison, étant aux yeux de Breton la pierre de touche de la libération poétique qu'il prône. Tous s'y adonnent, mais certains des textes qu'il présente comme jaillis spontanément, par exemple ceux du *Poisson soluble*, ont un degré de cohérence et une qualité syntaxique qui permettent de mettre en doute le fait qu'il s'agisse vraiment d'automatismes à l'état pur. Quant aux « poèmes » dont les incohérences authentifient l'origine, ni les siens, ni ceux de ses amis ne justifient l'enthousiasme de leurs auteurs.

Breton s'impose davantage par sa prose, celle de *Nadja* ou de *L'Amour fou*, où il donne la mesure de son pouvoir poétique en opérant la transmutation magique du réel ordinaire en un monde de signes et de sens. Certaines de ses pages sont des poèmes en prose qui fascinent par la fulgurance du style autant que par leur étrangeté.

Il n'en reste pas moins que son rôle essentiel fut celui de chef de groupe, malgré les querelles et les exclusions nombreuses, malgré l'adhésion au parti communiste qui détourna certains de ses amis du mouvement, et son exclusion de ce même parti précédée de la rupture avec Aragon, il resta jusqu'au bout la figure centrale d'un courant qui avait largement dépassé les seuls domaines de la poésie pour changer, comme il le souhaitait, sinon la vie, du moins la plupart des domaines de l'expression artistique.

VIGILANCE

À Paris la tour Saint Jacques chancelante
Pareille à un tournesol
Du front vient quelquefois heurter la Seine et son ombre glisse
    imperceptiblement parmi les remorqueurs
À ce moment sur la pointe des pieds dans mon sommeil
Je me dirige vers la chambre où je suis étendu
Et j'y mets le feu
Pour que rien ne subsiste de ce consentement qu'on m'a arraché
Les meubles font alors place à des animaux de même taille qui me
    regardent fraternellement
Lions dans les crinières desquels achèvent de se consumer les
    chaises
Squales dont le ventre blanc s'incorpore le dernier frisson des
    draps
À l'heure de l'amour et des paupières bleues
Je me vois brûler à mon tour je vois cette cachette solennelle de
    riens
Qui fut mon corps
Fouillée par les becs patients des ibis du feu
Lorsque tout est fini j'entre invisible dans l'arche
Sans prendre garde aux passants de la vie qui font sonner très loin
    leurs pas traînants
Je vois les arêtes du soleil
À travers l'aubépine de la pluie
J'entends se déchirer le linge humain comme une grande feuille
Sous l'ongle de l'absence et de la présence qui sont de connivence
Tous les métiers se fanent ne reste d'eux qu'une dentelle parfumée
Une coquille de dentelle qui a la forme parfaite d'un sein
Je ne touche plus que le cœur des choses je tiens le fil

Clair de terre
© Éditions Gallimard

ANTONIN ARTAUD

(1896-1948)

Dépossédé, comme Nerval, lui aussi peut se nommer *El
Desdichado*. Des forces mauvaises lui ont dérobé son royaume
intérieur, la pleine maîtrise de son esprit. Il exprime dans
L'Ombilic des limbes et *Le Pèse-nerfs* l'intolérable souffrance que lui
fait subir le vertige de cette faille ouverte en lui ; sa raison va
bientôt s'y perdre. De façon plus explicite encore, ses lettres à
Jacques Rivière décrivent l'impuissance du créateur qu'il devrait
être et qu'il serait, si une force maligne ne lui faisait obstacle jour
après jour. C'est là aussi qu'il renie, comme indignes de lui, les
pages que le critique a pourtant accueillies avec bienveillance et
intérêt. Il a cette formule déchirante et hautaine qui exprime à la
fois la cassure de l'être et le courage de l'orgueil : « J'ai, pour me
sauver du jugement des autres, toute la distance qui me sépare de
moi-même. »
   Il est d'abord lié aux surréalistes qui, assez vite, entrent en
conflit avec lui, l'expulsent de leur revue et de leur mouvement,
ajoutant à cela les insultes à son égard qu'ils impriment dans la
brochure intitulée *Au grand jour*. Il se tourne bientôt vers le
théâtre. Acteur, auteur et surtout théoricien, il réunit en 38, dans
Le Théâtre et son double, les textes écrits de 31 à 33. Sa conception
du « théâtre de la cruauté » marque durablement la plupart des
recherches théâtrales ultérieures. L'échec de sa propre tentative de
théâtre total avec *Les Cenci* accroît son amertume. Le peyolt
auquel il s'adonne au cours d'un voyage au Mexique, à l'exemple
des Indiens Tarahumaras, porte son délire à un paroxysme qui va
entraîner son internement.

Libéré neuf ans plus tard de l'asile de Rodez, il compose des textes d'une extrême violence où la rage accumulée contre la société se traduit en des termes atroces. Cette outrance, écho de la douleur physique et mentale dont il est la proie, l'état de déréliction et de misère matérielle où il est réduit, font de lui une moderne incarnation du poète maudit. Certains voient dans son malheur, comme l'auraient fait les romantiques, le signe indiscutable du génie. Il n'est pas assuré que la postérité ratifiera le jugement de ses fervents admirateurs, mais nul ne peut nier que ses écrits ont la force de communiquer, comme jadis la sibylle inspirée en proie au dieu, l'horreur sacrée qui le hantait.

Une grande ferveur pensante et surpeuplée portait mon moi comme un abîme plein. Un vent charnel et résonnant soufflait, et le soufre même en était dense. Et des radicelles infimes peuplaient ce vent comme un réseau de veines, et leur entrecroisement fulgurait. L'espace était mesurable et crissant, mais sans forme pénétrable. Et le centre était une mosaïque d'éclats, une espèce de dur marteau cosmique, d'une lourdeur défigurée, et qui retombait sans cesse comme un front dans l'espace, mais avec un bruit comme distillé. Et l'enveloppement cotonneux du bruit avait l'instance obtuse et la pénétration d'un regard vivant. Oui, l'espace rendait son plein coton mental où nulle pensée encore n'était nette et ne restituait sa décharge d'objets. Mais, peu à peu, la masse tourna comme une nausée limoneuse et puissante, une espèce d'immense influx de sang végétal et tonnant. Et les radicelles qui tremblaient à la lisière de mon œil mental, se détachèrent avec une vitesse de vertige de la masse crispée du vent. Et tout l'espace trembla comme un sexe que le globe du ciel ardent saccageait. Et quelque chose du bec d'une colombe réelle troua la masse confuse des états, toute la pensée profonde à ce moment se stratifiait, se résolvait, devenait transparente et réduite.

Et il nous fallait maintenant une main qui devînt l'organe même du saisir. Et deux ou trois fois encore la masse entière et végétale tourna, et chaque fois, mon œil se replaçait sur une position plus précise. L'obscurité elle-même devenait profuse et sans objet. Le gel entier gagnait la clarté.

L'Ombilic des limbes
© Éditions Gallimard

L'ARBRE

Cet arbre et son frémissement
forêt sombre d'appels,
de cris,
mange le cœur obscur de la nuit.

Vinaigre et lait, le ciel, la mer,
la masse épaisse du firmament,
tout conspire à ce tremblement,
qui gîte au cœur épais de l'ombre.

Un cœur qui crève, un astre dur
qui se dédouble et fuse au ciel,
le ciel limpide qui se fend
à l'appel du soleil sonnant,
font le même bruit, font le même bruit,
que la nuit et l'arbre au centre du vent.

L'Ombilic des limbes, Bilboquet
© Éditions Gallimard

ARAGON

(1897-1982)

Aragon peut être comparé à Hugo, bien qu'il n'ait ni son envergure spirituelle, ni sa stature de prophète. Une exceptionnelle longévité créatrice leur permet de participer à plusieurs courants littéraires de leur siècle sans jamais se limiter à aucun d'entre eux. Une volonté affichée de prendre part aux luttes de leur temps et de mettre leur plume au service des causes qu'ils jugent bon de défendre, engagement qui les rend l'un et l'autre étrangers au repli hautain de la tour d'ivoire et à la recherche d'une langue inaccessible au profane, justifie aussi ce rapprochement. Les deux écrivains ont encore en commun une diversité de talents qui les fait l'un et l'autre grands prosateurs aussi bien que poètes. Une même connaissance de la poésie du passé, dont ils assument l'héritage, modèle leurs œuvres respectives : Hugo magnifie la ballade médiévale et restaure l'épopée ; Aragon se veut le disciple des troubadours et particulièrement de cet Arnaud Daniel que cite Dante, et s'efforce, à son exemple, de perpétuer par son chant l'éclat et la présence d'une culture menacée par l'occupant pour contribuer comme lui à défendre sa langue, cette patrie essentielle. Le Moyen Âge n'est pas sa seule source d'inspiration, on sent à chaque instant dans ses poèmes affleurer les souvenirs de Villon, de Ronsard, de Nerval, d'Apollinaire et de tant d'autres dont il s'est nourri.

Ce parallèle se fonde enfin sur leur commun attachement aux rythmes traditionnels, même si Aragon ne se borne pas aux mètres habituels, et s'il use, en se jouant, du vers de onze, ou treize, ou quatorze syllabes. Car il est indéniablement, comme Hugo, un poète-virtuose que n'arrête aucune difficulté prosodique. Sensible aux ressources qu'offrent les formes codifiées léguées par ses prédécesseurs – à cet égard il faut lire par exemple son éloge du sonnet – il ne renonce jamais à elles.

Aragon poète fut d'abord Aragon surréaliste, ce jeune homme doué dont la verve est manifeste dès les premiers écrits, en particulier avec le *Paysan de Paris*, exemple le plus convaincant de ce merveilleux quotidien que cherchent désormais les transfuges de Dada. « J'annonce au monde, écrit-il dans le *Discours de l'imagination*, ce fait divers de première grandeur : ... un vertige de plus est donné à l'homme, le Surréalisme, fils de la frénésie et de l'ombre. » Ou encore : « Je vous apporte un stupéfiant venu des limites de la conscience, des frontières de l'abîme... Le vice appelé Surréalisme est l'emploi déréglé et passionnel du stupéfiant *image*... » La rencontre de Breton avec qui il fonde la revue *Littérature* l'a en effet détourné du dadaïsme et lancé dans la nouvelle aventure de la poésie. Commence alors pour lui la période des « cadavres exquis » et des sommeils hypnotiques auxquels il s'adonne avec ses amis et qu'il célébrera plus tard dans le *Roman inachevé* :

> *Nous étions trois ou quatre au bout du jour assis*
> *À marier les sons pour rebâtir les choses*
> *Sans cesse procédant à des métamorphoses.*

Son adhésion au parti communiste en 27 va peu à peu l'éloigner de ce groupe de poètes. Après la parution du *Traité du style* où il raille à la fois l'ordre bourgeois et l'écriture automatique, la rupture avec Breton est définitive. C'est alors qu'il se tourne vers « le monde réel » et publie, sous ce titre général, trois romans, *Les Cloches de Bâle*, puis *Les Beaux Quartiers* et *Les Voyageurs de l'Impériale*. À cette époque en effet, et jusqu'aux années 40, il privilégie le roman. Mais durant l'Occupation, il redonne toute sa place à la poésie, car il fait partie de ces poètes résistants pour qui l'écriture est un combat, comme en témoignent *Le Crève-cœur* en 1941 ou *La Diane française* en 44. Les recueils de cette période contribueront pour une large part à faire de lui le plus populaire des poètes.

Une autre rencontre, en 28, celle d'Elsa Triolet, s'inscrit dans sa

vie comme un commencement absolu. Il devient le chantre de
« l'amour unique » dont parlait Apollinaire, mais à la différence de
ce dernier, et sans doute de tous ceux qu'a inspirés avant lui la
fin'amor, il fait d'un seul visage le centre rayonnant de cette
célébration. Il est désormais le grand poète lyrique qui, dans un
constant renouvellement d'images et de formes, scande toute son
œuvre avec le nom d'Elsa. De la simple évocation familière en
distiques (« Et je pensais qu'un jour pareil, dans pas longtemps / Tu
ne reviendrais plus vers moi le cœur battant »...) jusqu'aux
entreprises les plus ambitieuses, comme le *Fou d'Elsa*, long poème
épique où il retrace la chute de Grenade au XVe siècle, c'est elle qui
vivifie son inspiration. Poète de l'amour quasi intemporel et
pourtant incarné, il est aussi, comme il le revendique, celui du *bel
canto*. Toute son œuvre fait entendre ce « beau chant » qui semble
naître en lui spontanément, avec une étonnante profusion. On le
lui reproche parfois comme si la poésie était à présent condamnée
à renoncer au plaisir du verbe, et le poète à se défier de la lyre.

RICHARD II QUARANTE

Ma patrie est comme une barque
Qu'abandonnèrent ses haleurs
Et je ressemble à ce monarque
Plus malheureux que le malheur
Qui restait roi de ses douleurs

Vivre n'est plus qu'un stratagème
Le vent sait mal sécher les pleurs
Il faut haïr tout ce que j'aime
Ce que je n'ai plus donnez-leur
Je reste roi de mes douleurs

Le cœur peut s'arrêter de battre
Le sang peut couler sans chaleur
Deux et deux ne fassent plus quatre
Au Pigeon-Vole des voleurs
Je reste roi de mes douleurs

Que le soleil meure ou renaisse
Le ciel a perdu ses couleurs
Tendre Paris de ma jeunesse
Adieu printemps du Quai-aux-Fleurs
Je reste roi de mes douleurs

Fuyez les bois et les fontaines
Taisez-vous oiseaux querelleurs
Vos chants sont mis en quarantaine
C'est le règne de l'oiseleur
Je reste roi de mes douleurs

Il est un temps pour la souffrance
Quand Jeanne vint à Vaucouleurs
Ah coupez en morceaux la France
Le jour avait cette pâleur
Je reste roi de mes douleurs

Le Crève-cœur © Éditions Gallimard

Marguerite Marie et Madeleine
Il faut bien que les sœurs aillent par trois
Aux vitres j'écris quand il fait bien froid
Avec un doigt leur nom dans mon haleine

Pour le bal de Saint-Cyr elles ont mis
Trois des plus belles robes de Peau d'Âne
Celle couleur de la route océane
Celle de vent celle d'astronomie

Comment dormir à moins qu'elles ne viennent
Me faire voir leurs souliers de satin
Qui vont danser danser jusqu'au matin
Pas des patineurs et valses de Vienne

Marguerite Madeleine et Marie
La première est triste à quoi songe-t-elle
La seconde est belle avec ses dentelles
À tout ce qu'on dit la troisième rit

Je ferme les yeux je les accompagne
Que les Saint-Cyriens avec leurs gants blancs
Que les Saint-Cyriens se montrent galants
Ils offriront aux dames du champagne

Chacune est un peu pour eux Cendrillon
Tous ces fils de roi d'elles s'amourachent
Si jeunes qu'ils n'ont barbe ni moustache
Mais tout finira par un cotillon

La vie et le bal ont passé trop vite
La nuit n'a jamais la longueur qu'on veut
Et dans le matin défont leurs cheveux
Madeleine Marie et Marguerite

Le Roman inachevé © Éditions Gallimard

Je chante pour passer le temps
Petit qu'il me reste de vivre
Comme on dessine sur le givre
Comme on se fait le cœur content
À lancer cailloux sur l'étang
Je chante pour passer le temps

J'ai vécu le jour des merveilles
Vous et moi souvenez-vous en
Et j'ai franchi le mur des ans
Des miracles plein les oreilles
Notre univers n'est plus pareil
J'ai vécu le jour des merveilles

Allons que ces doigts se dénouent
Comme le front d'avec la gloire
Nos yeux furent premiers à voir
Les nuages plus bas que nous
Et l'alouette à nos genoux
Allons que ces doigts se dénouent

Nous avons fait des clairs de lune
Pour nos palais et nos statues
Qu'importe à présent qu'on nous tue
Les nuits tomberont une à une
La Chine s'est mise en Commune
Nous avons fait des clairs de lune

Et j'en dirais et j'en dirais
Tant fut cette vie aventure
Où l'homme a pris grandeur nature
Sa voix par-dessus les forêts
Les monts les mers et les secrets
Et j'en dirais et j'en dirais

Oui pour passer le temps je chante
Au violon s'use l'archet
La pierre au jeu des ricochets
Et que mon amour est touchante
Près de moi dans l'ombre penchante
Oui pour passer le temps je chante

Je passe le temps en chantant
Je chante pour passer le temps

Le Roman inachevé
© Éditions Gallimard

Il n'aurait fallu
Qu'un moment de plus
Pour que la mort vienne
Mais une main nue
Alors est venue
Qui a pris la mienne

Qui donc a rendu
Leurs couleurs perdues
Aux jours aux semaines
Sa réalité
À l'immense été
Des choses humaines

Moi qui frémissais
Toujours je ne sais
De quelle colère
Deux bras ont suffi
Pour faire à ma vie
Un grand collier d'air

Rien qu'un mouvement
Ce geste en dormant
Léger qui me frôle
Un souffle posé
Moins Une rosée
Contre mon épaule

Un front qui s'appuie
À moi dans la nuit
Deux grands yeux ouverts
Et tout m'a semblé
Comme un champ de blé
Dans cet univers

Un tendre jardin
Dans l'herbe où soudain
La verveine pousse
Et mon cœur défunt
Renaît au parfum
Qui fait l'ombre douce

Le Roman inachevé
© Éditions Gallimard

Je n'ai plus l'âge de dormir
J'écris des rimes d'insomnie
Qui ne dort pas la nuit s'y mire
Signe couché de l'infini

Qui ne dort pas veiller lui dure
Des semaines et des années
Sa bouche n'est qu'un long murmure
Dans la chambre des condamnés

Je suis seul avec l'existence
Bien que tu sois à mon côté
Comme un dernier vers à la stance
Jusqu'au bout qu'on n'a point chanté

Ce qui m'étreint et qui me ronge
Soudain contre toi m'a roulé
Je retiens mon souffle et mes songes
Je crains d'avoir soudain parlé

Je crains de t'arracher à l'ombre
Et de te rendre imprudemment
À la triste lumière sombre
Qui ne t'épargne qu'en dormant

Comment cacher ce qui m'habite
Quand tu ne me regardes plus
Mon cœur bat mal mon cœur va vite
Comme un suicide irrésolu

Les heures nous sont lentes lentes
Les yeux ouverts les yeux fermés
Le temps pousse comme une plante
Et tremble comme une fumée

Pensée où vas-tu vagabonde
Prendre au fond des cieux triomphants
Le cerf-volant du bout du monde
Qui dit l'avenir aux enfants

Qui ne dort pas cherche une porte
Dans le mur des obsessions
Qui des deux sera la plus forte
L'ombre ou l'imagination

Qui ne dort pas la nuit s'y mire
Signe couché de l'infini
J'écris des rimes d'insomnie
Je n'ai plus l'âge de dormir.

Elsa

Mon sombre amour d'orange amère
Ma chanson d'écluse et de vent
Mon quartier d'ombre où vient rêvant
    Mourir la mer

Mon doux mois d'août dont le ciel pleut
Des étoiles sur les monts calmes
Ma songerie aux murs de palmes
    Où l'air est bleu

Mes bras d'or mes faibles merveilles
Renaissent ma soif et ma faim
Collier collier des soirs sans fin
    Où le cœur veille

Dire que je puis disparaître
Sans t'avoir tressé tous les joncs
Dispersé l'essaim des pigeons
    À ta fenêtre

Sans faire flèche du matin
Flèche du trouble et de la fleur
De l'eau fraîche et de la douleur
    Dont tu m'atteins

Est-ce qu'on sait ce qui se passe
C'est peut-être bien ce tantôt
Que l'on jettera le manteau
    Dessus ma face

Et tout ce langage perdu
Ce trésor dans la fondrière
Mon cri recouvert de prières
    Mon champ vendu

Je ne regrette rien qu'avoir
La bouche pleine de mots tus
Et dressé trop peu de statues
À ta mémoire

Ah tandis encore qu'il bat
Ce cœur usé contre sa cage
Pour Elle qu'un dernier saccage
La mette bas

Coupez ma gorge et les pivoines
Vite apportez mon vin mon sang
Pour lui plaire comme en passant
Font les avoines

Il me reste si peu de temps
Pour aller au bout de moi-même
Et pour crier-dieu que je t'aime
Tant

HENRI MICHAUX

(1899-1984)

On ne peut entrer dans cette œuvre déconcertante en la comparant à d'autres. Il faut même renoncer à voir en elle un avatar du surréalisme : Michaux a côtoyé ce mouvement mais n'y adhéra jamais. Certaines de ses pages peuvent ouvrir la voie au lecteur, en particulier celles de *Plume*. Le héros éponyme des courts récits qui composent en partie le recueil doit son originalité à l'insignifiance tragique de ses aventures. Broyé par les événements les plus ordinaires, rejeté, humilié, accusé, se sentant vaguement coupable, il persévère absurdement dans ses entreprises, jamais découragé, jamais révolté. Il semble d'ailleurs absent de sa propre vie et paraît s'en désintéresser. Ce portrait où l'humour de l'écrivain estompe son pessimisme métaphysique, propose au lecteur un *ecce homo* dérisoire. On peut voir que Plume emprunte certains traits à son auteur en lisant les *Quelques Renseignements sur cinquante neuf années d'existence*, autobiographie sommaire du poète ; il y caractérise son enfance en ces termes : « Indifférence, Inappétence, Résistance », et plus loin se décrit ainsi : « Secret, Retranché, Honteux de ce qui l'entoure... honteux de lui-même. Il continue à signer de son nom vulgaire, qu'il déteste, dont il a honte... peut-être le garde-t-il par fidélité au mécontentement et à l'insatisfaction. »

Une autre manière d'aborder l'écrivain est de voir en lui un explorateur-poète. Il voyage beaucoup en effet, pendant les quarante premières années de sa vie mais, comme il le dit lui-même, du moins au début, « il voyage contre ». C'est particulièrement clair dans *Ecuador*, journal d'un voyageur qui refuse l'exotisme : (« Indien ! Indien ! vous voulez me stupéfier avec ça. Un Indien, un homme quoi ! ») et finit par avouer : « Ce voyage est une gaffe. » Car il part surtout à sa propre recherche, espérant trouver ailleurs ce qui pourrait combler en lui un vide originel :

Ce n'est qu'un petit trou dans ma poitrine,
Mais il y souffle un vent terrible.

Le journal mêle aux remarques et aux impressions d'un observateur critique des textes qui, par leur disposition typographique, se présentent comme des poèmes. Mais plus que leur aspect, c'est leur violence incantatoire qui rompt de façon indiscutable avec la prose.

Michaux cultive aussi le voyage imaginaire. Moins, comme l'ont fait les utopistes, pour offrir une vision satirique ou idéalisée de la société, que pour rompre totalement avec le réel. C'est ainsi qu'il compose le *Voyage en Grande Garabagne* ou encore *Au Pays de la magie*. Auparavant il a visité un continent qui répondait à son attente, il en rend compte dans *Un barbare en Asie*. C'est là « enfin son voyage » ! L'Inde, surtout, car elle lui donne de voir de ses yeux « le premier peuple qui en bloc paraisse répondre à l'essentiel, qui dans l'essentiel cherche l'assouvissement... » Il y rencontre la pensée magique. Elle inspirera les affabulations géographiques déjà citées ou encore *Ici, Poddéma*, elle est surtout le point de départ d'une quête intérieure, qui, sous différentes formes, occupe désormais sa vie. À travers la revue *Hermès*, dans chacun de ses livres ou dans la découverte et la pratique de plus en plus assidue du dessin et de la peinture, il tente d'inventorier ce qu'il nommera « l'espace du dedans ». Plus tard, c'est dans le même but, qu'avec les expériences contrôlées de prises d'hallucinogènes, il expérimente sur lui les effets de la drogue, en particulier de la mescaline. Ainsi il consacre plusieurs ouvrages, comme *Misérable Miracle* ou *L'Infini turbulent*, à dresser, avec la rigueur d'une étude scientifique le bilan scrupuleux de chaque prise. Dans ces livres d'où la poésie semble a priori exclue, certaines pages cèdent pourtant à une sorte d'amplification spontanée du rythme et au déferlement inattendu d'images singulières et c'est bien alors une parole de poète qui se fait entendre.

Il appartient aussi à la catégorie insolite et peu représentée des moralistes-poètes. Un livre comme *Face aux verrous* propose une série d'aphorismes qu'il désigne sous le titre de « Tranches de savoir ». On y lit des confidences : « Je fus le vivant qui dit : "Je veux d'abord hiverner" », des notations que ne renierait pas le pessimisme du Grand Siècle : « Ce n'est pas l'homme autour de lui qui rend l'homme humain. Plus sur terre il y a d'hommes, plus il y a d'exaspération », des observations dont l'humour semble masquer à plaisir la pertinence : « Mendiant, mais gouverneur d'une gamelle ! », ou cette autre version : « Mort, moulu, mité et encore Charlemagne ! » Dans cette écriture condensée qui oscille entre la gravité de la maxime et la cocasserie du cadavre exquis, on pourrait croire qu'il n'est plus de place pour la poésie. Mais une constante de cette œuvre est de rompre par instants la prose par de brusques flambées poétiques, aussi voit-on surgir dans le même recueil des poèmes incontestables, comme celui qui peint les amants :

> ...*Étendus,*
> *Nous embrassons l'orage,*
> *nous embrassons l'espace,*
> *nous embrassons le flot, le ciel, les mondes,*
> *tout avec nous aujourd'hui tenons embrassé*
> *faisant l'amour sur l'échafaud.*

La hantise de la mort est l'un des thèmes majeurs du poète. Qu'il appelle celle-ci de ses vœux ou tente d'exorciser sa peur, il a des accents poignants. Ses poèmes ne font aucune concession aux thématiques habituelles, mais rejoignent Villon dans la fascination horrifiée d'une échéance proche.

C'est pourtant le même écrivain, qui, dès son premier recueil, avec un enjouement non feint, nous prend au jeu d'une langue imaginaire et savoureuse où il semble rivaliser tantôt avec Rabelais, tantôt avec Lewis Carrol. Par exemple lorsqu'il décrit un *Dimanche à la campagne* où « Jarrettes et Jarnetons s'avançaient sur la route débonnaire... » et *Le Grand Combat* dont il énumère les phases successives : « Il l'emparouille et l'endosque contre terre ; / Il le rague et le roupète jusqu'à son drâle ; Il le pratèle et le libucque et lui barufle les ouaillais ; / Il le tocarde et le

marmine, / Le manage rape à ri et ripe à ra . / Enfin il
l'écorcobalisse… » ou encore les mœurs étranges des *Ossopets* :
« Les Ematrus sont lichinés ou bien ils sont bohanés. C'est l'un ou
l'autre.» Et au grand étonnement de celui qui se contente d'en
rire, pour n'avoir pas compris que cet écrivain « écrit-contre »,
comme il voyage, ces textes en accompagnent d'autres où
l'expression de l'angoisse, de la révolte, d'une inappétence à la vie,
d'une insatisfaction fondamentale saisissent le cœur. S'il fallait
caractériser la démarche essentielle de Michaux poète, ou, pour
mieux dire, le chemin singulier qui fut le sien, on pourrait
reprendre ses propres termes dans le texte intitulé *Magie.* Après
avoir décrit ses nouveaux pouvoirs (mettre une pomme sur la
table, puis se mettre dans la pomme, ou encore se tenir au bord de
l'Escaut puis ne faire qu'un avec lui), il révèle enfin la méthode qui
rend possibles ces étonnantes affirmations et d'un trait en efface
soudain la gratuité : « …en un mot je puis vous le dire : *Souffrir* est
le mot. / Quand j'arrivai dans la pomme, j'étais glacé.»

Cependant l'ascèse rigoureuse à laquelle il se soumet, la
recherche qui domine toute sa vie, ne tendent pas à la possession
d'un pouvoir, encore moins d'une écriture. La quête spirituelle,
l'approfondissement intérieur du mystère comptent plus à ses yeux
que la poésie. Il voit surtout en elle une concession faite aux autres
et à soi-même, une sorte d'abdication quand le seul but doit être
de dissiper les prestiges mensongers de toute connaissance et
l'illusion de notre appartenance au monde : « Plus tu auras réussi
à écrire (si tu écris), plus éloigné tu seras de l'accomplissement du
pur, fort, originel désir, celui, fondamental, de ne pas laisser de
trace.»

REPOS DANS LE MALHEUR

Le Malheur, mon grand laboureur,
Le Malheur, assois-toi,
Repose-toi,
Reposons-nous un peu toi et moi,
Repose,
Tu me trouves, tu m'éprouves, tu me le prouves.
Je suis ta ruine.

Mon grand théâtre, mon havre, mon âtre
Ma cave d'or,
Mon avenir, ma vraie mère, mon horizon.
Dans ta lumière, dans ton ampleur, dans mon horreur,
Je m'abandonne.

Plume
© Éditions Gallimard

MA VIE

Tu t'en vas sans moi, ma vie.
Tu roules,
Et moi j'attends encore de faire un pas.
Tu portes ailleurs la bataille.
Tu me désertes ainsi.
Je ne t'ai jamais suivie.

Je ne vois pas clair dans tes offres.
Le petit peu que je veux, jamais tu ne l'apportes.
À cause de ce manque, j'aspire à tant.
À tant de choses, à presque l'infini...
À cause de ce peu qui manque, que jamais tu n'apportes.

La Nuit remue
© Éditions Gallimard

PETIT

Quand vous me verrez,
Allez,
Ce n'est pas moi.

Dans les grains de sable,
Dans les grains des grains,
Dans la farine invisible de l'air,
Dans un grand vide qui se nourrit comme du sang,
C'est là que je vis.

Oh ! je n'ai pas à me vanter : Petit ! petit !
Et si l'on me tenait,
On ferait de moi ce qu'on voudrait.

La Nuit remue
© Éditions Gallimard

EMPORTEZ-MOI

Emportez-moi dans une caravelle,
Dans une vieille et douce caravelle,
Dans l'étrave, ou si l'on veut, dans l'écume,
Et perdez-moi, au loin, au loin.

Dans l'attelage d'un autre âge.
Dans le velours trompeur de la neige.
Dans l'haleine de quelques chiens réunis.
Dans la troupe exténuée de feuilles mortes.

Emportez-moi sans me briser, dans les baisers,
Dans les poitrines qui se soulèvent et respirent,
Sur les tapis des paumes et leur sourire,
Dans les corridors des os longs, et des articulations.

Emportez-moi, ou plutôt enfouissez-moi.

La Nuit remue
© Éditions Gallimard

QU'IL REPOSE EN RÉVOLTE

Dans le noir, dans le soir sera sa mémoire
dans ce qui souffre, dans ce qui suinte
dans ce qui cherche et ne trouve pas
dans le chaland de débarquement qui crève sur la grève
dans le départ sifflant de la balle traceuse
dans l'île de soufre sera sa mémoire.

Dans celui qui a sa fièvre en soi, à qui n'importent les murs
Dans celui qui s'élance et n'a de tête que contre les murs
dans le larron non repentant
dans le faible à jamais récalcitrant
dans le porche éventré sera sa mémoire.

Dans la route qui obsède
dans le cœur qui cherche sa plage
dans l'amant que son corps fuit
dans le voyageur que l'espace ronge

Dans le tunnel
dans le tourment tournant sur lui-même
dans l'impavide qui ose froisser le cimetière.

Dans l'orbite enflammée des astres qui se heurtent en éclatant
dans le vaisseau fantôme, dans la fiancée flétrie
dans la chanson crépusculaire sera sa mémoire.

Dans la présence de la mer
dans la distance du juge
dans la cécité
dans la tasse à poison.

Dans le capitaine des sept mers
dans l'âme de celui qui lave la dague
dans l'orgue en roseau qui pleure pour tout un peuple
dans le jour du crachat sur l'offrande.

Dans le fruit d'hiver
dans le poumon des batailles qui reprennent
dans le fou dans la chaloupe

Dans les bras tordus des désirs à jamais inassouvis
sera sa mémoire.

La Vie dans les plis
© Éditions Gallimard

FRANCIS PONGE

(1899-1977)

Prendre le parti des choses comme le fait Ponge, c'est privilégier l'humble univers des objets, le préférer à celui des hommes. Se vouloir le porte-parole de ce monde muet, le mettre en lumière, c'est lui rendre une dignité, une autonomie, une présence dont la tradition humaniste l'a privée. Le poète va donc choisir les matériaux les plus ordinaires et s'efforcer de leur conférer une existence propre en les nommant.

Il s'en est lui-même expliqué : « Ce sont donc des descriptions-définitions-objets-d'art-littéraires que je prétends formuler c'est-à-dire des définitions qui... renvoient... à un ordre de connaissances assez communes, habituelles et élémentaires... » Il illustre son propos avec l'exemple d'un galet, ramassé par hasard. Il va s'agir de rendre visibles ses qualités propres et pour cela « de ne rien dire qui ne convienne qu'à lui seul ». Comment ? En cherchant des mots « tels qu'ils soient conducteurs de l'esprit (comme on dit conducteur de la chaleur ou de l'électricité) », que ces mots existent ou qu'il faille les créer. Ce choix doit entraîner pour chaque objet une forme particulière de poème : « C'est-à-dire que si j'envisage une rhétorique, c'est une rhétorique par objet. » De là pourra naître un texte qui par l'exacte adéquation de ses termes à l'objet décrit et aussi sa perfection formelle imposera son évidence. Les conséquences de ce « parti pris » concernent d'abord l'homme lui-même : « Du fait seul de vouloir rendre compte du contenu entier de leurs notions, je me fais tirer, par les objets, hors du vieil humanisme, hors de l'homme actuel et en avant de lui. J'ajoute à l'homme les nouvelles qualités que je nomme. »

Elles concernent aussi la définition de ce qu'on a, jusque-là, appelé poésie ou domaine de la poésie. Ponge affirme à plusieurs reprises : « Je ne me veux pas poète… j'utilise le magma poétique mais pour m'en débarrasser »… ou encore : « Pour moi, je suis de plus en plus convaincu que mon affaire est plus scientifique que poétique. » La véritable fonction de la poésie étant à ses yeux « de nourrir l'esprit de l'homme en l'abouchant au cosmos », il attend que par elle « le monde envahisse à ce point l'esprit de l'homme qu'il en perde à peu près la parole, puis réinvente un jargon » car la véritable poésie n'a rien à voir avec « ce qu'on trouve actuellement dans les collections poétiques. Elle est ce qui ne se donne pas pour poésie ». À ce compte, on le voit bien, ses dénégations ne sont pas à prendre au pied de la lettre : si Ponge ne se veut nullement poète au sens habituel, c'est pour se reconnaître tel dans l'acception nouvelle qu'il donne à ce terme.

D'où l'importance capitale attachée aux mots et à la forme. Ce n'est pas un hasard s'il écrit un *Pour Malherbe*. Il se sent une réelle affinité avec son l'œuvre puisque « la parole (chaque parole) y a sa dimension juste ». Aussi l'oppose-t-il à ceux qu'il nomme « les Mauvais (de Ronsard à Michaux) » (!) La différence avec ces poètes honnis, c'est que chez Malherbe « il ne s'agit pas des mouvements de son cœur, mais de la vibration de la parole tendue », expression révélatrice de l'art poétique personnel de Ponge. La parole, comme l'arc qui porte la flèche à son but, doit être nécessaire, fournir l'exact équivalent verbal de la chose en elle-même et des impressions qu'elle suscite en nous. Ce travail sur le langage exige une attention scrupuleuse et passionnée aux mots. De leur précision et de leur justesse dépend leur capacité à faire parler l'objet. C'est ce que Ponge nomme « la rage de l'expression ». L'enjeu de ce difficile et patient effort est de faire apparaître « les qualités différentielles des choses ».

La lecture de ces propos inspire respect et admiration. La passion des mots, la foi en leur pouvoir a toujours été l'apanage des poètes. Mais en quel sens peut-on dire de cet écrivain original qu'il est poète ? Sa volonté, exprimée à plusieurs reprises, d'inscrire ses pas dans ceux de Rimbaud ou de Lautréamont pourrait marquer son appartenance à la lignée prométhéenne. Cependant son œuvre ne paraît pas s'y rattacher, elle offre plutôt un avatar original du courant placé par Bénichou sous le signe de Narcisse : autant que la contemplation de sa propre image dans la clôture des mots, celle de l'objet au miroir du langage referme le poème sur lui-même et ne semble pas fonder cette ouverture vers l'avenir que le poète en attendait.

LA BOUGIE

La nuit parfois ravive une plante singulière dont la lueur décompose les chambres meublées en massifs d'ombre.

Sa feuille d'or tient impassible au creux d'une colonnette d'albâtre par un pédoncule très noir.

Les papillons miteux l'assaillent de préférence à la lune trop haute, qui vaporise les bois. Mais brûlés aussitôt ou vannés dans la bagarre, tous frémissent aux bords d'une frénésie voisine de la stupeur.

Cependant la bougie, par le vacillement des clartés sur le livre au brusque dégagement des fumées originales encourage le lecteur, – puis s'incline sur son assiette et se noie dans son aliment.

Le Parti pris des choses
© Éditions Gallimard

LE PAIN

La surface du pain est merveilleuse d'abord à cause de cette impression quasi panoramique qu'elle donne : comme si l'on avait à sa disposition sous la main les Alpes, le Taurus ou la Cordillère des Andes.

Ainsi donc une masse amorphe en train d'éructer fut glissée pour nous dans le four stellaire, où durcissant elle s'est façonnée en vallées, crêtes, ondulations, crevasses... Et tous ces plans dès lors si nettement articulés, ces dalles minces où la lumière avec application couche ses feux, – sans un regard pour la mollesse ignoble sous-jacente.

Ce lâche et froid sous-sol que l'on nomme la mie a son tissu pareil à celui des éponges : feuilles ou fleurs y sont comme des sœurs siamoises soudées par tous les coudes à la fois. Lorsque le pain rassit ces fleurs fanent et se rétrécissent : elles se détachent alors les unes des autres, et la masse en devient friable...

Mais brisons-la : car le pain doit être dans notre bouche moins objet de respect que de consommation.

Le Parti pris des choses
© Éditions Gallimard

RESSOURCES NAÏVES

L'esprit, dont on peut dire qu'il s'abîme d'abord aux choses (qui ne sont que *riens*) dans leur contemplation, renaît, par la nomination de leurs qualités, telles que lorsqu'au lieu de lui ce sont elles qui les proposent. Hors de ma fausse personne c'est aux objets, aux choses du temps que je rapporte mon bonheur lorsque l'attention que je leur porte les forme dans mon esprit comme des compos de qualités, de façons-de-se-comporter propres à chacun d'eux, fort inattendus, sans aucun rapport avec nos propres façons de nous comporter jusqu'à eux. Alors, ô vertus, ô modèles possibles-tout-à-coup, que je vais découvrir, où l'esprit tout nouvellement s'exerce et s'adore.

1927

Proèmes,
© Éditions Gallimard

JACQUES PRÉVERT

(1900-1977)

Tout n'est pas d'une égale qualité, ni toujours de bon goût dans l'œuvre de Prévert. Il a souvent confondu la gouaille avec l'inspiration, et le coq à l'âne avec la « méprise » verlainienne. Mais les raisons des détracteurs de cette poésie dite populaire sont souvent suspectes. Ils la rejettent parce qu'elle est d'emblée accessible. Ceux qui ne conçoivent la poésie qu'hermétique ou ésotérique ont lieu, en effet, d'être réticents. Le vers libre adapté avec souplesse à un style quasi parlé, le recours au jeu de mots, un sens toujours clair, mettent les poèmes de Prévert à la portée de tous. Mais c'est surtout à l'heureux compromis qu'ils proposent entre la fantaisie surréaliste (le poète fut d'abord influencé par ce mouvement) et la réalité familière la plus humble, celle de la misère et des quartiers sordides de Paris que le poète doit son audience auprès d'un très large public. Il est vrai de dire que ses poèmes en furent aussi redevables à la musique composée par Kosma pour certains d'entre eux, et au talent des interprètes. Ce poète si fraternel avec les petites gens, dont il évoque les misères et les joies, nous touche par sa sincérité, son absence de pose, et une humilité non feinte. Il participe vraiment à la vie des hommes, épouse leur haine de la guerre, leur indignation devant l'injustice, leur refus de la misère. Contempteur plein d'humour des institutions établies, Église, Justice ou Armée, il a des réquisitoires souvent savoureux contre les bourgeois égoïstes et ceux qui servent leurs seuls intérêts, mais ce qui demeure le plus convaincant dans son œuvre, c'est un mélange de tendresse, de spontanéité et de verve qui a peu d'équivalents.

SABLES MOUVANTS

Démons et merveilles
Vents et marées
Au loin déjà la mer s'est retirée
Et toi
Comme une algue doucement caressée par le vent
Dans les sables du lit tu remues en rêvant
Démons et merveilles
Vents et marées
Au loin déjà la mer s'est retirée
Mais dans tes yeux entr'ouverts
Deux petites vagues sont restées
Démons et merveilles
Vents et marées
Deux petites vagues pour me noyer.

Paroles
© Éditions Gallimard

CHANSON DU GEÔLIER

Où vas-tu beau geôlier
Avec cette clé tachée de sang
Je vais délivrer celle que j'aime
S'il en est encore temps
Et que j'ai enfermée
Tendrement cruellement
Au plus secret de mon désir
Au plus profond de mon tourment
Dans les mensonges de l'avenir
Dans les bêtises des serments
Je veux la délivrer
Je veux qu'elle soit libre
Et même de m'oublier
Et même de s'en aller
Et même de revenir
Et encore de m'aimer
Ou d'en aimer un autre
Si un autre lui plaît
Et si je reste seul
Et elle en allée
Je garderai seulement
Je garderai toujours
Dans mes deux mains en creux
Jusqu'à la fin des jours
La douceur de ses seins modelés par l'amour.

Paroles
© Éditions Gallimard

COMPLAINTE DE VINCENT

À Paul Éluard

À Arles où roule le Rhône
Dans l'atroce lumière de midi
Un homme de phosphore et de sang
Pousse une obsédante plainte
Comme une femme qui fait son enfant
Et le linge devient rouge
Et l'homme s'enfuit en hurlant
Pourchassé par le soleil
Un soleil d'un jaune strident
Au bordel tout près du Rhône
L'homme arrive comme un roi mage
Avec son absurde présent
Il a le regard bleu et doux
Le vrai regard lucide et fou
De ceux qui donnent tout à la vie
De ceux qui ne sont pas jaloux
Et montre à la pauvre enfant
Son oreille couchée dans le linge
Et elle pleure sans rien comprendre
Songeant à de tristes présages
Et regarde sans oser le prendre
L'affreux et tendre coquillage
Où les plaintes de l'amour mort
Et les voix inhumaines de l'art
Se mêlent aux murmures de la mer
Et vont mourir sur le carrelage
Dans la chambre où l'édredon rouge
D'un rouge soudain éclatant
Mélange ce rouge si rouge
Au sang bien plus rouge encore
De Vincent à demi mort
Et sage comme l'image même
De la misère et de l'amour
L'enfant nue toute seule sans âge
Regarde le pauvre Vincent

Foudroyé par son propre orage
Qui s'écroule sur le carreau
Couché dans son plus beau tableau
Et l'orage s'en va calmé indifférent
En roulant devant lui ses grands tonneaux de sang
L'éblouissant orage du génie de Vincent
Et Vincent reste là dormant rêvant râlant
Et le soleil au-dessus du bordel
Comme une orange folle dans un désert sans nom
Le soleil sur Arles
En hurlant tourne en rond.

Paroles
© Éditions Gallimard

BARBARA

Rappelle-toi Barbara
Il pleuvait sans cesse sur Brest ce jour-là
Et tu marchais souriante
Épanouie ravie ruisselante
Sous la pluie
Rappelle-toi Barbara
Il pleuvait sans cesse sur Brest
Et je t'ai croisée rue de Siam
Tu souriais
Et moi je souriais de même
Rappelle-toi Barbara
Toi que je ne connaissais pas
Toi qui ne me connaissais pas
Rappelle-toi
Rappelle-toi quand même ce jour-là
N'oublie pas
Un homme sous un porche s'abritait
Et il a crié ton nom
Barbara
Et tu as couru vers lui sous la pluie
Ruisselante ravie épanouie
Et tu t'es jetée dans ses bras
Rappelle-toi cela Barbara
Et ne m'en veux pas si je te tutoie
Je dis tu à tous ceux que j'aime
Même si je ne les ai vus qu'une seule fois
Je dis tu à tous ceux qui s'aiment
Même si je ne les connais pas
Rappelle-toi Barbara
N'oublie pas
Cette pluie sage et heureuse
Sur ton visage heureux
Sur cette ville heureuse
Cette pluie sur la mer
Sur l'arsenal

Sur le bateau d'Ouessant
Oh Barbara
Quelle connerie la guerre
Qu'es-tu devenue maintenant
Sous cette pluie de fer
De feu d'acier de sang
Et celui qui te serrait dans ses bras
Amoureusement
Est-il mort disparu ou bien encore vivant
Oh Barbara
Il pleut sans cesse sur Brest
Comme il pleuvait avant
Mais ce n'est plus pareil et tout est abîmé
C'est une pluie de deuil terrible et désolée
Ce n'est même plus l'orage
De fer d'acier de sang
Tout simplement des nuages
Qui crèvent comme des chiens
Des chiens qui disparaissent
Au fil de l'eau sur Brest
Et vont pourrir au loin
Au loin très loin de Brest
Dont il ne reste rien.

Paroles
© Éditions Gallimard

ROBERT DESNOS

(1900-1944)

Les jeux surréalistes semblent faits exprès pour lui, taillés à la mesure de ce médium exceptionnel. Il y aura chez d'autres membres du groupe quelques « sommeils » approximatifs : on peut en effet mettre en doute, pour ceux d'entre eux qui demeurent à chaque instant conscients des lois de la syntaxe, la profondeur de l'état d'hypnose où ils se prétendent plongés ! On imagine qu'il ne fut pas impossible de tricher parfois avec l'écriture automatique : Desnos, si l'on en croit les témoignages de ses amis, s'endort à volonté et profondément. Il s'adonne alors, sans aucun subterfuge, aux exercices proposés. Son inventivité sans limites lui dicte des formules et des images qui témoignent de ses dons personnels de rêveur inspiré, au moins autant que de l'efficacité de cette méthode. Du reste parmi les textes que l'histoire littéraire a retenus de la première période du surréalisme, on voit assez vite que ceux de Desnos ne valent pas seulement comme documents mais qu'ils existent pour eux-mêmes. Autour de lui tous s'accordent à reconnaître qu'il est le plus doué d'entre eux pour « la dictée psychique » telle que la conçoit Breton. Certes on peut imaginer que sa nature de poète se serait manifestée à n'importe quelle époque, tant la poésie est chez lui spontanée ; pourtant l'expérience surréaliste, dans laquelle il s'est engagé après avoir été séduit par Dada, est déterminante dans la mesure où elle l'incite d'abord à inventorier ses ressources profondes, à mettre en œuvre les matériaux du rêve qui s'offrent en lui à foison. Après sa rupture avec le groupe en 1930, il paraît renoncer à la poésie et s'intéresse à d'autres formes d'expression comme la radio ou le cinéma.

Toutefois c'est à cette époque qu'il écrit *La Complainte de Fantomas*. Malgré les distances prises vis-à-vis du surréalisme, il n'a jamais renoncé à écrire ; d'ailleurs on peut dire de lui que, quoi qu'il fasse, il vit en poésie. Ce qui le caractérise aussi c'est sa désinvolture vis-à-vis de ses propres écrits. On peut penser que la nonchalance du poète Desnos, sa manière de ne jamais se prendre au sérieux, ajoutent un charme certain à son œuvre. Cependant cette négligence a bien failli en provoquer la disparition au moins en grande partie, tant il se souciait peu des éditions quasi confidentielles qui furent faites durant sa vie ou des poèmes qu'il distribuait généreusement à ses amis. C'est après sa mort au camp de Terezin – les survivants ont témoigné de son courage souriant, de sa gentillesse naturelle, de sa cordialité à l'égard de tous – que ces poèmes furent rassemblés. On ne s'étonne pas de trouver sous sa plume ces *Chantefables* directement accessibles aux enfants avec lesquels il est de plain-pied. Il sait allier candeur et humour un peu à la manière de Max Jacob.

Ce qui est manifeste à travers l'ensemble de son œuvre c'est qu'il est un grand lyrique. Il utilise parfaitement l'ample rythme de l'alexandrin où il excelle, car il est revenu au mètre classique, à la versification traditionnelle, à la rime. Il n'a pas renoncé pour autant aux formes plus récentes qu'il maîtrise aussi bien : ses poèmes en prose, quelles que soient leur disposition et leur longueur, s'imposent d'emblée au lecteur qui ne songe pas à contester leur nature de poèmes. Comme tout lyrique, il célèbre l'amour, celui de la femme dont il est éperdument épris, et aussi de la « Mystérieuse », la fantôme qui hante ses nuits, et dont il relate les apparitions successives. « *Amour fou* » qui est sans doute, avec la *Nadja* de Breton, le plus bel exemple des créations bouleversantes de l'imaginaire surréaliste. Son engagement dans la Résistance l'ouvre à une autre inspiration, plus largement tournée vers les angoisses et les espoirs des hommes, mais jamais il ne renonce à la fantaisie et à la tendresse qui font de lui une des figures les plus humaines et les plus attachantes parmi les poètes de ce siècle.

J'AI TANT RÊVÉ DE TOI

J'ai tant rêvé de toi que tu perds ta réalité.

Est-il encore temps d'atteindre ce corps vivant et de baiser sur cette bouche la naissance de la voix qui m'est chère ?

J'ai tant rêvé de toi que mes bras habitués, en étreignant ton ombre, à se croiser sur ma poitrine ne se plieraient pas au contour de ton corps, peut-être.

Et que, devant l'apparence réelle de ce qui me hante et me gouverne depuis des jours et des années, je deviendrais une ombre sans doute.

Ô balances sentimentales.

J'ai tant rêvé de toi qu'il n'est plus temps sans doute que je m'éveille. Je dors debout, le corps exposé à toutes les apparences de la vie et de l'amour et toi, la seule qui compte aujourd'hui pour moi, je pourrais moins toucher ton front et tes lèvres que les premières lèvres et le premier front venus.

J'ai tant rêvé de toi, tant marché, parlé, couché avec ton fantôme qu'il ne me reste plus peut-être, et pourtant, qu'à être fantôme parmi les fantômes et plus ombre cent fois que l'ombre qui se promène et se promènera allègrement sur le cadran solaire de ta vie.

Corps et biens
© Éditions Gallimard

LES ESPACES DU SOMMEIL

Dans la nuit il y a naturellement les sept merveilles du monde
et la grandeur et le tragique et le charme.
Les forêts s'y heurtent confusément avec des créatures de
légende cachées dans les fourrés.
Il y a toi.
Dans la nuit il y a le pas du promeneur et celui de l'assassin et
celui du sergent de ville et la lumière du réverbère et celle de la
lanterne du chiffonnier.
Il y a toi.
Dans la nuit passent les trains et les bateaux et le mirage des
pays où il fait jour. Les derniers souffles du crépuscule et les
premiers frissons de l'aube.
Il y a toi.
Un air de piano, un éclat de voix.
Une porte claque. Une horloge.
Et pas seulement les êtres et les choses et les bruits matériels.
Mais encore moi qui me poursuis ou sans cesse me dépasse.
Il y a toi l'immolée, toi que j'attends.
Parfois d'étranges figures naissent à l'instant du sommeil et
disparaissent.
Quand je ferme les yeux, des floraisons phosphorescentes
apparaissent et se fanent et renaissent comme des feux d'artifice
charnus.
Des pays inconnus que je parcours en compagnie de créatures.
Il y a toi sans doute, ô belle et discrète espionne.
Et l'âme palpable de l'étendue.
Et les parfums du ciel et des étoiles et le chant du coq d'il y a
2 000 ans et le cri du paon dans les parcs en flamme et des baisers.
Des mains qui se serrent sinistrement dans une lumière blafarde
et des essieux qui grincent sur des routes médusantes.
Il y a toi sans doute que je ne connais pas, que je connais au
contraire.
Mais qui, présente dans mes rêves, t'obstines à s'y laisser
deviner sans y paraître.
Toi qui restes insaisissable dans la réalité et dans le rêve.

Toi qui m'appartiens de par ma volonté de te posséder en illusion mais qui n'approches ton visage du mien que mes yeux clos aussi bien au rêve qu'à la réalité.

Toi qu'en dépit d'une rhétorique facile où le flot meurt sur les plages, où la corneille vole dans des usines en ruines, où le bois pourrit en craquant sous un soleil de plomb,

Toi qui es à la base de mes rêves et qui secoues mon esprit plein de métamorphoses et qui me laisses ton gant quand je baise ta main.

Dans la nuit, il y a les étoiles et le mouvement ténébreux de la mer, des fleuves, des forêts, des villes, des herbes, des poumons de millions et millions d'êtres.

Dans la nuit il y a les merveilles du monde.

Dans la nuit il n'y a pas d'anges gardiens mais il y a le sommeil.

Dans la nuit il y a toi.

Dans le jour aussi.

Corps et biens
© Éditions Gallimard

COMME UNE MAIN À L'INSTANT DE LA MORT

Comme une main à l'instant de la mort et du naufrage se dresse
comme les rayons du soleil couchant, ainsi de toutes parts
jaillissent tes regards.
Il n'est plus temps, il n'est plus temps peut-être de me voir,
Mais la feuille qui tombe et la roue qui tourne te diront que rien
n'est perpétuel sur terre,
Sauf l'amour,
Et je veux m'en persuader.
Des bateaux de sauvetage peints de rougeâtres couleurs,
Des orages qui s'enfuient,
Une valse surannée qu'emportent le temps et le vent durant les
longs espaces du ciel.
Paysages.
Moi je n'en veux pas d'autres que l'étreinte à laquelle j'aspire,
Et meure le chant du coq.
Comme une main à l'instant de la mort se crispe, mon cœur se
serre.
Je n'ai jamais pleuré depuis que je te connais.
J'aime trop mon amour pour pleurer.
Tu pleureras sur mon tombeau,
Ou moi sur le tien.
Il ne sera pas trop tard.
Je mentirai. Je dirai que tu fus ma maîtresse
Et puis vraiment c'est tellement inutile,
Toi et moi, nous mourrons bientôt.

Corps et biens
© Éditions Gallimard

JEAN TARDIEU

(1903-1975)

Comment échapper à l'insuffisance du langage et capter la réalité qui est pareille, selon lui, « à ces fleuves cachés ou perdus au pied des montagnes » puisque « comme eux l'aspect des choses plonge et se joue entre la présence et l'absence » ? On peut ruser avec les mots en les détournant de leur emploi ordinaire, tout en prenant ceux du langage parlé. Le poète doit alors mêler le saugrenu au familier. En effet l'humour dont il fait preuve, s'il témoigne d'un goût du jeu incontestable, est surtout pour lui une manière de conjurer le caractère insaisissable de tout ce qui en nous et hors de nous se dérobe à notre prise.

D'où certains poèmes narquois comme la célèbre « Môme néant » :

Quoi qu'a dit ?
– A dit rin

Quoi qu'a fait ?
– A fait rin.

À quoi qu'a pense ?
– A pense à rin.

Pourquoi qu'a dit rin ?
Pourquoi qu'a fait rin ?

Pourquoi qu'a pense à rin ?
– A'xiste pas.

D'où les dialogues de Monsieur et Monsieur, dans le recueil qui porte ce titre ; l'auteur caractérise lui-même les deux marionnettes qu'il anime : « C'est comme si Personne avec Rien dialoguait ». Dans l'Argument il s'est expliqué en ces termes : « C'est au carrefour du Burlesque et du Lyrique... que je m'étais caché pour écrire ces poèmes. »

Ce carrefour lui est familier puisque son œuvre emprunte tour à tour les deux voies qu'il y distingue. L'une et l'autre sont pour lui des moyens de dissiper l'angoisse. Celle de l'oppressante présence d'un réel foisonnant peut être un moment jugulée si l'on parvient, avec des mots, à transformer l'apparence des choses jusqu'à les faire disparaître. Mais le vide suscite une autre angoisse, celle qui naît du souvenir de ce réel, tout à l'heure banni, et dont l'absence devient soudain douloureuse. Le poème lyrique répond pleinement à « cette angoisse en forme de cycle... les mots, choses semblables aux choses, passent, aussitôt formée l'image qu'ils révèlent ; le rythme qui les apporte abolit à son tour les images et la gangue de toute signification logique, s'il contente par ses temps forts le désir de solidité, et par ses flottements l'appel vers une disparition générale. »

Ainsi la voix du poète imite le cheminement des eaux souterraines avec leurs pertes et leurs résurgences et son chant ne peut être que fragmentaire et discontinu. Comme l'écrit Émilie Noulet dans son livre sur lui : « Silence plein, sens étouffé, ce sont peut-être les deux pôles de l'œuvre de Jean Tardieu. »

JOURS PÉTRIFIÉS

Les yeux bandés les mains tremblantes
trompé par le bruit de mes pas
qui porte partout mon silence
perdant la trace de mes jours
si je m'attends ou me dépasse
toujours je me retrouve là
comme la pierre sous le ciel.

Par la nuit et par le soleil
condamné sans preuve et sans tort
aux murs de mon étroit espace
je tourne au fond de mon sommeil
désolé comme l'espérance
innocent comme le remords

Un homme qui feint de vieillir
emprisonné dans son enfance,
l'avenir brille au même point,
nous nous en souvenons encore,
le sol tremble à la même place,

le temps monte comme la mer.

Le Témoin invisible
© Éditions Gallimard

RENÉ CHAR

(1907-1988)

« Le poète doit tenir la balance égale entre le monde physique de la veille et l'aisance redoutable du sommeil, les lignes de la connaissance dans lesquelles il couche le corps subtil du poème allant indistinctement de l'un à l'autre de ces états différents de la vie. » C'est en 1950 que Char écrit ces lignes. Plus tard il dira aussi : « La nuit porte nourriture, le soleil affine la partie nourrie. » Il ne cesse en effet d'élaborer un art poétique personnel. On voit qu'il s'attache, sans renier sa période surréaliste, à prendre désormais en compte la part diurne de l'homme. Il connaît bien lui-même « l'aisance redoutable » à laquelle il fait allusion, et il a pu mesurer le danger qu'il y a pour le poète à privilégier la dictée incontrôlée. Il prend donc ses distances avec les méthodes prônées par le groupe et qu'il a pratiquées, et leur préfère une quête solitaire, « parce que ce que nous cherchions n'était pas découvrable à plusieurs » explique-t-il, ajoutant ce bilan assez critique : « Le surréalisme a accompli son voyage... Ce n'est pas à moi qu'il appartient [de l'examiner]... dans ses effets, les détestables et les autres. » Sans renoncer jamais aux ressources du rêve, il veut faire du poète « un homme du quotidien », réduire les ambitions démesurées qui furent celles de ses amis et souligner l'importance d'un travail personnel et conscient sur le matériau verbal (« le poète n'a pas de mission, à tout prendre il a une tâche »). Tout en conservant certains des acquis de son expérience antérieure, c'est au réel qu'il s'attache désormais. Comme il le dit dans *La Parole en archipel* : « Le réel quelquefois désaltère l'espérance. »

Cependant l'Histoire va d'abord le contraindre à affronter la plus cruelle des réalités. On le voit concerné par la tragédie de la guerre d'Espagne (il dédie aux enfants de ce pays, en 37, son *Placard pour le chemin des écoliers)*, et on connaît sa participation à la Résistance. Ce temps va modeler sa trajectoire personnelle et marquer durablement sa conception de la poésie. *Les Feuillets d'Hypnos* en témoignent. Ce sont des notes « affectées par l'événement » qu'il rédige au milieu des maquisards de Provence dont il est le capitaine. C'est là qu'il affirme : « Le poète ne peut pas demeurer longtemps dans la stratosphère du Verbe. Il doit se lover dans de nouvelles larmes et pousser plus avant dans son ordre. » Le même recueil propose cette définition essentielle : « Le poète conservateur des infinis visages du vivant. »

Mais ces approches successives ne sont pas la marque d'une doctrine sûre d'elle-même, plutôt d'intuitions fulgurantes à travers lesquelles il poursuit une recherche jamais aboutie : « Magicien de l'insécurité, le poète n'a que des satisfactions adoptives. Cendre toujours inachevée. » Son souci majeur est d'atteindre la réalité, non celle que nous croyons percevoir mais celle que le verbe poétique seul est capable de dévoiler. Effort qui exige en lui vigilance et attention permanentes. En cela il n'œuvre pas pour une appropriation égoïste sur laquelle se refermerait le poème, mais pour les autres hommes (« redonnez-leur ce qui n'est plus présent en eux »). Pour eux, sans « l'énergie disloquante de la poésie » il n'y aurait pas d'accès à cette autre réalité. Cet effort d'arrachement exige une parole discontinue, fragmentaire, qu'il qualifie de « saxifrage » puisqu'elle est capable de briser le granit des apparences. S'il intitule l'un de ses recueils *Le Poème pulvérisé*, c'est qu'il compare chaque poème à la poussière lumineuse que fait naître la réfraction d'un rayon de soleil sur l'objet qu'il transfigure. Chez lui l'aspect prométhéen de la poésie l'emporte sur l'orphique, car l'ego est destiné à s'effacer quand la poésie dont le dessein est « de nous rendre souverain tout en nous impersonnalisant » nous délivre de la vision limitée qui était la nôtre. Si la forme qui prévaut dans cette œuvre est l'aphorisme, c'est que ce dernier permet, par le heurt des contraires et l'extrême resserrement de l'expression, cet effet qu'on pourrait appeler d'obscurité fulgurante. On en a un exemple avec les présocratiques, en particulier chez Héraclite que le poète met au

rang de ceux qui l'ont inspiré. Vivre en homme ordinaire et parler
en poète, goûter l'instant en ayant une constante ouverture sur
l'avenir, mener une œuvre en solitaire par solidarité avec les autres,
s'arc-bouter dans le refus du compromis avec le monde et
acquiescer à toute beauté, ce sont là les contraires qui rendent
crédible celui qui écrivait : « Si nous habitons un éclair, il est au
cœur de l'éternel. »

ENVOÛTEMENT À LA RENARDIÈRE

Vous qui m'avez connu, grenade dissidente, point du jour
déployant le plaisir comme exemple, votre visage – tel est-il, qu'il
soit toujours –, si libre qu'à son contact le cerne infini de l'air
se plissait, s'entrouvrant à ma rencontre, me vêtait des beaux
quartiers de votre imagination. Je demeurais là, entièrement
inconnu de moi-même, dans votre moulin à soleil, exultant à la
succession des richesses d'un cœur qui avait rompu son étau. Sur
notre plaisir s'allongeait l'influente douceur de la grande roue
consumable du mouvement, au terme de ses classes.

À ce visage – personne ne l'aperçut jamais –, simplifier la beauté
n'apparaissait pas comme une atroce économie. Nous étions
exacts dans l'exceptionnel qui seul sait se soustraire au caractère
alternatif du mystère de vivre.

Dès lors que les routes de la mémoire se sont couvertes de la
lèpre infaillible des monstres, je trouve refuge dans une innocence
où l'homme qui rêve ne peut vieillir. Mais ai-je qualité pour
m'imposer de vous survivre, moi qui dans ce Chant de Vous me
considère comme le plus éloigné de mes sosies ?

Fureur et mystère
© Éditions Gallimard

LE DEVOIR

L'enfant que, la nuit venue, l'hiver descendait avec précaution de la charrette de la lune, une fois à l'intérieur de la maison balsamique, plongeait d'un seul trait ses yeux dans le foyer de fonte rouge. Derrière l'étroit vitrail incendié l'espace ardent le tenait entièrement captif. Le buste incliné vers la chaleur, ses jeunes mains scellées à l'envolée de feuilles sèches du bien-être, l'enfant épelait la rêverie du ciel glacé :

« Bouche, ma confidente, que vois-tu ?

— Cigale, je vois un pauvre champignon au cœur de pierre, en amitié avec la mort. Son venin est si vieux que tu peux le tourner en chanson.

— Maîtresse, où vont mes lignes ?

— Belle, ta place est marquée sur le banc du parc où le cœur a sa couronne.

— Suis-je le présent de l'amour ? »

Dans la constellation des Pléiades, au vent d'un fleuve adolescent, l'impatient Minotaure s'éveillait.

Fureur et mystère
© Éditions Gallimard

ÉVADNÉ

L'été et notre vie étions d'un seul tenant
La campagne mangeait la couleur de ta jupe odorante
Avidité et contrainte s'étaient réconciliées
Le château de Maubec s'enfonçait dans l'argile
Bientôt s'effondrerait le roulis de sa lyre
La violence des plantes nous faisait vaciller
Un corbeau rameur sombre déviant de l'escadre
Sur le muet silex de midi écartelé
Accompagnait notre entente aux mouvements tendres
La faucille partout devait se reposer
Notre rareté commençait un règne
(Le vent insomnieux qui nous ride la paupière
En tournant chaque nuit la page consentie
Veut que chaque part de toi que je retienne
Soit étendue à un pays d'âge affamé et de larmier géant)

C'était au début d'adorables années
La terre nous aimait un peu je me souviens.

Fureur et mystère
© Éditions Gallimard

LE THOR

Dans le sentier aux herbes engourdies où nous nous étonnions, enfants, que la nuit se risquât à passer, les guêpes n'allaient plus aux ronces et les oiseaux aux branches. L'air ouvrait aux hôtes de la matinée sa turbulente immensité. Ce n'étaient que filaments d'ailes, tentation de crier, voltige entre lumière et transparence. Le Thor s'exaltait sur la lyre de ses pierres. Le mont Ventoux, miroir des aigles, était en vue.

Dans le sentier aux herbes engourdies, la chimère d'un âge perdu souriait à nos jeunes larmes.

Fureur et mystère
© Éditions Gallimard

JACQUEMARD ET JULIA

Jadis l'herbe, à l'heure où les routes de la terre s'accordaient dans leur déclin, élevait tendrement ses tiges et allumait ses clartés. Les cavaliers du jour naissaient au regard de leur amour et les châteaux de leurs bien-aimées comptaient autant de fenêtres que l'abîme porte d'orages légers.

Jadis l'herbe connaissait mille devises qui ne se contrariaient pas. Elle était la providence des visages baignés de larmes. Elle incantait les animaux, donnait asile à l'erreur. Son étendue était comparable au ciel qui a vaincu la peur du temps et allégi la douleur.

Jadis l'herbe était bonne aux fous et hostile au bourreau. Elle convolait avec le seuil de toujours. Les jeux qu'elle inventait avaient des ailes à leur sourire (jeux absous et également fugitifs). Elle n'était dure pour aucun de ceux qui perdant leur chemin souhaitent le perdre à jamais.

Jadis l'herbe avait établi que la nuit vaut moins que son pouvoir, que les sources ne compliquent pas à plaisir leur parcours, que la graine qui s'agenouille est déjà à demi dans le bec de l'oiseau. Jadis, terre et ciel se haïssaient mais terre et ciel vivaient.

L'inextinguible sécheresse s'écoule. L'homme est un étranger pour l'aurore. Cependant à la poursuite de la vie qui ne peut être encore imaginée, il y a des volonté qui frémissent, des murmures qui vont s'affronter et des enfants sains et saufs qui *découvrent*.

Fureur et mystère
© Éditions Gallimard

JOUVENCE DES NÉVONS

Dans l'enceinte du parc, le grillon ne
se tait que pour s'établir davantage.

Dans le parc des Névons
Ceinture de prairies,
Un ruisseau sans talus,
Un enfant sans ami
Nuancent leur tristesse
Et vivent mieux ainsi.

Dans le parc des Névons
Un rebelle s'est joint
Au ruisseau, à l'enfant,
À leur mirage enfin.

Dans le parc des Névons
Mortel serait l'été
Sans la voix d'un grillon
Qui, par instant, se tait.

Les Matinaux
© Éditions Gallimard

PATRICE DE LA TOUR DU PIN

(1911-1975)

Comment donner, au moyen de quelques fragment, une idée de cette œuvre qui se prête moins que toute autre à la juxtaposition de morceaux choisis ? Elle se présente en effet comme *Une Somme de poésie*, suivant le titre général de l'édition posthume qui regroupe la totalité des recueils publiés auparavant. Dans cette dernière, conformément au dessein du poète qui a lui-même conçu la disposition en trois volumes, les poèmes s'ordonnent non en fonction de leur date de parution mais suivant leur place dans le cheminement d'une vie, depuis l'adolescence jusqu'à l'âge mûr. Leur succession permet surtout de découvrir les différents moments d'un apprentissage spirituel. Ainsi répartis, ils forment une œuvre unique, cohérente et homogène, une Somme au sens philosophique ou théologique du terme.

Trois « jeux » la constituent, *Le Jeu de l'homme en lui-même, Le Jeu de l'homme devant les autres, Le Jeu de l'homme devant Dieu*. Ces sous-titres intriguent le lecteur : il peut voir dans le terme de jeu une allusion à des variations sur le langage, il doit l'entendre surtout en son sens médiéval : le jeu c'est le théâtre (comme ce *Jeu d'Adam*, première œuvre dramatique de notre littérature qui embrasse l'histoire humaine, du Paradis terrestre à l'annonce du Jugement dernier). Le rapprochement n'est pas arbitraire puisque le poète met en scène et fait dialoguer dans son texte des personnages imaginaires, aux noms étranges, incarnations de ses voix intérieures ou des moments de son histoire. Ainsi peut-on y lire, par exemple, *L'office secret de Lorentin, le Poème de Lydiverguen, la Prière de Gorphoncelet*, ou encore *L'aventure de Jean de Flaterre*.

Dès son premier livre paru en 1933 sous le beau titre de *La Quête de joie*, Patrice de la Tour du Pin fait intervenir l'une de ces figures singulières qui lui renvoient sa propre image, en la personne du tentateur Ullin. En lui s'incarne le désir de percer les mystères de la vie et de la mort et de satisfaire les pures exigences intellectuelles, loin des égarements de la sensibilité. Il propose, en effet, un chemin de connaissance et de silence qui ignorerait les facilités du poème et se refermerait sur soi dans une jouissance orgueilleuse. Mais le poète repousse l'invite, il n'accepte pas de vivre « sans prendre part ». Son itinéraire personnel l'ouvre de plus en plus aux autres, et d'abord à l'amour : « Vois-tu, pour tout ce qui n'est pas éternel, / C'est vraiment la mesure de toutes choses »... Cependant un plus haut désir le sollicite : « Laisse tes autres sens pour la gravitation dans la lumière. » Ce livre est accueilli avec enthousiasme par le monde des lettres, Gide, Montherlant, Supervielle et d'autres expriment leur admiration pour cette poésie jaillissante et neuve. Un poème, *Les Enfants de Septembre*, contribue entre tous à la célébrité de l'auteur. Ces mystérieux « enfants » que poursuit le poète :

> *...Je relevai la trace, incertaine parfois,*
> *Sur le bord d'un layon, d'un enfant de Septembre...*

ces présences qu'il entrevoit ou qu'il devine, comme il les sent proches et fraternelles :

> *Et je me dis : je suis un enfant de Septembre,*
> *Moi-même, par le cœur, la fièvre et l'esprit...*

Son goût pour les paysages de brume, pour les marais où il suit le vol des oiseaux migrateurs, pour les forêts touffues qui le fascinent est un élément essentiel de sa personnalité. Il vit depuis l'enfance sur sa terre du Bignon-Mirabeau « [l']obscur et bas pays troué de chapelets d'étangs », dont il connaît tous les recoins sauvages aussi bien que les labours. Son œuvre est marquée par cette intimité avec la nature et il s'efforce d'en traduire la beauté et les rythmes secrets. Les images qui en jaillissent sont aussi le reflet de son paysage intérieur : ainsi les fonds mystérieux du lac immobile se confondent avec l'énigmatique profondeur de l'homme :

Tourné vers les forêts d'algues aux profondeurs,
Afin de contempler,
Tout ensemble et dans un même espace,
Le flux et le reflux continuel de la Grâce,
La lumière jouant ses milliers de reflets.

Car *La Quête de joie* exprime aussi la foi catholique du poète. *Le Premier Jeu,* « ce long chapitre originel » qui intègre plus tard la *Quête* à un ensemble plus vaste, fait mieux comprendre encore que les diverses figures symbolisant les affrontements et les débats intérieurs convergeaient vers cette ouverture aux autres, et, au-delà, à l'Autre divin. Déjà dans les pages de prose qui s'entremêlent aux poèmes, en proposant « une vie recluse en poésie », il souligne que la base de son projet n'est pas la poésie elle-même, mais qu'il la subordonne à l'homme, « cet hybride de la terre et du ciel ». C'est lui qu'il espère approcher en creusant ses propres énigmes. Pour lui « tout homme est une histoire sacrée ».

Le Deuxième Jeu, fait de récits et de méditations en prose entrecoupés de poèmes, relate, de *La Fin de la vie privée* à *La Terre promise* en passant par *L'Exode,* le long cheminement de celui qui veut partager avec d'autres son expérience de la présence divine. La parole poétique se veut la transcription d'une autre Parole : « Si longues les douleurs pour mettre un mot au monde, / Mais qu'il soit de ton souffle et pourtant de ma voix ! » Cependant le poète a pris la mesure de sa pauvreté ; il note alors : « L'acte poétique s'était dénudé jusqu'à se réduire à la prière, perdant tous ses charmes et ses pouvoirs de magie verbale. » Son écriture reconnaît désormais sa dépendance : « C'est moi ton mot... Avant de parler, j'étais dit. » Et cette humilité ouvre une voie nouvelle.

Dans *Le Troisième Jeu* le poète fait au lecteur une promesse : « suis-moi sans défaillance / Nous mènerons jusqu'au divin la quête de reconnaissance ». Il va célébrer le Dieu qu'il connaît et parler au nom des autres hommes, car ils peuvent prendre à leur compte des paroles de foi qui ne sont pas le fruit d'une autonomie orgueilleuse :

Je livre à mes amis la vie de ma parole
Semis de ton semis...
Qu'elle croisse où tu veux dans les cœurs qui t'ignorent,...

Dans le chapitre d'où ces vers sont extraits et qui a pour titre *L'Auberge de l'agonie* il s'adresse « au client » anonyme qu'il invite à entrer en disant : « Ne te méprends pas sur l'enseigne, / C'est ton agonie qu'elle dit. » Il faut en effet que le plus indifférent se sente concerné, puisque le seul but du poète désormais est de communiquer aux hommes l'élan spirituel qui l'inspire. Il s'efforce d'élaborer ce qu'il nomme, en usant d'un néologisme qui lui est propre, une « théopoésie ». Voici comment il explique ce terme : « J'ai déjà dit que Dieu était pour moi l'Inter-essant, et vous savez que la poésie est mon mode habituel de traduction de la vie, mais tout se passe en moi comme si la vie me demandait d'être traduite et Dieu d'être signifié par moi. » Aussi les poèmes se font méditation sur la Semaine Sainte ; des hymnes, des psaumes, des prières prennent place dans ce livre qui déroule encore dans les derniers chapitres les liturgies de Carême ou de Pâques.

On comprend qu'après Vatican II l'Église catholique ait choisi ce laïc pour coopérer à la traduction française du bréviaire romain. On sait que Patrice de La Tour du Pin se consacra avec ferveur à cette tâche de traducteur, si proche du projet de son *Troisième Jeu* auquel il travaillait dans le même temps. Par là il ne dérogeait pas à sa mission de poète mais prenait place dans la longue lignée de ceux qui, depuis Marot, ont enrichi le domaine français des ressources du lyrisme biblique.

PRÉLUDE

à A.-H. de B.

Tous les pays qui n'ont plus de légende
Seront condamnés à mourir de froid...

Loin dans l'âme, les solitudes s'étendent
Sous le soleil mort de l'amour de soi.
À l'aube on voit monter dans la torpeur
Du marais, des bancs de brouillard immenses
Qu'emploient les poètes, par impuissance,
Pour donner le vague à l'âme et la peur.

Il faut les respirer quand ils s'élèvent
Et jouir de ce frisson inconnu
Que l'on découvre à peine dans les rêves,
Dans les paradis parfois entrevus ;
Les médiocres seuls, les domestiqués
Ne pourront comprendre son amertume :
Ils n'entendent pas, perdu dans la brume,
Le cri farouche des oiseaux traqués.

C'était le pays des anges sauvages,
Ceux qui n'avaient pu se nourrir d'amour ;
Comme toutes les bêtes de passage,
Un secret les menait toujours ;
Parfois ils restaient au sein des élus,
Abandonnant la fadeur de la terre,
Mais ils sentaient battre dans leurs artères
Le regret des cieux qu'ils ne verraient plus !

Alors ils s'en allaient des altitudes
Poussés par l'orgueil et la lâcheté ;
On ne les surprend dans les solitudes
Que si rarement ; ils ont tout quitté,
Leur légende est morte dans les bas-fonds,
On les rencontre dans les yeux des femmes,
Et ceux des enfants qui passent dans l'âme,
En fin septembre, tels des vagabonds.

On les voit furtifs qui rôdent dans l'ombre
Et ne doivent pas s'arrêter très loin ;
Ils vont se baigner par les nuits très sombres
Pour que leur ébats n'aient pas de témoins.
– Mais plus rare et solitaire le cri
Plus effrayant qui brise la poitrine,
Et va se perdre aux cimes de l'esprit
Comme un appel lointain de sauvagine.

Tous les hameaux l'entendront dans la crainte,
Le soir, passés les jeux de la chair ;
Il s'étendra sur la lande, la plainte
D'une bête égorgée en plein hiver ;
Ou bien ce cri de peur dans l'ombre intense
Qui déchire brusquement les étangs,
Quand s'approchent les pas des poursuivants
Et font rejaillir l'eau dans le silence.

Si désolant sera-t-il dans les plaines
Que tressailliront les cœurs des passants ;
Ils s'arrêteront pour reprendre haleine
Et dire : c'est le chant d'un innocent !
Passé l'appel, résonneront encore
Les échos, jusqu'aux profondeurs des moelles,
Il prendra son vol, comme un son de cor,
Vers le gouffre transparent des étoiles !

Toi, tu sauras que ce n'est pas le froid
Qui déchaîne un cri pareil à cette heure ;
Moins lamentable sera ton effroi,
Tu connais les fièvres intérieures,
Dans les ventres sourds, pliés à se tordre,
L'aube du désir chez les impuissants,
Et tu diras que ce cri d'innocent,
C'est l'appel d'un fauve qui voudrait mordre !

La Quête de joie
© Éditions Gallimard

ENFANTS DE SEPTEMBRE

à Jules Supervielle

Les bois étaient tout recouverts de brumes basses,
Déserts, gonflés de pluie et silencieux ;
Longtemps avait soufflé ce vent du Nord où passent
Les Enfants Sauvages, fuyant vers d'autres cieux,
Par grands voiliers, le soir, et très haut dans l'espace.

J'avais senti siffler leurs ailes dans la nuit,
Lorsqu'ils avaient baissé pour chercher les ravines
Où tout le jour, peut-être, ils resteront enfouis ;
Et cet appel inconsolé de sauvagine
Triste, sur les marais que les oiseaux ont fuis.

Après avoir surpris le dégel de ma chambre,
À l'aube, je gagnai la lisière des bois ;
Par une bonne lune de brouillard et d'ambre,
Je relevai la trace, incertaine parfois,
Sur le bord d'un layon, d'un enfant de Septembre.

Les pas étaient légers et tendres, mais brouillés,
Ils se croisaient d'abord au milieu des ornières
Où dans l'ombre, tranquille, il avait essayé
De boire, pour reprendre ses jeux solitaires
Très tard, après le long crépuscule mouillé.

Et puis, ils se perdaient plus loin parmi les hêtres
Où son pied ne marquait qu'à peine sur le sol ;
Je me suis dit : il va s'en retourner peut-être
À l'aube, pour chercher ses compagnons de vol,
En tremblant de la peur qu'ils aient pu disparaître.

Il va certainement venir dans ces parages
À la demi-clarté qui monte à l'orient,
Avec les grandes bandes d'oiseaux de passage,
Et les cerfs inquiets qui cherchent dans le vent
L'heure d'abandonner le calme des gagnages.

Le jour glacial s'était levé sur les marais ;
Je restais accroupi dans l'attente illusoire,
Regardant défiler la faune qui rentrait
Dans l'ombre, les chevreuils peureux qui venaient boire
Et les corbeaux criards aux cimes des forêts.

Et je me dis : je suis un enfant de Septembre,
Moi-même, par le cœur, la fièvre et l'esprit,
Et la brûlante volupté de tous mes membres,
Et le désir que j'ai de courir dans la nuit
Sauvage, ayant quitté l'étouffement des chambres.

Il va certainement me traiter comme un frère,
Peut-être me donner un nom parmi les siens ;
Mes yeux le combleraient d'amicales lumières
S'il ne prenait pas peur, en me voyant soudain
Les bras ouverts, courir vers lui dans la clairière.

Farouche, il s'enfuira comme un oiseau blessé,
Je le suivrai jusqu'à ce qu'il demande grâce,
Jusqu'à ce qu'il s'arrête en plein ciel, épuisé,
Traqué jusqu'à la mort, vaincu, les ailes basses,
Et les yeux résignés à mourir, abaissés.

Alors, je le prendrai dans mes bras, endormi,
Je le caresserai sur la pente des ailes,
Et je ramènerai son petit corps, parmi
Les roseaux, rêvant à des choses irréelles,
Réchauffé tout le temps par mon sourire ami...

Mais les bois étaient recouverts de brumes basses
Et le vent commençait à remonter au Nord,
Abandonnant tous ceux dont les ailes sont lasses,
Tous ceux qui sont perdus et tous ceux qui sont morts,
Qui vont par d'autres voies en de mêmes espaces !

Et je me suis dit : Ce n'est pas dans ces pauvres landes
Que les enfants de Septembre vont s'arrêter ;
Un seul qui se serait écarté de sa bande
Aurait-il, en un soir, compris l'atrocité
De ces marais déserts et privés de légende ?

La Quête de joie © Éditions Gallimard

LA QUÊTE DE JOIE

à A.L.T.P.

Il dit : « Il faut partir pour conquérir la Joie.
Vous irez deux par deux pour vous garder du mal,
Par les forêts, les fleuves, par toutes les voies
Ouvertes sur les solitudes de lumière ;
Vos bonheurs assouvis sentent déjà la cendre ;
Vous chasserez de nuit, de jour, jusqu'aux frontières
De l'âme où vous n'avez jamais osé descendre ;
Il vous faudra forcer au fond de leurs retraites,
Jusqu'au ciel de la mort, étrangement hanté,
Tout scintillants comme des joyaux de beauté,
Les Anges Sauvages de l'éternelle Fête.
Allez, vous sentirez en vous-mêmes leurs traces
Parmi les pentes d'ombre de l'autre versant,
Où le seul vent du Nord, tumultueux, les chasse
Par vols immenses, vers le Précieux Sang.

Allez, envolez-vous tels des oiseaux de proie,
Vers ces marais noyés de brouillard et de fange,
Et vous découvrirez après la mort d'un ange,
Tout ce qu'un cœur scellé peut contenir de Joie... »

Alors, ils ont suivi le fil des grandes routes
Pour s'enfoncer profondément dans les déserts,
Et bousculés de-ci, de-là, sans qu'ils s'en doutent,
Par le vent animal et fou de haute mer :
Ils ont sonné les débuchés dans la lumière,
D'un bout du monde à l'autre un lancé triomphal,
Quand leurs meutes levaient un ange solitaire
Loin dans l'âme... Jamais le hallali final
Et la mort...
                Ils se croisaient en se disant « Liesse ! »
Mais leurs regards déçus démentaient ce bonheur ;
C'était leur mot de passe : il leur tordait le cœur !

Quête de Joie ! Quête de Joie ! dans leur détresse,
Ils rêvaient de trouver ces philtres enchantés
Où l'on descend aux paradis par lâcheté...

On les rencontre encor, surgissant du ciel sombre,
Tels des rôdeurs, des fous vagants des grands chemins,
Solitaires, ayant abandonné leurs chiens
De meute, haletants jusqu'à la mort dans l'ombre ;
Ils ont erré dans les déserts de la souffrance,
Dans les âmes les plus hautes et les plus claires,
Dans les plaines encor vierges de l'enfance,
Parmi la pauvreté de l'esprit, volontaire,
Où les bouffées de Dieu montent comme des vagues,
Où les amours de soi rôdent comme des loups...

Dans le choc lumineux et brutal des dégoûts,
Ils ont bien pris cet ange qui partout divague,
« L'Angélus Communis », si triste et si petit
Qu'il se laisse attraper sans déployer les ailes ;
Mais ils n'ont pas couru ce grand ange rebelle
Qui déchaîne à son passage l'âme et l'esprit,
Et bouleverse le corps comme une tempête...

On les attend toujours, mais ils ont disparu ;
Ils ont été traînés aux obscures retraites
Par des brouillards mortels où leurs pas sont perdus ;
D'autres sont descendus aux vallées les plus vaines,
D'autres, le cœur rongé de désirs impuissants,
Se sont aventurés aux sources du Vrai Sang ;
Mais ils sont morts d'amour au fond de quelle impasse !
Et ceux qui revenaient, entraînant leurs conquêtes,
Ont été bousculés par la grande tempête
De décembre, qui fit tout trembler sur les cimes...

Mort de folie – dans un ravin, en fin décembre ;
Mort de froid et de vertige – sur les abîmes ;
Mort de fièvre – dans un marais, en fin décembre ;
Mort d'orgueil – si loin, sur les hauteurs de l'esprit
Après avoir blessé un ange ; mort en mer,

Mosuer, un héros, un grand ami, surpris
Par le vent ; un autre foudroyé dans les airs
Si près de la lumière qu'on l'a retrouvé
Aveugle ; mort n'importe où, Foulc, presqu'arrivé,
Dont la sauvagerie ressemblait à la mienne...

Morts ! ils ont forcé les limites lointaines,
Le ciel tout boursouflé de soleil, qui flamboie
Si tristement...
                    Quête de Joie ! Quête de Joie !

La Quête de joie
© Éditions Gallimard

LÉGENDE

Va dire à ma chère Île, là-bas, tout là-bas,
Près de cet obscur marais de Foulc, dans la lande,
Que je viendrai vers elle ce soir, qu'elle attende,
Qu'au lever de la lune elle entendra mon pas.

Tu la trouveras baignant ses pieds sous les rouches [1],
Les cheveux dénoués, les yeux clos à demi,
Et naïve, tenant une main sur sa bouche
Pour ne pas réveiller les oiseaux endormis.

Car les marais sont tout embués de légende,
Comme le ciel que l'on découvre dans ses yeux,
Quand ils boivent la bonne lune sur la lande
Ou les vents tristes qui dévalent des Hauts-Lieux.

Dis-lui que j'ai passé des aubes merveilleuses
À guetter les oiseaux qui revenaient du Nord,
Si près d'elle, étendue à mes pieds et frileuse
Comme une petite sauvagine qui dort.

Dis-lui que nous voici vers la fin de septembre,
Que les hivers sont durs dans ces pays perdus,
Que devant la croisée ouverte de ma chambre,
De grands fouillis de fleurs sont toujours répandus.

Annonce-moi comme un prophète, comme un prince,
Comme le fils d'un roi d'au-delà de la mer ;
Dis-lui que les parfums inondent mes provinces
Et que les Hauts-Pays ne souffrent pas l'hiver.

---

1. roseaux (en Poitou).

Dis-lui que les balcons ici seront fleuris,
Qu'elle se baignera dans des étangs sans fièvre,
Mais que je voudrais voir dans ses yeux assombris
Le sauvage secret qui se meurt sur ses lèvres,

L'énigme d'un regard de pure transparence
Et qui brille parfois du fascinant éclair
Des grands initiés aux jeux de connaissance
Et des coureurs du large, sous les cieux déserts...

La Quête de joie
© Éditions Gallimard

JEAN-PAUL DE DADELSEN

(1913-1957)

Son œuvre poétique est inachevée et presque entièrement inédite à sa mort. Quelques poèmes, dont le plus important est ce *Bach en automne* que son ami Albert Camus publie à la NRF en 55, ont paru dans des revues, mais Dadelsen retouchait sans cesse ce qu'il avait écrit, et lorsqu'il se décidait à confier un texte à l'éditeur, il n'en était jamais pleinement satisfait et disait avec humour ne voir en lui qu'un état « provisoirement définitif » du poème. Son œuvre de poète, regroupée pour l'essentiel dans l'édition préparée par François Duchêne, tient en un volume de la collection Poésie/Gallimard. Celui qui la découvre est frappé par la force et l'originalité de son auteur. Constitué de plusieurs poèmes composés à des dates différentes, le volume paraît sous le titre de *Jonas*. C'est celui qu'il voulait lui-même donner au grand roman symbolique qu'il rêvait d'écrire et dans lequel ces poèmes devaient s'insérer. La figure du prophète avalé par la baleine n'a pas ici une simple valeur d'ornement pittoresque, elle occupe sans doute la première place dans l'imaginaire du poète parce qu'elle traduit symboliquement sa vision de la condition humaine. Il voit en nous les habitants de la mort, naviguant sans l'avoir voulu vers un autre rivage. Pour un temps, nous sommes tous des Jonas captifs du ventre de la baleine et promis à une destination inconnue où commencera un autre parcours. Ce poète sans théorie ni art poétique, comme le souligne Henri Thomas dans sa préface, « ne vient à la suite de personne », son inspiration essentiellement religieuse au sens le plus large du terme, et lestée de la plus humaine des réalités, nous fait entendre une voix singulière et prenante.

UN CHANT DE SALOMON

Autour de nos reins les parois de la nuit sont rondes et sonores.
Dans la rumeur des artères heureuses et du sang contenté le cœur
Écoute s'ouvrir l'espace intérieur.

Les yeux fermés, regarde, telle une image dans une eau sombre,
À l'inverse de la fuite des mondes tournoyer des constellations
    obscures
Sous les voûtes de notre sang.
Les ténèbres du temple charnel sont vastes comme les profondeurs
    des cieux.

Noire, silencieuse, sourde jumelle du ciel visible, sœur de Rigel,
Sous nos paupières fermées écoute gonfler les jardins intérieurs,
Femme, porte du temps !

La palme vers le ciel sucré darde ses fruits nocturnes.
À l'homme tendu vers sa perte ouvre tes grottes marines,
Fais perdre pied à ce nageur
Pour qu'il t'éclabousse des voies lactées de ta descendance.

Mais déjà le premier oiseau pépie sur la branche confuse.
Les monts lavés naissent du safran oriental.
Il va faire jour encore.

Voici l'heure de cette trêve furtive
Où ni le ciel ne clame vers nous ni la terre ne nous attire
Et dans l'arbre qui dort sans rêves
La brise distraitement chuchote le nom de la patrie spirituelle.

Tourne vers ton souverain condamné
Ton masque de poupée qui sourit. Ô seule forte et seule sage,
Ô seule école de la mort !

Jonas
© Éditions Gallimard

INVOCATION LIMINAIRE

Ils ont habité avec nous dans la gueule de la baleine.
La baleine les a crachés sur l'autre rivage :
Les timides.
Les gauchers.
Celui qui était albinos et bègue.
Les myopes. Les méfiants, les malins.
Et ce grand garçon qui avait toujours soif,
toujours sommeil.

Regardent-ils parfois par-dessus notre épaule ?
Depuis qu'ils sont partis, nous n'avons vu personne.

. . . .

Ombre,
qui regardes par-dessus mon épaule
que puis-je faire pour toi ?
Il n'y a point ici d'ombre, mais seulement
la peine et le travail des hommes vivants,
la longueur du temps, la résistance de la seule matière.
Mais qui dira
si les ombres parmi nous
ne sont pas à leur tour penchées
sur ce même travail inépuisable ?

Ombre, que puis-je pour toi ?
Avec mes yeux bornés, mes yeux vivants,
avec mes mains obtuses, vivantes,
avec ce corps, avec ce temps qui m'est laissé,
Ombre, veux-tu que je regarde
pour toi
ces visages, ces paysages ?
veux-tu que je touche
pour toi
ces fleurs, ces cheveux, ces choses ?

veux-tu que j'essaie
avec toi
de soulever un peu du lourd fardeau accumulé ?

. . . .

Ombre de mon frère,
cendre de mon frère, qui fut homme,
c'est pour toi aussi qu'est dite la parole
la parole où l'on met genou en terre et
battent les prétoriens tambours :

ET HOMO FACTUS EST
Et fut fait
cendre, fut fait
peur, fut fait
pesanteur et ténèbre, fut fait
proie dans la gueule de la baleine, fut fait
doute, fut fait désespoir.

Seigneur des armées,
Seigneur des soldats,
Seigneur qui nous jeta dans la gueule de la baleine,
donne-nous aujourd'hui
non pas encore ta paix, mais
notre quotidienne nourriture d'erreur, de confusion,
d'aveuglement, d'injustice,
afin que, mâchant notre pain de poussière et de vent,
nous nous rappelions chaque jour
que l'Éternel n'est pas une poupée faite de main d'homme,
qu'Il n'est pas un fantôme docile à notre appel,
qu'Il ne donne, même contre Caïn, nulle victoire,
qu'Il n'est pas justice, pas ordre,
pas amour au sens de notre langage cannibale,
n'est pas vie, n'est pas dieu,
n'est rien de ce que dit une parole humaine.

Seigneur, donne-nous notre peine quotidienne
afin qu'elle soit pesée avec les cendres de nos frères.

Ombre,
que je ne vois pas, qui ne me parle pas,
que puis-je, sinon
dire que tu fus peur et courage,
amour et solitude,
homme que nous avons, si mal, aimé.

Jonas

CLAUDE ROY

(1915-1997)

Claude Roy n'a pas laissé tarir en lui la source rêveuse de l'enfance où il confie qu'il était un « petit imaginêtre ».

> *En ce temps-là j'avais douze ans*
> *et je les ai toujours glissés sous les années d'après*
> *comme des draps bien pliés et rangés*
> *qui sentent la lavande en grains*
> *dans une armoire à souvenirs*
> *dont les portes sont souvent fermées.*

Dans son *Bestiaire des animaux à l'aise dans leur peau*, il compare la certitude que nous donnent ces derniers de n'être qu'eux-mêmes (« La fourrure du chat tient le chat tout entier ») à sa propre porosité au monde qui l'entoure : « Mais moi je m'évapore et me perds et me trouve / Et ne suis jamais sûr d'être ce que je suis. » Ce qui frappe chez lui, c'est le don de symbiose avec ces vies humbles dont il est le témoin passionné, ainsi son attention à l'appel du crapaud (en « do mineur couleur d'eau »), l'oreille qu'il prête à « la voix minime du grillon », et, par-dessus tout, au chant des oiseaux. Par bien des aspects la tendresse amusée qu'il exprime à leur égard rappelle l'attitude de celui dont il fut proche, le Supervielle des *Amis inconnus*. S'il se définit lui-même comme poète mineur – nous dirions plutôt qu'il va « chantant sur le mode mineur » – il n'en aborde pas moins avec gravité certains des thèmes essentiels du lyrisme, le temps, l'amour, la mort. Son sens du tragique, l'angoisse devant le leurre du temps imparti aux humains n'interdit pas l'humour comme on peut le voir par exemple dans cet *Adagio un poco metafisico* : « Je ne / suis je le concède qu'un *ciron* / peu sérieux un humain assez usagé... Je ne / dis pas que l'Univers tient un grand compte / de l'existence précaire de Claude Roy / mais moi je *considère* l'Univers / et cela fait passer le temps », mais malgré le sourire qui tempère la détresse, il a les accents d'un homme dont les jours sont menacés, même si la pudeur de l'expression voile l'angoisse très réelle. On le perçoit d'abord dans ses poèmes des années quarante où, participant aux combats de la Résistance, il vit dans l'imminence d'une arrestation, plus tard dans ceux des années quatre-vingt, quand un cancer au poumon rend sa survie improbable ; il est désormais « ce voyageur en partance / qui ne sait pas l'heure de son train / et qui a oublié où il va », celui qui résume son destin en deux mots : « Inachevé / j'inachèverai. »

Deux forces l'aident à supporter la précarité de chaque instant dérobé à la mort : l'amour de Loleh, sa femme, et la confiance dans le pouvoir des mots. Cette femme dont il ne se lasse pas de redire la douceur mystérieuse :

> *Songeuse retirée rieuse tempérée*
> *flexible détournée distraite méditée*
> *le doux beau front bombé et sa pâleur d'opale*
> *les yeux de grand hiver et de brasero lent...*

avec des accents qui rappellent Aragon ou Éluard. Et cette voix écoutée en lui, modeste et puissante :

> *Voix simple qui ne dit que ce qu'elle aime et nomme*
> *aussi nue qu'une main toute habillée d'air pur,*
> *...et qui a tous les jours raison contre la mort.*

ABSENCE

Ma vive où que tu sois si loin que presque morte
si loin de mon sommeil de ma main de mes yeux
dans le noir et le noir et la nuit qui t'emporte
si loin de notre été menteur mélodieux

Mon ombre te surprend dans tes changeants séjours
Si l'on te dit mon nom il glisse à travers toi
Mais la nuit donne un poids aux mots légers du jour
rôdeur aux pas absents je rentre par le toit

Mots d'amour chuchotés dans l'ombreuse épaisseur
vous éveillez un soir un parfum d'autrefois
Étoiles vous buvez dans la main du dormeur
l'eau des sources perdues aux profondeurs des bois

L'hésitante chanson de la mer au rivage
la fraîcheur aux pieds nus des dalles sans couleur
l'odeur de tes cheveux tes bras ta gorge sage
le lit comme un navire au port du lent bonheur

tout cela qui n'est plus feint d'exister encore
Nous croisons nos regards au-delà des distances
au-delà de l'oubli du temps et de la mort
qui nous retrouvera dans le même silence.

Poésies
© Éditions Gallimard

SOLEIL ET VENT

Dans le silence et la respiration de l'eau
une voix très basse se mélange au vent
Si on prête l'oreille on devine des mots
mais ce que dit la voix est en langue étrangère

Voix qui parle et se tait   et qu'on ne comprend pas
dans le feu sous la cendre   au creux noir de l'hiver
dans l'averse d'avril qui caresse le toit
dans la bouilloire pensive qui marmonne les heures

Voix envolée   voix qui murmure et qui s'endort
voix de feuillage frais de sommeil et de brume
Ce n'est que presque toi qui parles à toi peut-être
sans comprendre pourtant la phrase chuchotée

Plus tard   à midi juste   à l'aigu du soleil
des mots t'habiteront pour la première fois
et la clarté du jour aura   sans avoir l'air
traduit et mis au clair ce qu'on avait cru taire

les mots de nuit de vent d'absence et de désert

Les Pas du silence
© Éditions Gallimard

PIERRE EMMANUEL

(1916-1984)

Depuis ses premiers recueils de poèmes Pierre Emmanuel n'a cessé d'interroger les grandes figures de la légende ou de la Bible. À son propos, Jean Onimus, dans *Expérience de la poésie*, écrit ceci : « Cet homme ne peut se passer d'Orphée, d'Ève, de Jacob, des Sodomites et de Babel... tant il est vrai que le mythe est un masque qui, posé sur le mystère, lui donne un visage ; visage d'énigme certes, mais seule clarté dans notre nuit. » On pourrait dire que par là il continue les grands poètes romantiques, et qu'en bien des points sa méditation sur le mystère de la création et de notre présence au monde rejoint celle de Hugo. Mais il y ajoute l'exploitation consciente et élargie des ressources de l'image que le symbolisme a mises en lumière. Pour ce dernier, comme on le sait, le symbole éclaire les rapports mystérieux entre diverses faces du réel, et tisse, entre les éléments disparates du monde sensible, une unité que la diversité des apparences cèle au non-initié, et le poète se contente le plus souvent d'explorer ces correspondances transversales. Pierre Emmanuel ne se borne jamais à ce scintillement de surface. Il recherche autre chose. Il a, suivant le titre de l'un de ses essais, *Le Goût de l'Un*. L'image est pour lui un véritable chemin de connaissance, elle permet une approche des profondeurs, et parfois leur saisie totalisante : « Ce que je sais par expérience, écrit-il dans *Autobiographies*, c'est que la pensée par images met en jeu, du physique au mental, toute la hiérarchie de l'être : elle n'est pas détachée de l'objet, mais engagée dans l'existence concrète et de proche en proche elle englobe l'univers, l'homme s'y pense avec le monde qui l'entoure, il est ensemble tout et partie. »

Ce poète difficile ne se veut pas hermétique. Il en donne la raison : « Si la Parole divine est sans orgueil, de quel droit l'orgueil du verbe humain ? : l'hermétisme est idolâtrie pure. » Sa pratique de la Bible l'a éclairé sur l'importance des mots qui sont pour lui la substance même de l'homme. À ses yeux il importe donc d'éviter deux fautes majeures : enfermer la parole dans un système de symboles en écho, ou la réduire à une simple fonction descriptive : il récuse également la clôture du verbe sur lui-même, chère aux initiés de toutes obédiences, et les mots dilapidés au seul profit d'un inventaire du réel. Les essais en prose qui accompagnent toute sa création poétique éclairent pleinement sur ce point le sens de sa démarche. Un poète qu'il vénère, Pierre-Jean Jouve, a très tôt perçu l'originalité de celle-ci... C'est lui qui l'encourage d'abord à se détacher de sa première manière, trop marquée par des influences extérieures, et lui enseigne à être attentif à sa propre intériorité, à tout ce qui sourd du moi profond. La patiente écoute à laquelle il se consacre alors s'apparente à une ascèse rigoureuse : elle va porter ses fruits puisqu'une œuvre naît de cet effort, puissante et neuve.

L'un de ses premiers recueils, *Le Tombeau d'Orphée*, lui vaut d'emblée la célébrité. Orphée, à travers sa légende, traduit l'affrontement par le poète de l'inacceptable mort. Vouloir arracher Eurydice au gouffre et la ramener à la lumière c'est vouloir substituer à l'aimée le leurre d'une emprise de la parole. Accepter de porter en soi son absence, c'est devenir cet être double, épouser à jamais la mystérieuse altérité du moi et connaître le chant que seul révèle la mort traversée :

> *Alors*
> *Orphée avec fureur pénètre au corps de dieu*
> *il traverse la faute, et sent la mort du Christ*
> *roidir ses membres,*
> *mais va et chante !*

Orphée est l'inspiré, il puise aux ténèbres intérieures qu'il affronte seul, la puissance de sa parole. Et s'il n'incarne pas, comme ce fut parfois le cas pour la Renaissance, une autre figure du Christ, il traduit le pouvoir du poète, digne, en opposant à la mort la force de son chant, d'éprouver en lui-même les prémices de la Résurrection telle qu'elle est annoncée dans l'Évangile.

Car Pierre Emmanuel est un poète chrétien. Son pseudonyme, comme il le dit lui-même, est fait de deux composantes opposées et complémentaires : il allie l'opacité et la pesanteur de la matière à la présence en elle du verbe. « Ce nouveau nom tranchait mes liens avec une vie qui m'était devenue odieuse : il me libérait, mais en me définissant, il m'intimait un ordre... du moins n'ai-je voulu rien d'autre, depuis que je connais la portée du langage humain, que d'être le poète de la parole, du Verbe reçu puis donné. » Il va s'attacher de livre en livre à retracer de façon symbolique l'épopée tragique du genre humain. Hugo ou d'Aubigné ont seuls de tels accents parmi les poètes français. En effet une veine épique anime la plus grande partie de cette œuvre, et la vision de l'histoire humaine qu'elle propose à travers le légendaire biblique, par exemple dans *Babel* et surtout dans la grande fresque de *Jacob*, lui donne une ampleur inégalée dans ce siècle. Il y a chez Pierre Emmanuel une étonnante diversité de registres puisqu'il fut aussi un poète de la Résistance. Chez lui l'engagement militant n'empêche pas les recueils de cette époque de dépasser par l'ampleur de leur lyrisme les circonstances qui présidaient à leur parution. Enfin le lyrisme familier trouve son expression dans *La Chanson du dé à coudre*, et dans des poèmes d'une spiritualité tout intérieure, comme ceux d'*Évangéliaire*. La très grande maîtrise technique du poète, qui se manifeste aussi bien dans le vers régulier que dans les formes prosodiques les plus modernes, lui permet en effet de varier à son gré les sujets et les tons. Cependant l'impression qui prévaut chez son lecteur, c'est d'être le témoin d'une grande aventure intérieure dont la poésie est l'instrument, et que cette aventure, assurément très singulière, propose au lecteur un chemin d'initiation.

DÉDICACE D'ORPHÉE

Me voici revenu de la rive incertaine
où lamente la lyre abandonnée d'Orphée :
le vent d'en-bas m'emplit de vertige les veines
et mon double brumeux ne s'est point dissipé.

Après avoir usé ma ressemblance humaine
les lunes mauves de l'Enfer m'ont patiné.
Mes yeux ? deux diamants d'hiver ou deux fontaines
qui fixent un soleil immuable et glacé.

Tel l'arbre aux pas profonds, aveugle de murmures
secoue dans le sommeil ses nocturnes verdures
où les soleils défunts mûrissent oubliés :

Le même arbre de jour, que la lumière outrage
sans feuilles, sans oiseaux, flagellant les nuages
maudit de ses grands bras anathèmes l'été.

Sodome
© Éditions du Seuil, 1953

AU NOM SECRET

I a pas que Dieu al mond e Dieu i es pas.
Joan LARZAC.

Ô mon amour je tiens parmi les hommes
Ton nom scellé mais ne chante que toi
Comme sous l'herbe une source chatoie
Que sans jamais te nommer je ne nomme
Que toi en tout ce qui tient nom de moi

Rends-moi présent Que je cesse d'attendre
Ce qui m'entoure en attente de moi
Donne à mon œil d'être humble envers mes doigts
Pour que je prenne ici au lieu de tendre
Filet troué le regard au-delà

Que de mes mains je modèle un langage
Souffle pétri qui m'engouffre et m'accroît
Plus s'ouvre un cœur plus il est à l'étroit
Ainsi du monde où lève ton image
Qui le nourrit en l'affamant de toi

La Face humaine
© Éditions du Seuil, 1965

ECCE ANCILLA

L'âme du monde empreint ce visage rieur
La sagesse éternelle éclaire un front sans ride
L'expérience de l'insondable douleur
Est dans ces yeux tel un point d'or dans le ciel vide

Cette virginité qui fait de chaque instant
Pour la somme des temps l'instant de l'Origine
Recueille un Orient immensément latent
De l'Un sans ombre au Tout que le nombre illumine

Le Oui de la servante au seuil de la maison
Répond au Toi qui entre toutes la désigne
Et syllabe scellant un parfait abandon
Inscrit l'orbe sans bords dans son œuf qui l'assigne

L'enfant qui nous naîtra de ce ventre auroral
Est de toujours l'Instaurateur de toute chose
Je cosmique dont le commandement royal
Est accompli dans le silence de la rose

Tu

RENÉ GUY CADOU

(1920-1951)

Dans le texte liminaire d'*Hélène ou le règne végétal*, le poète explique qu'il n'est pas le seul maître d'œuvre : « Je n'ai pas écrit ce livre. Il m'a été dicté au long des mois par une voix souveraine et je n'ai fait qu'enregistrer, comme un muet, l'écho durable qui frappait à coup redoublés l'obscur tympan du monde. » Il reprend la même affirmation en disant : « Ces poèmes m'arrivent de bien plus loin que moi-même. » Pour le lecteur sensible dans cette œuvre aux « étonnantes vibrations » répercutées jusqu'à lui à travers le poète et dont parle cette préface, il est clair que René Guy Cadou renoue, à sa manière humble et discrète, avec la conception platonicienne du poète. Il est bien ce maillon de la chaîne par laquelle se transmet aux hommes l'inspiration donnée par le dieu. Aussi, malgré la brièveté de sa vie, laisse-t-il une œuvre poétique incontestable, car chacun de ses poèmes est doté de cette résonance particulière qui le prolonge et l'amplifie. Il est difficile de n'être pas touché au cœur par une voix d'où la poésie jaillit, comme d'une source, voix toute simple qui célèbre la vie quotidienne avec tendresse, sans élever le ton :

> – Ô père ! J'ai voulu que ce nom de Cadou
> Demeure un bruissement d'eau claire sur les cailloux !
> Plutôt que le plain-chant la fugue musicale...

Cet homme qui va « Les yeux vagues ainsi qu'un veilleur de frontière / De songerie malade et de sens abîmés »... rejoint les rêveurs éveillés qui l'ont précédé et dont il se réclame.

Pleinement conscient de sa dette envers eux, il aime à nommer dans ses vers les poètes qu'il admire. Il compose même une « anthologie » où il les évoque avec ferveur. Le nom de Max Jacob, dont il se plaît à rappeler la foi naïve et le destin tragique, revient plus souvent que tout autre. Ce qui fait son originalité, même si l'on retrouve chez lui certains accents d'Aragon ou de Supervielle, c'est son amour de la terre, son sens des odeurs et des saisons, héritage de l'enfance à jamais intact en lui. L'un de ses poèmes s'intitule « Pourquoi n'allez-vous pas à Paris » ? et le dialogue qui suit réitère la question, à laquelle il répond d'abord :

> *Mais l'odeur des lys ! Mais l'odeur des lys !*

avant d'expliquer :

> *Mais moi seul dans la grande nuit mouillée*
> *L'odeur des lys et la campagne agenouillée...*

Ce « règne végétal » est à entendre aussi au sens d'une royauté de la femme par qui le monde retrouve sa première innocence.

> *Je te vois mon Hélène au milieu des campagnes*
> *Innocentant les crimes roses des vergers*
> *Ouvrant les hauts battants du monde afin que l'homme*
> *Atteigne les comptoirs lumineux du soleil...*

Ce chant d'amour, adressé à la femme réelle ou rêvée, rétablit celle-ci au cœur d'un jardin qui n'est plus l'*hortus conclusus* de Guillaume de Lorris, mais la nature tout entière, miraculeusement offerte à l'homme en son unité retrouvée.

J'AI TOUJOURS HABITÉ

J'ai toujours habité de grandes maisons tristes
Appuyées à la nuit comme un haut vaisselier
Des gens s'y reposaient au hasard des voyages
Et moi je m'arrêtais tremblant dans l'escalier
Hésitant à chercher dans leurs maigres bagages
Peut-être le secret de mon identité
Je préférais laisser planer sur moi comme une eau froide
Le doute d'être un homme Je m'aimais
Dans la splendeur imaginée d'un végétal
D'essence blonde avec des boucles de soleil
Ma vie ne commençait qu'au-delà de moi-même
Ébruitée doucement par un vol de vanneaux
Je m'entendais dans les grelots d'un matin blême
Et c'était toujours les mêmes murs à la chaux
La chambre désolée dans sa coquille vide
Le lit-cage toujours privé de chants d'oiseaux
Mais je m'aimais ah ! je m'aimais comme on élève
Au-dessus de ses yeux un enfant de clarté
Et loin de moi je savais bien me retrouver
Ensoleillé dans les cordages d'un poème.

Hélène ou le règne végétal
© Seghers

Je t'attendais ainsi qu'on attend les navires
Dans les années de sécheresse quand le blé
Ne monte pas plus haut qu'une oreille dans l'herbe
Qui écoute apeurée la grande voix du temps

Je t'attendais et tous les quais toutes les routes
Ont retenti du pas brûlant qui s'en allait
Vers toi que je portais déjà sur mes épaules
Comme une douce pluie qui ne sèche jamais

Tu ne remuais encor que par quelques paupières
Quelques pattes d'oiseaux dans les vitres gelées
Je ne voyais en toi que cette solitude
Qui posait ses deux mains de feuille sur mon cou

Et pourtant c'était toi dans le clair de ma vie
Ce grand tapage matinal qui m'éveillait
Tous mes oiseaux tous mes vaisseaux tous mes pays
Ces astres ces millions d'astres qui se levaient

Ah que tu parlais bien quand toutes les fenêtres
Pétillaient dans le soir ainsi qu'un vin nouveau
Quand les portes s'ouvraient sur des villes légères
Où nous allions tous deux enlacés par les rues

Tu venais de si loin derrière ton visage
Que je ne savais plus à chaque battement
Si mon cœur durerait jusqu'au temps de toi-même
Où tu serais en moi plus forte que mon sang.

Hélène ou le règne végétal
© Seghers

Les chevaux de l'amour me parlent de rencontres
Qu'ils font en revenant par des chemins déserts
Une femme inconnue les arrête et les baigne
D'un regard douloureux tout chargé de forêts

Méfie-toi disent-ils sa tristesse est la nôtre
Et pour avoir aimé une telle douleur
Tu ne marcheras plus tête nue sous les branches
Sans savoir que le poids de la vie est sur toi

Mais je marche et je sais que tes mains me répondent
Ô femme dans le clair prétexte des bourgeons
Et que tu n'attends pas que les fibres se soudent
Pour amoureusement y graver nos prénoms

Tu roules sous tes doigts comme des pommes vertes
De soleil en soleil les joues grises du temps
Et poses sur les yeux fatigués des villages
La bonne taie d'un long sommeil de bois dormant

Montre tes seins que je voie vivre en pleine neige
La bête des glaciers qui porte sur le front
Le double anneau du jour et la douceur de n'être
Qu'une bête aux yeux doux dont on touche le fond

Telle tu m'apparais que mon amour figure
Un arbre descendu dans le chaud de l'été
Comme une tentation adorable qui dure
Le temps d'une seconde et d'une éternité.

Hélène ou le règne végétal
© Seghers

OLIVIER LARRONDE

(1927-1966)

Deux recueils de son vivant : *Les Barricades mystérieuses* et *Rien voilà l'ordre*, un recueil posthume : *L'Arbre à lettres*. L'impeccable maîtrise du verbe, l'art, qui semble inné, d'un savant agencement de mots où l'apparente clarté dérobe le sens en offrant plusieurs prises, le jeu des sonorités qui se font écho, tout étonne chez ce jeune poète. Son appartenance à la lignée mallarméenne est manifeste. On admire qu'il s'établisse d'emblée sur un territoire que le Maître lui-même dut conquérir peu à peu. Tous les orages intérieurs, charnels et spirituels, d'une jeunesse sensuelle dont les idoles furent Cocteau et Jean Genet, sont traduits, ou voilés, dans le style de préciosité ardente propre aux symbolistes. Des violences baudelairiennes parfois, mais aucune trace apparente, dans les textes essentiels, des tumultes du monde extérieur dont témoignent si abondamment ses contemporains.

Chaque poème fait obstacle, par la perfection ciselée de sa structure, à toute approche superficielle, et fait songer à l'hermétisme classique dont Scève, par exemple, fut un modèle. L'épure de chacun d'eux semble cependant moins redevable à un culte de la forme entraînant la clôture, qu'à la passion torturante de Narcisse pour sa propre image. Penché sur son reflet, il oppose un refus hautain à ce qui l'arracherait au double désirable de lui-même dont il est captif.

De ce refus témoigne aussi le titre de son œuvre essentielle *Rien voilà l'ordre*. Il sonne comme une affirmation du néant du monde. Il est aussi l'anagramme de son nom. Par l'éclatement des lettres qui le désignaient et se regroupent pour ce constat désespéré, c'est sa vie même que le poète met en jeu dans sa démarche.

MA BOUCHE...

Ma bouche
            est-ce trahir le silence des voiles
Que donner forme au souffle à la mort nous poussant
Comme, battant des nuits, ma paupière en sa toile
Livre un trésor de gel en perles de néant ?

Non : tout s'est asservi dans l'ouvrage du gel
Exercé dans l'éclat de la perle profonde
Tu parles diaphane en armant sur l'autel
Du vide les cristaux de neige où il se fonde.

Sur les degrés de l'air à mes noces de mante
La somptueuse fange a trempé tes vigueurs
Forgeron ! C'est nommer cette mort qui l'aimante
D'arracher un silence au Cancer de mon cœur.

Mes souffles m'enfleront, enchaînés, jusqu'au port
Où poignant en éclats toute une aube acérée,
Le torrent de ton bras où se lave la mort
Meurtrir l'ombre de chair de mon ombre atterrée.

Rien voilà l'ordre
© Éditions Gallimard

PIERRE SEGHERS

(1906-1987)

Comment accepter les limites qu'imposent au choix de textes aimés les dimensions d'un volume ? Dans une anthologie des poètes, le mot « fin » semble particulièrement incongru, tant il est évident que la poésie, « chose ailée », poursuit d'un mouvement continu sa traversée du temps.

On peut témoigner de cet inachèvement à l'aide de quelques pages blanches qui évoquent bien la promesse des cahiers de jadis.

Ou encore, tâcher de couronner l'ensemble par l'évocation d'une œuvre qui donnerait à entendre sinon Orphée, Prométhée et Narcisse enfin unis dans un seul chant, du moins le poète le plus ouvert à toutes les formes d'inspiration de son temps.

En la dernière année d'un vingtième siècle où les poètes n'ont pas manqué, il semble bien que le miracle d'une diversité quasi exhaustive des registres dans la voix d'un seul ne s'est pas réalisé. Et pourtant notre époque est riche d'autant de personnalités poétiques puissantes que les précédentes. Mais qui pourrait aujourd'hui, comme le firent Ronsard ou Victor Hugo pour les lecteurs de leur siècle, incarner à lui seul la Poésie ? Il m'a paru qu'aucun poète, même parmi les plus grands, ne pouvait y prétendre.

J'ai donc choisi, en négligeant pour une fois la stricte chronologie, de refermer ce livre sur celui qui fut durant sa vie, au sens le plus fervent et le plus généreux du terme, à la fois le serviteur de la poésie sous toutes ses formes, et lui-même poète, l'éditeur Pierre Seghers.

C'est dans la collection *Poètes d'aujourd'hui*, sa collection, que les étudiants des années cinquante ont lu les poètes du début du XXᵉ siècle et d'autres, plus anciens qu'ignoraient alors les manuels scolaires. Le professeur de lettres orientait le choix, ou, plus souvent encore, le seul plaisir d'entrer dans des territoires inconnus, (ainsi pour O. V. de L. Milosz que son nom étrange désignait à l'attention). Mais pas un volume de cet éditeur ne laissait indifférent.

De lui nous ignorions tout. Que sa maison d'édition avait été fondée à Villeneuve-lès-Avignon, qu'il avait activement participé à la Résistance aux côtés d'Éluard et d'Aragon, qu'il était certainement la source où s'approvisionnaient en poésie ceux qui, dès 45, récitaient leurs poèmes dans les grandes réunions festives qui suivirent la Libération. Ce n'est que bien plus tard que nous avons découvert le poète Seghers, celui qui avait soufflé à son double d'assumer le risque (risque qu'à cette époque nous étions loin de mesurer – qui a jamais prospéré en éditant des poètes ?) de faire partager sa passion à des centaines d'autres lecteurs. Sans le connaître, nous étions conscients de notre dette à son égard : toutes les rencontres d'au-delà de Mallarmé, dans ce no man's land de la littérature contemporaine où l'école, à cette époque, s'aventurait rarement, n'auraient pu se faire sans son entremise. Un poète épris de poésie au point de sacrifier parfois sa propre création pour mieux se consacrer à d'autres poètes, ceux qui furent ses amis proches mais aussi ceux du domaine étranger et ceux du passé. Plus tard il fit même entrer la chanson dans sa collection. Elle était la parente pauvre, à peine reconnue, malgré la persistance de cette veine dans la tradition française. Des interprètes – compositeurs tels que Charles Trenet, Georges Brassens, Léo Ferré, Guy Béart et quelques autres, en proposant à un très large public des textes qu'ils écrivaient eux-mêmes, ou des poèmes empruntés aux poètes anciens ou récents que leur musique imposait à la mémoire, ont maintenu très vivante cette tradition en l'actualisant. Et Pierre Seghers, en accordant à quelques-uns d'entre eux un droit de cité dans sa collection, contribua à abolir les frontières anciennes. Lui-même composa plusieurs volumes de chansons dont certaines devinrent célèbres par la grâce d'une rencontre entre un texte et un interprète. Mais le public, souvent, admirait le chanteur, comme le dit Trenet, « en oubliant le nom de l'auteur » (même si son texte « courait dans les rues »).

Dans le même temps, il continuait à écrire dans un autre registre, et les recueils qui jalonnaient son parcours presque tous les deux ans, recueils aujourd'hui épuisés, élargissaient le cercle de ses lecteurs et faisaient de lui un poète reconnu et célébré. Un volume, *Le Temps des merveilles*, paru en 78 offre un choix de ses œuvres depuis 38. Ces quarante ans de création permettent de mieux connaître son cheminement poétique. Il y a chez lui une incontestable maîtrise des formes, des plus traditionnelles aux plus modernes, mais surtout un continuel jaillissement. Qu'il dise les années noires de la guerre, l'énigme de vivre, l'amour ou la fuite des années, la générosité du verbe et une sincérité souvent douloureuse donnent à ses poèmes un poids de vérité. La poésie est pour lui le seul accès au réel et à lui-même, le seul moyen de questionner inlassablement, et de trouver, peut-être, des réponses :

Dis-moi ma vie, pourquoi réponds-tu à mes questions par des images
Pourquoi ces leurres agités pour nous dérober notre temps...

Il note dans le même recueil que « chacun porte en lui sa musique... » Celle qu'il fit entendre donne la mesure de la gravité d'un poète qui savait jouer avec le langage mais qui demeure surtout, comme il l'écrit, un « homme de prière penché sur lui-même et les mots, artiste de la rigueur, même s'il suit en lui la fuite des nuages »...

POÈTE

Au monstre des secrets je plie sans jamais rompre
Jusqu'à l'existence et la voix,
Je me lie à mon temps qui roule entre mes doigts
Comme un bracelet d'or ou d'ambre.

Je sens autour de moi la vie morte, passée
Mon sang la polit chaque jour
Tel un bijou dans sa coquille de détours
Aussi fluide que la pensée.

Ce qui fut m'est léger. J'invente, j'imagine
Je tresse la nuit, le soleil
Je réponds en offrant les champs et les abeilles
L'espoir, le jour que je devine.

Sur mes chariots la vie balance ses navires
De foin, de mers et de parfums
Et je feins d'oublier le début et la fin
Il n'est de réel que de dire.

Le Domaine public
© Seghers

LA VIE

Ainsi passe la vie, de l'un à l'autre va
Se fait et se défait, s'invente, se prolonge
S'endort dans des maisons que bâtissent les songes
Se rêve et s'éveillant ne se reconnaît pas.

Ainsi passe la vie. Quand le soleil va naître
Il partage déjà ses hautes graminées
Ses nuages, ses fleurs, ses défuntes années
Son devenir de feux passant dans nos fenêtres.

Ainsi passe la vie. On entend des bourdons
Tracer dans la lumière un sillage illusoire
Pour lui seul le poète écoute ses histoires
Et plonge au cœur des fleurs pour apprendre leurs noms.

Ainsi passe la vie à surprendre un langage
Inaudible et pourtant comme l'herbe vivant
De l'éternel azur qui n'est fait que de vents
De silence, d'attente et d'autres paysages...

Les Mots couverts
© Seghers

TABLE

XIVe-XVe SIÈCLES

XVIᵉ SIÈCLE

XVIIᵉ SIÈCLE

XVIIIe SIÈCLE

XIXe SIÈCLE

XXᵉ SIÈCLE

Imprimé en Italie par
« La Tipografica Varese S.p.A. » – Varese

Numéro d'édition : 439
Dépôt légal : mai 2003